Curtin's
**California
Land Use** *and*
Planning Law

Publisher's Note

Before you rely on the information in this book, be sure you are aware that some changes in the statutes or case law may have gone into effect since the date of publication. The book, moreover, provides general information about the law. Readers should consult their own attorneys before relying on the representations found herein.

Curtin's California Land Use *and* Planning Law

TWENTY-EIGHTH EDITION

2008

Cecily T. Talbert

Curtin's
California Land Use *and* Planning Law

TWENTY-EIGHTH EDITION 2008

Copyright © 2008
by Bingham McCutchen LLP

All rights reserved.

Printed in the United States of America.
No part of this publication may be reproduced,
stored in a retrieval system, or transmitted,
in any form or by any means, electronic,
mechanical, photocopied, recorded, or
otherwise, without the prior written
approval of the authors and the publisher.

Solano Press Books
Post Office Box 773
Point Arena, California 95468

tel: 800 931-9373
fax: 707 884-4109
email: spbooks@solano.com

Cover and book design
    by Solano Press
Cover photographs by
    Julie Shell and Jon Handel
Index by Daniel McNaughton,
    Chicago, Illinois

ISBN 978-0-923956-52-3

This book may be cited as follows:
Cecily T. Talbert, *Curtin's California
Land Use and Planning Law*
(Solano Press, 28th ed. 2008) ___.

NOTICE

This book is designed to assist you in understanding land use and planning law. It is necessarily general in nature and does not discuss all exceptions and variations to general rules. Also, it may not reflect the latest changes in the law. It is not intended as legal advice and should not be relied on to address legal problems. You should always consult an attorney for advice regarding your specific factual situation.

In Memoriam

Daniel J. Curtin, Jr.
(1933–2006)

In the fall of 2006, Daniel J. Curtin, Jr. passed away unexpectedly from natural causes. He was 73.

This year's edition is dedicated to Dan's memory and spirit. Widely regarded as the "Dean" of land use and local government law, Dan received countless honors and awards for his leadership and service, including the Jefferson Fordham Lifetime Achievement Award from the State and Local Government Law Section of the American Bar Association; the International Municipal Lawyers Association Charles S. Rhyne Award for Lifetime Achievement in Municipal Law; the American Planning Association's Distinguished Leadership Award, recognizing more than two decades of writing and teaching and his support for planning ideas and education; and was named Honorary Life Member of the California Park and Recreation Society for his contributions to parklands.

He served as Chair of the State and Local Government Law Section of the American Bar Association in 2001–2002, and was past Chair of the Land Development, Planning and Zoning Section of the International Municipal Lawyers Association. Also, he was past Vice-Chair of the Executive Committee of the Real Property Law Section of the State Bar of California. He served as President of the City Attorneys' Department of the League of California Cities, as a member of the Board of Directors of the League, and as Regional Vice President of the International Municipal Lawyers Association. He was recognized on numerous "Best Lawyers" lists for the state and nation.

During his legal career, Dan shaped the general plan as the center point for land use decisionmaking. In *Lesher Communications v. City of Walnut Creek*, 52 Cal. 3d 551 (1990), the California Supreme Court adopted Dan's phrase that describes the general plan as the "constitution for all future development." Later, in *DeVita v. County of Napa*, 9 Cal. 5th 763 (1995), the court accepted the notion of "vertical consistency" that Dan had been teaching for years: that all key development decisions must be consistent with the general plan. Other notable decisions involving Dan include *Associated Home Builders, Inc. v. City of Walnut Creek*, 4 Cal. 3d 633 (1971), wherein the court upheld a city's police power to require developers to dedicate land or pay fees for park and recreation purposes.

Along with this text, Dan authored the *Subdivision Map Act Manual*, published by Solano Press, the *Subdivision Map Act and the Development Process*, published by California Continuing Education of the Bar, as well as hundreds of articles. He was a frequent lecturer for University of California Extension and Continuing Education of the Bar (CEB) and was an adjunct professor for the University of San Francisco Law School teaching Land Use Law. He also traveled extensively to provide land use expertise to the international community and to several developing nations.

A native San Franciscan, Dan was raised by Irish-immigrant parents. He earned his A.B. and J.D. from the University of San Francisco. After serving as an officer in the U.S. Army for eight years, Dan worked as Assistant Secretary for the California State Senate, as Counsel to the Assembly Committee on Local Government, and Deputy City Attorney for Richmond. From 1965 to 1982, Dan served as City Attorney of Walnut Creek. Dan then entered private practice and, in 1984, joined Van Voorhis & Skaggs, which later became part of Bingham McCutchen, LLP, where he continued to practice until his death. Dan visited over 65 countries, including several trips to his beloved Ireland, and voyaged on 39 cruises, typically with many family members in tow.

While Dan's accolades and accomplishments are long, the list of planners and land use practitioners he guided and befriended is even longer. His skills as a mentor were legendary and Dan counted as friends virtually every planning director and city attorney in the state, as well as planning experts around the country and the world. He had an exceptional memory, often surprising people who had not seen him for many years by asking about their close relatives or children by name. Anyone involved in local government or land use in California knew of Dan or had been influenced by his work and teachings.

In a fitting tribute, the California League of Cities described Dan's most important contribution to the land use field:

> Dan's lasting professional legacy truly rests with his peers who loved and respected him. Dan was a mentor and a friend to two generations of land use professionals. He reveled in mentoring young attorneys and planners and making them feel part of his circle. He would take an interest in their careers and go out of his way to cite their work. Dan made his numerous friends feel like they were the most important person in his life. He loved hosting dinners at conferences and hearing about everyone's practices and his invitees relished the heady conversations and the wisdom he could share. His gracious, old-school style of lawyering and living—always courteous, respectful, and inquiring about family—will be enormously missed.

> The state of California is fortunate that Dan Curtin was so generous with his talent and shared his knowledge so freely. He trained countless lawyers, planners, commissioners, and elected officials. Many have asked, "who will replace him?" The answer is that this responsibility falls upon us all. He was a moral compass for the legal and planning profession. And now we must make our way without him.

Dan is survived by his younger sister, Kathleen Curtin, and his five children and eight grandchildren. Myrtle Rose, his wife of 46 years, passed away in 2005. Dan is deeply missed by the legion of colleagues for whom he was such a valued inspiration, resource, and most of all, friend.

Chapters at a Glance

1	Overview	1
2	General Plan	9
3	Specific Plan	39
4	Zoning	43
5	Subdivisions	79
6	California Environmental Quality Act (CEQA)	147
7	Federal and State Wetland Regulation	173
8	Endangered Species Protections	207
9	Design Review, Historic Preservation, Williamson Act, TDR, Water Supply, Coastal Development, and Other Development Regulations	233
10	Vested Rights—Development Agreements and Vesting Tentative Maps	269
11	Necessity for Findings	283
12	Takings	289
13	Exactions: Dedications and Development Fees	339
14	Initiative and Referendum	385
15	What Is Growth Management?	419
16	Local Agency Formation Commissions: Local Agency Boundary Changes	435
17	Rights of the Regulated and of the Citizens	455
18	Legal Liability of Local Agency and Its Personnel	469
19	Enforcement of Land Use Laws	475
20	Affordable Housing	483
21	Land Use Litigation	525
22	Conclusion	583

Contents

Preface xix
Conventions
in This Book xxii

1 Overview / 1

Police Power 1
Legislative Preemption 4
**State Statutory Framework
for Land Use Decisions** 5
City Council 6
Planning Commission 6
Planning Staff 7
Public Meetings 8

2 General Plan / 9

**The General Plan Before
1971—Advisory Status** 9
**The General Plan Today—
Constitution for Development** 9
  Introduction
  General Plan—The Constitution
  General Plan—Purposes and Contents;
  General Plan Guidelines
  Legal Adequacy of the General Plan
    Description of the mandatory elements •
    Optional (permissive) elements • Organization
  Legal Implications of Failure to Have
  a Legally Adequate General Plan
    CEQA • Charter cities
  Internal (Horizontal) Consistency
  Consistency Between General Plan and Other Land
  Use and Development Actions (Vertical Consistency)
  Consistency with Airport Land Use Plan
  Procedure for Adoption and Amendment
  Implementation and Annual Report
  Checklist for General Plan Adequacy
    Is it complete? • Is it informational, readable, and
    available to the public? • Is it internally consistent? •
    Is it consistent with state policy? • Does it cover all
    territory within and outside its boundaries that relate
    to its planning? • Is it long-term in perspective? • Does
    it address all locally relevant issues? • Is it current? •
    Does it contain the statutory criteria required by state
    law as interpreted by the courts? • Are the diagrams
    or maps adequate? • Does it serve as a yardstick? •
    Does it contain an action plan or implementation plan? •
    Is it horizontally consistent? • Was it adopted correctly?

  Adoption of General Plans by New Cities
  The General Plan as a Source of
  Dedications and Development Fees
  The General Plan as a Tool in Growth
  Management and Other
  Innovative Land Use Controls
  Judicial Review of the
  Adequacy of the General Plan
Conclusion 37

3 Specific Plan / 39

Overview 39
Contents 39
Adoption 40
Interplay with CEQA 40
Judicial Review 41

4 Zoning / 43

Zoning Defined 43
Application to Charter Cities 43
Judicial Review 43
  Presumption of Validity
  Limited Role of Court
  Review—Policy Issue
**Enactment of
Zoning Regulations** 45
  In General
  The Ordinance Must Be Reasonably
  Related to the Public Welfare
  Zoning Must Be Consistent
  with the General Plan
  Zoning Must Be Consistent
  with Airport Land Use Plan
  Due Process Requirements
  Sufficiency of Standards—
  Vagueness and Uncertainty
  Adoption of a Zoning Ordinance
  Motives
  Zoning by Initiative and/or Referendum
  No Formal Rules of Evidence;
  Effect of Procedural Errors

Contents

**Zoning and the
First Amendment** 53
   Regulation of Adult Businesses
   Protection of Religious Exercise

**Administrative Zoning Relief—
Variances—Conditional Use Permits** 59
   In General
   Variances
   Conditional Use Permit
   Nonconforming Uses—Amortization

Other Types of Zoning 65
   Form-Based Zoning
   Prezoning
   Interim Ordinance
   Conditional Zoning
   Specific Plan as Zoning
   Planned-Unit Development

**Inclusionary Zoning/
Housing Programs** 69

**Relationship of General Plan and
Zoning to Redevelopment Law** 70
   Conformity of the Redevelopment
   Plan to the General Plan
   Status of Zoning Classifications
   After Redevelopment Plan Adoption

**Applicability of Zoning
to the Federal and
State Governments** 72
   Federal Government
   State Government

**Applicability of Zoning to Joint
Powers Agencies, School Districts,
County, and Other Local Districts** 73

**Applicability of
Zoning to Indian Lands** 75

5 Subdivisions / 79

Overview 79
   The Subdivision Map Act
      Need for a local ordinance; applicable
      to charter cities • Preemption

**Subdivisions
Covered by the Map Act** 81
   What Is a Subdivision?

**What Type of
Map Is Required?** 85
   General Rule: Tentative
   and Final Map or Parcel Map?
   Counting Parcels
      Successive subdivisions • Remainder
      parcels • Conveyances to public
      entities and public utilities

**Important Exemptions
to Mapping Requirements** 87
   Lot Line Adjustments
   "Second" Units
   Conveyances to or from Public
   Entities and Public Utilities
   Financing and Leasing of Certain Units
   Condominium, Stock Cooperatives,
   and Community Apartment Projects
      Conversions • Three-dimensional divisions
   Agricultural Leases
   Other Exemptions
   Map Waivers
      Condominium projects • Mobile home parks
      conversions • Other parcel map waivers

Tentative Map Processing 92
   Tentative Maps
      Necessity for tentative maps • Local
      ordinances • Other regulations • Applicable
      time periods to act upon the tentative map
   Time Limits Imposed by
   the Permit Streamlining Act
      Notice and hearing; processing • Life of tentative
      maps • Development agreements • Discretionary
      extensions • Statutory extensions • Moratoria •
      Litigation stays • Summary • Conditions imposed
      on extensions • Expiration of other permits
      issued in conjunction with a tentative map
   Effect of Approval of Map on the
   Right to Develop—Vested Rights
   Vesting Tentative Map
      Background • Procedures
   Effect of Annexation to City Upon Maps
   Effect of Incorporation into
   a Newly Incorporated City

Conditions to Map Approval 107
   In General
   Conditions Imposed Through
   the Subdivision Process
   Specific Conditions Allowed by
   the Map Act and Local Ordinance
      Parkland dedication • Adequate water supply •
      School site dedication • Reservations • Street and
      bicycle path dedications • Dedication for local
      transit facilities • Fees for drainage and sewer
      facilities • Fees for bridges and major thoroughfares •
      Groundwater recharge • Supplemental improvements—
      reimbursement agreements • Soils investigations
      and reports • Setting of monuments • Grading and
      erosion control requirements • Public access to public
      resources and dedication of public easements along
      banks of rivers and streams • Energy conservation •
      Dedication for solar access easements • Indemnification •
      Off-site improvements • Standards and criteria for
      public improvements: residential subdivisions

Contents

Conditions Imposed Under City's Authority to Regulate "Design" and "Improvement" and Ensure General and Specific Plan Consistency

Map Act Requirements vs. General Plan Standards

Conditions That May Be Imposed Through the CEQA Process

Condominium, Stock Cooperative, and Community Apartment Project Conversions

Timing of Conditions and Subsequent Conditions

Refunds

Reconveyances

Grounds for Map Approval or Denial 121

Grounds for Approval

Grounds for Denial

Findings for Approval or Denial

Appeals and Judicial Review 123

Appeals

Judicial Review

Exhaustion of administrative remedies • Statute of limitations

Final Maps and Parcel Maps 126

Final Maps

Form and filing of final maps • Procedures for approval

Final Map Is Deemed Valid When Recorded

Filing of certificates and security for tax liens • Subdivider to provide evidence of consent of record title holders • Recorder has 10 days to accept or reject map for filing • Condominium, stock cooperatives, and community apartment project conversions • Dedications of streets, utilities, and other property • Improvement agreements

Improvement Security

Types of security • How much security is required? • Rights and requirements • Releasing security • Remedies

Parcel Maps

Local ordinance requirements • Parcel map requirements • Special case: four or fewer parcels and no dedications or improvements

Correction and Amendment of Maps 135

Grounds

Errors and omissions • Changed circumstances

Amendment Procedure

Changes Affecting Property Rights

Enforcement 136

Prohibition

Remedies of Private Persons

Remedies of a City

Certificates of Compliance

Exclusions and Reversions 139

Antiquated Subdivisions 140

Antiquated Subdivisions— Legally Created Parcels?

Maps Before 1929

Maps After 1893 Generally

U.S. Survey Maps and Federal Patents

Merger and Unmerger

Merging Parcels Under One Ownership

Presumption of Legal Parcels

Unmerger or Deemed Not to Have Merged

6 California Environmental Quality Act (CEQA) / 147

Overview 147

Definition of a Project Under CEQA 148

Approval

Environmental Change

Process 151

Determining If the Activity Is Exempt from CEQA

Preparation of an Initial Study

Adoption of a Negative Declaration

Preparation of an EIR

EIR Procedure

Scoping • Draft EIR • Final EIR

Contents of an EIR

Project description • Water supply • Evaluation of environmental impacts • Cumulative impacts • Mitigation • Project alternatives • Range of alternatives • Extent of discussion • Growth inducement

Recirculation of an EIR

Project Approval and Findings

Mitigation Monitoring and Reporting Programs

Supplemental and Subsequent EIRs

Use of an Addendum

EIR Deadlines and Required Notices

Judicial Challenges to Agency Action 172

Time Limits for Judicial Challenges

Judicial Review

Contents

7 Federal and State Wetland Regulation / 173

Introduction … 173
A Brief History of the Federal Program … 174
How "Wetlands" Are Defined Under the CWA … 175
Legal Definition of Wetlands … 175
Scientific/Technical Definition of Wetlands … 181
Activities Regulated by the Corps … 184
Statutory Exemptions … 185
Corps' Permitting Process … 186
    Nationwide Permits
Corps' Individual Permitting Process … 192
Alternatives Analysis Under EPA's 404(b)(1) Guidelines … 193
Project Purpose and Wetlands Avoidance (Sequencing) … 194
    Practicability
    Availability
    Mitigation
EPA's Role in the Permit Evaluation Process … 199
Other Federal Statutes … 200
    Section 401 of the Clean Water Act • National Environmental Policy Act • Endangered Species Act • Fish and Wildlife Coordination Act • Section 302 of the Marine Protection, Research and Sanctuaries Act of 1972 • National Historic Preservation Act of 1966 • Land Sales Full Disclosure Act • Coastal Zone Management Act of 1972 • Food Security Act of 1985
Regulatory Guidance Letters … 201
State Statutory Authority … 202
    Porter-Cologne Water Quality Control Act • Streambed Alteration Agreement • Navigation Dredging Permit • Coastal Zone Management
Enforcement … 204
    Criminal, Civil, and Administrative Penalties
        Class I administrative penalties • Class II administrative penalties
    The Enforcement Process and After-the-Fact Permits
Practical Considerations … 206

8 Endangered Species Protections / 207

Introduction … 207
Listing Process … 208
    Listing of a Species as Threatened or Endangered
    Designation of "Critical Habitat"
Consultation Process … 214
    Procedure
        Agency action • "May affect" trigger • Biological opinion • Reinitiation of consultation
Exemptions from the Endangered Species Act Requirements … 220
Prohibitions Against Takings … 222
Habitat Conservation Plans … 226
Judicial Review and Enforcement … 228
California Endangered Species Act … 230
    The CESA Listing Process
    "Take" Under CESA
    Incidental Take Permits Under CESA

9 Design Review, Historic Preservation, Williamson Act, TDR, Water Supply, Coastal Development, and Other Development Regulations / 233

Introduction … 233
Design Review … 233
Historic Preservation … 236
    Federal Level
    State Level
    Local Level
Preservation of Agricultural Lands by Williamson Act Contract … 238
Coastal Development … 242
    The California Coastal Act of 1976
    The California Coastal Commission
    Composition
    Constitutionality
    The Coastal Zone
    Development and Permitting
    Local Coastal Programs
    Appeals
    Judicial Review of Commission Decisions
    Other Coastal Commission Responsibilities
    The San Francisco Bay Conservation and Development Commission
    Composition
    Jurisdiction
    Permitting Authority

Contents

Transfer of Development Rights 249
Water Supply Planning 250
   Senate Bill 610—
   Water Supply Assessment
   Senate Bill 221—
   Water Supply Verification
Storm Water Quality Requirements for California Cities 262
Congestion Management and Land Use 263
   Introduction
   Adoption of a CMP
   Failure to Comply with the CMP
Prevailing Wage Concerns on Private Development Projects 265
Public Bidding Concerns on Private Development Projects 267

10 Vested Rights—Development Agreements and Vesting Tentative Maps / 269

Vested Rights 269
   The Avco Rule
   Refinements of the Avco Rule
Development Agreements 273
Vesting Tentative Maps 279
Vesting Tentative Maps vs. Development Agreements 280

11 Necessity for Findings / 283

Background 283
***Topanga:* The Cornerstone for Adjudicatory Findings Under Code of Civil Procedure Section 1094.5** 283
Purpose of Findings 283
Evidence in the Record to Support Findings 284
When Are Findings Required? 286
   Legislative Acts
   Nonlegislative Acts
   Dedications or Ad Hoc Impact Fees

12 Takings / 289

Takings 289
   Overview
   Federal Constitutional Standard
   Denial of Economically Viable Use

Temporary Takings—Interim Ordinances, Moratoria, and Other Growth Management Measures 301
   "Partial" Takings; Segmentation—the Relevant Parcel Issue 306
Remedies for Excessive Land Use Regulation—Damages 309
Measurement of Damages 313
   Permanent Takings
   Temporary Takings
The Importance of Properly Calculating Damages 316
   Duration of Temporary Taking
   Measuring Compensation
   Summary
The Ripeness Issue—When Is a "Takings" Claim Ripe for Judicial Determination? 320
   The Final Determination of the Agency
   Seeking Compensation Through State Procedures
The Illegal Condition Must First Be Challenged in Court as Invalid Before Damages Are Sought for Inverse Condemnation 328
   The Direction of the California Courts After the First English, Nollan, Lucas, and Dolan Decisions
Civil Rights Action 330
Damages Resulting from Constitutional Violations—Due Process and Equal Protection 332

13 Exactions: Dedications and Development Fees / 339

Overview 339
The Proper Exercise of Police Power 340
Development: A Privilege or a Right? 340
Test of Reasonableness/Nexus Requirement 342
   In General
   U.S. Supreme Court Case Law—The Nollan and Dolan Decisions
     Nollan v. California Coastal Commission • Dolan v. City of Tigard • What does Dolan mean in California?

Contents

Applicability of the Nollan/Dolan Test
to Impact Fees: Ehrlich v. Culver City
  Factual situation • Judicial proceedings • The decision:
  new distinction—legislatively formulated vs. ad hoc
  development fees • $280,000 recreational mitigation
  fee • Art in public places fee • Mitigation Fee Act

Summary of Impacts of Ehrlich

San Remo Hotel Reaffirms Ehrlich 355

**California's "Nexus Legislation"—
The Mitigation Fee Act** 358
  Documenting the Nexus

Double Taxation 360

Equal Protection 361

**Opportunities for
Dedications or Fees** 362
  In General
  The General Plan
  Subdivision Process
  Building Permits

School District Facilities Fee 365
  Background
    Leroy F. Greene School Facilities Act of 1998 (SB 50) •
    Nonprofit private university is not exempt from
    school • Redevelopment construction is not exempt
    from school fees • Level of scrutiny for school fees
  Habitat Conservation Plans
  CEQA

**Special Requirements
Relating to Imposition of Fees** 370
  Waiting Period Before Fees Become
  Effective; Public Hearing Required
  When Fees Are Required to Be Paid
  Reasonableness of
  Development Fee Amount
  Fees Cannot Be Levied for
  Maintenance and Operation

**Dedication of Land—
Reconveyance to Subdivider** 372

Development Fee or a Tax? 372
  Historical Background
  Effect of Jarvis Initiatives—Proposition 13 (1978),
  Proposition 62 (1986), and Proposition 218 (1996)
    Proposition 218 • Impacts on local general taxes •
    Impacts on local special taxes • Impacts on special
    assessments • Impacts on fees and charges •
    Possible impacts on new development fees •
    Impacts on standby charges • Use of initiatives
  Conditions Attached to Land Use Approvals
  for Financing and Maintaining Public Facilities
    GHADs in particular • Burden
    of proof and interpretation

**Processing Fees—Land Use
and Building Permits** 382
Judicial Review 383
Conclusion 383

14 Initiative and Referendum / 385

Overview 385
The Initiative 386
The Referendum 387
  Procedural Requirements for
  Placing an Initiative or Referendum
  Measure on the Ballot
  Form of Petition
  Notice of Intention to Circulate;
  Ballot Title and Summary
  Publication and Posting
  Circulation; Signature
  Filing; Examination
  of Signatures
  Pre-Election Invalidation of Initiatives
  and Referenda for Failure to Comply
  with Procedural Requirements
  Action by Local Legislative Bodies
  on Initiatives and Referenda

**Limitations on the Use of
Initiative and Referendum** 396
  Constitutional Limitations
    Single subject rule •
    Cannot conflict with state law
  Judicial Limitations
    Cannot invade a duty imposed on an
    "agent of the state" • Cannot be an improper
    exercise of the police power • Cannot be
    inconsistent with the General Plan • Cannot
    affect non-legislative matters • Cannot impair
    an essential governmental function

**Initiatives and Referenda
Are Not Subject to the Same
Procedural Requirements
as City Council Measures** 404

**Pre-election Challenges
to Initiatives and Referenda** 408

**Initiatives Limiting Housing:
Burden of Proof** 411

**Conflicting Initiatives
on the Same Ballot** 412

**Restrictions on a City's
Role in Campaigns** 414

Conclusion 415

Contents

15 What Is Growth Management? / 419

    Types of Growth Management Measures 420
    California Growth Management Measures—Ballot Box Planning 422
    Problems with Certain Slow-Growth Measures 424
    Legality of Growth Management 424
        The Proper Exercise of the City's Police Power
        Planned Growth Ordinances
    Introduction to "Smart Growth" 427
    Barriers to Smart Growth 428
        APA's Growing Smart Legislative Guidebook
        ABAG's Smart Growth/Regional Livability Footprint Project
        Smart Growth Is Not Going Away
    Surviving Growth Management Regulations, Including Initiatives: Tools Developers Can Use 433
    Initiatives 433

16 Local Agency Formation Commissions: Local Agency Boundary Changes / 435

    Introduction 435
    Legislative Development of LAFCO Law 435
    Composition and Function of LAFCOs 437
    Spheres of Influence 438
        Municipal Service Review Requirement
    Boundary Changes 440
        Procedures for Boundary Changes
        Factors LAFCO Must Consider When Reviewing a Boundary Change Proposal
        Reconsideration Hearing
        Protest Proceedings
        Final Actions, Filings, and Notifications
        Processing Multi-County Changes of Organization or Reorganization
        Environmental Review

17 Rights of the Regulated and of the Citizens / 455

    In General 455
    Notice and Hearing 455
    The One Who Decides Must Hear 457
    Maintaining Separation Between Prosecutorial and Adjudicatory Function 458
    Ralph M. Brown Act 459
    Ex Parte Contacts 462
    Permit Streamlining Act 463
    Other Procedural Matters 468
    Developer Misrepresentations 468
    Standing to Sue 468

18 Legal Liability of Local Agency and Its Personnel / 469

    In General 469
    The California Tort Claims Act 469
        Liability of Public Employees and Entities
            Employees • Entities
        Immunity of Public Employees and Entities
    The Federal Civil Rights Act 471
        Color of Law
        Treatment of Public Entities Under Section 1983: Municipal Liability and Legislative Immunity

19 Enforcement of Land Use Laws / 475

    Introduction 475
    Administrative and Criminal Sanctions 475
        Misdemeanor
        Infraction
    Administrative Penalties 476
    Warrant 476
    Enforcement Under the Revenue and Taxation Code 477
    Enforcement Under the Subdivision Map Act 477
    Enforcement Under CEQA 477
    Enforcement Under the Business and Professions Code 478
    Possible Defenses to a City's Enforcement Action 478
        Denial of Due Process or Equal Protection
        Estoppel

Contents

20 Affordable Housing / 483

Introduction: The Affordable Housing Crisis In California 483

State Housing Element Law 484

Purpose of the Mandated Housing Element

Required Contents of the Housing Element

Regional Housing Needs Allocation Process

Preparing the Land Inventory and Identifying Adequate Sites

Analysis of Governmental and Non-Governmental Constraints

Consistency with General Plan, Preparation of Annual Report, and Notification Requirements

Special Provisions Regarding Housing Needs Within the Coastal Zone

Review and Certification of Housing Elements

Anti-Nimby Laws—Restrictions on the Disapproval of Certain Housing Projects 492

Affordable Housing Projects Under Government Code Section 65589.5(d)

Housing Development Projects Generally Under Government Code Section 65589.5(j)

Prioritization of Services to Certain Affordable Housing Projects

Special Treatment for Affordable Multi-Family Housing Projects

Other State Laws Designed to Facilitate Housing Production 497

Least Cost Zoning Law

Density Bonuses

Second Units

Community Redevelopment Law

Growth Management and Affordable Housing 503

Tension Between Environmental Protection and Affordable Housing

Special Legislative and Judicial Requirements for Growth Management Measures

Inclusionary Housing 506

Introduction

Judicial Treatment of Inclusionary Zoning

History of Inclusionary Housing—

The Pre-Nollan and Dolan Era

Inclusionary Housing in California in the Post-Nollan and Dolan Era

Legal Issues to Consider When Adopting and Implementing an Inclusionary Housing Program

Method of Enactment

Factual Record to Support Enactment and Application

Inclusion of "Safety Valve" Provisions

Provision of Incentives and Concessions to Developers

Relationship to the Costa-Hawkins (Anti-Rent Control) Act

Policy Issues to Consider When Crafting an Inclusionary Housing Program

Nature of the Program— Mandatory or Voluntary?

Determining the Classes and Size of Development That Will Be Subject to the Inclusionary Housing Program

Required Amount and Affordability Levels of Inclusionary Units

Timing Issues and Design Standards for Inclusionary Units

Preserving Affordability of Inclusionary Units

Rent and Price Limitations

Qualification of Beneficiaries

Length of Time That Inclusionary Units Must Remain Affordable

Enforcement and Monitoring Mechanisms

21 Land Use Litigation / 525

Introduction 525

Overview and Terminology 525

Types of Mandate Proceedings 526

Traditional Mandate Proceedings Under Section 1085 Challenge Legislative and Ministerial Acts

Legislative acts • Ministerial acts

Administrative Mandate Proceedings Under Section 1094.5 Challenge Administrative and Quasi-Judicial Decisions

Administrative Mandate Is the Exclusive Procedure for Challenging Administrative Decisions 530

Contents

Standards Courts Apply in Reviewing Land Use Decisions 531
    Standard of Judicial Review of Legislative Decisions
        The "arbitrary-and-capricious" standard of review • Individual legislator's motives are irrelevant • The intent and purpose of the legislative body is relevant • Due process and fair hearing requirements
    Standard of Judicial Review of Administrative Decisions
        "Excess of jurisdiction" • "Fair hearing" • "Proceeding in the manner required by law" • "Supported by the findings and evidence"
    Standard of Judicial Review of Agency Decisions with Both Legislative and Administrative Aspects
    Standard of Judicial Review of an Aspect of an Agency Decision That Interprets or Applies Law

Deadlines for Bringing Actions 539
    How to Find the Applicable Statute of Limitations

Process of a Mandate Proceeding 545
    Prerequisite to Litigation: Exhaustion of Administrative Remedies
        The common law exhaustion doctrine • The exhaustion requirement has two components • Issue exhaustion • Appeal exhaustion • Rehearing/Reconsideration • Exceptions to the exhaustion requirement • Codification of the exhaustion requirement
    Identifying the Proper Parties
        Petitioner • Beneficial interest • Citizen's action • Taxpayer suits • Respondent • Real party in interest
    Joining Other Causes of Action with a Writ Claim
    Preparation of the Record
    Discovery and Evidence Outside the Record
        Evidence outside the record generally is inadmissible and undiscoverable to determine whether a local agency's decision is valid • Evidence outside the record regarding issues other than the validity of a local agency's decision generally is admissible and discoverable • Evidence outside the record may be admissible in traditional mandate proceedings that challenge ministerial acts • Evidence regarding the decisionmaker's thought processes is not admissible or discoverable • Judicial notice of matters outside the record

    Setting a Briefing and Hearing Schedule
        Alternative writ • Noticed motion • Informal means of obtaining hearing date
    Summary Judgment
    Preparing the Briefs
    A Stay or Preliminary Injunction May Issue Pending a Final Decision on the Writ Petition
        Stays • TROs and preliminary injunctions
    Issuance of the Writ
    Appeal in a Writ of Mandate Case
        Time to appeal • Effect of appeal on judgment • Administrative mandate • Traditional mandate • Injunction

Litigation Under CEQA 568
    Special Procedures for CEQA Actions
    Contents of a CEQA Record
        Presenting comments to the local agency
    Standard of Judicial Review of CEQA Decisions
    Remedies in a CEQA Case

Litigation Under the Mitigation Fee Act 573
    Challenge to Imposition of Fees on a Development Project
    Challenge to Enactment or Increase of Certain Fees
    Remedy

The Anti-SLAPP Statute 579
    Application of the Anti-SLAPP Statute to the Land Use Context
        CEQA issues have also been addressed in SLAPP decisions

Attorneys' Fees in Land Use Cases 580

22 Conclusion / 583

Short Articles

Calculating the Life of a Tentative Map 99

Map Act Definitions of Design and Improvement 115

Nationwide Permits — Permit Number/Activity 187

Contents

List of Figures

Figure A
Certificate of Compliance
Flow Chart 137

Figure B
CEQA Flow Chart
for Local Agencies 156

Figure C
Lead Agency Decision
to Prepare an EIR 157

Figure D
Time Periods for Review of
Environmental Documents 165

Figure E
Scope of Corps
Regulatory Jurisdiction 177

Figure F
U.S. Army Corps of Engineers
Permitting Process 190

Figure G
LAFCO Proceedings 444

List of Tables

Table 1
Comparison of
SB 610 and SB 221 251

Table 2
A Comparison of California's
Vested Rights Statutes 281

Table 3
LAFCO Protest Proceedings—
Effect of Protests 447

Table 4
Statutes Applicable to
Common Land Use Decisions 542

Glossary / 585

Suggested Reading / 595

Table of Authorities / 599

Index / 631

Preface

For twenty-seven years, Dan Curtin authored this book as a handy desk reference for those interested in California land use and planning law. Beginning in 2000, Dan and I worked together drawing on our own and our partners' decades of experience representing both public agencies and private developers. Dan unexpectedly passed away in November 2006. Like the 2007 edition, this edition is dedicated to him. It covers all aspects of land use law, and is updated annually to reflect changes in statutes, case law, and practice.

This edition includes new or expanded discussions of several topics of interest, including:

- A comprehensive review of recent CEQA decisions, with a particular emphasis on the principles governing the adequacy of an EIR's analysis of water supply issues (chapter 6)
- Significant updates to chapter 7 (Wetlands) and chapter 8 (Endangered Species), including an analysis of the Corps' and the EPA's joint guidance concerning the *Rapanos* decision and federal wetlands jurisdiction
- Extensive review and analysis of affordable housing case law and legislation (chapter 20), with an extensive review of recent case law concerning density bonus incentives and concessions
- A thorough discussion of the circumstances under which administrative remedies must be exhausted and what constitutes a "remedy" (chapter 21)
- All of the significant 2007 California legislation, including flood control legislation in chapter 2 (General Plan) and chapter 4 (Zoning), strengthened housing element law in chapter 20 (Affordable Housing), and LAFCO law (chapter 16)
- All of the significant 2007 California land use case law

As in previous years, the 2008 edition has benefited from the contributions made by many of my partners and associates in Bingham McCutchen's Environmental and Land Use Groups. Barbara Schussman, a partner with our Land Use Group in Walnut Creek, authored chapter 6 (CEQA). Ms. Schussman has extensive experience litigating land use and environmental cases on behalf of public agencies and private entities, as well as providing comprehensive CEQA compliance advice. Her recent practice includes advising the Ports of Oakland and Stockton for their maritime projects, defending the Ports in CEQA litigation regarding expansion of their projects, and advising Stanford University in securing land use entitlements for the coming decade of campus growth. Ms. Schussman received her law degree in 1989 from Boalt Hall School of Law at the University of California, Berkeley, where she was elected to the Order of the Coif. She received her bachelor's degree in Communication Studies, magna cum laude, from the University of California, Los Angeles, where she was elected to Phi Beta Kappa.

This year's edition also has benefited from updated discussions on Federal and State Wetlands Regulation and the Endangered Species Protections (chapters 7 and 8) authored by Marc R. Bruner. Marc represents governmental entities and private companies in a wide variety of environmental and land use matters, focusing on litigation and counseling under the California Environmental Quality Act, the National Environmental Policy Act, the federal Clean Water Act, the Federal Endangered Species Act, and California laws and regulations regarding water quality and endangered species. Marc litigates in the state and federal courts, at both the trial and appellate level. He also advises clients in preparing environmental studies and processing environmental and land use permits and approvals for a broad range of public and private projects, including residential subdivisions, large commercial and mixed-use developments, airport and maritime expansion projects, industrial facilities, and major university campus projects. He speaks regularly on a variety of environmental and land use topics. Prior to joining the firm, Marc practiced environmental and land use law at Wilmer, Cutler & Pickering (now Wilmer Cutler Pickering Hale & Dorr) and Cutler & Stanfield (now Akin Gump) in Washington, D.C. He clerked for the Honorable Jose A. Cabranes, chief judge of the U.S. District Court for the District of Connecticut, from 1993 to 1994.

Additionally, this edition continues to benefit greatly from the discussion of Land Use Litigation (chapter 21), co-authored by two of Bingham McCutchen's top land use litigators, Geoffrey Robinson and Marie Cooper. Mr. Robinson and Ms. Cooper have brought their collective 40-plus years of land use litigation experience to bear in this practical and informative approach to land use litigation. Mr. Robinson is a partner in Bingham McCutchen's Walnut Creek office. He graduated with distinction from the University of California, Berkeley in 1978 and attended law school at the University of Virginia and Hastings College of the Law, from which he received his law degree with honors in 1983. After serving as an extern and a law clerk in two federal courts, Mr. Robinson has represented clients in civil litigation and administrative proceedings involving real estate, planning and zoning laws, CEQA, development fees and exactions, and Mello-Roos community facilities financing. Ms. Cooper, counsel in Bingham McCutchen's Walnut Creek office, graduated Order of the Coif from Boalt Hall School of Law in 1984. After serving as an extern for the California Supreme Court, Ms. Cooper has focused her practice on land use litigation and transactional work, at both the trial and appellate court levels. She frequently addresses issues arising under the planning and zoning laws, CEQA, and water rights law. She also has substantial experience challenging and defending land use entitlements, general plan and zoning enactments, fees and dedications, proceedings under the Cortese-Knox-Hertzberg Act, initiatives and referenda, and in inverse condemnation actions. Ms. Cooper also assisted in updating chapter 9 (Design Review and Other Development Regulations) and chapter 16 (LAFCOs).

I also wish to thank the following individuals in the Walnut Creek office of Bingham McCutchen for their contributions to this 2008 edition: Camarin Madigan, associate attorney, for her extensive efforts in reviewing and editing the entire text of this edition, as well as for her assistance in revising and updating chapters 2 (General Plan), 4 (Zoning), 9 (Design Review and Other Development Regulations), 10 (Vested Rights), 12 (Takings), 13 (Exactions), 14 (Initiatives and Referendum), 16 (LAFCOs), 17 (Rights of the Regulated), 18 (Legal Liability of Local Agency and Its Personnel), and 19 (Enforcement of Land Use Laws); Matthew Gray, partner, for his assistance in updating chapter 5 (Subdivision Map Act); Joshua Safran, associate attorney, for his assistance in updating chapter 9 (Design Review and Other Development Regulations) and 20 (Affordable Housing); Nadia Costa, associate attorney, for her assistance in updating chapters 16 (LAFCOs) and 20 (Affordable Housing); Marcos Getchell, our legal assistant, for compiling new land use legislation and cite-checking; Marsha Curtis, Administrative Assistant, for preparing all of the revised text; Sam DeSa, our intern, for preliminary research and editing; and Cynthia Nall, Office Administrator, for production and scheduling.

This book is not a substitute for the guidance and advice of an attorney, especially in complex matters in which refinements and interpretations of the law are essential before final conclusions are drawn about planning and development processes, property rights, due process, and procedural matters.

In addition, although legal reference points are essential, in matters pertaining to local public planning and the development process, there is no substitute for an understanding of how the planning process works at the city and county levels. Much of the process is delineated by California law and indeed most of the process is mandated. The law does not say a great deal, however, about what local planning policies should be or how a city or county should organize its land uses. That is a local task. But the law does require cities and counties to prepare, adopt, and update general plans before making land use and land use-related decisions, and it requires that certain procedures be followed to carry out public policies, protect private rights, and ensure due process prior to making decisions. I hope you find this book a helpful guide to better understanding how those mandates and procedures may be applied at the local level.

Cecily T. Talbert
December 2007

Conventions in This Book

For brevity and readability, this text uses the following conventions:

- When the word "city" is used, it also means "county"; "city council" also means "county board of supervisors." The text will note instances where there is a substantive distinction between how land use and planning law affects cities and counties.
- All references to the Legislature are to the California State Legislature, unless otherwise indicated.

Code references are to the California Code, unless otherwise indicated.

Overview

Police Power

The legal basis for all land use regulation is the police power of the city to protect the public health, safety, and welfare of its residents. *See Berman v. Parker*, 348 U.S. 26, 32–33 (1954). A land use regulation lies within the city's police power if it is reasonably related to the public welfare. *See Associated Home Builders, Inc. v. City of Livermore*, 18 Cal. 3d 582, 600–01 (1976).

As Justice William O. Douglas, speaking for the United States Supreme Court, stated about the police power:

> An attempt to define its reach or trace its outer limits is fruitless, for each case must turn on its own facts. The definition is essentially the product of legislative determinations addressed to the purposes of government, purposes neither abstractly nor historically capable of complete definition....
>
> Public safety, public health, morality, peace and quiet, law and order—these are some of the more conspicuous examples of the traditional application of the police power to municipal affairs. Yet they merely illustrate the scope of the power and do not delimit it. The concept of the public welfare is broad and inclusive.... The values it represents are spiritual as well as physical, aesthetic as well as monetary. It is within the power of the legislature to determine that the community should be beautiful as well as healthy, spacious as well as clean, well balanced as well as carefully patrolled.

Berman, 348 U.S. at 32–33 (citations omitted)

This statement is recognized by California courts as "a correct description of the authority of a state or city to enact legislation under the police power." *Metromedia, Inc. v. City of San Diego*, 26 Cal. 3d 848, 861 (1980).

The police power, even though recognized by common law, is set forth in the California Constitution, which confers on cities the power to "make and enforce within [their] limits all local police, sanitary and other ordinances and regulations not in conflict with general laws." Cal. Const. art. XI, § 7.

The California Supreme Court has stated:

> Under the police power granted by the Constitution, counties and cities have plenary authority to govern, subject only to the limitation that they exercise this power within their territorial limits and subordinate to state law. [Citation

The legal basis for land use regulation is the police power of a city to protect the public health, safety, and welfare of its residents.

The police power, even though recognized by common law, is set forth in the California Constitution.

omitted.] Apart from this limitation, the "police power [of a county or city] under this provision...is as broad as the police power exercisable by the Legislature itself."

Candid Enters., Inc. v. Grossmont Union High Sch. Dist., 39 Cal. 3d 878, 885 (1985)

Land use regulations are a manifestation of the local police powers conferred by the California Constitution, not an exercise of authority delegated by statute.

Land use regulations are a manifestation of the local police powers conferred by the California Constitution, not an exercise of authority delegated by statute. *See Scrutton v. County of Sacramento*, 275 Cal. App. 2d 412, 417 (1969). For example, state zoning laws pertaining to adoption of local zoning regulations are not intended as specific grants of authority, but as minimum standards to be observed in local zoning practices. As stated by the California Supreme Court:

> We have recognized that a city's or county's power to control its own land use decisions derives from this inherent police power, not from the delegation of authority by the state. *See, e.g., Candid Enters., Inc. v. Grossmont Union High Sch. Dist.*, 39 Cal. 3d 878, 885–86 (1985) (upholding a school facilities impact fee imposed by a county without statutory authorization); *Birkenfeld v. City of Berkeley*, 17 Cal. 3d 129, 140–42 (1976) (upholding city rent control initiative despite lack of express statutory authority).

DeVita v. County of Napa, 9 Cal. 4th 763, 782 (1995). *See also Big Creek Lumber Co. v. City of Santa Cruz*, 38 Cal. 4th 1139, 1151 (2006) (land use regulation in California historically a function of local government under the grant of police power contained in the California Constitution)

The police power allows cities to tailor regulations to suit the interests and needs of a "modern, enlightened and progressive community" even as those interests and needs change.

The police power is an elastic power. It allows cities to tailor regulations to suit the interests and needs of a "modern, enlightened and progressive community" even as those interests and needs change. *Rancho La Costa v. County of San Diego*, 111 Cal. App. 3d 54, 60 (1980). Regulations are sustained under current complex conditions that but a short time ago might have been condemned as arbitrary and unreasonable. *See Village of Euclid v. Ambler Realty Co.*, 272 U.S. 365, 387 (1926).

In the 1970s, Justice Douglas, speaking for the United States Supreme Court, upheld a village's zoning ordinance relating to land use restrictions on single-family dwelling units. His opinion identified the interests that supported the village's exercise of its police power at the time:

> A quiet place where yards are wide, people few, and motor vehicles restricted are legitimate guidelines in a land use project addressed to family needs. This goal is a permissible one within *Berman v. Parker, supra*. The police power is not confined to elimination of filth, stench, and unhealthy places. It is ample to lay out zones where family values, youth values, and the blessings of quiet seclusion and clean air make the area a sanctuary for people.

Village of Belle Terre v. Boraas, 416 U.S. 1, 9 (1974)

Today, many cities face needs and interests different than those identified in *Village of Belle Terre*. Regulations permitting smaller yards, denser housing, and narrower streets, so as to provide more housing within already developed areas, now address some cities' changing needs. Such regulations are as proper an exercise of a city's police power as were those in *Village of Belle Terre*, thanks to the elasticity of that power. However, a city's police powers may be limited by the California State Legislature. *See* Legislative Preemption, in this chapter.

An expansive range of interests can support a city's exercise of its police power. The California Supreme Court has held that aesthetic reasons alone can justify the exercise of the police power. *Ehrlich v. City of Culver City*, 12 Cal. 4th 854, 881–82 (1996) (upholding a city's public art fee ordinance); *Metromedia, Inc. v. City of San Diego*, 26 Cal. 3d 848, 858–59 (1980) (upholding in part a city's total ban of offsite advertising signs).

The United States Supreme Court also upheld land use regulations citing aesthetics as a valid rationale. In upholding a local ordinance prohibiting the posting of signs on public property, the Court stated that aesthetic concerns are substantial governmental interests properly addressed under a city's police power. *See City Council v. Taxpayers for Vincent*, 466 U.S. 789, 805 (1984). Similarly, in upholding New York City's Landmark Preservation Law, the Court approved of the city's use of its police power to enhance the quality of life by preserving "desirable aesthetic features of a city." *Penn Cent. Transp. Co. v. City of New York*, 438 U.S. 104, 129 (1978).

The United States Supreme Court has upheld land use regulations citing aesthetics as a valid rationale.

A city's ability to limit big-box retail stores was recently upheld on police power grounds in *Wal-Mart Stores, Inc. v. City of Turlock*, 138 Cal. App. 4th 273 (2006). Wal-Mart challenged a city zoning ordinance prohibiting the development of discount superstores as exceeding the police power. The court held that the police power empowers cities to "control and organize development within their boundaries as a means of serving the general welfare." *Id.* at 303.

Courts have held that regulations affecting economic interests in real property also are an appropriate exercise of the police power. *See, e.g., Birkenfeld v. City of Berkeley*, 17 Cal. 3d 129, 158 (1976) (regulations implementing local rent control laws are valid); *Griffin Dev. Co. v. City of Oxnard*, 39 Cal. 3d 256, 261–62 (1985) (regulations relating to condominium conversions are proper).

Although it did not directly address the police power, the United States Supreme Court, in *Kelo v. City of New London*, demonstrated the breadth of this power in holding that a city may condemn land for the purpose of economic development. 545 U.S. 469 (2005).

Protection of a city's "character," "stability," and "soul" has served to justify invocation of the police power. In *Ewing v. City of Carmel-by-the-Sea*, homeowners challenged the constitutionality of a zoning ordinance prohibiting transient commercial use of residential property for remuneration for less than 30 consecutive days. 234 Cal. App. 3d 1579 (1991). The homeowners claimed the ordinance was a taking, was void as arbitrary and vague, and violated their right of privacy. In ruling for the city, the court held that the ordinance was a proper exercise of the city's land use authority under its police power "to enhance and maintain the residential character of the city." *Id.* at 1590. The court stated that this is a wholly proper purpose of zoning:

Protection of a city's "character," "stability," and "soul" has served to justify invocation of the police power.

> It stands to reason that the "residential character" of a neighborhood is threatened when a significant number of homes—at least 12 percent in this case, according to the record—are occupied not by permanent residents but by a stream of tenants staying a weekend, a week, or even 29 days.... [Transient] rentals undoubtedly affect the essential character of a neighborhood and the stability of a community. Short-term tenants have little interest in public agencies or in the welfare of the citizenry. They do not participate in local government, coach little league, or join the hospital guild. They do not lead a Scout

troop, volunteer at the library, or keep an eye on an elderly neighbor. Literally, they are here today and gone tomorrow without engaging in the sort of activities that weld and strengthen a community.

Id. at 1591

In holding that the ordinance was related to a legitimate governmental goal, the court continued:

> Blessed with unparalleled geography, climate, beauty, and charm, Carmel naturally attracts numerous short-term visitors. Again, it stands to reason that Carmel would wish to preserve an enclave of single-family homes as the heart and soul of the city. We believe that this reason alone is "sufficiently cogent to preclude us from saying, as it must be said before the ordinance can be declared unconstitutional, that such provisions are clearly arbitrary and unreasonable, having no substantial relation to the public health, safety, morals or general welfare." [Citation omitted.]

Id. at 1591–92

Judicial review of a city's exercise of its police power is closely circumscribed. The California Supreme Court established the following rule:

> It is a well settled rule that determination of the necessity and form of regulations enacted pursuant to the police power "is primarily a legislative and not a judicial function, and is to be tested in the courts not by what the judges individually or collectively may think of the wisdom or necessity of a particular regulation, but solely by the answer to the question is there any reasonable basis in fact to support the legislative determination of the regulation's wisdom and necessity?"

Consolidated Rock Prods. Co. v. City of Los Angeles, 57 Cal. 2d 515, 522–23 (1962)

The California Supreme Court has stated that a land use restriction withstands constitutional attack if it is fairly debatable that the restriction in fact bears a reasonable relation to the general welfare.

Predictably, this test has resulted in substantial judicial deference when reviewing a city's decision to exercise the police power. *See Remmenga v. California Coastal Comm'n*, 163 Cal. App. 3d 623, 629 (1985); *Santa Monica Beach Ltd. v. Superior Court*, 19 Cal. 4th 952, 962–63 (1999) (advocating a hands-off policy for reviewing local legislative acts). Indeed, so long as "it is fairly debatable that the restriction in fact bears a reasonable relation to the general welfare," a land use regulation should withstand constitutional attack. *Associated Home Builders, Inc. v. City of Livermore*, 18 Cal. 3d 582, 601 (1976).

In exercising the police power, the city must act within all applicable statutory provisions so there will be no "conflict with general laws." The city's actions also must meet constitutional principles of due process: they must be reasonable and nondiscriminatory, and not arbitrary or capricious. *See, e.g., G & D Holland Constr. Co. v. City of Marysville*, 12 Cal. App. 3d 989, 994 (1970).

Legislative Preemption

As broad as its police power is, a city cannot act where the California State Legislature has enacted laws which completely occupy the field. *See, e.g., Morehart v. County of Santa Barbara*, 7 Cal. 4th 725, 747 (1994); *People ex rel. Deukmejian v. County of Mendocino*, 36 Cal. 3d 476, 483–85 (1984). Under the California Constitution, a city's ordinance cannot conflict with the state's general laws that preempt the subject matter.[1] A conflict exists between a local ordinance and state

---

1. For an excellent discussion of preemption, *see Preemption of Local Land Use Authority in California* (Governor's Office of Planning and Research, 1989).

law if the ordinance "duplicates, contradicts or enters an area fully occupied by general law, either expressly or by legislative implication." *Viacom Outdoor, Inc. v. City of Arcata*, 140 Cal. App. 4th 230, 236 (2006). For example, the recently expanded Housing Accountability Act directs local jurisdictions with regards to housing elements and affordable housing, and preempts a city's discretion to deny certain types of affordable housing projects. Gov't Code § 65589.5. Another example is Government Code section 65858 relating to interim ordinances, which preempts the field of "moratorium" ordinances. *See Bank of the Orient v. Town of Tiburon*, 220 Cal. App. 3d 992, 1001 (1990) (city's interim moratorium ordinance may not exceed the two-year maximum prescribed in state law). *See also Morehart*, 7 Cal. 4th at 761 (county's zoning ordinances relating to merger of antiquated lots were impliedly preempted by the merger provisions of the Subdivision Map Act). The scope of the state's preemption can be broad. For example, the Legislature has adopted health and safety policies and criteria for establishment of certain types of selected residential uses that preempt local zoning. *See* Health & Safety Code § 1597.40(a) (preempting local zoning and other regulations with respect to family day care homes); Health & Safety Code § 1566.3 (preempting local zoning with respect to residential facilities serving six or fewer mentally disabled or handicapped persons). However, preemption may not be found where the Legislature has not fully occupied a subject matter. For example, in *Viacom Outdoor, Inc. v. City of Arcata*, the city's demand that the owner obtain a permit to rebuild storm-damaged billboards pursuant to its building and sign codes was not preempted by state law because the state law (the California Outdoor Advertising Act) did not categorically prohibit local legislation and explicitly invited augmentation from local authorities. 140 Cal. App. 4th at 246.

The scope of the state's preemption can be broad. However, preemption may not be found where the Legislature has not fully occupied a subject matter.

Under the Supremacy Clause of the United States Constitution, Congress may preempt both state and local law through federal regulation. For example, the Federal Telecommunications Act (47 U.S.C. § 253) precludes states and cities from passing laws that would prohibit any entity from providing telecommunications services. In *Qwest Communications, Inc. v. City of Berkeley*, the city's telecommunications ordinance was pre-empted by section 253 because it burdened city service providers with regulations and requirements that had the effect of prohibiting companies from providing telecommunication services in the city. 433 F. 3d 1253, 1257–58 (9th Cir. 2006).

Under the Supremacy Clause of the United States Constitution, Congress may preempt both state and local law through federal regulation.

State Statutory Framework for Land Use Decisions

The following state laws provide most of the legal framework within which a city must exercise its police power in the context of land use regulation:

- Establishment of local planning agencies, commissions, and departments. Gov't Code § 65100 *et seq.*
- General and specific plans. Gov't Code § 65300 *et seq.*
- Zoning regulations. Gov't Code § 65800 *et seq.*
- Subdivision Map Act. Gov't Code § 66410 *et seq.*
- Development agreements. Gov't Code § 65864 *et seq.*
- California Environmental Quality Act. Pub. Res. Code § 21000 *et seq.*; Cal. Code Regs. tit. 14, §§ 15000–15387 (also known as the CEQA Guidelines)

CEQA = California Environmental Quality Act

- Ralph M. Brown Act. Gov't Code § 54950 *et seq.* (also known as the Open Meeting Act, or simply the Brown Act)
- Permit Streamlining Act. Gov't Code § 65920 *et seq.*
- Mitigation Fee Act. Gov't Code § 66000 *et seq.*

The City Council

The city council of a general law city is made up of five council members, one of whom is the mayor.[2] Gov't Code §§ 36501, 34900, 36801. The mayor has the duty of presiding at all meetings of the city council. Gov't code § 36802. In a chartered city, organization and power of the city's government is subject to control by the city's charter, which may provide for a different number of council members. Cal. Const. Art. XI § 5(a); *Socialist Party v. Uhl*, 155 Cal. 776 (1909).

The city council makes three types of decisions: legislative, quasi-judicial, and ministerial. Legislative acts are general policy decisions, such as general plan revisions (*see* chapter 2) and zoning ordinances (*see* chapter 4). Legislative acts are binding only when they are approved by the city council. Quasi-judicial acts are decisions that apply legislative policy to individual development projects. These decisions are generally made by the city council or the planning commission. Ministerial acts are those acts in which the city has no discretion, such as the mandatory issuance of a permit if certain conditions are met. Because they involve no discretion, ministerial decisions are often delegated to city staff.

The Planning Commission

The planning commission is a permanent committee of five or more citizens who have been appointed by the city council, or the mayor in some cities, to review and act on matters related to planning and development.

*A city need not create a planning commission. Gov't Code § 65101. In fact, in some jurisdictions, especially smaller ones, there is no planning commission and the city council serves in that capacity. Gov't Code §§ 65100, 65101.

The planning commission holds regularly scheduled public hearings to consider land use matters, such as the general plan, specific plans, zonings and rezonings, use permits, and subdivisions.[3] Depending upon a city's local ordinance, planning commission membership may change at the pleasure of the mayor or council, or at the expiration of fixed terms.[4] In general law cities with an elected mayor, the mayor appoints, but such appointments must be approved by the council. Gov't Code § 40605; 89 Ops. Cal. Atty. Gen. 178, Opinion No. 05-914 (Aug. 14, 2006).

A city council may assign any or all of the following tasks to its planning commission:

---

2. The governing body of a county is generally the board of supervisors. Cal. Const. Art. XI § 1(b); Gov't Code § 23005.
3. In some cities, some of these matters also may be considered by a zoning administrator or a design or architectural review board.
4. Suggested reading material for planning commissioners includes:
   - *The Planning Commissioner's Book* (Governor's Office of Planning and Research, 1998)
   - *Planning Commissioner's Handbook* (League of California Cities, 2004)
   - William Fulton and Paul Shigley, *Guide to California Planning* (Solano Press, 3rd ed. 2005)

OPR = Governor's Office of Planning and Research

- Assist in writing the general plan and community or specific plans, hold public hearings, and recommend action on proposed amendments to such plans. Gov't Code §§ 65103, 65353
- Investigate and make recommendations to the city council regarding reasonable and practical means for implementing the general plan or elements of the general plan, so that it will serve as an effective guide for orderly growth and development, preservation and conservation of open space and natural resources, and the efficient expenditure of public funds relating to the subjects addressed in the general plan. Gov't Code § 65400
- Provide an annual report to the city council on the status of the general plan and progress in its implementation, including progress in meeting the city's share of regional housing needs, local efforts to remove governmental constraints on housing, and compliance of the general plan with the guidelines in the Government Code. Gov't Code §§ 65584, 65583(c)(3), 65040.2
- Hold hearings and make recommendations on proposed changes to the city's zoning ordinances and zoning maps. Gov't Code § 65854
- Hold hearings and act on subdivision maps. Gov't Code § 66452.1
- Annually review the city's capital improvement program and the public works projects of other local agencies for consistency with the general plan. Gov't Code §§ 65401, 65403
- Consult with and advise public officials and agencies, utilities, organizations, and citizens regarding implementation of the general plan, and promote public interest in the general plan. Gov't Code § 65351
- Coordinate local plans and programs with those of other public agencies. Gov't Code § 65352
- Report to the city council on the conformity of proposed public land acquisition or disposal with the adopted general plan. Gov't Code § 65402
- Undertake special planning studies as needed. Gov't Code § 65101

Most often, the commission acts in an advisory capacity to the city council on land use matters. In some instances, the commission's decision on a project is referred to the city council as a recommendation for action (*e.g.*, general plan amendments and rezonings). In other instances, depending on state law and local ordinance provisions, it is considered a final action unless appealed to the council (*e.g.*, subdivisions, variances, and use permits). If a matter has been referred or appealed to the council, it may choose to follow the recommendation of the commission, reverse or modify the commission action, or send the project back to the commission for further review.

Planning Staff

A city's community development or planning department is the commission's and city council's staff. These city planners advise the commission or council on the city's general plan, specific plans, zoning ordinance, subdivision ordinance, and other land use regulations. In addition, they provide background information and recommendations on the proposals that are under consideration, answer technical questions, and make sure that meetings have been properly noticed. The commission and council also are advised by other members of the city's staff, including the city attorney's office and the public works department.

Most often, the commission acts in an advisory capacity to the city council on land use matters. In some instances, the commission's decision on a project is referred to the city council as a recommendation for action.

Public Meetings

The planning commission and city council hold regular meetings and special meetings as needed. Although usually held separately, such hearings may be jointly noticed and held, if both bodies agree to a joint hearing process.

The planning commission and city council hold regular meetings and special meetings as needed. Although usually held separately, such hearings may be jointly noticed and held, if both bodies agree to a joint hearing process. For the most part, state law requires public hearings before planning actions are taken. At its meetings, the planning commission weighs all city and planning proposals in light of federal, state, and local regulations and potential environmental effects; it also listens to testimony from citizens and other interested parties. If necessary, the commission or council generally (though not always) may continue a hearing to a later time to allow more information to be gathered or to take additional testimony. The commission and council usually consider several items at each hearing, considering each item separately and taking action before moving on to the next item on the agenda.

Pursuant to the Brown Act, all meetings, including study sessions and workshops, must be open and public.

Pursuant to the Brown Act, all meetings, including study sessions and workshops, must be open and public. Gov't Code § 54950 *et seq*. This means that a quorum of commissioners can discuss commission business only in a public meeting. For a more thorough discussion of the Brown Act and its restrictions for communications between members of the public and members of the commission or council, *see* chapter 17 (Rights of the Regulated and of the Citizens).

2
General Plan

The General Plan Before 1971–
Advisory Status [1]

The general plan is a city's basic planning document. It provides the blueprint for development throughout the community, and is the vehicle through which competing interests and the needs of the citizenry are balanced and meshed. The general plan addresses all aspects of development, including housing, traffic, natural resources, open space, safety, land use, and public facilities.

Before 1971, the general plan was considered to be an advisory document. Government Code section 65860 then read, "No county or city shall be required to adopt a general plan prior to the adoption of a zoning ordinance." In 1971, the Government Code was expanded to require that all land use approvals be consistent with a city's general plan. *See DeVita v. County of Napa*, 9 Cal. 4th 763, 772 (1995). Indeed, perhaps the most significant change in California planning law and practice in the past three decades is the key role played by a city's general plan.

The General Plan Today–
Constitution for Development
Introduction

In 1971, the general plan consistency doctrine was imposed in California when the Legislature directed that a city's zoning and subdivision approvals must be consistent with an adopted general plan. *See DeVita*, 9 Cal. 4th at 772 (citing this book).

The initial 1971 legislation[2] and subsequent amendments require cities to "engage in the discipline of setting forth their development policies, objectives and standards in a general plan composed of various elements of land use." 58 Ops. Cal. Atty. Gen. 21, 23 (1975). The general plan thus was

The general plan provides the blueprint for development throughout the community, and is the vehicle through which competing interests and the needs of the citizenry are balanced and meshed.

In 1971, the general plan consistency doctrine was imposed in California when the Legislature directed that a city's zoning and subdivision approvals must be consistent with an adopted general plan.

---

1. For a good history of planning law in California, starting with the adoption of the first planning law in 1927 by the Legislature, *see* the dissent by J. Arabian in *DeVita v. County of Napa*, 9 Cal. 4th 763, 808–13 (1995). *Also see* William Fulton and Paul Shigley, *Guide to California Planning* (Solano Press, 3rd ed. 2005) for an excellent discussion of how planning really works in California.
2. 1971 Cal. Stat. ch. 1446 (McCarthy legislation).

transformed from an "interesting study" to the basic land use charter that embodies fundamental land use and planning decisions and governs the direction of future land use in a city's jurisdiction. *See City of Santa Ana v. City of Garden Grove*, 100 Cal. App. 3d 521, 532 (1979); *see also DeVita*, 9 Cal. 4th at 763. Today, the general plan requirements are set forth in Government Code section 65300 *et seq.*

General Plan—The Constitution

> *In 1990, the California Supreme Court finally held that the general plan was the constitution for all future development.*

Although the consistency doctrine has been in effect since 1971,[3] it was not until 1990 that the California Supreme Court finally held that the general plan was the "constitution for all future development." *Lesher Communications, Inc. v. City of Walnut Creek*, 52 Cal. 3d 531, 540 (1990). The Court confirmed the general plan as the single most important planning document. *See also Citizens of Goleta Valley v. Board of Supervisors*, 52 Cal. 3d 553, 570–71 (1990).

In *Lesher*, the California Supreme Court struck down a growth management initiative that conflicted with the City of Walnut Creek's general plan. 52 Cal. 3d at 544. *Lesher* thus marked the first occasion where the Court squarely addressed the general plan's position in the planning hierarchy, and especially its interplay with the initiative process.

Lesher arose from a challenge to Measure H, a traffic-based growth management initiative adopted by Walnut Creek voters in 1985. The trial court had determined that Measure H was not a general plan amendment but rather a zoning ordinance or other land use regulation. As a mere regulation, Measure H was required to be consistent with the city's general plan. Because it was not consistent, the trial court declared it invalid. This holding was overturned on appeal. The Court of Appeal agreed that Measure H was inconsistent with the city's general plan, but interpreted it as a general plan amendment in order to give the greatest possible protection to the initiative process. The California Supreme Court rejected this interpretation and struck down the initiative, thereby upholding the trial court's decision.

The Court began its decision by emphasizing that all laws are subject to the same constitutional and statutory limitations and rules of construction, whether enacted by the local legislative body or the electorate. Focusing on the absence of any ballot materials that labeled Measure H a general plan amendment, as well as the detailed scope and self-executing nature of its text (resembling a zoning ordinance), the Court ruled that Measure H was a land use regulation subordinate to the city's general plan and therefore invalid under the consistency doctrine. "The tail does not wag the dog," pronounced the Court. *Lesher*, 52 Cal. 3d at 541.

> *Under* Lesher, *any subordinate land use action that is not consistent with a city's current general plan is invalid at the time it is passed.*

Therefore, under *Lesher*, any subordinate land use action, such as a zoning ordinance, tentative map, or development agreement, that is not consistent with a city's current general plan is "invalid at the time it is passed." *Id.* at 544. A court's only task is to determine whether a conflict exists. It does

---

3. *See* Daniel J. Curtin, Jr., "The Comprehensive Plan as Constitution: General Lessons from Recent California Zoning Initiative Cases," *Zoning and Planning Law Handbook* (Kenneth H. Young, ed., Clark, Boardman, and Callaghan, 1992). *See also* Daniel J. Curtin, Jr., "Ramapo's Impact on the Comprehensive Plan," 35 *Urban Lawyer*, no. 135 (Winter 2003).

not matter how the conflict arises; if it is present, under state law, the city's action is void.

In *Goleta Valley*, the Court reiterated its statements in *Lesher* that the general plan is the "'constitution for all future developments' within the city or county" to which any local decision affecting land use and development must conform. 52 Cal. 3d at 570. In light of the importance attached to general plans, the Court also noted that planning efforts must remain current: "Local agencies must periodically review and revise their general plans as circumstances warrant...." *Id.* at 572.

The supremacy of the general plan was reinforced in *Mira Mar Mobile Community v. City of Oceanside*, where a court held that a local coastal program had become part of the city's general plan and therefore had become part of the "constitution" for future development in that community. 119 Cal. App. 4th 477, 494 (2004). In *Friends of Lagoon Valley v. City of Vacaville*, the court emphasized that a general plan provides "a charter for future development" and sets forth "a city or county's fundamental policy decisions about such development." 154 Cal. App. 4th 807, 815 (2007) (citing *Federation of Hillside and Canyon Assns. v. City of Los Angeles*, 126 Cal. App. 4th 1180, 1194 (2004)). The court conceded that these policies "typically reflect a range of competing interests," but then stated that a city's land use decisions must nevertheless be consistent with the policies expressed in that city's general plan. *Id.*

PRACTICE TIP

Since the general plan is a city's constitution for all future development, before purchasing property, check the text and diagrams of the general plan, as well as all of the local land use policies and regulations affecting the property.

General Plan—
Purposes and Contents;
General Plan Guidelines

Under state planning law, a city's general plan must include a comprehensive, long-term plan for the physical development of both the city and any land outside the city's boundaries that the city determines relates to its planning. Gov't Code § 65300. The general plan shall consist of a "statement of development policies," and must include diagrams and text setting forth "objectives, principles, standards, and plan proposals." Gov't Code § 65302. The general plan must consist of seven mandatory elements—land use, circulation, housing, conservation, open space, noise, and safety—and any optional element that a city chooses to adopt. Gov't Code § 65302.

The general plan must consist of seven mandatory elements and any optional element that a city chooses to adopt.

The Governor's Office of Planning and Research (OPR) must develop and adopt guidelines for the preparation and content of the seven mandatory elements. Gov't Code § 65040.2. These general plan guidelines must include guidelines for associated environmental justice matters, and advice for collaborative land use planning of adjacent civilian and military lands and facilities, as well as advice for addressing the effects of civilian development on military readiness activities. In 2003, OPR issued a revised edition of the General Plan Guidelines, which added the following:

OPR = Governor's Office of Planning and Research

- Guidance for addressing environmental justice in the general plan
- Guidance on developing optional water and energy elements
- Expanded guidance on public participation in the development of the general plan
- Revised and expanded housing element guidelines

- Expanded guidance on consolidation of individual general plan elements
- Suggested reporting formats for the annual general plan progress report[4]

In 2004, the Legislature added a requirement that the Guidelines also contain advice for consulting with California Native American tribes for preservation of Native American places, features, and objects. Gov't Code § 65040.2(g). The courts have held that the guidelines are merely advisory and not mandatory; however they provide assistance to a court in determining compliance with the general plan laws. *See Twain Harte Homeowners Ass'n v. County of Tuolumne*, 138 Cal. App. 3d 664 (1982).

Except for mandating development and adoption of a general plan, specifying the elements to be included, and imposing on cities the general requirement that land use decisions be guided by that plan, the Legislature has not preempted the decision-making power of local legislative bodies as to the specific contours of the general plan or actions taken under it. *See DeVita v. County of Napa*, 9 Cal. 4th at 763, 783 (1995).

In sum, the preparation, adoption, and implementation of a general plan serves to:

- Identify the community's land use, circulation, housing, environmental, economic and social goals and policies as they relate to land use and development
- Provide a basis for local government decisionmaking, including decisions on development approvals and exactions
- Provide citizens with opportunities to participate in the planning and decision-making processes of their community
- Inform citizens, developers, decisionmakers, and other cities of the ground rules that guide development within the community

Thus, the general plan bridges the gap between community values, visions, and objectives on the one hand, and physical decisions such as subdivisions and public works projects on the other.

Legal Adequacy of the General Plan

To be legally adequate, a plan must show substantial compliance with the statutory requirements for general plans.

The key to the validity of the general plan is legal adequacy. To be legally adequate, a plan must show "substantial compliance with the statutory requirements" for general plans. *See Camp v. Board of Supervisors*, 123 Cal. App. 3d 334, 348 (1981). On this point the court in *Garat v. City of Riverside* stated:

[T]he standards of adequacy are defined by the statutes related to general plans. Turning to those statutes, the following statutory requirements, for example, are necessary for an adequate general plan:

a. A general plan must be "comprehensive" and "long-term." (Gov't Code § 65300).

b. The plan and its elements and parts must comprise "an integrated, internally consistent and compatible statement of policies...." (Gov't Code § 65300.5).

---

4. For further discussion on these and other changes, *see* the Introduction to OPR's General Plan Guidelines (2003), page 8 *et seq.*

c. The plan must address all the elements specified in section 65302, *i.e.*, land use, circulation, housing, conservation, open space, noise, and safety. (Gov't Code §§ 65301, 65302). The degree of specificity and level of detail shall reflect local conditions and circumstances. (Gov't Code § 65301).

d. The required elements must meet the criteria, if any, set out in section 65302. For example, the components of the circulation element must be correlated with the land use element. (Gov't Code § 65302(b)).

It follows that even though a plan or its parts may not, from a court's subjective point of view, be "satisfactory" or "suitable," unless there is a statutory requirement on point, such unsatisfactoriness or unsuitability may not form a basis for concluding that the plan is legally inadequate.

2 Cal. App. 4th 259, 293 (1991) (overruled on other grounds in *Morehart v. County of Santa Barbara*, 7 Cal. 4th 725, 743 n.11 (1994))

There is a presumption that a city's general plan is valid and that official duties have been regularly performed. Therefore, the burden is on those challenging the plan to demonstrate that the plan is inadequate, except in the case of growth management provisions, where the burden of proof is shifted to the city. *See Hernandez v. City of Encinitas*, 28 Cal. App. 4th 1048, 1072 (1994). The challenger also must demonstrate the existence of a nexus between any plan inadequacies and the project or action being challenged. *See Garat*, 2 Cal. App. 4th at 293.

There is a presumption that a city's general plan is valid and that official duties have been regularly performed.

Pursuant to 2007 legislation, each city within the Sacramento-San Joaquin Valley must, within 24 months of the Central Valley Flood Protection Board's adoption of a specified flood protection plan, amend its general plan to address flood protection. Gov't Code § 65302.9(a).

Description of the mandatory elements. Government Code section 65302 mandates that a general plan contain seven mandatory elements: land use, circulation, housing, conservation, open space, noise, and safety.[5]

According to Government Code section 65302, a general plan must contain seven mandatory elements: land use, circulation, housing, conservation, open space, noise, and safety.

Land use element. The land use element of a general plan must identify the proposed general distribution and intensity of uses of the land for housing, business, industry, open space, natural resources, public facilities, waste disposal sites, and other categories of public and private uses. This element serves as the central framework for the entire plan and is intended to correlate all land use issues into a set of coherent development policies. Its goals, objectives, policies, programs, diagrams, and maps relate directly to the other elements. *See* Gov't Code § 65302(a).

While all general plan elements generally carry equal weight legally, in practice the land use element is the most visible and frequently used. *See Sierra Club v. Board of Supervisors*, 126 Cal. App. 3d 698, 708 (1981).

The land use element must include standards of population density (measured in numbers of persons) and building intensity (using measures such as site coverage, floor-to-area ratio, building type and size, or units per acre). *See Twain Harte Homeowners Ass'n v. County of Tuolumne*, 138 Cal. App. 3d 664, 696–97 (1982); *Camp v. Board of Supervisors*, 123 Cal. App. 3d 334, 349 (1981). The land use element also must identify areas subject to flooding and parcels designated for timberland production. With the passage of 2007 legislation, flood areas

---

5. *See* chapter 4 of OPR's General Plan Guidelines (2003) for a detailed discussion of the seven mandatory elements of the general plan.

must include those identified by flood plain maps prepared by the Federal Emergency Management Agency or the State Department of Water Resources. Gov't Code § 65302(a). In addition, the law requires general plans to account for growth of military activities at bases, ports, airports, or other training installations. Gov't Code § 65302(a)(2). Legislation passed in 2004 provides that the text and diagrams in the land use element may express community intentions regarding urban form and design. Gov't Code § 65302.4.[6] For a discussion of form-based zoning, *see* chapter 4 (Zoning).

Circulation element. The circulation element must identify the general location and extent of existing and proposed major thoroughfares, transportation routes, terminals, and other local public utilities and facilities. It serves as an infrastructure plan and must correlate with the remaining elements of the plan, including the land use element. *See Concerned Citizens of Calaveras County v. Board of Supervisors*, 166 Cal. App. 3d 90, 94 (1985).

The circulation element both determines and constrains the pattern and extent of development.

The circulation element both determines and constrains the pattern and extent of development. Generally, this element contains detailed maps, standards for operation (*e.g.*, traffic level of service), policies (*e.g.*, promoting disabled accessibility), and financing plans. Specific circulation components addressed by this element may include, among many others, public transit, bicycle facilities, parking, truck routes, sewage transport and treatment, electric and gas transmission lines, drainage facilities, and waterways. Gov't Code § 65302(b).

While cities generally have considerable flexibility in drafting elements of the general plan, the housing element must comply with the elaborate statutory provisions of article 10.6 of the Government Code.

Housing element.[7] While cities generally have considerable flexibility in drafting the elements of the general plan, the housing element must comply with the elaborate statutory provisions of article 10.6 of the Government Code (Gov't Code § 65580 *et seq.*). Government Code section 65583 establishes the required contents of a housing element. Among other things, the housing element must contain an assessment of the jurisdiction's existing and projected housing needs. This needs assessment must include the jurisdiction's fair share of regional housing needs in accordance with Government Code section 65584. Gov't Code § 65583(a). It must also contain a land inventory (Gov't Code § 65583(a)(3)), and must identify adequate sites to provide for the needs of households at all income levels. The element also must contain an analysis of governmental and nongovernmental constraints, and include a statement of the community's goals, policies, quantified objectives, financial resources, and scheduled programs for the preservation, improvement, and development of housing. Gov't Code § 65583. In adopting a housing element, a city must consider economic, environmental, and fiscal factors, as well as community goals set forth in the general plan. Gov't Code § 65580(e).

---

6. *See* Rebecca Retzlaff, "California Enacts Form-Based Zoning Legislation," *Zoning Practice*, pages 10–11 (APA, January 2005) (discussing California's form-based zoning law which seeks to integrate streets, open space, housing, commercial development, and neighborhoods, rather than grouping similar and related land uses). *See also* Carla M. Moynihan, "Implementing Form-Based Zoning in Your Municipality," 47 *Municipal Lawyer* 15 (IMLA July/August 2006); Robert J. Sitkowski & Brian W. Ohm, *Form-Based Land Development Regulations*, 38 The Urban Lawyer 163 (Winter 2006); William Fulton, "Transition Away from Suburbia Bolsters Form-Based Zoning Movement," 21 *Cal. Plan. & Dev. Rep.* 1 (April 2006); Michael Moore, "Form-Based Zoning Is Not the (Whole) Answer," *APA Northern News*, page 1 (May/June 2006).

7. For a detailed discussion of the issues of affordable housing and requirements under state housing element law, *see* chapter 20.

In evaluating the adequacy of a housing element, a court will limit its review to determining whether a city has "substantially complied" with the statutory requirements, and will not engage in an examination of the merits. *Hernandez v. City of Encinitas*, 28 Cal. App. 4th 1055 (1994) (a city's housing element withstood attack by low-income and homeless petitioners since it complied with statutory requirements). *But see Hoffmaster v. City of San Diego*, 55 Cal. App. 4th 1098, 1111 (1997) (providing guidance regarding what constitutes "substantial compliance").

In enacting these requirements, the Legislature declared that the availability of housing is a matter of "vital statewide importance," and "the early attainment of decent housing and a suitable living environment for every Californian, including farmworkers, is a priority of the highest order." Gov't Code § 65580(a). The housing "goal requires cooperative participation between government and the private sector," and among all levels of government, and the use of state and local governmental power "to facilitate the improvement and development of housing...[for] all economic segments of the community." Gov't Code §§ 65580(b)–(d).

At least one court has highlighted the role of the housing element by describing the Legislature's intent to ensure that cities recognize their responsibility to adopt housing elements that contribute to the attainment of state housing goals. *See Committee for Responsible Planning v. City of Indian Wells*, 209 Cal. App. 3d 1005, 1013 (1989).

In some respects, the housing element has been elevated above other required elements of the general plan. Under Government Code section 65589.5(d), a city may not deny specific types of affordable housing projects or condition approval of such a project in a manner that makes the project infeasible unless certain findings are made, such as the project would have a specific adverse impact upon the public health and safety that cannot be satisfactorily mitigated without rendering it unaffordable. For further discussion on the Housing Element, Density Bonus, and Anti-Nimby laws, *see* chapter 20 (Affordable Housing).

In some respects, the housing element has been elevated above other required elements of the general plan.

The housing element shall be reviewed "as frequently as appropriate" in order to evaluate progress made and any changes in conditions affecting a city's housing needs. It must be revised as necessary, but not less often than once every five years. Gov't Code § 65588(a), (b). Although the timetable for cities to revise their housing elements is set forth in Government Code sections 65588 and 65588.1, failure to comply with the timetable will not automatically invalidate a general plan or its housing element. *See San Mateo County Coastal Landowners' Ass'n v. County of San Mateo*, 38 Cal. App. 4th 523, 544 (1995) (to invalidate a housing element on the basis that it has not been timely revised, plaintiff must show how the failure to timely revise is connected to a substantive deficiency in the general plan or the housing element). This revision schedule is unique to the housing element; the remainder of the general plan need be reviewed only periodically and updated only when warranted by changing circumstances. Gov't Code § 65103(a); *see also Citizens of Goleta Valley v. Board of Supervisors*, 52 Cal. 3d 553, 572 (1990); *Garat v. City of Riverside*, 2 Cal. App. 4th 259, 298 (1991).

The housing element shall be reviewed "as frequently as appropriate" in order to evaluate progress made and any changes in conditions affecting a city's housing needs, but not less often than once every five years.

Special attention is given and detailed provisions are applied to housing needs within the state's coastal zone. Gov't Code §§ 65588(d), 65590, 65590.1.

Conservation element. The conservation element of the general plan must address the identification, conservation, development, and use of natural resources including water, forests, soils, waterways, wildlife, and mineral deposits. Gov't Code § 65302(d). This element may consider issues such as flood control, water and air pollution, erosion, conversion of farmland, endangered species, and timing and impact of mining and logging activities. Moreover, under flood control legislation enacted in 2007, any revision to this element that occurs after January 1, 2009 must identify the following: rivers, creeks, streams, flood corridors, riparian habitat, and land that may accommodate floodwater for purposes of groundwater recharge and storm water management. Gov't Code § 65302(d). While there may be some overlap with other elements of the plan, such as the open space and safety elements, the conservation element's primary focus is on natural resources. The portion of the conservation element addressing water issues must be developed in coordination with all local agencies that deal with water in that community.

The conservation element must include mineral resource management policies to address the conservation and development of identified mineral deposits designated by the state geologist as being of statewide or regional significance. The goal is to balance the value of those deposits against competing land uses that may prevent future access to the minerals, and to minimize the impact of mining activities. Pub. Res. Code § 2761 *et seq.*

Open space element. The open space element is the plan for the "comprehensive and long-range preservation and conservation of open space land...." Gov't Code § 65563. Under the Government Code, "open space" includes open space for the preservation of natural resources, for the managed production of resources, for outdoor recreation, for public health and safety, in support of military installations, and protection of Native American artifacts, sites, and remains. Gov't Code § 65560(b).

Legislation passed in 2004 added a requirement that open space for preservation of Native American historical, cultural, and sacred sites be addressed in an open space plan. Gov't Code § 65560(b)(5). Where land designated or proposed to be designated as open space contains such sites, the city must consult with the tribe as to the level of confidentiality required to protect the site and as to the treatment of the site in any management plan. Gov't Code § 65562.5.

State law mandates an ambitious and detailed planning effort for open space that is comparable only to the requirements for the housing element. The open space element "shall contain an action program consisting of specific programs which the legislative body intends to pursue...." Gov't Code § 65564. That action program must include the adoption of an open space zoning ordinance consistent with the element (Gov't Code § 65910) that, among other things, designates exclusive agricultural zones, large-lot zones, and special overlay requirements for hazard areas, but without taking or damaging private property without compensation. Gov't Code §§ 65910, 65912. The open space element also must contain goals and policies for preserving and managing open space and an inventory of all open space property, whether privately or publicly owned. Gov't Code §§ 65560, 65563, 65564; *see also Save El Toro Ass'n v. Days*, 74 Cal. App. 3d 64, 72 (1977).[8]

The primary purpose of the open space element is "[t]o assure that cities and counties recognize that open space land is a limited and valuable resource which must be conserved wherever possible," and to discourage "premature and unnecessary conversion of open space land to urban uses...and non-contiguous development patterns...." Gov't Code §§ 65561(a)–(b). To this end, building permits, subdivision maps, and open space zoning ordinances that are inconsistent with the local open space plan are specifically forbidden. Gov't Code § 65567.

Noise element. The noise element must identify and appraise noise problems in the community. To the extent practicable, current and projected noise levels are calculated and mapped for roadways, railroads, airports, industrial plants, and other major noise sources. Gov't Code § 65302(f).

The noise element must identify and appraise noise problems in the community.

Projected noise levels are used as a guide for establishing a pattern of land uses in the land use element that minimizes the exposure of community residents to excessive noise. Implementation measures and possible solutions to noise problems must be included in the noise element. Gov't Code § 65302(f); *see also Camp v. Board of Supervisors*, 123 Cal. App. 3d 334, 352 (1981). These measures may involve sound barriers to shield noise-sensitive land uses (*i.e.*, hospitals, schools, and housing), restricted operating hours for stationary noise generators, protective building design, and location of new roadways. Noise element guidelines issued by the State Office of Noise Control, as well as the state's noise insulation standards, must be considered and applied during preparation of the noise element. Gov't Code § 65302(f).

Safety element. The safety element must establish policies and programs to protect the community from risks associated with seismic, geologic, flood, and wildfire hazards. Known seismic and other geologic hazards (*i.e.*, landslide areas) must be mapped, and issues such as emergency evacuation routes and water supply for fire fighting must be addressed. Gov't Code § 65302(g).

The safety element must establish policies and programs to protect the community from risks associated with seismic, geologic, flood, and wildfire hazards.

Moreover, concern about vulnerabilities in the Sacramento-San Joaquin Valley region triggered a spate of flood legislation in 2007, adding a number of requirements. Gov't Code § 65302(g)(2). In addition to identifying various hazards, the safety element now must establish a set of comprehensive goals, policies, and objectives that would protect a given community from the unreasonable risks of flooding. *Id.* A public entity, prior to revising its safety element, also must consult with the Department of Conservation's Division of Mines and Geology and with the Office of Emergency Services. The public entities must submit a draft of the amended safety element to such agencies for review. Further, each city and county located within the boundaries of the Sacramento and San Joaquin Drainage District must submit a draft of the safety element to the newly created Central Valley Flood Protection Board, as well as to every local agency that provides flood protection to territory in the city or county. *Id.*

Consistent with the goals of the safety element, a statewide program has been established to identify and work to mitigate potentially hazardous buildings

---

8. For a discussion of fees in the context of open space programs, *see Funding Open Space Acquisition Programs: A Guide for Local Agencies in California* (Institute for Local Government, League of California Cities, 2005).

located within dangerous seismic areas. Gov't Code §§ 8875–8876. The program requires local building departments to identify potentially hazardous buildings within their jurisdictions, including the current building use and daily occupancy load. It also requires that building owners be notified that the building is considered to be at risk in an earthquake. Building departments must establish mitigation programs for identified buildings which may include measures to strengthen buildings, and a variety of incentives including low-cost seismic rehabilitation loans. Gov't Code § 8875.2. The program does not require the state or any local government to assume the cost associated with compliance. It also gives such governments immunity from liability for action or inaction under the program. Gov't Code § 8875.3.

The safety element is the major tool for identifying hazards that should be considered in preparing the land use element and other elements of the general plan, and should be consulted before making land use decisions. The policies and programs in the safety element usually are supported by detailed maps of fault zones, mudslides, watercourse and oceanside flooding, dam collapse inundation areas, ground subsidence, vegetation density/slope combinations for fire risk, and other safety-related concerns. Some cities expand the safety element to cover a broad range of safety-related issues that may be locally relevant, such as the use, transport, and disposal of hazardous materials, power failure, and vehicle accidents.

Each city is required to consult with the Division of Mines and Geology of the Department of Conservation and to include in the safety element information available from both the Division and the Office of Emergency Services. Gov't Code § 65302(g). A city must submit a copy of the draft element or amendment to the Division for its review and comment at least 45 days prior to the adoption or amendment of the safety element. Gov't Code § 65302.5. The Division is authorized to report its findings to the city's planning commission for its consideration within 30 days of receipt of the draft element or amendment. *Id.*

The Division's findings must be considered by a city prior to final adoption of the element or amendment, unless such comments are not available within the 45-day period, or where the Division has indicated it will not review the element. After the safety element is adopted, a copy of the adopted element or amendment must be submitted to the Division.

In addition, any county containing a "state responsibility area" and any city or county containing a very high fire hazard severity zone must submit its safety element for review and comment by the State Board of Forestry and Fire Protection and any local agencies that provide fire protection to the city or county. Gov't Code §§ 65302.5(a)(1)–(a)(2). The city or county must submit its existing safety element for such review by dates established in Government Code section 65302.5(a)(2). Where a city or county proposes to adopt a new safety element or amend its safety element, it shall submit the draft element or proposed amendment to the reviewing Board and local fire agencies at least 90 days prior to adoption or amendment. Gov't Code §§ 65302.5(a)(1)–(a)(2). The Board shall, and the local agency may, report recommendations to the city's planning commission or the county's board of supervisors within 60 days of receipt of the existing or draft safety element. Gov't Code § 65302.5(a)(3).

Prior to its adoption of a draft safety element or draft amendment, the city or county shall consider the Board's and the local agency's recommendations. If the city or county declines to accept some or all of the recommendations, it must communicate its reasons in writing to the Board or the local agency. Gov't Code § 65302.5(b). If the Board's or local agency's recommendations are not available within the above timeframes, the city or county may act without them. Gov't Code § 65302.5(c).

Statutory criteria for mandatory elements. To be legally adequate, the mandatory elements of the general plan must meet the minimum requirements contained in state law. *See Hernandez v. City of Encinitas*, 28 Cal. App. 4th 1048, 1070 (1994); *Buena Vista Gardens Apartments Ass'n v. City of San Diego*, 175 Cal. App. 3d 289, 298 (1985); *Concerned Citizens of Calaveras County v. Board of Supervisors*, 166 Cal. App. 3d 90, 95 (1985); *Twain Harte Homeowners Ass'n v. County of Tuolumne*, 138 Cal. App. 3d 664, 696 (1982); *Camp v. Board of Supervisors*, 123 Cal. App. 3d 334, 352 (1981). Thus, it is imperative that a city make sure that statutory criteria are contained in the mandatory elements.

To be legally adequate, the mandatory elements of the general plan must meet the minimum requirements contained in state law.

In *Camp*, the court addressed the fatal inadequacies of the county's noise element:

> The so-called "noise element" of the Mendocino County General Plan is set out in a separate pamphlet which shows that it was adopted by the Board in 1976.... It includes no "noise exposure information... presented" in the technical nomenclature ("CNEL" and "Ldn") required... [and] shows nothing "determined by monitoring" with regard to "areas deemed noise sensitive" as required by the next paragraph of the statute.... For these reasons and others, it does not substantially comply with the requirements of section 65302, subdivision (g).
>
> The County asserts that it is "certainly adequate for [a] quiet rural county such as Mendocino," but the test is neither geographical nor subjective: it is purely statutory, and the County has failed it.

123 Cal. App. 3d at 352

In *Twain Harte*, the court found the county's general plan legally inadequate for several reasons. It provided no basis for correlation between the measure of dwelling units per acre and numbers of people, and no standards for building intensity for the nonresidential areas of the county. 138 Cal. App. 3d at 669 (1982). The land use element failed to include standards of population density and building intensity as required by Government Code section 65302(a), and the circulation element was fatally flawed because the court could not determine from the evidence whether the circulation element was correlated with the land use element, as required by Government Code section 65302(b). *Id.* at 700–02.

In *Concerned Citizens*, the court stated that the correlation between the land use and circulation elements required by Government Code section 65302(b) could not be achieved if the general plan called for solving traffic deficiencies by simply asking other governmental agencies for money. 166 Cal. App. 3d at 99.

In *Buena Vista Gardens*, the court held that a permit for a planned residential development could not be approved until the city demonstrated that its plan included housing development programs to "conserve and improve the condition of existing affordable housing stock" as required by Government Code section 65583(c)(4). 175 Cal. App. 3d at 303.

Thus, it is imperative that a city ensure that all of the statutory criteria are contained in the mandatory elements of its general plan.

Optional (permissive) elements. In addition to the seven mandatory elements, the general plan may include any other elements or address any other subjects that, in the judgment of a city, relate to the physical development of the city. Gov't Code § 65303.[9]

Once an optional element has been adopted, it becomes a full-fledged part of the general plan, with the same legal force and effect as the mandatory elements. The requirements of internal consistency among all general plan elements, and of consistency between the general plan and other land use decisions, apply equally to optional elements. *See* 58 Ops. Cal. Atty. Gen. 21, 25 (1975).

It is possible in certain instances for a city to expand its authority by adopting an element to its general plan. For example, if a city adopts a certified geothermal element, state agencies then may delegate their responsibility for environmental review of exploratory wells to the city as lead agency. Pub. Res. Code § 3715.5. Similarly, primary permitting powers for large geothermal plants may be delegated to the city upon its request. Pub. Res. Code § 25540.5.

Optional general plan elements have been adopted by cities on a wide variety of topics. Any subject is appropriate when there is a concern in the community to study and plan regarding an issue not addressed in sufficient detail in the mandatory elements. Some of the more common areas of concern have been air quality, recreation, design, economic development, infrastructure, energy, historic preservation, and redevelopment. Elements addressing more unique subjects also have been adopted, such as tourism, urban forest, law enforcement, quality of life, arts, and agriculture. For examples of such optional elements, *see* pages 58–69 of Governor's Office of Planning and Research, *California Planners' 2007 Book of Lists*.

Organization. All elements of the general plan have equal legal status. In *Sierra Club v. Board of Supervisors*, the court declared void a precedence clause giving one element priority over another. 126 Cal. App. 3d 698, 704 (1981). Despite this general rule, changes to the law in 2004 have limited a city's discretion to deny certain affordable housing projects, resulting in an elevation of the housing element over the other elements of a general plan. As discussed above, and in chapter 20 (Affordable Housing), even if an affordable housing project is inconsistent with a city's zoning ordinance and general plan land use designation, such inconsistency may not be the basis for denying the project if it is proposed on a site that is identified for very low-, low-, or moderate-income households in the city's housing elements, and is consistent with the density specified in the housing element. Gov't Code § 65589.5(d)(5). However, each city is accorded great flexibility in designing the general plan's structure, as long as it satisfies the minimum requirements as to content, format, and procedure. Gov't Code §§ 65300.7, 65300.9; *see also Camp v. Board of Supervisors*, 123 Cal. App. 3d 334, 348 (1981).

Two or more state-mandated elements may be combined in a single element. Gov't Code § 65301(a). A combined element should explicitly set forth the relationship between its contents and planning requirements.

---

9. *See* chapter 6 of OPR's General Plan Guidelines (2003) for a detailed discussion of optional elements.

In addition to the text, the general plan "shall include a diagram or diagrams." Gov't Code § 65302. This requirement suggests that specificity as to individual parcels is not required because a "map" is considered to represent precision, whereas "diagram" represents approximation. *See* 67 Ops. Cal. Atty. Gen. 75 (1984). In one case, for example, the California Supreme Court noted the distinction between a circle drawn on a general plan, designating an area for potential commercial development, and the more precise location of a commercial "zone." *United Outdoor Adver. Co. v. Business, Transp. and Hous. Agency,* 44 Cal. 3d 242 (1988).

> Unlike a zone, which delimits a well defined geographic area, the circle on the General Plan no more represents the precise boundary of a present or future commercial area than the dot or square on a map of California represents the exact size and shape of Baker or any other community.

Id. at 250

While some cities adopt their elements individually, this practice may create a number of problems, particularly if the elements have been prepared and adopted over many years without any correlation. At the very least, it makes internal consistency difficult to maintain, results in needless duplication and bulk, and usually results in a plan that is difficult to use and review.

Legal Implications of Failure to Have a Legally Adequate General Plan

Since 1971, cities have been required to have a legally adequate general plan with all of the mandatory elements. What happens if a city does not have a valid general plan? What if the general plan lacks a noise element, or an element does not meet the mandatory statutory criteria, is not current, or is internally inconsistent?

Where a city's general plan is found to be inadequate, a land use approval is vulnerable whenever the inadequacy is relevant to the challenged approval. That is, if the challenger can establish a nexus between the claimed deficiency or inadequacy and the approval being challenged, the approval may be set aside. *See Flavell v. City of Albany,* 19 Cal. App. 4th 1846 (1993); *Garat v. City of Riverside,* 2 Cal. App. 4th 259 (1991); *Neighborhood Action Group v. County of Calaveras,* 156 Cal. App. 3d 1176, 1187 (1984). For example, if the defects in the general plan are related to a proposed land use action, such as a rezoning, the city cannot find that the new zoning is consistent with the general plan. Therefore, the rezoning could be declared invalid when passed—void *ab initio*—if successfully challenged in court. *See Sierra Club v. Board of Supervisors,* 126 Cal. App. 3d at 698, 704 (1981); *see also Lesher Communications, Inc. v. City of Walnut Creek,* 52 Cal. 3d 531, 541 (1990) (citing *Sierra Club*); 73 Ops. Cal. Atty. Gen. 78 (1990).

The requirement that a city's general plan be adequate as a prerequisite to undertaking any land use approval has been emphasized repeatedly by the courts. *See Resource Defense Fund v. County of Santa Cruz,* 133 Cal. App. 3d 800, 806 (1982); ("Since consistency with the general plan is required, absence of a valid general plan, or valid relevant elements or components thereof, precludes any enactment of zoning ordinances and the like."); *see also Kings County Farm*

Bureau v. City of Hanford, 221 Cal. App. 3d 692, 745 (1990) (project approval overturned based on inadequacy of general plan elements related to the project); *Neighborhood Action Group v. County of Calaveras*, 156 Cal. App. 3d at 1188 (issuance of a conditional use permit authorizing a project which would create noise impacts was beyond the county's authority if the noise element of the county's general plan does not conform to the statutory criteria); *City of Carmel-by-the-Sea v. Board of Supervisors*, 137 Cal. App. 3d 964, 974 (1982) (due to inadequacy of general plan, use permit to constrict resort hotel was necessarily void).

In 1991, however, one court upheld a land use initiative against a challenge based on an allegedly inadequate general plan. *See Garat*, 2 Cal. App. 4th at 298. The court held there were no statutory requirements that the general plan be updated at any particular time, except for the housing element, or that it be organized or kept in any particular format or location. In addition, the court held that since the petitioner did not prove a nexus between other alleged inadequacies in the general plan and the initiative, the challenge failed. *Id. See also Flavell*, 19 Cal. App. 4th at 1852 (1993) (claim failed since the challenger did not prove a nexus between the alleged inadequacy of the housing element (not timely revised), and the adoption of a zoning ordinance relating to residential off-street parking requirements).

Subdivision approvals also must be consistent with an adequate general plan. If one mandatory element is missing, or if a relevant element is inadequate, a city cannot legally find the subdivision to be consistent with the general plan; thus, no valid subdivision approval will occur.

Subdivision approvals also must be consistent with an adequate general plan. Gov't Code § 66473.5. If one of the mandatory elements is missing, or if a relevant element is inadequate, a city cannot legally find the subdivision to be consistent with the general plan; thus, no valid subdivision approval will occur. For example, in *Camp v. Board of Supervisors*, the court said the county could not approve subdivisions because some of its general plan elements were inadequate under state law. 123 Cal. App. 3d 334, 349 (1981). *See also Friends of "B" St. v. City of Hayward*, 106 Cal. App. 3d 988, 999 (1980) (city could not proceed with a public works project because it was missing its noise element, and the project therefore could not conform to an officially adopted general plan); *Save El Toro Ass'n v. Days*, 74 Cal. App. 3d 64, 74 (1977) (city could not approve any subdivisions as its ordinances were not sufficient to constitute a comprehensive and long-range open space plan as required by Government Code section 65563 due to its failure to prepare maps to be used in conducting an inventory of the open space resources available).

EIR = Environmental impact report

Environmental review of a land use proposal also may be hampered by the legal inadequacy of a general plan.

The California Environmental Quality Act. Environmental review of a land use proposal also may be hampered by the legal inadequacy of a general plan. If a general plan lacks a mandatory element, an environmental impact report (EIR) on a project is "prepared in a vacuum." On this point, a court stated: "The lack of a noise element in the general plan resulted in a subversion of CEQA, because a necessary foundation as to the level of acceptable noise made the EIR deficient." *Guardians of Turlock's Integrity v. City Council*, 149 Cal. App. 3d 584, 593 (1983).

Charter cities. Charter cities have considerable autonomy when it comes to certain types of land use regulation. Where a regulation relates to a municipal affair, a charter city's own charter provisions or ordinances are controlling even where there is conflict with state law. Only where regulation is a matter of statewide concern must the charter city follow state law.

Much of the State Planning and Zoning Law does not apply to charter cities unless either a specific section provides otherwise or the charter city has expressly adopted the Planning and Zoning Law through its charter or an ordinance. Gov't Code § 65700. State law does require, however, that even a charter city adopt a general plan that includes all of the mandatory elements identified above. Gov't Code §§ 65700, 65300.

With the exception of Los Angeles, charter cities are exempt from the requirement that zoning be consistent with the general plan, unless the charter city requires such consistency by its charter or by local ordinance. Gov't Code §§ 65803, 65860(d); *see also Garat v. City of Riverside*, 2 Cal. App. 4th 259, 281 (1991); *City of Irvine v. Irvine Citizens Against Overdevelopment*, 25 Cal. App. 4th 868, 874 (1994) (although Irvine is a charter city, because it had adopted a consistency rule, it was subject to the consistency requirement). Similar to the City of Irvine, almost 25 percent of charter cities have adopted a consistency rule. Notwithstanding the consistency exemption for charter cities, 2007 flood protection legislation requires all cities in the Sacramento-San Joaquin Valley, including charter cities, to amend their zoning ordinances so that they are consistent with the flood protection goals and policies of each city's respective general plan. Gov't Code § 65860.1. Additionally, all subdivisions and all public works projects within a city, whether or not the city is a charter city, must be consistent with the general plan, or they will be subject to legal attack. *See Friends of "B" St.*, 106 Cal. App. 3d at 999.

With the exception of Los Angeles, charter cities are exempt from the requirement that zoning be consistent with the general plan, unless the city requires such consistency by its charter or by local ordinance.

Internal (Horizontal) Consistency

A general plan must be integrated and internally consistent, both among the elements and within each element. Gov't Code § 65300.5. This applies to any optional elements adopted by a city as well as the mandatory elements. If there is internal inconsistency, the general plan is legally inadequate and the required finding of consistency for land use approvals cannot be made. This section applies to charter cities. *See Garat v. City of Riverside*, 2 Cal. App. 4th 259, 286 (1991). *See also Concerned Citizens of Calaveras County v. Board of Supervisors*, 166 Cal. App. 3d 90, 97–98 (1985) (general plan found to be internally inconsistent where one portion of the circulation element indicated that roads were sufficient for projected traffic increases, while another section of the same element described increased traffic congestion as a result of continued subdivision development).

A general plan must be integrated and internally consistent, both among the elements and within each element. This applies to any optional elements adopted by a city as well as the mandatory elements.

Because the adoption or amendment of a general plan is a legislative act presumed to be valid, cities need not make explicit findings to support their actions. A court therefore cannot find a general plan to be internally inconsistent unless, based on the evidence before the city council, a reasonable person could not conclude that the plan was internally consistent. *Federation of Hillside & Canyon Ass'ns v. City of Los Angeles*, 126 Cal. App. 4th 1180 (2004).

Internal consistency also requires that diagrams in the land use, circulation, open space, and natural resource elements reflect the written policies and programs of those elements. *See generally Citizens Ass'n for Sensible Dev. of Bishop Area v. County of Inyo*, 172 Cal. App. 3d 151 (1985); *Environmental Council v. Board of Supervisors*, 135 Cal. App. 3d 428 (1982); *Karlson v. City of Camarillo*, 100 Cal. App. 3d 789 (1980).

The internal consistency requirement may not be evaded by incorporating a subordination or precedence clause, such as "in the event of a conflict, the land use element controls." *See Sierra Club v. Board of Supervisors*, 126 Cal. App. 3d 698, 708 (1981) (expressly rejecting use of a precedence clause, where the county general plan's land use and open space elements designated conflicting land uses for the same property).

As discussed earlier in this chapter, housing legislation passed in 2004 deviates somewhat from these previously accepted principles relating to the equality of elements in a general plan and the requirement that a general plan be internally consistent by providing that if a development project is proposed on a site that is identified for very low, low-, or moderate-income households in the jurisdiction's housing element, and is consistent with the density specified in the housing element, it may not be disapproved on the basis that it is inconsistent with both the jurisdiction's zoning ordinance and general plan land use designation. Gov't Code § 65589.5(d)(5). Thus, this section essentially may trump land use designations elsewhere in the general plan, thereby permitting internal inconsistency in such circumstances.

Consistency Between General Plan and Other Land Use and Development Actions (Vertical Consistency)

Since the general plan is the constitution for all future development, any decision by a city affecting land use and development must be consistent with the general plan. *See Friends of Lagoon Valley*, 154 Cal. App. 4th at 815; *Citizens of Goleta Valley v. Board of Supervisors*, 52 Cal. 3d 553, 570 (1990).

"An action, program or project is consistent with the general plan if, considering all its aspects, it will further the objectives and policies of the general plan and not obstruct their attainment." Governor's Office of Planning and Research, *General Plan Guidelines* (2003), page 164. *See also Corona-Norco Unified Sch. Dist. v. City of Corona*, 17 Cal. App. 4th 985, 994 (1993); *City of Irvine v. Irvine Citizens Against Overdevelopment*, 25 Cal. App. 4th 868, 879 (1994). To be consistent, an action, program, or project must be "in agreement or harmony" with the general plan. *Friends of Lagoon Valley*, 154 Cal. App. 4th at 817 (upholding the City's approval of the Lower Lagoon Valley Policy Plan Implementation Project and the City's finding that the Project was consistent with its general plan).

As discussed above, charter cities are exempt from the mandate that zoning be consistent with the general plan, unless the city's charter provides otherwise. Gov't Code § 65803. *See Garat v. City of Riverside*, 2 Cal. App. 4th at 282 (where city regulations did not provide for consistency); *City of Irvine v. Irvine Citizens Against Overdevelopment*, 25 Cal. App. 4th at 868 (where city ordinance did require consistency). However, this exemption applies only to zoning and not to consistency requirements for subdivision map approval, public works construction, or for other subordinate land use or development approvals.

Reviewing courts generally defer to cities' superior abilities to interpret and apply the general plan policies they have authored. "When we review an agency's decision for consistency with its own general plan, we accord great deference to the agency's determination. This is because the body which adopted the general plan policies in its legislative capacity has unique competence to interpret those policies when applying them in its adjudicatory capacity." *Save Our Peninsula Comm. v. County of Monterey*, 87 Cal. App. 4th 99, 142 (2001) (citing *City of Walnut Creek v. County of Contra Costa*, 101 Cal. App. 3d 1012, 1021 (1980)). The court's review of a city's interpretation of its general plan is highly deferential because "policies in a general plan reflect a range of competing interests, the [city] must be allowed to weigh and balance the plan's policies when applying them, and it has broad discretion to construe its policies in light of the plan's purpose." *Friends of Lagoon Valley*, 154 Cal. App. 4th at 816; *see also Anderson First Coalition v. City of Anderson*, 130 Cal. App. 4th 1173 (2005); *San Franciscans Upholding the Downtown Plan v. City and County of San Francisco*, 102 Cal. App. 4th 656, 668 (2002).

It is the city's responsibility to determine whether proposed land use development approvals are consistent with the general plan. A determination regarding such consistency is a legislative decision, and will not be set aside by a court unless the city has acted arbitrarily, capriciously, or without evidentiary support, or has failed to follow proper procedures, such as failing to give notice as required by law. *See San Franciscans Upholding the Downtown Plan v. City and County of San Francisco*, 102 Cal. App. 4th at 668 (claim that redevelopment plan amendments were inconsistent with the general plan reviewed under arbitrary and capricious standard); *No Oil, Inc. v. City of Los Angeles*, 196 Cal. App. 3d 223, 233 (1987) (judicial review of a zoning ordinance's consistency with the general plan is limited to a determination of whether the agency's action was arbitrary, capricious, or entirely without evidentiary support); *Mitchell v. County of Orange*, 165 Cal. App. 3d 1185, 1191–92 (1985) (county's determination that a specific plan is consistent with its general plan is legislative, and the reviewing court is limited to an examination of whether the action was arbitrary and capricious).

It is the city's responsibility to determine whether proposed land use development approvals are consistent with the general plan.

Although a city's decision regarding consistency of an action with the general plan is legislative, the decision necessitates some level of factual determinations. *See Building Indus. Ass'n v. City of Oceanside*, 27 Cal. App. 4th 744, 761 (1994); *Building Indus. Ass'n v. Superior Court*, 211 Cal. App. 3d 277, 291 (1989). A court will defer to a city's interpretation of its own general plan and factual findings unless "based on the evidence before [the] city council, a reasonable person could not have reached the same conclusion." *No Oil*, 196 Cal. App. 3d at 243 (upholding city's specific finding of consistency between general plan and ordinance establishing oil drilling zones).

Although a city's decision regarding consistency of an action with the general plan is legislative, the decision necessitates some level of factual determinations.

Notwithstanding such purported judicial deference, at least three appellate courts have overturned a city or county's finding that a land use approval was consistent with the agency's general plan. In *Families Unafraid to Uphold Rural El Dorado County v. County of El Dorado*, the court overturned the county's finding that a planned development was consistent with the general plan, stating that it was "readily apparent that the [Low Density Residential] designation for [the development] is inconsistent with the Draft General Plan...." 62 Cal. App. 4th 1332, 1341 (1998). Despite the usual deference of courts to consistency determinations, the county was unable to overcome the "specific, mandatory and fundamental inconsistencies" of the project with the land use policies of the general plan. *Id.* at 1342.

Even if there is no direct conflict, at least one appellate court has found a land use approval inconsistent where it did not implement or advance the goals of the general plan. In *Napa Citizens For Honest Gov't v. County of Napa Bd. of Supervisors*, the court overturned the county's determination that an updated specific plan was consistent with the general plan. 91 Cal. App. 4th 342 (2001). While the specific plan did not directly conflict with any stated goals or policies of the general plan, it did not, as the county conceded, actually implement general plan goals and policies, nor did it require any specific action that would further such goals and policies. The specific plan in question included a circulation element that contained no specific highway improvements, nor any detailed statement of goals or policies. In addition, it contained no specific action which would further the housing goals and policies within the general plan. *Id.* at 379–381.

Although courts generally will defer to an agency's factual findings of consistency with a general plan, project approvals may be overturned if a court determines that no reasonable person could have reached the same conclusion on the relevant evidence.

Although courts generally will defer to an agency's factual findings of consistency with a general plan, project approvals may be overturned if a court determines that no reasonable person could have reached the same conclusion on the relevant evidence (the "arbitrary and capricious" standard of review). In *Endangered Habitats League, Inc. v. County of Orange*, the court overturned a set of project approvals due to their inconsistency with the general plan. 131 Cal. App. 4th 777 (2005). The court found that the project's traffic impacts were in conflict with mandatory requirements of the general plan. The court also found that the provisions of the proposed specific plan amendment which allowed a "balancing" of specific plan requirements and exempted the project from such mandatory specific plan requirements were in conflict with the general plan. Stating that the language of the general plan was "unambiguous," the court rejected the county's consistency arguments.

The Subdivision Map Act does not require an exact match between the tentative map and the general plan or specific plan.

In the subdivision context, Government Code section 66473.5 requires that approvals of tentative maps be consistent with a city's general plan. However, the Subdivision Map Act (Gov't Code § 66410 *et seq.*) does not require an exact match between the tentative map and the general plan or specific plan. The tentative map only need be in agreement or harmony with the general or specific plan. *See Sequoyah Hills Homeowners Ass'n v. City of Oakland*, 23 Cal. App. 4th 704, 717–18 (1993) (city's determination that the map was consistent with 14 of 17 general plan policies was held legally adequate); *Greenbaum v. City of Los Angeles*, 153 Cal. App. 3d 391, 408 (1984). As to consistency, the *Sequoyah Hills* court held that a given project including a map need not be in perfect conformity with each and every general plan policy.

> Indeed, it is beyond cavil that no project could completely satisfy every policy stated in the [Oakland Comprehensive Plan], and that state law does not impose such a requirement (*Greenbaum v. City of Los Angeles*, 153 Cal. App. 3d at 406–07; 59 Ops. Cal. Atty. Gen. 129, 131 (1976)). A general plan must try to accommodate a wide range of competing interests—including those of developers, neighboring homeowners, prospective homebuyers, environmentalists, current and prospective business owners, jobseekers, taxpayers, and providers and recipients of all types of city-provided services—and to present a clear and comprehensive set of principles to guide development decisions. Once a general plan is in place, it is the province of elected city officials to examine the specifics of a proposed project to determine whether it would be "in harmony" with the policies stated in the plan. [Citation omitted.] It is, emphatically, not the role of the courts to micromanage these development decisions.

Our function is simply to decide whether the city officials considered the applicable policies and the extent to which the proposed project conforms with those policies, whether the city officials made appropriate findings on this issue, and whether those findings are supported by substantial evidence. (Code Civ. Proc. § 1094.5(c); *Youngblood v. Board of Supervisors*, 22 Cal. 3d 644, 651 (1978)).

Sequoyah Hills Homeowners Assn. v. City of Oakland, 23 Cal. App. 4th at 719–20; *but see Families Unafraid to Uphold Rural El Dorado County v. County of El Dorado*, 62 Cal. App. 4th 1332 (1998) (holding that the county's findings of consistency between a proposed residential subdivision and the county's draft general plan were not supported by substantial evidence).

There are at least two exceptions to the Subdivision Map Act's consistency requirement. In *Corona-Norco Unified School District v. City of Corona*, the court held that Government Code section 65996 creates an express exception to the general requirement of consistency by precluding a city from denying approval of a development project under the Map Act based on inadequate school facilities. 13 Cal. App. 4th 1577, 1584 (1993). Although the court stated that it did not "mean to diminish the importance of the consistency doctrine in the planning process," the Legislature made clear "that development takes precedence to the adequacy of school facilities." *Id.* at 1585.

In addition, under Government Code section 65589.5(d), a city may not disapprove a housing development on the basis that such development is inconsistent with the city's general plan and zoning designation so long as the proposed project is on a site identified for very low-, low-, or moderate-income households in the city's housing element and is consistent with the density specified in the housing element, even if the project is inconsistent with the city's general plan and zoning designation.

Finally, consistency is required only in the context of approvals for future development. For example, as to public works projects, a city is not required to bring existing public works projects, including neighborhoods and streets, into compliance with the general plan. *See Friends of H Street v. City of Sacramento*, 20 Cal. App. 4th 152, 169 (1993) (requirements of general plan compliance were not applicable to the maintenance and operation of an existing street completed before the consistency mandate came into effect).

Consistency is required only in the context of approvals for future development—a city is not required to bring existing public works projects into compliance with the general plan.

Consistency with Airport Land Use Plan

General plans must be consistent with any Airport Land Use Plan (ALUP) adopted by a county airport land use commission pursuant to Public Utilities Code section 21675, unless the city overrules the commission and makes certain findings. Gov't Code § 65302.3(a); *Muzzy Ranch v. Solano County Airport Land Use Com'n*, 41 Cal. 4th 372, 384 (2007). If a city does not concur with any aspect of the ALUP, it may overrule the commission's ALUP by a two-thirds vote if it makes specific findings that the decision to overrule the ALUP is consistent with the purposes of protecting public health, safety, and welfare, minimizing the public's exposure to excessive noise, and minimizing safety hazards within areas around the public airport. *See* Pub. Util. Code §§ 21670, 21676. At least 45 days prior to such decision, the city shall provide a copy of the

ALUP = Airport Land Use Plan

proposed decision and findings to the commission and the Division of Aeronautics of the State Department of Transportation. The commission and the division may provide comments to the local agency governing body within 30 days of receiving the proposed decision and findings. If the commission's or division's comments are not available within this time limit, the city may overrule the ALUP without receiving them. These comments are merely advisory to the city; however, the city must include them in the final record of any final decision to overrule the ALUP. *See California Aviation Council v. City of Ceres*, 9 Cal. App. 4th 1384 (1992) (a city's ordinance approving a portion of a specific plan that was inconsistent with the local ALUP was invalid, because the city did not make the specific findings required by Public Utilities Code section 21676(b)); Governor's Office of Planning and Research, *Governor's Strategy Growth Report*, pages 72–73 (1993) (discussing airport land use commissions); Peter M. Detwiler, *Airport Land Use Commissions: Common Sense, Uncommon Confusion*, 3 CEB Land Use & Env. Forum 36 (Winter 1994). The general plan must be amended as necessary within 180 days of any amendment to the ALUP. Gov't Code § 65302.3(b).

A county airport land use commission may not "exempt" a general or specific plan from this consistency requirement where a conflict otherwise exists. The California Attorney General recently opined that allowing a city's or county's plan to simply be "exempted" from consistency with the more stringent requirements of an ALUP would undermine the legislative intent behind the detailed procedure provided in the Public Resources Code for resolving conflicts between a city or county's plan and an ALUP. 87 Ops. Cal. Atty. Gen. 102 (2004).

Procedure for Adoption and Amendment[10]

When adopting or amending a general plan, a city must follow the procedures set forth in Government Code section 65350 *et seq*. The planning commission must hold a public hearing on the adoption or amendment and make a written recommendation to the city council. Gov't Code §§ 65353(a); 65354. The commission's recommendation for approval must be made by an affirmative vote of not less than a majority of its total membership; thus, if a planning commission consists of seven members, there must be four affirmative votes to recommend approval to the city council. Gov't Code § 65354. Unless an applicant appeals a planning commission's denial of a request for a general plan amendment, the request will not be automatically heard by the council. Accordingly, a city with a planning commission that has the authority to consider and recommend approval or disapproval of a general plan amendment must provide a procedure to appeal the action of the planning commission to the city council. Gov't Code § 65354.5.

Once it receives the recommendation of the planning commission, and prior to adopting or amending the general plan, the city council must hold at least one public hearing. The city council may approve, modify, or disapprove the recommendation of the planning commission, but any substantial modification made

---

10. *See* chapter 3 of OPR's General Plan Guidelines (2003) for a detailed discussion of preparing and amending the general plan.

to the proposed plan or amendment that was not previously considered by the commission must be referred back for its recommendation. Gov't Code § 65356.

A general plan is adopted or amended by resolution. Gov't Code § 65356. Because the nature of the resolution is legislative, it does not take effect until the 30-day period for referendum has elapsed. *See Midway Orchards v. County of Butte*, 220 Cal. App. 3d 765, 780 (1990). For a detailed discussion of the referendum process, *see* chapter 14 (Initiative and Referendum).

For a discussion of the additional requirements that apply when adopting or amending a general plan's housing element, *see* the earlier discussion in this chapter on the housing element and the discussion in chapter 20 (Affordable Housing). For a thorough discussion of the environmental review process required by CEQA and applicable to all discretionary land use actions, including adoption and amendment of general plans, *see* chapter 6 (CEQA).

A mandatory element of the general plan may be amended only four times during any calendar year. Gov't Code § 65358(b). However, more than one change can be made at a time and will be considered a single amendment to the general plan. *Id.*; *see also* 66 Ops. Cal. Atty. Gen. 258 (1983). Further, amendments for affordable housing projects are exempt from this restriction. Gov't Code § 65358(c).

Prior to legislative approval, a city shall refer a proposal to adopt or substantially amend a general plan to the following agencies:

- Any county and city within or abutting the area covered by the proposal
- Any special district that may be significantly affected by the proposed action as determined by the planning agency
- Any elementary, high school, or unified school district within the area covered by the proposed action
- The local agency formation commission
- Any area-wide planning agency whose operations may be significantly affected by the proposed action
- Any federal agency if lands within its jurisdiction may be significantly affected by the proposed action
- Any public water system with 3,000 or more service connections that serves customers within the area covered by the proposal
- The Bay Area Air Quality Management District for proposed action within its boundaries
- Any branch of the military with installations within 1,000 feet of the proposed action or if the action is within special use airspace or beneath a low level flight path
- Any Native American tribe with traditional lands located within the city or county's jurisdiction

Gov't Code § 65352

Generally, these agencies have 45 days to comment. Although the provision uses the word "shall," this section is directory, not mandatory (Gov't Code § 65352(c)(1)) and failure to comply does not invalidate the adoption or amendment of the plan.

Cities and counties also must refer a "proposed action" (general plan, specific plan, or zoning) to one another pursuant to Government Code section 65919

PRACTICE TIP

If a planning commission consists of seven members, there must be four affirmative votes to recommend approval of the general plan to the city council. For example, a 3–2 vote where two members are absent will not be sufficient even if that vote is sufficient to approve a tentative map.

et seq. Thus, before acting on the proposed action, a county must refer it to the affected cities for comment and vice-versa. Gov't Code § 65919.3. If a housing element or an amendment to it is to be adopted, the draft first must be referred to HCD for its review and comment. Gov't Code § 65585(b). A 90-day review period is provided for an element; for an amendment, the review period is 60 days.

Copies of the general plan and amendments shall be made available for inspection by the public one working day following adoption. Within two working days after a request, copies shall be furnished to those so requesting. Gov't Code § 65357(b); *see also City of Poway v. City of San Diego*, 229 Cal. App. 3d 847, 862 (1991) (a general plan amendment was ineffective because it was not timely made available to the public).

> HCD = Department of Housing and Community Development

Implementation and Annual Report

The planning agency must investigate and make recommendations to the city regarding reasonable and practical means for implementing the general plan or one of its elements so that the plan will serve as an effective guide for orderly growth and development, preservation and conservation of open space and natural resources, and the efficient expenditure of public funds relating to the subjects addressed in the general plan. The planning agency must render an annual report by April 1 of each year (rather than October 1, as was previously required) to the city council, OPR, and HCD, through the use of forms and definitions adopted by HCD, on the status of the plan and the progress in its implementation. Specifically, the report must include the progress in meeting its share of regional housing needs as determined by Government Code section 65584.01; the progress on local efforts to remove governmental constraints to the maintenance, improvement, and development of housing pursuant to Government Code section 65583(c)(3); the degree to which its approved general plan complies with the guidelines developed and adopted pursuant to Government Code section 65040.2; and the date of the last revision to the general plan. Gov't Code § 65400.

A general plan may be amended by initiative. *See DeVita v. County of Napa*, 9 Cal. 4th 763, 777 (1995) (upholding a land use element amendment by initiative). However, the *DeVita* court said it was not determining whether an initiative that later amends or conflicts with the housing element is valid. *Id.* at 793 n.11. A general plan adoption or amendment also is subject to the referendum process. *See Yost v. Thomas*, 36 Cal. 3d 561, 570 (1984).

> *A general plan may be amended by initiative. A general plan adoption or amendment also is subject to referendum.*

Checklist for General Plan Adequacy

The following is a brief questionnaire that highlights the various issues that may be raised in a challenge as to the legal adequacy of a general plan. For a more detailed discussion of judicial review of general plans, *see* chapter 21 (Land Use Litigation).

Is it complete? The seven mandatory elements must be addressed. Gov't Code § 65302; *see also Camp v. Board of Supervisors*, 123 Cal. App. 3d at 349.

Is it informational, readable, and available to the public? The courts have suggested that a general plan must set forth the required elements in a logical, understandable manner in order to be in substantial compliance. *See Kings County Farm Bureau v. City of Hanford*, 221 Cal. App. 3d at 743–44 (citing *Camp*). However, there is no requirement that a general plan be organized or kept in any particular format or location. *See Garat*, 2 Cal. App. 4th at 296.

The courts appear to be concerned with public availability of general plans and their amendments, which is required by Government Code section 65357. A general plan amendment that was not contained in a city's public version of its general plan was held to be ineffective. *See City of Poway v. City of San Diego*, 229 Cal. App. 3d 847, 861 (1991). A deficient element cannot be saved by consideration of documents that are not relied upon in the discussion of that element. *See Kings County Farm Bureau*, 221 Cal. App. 3d at 744.

Is it internally consistent? The data, assumptions, and projections (*e.g.*, for population, housing, jobs) used in various parts of the plan must be consistent with one another. Gov't Code § 65300.5; *see also Concerned Citizens of Calaveras County v. Board of Supervisors*, 166 Cal. App. 3d 90 (1985); *Sierra Club v. Board of Supervisors*, 126 Cal. App. 3d 698 (1981).

The data, assumptions, and projections used in various parts of the plan must be consistent with one another.

Is it consistent with state policy? The plan must comport with legislative policies relating to:

- California Coastal Act. Pub. Res. Code § 30000 *et seq.*
- Open space. Gov't Code § 65561
- Housing. Gov't Code § 65580. *See* HCD's "Housing Element Review Worksheet," 2001.
- Surface mining—Surface Mining and Reclamation Act (SMARA). Pub. Res. Code § 2712
- Airport land use plans adopted pursuant to Public Utilities Code § 21675. Gov't Code § 65302.3[11]

See OPR's General Plan Guidelines, chapter 10 (Special General Plan Considerations) (2003).

Does it cover all territory within its boundaries and outside its boundaries that relate to its planning? For purposes of determining the adequacy of a general plan, "territory" covers "any land outside its boundaries that in the planning agency's judgment bears relation to its planning." Gov't Code § 65300.

For purposes of determining the adequacy of a general plan, territory covers any land outside its boundaries that in the planning agency's judgment bears relation to its planning.

Is it long-term in perspective? The plan must be long-term. Gov't Code § 65300. However, at least one court has emphasized that, with the exception of the housing element, there is no statutory requirement that a general plan be updated at any given interval or in connection with a specific event. *See Garat v. City of Riverside*, 2 Cal. App. 4th at 296.

Does it address all locally relevant issues? The degree of detail in the discussion must reflect local conditions and circumstances. Gov't Code § 65301(c).

Is it current? Each city shall "periodically review, and revise, as necessary, the general plan." Gov't Code § 65103(a); *see also Citizens of Goleta Valley v. Board of*

---

11. For exceptions to this consistency requirement, *see* Consistency with Airport Land Use Plan, this chapter.

Supervisors, 52 Cal. 3d 553 (1990). The California Supreme Court stated that there is an implied duty to keep the general plan current. *See DeVita v. County of Napa*, 9 Cal. 4th at 792 (citing *Garat*). While the court confirmed in *Garat* there is no statutory requirement that a general plan be updated at any given interval or in connection with a specific event (except for the housing element, which must be updated no less than once every five years), this statement was qualified in footnote 28 of the opinion:

> This conclusion does not preclude a court from looking at the results of a public entity's failure to update its entire plan or any parts thereof, *i.e.*, the failure to update a plan and/or its parts may cause a general plan or mandatory element to not be in compliance with the statutory requirements ("legally inadequate") which, in turn, if properly challenged in a timely manner, may subject the entity to an attack on its validity pursuant to those proceedings provided in section 65750 *et seq*.

2 Cal. App. 4th at 296 n.28

The OPR must notify a city that its general plan has not been revised within eight years and must notify the Attorney General if a city has not revised its general plan within ten years.

Other elements must be updated to reflect changed circumstances. The OPR must notify a city that its general plan has not been revised within eight years and must notify the Attorney General if a city has not revised its general plan within ten years. Gov't Code § 65040.5.

Does it contain the statutory criteria required by state law as interpreted by the courts? For example:

- Does the land use element identify areas that are subject to flooding? Gov't Code § 65302(a)
- Are noise contours shown for all of the listed sources? *See Camp v. Board of Supervisors*, 123 Cal. App. 3d at 351–52
- Does it contain adequate standards of population density and building intensity for the various districts? *See Twain Harte Homeowners Ass'n v. County of Tuolumne*, 138 Cal. App. 3d at 699
- Is the circulation element fiscally responsible? *See Concerned Citizens of Calaveras County v. Board of Supervisors*, 166 Cal. App. 3d at 101–03
- Is the circulation element correlated with the land use element? Gov't Code § 65302(b)
- Does the general plan clearly specify allowable uses for each land use district? Gov't Code § 65302(a)
- Are the density ranges specific enough to provide guidelines in making consistency findings where necessary, *e.g.*, regarding zoning, use permits, subdivision? Gov't Code § 65302(a)
- Does the housing element contain a program to conserve and improve the condition of the existing affordable housing stock? *See Hernandez v. City of Encinitas*, 28 Cal. App. 4th at 1069; *Buena Vista Gardens Apartments Ass'n v. City of San Diego*, 175 Cal. App. 3d at 303 (1985)
- Has the city adopted an analysis and program for preserving assisted housing developments as part of its housing element? Gov't Code § 65583(a)(8)
- Does the housing element comply with the statutory mandate to identify adequate sites that will be available to accommodate the city's share of regional housing needs, including through an action program for development of emergency shelters and transitional housing for the homeless? Gov't

Code § 65583(c)(1); *see also Hoffmaster v. City of San Diego*, 55 Cal. App. 4th 1098, 1109 (1997)

Are the diagrams or maps adequate?

- Do the diagrams or maps show proposed land uses for the entire planning area? Gov't Code § 65302
- Is the land use map linked directly to the text of the general plan?
- Are the maps and text consistent? Gov't Code § 65300.5

Does it serve as a yardstick? Can one take an individual parcel and check it against the plan and then know which uses would be permissible?

Does it contain an action plan or implementation plan? For example: "Every local open space plan shall contain an action program consisting of specific programs that the legislative body intends to pursue in implementing its open space plan." Gov't Code § 65564.

Is it horizontally consistent? Is it integrated and internally consistent among the elements and within each element? Gov't Code § 65300.5.

Was it adopted correctly?

- Did it receive proper environmental review? Gov't Code § 65350
- Was the draft housing element or amendment thereto sent to HCD for its review before adoption? Gov't Code § 65585(b)
- Was there consultation with Native American tribes for the preservation of Native American features, places, or objects within the city's jurisdiction? Gov't Code § 65352.3; *see also* Gov't Code § 65562.5
- Was there consultation on the safety element with the Division of Mines and Geology and the State Board of Forestry and Fire Protection and local agencies, if required? Gov't Code §§ 65302(g)

Adoption of General Plans by New Cities

A newly incorporated city must adopt a general plan within 30 months following its incorporation. During that time, the city is not subject to the requirement that it have an adopted general plan or that its land use approvals be consistent with the general plan so long as it is proceeding in a timely fashion with preparation of the general plan, and the planning agency makes certain findings when approving projects and taking other actions. Gov't Code § 65360.

A new city in the process of preparing a general plan may apply to the Director of OPR for an extension of time of up to two years. Gov't Code § 65361(a), (c). OPR will grant an extension if the city makes certain findings explaining why the general plan was not previously adopted or amended (*e.g.*, coordination problems with another agency, natural disaster, difficulty recruiting staff, extensive public review). Gov't Code § 65361(a). One additional extension, which shall not exceed one year, may be granted upon a showing of substantial progress. Gov't Code § 65361(f).

OPR may not grant an extension for the preparation or adoption of a housing element except in the case of a new city. Gov't Code §§ 65361(b),

A newly incorporated city must adopt a general plan within 30 months following its incorporation.

65587(a). Projects approved during the extension period must still be consistent with the adopted general plan and those portions of the general plan for which the extension was granted, except as provided by the conditions imposed by the OPR director. Gov't Code §§ 65361(d), (e).

Land use approvals that predate the extension are not protected, as the extension is not retroactive. An approval granted before the extension can be attacked based on the general plan in effect at the time of the approval. *See Neighborhood Action Group v. County of Calaveras*, 156 Cal. App. 3d 1176, 1191 (1984); *Resource Defense Fund v. County of Santa Cruz*, 133 Cal. App. 3d 800, 812 (1982).

The extension can serve to prevent a court-ordered, city-wide moratorium on project approvals resulting from a legal challenge to some individual approval. However, OPR may attach conditions to the extension that might restrict a city's ability to approve development during the extension period. For example, OPR could require that any development be consistent with the general plan proposal being considered or studied. In *Harroman Co. v. Town of Tiburon*, the court held that a tentative subdivision map must be evaluated against a draft general plan being prepared under an OPR extension, rather than against the existing general plan. 235 Cal. App. 3d 388, 395–96 (1991). *See also Families Unafraid to Uphold Rural El Dorado County v. El Dorado County Bd. of Sup'rs.*, 62 Cal. App. 4th at 1336. Under a law passed in 1996, during the extension period, development approvals generally must be consistent with those portions of the general plan for which an extension has been granted. Gov't Code § 65361(e). Moreover, OPR could bar approvals that vest development rights or limit individual general plan amendments.

The General Plan as a Source of Dedications and Development Fees

The city, under the umbrella of its police power, can look to its zoning ordinance, subdivision ordinance, and use permit regulations for many of the standard types of dedications or development fees. However, more cities now are relying on the general plan or applicable specific plan to support such requirements. The goals and policies contained in general plans have been upheld as a basis for dedication requirements. *See J.W. Jones Cos. v. City of San Diego*, 157 Cal. App. 3d 745, 757–58 (1984).

The general plan is the most comprehensive statement of a city's interest and welfare. Thus, the plan can assist in defending a condition judicially attacked as beyond the city's police power. If the condition is mandated by the plan, that mandate evinces that the condition substantially advances a legitimate state interest. *See* Edward J. Sullivan and Isa Lester, "The Role of the Comprehensive Plan in Infrastructure Financing," 37 *Urb. Law.* 53 (2005) (arguing that by incorporating a comprehensive financing scheme into its comprehensive plan, a local government will reduce its exposure to Takings Clause challenges). *See also* Daniel J. Curtin, Jr. and Jonathan D. Witten, "Windfalls, Wipeouts, Givings, and Takings in Dramatic Redevelopment Projects: Bargaining for Better Zoning on Density, Views, and Public Access," 32 *B.C. Envtl. Aff. L. Rev.* 325 (2005).

The power to impose a condition of approval need not be expressed by the specific enactment of an ordinance or regulation. Thus, a city's requirement that smoke detectors be installed in all units in a condominium conversion was upheld based on the objectives of the city's general plan to "promote safe housing for all." *Soderling v. City of Santa Monica*, 142 Cal. App. 3d 501, 506 (1983). The court said such a condition was valid to achieve the goals of the city's general plan. *Id.*; *see also J.W. Jones Cos. v. City of San Diego*, 157 Cal. App. 3d at 757–58.

Cities have amended their general plans to adopt goals and policies relating to the need for fire stations, police stations, libraries, and child day care centers, for example, in order to support subsequent ordinances requiring developers to pay a fee for those purposes. These requirements are valid if they are reasonably related to the burden created by the proposed development. *See Dolan v. City of Tigard*, 512 U.S. 374, 390–91 (1994). For a thorough discussion of exactions and fees, *see* chapter 13 (Exactions).

The General Plan as a Tool in Growth Management and Other Innovative Land Use Controls

There are practical as well as legal reasons for growth management measures to be tied directly to the general plan. A growth management program will be more effective, and perhaps subject to fewer legal challenges, if it is linked directly to the general plan rather than adopted independently.

Growth management regulations based on the police power must promote the general welfare of the community. The general plan represents the most comprehensive statement of the community's welfare relative to environmental and land use matters. Thus, the data and policies in the general plan supporting the growth management objectives can provide a rationale upon which the regulations rest.

The general plan contains projections of future population that form the basis for proposed land uses and facilities. Population projections set forth in the general plan can give legitimacy to specific measures that regulate population growth by either an absolute growth limit or an annual growth rate.

The general plan also is a forum for balancing competing interests and objectives in deciding the future of the city. The city's desire to regulate growth may conflict with its obligation to provide adequate housing opportunities. The general plan is the most appropriate mechanism for making the necessary trade-offs between these two competing objectives. For a discussion of the general plan as a tool to regulate development, *see* Daniel J. Curtin, Jr., "Symposium 2005: Regulating Big Box Stores: The Proper Use of the City or County's Police Power and Its Comprehensive Plan—California's Experience," 6 *Vt. J. Envtl. L.* 31 (2005) (discussing use of the general plan as a guide when deciding whether to permit or deny big box development).

Judicial Review of the Adequacy of the General Plan

Since they are legislative acts, general plans are subject to judicial review in an action for ordinary mandate. *See* chapter 21 (Land Use Litigation) for a detailed discussion of this topic. The court generally considers whether the adoption or amendment of the general plan was arbitrary, capricious, or entirely lacking in evidentiary support. *See Environmental Council v. Board of Supervisors*, 135 Cal. App. 3d 428, 436 (1982). The court determines whether the plan substantially

A growth management program will be more effective, and perhaps subject to fewer legal challenges, if it is linked directly to the general plan rather than adopted independently.

Since they are legislative acts, general plans are subject to judicial review in an action for ordinary mandate.

complies with the statutory criteria. Substantial compliance is achieved when there is actual compliance with the "'substance essential to every reasonable objective of the statute', as distinguished from 'mere technical imperfections of form.'" *Camp v. Board of Supervisors*, 123 Cal. App. 3d at 348; *Hernandez v. City of Encinitas*, 28 Cal. App. 4th 1048, 1058 (1994) (citing Gov't Code § 65587(b) and uncodified section 44 of Chapter 1009 of the 1984 statutes).

However, the housing element, because it is subject to more detailed requirements, faces closer judicial scrutiny. *See Hernandez*, 28 Cal. App. 4th at 1059.

Actions and remedies relating to general plan adequacy generally are governed by Government Code sections 65750–65763. *See Garat v. City of Riverside*, 2 Cal. App. 4th at 303. Housing element challenges also are subject to Government Code sections 65587(b) and (c). The action must be brought pursuant to Code of Civil Procedure section 1085 (traditional mandamus) generally within 90 days after the adoption or amendment of the general plan. Gov't Code § 65009(c); *see also A Local & Reg'l Monitor (ALARM) v. City of Los Angeles*, 16 Cal. App. 4th 630, 649 (1993). There are exceptions related to the development of low- or moderate-income housing. Gov't Code § 65009. Challenges also may be brought after the 90-day period when a project approval is claimed to be inconsistent with relevant portions of the general plan because those portions are inadequate. *See Garat*, 2 Cal. App. 4th at 289.

In the event of a judicial determination that the plan is inadequate, the Government Code specifies the types of municipal actions (*e.g.*, rezonings, subdivision approvals) that may be suspended, and specifies time limits to be imposed on the preparation of an adequate plan. Gov't Code §§ 65755, 65754. The law also details other relief the court may grant during the life of the suit. Gov't Code § 65753.

In *Committee for Responsible Planning v. City of Indian Wells*, a court enunciated the circumstances under which development may be allowed to proceed after a judicial determination of general plan inadequacy. 209 Cal. App. 3d 1005 (1989). After finding the city's general plan inadequate, the court issued a writ of mandate prohibiting the issuance of building permits and discretionary land use approvals until the city brought its general plan into compliance with state law.

After judgment, a developer intervened, and moved for an order allowing approval of its 29-unit subdivision on the basis that under Government Code section 65755, a project approval could still be granted so long as it did not "significantly impair" a city's ability to adopt or amend its general plan. The developer argued that in order to significantly impair adoption or amendment of a special plan, a project must be of such size or nature that it would necessarily and significantly reduce the city's options in drafting a general plan. The court rejected this argument, and, noting the special importance of the housing element, deferred to the trial court's determination that the moratorium was necessary to prevent development that might frustrate the ability to implement a new housing element, because of the limited area available for new housing. *Id.* at 1013–14. The court compared the Legislature's emphasis on the need for an adequate general plan to its intent that CEQA be applied to afford the fullest possible protection to the environment, and held that the definition of "significant" in CEQA should apply to Government Code section 65755 as well. Based on this analogy, the court adopted CEQA's "significant effect" definition as

In the event of a judicial determination that the plan is inadequate, the Government Code specifies the types of municipal actions that may be suspended, and specifies time limits to be imposed on the preparation of an adequate plan.

being "a substantial, or potentially substantial, adverse change in the environment." Pub. Res. Code § 21068. Of key importance in the *Indian Wells* case was the city's recent approval of a resort containing 4,500 hotel rooms, which would generate a substantial need for affordable housing for the resort's employees.

Conclusion

The general plan is the most important legal planning tool for a city to utilize in its efforts to regulate development. It is the constitution for all future development. The goals and policies of the general plan can be used not only in managing growth but also in imposing dedications and impact fees on new projects, especially those not directly authorized under state law. Examples include dedications for libraries, police stations, and fire station sites, and fees for affordable housing or child day care centers, provided that the general plan contains the legally required nexus.

However, all of this presupposes the existence of a legally adopted general plan. Cities must ensure that their general plans meet the test of state law as enunciated by the courts, and should refer to the 2003 edition of the OPR's General Plan Guidelines for assistance. Since the general plan is the constitution for all development, the plan can be of major legal assistance to cities in drafting all ordinances and regulations and for making proper land use decisions.

The goals and policies of the general plan can be used not only in managing growth but also in imposing dedications and impact fees on new projects, especially those not directly authorized under state law.

3

Specific Plan

Overview

The specific plan is just a step below the general plan in the land use approval hierarchy, and is used to systematically implement the general plan in particular geographical areas. Gov't Code § 65450. Zoning ordinances, subdivisions, public works projects, and development agreements all must be consistent with an applicable adopted specific plan. Gov't Code §§ 65455, 65867.5. Thus, it is important for a property owner or developer to check with the city planning or community development department to determine whether a specific plan covering the property has been adopted.

PRACTICE TIP

A property owner or developer should always check with the local planning department to see if a specific plan covers the property since that plan will govern the property's future development and use.

Contents

State law requires that a specific plan include text and a diagram or diagrams that specify all of the following in detail:

- Distribution, location, and extent of the uses of land, including open space, within the area covered by the plan
- Proposed distribution, location, extent and intensity of major components of public and private transportation, sewage, water, drainage, solid waste disposal, energy, and other essential facilities proposed to be located within the area covered by the plan and needed to support the land uses described in the plan
- Standards and criteria by which development will proceed and, where applicable, standards for conservation, development, and utilization of natural resources
- A program of implementation measures including regulations, programs, public works projects, and financing measures necessary to carry out the matters listed above

Gov't Code § 65451(a)

The specific plan also must include a statement of the relationship between the specific plan and the general plan. Gov't Code § 65451(b). In *Napa Citizens for Honest Gov't v. County of Napa Bd. of Supervisors*, the court reviewed a specific plan for consistency with the county's general plan. 91 Cal. App. 4th 342 (2001). The specific plan in question did not directly conflict with the general plan, but nevertheless was determined by the court to be incompatible with

The specific plan must include a statement of the relationship between the specific plan and the general plan.

certain goals and policies of the general plan. The court acknowledged that a county's conclusion that a specific plan is consistent with its general plan "carries a strong presumption of regularity that can be overcome only by a showing of abuse of discretion." *Id.* at 357. Despite this stated deference, the court invalidated the specific plan. In declaring the specific plan inconsistent with the general plan, the court noted that the specific plan frustrated the general plan's goals and policies by failing to include definite affirmative commitments to mitigate the specific plan's adverse effects. *Id.* at 366. The court stated that the consistency doctrine requires that a specific plan do more than simply recite goals and policies that are consistent with those set forth in the county general plan, making clear that an outright conflict is not required for a finding of inconsistency. *Id.* In fact, a project is consistent with the general plan if, considering all its aspects, it will further the objectives and policies of the general plan and not obstruct their attainment. *Id.* at 378.

The specific plan also may address any other subjects that, in the judgment of the city, are necessary or desirable for implementation of the general plan. Gov't Code § 65452. Additionally, cities are increasingly adopting more comprehensive and detailed specific plans by ordinances and declaring such plans to constitute the zoning for areas. *See* chapter 4.

Adoption

The procedures for adopting and amending a specific plan are essentially the same as for a general plan, except that it may be amended as often as necessary, and may be adopted by ordinance or resolution. The adoption or amendment of a specific plan, like a general plan, is a legislative act. *See Yost v. Thomas*, 36 Cal. 3d 561, 570 (1984). To defray the cost of preparation of the specific plan, cities may impose a specific plan fee upon persons seeking governmental approvals that are required to be consistent with the specific plan. Gov't Code § 65456(a).

Specific plans, like general plans, must be consistent with any applicable county Airport Land Use Plans (ALUPs) adopted pursuant to Public Utilities Code section 21675, unless the city overrules the airport land use commission and makes certain findings. The Attorney General has opined that allowing a specific plan to be exempted from compliance with more stringent land use compatibility standards in a local ALUP would undermine the legislative intent behind the detailed procedure in the Public Resources Code for resolution of inconsistencies. 87 Ops. Cal. Atty. Gen. 96 (2004). For a discussion of how to address conflicts between a specific plan and an ALUP, *see* chapter 2 (General Plan).

Interplay with CEQA

To assist and encourage cities and developers to use specific plans for development of housing, State law exempts certain residential development projects from further CEQA requirements if they are undertaken to implement and are consistent with a specific plan for which an EIR has been certified. Gov't Code § 65457; *see also* Dills, Allen, and Sher, California Environmental Quality Act Revision Act of 1993, Pub. Res. Code §§ 21156–21159.9 (use of Master Environmental Impact Report process applicable to specific plan adoptions);

Stephen L. Kostka and Michael H. Zischke, *Practice Under the California Environmental Quality Act*, chapter 5 (Cal. Cont. Ed. Bar, 2008). For a more thorough discussion of the requirements of CEQA, *see* chapter 6 (CEQA).

For a more detailed discussion of specific plans, *see* Governor's Office of Planning and Research, *The Planner's Guide to Specific Plans*, January 2001.

Judicial Review

Because the adoption of a specific plan is a legislative act, it is reviewed by the courts in traditional mandate proceedings. Judicial review is generally limited to an examination of the proceedings before the city to determine whether its adoption of the specific plan was arbitrary or capricious, entirely lacking in evidentiary support, or whether it failed to follow the procedures and give the notices required by law. *See Mitchell v. County of Orange*, 165 Cal. App. 3d 1185, 1191–92 (1985); Code Civ. Proc. § 1085. This "arbitrary and capricious" test also applies to challenges to a specific plan's conformance with a general plan. *Id. See also Kawaoka v. City of Arroyo Grande*, 17 F. 3d 1227, 1238 (9th Cir. 1994) (applying the arbitrary and capricious test, the court held that a general plan's requirement that a specific plan be prepared before land was converted to residential use was not arbitrary; nor was requiring payment of a fee for preparation of a specific plan unconstitutional). Any lawsuit challenging the adoption or amendment of a specific plan must be brought within 90 days after the city council's decision. Gov't Code § 65009.

Any lawsuit challenging the adoption or amendment of a specific plan must be brought within 90 days after the city council's decision.

Once a specific plan is adopted, courts give substantial deference to a city's determination of whether a particular project is consistent with that specific plan. *Sierra Club v. County of Napa*, 121 Cal. App. 4th 1490, 1497 (2004). In *Sierra Club*, the petitioners challenged the county's issuance of a use permit for development of a winery. The EIR for the project concluded that the project would result in the loss of some seasonal wetlands. Petitioners claimed the project was inconsistent with a policy in an applicable specific plan providing that wetlands shall be protected in their natural state unless shown to be infeasible. *Id.* at 1506.

In upholding the county's approval of the use permit, the court deferred to the county's conclusion that preservation of the wetlands was not "feasible," finding there was substantial evidence in the record to support that conclusion. It also noted that the "agency had discretion to approve a plan even though the plan is not consistent with all of the specific plan's policies. It is enough that the proposed project will be compatible with the objectives, policies, general land uses and programs specified in the applicable plan." *Id.* at 1511–12.

For a more thorough discussion of judicial review, *see* chapter 21 (Land Use Litigation).

4

Zoning

Zoning Defined

In general terms, zoning is the division of a city into districts and the application of different regulations in each district. A zoning regulation is often city-wide, such as a city-wide building height limit. *See Taschner v. City Council*, 31 Cal. App. 3d 48, 62 (1973). Zoning regulations are generally divided into two classes: (1) those that regulate the height or bulk of physical structures within certain designated districts—in other words, those regulations that have to do with structural and architectural design of the buildings; and (2) those that prescribe the use to which buildings within certain designated districts may be put. "[Z]oning is a separation of the municipality into districts, and the regulation of buildings and structures, according to their construction, and the nature and extent of their use, and the nature and extent of the uses of land." *O'Loane v. O'Rourke*, 231 Cal. App. 2d 774, 780 (1965).

The Legislature has given cities maximum control over zoning matters while ensuring uniformity of, and public access to, zoning and planning hearings. *See Beck Dev. Co. v. Southern Pac. Transp. Co.*, 44 Cal. App. 4th 1160, 1187–88 (1996).

PRACTICE TIP

Because the State Zoning Law does not apply to charter cities that have not adopted it by charter or ordinance, one should call the City Clerk to see if the city is in fact a charter city or consult the latest issue of *California Planners' Book of Lists* published by the Governor's Office of Planning and Research.

Application to Charter Cities

The State Zoning Law (Gov't Code § 65800 *et seq*.) applies to general law cities and all counties. The State Zoning Law does not apply to a charter city, however, except to the extent a city adopts it by charter or ordinance, or the Legislature has specifically required its application. Gov't Code § 65803. For example, Government Code section 65804, requiring cities to implement minimum procedural standards for the conduct of zoning hearings, is specifically applicable to charter cities. *See also* Gov't Code § 65589.5 (restricting a city's power to disapprove affordable housing).

The State Zoning Law does not apply to a charter city, except to the extent that a city adopts it by charter or ordinance or the Legislature has specifically required its application.

Judicial Review [1]
Presumption of Validity

A zoning ordinance is a legislative act and, unlike administrative decisions, does not require explicit findings. A zoning ordinance is valid if it is reasonably related

---

1. For a detailed discussion of judicial review, *see* chapter 21 (Land Use Litigation).

to the public welfare. *See Arnel Dev. Co. v. City of Costa Mesa*, 28 Cal. 3d 511, 522 (1980). Such an ordinance comes before the court with every presumption in its favor, including a presumption of constitutionality. *See Lockard v. City of Los Angeles*, 33 Cal. 2d 453, 460 (1949).

Because zoning is legislative, it is reviewed in ordinary mandate proceedings.

Because zoning is legislative, it is reviewed in ordinary mandate proceedings. Generally, the burden rests with the party challenging the constitutionality of an ordinance to present the evidence and documentation that a court will require in undertaking a constitutional analysis. *See Associated Home Builders, Inc. v. City of Livermore*, 18 Cal. 3d 582, 601 (1976). There is an exception, however. When a city adopts an ordinance directly limiting the number of dwelling units, the burden of proof reverts to the city to justify its action. Evid. Code § 669.5. This applies to ordinances adopted by the city council or the voters through the initiative process. *See Lee v. City of Monterey Park*, 173 Cal. App. 3d 798, 806–07 (1985); *Bldg. Indus. Ass'n v. City of Camarillo*, 41 Cal. 3d 810, 818 (1986); *but see Hernandez v. City of Encinitas*, 28 Cal. App. 4th 1048, 1074–75 (1994) (Evidence Code section 669.5 did not apply to challenges to a city's housing element and its implementing regulations).

Limited Role of Court Review—Policy Issue

As long as the ordinance bears a reasonable relationship to the public welfare, courts have consistently refused to substitute judicial judgment for the legislative decisions made by a city.

Because of the broad construction of the police power as it relates to land use regulations, including zoning, the courts have consistently taken a "hands off" approach when reviewing the validity of such regulations. The courts have recognized the separation of powers between the legislative and judicial branches, and as long as the ordinance bears a reasonable relationship to the public welfare, courts have consistently refused to substitute judicial judgment for the legislative decisions made by a city. As the United States Supreme Court stated:

> It is not our function to appraise the wisdom of its decision.... In either event, the city's interest in attempting to preserve the quality of urban life is one that must be accorded high respect. Moreover, the city must be allowed a reasonable opportunity to experiment with solutions to admittedly serious problems.

Young v. Am. Mini Theatres, Inc., 427 U.S. 50, 71 (1976)

A California court described the judiciary's role in considering the validity of zoning regulations as follows:

> [a.] The wisdom of the [zoning regulation] is a matter for legislative determination, and even though a court may not agree with that determination, it will not substitute its judgment for that of the zoning authorities if there is any reasonable justification for their action.
>
> [b.] In passing upon the validity of legislation,... the rule is well settled that the legislative determination that the facts exist which make the law necessary, must not be set aside by the courts, unless the legislative decision is clearly and palpably wrong and the error appears beyond reasonable doubt from facts or evidence which cannot be controverted....
>
> [c.] In considering the scope... of appellate review,... [it] must be kept in mind that the courts are examining the act of a coordinate branch of the government—

the legislative—in a field in which it has paramount authority and, are not reviewing the decision of a lower tribunal or a fact-finding body.

[d.] Courts have nothing to do with the wisdom of laws and regulations, and the legislative power must be upheld unless manifestly abused so as to infringe on constitutional guaranties....

[e.] The only function of the courts is to determine whether the exercise of legislative power has exceeded constitutional limitations....

[f.] [T]he function of this court is to determine whether the record shows a reasonable basis for the action of the zoning authorities, and, if the reasonableness of the ordinance is fairly debatable, the legislative determination will not be disturbed.

Carty v. City of Ojai, 77 Cal. App. 3d 329, 333 (1978)

Enactment of Zoning Regulations

In General

Every city in California has an existing zoning ordinance. The effect of that zoning ordinance on real property can be changed by a city's adoption of an amending ordinance.

There are two basic types of substantive amendments to zoning ordinances: (1) reclassification of the zoning applicable to a specific property, designating a change from one district to another district, commonly called "rezoning"; and (2) changes in the permitted uses or regulations on property within particular zones or citywide, commonly called "text amendments." The first type of amendment usually involves a change in the zoning map, without any change in the text of the basic zoning ordinance. The second type of amendment usually involves amending the text of the zoning ordinance, but not the zoning map.

The Ordinance Must Be Reasonably Related to the Public Welfare

Zoning ordinances, as with other land use regulations, must be reasonably related to the public welfare. *See Associated Home Builders, Inc. v. City of Livermore*, 18 Cal. 3d at 604; *City of Del Mar v. City of San Diego*, 133 Cal. App. 3d 401, 409 (1982); *Arnel Dev. Co. v. City of Costa Mesa*, 126 Cal. App. 3d 330, 336 (1981). Consistently, courts have construed broadly what constitutes a reasonable relationship. For example, maintaining the character of residential neighborhoods is a proper purpose. In *Ewing v. City of Carmel-by-the-Sea*, an ordinance prohibiting transient commercial use of single-family homes was upheld based on the existence of a reasonable relationship to the public welfare. 234 Cal. App. 3d 1579, 1592 (1991).

The courts have interpreted the relationship to the public welfare to include not only the public welfare of the citizens of the city but also of the affected region, if necessary. In *Associated Home Builders, Inc. v. City of Livermore*, the California Supreme Court set forth the "*Livermore* test:" a three-step analysis for determining whether a land use regulation bears a reasonable relationship to the regional welfare. 18 Cal. 3d at 604. First, the court must forecast the probable effect and duration of the restriction. Second, the court

The court must determine whether the regulation, in light of its probable effect, represents a reasonable accommodation of the competing interests.

must identify the competing interests affected by the restriction, *e.g.*, open space versus affordable housing. Finally, the court must determine whether the regulation, in light of its probable effect, represents a reasonable accommodation of the competing interests. In all cases, the regulation must have a "real and substantial" relationship to the public welfare.

Numerous courts have applied the *Livermore* test to determine whether a zoning ordinance is valid, reaching varied results. For example, in *Arnel*, the court struck down a rezoning initiative aimed at defeating a multi-family housing project as an improper exercise of the police power. The record demonstrated that the initiative discriminated against a particular piece of property, and failed to consider the competing interest of the community in the development of affordable housing. 126 Cal. App. 3d at 337–38. Conversely, in *Del Mar*, the court upheld the San Diego North City West Housing Development Plan, concluding that the regulation bore a substantial and reasonable relationship to the public welfare. 133 Cal. App. 3d at 415.

The California Supreme Court upheld the City of Santa Monica's antidemolition ordinance against an attack that it operated to deprive a landowner of property without due process of law by restricting his right to go out of the rental business. *See Nash v. City of Santa Monica*, 37 Cal. 3d 97 (1984). The Court stated that the applicable legal test "requires the regulation be 'procedurally fair and reasonably related to a proper legislative goal. The wisdom of the legislation is not at issue in analyzing its constitutionality....'" *Id*. at 108–09. The Court stated that the city's ordinance met the *Livermore* test. *Id*. at 109.

In *Hernandez v. City of Hanford*, the city adopted a zoning ordinance that prohibited the sale of furniture in a planned commercial district, with a limited exception for large department stores. 41 Cal. 4th 279 (2007). The California Supreme Court upheld the zoning ordinance's general prohibition on the sale of furniture. Although the ordinance concededly intended, at least in part, to regulate competition, the Supreme Court held that the ordinance was adopted to promote the legitimate public purpose of preserving the economic viability of the Hanford downtown business district. *Id*. at 298. The ordinance was not adopted to serve any impermissible private anti-competitive purpose. Additionally, the Supreme Court held that the ordinance did not violate the equal protection clause because it survived the rational basis test, even though it served the dual purpose of protecting the city's downtown economic health and attracting large department stores. *Id*. at 300.

Zoning Must Be Consistent with the General Plan

Zoning ordinances must be consistent with the general plan and any applicable specific plan.

Zoning ordinances must be consistent with the general plan and any applicable specific plan. Gov't Code § 65860(a). This provision does not apply to charter cities, with the exception of Los Angeles. Gov't Code §§ 65803, 65860(d). However, a charter city can, on its own, require consistency by charter or by ordinance. *See Verdugo Woodlands Homeowners Ass'n v. City of Glendale*, 179 Cal. App. 3d 696 (1986); *City of Irvine v. Irvine Citizens Against Overdevelopment*, 25 Cal. App. 4th 868 (1994) (where the charter city of Irvine required consistency); *Garat v. City of Riverside*, 2 Cal. App. 4th 259 (1991) (the charter of the City of Riverside did not require consistency).

A zoning ordinance is consistent with a city's general plan only if:

- The city has officially adopted such a plan, and
- The various land uses authorized by the ordinance are compatible with the objectives, policies, general land uses, and programs specified in such a plan

Gov't Code § 65860(a)

Under new 2007 legislation, each city located within the Sacramento-San Joaquin Valley will be required to amend its zoning ordinances so that they are consistent with the flood protection goals and policies of the city's general plan. Gov't Code §§ 65302.9(a), 65860.1.

Applying the consistency test set forth in the Governor's Office of Planning and Research, *General Plan Guidelines* (2003) page 166, a zoning ordinance is consistent with a city's general plan where, considering all of its aspects, the ordinance furthers the objectives and policies of the general plan and does not obstruct their attainment. *See City of Irvine*, 25 Cal. App. 4th at 879.

A zoning ordinance is consistent with a city's general plan where, considering all of its aspects, the ordinance furthers the objectives and policies of the general plan and does not obstruct their attainment.

Any resident or property owner within a city may bring an action in superior court to enforce compliance with the consistency requirement. Such actions or proceedings are governed by Code of Civil Procedure section 1084 *et seq*. Except for certain exceptions in Government Code section 65009(d) expressly relating to housing projects for low-income persons and families, any actions or proceedings must be taken within 90 days of the enactment of any new zoning ordinance or the amendment of any existing zoning ordinance, and any such action also must be served on a city within this 90-day period. Gov't Code § 65860(b). The purpose of this remedy is to "compel amendment of a nonconforming zoning ordinance to bring it into compliance with the general plan." *Gonzalez v. County of Tulare*, 65 Cal. App. 4th 777, 785 (1998). Also, a city can avail itself of this statute of limitations period in a pre-election challenge to an initiative or referendum related to zoning. *See City of Irvine*, 25 Cal. App. 4th at 879.

A city's findings that the zoning ordinance is consistent with its general plan can be reversed only if it is based on evidence from which no reasonable person could have reached the same conclusion. *See A Local & Reg'l Monitor v. City of Los Angeles*, 16 Cal. App. 4th 630, 648 (1993).

The courts have stated that a zoning ordinance inconsistent with the general plan at the time of enactment is "void *ab initio*," meaning invalid when passed. *See Lesher Commc'ns, Inc. v. City of Walnut Creek*, 52 Cal. 3d 531, 541 (1990); *City of Irvine*, 25 Cal. App. 4th at 879; *Bldg. Indus. Ass'n v. City of Oceanside*, 27 Cal. App. 4th 744, 762 (1994); *deBottari v. City Council*, 171 Cal. App. 3d 1204, 1212 (1985). However, while an inconsistent ordinance is void when adopted, its invalidity still must be determined judicially in an appropriate legal action, and any such action is governed by the appropriate statute of limitations. *See Gonzalez*, 65 Cal. App. 4th at 785–91. If a zoning ordinance becomes inconsistent with a general plan by reason of an amendment to the plan, or to any element of the plan, the ordinance must be amended within a reasonable time so that it is consistent with the amended general plan. Gov't Code § 65860(c).

The courts have stated that a zoning ordinance inconsistent with the general plan at the time of enactment is "void ab initio," *meaning invalid when passed.*

Since general plan consistency is required, the absence of a valid general plan, or the failure of any relevant elements thereof to meet statutory criteria, precludes the enactment of zoning ordinances and the like. *See Res. Def. Fund v.*

County of Santa Cruz, 133 Cal. App. 3d 800, 806 (1982).[2] For further discussion of general plan consistency, *see* chapter 2 (General Plan).

Zoning Must Be Consistent with Airport Land Use Plan

Just as a city's general plan must be consistent with any ALUP that overlaps with the city's planning area, so too must a city's zoning be consistent with any applicable ALUP.

ALUP = Airport Land Use Plan

Just as a city's general plan must be consistent with any Airport Land Use Plan (ALUP) that overlaps with the city's planning area, so too must a city's zoning be consistent with any applicable ALUP, unless the city overrules the airport land use commission and makes certain findings. Pub. Util. Code § 21676(b). Prior to adoption or approval of a zoning ordinance or building regulation within the planning boundary established by the ALUP, a city must first refer the proposed action to the commission that adopted the relevant ALUP. Pub. Util. Code § 21676(b). In the event the commission finds the zoning regulation to be inconsistent with its ALUP, and upon making specific findings, the city may overrule the commission by a two-thirds vote. Pub. Util. Code § 21676(b). The timeframes, procedures, and findings requirements for overruling a commission's findings of inconsistency in order to approve a zoning regulation are the same as those for overruling an ALUP to amend a general plan and are explained in chapter 2 (General Plan). *See also* Pub. Util. Code § 21676(b). For a comprehensive discussion of Airport Land Use Commissions, how they devise Airport Land Use Plans, and how they determine consistency with local agencies' proposed general plans and zoning regulations, *see* The California Airport Land Use Planning Handbook, California Department of Transportation, Division of Aeronautics, January 2002 (available at www.dot.ca.gov/hp/planning/aeronaut/htmfile/landuse.php).

Due Process Requirements

Rezonings, no matter how small the parcel, and text amendments are legislative acts and are not administrative or quasi-judicial in nature.

Rezonings, no matter how small the parcel, and zoning text amendments are legislative acts and are not administrative or quasi-judicial in nature. *See Arnel Dev. Co. v. City of Costa Mesa*, 28 Cal. 3d 511, 514 (1980). As a general rule, procedural due process requirements of notice and hearing to nearby property owners only apply in quasi-judicial or adjudicatory hearings and not in the adoption of general legislation. *See Horn v. County of Ventura*, 24 Cal. 3d 605, 612 (1979). However, notice and hearing are statutorily required where zoning ordinance amendments change property from one zone to another, or impose or delete certain regulations listed in Government Code section 65850. For more detail, *see* the requirements set forth in Government Code section 65854 *et seq*. Any other amendment to a zoning ordinance may be adopted as other ordinances are adopted (Gov't Code § 65853), although special provision is made for notice and hearing on interim ordinances, such as urgency measures. Gov't Code § 65858.

Although the State Zoning Law requires both a hearing before the planning commission, if there is one, and a hearing before the city council prior to the enactment of certain amendments to zoning ordinances, it requires only that

---

2. The Attorney General opined that a county may incorporate land use designations and other provisions of its zoning ordinances into its general plan and then repeal its zoning ordinances and replace them with a single ordinance that requires all land use activity to conform to the general plan. *See* 81 Ops. Cal. Atty. Gen. 57 (1998).

minimum due process standards be observed in conducting those hearings. Gov't Code § 65804. This applies to all zoning authorities, including charter cities.

Government Code section 65804 requires that every city:

- Develop and publish procedural rules governing the conduct of hearings so that all interested parties shall have advance knowledge of the procedures to be followed
- Keep and provide a record of the hearings when a matter is contested and a request is made in writing prior to the date of hearing
- Make public any planning commission's staff report prior to a hearing; and
- Prepare a staff report with recommendations and the basis for the recommendations, which shall be included in the record of the hearing, when a hearing is held on an application for a change of zone for parcels of at least 10 acres

Proposed zoning amendments must be submitted to the planning commission and given a noticed public hearing. Gov't Code § 65854. After the hearing, the planning commission must render its decision in the form of a written recommendation to the city council that includes the reasons for the recommendation and the relationship of the proposed amendment to applicable general and specific plans. Gov't Code § 65855.

Except in limited circumstances, upon receipt of the recommendation of the planning commission, the city council must hold a public hearing on the proposed amendment. Gov't Code § 65856. Following a noticed hearing, the city council may approve, modify, or disapprove the planning commission's recommendation. A zoning ordinance adopted without the required notice and hearing will be void. *See Sounhein v. City of San Dimas*, 11 Cal. App. 4th 1255, 1260 (1992).

If the city council wants to modify a recommendation not previously considered by the planning commission, it is required to refer the modification back to the planning commission for a report and recommendation. However, the planning commission is not required to hold a public hearing regarding the modification under consideration. Failure of the planning commission to report within 40 days after the referral was made shall be considered an approval of the proposed modification. Gov't Code § 65857.

Sufficiency of Standards— Vagueness and Uncertainty

A land use ordinance, including a zoning ordinance, cannot be so vague or uncertain that a person of common intelligence and understanding must guess as to its meaning. If this occurs, due process of law could be violated. *See People v. Gates*, 41 Cal. App. 3d 590, 601–02 (1974); *see also Associated Home Builders, Inc. v. City of Livermore*, 18 Cal. 3d at 596 (upholding the general terms of a growth management initiative against a vagueness challenge). However, the California courts have stated that a substantial amount of vagueness is permitted in land use ordinances.

The leading case on this issue is *Novi v. City of Pacifica*, where the court held that a city's land use ordinance, which precluded uses that were detrimental to the "general welfare" as well as developments that were "monotonous" in design and external appearance, was not unconstitutionally vague, either facially or as applied. 169 Cal. App. 3d 678 (1985). Novi was a developer who sought to construct a 48-unit condominium project. The project was turned down because it would have violated the city's anti-monotony ordinance. Novi argued that the city's ordinance lacked objective criteria for reviewing the element of monotony, and that such criteria are required for aesthetic land use regulations. The court disagreed, however, stating:

> In fact, a substantial amount of vagueness is permitted in California zoning ordinances: "[I]n California, the most general zoning standards are usually deemed sufficient. 'The standard is sufficient if the administrative body is required to make its decision in accord with the general health, safety, and welfare standard.' [citations omitted] 'California courts permit vague standards because they are sensitive to the need of government in large urban areas to delegate broad discretionary power to administrative bodies if the community's zoning business is to be done without paralyzing the legislative process.'" (alteration in original) [citations omitted].
>
> Here, subdivision (g) of section 9-4.3204 requires "variety in the design of the structure and grounds to avoid monotony in the external appearance." The legislative intent is obvious: the Pacifica city council wishes to avoid "ticky-tacky" development of the sort described by songwriter Malvina Reynolds in the song, "Little Boxes." No further objective criteria are required, just as none are required under the general welfare ordinance. Subdivision (g) is sufficiently specific under the California rule permitting local legislative bodies to adopt ordinances delegating broad discretionary power to administrative bodies.

Id. at 682

Relying on *Novi*, another court held that a view protection ordinance was not unconstitutionally vague, finding that such an ordinance supported a building permit denial. See *Ross v. City of Rolling Hills Estates*, 192 Cal. App. 3d 370, 376 (1987); *see also Hotel & Motel Ass'n of Oakland v. City of Oakland*, 344 F. 3d 959 (9th Cir. 2003) (an ordinance improving conditions in and around hotels was not vague; a party challenging the facial validity of an ordinance on vagueness grounds outside the domain of the First Amendment must demonstrate that the "enactment is impermissibly vague in all of its applications"); *Personal Watercraft Coalition v. Marin County Board of Supervisors*, 100 Cal. App. 4th 129, 140 (2002) (prohibition of personal watercraft in specific area was not unconstitutionally vague); *Briggs v. City of Rolling Hills Estates*, 40 Cal. App. 4th 637, 643 (1995) (a "neighborhood compatibility" ordinance protecting privacy was not unconstitutionally vague); *City of Los Altos v. Barnes*, 3 Cal. App. 4th 1193, 1203 (1992) (specific land use ordinances were not unconstitutionally vague); *Ewing v. City of Carmel-by-the-Sea*, 234 Cal. App. 3d at 1595 (ordinance that prohibited rental of residential property for fewer than 30 days was not unconstitutionally vague).

Adoption of a Zoning Ordinance

If the city council approves, or approves as modified, a proposed zoning amendment, the council must introduce it at a regular or adjourned regular meeting and then adopt the amendment by ordinance at a subsequent meeting. Gov't Code §§ 36934, 65850. In contrast, county boards of supervisors are authorized to adopt a rezoning ordinance with only one reading after a noticed public hearing. Gov't Code § 25131.

The amendment of a zoning ordinance is a legislative rather than a quasi-judicial function; therefore, findings are not required unless state law or local ordinance so provides. *See Arnel Dev. Co. v. City of Costa Mesa*, 28 Cal. 3d 511, 514 (1980). For example, state law requires findings when a city limits the number of housing units through general plan or zoning adoption—both of which are legislative acts. Gov't Code §§ 65302.8, 65863.6.

A California court held that Government Code section 65030.2, which contains a policy statement that land use decisions be made with "full knowledge of their economic and fiscal implications," creates no duty to prepare a financing plan for a public facility prior to approving a rezoning. *See Towards Responsibility in Planning v. City Council*, 200 Cal. App. 3d 671, 677–78 (1988). The court declined the plaintiffs' request to treat the policy statement as a substantive requirement. Instead, the court concluded that rezoning is a legislative act, and that review of such acts is limited to a determination of whether it was arbitrary and capricious or without any evidentiary basis. *Id*. For further discussion, *see* chapter 11 (Necessity for Findings).

Motives

As a general rule, motives of the city council or local officials in amending or declining to amend a zoning ordinance are irrelevant to any inquiry concerning its reasonableness. *See Cormier v. County of San Luis Obispo*, 161 Cal. App. 3d 850, 858 (1984). For further discussion of this principle, *see* chapter 21 (Land Use Litigation).

The issue of motives of an individual member of a board of supervisors was discussed in *County of Butte v. Bach*:

> The Bachs suggest that, by advancing the interests of the neighbors who opposed commercial use of the corner lots, Supervisor Wheeler, and by attribution the County of Butte, acted improperly. The implication is that Wheeler's affiliation with the cause of those constituents who opposed the commercial use is an illicit motivation for her official acts in the course of the controversy. With few exceptions, *e.g.*, racially discriminatory animus, none of which are made out in this case, the motive of officials enacting a zoning ordinance is immaterial. (Citation omitted.) Absent such an unconstitutional motivation, we discern no legal impropriety in an elected official siding with one faction in what is, so long as the alternative chosen is not unreasonable, ultimately a political contest. (Citation omitted.)

172 Cal. App. 3d 848 (1985) at 862 n.1

Motives also are irrelevant to an inquiry concerning other land use decisions, including nonlegislative ones. In fact, the subjective motives or mental processes of city council members are subject to the legislative privilege. *See Kleitman v. Superior Court*, 74 Cal. App. 4th 324, 335–36 (1999). Thus, a showing of individual bias or prejudice based upon prior statements of an individual legislator is irrelevant. *See City of Fairfield v. Superior Court*, 14 Cal. 3d 768, 773 (1975). Discovery to learn whether local legislators arrived at their position before the hearing also is barred as irrelevant. Such positions do not disqualify one from voting or invalidate the decision. *Id*. at 780. Discovery into council members' legislative motives or mental processes to support a claim of a general plan's invalidity is not permitted. *See City of Santa Cruz v. Superior Court*, 40 Cal. App. 4th 1146, 1148 (1995).

Acquisition of information outside the hearing does not disqualify or invalidate the actions in the hearing.

Further, acquisition of information outside the hearing does not disqualify or invalidate the actions in the hearing. *See Board of Supervisors v. Superior Court*, 32 Cal. App. 4th 1616, 1627 (1995) (citing *City of Fairfield v. Superior Court*). The Attorney General opined that a city council member who signed a petition opposing a land use project is not disqualified from participating in the council proceeding during which the application for a conditional use permit for the project is considered. *See* 78 Ops. Cal. Atty. Gen. 77 (1995) (citing *City of Fairfield v. Superior Court*).

Subject to the limited exceptions discussed below, a government official's motive for voting on a land use issue is irrelevant to assessing the validity of the action. For example, in *Breneric Assocs. v. City of Del Mar*, the court rejected allegations of hostile feelings of design review board members and the city council in denying a design review permit. 69 Cal. App. 4th 166, 184 (1998).

In another case, a court said that nothing illegal transpired when one city council member did everything he could to delay a project and then have it denied. *See Stubblefield Constr. Co. v. City of San Bernardino*, 32 Cal. App. 4th 687, 710–11 (1995).

A limited exception to the general rule has been recognized when the facts reveal that a zoning action was taken for an unlawful purpose. For example, when the police power has been exercised in such a manner as to oppress or discriminate against an individual or individuals or against a particular parcel of land, it will be overturned. *See G & D Holland Constr. Co. v. City of Marysville*, 12 Cal. App. 3d 989, 994 (1970); *Kissinger v. City of Los Angeles*, 161 Cal. App. 2d 454 (1958).

In order to successfully claim a due process violation due to bias or improper motives, there must be a sufficient showing that a party's rights were prejudiced by the bias.

In order to successfully claim a due process violation due to bias or improper motives, there must be a sufficient showing that a party's rights were prejudiced by the bias. *See Sladovich v. County of Fresno*, 158 Cal. App. 2d 230, 239–40 (1958). For instance, in *Arnel Dev. Co. v. City of Costa Mesa*, the court held an initiative rezoning ordinance to be invalid as discriminatory, stating that motives and legislative purpose are factors to be considered in determining whether a zoning ordinance is invalid as discriminatory. 126 Cal. App. 3d at 337. The court looked at the ballot arguments, in part, to determine that the initiative ordinance discriminated against a particular parcel of land.

In *Nasha v. City of Los Angeles*, the court set aside the decision of the planning commission and ordered a new hearing after it was disclosed that one of the commissioners wrote an unsigned article in a newsletter that was hostile to the project. 125 Cal. App. 4th 470 (2004). The court held that authorship of such an article while the matter was pending before the commission showed an unacceptable probability of actual bias and was sufficient to preclude the Commissioner from serving as a "reasonably impartial, noninvolved reviewer." *Id.* at 484.

For a discussion of the admissibility of such evidence in court proceedings and discovery regarding a legislator's motives, *see* chapter 21 (Land Use Litigation).

Zoning by Initiative and/or Referendum

Under California law, all zoning ordinances are subject to initiative and referendum. *See Arnel Dev. Co. v. City of Costa Mesa*, 126 Cal. App. 3d at 336. While an initiative ordinance must comply with the substantive law, it need not comply with procedural requirements such as findings, notice, and hearing. *See Building Indus. Ass'n v. City of Camarillo*, 41 Cal. 3d 810, 815 (1986). However, when a referendum petition on a zoning ordinance will cause an inconsistency with the general plan, it cannot be processed. *See deBottari v. City Council*, 171 Cal. App. 3d 1204, 1213 (1985). In *City of Irvine v. Irvine Citizens Against Overdevelopment*, a proposed referendum on a prezoning was held invalid, since it would cause an inconsistency with the general plan if adopted. 25 Cal. App. 4th 868, 879 (1994). *See also Lesher Commc'ns, Inc. v. City of Walnut Creek*, 52 Cal. 3d 531, 541 (1990). For further discussion of this subject, *see* chapter 14 (Initiative and Referendum).

No Formal Rules of Evidence; Effect of Procedural Errors

Under Government Code section 65010(a), formal rules of evidence and procedure applicable in judicial actions and proceedings do not apply to any proceedings under the Planning and Zoning Law (Gov't Code § 65000 *et seq.*), except to the extent a city provides otherwise by charter, ordinance, resolution, or rule of procedure.

Government Code section 65010 is the "curative" statute for procedural errors in any action under the Planning and Zoning Law. Section 65010 applies to cure procedural errors so long as there has been no denial of due process. *See Mack v. Ironside*, 35 Cal. App. 3d 127, 130 (1973); *City of Sausalito v. County of Marin*, 12 Cal. App. 3d 550, 557 (1970). This statute makes it extremely difficult to invalidate land use decisions based upon mere procedural errors. It provides that no action regarding any planning or zoning matter by a city may be held void or invalid, or be set aside by any court, on grounds of improper admission or rejection of evidence or by reason of any error in matters pertaining to petitions, applications, notices, findings, records, hearings, reports, recommendations, appeal, or any other matters of procedure.

Government Code section 65010 is the "curative" statute for procedural errors in any action under the Planning and Zoning Law. Section 65010 applies to cure procedural errors so long as there has been no denial of due process.

The court may invalidate a decision, however, when after an examination of the entire case including the evidence, it determines (1) that the error was prejudicial, (2) that the complaining party suffered substantial injury as a result of the error, and (3) that a different result would have been probable if such error had not occurred. Gov't Code § 65010(b).

Zoning and the First Amendment

Regulation of Adult Businesses [3]

Zoning ordinances regulating adult businesses, such as adult motion picture theaters and adult bookstores and arcades, will be upheld as not violating the First Amendment Freedom of Speech Clause of the United States Constitution if the ordinance is a content-neutral "time, place, and manner" regulation designed to serve a substantial governmental interest, and if it allows for reasonable alternative avenues of communication. *See City of Renton v. Playtime Theatres, Inc.*, 475 U.S. 41 (1986); *Young v. American Mini Theatres, Inc.*, 427 U.S. 50, 58 (1976).

---

3. *See* Daniel R. Mandelker and Rebecca Rubin, eds., *Protecting Free Speech and Expression: The First Amendment and Land Use Law* (Sect. of State and Local Gov't Law, ABA, 2001).

In 1992, the California Supreme Court upheld such a zoning ordinance where a city sought to close an adult bookstore and arcade. *See City of National City v. Wiener*, 3 Cal. 4th 832, 843 (1992). That ordinance prohibited any adult business from locating within 1,500 feet of another adult business, 1,500 feet of a school or public park, or 1,000 feet of any residentially zoned property. There was no limit on the total number of adult businesses that could locate in National City, nor on the hours they could operate. The ordinance also provided that adult businesses were not subject to the distance requirements and could locate anywhere within the city's 572 acres of commercially zoned property if the business was located in a retail shopping center. The Court concluded that the ordinance was content-neutral because it was not aimed at the content of materials sold. In addition, the "substantial government interest" requirement was satisfied based on adult businesses being a source of urban decay. Moreover, reasonable alternative avenues of communication were provided. The argument that current sites were not available for rent did not establish constitutional infirmity. "The inquiry for First Amendment purposes is not concerned with economic impact." *Id*. at 847.

An ordinance that keeps adult businesses a reasonable distance from residential areas may be a constitutional time, place, and manner restriction that does not violate the First Amendment.

An ordinance that keeps adult businesses a reasonable distance from residential areas may be a constitutional time, place, and manner restriction that does not violate the First Amendment. However, such a restriction is not per se constitutional, and can be enforced only if the restriction is reasonably related to preventing undesirable secondary effects, such as neighborhood blight or crime. For example, in *Gammoh v. City of Anaheim*, a court found the denial of a permit unconstitutional after finding that the applicant adult business could not create any secondary effects upon a single undeveloped residential parcel located within an industrial zone. 73 Cal. App. 4th 186, 191 (1999).

While a city must demonstrate that there is a reasonable relationship between the restriction and the purported secondary effects, the United States Supreme Court has made it clear that this burden is not a heavy one.

However, while a city must demonstrate that there is a reasonable relationship between the restriction and the purported secondary effects, in *City of Los Angeles v. Alameda Books, Inc.*, the United States Supreme Court made it clear that this burden is not a heavy one. 535 U.S. 425 (2002). In 1977, the City of Los Angeles conducted a study concluding that concentration of adult entertainment establishments was associated with higher crime rates. In response, in 1983, the city enacted a zoning ordinance prohibiting more than one adult operation from occupying a single structure. Alameda Books, Inc., which shared building space with another adult entertainment business, sued to have the ordinance declared unconstitutional. The Ninth Circuit affirmed the grant of summary judgment in favor of Alameda Books by the trial court. Specifically, the Ninth Circuit found that the city could not reasonably rely on the 1977 study to show that the ordinance was designed to reduce crime.

The United States Supreme Court, in ruling for the city, reversed and remanded. The Court found that it was reasonable for the city to conclude from the 1977 report that the reduction of adult businesses in a single locale would help reduce crime. The city could have rationally concluded that a number of adult operations in one single establishment drew the same dense foot traffic as would separate establishments in close proximity. This is a reasonable conclusion drawn from the 1977 report, although other conclusions were also possible. The Ninth Circuit imposed too high a burden by requiring the city to prove that its conclusion was the only one to be drawn from the 1977 study.

Alameda Books failed to provide evidence that refuted the city's interpretation of the study. Therefore, the city had satisfied the evidentiary requirement to survive summary judgment.

In arriving at its decision, the Court relied on its earlier decision in *Renton v. Playtime Theatres, Inc.*, wherein it upheld the validity of a municipal zoning ordinance prohibiting any adult movie theater from locating within 1,000 feet of any residential zone, family dwelling, church, park, or school. 475 U.S. 41 (1986).

The Court stated that in *Renton*, it specifically refused to set such a high bar for municipalities that want to address merely the secondary effects of protected speech. It held that a municipality may rely on any evidence that is "reasonably believed to be relevant" for demonstrating a connection between speech and a substantial, independent government interest. A city may not rely on shoddy data or reasoning, and its evidence must fairly support its rationale for its ordinance. However, if the plaintiffs fail either to demonstrate that the city's evidence does not support its rationale or furnish evidence that disputes the city's factual findings, the city meets the standard set forth in *Renton*. If the plaintiffs succeed in casting doubt on a city's rationale in either manner, the burden shifts back to the city to supplement the record with evidence renewing support for a theory that justifies its ordinance. The Court then stated that this case was at a very early stage in this process, noting that it arrived on a summary judgment motion by the respondents defended only by complaints that the 1977 study failed to prove that the city's justification for its ordinance was necessarily correct. Therefore, the Court concluded that the city, at this stage of the litigation, had complied with the evidentiary requirement in *Renton*.

In Renton *the Court held that a municipality may rely on any evidence that is "reasonably believed to be relevant" for demonstrating a connection between speech and a substantial, independent government interest.*

In *Isbell v. City of San Diego*, the plaintiff adult business owner claimed that the city's zoning ordinance, which prohibited adult businesses within 1000 feet of each other or any residential zone, school, church, public park, or social welfare institution, failed to offer reasonable alternative avenues of expression. 258 F. 3d 1108 (9th Cir. 2001). The Ninth Circuit first found that the methods used by both parties to compute the number of available alternative sites within the city were fatally flawed, and calculated a number of sites based on evidence in the record. It then held that the city's failure to analyze the supply and demand of adult businesses and to conduct other inquiries pursuant to a comprehensive and collective analysis failed to establish that reasonable alternative avenues of communication existed in the city under the ordinance.

The plaintiff next argued that because the freeway running between his property and the residential neighborhood 900 feet away would alleviate any secondary effects of his business, the 1000-foot rule served no valid purpose in his case and thus violated the First Amendment. The Ninth Circuit rejected this contention. Noting that any application of the 1000-foot rule would have varying effects in each situation, it held that if each situation must be examined and exceptions tailored, there would be nothing left of the 1000-foot rule approved by the United States Supreme Court in *American Mini Theatres*. Thus, the city could apply the rule without exception.

Finally, the plaintiff contended that the ordinance violated the Equal Protection Clause by applying variance standards that were more stringent for adult entertainment businesses than for non-adult businesses, since the city could take into account the mitigating effect that barriers such as freeways have on the secondary effects of a non-adult business, but could not do so with respect to an adult entertainment business. The court concluded that since the regulation of adult businesses is not a regulation of content and therefore may survive an equal protection challenge if it has a rational basis, the fact that the secondary effects of adult businesses are arguably more extreme than those of other businesses was enough to justify the more stringent review of variance applications for adult businesses.

In *City of Littleton, Colo. v. Z.J. Gifts D-4, LLC*, the owner of an adult business attacked a city's licensing requirement for adult business as unconstitutional on its face, claiming that the city's ordinance did not provide sufficiently prompt judicial review of license denials. 541 U.S. 774, 776–77 (2004). The Littleton ordinance called for applicants to take claims of improperly denied licenses to the Colorado state courts. The Tenth Circuit Court of Appeals agreed with the business owner, holding that Colorado law did not "assure that [the city's] license decisions will be given expedited [judicial] review" and hence, did not assure the prompt judicial decision that is required when First Amendment expression is implicated. *Id.* at 777.

On appeal to the United States Supreme Court, the city made two arguments in defense of its ordinance. First, it claimed that the First Amendment requires only prompt access to judicial review of adult-oriented business license denials or zoning decisions, not a prompt final judicial determination. The city noted there was nothing to stop business owners from going to court immediately to seek review of license denials. Second, the city claimed that, even if there were a requirement of prompt judicial determination, Colorado law satisfied that requirement.

The Supreme Court reversed the Tenth Circuit and upheld the city's ordinance. The Court, however, rejected the city's argument that a requirement for prompt judicial review somehow did not include a prompt judicial determination. "A delay in issuing a judicial decision, no less than a delay in obtaining access to a court, can prevent a license from being 'issued within a reasonable period of time.'" *Id.* at 781. But the Court agreed with the city that Colorado's ordinary "judicial review" rules were adequate to satisfy this "prompt judicial determination" requirement in any event. It reasoned that state courts have great flexibility to accelerate procedures and are presumed to know when they must exercise such power to protect against "unconstitutional suppression of protected speech." *Id.* at 782. The Court also noted that Littleton's ordinance imposed objective, nondiscretionary licensing criteria unrelated to the content of the expressive materials in the adult business. The use of such objective criteria meant there was not grave danger of suppression of any type of adult material. These circumstances indicated that Colorado's ordinary rules of judicial review were adequate to protect First Amendment interests. *Id.* at 784.

For further discussion of the intersection between adult entertainment zoning ordinances and the First Amendment, *see* Jules B. Gerard, *Local Regulation of Adult Businesses* (West, 2005) and Gov't Code § 65850.4 (regarding adoption of zoning ordinances to regulate sexually oriented businesses; authorizing cities to consider secondary effects of adult businesses on adjacent cities and to enter into joint powers authority and other cooperative agreements with adjacent cities for the purpose of regulating such effects).

In City of Littleton, *the Supreme Court rejected the city's argument that a requirement for prompt judicial review somehow did not include a prompt judicial determination.*

Protection of Religious Exercise

Courts have grappled with the question of what constitutes the proper standard of review in cases involving claims of infringement on the free exercise of religion. Prior to 1990, courts generally reviewed government actions that imposed substantial burdens on the exercise of religion under the strict scrutiny test; *i.e.*, a regulation must be the least restrictive means of furthering a compelling governmental interest. In 1990, the United States Supreme Court in large part eliminated this heightened scrutiny for cases involving the free exercise of religion. In *Employment Div. v. Smith*, the Court upheld a state law of general applicability criminalizing the use of peyote, which was used to deny unemployment benefits to Native American church members who lost their jobs because of such use. 494 U.S. 872 (1990). In so deciding, the Court declined to apply a balancing test that would have asked whether the law substantially burdened the religious use of peyote and, if so, whether that burden was justified by a compelling government interest. *Id.* at 885.

In response to the Court's decision, Congress enacted the Religious Freedom and Restoration Act of 1993 (RFRA). RFRA prohibited the government from imposing a substantial burden on a person's free exercise of religion unless the government could demonstrate that the burden furthered a compelling governmental interest and used the least restrictive means in doing so.

The Catholic Archbishop of San Antonio, Texas, invoked RFRA in the *City of Boerne v. Flores*, 521 U.S. 507 (1997). The Archbishop applied for a building permit to enlarge a church to accommodate its growing parish. The city denied the application based on a local preservation ordinance that required the city's landmark commission to preapprove construction affecting historic landmarks, such as the church. The Archbishop argued that the preservation ordinance constituted a substantial burden under RFRA. In ruling for the city, the Court held that RFRA's coverage of state and local governments exceeded Congressional authority and struck down the law as unconstitutional. *Id.* at 536.

In 2000, Congress passed the Religious Land Use and Institutionalized Persons Act (RLUIPA), 42 U.S.C. §§ 2000cc *et seq.* RLUIPA was drafted in light of recent pronouncements of the Court's federalism doctrine. Under RLUIPA, a government may not "impose or implement a land use regulation in a manner that imposes a substantial burden" on religious exercise unless the government demonstrates that the imposition of the burden is "in furtherance of a compelling governmental interest" and is the "least restrictive means of furthering" that interest. *Id.* at § 2000cc.

While RLUIPA does not itself define "substantial burden," the Ninth Circuit Court of Appeals, in 2004, clarified what must be shown to demonstrate a "substantial burden" on religious exercise under RLUIPA. *See San Jose Christian College v. City of Morgan Hill*, 360 F. 3d 1024, 1035 (9th Cir. 2004). The Ninth Circuit held that "for a land use regulation to impose a 'substantial burden,' it must be 'oppressive' to a 'significantly great' extent. That is, a 'substantial burden' on 'religious exercise' must impose a significantly great restriction or onus upon such exercise." *Id.* at 1034. The court held that the ordinance at issue imposed no restriction whatsoever on the college's exercise of religion; it merely required the college to submit a *complete* application for rezoning, as it

Courts have grappled with the question of what constitutes the proper standard of review in cases involving claims of infringement on the free exercise of religion.

RFRA = Religious Freedom and Restoration Act of 1993
RLUIPA = Religious Land Use and Institutionalized Persons Act

In 2000, Congress passed the Religious Land Use and Institutionalized Persons Act. RLUIPA was drafted in light of recent pronouncements in the Court's federalism doctrine.

required of all applicants. *Id.* at 1035. Because the college was not precluded from using other sites within the city and the city would have imposed the same application requirements on any other applicant similarly seeking approval of a rezone, the court found no "substantial burden." *Id.*[4] Two years later, the Ninth Circuit did find a county's denial of a conditional use permit for construction of a temple constituted a substantial burden under RLUIPA. *See Guru Nanak Sikh Society of Yuba City v. County of Sutter,* 456 F. 3d 978 (9th Cir. 2006). In *Guru Nanak,* the county twice denied the group's use permit application: once due to noise and traffic concerns, when the temple was proposed as an infill project on a residentially-zoned site, and later, due to concerns of leapfrog development when proposed on a larger, agriculturally-zoned site. The court found that denial of the second application lessened to a significantly great extent the possibility the group ever would be permitted to construct a temple, and that the county had not asserted any compelling interest for its action. *Id.* at 992. The court explained that unlike *San Jose Christian,* where there was no evidence that the desired religious institution could not be obtained merely by submitting a complete application, the applicant in *Guru Nanak* had no reason to believe that a further application would be accepted. *Id.*

If a claimant demonstrates that a regulation constitutes a substantial burden on its religious exercise, the burden shifts to the government to prove that the burden is the least restrictive means of furthering a compelling governmental interest. RLUIPA contains a broad definition of "religious exercise," which includes the "use, building, or conversion of real property for the purpose of religious exercise." 42 U.S.C. § 2000cc-5(7)(B). Under RLUIPA, the exercise of religion does not have to be "compelled by, or central to, a system of religious belief." *Id.* at § 2000cc-5(7)(A).

RLUIPA also includes a nondiscrimination provision that renders a city strictly liable for implementing a land use regulation that discriminates against religious uses regardless of the justifications offered by the city. *See Midrash Sephardi, Inc. v. Town of Surfside,* 366 F. 3d 1214, 1229 (11th Cir. 2004). This provision operates independently from the "substantial burden" provision of RLUIPA. In *Midrash,* the nondiscrimination provision of RLUIPA was violated where the Town of Surfside imposed certain zoning restrictions on synagogues and churches but not on similar nonreligious assemblies or institutions like private clubs and lodges. *Id.* at 1231.

In California, Government Code sections 25373 and 37361 provide statutory exemptions from local landmark preservation laws for noncommercial property owned by religious organizations. The legality of these exemptions was upheld following a challenge by the City and County of San Francisco and several organizations concerned with landmark preservation under the state and federal constitutions. *See East Bay Asian Local Dev. Corp. v. State of California,* 24 Cal. 4th 693 (2000). The court in finding that the exemptions did not constitute an endorsement of religion, held that the it is lawful for a state to act to reduce a burden on the religious freedom of those within its jurisdiction, particularly when it is the state itself that is imposing the burden. *Id.*

---

4. *See also* Daniel J. Curtin, Jr. and Joshua Safran, "Denial of Religious College's Rezoning Bid Was Not Illegal," *San Francisco Daily Journal,* May 12, 2004, page 5.

Despite the holding in *East Bay Asian Dev. Corp.*, RLUIPA has forced cities to walk the fine line between the Free Exercise Clause and the Establishment Clause of the First Amendment. RLUIPA provides religious groups with a powerful weapon with which to challenge zoning ordinances, requiring cities to be more flexible when responding to zoning applications from religious groups. Given this reality, many cities have or should revise their ordinances to avoid lengthy and expensive lawsuits. However, cities must also be careful not to favor religious groups too much, or they may face lawsuits alleging the endorsement of religion in violation of the Establishment Clause. Cities should develop a detailed record in administrative actions involving religious institutions, both for the purpose of detailing findings of "substantial burden" and "compelling government interest," as well as to include evidence regarding steps taken to explore alternative means of solving the problems that the proposed religious activity may pose. Local governments also may want to develop a more detailed record in cases not involving religious groups, to assist them in fighting claims of discrimination in cases that do involve religious organizations.[5]

Administrative Zoning Relief—Variances—Conditional Use Permits

In General

Variances and conditional use permits (CUPs) are methods by which a property owner may seek relief from the strict terms of a comprehensive zoning ordinance. While the amendment of a zoning regulation is a legislative function, the granting of variances and use permits are quasi-judicial, administrative functions. Variances and use permits run with the land. *See County of Imperial v. McDougal*, 19 Cal. 3d 505, 510 (1977). Therefore, a city cannot condition a use permit on its nontransferability. *See Anza Parking Corp. v. City of Burlingame*, 195 Cal. App. 3d 855, 860 (1987). In addition, variances and conditional use permits must be consistent with a city's general plan. *See Neighborhood Action Group v. County of Calaveras*, 156 Cal. App. 3d 1176, 1187 (1984); *City of Carmel-by-the-Sea v. Board of Supervisors*, 137 Cal. App. 3d 964, 992 (1982).

The Government Code provides that any restriction imposed by a municipal entity on an owner's ability to convey real property or a leasehold interest

Variances and conditional use permits are methods by which a property owner may seek relief from the strict terms of a comprehensive zoning ordinance.

CUP = Conditional use permit

---

5. For good overviews of RLUIPA and recommendations on how to successfully navigate its provisions, *see* Alan C. Weinstein, "Recent Developments Concerning RLUIPA" in *Current Trends and Practical Strategies in Land Use Law and Zoning* 1 (Patricia E. Salkin ed., 2004); Alan C. Weinstein, "RLUIPA: Where are we now? Where are we heading?," 56 *Planning & Environmental Law*, no. 2, page 3 (2004); Robert B. Hall, "Zen and the Art of Zoning—Constitutional Challenge to RLUIPA," 13 *California Land Use Law & Policy Reporter*, no. 6 (March 2004); Helene Leichter, "Zoning Churches: An Update on Religious Land Use Litigation," *Western City*, page 27 (July 2004); Anthony R. Picarello, Jr., "RLUIPA Is Constitutional," Marci A. Hamilton, "RLUIPA Is Unfair, Unwise, and Unconstitutional," and Lora Lucero, "Where Does APA Stand on RLUIPA?," point/counterpoint commentaries in 56 *Planning and Environmental Law*, no. 4, pages 3–14 (APA, April 2004); Sara Smolik, "The Utility and Efficacy of the RLUIPA: Was It a Waste?," 31 *Boston Col. Env'tl Aff. L. Rev.*, no. 3, page 723 (2004) (analyzing the constitutionality of RLUIPA and discussing whether RLUIPA serves the purpose for which it was designed); James L. Dam, "Churches Use New Federal Statute to Win Zoning Cases," *Lawyers Weekly*, August 20, 2001; Amanda Hills, "Zoning of Religious Land Use and Institutionalized Persons Act of 2000," *Trends in Land Use Law from A to Z*, chapter 5 (Patricia E. Salkin, ed., State and Local Gov't Law Sec., ABA, 2001).

in real property shall be set forth in a recorded document in order to impart notice of the restriction. Gov't Code § 27281.5. This provision has been held to require recordation of a conditional use permit that placed restrictions on the occupancy of units in a particular apartment building. *1119 Delaware v. Continental Land Title Co.*, 16 Cal. App. 4th 992, 999–1000 (1993) (CUP required that at least one occupant of each unit be at least 62 years of age or physically handicapped). A zoning ordinance of general application, however, is considered to impart constructive notice of its terms to the public and need not be recorded against an owner's title to be enforceable. *Id.* at 1002; *see also City of W. Hollywood v. Beverly Towers, Inc.*, 52 Cal. 3d 1184, 1194 (1991).

Variances [6]

A variance is a permit issued to a landowner by an administrative agency to build a structure or engage in some action not otherwise permitted under the current zoning regulations.

A variance is a permit issued to a landowner by an administrative agency (*e.g.*, zoning administrator, board of zoning adjustment, planning commission, or the city council acting as an administrative agency) to build a structure or engage in some action not otherwise permitted under the current zoning regulations. The statutory justification for a variance is that the owner otherwise would suffer unique hardship under the general zoning regulations because this particular parcel is different from the others to which the regulation applies due to its size, shape, topography, location, or surroundings. Gov't Code § 65906. This section is applicable to all cities and counties except charter cities, and can be supplemented by harmonious local legislation. *See Topanga Ass'n for a Scenic Community v. County of Los Angeles*, 11 Cal. 3d 506, 511 (1974).

Variances allow deviations from regulations on physical standards such as lot sizes, floor area ratios for buildings, and off-street parking requirements.

Variances may not be granted to authorize a use that is not otherwise authorized by the zoning regulations. Rather, variances allow deviations from regulations on physical standards such as lot sizes, floor area ratios for buildings, and off-street parking requirements. The concept is not that the basic zoning provision is being changed, but that the property owner is allowed to use its property in a manner basically consistent with the established regulations, with minor variations that will place the owner in parity with other property owners in the same zone. Variances are, in effect, constitutional safety valves to permit administrative adjustments when application of a general regulation would be confiscatory or produce unique hardship.

Some basic principles that must be applied in the consideration of an application for a variance are:

- Circumstances surrounding the applicant's situation must be unique in that they create disparities between the applicant's property and other properties in the area. The unique circumstances must cause unique hardship to the property owner to justify the authorization of a variance. Generally, such circumstances have been limited to physical conditions of the property. But in *Craik v. County of Santa Cruz*, the court held for the first time that a grant of variance did not require a showing of physical disparity. 81 Cal. App. 4th 880, 890 (2000). In this case, the court rejected an argument based on statements made in an OPR handbook requiring physical disparities, stating that there was no authority to support that a physical disparity is a precondition for a variance.

PRACTICE TIP

State law on variances is not applicable to a charter city unless the city adopts it.

OPR = Governor's Office of Planning and Research

6. *See The Variance* (Governor's Office of Planning and Research, July 1997).

- A variance may not be granted if it will adversely affect the interests of the public or the interests of other residents and property owners within the vicinity of the premises in question.
- A variance must be consistent with the objectives of the general plan and the zoning ordinance.
- The mere existence of a peculiar situation that will result in unnecessary hardship to the applicant if the ordinance is enforced does not necessarily require the granting of a variance.
- A variance must not grant a "special privilege" inconsistent with the limitations on other nearby properties.

The variance criteria contained in Government Code section 65906 prevail over any inconsistent requirements in local ordinances. A variance can be sustained only if all applicable legislative requirements of Government Code section 65906 are met. *See Topanga*, 11 Cal. 3d 506, 518 (1974).

In *Orinda Ass'n v. Bd. of Supervisors*, the court invalidated a height variance as a kind of special privilege explicitly prohibited by Government Code section 65906. 182 Cal. App. 3d 1145 (1986). The court held there were no facts sufficient to justify a variance, and there was no affirmative showing that the subject property differed substantially and in relevant aspects from other parcels in the applicable zones. *Id.* at 1160.

Conditional Use Permit

The second administrative method of providing relief from the strict terms of a comprehensive zoning ordinance is a conditional use permit. Unlike the variance procedure, the State Zoning Law is silent with respect to the proper criteria to evaluate whether a CUP should be issued. Rather, this is determined by local ordinance. Gov't Code § 65901. Typically, following a list of permitted uses in each zone, a local zoning ordinance will provide for other uses that are not permitted as a matter or right, but for which a CUP must be obtained. The CUP is well recognized by zoning administrators and the courts as a necessary and proper method to provide flexibility and alleviate hardship. *See Groch v. City of Berkeley*, 118 Cal. App. 3d 518 (1981); *Upton v. Gray*, 269 Cal. App. 2d 352 (1969). However, it must be issued pursuant to proper procedures. "The decision to allow a conditional use permit is an issue of vital public interest. It affects the quality of life of everyone in the area of the proposed use." *Penn-Co v. Board of Supervisors*, 158 Cal. App. 3d 1072, 1084 (1984). In *League of Residential Neighborhood Advocates v. City of Los Angeles*, a settlement agreement granting a CUP for a synagogue in an area zoned residential was held invalid because it did not provide for the required public hearing and it permitted the city to disregard its own zoning ordinance. 498 F.3d 1052, 1057 (9th Cir. 2007).

A CUP or other similar permit does not expire automatically even when a condition to the CUP provides for such expiration or the local code provides for an automatic expiration. For instance, in *Cmty. Dev. Comm'n v. City of Fort Bragg*, the court held that a CUP cannot be revoked without notice and hearing despite an automatic expiration condition, and that such revocation must be reasonable. 204 Cal. App. 3d 1124, 1131–32 (1988).

Until a CUP is issued and relied upon, no right has vested. Therefore, the initial denial of an application for a CUP is subject to judicial review under the substantial evidence test. However, the grant of a CUP with subsequent reliance on the permit by the permit holder creates a fundamental vested property right that subjects a CUP revocation to judicial review under the independent judgment test. *See Malibu Mountains Recreation, Inc. v. County of Los Angeles*, 67 Cal. App. 4th 359, 367 (1998); *see also Bauer v. City of San Diego*, 75 Cal. App. 4th 1281, 1294 (1999) (once a right to a CUP vests, the permittee is entitled to all the protections of due process before the permit may be revoked). For a more detailed discussion of the proper standard of judicial review of agency decisions, *see* chapter 21 (Land Use Litigation).

The types of uses subject to obtaining a CUP are quite varied. The courts generally have upheld the issuance of a CUP by a city if all applicable laws are followed. Examples of CUPs that have been upheld include the following:

- Farm equipment repair shop. *Upton v. Gray*, 269 Cal. App. 2d 352 (1969)
- Synagogue in residential zone. *Stoddard v. Edelman*, 4 Cal. App. 3d 544 (1970)
- Mobile home park in residential-agricultural (R-A) zone. *Jones v. City Council*, 17 Cal. App. 3d 724 (1971)
- Airplane hangar in residential zone. *Mitcheltree v. City of Los Angeles*, 17 Cal. App. 3d 791 (1971)
- Planned residential development. *Concerned Citizens of Palm Desert, Inc. v. Board of Supervisors*, 38 Cal. App. 3d 257 (1974)
- Cemetery. *Essick v. City of Los Angeles*, 34 Cal. 2d 614 (1950)
- Extraction of minerals (sand and gravel quarry). *Rapp v. County of Napa Planning Comm'n*, 204 Cal. App. 2d 695 (1962)
- Erection of a radio tower. *McManus v. KPAL Broad. Corp.*, 182 Cal. App. 2d 558 (1960)

The following cases have upheld the denial of CUPs for the following proposed uses:

- Automobile service station. *Van Sicklen v. Browne*, 15 Cal. App. 3d 122 (1971)
- Used car business. *Felice v. City of Inglewood*, 84 Cal. App. 2d 263 (1948)
- Use of a bus for a restaurant. *Melton v. City of San Pablo*, 252 Cal. App. 2d 794 (1967)
- Storage yard for houses. *Snow v. City of Garden Grove*, 188 Cal. App. 2d 496 (1961)
- Three-story home in a single-family zone, because of view impairment and towering effect. *Saad v. City of Berkeley*, 24 Cal. App. 4th 1206 (1994)

In granting a new CUP, a city need not consider evidence of purported violations of an original CUP. Instead, a city can revoke the original CUP if there were violations, but such violations are not relevant to the application for a new CUP. *See Baird v. County of Contra Costa*, 32 Cal. App. 4th 1464, 1470 (1995) (upholding grant of CUP to expand an addiction treatment facility).

Where a city's CUP requirement implicates speech rights, it must also circumscribe the zoning administrator's discretion in deciding whether to grant or deny the CUP. *Vo v. City of Garden Grove*, 115 Cal. App. 4th 425 (2004). The plaintiffs in *Vo* sought to enjoin preliminarily the city's ordinance requiring, among other things, that they obtain CUPs to continue operating cyber-cafes. Plaintiffs claimed the CUP requirement violated the First Amendment.

The court upheld an injunction against the CUP requirement. The court agreed with plaintiffs that First Amendment activity was implicated by the regulation of cyber-cafes. The court noted that the city's code would allow the zoning administrator to deny the CUPs based on such ambiguous criteria as the "general welfare" of the community. *Id.* at 438. This gave the zoning administrator unfettered discretion to make decisions on any basis and left open the possibility that the city could, for example, require installation of content filtering software on the basis that such filters would advance the "general welfare." The potential for an impact upon First Amendment expression required "precise standards capable of objective measurement" that were missing in the city's CUP requirement. *Id.* at 437.

A requirement that a CUP be obtained may raise takings concerns. However, in *Allegretti & Co. v. County of Imperial*, a landowner's claim that the county's CUP requirement constituted inverse condemnation was rejected. 138 Cal. App. 4th 1261 (2006). Allegretti filed for a CUP to re-drill an inoperable well. The county approved the CUP but limited the draw of groundwater. Allegretti argued that the limitation constituted a taking, however the court concluded that the CUP was not a physical taking since the county did not divert any water or invade the property. *Id.* at 1273. Further, the CUP was not a regulatory taking since it did not unreasonably impair the value or use of the property but merely resulted in a reduction in profit. *Id.* at 1278–79. For more discussion on takings, *see* chapter 12 (Takings).

Nonconforming Uses— Amortization [7]

A nonconforming use describes a lawful use existing on the effective date of a new zoning restriction that has continued since that time without conformance to the ordinance. While the policy of the law is for elimination of nonconforming uses, as a general rule, a new zoning ordinance may not operate constitutionally to compel immediate discontinuance of an otherwise lawfully established use or business. *See City of Los Angeles v. Wolfe*, 6 Cal. 3d 326, 337 (1971); *Livingston Rock & Gravel Co. v. County of Los Angeles*, 43 Cal. 2d 121, 127 (1954). However, if an activity constitutes a public nuisance, it can be removed immediately as long as due process protections are provided. *Id; see also City of Bakersfield v. Miller*, 64 Cal. 2d 93, 103 (1966).

Zoning laws look to the future and the eventual elimination of nonconforming uses to effectuate change or to accommodate changed circumstances. Thus, the legal means of terminating a nonconforming use is a prime concern of zoning law, and a city can provide a period of time to eliminate nonconforming uses. *See Nat'l Adver. Co. v. County of Monterey*, 1 Cal. 3d 875, 880 (1970). Given the objective of zoning to eliminate nonconforming uses, courts generally follow a strict policy against the extension or enlargement of nonconforming uses.

As a general rule, a new zoning ordinance may not operate constitutionally to compel immediate discontinuance of an otherwise lawfully established use or business.

---

7. *See* Jay Campbell, "Amortization in the Twenty-Second Century," 24 *Zoning & Planning Law Report*, no. 2 (Feb. 2004).

See County of San Diego v. McClurken, 37 Cal. 2d 683, 686–87 (1951). The spirit of a zoning ordinance with a provision permitting continued nonconforming uses is to allow, but not increase, the nonconforming use. Intensification or expansion of an existing nonconforming use, or moving the use to another location on the property, is not permitted. For a general discussion of this subject, *see Hansen Bros, Enters., Inc. v. Bd. of Supervisors*, 12 Cal. 4th 533 (1996).

California courts have relied upon a case-by-case balancing approach to determine when a city can properly terminate a nonconforming use.

California courts have relied upon a case-by-case balancing approach to determine when a city can properly terminate a nonconforming use. The courts have upheld termination provisions where a reasonable period of time to recover the permit holder's investment is allowed. *See Livingston Rock & Gravel Co. v. County of Los Angeles*, 43 Cal. 2d at 127 (upholding a period commensurate with the investment involved); *Sabek, Inc. v. County of Sonoma*, 190 Cal. App. 3d 163, 168 (1987) (upholding loss of nonconforming status when remodeling costs were more than 15 percent of a structure's appraised value); *City of Los Angeles v. Gage*, 127 Cal. App. 2d 442, 460 (1954) (constitutionality of a termination period depends upon the relative importance to be given to the public gain and the private loss).

The leading case discussing elimination of nonconforming uses with a proper amortization period is *Metromedia, Inc. v. City of San Diego*, 26 Cal. 3d 848 (1980). This case involved an action by owners of billboards to enjoin the enforcement of a city ordinance banning all off-site advertising billboards, and requiring the removal of existing billboards following expiration of an amortization period. The California Supreme Court stated that the amortization period, which ranged from one to four years depending on the depreciated value of the sign, was not unreasonable on its face. Moreover, the owners had the burden of proving the invalidity of the amortization period as it applied to each structure. The Court laid down the following rule:

> The California cases have firmly declared that zoning legislation may validly provide for the eventual termination of nonconforming uses without compensation if it provides a reasonable amortization period commensurate with the investment involved.

Id. at 882

This rule was not changed by the United States Supreme Court decisions in *First English Evangelical Lutheran Church v. County of Los Angeles*, 482 U.S. 304 (1987), and *Nollan v. California Coastal Comm'n*, 483 U.S. 825 (1987). *See also Tahoe Reg'l Planning Agency v. King*, 233 Cal. App. 3d 1365, 1393–1400 (1991).

In terms of defining what constitutes a "reasonable" amortization period, the court in *City of Salinas v. Ryan Outdoor Adver., Inc.* stated that the reasonableness of the amortization period depends on the interplay of many factors, including the depreciated value of the structures to be removed, their remaining useful life, and the harm to the public if they are left standing. 189 Cal. App. 3d 416, 424 (1987).

With respect to "on-premises signs," the Legislature has provided, with some exceptions, that cities cannot terminate nonconforming signs without payment.

With respect to "on-premises signs," the Legislature has provided, with some exceptions, that cities cannot terminate nonconforming signs without payment. Bus. & Prof. Code § 5490 *et seq.* The court in *Denny's Inc. v. City of Agoura Hills* reviewed this statutory provision. 56 Cal. App. 4th 1312 (1997). It held that Business and Professions Code section 5499 bars local ordinances that proscribe on-premises signs or advertising displays based on their height or size if "nontemporary" topographic features, including natural or man-made features, would cause a sign or display that conformed to the ordinance to be less visible or less effective in communicating to the public. *Id.* at 1323.

Other Types of Zoning

Form-Based Zoning

Increasingly, cities are incorporating form-based zoning principles into their zoning regulations. Form-based codes place primary emphasis on the design and physical form of buildings, streetscapes, and public places, with less emphasis than conventional land use regulations on allowed uses inside the buildings. In contrast to traditional zoning, form-based zoning regulates building types, dimensions, parking locations, and design features. Often, form-based codes are applied through regulating plans that map a community with geographic designations based on scale, character, intensity, and form of development instead of differences in land uses. Form-based development regulations commonly include a regulating plan (showing sites for buildings, street types, and possibly design features), urban regulations (addressing height, bulk, area coverage, and use standards), street regulations (including street and sidewalk dimensions), landscape regulations and architectural regulations (concerning building styles and materials).[8] Many form-based regulations are presented in or illustrated by graphical diagrams and drawings.

Form-based codes place primary emphasis on the design and physical form of buildings, streetscapes, and public places, with less emphasis than conventional land use regulations on allowed uses inside the buildings.

Form-based advocates believe that this approach makes sense in many California locations where one key planning task is managing the transition from suburban to urban development.[9] Further, technological advances that minimize certain environmental effects may help alleviate what were formerly considered incompatible uses. Several cities in California have adopted or incorporated form-based ideas into their zoning codes including the cities of Petaluma, Hercules, and Azusa, as well as Contra Costa County.[10]

LAFCO = Local Agency Formation Commission

Prezoning

A city may prezone unincorporated territory outside its limits for the purpose of determining zoning that will apply to such property in the event of subsequent annexation to the city. Gov't Code § 65859. In fact, pursuant to the Cortese-Knox-Hertzberg Local Government Reorganization Act of 2000, a local agency formation commission (LAFCO) shall require as a condition of annexation that a city prezone the territory to be annexed. Gov't Code § 56375(a). For a detailed discussion of LAFCOs, *see* chapter 16. Prezoning becomes effective at the same

A city may prezone unincorporated territory outside its limits for the purpose of determining zoning that will apply to such property in the event of subsequent annexation to the city.

---

8. For an excellent discussion of form-based regulations, *see* Robert J. Sitkowski and Brian W. Ohm, "Form-Based Land Development Regulations," 38 *The Urban Lawyer* 163 (Winter 2006).
9. *See* William Fulton, "Transition Away from Suburbia Bolsters Form-Based Zoning Movement," 21 *Cal. Plng. & Dev. Rep.* 1 (April 2006).
10. *See* Rebecca Retzlaff, "California Enacts Form-Based Zoning Legislation," *Zoning Practice*, pages 10–11 (APA, January 2005) (discussing California's form-based zoning law which seeks to integrate streets, open space, housing, commercial development, and neighborhoods, rather than grouping similar and related land uses). *See also* Carla M. Moynihan, "Implementing Form-Based Zoning in Your Municipality," 47 *Municipal Lawyer* 15 (IMLA July/August 2006); Michael Moore, "Form-Based Zoning Is Not the (Whole) Answer," *APA Northern News*, page 1 (May/June 2006).

time the annexation becomes effective. Gov't Code § 56375. Prezoning must also be consistent with the city's general plan. *See City of Irvine v. Irvine Citizens Against Overdevelopment*, 25 Cal. App. 4th 868, 879 (1994).

Interim Ordinance

There are times when a property owner will submit a land use proposal or request a building permit for use of property that may be in conflict with a contemplated general plan, specific plan, or zoning proposal that the city is considering, studying, or intending to study within a reasonable period of time. In these types of situations, Government Code section 65858 authorizes a city to adopt, as an urgency measure, an interim ordinance prohibiting such uses that may be in conflict with a general plan, specific plan, or zoning proposal that the city is considering, without following the procedures otherwise required for the adoption of a zoning ordinance. However, such an urgency measure requires a four-fifths' vote of the city council for adoption. No notice or hearing is required for the first adoption. *See Beck Dev. Co. v. Southern Pac. Transp. Co.*, 44 Cal. App. 4th 1160 (1996).

> **PRACTICE TIP**
>
> No notice or hearing is required for the first adoption of an interim ordinance.

Interim urgency ordinances have statutory time limitations. Gov't Code § 65858. If an interim ordinance is initially adopted without notice and hearing, it is effective for only 45 days from the date of adoption. However, after notice and hearing, the city council may extend such interim ordinance for 10 months and 15 days and subsequently extend the interim ordinance for an additional one year. However, like the ordinance itself, extensions require a four-fifths' vote for adoption. Additionally, not more than two extensions may be adopted for a total extension of two years. Alternatively, an interim ordinance may be adopted initially by a four-fifths' vote following notice and hearing, in which case it is effective for 45 days and can be extended, after notice and hearing, by a four-fifths' vote for 22 months and 15 days. Gov't Code § 65858(b). Under either approach, interim "urgency" ordinances are limited by statute to a two-year period.

Interim urgency ordinances have statutory time limitations. If an interim ordinance is initially adopted without notice and hearing, it is effective for only 45 days from the date of adoption. However, subject to conditions, it may be extended for 10 months and 15 days.

Before adopting or extending an interim ordinance, the city council must make a finding that there is a current and immediate threat to the public health, safety, or welfare, or that the approval of additional subdivisions, use permits, variances, building permits, or the like would result in such a threat. The proper findings must be contained in the ordinance. *See 216 Sutter Bay Assocs. v. County of Sutter*, 58 Cal. App. 4th 860, 868 (1997) (upholding interim ordinance that recited facts that "may reasonably be held to constitute" an urgency). Ten days prior to the expiration of the ordinance, the city council must issue a written report describing the measures taken to alleviate the condition that led to the adoption of the ordinance. Gov't Code § 65858(d).

Extensions of an interim ordinance beyond 45 days that have the effect of denying approvals needed for development of projects with a significant component of multi-family housing are prohibited unless specific findings are made and supported by substantial evidence.

Extensions of an interim ordinance beyond 45 days that have the effect of denying approvals needed for the development of projects with a "significant component" (at least one-third of the total project square footage) of multi-family housing are prohibited unless specific findings are made and supported by substantial evidence. Those findings include a conclusion that continued approval of multi-family housing projects would have a specific, adverse impact on public health or safety, that the interim ordinance is necessary to avoid that impact, and that there is no feasible alternative to satisfactorily avoid or mitigate such impact. The ban on extensions does not, however, apply to demolition, conversion, redevelopment, or rehabilitation of lower income multi-family housing. Gov't Code §§ 65858(e), (g), (h).

Since the purpose of an interim ordinance is to preserve the status quo by prohibiting a use of land that may be inconsistent with a contemplated general plan, specific plan, or zoning proposal currently under consideration, an interim ordinance cannot be used to authorize construction. This authorization can only be accomplished after notice and hearing under the State Zoning Law. *See Silvera v. City of S. Lake Tahoe*, 3 Cal. App. 3d 554, 558 (1970). Nor can an interim ordinance be used to halt a use already in existence. *See Kieffer v. Spencer*, 153 Cal. App. 3d 954, 963 (1984). However, a court has held that an interim ordinance may be used to cancel a development agreement prior to the expiration of the 30-day period between approval of the agreement and its effective date. *See 216 Sutter Bay Assocs. v. County of Sutter*, 58 Cal. App. 4th at 870–71.

Although Government Code section 65858 provides that an interim ordinance can be used to prohibit uses of property, it cannot be used to prohibit the processing of a development application. *See Building Indus. Legal Defense Found. v. Superior Court*, 72 Cal. App. 4th 1410, 1420 (1999) (city's interim ordinance was invalid to the extent that it applied to processing a development application).

The United States Supreme Court's decision in *Tahoe-Sierra Preservation Council, Inc. v. Tahoe Regional Planning Agency* reaffirmed the ability of cities to use temporary development moratoria as a planning tool without necessarily having to compensate property owners for the time period during which development is banned. 535 U.S. 302 (2002). In particular, the Court cited California, among other states, which had enacted statutory provisions for interim ordinances, including moratoria, with specific time limits. *Id.*

Government Code section 65858 preempts the entire field of interim zoning moratoria. *See Bank of the Orient v. Town of Tiburon*, 220 Cal. App. 3d 992, 1004 (1990) (the people, via an initiative, could not add an additional year to the two-year moratorium the town council had earlier imposed). Under Government Code section 65858, a city may impose a moratorium for a maximum of two years. However, upon termination of a prior interim ordinance, the city council may adopt another interim ordinance if the new interim ordinance arises from an event, occurrence, or set of circumstances different from that which led to the adoption of the prior interim ordinance. Gov't Code § 65858(f).

Although *Tahoe-Sierra* reaffirmed a city's ability to impose a temporary moratorium through such planning tools as Government Code section 65858, a slight risk remains that a moratorium that constitutes an improper land use regulation may effect a temporary taking, and that money damages for such taking might have to be paid. *See First English Evangelical Lutheran Church v. County of Los Angeles*, 482 U.S. 304, 321 (1987).

Tahoe-Sierra makes clear that unless the regulation eliminates *all* economically beneficial uses of the land, the more flexible ad hoc analysis enunciated in *Penn Central* applies. 535 U.S. at 321. Therefore, it is good practice to allow some use of the property while the interim period is in effect and to insert a "safety valve" provision to allow the owner to apply for an exception. For a detailed discussion of takings jurisprudence, *see* chapter 12 (Takings).

PRACTICE TIP

To avoid a temporary takings claim, cities should allow property owners some use of the property during the period the interim ordinance is in effect, as well as inserting a "safety valve" provision to allow owners to apply for an exception.

Under Government Code section 65858, a city may impose a moratorium for a maximum of two years.

Tahoe-Sierra *makes clear that unless the regulation eliminates* all *economically beneficial uses of the land, the more flexible ad hoc analysis enunciated in* Penn Central *applies.*

Conditional Zoning

Conditional zoning describes a zoning change that permits use of a particular property subject to conditions not generally applicable to land similarly zoned.

"Conditional zoning" describes a zoning change that permits use of a particular property subject to conditions not generally applicable to land similarly zoned. See *Scrutton v. County of Sacramento*, 275 Cal. App. 2d 412, 417 (1969). Although the term "contract zoning" has sometimes been used synonymously with "conditional zoning" the *Scrutton* court stated that the phrase "contract zoning" has no legal significance and simply refers to a reclassification of land use in which the landowner agrees to perform conditions not imposed on other landowners. *Id.* at 419.

In *Scrutton*, a landowner filed an application to have property rezoned from agricultural to multiple-family residential to permit development of residential apartments. The planning commission recommended approval of the application subject to certain conditions, which included dedication and improvement of certain streets adjacent to the parcel. The board of supervisors, after a hearing, approved the planning commission's recommendation. Before adopting a rezoning ordinance, however, the board tendered a deed and contract for the owner's signature and would not formally adopt the rezoning ordinance until the owner returned the executed deed and contract. The owner refused to sign, and filed an action for declaratory relief against the county on the theory that the imposition of such conditions to a rezoning was improper.

The court upheld both the county's action and the conditional rezoning as a proper exercise of the same police power that supports the imposition of conditions on approval of subdivisions, building permits, and zoning variances. *Id.* at 418. However, the court also found that the conditions cannot require an automatic reversion of the land to its former zoning if the conditions are not met. Such a reversion would be a zoning amendment that would be invalid for failure to comply with the notice and hearing procedures of the State Zoning Law. *Id.* at 420.

Specific Plan as Zoning

A specific plan, provided it is sufficiently comprehensive and detailed as to regulations of the use of property within the plan area, may be adopted by ordinance as zoning for the plan area.

A specific plan, provided it is sufficiently comprehensive and detailed as to regulations of the use of property within the plan area, may be adopted by ordinance as zoning for the plan area. A specific plan can create new zoning regulations for unique areas and developments, such as mixed use districts and master planned communities, where other conventional zoning districts are too restrictive to achieve the desired planning results. In some cities, local ordinances mandate that specific plans be adopted into the zoning code by ordinance to become either the base zone or an overlay zone for the specific plan area.

Planned-Unit Development

PUD = Planned-unit development

Planned-unit development (PUD or PD) has dual characteristics: it is simultaneously a type or method of development and a zoning classification. As a method of development, it normally consists of individually owned lots with common areas (open space, recreation, and, sometimes, street improvements) that are owned in common by the lot owners. As a zoning classification, it allows a single zoning district to combine a variety of uses (residential, commercial, and even industrial) that are otherwise generally not permitted within the same zoning district. The term "planned-unit development" is often synonymous with such terms as "cluster development," "planned development," "master-planned community," and the like. The planned-unit development concept has been approved by the California courts. *See Orinda Homeowners Comm. v. Board of Supervisors*, 11 Cal. App. 3d 768, 773 (1970).

Depending upon the local ordinance, the plan of development (either the general or precise development plan) for a PUD may constitute the zoning restrictions for the property after the plan has been approved by a city. Thus, any substantial change or alteration in the physical configuration of the property may amount to a rezoning that must be accomplished pursuant to provisions of state statutes governing local zoning ordinances, such as notice and public hearing. However, in certain cities, depending on the local ordinance, the plan is adopted through a quasi-judicial permit process, and cannot be amended by ordinance. Instead, the plan and its conditions can be amended only by the method prescribed in the enabling PUD ordinance or by a method set forth in the conditions of approval. *See W.W. Dean & Assoc. v. City of South San Francisco*, 190 Cal. App. 3d 1368, 1374, 1380 (1987); *Lincoln Property Co. No. 41 v. Law, Inc.* 45 Cal. App. 3d 230 (1975).

Depending upon the local ordinance, the plan of development for a PUD may constitute the zoning restrictions for the property after the plan has been approved by a city.

Inclusionary Zoning/Housing Programs

Inclusionary housing programs provide mechanisms for cities to ensure that new development creates affordable housing options. Inclusionary housing programs have been in effect since the early 1970s, and are growing in popularity today as more jurisdictions view them as innovative ways to increase the supply of affordable housing as well as combat exclusionary zoning practices. In general, cities enact such programs pursuant to their local police power, and they are typically effectuated through inclusionary housing ordinances, zoning codes, policy statements, or a city's housing element. In general, an "inclusionary" housing program is one that requires a residential developer to set aside a specified percentage of new units (often 10–15 percent) for very low-, low-, or moderate-income households in conjunction with the development of market rate units.[11]

Inclusionary housing programs provide mechanisms for cities to ensure that new development creates affordable housing options.

In California, by 2000, at least 108 cities and 13 counties had adopted various inclusionary housing programs, a majority of which are mandatory.[12] Dozens more cities and counties are considering adopting such a program. Examples of creative inclusionary housing programs also can be found across the nation in Colorado, Florida, Maryland, Massachusetts, Minnesota, New

---

11. However, the term "inclusionary housing" or "inclusionary zoning" can include a variety of methods designed to create more affordable housing. Some examples include density bonuses, reduced development standards, and imposition of fees on developers to fund affordable housing projects. *See* Laura M. Padilla, "Reflections on Inclusionary Housing and a Renewed Look at Its Viability," 23 *Hofstra L. Rev.* 539, 551–52 (1995).

12. *See* Cecily T. Talbert, Nadia L. Costa, and Alison L. Krumbein, "Recent Developments in Inclusionary Zoning," 38 *Urb. Law.*, no. 3 (Summer 2006); Cecily T. Talbert and Nadia L. Costa, "Current Issues in Inclusionary Zoning," 37 *Urb. Law.*, no. 3, page 513 (Summer 2005). *See generally Expanding Opportunity: New Resources to Meet California's Housing Needs* (Policy Link, Winter 2005); *Inclusionary Zoning: The Essential PAS Information Packet* (APA Planning Advisory Service, March 2003); *California Inclusionary Housing Reader* (Institute for Local Self Government, Winter 2003); *Inclusionary Housing in California: 30 Years of Innovation* (Non-Profit Housing Association of Northern California, 2003, www.nonprofithousing.org).

Jersey, New Mexico, and Virginia. The inclusionary housing philosophy has also been supported internationally. *See In the Matter of Article 26 of the Constitution and In the Matter of Part V of the Planning and Development Bill 1999*, Supreme Court of Ireland, August 28, 2000 (unanimously upholding a national 20 percent affordable housing statute, which allows the local agency, as a condition of approval, to require the developer to enter into an agreement whereby it gives up to 20 percent of the land for affordable housing or provide several sites or houses actually built for such purposes). For a full discussion of inclusionary zoning, *see* chapter 20 (Affordable Housing).

Relationship of General Plan and Zoning to Redevelopment Law [13]

When a city decides to redevelop an area under the California Community Redevelopment Law, it must comply with both redevelopment and land use law.

When a city decides to redevelop an area under the California Community Redevelopment Law (Health & Safety Code § 33000 *et seq*.), it must comply with both redevelopment and land use law. The community must have a valid general plan that meets the requirements and contains all the mandatory elements of Government Code section 65302, whether or not it is a charter city. The complete general plan, as described, should be legally effective when an area is "designated for redevelopment." Health & Safety Code §§ 33300, 33331.

Under the Community Redevelopment Law, cities may designate certain "blighted" areas that constitute physical and economic liabilities as requiring redevelopment in order to improve the health, safety, and general welfare of the people in those communities. Health & Safety Code § 33030; *Blue v. City of Los Angeles*, 137 Cal. App. 4th 1131, 1149 (2007) (a determination of blight is a prerequisite to invoking redevelopment). Redevelopment has become an increasingly popular and widespread tool for cities to facilitate revitalization. However, concerns of redevelopment abuses, including the use of eminent domain within redevelopment areas, and the local redevelopment agency's retention and use of tax increment generated by redevelopment projects, has brought redevelopment under increasing legislative scrutiny.

In 2006, the Legislature enacted several new laws designed to narrow the definition of what constitutes a blighted area.

In 2006, the Legislature enacted several new laws designed to narrow the definition of what constitutes a "blighted area," limit the inclusion of non-blighted parcels in redevelopment project areas, and require redevelopment agencies to make more specific findings regarding the physical and economic conditions that cause an area to be blighted. Health & Safety Code §§ 33030, 33031, 33320.1. The revised statutes also require new blight findings be made when a redevelopment agency extends the time period for eminent domain authority within a project area. Health & Safety Code §§ 33333.2, 33333.4. These revisions expand the ability of opponents to challenge redevelopment decisions and the attorney general's office to intervene in redevelopment controversies. *See, e.g.,* Health & Safety Code §§ 33500, 33501, 33501.1.

Two appellate courts recently made fact-based decisions interpreting these new laws. In *N.L. Neilson and Assoc. For Legal Desert Development, et al. v. City of California City*, the city's redevelopment agency approved redevelopment plans that resulted in the building of an automobile test track facility on desert land.

---

13. *See* David F. Beatty *et al., Redevelopment in California* (Solano Press, 2004), for an excellent discussion of California redevelopment law.

145 Cal. App. 4th 633, 634 (2007). In approving the redevelopment plans, the agency determined that 24.4 square miles of vacant land were urbanized and blighted based on "the existence of subdivided lots of irregular form and shape and inadequate size for proper usefulness and development that are in multiple ownership." *Id.* The court rejected the agency's finding of blight, and determined the agency was in error because the lots' lack of access to the right-of-way did not reflect the usual and ordinary meaning of irregular "form and shape" as used in the statute. Health & Safety Code § 33031(a)(4).

In *Blue*, the city adopted a redevelopment plan and made a determination of blight based upon an assessment which demonstrated that 50 percent of the buildings in the project area were in need of rehabilitation. 137 Cal. App. 4th at 1143. The court held that the city had substantial evidence that physical blight existed as defined by Health & Safety Code section 33031(a)(1) and, additionally, that the blight could not have been reasonably eliminated without the redevelopment agency's intervention. *Id.* at 1152.

Conformity of the Redevelopment Plan to the General Plan

A redevelopment plan must be consistent with the city's general plan. Health & Safety Code § 33331. The preliminary plan must illustrate this consistency, the planning commission must report on the proposed redevelopment plan's conformity with the general plan, and the city council must include a supportable finding of consistency in the ordinance adopting the redevelopment plan. Health & Safety Code §§ 33324(d), 33346, 33367(d)(4).

A redevelopment plan must be consistent with the city's general plan, and the preliminary plan must illustrate this.

Additionally, a redevelopment plan must contain building use limitations. Health & Safety Code § 33333(b). The redevelopment plan is required to conform to the general plan, but there is no concomitant requirement to conform with applicable zoning use classifications; a redevelopment plan's use designations can differ from zoning use classifications applicable to property in the project area. Thus, the effect of a redevelopment plan adoption may be to restrict development that is otherwise permitted under applicable zoning.

Status of Zoning Classifications After Redevelopment Plan Adoption

The question of a city's land use regulatory power in a redevelopment project area was addressed in *Kehoe v. City of Berkeley*, 67 Cal. App. 3d 666 (1977). In *Kehoe*, the court held that regulation of the issuance of demolition permits within a redevelopment project is preempted by the State Community Redevelopment Law. Therefore, building and zoning ordinances that conflict with the controlling State Community Redevelopment Law must give way to the state statute. Moreover, the court stated that a redevelopment plan may not be amended by a building or zoning ordinance. *Id.* at 674.

Since the State Community Redevelopment Law requires that the use designations for a redevelopment plan conform to the land use element of a general plan, a zoning ordinance permitting a use that conflicts with the general plan (and hence the redevelopment plan) must give way and cannot allow uses that are restricted or prohibited by the general plan.

Applicability of Zoning to the Federal and State Governments

Federal Government

Under the Supremacy Clause and the Property Clause of the United States Constitution, Congress has preemptive power over state and local control of federal lands.

Under the Supremacy Clause (art. VI, § 2) and the Property Clause (art. IV, § 3) of the United States Constitution, Congress has preemptive power over state and local control of federal lands. *See Mayo v. United States*, 319 U.S. 441, 445 (1943). Even a federal government lessee, such as an oil company, is not required to obtain a permit from a city in compliance with zoning ordinances governing oil explorations and extraction activities. *See Ventura County v. Gulf Oil Corp.*, 601 F. 2d 1080, 1085 (9th Cir. 1979). The United States Postal Service need not comply with local zoning regulations in constructing a post office on land owned or leased by the United States. *See* 68 Ops. Cal. Atty. Gen. 310 (1985).

NEPA = National Environmental Policy Act

However, reference should be made to the National Environmental Policy Act (NEPA) (42 U.S.C. § 4321 *et seq.*), the Intergovernmental Coordination Act of 1968 (31 U.S.C. § 6506), and the Intergovernmental Coordination Executive Order (Exec. Order No. 12,372, reprinted in 31 U.S.C. § 6506). Both NEPA and the intergovernmental coordination statute/order require federal agencies to solicit and consider local views on their projects, at least with respect to those of a size with the potential to produce serious conflicts.

In 1988, the court held that a county can apply its building codes to construction of an office building to be leased in its entirety by the federal government, and that the builder cannot share in the sovereign immunity of the United States. *See Smith v. County of Santa Barbara*, 203 Cal. App. 3d 1415, 1419 (1988). The court also noted that the Intergovernmental Coordination Act does not preempt land use regulations but, in fact, encourages cooperation with local zoning and land use practice. *Id.* at 1424. *See also Maryland-Nat'l Capital Park Planning Comm'n v. U.S. Postal Serv.*, 487 F. 2d 1029, 1037 (D.C. Cir. 1973) (NEPA requires close scrutiny of federal projects deviating from local land use regulations); *Town of Groton v. Laird*, 353 F. Supp. 344, 351 (D. Conn. 1972) (NEPA should not be used to shore up exclusionary zoning in a Navy housing program).

The United States Supreme Court ruled that states may impose environmental controls on activities occurring on federal lands.

The United States Supreme Court ruled that states may impose environmental controls on activities occurring on federal lands. *See California Coastal Comm'n v. Granite Rock Co.*, 480 U.S. 572 (1987). In *Granite Rock*, the Court held that the California Coastal Commission could require a private company to obtain a permit for its limestone mining operations in the Big Sur region of the federally owned Los Padres National Forest. *Id.* at 588–89. The decision represented a victory for states, particularly western states with substantial acreage owned by the federal government, by allowing them to subject private mining operations conducted on federal lands to environmental regulations.

For an interesting discussion on the intersection between federal law and a city's power to regulate telecommunications services and facilities, *see* Paul Valle-Riestra, *Telecommunications: The Local Government Role in Managing the Connected Community* (Solano Press, 2002).

State Government

In general, the state is exempt from a city's zoning regulations. *See Hall v. City of Taft*, 47 Cal. 2d 177, 184 (1956). For example, the Regents of the University of

California, a state agency, in constructing improvements solely for educational purposes, is exempt from local building codes and zoning regulations, and also is to be specifically exempt from payment of local permit and inspection fees. It is not relevant that the affected city is a charter city, nor does it matter whether the property involved is owned or leased by the Regents. *Regents of Univ. of Cal. v. City of Santa Monica*, 77 Cal. App. 3d 130, 136–37 (1978).

However, the same general rule does not apply to a city's subdivision powers. Gov't Code § 66428. The Attorney General determined that a city's subdivision ordinance applied to the California Department of Transportation (Caltrans) when it desired to dispose of real property. It can be stated as a general rule that a city's subdivision regulations apply so long as they do not affect the fundamental purposes and functions of the state. *See* 62 Ops. Cal. Atty. Gen. 410 (1979); *see also* 75 Ops. Cal. Atty. Gen. 98 (1992) (University of California construction of for-sale on-campus homes to provide faculty housing is considered to be part of the state's function in providing education and, therefore, is not bound by the Subdivision Map Act).

> *It can be stated as a general rule that a city's subdivision regulations apply so long as they do not affect the fundamental purposes and functions of the state.*

Cities may assess only certain capital facilities fees on the state. Government Code section 54999.1(d) limits the imposition of such fees to facilities that provide water, light, heat, communications, power, or garbage service for flood control, drainage or sanitary purposes, or for sewage collection, treatment, or disposal.

Applicability of Zoning to Joint Powers Agencies, School Districts, and County and Other Local Districts

All local agencies, except the state, a city or a county, and other specifically named agencies such as the San Francisco Bay Area Rapid Transit District, must comply with local zoning ordinances. Gov't Code § 53090 *et seq*. Government Code section 53091 does not mandate compliance with applicable general plans but does contemplate compliance with building and zoning ordinances. *Friends of the Eel River v. Sonoma County Water Agency*, 108 Cal. App. 4th 859 (2003). Zoning ordinances do not apply, however, to the location or construction of facilities for the production, generation, storage, or transmission of water, or facilities for the production or generation of electricity. Gov't Code § 53091. Moreover, the governing board of a local agency (such as a water district) can override otherwise applicable zoning ordinances by a four-fifths' vote if it determines by resolution that there is no feasible alternative to a project for facilities not related to the storage or transmission of water or electricity, such as warehouses, administrative buildings, or automotive storage and repair buildings. Gov't Code § 53096(a); *Delta Wetlands Props. v. County of San Joaquin*, 121 Cal. App. 4th 128 (2004) (clarifying that exemptions allowed by §§ 53091 and 53096 extend only to local agencies and not to private parties); *see also City of Lafayette v. East Bay Mun. Util. Dist.*, 16 Cal. App. 4th 1005, 1014–16 (1993) (absolute and qualified exemptions from local zoning regulations inapplicable to a water district's proposed facility for a maintenance storage center); *see also* 78 Ops. Cal. Atty. Gen. 31 (1995) (relating to water district's need to comply with building and zoning ordinances, with certain exceptions).

> *All local agencies, except the state, a city or a county, and other specifically named agencies such as the San Francisco Bay Area Rapid Transit District, must comply with local zoning ordinances.*

CEQA = California Environmental Quality Act
JPA = Joint powers agency
MERA = Marin Emergency Radio Authority

Government Code section 53094 allows a school district, by a two-thirds vote, to render a city zoning ordinance inapplicable to classroom facilities, except when the proposed use of the property by the school district is for non-classroom facilities.

A joint powers agency (JPA) may be exempt from local land use regulation, depending upon its membership and which constituent member is designated by the JPA to supply the JPA's procedural restrictions. *Zack v. Marin Emergency Radio Auth.*, 118 Cal. App. 4th 617, 628 (2004). The JPA at issue in *Zack* was the Marin Emergency Radio Authority (MERA), which included over two dozen cities and districts within Marin County as well as the county itself. MERA sought to place an emergency radio antenna in the Town of Tiburon, and the trial court halted the project, concluding that it first had to comply with the town's land use ordinances.

The appellate court reversed. It noted that under the Joint Exercise of Powers Act, the exercise of "common power" specified in a JPA "is subject to the restrictions upon the manner of exercising the power of one of the contracting parties, which party shall be designated in the agreement." *Id.* at 628 (citing Gov't Code § 6509). The plaintiffs had not shown that any member of MERA lacked the implied power to construct an emergency radio system. MERA was therefore exercising a "common power" in executing the project. *Id.* at 637. MERA had designated Marin County as the member agency whose procedures would govern the exercise of common power under the JPA. Because the county is not subject to the town's land use regulation, neither was MERA. *Id.* at 638.

Government Code section 53094 allows a school district, by a two-thirds vote, to render a city zoning ordinance inapplicable to classroom facilities, except when the proposed use of the property by the school district is for non-classroom facilities. Gov't Code § 53094. However, a 2001 amendment to this section requires more extended communication and coordination between school districts and local agencies, and adds procedural requirements to a school district's ability to render local zoning inapplicable. When a city notifies a school district of a proposed general plan adoption or amendment, the revised law allows the district to request a meeting with the planning agency. Conversely, when a school district is preparing a facility needs analysis, master plan, or other long-range plan for school siting, it must notify the appropriate planning agencies, which may then request a meeting with the district. If either agency requests a meeting, the parties must meet within 45 days to discuss school siting-related issues. Before a school district can override a local zoning ordinance, it must first comply with these expanded coordination requirements. The district also must comply with pre-existing CEQA requirements regarding school site review before overriding local zoning. Gov't Code §§ 53094, 65352.2. For example, in *City of Santa Cruz v. Santa Cruz Bd. of Educ.*, the court held that a school athletic field was a "classroom facility" for the purpose of exemption from a city's zoning ordinance and, therefore, the installation of new lights was exempt pursuant to a two-thirds vote by the school board. 210 Cal. App. 3d 1, 9 (1989).

Cities are exempt from zoning regulations with respect to property that one such entity may own within the territory of the other. Gov't Code §§ 53090–53091; 40 Ops. Cal. Atty. Gen. 243 (1962). Note also that a city is not bound by its own zoning ordinance. *See Sunny Slope Water Co. v. City of Pasadena*, 1 Cal. 2d 87, 98 (1934). Moreover, the court held that nonconformance with a county's general plan did not prevent a city from constructing a public project, because Government Code section 65402(b) requires only that the county where the project is located have an opportunity to review and report on whether the location, purpose, and extent of the acquisition or disposition of a public structure is in conformity with the general plan. *See Lawler v. City of Redding*, 7 Cal. App. 4th 778, 783 (1992). The court further held that, under a fair reading of Government Code sections 53090–53091, there is intergovernmental immunity from building and zoning regulations, including compliance with county general plans. *Id*. at 783–84.

However, a different rule applies to a city's subdivision powers. Government Code section 66428 provides that a parcel map may be required for land conveyed to or from a governmental agency, including the state, if a showing is made that public policy necessitates such a map.

Applicability of Zoning to Indian Lands

Indian tribes enjoy attributes of sovereignty over both their members and their territory. That sovereignty "is dependent on, and subordinate to, only the Federal government, not the States." *California v. Cabazon Band of Mission Indians*, 480 U.S. 202, 207 (1987). As a general rule, state laws cannot be applied to tribal Indians on Indian lands except where Congress has expressly provided that such laws shall apply. *See Gobin v. Snohomish County*, 304 F. 3d 909, 914 (9th Cir. 2002).

In the area of land use regulation, it has long been recognized that "any concurrent jurisdiction the states might inherently have possessed to regulate Indian use of reservation lands has long ago been preempted by extensive Federal policy and legislation." *Santa Rosa Band of Indians v. Kings County*, 532 F. 2d 655, 658 (9th Cir. 1975). Federal law, with its power to regulate Indian affairs, has not given cities or counties any general authority to enforce local land use regulation on Indian lands. Courts have interpreted federal laws relating to Indian lands as making "tribal government over the reservation more or less the *equivalent* of a county or local government in other areas within the state, empowered... to regulate matters of local concern within the area of its jurisdiction." *Id*. at 661 (emphasis added). Thus, tribes have been held to have power to impose their own building, health, and safety regulations on reservation lands, *see Cardin v. De La Cruz*, 671 F. 2d 363, 366 (9th Cir. 1982), and county building codes and ordinances have been held not to apply on those lands. *Santa Rosa Band of Indians*, 532 F. 2d at 661 (zoning ordinance and building code held not to apply); *see also Segundo v. City of Rancho Mirage*, 813 F. 2d 1387, 1393–94 (9th Cir. 1987).

As a general rule, state laws cannot be applied to tribal Indians on Indian lands except where Congress has expressly provided that such laws shall apply.

Mere ownership of land by an Indian tribe, however, is not sufficient to insulate it from local land use regulation. The California Attorney General opined that local ordinances pertaining to land use and planning, building standards, and health and sanitation regulations applied to a low-income housing project owned by an Indian tribe and occupied by Native Americans but located outside of the tribe's reservation and on land not held in trust for the tribe by the United States. 83 Ops. Cal. Atty. Gen. 190, 193–94 (2000). For an explanation of the various classification of Indian lands, *see* Conference of Western Attorneys General, *American Indian Law Deskbook*, chapters 2–3 (2nd ed., 1998).

Mere ownership of land by an Indian tribe is not sufficient to insulate it from local land use regulation.

The issue of the role, if any, state and local governments should play with respect to Indian lands has become a particularly charged topic in light of the growth in Indian gaming in California.

IGRA = The Indian Gaming Regulatory Act

TEIR = Tribal Environmental Impact Report

The regulatory framework for Indian gaming was established by the Indian Gaming Regulatory Act (IGRA), passed by Congress in 1988. 25 U.S.C. § 2701 *et seq.* The IGRA divides gaming into three classes. 25 U.S.C. § 2710. Class I gaming consists of social games for prizes of minimal value or traditional Indian games in connection with a tribal ceremony or celebration, and is not regulated by the IGRA. 25 U.S.C. §§ 2703(6), 2710. Class II gaming includes bingo and certain card games, and while subject to the IGRA, remains within the jurisdiction of individual Indian tribes for regulatory purposes. 25 U.S.C. §§ 2703(7), 2710. Class III gaming, which includes casino-style games like slot machines, blackjack, craps, and roulette, is allowed: a) to the extent such games are allowed by the state where the Indian land is located;[14] b) is on land within a reservation or land that is either held in trust for an Indian tribe by the United States or held by a tribe or individual subject to restrictions by the United States upon alienation and over which the tribe exercises governmental power; and c) is subject to a compact to be negotiated between the tribe and the state and then approved by the Secretary of the Interior. 25 U.S.C. § 2710(d)(1)(B).

The IGRA requires states to negotiate with Indian tribes in good faith to enter into tribal-state compacts to allow gaming. 25 U.S.C. § 2710(d)(3). If the state fails to negotiate in good faith, a tribe may after 180 days bring an action in federal district court. 25 U.S.C. § 2710(d)(7). If the court finds that the state has failed to negotiate in good faith, it shall order the state and the tribe to conclude a compact within a 60-day period. 25 U.S.C. § 2710(d)(7)(B)(iii).

The California Legislature has ratified dozens of tribal-state compacts allowing Class III gaming on Indian lands within the state pursuant to the IGRA.

The California Legislature has ratified dozens of tribal-state compacts allowing Class III gaming on Indian lands within the state pursuant to the IGRA. Indian gaming has generated $5.1 billion per year in California. *See Indian Gaming in California*, Institute of Governmental Studies Hot Topic, University of California at Berkeley (August 2004) (available at www.igs.berkeley.edu).

In recent years, California's Governor negotiated several new and amended tribal-state compacts. These newer compacts have resulted in substantial increases in casino revenues to be paid to the state. They also have given local governments significantly more leverage to force tribes to address the effects of their gaming operations by requiring that:

- A tribe must prepare a Tribal Environmental Impact Report (TEIR) before commencing a new project. A project is defined as any activity occurring on Indian Lands to serve the tribe's gaming activities that may cause a direct or indirect physical change in the off-reservation environment.
- The TEIR must include detailed information about the significant effects, mitigation, and alternatives to the project.
- Failure to prepare a TEIR could result in the state obtaining an injunction to stop the project.
- Tribes must meet and negotiate with local governments and adopt an enforceable written agreement that addresses off-reservation impacts, including public safety, gambling addiction, and environmental impacts.

14. Although casino-style gaming is generally prohibited under the California Constitution, state voters in 2000 passed Proposition 1A, which expressly allowed gaming by Indian tribes on Indian lands in accordance with federal law. Cal. Const., art. IV, § 19(f).

See, e.g., Tribal-State Gaming Compact Between the Coyote Valley Band of Pomo Indians and the State of California, §§ 11.1, 11.2 (available at www.governor.ca.gov); *see also* California State Ass'n of Counties, CSAC Comparison of the Five Tribal-State Compacts (Aug. 23, 2004) (available at www.csac.counties.org/legislation/Indian_ gaming/compacts_summary.pdf).

Taking advantage of the terms found in these newer compacts, cities are negotiating memoranda of understanding (MOUs) with local tribes to address anticipated impacts from casinos. Negotiation and execution of these MOUs has been held to be an administrative act by cities and not subject to referendum, given that only the federal and state governments have legislative power over Indian affairs. *Worthington v. City Council of the City of Rohnert Park*, 130 Cal. App. 4th 1132, 1139–40 (2005); *see also Citizens to Enforce CEQA v. City of Rohnert Park*, 131 Cal. App. 4th 1594 (2005) (holding an MOU such as the one in *Worthington* did not trigger environmental review under CEQA).

In deference to tribal sovereignty, none of the following shall be deemed a project for purposes of CEQA: execution of the compacts, execution of the required agreements between tribes and local governments, on-reservation impacts resulting from the compacts, and the sale of any compact assets. *See* Gov't Code §§ 12012.40, 12012.45.[15] Therefore, while the language of certain compacts may impose requirements for environmental study, CEQA itself cannot ensure the disclosure, avoidance, or mitigation of impacts associated with Indian gaming.

Believing that the potential for impacts from Indian gaming is greatest where casinos are proposed in urban areas, the California Governor took steps in 2005 to severely limit the development of casinos in more densely populated areas. The Governor issued a proclamation stating that he would oppose proposals for the federal acquisition of lands in any urbanized areas where the lands sought to be acquired in trust are to be used for gaming activities.

Taking advantage of the terms found in these newer compacts, cities are negotiating MOUs with local tribes to address anticipated impacts from casinos.

MOU = Memorandum of understanding

---

15. Voters rejected two ballot initiatives relating to Indian gaming that appeared on the November 2004 ballot. Each sought amendments to the California Constitution that would have set different requirements for revenue payments of Indian gaming operations. Notably, both initiatives contemplated including requirements that the tribes conduct some environmental review in connection with their gaming activities.

5

Subdivisions

Overview

The Subdivision Map Act[1]

The Map Act vests in a city the power to regulate and control the design and improvement of subdivisions within its boundaries. Gov't Code § 66411.

Each city must adopt an ordinance regulating and controlling subdivisions for which the Map Act requires a tentative and final or parcel map. Gov't Code § 66411. The authority for a city to regulate land use, including subdivisions, flows from the general police power. Cal. Const. art. XI, § 7. However, the Map Act sets forth certain mandates that must be followed for subdivision processing. A city can impose conditions on the subdivision process when the Map Act is silent. *Soderling v. City of Santa Monica*, 142 Cal. App. 3d 501, 506–07 (1983) (holding that smoke detectors can be required in a condominium conversion map process); *see also Ayres v. City Council of Los Angeles*, 34 Cal. 2d 31, 37 (1949) (finding that certain street improvement conditions could be imposed even though they were not expressly provided for in the Map Act and local city ordinances). However, a city cannot regulate contrary to specific provisions contained in the Map Act. *Shelter Creek Dev. Corp. v. City of Oxnard*, 34 Cal. 3d 733, 735–36 (1983) (holding that a city cannot override a specific provision in the Map Act grandfathering certain stock cooperative conversions).

The Map Act's primary goals are:

- To encourage orderly community development by providing for the regulation and control of the design and improvement of the subdivision, with a proper consideration of its relation to adjoining areas
- To ensure that the areas within the subdivision that are dedicated for public purposes will be properly improved by the subdivider so that they will not become an undue burden on the community
- To protect the public and individual transferees from fraud and exploitation

61 Ops. Cal. Atty. Gen. 299, 301 (1978); 77 Ops. Cal. Atty. Gen. 185 (1994)

The Map Act vests in a city the power to regulate and control the design and improvement of subdivisions within its boundaries.

A city cannot regulate contrary to specific provisions contained in the Map Act.

---

1. *See also* Daniel J. Curtin, Jr. and Robert E. Merritt, *California Subdivision Map Act and the Development Process* (Cal. Cont. Ed. Bar, 2nd ed. 2001) (Dec. 2005 Update); Daniel J. Curtin, Jr. and Robert E. Merritt, *Subdivision Map Act Manual* (Solano Press, 2003).

The Map Act is applied in conjunction with other state land use laws, such as the general plan and the specific plan (Gov't Code § 65300 *et seq.*), zoning (Gov't Code § 65800 *et seq.*), the California Environmental Quality Act (CEQA) (Pub. Res. Code § 21000 *et seq.*), and the Permit Streamlining Act (Gov't Code § 65920 *et seq.*).

CEQA = California Environmental Quality Act

The Map Act must be distinguished from the Subdivided Lands Act. Bus. & Prof. Code § 11000 *et seq.* The Map Act provides for regulation of land divisions by a city and is interpreted and enforced by the city. The Subdivided Lands Act is a consumer protection statute primarily intended to ensure that adequate disclosures are made. This statute regulates public offerings of land in subdivisions for sale or lease, and is interpreted and enforced by the California Department of Real Estate. An excellent discussion on the differences between the two acts is found in both *Daro v. Superior Court*, 151 Cal. App. 4th 1079, 1093–94 (2007) and *California Coastal Comm'n v. Quanta Inv. Corp.*, 113 Cal. App. 3d 579, 588 (1980).[2]

Each city must, by ordinance, regulate and control subdivisions for which the Map Act requires a tentative and final map or a parcel map.

Need for a local ordinance; applicable to charter cities. Each city must, by ordinance, regulate and control subdivisions for which the Map Act requires a tentative and final map or a parcel map. In addition, a city may, by ordinance, regulate other subdivisions, provided that such regulations are not more restrictive than the regulations for those subdivisions for which a tentative and final or parcel map are required by the Map Act, with certain exceptions. Gov't Code § 66411. *See also City of Tiburon v. Northwestern Pac. R.R. Co.*, 4 Cal. App. 3d 160 (1970). The Map Act applies to charter cities. *Santa Clara County Contractors and Homebuilders Ass'n v. City of Santa Clara*, 232 Cal. App. 2d 564 (1965).

The courts have been reluctant to hold that local subdivision ordinances are preempted by the Map Act. However, a city cannot regulate contrary to specific Map Act provisions.

Preemption. The courts have been reluctant to hold that local subdivision ordinances are preempted by the Map Act. *See Griffin Dev. Co. v. City of Oxnard*, 39 Cal. 3d 256, 261–62 (1985) (the Map Act does not preempt a city's condominium conversion ordinance); *Santa Monica Pines, Ltd. v. Rent Control Bd.*, 35 Cal. 3d 858 (1984) (a city has independent authority from the police power to regulate subdivisions); *The Pines v. City of Santa Monica*, 29 Cal. 3d 656, 659–60 (1981) (the Map Act does not preempt local revenue taxes); *Benny v. City of Alameda*, 105 Cal. App. 3d 1006, 1010–11 (1980) (a tentative subdivision map application can be conditioned on receiving prior land use approval, including zoning). For instance, one court upheld a "removal permit" requirement that was imposed by the voters after the plaintiff's map had been approved. *McMullan v. Santa Monica Rent Control Bd.*, 168 Cal. App. 3d 960, 963 (1985). "While the [Map] act may be the final word respecting the subdivision process, it does not purport and may not be understood to be preemptive of all land use regulation." *Id.* at 963.

However, a city cannot regulate contrary to specific Map Act provisions. *Shelter Creek*, 34 Cal. 3d at 738. For example, in *Griffis v. County of Mono*, the court held that a local ordinance that limited the maximum duration of a map extension to one year was not valid since the Map Act allows extensions of up to three years. 163 Cal. App. 3d 414, 420 (1985). Another court found an

---

2. *See Forming California Common Interest Development*, chapter 3 (Cal. Cont. Ed. Bar, 2006) for a discussion of the Subdivided Lands Act.

implied preemption based on the merger provision of the Map Act, and held invalid local zoning ordinances requiring merger under certain circumstances upon application of a development permit. *Morehart v. County of Santa Barbara*, 7 Cal. 4th 725, 748 (1994).

Subdivisions Covered by the Map Act
What Is a Subdivision?

A subdivision is defined in the statute as:

> [T]he division, by any subdivider, of any unit or units of improved or unimproved land, or any portion thereof, shown on the latest equalized county assessment roll as a unit or as contiguous units, for the purpose of sale, lease, or financing, whether immediate or future.

Gov't Code § 66424

The Map Act distinguishes between a subdivision consisting of five or more parcels and one consisting of four or fewer parcels. In general, a subdivision of five or more parcels requires a tentative and a final map; a subdivision of four or fewer requires just a parcel map.

"the division..." In order to achieve the purposes of the Map Act, the courts have broadly defined what is covered under this definition. Several Attorney General opinions have attached importance to divisions that award the right to exclusive occupancy in determining a subdivision under the Map Act. *See* 39 Ops. Cal. Atty. Gen. 82 (1962); 17 Ops. Cal. Atty. Gen. 79 (1951).

Divisions created by deeds, leases, and deeds of trust are clearly ones that fall under Government Code section 66424. Other divisions are less certain. For example, do easements create divisions? It can be argued that a non-exclusive easement is not a division because of the lack of any right to exclusive occupancy. However, an exclusive easement may be subject to the Map Act because it gives the right of exclusive occupancy similar to a fee interest. *But see Robinson v. City of Alameda*, 194 Cal. App. 3d 1286 (1987) (holding that an agreement allowing exclusive use of a portion of land for an indefinite term after sale was not subject to the Map Act). Divisions also can be created via an agency's exercise of eminent domain under certain conditions. *See* 86 Ops. Cal. Atty. Gen. 70 (2003) (opining that a public agency which condemned and acquired most of a 640-acre parcel to create a reservoir, leaving the parcel's two remaining areas divided by water, lawfully created two parcels because the division met the conclusive presumption of legality under Government Code section 66412.6).

"...by any subdivider..." The term "subdivider" is defined broadly by the Map Act. Any person, firm, corporation, partnership, or association (but not their consultants or employees) who will divide land for itself or others is a subdivider. Gov't Code § 66423. Governmental agencies such as the Department of Transportation (Caltrans) and public agencies such as agricultural associations are also considered subdividers and subject to the provisions of the Map Act in certain situations. 62 Ops. Cal. Atty. Gen. 136 (1979); 62 Ops. Cal. Atty. Gen. 140 (1979). However, the Attorney General has said a tax collector is not a subdivider. Thus, the Map Act does not apply to a sale of a portion of a tax-deeded parcel conducted by the tax collector. 64 Ops. Cal. Atty. Gen. 814 (1981).

In general, a subdivision of five or more parcels requires a tentative and a final map; a subdivision of four or fewer requires just a parcel map.

Any person, firm, corporation, partnership, or association (but not their consultants or employees) who will divide land for itself or others is a subdivider.

Caltrans = Department of Transportation

"…of any unit or units of improved or unimproved land, or any portion thereof…" The Map Act does not make a distinction between improved and unimproved land. Land as defined by Civil Code section 659 includes free or occupied space for an indefinite distance upwards as well as downwards. Thus a division of airspace, such as the sale of a floor in a high rise building, would be subject to the Map Act.[3]

"…shown on the latest equalized county assessment roll as a unit…" Reference to the assessor's roll provides a convenient method of identifying the property being divided and its ownership during a given period of time. 59 Ops. Cal. Atty. Gen. 581 (1976). It often is misunderstood as permitting the owner to convey assessor's parcels without first obtaining a subdivision map. The assessor's parcel designations have no effect on application of the Map Act, and owners may not divide land along the lines of the assessor's parcels for the purpose of sale, lease, or financing without obtaining a subdivision map. The function and purpose of the assessor is to raise revenue, not to regulate the division of land. 62 Ops. Cal. Atty. Gen. 147 (1979) (a property owner may not rely on county assessor's assignment of two separate parcel numbers as compliance with Map Act in proposed sale of one of the areas given a separate parcel number); 59 Ops. Cal. Atty. Gen. 581 (1976) (when three legally subdivided lots are subsequently combined as one assessment parcel, no new parcel map need be processed before conveyance of the lots).

> **PRACTICE TIP**
> The fact that a parcel of land appears on an assessor's roll does not mean that the parcel was validly created pursuant to the Map Act.

When property is subdivided, the new parcels do not appear on the latest equalized assessment roll until the roll comes into existence on August 20. Rev. & Tax. Code §§ 2050, 2052; 55 Ops. Cal. Atty. Gen. 414 (1972). The purchaser of a unit of land created under the Map Act may divide the property one or more times before completion of the equalized assessment roll for that unit, and may not be prevented by local ordinance from making consecutive subdivisions of the unit. Gov't Code § 66424.1.

In order to ensure local requirements are satisfied, recent legislation has restricted the ability of assessors to assign parcel numbers. Thus, even after property has been subdivided, an assessor may not assign parcel numbers until the required map has been recorded. If the requirement for a parcel map is waived, the assessor may not assign parcel numbers until the applicant provides a copy of the finding required to justify such waiver. Rev. & Tax. Code § 327.5.

Property that will be divided must be contiguous as shown on the assessor's roll.

"…or as contiguous units…" Property that will be divided must be contiguous as shown on the assessor's roll. The Map Act expressly provides that property is contiguous even though separated by roads, streets, utility easements, or railroad rights-of-way. Gov't Code § 66424. Note that the list in Government Code section 66424 might not be exclusive, but merely illustrative. For example, the Attorney General has stated that parcels on two sides of a canal owned in fee by the Federal Bureau of Reclamation are considered to be contiguous. 61 Ops. Cal. Atty. Gen. 299 (1978).

"…for the purpose of sale, lease, or financing, whether immediate or future." The division must be for the purpose of sale, lease, or financing, whether immediate

---

3. The Map Act does not apply to the leasing or financing of apartments, offices, stores, or similar space within buildings. Gov't Code § 66412(a).

or future. According to the Attorney General, partitions are considered a division for the purpose of sale and thus governed by the Map Act. *See* 64 Ops. Cal. Atty. Gen. 762 (1981); Code Civ. Proc. § 872.040; *Pratt v. Adams*, 229 Cal. App. 2d 602, 605 (1964).

> The conversion and exchange of property interest in a partition action may be considered a "sale" in the broad sense of the term.... [C]wnership and title to partitioned property is changed and transferred among the owners in consideration for each's mutual undertaking. Accordingly, a division under the partition action statutory scheme may be said to be "for the purpose of sale" and thus constitute a "subdivision" for purposes of section 66424 and the requirements of the Act.

64 Ops. Cal. Atty. Gen. 762, 766–67 (1981)

Gifts also can fall under the definition of subdivision. For instance, in *Pescosolido v. Smith*, the court held that bona fide gifts of distinct, independently developable and salable parcels are encompassed under Government Code section 66424. 142 Cal. App. 3d 964, 972 (1983). The Pescosolidos conveyed parcels of land to their children for estate planning, tax, and college financing purposes. Although they testified that it was not their intent to sell the property given to their children, the evidence showed an intent by some of the children to sell parcels. The court held that the transfer was a "sale" for purposes of the Map Act because the court found that the ultimate purpose of the gift was to sell the property in the future and "it was the intent of the Pescosolidos to circumvent the map filing and approval provisions required under the Subdivision Map Act...." *Id.* at 970.

Gifts also can fall under the definition of subdivision.

However, an agreement allowing use of a portion of land after sale for an indefinite term was found not to be subject to the Map Act. *Robinson v. City of Alameda*, 194 Cal. App. 3d 1286, 1288–89 (1987). In that case, the Robinsons owned two parcels of land, Parcel A and Parcel B. They sold Parcel B, but reserved the exclusive right to use a portion of Parcel B until they sold Parcel A or until both of them died. The court held that the Robinsons' interest in Parcel B was not a sale because they had no ownership interest in the portion of Parcel B. Additionally, it was not a lease because a lease by definition must be for a definite period of time, and the term of "until the Robinsons sold Parcel A or died" was not a definite period of time. *Id.*

An agreement allowing use of a portion of land after sale for an indefinite term was found not to be subject to the Map Act in Robinson v. City of Alameda.

The *Robinson* decision appears inconsistent with the *Pescosolido* decision in that neither the Robinsons nor the Pescosolidos had any immediate intention to sell, lease, or finance their respective properties. Yet, the gift in *Pescosolido* was held to be subject to the Map Act because of future purpose of sale, while the court in *Robinson* failed to look at the purpose of conveyance. This is the result of the *Robinson* court taking a narrow view of what constituted a "sale" or "lease," and basing its holding on the ground that the interest reserved was neither.

A deed approving a non-exclusive easement authorizing construction of a garage for the easement-holder's use on a portion of the burdened property has been held not to require compliance with the Map Act. *Blackmore v. Powell*, 150 Cal. App. 4th 1593, 1603–04 (2007). Although it found that exclusive use of the garage (which occupied approximately ten percent of the otherwise non-exclusive easement area) was a necessary incident of the easement, the court nonetheless held that the easement was "merely the right to use a portion of appellant's property in a restricted manner, and [did] not divide or sever the property into distinguishable possessory estates or interests." *Id.* at 1599, 1604. The easement was "too restricted in scope to constitute a subdivision under the Act." *Id.* at 1605.

Leases are subdivisions under Government Code section 66424. However, it is not always easy to spot a lease. In making this assessment, the focus should be more on the substance rather than the form of the instrument. For example, the Attorney General opined that an agreement called a "permit" authorizing the construction and use of a house, mobile home, or camping facilities on lots owned by a fraternal organization was covered under the Map Act because the permit was actually a lease. 57 Ops. Cal. Atty. Gen. 556 (1974). Even though the instrument stated "THIS IS A PERMIT AND NOT A LEASE" on its face, the Attorney General found:

> The contents and the effect of said conveyance will prove its legal nature. No particular or set language such as "let" or "demise" or the usual words of hiring is necessary to constitute a given writing as a lease. Any words sufficient to express the intent of the parties that one party shall divest himself of the possession, and the other come into possession for a determinate time...will, by construction of law, amount to a lease.

Id. at 558

While there are no published cases involving financing, it seems clear that divisions are created by the execution and recording of mortgages, deeds of trust, and land installment contracts. *See* 58 Ops. Cal. Atty. Gen. 408 (1975). This makes sense given that if the financing instrument is foreclosed, a division in ownership will result. There has been a question whether release provisions in a deed of trust by which the lender agrees to reconvey portions of the land as payments create subdivisions. While no court has considered this question, the better view is that these agreements, alone, do not create subdivisions; however, a subdivision will happen upon actual reconveyance of one or more parcels, and a map must be processed before this occurs. To address this concern, as a practical matter, release agreements should be drafted to condition reconveyance on compliance with the Map Act and local subdivision ordinances.

Whether a devise of property, alone, will constitute a division is another unresolved question. However, in *Wells Fargo Bank v. Town of Woodside*, the court held that a local subdivision ordinance cannot require the filing of a map for a parcel created as a probate homestead by the probate court. The court based its holding on preemption—that the Probate Law superseded the local subdivision ordinance. 33 Cal. 3d 379 (1983).

The Attorney General has opined that the creation of a conservation easement pursuant to Civil Code section 815 *et seq.* in which the owner maintains ownership and possession of the land does not, in itself, constitute a subdivision requiring compliance with the Subdivision Map Act. While the grant of a conservation easement may involve identifying a portion of a larger tract of land upon which enforceable use restrictions will be placed, the grant does not constitute a division of the land within the meaning of the Act, according to the Attorney General. The mere granting of a conservation easement neither

PRACTICE TIP
Release agreements should be drafted to condition reconveyance of parcels on compliance with the Map Act and local subdivision ordinances.

PRACTICE TIP
There is considerable incentive to avoid final maps and subdivide using parcel maps when possible. Generally, the city will impose fewer fees and other exactions when a parcel map is processed. Also, processing a parcel map is generally simpler and less time-consuming.

conveys the land subject to the easement, nor expresses any future intent to convey it, as a separate unit. 90 Ops. Cal. Atty. Gen. 69 (2007).

What Type of Map Is Required?
General Rule: Tentative and Final Map or Parcel Map?

The general rule is that a tentative and final map are required for all subdivisions creating five or more parcels, five or more condominiums, a community apartment project containing five or more parcels, or the conversion of a dwelling to a stock cooperative containing five or more dwelling units, unless specifically excepted. Gov't Code § 66426. However, there are five exceptions that allow a parcel map instead of a tentative and final map regardless of the number of parcels created. These are:

- Divisions of less than five acres where each parcel abuts upon a maintained public street and no dedications or improvements are required by the local agency.
- Twenty-acre-plus parcels with approved access to a maintained public street.
- Industrial and commercial developments with approved access to public streets, where the street alignment and width have been approved by the local agency.
- Parcels that consist of not less than 40 acres or not less than a quarter of a quarter-section.
- A division solely for the creation of an environmental subdivision pursuant to Government Code section 66418.2. An environmental subdivision allows a landowner to sell property for off-site mitigation based on defined criteria such as a subdivision for biotic and wildlife purposes. The division must be at least 20 acres, or less than 20 acres but contiguous to other property also qualifying as an environmental subdivision with a total of at least 20 acres.

Gov't Code § 66426

A tentative and final map are required for all subdivisions creating five or more parcels or condominiums, a community apartment project containing five or more parcels, or the conversion of a dwelling to a stock cooperative containing five or more dwelling units, unless specifically excepted.

Counting Parcels

Successive subdivisions. When counting parcels to determine whether a final map or a parcel map is required, all previous subdivisions by the same subdivider are included. *Bright v. Board of Supervisors*, 66 Cal. App. 3d 191 (1977). The *Bright* case illustrates this point. In 1966, Bright acquired title to one parcel, Parcel A, which he held as separate property. An adjoining parcel, Parcel B, was acquired in 1968 by Bright and his wife as joint tenants. In 1973, Bright transferred a portion of Parcel B to his wife as her separate property, thereby creating a new parcel, Parcel C. He then applied for a tentative parcel map to divide Parcel A into four lots. *Id.* at 193. The county refused to process the parcel map, stating a final map instead was required. On appeal, the court agreed. Since Bright was the owner of two contiguous lots, Parcels A and B, the division of Parcel B into Parcel C must be taken into account when dividing Parcel A. Thus, six parcels were created by this division. *Id.* at 195.

When counting parcels to determine whether a final map or a parcel map is required, all previous subdivisions by the same subdivider are included.

The subdivider may not avoid the tentative and final map requirements by subdividing one parcel four times using a parcel map and then, through agents, repeating the process over and over again. This practice, known as "quartering" or "4 x 4" is illegal. If discovered, it will be prosecuted by cities because it can result in a subdivision of numerous lots without compliance with the more stringent requirements applicable to final maps.

A form of quartering was attempted in *Pratt v. Adams*, 229 Cal. App. 2d 602 (1964). The plaintiffs tried to circumvent the requirement of a final map by partitioning land held in joint tenancy into 12 parcels, and then dividing each parcel four or fewer times resulting in 38 parcels. The court held that the division of the land into 38 parcels was part of a general scheme to multiply the number of parcels, and required a tentative and final map:

> [This] is a case where the permit is sought as the culmination of a plan to circumvent the law by one of the planners. The courts will not assist, by equitable process, the fulfillment of this plan.

Id. at 606

The action by a subdivider in creating divisions also includes divisions by its agent. The Attorney General has indicated that an agency relationship will be found in cases where the parties may not be dealing at "arm's length":

> If there is evidence that the transfer is not an "arm's length transaction," for example, a sale for inadequate consideration, a transfer to a close relative or business associate, retention of control or financial interest, or generally a transfer which is part of a conspiracy to evade the Subdivision Map Act, the total number of lots should be treated as a subdivision.

55 Ops. Cal. Atty. Gen. 414, 417–18 (1972)

Quartering may be tempting for subdividers, but it can result in a criminal prosecution under the Map Act. Gov't Code § 66499.31. It may also result in severe penalties under the Subdivided Lands Act, which governs the offering of subdivided lands for sale or lease and is administered by the California Department of Real Estate. *See* Bus. and Prof. Code § 11000 *et seq.*

PRACTICE TIP

"Quartering" or "4 x 4" is illegal and can result in a criminal prosecution under the Map Act.

Remainder parcels. When a subdivider only divides a portion of a parcel of land, the Map Act allows the subdivider to designate the undivided portion as a "remainder" parcel so long as that portion is not divided for the purpose of sale, lease, or financing immediately or in the future. If the gross area of the remainder parcel is five acres or more, the subdivider may omit from the map the portion of land that is not divided for the purpose of sale, lease, or financing. In that case, the location need only be indicated by deed reference to the existing boundaries of the remainder parcel. Gov't Code §§ 66424.6(a), 66434(e) (final maps), § 66445(d) (parcel maps). A parcel designated as "not a part" is considered to be a remainder parcel. Gov't Code §§ 66434(e), 66445(d)(3). If the subdivider elects to designate a remainder:

- The designated remainder shall not be counted as a parcel when determining whether a final map or parcel map is required.
- A city may not require construction of improvements or payment of fees associated with improvements on the remainder parcel until a permit or other approval for development of the remainder parcel is issued.
- If a city has an ordinance that authorizes agreements, the construction of the improvements will be done pursuant to the terms of the agreement.
- If there is no agreement, a city may require construction of improvements or payment of fees within a reasonable time after final map approval and

prior to the issuance of a permit if the improvements are necessary for the public health and safety or necessary for the orderly development of the surrounding area.

Gov't Code § 66424.6(a)

A subdivider must not designate a remainder parcel with the present intent to sell that remainder parcel. As the court in *Pescosolido v. Smith* stated:

> [T]he phrase "for the purpose of sale…whether immediate or future" in the definition provided by Government Code section 66424 must encompass the ultimate purpose for which the particular land division is done.

142 Cal. App. 3d 964, 972 (1983)

The Attorney General issued an opinion stating that two or more remainder parcels may not be designated when a developer subdivides portions of more than one parcel with the intention of further dividing the remainder parcels in a subsequent phase. Only one remainder parcel may result from the division of each unit of land when a subdivider creates a subdivision. 77 Ops. Cal. Atty. Gen. 185 (1994).

The remainder parcel may eventually be sold without any subsequent filing of a parcel map or a final map. However, a city may require a certificate or conditional certificate of compliance. Gov't Code § 66424.6(d).[4]

Conveyances to public entities and public utilities. Conveyance of a parcel of land to a governmental agency, public entity, or public utility is not counted when counting parcels and determining which type of map to file. Gov't Code § 66426.5. A "conveyance" includes a fee interest, a leasehold interest, an easement, or a license. For example, if the division results in five parcels, but one parcel will be conveyed to a public utility, the subdivider will only be required to file a parcel map.

Important Exemptions to Mapping Requirements

All divisions of property that fall under the definition of subdivision in Government Code section 66424 are covered under the Map Act, unless specifically exempted by statute. The following exemptions are most commonly utilized.

Lot Line Adjustments

Lot line adjustments are exempt from the Map Act.[5] Gov't Code § 66412(d).

The Legislature has significantly revised the lot line adjustment procedure, limiting the manner in which they can be used as follows:

- A lot line adjustment can only be between four or fewer parcels. Under prior law, there was no limit as to the number of parcels involved in a lot line adjustment.

> *A subdivider must not designate a remainder parcel with the present intent to sell that remainder parcel.*

> *Conveyance of a parcel of land to a governmental agency, public entity, or public utility is not counted when counting parcels and determining which type of map to file.*

PRACTICE TIP

Under a lot line adjustment procedure, the number of lots on a property can be decreased (e.g., from 4 to 2). A city can deny a lot line adjustment if the resulting parcels do not conform to its general plan, any applicable coastal plan, and zoning and/or building ordinances.

---

4. For a practical discussion of how and why certificates of compliance may be used by land owners, buyers, and public agencies, *see* Robert E. Merritt and Tedra E. Fox, "Using Certificates of Compliance to Help Clients Under the Subdivision Map Act," 26 *Real Property Law Reporter* (Cal. Cont. Ed. Bar, July 2003).

5. However, lot line adjustments are not exempt from the requirements of the California Coastal Act (Pub. Res. Code § 30000 *et seq.*) because the Coastal Act defines "development" more broadly than the Map Act. *La Fe, Inc. v. County of Los Angeles*, 73 Cal. App. 4th 231, 239 (1999).

> **PRACTICE TIP**
>
> After completion of a lot line adjustment, make sure that any deed of trust encumbering the affected parcels is amended to reflect the adjustment.

- The parcels must be adjoining. Under prior law, the parcels need only have been "adjacent," which had been interpreted to mean "near or close to." *San Dieguito Partnership, L.P. v. City of San Diego*, 7 Cal. App. 4th 748, 757 (1992).
- The new parcels must conform to the local general plan, applicable specific plan, any applicable coastal plan, and zoning and building ordinances. In contrast, prior law required only conformance to zoning and building laws.

A city still is prohibited from requiring a tentative, final, or parcel map as a condition of approval of a lot line adjustment. The city may only require conditions (1) to conform to the local general plan, applicable specific plan, applicable coastal plan, and zoning and building ordinances, (2) to require the prepayment of real property taxes, and (3) to facilitate the relocation of existing utilities, infrastructure, or easements.

The lot line adjustment must be reflected in a recorded deed, to show the lot line adjustment in the chain of title. No record of survey can be required unless required by Business and Professions Code section 8762. Gov't Code § 66412(d); 77 Ops. Cal. Atty. Gen. 231 (1994).

If one or more of the parcels affected by a lot line adjustment is encumbered by a deed of trust, a mortgage, or a lien for a special assessment imposed by a special district, the instrument should be amended to reflect the new lot lines. Otherwise, an illegal lot may be created if the lender forecloses. One court has held that language in a deed of trust encumbering "all the improvements now or hereafter erected on the property, and all easements, rights, appurtenances... and all fixtures now or hereafter a part of the property," was sufficient to automatically add property acquired in a lot line adjustment to the encumbered parcel. *Hellweg v. Cassidy*, 61 Cal. App. 4th 806, 809 (1998). However, this kind of language should not be relied upon to protect against the creation of an illegal lot. The better practice is to amend the financing instrument so the encumbered property conforms to the new parcels created by the lot line adjustment.

Many cities require recording of a drawing or plat showing the lot line adjustment and a certificate of compliance to finalize the lot line adjustment. The local subdivision ordinance should be consulted to determine whether this is required.

"Second" Units [6]

The Map Act exempts the construction, financing, or leasing of second units.

The Map Act exempts the construction, financing, or leasing of "second" units. However, if the unit is sold or transferred, the Map Act applies. Gov't Code § 66412.2. A "second" unit is defined as an attached or detached residential dwelling providing complete independent living facilities for one or more persons. Gov't Code § 65852.2(i)(4). It must contain permanent provisions for living, sleeping, eating, cooking, and sanitation on the same parcel as the main residential unit is located. A "second" unit also is an efficiency unit as defined by Health and Safety Code section 17958.1, and a manufactured home as defined by Health and Safety Code section 18007. Gov't Code § 65852.2(i)(4). Legislation passed in 2007 repealed provisions concerning so-called "granny" units, but specified that units approved pursuant to the law prior to 2007 are valid. Gov't Code § 65852.1.

---

6. *See* California State Department of Housing and Community Development, Division of Housing Policy Development, Report on Second Units (Dec. 1990).

Conveyances to or from Public Entities and Public Utilities

The Map Act exempts from the requirement of a parcel map land conveyed to or from a governmental agency, public entity, public utility, or land conveyed to a subsidiary of a public utility for conveyance to the public utility for rights-of-way, unless a showing is made in an individual case on substantial evidence that public policy necessitates a parcel map. Gov't Code § 66428(a)(2). The law has been clarified to provide that the conveyance may be for a fee interest, easement, leasehold interest, or license.

Some local ordinances require notice to the city of conveyances of this nature. By receiving notice before the conveyance, this provides an opportunity for the city to hold a hearing to determine whether public policy necessitates a map.

This exemption, however, is only from a parcel map requirement. Divisions requiring final maps are not exempted. But since parcels conveyed to governmental agencies, public entities, and public utilities are not counted under Government Code section 66426.5, this raises the issue whether only conveyances *from* those entities could trigger a final map requirement.

The Attorney General has opined that the Map Act will not apply if the public agency is engaged in performing its official functions. For example, the University of California was not bound by the Map Act when it was constructing for-sale on-campus homes as part of its program to provide faculty housing since such a program helped fulfill the university's educational mission and purpose. 75 Ops. Cal. Atty. Gen. 98 (1992).

Even though a map may not be required, dedications and improvements may still be required. The legislative history of the Map Act makes clear that the intent was only to exempt the mapping requirement and not place the transfer outside the Map Act entirely. *See* 1977 Cal. Stat. ch. 234, § 19 (uncodified); 62 Ops. Cal. Atty. Gen. 140 (1979) (determining that local merger ordinance, authorized by Government Code section 66424.2 (later repealed, *see* Gov't Code § 66451.10 *et seq*.), applies to California Department of Transportation); 62 Ops. Cal. Atty. Gen. 136 (1979) (finding District Agricultural Association subject to provisions of Map Act in subdivision and sale of its property).

Even though a map may not be required, dedications and improvements may still be required.

Financing and Leasing of Certain Units

Financing and leasing of apartments, offices, stores, or similar space within apartment buildings, industrial buildings, commercial buildings, mobile home parks, or trailer parks are expressly exempt from the Map Act. Gov't Code § 66412(a).

The financing or leasing of (1) existing separate commercial or industrial buildings on a single parcel or (2) any parcel of land in conjunction with the construction of commercial or industrial buildings on a single parcel is exempt, unless the project is not subject to review under other city ordinances regulating design and improvement. Gov't Code § 66412.1. It is uncertain what types of local ordinances would qualify as regulating design and improvement. A building permit probably would not suffice because it is a ministerial permit that

Financing and leasing of apartments, offices, stores, or similar space within apartment buildings, industrial buildings, commercial buildings, mobile home parks, or trailer parks are expressly exempt from the Map Act.

only requires compliance with the relevant building code. However, regulations that involve exercise of discretion by a city (*e.g.*, design review) would probably qualify. The exemptions under Government Code section 66412.1 apply only to "leasing" and "financing," not to sale.

Condominium, Stock Cooperatives, and Community Apartment Projects

Conversions.[7] Conversions of a community apartment to a condominium are exempt from the Map Act under limited circumstances. The following requirements must be met for the exemption to apply:

- At least 75 percent of the units in the project were occupied by record owners of the project on March 31, 1982.
- A final or parcel map of the project was properly recorded after January 1, 1964, with all of the conditions of the map remaining in effect after the conversion.
- The city certifies that these requirements were satisfied if the city provides for that certification.
- Subject to Civil Code section 1351(e), all conveyances and other documents necessary to complete the conversion are signed by the required number of owners in the project as specified in the bylaws or other organizational documents. If the bylaws or organizational documents do not specify the number of owners, then a majority of owners is required to sign the documents.

Gov't Code § 66412(g)

Likewise, conversions of a stock cooperative into a condominium are exempt if certain conditions are met:

- At least 51 percent of the units in the cooperative were occupied or individually owned by stockholders of the cooperative on January 1, 1981. A cooperative unit is "individually owned" if the stockholder of that unit owns or partially owns an interest in only one unit in the cooperative.
- No more than 25 percent of the shares of the cooperative were owned by any one person on January 1, 1981.
- At the time of conversion, a person renting a unit in a cooperative shall be entitled to all tenant rights under state or local law, including, but not limited to, rights respecting first refusal, notice, and displacement and relocation benefits.
- If a city so provides, a certification by the city that these requirements were satisfied.
- Subject to Civil Code section 1351(e), all conveyances and other documents necessary to complete the conversion and signed by the required number of owners in the project as specified in the bylaws or other organizational documents. If the bylaws or organizational documents do not specify the number of owners, then a majority of owners is required to sign the documents.

Gov't Code § 66412(h)

---

7. See F. Scott Jackson, *Forming California Common Interest Developments*, "Condominium Conversions," chapter 4 (Cal. Cont. Ed. Bar, 2007).

Because of the occupancy requirements dating back to 1981 and 1982, these exemptions are of limited applicability today. Also, a city may regulate condominium conversions by adopting other ordinances under its police power, such as zoning and rent control ordinances, or by taxing them under its taxing power. For instance, in *Santa Monica Pines, Ltd. v. Rent Control Bd.*, the Court stated the Map Act did not preempt a city's right to regulate conversion in connection with its rent control law. 35 Cal. 3d 858 (1984); *see also The Pines v. City of Santa Monica*, 29 Cal. 3d 656 (1981) (upholding a city's revenue tax).

Three-dimensional divisions. A final or parcel map is required for a condominium project depending on the number of units created, although the division of air space need not be shown on the map. Gov't Code §§ 66426, 66427. However, another map is not required in a division of a condominium project into three-dimensional units if there was a previously approved parcel or final map and the following requirements are met:

- The total number of units does not increase above the number approved on the final or parcel map.
- A perpetual estate or an estate for years in the remainder of the property is held by the condominium owners or by an association, and the estate in the remainder of the property is the same as the duration of the estate in the condominiums.
- The three-dimensional portions are described on a condominium plan.

Gov't Code § 66427

A final or parcel map is required for a condominium project depending on the number of units created, although the division of air space need not be shown on the map.

Agricultural Leases

A lease of agricultural land for agricultural purposes is exempt from Map Act requirements. "Agricultural purposes" means the cultivation of food or fiber, or the grazing or pasturing of livestock. Gov't Code § 66412(k). What constitutes "agricultural land" is not defined by the Map Act. However, it is likely that agricultural land would include land designated as agricultural by a local zoning ordinance, general plan, or specific plan. Moreover, if a Williamson Act contract is involved, this contract likely is sufficient to establish the land as agricultural.

A lease of agricultural land for agricultural purposes is exempt from Map Act requirements.

Other Exemptions

- The construction of removable commercial buildings having a floor area of less than 100 square feet, if so provided by local ordinance. Gov't Code § 66412.5
- The leasing of, or the granting of an easement for, wind-powered electrical generation devices if the project is subject to discretionary action by the city. Gov't Code § 66412(i)
- Dedication of land for cemetery purposes under the Health and Safety Code. Gov't Code § 66412(c)
- Mineral, oil, or gas leases. Gov't Code § 66412(b)
- The leasing, licensing, granting of an easement, use permit, or similar right on a portion of a parcel to a telephone corporation, exclusively for the placement and operation of cellular radio transmission facilities, if the project is subject to discretionary action by the city. Gov't Code § 66412(j)

PRACTICE TIP

If a parcel map will be filed, check the local ordinance to see if a tentative parcel map is also required.

Map Waivers

Condominium projects. A city may waive the requirement for a tentative and final map or a parcel map for construction of a condominium project on a single parcel. To do so, a city must enact an ordinance that provides a procedure for the waiver. The ordinance shall require a finding by the city council that the division of land complies with the Map Act and other local ordinances including, but not limited to, area, improvement and design, floodwater drainage control, appropriate improved public roads, sanitary disposal facilities, water supply availability, and environmental protection. Gov't Code § 66428(b).

A city may waive the requirement for a tentative and final map or a parcel map for construction of a condominium project on a single parcel.

Mobile home parks conversions. The requirement for a tentative and final map or a parcel map may be waived in a mobile home conversion if at least two-thirds of the owners who are tenants in the mobile home park sign a petition showing their intent to purchase the park for a conversion to resident ownership. Additionally, a field survey must be performed. However, the requirement for a map cannot be waived if:

- There are design or improvement requirements necessitated by significant health and safety concerns.
- A city determines that there is an exterior boundary discrepancy that would require a map.
- The existing parcels were not created by a recorded final or parcel map.
- The conversion would result in more units or interests than existed prior to the conversion.

Gov't Code § 66428.1

Other parcel map waivers. The requirement of a parcel map can be waived pursuant to local ordinance. Every city is required to enact such a waiver ordinance. Gov't Code § 66428(b). A city must act upon a waiver application within 60 days of the application being deemed complete. Gov't Code § 66451.7. Before waiving a parcel map, a city must make certain specified findings, including, but not limited to, a finding that the proposed division of land complies with the Map Act and any local subdivision ordinance, and that the subdivision meets requirements relating to area, improvement and design, floodwater drainage control, public road improvements, sanitary disposal facilities, water supply availability, and environmental protection. Note that a city may still require a tentative map even if a parcel map is waived. Gov't Code § 66428(b).

The requirement of a parcel map can be waived pursuant to local ordinance. Every city is required to enact such a waiver ordinance.

Tentative Map Processing

Tentative Maps

Necessity for tentative maps. When a final map is required, a tentative map is always required. Gov't Code § 66426. Contrast this with situations involving only parcel maps, which do not require a tentative map under the Map Act. However, local ordinances may, and often do, still require a tentative map.

When a final map is required, a tentative map is always required.

A subdivider may file a vesting tentative map for a parcel map subdivision even though the local ordinance does not require a tentative map. Gov't Code § 66428(c).

Local ordinances. When processing a tentative and a final subdivision map, or a parcel map, it is imperative to consult the city's general plan, specific plans (if any), any applicable coastal plans, local ordinances, and procedures. The local subdivision ordinance specifies which type of governmental review is required and identifies the "advisory agency." In some cities, the advisory agency that approves the map is the planning commission, whose decision can be appealed to the city council; in other cities, the planning commission is purely advisory to the city council. In yet other cities, the approving body can be a city official or a committee of city officials.

It is important to determine when filing of the tentative map may be accomplished. Some cities require that all land use approvals be obtained before a tentative map is accepted for filing. *Benny v. City of Alameda*, 105 Cal. App. 3d 1006, 1009–10 (1980).

It is important to determine when filing of the tentative map may be accomplished. Some cities require that all land use approvals be obtained before a tentative map is accepted for filing.

Other regulations. Before a city accepts as complete an application for any development project, the applicant must submit a signed statement indicating whether the project and any alternatives are located on a site that is included on any of the local lists prepared by the California Integrated Waste Management Board of all solid waste disposal facilities from which there is a known migration of hazardous waste. Gov't Code §§ 65962.5(d), (f) ("Cortese List"). The Secretary for Environmental Protection maintains a statewide list and is responsible for distributing this information to any persons upon request. Gov't Code § 65962.5(e). The form of the Hazardous Waste and Substance Statement is contained in Government Code section 65962.5(f). *See Beck Dev. Co. v. Southern Pac. Transp. Co.*, 44 Cal. App. 4th 1160, 1202 (1996) (discussing this list).

In addition, a city must include in the information list for development projects, or on the application form for a building permit, specified requirements concerning compliance with statutes regulating hazardous materials and air pollution, the handling of acutely hazardous materials, and the emission of hazardous air emissions. Gov't Code § 65850.2. A city is prohibited from finding an application complete, approving a development project, or issuing a building permit for a project that requires only a building permit if the project meets specified requirements concerning hazardous materials and emissions, unless the owner or authorized agent complies with certain provisions, including submitting a risk management and prevention program (RMPP) if the administering agency makes a specified determination. This section, however, does not apply to applications solely for residential construction. Gov't Code § 65850.2(i).

RMPP = Risk Management and Prevention Program

Applicable time periods to act upon the tentative map. Under the Map Act, a city has 30 days to determine whether an application is complete if the application contains a statement that it is an application for a development permit. If the city does not respond within that time period, the application is "deemed complete" under the Permit Streamlining Act. Gov't Code § 65943(a).

A city has 30 days to determine whether an application is complete if the application contains a statement that it is an application for a development permit.

Once the application is complete, the Map Act sets forth certain statutory time periods for reporting and acting upon maps, depending on which advisory agency is charged with approving the map. Gov't Code §§ 66452.1, 66452.2. However, even if a city fails to act within these time limits, the map might not automatically be approved under Government Code section 65920 *et seq*. Constitutional due process of notice and opportunity for hearing negates automatic approval under the provisions of the Map Act. *Horn v. County of Ventura*, 24 Cal. 3d 605, 615 (1979).

In addition, there must be an express finding of consistency with the applicable general plan as a prerequisite for approval of the tentative map, thereby precluding automatic approval. *Woodland Hills Residents Ass'n, Inc. v. City Council*, 44 Cal. App. 3d 825 (1975). Other courts, however, have held that automatic approval is proper under certain circumstances. But, in *Pongputmong v. City of Santa Monica*, the court held that a tentative map could not be approved by operation of law pursuant to Government Code sections 66452.1(b) and 66452.4 since the application did not comply with the city's law. 15 Cal. App. 4th 99 (1993). In *Orsi v. City Council of Salinas*, the court found notice was proper because of automatic approval of a project including a tentative map under both the Permit Streamlining Act and Government Code section 66452.4. 219 Cal. App. 3d 1576 (1990). In that case, public hearings had been held on the project and the court found it consistent with the general plan even though no specific findings were made. *See also Selinger v. City Council*, 216 Cal. App. 3d 259 (1989). If the map is automatically approved, it is entitled to the same treatment as if it were approved in a timely manner. 81 Ops. Cal. Atty. Gen. 166 (1998).

A city also must comply with the time periods for environmental review provided for in Public Resources Code section 21151.5 and CEQA. In *Sunset Drive Corp. v. City of Redlands*, the court held that a city can be subject to a writ of mandate and monetary damages for failing to complete and certify an EIR within one year after a complete application is accepted. 73 Cal. App. 4th 215, 222, 225 (1999); Pub. Res. Code § 21151.5. The time periods contained in the Map Act, including the basic time periods, commence after certification of the environmental impact report, adoption of a negative declaration, or an exemption determination. Gov't Code §§ 66452.1(c), 66452.2(c).

A city cannot disapprove a map based only on a failure to comply with the time limits specified in chapter 3 of the Map Act. Gov't Code § 66451 *et seq.*

Time Limits Imposed by the Permit Streamlining Act

In addition to the time limits contained within the Map Act, the time limits contained in the Permit Streamlining Act (Gov't Code § 65920 *et seq.*) must be followed. The Permit Streamlining Act requires that a city approve or disapprove a tentative map or a parcel map within the time limits set forth in the Act. Generally, this is a 180-day period if an environmental impact report is required and 60 days if a negative declaration is issued, with certain exceptions. Gov't Code § 65950. If the city does not approve or disapprove a map within the time limits, the Permit Streamlining Act states that failure to do so shall be deemed approval of the project, provided that the prescribed public notice requirements have been met. There is no common law right to waive the time limits of the Permit Streamlining Act. In 1998, the Legislature made this clear when it expressly cited *Bickel v. City of Piedmont*, which found that an applicant had a common law right to waive the time limitations of the Act. 16 Cal. 4th 1040 (1997). The Legislature expressly stated its intent to clarify that the Permit Streamlining Act does not provide for a common law right of waiver.

However, the provisions of the Permit Streamlining Act do not apply to administrative appeals. Gov't Code § 65922(b). The Permit Streamlining Act also does not apply if map approval is contingent on a general plan amendment, rezoning, or other land use legislation. *Land Waste Mgmt. v. County of Contra Costa Bd. of Supervisors*, 222 Cal. App. 3d 950, 959 (1990); *Landi v. County of Monterey*, 139 Cal. App. 3d 934, 936 (1983). For a more detailed discussion of the Permit Streamlining Act, *see* chapter 17 (Rights of the Regulated and of the Citizens).

Notice and hearing; processing. It is advisable in all subdivision approval processes, whether they involve tentative or parcel map approval or any other discretionary approval under the Map Act, such as an extension of a tentative map or the issuance of a conditional certificate of compliance, that notice be given and an opportunity for hearing be provided. In fact, the California Supreme Court has held that the due process requirements of the United States and California Constitutions require notice and opportunity for hearing if map approval will constitute a substantial or significant deprivation of the property rights of other landowners. *Horn v. County of Ventura*, 24 Cal. 3d 605, 612 (1979). *See also Kennedy v. City of Hayward*, 105 Cal. App. 3d 953, 962 (1980). In general, notice must be given pursuant to Government Code sections 65090 through 65091, and 66451.3(a).

> **PRACTICE TIP**
>
> Even if the local subdivision ordinance is silent as to notice requirements, one should be sure the city gives proper notice.

In *Cohan v. City of Thousand Oaks*, the court held that the cumulative procedural errors committed by a city impaired the adequacy of the appeal hearing on the owners' subdivision, thus violating their due process rights. 30 Cal. App. 4th 547, 559–60 (1994). Some of the errors involved (1) the council itself appealing the planning commission's decision without following either the Ralph M. Brown Act or the city's own ordinance provisions, (2) the failure to inform the owners of the grounds for the appeal, and (3) the unfair placement of the burden on the owners to convince the council of the correctness of the planning commission's decision. The court held that ignoring laws and regulations meant to ensure a fair process "stands due process on its head." *Id.* at 560. Another case also highlights the importance of adhering to applicable procedures. In *Breakzone Billiards v. City of Torrance*, the court distinguished *Cohan* and upheld a councilperson's appeal of a planning commission's approval of a conditional use permit because the city's ordinance provisions were followed. 81 Cal. App. 4th 1205 (2000).

Specific requirements apply when school districts and other agencies are affected. For example, a city must refer all maps to school districts that could be affected by the subdivision. Gov't Code § 66455.7. A city must also refer all maps to any water supplier that is, or may become, a public water system that may supply water for the subdivision, and also to Caltrans if Caltrans files a map with a city indicating territory in which it desires to make a recommendation. Gov't Code §§ 66455.3, 66455. There is a similar provision allowing the State Department of Water Resources to file a map of any territory within one mile of any facility of the State Water Resources Development System. If this occurs, the city must refer maps to the department for recommendations. Gov't Code § 66455.1. Furthermore, local agencies may make recommendations concerning proposed subdivisions in adjoining cities or unincorporated areas if the subdivision is located within the local agency's planning area and the local agency files a map with the neighboring jurisdiction that shows the territory for which it desires to make recommendations. Gov't Code § 66453. All such referrals to the recommending agency or district must be transmitted within five days after the map application is deemed complete. Such agencies and districts have 15 days after receiving a copy of the proposed map to provide their comments;

A city must refer all maps to school districts that could be affected by the subdivision, and must also refer all maps to any water supplier that is, or may become, a public water system that may supply water for the subdivision.

the applicable city or county must consider the recommendations before acting. Gov't Code §§ 66453, 66455.1, 66455.7.

Any report or recommendation on a tentative map by the city staff shall be in writing and a copy served on the subdivider three days prior to any hearing, or prior to action on the map. Also, if there is a residential condominium conversion at issue, all tenants must receive the staff report. Gov't Code § 66452.3.

Life of tentative maps

Initial life. The Map Act mandates an initial two-year life. By local ordinance, a city can extend that initial life for up to an additional 12 months. Gov't Code § 66452.6(a).

Multiple final maps. This extension applies only when the subdivider files multiple final maps. Gov't Code § 66456.1. The life of tentative maps can be extended by 36 months if the subdivider is required to construct, improve, or finance the construction of public improvements of $178,000[8] or more outside of the boundaries of the tentative map. Gov't Code § 66452.6. This provision does not apply, however, if the improvements are public rights-of-way that abut the boundaries of the property to be subdivided, and that are reasonably related to the development of that property. Each 36-month extension affects the remaining portions of the tentative map upon the filing of each final map authorized by Government Code section 66456.1. Such an extension shall not extend the tentative map more than 10 years from its initial approval, taking into account the initial life of a map, but not any other mandatory or discretionary extensions.

The filing of a phased final map that does not conform to the tentative map's requirements would not entitle the map to a 36-month extension under section 66452.6(a)(1). *See Ailanto Props., Inc. v. City of Half Moon Bay*, 142 Cal. App. 4th 572 (2006). In *Ailanto*, an applicant filed, and the city rejected, a phased final map that did not include a coastal development permit required by the tentative map. The court found that the 36-month extension would not apply. The court stated that implicit in the extension provision is the requirement that the final map substantively complies with the Map Act. Thus, timely delivery of a final map that did not conform with the tentative map would not be an effective filing; to conclude otherwise would permit an applicant to file nonconforming maps simply to secure an extension.

Development agreements. A tentative map for property subject to a development agreement authorized by Government Code sections 65864 and 65869.5 may be extended for the period of time provided for in the agreement, but not beyond the duration of the agreement. Gov't Code § 66452.6(a).

Discretionary extensions. Upon application by the subdivider, a city may extend the time at which the map expires for a period or periods not to exceed a total of five years. Gov't Code § 66452.6(e). These are called the discretionary

---

8. The amount of $178,000 is automatically increased each year according to the adjustment for inflation set forth in the statewide cost index for class B construction, as determined by the State Allocation Board at its January meeting. The effective date of the annual adjustment is March 1. The adjustment amount applies to tentative and vesting tentative maps whose applications were received after the effective date of the adjustment. Gov't Code § 66452.6(a)(2).

extensions. *See Griffis v. County of Mono*, 163 Cal. App. 3d 414 (1985) (an ordinance restricting extensions to a one-year period was invalid). The application for extension must be filed prior to the expiration date. Once an application for an extension is timely filed, the map is automatically extended for 60 days or until the city acts on the extension, whichever occurs first.

An application to extend the life of a tentative map may be approved even after the automatic 60-day extension period has expired, so long as the application itself is filed prior to the expiration date. The issue of whether a timely filed application for an extension may be approved after the map's expiration date was addressed in *Bodega Bay Concerned Citizens v. County of Sonoma*, where the Board of Supervisors failed to consider a subdivider's timely filed application for extension of a tentative map until nearly one month after the map's expiration date. 125 Cal. App. 4th 1061 (2005). A citizen's group challenged the decision on the ground that the Board lacked the authority to grant the extension because the map had already expired. The appellate court disagreed and held that the Board may approve a timely application for an extension of a tentative map after the map has otherwise expired. The court based its holding in part upon Government Code section 66452.6(d), which allows local agencies to take action on "timely filings," even after expiration of the tentative map. According to the court, the statutory authority of an agency to act is expressed broadly and without limitation. Consequently, an agency may extend a tentative map after it has otherwise expired, where an application for extension is timely filed, so long as the aggregate five-year period is not exceeded.

An application to extend the life of a tentative map may be approved even after the automatic 60-day extension period has expired, so long as the application itself is filed prior to the expiration date.

Statutory extensions. Recognizing the severe impact of a recession on developers, the Legislature in 1993, and again in 1996, extended the lives of tentative, vesting tentative, and parcel maps. The 1993 amendment added Government Code section 66452.11, which provided for a 24-month extension for all approved tentative maps that had not expired on the effective date, September 13, 1993. The extension was automatic, required no action by the city that approved the tentative maps, and provided no opportunity for the imposition of additional conditions of approval. This extension is in *addition* to all other extensions allowed or required by Government Code sections 66452.6 and 66463.5. Although not expressly stated, by extending the life of tentative maps, the 1993 amendment extended the rights conferred by a vesting tentative map, which last for at least one year beyond the recording of a final map.

The 1996 amendment is virtually identical to the 1993 amendment. The 1996 amendment provides for a 12-month extension in *addition* to all other extensions, for all tentative, vesting tentative, and parcel maps that had not expired as of May 14, 1996. Gov't Code §§ 66452.6, 66463.5.

Both the 1993 and 1996 extensions also apply to "any legislative, administrative, or other approval by any agency of the State of California that pertains to a development project included in a map that is extended pursuant to" this new law. Gov't Code §§ 66452.11(c), 66452.13(c). The effect of this language is to extend related approvals issued by acknowledged state agencies such as the Coastal Commission, Department of Fish and Game, and the Regional Water Quality Control Boards. Note, however, that cities and counties are not agencies of the state, and their related approvals are not extended.

Moratoria. The life of a tentative map does not include periods of time during which a development moratorium is in effect after the approval of the tentative map—provided, however, the length of the moratorium does not exceed five years. Gov't Code § 66452.6(b)(1). In 2006, a court of appeal clarified that the length of any moratorium-related tolling of the expiration of a vesting tentative map under section 66452(b)(1) was limited to five years, regardless of the duration of the development moratorium. *Ailanto Props., Inc. v. City of Half Moon Bay*, 142 Cal. App. 4th 572 (2006). The court noted that interpreting section 66452.6(b)(1) to mean that development moratoria would expire after five years, regardless of whether the reasons for the moratoria were still in effect, would lead to absurd practical results. The court also rejected Ailanto's arguments that multiple moratoria could lead to multiple tolling periods.

Development moratoria include a water and/or sewer moratorium, as well as other actions of public agencies that regulate land use, development, or the provision of services to the land. Thus, where a public agency with the authority to approve the tentative map, thereafter prevents, prohibits, or delays the approval of a final or parcel map, the life of the map is tolled. Gov't Code § 66452.6(f). Once the moratorium is lifted, the map will be valid for the shorter of five years or the period of time that remained on the map when the moratorium was imposed, but in any event, no less than 120 days. Gov't Code § 66452.6(b).

For a discussion of a development moratorium's effect on a tentative map, see *Ailanto Props.*, 142 Cal. App. 4th 572 (2006), and *Native Sun/Lyon Communities v. City of Escondido*, where the court held that a city's development moratorium met the terms of Government Code section 66452.6(b)(1), and the map was extended. 15 Cal. App. 4th 892 (1993).

Litigation stays. The life of the tentative map also may be tolled during the time in which a lawsuit challenging the approval or disapproval of the tentative map is, or was, pending. A litigation stay is not automatic; it requires approval from the local agency prior to the expiration of the tentative map. The subdivider may apply for the litigation stay after the local agency is served with the lawsuit. Within 40 days following the application for the stay, the agency must either stay the time period for up to five years or deny the request. The agency may adopt local procedures for reviewing such requests. Gov't Code §§ 66452.6(c), 66463.5(e).

In *Friends of Westhaven and Trinidad v. County of Humboldt*, the court held that a subdivider's application for a litigation stay must be submitted prior to expiration of the tentative map, even if litigation is still pending. 107 Cal. App. 4th 878 (2003). The subdivider in this case received initial tentative map approval for two years. Litigation over the map ensued, and the case was resolved more than four months after the tentative map had expired. The subdivider waited until after the litigation had ended to apply for the stay. Although the county approved the request, the court overturned the extension, agreeing with project opponents that the stay request was not timely because the tentative map already had expired. *Id.*

Summary. The Map Act authorizes a maximum life of 15 years for a tentative map filed after May 14, 1996, so long as the life of the map does not exceed an aggregate of mandatory extensions of up to 10 years and discretionary extensions

Calculating the Life of a Tentative Map

① Determine the Initial Life of the Map

- Identify the date the tentative map was *approved or conditionally approved* by the local agency.
- The tentative map will expire 24 months after this date, *unless* the local agency's ordinance extends the life up to an additional 12 months. Gov't Code § 66452.6(a)(1).

② Check for Special Extensions Granted by the State Legislature

- If an approved tentative map had not expired as of *September 13, 1993*, its expiration date is automatically extended by 24 months. § 66452.11.
- If an approved tentative map had not expired as of *May 14, 1996*, its expiration date is automatically extended by 12 months. § 66452.13.

③ Determine If the Automatic Extension for Phased, Final Maps Applies

- To qualify for this automatic extension, the following two conditions must be met:
  - The subdivider must be authorized to file multiple final maps (§ 66456.1); and
  - The subdivider must be required to expend a minimum amount on public improvements[1] outside the tentative map boundary, *excluding* public right-of-way improvements that abut the property and are reasonably related to the property's development (§ 66452.6(a)(1)).
- If the conditions are met, *each time* a phased final map is filed before the tentative map expires, the life of the tentative map is extended for *36 months from the later of:* (1) the date of the tentative map's expiration; or (2) the date of the previously filed final map. § 66452.6(a)(1).
- These extensions cannot extend the tentative map more than ten years from the date of its approval or conditional approval.[2] § 66452.6(a)(1).

④ Determine If the Local Agency Has Granted Any Discretionary Extensions

- If the subdivider applies for a discretionary extension before the tentative map expires, the local agency may approve an extension(s) up to a total of five years. § 66452.6(e).
- While the extension application is pending, the tentative map is automatically extended for 60 days *or* until the agency approves or denies the application, whichever comes first. § 66452.6 (e).

⑤ Apply the Tolling Period for Development Moratoria, If Applicable

- If a development moratorium is imposed after the tentative map is approved, do not include the moratorium period when calculating the life of the map. The tolling period resulting from the moratorium cannot exceed five years. § 66452.6(b)(1).
- If the remaining time on the map is less than 120 days when the moratorium is lifted, the map is valid for 120 days after the moratorium ends. § 66452.6(3).
- Development moratoriums include sewer and water moratoriums, and other public agency actions that delay or prohibit the approval of the final map. § 66452.6(f). They also include periods when map conditions cannot be satisfied because they require local agency action or acquisition of real property from a public agency. If the latter condition is involved, the tolling period cannot extend beyond January 1, 1992. *See* § 66452.6(f)(1) for specific limitations.
- The moratorium tolling period can be extended up to an additional three years (but not beyond January 1, 1992) when litigation is pending over the existence or applicability of a moratorium to the property. *See* § 66452.6(b)(2) for specific requirements.

MAXIMUM LIFE OF A MAP

- For tentative maps filed after May 14, 1996, the Map Act permits a maximum life of 15 years (5 years of discretionary extensions and 10 years of automatic extensions for phased final maps).
- This does not include tolling periods for pending litigation, development moratoriums, and maps covered by a development agreement.

⑥ Apply the Tolling Period for Pending Litigation, If Applicable

- If a lawsuit is filed involving the map's approval or conditional approval, the subdivider may apply to the local agency for a "stay" while the lawsuit is pending. If the local agency approves the stay, the map's life will be tolled for up to five years. § 66452.6(c).

⑦ Check to See If the Map Is Covered by a Development Agreement

- Tentative maps on property subject to a development agreement authorized by §§ 65864 and 65869.5 may be extended for the period of time provided in the agreement, but not beyond the term of the agreement. § 66452.6(a)(1).

NOTES

1. Public improvements include traffic controls, roads, bridges, over crossings, flood control or storm drain facilities, sewer facilities, water facilities, and lighting facilities. § 66452.6(a)(3).

2. However, an appellate court held the Map Act does not dictate the order in which discretionary and automatic extensions are used. The court rejected the argument that extensions beyond the tenth anniversary of the map may only be granted under the city's discretionary authority. *California Country Club Homes Ass'n, Inc. v. City of Los Angeles,* 18 Cal. App. 4th 1425 (1993).

not exceeding 5 years. Gov't Code § 66452.6(e). *See, e.g., California Country Club Homes Ass'n, Inc. v. City of Los Angeles,* 18 Cal. App. 4th 1425, 1436–37 (1993) (the Map Act does not dictate the order in which discretionary and mandatory extensions must be used). The life of a tentative map could be extended even further by the tolling provisions triggered by development moratoria or litigation. Gov't Code §§ 66452.6(b), (c).

Following are the rules that determine the life of a tentative map:

- A map has an initial life of two years plus any additional time, to a maximum of three years, allowed by local ordinance.
- A map is automatically extended by three years upon the filing of each phased final map (to a maximum of ten years) by a subdivider required to make substantial off-site public improvements as a condition of approval of the map.
- A map may be extended for up to five years, at the discretion of the city, in addition to the initial life and the automatic extension.
- A map may be extended by various tolling provisions triggered by development moratoria or litigation by up to five years.
- If a map had not expired on September 13, 1993, it was automatically extended by two years in addition to any other extension.
- In addition to any other extension, if a map had not expired on May 14, 1996, it was automatically extended one year.

Even though granting an extension is a discretionary act under Government Code section 66452.6(e), cities may not impose additional conditions other than those related to the length of time a map is valid.

Conditions imposed on extensions. Even though granting an extension is a discretionary act under Government Code section 66452.6(e), cities may not impose additional conditions other than those related to the length of time a map is valid. *See El Patio v. Permanent Rent Control Bd.*, 110 Cal. App. 3d 915, 928 (1980); *see also Bodega Bay Concerned Citizens v. County of Sonoma*, 125 Cal. App. 4th 1061 (2005). A subdivider may agree to a new condition that a city imposes as a condition to an extension of the tentative map. However, if the subdivider chooses to do so, it may not later challenge the validity of that condition. *Rossco Holdings, Inc. v. State of California*, 212 Cal. App. 3d 642 (1989) (citing *County of Imperial v. McDougal*, 19 Cal. 3d 505 (1977)) (landowner cannot challenge condition on a permit after acquiescing to the condition by specific agreement, or by failure to challenge validity and accepting the benefits); *Pfeiffer v. City of La Mesa*, 69 Cal. App. 3d 74 (1977) (landowner waives right to assert invalidity of conditions and sue public entity for costs of compliance after acceptance of building permits and compliance with conditions).

If a subdivider does not agree to a new condition, a city can deny the extension within its discretion under the reasonable exercise of the police power.

If a subdivider does not agree to a new condition, a city can deny the extension within its discretion under the reasonable exercise of the police power. If the city does so, the tentative map will expire and the subdivider will have to obtain a new tentative map that may have new conditions. Alternatively, unless the tentative map is a vesting tentative map, a city could permit the extension, but attach a new condition to a later approval, such as the issuance of a building permit, if permitted by its local regulations or ordinances. *See McMullan v. Santa Monica Rent Control Bd.*, 168 Cal. App. 3d 960 (1985).

PUD = Planned-unit development

Expiration of other permits issued in conjunction with a tentative map. Unless an earlier expiration appears on the face of the permit, any permit issued in conjunction with a tentative subdivision map for a planned-unit development (PUD) shall expire no earlier than the approved tentative map, or any extension thereof, whichever occurs later. Gov't Code § 65863.9, 66452.12(a).

A local coastal development permit issued by a city in conjunction with a tentative subdivision map for a planned-unit development shall expire no earlier than the approved tentative map, and any extension of the map shall be in accordance with the applicable local coastal program, if any, that is in effect. Gov't Code § 65863.9.

For easy reference, a step-by-step approach to calculating the life of a tentative map is presented on page 99.

Effect of Approval of Map on the Right to Develop—Vested Rights

Approval of a final map or a parcel map does not in itself confer a vested right to develop. *Avco Community Developers, Inc. v. South Coast Reg'l Comm'n*, 17 Cal. 3d 785, 739–94 (1976); *Consaul v. City of San Diego*, 6 Cal. App. 4th 1781, 1793 (1992); *Oceanic California, Inc. v. North Cent. Coast Reg'l Comm'n*, 63 Cal. App. 3d 57, 72–73 (1976). Zoning can still be changed, or other police power ordinances can be adopted, after even final maps, conditional use permits, PUDs, zoning, rezoning, grading, or other permits have been granted. *See Hafen v. County of Orange*, 128 Cal. App. 4th 133 (2005) (upholding zoning changes after tentative map approval because developer had not obtained a vested right to develop). There is no vested right to develop until actual building or other permits for identifiable buildings have been issued, and substantial work has been done thereafter in reliance on those permits. *Avco*, 17 Cal. 3d at 791. *See also Hafen*, 128 Cal. App. 4th at 142–43; *Golden State Homebuilding Ass'n v. City of Modesto*, 26 Cal. App. 4th 601, 611–12 (1994).

Approval of a final map or a parcel map does not in itself confer a vested right to develop.

Also, no contract regarding dedications will deprive the city of its rezoning power. *Call v. Feher*, 93 Cal. App. 3d 434, 441 (1979). For example, a condominium converter has no vested right through approval of a tentative or final map to bypass a later-enacted police power regulation including rent control provisions. *Santa Monica Pines, Ltd. v. Rent Control Bd.*, 35 Cal. 3d 858, 868–69 (1984); *People v. H & H Props.*, 154 Cal. App. 3d 894, 899–900 (1984); *see also Palmer v. Board of Supervisors*, 145 Cal. App. 3d 779, 783 (1983) (filing of a map is insufficient to exempt property from a subsequent zone change even though the original tentative map was improperly denied); *McMullan v. Santa Monica Rent Control Bd.*, 168 Cal. App. 3d 960, 962–63 (1985) (denial of a condominium conversion permit by the Rent Control Board was a proper exercise of the police power even though map approval was granted).

No contract regarding dedications will deprive the city of its rezoning power.

The courts have carved out several narrow exceptions to the vested rights rule. For example, the California Supreme Court held that a final map and a Department of Real Estate's issuance of a public report is all that is needed to allow a condominium converter to proceed, without complying with a later-enacted land use regulation. *City of W. Hollywood v. Beverly Towers, Inc.*, 52 Cal. 3d 1184 (1991). In another case, the court held that property owners could claim estoppel since the city had issued administrative regulations that were relied upon by the owners in proceeding with a condominium conversion—even though the city later enacted an ordinance that would have prevented the conversion. *Hock Inv. Co. v. City and County of San Francisco*, 215 Cal. App. 3d 438, 448–49 (1989).

The policy underlying the rule restricting vested rights was set forth by the California Supreme Court:

> If we were to accept the premise that the construction of subdivision improvements or the zoning of the land for a planned community are sufficient to afford a developer a vested right to construct buildings on the land in accordance with the laws in effect at the time the improvements are made or the zoning enacted, there could be serious impairment of the government's right to control land use policy.... Thus tracts or lots in tracts which had been subdivided decades ago, but upon which no buildings have been constructed could be free of all zoning laws enacted subsequent to the time of the subdivision improvement, unless facts constituting waiver, abandonment, or opportunity for amortization of the original vested right could be shown.

Avco Cmty. Developers, Inc. v. South Coast Reg'l Comm'n, 17 Cal. 3d at 797–798

In response to the Avco *decision and other similar decisions, the Legislature adopted the Development Agreement Act.*

In response to the *Avco* decision and other similar decisions, the Legislature adopted the Development Agreement Act. Gov't Code § 65864 *et seq*. This statute provides that a city and a developer may enter into an agreement whereby the developer is insulated from future land use actions by the city that might otherwise prevent the developer from completing the approved development. Also as a result of *Avco*, the Legislature adopted the Vesting Tentative Map statute. Gov't Code § 66498.1 *et seq*. For further discussion of vested rights, *see* chapter 10 (Vested Rights). *See also* David L. Callies, Daniel J. Curtin, Jr., and Julie Tappendorf, *Bargaining for Development: A Handbook on Development Agreements, Annexation Agreements, Land Development Conditions, Vested Rights and the Provision of Public Facilities* (Environmental Law Institute, 2003).

Vesting Tentative Map

Background. In 1984, the Legislature added Chapter 4.5 (Development Rights) to the Map Act, establishing a new form of tentative map for subdivisions in California—the "vesting tentative map." Gov't Code § 66498.1 *et seq*.

The approval of a vesting tentative map expressly confers a vested right to proceed with a development in substantial compliance with the ordinances, policies, and standards in effect at the time the application for approval of the vesting tentative map is deemed complete.

The approval of a vesting tentative map expressly confers a vested right to proceed with a development in substantial compliance with the ordinances, policies, and standards in effect at the time the application for approval of the vesting tentative map is deemed complete. Gov't Code § 66498.1(b). However, if a city has initiated proceedings changing its general or specific plan, zoning, or subdivision ordinances, by ordinance, resolution, or motion, and has published notice of this change, or if the subdivider has requested changes in connection with the same development project, the city may apply these new standards to any map for which an application has not been deemed complete. Gov't Code §§ 66474.2(b), (c). As stated by the court in *Bright Dev. Co. v. City of Tracy*:

> The Subdivision Map Act (Act) permits a subdivider to file a "vesting tentative map" whenever the Act requires a tentative map. This procedure is intended to provide greater statutory protection to subdividers than was afforded under the common law vested rights doctrine. (Gov't Code §§ 66498.1–66498.9; California Subdivision Map Act Practice (Cont. Ed. Bar 1987) § 6.31; Curtin, Subdivision Map Act Manual (1992), p. 13.).

20 Cal. App. 4th 783, 792 (1993)

In adopting this statute, the Legislature stated:

By the enactment of this article, the Legislature intends to accomplish all of the following objectives:

(a) To establish a procedure for the approval of tentative maps that will provide certain statutorily vested rights to a subdivider.

(b) To ensure that local requirements governing the development of a proposed subdivision are established in accordance with Section 66498.1 when a local agency approves or conditionally approves a vesting tentative map. The private sector should be able to rely upon an approved vesting tentative map prior to expending resources and incurring liabilities without the risk of having the project frustrated by subsequent action by the approving local agency....

Gov't Code § 66498.9. *See also Bright Dev. Co.*, 20 Cal. App. 4th at 792–93

The primary exception to these vesting provisions provides that a city may condition or deny a permit, approval, extension, or entitlement if it determines any of the following: (1) a failure to do so would place the residents of the subdivision or the immediate community, or both, in a condition dangerous to their health or safety or both; (2) the condition or denial is required in order to comply with state or federal law. Gov't Code § 66498.1(c). *See also N.T. Hill, Inc. v. City of Fresno*, 72 Cal. App. 4th 977, 981 (1999).

These statutes went into effect on January 1, 1986 for residential developments. As of that date, cities were required to have their own implementing procedures in effect. Gov't Code § 66498.8. The vesting tentative map statute became applicable to all subdivisions as of January 1, 1988, including commercial and industrial subdivisions; by that date, a city's implementing procedures should have been amended to so provide. Gov't Code § 66498.7. This statute is also applicable to parcel map filings. Gov't Code §§ 66428, 66463.5(g).

The vesting tentative map statute represents one of the Legislature's responses to the long debate regarding the precise nature of vested rights for developers in California. *See, e.g., Avco Community Developers, Inc. v. South Coast Reg'l Comm'n*, 17 Cal. 3d at 791 ("[I]f a property owner has performed substantial work and incurred substantial liabilities in good faith reliance upon a permit issued by the government, he acquires a vested right to complete construction in accordance with the terms of the permit.") Until the enactment of this statute, a developer's only means of obtaining assurance from a city that its project, for which a tentative map had been approved, would not be thwarted by subsequent changes in the city's land use laws (*e.g.*, by a subsequent rezoning by the city council or by initiative) was through the approval of an agreement pursuant to the authority of the Development Agreement statute. Gov't Code § 65864 *et seq*. Without such an agreement, the developer risked expending great sums of money for preliminary work, while being subject to the vagaries of the common law test for vested rights. The vesting tentative map statute offers developers a degree of assurance not previously available.

Until *Bright Development*, no appellate court cases discussed what was meant by the provisions to freeze in place those ordinances, policies, and standards in effect at the time the vesting tentative map application was accepted as or deemed complete. In *Bright Development*, Bright filed a vesting tentative map application with the city, which was deemed complete and approved by the city. A dispute later arose concerning whether Bright was required at its own expense to underground existing off-site utilities in the subdivision.

At the time Bright's vesting tentative map application was deemed complete, the city did not have in effect an ordinance, policy, or standard that required Bright, at its own expense, to underground existing off-site utilities fronting the development. Accordingly, the city's action in imposing the off-site undergrounding requirement on Bright was illegal since it violated the provisions of the vesting tentative map statute. The court noted:

> The Legislature enacted these provisions to freeze in place those "ordinances, policies and standards in effect" at the time the vesting tentative map application is deemed complete. (Cal. Subdivision Map Act Practice, *supra*, § 6.31.) These provisions enable the private sector to rely on vesting maps to plan and budget development projects. (Gov't Code § 66498.9, subd. (b).) "The vesting tentative map statute now offers developers a degree of assurance, not previously available, against changes in regulations." (Longtin's California Land Use (2d ed. 1987) § 6.50[2]; Subdivision Map Act Manual, *supra*, pp. 13, 15.)

20 Cal. App. 4th at 793

Relying on Bright Development, *the* Kaufman & Broad *court held that a city's open-ended fee policy conflicted with the intent of the vesting tentative map.*

Relying on *Bright Development*, a court held that a city's open-ended fee policy conflicted with the intent of the vesting tentative map. *Kaufman & Broad Cent. Valley, Inc. v. City of Modesto*, 25 Cal. App. 4th 1577, 1586–87 (1994). In *Kaufman & Broad*, the application for a vesting tentative subdivision map for a 31-acre residential development was deemed complete on June 22, 1988. At that time, the fee per unit was $1,434. The planning commission, on October 3, 1988, approved the developer's vesting tentative map for 134 lots, subject to a new fee escalator condition that was added to all new vesting tentative maps resulting from a new council policy adopted on August 16, 1988. That condition read as follows: "'The Capital Facilities Fee payable at the time of the issuance of a building permit for any construction in this subdivision map (parcel map) shall be based on the rates in effect at time of issuance of the building permit.'" *Id.* at 1581.

When the developer applied for building permits to construct individual units, the city charged capital facilities development fees of $4,890 per unit, which was the fee in effect at that time. The developer paid the fees under protest and filed a complaint and petition for writ of mandate, seeking reimbursement of all fees paid in excess of $1,434 per unit, the rate in effect when the vesting tentative subdivision map was deemed complete.

The issues were whether the city was entitled to attach the fee escalator condition to its approval of Kaufman's vesting tentative map application and, if so, whether the condition permitted imposition of fees in excess of those in effect when the map application was deemed complete. The court ordered the city to refund the fees for individual units in excess of those in effect when the vesting tentative map was deemed complete. "[D]ue process notice requirements implicit in the vesting tentative map statutes limit increases in developer's fees to those for which adequate standards for determining the scope and extent of the fee increases are in place at the time the vesting tentative map is deemed complete." *Id.* at 1579–80. In so doing, the court held that the city's open-ended fee policy conflicted with the intent of the vesting tentative map statutes, which were intended to create a vested right arising earlier in the development process and affording greater protection than the common law. *Id.* at 1588 (citing Curtin and Merritt, *California Subdivision Map Act Practice*, sections 6.28, 6.31, pages 146–52 (Cal. Cont. Ed. Bar, 1987); Daniel J. Curtin, Jr., *California Land Use and Planning Law*, pages 187–188 (Solano Press, 14th ed. 1994)).

In addition, the court found that the "vesting tentative map statutes also incorporate a notice requirement consistent with due process." *Id.*

> The private sector should be able to rely upon an approved vesting tentative map prior to expending resources and incurring liabilities without the risk of having the project frustrated by subsequent action by the approving local agency...." (§ 66498.9, subd. (b).). It follows that a developer is entitled to actual or constructive notice of the ordinances, policies, and standards with which it will be expected to comply.... Quite obviously one cannot rely on what one does not know or cannot reasonably discover.

Id. (quoting *Bright Dev. Co. v. City of Tracy*, 20 Cal. App. 4th at 799)

With respect to timing of the notice, the court stated:

> The City argues at some length that Kaufman & Broad had actual or constructive notice of the fee increases later in the development process, both when the increases were approved and again when it acquired River Terrace. Be that as it may, the critical point in the process for the purposes of the vesting tentative map statutes is the date on which the map application is complete. Consequently, any notice Kaufman & Broad might have received afterward is of no particular significance to the present discussion.

Id. at 1589–90

Although the city's fee policy contemplated future increases in the amount of the fees, it did not foretell the comprehensive re-evaluation of the fee structure that the city later conducted. Government Code section 66498.1 conferred on the developer the vested right to develop its subdivision subject only to the capital facilities fees in effect when its vesting tentative map application was deemed complete.

This raises the question of what happens if a city changes the land use by a general plan amendment or adoption, amendment to a specific plan, or by a rezoning, after an application has been accepted as or deemed complete. From the holdings in *Bright Development* and *Kaufman & Broad*, and from the unambiguous language of the statute, it seems clear that there is no effect on the rights granted.

At present, there are no published court decisions on point. However, at least one superior court has held the "vesting effect" of the 1984 statute prohibits application of a later change in land use law to property subject to the vesting tentative map. In 1987, the Superior Court of Contra Costa County held that an initiative imposing a retroactive freeze on rezonings that increase density may not be applied to nullify a vested right to develop in accordance with a vesting tentative map. *Davidon Homes v. City of Pleasant Hill*, No. 297988 (Superior Court, Contra Costa County, April 3, 1987). The city did not appeal this trial court decision, and thus the decision cannot be cited as precedent in any other litigation.

As discussed above, the vesting tentative map statute gives subdividers who obtain approval of a vesting tentative map a statutory right to proceed with development in substantial compliance with the local ordinances, policies, and standards in effect at the time the map application is found complete. In *Davidon Homes*, the city had rezoned the project site and later approved a vesting tentative map for a 69-unit residential subdivision. Three weeks after the map was approved, an initiative that contained a retroactive limitation on rezonings was enacted. The city then refused to process Davidon's final map, claiming that the subdivision conflicted with the initiative's density limitations, and that the initiative operated to revoke the vested rights granted through the map. Based upon the vesting tentative map statute, the court rejected that argument, and Davidon was allowed to proceed.

Procedures. The vesting tentative map process begins when a subdivider files a tentative or parcel map with the words "vesting tentative map" printed conspicuously on the face of the map. Gov't Code § 66452(c).

When these prerequisites are met, a city must process the vesting tentative map and cannot deny it solely because it is an application for a vesting tentative map. The statute requires that vesting tentative maps be treated the same as tentative maps, except as otherwise provided by the Map Act or local ordinance adopted pursuant thereto. Gov't Code § 66452; *see McPherson v. City of Manhattan Beach*, 78 Cal. App. 4th 1252, 1259 (2000).

The rights conferred by a vesting tentative map last for not less than one year, and no more than two years after the final map has been recorded, although they may be extended. Gov't Code §§ 66498.5(b), (c).

In adopting its implementing procedures, a city may require the subdivider to supply additional information before the map is processed. However, a city may not require more information than that related to ordinances, resolutions, policies, or standards for the design, development, or improvement relating to the conferred rights, except where necessary (1) to permit the city to make the determination whether an environmental impact report or negative declaration is required pursuant to Public Resources Code section 21080.1 (CEQA), or (2) to comply with federal or state requirements. Gov't Code § 66498.8(d).

If a subdivider files a vesting tentative map for a subdivision where the intended development is inconsistent with the zoning ordinance in existence at that time, that inconsistency must be noted on the map. A city may deny a vesting tentative map or approve it conditioned on the subdivider, or its designee, obtaining the necessary change in the zoning ordinance to eliminate the inconsistency. If the change in the zoning ordinance is obtained, then the approved or conditionally approved vesting tentative map, notwithstanding Government Code section 66498.1(b), confers the vested right to proceed with the development in substantial compliance with the change in the zoning ordinance and the map as approved. Gov't Code § 66498.3(a).

If the ordinances, policies, or standards described in Government Code section 66498.1(b) are changed subsequent to the approval or conditional approval of a vesting tentative map, the subdivider, or his or her assignee, at any time prior to the expiration of the vesting tentative map pursuant to Government Code sections 66498.5(b), (c), and (d) may apply for an amendment to the vesting tentative map to secure a vested right to proceed with the changed ordinances, policies, or standards. An application shall clearly specify the changed ordinances, policies, or standards for which the amendment is sought. Gov't Code § 66498.2.

> **PRACTICE TIP**
>
> When filing an application for a vesting tentative map, make sure that (1) "Vesting Tentative Map" is printed conspicuously on the face of the map; (2) all other requirements for processing a tentative map are complete; and (3) the Cortese List statement (Gov't Code § 65962.5) is signed.

> **PRACTICE TIP**
>
> Since the rights vested continue for some time, from a practical standpoint, it is advisable for a subdivider to retain a complete set of the local ordinances, policies, and standards in effect when the vesting tentative map application is complete. Otherwise, should a dispute arise years later, it may be difficult to determine the operative law.

Effect of Annexation to City Upon Maps

If a subdivision is annexed to a city after a final map has been approved and filed for record, the final map as approved by the county and any related agreements shall continue to govern. Gov't Code § 66413(a). However, if a tentative or vesting tentative map has been approved by the county and no final map has been approved, or if a parcel map has not been finalized, and the subdivision is annexed to a city, all procedures and regulations of the annexing city shall govern. This means that the map shall comply with the city's regulations on the effective date of the annexation. Gov't Code § 66413(b).

Any subdivider may file with a city a tentative map of a proposed subdivision of unincorporated territory adjacent to such a city. The city may approve it conditioned upon annexation of the property to the city. Gov't Code § 66454.

Effect of Incorporation into a Newly Incorporated City

If an area in a subdivision or proposed subdivision is incorporated into a newly incorporated city, the newly incorporated city is required to approve the final map if:

- The final map meets the conditions of the tentative or vesting tentative map and all of the requirements for approval of final maps under the Map Act;
- The county board of supervisors approved the tentative or vesting tentative map prior to the date of the incorporation election; and
- The application for the tentative or vesting tentative map was submitted prior to the date the first signature was affixed on the petition for incorporation pursuant to Government Code section 56704 (regardless of the first signature's validity) or the date a resolution was adopted pursuant to Government Code section 56800, whichever occurs first.

Gov't Code § 66413.5(a) and (f); *City of Goleta v. Superior Court*, 40 Cal. 4th 270, 276–77 (2006). Where these conditions are not satisfied, a city retains discretion over a final map that relates to a county-approved tentative map, notwithstanding Government Code section 66474.1. *Id.* at 276–77.

An approved tentative or vesting tentative map will not limit a newly incorporated city from imposing reasonable conditions on subsequent required approvals or permits necessary for the development consistent with Government Code section 66474.2. Gov't Code § 66413.5(e). Furthermore, the newly incorporated city may condition or deny a permit, approval, or extension or entitlement if: (1) failure to do so would place the residents of the subdivision or the immediate community in a condition dangerous to their health and/or safety; and (2) the condition or denial is necessary to comply with state or federal law. Gov't Code § 66413.5(c).

Conditions to Map Approval
In General

There is probably no issue in subdivision law that has generated more controversy than that of dedications and the imposition of impact fees. The concept is simple—a subdivider, in return for obtaining a map to sell, lease, or finance property and thus develop it, agrees to donate to the city an amount of land or money needed to provide certain services necessitated by the influx of new residents into the community that this development will attract. *Trent Meredith, Inc. v. City of Oxnard*, 114 Cal. App. 3d 317, 361 (1981).[9]

However, determining how far a city can go in imposing conditions in a particular case can be considerably more difficult. The authority for a city to impose conditions is the police power, and the test of its proper exercise is reasonableness. In general, cities must show through individualized findings that: (1) there is a "nexus" between the condition imposed and the state interest advanced; and (2) the condition imposed is "roughly proportional" to the subdivision's impacts. For more discussion on the "nexus" and "rough proportionality" tests set forth in the United States Supreme Court's *Nollan/Dolan* decisions, *see* chapter 12 (Takings) and chapter 13 (Exactions).

Conditions Imposed Through the Subdivision Process

In Ayres v. City Council, *the California Supreme Court held that dedication conditions can be imposed on a subdivision even though they are not expressly set forth in the Map Act or local ordinance.*

In the seminal dedication case of *Ayres v. City Council of Los Angeles*, 34 Cal. 2d 31 (1949), the California Supreme Court held that dedication conditions can be imposed on a subdivision even though they are not expressly set forth in the Map Act or local ordinance. In determining which conditions to impose on a subdivision, cities generally look to three sources:

- The Map Act, which allows specific conditions to be imposed on subdivision maps either through the statutory authority of the Map Act itself, or by a local enabling ordinance adopted by the city.
- CEQA and Government Code section 66474(e), which allow conditions to be imposed that will mitigate a subdivision's environmental impacts.
- The city's general plan, or an applicable specific plan, to ensure that the subdivision, including its design and improvements, are consistent with such plans.

All of these sources fall within the purview of the city's general police power.

Specific Conditions Allowed by the Map Act and Local Ordinance

The Map Act identifies numerous conditions that can be imposed on the approval of subdivision maps.

The Map Act identifies numerous conditions that can be imposed on the approval of subdivision maps. Some of these conditions are permissive, and the city must first adopt a local enabling ordinance, following the criteria set forth in the Map Act, before imposing the condition on subdividers. Other conditions are mandatory, and must be imposed pursuant to the authority of the Map Act alone. *See, e.g.*, the requirements for public access to waterways (sections 66478.1–14), energy conservation (section 66473.1), and proof of an adequate water supply for subdivisions that meet a certain size threshold (section 66473.7).

---

9. *See* David L. Callies, Daniel J. Curtin, Jr., and Julie Tappendorf, *Bargaining for Development: A Handbook on Development Agreements, Annexation Agreements, Land Development Conditions, Vested Rights and the Provision of Public Facilities* (Environmental Law Institute 2003).

Parkland dedication Gov't Code § 66477 (Quimby Act). A city may, by ordinance, require the dedication of land or payment of fees for park or recreational purposes. Gov't Code § 66477. *Associated Home Builders, Inc. v. City of Walnut Creek*, 4 Cal. 3d at 641 (1971). However, before such a condition can be validly attached to the approval of a map, certain criteria must be met:

- The ordinance must be in effect for a period of 30 days before filing of the tentative or parcel map.
- The ordinance must include definite standards for determining the proportion of the subdivision to be dedicated and the amount of the fee to be paid. The dedication or payment shall not exceed a proportionate amount necessary to provide three acres of park area per 1,000 subdivision residents, with certain exceptions.
- The land or fees are to be used only for the purpose of developing new, or rehabilitating existing, park or recreational facilities to serve the subdivision, and the amount and location of land to be dedicated or amount of fees paid shall bear a reasonable relationship to the use of the park and recreational facilities by the future inhabitants of the subdivision. There is no strict limitation on this criteria. Fees are justified if used for park and recreational facilities generally, but not exclusively, available to subdivision residents. *Associated Home Builders*, 4 Cal. 3d at 640 n.5
- A city must have a general plan or specific plan containing policies and standards for park and recreational facilities in accordance with definite principles and standards.
- A city shall develop a schedule specifying how, when, and where it will use the land or fees or both to develop park or recreational facilities. Any fees collected under the ordinance shall be committed within five years after payment of the fees or the issuance of building permits on one-half of the lots created by the subdivision, whichever occurs later. If the fees are not committed, they shall be distributed and paid to each record owner of the subdivision in the same proportion that the size of each lot bears to the total area of all lots in the subdivision.
- Only the payment of fees may be required for subdivisions containing 50 or fewer parcels.
- Subdivisions of fewer than five parcels that are not used for residential purposes shall be exempt unless a building permit for a residential structure is requested for one of the parcels within four years. The Quimby Act is not applicable to commercial and industrial subdivisions or condominium projects or stock cooperatives that consist of subdivision of airspace in an existing apartment building more than five years old when no new dwelling units are added.
- A city may provide developers of planned developments, real estate developments (Bus. & Prof. Code § 11003), community apartment projects, condominium projects, and stock cooperatives that contain private recreational open space credit for the value of that private open space. Gov't Code § 66477(e). However, unless a city has adopted legislation providing a credit for private open space, it has no clear, present, and ministerial duty to provide a specific amount of credit. *See Branciforte Heights, LLC v. City of Santa Cruz*, 138 Cal. App. 4th 914, 938–939 (2006) (noting that the court did not

A city may, by ordinance, require the dedication of land or payment of fees for park or recreational purposes.

A city may provide developers of planned developments, real estate developments, community apartment projects, condominium projects, and stock cooperatives that contain private recreational open space credit for the value of that private open space.

reach the question of whether a city could be compelled to enact an ordinance providing some credit for private open space consistent with Gov't Code § 66477(e).

- If the subdivider provides park and recreational improvements to the dedicated land, the value of the improvements, together with any equipment located thereon, shall be a credit against the payment of fees or dedication of land required by the ordinance. Gov't Code § 66477(a)(9). A city, as a condition of regulating and approving a subdivision, may not lawfully require the dedication of land improved for park and recreational purposes without credit being given to the subdivider for the value of the recreational improvements that are provided by the subdivider. 73 Ops. Cal. Atty. Gen. 152 (1990). However, this does not limit a city's use of other means by which it may obtain recreational fees and land, improvements, and fees for parks.

- Funds obtained as in-lieu fees under Government Code section 66477 may be used to purchase, construct, or acquire land for a theater for cultural activities. 81 Ops. Cal. Atty. Gen. 293 (1998)

A condition requiring verification of water supply must be imposed on certain tentative maps.

Adequate water supply Gov't Code § 66473.7. A condition requiring verification of water supply must be imposed on certain tentative maps. This requirement applies to proposed residential developments of more than 500 dwelling units. This requirement also applies when the public water system that will serve the subdivision has fewer than 5,000 service connections and the proposed residential development would account for an increase of ten percent or more in the number of the public water system's existing service connections. This law is discussed in more detail in chapter 9 (Design Review and Other Development Regulation).

School site dedication Gov't Code § 66478. The provision in the Map Act for school site dedication is not a true dedication provision. Gov't Code § 66478. Instead, it is basically a reservation requirement for an elementary school site with a right to purchase at a later date. Its use appears to be minimal, since cities and school districts rely on other laws to require dedications. For further discussion regarding these laws, *see* chapter 13 (Exactions).

Conditions related to school *fees* are discussed below, as well as in chapter 13 (Exactions).

The Map Act provides that a city may impose by ordinance a requirement that real property within the subdivision be reserved for parks, recreational facilities, fire stations, libraries, or other public uses.

Reservations Gov't Code § 66479 *et seq.* The Map Act provides that a city may impose by ordinance a requirement that real property within the subdivision be reserved for parks, recreational facilities, fire stations, libraries, or other public uses. As with parkland dedication, the ordinance must follow certain criteria contained in the statute.

The reserved area must be of a size and shape to permit the balance of the property to develop in an orderly, efficient manner. Upon approval of the final map, a city must enter into a binding agreement with the subdivider to acquire the reserved area within two years after the completion and acceptance of all improvements, unless this time period is mutually extended. The purchase price shall be the market value at the time of filing of the tentative map, plus the taxes against the reserved area from the date of reservation, and maintenance costs (including interest costs) on any loans covering the reserved area. If the city does not agree, the reservation automatically terminates.

Street and bicycle path dedications Gov't Code §§ 66475, 66475.1. Dedications for streets, alleys, including access rights and abutters' rights, drainage, public utilities, and other public easements can be imposed by ordinance. Gov't Code § 66475. When a subdivider is required to dedicate roadways, the subdivider also may be required to dedicate land for bicycle paths. Gov't Code § 66475.1.

Dedication for local transit facilities Gov't Code § 66475.2. A city may, by local ordinance, require dedication of land for local transit facilities, such as bus turnouts, benches, shelters, landing pads, and similar items that directly benefit the residents of a subdivision. However, only payment of fees in lieu of a dedication can be required for divisions in airspace of existing buildings into condominium projects, stock cooperatives, or community apartment projects.

A city may, by local ordinance, require dedication of land for local transit facilities, such as bus turnouts, benches, shelters, landing pads, and similar items that directly benefit the residents of a subdivision.

Fees for drainage and sewer facilities Gov't Code § 66483. This section details the requirements for payment of fees to defray actual or estimated costs of constructing planned drainage facilities and sanitary sewer facilities for local or neighborhood areas. The local ordinance requirement must meet certain criteria. A city must have a general drainage or sanitary sewer plan, and the fees shall be paid into a "planned local drainage facilities fund" and "a planned local sanitary sewer fund." The fees that are required must be fairly apportioned within the areas, either on the basis of benefits conferred or on the need for the facilities created by the proposed subdivider. Disposition of surplus money is covered by Government Code sections 66483.1 and 66483.2.

In interpreting this section, the Attorney General has stated that a city, in regulating a subdivision, must comply with its requirements when enacting a drainage fee ordinance. But if it desires to use some other police power authority or taxation power, it need not follow the requirement of Government Code section 66483. Also, in calculating the maximum possible drainage fee under this section, the total acreage in the drainage area is to be the basis of the calculation. 66 Ops. Cal. Atty. Gen. 120 (1983).

Fees for bridges and major thoroughfares Gov't Code § 66484. A local ordinance may require the payment of a fee as a condition of approval or as a condition of issuing a building permit for purposes of defraying the actual or estimated costs of constructing bridges over waterways, railways, freeways, and canyons, or constructing major thoroughfares. Again, the ordinance must meet certain criteria and must refer to the circulation element. This section reads as an assessment district procedure and provides for a majority protest.

Groundwater recharge Gov't Code § 66484.5. A city may adopt an ordinance requiring, among other things, the payment of a fee or other consideration as a condition to approval of a final map or parcel map, or the issuance of a building permit to defray the cost of constructing planned recharge facilities for the replacement of surface waters into underground aquifers if the specified conditions are satisfied.

Supplemental improvements—reimbursement agreements Gov't Code § 66485 *et seq.* These sections allow a local ordinance to require that improvements be installed by the subdivider, for the subdivision's benefit, that contain supplemental size, capacity, number, or length for the benefit of property not within the subdivision. Supplemental length may include minimum-sized offsite sewer lines necessary to reach a sewer outlet in existence at that time. If a supplemental improvement requirement is imposed, a city shall enter into an agreement with the subdivider for reimbursement of the difference in cost. To pay costs of reimbursement, a city may collect a reasonable charge from persons or public agencies outside the subdivision for their use of supplemental improvements installed by the subdivider. For example, a city can collect reimbursement from a school district that is benefited by supplemental improvements to a storm drainage system. Gov't Code § 66487; 71 Ops. Cal. Atty. Gen. 163 (1988). Or a water district organized under the California Water District Law (Water Code § 3400 *et seq.*) can enter into an agreement with land developers for construction of oversized water facilities in support of anticipated growth in the area and enter into agreements with subsequent developers to reimburse the first developer for construction costs of the oversized facilities. 307 Ops. Cal. Atty. Gen. 172 (2005).

Soils investigations and reports Gov't Code §§ 66490, 66491. These sections require that the preliminary soils report be prepared by a registered civil engineer and must be based on adequate test borings. By local ordinance, a city may allow the report to be waived if it determines that it knows the qualities of the soils in the subdivision. In addition, by ordinance, a soils investigation may be required for each lot. If the preliminary report indicates the presence of critically expansive soils or other soils problems that, if not corrected, may lead to structural defects, then corrective action must be recommended. A city may approve the subdivision if recommended action is proposed to prevent structural damage to each structure and such action is imposed as a condition to issuance of a building permit. *See* Alquist-Priolo Special Studies Zones Act, Pub. Res. Code § 2621 *et seq.*

The state geologist is required to map earthquake fault zones. Pub. Res. Code § 2622. The State Mining and Geology Board establishes policy and criteria for approval of real estate development and structures for human occupancy in these special zones. Each development and structure must be approved for a city according to these criteria. Pub. Res. Code § 2623. Applications for all real estate developments and structures for human occupancy within earthquake fault zones must be accompanied by a geologist's report.

Setting of monuments Gov't Code § 66495 *et seq.* A city must require that at least one exterior boundary line of the land being subdivided be adequately monumented or referenced before the map is recorded. However, a city may, by ordinance, require additional monuments to be set.

Grading and erosion control requirements Gov't Code § 66411. The local ordinance must provide for proper grading and erosion control, including the prevention of sedimentation or damage to off-site property.

Public access to public resources and dedication of public easements along banks of rivers and streams Gov't Code § 66478.1 *et seq.* Before approving a map, a city must require that there will be public access through the subdivision to public waterways, rivers, streams, coastlines, shorelines, lakes, and reservoirs, and must require dedication of public easements along banks of rivers and streams. This is based on definitive legislative policy:

> The Legislature finds and declares that the public natural resources of this state are limited in quantity and that the population of this state has grown at a rapid rate and will continue to do so, thus increasing the need for utilization of public natural resources. The increase in population has also increased demand for private property adjacent to public natural resources through real estate subdivision developments which resulted in diminishing public access to public natural resources.

Gov't Code § 66478.2

For a list of some of the navigable waters and public waterways, *see* Harbors and Navigation Code sections 100–107.

In interpreting Government Code sections 66478.1–66478.14, a court held that this law requires owners of a subdivision along a river not only to provide reasonable access to the riverbanks, but also to allocate a piece of the private land for public use. The court struck down an alternative access plan accepted by the city because it only provided access to an easement along the wrong part of the riverbank. *Kern River Pub. Access Com. v. City of Bakersfield*, 170 Cal. App. 3d 1205, 1214–15 (1985).

Energy conservation Gov't Code § 66473.1. The design of a subdivision shall provide, to the extent feasible, for future passive or natural heating or cooling opportunities. The law shall not, however, be construed to require a reduction in allowable densities. This requirement does not apply to condominium projects that consist of the subdivision of air space in an existing building when no new structures are added. 64 Ops. Cal. Atty. Gen. 328 (1981).

Dedication for solar access easements Gov't Code § 66475.3. This section gives a city the authority to require dedication of solar access easements as a condition of approval of a tentative map. However, an ordinance must be adopted to this effect that follows the criteria set forth in the section.

Indemnification Gov't Code § 66474.9. A city may require, as a condition to a map application or approval, that the subdivider defend, indemnify, and hold harmless the city against any claim or action brought within the 90-day time period provided for in Government Code section 66499.37 to attack an approval by the city concerning a subdivision. Gov't Code § 66474.9(b)(1). Such condition may require indemnification of any agent, officer, and employee of the city, as well as indemnification of the city, the legislative body, and the planning commission or other advisory body. *Id*. However, a city may not condition map approval on a requirement that the subdivider indemnify it against a claim based on the city's action or inaction in reviewing, approving, or denying the map. Gov't Code § 66474.9(a). Any condition adopted under Government Code section 66474.9(b)(1) must include a requirement that the city promptly notify the subdivider of a claim against the city and that the city cooperate fully in the defense. Gov't Code § 66474.9(b)(2). In *Topanga Ass'n for a Scenic Community* *v. County of Los Angeles*, the court said that this section properly authorized the Board of Supervisors to require the developer to defend a legal action challenging the Board's approval of a map. 214 Cal. App. 3d 1348 (1989). *See also* 85 Ops. Cal. Atty. Gen. 21 (2002) (county may require applicant to pay for defense of lawsuit challenging issuance of Coastal Development Permit); P. Dallarda and K. Cold, "Developers to the Rescue: Indemnifying Public Entities for Litigation Arising Out of the Decision to Issue Development Permits," 11 *Cal. Land Use Law & Policy Rptr.* 293 (2001).

A city cannot postpone or refuse approval of a final map if a subdivider fails to construct or install off-site improvements on land owned by a third party.

Off-site improvements Gov't Code § 66462.5. A city cannot postpone or refuse approval of a final map if a subdivider fails to construct or install off-site improvements on land owned by a third party. A court held that Government Code section 66462.5 only applies when approval of a final map is delayed or refused because the off-site improvements have not been completed. *Hill v. City of Clovis*, 80 Cal. App. 4th 438, 446–47 (2000). The city must act to acquire the land within 120 days of the filing of the final map or the condition is waived, unless the city, prior to final map approval, requires the subdivider to enter into an agreement to complete the off-site improvements at such time as the city acquires an interest in land that will permit the improvements to be made. In response to the *Hill* case, the Legislature amended the statute to provide that the waiver shall occur whether or not the city has postponed or refused approval of the final map. *See* Gov't Code § 66462.5(b). Note that this section is not applicable to parcel maps.

The legality of a city's consent to private condemnation of sewer and storm drainage easements, which was imposed as a condition of tentative map approval, was upheld in *L&M Professional Consultants, Inc. v. Ferreira*, 146 Cal. App. 3d 1038, 1059–60 (1983).

PRACTICE TIP

A subdivider should become familiar with the dedication and fee requirements of a city's subdivision ordinance, and verify their consistency with the general plan.

Standards and criteria for public improvements: residential subdivisions Gov't Code § 65913.2. A city is prohibited from imposing on the developer of a residential subdivision more stringent standards and criteria for public improvements pursuant to the Map Act than those currently being applied by the city to its own publicly financed improvements located in similarly zoned districts within that city. In other words, a city cannot impose standards for improvements on a developer that exceed the city's own standards for constructing the same improvements with public funds.

If a city imposes engineering or surveying conditions on a tentative or a parcel map, those conditions must be reviewed by the city's engineer or surveyor to determine compliance with generally accepted engineering or surveying practices. Gov't Code § 66474.10.

Conditions Imposed Under City's Authority to Regulate "Design" and "Improvement" and Ensure General and Specific Plan Consistency

The Map Act vests in cities the power to regulate and control the "design" and "improvement" of subdivisions. Gov't Code § 66411. These terms are broadly defined by Government Code sections 66418–19.

Map Act Definitions of "Design" and "Improvement"	
Design	**Improvement**
(1) street alignments, grades, and widths; (2) drainage and sanitary facilities and utilities, including alignments and grades thereof; (3) location and size of all required easements and rights-of-way; (4) fire roads and firebreaks; (5) lot size and configuration; (6) traffic access; (7) grading; (8) land to be dedicated for park or recreational purposes; and (9) *other specific physical requirements in the plan and configuration of the entire subdivision as may be necessary to ensure consistency with, or implementation of, the general plan or any applicable specific plan as required pursuant to section 66473.5.*	(a) any street work and utilities to be installed, or agreed to be installed, by the subdivider on the land to be used for public or private streets, highways, ways and easements, as are necessary for the general use of the lot owners in the subdivision and local neighborhood traffic and drainage needs as a condition precedent to the approval and acceptance of the final map thereof; and (b) such other specific improvements or types of improvements, *the installation of which, either by the subdivider, by public agencies, by private utilities, by any other entity approved by the local agency, or by a combination thereof, is necessary to ensure consistency with, or implementation of, the general plan or any applicable specific plan.*

The "McCarthy Legislation," passed in 1971, requires that a city, in approving a map, must make a finding that the subdivision, together with the provisions of its "design" and "improvement," are consistent with the general plan or any applicable specific plan. Gov't Code § 66473.5. This legislation, in addition to stressing the role of the general plan, expanded the power of cities to condition development. 58 Ops. Cal. Atty. Gen. 41 (1975).

The Attorney General has discussed the implications of this legislation, and concluded that a city is not limited to the traditional dedication requirements such as streets and parks, but, with proper general plan and regulatory ordinances, such dedication principles could be applied to other matters. 59 Ops. Cal. Atty. Gen. 129 (1976). The key portion of both definitions is the connection to the general plan. For example, the term "design" includes such other specific physical requirements in the plan and configuration of the entire subdivision as may be necessary to ensure consistency with or implementation of the general plan. The definition of "improvement" contains similar language. The Attorney General stated that the 1971 legislation, read together with the California Supreme Court's *Associated Home Builders* decision in upholding parkland dedication, clearly indicated that the Legislature intended that cities have greater power than they had previously. *Id.* at 132–36 (citing *Associated Home Builders, Inc. v. City of Walnut Creek*, 4 Cal. 3d 633 (1971)). *See also Ayres v. City Council*, 34 Cal. 2d 31, 35, 37 (1949) (even before the McCarthy Legislation, the California Supreme Court, in rejecting subdivider petitioner's objections to the imposition of dedication/improvement "conditions on the ground that they were not expressly provided by the Subdivision Map Act nor by city ordinance," upheld such conditions as valid).

Courts have used these broader definitions to uphold the validity of conditions attached through the subdivision process. For example, one court found valid the conditions of approval imposed upon a condominium conversion that required building repairs and installation of smoke detectors in each unit. *Soderling v. City of Santa Monica*, 142 Cal. App. 3d at 509. The court pointed out that under these definitions of design and improvement, and in order to achieve one of the objectives of the city's general plan, "to promote safe housing for all," these conditions were valid, and the power to impose them need not be exercised by the specific enactment of an ordinance or the promulgation of a regulation. *See also Ayres v. City Council of Los Angeles*, 34 Cal. 2d at 37 (finding that subdivision map conditions, even though not authorized in the Map Act or local ordinance, are lawful if they are not inconsistent with the Map Act and local ordinances and are reasonably required by the subdivision type and use).

Following the Attorney General's expansive interpretation of the McCarthy Legislation in the 1970s, and the *Soderling* opinion in 1983, the California Legislature amended the Map Act in 1984 to limit the definition of "design" to "specific *physical* requirements" rather than "specific requirements" in general (SB 2166). However, this amendment appears to have had little practical effect since: (1) it left untouched the Map Act's broad definition of "subdivision"; and (2) Government Code section 66473.5 requires that *subdivisions*, together with their *design and improvements*, be consistent with a city's general plan and any applicable specific plan. *See also DeVita v. County of Napa*, 9 Cal. 4th 763, 772–73 (1995) (referring to the McCarthy Legislation, the California Supreme Court observed that, "For the first time, proposed *subdivisions* and their *improvements* were required to be consistent with the general plan.... Thus after 1971 the general plan truly became, and today remains, a 'constitution' for future development.") (emphasis added).

Accordingly, utilizing the definitions of "design" and "improvement," and the independent treatment of "subdivision" under the law, a city has the authority, in proper circumstances, to require as a condition of subdivision approval the dedication of land or the payment of fees for various improvements not otherwise mentioned in the Map Act, such as child day care centers, public art, police stations, fire stations, and libraries. In addition, a city can require that certain "inclusionary" dwelling units be set aside for low- and moderate-income housing, and can impose deed restrictions to ensure that they remain so for a number of years. This authority is based on the principle that if a city's general plan requires these types of improvements, the subdivision must provide for them. Otherwise, the city must deny the map since it will not be consistent with the general plan. Gov't Code § 66474.

It is clear that if a city has the power to deny a map because it is not consistent with the general plan, then a city may impose conditions on map approval that would ensure the map's consistency with the general plan. This is predicated on the theory that the power to reject for a given factor implies the power to accept with conditions to obviate that factor. *See City of Buena Park v. Boyar*, 186 Cal. App. 2d 61 (1960).

Map Act Requirements vs. General Plan Standards

If a dedication or fee condition is attached to a subdivision map approval based solely on the statutory authority of the Map Act, then the Map Act's criteria for that condition governs. For example, if a city wants to impose a condition requiring parkland dedication or payment of in-lieu park fees as part of the subdivision process, a city, by ordinance, may do so. Gov't Code § 66477; *see also Associated Home Builders, Inc. v. City of Walnut Creek*, 4 Cal. 3d 633, 640–41 (1971). Therefore, if the city attaches this condition to the approval of a map, it must adhere to the limitation of three to five acres per 1,000 residents as set forth in the Map Act.

However, a different rule applies if a dedication or fee is attached to a non-subdivision approval, such as an application for rezoning or a conditional use permit. In such situations, the imposition of dedications or fees is governed by a city's general police power, and subject to the Supreme Court's "nexus" and "rough proportionality" tests. Consequently, if a city's general plan calls for six or seven acres per 1,000 residents, then a city may impose this higher standard under its general police power if this condition is attached to a non-subdivision approval, rather than a subdivision map approval, and the city has adopted a regulation to that effect. 73 Ops. Cal. Atty. Gen. 152, 156 (1990).

Conditions That May Be Imposed Through the CEQA Process

The California Environmental Quality Act of 1970 (Pub. Res. Code § 21000 *et seq.*) has a peculiar impact upon the application of Government Code section 66474(e), which states, in part, that a city shall deny a subdivision if it finds that the design of the subdivision or the proposed improvements are likely to cause substantial environmental damage or substantially injure fish or wildlife or their habitats. An environmental impact report (EIR) that comments upon the amount of substantial environmental damage or injury to fish or wildlife caused by the subdivision could constitute the basis for a finding on those matters that would necessitate the denial of the subdivision map. CEQA requires that an EIR be prepared by a city before it approves a private project having a significant effect on the environment if the city has discretion to either approve or disapprove the project.

EIR = Environmental impact report

It is clear that if the EIR points out negative impacts, the city may impose conditions to mitigate those impacts based on Government Code section 66474(e). The imposition of mitigating conditions is based on the theory that the power to reject because of a specific impact implies the power to accept with conditions that would obviate that impact. *See City of Buena Park v. Boyar*, 186 Cal. App. 2d 61, 66–7 (1960). A city cannot use its CEQA powers to attach conditions to approval (Pub. Res. Code § 21004), but that does not limit the city in the subdivision approval process since it is relying on its powers under Government Code section 66474(e).

The imposition of mitigating conditions is based on the theory that the power to reject because of a specific impact implies the power to accept with conditions that would obviate that impact.

There are special rules relating to school impact fees, since a city cannot levy these fees as a CEQA mitigation. Gov't Code § 65996(b). A line of cases had held that this prohibition did not apply to *legislative*, as opposed to adjudicatory, actions. For example, it did not apply to general plan amendments or rezonings. *Mira Dev. Corp. v. City of San Diego*, 205 Cal. App. 3d 1201, 1217 (1988). *See also Murrieta Valley Unified Sch. Dist. v. County of Riverside*, 228 Cal. App. 3d 1212, 1230–31 (1991); *William S. Hart Union High Sch. Dist. v. Reg'l Planning Comm'n*, 226 Cal. App. 3d 1612, 1625 (1991). Relying on these decisions, many cities required payment of school fees in excess of the statutory limits as a condition to granting rezoning, general plan amendments, and other legislative approvals.

In 1998, however, the Legislature enacted the Leroy F. Greene School Facilities Act (SB 50), 1998 Cal. Stat. ch. 407 (the "1998 Act"), which significantly amended the statutory scheme for school fees. Most important, it appears to have eliminated the rule of the *Mira-Hart-Murrieta* trilogy—i.e., that the statutory limitations on school impact fees and mitigation apply only to adjudicative, not legislative, actions.

The 1998 Act included a $9.2 billion state bond measure, which was approved by the voters as Proposition 1A in the November 3, 1998 general election. The approval of Proposition 1A made operative, effective November 4, 1998, other provisions of SB 50 that amended the school facilities law. The 1998 Act amended Government Code section 65995(a) to prohibit state or local agencies from imposing school impact mitigation fees, dedications, or other requirements in excess of those provided in the statute in connection with "any legislative or adjudicative act...by any state or local agency involving...the planning, use, or development of real property...."

The legislation also amended Government Code section 65996(b) to prohibit local agencies from using the inadequacy of school facilities as a basis for denying or conditioning approvals of any "legislative or adjudicative act...involving... the planning, use or development of real property...." The express inclusion of "legislative" approvals in the statute evidences a legislative intent to overturn the *Mira-Hart-Murrieta* line of cases. For further discussion of this legislation, *see* chapter 13 (Exactions).

A court has held that Government Code section 66474(e) provides for environmental review separate from and independent of the requirements of CEQA.

Further, a court has held that Government Code section 66474(e) provides for environmental review separate from and independent of the requirements of CEQA. *Topanga Ass'n for a Scenic Community v. County of Los Angeles*, 214 Cal. App. 3d 1348, 1355–56 (1989). In *Topanga*, the court held that the finding required by that section is in addition to the requirements for the preparations of an EIR or a negative declaration. It further stated that this section requires disapproval of a project upon a finding that it is likely to cause substantial environmental damage; it does not require a finding of no substantial environmental damage as a condition of approval of a project. Finally, the court held that the term "substantial environmental damage" as used in Government Code section 66474(e) is the equivalent of "significant effect on the environment," which is defined in Public Resources Code section 21068 as "a substantial, or potentially substantial, adverse change in the environment." 68 Ops. Cal. Atty. Gen. 108, 111 n.2 (1985). However, the court held that the county made a proper finding of no substantial damage when it found:

> The design of the subdivision and the proposed improvements will not cause substantial environmental damage or substantial and avoidable injury to fish or wildlife or their habitat, since the project is not located in a Significant Ecological Area and the initial study for the project shows that the proposed development will not have a significant effect on the environment.

Topanga, 214 Cal. App. 3d at 1356

Condominium, Stock Cooperative, and Community Apartment Project Conversions

Since condominium and stock cooperative conversions are governed by the Map Act, a city may be able to require dedications when a conversion is proposed. One of the leading condominium conversion cases is *Norsco Enters. v.*

City of Fremont, 54 Cal. App. 3d 488 (1976), which held that a city could require parkland dedication fees for condominium conversion even though no new residences had been added.

> Moreover, we find no unconstitutional legislative discrimination, as claimed by Norsco, in classifying differently, existing apartment buildings with rental units and similar apartment buildings for which the owner seeks municipal authorization for subdivision into condominium units....
>
> It seems not unreasonable that an apartment house owner seeking, for his presumable economic advantage, the City's permission to convert his already occupied rental units into condominiums, be assessed a reasonable amount for additional park and recreational facilities in the neighborhood.

Id. at 497–98

After this decision, the Legislature amended the law to provide that dedication cannot be required under these circumstances. Gov't Code § 66477. However, the principle that reasonable conditions can be imposed on condominium conversions enunciated in *Norsco* remains and might be applicable in other contexts.

For instance, in *Soderling v. City of Santa Monica*, the court held that since condominium conversion projects are subdivisions, a denial of map approval is required when there is a failure to fulfill design conditions authorized by local ordinance. 142 Cal. App. 3d 501, 506–07 (1983). That same year, the court held that a city acted properly in denying a conversion since it did not comply with present zoning. *Rasmussen v. City Council*, 140 Cal. App. 3d 842 (1983). Further, the court stated that a council finding that there may be a "domino effect" on other apartments was reasonable grounds for denial.

> *In* Soderling, *the court held that since condominium conversion projects are subdivisions, a denial of map approval is required when there is a failure to fulfill design conditions authorized by local ordinance.*

In addition, there are two important Attorney General opinions on condominium conversions. The first stated that cities possess powers necessary under the Map Act to set up condominium conversion restrictions. 58 Ops. Cal. Atty. Gen. 41 (1975). The second stated that the Map Act requires the processing of tentative and final subdivision maps to convert an existing apartment or house to a condominium, even though the condominium will be located on a single lot created by an earlier approved final subdivision map. 62 Ops. Cal. Atty. Gen. 410 (1979).

Timing of Conditions and Subsequent Conditions

Under the so-called "one bite at the apple" rule, in determining whether to approve or disapprove an application for a tentative map, a city may impose only those ordinances, policies, and standards that are already in effect at the time the application for the tentative or parcel map has been deemed complete pursuant to Government Code section 65943 (the Permit Streamlining Act). Gov't Code § 66474.2(a). However, in certain circumstances, if the city has formally taken steps to change its requirements, it can attach the new requirements that are in effect at the time of approval. Gov't Code § 66474.2.

> *A city may impose only those ordinances, policies, and standards that are already in effect at the time the application for the tentative or parcel map has been deemed complete pursuant to the Permit Streamlining Act.*

Further, conditions that could have been placed on a tentative map, but were not, may not be placed on a subsequent building permit or other type of permit for residential construction with the following exceptions:

- More than five years have passed since the final map was recorded
- The condition is necessary to protect public health and safety
- The condition is necessary to comply with state or federal law
- The condition is necessary to ensure compliance with applicable zoning ordinances

Gov't Code § 65961; *see also Beck Dev. Co. v. Southern Pac. Transp. Co.*, 44 Cal. App. 4th 1160, 1199–1200 (1996).

In *Laguna Village, Inc. v. County of Orange*, the court held that Government Code section 65961 did not preclude the imposition of school impact fees at the time of issuance of the building permit, even though a map had been approved. 166 Cal. App. 3d 125 (1985). *See also Golden State Homebuilding Ass'n v. City of Modesto*, 26 Cal. App. 4th 601, 608 (1994) (a city could lawfully condition issuance of building permits on development fees not yet established at the time of map approval). The court explicitly held that Government Code section 65961 did not protect the subdivider. *Laguna Village Inc.*, 166 Cal. App. 3d at 131. The "one-bite-of-the-apple" rule of section 65961 likewise provides no protection against zoning changes that occur after approval of a tentative map. *Hafen v. County of Orange*, 128 Cal. App. 4th 133, 142–43 (2005) (approval of a tentative map does not insulate developer from future zoning changes unless vested rights have been obtained).

Refunds

After a map has been recorded, the Map Act provides the exclusive procedures for obtaining refunds of unused and unnecessary subdivision fees after reversion to acreage, refunds of park fees, and storm drainage and sanitary sewer fees.

After a map has been recorded, the Map Act provides the exclusive procedures for obtaining refunds of unused and unnecessary subdivision fees after reversion to acreage (Gov't Code §§ 66499.17, 66499.19), refunds of park fees (Gov't Code § 66477(a)(6)), and storm drainage and sanitary sewer fees (Gov't Code § 66483.2). A request for a refund of development fees can be denied if the developer fails to comply with statutory refund procedures. *B&P Dev. Corp. v. City of Saratoga*, 185 Cal. App. 3d 949 (1986). However, fees may be refunded if the subdivision map was not recorded. *See Wright Dev. Co. v. City of Mountain View*, 53 Cal. App. 3d 274, 276 (1975).

Reconveyances

If a property is dedicated in fee to a local agency for a public purpose, and the agency determines that the purpose no longer exists, it must reconvey the property back to the subdivider or its successor in interest. Gov't Code § 66477(a). This rule does not apply to: (1) land dedicated for open space, parks, or schools; (2) land that was required to be dedicated before January 1, 1990; or (3) any portion of the land that is required for the public purpose or for public utilities. Gov't Code § 66477(a)–(e). The subdivider may pay a fee and request that the local agency determine whether the public purpose for which the land was dedicated still exists. Gov't Code § 66477(b). The determination may be based on a capital improvement plan, a general or specific plan, the subdivision map, or other public documents that identify the need for the dedication.

The law also provides that the city must give the subdivider 60 days notice prior to vacating, leasing, selling, or otherwise disposing of the property, unless it will be used for the same public purpose for which it was dedicated. Gov't Code § 66477(d).

Grounds for Map Approval or Denial
Grounds for Approval

Before a tentative map or a parcel map is approved, a city must find that the proposed subdivision, together with the provisions for its design and improvement, is consistent with the general plan and any applicable specific plan. Gov't Code § 66473.5; *see also Woodland Hills Residents Ass'n, Inc. v. City Council*, 44 Cal. App. 3d 825, 832–33 (1975). However, the law does not require an exact match. The map need only be "in agreement with or in harmony with the general plan." *Sequoyah Hills Homeowners Ass'n v. City of Oakland*, 23 Cal. App. 4th 704, 707 (1993). In addition, a city should make a "housing balance finding," and a finding relating to future passive or natural heating or cooling opportunities. Gov't Code §§ 66412.3, 66473.1.

The importance of the consistency finding is reflected in the language of *Woodland Hills Residents Ass'n, Inc. v. City Council*:

> As plaintiffs suggest, the legislative history of the Subdivision Map Act illuminates the Legislature's acute awareness that approval of subdivisions which are inconsistent with a locality's general plan "subverts the integrity... of the local planning process." (Subcommittee on Premature Subdivisions, Staff Recommendations for Legislative Action (January 15, 1971), p. 4.) To preserve the integrity of the "general plan" concept, the Legislature enacted Government Code sections 66473.5 and 66474.60, subd. (c)..., mandating that a subdivision map may not be approved unless the appropriate agencies first find that the subdivision is consistent with the applicable general plan. Plaintiffs argue, with much force, that once a general plan has been formulated, the public has an overriding interest in the faithful enforcement of the guidelines established by the plan as applied to proposed subdivisions.

23 Cal. 3d 917, 936 (1979)

However, any policies in the general plan related to school facilities are preempted by Government Code section 65996(a), which provides that the school facilities legislation is the exclusive method of mitigating school impacts. This section prevails over Government Code section 66473.5, since the former is more specific and was adopted later; therefore, a city cannot use the general plan consistency rule to deny a map where it does not comply with a school facilities policy. *See Corona-Norco Unified Sch. Dist. v. City of Corona*, 13 Cal. App. 4th 1577, 1585–86 (1993).

If a map is inconsistent with a city's general plan or if general plan elements relevant to the map are legally inadequate, the map is vulnerable to a legal challenge. *See, e.g., Camp v. Board of Supervisors*, 123 Cal. App. 3d 334, (1981). However, as with zoning consistency, a city's consistency finding will not be disturbed unless it is based on evidence from which no reasonable person could have reached the same conclusion. *Corona-Norco Unified Sch. Dist. v. City of Corona*, 17 Cal. App. 4th 985, 992 (1993). *See also Sequoyah Hills Homeowners*, 23 Cal. App. 4th 704 (1993).

When a proposed adoption or amendment to a general plan is at issue, the Governor's Office of Planning and Research conditions with respect to an extension of time to adopt or amend a general plan pursuant to Government Code section 65361 can require that tentative maps be consistent with the proposed general plan if the proposed general plan has been approved by the planning commission. *Harroman Co. v. Town of Tiburon*, 235 Cal. App. 3d 388, 393–94 (1991).

Also, before a final map is approved for a residential condominium conversion, special findings must be made relating to tenant notices. Those findings are contained in Government Code section 66427.1.

Grounds for Denial

In approving or disapproving a map, a city shall apply only those ordinances, policies, or standards in effect at the time the application was deemed complete, with certain exceptions. Gov't Code § 66474.2.

No city shall disapprove a tentative, final, or parcel map in order to comply with the time limits specified in chapter 3 of the Map Act (Gov't Code § 66451 *et seq*.), unless there are reasons for disapproval other than the failure to timely act in accordance with the time limits. Gov't Code § 66451.4.

If a city makes any of the following findings with respect to a tentative map or a parcel map, it must deny approval of the map. Gov't Code § 66474.

- The proposed map or the design or improvements of the proposed subdivision are inconsistent with the applicable general and specific plans (*Woodland Hills*, 44 Cal. App. 3d at 825), or with a draft general plan being prepared under an OPR extension (*Harroman*, 235 Cal. App. 3d at 388; *see also* Gov't Code § 65361(e)).

- The site is not physically suited for the proposed type or density of development (*Carmel Valley View, Ltd. v. Board of Supervisors*, 58 Cal. App. 3d 817, 822–23 (1976) (upholding the disapproval of a map because a site was not physically suited for the proposed development)). However, where such a finding has been made, the city may approve the map on conditions that will reduce the density. 56 Ops. Cal. Atty. Gen. 274 (1973).

- The design or proposed improvements are likely to cause substantial environmental damage, or substantially and unavoidably injure fish, wildlife, or their habitats, or cause serious public health problems. Regarding assessment of environmental impacts (Gov't Code § 66474(e)), *see* the California Environmental Quality Act of 1970 (Pub. Res. Code §§ 21000–21178.1) and 59 Ops. Cal. Atty. Gen. 129 (1976). Notwithstanding Government Code section 66474(e), a city may approve a map if an EIR was prepared and appropriate findings are made that specific economic, social, or other considerations make infeasible the mitigation measures or project alternatives identified in the EIR. Gov't Code § 66474.01.

- The design or the types of subdivision improvements will conflict with public easements for access through or use of property within the proposed subdivision. A city may approve the map if alternative public easements will be provided.

In addition to these specific grounds for denial contained in Government Code section 66474, a city must disapprove a map if the design of the subdivision does not provide for, to the extent feasible, future passive or natural heating or cooling opportunities. Gov't Code § 66473.1; 64 Ops. Cal. Atty. Gen. 328 (1981). Also, a city must disapprove a map for the applicant's failure to perform any of the requirements or conditions imposed by the Map Act or local ordinance pursuant thereto. Gov't Code § 66473.

In approving or disapproving a map, a city shall apply only those ordinances, policies, or standards in effect at the time the application was deemed complete, with certain exceptions.

OPR = Governor's Office of Planning and Research

A city must disapprove a map for the applicant's failure to perform any of the requirements or conditions imposed by the Map Act or local ordinance pursuant thereto.

A city must disapprove a map if the property is subject to a Williamson Act contract, open space easement, agricultural conservation easement, or conservation easement if the resulting parcels would be too small to sustain their agricultural use or will result in residential development not incidental to the agricultural uses. Gov't Code § 66474.4(a). Absent specific findings to the contrary, a parcel is too small to sustain agricultural use if it is less than 10 acres of prime agricultural land, or less than 40 acres of nonprime agricultural land. Gov't Code § 66474.4(b).

For further discussion of the Williamson Act, *see* chapter 9 (Design Review and Other Development Regulations).

Finally, a city may disapprove a tentative map if discharge of waste from the proposed subdivision would violate existing requirements prescribed by a regional water quality control board. Gov't Code § 66474.6.

Findings for Approval or Denial

In approving or denying a map, a city must make findings that meet the test set forth in *Topanga Ass'n for a Scenic Cmty. v. County of Los Angeles*, 11 Cal. 3d 506 (1974). These findings are the legal footprints that a city must leave behind to explain how it progressed from the facts presented through established policies to the decision to grant or deny a map. Not only must findings be made, but more importantly, there must be evidence in the record to justify these findings. Evidence can be in the form of staff reports, written and oral testimony, exhibits, and the like.

PRACTICE TIP
If a subdivision is approved, it is incumbent upon the subdivider to make sure that a city makes the appropriate findings, especially if there has been controversy. Otherwise, if the map approval is later invalidated because of lack of appropriate findings, the subdivider is the real loser.

Additionally, pursuant to 2007 legislation, each city in the Sacramento-San Joaquin Valley shall make certain general amendments to provide for increased flood protection and thereafter deny approval of a tentative map for any subdivision located in the flood hazard zone unless the city makes one of three findings related to adequacy of flood protection. Gov't Code § 66474.5.

For a more detailed discussion of findings, *see* chapter 11 (Necessity for Findings). For an excellent discussion on findings, *see* Governor's Office of Planning and Research, *Bridging the Gap: Using Findings in Local Land Use Decisions* (2nd ed., 1989).

Appeals and Judicial Review

Appeals

Under the Map Act, the subdivider may appeal the action of the advisory agency, *e.g.*, a planning commission. Gov't Code § 66452.5(a). In addition, tenants in condominium conversions have the same right to appeal. The Map Act provides a limited right of appeal of interested persons to appeal findings made by an advisory agency or appeals board concerning general and specific plan consistency, suitable siting, environmental concerns, and other items listed under Government Code sections 66474, 66474.1, and 66474.6. Gov't Code § 66474.7. In addition, the Map Act provides that any interested person adversely affected by a decision of the advisory agency may file an appeal with the city council. Gov't Code § 66452.5(d). Then, upon filing of the appeal, the city council shall set the matter for hearing and act on the appeal. For a general discussion on appeals, *see* 73 Ops. Cal. Atty. Gen. 338 (1990). Note that a city planning director can be an "interested person adversely affected" under Government Code section 66452.5(d), and may appeal a planning commission decision to the city council even without an enabling ordinance to that effect. 71 Ops. Cal. Atty. Gen. 326 (1988). *But see Cohan v. City of Thousand Oaks*, 30 Cal. App. 4th 547, 559–60 (1994) (a city council is not an interested person permitted to appeal a planning commission's approval of a tentative map). However, the *Cohan* court limited the holding as not invalidating all appeals taken by a city council or other governing body to itself from a decision of a subordinate agency. The court emphasized that such a procedure should, however, be authorized by the ordinances or rules that govern appeals to such entity. These rules are necessary to ensure fairness and due process. "A fair trial in a fair tribunal is a basic requirement of due process." *Bullock v. City and County of San Francisco*, 221 Cal. App. 3d 1072, 1091 (1990). In *Cohan*, the city council disregarded the procedural and substantive due process rights of the developer. It was the cumulative effects of the council's actions that caused the court to nullify the council's appeal to itself. 30 Cal. App. 4th at 561.

However, one court held that when a city code specifically permitted filing of an appeal from a planning commission's decision by a city council member, such an appeal did not violate due process. *Breakzone Billiards v. City of Torrance*, 81 Cal. App. 4th 1205, 1239–41 (2000) (citing *Withrow v. Larkin*, 421 U.S. 35, 53, 56–57 (1975)). On appeal, the city council is not bound by the findings of the advisory agency and may hear the matter *de novo* and make its own determinations based on any relevant testimony or documents produced before it. Gov't Code § 66452.5(d); *see also Langrutta v. City Council*, 9 Cal. App. 3d 890, 895 (1970).

Judicial Review

Exhaustion of administrative remedies. Before judicial relief is sought, all administrative remedies must be exhausted. If there is a failure to exhaust, there can be no judicial review. *Sea & Sage Audubon Soc'y, Inc. v. Planning Comm'n*, 34 Cal. 3d 412, 417–18 (1983); *Tahoe Vista Concerned Citizens v. County of Placer*, 81 Cal. App. 4th 577, 589–90 (2000); *Coalition for Student Action v. City of Fullerton*, 153 Cal. App. 3d 1194, 1197–98 (1984); Gov't Code § 65009. If a city seeks to invoke the doctrine of exhaustion, it must include a notice to this effect in its public hearing notice. Gov't Code § 65009(b)(2). If a city fails to do so, it may lose this defense in a court challenge. *Kings County Farm Bureau v. City of Hanford*, 221 Cal. App. 3d 692, 740 (1990). For further discussion of judicial review of tentative map approvals, *see* chapter 21 (Land Use Litigation).

Statute of limitations. Any action to attack a decision concerning a subdivision must be commenced and summons must be served within 90 days after the date of such decision. Gov't Code § 66499.37. *See also Maginn v. City of Glendale*, 72 Cal. App. 4th 1102, 1104 (1999) (statute of limitations to be strictly enforced); *Sprague v. County of San Diego*, 106 Cal. App. 4th 119 (2003) (dismissing case because summons was served late, although suit was filed on time). The time period runs from the date of the decision. For example, the time to attack conditions imposed by a tentative map runs from approval of the tentative map, not from final map approval. *Soderling v. City of Santa Monica*, 142 Cal. App. 3d at 505. The 90-day period applies to a failure to issue a certificate of compliance, as well as to map approvals, denials, conditions, and subdivision improvement agreements. *Hunt v. County of Shasta*, 225 Cal. App. 3d 432, 446 (1990). *See also Anthony v. Snyder*, 116 Cal. App. 4th 643 (2004) (holding that a lawsuit over a subdivision improvement agreement amounted to an action "concerning a subdivision" and therefore the 90-day limitations period applied); *Stell v. Jay Hales Dev. Co.*, 11 Cal. App. 4th 1214, 1228–29 (1992). The denial of an application to grant an extension for the life of a tentative map also triggers the 90-day statute of limitations. *Presenting Jamul v. Board of Supervisors*, 231 Cal. App. 3d 665, 670 (1991). As the court in *Jamul* stated, the broad language of Government Code section 66499.37 applies whenever "'the conduct of a local agency under the Subdivision Map Act is called into question,' even where it allegedly exercised no discretion under the act." *Id*. at 672 (citation omitted).

In *Hensler v. City of Glendale*, the California Supreme Court addressed a claim that the application of a ridgeline ordinance in a condition of approval of the owner's subdivision map constituted a "taking" requiring just compensation. The court held that this claim was barred by the 90-day statute of limitations of the Map Act, because the ridgeline ordinance was part of the city's subdivision regulations. 8 Cal. 4th 1 (1994). In contrast, a court of appeal has ruled that a developer could sue for inverse condemnation within the five-year period applicable for such claims, where the challenged condition was imprecisely drafted in that a condition the city sought to enforce was not contained in the language of the tentative map. The court reasoned that such a vague map condition is not subject to the Map Act's 90-day statute of limitations. *Uniwill L.P. v. City of Los Angeles*, 124 Cal. App. 4th 537 (2004).

A claim alleging a breach of a subdivision-related development agreement is generally subject to the statute of limitations period for contract claims. However, those portions of the claim that could be challenged directly under the Map Act are subject to the shorter 90-day limitations period of section 66499.37. *Legacy Group v. City of Wasco*, 106 Cal. App. 4th 1305 (2003). In *Legacy*, a developer sued the city for breaching a development agreement by refusing to approve final subdivision maps, and for halting payments on improvements made to the property. The city argued the suit was time barred by the Map Act. The court held that the claim challenging denial of the maps was subject to the Map Act's 90-day limitations period, but found the remaining claims were subject to the statute of limitations for contract claims. The court observed that this rule "precludes the parties from avoiding the application of section 66499.37 to decisions arising under the [Map Act] simply by restating as contractual covenants the responsibilities imposed on local government by the [Map Act]." *Id.* at 1313.

The statute of limitations period applicable to a claim challenging excessive fees imposed as a condition to the approval of a tentative map or parcel map under the Quimby Act depends on the manner in which the fee is challenged. When a party avails itself of the fee protest procedures of Government Code section 66020 to challenge allegedly excessive fees imposed upon a development project, the limitations period is the one established by section 66020 (180 days). However, where a party does not comply with the fee protest procedures of section 66020, a traditional mandate action must be brought within

A claim alleging a breach of a subdivision-related development agreement is generally subject to the statute of limitations period for contract claims.

the 90-day limitations period specified by Government Code § 66499.37. *See Branciforte Heights, LLC*, 138 Cal. App. 4th at 928–29 (developer's compliance with the protest procedures set forth in section 66020 made 180-day statute of limitations applicable, rather than the 90-day period in a traditional mandate action). For a more detailed discussion of Government Code section 66020, *see* chapter 21 (Land Use Litigation).

Final Maps and Parcel Maps

Final Maps

The Map Act contains detailed provisions governing the content and form of the final map.

Form and filing of final maps. The Map Act contains detailed provisions governing the content and form of the final map. Gov't Code § 66433 *et seq*. These sections establish the persons who are qualified to prepare the final map, the standard for preparation, and the various certificates and acknowledgments required for the final map.

The final map must be prepared under the direction of a registered civil engineer or a licensed land surveyor and be based on a survey.

The final map must be prepared under the direction of a registered civil engineer or a licensed land surveyor and be based on a survey. Gov't Code § 66434. Detailed requirements for its format are also contained in Government Code section 66434. Only final and parcel maps (not tentative maps) may be filed for recording in the county recorder's office. Gov't Code § 66429. The written consent of all parties having any record title interest in the real property proposed to be subdivided must be obtained as a prerequisite to the recordation of a final or parcel map. Gov't Code § 66430.

Various certificates, statements, and acknowledgments must accompany the final map under Government Code sections 66435–66443, including:

- A statement signed and acknowledged by all parties having any record title interest in the property consenting to preparation and recordation of the final map must appear on the map. Excluded from this requirement are various lienholders, parties owning easements, rights-of-way, owners of beneficial interests or trustees under deeds of trust (but not both), and holders of other interests that cannot ripen into a fee. Gov't Code § 66436
- Certain statements of dedication, including dedications of interests in real property for specified public purposes, such as streets and public utility easements. Gov't Code § 66439
- A certificate or statement for execution by the clerk of each approving legislative body, stating that the body approved the map and accepted any real property offered for dedication for public use. Gov't Code § 66440
- The certificate or statement of a city engineer or county surveyor. Gov't Code § 66442(a). It must state that the official has examined the map, that the subdivision is substantially the same as it appeared on the tentative map, that there has been compliance with all applicable provisions of the Map Act and local ordinances, and that the official is satisfied that the map is "technically correct." This certificate or statement must be completed and filed with the appropriate legislative body within 20 days from the date the final map is submitted to the official by the subdivider for approval. Gov't Code § 66442(b)

Multiple final maps may be filed before expiration of the tentative map if (1) at the time the tentative map is filed, the subdivider informs the city of its intent to file multiple final maps, or (2) the city and the subdivider later concur in the filing of multiple final maps. Gov't Code § 66456.1. The right of a subdivider to file multiple final maps under this section does not limit a city's authority to impose reasonable conditions relating to the filing of multiple final maps. Gov't Code § 66456.1.

Procedures for approval. It is important to file a final map with a city before the tentative map expires. The expiration of the tentative map terminates all proceedings, and no final map or parcel map can be filed without first processing a new tentative map. Once a timely filing is made, subsequent actions of the city, including but not limited to processing, approval, and recording, may lawfully occur after the date of expiration of the tentative map. Gov't Code § 66452.6(d). Delivery to the county surveyor or city engineer shall be deemed a timely filing for purposes of this section. The Map Act does not indicate what constitutes a "timely filing." It usually goes beyond presenting the map to the city, and includes such things as improvement agreements, bonds, evidence of other agency approvals, and a completed plan check. One must look at the local ordinances or procedures for specific requirements by a city in order for the map to be "timely filed."

In *McPherson v. City of Manhattan Beach*, the court clarified that Government Code section 66452.6(d) was intended to protect the subdivider if the city failed to record the map through no fault of the subdivider. 78 Cal. App. 4th 1252 (2000). In *McPherson*, the developer filed a final parcel map with the city engineer, but did not pay the requisite property taxes or submit data for monument inspection approval. After the tentative map expired, the developer paid the taxes and submitted the monument data. The court held that under the unique circumstances of this case, delivery of the final parcel map to the city engineer did not constitute a timely filing. *See also Ailanto Props., Inc. v. City of Half Moon Bay*, 142 Cal. App. 4th 572 (2006) (following *McPherson* and holding that filing a phased final map that does not conform to the tentative map's requirements would not entitle the map to a 36-month extension under Government Code section 66452.6(a)(1); implicit in the extension provision is the requirement that the final map substantively complies with the Map Act).

The approval of a final map is ministerial if the final map is in substantive compliance with a properly approved tentative map, and the subdivider has satisfied the conditions of approval attached to the tentative map. *Youngblood v. Board of Supervisors*, 22 Cal. 3d 644, 656 (1978); *see also* Government Code section 66474.1. The developer is entitled to acceptance and approval of the final map, without the imposition of new or altered conditions, particularly those that are of a technical nature. *Anthony v. Snyder*, 116 Cal. App. 4th 643, 660, 664 (2004) (holding that the developer has a right to rely on the conditions established during tentative map approval). Accordingly, it is essential to make sure the final map is timely filed. *Santa Monica Pines, Ltd. v. Rent Control Bd.*, 35 Cal. 3d 858, 863 (1984); Gov't Code §§ 66458, 66474.1.

However, final maps cannot be ministerially approved if the map conditions are not fulfilled. The Map Act requires disapproval of a map if it fails to meet or perform any of the conditions imposed by the Map Act or local ordinance. Gov't Code § 66473; *see also Soderling v. City of Santa Monica*, 142 Cal. App. 3d at 507; *Kriebel v. City Council*, 112 Cal. App. 3d 693, 703 (1980) (observing that "[a]pproval of the final map in effect is a confirmation that the tentative map requirements have been fulfilled"). The disapproval of a final map must be

PRACTICE TIP

The Map Act does not indicate what constitutes a "timely filing" pursuant to Government Code section 66452.6(d). One must look at the local ordinances or procedures for specific requirements in order to determine what constitutes a map being "timely filed."

PRACTICE TIP

Approval of a final map by the city council is ministerial; it has no discretion to deny the map or place additional conditions on its approval.

accompanied by a finding that identifies the conditions that have not been met. Gov't Code § 66473. A local ordinance that implements the Map Act is required to set forth a procedure for waiving the requirements of Government Code section 66473 when the failure of a map is due to a technical or inadvertent error that does not materially affect the map's validity.

The city council may delegate, by ordinance, the authority to approve or disapprove a final map to the city or county engineer, surveyor, or other designated official. Gov't Code § 66458(d). The ordinance that permits an official to approve or disapprove final maps must require the official to notify the city council when he or she is reviewing a map, contain specified time limits, provide notice of pending approval or disapproval by the official, state that the official's decisions may be appealed to the city council, and require periodic legislative review of the delegation of authority. Gov't Code § 66458(d).

If the city council or a designated official does not approve or disapprove the map within the prescribed time, or within any authorized extension, and the map conforms to all requirements and rulings, it shall be deemed approved, and the city clerk shall certify or state its approval thereon. Gov't Code § 66458(b). Here, in contrast to the tentative map, automatic approval does occur, since approval is ministerial and the principles of *Horn* are not applicable. *See Horn v. County of Ventura*, 24 Cal. 3d 605, 615 (1979).

A newly incorporated city may have discretion to disapprove a final map despite its substantial conformance with a county-approved tentative map depending on the timing and sequence of incorporation proceedings relative to the processing of the map. Gov't Code § 66413.5; *City of Goleta v. Superior Court*, 40 Cal. 4th 270, 276–77 (2006). For further discussion of the effect of incorporation upon a subdivision map, *see* Tentative Map Processing—Effect of Incorporation, this chapter.

Final Map Is Deemed Valid When Recorded

Unless otherwise provided by the county, if the final map or parcel map is not subject to Government Code section 66493 (relating to security for taxes), after the city's approval of a final map or parcel map, the city clerk shall transmit the map to the county recorder. Gov't Code § 66464(a). Once a final map or parcel map is recorded by the county recorder, it is deemed valid and imparts constructive notice to parties of interest. Gov't Code § 66468. Certain steps must occur, however, before the county records the final or parcel map.

Filing of certificates and security for tax liens. If at the time the final map is to be recorded, the subject property is subject to a lien for taxes (or special assessments collected as taxes) and those taxes are not yet payable, the subdivider must file the following two items with the clerk of the board of supervisors of the county where any part of the subdivision is located:

- A certificate of statement prepared by the appropriate state or local official, which estimates the amount of taxes or assessments subject to the lien. Gov't Code § 66493(a)(1); and
- Security conditioned upon the payment of all state, county, municipal, and local taxes and the current installment of principal and interest of all special

assessments collected as taxes that are not yet payable. Gov't Code § 66493(a)(2). The security requirement may be waived by the county after consultation with the tax collector for a final parcel map of four or fewer parcels. Gov't Code § 66493(d)

Upon receipt of the certificate and security, the clerk of the board of supervisors then transmits the final map or parcel map to the county recorder for recording. Gov't Code § 66464(b). Other county officials also may transmit the final or parcel map to the county recorder if authorized to do so by the board of supervisors. Gov't Code § 66494.1.

If the subdivided property has no tax liens, the subdivider must simply file a certificate or statement with the county where any part of the subdivision is located. The certificate or statement must show that county records indicate there are no liens against the property for unpaid taxes or special assessments, except for those taxes not yet payable. The certificate should be filed prior to submitting the final or parcel map to the legislative body. Gov't Code § 66492.

If the subdivided property has no tax liens, the subdivider must simply file a certificate or statement with the county where any part of the subdivision is located.

Subdivider to provide evidence of consent of record title holders. If a final or parcel map is not subject to the liens described in Gov't Code § 66493, then the appropriate city or county official can transmit the map directly to the county recorder. Gov't Code § 66464(a),(c). The subdivider must demonstrate that all parties with a record title interest in the subdivided property have consented in writing to the filing before the map is recorded. Gov't Code § 66465.

Recorder has 10 days to accept or reject map for filing. The county recorder has 10 days to examine the parcel or final map and make a determination about whether it should accept or reject it for filing (in this context, filing is the same as "recording"). Gov't Code § 66466. If the county recorder rejects the map, it must within 10 days mail a written notice of the reasons for the rejection to the city engineer or county surveyor and subdivider. It must also return the map to the city or county clerk so that the map can be placed on the agenda of the legislative body's next regular meeting.

If the county recorder rejects the map, it must within 10 days mail a written notice of the reasons for the rejection to the city engineer or county surveyor and subdivider.

The legislative body has 15 days after the meeting to rescind its approval and return the map to the subdivider, unless the subdivider demonstrates that the reason for the rejection by the recorder has been removed. The legislative body may continue the matter with the subdivider's consent, but the prior approval of the map shall be treated as rescinded during the continuation period. If the city or county determines that the map should be returned to the county recorder, the county recorder has a new 10-day period to decide whether to accept or reject the map for filing. After the map is filed, the surveyor or engineer who prepared the map must transmit a copy of the map with the recording information to the county surveyor, unless the county already requires automatic transmittal of the map to the surveyor. Gov't Code § 66466(f).

Condominium, stock cooperatives, and community apartment project conversions. The Map Act has several additional requirements for a final map for a conversion. A city council shall not approve a final map for conversion until it makes six findings relating to different types of notices to tenants, including:

- Each tenant has received written notification of the intention to convert 60 days prior to the filing of a tentative map.

- Each tenant has received all applicable notices required by the Map Act.
- Each tenant has received 10 days' written notice regarding the submittal of an application for a public report to the Department of Real Estate.
- Each tenant will be given written notification within 10 days of final map approval.
- Each tenant will be given 180 days' written notice of the intention to convert prior to termination of tenancy.
- Each tenant will be given notice of the exclusive right to contract for the purchase of his or her unit, for a period of 90 days.

Gov't Code § 66427.1

The final map must contain a certificate containing statements of dedication and offers to dedicate property for use as streets, utilities, or other public uses.

Dedications of streets, utilities, and other property. The final map must contain a certificate containing statements of dedication and offers to dedicate property for use as streets, utilities, or other public uses. If a street is not offered for dedication, and there is a statement on the map to that effect, use of that street by the public will be with permission only. The offer of dedication includes public utility facilities located on or under the property only if there is a statement that the dedication includes these facilities. Gov't Code § 66439. Statements of dedication and offers to dedicate can also be done by separate instrument.

Once an offer of dedication is made, the city or a city official designated by ordinance must accept, accept subject to improvement, or reject all offers of dedication. Gov't Code § 66477.1. If the offer of dedication for streets, paths, alleys, public utility easements, rights-of-way for local transit facilities that directly benefit the residents of a subdivision, or storm drainage easements, is rejected, the offer will still remain open and a city may accept the offer in the future without any further action by the subdivider. Many cities will reject the offer when the final map is filed, and rescind that rejection and accept the offer once the improvements have been made. In this situation, the offer remains outstanding and cannot be revoked. However, no public interest is created until the offer of dedication is unconditionally accepted. *Mikels v. Rager*, 232 Cal. App. 3d 334, 354 (1991). Other cities will accept the dedication at the time of the final map approval subject to an agreement that the developer will pay for all the improvements. However, the offer will terminate without action by a city if all of the following conditions are satisfied:

No public interest is created until the offer of dedication is unconditionally accepted.

- The offer was made by filing a map.
- No acceptance of the dedication was made and recorded within 25 years after the map was filed.
- The property was not used for the purpose for which the dedication was proposed within 25 years after the map was filed.
- The property was sold to a third person after the map was filed and used free of the dedication.

Code Civ. Proc. § 771.010

A legal action is still required to clear title under these circumstances. Code Civ. Proc. § 771.020. Otherwise the offer will remain open.

Improvement agreements. When the final map is submitted for approval, all conditions must be satisfied. If the conditions for improvements will not be satisfied until after filing of the final map (which is often the case), the subdivider must enter into an improvement agreement with the city. The agreement must provide that the subdivider will complete the improvements at the subdivider's expense. Gov't Code § 66462(a). There is no right to a final map until the parties have entered into the agreement. *South Cent. Coast Reg'l Comm'n v. Charles A. Pratt Constr. Co.*, 128 Cal. App. 3d 830, 834 (1982). If a city enters into an improvement agreement, it must require that performance be guaranteed by security.

Improvement Security

Types of security. A city can require by ordinance that a subdivider post bonds, cash deposits, instruments of credit, a lien upon the property, or any other form of security acceptable to the city to secure completion of subdivision improvements. Gov't Code § 66499. The security ensures the faithful performance of the terms of the agreement and the securing of payment for labor, materials, and improvements, along with a guaranty and warranty for one year, plus costs, including reasonable attorneys' costs. Gov't Code §§ 66499.3, 66499.4. Courts will not interfere with a city's exercise of discretion in accepting or rejecting the security unless there is a showing of fraud, arbitrary action, or a clear abuse of discretion. Also, a city may adopt financial size criteria for insurers with respect to performance bonds. 74 Ops. Cal. Atty. Gen. 89 (1991). In addition, a city may have the obligation to ensure that the surety is sufficient. *Walt Rankin & Assocs., Inc. v. City of Murrieta*, 84 Cal. App. 4th 605, 627–28 (2000).

A city can require by ordinance that a subdivider post bonds, cash deposits, instruments of credit, a lien upon the property, or any other form of security acceptable to the city to secure completion of subdivision improvements.

How much security is required? A city will determine the amount of security required for performance of an agreement to complete improvements. Gov't Code § 66499.3. The amounts required by Government Code section 66499.3 are:

A city will determine the amount of security required for performance of an agreement to complete improvements.

- The amount for faithful performance (performance bond) must be no less than 50 percent or more than 100 percent of the total estimated cost of the improvement or the act to be performed.
- The amount for payment to the contractor, subcontractors, laborers, and anyone providing equipment must be no less than 50 percent or more than 100 percent of the total estimated cost of the improvement or the performance of the required act.
- The amount must equal the amount determined by the city to fulfill the obligations for one year after completion of the improvement arising under a guaranty and warranty against defective work, labor, and materials.

Some nonprofit organizations are exempt from the first two requirements listed above if certain conditions are met relating to how letters of credit are secured and how the contractor is paid. Gov't Code § 66499.3(c). In addition to the face amount, the security must be sufficient to cover any costs, reasonable expenses, and fees, including attorneys' fees, that the city would have if it successfully enforced the security. Gov't Code § 66499.4.

Rights and requirements. Once the improvement work begins, the subdivider and the entity that furnished the security (surety) are liable until all subdivision improvements are completed and accepted by the city. Therefore, subdividers and sureties must maintain and repair improvements after completion until all improvements guaranteed by the security are accepted by the city. *See County of Kern v. Edgemont Dev. Corp.*, 222 Cal. App. 2d 874, 879–80 (1963). A city's right to damages against a subdivider and the surety is not necessarily affected by modifications to an improvement agreement. *City of Sacramento v. Trans Pac. Indus., Inc.*, 98 Cal. App. 3d 389, 400–01 (1979).

A local agency is entitled to damages under a performance bond when a subdivider who is contractually responsible for constructing public improvements fails to perform, even if the agency incurs no out-of-pocket expense. In *City of Merced v. American Motorists Ins. Co.*, a developer entered into a subdivision agreement with the city under which it agreed to obtain a performance bond for deferred work identified in the agreement. 126 Cal. App. 4th 1316 (2005). After completing construction of numerous residential units, the developer became insolvent. The insolvent developer then conveyed the remaining undeveloped property to another developer, who agreed to perform the first developer's deferred work. The city promised to obtain the bond proceeds and pay them to the second developer to defray the costs of completing the first developer's obligations. The city then sued to enforce the first developer's deferred work obligations.

The bonding company argued that the city should not be able to enforce the performance bond against it since the city was not damaged by the first developer's refusal to perform because the second developer agreed to timely perform the deferred work at no cost to the city. The appellate court disagreed and held that the city's damages were not limited to its actual costs. The city maintained a contractual right to expect the first developer to perform the deferred work, despite the city's agreement with the second developer. According to the court, the city was damaged once the first developer refused to perform. Thus, its damages are measured by the first developer's share of the uncompleted portion of the deferred work, and the surety is liable under the performance bond up to the bond amount.

There is conflicting authority as to whether the surety is liable under an improvement agreement when the subdivider has not actually commenced construction. In *County of Yuba v. Central Valley Nat'l Bank, Inc.*, the court held that if the project is abandoned after a final map has been recorded, even though an improvement agreement has been entered into by the subdivider and the city, the surety is exonerated as long as no construction has begun. 20 Cal. App. 3d 109 (1971). If this occurs, the city cannot collect the amount of the bond or force the surety to install the improvements. The city may be able to proceed under Government Code section 66499.11 *et seq*. and "revert the subdivision to acreage," which has the practical effect of rescinding the subdivision map.

Conversely, in *City of Los Angeles v. Amwest Surety Ins. Co.*, the court held that the surety remained liable on the bond after the subdivider abandoned the project even though very minimal construction actually began. 63 Cal. App. 4th 378 (1998). The court distinguished *Yuba* based on the language of the security instrument, the fact that in *Amwest* the improvements were needed because the parcel was going to be developed by another developer, the money derived from the bond would be used to benefit the new development, and the parcel would not automatically revert to acreage because a reversion to acreage is a discretionary, not a ministerial action.

It appears that the courts are limiting *Yuba* to its facts; thus, a surety will likely remain liable under an improvement agreement even if the subdivider has not begun construction.

Releasing security. The Map Act allows a partial or complete release of the security for public improvements. Gov't Code § 66499.7. The security given for the faithful performance of an act (performance guarantee) must be released once the improvement is finally completed and accepted. Additionally, a city may establish rules that permit a partial release of the security as the work progresses. Gov't Code § 66499.7(a). The Map Act sets forth a detailed process for such partial release of performance security. For example, the subdivider may provide written notice to the city when it believes the required work has been completed. Gov't Code § 66499.7(b). The city then has 45 days to review and comment or approve the completion of the work. Gov't Code § 66499.7(b). If the city concludes that all required work has not been completed, it must provide a list of outstanding obligations to the subdivider. Gov't Code § 66499.7(b). The subdivider has 45 days from the date of receipt of the list to provide cost estimates to the city for all remaining work. Gov't Code § 66499.7(c). The city then has 45 days to review, comment, and approve, modify, or disapprove the subdivider's cost estimates. Gov't Code § 66499.7(d). If the city approves the cost estimate, it shall release all performance security except for security in an amount up to 200 percent of the cost estimate of the remaining work. Unless the city allows for earlier release, the process of partially releasing performance security must take place when the cost estimate of the remaining work does not exceed 20 percent of the original performance security. Gov't Code § 66499.7(d). If the obligation must be approved by another agency other than the city, the city cannot release the security until the obligation is performed to the satisfaction of the other agency. The other agency has two months after completion to determine its satisfaction or dissatisfaction. If it reaches no decision after two months, the obligation shall be deemed to be satisfied. Gov't Code § 66499.8. The security given for labor and materials must be released (1) if no liens have been filed and the time has expired for a lien to be recorded pursuant to Civil Code section 3114 *et seq.*, and (2) the city has accepted the work. Gov't Code § 66499.7(h). If liens have been filed, upon expiration of the period for recording of liens, the city will hold an amount equal to the amount of the liens and release the remainder, provided the lien holders have given notice in writing to the city. Gov't Code § 66499.7(h). However, the release provisions do not apply to the release of the portion of security that covers any warranty or guaranty by the subdivider or reasonable costs and attorneys' fees pursuant to Government Code section 66499.9. Gov't Code § 66499.7(i).

Remedies. If a developer does not satisfy its obligations under the improvement agreement, the method of recovery depends on the type of security that is furnished. If the security is cash or negotiable bonds and is conditioned on payments to the contractor, subcontractor, and other persons furnishing labor, materials, or equipment, a city may recover from the holder of the deposit. If the security is a surety bond, a city may recover from the surety and sue if necessary to enforce the bond. If an irrevocable standby letter of credit is used, a city may draw on the letter of credit. Gov't Code § 66499.10. Although the

Map Act authorizes a cause of action by a city against the financial institution obligated by the letter of credit, this should not be necessary in order for the city to collect on an irrevocable standby letter of credit.

The liability of a surety that issues a labor and materials bond for public improvements may extend to the benefit of contractors in addition to the city. *Sukut-Coulson, Inc. v. Allied Canon Co.*, 85 Cal. App. 3d 648, 651 (1978). This is because provisions of the Civil Code that would provide an appropriate remedy are not applicable to privately funded public improvements. *Id.* at 654; *see* Civ. Code § 3109 *et seq.*, § 3179 *et seq.*

Parcel Maps

Local ordinance requirements. Parcel map procedures and approvals are left up to the local ordinance, except as specifically provided in the Map Act. Gov't Code § 66463(a). However, even though notice and hearing requirements for parcel maps are not specifically set forth in the Map Act, constitutional prerequisites must be followed. *Horn v. County of Ventura*, 24 Cal. 3d 605, 616 (1979). For notice procedures, *see* Government Code sections 66451.3(a), 65090, 65091.

Parcel map requirements. When a parcel map is submitted, a city is more limited than with a tentative and final map in imposing fees and exactions. A city may only impose requirements for the dedication of rights-of-way, easements, and the construction of reasonable offsite and onsite improvements for the parcels that are being created. Gov't Code § 66411.1(a).

An important difference between final and parcel map conditions is that a city generally may not require that improvements be completed for subdivisions of four or fewer parcels until a permit for development is issued. However, satisfaction of conditions can be required at an earlier time upon a finding by the city that an earlier fulfillment of the construction improvements is necessary for the public health and safety or orderly development of the surrounding area. The completion of improvements can also be required earlier by agreement. Gov't Code § 66411.1; *see also* 78 Ops. Cal. Atty. Gen. 158 (1995).

While in subdivisions of five or more parcels security must be provided by the subdivider to ensure construction of the required improvements, cities *may*, by local ordinance, require similar security for subdivisions of four or fewer parcels. Such security may be in the form of bonds, money, or an instrument of credit. Gov't Code § 66411.1(a); *see also* 62 Ops. Cal. Atty. Gen. 175, 178 (1979).

Provisions regarding offers of dedication, approval of parcel maps, and the time limitations for a city to act on the parcel map are the same as for final maps. Gov't Code § 66463. Dedications or offers of dedication can be made either by a statement on the parcel map or by a separate written instrument recorded before or concurrently with the parcel map. Gov't Code § 66447. A subdivider may file multiple parcel maps if notice is given at the time of the filing of a tentative map or at a later date if the city concurs. Gov't Code § 66463.1.

Special case: four or fewer parcels and no dedications or improvements. Ordinarily, the map must be signed by all parties who have a record title interest in property to be subdivided. There must also be a statement that all of those parties consented to the preparation and recordation of the parcel, unless the local ordinance provides for a different statement. A special case exists if there is a division of four or fewer parcels and no dedications or improvements are required. In that case, only the subdivider must sign the map. If the subdivider does not own the property, the city may require that the subdivider provide the city with evidence that owners have consented to the division. Gov't Code § 66445(e).

Correction and Amendment of Maps
Grounds

Errors and omissions. After a final map or parcel map has been filed for recording, it may be amended in a limited number of situations by means of a certificate of correction or an amending map prepared by a civil engineer or licensed land surveyor. Gov't Code §§ 66469, 66470. An existing map may be amended to correct an error or omission in a course or distance on the map, or in the description of the real property shown on the map (Gov't Code §§ 66469(a)–(c)), but an existing course or distance may be corrected only if the error is ascertainable from data shown on the map (Gov't Code § 66469). A map also may be amended to indicate monuments that are set after the death, disability, or retirement of the engineer or surveyor responsible for setting the monuments (Gov't Code § 66469(d)), or to show the proper location or character of a monument that has been changed (Gov't Code § 66469(e)). Map amendments also are permitted under a catch-all provision to correct any other type of map error or omission if approved by either the county surveyor or the city engineer, provided the correction does not affect a property right. Gov't Code § 66469(g). Examples provided in Government Code section 66469(g) include correction of lot numbers, acreage, street names, and identification of adjacent record maps.

After a final map or parcel map has been filed for recording, it may be amended in a limited number of situations by means of a certificate of correction or an amending map prepared by a civil engineer or licensed land surveyor.

Changed circumstances. A recorded final map or parcel map may be amended if a city enacts an authorizing ordinance and makes certain specified findings. Gov't Code § 66472.1. To support the amendment, a city must find that:

- Changed circumstances make any or all map conditions no longer appropriate or necessary.
- The modifications do not impose an additional burden on the existing fee owner.
- The modifications do not alter any right, title, or interest in the property shown on the recorded map.
- The modified map does not contain any of the grounds for denying a map under Government Code section 66474.
- The modifications must be set for public hearing as provided in Government Code section 66451.3, and the hearing must be confined to consideration of and action on the proposed modifications. Gov't Code § 66472.1.

A recorded final map or parcel map may be amended if a city enacts an authorizing ordinance and makes certain specified findings.

Amendment Procedure

The amending map or certificate of correction must be prepared and signed by a registered civil engineer or licensed land surveyor in accordance with the standards applicable to a final map or a parcel map. Gov't Code § 66470. Each of the fee owners of property affected by the correction or omission at the time the original map was recorded must be listed on the amending map or "certificate of correction," but need not sign this document. Gov't Code § 66470. Within 60 days after recordation of a certificate of correction, the recorder must transmit a certified copy to the county engineer or surveyor, who must maintain an index of recorded certificates of correction. Gov't Code § 66470. After the corrected map or certificate of correction has been prepared, it must be submitted to the city engineer or county surveyor for certification that the changes made from the previously recorded map are only those specifically permitted by Government Code section 66469. Gov't Code § 66471. The amending map or certificate must then be filed with the recorder. The recorder must index the names of the fee owners and appropriate tract designation in the general index and map index. Gov't Code § 66472. On recordation, the original map is deemed to have been conclusively corrected, and the amending map or certificate imparts constructive notice of all corrections as though set forth in the original map. Gov't Code § 66472.

Changes Affecting Property Rights

An amendment to a recorded final map or parcel map is not permitted by Government Code sections 66469(f) or 66472.1 if it would affect existing property rights.

An amendment to a recorded final map or parcel map is not permitted by Government Code sections 66469(f) or 66472.1 if it would affect existing property rights. The Map Act contains no provision for amending a map when a property right is affected. In this situation, a subdivider might be able to effect an amendment by means of a lot line adjustment, which is excluded from Map Act regulation. Gov't Code § 66412(d).

Otherwise, even when the consent of all affected parties can be obtained, a subdivider may be required to process a new map in order to make amendments or corrections. When multiple legal parcels are involved, a subdivider might be able to correct an error or omission affecting a property right by filing a new final map or parcel map on only the affected property. Gov't Code § 66499.20½ (permitting merger and resubdivision of the property); Gov't Code §§ 66424, 66424.6 (permitting subdivision of a portion of a larger parcel).

Enforcement

Prohibition

The Map Act prohibits the sale, lease, or financing of any parcels, or commencement of construction, except for model homes, on any parcel or parcels of real property for which a map is required before the map is filed.

The Map Act prohibits the sale, lease, or financing of any parcels, or commencement of construction, except for model homes, on any parcel or parcels of real property for which a map is required before the map is filed. The Map Act also prohibits occupancy before the map is filed in compliance with the Map Act and local ordinance. Gov't Code § 66499.30.

However, this prohibition does not prohibit an offer or contract to sell, lease, or finance property or to construct improvements thereon so long as it is expressly conditioned upon the approval and filing of the final map or parcel map. Gov't Code § 66499.30(e). In *Black Hills Invs., Inc. v. Albertsons, Inc.*, the court held that contracts for the sale of unsubdivided real property, which did not expressly condition the sale upon the recordation of a parcel map, were illegal and therefore void, not voidable. 146 Cal. App. 4th 883, 893–94 (2007). The *Black Hills* contract allowed the seller to waive the condition, which the court reasoned could have resulted in a violation of the Map Act. Therefore, the contract was void, not voidable. *Id.*

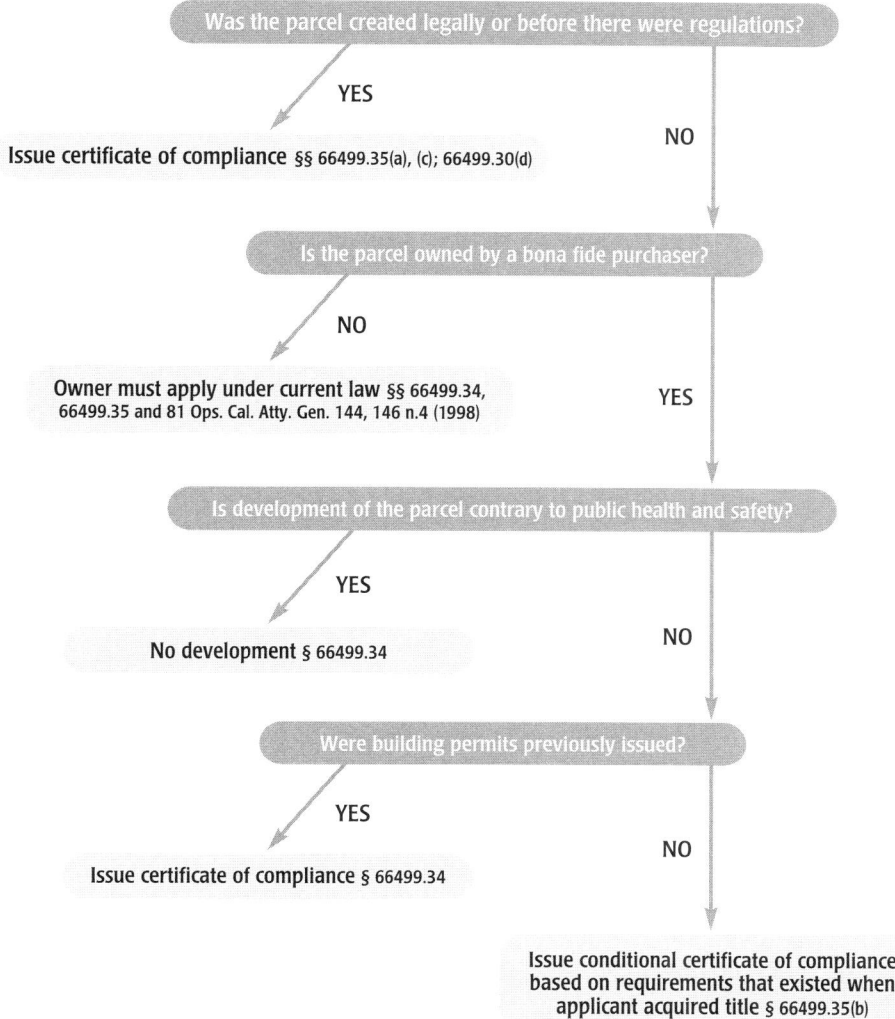

**Figure A
Certificate of
Compliance Flow Chart**

Remedies of Private Persons

Any deed of conveyance, sale, or contract to sell that results in a violation of the Map Act is voidable at the sole option of the grantee, buyer, or person contracting to purchase within one year after the date of discovery of the violation. However, the deed of conveyance, sale, or contract of sale is binding upon any successor in interest of the grantee, buyer, or person contracting to purchase. Gov't Code § 66499.32(a). Nevertheless, any such grantee, or the successor in interest of real property that has been divided in violation of the Map Act, may, within one year of the date of discovery of such violation, bring an action to recover any damages suffered by reason of such division. Gov't Code § 66499.32(b). However, the grantee or successor in interest cannot bring such an action if a certificate of compliance has been issued, which serves to defeat a contention that the Map Act has been violated. *LeGault v. Erickson*, 70 Cal. App. 4th 369, 374 (1999).

In addition, any private individual has a right to bring a lawsuit to restrain or enjoin a violation of the Map Act. Gov't Code § 66499.33.

Any deed of conveyance, sale, or contract to sell that results in a violation of the Map Act is voidable at the sole option of the grantee, buyer, or person contracting to purchase within one year after the date of discovery of the violation.

Remedies of a City

There are several remedies available to a city for Map Act violations. First, it can bring a suit for declaratory relief or an action to restrain or enjoin a violation of the Map Act in superior court. Gov't Code § 66499.33; *City of Tiburon v. Northwestern Pac. R.R. Co.*, 4 Cal. App. 3d 160, 175–76 (1970). A city also may request that a criminal complaint be filed in court. Gov't Code § 66499.31. However, the most practical enforcement tool for a city is to withhold permits and approvals necessary to develop any property that has been divided in violation of the Map Act after making the necessary finding that the development is contrary to the public health or public safety. Gov't Code § 66499.34. As soon as a city has knowledge that there is a violation, it must process a notice of violation pursuant to Government Code section 66499.36.

Certificates of Compliance[10]

Any owner or vendee (*i.e.*, a person contracting to acquire property) may request that a city determine whether the property complies with the provisions of the Map Act and the local subdivision ordinance. Gov't Code § 66499.35. *See County of San Luis Obispo v. Superior Court*, 90 Cal. App. 4th 288 (2001). When such request is made, the city must issue a certificate of compliance or a conditional certificate of compliance. 74 Ops. Cal. Atty. Gen. 149 (1991); *see also Lakeview Meadows Ranch v. County of Santa Clara*, 27 Cal. App. 4th 593, 598–600 (1994); *Hunt v. County of Shasta*, 225 Cal. App. 3d 432, 438–39 (1990). If the city determines that the property complies with the provisions of the Map Act and local subdivision ordinances, it must issue a certificate of compliance. Gov't Code § 66499.35(a). If the city determines that the property does not comply, it must issue a conditional certificate of compliance. Gov't Code § 66499.35(b). Where property does not comply because parcels have been illegally created, the city may only issue a conditional certificate of compliance. *Fishback v. County of Ventura*, 133 Cal. App. 4th 896 (2005). A court described the legislative intent behind the certificate of compliance procedure:

> The Legislature in enacting a comprehensive scheme to regulate the creation and control of subdivisions and other divisions of land, past and present, and in an obvious effort to provide a fair and equitable scheme to settle the validity of divisions of land occurring in decades past under earlier provisions of law, also provided a means whereby land owners could request that a local government make a determination about the validity of any prior division of land. That means is presently embodied in Gov't Code § 66499.35.

Stell v. Jay Hales Dev. Co., 11 Cal. App. 4th 1214 (1992)

Government Code section 66499.35 allows two different standards of conditions to be imposed in issuing a conditional certificate of compliance. If the one who seeks the certificate is the one who initially violated the law and that person is the current owner, a city may impose such conditions as would be applicable to a current division of property. However, if the one who is requesting the certificate is not the violator, a city may impose only those conditions

> **PRACTICE TIP**
> A city must issue either a certificate of compliance or a conditional certificate of compliance. It cannot refuse to act.

> **PRACTICE TIP**
> Certificates of compliance determine only whether the parcel conforms to the requirements of the Map Act and local ordinances. They do not grant any right to develop the parcel.

---

10. *See* Robert E. Merritt and Tedra E. Fox, "Using Certificates of Compliance to Help Clients Under the Subdivision Map Act," 26 *Real Property Law Reporter* 139 (Cal. Cont. Ed. Bar, July 2003).

established by the Map Act or local ordinance that would have been applicable to the division at the time the applicant acquired its interest. Gov't Code § 66499.35(b). The two different standards were established on the assumption that conditions in effect at the current time would be more strict as compared to those in effect earlier. The Attorney General has opined that the conditions imposed could include the requirement that the subdivider apply for a subdivision map to legally create the parcel. 81 Ops. Cal. Atty. Gen. 144, 146 n.4 (1998).

Certificates of compliance and conditional certificates of compliance must include the following notice:

> This certificate relates only to issues of compliance or noncompliance with the Subdivision Map Act and local ordinances enacted pursuant thereto. The parcel described herein may be sold, leased, or financed without further compliance with the Subdivision Map Act or any local ordinance enacted pursuant thereto. Development of the parcel may require issuance of a permit or permits, or other grant or grants of approval.

Gov't Code § 66499.35(f)(1)(e)

To reiterate, certificates of compliance determine only whether the parcel conforms to the requirements of the Map Act and local subdivision ordinances. They do *not* grant any right to develop the parcel. *See Gardner v. County of Sonoma*, 29 Cal. 4th 990 (2003). If the parcel has been illegally created, a city may only issue a conditional certificate of compliance. *Fishback*, 133 Cal. App. 4th 896 (2005).

Exclusions and Reversions

Exclusions are governed by Government Code section 66499.21 *et seq*. and are rarely used. This procedure removes land from an existing subdivision and requires judicial action. It requires notice and a court hearing. A two-prong test must be met to exclude a parcel from a recorded subdivision map: (1) petitioners must prove to the court that the exclusion of the property is a necessity; and (2) there must not be a reasonable objection to the exclusion. The court granted a petition for exclusion in *Van't Rood v. County of Santa Clara*, after finding that the petitioners had never consented to the contested parcel map, they were not afforded due process before their parcels were "merged" by the map, and the county had no reasonable grounds for objecting to the exclusion. 113 Cal. App. 4th 549 (2003).

Exclusions remove land from an existing subdivision and require judicial action.

A reversion to acreage eliminates the subdivision entirely. Gov't Code § 66499.11 *et seq*. It requires city approval after public hearing, with findings (1) that the dedications to be vacated are unnecessary, and (2) that the owners have consented, or that no improvements have been made, or that no lots have been sold. Gov't Code § 66499.16. However, an alternative procedure is more commonly used today. This allows the filing of a new map over the old map that merges and re-subdivides without reverting to acreage. This accomplishes, in one clean step by filing of a street map, the merger, re-subdivision, and abandonment of all streets and easements not shown on the map. These procedures only are applicable to property on which a previously recorded subdivision existed. Gov't Code § 66499.20½; *Negron v. Dundee*, 221 Cal. App. 3d 1502 (1990). The background of this law is discussed in *Gomes v. County of Mendocino*, 37 Cal. App. 4th 977 (1995). The *Gomes* court stated:

A reversion to acreage eliminates the subdivision entirely.

Article 1 of chapter 6 of the Act provides a procedure for the reversion of previously subdivided property to unsubdivided acreage, initiated either by the legislative body of the local agency or by petition of the owners of the property within the subdivision. ([Gov't Code] §§ 66499.11–66499.20¼.) According to one commentator, these formal reversion proceedings typically are initiated by local agencies to eliminate a previously approved subdivision map when the improvements required as map conditions have not been constructed within applicable time limits or when no subdivision lots have been sold. (Curtin *et al.*, Cal. Subdivision Map Act Practice (Cont. Ed. Bar 1987) § 9.1, p. 209.)

Also appearing in the same article is Government Code section 66499.20½, the statute at issue in this case. The statute states in pertinent part:

> Subdivided lands may be merged and resubdivided without reverting to acreage by complying with all the applicable requirements for the subdivision of land as provided by this division and any local ordinance adopted pursuant thereto. The filing of the final map or parcel map shall constitute legal merging of the separate parcels into one parcel and the resubdivision of such parcel, and the real property shall thereafter be shown with the new lot or parcel boundaries on the assessment roll....

Curtin suggests that this merger and resubdivision procedure is more commonly used than the formal reversion to acreage process because it enables an owner to resubdivide property for development in one relatively simple step. Curtin *et al.*, *California Subdivision Map Act Practice*, *supra*, section 9.4, page 212.

Id. at 981–82

Note that the reversion procedure is the exclusive method to obtain refunds of unused and unnecessary fees after recordation of a map, except for parkland dedication funds and storm drainage and sanitary sewer fees.

Note that the reversion procedure is the exclusive method to obtain refunds of unused and unnecessary fees after recordation of a map, except for parkland dedication funds (Gov't Code § 66477(b)), and storm drainage and sanitary sewer fees (Gov't Code § 66483.2). See *B&P Dev. Corp. v. City of Saratoga*, 185 Cal. App. 3d 949, 961–62 (1986).

Antiquated Subdivisions

Antiquated Subdivisions— Legally Created Parcels?

California's first statewide Map Act was enacted in 1893. In *Gardner v. County of Sonoma*, the California Supreme Court examined whether a subdivision map recorded prior to 1893 could create legal lots. 29 Cal. 4th 990 (2003). The map in question was recorded in 1865 and showed a 1,000-acre property divided into 90 lots. A 158-acre portion was conveyed intact through successive owners until it reached the plaintiffs. The plaintiffs applied to the county for certificates of compliance to certify that the 12 lots shown on their property were valid under the Map Act, but the county only would recognize the land as a single parcel.

The California Supreme Court found that the map, despite its purported accuracy and the fact that it was adopted as the county's official map,[11] did not give rise to legally cognizable parcels. The map did not satisfy either of the two main conditions required to establish a subdivision prior to 1893:

---

11. The court noted that the county's adopted map was not technically an "official map" for purposes of the Map Act because it did not meet the requirements of Gov't Code § 66499.50 *et seq.*

(1) Approval or exemption under a preexisting statute.

(2) Separate conveyance of the parcels.

If the map had been approved pursuant to, or exempted from, a statute governing local Sonoma County subdivisions in effect at the time the subdivision was established, it would have been grandfathered in under Sections 66499.30(d) and 66412.7. Because few local subdivision statutes existed prior to 1893, this occurrence would be extremely rare.[12] In the case of the Gardner map, the court found no legislation that authorized the creation of subdivided parcels in Sonoma County by map recordation before 1893. If the individual parcels had been separately conveyed from the surrounding land through a deed or patent after the map was recorded, they might have become eligible for legal status under the common law. The Gardners did not qualify for this consideration because their 158-acre portion of the map was conveyed intact through the years. *Gardner*, 29 Cal. 4th at 1001.

In holding that the 1865 map did not create legal parcels, the court cited strong public policy reasons for its decision:

> [I]f we were to adopt plaintiffs' position and hold that local agencies must issue a certificate of compliance for any parcel depicted on an accurate, antiquated subdivision map, we would, in effect, be permitting the sale, lease, and financing of parcels: (1) without regard to regulations that would otherwise require consistency with applicable general and specific plans... and require consideration of potential environmental and public health consequences...; (2) without consideration of dedications and impact mitigation fees that would otherwise be authorized by the Act; and (3) without affording notice and an opportunity to be heard to interested persons and landowners likely to suffer a substantial or significant deprivation of their property rights.

Id. at 1005 (internal citations omitted)

Maps Before 1929

In a footnote in the *Gardner* decision, the California Supreme Court left open the question of whether maps filed before 1929 can, by themselves, create legal lots. *Id.* at 1001 n.7. This date is significant because it was not until the 1929 amendments to the Map Act that cities and counties were given authority to regulate subdivisions. The court said it had no reason to resolve this question in *Gardner* because the map at issue predated the earliest statewide Map Act statute (1893).

In a footnote in the Gardner *decision, the Supreme Court leaves open the question of whether maps filed before 1929 can, by themselves, create legal lots.*

Maps After 1893 Generally

If a subdivision map was filed after the first Map Act was enacted in 1893, its validity is determined by whether it met the requirements of the version of the Map Act that was in effect at the time the subdivision was established. Gov't Code §§ 66451.10, 66499.30; 74 Ops. Cal. Atty. Gen. 149 (1991). For example, if a map was filed in 1935, the Map Act in effect in that year is the governing law and the map must have conformed to that law.

If a subdivision map was filed after the first Map Act was enacted in 1893, its validity is determined by whether it met the requirements of the version of the Map Act that was in effect at the time the subdivision was established.

---

12. Daniel J. Curtin, Jr. and Robert E. Merritt, *California Subdivision Map Act and the Development Process*, section 2.37 (Cal. Cont. Ed. Bar, 2nd ed. 2001) (Dec. 2005 Update).

U.S. Survey Maps and Federal Patents

In *John Taft Corp. v. Advisory Agency*, the court held that a United States Government Survey Map is insufficient to create legal parcels. 161 Cal. App. 3d 749 (1984). A patent (a grant of land) for more than 140 acres of land, including the three parcels at issue in this case, was granted to the landowner in 1895. While the survey described the land as separate parcels on a U.S. Survey Map, the patent was for the entire 140 acres. A subsequent landowner attempted to sell the separately described parcels and the court held that the U.S. Survey Map did not "create" parcels, and any transfer of these parcels was an illegal land division in violation of the Map Act. *Id.* at 757.

Conversely, a federal patent that itself divides the land can create legal parcels. In *Lakeview Meadows Ranch v. County of Santa Clara*, the parcel at issue was separately conveyed by the patent, and the court held that the patent created a parcel of land. 27 Cal. App. 4th 593, 597 (1994).

The Attorney General has followed the reasoning of *Taft* and *Lakeview Meadows*, and stated that a patent that granted land depicted on a United States Government Survey Map as contiguous "lots" does not create separate lots that must be recognized by a county. 81 Ops. Cal. Atty. Gen. 144 (1998).

Merger and Unmerger

Merging Parcels Under One Ownership. Under certain circumstances, contiguous legal parcels owned by the same person can be combined into one parcel. This is described as "merger."

For purposes of the Map Act's merger provisions, common ownership of contiguous parcels is determined not only by looking to proper title, but also by considering other indicators, including possession of or control over the affected property, whether a transfer occurred shortly before the planned merger, whether it occurred between family members, and the purpose of any recent transfer in title. *Kalway v. City of Berkeley*, 151 Cal. App. 4th 827, 834 (2007) (holding that parcels were in substance under common ownership at time city recorded notice of intent to determine status despite recent grant deed of parcel from landowner to his wife in effort to avoid merger).

Merger can occur by filing a final map or parcel map, which has the effect of creating a new subdivision. Gov't Code § 66499.20½. In addition, a city can adopt an ordinance permitting owner-initiated mergers. The ordinance must require recordation of an instrument evidencing the merger. Gov't Code § 66499.20¾. Finally, some jurisdictions permit a *de facto* merger using the lot line adjustment procedure by permitting lot lines dividing two or more parcels to be moved to correspond to the boundary lines of the parcels. Gov't Code § 66412(d).

The merger provisions of the Map Act provide the sole and exclusive authority for the merger of contiguous parcels initiated by a local agency. However, prior to 1983, merger was left largely to local law. *Moores v. Mendocino County*, 122 Cal. App. 4th 883 (2004). In the *Moores* case, the court upheld the county's determination that four contiguous parcels were automatically merged by the county's merger ordinance adopted in 1981. The plaintiffs unsuccessfully argued that a merger had not occurred because the county did not follow its own local notice procedures enacted a year later in 1982. However, the court held that the "[c]ounty's subsequent enactment of an ordinance providing for recording of notice and a hearing did not result in unmerging parcels already automatically merged the previous year by operation of law." *Id.* at 890. Furthermore, the court observed that because the automatic merger of the parcels occurred as a result of a legislative enactment, due process did not require notice and an opportunity for a hearing. The court said the intent of Government Code sections 66451.301 and 66451.302 was to preserve such mergers "accomplished through local law by exempting them from the requirement of recorded notice, and allowing the more informal notice outlined in Section 66451.302." *Id.* The County of Mendocino properly followed Government Code section 66451.302's required notice when it sent a form letter to the plaintiffs informing them that their parcels may have merged unless they qualified for one of the exemptions in section 66451.301. *Id.* at 891.[13]

The fact that the Map Act has provided exclusive authority for the merger of parcels since 1983 does not abrogate or limit the authority of a city to approve lot line adjustments, reversions to acreage, or parcel or final maps that combine lots and create fewer parcels. Gov't Code § 66451.10. Merger is not effective until notice of merger is filed for record with the county recorder. Before recording this notice, a city shall send by certified mail a notice of intention to determine status (Gov't Code § 66451.13), and the owner may request a hearing on determination of status (Gov't Code § 66451.14). The detailed requirements for parcel merger are contained in Government Code section 66451.11. Generally stated, the parcels must be contiguous, held by the same owner, and one of the parcels must not conform to the local standards for minimum parcel size. In addition:

- At least one of the parcels does not contain a structure for which a building permit was required, or contains only an accessory structure; and
- It comprises less than 5,000 square feet at the time of merger; or
- It was not created in compliance with applicable laws and ordinances in effect at the time of creation; or
- It does not meet current standards for sewage disposal and water supply; or
- It does not meet slope stability standards; or
- It has no legal access; or
- Its development would create health or safety hazards; or
- It is inconsistent with the general plan or specific plan in areas other than minimum parcel size.

The issue of merger was addressed in *Stell v. Jay Hales Dev. Co.*, 11 Cal. App. 4th 1214 (1992). In *Stell*, a landowner subdivided a single lot within a subdivision in 1960 that had conditions and restrictions stating that the lots contain not more than one single-family dwelling and limiting houses to one story in height. Both halves of that lot were sold to the defendant's predecessor in interest, and then the back half was conveyed to the defendant in 1989, who

Merger is not effective until notice is filed for record with the county recorder.

---

13. For a discussion of the legislative history of the merger law, *see Games v. County of Mendocino*, 37 Cal. App. 4th 977 (1995); Governor's Office of Planning and Research, Merger and Local Governments (1986).

began building a two-story house after obtaining the proper permits from the city as well as a certificate of compliance on the back half of the lot. Plaintiffs contended that the divided lot was not lawfully subdivided in 1960 and, by operation of law, the two parcels comprising that lot were merged.

The court, after reviewing the history of merger law, held there was no merger by operation of law when the defendant's predecessor in interest became the owner of the contiguous parcels because there was no notice and hearing held by the city. *Id.* at 1227–28. The court stated that because the city issued and recorded the certificate of compliance for the lot, the city did not see fit to attempt any merger of the two parcels. The court stated that if the plaintiffs did not agree with the city's decision to issue the certificate of compliance, they should have filed a lawsuit within the 90-day statute of limitation period under Government Code section 66499.37.

In 1994, the California Supreme Court struck down a local zoning ordinance requiring a merger of certain contiguous parcels in common ownership as a prerequisite to a development application involving one of the parcels. The court found that the local zoning regulations conflicted with the requirements of the merger provisions of the Map Act, and that the Map Act preempted such conflicting local laws. *Morehart v. County of Santa Barbara*, 7 Cal. 4th 725, 759 (1994); Gov't Code § 66451.10 *et seq.*

In *Morehart*, the court reviewed the legislative history and intent of the Map Act merger provisions. Section 66451.11 enumerates specific and limited grounds for a local agency to require merger of parcels (*e.g.*, failure to meet standards for sewage disposal, water supply, or vehicular access). The court held that these standards were intended to limit the conditions under which merger may be required, and that the county ordinance was invalid because it went beyond these standards and required merger to meet local density standards. The court found a "paramount state concern that statewide uniform standards govern the use of compulsory merger as a means of controlling development." 7 Cal. 4th at 760. This paramount concern was sufficient to find *implied* preemption of the local ordinances. In describing the relationship between the county's zoning and subdivision authority, the court stated that the Map Act does not "affect the applicability of zoning ordinances requiring minimum parcel size for development so long as the requirements are not conditioned upon parcel merger." *Id.*

Presumption of Legal Parcels

Any parcel created prior to March 4, 1972, is conclusively presumed to be a legally created parcel if it resulted from a division of land where fewer than five parcels were created, and no ordinances were in effect that regulated the division of land creating fewer than five parcels.

The Map Act contains a strong presumption for legally created parcels. Any parcel that was created prior to March 4, 1972, is conclusively presumed to be a legally created parcel if the parcel resulted from a division of land where fewer than five parcels were created, and no legal ordinances were in effect that regulated the division of land creating fewer than five parcels. Gov't Code § 66412.6(a). The presumption also exists for a parcel created before March 4, 1972 if a subsequent purchaser acquired the parcel for consideration without any actual or constructive knowledge of a violation of the Map Act or any applicable local ordinance. In that case, the owner must obtain a certificate of compliance or a conditional certificate of compliance before obtaining any grant of approval for development of the parcel. Gov't Code § 66412.6(b).

The Attorney General applied Government Code section 66412.6 to find that an agency had created two legal parcels under the Map Act when it acquired, through eminent domain, a significant portion of a 640-acre parcel to create a reservoir. 86 Ops. Cal. Atty. Gen. 70 (2003). The reservoir left two remaining areas of the parcel separated by 700 feet of water. Because the division occurred prior to March 4, 1972, and there was no local subdivision ordinance in effect at the time for four or fewer parcels, the Attorney General concluded the parcels were legally created for purposes of the Map Act. The Attorney General also found that the legal status of the two parcels was unaffected by the owner later obtaining a timberland production zone classification over the parcels, which required them to be managed contiguously as a single unit. *Id.*

Unmerger or Deemed Not to Have Merged

Government Code section 66451.30 *et seq.* provides a procedure for the unmerger of certain contiguous parcels. Parcels for which no notices of merger were recorded as of January 1, 1984, shall be deemed not to have been merged if, as of that date, certain findings can be made. Gov't Code § 66451.30. This section was enacted to reverse an automatic merger before the law was changed requiring a hearing and recording of merger. It has limited application.

For an excellent discussion of merger, *see* Governor's Office of Planning and Research, *Merger and Local Governments* (1986). *See also* Robert E. Merritt *et al.*, "Antiquated Subdivisions," 5 *Land Use & Env. Forum* 39–53 (Cal. Cont. Ed. Bar, Winter 1996).

Government Code section 66451.30 et seq. *provides a procedure for the unmerger of certain contiguous parcels.*

6

California Environmental Quality Act (CEQA)

by Barbara Schussman

Overview

The California Environmental Quality Act (CEQA) requires government agencies to consider the environmental consequences of their actions before approving plans and policies or committing to a course of action on a project. In enacting CEQA, the Legislature explained that this process is intended to: (1) inform government decisionmakers and the public about the potential environmental effects of proposed activities; (2) identify the ways that environmental damage can be avoided or significantly reduced; (3) prevent significant, avoidable environmental damage by requiring changes in projects, either by the adoption of alternatives or imposition of mitigation measures; and (4) disclose to the public why a project was approved if that project would have significant environmental effects.[1] Pub. Res. Code §§ 21000, 21001.

Consistent with these purposes, CEQA applies to most state, regional, and local agency decisions to carry out, authorize, or approve projects that could have adverse effects on the environment. CEQA requires that public agencies inform themselves about the environmental effects of proposed actions, consider all relevant information before they act, give the public an opportunity to comment on the environmental issues, and avoid or reduce potential harm to the environment when feasible.

To ensure their validity, an agency's actions should comply with CEQA's statutory provisions as well as the state environmental guidelines that have been adopted by the Secretary of Resources and incorporated into the California Code of Regulations, title 14, section 15000 *et seq.* ("Guidelines").[2]

CEQA requires government agencies to consider the environmental consequences of their actions before approving plans and policies or committing to a course of action on a project.

CEQA = California Environmental Quality Act

CEQA applies to most state, regional, and local agency decisions to carry out, authorize, or approve projects that could have adverse effects on the environment.

---

1. For a more detailed summary of CEQA and its application, *see* Stephen L. Kostka and Michael H. Zischke, *Practice Under the California Environmental Quality Act* (Cal. Cont. Ed. Bar, 2nd ed. 2008, supplemented annually); Michael H. Remy *et al.*, *Guide to the California Environmental Quality Act* (Solano Press, 11th ed. 2007); Ronald E. Bass *et al.*, *CEQA Deskbook: A Step-by-Step Guide on How to Comply with the California Environmental Quality Act* (Solano Press, 2nd ed. 1999–2000).
2. At a minimum, the courts should afford great weight to the Guidelines. *See Laurel Heights Improvement Ass'n v. Regents of Univ. of Cal.*, 47 Cal. 3d 376, 391 n. 2 (1988). However, if a guideline is inconsistent with CEQA's statutory provisions or case law it may be invalidated. *See Communities for a Better Environment v. California Resources Agency*, 103 Cal. App. 4th 98 (2002).

The CEQA process begins with a preliminary review of the proposal to determine whether CEQA applies to the agency action, or whether the action is instead exempt.

The CEQA process begins with a preliminary review of the proposal to determine whether CEQA applies to the agency action, or whether the action is instead exempt. Guidelines §§ 15060–15061. If the agency determines that the activity is not subject to CEQA, it may file a notice of exemption, and no further action to comply with CEQA is required. Guidelines §§ 15061, 15062. If the agency determines that the activity is a project subject to CEQA, the agency then must prepare either an environmental impact report (EIR) or a negative declaration. Pub. Res. Code §§ 21080, 21002.1.

EIR = Environmental impact report

Definition of a Project Under CEQA

CEQA applies to discretionary projects proposed to be carried out or approved by a public agency.

CEQA applies to discretionary actions proposed to be carried out or approved by a public agency.[3] Pub. Res. Code § 21080(a). An action is discretionary if the public agency is required to exercise judgment in deciding whether to approve or disapprove the particular activity, as distinguished from situations where the public agency merely has to determine whether there has been conformity with objective standards in applicable ordinances or other laws. Pub. Res. Code § 21080; Guidelines § 15357. "The statutory distinction between discretionary and purely ministerial projects implicitly recognizes that unless a public agency can shape the project in a way that would respond to concerns raised in an [environmental impact report], or its functional equivalent, environmental review would be a meaningless exercise." *Mountain Lion Found. v. Fish & Game Comm'n*, 16 Cal. 4th 105, 117 (1997). Thus, CEQA does not apply to proposed agency actions that are ministerial, rather than discretionary. *See Native American Sacred Site & Envtl. Protection Ass'n v. City of San Juan Capistrano*, 120 Cal. App. 4th 961 (2004) (because cities have a mandatory duty to place a voter-sponsored initiative on the ballot or adopt the initiative by ordinance, a city's decision to adopt the initiative by ordinance is ministerial and is not subject to CEQA); *San Bernardino Assoc. Governments v. Superior Ct.*, 135 Cal. App. 4th 1106 (2006) (county's decision to place transportation agency's measure on ballot was ministerial); *compare Friends of Sierra Madre v. City of Sierra Madre*, 25 Cal. 4th 165 (2001) (city's decision to place a city-sponsored initiative on the ballot is a discretionary action subject to CEQA).

CEQA also does not apply to activities that are not proposed for approval, or that will not directly or indirectly result in a change to the environment.

CEQA also does not apply to activities that are not proposed for approval, or that will not directly or indirectly result in a change to the environment. CEQA defines a "project" as:

> An activity that may cause either a direct physical change in the environment, or a reasonably foreseeable indirect physical change in the environment and that is any of the following:
> - An activity directly undertaken by any public agency

---

3. The agency that is responsible for carrying out the mandates of CEQA is called the "lead agency." If a project will be carried out by a public agency, that agency will be the lead agency. Guidelines § 15051; *see also Planning & Conserv. League v. Dep't of Water Resources*, 83 Cal. App. 4th 892, 905 (2000) (if several agencies are involved in a project, the agency with principal responsibility for carrying out the project is the lead agency). For a private project, the lead agency is the public agency with the greatest responsibility for supervising or approving the project as a whole. Guidelines § 15051(b).

- An activity undertaken by a person that is supported, in whole or in part, through contracts, grants, subsidies, loans, or other forms of assistance from one or more public agencies
- An activity that involves the issuance to a person of a lease, permit, license, certificate, or other entitlement for use by one or more public agencies

Pub. Res. Code § 21065; Guidelines § 15378(a)

Approval

CEQA compliance must occur before a public agency approves a project. The term "approval" refers to a public agency decision that "commits [it] to a definite course of action in regard to a project." Guidelines § 15352(a). Public agency approval of private projects is deemed to occur "upon the earliest commitment to issue or the issuance by the public agency of a discretionary contract, grant, subsidy, loan or other form of financial assistance, lease, permit, license, certificate, or other entitlement for use of the project." Guidelines § 15352(b). Approval of an agreement between a public agency and a private entity that is conditioned upon future CEQA compliance may not constitute "approval of a project" under CEQA where the agreement recognizes changes to the project may be made due to CEQA review, the agency does not commit itself to move forward with the project, and the agency does not limit its discretion in conducting its part of the CEQA analysis. *Concerned Citizens v. McCloud Community Services Dist.*, 147 Cal. App. 4th 181 (2007). By contrast, approval of an agreement that is not conditioned on CEQA compliance and requires an agency to construct public works improvements that may have an effect on the environment is a project under CEQA. *County of Amador v. City of Plymouth*, 149 Cal. App. 4th 1089 (2007).

For projects to be carried out by a public agency, approval does not occur until the agency is legally committed to proceed with the project. *See City of Vernon v. Board of Harbor Comm'rs*, 63 Cal. App. 4th 677, 688 (1998) (statement of intent signed by agency's director did not constitute project approval, because statement did not legally bind agency to approve the project, nor did the agency commit to a definite course of action by merely advocating for a project or acting as a proponent for a project). *See also Pala Band of Mission Indians v. County of San Diego*, 68 Cal. App. 4th 556, 576 (1998) (designation of potential waste disposal sites as "tentatively reserved" in county waste management plan did not trigger duty to prepare EIR, because commitment to develop one or more of the sites could only arise after county found them consistent with general plan and designated them reserved); *Kaufman & Broad-South Bay, Inc. v. Morgan Hill Unified Sch. Dist.*, 9 Cal. App. 4th 464, 474 (1992) (formation of community facilities district to provide funding for district activities was not a project, because agency was not committed to definite course of action relating to expenditure of funds); *Residents Ad Hoc Stadium Com. v. Board of Trustees*, 89 Cal. App. 3d 274, 291 (1979) (in preparing EIR for proposed athletic stadium, agency did not have to consider other potential capital improvements in university's master plan, because other components were not proposed for approval). *But see County of Amador v. El Dorado County Water Agency*, 76 Cal. App. 4th 931, 950 (1999) (approval of a water supply program before adopting a revised general plan precludes proper review of significant growth issues).

CEQA compliance must occur before a public agency approves a project.

For projects to be carried out by a public agency, approval does not occur until the agency is legally committed to proceed with the project.

Environmental Change

To constitute a project under CEQA, the activity also must be one that might result in a physical change in the environment. Pub. Res. Code § 21065; Guidelines § 15378(a). The term "environment" is defined as:

> The physical conditions within the area that will be affected by a proposed project, including land, air, water, minerals, flora, fauna, noise, and objects of historic or aesthetic significance, both within and beyond the project boundaries.

Pub. Res. Code § 21060.5; Guidelines § 15360. CEQA covers "tangible physical manifestations that are perceptible by the senses,"... "matters that can be seen, felt, heard, or smelled." *Martin v. City and County of San Francisco*, 135 Cal. App. 4th 392, 403 (2006) (project that affects only the interior of a house, even where the house is located in an historic district defined in part by the residential interiors, is not subject to CEQA). Impacts to a limited number of individual users of project facilities do not constitute impacts on the environment. *Eureka Citizens for Responsible Gov't v. City of Eureka*, 147 Cal. App. 4th 357 (2007).

The action reviewed under CEQA is the development or other physical activities that will result from the approval, not the approval itself. Guidelines § 15378 (discussion following). A public agency action that will not have an immediate effect on the environment but might culminate in a physical impact to the environment is a project under CEQA. *See Fullerton Joint Union High Sch. Dist. v. State Bd. of Educ.*, 32 Cal. 3d 779, 795 (1982). Thus, general plan amendments and other legislative policy enactments may be "projects" subject to CEQA even if further discretionary approvals will be necessary before development causing physical changes to the environment can occur. In *Christward Ministry v. Superior Court*, for example, the City of San Marcos argued that an EIR was not required for a general plan amendment relating to the siting of a landfill, because an EIR would be required for the development of the landfill itself. 184 Cal. App. 3d 180, (1986). The court rejected the city's argument, stating that general plans, though not directly effecting a physical change in the environment, do have an ultimate effect upon physical changes, and therefore require environmental review, where appropriate. Further, preparation of an EIR at the general plan stage comports with the policy that environmental consequences be considered at the earliest possible time. *Id.* at 193–94. *See also Muzzy Ranch Co. v. Solano County Airport Land Use Comm'n*, 41 Cal. 4th 372, 383 (2007) (adoption of an airport land use plan is a "project" under CEQA even if the plan merely freezes existing laws and even if future actions must be taken by other agencies); *but see Friends of Sierra Railroad v. Tuolumne Park & Recreation Dist.*, 147 Cal. App. 4th 643 (2007) (where development proposals have not yet been submitted, an action to transfer land may not be a "project" requiring CEQA review because not enough information is known to conduct a meaningful review).

The action reviewed under CEQA must encompass all components of the activity that is being approved. The term "project" refers to the whole of an action. Guidelines § 15378. A public agency may not divide a single project into smaller individual subcomponents in order to avoid responsibility for considering the environmental impact of the project as a whole. *See Orinda Ass'n v. Board of Supervisors*, 182 Cal. App. 3d 1145, 1171 (1986). The project includes reasonably foreseeable consequences of the proposed approval (*Bozung v. Local Agency Formation Comm'n*, 13 Cal. 3d 263, 279–81, 289 (1975); *Laurel Heights Improvement Ass'n v. Regents of the Univ. of Cal.*, 47 Cal. 3d 376, 395–398 (1988) (*Laurel Heights I*); improvements necessary for the provision of public services to the project (*Santiago County Water Dist. v. County of Orange*, 118 Cal. App. 3d 818, 829–30 (1981)); and components that are an integral part of the project (*No Oil, Inc. v. City of Los Angeles*, 196 Cal. App. 3d 223, 237 (1987)).

Process

If an agency determines that a proposed activity is a project under CEQA, it will usually take the following three-step approach: (1) determine whether the project is statutorily or categorically exempt from CEQA; (2) if the project is not exempt, prepare an initial study to determine whether the project may result in significant environmental effects; and (3) prepare a negative declaration, mitigated negative declaration, or EIR, depending upon the results of the initial study. For a more detailed discussion of these three steps, *see Gentry v. City of Murrieta*, 36 Cal. App. 4th 1359, 1371–72 (1995).

Determining If the Activity Is Exempt from CEQA

If it can be seen with certainty that a project will not have a significant effect on the environment, it is exempt from further CEQA review. Guidelines § 15061(b)(3). Such a determination is known as the "common sense" exemption. This exemption can be relied upon only if substantial evidence in the record supports the determination that it applies. *Davidon Homes v. City of San Jose*, 34 Cal. App. 4th 106, 114 (1997). Such a decision need not necessarily be supported by detailed or extensive fact finding, at least where a project is consistent with existing general plan and zoning designations, and future effects will themselves require analysis under CEQA. *Muzzy Ranch*, 41 Cal. 4th at 388–89. Alternatively, a project may fit within a category of projects that expressly are excluded as exempt from CEQA compliance either by CEQA or the Guidelines. *See, e.g.*, Pub. Res. Code §§ 21080(b), 21080.01–21080.03, 21080.05–21080.08, 21080.7–21080.33, 21159.21–21159.24; Guidelines §§ 15062, 15260–15285, 15300–15332.

Statutory exemptions cover a wide range of activities, some limited to one particular project and some having more widespread application.[4] Several of the statutory exemptions provide limited environmental review for projects that are consistent with a previously adopted general plan, community plan, specific plan, or zoning ordinance. Gov't Code § 65457(a) (residential development or any zoning change undertaken to implement a specific plan); Pub. Res. Code § 21083.3 (limited environmental review of development proposals consistent

If it can be seen with certainty that a project will not have a significant effect on the environment, it is exempt from further CEQA review.

Statutory exemptions cover a wide range of activities, some limited to one particular project and some having more widespread application.

---

4. Most of CEQA's statutory exemptions are listed in Article 18 of the CEQA Guidelines, sections 15260–15285. However, because statutory exemptions may be found in various codes, all statutes regulating approval or development of a proposed project should be reviewed carefully to determine whether the project is exempt from CEQA. For examples of additional statutory exemptions that are not found in Article 18 of the CEQA Guidelines, *see* Stephen L. Kostka and Michael H. Zischke, *Practice Under the Environmental Quality Act*, section 5.5 (Cal. Cont. Ed. Bar, 2nd ed. 2008, supplemented annually).

with a previously adopted planning or zoning action). *See also* Pub. Res. Code § 21158.5(a) (limited environmental review of multiple family residential developments of not more than 100 units, and mixed use residential developments of not more than 100,000 square feet); Pub. Res. Code § 21080.14 (development of up to 100 units of low- and moderate-income housing). Prior to conducting CEQA review of any project that is consistent with a prior planning action, each of these code sections should be reviewed carefully to determine whether all of the necessary conditions can be met.

Categorical exemptions are classes of projects that the Secretary of Resources has found do not have a significant effect on the environment.

Categorical exemptions are classes of projects that the Secretary of Resources has found do not have a significant effect on the environment. Pub. Res. Code § 21084(a); Guidelines § 15300. The categorical exemptions are set out in Article 19 of the CEQA Guidelines, sections 15301–15332. The categorical exemptions are not absolute. A categorical exemption generally will not apply if (1) there is a reasonable possibility of a significant effect on the environment due to unusual circumstances; (2) significant cumulative impacts from projects of the same type will result; or (3) the project will have impacts on a uniquely sensitive environment. Guidelines § 15300.2. The Guidelines also list several specific exceptions to the categorical exemptions. Guidelines § 15300.2. Effects common to projects generally within a categorical exemption are not considered "unusual circumstances" triggering an exception. *See Fairbank v. City of Mill Valley*, 75 Cal App. 4th 1243, 1260 (1999) (traffic and parking effects from small commercial structure in downtown area not considered unusual circumstances). *See also Turlock Irrigation Dist. v. Zanker*, 140 Cal. App. 4th 1047 (2006) (no significant effect due to unusual circumstances shown from water district's conservation measures); *San Lorenzo Valley Community Advocates for Responsible Education v. San Lorenzo Valley Unified School Dist.*, 139 Cal. App. 4th 1356 (2006) (traffic and parking effects associated with school closure and transfer of students not unusual circumstances).

The project must qualify for statutory or categorical exemptions without modification; an agency cannot adopt mitigation measures in order to ensure that a project fits within a categorical exemption. *Salmon Protection and Watershed Network v. County of Marin*, 125 Cal. App. 4th 1098 (2004).

CEQA does not contain any required procedures for making an exemption determination.

CEQA does not contain any required procedures for making an exemption determination. *See City of Pasadena v. State of California*, 14 Cal. App. 4th 810, 819–20 (1993); *San Lorenzo Valley Community Advocates for Responsible Education*, 139 Cal. App. 4th 1356; *Apartment Ass'n of Greater Los Angeles v. City of Los Angeles*, 90 Cal. App. 4th 1162, 1772–73 (2001) (initial study not required for determination that city's housing code enforcement program is exempt). Neither CEQA nor the CEQA Guidelines require findings documenting the basis for an exemption. *See CalBeach Advocates v. City of Solana Beach*, 103 Cal. App. 4th 529, 540 (2002). However, the agency should ensure the record demonstrates that the project falls within the claimed exemption. *See Magan v. County of Kings*, 105 Cal. App. 4th 468, 475 (2002). *See also Save Our Carmel River v. Monterey Peninsula Water Mgmt. Dist.*, 141 Cal. App. 4th 677 (2006) (replacement project exemption determination must be based on evidence from which agency can compare the replacement structure and the existing structure to verify that replacement structure will be on the same site with substantially the same purpose and capacity as the structure it replaces).

An agency's determination that the project fits within a categorical exemption includes an implied finding that none of the exceptions identified in the Guidelines is applicable. The burden then shifts to the challenging party to produce evidence showing that one of the exceptions applies to take the project out of the exempt category. *Banker's Hill v. City of San Diego*, 139 Cal. App. 4th 249 (2006). Two appellate districts are split as to whether the decision to apply an exception is subject to the substantial evidence standard or the "fair argument" test, in which an exemption cannot stand if the challenger presents evidence supporting a fair argument that an exception applies. *Compare Save Our Carmel River*, 141 Cal. App. 4th 677 (applying the substantial evidence test); *with Banker's Hill*, 139 Cal. App. 4th 249 (applying fair argument test to determine whether an infill housing project would have a significant effect on the environment due to unusual circumstances).

An agency may elect to file a notice of exemption. A notice of exemption contains a brief project description; the location of a project; a finding that the project is exempt from CEQA, including a citation to the appropriate exemption; and a brief statement of the reasons to support the finding that the project is exempt. Guidelines § 15062(a). If a notice of exemption is properly filed, it will trigger a 35-day statute of limitations for challenging the agency's decision that the project is exempt from CEQA. Pub. Res. Code § 21167(d); Guidelines § 15062(d). Further, the statute of limitation bars challenges to subsequent approvals for project components that are within the scope of the project determined to be exempt. *Madrigal v. City of Huntington Beach*, 147 Cal. App. 4th 1375 (2007) (challenge to grading permit barred where subject fill activity was within scope of original project approval). If the notice of exemption is not filed, the time period for challenging the action under CEQA is normally 180 days following the agency's approval. Pub. Res. Code § 21167(d); Guidelines § 15062(d).

If a notice of exemption is properly filed, it will trigger a 35-day statute of limitations for challenging the agency's decision that the project is exempt from CEQA.

Preparation of an Initial Study

If the project is not exempt, the public agency usually undertakes an "initial study." An initial study is:

> A preliminary analysis prepared by the lead agency (usually the city or the county having primary jurisdiction over the project) to determine whether an EIR must be prepared, or if a negative declaration will be sufficient.

Guidelines §§ 15063, 15365; Pub. Res. Code §§ 21080.1, 21080.3

The purpose of the initial study is to determine whether there may be a significant environmental impact. Pub. Res. Code § 21080(c); Guidelines §§ 15063– 15065. Appendix G to the CEQA Guidelines provides a suggested checklist for initial studies. In conducting the initial study, many agencies rely on a checklist, but, in doing so, they should disclose the data or evidence upon which the persons conducting the study relied. Mere conclusions as to the absence of the possibility of a significant effect are inadequate to support a negative declaration. *See Citizens Ass'n for Sensible Dev. of Bishop Area v. County of Inyo*, 172 Cal. App. 3d 151, 171 (1985); *Sundstrom v. County of Mendocino*, 202 Cal. App. 3d 296, 305–06 (1988).

The purpose of the initial study is to determine whether there may be a significant environmental impact.

Where the proposed project would result in the adoption of revised policies that may result in adverse effects, those effects must be considered in the initial study. *See Lighthouse Field Beach Rescue v. City of Santa Cruz*, 131 Cal. App. 4th 1170 (2005). Indirect effects of a project also must be determined. *City of Arcadia v. State Water Resources Control Bd.*, 135 Cal. App. 4th 1392 (2006) (State Board's functional equivalent document should have evaluated potential construction and air quality effects from pollution control equipment likely to be installed in order to comply with "zero trash" water run-off standard). For a detailed discussion of the law on the initial studies, *see Gentry v. City of Murrieta*, 36 Cal. App. 4th 1359, 1376 (1995).

Adoption of a Negative Declaration

If the initial study concludes that there will not be a significant effect on the environment, the agency can prepare a negative declaration and forego further CEQA compliance.

If the initial study concludes that there will not be a significant effect on the environment, the agency can prepare a negative declaration and forego further CEQA compliance. Pub. Res. Code § 21080(c); Guidelines § 15070 *et seq.* (negative declaration process). A negative declaration is a written statement that an EIR is not required because a project will not have a significant adverse impact on the environment. Pub. Res. Code §§ 21064, 21080(c).

An agency may attach conditions to a negative declaration for the purpose of mitigating potential environmental effects. Such a negative declaration is referred to as a "mitigated negative declaration." Guidelines § 15070(b); Pub. Res. Code § 21064.5. A mitigated negative declaration states that revisions in the project made or agreed to by the applicant would avoid the potentially significant adverse impacts, and that there is no substantial evidence that the project, as revised, will have a significant effect on the environment. Pub. Res. Code § 21064.5; Guidelines § 15070(b)(2).

As a general rule, an agency may not adopt a negative declaration, and must instead prepare an EIR, if it can be fairly argued on the basis of substantial evidence that the project may have a significant environmental impact.

As a general rule, an agency may not adopt a negative declaration, and must instead prepare an EIR, if it can be fairly argued on the basis of substantial evidence that the project may have a significant environmental impact. *See No Oil, Inc. v. City of Los Angeles*, 13 Cal. 3d 68, 74–75 (1974); Guidelines § 15064(f)(1). Even where a project may result in a net benefit to the environment, if any adverse environmental impacts also may result then an EIR must be prepared in order to explore potential mitigation measures and alternatives that would reduce or avoid such impact. *County Sanitation Dist. No. 2 v. County of Kern*, 127 Cal. App. 4th 1544 (2005).

Substantial evidence means enough relevant information and reasonable inferences from this information that a fair argument can be made to support a conclusion, even though other conclusions may be reached. Guidelines § 15384(a). Reports prepared by experts, if based on fact, normally constitute substantial evidence. *See Architectural Heritage Ass'n v. County of Monterey*, 122 Cal. App. 4th 1095 (2004); *Sierra Club v. California Dept. of Forestry*, 150 Cal. App. 4th 370 (2007).

Argument, speculation, inaccurate information, unsubstantiated opinion, or social or economic impacts unrelated to physical changes to the environment do not constitute substantial evidence.

Argument, speculation, inaccurate information, unsubstantiated opinion, or social or economic impacts unrelated to physical changes to the environment do not constitute substantial evidence. Pub. Res. Code §§ 21080(e), 21082.2(c). Similarly, the existence of public controversy over the environmental effects of a project does not, in and of itself, require preparation of an EIR if there is no substantial evidence before the agency that the project may have a significant effect on the environment. Pub. Res. Code § 21082.2(b); Guidelines § 15064(f)(4). *See also Bowman v. City of Berkeley*, 122 Cal. App. 4th

572 (2004) (differences of opinion regarding aesthetic effects in an urban area do not trigger preparation of an EIR). A significance determination requires the agency to exercise discretion. *See, e.g., Citizen Action to Serve All Students v. Thornley*, 222 Cal. App. 3d 748, 755 (1990).

A negative declaration must include a project description, the project location, the name of the project proponent, a finding of no significant effect on the environment, an attached copy of the initial study, and any mitigation measures that have been included in the project. Guidelines § 15071. The agency prepares the negative declaration and notifies the public that it is available for review, receives and considers comments on the negative declaration, considers and adopts the negative declaration, makes any necessary findings regarding mitigation measures, adopts a mitigation and monitoring program for any mitigation measures, and usually posts a notice of determination. Pub. Res. Code §§ 21092(b), 21092.2; Guidelines §§ 15072(a), 15075(a). It is important that the negative declaration also be provided to the State Clearinghouse for review by relevant state agencies prior to its approval. *See Fall River Wild Trout Found. v. County of Shasta*, 70 Cal. App. 4th 482, 490 (1999). If a fair argument based on substantial evidence can be made that significant impacts to biological resources may occur, the agency must consult with the Department of Fish and Game before conducting its initial study, and subsequently must notify CDFG of its intent to adopt a negative declaration. *Mejia v. City of Los Angeles*, 130 Cal. App. 4th 322 (2005).

CDFG = California Department of Fish and Game

Any mitigation measures that will be incorporated into the project must be identified before the proposed negative declaration and initial study are released for public review. Pub. Res. Code § 21064.5; Guidelines § 15070(b). When a negative declaration has been substantially revised after public notice of its availability, but prior to its adoption, it must be recirculated before the agency may adopt it. Guidelines section 15073.5 states that recirculation is required upon (1) the identification of a new, avoidable significant effect that can be reduced to a less-than-significant level only through the adoption of mitigation, and (2) a determination that originally proposed mitigation is not sufficient to reduce a project's impact to a less-than-significant level, and that additional mitigation or project revisions are necessary. The section also provides detailed guidance as to how a negative declaration should be recirculated prior to its approval.

Any mitigation measures that will be incorporated into the project must be identified before the proposed negative declaration and initial study are released for public review.

Preparation of an Environmental Impact Report

If the project is one that the agency determines may have a significant effect on the environment, an EIR must be prepared. Pub. Res. Code §§ 21002.1, 21061, 21080, 21080.1 *et seq.*; Guidelines §§ 15080–15081.5. An agency is required to prepare an EIR only for the project that it is considering. However, CEQA provides several optional tools for streamlining environmental review of a series of projects.

If the project is one that the agency determines may have a significant effect on the environment, an EIR must be prepared.

A master EIR is designed to provide for analysis of broad policy issues, such as cumulative and growth-inducing impacts, to limit the environmental review of subsequent projects. Pub. Res. Code § 21156. The Public Resources Code, starting with section 21157.1, outlines the procedure for reviewing subsequent projects after a master EIR has been prepared. During the first five years after certification of a master EIR, an agency need not review the adequacy

CURTIN'S CALIFORNIA LAND USE AND PLANNING LAW

**Figure B
CEQA Flow Chart for Local Agencies**

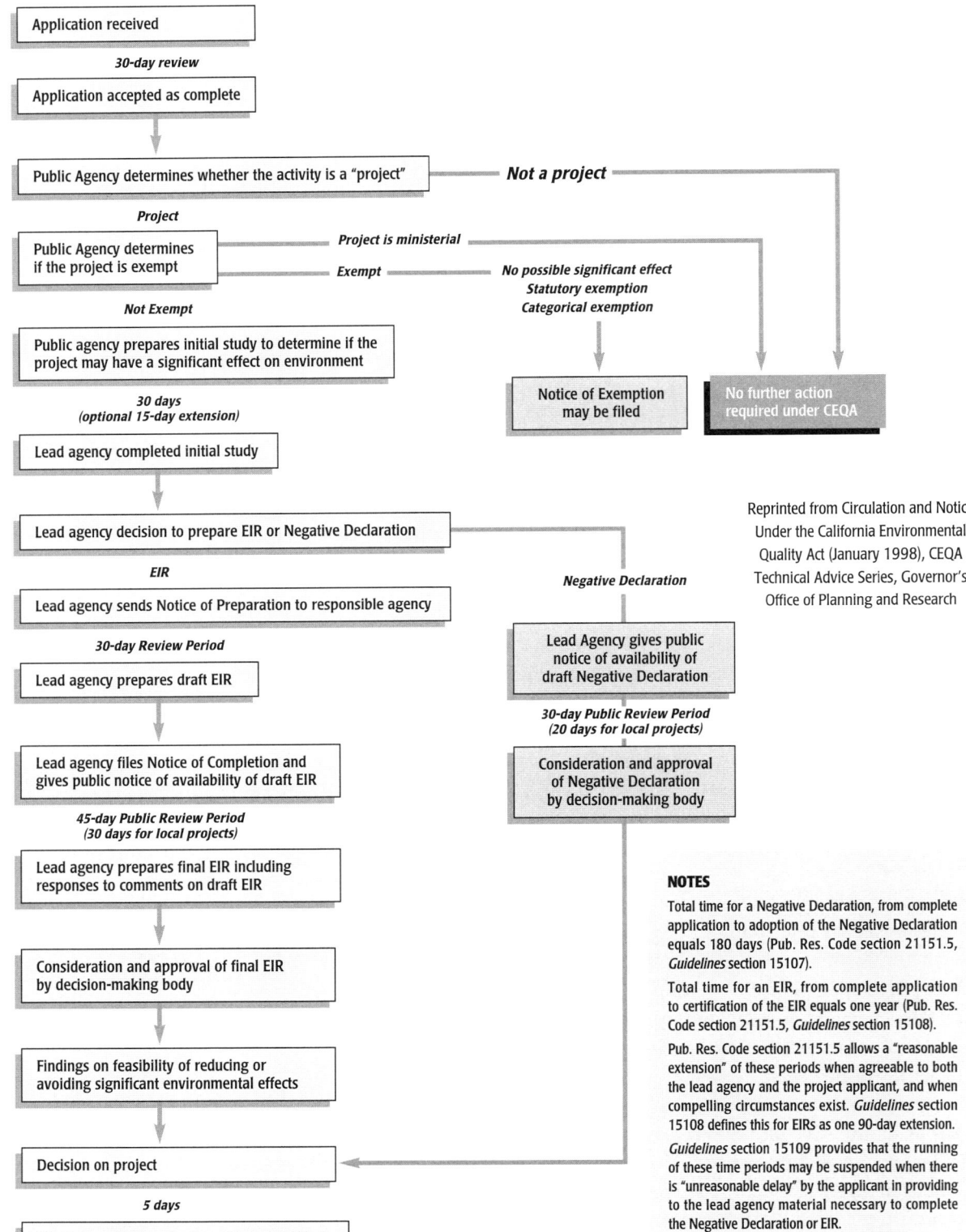

Reprinted from Circulation and Notice Under the California Environmental Quality Act (January 1998), CEQA Technical Advice Series, Governor's Office of Planning and Research

NOTES

Total time for a Negative Declaration, from complete application to adoption of the Negative Declaration equals 180 days (Pub. Res. Code section 21151.5, *Guidelines* section 15107).

Total time for an EIR, from complete application to certification of the EIR equals one year (Pub. Res. Code section 21151.5, *Guidelines* section 15108).

Pub. Res. Code section 21151.5 allows a "reasonable extension" of these periods when agreeable to both the lead agency and the project applicant, and when compelling circumstances exist. *Guidelines* section 15108 defines this for EIRs as one 90-day extension.

Guidelines section 15109 provides that the running of these time periods may be suspended when there is "unreasonable delay" by the applicant in providing to the lead agency material necessary to complete the Negative Declaration or EIR.

Figure C
Lead Agency Decision to Prepare an EIR

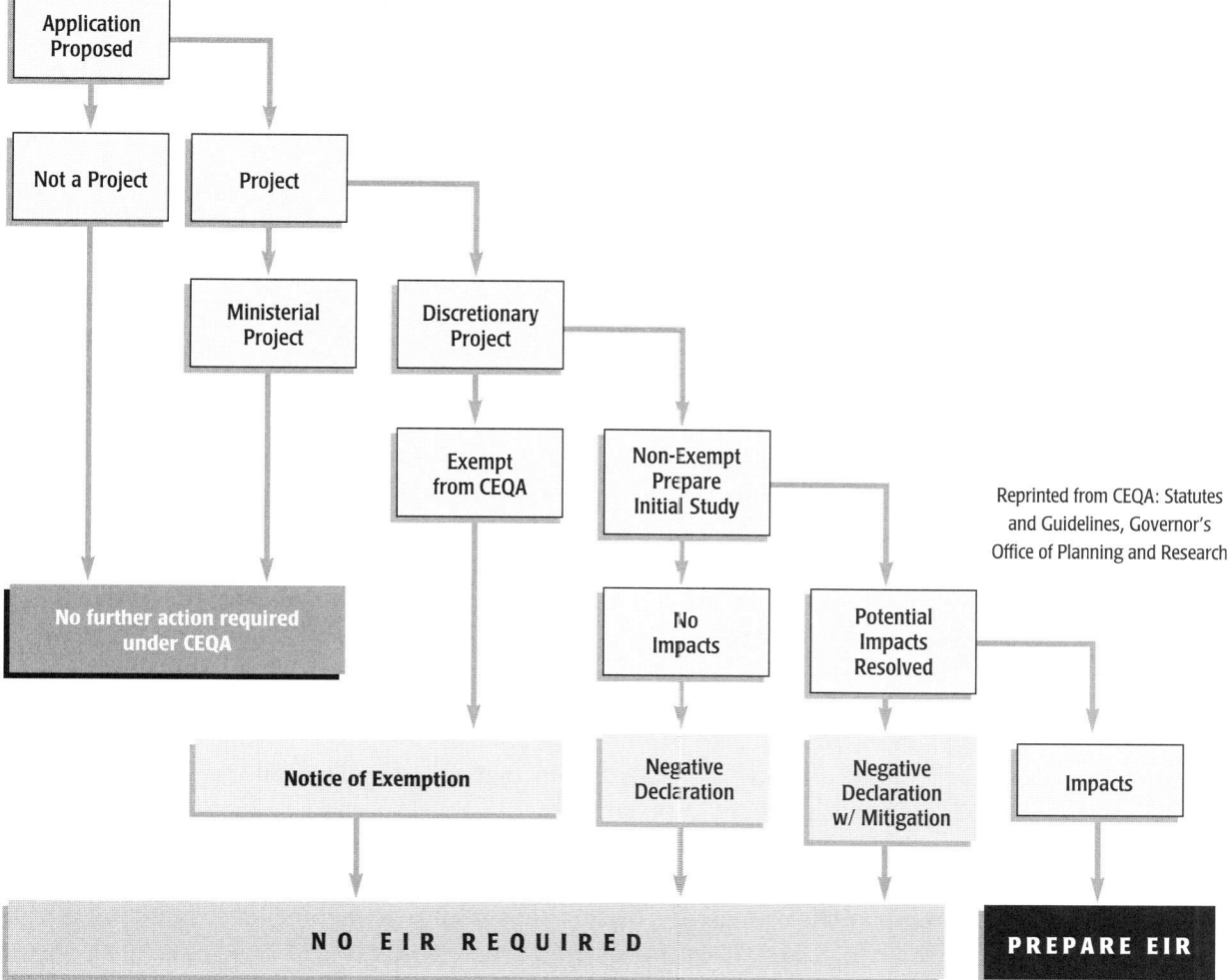

Reprinted from CEQA: Statutes and Guidelines, Governor's Office of Planning and Research

of the master EIR for projects included therein; after five years, the agency must determine whether a subsequent or supplemental EIR is needed. Pub. Res. Code § 21157.6.

Program EIRs generally can be used for the same types of actions as master EIRs. Guidelines § 15168. They can be used to study a broad planning decision or a series of projects that may have related impacts. If the program EIR is sufficiently comprehensive, the agency may dispense with further environmental review for later activities within the program that are covered in the program EIR. Guidelines § 15168(c). A program EIR also may be used to focus or simplify later environmental review or as the basis of a tiered EIR.

In determining whether a program EIR can be used for a later activity, the decision-making agency first should consider whether the project at issue is within the geographic scope of the plan, program, or group of projects evaluated

Program EIRs can be used to study a broad planning decision or a series of projects that may have related impacts.

in the program EIR. Guidelines § 15168. The agency then must determine whether the later activity would have environmental effects that were not examined in the program EIR. Guidelines § 15168(c)(1). A written checklist should be used to document the evaluation of any site specific operations. Guidelines § 15168(c)(3). However, unlike an initial study for a new project that has not undergone any review at all, the question the agency asks in reviewing whether a project is within the scope of a program EIR is will there be any new or substantially more severe impacts compared to the impacts discussed in the program EIR. *See* Guidelines §§ 15168(c)(2); 15162. If substantial evidence supports the agency's determination that no new or substantially more severe impacts will occur, the agency can approve the later activity based upon the program EIR; no further environmental review is required. *Citizens for Responsible Equitable Environmental Development v. City of San Diego Redevelopment Agency*, 134 Cal. App. 4th 598 (2005).

If a project is consistent with existing land use regulations, including a city's general plan, lead agencies should consider reliance upon an EIR prepared for the general plan, community plan, or zoning ordinance.

If a project is consistent with existing land use regulations, including a city's general plan, lead agencies should consider reliance upon an EIR prepared for the general plan, community plan, or zoning ordinance. *See* Pub. Res. Code § 21083.3; Guidelines § 15183. Under Guidelines section 15183(a), projects that are consistent with the development density established by existing general plan policies for which an EIR has been certified "shall not require additional environmental review, except as might be necessary to examine whether there are project-specific effects which are peculiar to the project or its site." *See Wal-Mart Stores, Inc. v. City of Turlock*, 138 Cal. App. 4th 273 (2006) (project opponent did not present evidence of a reasonably foreseeable project-specific significant change in the environment that was peculiar to a zoning ordinance to ban big box supercenters).

Tiering, under CEQA, means that where the general matters relevant to a project are covered in one or more previously prepared EIRs or negative declarations, future environmental documents may incorporate and build upon the earlier ones.

Tiering, under CEQA, means that where the general matters relevant to a project are covered in one or more previously prepared EIRs or negative declarations, future environmental documents may incorporate and build upon the earlier ones. Pub. Res. Code §§ 21068.5, 21093; Guidelines §§ 15152, 15385. Later EIRs or negative declarations need not examine environmental effects that the lead agency finds were mitigated or avoided as a result of the prior approval, or that were reviewed in the previous EIR or negative declaration in sufficient detail to allow those effects to be mitigated when the later project is approved. *See Gilroy Citizens for Responsible Planning v. City of Gilroy*, 140 Cal. App. 4th 911 (2006) (EIR appropriately tiered from prior EIR for general plan and prior negative declaration for retail center).

Tiering does not, however, allow deferral of review when a specific project is involved. In *Stanislaus Natural Heritage Project v. County of Stanislaus*, the court rejected an EIR for a 5,000 unit resort and residential project because the EIR did not analyze the impact of supplying water to most of the project. 48 Cal. App. 4th 182 (1996). Instead, the EIR indicated that the source of water was uncertain and concluded that this was a significant impact until a firm water supply could be established. The EIR also included a mitigation measure stating that development would not proceed until adequate water supply had been identified and evaluated under CEQA. The court held that the EIR did not need to identify a specific water source, but that the EIR must adequately disclose the impacts of supplying water to the site. *Id.* at 194–206.

EIR Procedure

Scoping. The first step in preparing an EIR is to determine the scope of the EIR in consultation with agencies, the public, and the applicant. Guidelines §§ 15082, 15083. To do this, the agency prepares a notice of preparation of an EIR describing the project and soliciting comments on the scope of the EIR. The notice should be sent to specified public agencies, including responsible agencies, trustee agencies, and the Governor's Office of Planning and Research. Pub. Res. Code §§ 21080.4, 21092.4, 21104.2; Guidelines § 15082(a). Many agencies also publish the notice and solicit comments from members of the public. Written responses are due 30 days after receipt of the notice of preparation. Guidelines § 15082(b). Agencies also can hold scoping meetings with other agencies or members of the public. Guidelines § 15082(c). An agency is required to hold at least one scoping meeting in several instances, such as when a project is of statewide, regional, or areawide significance. Pub. Res. Code § 21083.9(a).

Draft EIR. Following the scoping process, either the agency must prepare a draft EIR or the applicant's consultant may prepare the CEQA documents, so long as the agency independently reviews, evaluates, and exercises judgment over the document and the issues it raises and addresses. *See Friends of La Vina v. County of Los Angeles*, 232 Cal. App. 3d 1446, 1452 (1991); Pub. Res. Code § 21082.1; Guidelines § 15084. The final responsibility to provide an adequate EIR lies with the lead agency. *See Mission Oaks Ranch, Ltd. v. County of Santa Barbara*, 65 Cal. App. 4th 713, 723–24 (1998).

The draft EIR is circulated to the public and to public agencies for review and comment. *See* Figure D, page 165 (Time Periods for Review of Environmental Documents), and Guidelines section 15105 for timing of review. Notice of availability of the draft EIR must be provided by newspaper publication, posting on or off-site in the area where the project will be located, or direct mailing to the owners or occupants of contiguous properties. Pub. Res. Code § 21092(b)(3); *see also Gilroy Citizens for Responsible Planning v. City of Gilroy*, 140 Cal. App. 4th 911 (2006) (newspaper notice published 42 days before expiration of 45-day comment period insufficient; however, substantial evidence of mailing notice found based upon evidence of intent to mail combined with testimony of staff that notice was timely mailed and absence of contrary evidence). After receiving the comments, the agency must prepare responses to significant issues raised by the reviewers and, in some instances, revise the EIR. Pub. Res. Code §§ 21091–21092; Guidelines §§ 15085–15089.

Final EIR. The final EIR consists of:
- The draft EIR
- Comments and recommendations received on the draft EIR
- The responses of the lead agency to the significant environmental points raised in the review and consultation process
- A list of persons and agencies commenting on the draft EIR
- Any other information added by the lead agency

Guidelines § 15132

CEQA provides a once-around review system. There is no duty to make the final EIR available for public review and comment, but agencies may elect

---

The first step in preparing an EIR is to determine the scope of the EIR in consultation with agencies, the public, and the applicant.

PRACTICE TIP

The interactive CEQA flowchart (available at http://ceres.ca.gov/ceqa/flowchart/index.html) is an excellent resource.

to do so. At least 10 days before certifying a final EIR, the lead agency must provide any public agency that commented on the EIR with a written response to that agency's comments. Guidelines § 15088(b). This requirement may be met by providing the commenting agency with a copy of the final EIR or by making a separate response. Pub. Res. Code § 21092.5.

CEQA requires the agency to complete and certify the EIR within one year of the time the application is complete.

CEQA requires the agency to complete and certify the EIR within one year of the time the application is complete. Pub. Res. Code § 21151.5(a). In fact, one court has concluded that the agency was required to meet this deadline even though the applicant, rather than the city, had prepared the proposed draft EIR. The court stated that if the applicant fails to fulfill its responsibility to timely prepare a satisfactory draft EIR, the agency must take control of the preparation process. *See Sunset Drive Corp. v. City of Redlands*, 73 Cal. App. 4th 215, 223 (1999).

Contents of an Environmental Impact Report

To be complete, an EIR must contain the following:

- **Table of contents or index.** Guidelines § 15122
- **Summary of the proposed actions and their consequences.** Guidelines § 15123
- **Project description.** Guidelines § 15124
- **Environmental setting.** A description of the environment in the vicinity of the project as it exists before the commencement of the project, at the time the notice of preparation is published, or if no notice of preparation is published, at the time environmental analysis is commenced, from both a local and regional perspective. Guidelines § 15125. *See Save Our Peninsula Comm. v. County of Monterey*, 87 Cal. App. 4th 99, 125 (2001)
- **Evaluation of environmental impacts.** All phases of a project must be considered when evaluating its impact on the environment: planning, acquisition, development, and operation. Several of the subjects that must be discussed are listed below. Pub. Res. Code § 21100; Guidelines § 15126
- **Water supply assessment.** Water Code section 10911(b) requires that for certain large development projects, a water supply assessment must be included in any environmental document prepared for such projects, and findings must be made based on that assessment. Pub. Res. Code § 21151.9 (requiring compliance with Water Code section 10910 *et seq.*)
- **Significant environmental effects of the proposed project.** Guidelines § 15126.2
- **Effects not found to be significant.** Pub. Res. Code § 21100(c); Guidelines § 15128
- **Mitigation measures: Measures proposed to avoid or minimize the significant effects.** Guidelines § 15126.4
- **Cumulative impacts.** Pub. Res. Code § 21083(b); Guidelines § 15130
- **Alternatives to the proposed action.** Guidelines § 15126.6
- **Inconsistencies with applicable plans.** Guidelines § 15125(d)
- **A discussion of the growth-inducing impacts of the proposed action.** Pub. Res. Code § 21100 (b)(5); Guidelines § 15126.2(d)
- **Organizations and persons consulted.** Pub. Res. Code §§ 21104, 21153; Guidelines § 15129

Several of these EIR requirements have been discussed extensively in the case law and are described in the CEQA Guidelines.

Project description. The project description should extend to the entire activity that will ultimately result. All components of the project must be included. *See Santiago County Water Dist. v. County of Orange*, 118 Cal. App. 3d 818, 829 (1981) (EIR for mining operation should have included an examination of the extension of waterlines to serve the mine); *Whitman v. Board of Supervisors*, 88 Cal. App. 3d 397, 414–15 (1979) (EIR for oil facilities should have considered pipelines needed to serve the facility); *Ass'n for a Cleaner Environment v. Yosemite Community College Dist.*, 116 Cal. App. 4th 629 (2004) (college required to prepare initial study for closure, clean up, and transfer of shooting range where only some of the project components fit within categorical exemptions). Activities undertaken at the same time and location as the project that are required as conditions of project approval must be evaluated in the same EIR as the project, even if they theoretically could have occurred independent from the project. *Tuolumne County Citizens for Responsible Growth, Inc. v. City of Sonora*, 2007 WL 2834230 (2007).

The project description need not include information immaterial to a project's physical effects on the environment.

The project description also must include reasonably foreseeable future activities that are consequences of the project. *See Laurel Heights Improvement Ass'n v. Regents of the Univ. of Cal.*, 47 Cal. 3d 376, 394–95 (1988) (future planned expansion of project into entire building should have been considered); *City of Santee v. County of San Diego*, 214 Cal. App. 3d 1438, 1452 (1989) (foreseeable extended duration of temporary facilities should have been examined). The project description need not include, however, potential future projects that exist only in concept and are not linked to the project the agency is considering. *See Berkeley Keep Jets Over the Bay Committee v. Port of Oakland*, 91 Cal. App. 4th 1344, 1361 (2001). Further, where two proposed projects activities are independent of one another, they may be reviewed separately under CEQA, even though they may be similar. *Sierra Club v. Westside Irrigation Dist.*, 128 Cal. App. 4th 690 (2005) (transfers of water rights by two different agencies that could be implemented independently of one another and were not contingent on one another properly could be treated as separate projects).

The project description also must include reasonably foreseeable future activities that are consequences of the project.

Evaluation of environmental impacts. An EIR should be prepared with a sufficient degree of analysis to provide decisionmakers with information that enables them to evaluate and review possible environmental consequences intelligently. An evaluation need not be exhaustive, and disagreement among experts does not make an EIR inadequate. *See Citizens of Goleta Valley v. Board of Supervisors*, 52 Cal. 3d 553, 564 (1990). The courts have looked not for perfection but for adequacy, completeness, and a good faith effort at full disclosure of impacts. Thus, it is not required that the body acting on an EIR "correctly" resolve a dispute among experts. All that is required is that, in substance, the material in the EIR be responsive to the opposition and that it responds to the most significant questions presented. *See Ass'n of Irritated Residents v. County of Madera*, 107 Cal. App. 4th 1383 (2003); *Browning-Ferris Industries v. City Council*, 181 Cal. App. 3d 852, 862 (1986); *Greenbaum v. City of Los Angeles*, 153 Cal. App. 3d 391, 413 (1984). By contrast, an EIR that does not explain the basis for its conclusion may be deemed to not comply with CEQA's requirements. *See Protect the Historic Amador Waterways v. Amador Water Agency*, 116 Cal. App. 4th 1099 (2004); *Californians for Alternatives to Toxics v. Dept. of Food and Agriculture*, 136 Cal. App. 4th 1 (2006).

An EIR should be prepared with a sufficient degree of analysis to provide decisionmakers with information that enables them to evaluate and review possible environmental consequences intelligently.

In determining whether a project will result in a significant effect, the EIR normally should compare the effects of the proposed project to the physical condition of the project site at the time the notice of preparation of an EIR is prepared. Guidelines § 15125(a). In some cases, it may be appropriate for an EIR to compare impacts to both the hypothetical conditions that could occur if development of the project site proceeded under a current plan and to conditions that would occur on the site without any project. *Woodward Park Homeowners Ass'n v. City of Fresno*, 150 Cal. App. 4th 683, 708 (2007). But an EIR cannot exclusively compare impacts to those that might occur under existing plans and zoning. *Id.*

If evidence is submitted to the decision-making body supporting a fair argument that a significant impact could occur, and the agency fails to consider the impact, then certification of an EIR may be overturned.

If evidence is submitted to the decision-making body supporting a fair argument that a significant impact could occur, and the agency fails to consider the impact, then certification of an EIR may be overturned. *Bakersfield Citizens for Local Control v. City of Bakersfield*, 124 Cal. App. 4th 1184 (2004). In *Bakersfield*, opponents of two WalMart supercenters submitted studies and reports indicating the centers could over saturate the market, resulting in store closures and long-term vacancies in nearby retail areas. The city responded that such evidence showed an economic impact, not within CEQA's purview. The court ruled that when faced with evidence, the city was required to determine whether indirect physical effects, such as urban decay or deterioration, may occur. By contrast, where an EIR does consider the potential for such effects, the agency's determination will be upheld so long as it is supported by evidence in the record, even if the evidence also would support the opposite determination. *See Gilroy Citizens for Responsible Planning*, 140 Cal. App. 4th 911 (2006); *Anderson First Coalition v. City of Anderson*, 130 Cal. App. 4th 1173 (2005).

An EIR must consider whether there is sufficient available water to serve project demand in both the near-term and in the long-term.

Water supply. An EIR must consider whether there is sufficient available water to serve project demand in both the near-term and in the long-term. The following general principles govern an EIR's analysis of water supply issues:

- CEQA's informational purposes are not satisfied by an EIR that ignores or assumes a solution to the problem of supplying water to proposed development. Decisionmakers must be supplied with sufficient facts to evaluate the pros and cons of supplying the water the project will need.
- An adequate environmental impact analysis for a long-range development proposal cannot be limited to water supply for the first stage of development.
- Future water supplies identified and analyzed in an EIR must bear a likelihood of actually proving available; speculative sources and unrealistic allocations do not provide an adequate basis for decisionmaking under CEQA.
- Where a full analysis leaves some uncertainty regarding the availability of anticipated future water sources, CEQA requires some discussion of possible replacement or alternative supply sources, and of the environmental consequences of resorting to these sources.

Vineyard Area Citizens for Responsible Growth v. City of Rancho Cordova, 40 Cal. 4th 412 (2007) (citing *Santiago County Water Dist. v. County of Orange*, 118 Cal. App. 3d 818 (1981); *Stanislaus Natural Heritage Project v. County of Stanislaus*, 48 Cal. App. 4th 182 (1996); *Santa Clarita Organization for Planning the Environment v. County of Los Angeles (SCOPE 1)*, 106 Cal. App. 4th 715 (2003); *Planning and Conservation League v. Dept. of Water Resources*, 83 Cal. App. 4th 892 (2000); *California*

Oak Foundation v. City of Santa Clarita, 133 Cal. App. 4th 1219 (2005); *Napa Citizens for Honest Gov't v. Napa County Bd. of Supervisors*, 91 Cal. App. 4th 342 (2001)).

Under these principles, CEQA does not require a definite water supply—rather CEQA's reporting requirements are satisfied when an EIR fully discloses the uncertainties, likely water sources, their impacts, and appropriate mitigation measures. *Vineyard Area Citizens*, 40 Cal. 4th at 434 (EIR's analysis of near-term supplies was sufficient, but the discussion of long-term supplies suffered from lack of evidentiary support); *Santa Clarita Organization for Planning the Environment v. County of Los Angeles (SCOPE 2)*, 2007 WL 2773399 at *10 (EIR revealing legal uncertainty but explaining why, as a practical matter, water supply was likely to remain in place, supported the conclusion that water supply would be sufficient). Further, where a small amount of uncertainty exists, an analysis of possible replacement sources may not be necessary if substantial evidence supports the conclusion that the uncertainty regarding future water supply is not substantial. *Id.* at *9 ("'Some uncertainty' is not the same as any conceivable certainty.")

> Under these principles, CEQA does not require a definite water supply—rather CEQA's reporting requirements are satisfied when an EIR fully discloses the uncertainties, likely water sources, their impacts, and appropriate mitigation measures.

Cumulative impacts. An EIR must discuss significant cumulative impacts. Cumulative impacts are two or more individual effects that, when considered together, are considerable or that compound or increase other environmental impacts. Guidelines § 15355. The individual effects may be changes resulting from a single project or a number of separate projects. Thus, an EIR's cumulative impacts discussion should encompass "past, present and probable future projects." Guidelines §§ 15130(b)(1)(A), 15355. The purpose of this requirement is to avoid "piecemeal" approval of projects without consideration of the total environmental effects the projects would have when taken together. *See San Joaquin Raptor/Wildlife Rescue Ctr. v. County of Stanislaus*, 27 Cal. App. 4th 713, 740 (1994).

The evaluation of cumulative impacts may be based upon a list of past, present, and probable future projects. Guidelines § 15130(b)(1)(A). Projects that have been approved or are under environmental review should be included in the analysis. *See Friends of the Eel River v. Sonoma County Water Agency*, 108 Cal. App. 4th 859 (2003) (finding the cumulative impacts analysis inadequate where water agency reviewed project for increased withdrawals from river, but did not also review pending diversion curtailment proposals for the same river system). When using a list approach, the EIR also should define the relevant area affected and provide a reasonable explanation for the geographic limitation used. *Compare Kings County Farm Bureau v. City of Hanford*, 221 Cal. App. 3d 692, 723–24 (1990) (no explanation why analysis of cumulative air quality impacts limited to Central Valley), *with East Bay Mun. Utility Dist. v. Department of Forestry & Fire Protection*, 43 Cal. App. 4th 1113, 1128–29 (1996) (EIR explained agency practice to define assessment area that "was small enough to detect impacts, but not so small as to reduce any impact to insignificance"). *See also Bakersfield Citizens for Local Control v. City of Bakersfield*, 124 Cal. App. 4th 1184 (2004) (EIR could not arbitrarily define project area so narrowly as to avoid discussion of cumulative effects).

Alternatively, the evaluation of cumulative impacts may be based on a summary of projections from an adopted general plan, related planning document, or previously adopted or certified environmental document that evaluates regional or area-wide conditions contributing to the cumulative impact. Guidelines § 15130(b)(1)(B); *Schaeffer Land Trust v. San Jose City Council*, 215 Cal.

App. 3d 612, 630–32 (1989); *see also Las Virgenes Homeowners Federation, Inc. v. County of Los Angeles*, 177 Cal. App. 3d 300, 307 (1986) (cumulative impacts analysis for a project may incorporate the information in an EIR prepared for a general plan or an adopted program).

It is improper for an EIR to conclude that a project's cumulative impacts are insignificant merely because the project contributes to an existing unacceptable environmental condition.

It is improper for an EIR to conclude that a project's cumulative impacts are insignificant merely because the project contributes to an existing unacceptable environmental condition. See *Los Angeles Unified School Dist. v. City of Los Angeles*, 58 Cal. App. 4th 1019, 1025–26 (1997); *Kings County Farm Bureau*, 221 Cal. App. 3d at 718. Rather, in assessing cumulative impacts, the determination of whether the project's contribution is cumulatively considerable should take into account both the project's incremental effect and the nature and severity of the pre-existing significant cumulative effect. *Communities for a Better Environment v. California Resources Agency*, 103 Cal. App. 4th 98, 119–120 (2002).

An EIR must describe feasible mitigation measures to minimize the project's significant environmental impacts.

Mitigation. An EIR must describe feasible mitigation measures to minimize the project's significant environmental impacts. Pub. Res. Code §§ 21002.1(a), 21100(b)(3); Guidelines § 15126.4(a). The EIR also must analyze any significant effects of the mitigation measures it describes. Guidelines § 15126.4(a)(1)(D); *see also Stevens v. City of Glendale*, 125 Cal. App. 3d 986, 995 (1981).

Generally, mitigation measures should be described specifically in the EIR and not left for future formulation.

Generally, mitigation measures should be described specifically in the EIR and not left for future formulation. Guidelines § 15126.4(a)(1)(B). See *Endangered Habitats League, Inc. v. County of Orange*, 131 Cal. App. 4th 777 (2005) (mitigation that does no more than require a report to be prepared and followed, or allows approval by a county department without setting any standards, is insufficient); *San Joaquin Raptor Rescue Center v. County of Merced*, 149 Cal. App. 4th 645 (2007) (mitigation calling for future formulation of habitat management plan improper). However, the measures may specify "performance standards" that would mitigate the environmental effects, and that could be met in more than one way. Guidelines § 15126.4(a)(1)(B). In *Sacramento Old City Association v. City Council*, for example, the court upheld an EIR that set forth a menu of possible mitigation measures to offset parking and traffic impacts, even though the EIR did not specify which mitigation measures the agency would adopt. 229 Cal. App. 3d 1011, 1032 (1991).

In some cases, payment of fees into established fee programs designed to fund offsite infrastructure projects and regional improvements may be an effective approach to reducing a project's effects.

In some cases, payment of fees into established fee programs designed to fund offsite infrastructure projects and regional improvements may be an effective approach to reducing a project's effects. Accordingly, an agency carrying out its own development activities should consider the feasibility of voluntary payments into such programs, as well as the effectiveness of such programs, before it approves a project that will contribute to regional traffic congestion or other significant offsite environmental effects. See *City of Marina v. Bd. of Trustees of the Cal. St. Univ.*, 39 Cal. 4th 341 (2006); *see also County of San Diego v. Grossmont-Cuyamaca Community College District*, 141 Cal. App. 4th 86 (2006). Payment into regional traffic fees may also be sufficient to reduce a private project's contribution to a cumulative impact. Time-specific schedules for implementation of mitigation measures to be implemented under the fee program are not required; rather "all that is required by CEQA is that there be a reasonable plan for mitigation." *Save Our Peninsula Comm. v. County of Monterey*, 87 Cal. App. 4th 99, 141 (2001) (discussing mitigation of traffic impacts).

Figure D
Time Periods for Review
of Environmental Documents

Action Guidelines	Effect	Time Period	Relevant Statutes
Review of application for completeness	If no determination is made within this period, it will be deemed complete.	30 days	Guidelines § 15101
Lead agency acceptance of a project as complete	Begins maximum one-year period to complete environmental review for certain projects.	1 year	Guidelines § 15108
Initial study	Provides 30 days to determine whether an EIR or negative declaration will be required.	30 days	Guidelines § 15102
Notice of preparation	Provides 30 days from receipt of NOP for agencies to review and comment.	30 days	Guidelines § 15103
Convening of scope and content meetings	Requires a meeting requested by an agency or by the applicant to be convened within 30 days of the request.	30 days	Guidelines § 15104
Public review	When an environmental document is submitted to the Clearinghouse, the public review period shall be at least as long as the review set by the Clearinghouse.	EIR: 30–60 days ND: 20–30 days	Guidelines § 15105
Review by state agencies	Provides standard 45 days for EIRs and standard 30 days for negative declarations.	EIR: 45 days ND: 30 days	Guidelines § 15105
Completion and certification of negative declaration	For a private project, the negative declaration must be completed in 180 days.	180 days	Pub. Res. Code § 21100.2(a)(1)(B)
Approval or disapproval of a project based on a negative declaration	A private project must be approved or disapproved within 60 days of the certification of the negative declaration.	60 days	Gov't Code § 65950(a)(2)
Completion and certification of EIR	For a private project, an EIR must be completed within one year. May be extended once for up to 90 days.	1 year	Guidelines § 15108
Approval or disapproval of a project based on an EIR	A private project must be approved or disapproved within 180 days of the certification of the EIR.	180 days	Gov't Code § 65950(a)(1)
Notice of determination—filing	Provides that the notice shall be filed within 5 days after project approval.	5 days	Guidelines § 15094(a)
Notice of determination	Filing and posting starts a 30-day statute approval of the project.	30 days	Guidelines § 15094(f)
Suspension of time limits	Unreasonable delay of document preparation caused by the applicant allows suspension of time period in Guidelines, §§ 15107 and 15108.	varies	Guidelines § 15109
Projects with federal involvement	Time limits may be waived or superseded by federal time requirements.	varies	Guidelines § 15110

NOTE: Related time periods for project approval are contained in Chapter 4.5 of the Government Code beginning at section 65920. These generally run concurrently with certain CEQA time periods.

However, if implementation of a mitigation plan cannot reasonably be assured, an agency can find the impact will remain significant and unavoidable. *See Federation of Hillsides & Canyon Ass'ns v. City of Los Angeles*, 126 Cal. App. 4th 1180 (2004) (traffic mitigation within control of other agencies).

The EIR must contain a meaningful discussion of project alternatives.

Project alternatives. The EIR must contain a meaningful discussion of project alternatives. *See Laurel Heights I*, 47 Cal. 3d at 403; Guidelines § 15126.6(a). The number of alternatives required to be analyzed in an EIR is subject to a "rule of reason." Guidelines § 15126.6(f); *Citizens of Goleta Valley v. Board of Supervisors*, 52 Cal. 3d 553, 565–66 (1990) (*Goleta II*). Alternatives that are not reasonable or feasible need not be discussed at length. Guidelines § 15126.6(a); *Village Laguna, Inc. v. Board of Supervisors*, 134 Cal. App. 3d 1022, 1028–29 (1982); *Goleta II*, 52 Cal. 3d at 574. Alternatives that do not offer substantial environmental advantages over the project also can be rejected from consideration. Guidelines § 15126.6. In addition, alternatives that do not accomplish most of the basic objectives of the project can be excluded from the analysis. *See Save Our Residential Env't v. City of W. Hollywood*, 9 Cal. App. 4th 1745, 1752–53 (1992); *but see San Bernardino Valley Audubon Soc'y v. County of San Bernardino*, 155 Cal. App. 3d 738, 750 (1984) (reasonable alternatives must be considered, "even if they substantially impede the project or are more costly"); Guidelines § 15126(d)(1).

The CEQA Guidelines require that a range of reasonable alternatives be considered sufficient to permit a reasonable choice of alternatives so far as environmental aspects are concerned.

Range of alternatives. The courts and CEQA Guidelines require that a "range of reasonable alternatives" be considered. *See Goleta II*, 52 Cal. 3d at 566; *Residents Ad Hoc Stadium Com. v. Board of Trustees*, 89 Cal. App. 3d 274, 287–88 (1979); Guidelines § 15126.6(c). The range must be sufficient "to permit a reasonable choice of alternatives so far as environmental aspects are concerned." *San Bernardino Valley Audubon Soc'y*, 155 Cal. App. 3d at 750–51; Guidelines §§ 15126.6(c), (f). Several cases support the view that not every alternative need be considered (even if it is reasonable) so long as the EIR's range of alternatives is itself reasonable. Numerous variations on the same theme need not be discussed. *See Village Laguna, Inc.*, 134 Cal. App. 3d at 1028–29 (EIR that discussed density alternatives of 7,500, 10,000, 20,000 and 25,000 units was not deficient for failure to discuss intermediate 16,000 unit alternative). The EIR may evaluate "prototypical" alternatives that demonstrate the advantages and disadvantages of a wider range of suggested alternatives. *See Save San Francisco Bay Ass'n v. San Francisco Bay Conserv. and Dev. Comm'n*, 10 Cal. App. 4th 908, 922 (1992).

One of the alternatives studied must be the no-project alternative.

One of the alternatives studied, however, must be the "no project" alternative. Guidelines § 15126.6(e). The no-project analysis should discuss existing conditions as well as what would reasonably be expected to occur in the foreseeable future if the project were not approved, based on current plans and consistent with available infrastructure and community services. Guidelines § 15126.6(e); *but see Planning & Conserv. League v. Dep't of Water Resources*, 83 Cal. App. 4th 892, 913 (2000) (existing water contracts that "plausibly" could be interpreted to require reduced entitlements must be studied as part of the no-project alternative).

Consideration of alternative sites also may be required for both public and private development projects. *See Goleta II*, 52 Cal. 3d at 574–75. Whether alternative sites should be considered depends upon a variety of factors, including site ownership, whether the site is within the lead agency's jurisdiction, and current land use designations in a general plan or local coastal program. *Id.* at 573–75.

If a development project is consistent with an adopted plan, evaluation of off-site alternatives may be unnecessary. *Mira Mar Mobile Cmty v. City of Oceanside*, 119 Cal. App. 4th 477 (2004).

Extent of discussion. The CEQA Guidelines require that an EIR include sufficient information about each alternative "to allow meaningful evaluation, analysis and comparison with the proposed project." Guidelines § 15126.6(d). A matrix may be used to summarize comparisons. Guidelines § 15126.6(d). However, as with the range of alternatives, there are no clear rules regarding the level of detail that must be provided. The extent of the analysis is subject to a rule of reason. *See Goleta II*, 52 Cal. 3d at 565.

The CEQA Guidelines require that an EIR include sufficient information about each alternative to allow meaningful evaluation, analysis and comparison with the proposed project.

Growth inducement. An EIR should discuss the "ways in which the proposed project could foster economic or population growth, or the construction of additional housing, either directly or indirectly, in the surrounding environment." Guidelines § 15126.2(d). This discussion should include projects that could remove obstacles to growth and projects that might facilitate other activities that could significantly affect the environment. If a project will create jobs and bring people into the area, the EIR must discuss the resulting housing needs and, if more housing will be required, its probable location. *Napa Citizens for Honest Gov't v. County of Napa Bd. of Supervisors*, 91 Cal. App. 4th 342 (2001). The CEQA Guidelines caution "It must not be assumed that growth in any area is necessarily beneficial, detrimental, or of little significance to the environment." Guidelines § 15126.2(d); *see also Defend the Bay v. City of Irvine*, 119 Cal. App. 4th 1261 (2004) (upholding city's analysis of jobs-housing balance).

Recirculation of an EIR

Normally, lead agencies are not required to provide an opportunity to review and comment on the final EIR. Guidelines §§ 15088.5(b), (e), 15089(b). However, when significant new information is added to an EIR after notice and consultation have occurred, but prior to certification, the agency must recirculate the final EIR for public comment. Pub. Res. Code § 21092.1. In *Laurel Heights Improvement Association v. Regents of University of California*, (*Laurel Heights II*), the California Supreme Court concluded that recirculation of a final EIR is required in four situations:

When significant new information is added to an EIR after notice and consultation have occurred, but prior to certification, the agency must recirculate the final EIR for public comment.

- When the new information shows a new, substantial environmental impact
- When new information shows a substantial increase in the severity of an environmental impact (unless mitigation measures reduce that impact to insignificance)
- When new information shows a feasible alternative or mitigation measure that clearly would lessen environmental impacts, but it is not adopted
- When the draft EIR was so fundamentally inadequate and conclusory that meaningful public review and comment were precluded

6 Cal. 4th 1112, 1129–30 (1993)

Guidelines section 15088.5(a) reflects *Laurel Heights II* and similarly defines "significant new information" for purposes of determining whether recirculation is required. The analysis of whether new information or project changes trigger a need for recirculation need not appear in the final EIR itself. It is sufficient that the decision not to recirculate the EIR is supported by evidence in the record. *Western Placer Citizens for An Agricultural and Rural Environment*, 144 Cal. App. 4th 890 (2006) (rejecting argument that the final EIR must be revised to include project changes proposed after the final EIR was prepared but prior to certification).

Project Approval and Findings

After the final EIR is complete, the agency determines whether to approve the project. CEQA contains explicit requirements pertaining to approval of projects that have significant environmental impacts. Most importantly, agencies should not approve projects as proposed if there are feasible alternatives or feasible mitigation measures available that would substantially lessen the significant environmental effects of such projects unless (1) the agency finds that changes or alterations have been required in, or incorporated into the project to mitigate significant impacts; (2) such changes are within the responsibility of another agency and have been or can and should be adopted by that agency; or (3) specific economic, social, or other considerations make the mitigation measures or project alternatives identified in the EIR infeasible. Pub. Res. Code §§ 21002, 21081; Guidelines §§ 15091–15094.

CEQA does not, however, provide independent authority to require mitigation measures as project conditions:

> In mitigating or avoiding a significant effect of a project on the environment, a public agency may exercise only those express or implied powers provided by law other than this division. However, a public agency may use discretionary powers provided by such other law for the purpose of mitigating or avoiding a significant effect on the environment subject to the express or implied constraints or limitations that may be provided by law.

Pub. Res. Code § 21004; *see also Sierra Club v. California Coastal Commission*, 35 Cal. 4th 839 (2005) (CEQA does not expand Coastal Commission's authority to consider or require mitigation for impacts that would result from elements of the project outside the coastal zone)

In order to approve a project that would have significant environmental effects after mitigation, the lead agency must adopt findings identifying the specific considerations that make infeasible the environmentally superior alternatives. Pub. Res. Code § 21002.1(b); Guidelines § 15092. Evidence supporting the agency's ultimate findings of the infeasibility of alternatives studied in the EIR can be set forth elsewhere in the record; it need not appear in the EIR itself. *See Sierra Club v. County of Napa*, 121 Cal. App. 4th 1490 (2004); *San Franciscans Upholding the Downtown Plan v. City and County of San Francisco*, 102 Cal. App. 4th 656, 679–80 (2002). However, an applicant's bald claims that an alternative is infeasible is not sufficient to support rejection of the alternative; the lead agency must independently analyze the alternatives to determine their feasibility. *Preservation Action Council v. City of San Jose*, 141 Cal. App. 4th 1336 (2006). *See also Uphold Our Heritage v. Town of Woodside*, 147 Cal. App. 4th 587 (2007) (that applicant refuses to implement an alternative is not relevant; question in evaluating economic feasibility of alternatives is whether the cost of the alternative when compared with the cost of the project is so great that a reasonably prudent property owner would not proceed with the alternative).

CEQA allows agencies to approve projects that damage the environment. If economic, social, or other considerations make it infeasible to mitigate the significant effects of a project on the environment, the project nevertheless may be carried out. Pub. Res. Code § 21002; Guidelines § 15091. In that case, however, the decision-making body must adopt a Statement of Overriding Considerations to the effect that, although adverse impacts may result, specific overriding economic, legal, social, technological, or other considerations outweigh the project's significant, unmitigated impacts. Pub. Res. Code § 21081; Guidelines § 15093. These findings, which are adopted under Public Resources Code sections 21002.1 and 21081, must be supported by substantial evidence in the record. *See Sierra Club v. County of Contra Costa*, 10 Cal. App. 4th 1212, 1223 (1992).

The agency also must include the following provisions in the findings or resolution of approval, in addition to the findings on mitigation measures, alternatives, and overriding considerations as required by Public Resources Code section 21081 and Guidelines sections 15091–15093:

- The lead agency "shall certify" that the EIR has been completed in compliance with CEQA. Guidelines § 15090(a)(1)
- The lead agency "shall certify" that the final EIR "was presented to the decisionmaking body of the lead agency and that the decisionmaking body reviewed and considered the information contained in the final EIR prior to approving the project." Guidelines § 15090(a)(2)
- The lead agency must independently review and analyze the EIR. Pub. Res. Code § 21082.1(c)(1). As part of the certification of the EIR, it must "find that the report…reflects the independent judgment of the lead agency." Pub. Res. Code § 21082.1(c)(3); Guidelines § 15090(a)(3)

The agency must file a notice of determination within five working days after it approves the project. Guidelines § 15094(a). The notice must identify the project and include a brief description of the project, the date when the agency approved the project, the agency's determination whether the project will have a significant effect on the environment, a statement that an EIR was prepared and certified, whether mitigation measures were made a condition of approval of the project, whether findings were made, whether a statement of overriding considerations was adopted, and the address where a copy of the final EIR and the record of project approval may be examined. Guidelines § 15094(a). If a notice of determination is properly filed and posted, then the notice will start a 30-day statute of limitations on court challenges to the approval under CEQA. Guidelines § 15094(f).

Mitigation Monitoring and Reporting Programs

When an agency makes CEQA findings for any project that is approved subject to mitigation measures in an EIR, or when an agency adopts a mitigated negative declaration, the agency must impose a mitigation monitoring or reporting program to ensure implementation of the mitigation measures and project revisions that are required by the agency. Pub. Res. Code § 21081.6. *See also Federation of Hillside & Canyon Ass'ns v. City of Los Angeles*, 83 Cal. App. 4th 1252, 1261 (2000) (an agency must take steps to ensure that mitigation measures will be implemented). This requirement does not apply if the EIR does not recommend any mitigation measures, or if no mitigation measures are imposed. The statute does not require that the monitoring or reporting program be discussed in the EIR or mitigated negative declaration.

Guidelines section 15097(c) provides that "reporting" consists of a written compliance review that is to be submitted to the decision-making body or authorized staff person. The same section provides that "monitoring" is an ongoing periodic process of project oversight. The section explains that reporting is best suited to readily measurable or quantitative mitigation measures and to complex mitigation measures, particularly those to be implemented over a period of time. Monitoring or reporting programs must be "designed to ensure compliance during project implementation." Pub. Res. Code § 21081.6.

Reporting consists of a written compliance review that is to be submitted to the decision-making body or authorized staff person; monitoring is an ongoing periodic process of project oversight.

In *Rio Vista Farm Bureau Center v. County of Solano*, the court upheld a mitigation monitoring program for a countywide hazardous waste management plan. 5 Cal. App. 4th 351 (1992). The court stated that adequacy of a mitigation monitoring program must be assessed in accordance with a "rule of reason" that requires adherence to mitigation that is reasonably feasible. *Id.* at 376. The court upheld the plan in which the county committed to follow all CEQA, state law, and other applicable requirements for managing and disposing of hazardous waste, and described the federal, state, and local agencies that would monitor and report on hazardous waste practices or participate in implementing future projects. *Id.* at 376–77. *See also Christward Ministry v. County of San Diego*, 13 Cal. App. 4th 31, 49 (1993) (upholding a mitigation monitoring program that simply included a time for each measure to be implemented).

CEQA section 21081.6 itself does not give agencies the authority to modify mitigation measures if they later prove inadequate.

CEQA section 21081.6 itself does not give agencies the authority to modify mitigation measures if they later prove inadequate. However, an agency is not forever bound by mitigation measures that it adopts, at least where it is considering a subsequent discretionary approval for the same project or planning area. *See Napa Citizens*, 91 Cal. App. 4th at 375. In recognition that land use plans need to be modified as circumstances change and that "the vision of a region's citizens or its governing body may evolve over time," an agency deleting an earlier-adopted mitigation measure need only state a legitimate reason for deleting the measure and support that statement with substantial evidence. *Id.* at 345–46.

SEIR = Supplemental environmental impact report

Supplemental and Subsequent EIRs

Ordinarily, only one EIR or negative declaration is prepared for a project. Once an EIR has been prepared and a project has been approved, a public agency may not require additional environmental analysis. A supplemental or subsequent EIR (SEIR) may be required only if another discretionary approval for the same project is being considered and (a) there are substantial changes to the project; (b) there are substantial changes in the project's circumstances; or (c) new information that could not have been known at the time the EIR was certified becomes available and such changes or new information require major revisions to the previous EIR or negative declaration due to new significant environmental effects or a substantial increase in the severity of previously identified significant effects. Pub. Res. Code § 21166; Guidelines § 15162(a). *See also Cucamongans United for Reasonable Expansion v. City of Rancho Cucamonga*, 82 Cal. App. 4th 473, 478 (2000) (applying same once around rule to negative declarations).

An SEIR may be required only if there is a need to evaluate new significant environmental impacts that were not evaluated in the EIR for the project.

Project changes standing alone normally will not trigger the SEIR requirements. An SEIR may be required only if there is a need to evaluate new significant environmental impacts that were not evaluated in the EIR for the project. *See Fund for Envtl. Defense v. County of Orange*, 204 Cal. App. 3d 1538, 1544–45 (1988). However, the lead agency must provide a reasoned basis supporting its conclusion that project changes would not result in new or substantially more severe significant impacts. *American Canyon Community United for Responsible Growth v. City of American Canyon*, 145 Cal. App. 4th 1062 (2006) (where agency did not provide a reasoned basis for excluding portions of requested square footage from its analysis, the determination that project changes would not substantially increase traffic effects was not supported by substantial evidence). In addition, a city may be precluded from relying upon a prior mitigated negative declaration where the project at issue is considered to be a new project rather than a modification to a prior project. *Save Our Neighborhood v. Lishman*, 140 Cal. App. 4th 1288 (2006) (rejecting city's attempt to rely on an addendum to a prior mitigated negative declaration where the city initially treated the proposed project as a new project, the project was proposed by a new applicant, and there was no evidence that any of the prior plans and drawings had been re-used); *but see Mani Brothers Real Estate Group v. City of Los Angeles*, 153 Cal. App. 4th 1385, 1399–1400 (2007) (distinguishing *Save Our Neighborhood* on the ground the project originally had been analyzed in a negative declaration rather than in an EIR and criticizing the "new project" test as not providing an objective or useful framework).

Project changes standing alone normally will not trigger the SEIR requirements. An SEIR may be required only if there is a need to evaluate new significant environmental impacts that were not evaluated in the EIR for the project.

New information can trigger an SEIR only if the information was not known and could not have been known at the time the EIR was certified as complete, shows new or substantially more severe significant impacts or demonstrates the feasibility of mitigation measures or alternatives previously found infeasible, and is of substantial importance to the project. Pub. Res. Code § 21166(c); Guidelines § 15162(a)(3).

An agency's decision that an SEIR is not required will be upheld as long as it is supported by substantial evidence in the record. *See Bowman v. City of Petaluma*, 185 Cal. App. 3d 1065, 1071–72 (1986). Therefore, an explanation somewhere in the record as to why an SEIR is not required will assist a court reviewing the agency's determination.

An agency's decision that an SEIR is not required will be upheld as long as it is supported by substantial evidence in the record.

If the agency determines that an SEIR is warranted, it must be prepared and circulated for public review and comment in much the same manner as an original EIR. Guidelines § 15162(d).

Use of an Addendum

If none of the three triggers for an SEIR exist, then an agency may use an addendum to make changes or additions to the prior EIR or negative declaration. Guidelines §§ 15164(a), (b). The addendum does not need to be circulated for public review, but it can be included in the final EIR or adopted negative declaration, and the agency must consider it before making a decision on the project. Guidelines §§ 15164(c), (d). A brief explanation of the decision not to prepare an SEIR should be included in the addendum, the findings, or elsewhere in the record. Guidelines § 15164(e).

If none of the three triggers for an SEIR exist, then an agency may use an addendum to make changes or additions to the prior EIR or negative declaration.

EIR Deadlines and Required Notices

Various deadlines have been established by the Legislature for the EIR process. *See* Figure D (Time Periods for Review of Environmental Documents).

Also, a minimum of three notices must be prepared and properly filed in connection with the EIR. They are as follows:

- Notice of preparation of EIR. Pub. Res. Code § 21080.4; Guidelines § 15082
- Notice of completion of EIR. Pub. Res. Code § 21161; Guidelines § 15085
- Notice of approval or determination, which is filed and posted after the project is approved. Pub. Res. Code § 21152; Guidelines § 15094

Judicial Challenges to Agency Action

Time Limits for Judicial Challenges

> **PRACTICE TIP**
>
> Make sure the notice of determination is filed and posted promptly to get the statute of limitations running.

A 30-day statute of limitations on judicial challenges to a project approval begins to run on the date the notice of determination is filed and posted. Pub. Res. Code §§ 21152(a), (c), 21167(b); Guidelines § 15075(e); *Citizens of Lake Murray Area Ass'n v. City Council*, 129 Cal. App. 3d 436, 440–41 (1982). The notice must include a certification that the final EIR with comments and responses, if one was prepared, is available to the general public. Pub. Res. Code § 21152; *see also* Figure D (Time Periods for Review of Environmental Documents).

Absent the posting of a notice of determination, the statute of limitations to commence a lawsuit generally is 180 days. That period runs from the date of the decision to carry out or approve the project, or, if a project is undertaken without a formal decision, the statute runs from the date of commencement of the project. Pub. Res. Code § 21167(a); Guidelines § 15112(c)(5). However, the date of accrual may depend on the basis for the challenge. For example, in *Concerned Citizens of Costa Mesa, Inc. v. 32nd District Agricultural Association*, the project was substantially changed during construction, long after the EIR had been completed; the lawsuit was filed nearly a year after construction had begun. 42 Cal. 3d 929, 937–38 (1986). The California Supreme Court stated that the public reasonably could expect that the project under construction would be the project described in the EIR, and therefore the failure to file a later EIR concerning the changes expanded the time period so that the lawsuit could be filed within 180 days of the time the plaintiff knew, or should have known, that the project differed substantially from the one for which the EIR was prepared.

Filing additional notices of determination for subsequent discretionary determinations implementing a previously approved project does not reopen the statute of limitations to challenge the original CEQA document. *Citizens for a Megaplex-Free Alameda v. City of Alameda*, 149 Cal. App. 4th 91 (2007).

Judicial Review

For a detailed discussion regarding judicial review of CEQA decisions, *see* chapter 21 (Land Use Litigation).

7

Federal and State Wetland Regulation

Introduction

Traditionally, land use regulation has been primarily a local responsibility. However, two major federal programs have taken on increasing importance over the past two decades. These are the federal wetlands regulatory program under the Clean Water Act (CWA), discussed in this chapter, and federal species protections under the Endangered Species Act (ESA), discussed in chapter 8. The state's role in addressing wetlands and species issues is also discussed.

Wetlands perform important functions such as flood control, erosion protection, and nutrient and pollutant removal. They also provide valuable fish and wildlife habitat, serving as spawning areas for many commercially important fisheries species, as well as playing a vital role in major waterfowl migration routes. In some areas of California, up to 90 percent of the historic wetlands have been lost to agricultural and urban development, leading to a heightened sense of public concern about further incremental losses.

The United States Army Corps of Engineers (Corps) is the federal agency with primary responsibility for regulating activities in wetlands, with the Environmental Protection Agency (EPA) having a more limited role. In California, in addition to the Corps, the State Water Resources Control Board and the nine Regional Water Quality Control Boards are the agencies with the greatest involvement in wetlands regulation. The California Coastal Commission also regulates the development of wetlands in the coastal zone, and other agencies, such as the San Francisco Bay Conservation and Development Commission, regulate wetlands within the geographic areas of their respective jurisdictions.

As often occurs where several agencies regulate a common resource, the various agencies responsible for wetlands regulation do not always agree on key issues, such as the definition of what constitutes a wetland, what role mitigation plays in the regulatory process, and whether particular projects should be allowed to proceed. Frequently, the responsibility for resolving these differences falls on the project proponent, and success in the permitting process may depend on guiding the agencies to a common conclusion. An understanding of their varying viewpoints, and how they have evolved, can be essential to achieving the desired outcome.

CWA = Clean Water Act
ESA = Endangered Species Act
Corps = United States Army Corps of Engineers
EPA = Environmental Protection Agency

The United States Army Corps of Engineers is the federal agency with primary responsibility for regulating activities in wetlands, with the Environmental Protection Agency having a more limited role.

LEDPA = Least Environmentally Damaging Practicable Alternative

This chapter presents an overview of the major aspects of the federal and state wetland regulatory programs. Following a brief history of the federal program, it addresses the legal and scientific considerations that govern what lands constitute wetlands for regulatory purposes. It then presents an overview of the wetlands permitting program, including both nationwide and individual permits. Next is a more detailed discussion of the application of the EPA's 404(b)(1) guidelines, which require that Corps permits be issued only for the "Least Environmentally Damaging Practicable Alternative" (LEDPA), and which have the most direct effect on the land use entitlement process. Federal enforcement mechanisms are also presented. Finally, other programs affecting development in wetlands are summarized.

For further discussion of these issues, *see* Paul D. Cylinder, Kenneth M. Bogdan, April I. Zohn, and Joel B. Butterworth, *Wetlands, Streams, and Other Waters: Regulation, Conservation, and Mitigation Planning* (Solano Press, 2004). *See also* www.epa.gov.owow/wetlands (2007).

A Brief History of the Federal Program

Modern wetlands regulation traces its roots to Sections 9 and 10 of the Rivers and Harbors Act of 1899, pursuant to which the Corps originally regulated streams and rivers to protect interstate commerce in navigable waterbodies.

Modern wetlands regulation traces its roots to Sections 9 and 10 of the Rivers and Harbors Act of 1899 (33 U.S.C. §§ 402–403), under which the Corps originally regulated streams and rivers to protect interstate commerce in navigable waterbodies. Section 9 of the Rivers and Harbors Act requires a permit to construct a dike or dam in navigable waters of the United States. 33 U.S.C. § 402. Section 10 regulates construction of structures or work that could interfere with navigation. Under this section, a permit is needed to build structures in navigable waters such as piers, breakwaters, bulkheads, revetments, power lines, and aids to navigation, as well as to perform activities including dredging, stream channelization, excavation, and filling. 33 U.S.C. § 403.

Initially, the Corps administered the Rivers and Harbors Act to protect only actual navigation and navigable capacity. Beginning in 1968, the Corps began to expand the focus of the program, by adopting regulations establishing a "public interest review standard" for Section 9 and 10 permits. 33 C.F.R. § 209.120. These regulations were upheld in *Zabel v. Tabb*, 430 F.2d 199, 201–02 (5th Cir. 1970), *cert. denied*, 401 U.S. 910 (1971). The regulations expanded the Corps' permit application review from issues related to navigation and navigability to include other factors, such as environmental concerns related to pollution and impacts on fish and wildlife.

In 1972, the Corps continued to shift from a narrow focus on navigation to a broader consideration of environmental values by publishing an expanded administrative definition of navigable waters under the Rivers and Harbors Act. This definition collected and codified key court cases determining federal jurisdiction over navigable waters. The Corps' administrative definition of navigable waters included:

- All waters presently used for commerce. *See Ball v. United States*, 77 U.S. 557 (1870)
- All waters used in the past for interstate commerce. *See Economy Light & Power Co. v. United States*, 256 U.S. 113 (1921)

- All waters susceptible to use in their ordinary condition or with reasonable improvements to transport interstate and foreign commerce. *See United States v. Appalachian Elec. Power Co.*, 311 U.S. 377 (1940)
- All waters subject to the ebb and flow of the tide. *See United States v. Moretti*, 478 F. 2d 418 (5th Cir. 1973)

Thus, despite retaining the term "navigable" in the definition, coverage of the regulatory program expanded beyond traditional concepts of navigability. The Corps maintains essentially the same jurisdictional definition of navigable waters today. 33 C.F.R. § 329.4; 33 C.F.R. Part 329.

It was in this context that Congress passed the Federal Water Pollution Control Act of 1972, commonly known as the Clean Water Act (CWA). The goal of the CWA is to "restore and maintain the chemical, physical, and biological integrity of the Nation's waters." 33 U.S.C. § 1251(a). To meet this objective, Section 301 of the CWA (33 U.S.C. § 1311) prohibits the discharge of any pollutants into navigable waters, except as allowed by permits issued under Sections 402 and 404 of the CWA. 33 U.S.C. §§ 1342, 1344. Section 402 of the CWA establishes the National Pollutant Discharge Elimination System (NPDES) program. Section 404 authorizes the Corps to issue permits for and regulate the discharge of "dredged or fill material[s] into waters of the United States." 33 U.S.C. § 1344.

NPDES = National Pollutant Discharge Elimination System

How "Wetlands" Are Defined Under the CWA

The definition of what constitutes a regulated wetland is often a complex mix of legal, scientific and policy considerations. On the legal front, the evolution of the modern wetland regulatory program out of the Rivers and Harbors Act permitting system has generated much discussion in the cases regarding the relationship of regulated wetlands to traditional concepts of navigability. On the scientific and technical level, detailed protocols have been established for answering the question "how wet is wet?" This line drawing exercise, frequently requiring the assistance of experts, is of critical importance given the emphasis of the permitting program on the amount of acreage of wetlands affected by a project.

The definition of what constitutes a regulated wetland is often a complex mix of legal, scientific and policy considerations.

The Legal Definition of Wetlands

Congress chose in 1972 not to create an entirely new definition of wetlands, but instead defined "navigable waters" in the CWA simply to mean "waters of the United States." 33 U.S.C. § 1362(7). Much of the subsequent—and current—controversy can be traced to the ambiguous legislative intent reflected in this definition. One view is that Congress intended the definition to expand the scope of navigable waters to include all waters subject to jurisdiction under the Commerce Clause of the United States Constitution. However, since Congress retained the term "navigable" and used it throughout the CWA, courts have continued to struggle with the implication that traditional notions of navigability still have a role in the federal regulation of wetlands.

The Corps' initial regulations under the CWA substantially retained the historic consideration of navigability by defining waters of the United States to match the Corps' jurisdiction under the Rivers and Harbors Act. In 1975, a federal district court found this definition to be too narrow, and upheld the

Natural Resources Defense Council's (NRDC) claims that the Corps' Section 404 jurisdiction over "waters of the United States" extended to the maximum extent permissible under the Commerce Clause. *See NRDC v. Callaway*, 392 F. Supp. 685, 686 (D.D.C. 1975).

In response to *NRDC v. Callaway*, in 1977 the Corps adopted regulations that defined waters of the United States to the effective limits of the Commerce Clause. 42 Fed. Reg. 31722 (June 22, 1977). In those regulations, found at 33 C.F.R. Part 328, the term "waters of the United States" is defined to include wetlands, as well as a broad range of other aquatic features. Under the regulations, the Corps' Section 404 jurisdiction extends to:

- All waters that are currently used, or were used in the past, or may be susceptible to use in interstate or foreign commerce, including all waters that are subject to the ebb and flow of the tide
- All interstate waters including interstate wetlands
- All other waters such as intrastate lakes, rivers, streams (including intermittent streams), mud flats, sand flats, wetlands, sloughs, prairie potholes, wet meadows, playa lakes, or natural ponds, the use, degradation, or destruction of which could affect interstate or foreign commerce
- All impoundments of waters otherwise defined
- Tributaries of waters identified in the preceding four bullets
- Territorial seas
- Wetlands adjacent to the waters in the preceding six bullets

33 C.F.R. § 328.3(a)

Under the Corps' regulations, the origin of a wetland—whether it is natural or artificial—is largely irrelevant. An area is treated as a wetland if it has physical wetlands characteristics. *See Leslie Salt Co. v. United States*, 896 F. 2d 354, 357–58 (9th Cir. 1990); *but see United States v. City of Fort Pierre*, 747 F. 2d 464, 465 (8th Cir. 1984) (Corps does not have jurisdiction over wetlands inadvertently created as a result of the Corps' own activity).

In 1985, the United States Supreme Court affirmed the Corps' power to regulate to the limits of the Commerce Clause in *United States v. Riverside Bayview Homes, Inc.*, 474 U.S. 121, 134 (1985). Bolstered by that ruling, during the late 1980s and 1990s the Corps adopted an ever expanding view of regulated wetlands, taking the position that Section 404 jurisdiction extends to waters and wetlands that are neither physically navigable nor connected in any way to navigable waters, so long as they provide habitat for migratory birds. The underlying legal theory was that hunting and bird watching are activities of interstate commerce. 51 Fed. Reg. 41216 (Nov. 13, 1986). This position, known as the "migratory bird rule," was upheld by several federal courts. *See Leslie Salt Co. v. United States*, 896 F. 2d at 360; *Hoffman Homes, Inc. v. U.S. EPA*, 999 F. 2d 256, 261–62 (7th Cir. 1993).

In 2001, the United States Supreme Court reined in the Corps' expansive approach. *Solid Waste Agency of Northern Cook County (SWANCC) v. U.S. Army Corps of Eng'rs*, 531 U.S. 159 (2001). The *SWANCC* case involved a proposed solid waste disposal operation on the site of a former sand and gravel pit mine. The site contained numerous seasonal and permanent ponds, which were neither connected nor adjacent to any navigable waters—rather, they were "isolated"

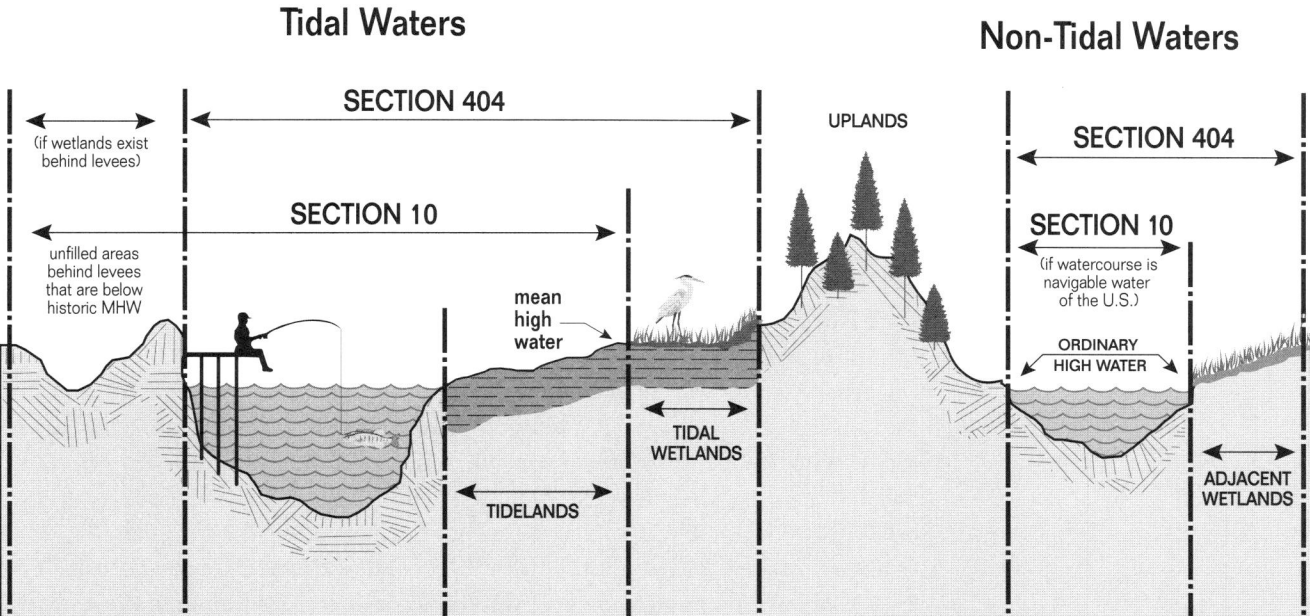

**Figure E
Scope of Corps Regulatory Jurisdiction**

Source: U.S. Army Corps of Engineers

waters. The Corps determined that the ponds were "waters of the United States" because they were periodically used by migratory birds. The project proponent challenged the Corps' jurisdiction over the site. The challenge failed before the district court and the Seventh Circuit, but found a more receptive audience at the Supreme Court.

The high court opinion begins back where the CWA started—with the definition of "navigable waters." The Court concluded, by a slim 5–4 majority, that the migratory bird rule did not fit within this definition because it stretched the concepts of navigability too far. The Court therefore invalidated the migratory bird rule and determined that the Corps lacked jurisdiction over isolated ponds at the pit mine. In distinguishing its earlier decision in *Riverside Bayview*, the Court explained that the wetlands at issue in that case were adjacent to, and therefore had a "significant nexus" to, navigable waters, whereas in *SWANCC* the ponds were isolated from any navigable waters. *Id.* at 167–68, 171–72. In holding that the migratory bird rule was inconsistent with the CWA's definition of navigable waters, the Court avoided the broader constitutional question of whether the rule violated the Commerce Clause. *Id.* at 174.

In January 2003, the Corps and the EPA published joint guidance concerning the scope of federal wetlands jurisdiction in light of *SWANCC*. 68 Fed. Reg. 1995 (Jan. 15, 2003). The guidance makes clear that the Corps now lacks the authority to regulate isolated, intrastate, non-navigable waters where the sole basis of jurisdiction is the use of those waters by migratory birds. The guidance further instructs Corps field staff to seek formal, project-specific approval from the Corps' headquarters in Washington, D.C. (the "phone home" rule) before asserting jurisdiction over such isolated waters on any *other* grounds (*e.g.*, recreational use by interstate or foreign travelers or industrial uses in interstate commerce, *see* 33 C.F.R. § 328.3(a)(3)).

Subsequent court decisions have provided inconsistent guidance on how to interpret the Supreme Court's decision in SWANCC.

Subsequent court decisions have provided inconsistent guidance on how to interpret the Supreme Court's decision in *SWANCC*. For example, the Fifth Circuit viewed *SWANCC* broadly, and held that a seasonal, intermittent stream did not constitute a "navigable water." *See Rice v. Harken Exploration Co.*, 250 F. 3d 264, 271 (5th Cir. 2001). The Sixth Circuit, on the other hand, ruled that *SWANCC* should be given narrow effect, and only operated to void the migratory bird rule. *See United States v. Rapanos*, 339 F. 3d 447 (6th Cir. 2003), *cert. denied*, 541 U.S. 972 (2004). The Ninth Circuit held that a connection to navigable waters can be maintained by intermittent flows in an irrigation canal. *See Headwaters, Inc. v. Talent Irr. Dist.*, 243 F. 3d 526 (9th Cir. 2001).

A fractured 4-1-4 decision of the Supreme Court in June 2006 failed to resolve these differences or otherwise clarify the line between jurisdictional and non-jurisdictional waters. *Rapanos v. United States*, 126 S. Ct. 2208 (2006). The Court was reviewing two decisions by the Sixth Circuit that had upheld the Corps' assertion of jurisdiction over wetlands remote and physically separated from navigable bodies of water. The first case, *United States v. Rapanos*, 376 F. 3d 629 (6th Cir. 2004), involved an enforcement action brought against a landowner who had filled wetlands to build a mall without a Corps permit. The wetland property was adjacent to a ditch that drained into a river and eventually to a lake. The second case, *Carabell v. U.S. Army Corps of Engineers*, 391 F. 3d 704 (6th Cir. 2004), centered on whether a Corps permit is required to fill wetlands separated by a manmade berm from a drainage ditch that led to a river. The landowner wanted to fill the wetlands to build condominiums, and sued after regulators denied the permit. In both cases, the Corps asserted jurisdiction over the wetlands because of their proximity to "tributary" ditches that eventually drained into navigable waters.

In voting to overturn the Sixth Circuit, the four most conservative members of the Court, in an opinion authored by Justice Scalia, opined that the Corps' previously broad jurisdictional approach to wetlands regulation should be severely curtailed. Justice Scalia's opinion reasoned that only bodies of water with a "continuous surface connection" to navigable waters should fall under the CWA's aegis.

In a separate opinion, Justice Kennedy joined the conservative members' decision to reverse the lower court, but on much narrower grounds, leaving intact much of the Corps' previously broad jurisdiction to regulate wetlands not directly adjacent and connected to navigable waters. In rejecting the conservative members' narrow view of the Corps' jurisdiction as inconsistent with the CWA, Justice Kennedy opined that regulators instead should focus on whether the wetlands at issue possess a "significant nexus" to currently or conceivably navigable waters. This fact-based inquiry requires consideration of hydrologic and ecological factors, based upon a determination of whether the wetlands may "significantly affect the chemical, physical and biological integrity of other covered waters more readily understood as 'navigable.'"

In another opinion, the four dissenting and more liberal justices would have simply upheld the lower court's decision and the Corps' historically expansive reach.

The decisions applying *Rapanos* have borne out Justice Roberts' prediction that "[l]ower courts and regulated entities will now have to feel their way on a case-by-case basis." 126 S.Ct. at 2236. In the first case to interpret *Rapanos*, a district court in Texas declined to follow Justice Kennedy's significant nexus test, emphasizing the lack of a consensus in *Rapanos*. Instead, the court generally followed Justice Scalia's approach in holding that an oil spill into a dry intermittent streambed that never reached a navigable-in-fact water did not violate the CWA. *United States v. Chevron Pipe Line Co.*, 473 F. Supp. 2d 605 (D. Tex. 2006).

In contrast, the Seventh Circuit, in remanding a wetlands case to the district court for further fact-finding, decided that Justice Kennedy's opinion was controlling. *United States v. Gerke Excavating*, 464 F. 3d 723 (7th Cir. 2006). Relying on *Gerke*, the Ninth Circuit also adopted Justice Kennedy's test in holding that a discharge to ponds adjacent to the navigable Russian River required a CWA permit. *Northern California River Watch v. City of Healdsburg*, 496 F. 3d 993 (9th Cir. 2007). The court emphasized that the pond water seeps into the river through both surface wetlands and an underground aquifer, thus establishing a significant nexus to the river. In another case, however, the Ninth Circuit determined that a non-navigable pond adjacent to a navigable slough was not subject to CWA jurisdiction because it was not a wetland. *San Francisco Baykeeper v. Cargill Salt Division*, 481 F. 3d 700 (9th Cir. 2007). The court reasoned that while *wetlands* adjacent to navigable waters fell under the CWA's coverage, other adjacent waters did not. The court similarly reasoned that Justice Kennedy's significant nexus test applied only to wetlands, and not to other waterbodies that failed to qualify as wetlands.

Meanwhile, the First Circuit has adopted yet another approach in the wake of *Rapanos*: in remanding a wetlands case to the district court for further proceedings, it rejected the reasoning in both *Chevron Pipe* and *Gerke*, stating that federal jurisdiction exists if *either* Justice Scalia's test ("continuous surface connection") *or* Justice Kennedy's test ("significant nexus") is satisfied. *United States v. Johnson*, 467 F. 3d 56 (1st Cir. 2006). The *Johnson* decision is notable for its lengthy analysis simply to determine which of the opinions in *Rapanos* has the force of law.

In June 2007, the Corps and EPA adopted joint guidance attempting to coalesce the competing tests in *Rapanos* and clarify federal wetlands jurisdiction.[1] Unfortunately, the guidance does little to resolve the significant uncertainties created by *Rapanos*.

The guidance establishes a two-tired approach, under which the Corps will categorically assert jurisdiction over some waters, and will apply the significant nexus on a case-by-case basis for other waters to determine whether jurisdiction exists. Under the guidance, the Corps will categorically assert jurisdiction over the following waters:

- **Traditional Navigable Waters:** These are waters that are "currently used, or were used in the past, or may be susceptible to use in interstate or foreign commerce, including all waters which are subject to the ebb and flow of the tide."

---

1. The guidance and accompanying documents are available on EPA's website at www.epa.gov/owow/wetlands/guidance/CWAwaters.html.

- **Wetlands "Adjacent" to Traditional Navigable Waters**: "Adjacent" means "bordering, contiguous, or neighboring." The guidance explains that wetlands need not have a "continuous surface connection" to be "adjacent," since only four justices in *Rapanos* endorsed this restrictive view.

- **Relatively Permanent Non-navigable Tributaries of Traditional Navigable Waters**: These are non-navigable water bodies with continuous flow, at least seasonally (typically three months), whose waters flow into a traditional navigable water.

- **Wetlands Directly Abutting Relatively Permanent Non-navigable Tributaries**: These wetlands have a continuous surface connection to a relatively permanent non-navigable tributary (*e.g.*, they are not separated by uplands or by a berm, dike, or similar feature).

For other tributaries and wetlands, the Corps will assert jurisdiction only after making a case-specific determination that there is a significant nexus to navigable waters, in accordance with Justice Kennedy's test. This fact-specific approach applies to the following waters:

- Non-navigable tributaries that are not relatively permanent
- Wetlands adjacent to non-navigable tributaries that are not relatively permanent
- Wetlands adjacent to, but not directly abutting, a relatively permanent non-navigable tributary

The guidance explains that determining whether a significant nexus exists requires consideration of hydrologic and ecological factors to assess the tributary's contribution to "restoring and maintaining the chemical, physical and biological integrity of the Nation's traditional navigable waters." In making this assessment, the Corps will consider the volume, duration and frequency of the flow of water in the tributary, and the proximity of the tributary to the navigable water, as well as the ecological relationship between the tributary and any adjacent wetlands. Other relevant factors include the extent to which the tributary and any adjacent wetlands affect the pollutant levels and water quality of downstream navigable waters, or provide nutrients and habitats for species in such waters. The guidance does not specify how these different considerations should be weighed, stating only that the effect on navigable waters must be "more than speculative or insubstantial" for a significant nexus to exist. Finally, the guidance explains that swales, erosional features such as gullies, and upland ditches generally will not qualify as jurisdictional waters.

The guidance attempts to bring "certainty and consistency" to jurisdictional determinations, but it fails to provide clear, objective factors that the public can rely on in attempting to answer the key question posed by Justice Kennedy's opinion: what constitutes a significant nexus to navigable waters to support the Corps' assertion of jurisdiction over wetlands? As the question-and-answer document accompanying the guidance explains, "it is likely that legal challenges to the scope of CWA jurisdiction will continue."

The status of federal wetlands jurisdiction in the wake of the *SWANCC* and *Rapanos* decisions is being closely monitored by the State Water Resources Control Board (SWRCB), which has asserted that isolated wetlands remain subject to state regulation under the Porter-Cologne Act (Water Code § 13000 et seq.).[2] In order to moderate the permitting burden that could have resulted from this position, on May 4, 2004, the SWRCB issued a statewide general permit for discharges to waters deemed by the Corps to be outside of federal jurisdiction. SWRCB, Order No. 2004-0004-DWQ (available at www.swrcb.ca.gov/resdec/wqorders/2004/wqo/wqo2004-0004.pdf). This general permit authorizes fills to isolated wetlands of not more than two-tenths of an acre in area, affecting no more than 400 linear feet of waters of the state, and involving dredging of no more than 50 cubic yards within waters of the state. Coverage under the general permit is obtained through the filing of a notice of intent. For larger fills to isolated wetlands, the SWRCB has asserted that individual waste discharge requirements must be obtained.

The SWRCB also has launched a program to develop a statewide "wetland and riparian area protection policy."[3] The SWRCB has explained that such a policy is needed to address the lack of clarity in the existing regulatory framework due to recent cases limiting the extent of federal wetlands jurisdiction, as well as the lack of statewide consistency in defining wetlands and evaluating impacts to wetlands functions. One of the options the SWRCB is considering is to regulate wetlands in the same manner as the Corps, but without the jurisdictional restrictions established by *SWANCC* and *Rapanos*. But the SWRCB is also considering another option that would go much further, by regulating not just the filling of wetlands, but any activities that could adversely affect wetlands or riparian areas—including, for example, clearing of vegetation or actions that increase the potential for invasive species.

In addition to this statewide policy effort by the SWRCB, the Regional Water Quality Control Boards for the San Francisco Bay and North Coast regions are in the process of formulating new regulatory protections for streams and wetlands. This effort will likely culminate in established methodologies (and perhaps even specific measures) for mitigating impacts to wetlands resulting from development. For more information, see www.waterboards.ca.gov/rwqcb2/streamandwetlands.htm and www.waterboards.ca.gov/northcoast/programs/basinplan/swspp.html.

Thus, the restrictions established by the Supreme Court on federal wetlands jurisdiction have generated increased efforts in California at the state and regional level not only to fill the gap but to increase the breadth and types of protections afforded to wetlands and other waters.

The Scientific/Technical Definition of Wetlands

The legal considerations outlined above merely set the stage for asking the frequently difficult question: what is the "point at which water ends and land

---

2. *See* January 25, 2001 Memorandum from SWRCB Chief Counsel Craig Wilson, Effect of *SWANCC v. United States* on the 401 Certification Program (available at www.swrcb.ca.gov/cwa401/docs/stateregulation_memorandum.pdf).
3. *See* SWRCB, March 2007 Informational Document, *Public Scoping Meeting for Proposed Wetland and Riparian Area Protection Policy* (available at www.swrcb.ca.gov/cwa401/docs/wrapp/info_doc.pdf).

begins?" *Riverside Bayview Homes*, 474 U.S. at 132. The Supreme Court has recognized that:

> Our common experience tells us that this is often no easy task: the transition from water to solid ground is not necessarily or even typically an abrupt one. Rather, between open waters and dry land may lie shallows, marshes, mudflats, swamps, bogs—in short, a huge array of areas that are not wholly aquatic but nevertheless fall far short of being dry land. Where on this continuum to find the limit of "waters" is far from obvious.

Id.

The Corps' regulations governing this determination define wetlands as:

> Those areas that are inundated or saturated by surface or ground water at a frequency and duration sufficient to support, and under normal circumstances do support, a prevalence of vegetation typically adapted for life in saturated soil conditions. Wetlands generally include swamps, marshes, bogs, and similar areas.

33 C.F.R. § 328.3(b)

Although the regulatory definition is simple, the field identification of wetlands can be quite complicated.

Although this regulatory definition is simple, the field identification of wetlands can be quite complicated. For this reason, the Corps has developed a series of technical manuals to provide guidance on determining what constitutes a jurisdictional wetland. Generally, these manuals use a three-part approach to define wetlands by the presence of:

- Permanent or periodic soil saturation or inundation (wetlands hydrology)
- Soils that exhibit anaerobic conditions in the upper part of the soils (hydric soils)
- Plants that grow in soils that are deficient in oxygen (hydrophytic vegetation)

Three major versions of the Corps' wetlands delineation manual were published in 1987, 1989, and 1991, respectively. All three versions follow the general three-part approach evaluating hydrology, soils, and vegetation, but differ in the details of their implementation (such as the number of days of inundation that are required before the hydrology is deemed to be wet). However, controversy surrounding the 1989 Manual led Congress to suspend its use until a 1991 version could be adopted. In the meantime, Congress directed that the 1987 manual be used on an "interim" basis. *See* Energy and Water Development Appropriations Act of 1992 (H.R. 2427). But the 1991 Manual only was proposed for public comment, and never was finalized. As a result of this history, the "interim" period has continued to the present, and the 1987 Manual is still in use.

The Corps is currently developing supplements to the 1987 Manual to address conditions that are specific to different regions of the country.

The Corps is currently developing supplements to the 1987 Manual to address conditions that are specific to different regions of the country. These "Regional Supplements" (available at **www.usace.army.mil/cw/cecwo/reg/reg_supp.htm**) are designed to address various situations that pose problems for delineating wetlands, such as soils with faint or no wetlands indicators or wetlands that periodically lack the requisite hydrology. The appropriate Regional Supplement is to be used in conjunction with the 1987 Manual, and where there are differences between the two documents, the Regional Supplement governs.

The Fourth Circuit, in discussing the legal status of the Corps' manuals, accepted the agency's description of the manuals as "technical guidance document[s]" reflecting only "internal procedures for agency field staff for identifying and delineating wetlands." *United States v. Ellen*, 961 F. 2d 462, 465–66 (4th Cir. 1992). Since the Corps' manuals were not promulgated through formal notice and comment rulemaking procedures, they are considered interpretative rather than legislative in nature, and do not have the status of regulations.

The 1987 Manual defines wetland vegetation as vegetation that, due to morphological, physiological, and/or reproductive adaptation(s), has the ability to grow, effectively compete, reproduce, and/or persist in aerobic soil conditions. The National List of Plant Species That Occur in Wetlands classifies approximately 7,000 plants into four categories of wetland indicator status:

- Obligate wetland plants that almost always occur in wetlands (greater than 99 percent of the time)
- Facultative wetland plants that usually occur in wetlands (67 percent to 99 percent of the time)
- Facultative plants that are equally likely to occur in wetlands or non-wetlands (34 percent to 66 percent of the time)
- Facultative upland plants that usually occur in non-wetlands but occasionally are found in wetlands (1 percent to 33 percent of the time)

To apply the hydrophytic vegetation criteria to a particular area, plant surveys must be performed and statistical formulas applied to determine whether the plant community as a whole is hydrophytic.

The 1987 Manual defines wetlands soils as soils classified as hydric or possessing characteristics associated with reducing soil conditions. The Natural Resources Conservation Service (NRCS) maintains national lists of hydric soils on soil maps; however, field investigation by soil scientists is needed to verify the mapping. The Manual provides examples of various field indicators of hydric soils.

The 1987 Manual defines an area as having wetlands hydrology when it is saturated to the surface or inundated at some point in time during the growing season of the prevalent vegetation, or is permanently inundated at depths of less than 6.0 feet. Hydrology can be determined from recorded data, aerial photographs, or field indicators. Field indicators include visual evidence of flooding, water marks, scoured areas, and plant adaptations.

Due to the scientific and technical expertise required by the 1987 Manual, most wetlands delineations are performed by biologists or other specialists hired by a developer or landowner and are presented to the Corps for review and approval. Generally, once a delineation has been accepted by the Corps, it remains valid for a period of two years. *See* Regulatory Guidance Letter No. 90-6, Aug. 14, 1990; 56 Fed. Reg. 2408 (January 22, 1991). However, individual districts may specify a longer period. For example, the San Francisco District generally certifies its delineations for five years.

The Corps recently adopted nationwide guidance for making, documenting, and approving jurisdictional determinations. *See* Regulatory Guidance Letter No. 07-01 (June 5, 2007). There is also an established administrative process for obtaining formal review of the Corps' jurisdictional determinations and permit denials. *See* 65 Fed. Reg. 16486 (March 28, 2000), codified at 33 C.F.R. Part 331.

Activities Regulated by the Corps

Under Section 404, the Corps is authorized to regulate placing "dredged materials" and "fill" into waters of the United States.

Under Section 404 of the CWA, the Corps is authorized to regulate placing "dredged materials" and "fill" into waters of the United States. Under definitions revised in 2002, the "discharge of dredged material" means adding into waters of the United States materials removed (dredged or excavated) from waters of the United States, including redeposit of dredged material other than incidental fallback. 33 C.F.R. § 323.3(c). The "discharge of fill material" means adding any material into the waters of the United States that has the effect of replacing any portion of the water of the United States with dry land, or that changes the bottom elevation of a water of the United States. 33 C.F.R. § 323.2(f).

The Corps issues permits for seven general classes of discharge of dredged and fill materials. These activities are listed in 33 C.F.R. section 320.1(b) and consist of the following:

- Dams or dikes in navigable waters of the United States (regulated in 33 C.F.R. § 321)
- Other structures or work including excavation, dredging, and/or disposal activities in navigable waters of the United States (regulated in 33 C.F.R. § 322)
- Activities that alter or modify the course, condition, location, or capacity of a navigable water of the United States (regulated in 33 C.F.R. § 322)
- Construction of artificial islands, installations, or other devices on the outer-continental shelf (regulated in 33 C.F.R. § 322)
- Discharges of dredged or fill material into waters of the United States (regulated in 33 C.F.R. § 323)
- Activities involving the transportation of dredged material for the purpose of disposal in ocean waters (regulated in 33 C.F.R. § 324)
- Nationwide general permits for certain categories of activities (described in 33 C.F.R. § 330)

Dredging a wetlands—as opposed to discharging dredged material into a wetlands—is not directly regulated under Section 404 of the CWA.

Dredging a wetlands—as opposed to *discharging* dredged material into a wetlands—is not directly regulated under Section 404 of the CWA. But an early court decision established that the term "discharge" could reasonably be construed to include the redeposition of soils dredged from a wetland by mechanized land-clearing activities. *See Avoyelles Sportsmen's League, Inc. v. Marsh*, 715 F. 2d 897, 923–24 (5th Cir. 1983); Regulatory Guidance Letter 90-5 (July 18, 1990). In 1993, in a significant departure from prior practice, the Corps adopted a rule requiring a permit for *any* such redeposit of soils. 58 Fed. Reg. 45008, 45035 (Aug. 25, 1993). The D.C. Circuit, however, invalidated the regulations, concluding that the definition of discharge "cannot reasonably be said to encompass the situation in which material is removed from the waters of the United States and a small portion of it happens to fall back." *National Mining Ass'n v. U.S. Army Corps of Eng'rs*, 145 F. 3d 1399, 1404 (D.C. Cir. 1998). The Court reasoned that because incidental fallback represents a net withdrawal, not an addition, of material into the wetland, it is not a discharge that can be regulated under the CWA.

In response, the Corps adopted a revised rule in 2001, which provided an exemption for "incidental fallback," defined as "the redeposit of small volumes of dredged material that is incidental to excavation activity in waters of the

United States when such material falls back to substantially the same place as the initial removal." 66 Fed. Reg. 4550 (Jan. 17, 2001). This revised rule, however, suffered the same fate as the 1993 rule. In January 2007, a district court struck down the Corps' definition of "incidental fallback," concluding that the volume of material being redeposited was irrelevant. *Nat' Ass'n of Home Builders v. U.S. Army Corps of Eng'rs.* Not Reported in F. Supp. 2d, 64 ERC 2050, 2007 U.S. Dist. LEXIS 6366 (D.D.C. Jan. 30, 2007). According to the court, the difference between incidental fallback and redeposit is best understood in terms of the time the material is held before being dropped to the earth and the distance between the place where the material is collected and the place where it is dropped. Because the Corps' definition did not address the timing issue and imposed an improper volume requirement, it was invalid.

Statutory Exemptions

The Corps does not have regulatory authority over all discharges of dredged or fill materials into waters of the United States. Six classes of discharges, which would otherwise be subject to Section 404, are exempted from regulation under the CWA. 33 U.S.C. § 1344(f). These exemptions are intended to avoid regulation of ordinary or minor actions, or to implement political compromises in the passage of the CWA. The exemptions include:

Six classes of discharges, which would otherwise be subject to Section 404, are exempted from regulation under the CWA.

- Normal farming, silviculture, and ranching activities, such as plowing, seeding, cultivating, minor drainage, harvesting for the production of food, fiber, and forest products, and upland soil and water conservation practices
- Maintenance, including emergency reconstruction of recently damaged parts of currently serviceable structures, such as dikes, dams, levees, groins, riprap, breakwaters, causeways, and bridge abutments or approaches and transportation structures
- Construction or maintenance of farm or stock ponds or irrigation ditches, or the maintenance of drainage ditches[4]
- Construction of temporary sedimentation basins on a construction site that does not include placement of fill materials into navigable waters
- Construction or maintenance of farm roads or forest roads, or temporary roads for moving mining equipment, where such roads are constructed and maintained in accordance with best management practices to assure that flow and circulation patterns and chemical and biological characteristics of the navigable waters are not impaired, that the reach of the navigable waters is not reduced, and that any adverse effect on the aquatic environment will be otherwise minimized
- Any activities for which a state administers an approved program for dredged or fill materials

33 U.S.C. § 1344(f); 33 C.F.R. § 323.4

These exemptions do not apply where the purpose of the discharge is to bring an area of navigable waters into a use to which it was not previously subject, or

---

4. In July 2007, the Corps issued detailed guidance on how to apply this statutory exemption with respect to the construction and maintenance of ditches. Regulatory Guidance Letter No. 07-02 (July 4, 2007).

where the discharge may impair the flow or circulation of navigable waters or reduce the reach of such waters. 33 U.S.C. § 1344(f)(2). As a result of this "recapture" provision, the "normal farming" exemption does not apply to deep ripping of soil for the purpose of converting ranch land to orchards and vineyards (*i.e.*, a different use). *See Borden Ranch P'ship v. U.S. Army Corps of Eng'rs*, 261 F. 3d 810, 815–16 (9th Cir. 2001), *judgment aff'd*, 537 U.S. 99 (2002). Similarly, the silviculture exemption does not apply to timber clearing that converts wetlands to non-wetland uses. *See United States v. Larkins*, 852 F. 2d 189, 192–93 (6th Cir. 1988).

The Corps' Permitting Process

Section 404 gives the Corps authority over the discharge of dredged or fill material into wetlands and other waters of the United States, and allows the Corps to issue permits for these activities.

Section 404 gives the Corps authority over the discharge of dredged or fill material into wetlands and other waters of the United States, and allows the Corps to issue permits for these activities. This regulatory authority is shared with the EPA, which also has authority to determine the scope of Section 404 jurisdiction over waters of the United States. In addition, the Corps must follow EPA-promulgated guidelines when reviewing Section 404 permit applications to determine whether the discharge of dredged or fill materials can be permitted. 40 C.F.R. Part 230. The EPA also has the authority to "veto" a Corps decision to issue a permit. 33 U.S.C. § 1344(c). Finally, the EPA can prohibit a discharge in certain areas even before a permit is filed where the result would cause an "unacceptable adverse effect" on municipal water supplies, shellfish beds or spawning areas, wildlife, or recreational areas. The EPA's role in the permitting process is discussed later in this chapter.

The Corps issues both "general" and "individual" permits. Individual permits are for specific projects following review of an individual application, while general permits are available for a listed category of activities in specific geographic regions or nationwide. General permits typically cover activities that involve only minimal impacts to aquatic resources.

Nationwide Permits

NWPs have been issued for a wide array of different activities involving discharges into waters of the United States. They are intended to allow dredging or filling to occur with little or no delay or paperwork.

Nationwide permits (NWPs) are the most important type of general permit involving wetlands. 33 C.F.R. § 320.1(c). They cover discrete classes of activities and are applicable throughout the nation (hence their name). NWPs have been issued for a wide array of different activities involving discharges into waters of the United States. They are intended to allow dredging or filling to occur with little or no delay or paperwork. 33 C.F.R. § 330.1; *see also Orleans Audubon Soc'y v. Lee*, 742 F. 2d 901, 904–05 (5th Cir. 1984). The regulations governing NWPs are codified at 33 C.F.R. Part 330.

NWP = Nationwide permit

In March 2007, the Corps reissued all of the existing NWPs, with a few revisions, and it issued six new NWPs (NWPs 45, 46, 57, 48, 49 and 50). 72 Fed. Reg. 11092 (March 12, 2007). The Corps also modified the general conditions that must be met to qualify for NWP coverage, which include requirements for when permittees must submit a pre-construction notification (PCN) to the Corps.

The existing NWPs are briefly summarized below. Details can be found in the March 12, 2007 issue of the Federal Register, or on the Corps' website (www.usace.army.mil/cw/cecwo/reg/nationwide_permits.htm).

Nationwide Permits

No.	Activity	No.	Activity
1	Aids to navigation*	26	Reserved
2	Structures in artificial canals within principally residential communities where the connection to navigable water has been previously approved	27	Wetland and riparian restoration and creation activities
		28	Modifications of existing marinas*
3	Maintenance activities	29	Single-family housing*
4	Fish and wildlife harvesting, enhancement, and attraction devices and activities*	30	Moist soil management for wildlife*
		31	Maintenance of existing flood control facilities
5	Scientific measurement devices*	32	Completed enforcement actions*
6	Survey activities, including core sampling and seismic exploratory activities*	33	Temporary construction, access, and dewatering
		34	Cranberry production activities*
7	Outfall structures	35	Maintenance dredging at existing basins
8	Oil and gas structures		
9	Structures in fleeting and anchorage areas*	36	Boat ramps*
		37	Emergency watershed protection and rehabilitation
10	Mooring buoys*		
11	Temporary recreational structures*	38	Cleanup of hazardous and toxic waste*
12	Utility line discharges	39	Residential, commercial, and institutional developments
13	Bank stabilization		
14	Linear transportation projects	40	Agricultural activities
15	U.S. Coast Guard-approved bridges	41	Reshaping existing drainage ditches
16	Return water from upland, contained disposal areas	42	Recreational facilities
		43	Stormwater management facilities
17	Hydro-power projects	44	Mining activities
18	Minor discharges	45	Repair of uplands damaged by discrete events
19	Minor dredging		
20	Oil spill cleanup*	46	Discharges in ditches
21	Surface coal mining activities	47	Pipeline safety program designated time sensitive inspections and repairs
22	Removal of vessels*		
23	Approved categorical exclusions	48	Existing commercial shellfish aquaculture activities
24	State-administered Section 404 programs*		
		49	Coal remining activities
25	Structural discharges	50	Underground coal mining activities

* Those NWPs with an asterisk have received Section 401 water quality certification from the SWRCB (see www.swrcb.ca.gov/cwa401/docs/generalorders/nwp2007rev.pdf). For the other NWPs, an individual certification must be obtained before permit coverage is effective.

As discussed above, to qualify for a particular NWP, an activity must comply with a series of general conditions. Many Corps district offices also impose additional regional conditions. The conditions are safeguards to ensure that an otherwise minor action does not cause unacceptable environmental impacts. The general conditions are summarized below:

1. No activity may cause more than a minimal adverse effect on navigation.
2. No activity may substantially disrupt the movement of aquatic species indigenous to the waterbody, including species that normally migrate through the area, unless the activity's primary purpose is to impound water.
3. Activities in spawning areas must be avoided during the spawning season to the maximum extent practicable. Destruction of important spawning areas is prohibited.
4. Activities in waters of the United States that serve as breeding areas for migratory waterfowl must be avoided to the maximum extent practicable.
5. Discharges of dredged or fill material in areas of concentrated shellfish populations are generally prohibited.
6. Discharges of dredged or fill material may not consist of unsuitable material or contain toxic pollutants in toxic amounts.
7. No discharge may occur in the proximity of a public water supply intake, unless the activity is for the repair or improvement of the intake or for adjacent bank stabilization.
8. Adverse effects on the aquatic system from accelerating or restricting water flows must be minimized to the maximum extent practicable.
9. The pre-construction course, condition, capacity, location, and flow of the waterbody generally must be maintained as is to the maximum extent practicable.
10. Fills within a 100-year floodplain must comply with FEMA-approved state or local floodplain management requirements.
11. Heavy equipment working in wetlands must be placed on mats or other measures must be taken to minimize soil disturbance.
12. Appropriate soil erosion and sediment controls must be used and maintained during construction, and all exposed soils and other fills must be permanently stabilized at the earliest practicable date.
13. Any temporary fills must be removed in their entirety and the affected areas revegetated and returned to the pre-construction elevation.
14. Any structure or fill must be properly maintained, including to ensure public safety.
15. Activities within the National Wild and Scenic River System (or in a river officially designated by Congress as a "study river" for possible inclusion in the system) are generally prohibited.
16. No activity or its operation may impair reserved tribal rights, including reserved water rights and treaty fishing and hunting rights.
17. No activity is authorized under any NWP that is likely to jeopardize the continued existence of a threatened or endangered species or a species proposed for such designation, or that is likely to destroy or adversely modify the critical habitat of such species. Non-federal permittees must notify the District Engineer if any listed species or critical habitat might be affected or is in the vicinity of the project, and shall not begin work on the activity until notified by the District Engineer that the ESA's requirements have

been satisfied and that the activity is authorized. An NWP does not authorize the "take" of a listed species.

18. No activity that may affect historic properties listed or eligible for listing in the National Register of Historic Places is authorized, until the District Engineer has complied with the provisions of 33 C.F.R. Part 325, Appendix C. The permittee must notify the District Engineer if the authorized activity may affect any historic properties that are listed, that are determined to be eligible for listing, or that the prospective permittee has reason to believe may be eligible for listing on the National Register of Historic Places. The permittee may not begin the activity until notified by the District Engineer that the requirements of the National Historic Preservation Act have been satisfied and that the activity is authorized.

19. For certain NWPs, discharges to "critical resource waters" (defined to include critical habitat for federally listed species, marine sanctuaries, and other sensitive areas) are prohibited.

20. General Condition No. 20 establishes detailed requirements for mitigation of impacts to wetlands and other waters of the United States. The activity must be designed and constructed to avoid and minimize adverse effects to the maximum extent practicable. If impacts cannot be avoided and if a pre-construction notification (PCN) is required (*see* No. 27 below), compensatory mitigation (*e.g.*, wetlands restoration) is generally required at a minimum 1:1 ratio to make up for any wetland losses exceeding 1/10 acre. When proceeding under an NWP, compensatory mitigation may not be used to increase the loss of wetlands acreage over the acreage limitation established by that NWP.

PCN = Pre-construction notification

21. A state (or Tribal) "water quality certification" must be obtained or waived. In California, the SWRCB has "pre-certified" a number of the NWPs; for the remaining NWPs, an individual certification is required from the appropriate Regional Water Quality Control Board. California regulations do not provide for a waiver of this certification requirement. *See* Title 23 Cal. Code Regs. § 3859 (requiring approval or denial of certification).

22. Where applicable, a Coastal Zone Management Act consistency certification must be obtained or waived. In California, the Coastal Commission has refused to pre-certify any of the NWPs. However, the issuance of a coastal development permit serves as a project-specific consistency certification. The Bay Conservation and Development Commission has taken a similar approach.

23. The activity must comply with any regional conditions added by the Division Engineer, as well as any additional conditions contained in the water quality certification or the Coastal Zone Management Act consistency determination.

24. Use of more than one NWP for a single project is prohibited unless the loss of wetlands is no greater than the limit of the NWP with the highest acreage limitation.

25. If the permittee sells the property associated with an NWP, the permittee must notify the Corps to validate the transfer of the NWP to the new owner.

26. Every permittee receiving an NWP verification from the Corps must submit a signed certification concerning the completed work and any required mitigation.

27. Where required by the terms of an NWP, the applicant must provide the Corps with a PCN, which the Corps then has 30 days to review. The specific

CURTIN'S CALIFORNIA LAND USE AND PLANNING LAW

**Figure F
U.S. Army Corps of Engineers
Permitting Process**

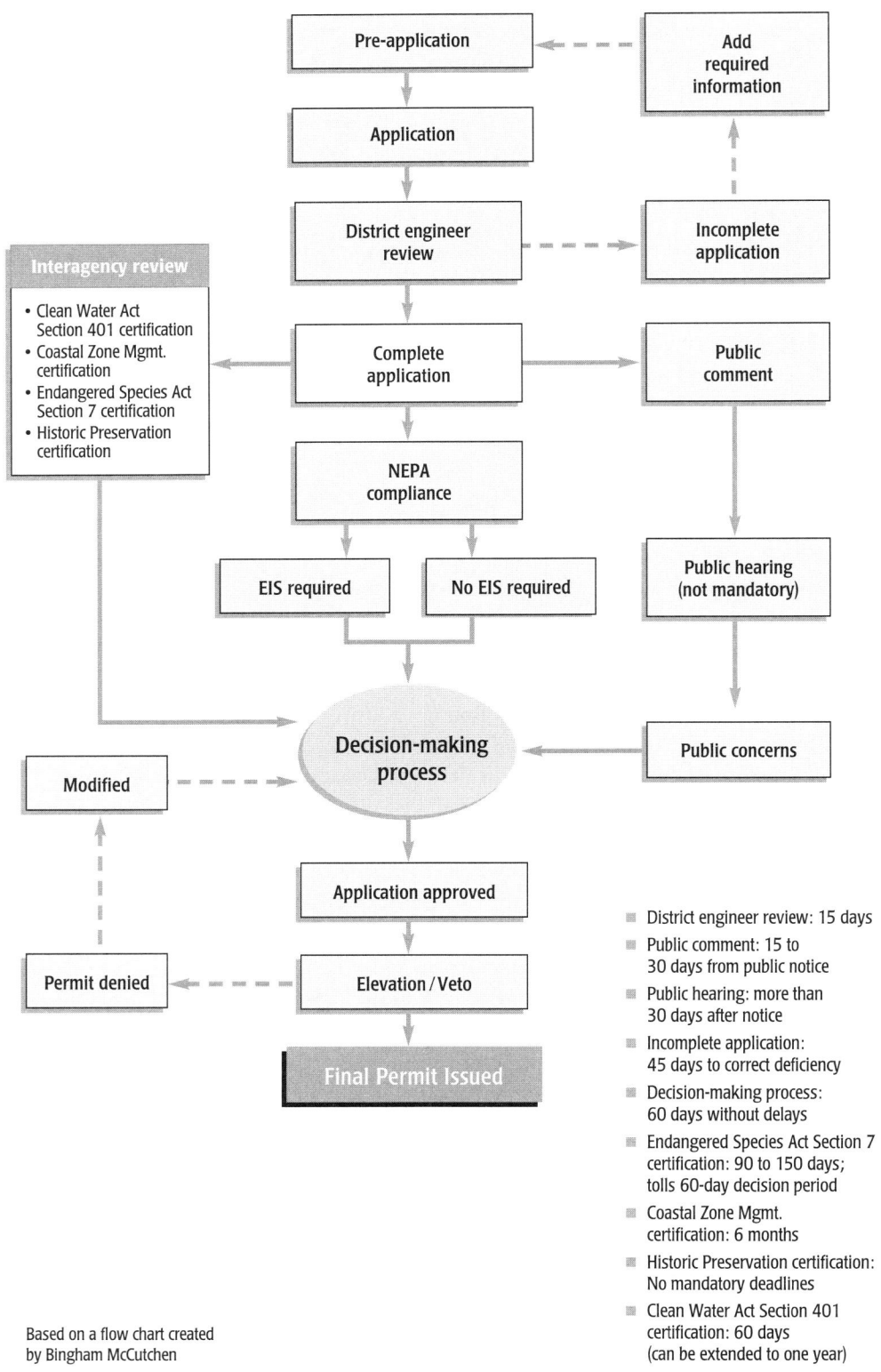

Based on a flow chart created by Bingham McCutchen

contents of the PCN vary depending upon which NWP is being used. This notice provides the Corps with an opportunity to impose special conditions on the project and/or require mitigation. In California, some regional conditions include an expanded notice requirement.

28. Finally, the activity covered by an NWP must be a single and complete project.

Historically, one of the most important and controversial general permits was NWP 26, which the Corps eliminated in March 2000. Originally, NWP 26 authorized the fill of up to 10 acres of wetlands, and did not require any PCNs for fills of less than one acre. The Corps later reduced those acreage thresholds to three acres and one-third acres, respectively, as well as restricting the use of NWP 26 to projects that would result in the fill of no more than 500 linear feet of streambed, regardless of the acreage involved.

One of the most important and controversial general permits was NWP 26, which the Corps eliminated in March 2000.

In March 2000, the Corps replaced NWP 26 with five activity-specific permits (NWPs 39, 41, 42, 43, and 44). In authorizing these new NWPs, the Corps reduced the acreage limit from three acres to one-half acre, required a PCN for activities affecting more than one-tenth acre, and restricted the use of an NWP to projects that fill no more than 300 linear feet of a water body. Furthermore, the conditions imposed by the Corps do not authorize the use of these five NWPs in designated "critical resource waters," which include critical habitat for a listed threatened or endangered species. By eliminating NWP 26 and replacing it with activity-specific permits, the Corps significantly reduced the scope of activities that can occur in or near wetlands under an NWP. Projects that would have been covered under the old NWP 26 may now require an individual Section 404 permit. In September 2006, a district court upheld the Corps' issuance of activity-specific permits to replace former NWP 26, concluding that the Corps acted within its authority and adequately explained the reasons for its actions. *Nat'l Assn of Home Builders v. U.S. Army Corps of Eng'rs*, 453 F. Supp. 2d 116 (D.D.C. 2006). The case is presently on appeal to the D.C. Circuit.

The National Association of Home Builders also has brought a lawsuit in the U.S. District Court for the District of Columbia challenging the Corps' issuance of the new NWP 46, adopted in March 2007, which regulates discharges to certain upland ditches. In all likelihood, the case will require application of the *Rapanos* decision and Justice Kennedy's significant nexus test.

For many NWPs involving more than one-half acre of fill, upon receipt of a PCN, the Corps immediately will furnish (via facsimile or overnight mail) a copy of the notification to the EPA, the Fish and Wildlife Service (Service), and other appropriate resource agencies. Generally, these agencies will then have 10 calendar days to contact the Corps and inform the District Engineer that they will be submitting comments. 72 Fed. Reg. 11195 (March 12, 2007). The District Engineer will then wait an additional 15 calendar days before making a decision on the PCN.

For many NWPs involving more than one-half acre of fill, upon receipt of a PCN, the Corps immediately will furnish a copy of the notification to the EPA, the Fish and Wildlife Service, and other appropriate resource agencies.

The Corps may require an individual permit on its own initiative, or at the request of the EPA or the Service, but the Corps has the sole discretion to make this decision. The Corps has considerable discretion to require an individual permit if the combined direct and indirect adverse impacts of any NWP activity are more than minimal. NWP applicants can submit a proposed mitigation plan with a PCN to expedite the process, and the Corps will consider such optional mitigation in determining whether the project's net effects are minimal. Consequently, the nature and extent of mitigation proposed in a PCN can be of critical importance in determining what action the Corps will take.

The Corps' Individual Permitting Process

Individual permits are required for any discharges of dredged or fill material into waters of the United States that are not authorized by an NWP or exempted. Unlike the NWP process, individual permit applications are subject to public notice and comment, and require preparation of an alternatives analysis by the applicant to demonstrate compliance with the EPA's 404(b)(1) Guidelines (which are discussed below). In addition, individual permits are also subject to specific procedures for compliance with the National Environmental Policy Act (NEPA).

The Corps must apply the EPA's regulations when making decisions on individual permit applications. 40 C.F.R. Part 230. The EPA's regulations are known as the Section 404(b)(1) Guidelines because that section of the CWA requires the EPA to develop criteria for the discharge of dredged or fill materials in environmentally sensitive areas such as wetlands.

The Corps individual permitting process is schematically outlined in Figure F. The minimum time schedule for processing an individual application is 60 days (33 C.F.R. § 325.2); however, the process usually takes considerably longer to complete. A complicated individual permit can take two or more years for processing. To avoid delays, prior to submitting an individual permitting application, the applicant should meet with the Corps, the Service, and the EPA to discuss the proposed activity, the type of permit required, and the information required to complete the application. *See* 33 C.F.R. § 325.1(b).

Applicants must use the Corps' standard application form and include a complete description of the proposed activity. 33 C.F.R. § 325.1(c). The regulations specify that the following information must be included in a standard application:

- Necessary drawings, sketches, or plans sufficient for the public notice (detailed engineering plans and specifications are not required)
- The location, purpose, and need for the proposed activity
- Scheduling of the activity
- The names and addresses of adjoining landowners
- The locations and dimensions of adjacent structures
- A list of the authorizations required by other federal, state, or local agencies for the work, including all approvals or denials already made

33 C.F.R. § 325.1(d)(1)

All activities the applicant plans to undertake that are reasonably related to the proposed project and for which a Corps permit is required must be included in the same application. 33 C.F.R. § 325.1(d)(2). For example, if a construction project involves structural fills in wetlands and bridges across navigable waterways, the permit application should include both of these activities. 33 C.F.R. § 325.1(d)(2). However, in *Wetlands Action Network v. U.S. Army Corps of Engineers*, the Ninth Circuit upheld a decision by the Corps to consider only the environmental effects of the first phase of a large multi-phase development project. 222 F. 3d 1105 (9th Cir. 2000). The court found that each phase of the project had "independent utility," and therefore the Corps could assess each phase separately. *Id.* at 1116. In addition, the court held that when assessing the environmental effects of the first phase, the Corps only needed to consider the effects of filling the wetlands and not the entire first phase of the project. *Id.* at 1117.

If the application includes dredging in navigable waters of the United States, the application must include a description of the type, composition, and quantity of material to be dredged, the method of dredging, and the site and plans for disposal of the dredged material. The Corps' jurisdiction extends to the dredge spoil disposal site, even if the spoils are disposed on uplands. 33 C.F.R. § 325.1(d)(3).

The 404(b)(1) Guidelines prohibit the discharge of fill material into waters of the United States where:

- There is a practicable, less environmentally damaging alternative. 40 C.F.R. § 230.10(a)
- The discharge violates water quality or toxic effluent standards or jeopardizes the continued existence of species listed as threatened or endangered under the ESA. 40 C.F.R. § 230.10(b)
- The discharge will have a significant adverse effect on aquatic resources. 40 C.F.R. § 230.10(c)
- Appropriate and practicable steps have not been taken to minimize the potential adverse impact on the aquatic system. 40 C.F.R. § 230.10(d)

The alternatives analysis required under the first prong of EPA's 404(b)(1) Guidelines is typically the most significant hurdle for the project applicant, and is discussed in greater detail below.

Before issuing an individual permit, the Corps also must apply its own public interest review factors. The Corps' public interest review balances the favorable aspects of the proposed activity against its reasonably foreseeable detriments. The specific evaluation factors include:

Before issuing an individual permit, the Corps must also apply its own public interest review factors.

- The relative extent of the public and private need for the proposed structure or work
- Where there are unresolved conflicts as to resource use, the practicability of using reasonable alternative locations and methods to accomplish the objective of the proposed structure or work
- The extent and permanence of the beneficial and detrimental effects that the proposed structure or work is likely to have on public and private uses of the affected area

33 C.F.R. § 320.4(a)(2)

Upon completion of the public interest review, and subject to other standards, the Corps' regulations state that a permit "will be granted unless the district engineer determines that it would be contrary to the public interest." 33 C.F.R. § 320.4(a)(1).

Alternatives Analysis Under EPA's 404(b)(1) Guidelines

Under the 404(b)(1) Guidelines, the Corps may not issue a permit if there is a "practicable alternative" to the proposed discharge. 40 C.F.R. § 230.10(a). The practicable alternatives test prohibits the discharge of dredged or fill materials to waters of the United States, including wetlands, if there is a *practicable alternative* to the proposed discharge that would have less adverse impact on the aquatic ecosystem, provided that the alternative does not have other, more adverse environmental impacts. 40 C.F.R. § 230.10(a). An alternative is "practicable" if it is "available and capable of *being done after taking into consideration cost, existing technology, and logistics in light of overall project purposes.*" (emphasis added). 40 C.F.R. §§ 230.3(q), 230.10(a)(2).

The practicable alternatives test applies on a case-by-case basis to individual permit applications, while it applies programmatically to general permits.

The practicable alternatives test is frequently the steepest hurdle a project proponent must overcome to obtain an individual permit from the Corps to fill wetlands. For projects involving the filling of wetlands, the 404(b)(1) process injects the Corps into land use decisions and creates what is effectively a federal land use entitlement process.

In evaluating practicable alternatives, the EPA Section 404(b)(1) Guidelines distinguish between water-dependent and non water-dependent projects. A water-dependent project is one that requires access to waters to achieve its *basic purpose*. 40 C.F.R. § 230.10(a)(2). A marina is an example of a water-dependent project. A non water-dependent project is one that does not need to be located in or adjacent to water to fulfill its basic purpose. Residential housing, shopping centers, restaurants, or office buildings are examples of non water-dependent activities. 40 C.F.R. § 230.10(a)(3); 45 Fed. Reg. 85339 (December 3, 1980).

A marina is an example of a water-dependent project. A non water-dependent project is one that does not need to be located in or adjacent to water to fulfill its basic purpose.

The Guidelines *presume* that alternative sites that do not require placing dredged and fill materials into waters of the United States are available for non water-dependent activities that result in a discharge into a special aquatic site. 40 C.F.R. § 230.10(a)(3). Special aquatic sites include wetlands, mudflats, vegetated shallows, coral reefs, and riffle and pool complexes in streams. 40 C.F.R. §§ 230.41–230.45. A non water-dependent project must overcome this presumption in an alternatives analysis to demonstrate compliance with the EPA 404(b)(1) Guidelines. The Guidelines also presume that a practicable alternative that does not involve a discharge into a special aquatic site has less impact on the aquatic ecosystem unless the applicant clearly demonstrates otherwise. 40 C.F.R. § 230.10(a)(3). An alternatives analysis is also required for water-dependent projects; however, there is no regulatory presumption that a less adverse project site exists.

The Corps and the EPA do not apply the Guidelines inflexibly in all cases. The Guidelines make clear that the degree of rigor depends on the situation.

The Corps and the EPA do not apply the Guidelines inflexibly in all cases. The Guidelines make clear that the degree of rigor depends on the situation. "[C]ompliance evaluation procedures will vary to reflect the seriousness of the potential for adverse impacts on the aquatic ecosystems posed by specific dredged or fill material discharge activities." 40 C.F.R. § 230.10; *see also Town of Norfolk v. U.S. Army Corps of Eng'rs*, 968 F. 2d 1438, 1445 (1st Cir. 1992) (issuance of permit proper despite lack of detailed alternatives analysis).

Project Purpose and Wetlands Avoidance (Sequencing)

A first critical step in the 404(b)(1) analysis is determining the project's purpose, since the statement of the project's purpose forms the basis for evaluating all of the alternatives. From the early days of the program, the Corps demonstrated that it would not always accept uncritically an applicant's statement of purpose. For example, in 1976, the Corps rejected a proposal to build a waterfront resort project on Marco Island, Florida. The developer claimed that its purpose was to build an integrated waterfront project, that the project was water-dependent, and that there were no practicable alternatives to the project. The Corps rejected these claims in its decision to deny the permit. It said that the "basic purpose" of the project was housing and that the project was not water-dependent because housing does not have to be located near water or in wetlands. *See Report on Application for Department of Army Permit, Marco Island* (April 15, 1976). Consequently, there were other "practicable" locations for accomplishing the basic project purpose. The courts upheld the Corps' decision. *See Deltona Corp. v. Alexander*, 504 F. Supp. 1280, 1283 (M.D. Fla. 1981); and *Deltona Corp. v. United States*, 657 F. 2d 1184, 1185 (Ct. Cl. 1981) (permit denial was not a taking requiring compensation).

When the EPA adopted the practicable alternatives test in 1980, the tenor, tone, and language of the rulemaking was consistent with the Corps' decision in *Deltona Corporation*. 45 Fed. Reg. 85338–85339 (December 24, 1980). In the preamble to the rule and in the rule itself, the EPA emphasized the importance of the basic project purpose in evaluating alternatives and the importance of avoiding wetlands in the development process. During the 1980s, there was considerable controversy over the application of these factors, with several changes of position by the Corps regarding the degree of deference to be given to the project applicant's statement of purpose, and the priority to be given to avoiding wetlands.

When the EPA adopted the practicable alternatives test in 1980, the tenor, tone, and language of the rulemaking was consistent with the Corps' decision in Deltona Corporation.

In 1990, this controversy was substantially resolved, and the role of the 404(b)(1) alternatives analysis was significantly magnified when the Corps and the EPA signed a Memorandum of Agreement (MOA) on the application of the practicable alternatives test. 55 Fed. Reg. 9210 (March 12, 1990). The MOA's stated objective was to unify the Corps and the EPA positions on how the test would be applied. Most importantly, it established a sequence for evaluating individual permit applications. Applicants must show first that there is no practicable alternative to avoid filling wetlands based on a comparison to available alternative sites. Then, if there is no practicable alternative with less impact to aquatic resources, the applicant must minimize impacts to the project through on-site avoidance and other means. Finally, applicants must provide compensatory mitigation for any lost aquatic values. The MOA effectively ended the former practice of mitigation buy-downs, where credit for mitigation was applied before the proposed project was tested against the other alternatives. Although the MOA is only a statement of goals by both agencies and does not have the force and effect of law, as a general matter, it is consistently applied by the Corps.

MOA = Memorandum of Agreement

This sequencing approach emphasizes a preference for preserving existing wetlands over building artificial wetlands, and gives only minimal weight to economic development and local land use planning goals. It historically has not distinguished between wetlands of high and low-value nor between pristine versus degraded wetlands, although more recent approaches taken by the Corps give increasing emphasis to assessing the functional values of particular wetlands. *See* RGL 02-2, Guidance on Compensatory Mitigation Projects for Aquatic Resource Impacts Under the Corps Regulatory Program Pursuant to Section 404 of the Clean Water Act and Section 10 of the Rivers and Harbors Act of 1899 (December 24, 2002) ("when possible, Districts should use a functional

Sequencing emphasizes a preference for preserving existing wetlands over building artificial wetlands, and gives only minimal weight to economic development and local land use planning goals.

assessment by qualified professionals to determine impacts and compensatory mitigation requirements.").

In evaluating alternatives, the agencies also consider the level of specificity in the project purpose statement, often described as the difference between the "basic" and the "overall" purpose. Generally, the basic project purpose is the fundamental goal to provide housing, transportation, or the like. The overall project purpose takes into account additional considerations, such as the benefits of locating a project near other associated developments, or the need for the project to be profitable in order to be viable.

In at least one case, the EPA asserted that considerations relating to the overall project purpose are subsumed in the basic project purpose, effectively eliminating consideration of a broader range of factors that could be used to reject alternatives. The EPA made this assertion in vetoing the permit for a controversial water supply project for Denver—the Two Forks Dam. In its veto, the EPA stated:

> The 404(b)(1) Guidelines use the terms "basic purpose" and "overall project purposes" *interchangeably*. [I]t is clear that the two terms are not intended to have distinct meanings.... As such, we have read both phrases to have the same meaning, which is a generic basic purpose test.

Two Forks Dam Section 404(c) Veto at 2, n. 1 (emphasis added)

The EPA described the project purpose as providing a dependable water supply for Denver. It rejected the applicant's request to include as a project purpose the provision of water at least cost.

The decision of the Ninth Circuit in *Sylvester v. U.S. Army Corps of Engineers* took a somewhat broader view, accepting a developer's assertion that it was necessary for a resort development to be located in association with an on-site, 18-hole golf course. 882 F. 2d 407 (9th Cir. 1989). Based on research conducted by the applicant demonstrating that such a golf course would be an essential element for the project's success, the court declined to set aside the proponent's project purpose statement, stating that "it would be bizarre if the Corps were to ignore the purpose for which the applicant seeks a permit and to substitute a purpose it deems more suitable." *Id.* at 409. The court continued, "Obviously, an applicant cannot define a project in order to preclude the existence of any alternative sites and thus make what is practicable appear impracticable.... [T]he applicant's purpose must be 'legitimate.'" *Id.*

Practicability

The EPA 404(b)(1) Guidelines require that the alternative selected be the "Least Environmentally Damaging Practicable Alternative." An alternative is "practicable" if it is "available and capable of being done after taking into consideration cost, existing technology, and logistics in light of overall project purposes." 40 C.F.R. § 230.3(q).

As a practical matter, the factors that come into play in a particular alternatives analysis will depend greatly upon the characteristics of the alternatives being evaluated. An alternative may be impracticable from a cost standpoint if the cost of its implementation is unreasonably greater than the cost of other alternatives, considering such elements as development costs, acquisition costs, infrastructure costs, and operating costs. *See Hough v. Marsh*, 557 F. Supp. 74 (D. Mass. 1982). Technological considerations affecting practicability could include such factors as access to a transportation system, water supplies, and other necessary infrastructure. Logistical considerations could include such factors as the need to rezone the alternative sites for the proposed use, existing barriers to the development such as the presence of improvements that would be difficult to move, etc. Sometimes these criteria overlap, such as where a logistical or technological barrier could be overcome with an adequate investment of money.

A project applicant frequently will submit a written alternatives analysis evaluating a reasonable range of alternatives and documenting the assertion that no practicable alternatives exist. The expected level of detail in these alternatives analyses has been steadily increasing. Corps field guidance indicates that the level of analysis should be proportionate to the scale of the project and its environmental impacts. Corps, 1993, Memorandum: Appropriate Level of Analysis Required for Evaluating Compliance with the Section 404(b)(1) Guidelines Alternatives Requirements (available at www.epa.gov/owow/wetlands/guidance/flexible.html). It also may be appropriate to rely on the alternatives analysis in a NEPA document. *See Town of Norfolk v. U.S. Army Corps of Eng'rs*, 968 F. 2d 1438 (1st Cir. 1992).

Given the relatively open-ended and subjective nature of the practicability determination, it is common for disagreements to arise, both between the applicant and the Corps, and between the Corps and the EPA. As with the other determinations in the permitting process, the Corps retains the ultimate discretion to make the practicability determination, subject to judicial review under an "arbitrary and capricious" standard, and/or an EPA veto.

Given the relatively open-ended and subjective nature of the practicability determination, it is common for disagreements to arise, both between the applicant and the Corps, and between the Corps and the EPA.

Availability

In addition to being practicable in view of costs, logistics, and technology, an alternative must be "available."

As a practical matter, a site not owned by an applicant cannot be available if the owner is unwilling to sell, although the Corps may assert that entities with eminent domain powers should be presumed to exercise those powers (if a "public purpose" can be shown) and therefore have access to a broader range of sites. Unavailability also might be determined by a law that prohibits site development.

A key question is "available as of what time?" In describing alternative sites, the Guidelines refer to an area not "presently" owned by the applicant as being an acceptable site if it could reasonably be obtained or used. 40 C.F.R. § 230.10(a)(2). This seems to imply that the availability test is judged when the Corps considers the application. However, this is not the EPA's view, and the Corps' view on the issue is not settled.

In *Bersani v. U.S. Army Corps of Engineers*, a developer sought a Section 404 permit to build a shopping mall on an 80-acre site, a portion of which contained a 49.5-acre wetland known as Sweedens Swamp. 850 F. 2d 36 (2d Cir. 1988), *cert denied*, 489 U.S. 1089 (1989). The Corps granted the permit based on a mitigation buy-down analysis. The EPA, however, objected to the issuance of the permit and used its veto power under Section 404(c). 33 U.S.C. § 1344(c). The EPA concluded that because a practicable alternative was "available" when the developer "entered" the market to buy shopping center property, it could deny the permit for noncompliance with the practicable alternatives test even though the alternative site was no longer on the market when the EPA vetoed the permit. The court deferred to the EPA's use of the "market entry approach" to determine availability under the practicable alternatives test, although the *Bersani* test is not mandated either by the CWA or the EPA 404(b)(1) Guidelines.

The Corps has not adopted the court-approved market entry approach for availability.

The Corps has not adopted the court-approved market entry approach for "availability." Given the problems with the market entry approach to the practicable alternatives test, it is unlikely that the Corps will use it unquestioningly. The *Bersani* opinion itself was a 2–1 decision, with the dissent arguing that Congress designed Section 404 "to preserve the environment consistent with reasonable accommodation to the economic and social needs of the public; it was not concerned with the identities or past activities of particular developers." *Bersani*, 850 F. 2d at 48.

Does the market entry approach to the practical alternatives test make sense? The market entry approach encourages buyers to look for properties that do not have wetlands, which arguably encourages avoidance. In a number of cases, the application of this approach has led to better decisions (use of lower cost sites with less aquatic impact). It makes very little sense, though, when applied to a developer who has owned property for a long time.

Mitigation

Corps regulations authorize the Corps to require compensatory mitigation for these unavoidable impacts to wetlands and other waters.

In many circumstances, despite the avoidance of impacts to the extent practicable through the 404(b)(1) Guideline analysis, some residual impacts to wetlands will remain. The Corps regulations authorize requiring compensatory mitigation for these unavoidable impacts to wetlands and other waters. 33 C.F.R. Parts 320–331. Generally mitigation will consist of on-site and/or off-site creation, enhancement, restoration, or preservation of wetlands.

NRC = National Research Council

A 2001 study prepared by the National Research Council (NRC) and published by the National Academy of Science, entitled "Compensating for Wetland Losses under the Clean Water Act," criticized a number of common compensatory mitigation practices, concluding that in many circumstances approved mitigation plans either were not carried out, or failed to produce anticipated benefits.

In December 2004, the San Francisco and Sacramento districts of the Corps published "Mitigation and Monitoring Proposal Guidelines" that respond to the criticisms made in the NRC report. Under the Guidelines, the ultimate goal of the mitigation plan is the successful replacement of all lost functions and values associated with regulated impacts to the waters of the United States. Elements of successful mitigation planning include appropriate mitigation site selection with a particular emphasis on self-sustaining natural hydrology that will support wetlands; development of a mitigation plan that will create, restore, or enhance the physical, chemical, or biological characteristics of the site with the goal of increasing wetland functions and values; monitoring, maintenance, and reporting; and contingency measures to address possible failures to produce the anticipated results. Generally, mitigation sites are required to be preserved "in perpetuity" through a conservation easement or other form of protection, and the permittee is usually required to provide a realistic endowment or other financial assurance to fund long-term activities.

In March 2006, the Corps and EPA jointly published a proposed rule on compensatory mitigation in the Federal Register. 59 Fed. Reg. 15520 (Mar. 28, 2006). The proposal incorporates many of the recommendations suggested in the 2001 NRC report, with the aim of improving the ecological success and sustainability of compensatory mitigation projects. The proposal emphasizes a watershed approach to compensatory mitigation, based largely on the strategic selection of compensatory mitigation sites. The proposal would establish broad protocols for formulating ecological performance standards and monitoring and management plans, while providing flexibility to the District Engineer and the project applicant to tailor the details to the particular project at issue.

EPA'S Role in the Permit Evaluation Process

Although the Corps issues the permits under Section 404 of the CWA, the EPA developed the 404(b)(1) Guidelines. Moreover, the EPA retains veto power over Section 404 permits and may designate specific areas as non-discharge sites. 33 U.S.C. § 404(c); 40 C.F.R. Part 231. The EPA will comment on individual permit applications and often will act as an agency "watchdog" to ensure compliance with the 404(b)(1) Guidelines and NEPA. In recent years, the EPA has been much more aggressive in its "watchdog" capacity, and increasingly has sought to expand the regulatory authority under Section 404. While the EPA rarely invokes its veto power under Section 404(c) (having vetoed only 11 permits, the most recent of which was in 1990), it often will comment extensively on the 404(b)(1) analysis and other elements of the permit process. These comments become part of the administrative record for purposes of judicial review, and therefore are available for use by project opponents in litigation.

In recent years, the EPA has been much more aggressive in its "watchdog" capacity, and increasingly has sought to expand the limits of its regulatory authority under Section 404.

In addition to its veto authority, pursuant to a 1992 Memorandum of Agreement (MOA) between the EPA and the Corps, the EPA also may seek to "elevate" proposed Corps permitting decisions with which the EPA disagrees. Once elevated, permitting decisions are then to be resolved between the agencies at higher levels within the respective agency hierarchies. *See* MOA between the Corps and the EPA (August 11, 1992, available at www.usace.army.mil/cw/cecwo/reg/mou/epa404q.htm).

In addition to its veto authority, pursuant to an MOA between the EPA and the Corps, the EPA may seek to elevate proposed Corps permitting decisions with which the EPA disagrees.

The EPA, however, may only seek to elevate permitting decisions on individual projects when they involve impacts to "aquatic resources of national importance" or "ARNIs." The MOA does not define this threshold term. In practice, there has been no limitation on what wetlands or other waters the EPA asserts are ARNIs. Rather, if the EPA objects to a permitting decision, it appears to automatically assert that the wetlands or other waters in question are ARNIs, irrespective of their biological or other values, simply because classifying them as such is necessary under the MOA to begin the elevation process. This seemingly automatic characterization, however, has been rejected in at least one Corps' decision. In a case involving a project in Stanislaus County, the Corps rejected the EPA's claim that seasonal wetlands and a creek with sparse riparian vegetation qualified as ARNIs. Consequently, the Corps' permitting decision was not elevated. *See* www.usace.army.mil/cw/cecwo/reg/diablo_q.pdf.

ARNI = Aquatic Resources of National Importance

Courts do not always accept that the EPA may second-guess the Corps in conducting a practicable alternatives analysis. While *Bersani* upheld the EPA's efforts to redo the Corp's practicable alternatives analysis, in *James City County v. U.S. EPA*, the court reversed EPA's second-guessing. 955 F. 2d 254 (4th Cir. 1992). The district court overturned the EPA's veto of a permit to build a dam and construct a water reservoir, determining that the EPA's conclusion that there were practicable alternatives to the project was arbitrary and capricious. *Id.* at 259. On remand, the EPA again vetoed the permit and its veto once again was overturned by the court. *See James City County v. U.S. EPA*, 12 F. 3d 1330, 1331 (4th Cir. 1993), *cert. denied*, 513 U.S. 823 (1994).

Other Federal Statutes

Numerous other federal statutes also are involved in the permitting process. An outline of the statute and its relationship to the Corps' permitting process follows.

Section 401 of the Clean Water Act
33 U.S.C. § 1341

- Section 401 of the CWA requires all permittees to obtain certification from the state that the activity associated with dredging or filling will comply with applicable state effluent limitations and water quality standards.
- In California, as discussed above, the water quality certification must be obtained from the appropriate Regional Water Quality Control Board, both for individual permits and for any NWPs that have not been "pre-certified."

National Environmental Policy Act
42 U.S.C. §§ 4321–4347

- For Corps individual permits, an environmental assessment (EA) must be prepared.
- For permits that are major federal actions having a significant effect on the human environment, an environmental impact statement (EIS) is required.
- The Corps guidelines concerning compliance with NEPA are codified at 33 C.F.R. Part 330 and 33 C.F.R. Part 325, Appendix B. The factor that determines the scope of analysis under NEPA is the specific activity requiring a Corps permit and those portions of the entire project over which the Corps has sufficient control and responsibility to warrant federal review. 33 C.F.R. Part 325, Appendix B, Paragraph 7(b)(1).

Endangered Species Act
16 U.S.C. § 1531 *et seq.*

- The Endangered Species Act (ESA) requires the Corps to consult with the United States Fish and Wildlife Service if any proposed action may affect a listed threatened or endangered species or designated critical habitat. For a detailed discussion of the ESA, *see* chapter 8 (Endangered Species Protections).
- A Corps permit will not be granted if the Service determines that the permitted activities will jeopardize the continued existence of threatened or endangered species, or adversely modify critical habitat for such species.

Fish and Wildlife Coordination Act
16 U.S.C. §§ 661–666(c)

- Prior to issuing a permit, the Corps must consult with the Service to prevent the direct and indirect loss of, or damage to, wildlife resources from the permitted activity.

In California, the water quality certification must be obtained from the appropriate RWQCB, both for individual permits and for those NWPs that have not been pre-certified.

EA = Environmental assessment
EIS = Environmental impact statement

- The Service has published guidelines that explain its consultation role under the Fish and Wildlife Coordination Act. 46 Fed. Reg. 7644 (January 23, 1981).

Section 302 of the Marine Protection, Research and Sanctuaries Act of 1972
16 U.S.C. § 1432

- Permits to dredge or fill will not be granted in areas designated as "marine sanctuaries" unless the dredge or fill activity is certified by the Secretary of Commerce.

National Historic Preservation Act of 1966
16 U.S.C. § 470

- The Advisory Council on Historic Preservation reviews and comments upon Corps permit applications that could have an effect upon historic properties listed, or eligible for listing, on the National Register of Historic Places.
- If the proposed activity will alter terrain so that significant historical or archeological data are threatened, the Secretary of the Interior may take action necessary to recover and preserve the data prior to commencement of the project.
- Obtaining the required cultural resource approvals can be a very complex and time-consuming process and may require extensive cultural resource surveys.
- The Corps' guidelines on its duties under the National Historic Preservation Act are codified at 33 C.F.R. Part 325, Appendix C.

If the proposed activity will alter terrain so that significant historical or archeological data are threatened, the Secretary of the Interior may take action necessary to recover and preserve the data prior to commencement of the project.

Land Sales Full Disclosure Act
15 U.S.C. § 1701 *et seq.*

- If a subdivision lot is part of a project that requires a Corps permit prior to sale of the property, the developer must state whether or not a permit for the development has been applied for, issued, or denied by the Corps.

Coastal Zone Management Act of 1972
16 U.S.C. § 1456(c)

- In the event the proposed project is located in California's coastal zone, approval from the California Coastal Commission is required before the Corps will issue a permit.

Food Security Act of 1985
16 U.S.C. §§ 3821–22

- The United States Department of Agriculture (USDA) has authority over certain activities in wetlands. Known as the "Swampbuster Provisions" of the Food Security Act, they deal with agricultural conversion of wetlands. Under USDA regulations, any person producing agricultural commodities on certain converted wetlands is ineligible for crop insurance and other USDA benefits. 7 C.F.R. § 400.47(c).

RGL = Regulatory Guidance Letter
USDA = United States Department of Agriculture

Regulatory Guidance Letters

In addition to the regulations published in the Federal Register, the Corps also issues Regulatory Guidance Letters (RGLs). RGLs are not subject to the same formal rulemaking procedures as regulations, and are intended to provide guidance to the Corps' District and Division Offices on specific issues that arise.

However, topics covered in RGLs often are incorporated into later Corps regulations. Many Corps offices continue to follow a particular RGL even after it has expired. Many of the RGLs (available at www.usace.army.mil/cw/cecwo/reg/rglsindx.htm) deal with clarifying activities that are regulated and the extent of Corps' jurisdiction.

State Statutory Authority

In California, several state agencies are charged with regulating activities that may impact wetlands or other waters under the Corps' jurisdiction. In addition, local agencies also may promulgate wetland protection programs under their planning and zoning powers. An outline of these state regulations follows.

Porter-Cologne Water Quality Control Act
Water Code § 13000 *et seq.*

The Porter-Cologne Water Quality Control Act regulates the discharge of waste that could affect the quality of the waters of the state.

- The Porter-Cologne Water Quality Control Act is California's comprehensive water pollution statute. It specifically regulates the discharge of waste "that could affect the quality of the waters of the state." Water Code § 13260(1). The Porter-Cologne Act defines waste as "sewage and any and all other waste substances, liquid, solid, gaseous, or radioactive, associated with human habitation, or of human or animal origin, or from any producing, manufacturing, or processing operation, including waste placed within containers of whatever nature prior to, and for purposes of, disposal." Water Code § 13050(d). It defines "waters of the state" as "any surface water or groundwater, including saline waters, within the boundaries of the state." Water Code § 13050(e). However, it does not mention, much less define, wetlands.

DFG = Department of Fish and Game
RWQCB = Regional Water Quality Control Board

- Under the Porter-Cologne Act, the discharge of a waste into a water of the state requires the discharger to first file with the appropriate Regional Water Quality Control Board (RWQCB) a "Report of Waste Discharge." Water Code § 13260(1). In turn, the RWQCB determines whether a permit (called "Waste Discharge Requirements") is required.

- Historically, the State Water Resources Control Board and the nine individual RWQCBs have taken the position that wetlands constitute "waters of the state" subject to the Porter-Cologne Act. Likewise, they have taken the position that any fill of wetlands is subject to the Report of Waste Discharge and Waste Discharge Requirements. Before *SWANCC* and *Rapanos*, in practice nearly every wetland fill was subject to Corps' jurisdiction under Section 404; the RWQCBs therefore obtained jurisdiction through the Section 401 water quality certification process, such that jurisdiction under the Porter-Cologne Act was not needed.

- But the Supreme Court's 2001 decision in *SWANCC*, which eliminated many isolated waters and wetlands from federal jurisdiction, suddenly brought to the fore the legal issue of state jurisdiction under the Porter-Cologne Act. In response to *SWANCC*, the State and Regional Boards have reiterated their position that the Porter-Cologne Act provides an independent basis for state regulation of wetland fill, and have begun demanding that landowners file Reports of Waste Discharge prior to filling any isolated waters or wetlands that now escape Corps regulation. The State Board also has issued a general permit for some of those discharges.

The State Board and several of the Regional Boards also are developing new programs to regulate projects that adversely affect streams, wetlands, and riparian habitats. Whether or not the Porter-Cologne Act actually confers regulatory jurisdiction over wetlands to the state is an open question, one that will likely have to be answered by the courts.

Streambed Alteration Agreement
Fish and Game Code § 1602

- The Department of Fish and Game (DFG) must be notified and given an opportunity to approve ordering any work that substantially diverts, alters, or obstructs the natural flow or substantially changes the bed, channel, or banks of any river, stream, or lake. Most waterways subject to the DFG's jurisdiction also will be subject to Corps regulations. However, not all areas subject to Corps regulations will require a streambed alteration agreement. For example, wetlands under Corps jurisdiction are not regulated by Section 1602, because they are not rivers, streams, or lakes. The DFG has specified that all waterways of the state, including intermittent streams, are subject to its jurisdiction. 14 Cal. Code Regs. § 720. If DFG does not grant or deny approval within 30 days of the notification, the applicant may proceed with the work.

Navigation Dredging Permit
Fish and Game Code § 5653

- A permit is required before using a vacuum or suction dredge in any river, stream, or lake of the state. Dredging activity also may be regulated by the Corps if the water body is navigable or dredged material is discharged into waters of the United States. The DFG may prohibit suction dredging in certain areas.

A permit is required before using a vacuum or suction dredge in any river, stream, or lake of the state.

Coastal Zone Management
Public Resources Code § 30600

- Developments proposed within the state's coastal zone must obtain a coastal development permit in addition to any other approvals or permits required. Pub. Res. Code § 30600. The Coastal Commission will not issue a permit unless the applicant can demonstrate that the development within the coastal zone minimizes adverse impacts to wetlands. Pub. Res. Code § 30233(a). Certain developments that are coastal-dependent (such as ports) may be sited in wetlands, provided the impact mitigation requirements of section 30233 are met. Obtaining a permit from the Coastal Commission does not eliminate the need to obtain the applicable permits from the Corps, but that permit does serve as the required certification of consistency with the coastal program, under the Coastal Zone Management Act.

Developments within the state's coastal zone must obtain a coastal development permit in addition to any other approvals or permits required.

- In 1994, the Coastal Commission released a guidance document entitled Procedural Guidance for Evaluating Wetland Projects in California's Coastal Zone. This guidance document addresses the full range of issues raised by the permitting process, including procedures for permit processing, the approach to be taken for wetland delineations, mitigation, etc. It should be noted that the Coastal Commission takes a more expansive approach to wetland delineations that is similar to, but not the same as, the Corps' 1987 Manual.

- In late 1995, the Coastal Commission released a more detailed guidance document on the evaluation of mitigation proposals, entitled Procedural

Guidance for Evaluating Wetland Mitigation Projects in California's Coastal Zone. The purposes of this guidance are (1) to give those required to develop compensatory wetlands mitigation a clear idea of what will be acceptable to the Commission, and (2) to give the Commission staff a methodology to evaluate the post-approval performance of wetland mitigation projects. Online versions of these and many other Coastal Commission publications are available at www.coastal.ca.gov/pubs.html.

Enforcement
Criminal, Civil, and Administrative Penalties

Section 309 of the CWA sets out the factors for determining the appropriate type and amount of penalty for violations of the CWA. 33 U.S.C. § 1319. Criminal, civil, or administrative penalties may be imposed. Each day of a violation is considered a separate offense for the purpose of assessing penalties. Each day that fill is placed in the wetland can be considered a separate offense and, if the Corps issues a cease-and-desist order for an unpermitted activity such as a wetland fill, each day that fill remains in the wetland in violation of the order is also a separate offense. *See United States v. Ciampitti*, 669 F. Supp. 684 (D. N.J. 1987); *United States v. Cumberland Farms*, 826 F. 2d 1151 (1st Cir. 1987). The government has the burden of proof in an enforcement case to show the existence of wetlands by a preponderance of the evidence. *See Stoeco Dev. Ltd. v. U.S. Army Corps of Eng'rs*, 792 F. Supp. 339, 340 (D. N.J. 1992).

Civil and criminal penalties are imposed in civil enforcement proceedings brought in United States District Court for the district in which the defendant is located or resides or is doing business. 33 U.S.C. § 1319(b). Such actions may be brought by either the Corps or the EPA. Criminal penalties may be sought for negligent or knowing violations, or violations that consist of knowing endangerment. 33 U.S.C. § 1319(c). For knowing violations, the government need not prove that the discharger knew that the site qualified as a wetlands subject to federal jurisdiction; rather, it need only prove that the discharger knew he was discharging dredged or fill material. *See United States v. Cooper*, 482 F. 3d 658, 665–66 (4th Cir. 2007) (holding that defendant was criminally liable for discharging sewage into a creek because he knowingly discharged the sewage, even if he may not have known that the creek was a navigable water).

Under the CWA, simple negligence can result in criminal penalties of up to $25,000 a day and one year in prison for first-time offenders, and up to $50,000 and two years in prison for repeat offenders. *See* 33 U.S.C. § 1319(c)(1); *United States v. Hanousek*, 176 F. 3d 1116 (9th Cir. 1999), *cert. denied*, 528 U.S. 1102 (2000). For knowing violations, criminal penalties can reach $500,000 per day and 30 years of imprisonment for repeat offenders. 33 U.S.C. § 1319(c)(2), (3). In theory, corporate officers can be held personally liable for criminal acts committed by subordinates without their knowledge. For a discussion of the "responsible corporate officer" doctrine, *see* Joshua Safran Reed, "Reconciling Environmental Liability Standards After Iverson and Bestfoods," 27 *Ecology L.Q.* 673 (2000).

The factors used to assess civil penalties for any particular violation are based on the seriousness of the violation, the economic benefit realized by the violator, any past history of violations, any good faith efforts to comply with the

Civil and criminal penalties are imposed in civil enforcement proceedings brought in United States District Court for the district in which the defendant is located or resides or is doing business.

applicable requirements, the economic impact of the penalty on the violator, and other matters as justice may require. 33 U.S.C. § 1319(d). A maximum civil penalty of $27,500 per day may be imposed for each violation. 40 C.F.R. pt. 19.

The EPA may also assess administrative penalties. Two classes of administrative penalties may be imposed for violations of permit conditions.

Class I administrative penalties are limited to a maximum of $11,000 per violation, and the total penalty amount is limited to $27,500. A violator will be provided a reasonable opportunity to be heard and to present evidence; however, the hearing is not subject to the procedural requirements of the Administrative Procedure Act.

Class II administrative penalties are limited to $11,000 per day during which the violation continues, with the total penalty capped at $137,500. A hearing on the record in accordance with the Administrative Procedure Act must be held.

Class II penalties are limited to $11,000 per day during which the violation continues; however, the maximum amount is limited to $137,500.

Administrative penalties also are assessed using a set of factors similar to those used for civil penalties. These factors include: the nature, circumstances, extent, and gravity of the violation, the violator's ability to pay the penalty, any prior history of violations, the degree of culpability, the economic benefit or savings resulting from the violation, and other such matters as justice may require. 33 U.S.C. § 1319(g)(3).

The Enforcement Process and After-the-Fact Permits

While neither the Corps nor the EPA has an active inspection program, other state and federal resource agencies cooperate in identifying possible violators upon learning of a violation. The enforcement process begins with the discovery of the unauthorized activity. Normally, the Corps will take the lead in investigating potential violations. The Corps, the EPA, or the Service will determine which agency takes the lead role in prosecuting a violation. 33 C.F.R. § 326.3(g). If the Corps has the lead role, it will make an initial investigation to confirm whether a violation exists and, if so, the identity of the responsible party. 33 C.F.R. § 326.3(b).

The Corps, the EPA, or the Service will determine which agency takes the lead role in prosecuting a violation.

If the Corps finds that a violation exists, it will issue a formal notification to the landowner or responsible party; if the activity is not complete, the Corps usually will issue a cease-and-desist order. 33 C.F.R. § 326.3(c). A cease-and-desist order is not judicially reviewable until either the Corps seeks formal enforcement action in court or civil penalties are assessed. *See Southern Pines Ass'n v. United States*, 912 F. 2d 713 (4th Cir. 1990); *Hoffman Group, Inc. v. U.S. EPA*, 902 F. 2d 567 (7th Cir. 1990); *Howell v. U.S. Army Corps of Eng'rs*, 794 F. Supp. 1072 (D. N.M. 1992). The Corps also may order initial corrective actions to stabilize the site. 33 C.F.R. § 326.3(d). The Corps then will determine if further enforcement action is warranted, or whether the matter should be resolved administratively or referred to the Department of Justice for prosecution. 33 C.F.R. § 326.5(a).

Once the enforcement procedures are completed, the Corps may accept an "after-the-fact" permit application. 33 C.F.R. § 326.3(e). This allows the Corps to decide whether it will grant authorization for the discharge of dredged or fill material.

In enforcement actions, the federal courts tend to uphold the Corps' conclusions concerning whether particular activities constitute the discharge of dredged or fill material into a water of the United States. For example, in *United States v. Deaton*, the court held that "sidecasting"—which is the process of dredging soil out of a ditch and casting it to the side of the ditch—constitutes a discharge requiring a Section 404 permit, notwithstanding the fact that the dredging did not add new material to the land, but simply relocated it slightly. 209 F. 3d 331 (4th Cir. 2000). In *Borden Ranch Partnership v. U.S. Army Corps of Engineers*, the court held that the act of deep ripping wetlands in the process of converting grazing land to vineyards and orchards created a discharge requiring a permit. 261 F. 3d 810, 814–15 (9th Cir. 2001).

The consequences for a serious violation of the CWA can be substantial. In the *Borden Ranch* case, the district court assessed a landowner a civil fine of $1.5 million for what the court deemed serious violations of the CWA and the landowner's lack of an earnest effort to comply with the CWA. The landowner's deep ripping of ranch land was conducted without a Section 404 permit despite repeated warnings from the Corps that a permit was required. On appeal, the Ninth Circuit upheld the lower court's liability and penalty findings. Significantly, the Ninth Circuit confirmed that each pass of the landowner's deep ripping machine through a wetland constituted a separate violation of the CWA, resulting in a total potential civil penalty of $8,950,000. *Id.* at 816.

Practical Considerations

Wetlands issues should be considered at each stage in the land development process: land acquisition, site planning, and permitting.

Wetlands issues should be considered at each stage in the land development process: land acquisition, site planning, and permitting. Efforts should be made to coordinate federal wetlands permits with other needed state and local permits.

In sum, the four key steps in the federal permitting process are:

- First, in any complex situation, determine the extent of wetlands and other waters of the United States on the lands in question. Information on wetlands can be compiled or sent to the Corps for its approval. 33 C.F.R. § 325.9. Once the Corps makes a "jurisdictional" determination, it is normally binding for at least two years. *See* RGL 90-6, Aug. 14, 1990; 56 Fed. Reg. 2411 (January 26, 1991). Reaching agreement with the Corps on the extent of its jurisdiction eliminates a major uncertainty in the permitting process.

- Second, the proposed project should be analyzed to determine whether it is possible to avoid filling wetlands and other waters of the United States. If such areas can be avoided practicably, this will eliminate a major permitting obstacle.

- Third, if total avoidance is not possible, attempts should be made to minimize the amount of fill. Activities should be carefully examined to determine if an NWP is applicable. The NWP process is typically much less difficult than the individual permit process.

- Fourth, if the activity requires an individual permit, the complexity of the process should be recognized and the applicant must be fully prepared to meet and achieve each of the critical regulatory hurdles discussed above.

8

Endangered Species Protections

Introduction

Protection of fish, wildlife, and plants has become increasingly important in California. Indeed, today it is difficult to avoid endangered species issues when developing land virtually anywhere in the state.

Congress passed the first legislation to protect endangered species in 1966. The 1966 Endangered Species Act (ESA) directed the Secretary of the Interior (Secretary) to carry out a federal program to protect endangered species and to prepare an official list of endangered species. It further directed the Departments of Interior, Agriculture, and Defense to preserve endangered species' habitats on their lands, consistent with the basic missions of these agencies. The 1966 ESA applied only to wildlife. Although the ESA has been amended several times since 1966, compilation of a list of species in need of protection was, and still is, the linchpin for applying the ESA's protections.

In California alone, there are approximately 300 federally listed species—more than any other state except Hawaii.

The ESA forms the basis for the federal protection of threatened or endangered plants, insects, fish, and wildlife. California has its own Endangered Species Act, which is discussed at the end of this chapter.

The United States Fish and Wildlife Service (Service) administers the federal ESA, although the National Oceanic and Atmospheric Administration Fisheries (NOAA Fisheries, also known as the National Marine Fisheries Service or NMFS) administers the ESA with respect to anadromous fish,[1] such as salmon and steelhead. The ESA has four major components:

- Provisions for listing species as threatened or endangered. 16 U.S.C. § 1533
- A requirement for consultation with the Service by federal agencies on federal projects, including federal approvals of private projects (such as the issuance of a federal permit or license). 16 U.S.C. § 1536
- Prohibitions against the "taking" of listed species. 16 U.S.C. § 1538

Today it is difficult to avoid endangered species issues when developing land virtually anywhere in the state.

ESA = Endangered Species Act
NOAA = National Oceanic and Atmospheric Administration

In California alone, there are approximately 300 federally listed species.

---

1. Anadromous fish are born in fresh water, migrate to the ocean to grow into adults, and then return to fresh water to spawn.

- Provisions for permits allowing the incidental taking of threatened or endangered species. 16 U.S.C. §§ 1536, 1539

The ESA's reach is not limited to the territorial boundaries of the United States. In considering listing actions, the Secretary is required to take into account the impacts of activities that occur outside the United States, and the ESA requires the Secretary to list species that are not found in the United States. The ESA also regulates the importation and exportation of species that are listed as threatened or endangered.

In its early years, the ESA focused largely on the consultation obligations of federal agencies. In recent years, the ESA has become of increasing concern to private developers, who can face serious penalties for violating the ESA's prohibition against the "taking" of an endangered or threatened species. The takings provisions were initially directed to shooting, trapping, and similar direct actions. But over the years the scope of the takings provisions has expanded to include indirect impacts caused by habitat destruction. Under this broad interpretation, the otherwise lawful action of a landowner in clearing or developing land can result in civil and criminal penalties.

The Listing Process

Listing of a Species as Threatened or Endangered

The listing of a species as threatened or endangered is a key component of the ESA. The ESA's protections extend to "any subspecies of fish or wildlife or plants, and any distinct population segment of any species of vertebrate fish or wildlife which interbreeds when mature." 16 U.S.C. § 1532 (16). The Secretary may list a species as threatened or endangered if the continued existence of the species is jeopardized by:

- The present or threatened destruction, modification, or curtailment of its habitat or range
- Overuse for commercial, recreational, scientific, or educational purposes
- Disease or predation
- The inadequacy of existing regulatory mechanisms, and/or
- Other natural or man-made factors concerning or affecting its continued existence

16 U.S.C. § 1533(a)(1)

An endangered species is "any species which is in danger of extinction throughout all or a significant portion of its range...." 16 U.S.C. § 1532(6). A threatened species is one "which is likely to become an endangered species within the foreseeable future throughout all or a significant portion of its range." 16 U.S.C. § 1532(20). The Service determines whether a species is endangered or threatened based on "the best scientific and commercial data available... after conducting a review of the status of the species and after taking into account those efforts, if any, being made by any State or foreign nation or any political subdivision of a State or foreign nation, to protect such species...." 16 U.S.C. § 1533(b)(1)(A). In making this determination, the Service is required to provide expert analysis to support its conclusions. *See*

Northern Spotted Owl v. Hodel, 716 F. Supp. 479, 482–83 (W.D. Wash. 1988) (overturning the Service's decision not to list northern spotted owl because its documents lacked any expert analysis supporting its conclusions; in fact, the expert opinion was entirely to the contrary).

The primary considerations the Service likely will take into account when determining whether to list a species are:

- Is the species under consideration a species or subspecies of fish, wildlife, or plant, or a distinct population segment of any species of vertebrate fish or wildlife, that interbreeds when mature?
- What is the range of the species, subspecies, or population segment?
- Is the species, subspecies, or population segment in danger of extinction in all or any part of its range?
- If it is in danger of extinction in only part of its range, is that a significant part of its range?
- If the species, subspecies, or population segment is not in danger of extinction in all or part of its range, is it likely to become an endangered species within the foreseeable future through all or part of its range?

As with other determinations under the ESA, the Service's listing decisions are judicially reviewable under an "arbitrary and capricious" standard. *See, e.g., Northwest Ecosystem Alliance v. U.S. Fish & Wildlife Service*, 475 F. 3d 1136 (9th Cir. 2007) (Service's denial of petition to list western gray squirrels in Washington as an endangered "distinct population segment" was not arbitrary and capricious, where Service found a lack of distinctive biological traits); *Nat'l Ass'n of Home Builders v. Norton*, 340 F. 3d 835 (9th Cir. 2003) (overturning as arbitrary and capricious Service's decision to list Arizona pygmy owl population as an endangered distinct population segment); *Alsea Valley Alliance v. Evans*, 161 F. Supp. 2d 1154, 1158–59 (D. Or. 2001) (arbitrary and capricious for NMFS to list coho salmon as a distinct population segment, but in the listing deny protections to hatchery born coho that are afforded wild coho).

Although the economic impacts of listing a species as threatened or endangered can be tremendous, by law these impacts may not be considered in the listing process. Only information concerning the species may be considered.

Although the economic impacts of listing a species as threatened or endangered can be tremendous, by law such impacts may not be considered in the listing process.

Generally, the Service initiates the listing process, although the ESA allows individuals to petition the Service to consider a species for listing. In California, a substantial portion of the listings have resulted from such petitions. The listing process begins with the publication of notice of a proposed rule in the Federal Register. 50 C.F.R. § 424.16. This notice must contain the complete text of the proposed rule, summarize the data on which the proposed listing is based, and show the relationship of the data to the rule being proposed. 50 C.F.R. § 424.16(b).

The Service then allows at least 60 days for the public to comment following publication of the proposed rule in the Federal Register. The Service must hold at least one public hearing if any person so requests within 45 days of publication of the proposed rule, and must provide at least 15 days notice in the Federal Register of the time and place of the hearing. 50 C.F.R. § 424.16(b)(3).

The Service may extend or reopen the public comment period upon a finding that there is good cause to do so. 50 C.F.R. § 424.16(c)(2). When new information becomes available after the close of the public comment period that is critical to the listing decision, the Service must provide an additional opportunity for public review and comment. *See Idaho Farm Bureau Fed'n v. Babbitt*, 58 F. 3d 1392 (9th Cir. 1995); *but see Kern County Farm Bureau v. Allen*, 450 F. 3d 1072 (9th Cir. 2006) (no duty to reopen comment period where new information was important, but not critical, to listing decision).

Within one year of publication of a proposed rule, the Service is required to publish in the Federal Register one of the following: (1) a final rule to implement the determination whether a species is endangered or threatened, (2) a finding that the determination will not be made, (3) a notice withdrawing the proposed rule "upon a finding that available evidence does not justify the action proposed by the rule," or (4) a notice extending the one-year period by an additional period of not more than six months because there is a "substantial disagreement among scientists knowledgeable about the species concerned regarding the sufficiency or accuracy of the available data relevant to the determination." 50 C.F.R. § 424.17(a).

Although the listing of an endangered or threatened species is a federal action, the requirements under the National Environmental Protection Act (NEPA) for conducting an environmental review do not apply to the listing process. *See Pacific Legal Found. v. Andrus*, 657 F. 2d 829, 835 (6th Cir. 1981).

In addition to its normal listing authority, the Service also has the authority at any time to take a listing action in response to any "emergency posing a significant risk to the well-being of a species of fish, wildlife or plant." 50 C.F.R. § 424.20. These emergency rules take effect immediately on publication in the Federal Register but cease to have force and effect after 240 days. 50 C.F.R. § 424.20.

One example of an emergency listing is the Mojave Desert population of the desert tortoise. The Service explained that a variety of factors, including disease and predation by ravens, were causing a significant and dramatic decline of the species, and that an emergency listing was required to protect the species while further actions were considered. 50 C.F.R. § 17.11.

The emergency listing of the desert tortoise caused serious problems for developers in Southern California and Las Vegas, and the action was challenged in *City of Las Vegas v. Lujan*, 891 F. 2d 927 (D.C. Cir. 1989). The court held that the ESA gave the Secretary considerable deference and latitude in the emergency listing of endangered species, and refused to grant a preliminary injunction to halt the emergency listing. The court said that its "scrutiny of such emergency regulation is...less exacting on the Secretary than it would be if he enacted precisely the same regulation...after a normal rulemaking." *Id.* at 932. *See also* 63 Fed. Reg. 3835 (January 27, 1998) (emergency listing of San Bernardino kangaroo rat); 65 Fed. Reg. 3096 (January 19, 2000) (emergency listing of Santa Barbara County population of California tiger salamander); 67 Fed. Reg. 47726 (July 22, 2002) (emergency listing of Sonoma County population of California tiger salamander).

Since the ESA was passed, the Service has listed hundreds of species yet has consistently faced a backlog of species to consider. In 1988, Congress noted that 950 species were prime candidates for listing for which the Service had taken no action. To address this issue, the ESA was amended in 1988 to allow any person to petition the Service to add a species to or remove a species from the list as threatened or endangered. Within 90 days of receiving the petition, the Service must make a finding on whether the petition presents substantial scientific or commercial information indicating that the petitioned action may be warranted. If the Secretary so finds, the Secretary promptly must begin a review of the status of the species. 16 U.S.C. § 1533(b)(3).

Within 12 months of receiving a petition for which the Secretary determines further action is warranted, the Secretary is required to publish in the Federal Register one of the following findings:

- That the petitioned action is not warranted
- That the petitioned action is warranted, in which case the Secretary shall promptly publish a proposed rule to that effect in the Federal Register, or
- That the action is warranted, but further action is precluded by other pending proposals considering whether various species are eligible or ineligible for listing

16 U.S.C. § 1533(b)(3); see *Center for Biological Diversity v. Norton*, 254 F. 3d 833, 838 (9th Cir. 2001) (designation of a species as a "candidate" for listing does not satisfy the requirement to make and publish one of the specific 12-month findings required by § 1533(b)(3))

The Secretary also is required to adopt a system to prioritize efforts for the species for which further action is warranted but precluded by other pending proposals. The goal is for the Secretary to list those species that are in the greatest danger of extinction. These are referred to as candidate species. The list of candidate species is updated periodically. The Service's most recent annual summary of candidate and proposed species can be found at 71 Fed. Reg. 53756 (Sept. 12, 2006).

Once a species is listed, the Secretary is required to develop a "recovery plan." A recovery plan provides for the conservation and survival of the species. 16 U.S.C. § 1533(f). In the past, the Secretary has asserted that insufficient funds were available to prepare recovery plans for all species. See *Defenders of Wildlife v. Lujan*, 792 F. Supp. 834, 836 (D.D.C. 1992) (action to force the Secretary to implement the portion of the gray wolf recovery plan calling for reintroduction to Yellowstone Park was moot as all funds were specifically withheld under a rider to the 1992 Appropriations Act). However, in 1997, the Secretary announced a goal of issuing recovery plans for all listed species by the end of 1998. As a result, a dramatic increase in the number of draft recovery plans released for public comment began in late 1997. Although the Secretary's goal for completing this task by the end of 1998 was not met, the effort is continuing, as scores of plans have been finalized or proposed in recent years.

Once a species is listed, the Secretary is required to develop a "recovery plan." A recovery plan provides for the conservation and survival of the species.

Designation of "Critical Habitat"

When a species is listed as endangered or threatened, the Service also is required to publish concurrently, absent "extraordinary circumstances," a designation of a "critical habitat" for the species. 16 U.S.C. § 1533(a)(3); see also *Conservation Council v. Babbitt*, 2 F. Supp. 2d 1280 (D. Hawaii 1998) (ordering the Service to designate critical habitat for several hundred listed plant species). The term "critical habitat" means:

- The specific areas within the geographical area currently occupied by a species, at the time it is listed in accordance with the ESA, on which are found those

When a species is listed as endangered or threatened, the Service also is required to publish concurrently, absent "extraordinary circumstances," a designation of a "critical habitat" for the species.

physical or biological features (1) essential to the conservation of the species, and (2) that may require special management considerations or protection
- Specific areas outside the geographical area occupied by a species at the time it is listed upon a determination by the Secretary that such areas are essential for the conservation of the species

50 C.F.R. § 424.02(d)

Unlike the listing determination, the designation of critical habitat must include consideration of economic factors.

Unlike the listing determination, the designation of critical habitat must include consideration of economic factors. 50 C.F.R. § 424.19. The designation of critical habitat for 15 vernal pool species in California and southern Oregon illustrates the difficulties facing the Service in addressing economic issues. The Service's designation in 2003 excluded certain lands based on economic grounds. In response to a lawsuit by environmentalists challenging the exclusions, the Service agreed to conduct a new economic analysis. The Service then issued a new designation in 2005, which was challenged again in court, by both environmentalists and the Home Builders Association of Northern California. In setting aside the determination, the court faulted the Service's economic determinations for not adequately explaining why two particular tracts of land were excluded and for not adequately considering the benefits that would result from a critical habitat designation.[2] In response, the Service again reevaluated its economic exclusions, and while it retained its 2005 designation, it published a detailed analysis in the Federal Register addressing the issues raised by the court. *See* 72 Fed. Reg. 30279 (May 31, 2007).

With respect to compliance with NEPA, there is some judicial disagreement as to whether this statute applies to the designation of critical habitat (as opposed to the listing of a species). *Compare Douglas County v. Babbitt*, 48 F. 3d 1495, 1502–03 (9th Cir. 1995) (critical habitat designations do not require NEPA compliance) *with Catron County v. U.S. Fish and Wildlife Serv.*, 75 F. 3d 1429, 1433–34 (10th Cir. 1996) (environmental impact statement may be needed to support critical habitat designation). The Ninth Circuit's decision (holding that NEPA does not apply) is the governing law in California.

The requirement to designate critical habitat concurrently with the final listing of a species can be deferred if the Secretary determines that it is essential that the species be listed promptly, even without a critical habitat designation, or if the Service determines that the critical habitat of the species is "not then determinable." 16 U.S.C. § 1533(b)(6)(C); 50 C.F.R. § 424.17(b). *See Enos v. Marsh*, 769 F. 2d 1363, 1370–71 (9th Cir. 1985) (decision not to define critical habitat is proper where essential biological features are unknown); 63 Fed. Reg. 54938 (October 13, 1998) (Service declined to designate critical habitat immediately for several listed plants in Southern California due to fear that designation will result in purposeful vandalism and eradication efforts by landowners).

The Service must state the reasons for not designating critical habitat, and may not delay designation of critical habitat for more than 12 months after publication of the final listing rule.

The Service must state "the reasons for not designating critical habitat." 50 C.F.R. § 424.12(a). The Service may not delay designation of critical habitat for more than 12 months after publication of the final listing rule. *See Northern Spotted Owl v. Lujan*, 758 F. Supp. 621, 625–26 (W.D. Wash. 1991) (Service

---

2. *See Home Builders Assn. of Northern California v. U.S. Fish and Wildlife Serv.*, 2006 U.S. Dist. LEXIS 80255 (E.D. Cal. Nov. 2, 2006), on reconsideration, 2007 U.S. Dist. LEXIS 5208 (E.D. Cal. Jan. 24, 2007).

abused its discretion when it decided not to designate critical habitat concurrently with the listing of the northern spotted owl, or to explain why critical habitat was not determinable); *but see Center for Biological Diversity v. U.S. Fish and Wildlife Service*, 450 F. 3d 930 (9th Cir. 2006) (Service was not required to designate critical habitat for endangered fish species listed in 1970, since ESA requirement to designate critical habitat concurrently with listing was not enacted until 1982 and did not apply to listings made before that date).

The controversy over designations of critical habitat intensified in 2000 and continues today, as environmental group plaintiffs succeed in case after case forcing the Service to designate critical habitat against its will. The resulting accumulation of court orders, most containing deadlines for Service compliance, have resulted in a profusion of critical habitat proposals and designations in California.

The controversy over designations of critical habitat intensified in 2000 and continues today, as environmental group plaintiffs succeed in case after case forcing the Service to designate critical habitat against its will.

Not surprisingly, legal challenges to critical habitat designations by both industry and environmental groups have followed. *See, e.g., New Mexico Cattle Growers Ass'n v. U.S. Fish and Wildlife Serv.*, 248 F. 3d 1277, 1283 (10th Cir. 2001) (Service's economic impact analysis failed to account for all economic impacts of critical habitat designation); *Home Builders Ass'n of N. Calif. v. Norton*, 293 F. Supp. 2d 1 (D.D.C. 2002) (court approved settlement whereby the Service voluntarily rescinded its critical habitat designation for the California red-legged frog and agreed to new rulemaking proceedings); *Home Builders Ass'n of N. Calif. v. U.S. Fish and Wildlife Serv.*, 268 F. Supp. 2d 1197 (E.D. Cal. 2003) (Service's designation of critical habitat for Alameda whipsnake inadequately justified); *Center for Biological Diversity v. Norton*, 240 F. Supp. 2d 1090 (D. Ariz. 2003) (Service was arbitrary and capricious in failing to designate full extent of Mexican spotted owl critical habitat where the Service contended that the habitat already was fully protected under Forest Service plans).

As a result of court orders and settlement agreements, the Service recently has designated or proposed to designate critical habitat for a number of listed species in California affecting hundreds of thousands of acres. Recent critical habitat designations include:

- 200,000 acres in 19 counties for the California tiger salamander. 70 Fed. Reg. 49739 (Aug. 23, 2005)
- Over 850,000 acres in 34 California counties and one Oregon county for four vernal pool crustaceans and 11 vernal pool plant species. 70 Fed. Reg. 49739 (Aug. 23, 2005); 72 Fed. Reg. 30279 (May 31, 2007)
- Over 450,000 acres in counties ranging from Butte to Ventura for the red-legged frog. 71 Fed. Reg. 19244 (Apr. 13, 2006)
- Over 150,000 acres in Northern California for the Alameda whipsnake. 71 Fed. Reg. 58176 (Oct. 2, 2006)
- A broad-reaching designation for west coast salmon and steelhead that includes riverine and estuarine habitats. 70 Fed. Reg. 52488 (Sept. 8, 2005)
- A proposal to designate over 400,000 acres for the Sierra Nevada bighorn sheep. 72 Fed. Reg. 40956 (July 25, 2007)
- A proposal to designate 20,000 acres in Northern California for the bay checkerspot butterfly. 72 Fed. Reg. 48178 (Aug. 22, 2007)

Given the combined effect of lawsuits by environmental groups to compel designations, and challenges to those designations once they have been made, the status of many of the Service's designations is in a state of flux. The Service maintains a website with species-by-species status reports that can be consulted for current information regarding critical habitat designations (*see* http://ecos.fws.gov/tess_public/StartTESS.do).

The Consultation Process

Section 7 of the ESA (16 U.S.C. § 1536) implements the protections that are afforded to listed species. Under Section 7, each federal agency must consult with the Service to ensure that any actions authorized, funded, or carried out by the agency are not likely to "jeopardize the continued existence of any endangered species or threatened species or result in the destruction or adverse modification of habitat...determined" by the Service to be "critical." 16 U.S.C. §§ 1532(5), 1536(a)(2). The consultation process applies only to actions taken by federal agencies, or actions by private parties that require federal agency permits, approval, or funding. It does not apply to private actions that do not require or involve a federal action, or to agency actions taken abroad. 51 Fed. Reg. 19926 (June 3, 1986); 50 C.F.R. § 402.01.

In 1998, the Service published a detailed handbook on the Section 7 process (available at www.fws.gov/endangered/consultations/s7hndbk/s7hndbk.htm).

Procedure

Agency action. Section 7 applies to all federal agency actions—"all activities or programs of any kind authorized, funded or carried out, in whole or in part, by federal agencies in the United States or upon the high seas." 50 C.F.R. § 402.02.

Examples of direct federal actions include the construction of a flood control dam by the Army Corps of Engineers (Corps), adoption of a new grazing policy by the Bureau of Land Management, and the EPA's registration of pesticides. The Ninth Circuit held that Section 7 also applies not only to the initial adoption by the Forest Service of a National Forest Land and Resource Management Plan, but also to the ongoing implementation of that plan. *See Pacific Rivers Council v. Thomas*, 30 F. 3d 1050, 1055–56 (9th Cir. 1994).

Examples of indirect, "non federal" actions that require Section 7 consultation include the construction of a dam by a private entity where a Clean Water Act (CWA) Section 404 permit is required from the Corps (*Riverside Irr. Dist. v. Andrews*, 758 F. 2d 508 (10th Cir. 1985)); development of a ski resort pursuant to a special use permit issued by the Forest Service (*Wilson v. Block*, 708 F. 2d 735 (D.C. Cir. 1983)); a federally financed state highway project (*National Wildlife Fed'n v. Coleman*, 529 F. 2d 359 (5th Cir.), *cert. denied*, 429 U.S. 979 (1976)); and operation of an oil refinery pursuant to an NPDES wastewater discharge permit issued by the EPA under Section 402 of the CWA (*Roosevelt Campobello Int'l Park Comm'n v. U.S. EPA*, 684 F. 2d 1041 (1st Cir. 1982)).

However, Section 7 consultation is required only for "discretionary" actions by federal agencies. The United States Supreme Court, in reversing the Ninth Circuit, determined that the EPA's transfer of water pollution control authority to Arizona under Section 402 of the Clean Water Act did not trigger consultation, since the EPA was legally compelled by that Act to effectuate the transfer if certain conditions were met. *National Ass'n of Home Builders v. Defenders of Wildlife*, 127 S. Ct. 2518 (2007).

Corps = Army Corps of Engineers
CWA = Clean Water Act
EPA = Environmental Protection Agency
NPDES = National Pollutant Discharge Elimination System

Section 7 consultation is required only for "discretionary" actions by federal agencies.

Section 7 consultation is also not triggered by a federal agency's *failure* to act. In *Western Watershed Project v. Matejko*, 468 F. 3d 1099 (9th Cir. 2006), the Ninth Circuit rejected the claim that consultation was required as a result of the Bureau of Land Management's refusal to exercise its discretion to regulate private water diversions. "We conclude that the duty to consult is triggered by affirmative actions; because there was no such 'action' here, there was no corresponding duty to consult." *Id.* at 1102. The Ninth Circuit reached a similar result in *California Sportfishing Protection Alliance v. Federal Energy Regulatory Commission*, 472 F. 3d 593 (9th Cir. 2006). There, the court rejected the claim that the listing of a new species triggered the need to consult concerning a private hydroelectric project that was operating under a federal license issued in 1980. The court stated: "The triggering mechanism for consultation is an agency action, not the listing of a species." *Id.* at 597.

However, once the requirement to consult is triggered by a discretionary action, the effects resulting from the *entirety* of the project—including those parts of the project that are nondiscretionary—must be evaluated. *See Nat'l Wildlife Fed'n v. Nat'l Marine Fisheries Serv.*, 481 F. 3d at 1233–34.

"May affect" trigger. Section 7's consultation requirement is triggered by the "action agency's" determination that the proposed federal action "may affect" a listed species or critical habitat. 50 C.F.R. § 402.14(a). The "action area" and the "effects of the action" constitute the "scope of the action" subject to consultation. *See National Wildlife Fed'n*, 529 F. 2d at 371.

Section 7's consultation requirement is triggered by the action agency's determination that the proposed federal action may affect a listed species or critical habitat.

"Action area" means:

[A]ll areas to be affected directly or indirectly by the Federal action and not merely the immediate area involved in the action.

50 C.F.R. § 402.02

The "effects of the action" are:

[T]he direct and indirect effects of an action on the species or critical habitat, together with the effects of other activities that are interrelated or interdependent with that action....

50 C.F.R. § 402.02

The Service uses a "but for" test in deciding whether activities are "interrelated" (are part of a larger action and depend on the larger action for their justification) or "interdependent" (have no independent utility apart from the action under consideration), and therefore should be included within the scope of the action. *See Sierra Club v. Marsh*, 816 F. 2d 1376, 1387 (9th Cir. 1987); *see also* 51 Fed. Reg. 19932 (June 3, 1986).

The Service uses a "but for" test in deciding whether activities are interrelated or interdependent, and therefore should be included within the scope of the action.

In *Riverside Irrigation District v. Andrews*, the court held that in reviewing an application for a Section 404 fill permit required in connection with dam construction, the Corps properly looked at the indirect impacts to whooping crane critical habitat located 150 miles downstream from the dam that would result from increased upstream consumptive water use enabled by the dam. 758 F. 2d 508 (10th Cir. 1985). In *National Wildlife Federation v. Coleman*, the court similarly held that the indirect effects of private development resulting from construction of highway interchanges were to be considered as impacts of a federal highway project. 529 F. 2d 359 (5th Cir. 1976).

The consultation process begins with the action agency's request to the Service for information on whether any species listed or proposed to be listed exist in the area of the proposed action. 16 U.S.C. § 1536(c)(1). The action agency then conducts a biological assessment to determine whether those species are likely to be affected by the proposed action. *Id.* If the action agency determines that the proposed action is likely to jeopardize the continued existence of any species or result in the destruction or adverse modification of any critical habitat, it must formally consult with the Service. 16 U.S.C. § 1536(a)(4).

The action agency has the responsibility to provide the best available scientific and commercial information about the potential impacts of the proposed federal action on the listed species and its critical habitat, if any.

The action agency has the responsibility to provide the best available scientific and commercial information about the potential impacts of the proposed federal action on the listed species and its critical habitat, if any. 50 C.F.R. §§ 402.14(c), (d). This includes information that can be obtained during the consultation. *See Roosevelt Campobello Int'l Park Comm'n*, 684 F. 2d at 1051 (a federal agency that "proceeds with [an] action in the face of inadequate knowledge or information does so with the risk that it has not satisfied the standard of" Section 7(a)(2)); *Conservation Law Found. v. Watt*, 560 F. Supp. 561, 572 (D. Mass. 1983), *aff'd on other grounds sub nom.*; *Massachusetts v. Watt*, 716 F. 2d 946 (1st Cir. 1983) (action agency has an "ongoing" duty to incorporate new information into consultation); *Resources Ltd. v. Robertson*, 35 F. 3d 1300, 1305 (9th Cir. 1993) (consultation invalid where consulting agency selectively withholds information about impacts to listed species); *but see Greenpeace Action v. Franklin*, 982 F. 2d 1342, 1355 (9th Cir. 1992) (action agency's reliance on "admittedly weak" scientific data upheld as the best information available); *Stop H-3 Ass'n v. Dole*, 740 F. 2d 1442, 1460 (9th Cir. 1984), *cert. denied sub nom., Yamasaki v. Stop H-3 Ass'n*, 471 U.S. 1108 (1985) (reliance on the Service's biological opinion was not arbitrary even though there was a disagreement among experts as to its conclusions).

Biological opinion. The Service is charged with formulating a biological opinion based on the best available information as to whether the action, including its direct and indirect effects, as well as the effects of any interrelated actions or interdependent activities—taken together with cumulative effects (future state or private activities, not involving federal activities, that are reasonably certain to occur within the action area)—is likely to jeopardize the continued existence of a species or destroy or adversely modify its critical habitat. 50 C.F.R. § 402.14(g).

If the Service finds that the action would jeopardize the continued existence of the species or adversely modify critical habitat, the Service must suggest reasonable and prudent alternatives to avoid the adverse impacts.

The Service then prepares a biological opinion identifying the effects of the action on the threatened or endangered species. If the Service finds that the action would jeopardize the continued existence of the species or adversely modify critical habitat, the Service must suggest reasonable and prudent alternatives to avoid the adverse impacts. 16 U.S.C. § 1536(b)(3). If there are no such alternatives, the agency may not proceed with the project unless the Endangered Species Committee grants an exception. 16 U.S.C. § 1536(h).

"Jeopardize the continued existence" means:

[T]o engage in an action that reasonably would be expected, directly or indirectly, to reduce appreciably the likelihood of *both the survival and recovery* of a listed species in the wild by reducing the reproduction, numbers, or distribution of the species.

50 C.F.R. § 402.02 (emphasis added)

"Destruction or adverse modification of critical habitat" means:

[A] direct or indirect alteration that appreciably diminishes the value of critical habitat for *both the survival and recovery* of a listed species. Such alterations include, but are not limited to, alterations adversely modifying any of those physical or biological features that were the basis for determining the habitat to be critical.

50 C.F.R. § 402.02 (emphasis added)

Thus, under both regulatory definitions, the proposed action must appreciably diminish the survival, and not simply the recovery, of the species. The "survival and recovery" standard is seen by many, particularly those on the conservation side of the debate, as a deficiency in the regulatory definitions, and not supportive of the ESA's overall purpose of conservation of endangered species and their habitats. Under this view, the ESA should protect against actions that threaten the recovery of a species, even if those actions do not threaten the species' survival. The Ninth Circuit has agreed with this position in two recent decisions.

In 2004, the Ninth Circuit invalidated the "survival and recovery" standard as applied to the adverse modification of critical habitat under 50 C.F.R. § 402.02. The court reasoned that such a standard effectively required only consideration of the survival of the affected species, not its recovery. This was inconsistent, in the court's view, with the ESA's definition of critical habitat—which references the "conservation" of the species, a term the statute elsewhere equates to recovery. The court followed decisions of other circuits in holding that "the regulatory definition of 'adverse modification' gives too little protection to designated critical habitat." *Gifford Pinchot Task Force v. U.S. Fish and Wildlife Serv.*, 378 F. 3d 1059, 1069–70 (9th Cir. 2004).

In 2007, the Ninth Circuit made clear that the requirement to consider the recovery of a species, as set out in the *Gifford Pinchot* case, also applies to consideration of whether an action will cause jeopardy. *Nat'l Wildlife Fed'n v. Nat'l Marine Fisheries Serv.*, 481 F. 3d at 1236–37. The court flatly rejected NMFS' claim that jeopardy is not triggered unless the action appreciably reduces *both* survival odds *and* the likelihood of recovery.

The Ninth Circuit's rulings in *Gifford Pinchot* and *National Wildlife Federation* throw into serious question the validity of many prior consultations that failed to consider recovery adequately, or even at all. *See, e.g., Oregon Natural Resources Council v. Allen*, 476 F. 3d 1031 (9th Cir. 2007) (Service voluntarily withdrew its biological opinion for part of a proposed timber harvest to consider recovery in accordance with *Gifford Pinchot*); *Natural Resources Defense Council v. Kempthorne*, 506 F. Supp. 2d 322 (E.D. Cal. 2007) (biological opinion for water pumping operations did not adequately consider the impact on recovery of the Delta smelt); *Center for Biological Diversity v. Bureau of Land Management*, 422 F. Supp. 2d 1115, 1136 (N.D. Cal. 2006) (overturning biological opinion for a federal recreation area management plan where species recovery goals were ignored); *Natural Resources Defense Council v. Rogers*, 381 F. Supp. 2d 1212 (E.D. Cal. 2005) (Section 7 consultations on Bureau of Reclamation water contract renewals were invalidated for failure to consider recovery).

In addition to recovery of the species, the evaluation of jeopardy in a biological opinion also must take into account the degree to which the environment has been degraded by past activities. In *National Wildlife Federation v. NMFS*, the Ninth Circuit rejected the view that jeopardy exists only if a project's effects are appreciably worse than the existing "baseline" conditions. 481 F. 3d 1224 (9th Cir. 2007). Under this view, the court stated that "a listed species could be gradually destroyed, so long as each step on the path to destruction is sufficiently modest." *Id.* at 1235. This decision will make it more difficult to make a no jeopardy finding where the baseline conditions are poor.

If the proposed action will result in incidental take of a listed species, but not jeopardy, the Service includes an incidental take statement.

If the proposed action will result in an "incidental take" of a listed species (*i.e.*, a take that is incidental to the carrying out of an otherwise lawful activity), but not jeopardy, the Service includes an "incidental take statement" in the biological opinion. The statement details the amount of take, those "reasonable and prudent" measures necessary to minimize such take, and mandatory terms and conditions to implement the reasonable and prudent measures. 50 C.F.R. § 402.14(i)(1). The Service also imposes reporting requirements on the federal agency or applicant, so that the Service can monitor the impacts of the incidental take. 50 C.F.R. § 402.14(i)(3). The incidental take statement, if complied with by the "action agency" and applicant, if any, insulates both from liability for a prohibited take of the listed species pursuant to Section 4(d) or Section 9 of the ESA. 50 C.F.R. § 402.14(i)(5).

Reasonable and prudent incidental take measures and implementing terms and conditions are restricted to minor changes that do not alter the basic design, location, scope, duration, or timing of the action.

Reasonable and prudent incidental take measures and implementing terms and conditions are restricted to minor changes that do not alter the basic design, location, scope, duration, or timing of the action. 50 C.F.R. § 402.14(i)(2).

In 2007, the Ninth Circuit authored an opinion that contains several important rulings on incidental take statements. *Oregon Natural Resources Council v. Allen*, 476 F. 3d 1031 (9th Cir. 2007). First, when the Service withdraws its biological opinion for a proposed action, any incidental take statements based on the opinion are no longer valid. Second, the Service must adequately explain why a numerical standard is impractical if it decides not to include such a standard in an incidental take statement. Third, an incidental take statement must contain an adequate threshold (numerical or otherwise) that, if exceeded, will trigger the reinitiation of consultation (which is discussed below). A statement that simply allows the take of "all spotted owls" associated with the project is therefore invalid, since it essentially shields the project from any requirement to reinitiate the Section 7 consultation process.

As with listing decisions, biological opinions are judicially reviewable under an "arbitrary and capricious" standard. *See, e.g., NRDC v. Kempthorne*, 506 F. Supp. 2d 322 (E.D. Cal. 2007) (invalidating biological opinion for coordinated water pumping operations under the Central Valley Project and State Water Project, after determining that the finding of no jeopardy to the Delta smelt was arbitrary and capricious).

Federal district courts have the authority to enjoin an agency from violating Section 7 of the ESA.

Further, federal district courts have the authority to enjoin an agency from violating Section 7 of the ESA. 16 U.S.C. § 1540(g)(1)(A). As part of that authority, the court may, to the extent necessary, temporarily dictate the actions the agency must take with regard to the activity that has resulted in violations of Section 7 of the ESA. *See Sierra Club v. Yeutter*, 926 F. 2d 429, 439–40 (5th Cir. 1991). The court may not, however, fashion an injunction that eviscerates the consultation process by effectively dictating the results of that process. *Id.* Congress, however, can alter the consultation process to accomplish its objectives more speedily. *See Robertson v. Seattle Audubon Soc'y*, 503 U.S. 429, 437 (1992) (Northwest Timber Compromise was constitutional and did not dictate results of pending litigation); *Mt. Graham Red Squirrel v. Madigan*, 954 F. 2d 1441, 1451–52 (9th Cir. 1992) (special act of Congress suspending ESA requirements with respect to one phase of a project did not require reinitiation of consultation with the Service).

Agencies are permitted to depart from the alternatives recommended in the Service's biological opinion without violating the ESA so long as the agency has taken alternative, reasonable, and prudent steps to ensure the continued existence of the endangered species. *See Tribal Village of Akutan v. Hodel*, 869 F. 2d 1185, 1192–94 (9th Cir. 1988); *see also Sierra Club v. Yeutter*, 926 F. 2d at 438–39 (Forest Service violated Section 7 by not taking the steps necessary to ensure that its conduct did not jeopardize the continued existence of the red-cockaded woodpecker).

FERC = Federal Energy Regulatory Commission

While an agency's departure from alternatives recommended in the biological opinion may be permitted if these steps are taken, the failure to consult with the Service (or reinitiate consultation, if necessary) violates the ESA. *Platte River Whooping Crane v. F.E.R.C.*, 876 F. 2d 109, 117 (D.C. Cir. 1989) (failure to consult on annual FERC relicensing); *Sierra Club v. Marsh*, 816 F. 2d 1376, 1384 (9th Cir. 1987) (failure to reinitiate consultation when mitigation lands were not transferred). However, where an agency's determination that a project will have "no effect" on a species is not arbitrary or capricious, that determination will be upheld. *Defenders of Wildlife v. Flowers*, 414 F. 3d 1066 (9th Cir. 2005).

While an agency's departure from alternatives recommended in the biological opinion may be permitted if these steps are taken, the failure to consult with the Service (or reinitiate consultation, if necessary) violates the ESA.

In deciding how to proceed with the Section 7 consultation process, both the Service and the other federal agencies must use the best available scientific and commercial information. *See Roosevelt Campobello Int'l Park Comm'n v. U.S. EPA*, 684 F. 2d at 1050 (failure to use "real time simulation studies" to assure low risk of oil spill with potential impact on endangered whales violates the ESA); *NRDC v. Kempthorne*, 506 F. Supp. 2d 322 (E.D. Cal. 2007) (agency's failure to reasonably estimate Delta smelt population and analyze most recent smelt abundance data made the take limits established in the biological opinion unreliable and unreasonable); *but see Village of False Pass v. Clark*, 733 F. 2d 605, 610 (9th Cir. 1984) (minor differences between the draft and final biological opinions did not fatally undermine the quality of the data).

For permitting applications where a private party seeks action by a federal agency, as a practical matter, the burden of satisfying the ESA usually falls on the applicant. It is generally advisable in such cases to work with the federal agency in the early part of the permitting process to identify potential problems, and to meet and consult informally with the Service at the earliest possible time. The applicant normally must identify the presence or absence of the endangered species and prepare the required studies and reports.

For actions where a private party seeks action before a federal agency, as a practical matter, the burden of satisfying the ESA usually falls on the applicant.

If possible, consideration should be given at the earliest stages to redesigning the project to avoid having an impact on threatened or endangered species, and to identifying suitable mitigation. It is even possible to engage in "early consultation" on the effect of a proposal on endangered species. 50 C.F.R. § 402.11. This allows an applicant to obtain advance approval of his or her plans before submitting the actual permit application. The early consultation results in a "preliminary biological opinion." 50 C.F.R. § 402.11(e).

The preliminary biological opinion will be confirmed as final if there have been no significant changes in the proposed action or in the information used in the early consultation. 50 C.F.R. § 402.11(f).

The mitigation measures set forth in a biological opinion must ensure that there will be no jeopardy to the continued existence of the species.

The mitigation measures set forth in a biological opinion must ensure that there will be no jeopardy to the continued existence of the species. *Pacific Coast Fed'n of Fishermen's Ass'ns v. Bureau of Reclamation*, 426 F. 3d 1082 (9th Cir. 2005) (delayed in-stream flow requirements insufficient to ensure near-term survival of Coho salmon in the Klamath River); *NRDC v. Kempthorne*, 506 F. Supp. 2d 322 (E.D. Cal. 2007) (biological opinion was inadequate where there was no reasonable degree of certainty that mitigation actions would take place). The degree of required mitigation can vary but the general objective is to ensure the short-term and long-term viability of the species in the area affected by the project. For animals and birds, habitat enhancement and habitat protection are likely mitigation measures. For plants, cultivation and protection of existing populations may be required.

Section 7 of the ESA also requires that federal agencies consult with the Service if a proposed action may affect designated critical habitat.

Section 7 of the ESA also requires that federal agencies consult with the Service if a proposed action may affect designated "critical habitat." 50 C.F.R. § 402.14(a). Any federal action occurring within these designated critical habitats triggers the consultation process under Section 7 of the ESA. This includes not only actions that a federal agency may carry out on its own, but also private actions that the agency funds or authorizes.

Reinitiation of consultation. Finally, there is the possible need to reinitiate consultation where discretionary federal involvement or control over the action has been retained or is authorized by law, and one or more of the following circumstances arises:

- The amount or extent of take specified in the incidental take statement is exceeded
- New information reveals effects of the action that may affect listed species or critical habitat in a manner or to an extent not previously identified
- The identified action is modified in a manner that causes an effect to the listed species or critical habitat that was not considered in the biological opinion
- A new species is listed or critical habitat designated that may be affected by the identified action

50 C.F.R. § 402.16. *See Envtl. Prot. Info. Ctr. v. Simpson Timber Co.*, 255 F. 3d 1073, 1081 (9th Cir. 2001) (Service not required to reinitiate consultation for a lumber company's permit for incidental take of the spotted owl, following the subsequent listing of two other species that could be affected by lumber company operations, where Service did not retain discretionary control over the permit); *Guardians v. Johanns*, 450 F. 3d 455 (9th Cir. 2006) (reinitiation required where annual monitoring demonstrated that grazing limits specified in the biological opinion were exceeded, and not all required monitoring was undertaken).

Exemptions from the Endangered Species Act Requirements

In 1978, the United States Supreme Court decided *Tennessee Valley Authority v. Hill*, 437 U.S. 153 (1978). In that case, the Tennessee Valley Authority had proposed to build a dam on the Little Tennessee River. The dam had been opposed by local interests for many years, but these efforts were largely unsuccessful. After nearly $100 million had been spent on the dam, a University of Tennessee ichthyologist discovered the tiny snail darter in the river. The Secretary designated the snail darter as an endangered species and designated the stretch of the Little Tennessee River in which the dam was located as "critical habitat."

Shortly thereafter, a group of scientists and local river users sued to halt completion and operation of the dam. The Court held that years of Congressional funding of the dam did not repeal by implication the mandate in the ESA to halt or reverse the trend toward extinction of species. The Court upheld a decision enjoining construction of the dam, finding that protection of endangered species had priority over the primary mission of the agency and completion of the dam. *Id.* at 154. Ultimately, the Tellico Dam was completed, as subsequent research found the snail darter could live in other streams, enabling the Service to modify its jeopardy opinion.

The *Hill* decision brought into sharp focus the tension between economic development and protection of endangered species. Consequently, Congress established the Endangered Species Committee—popularly known as the "God Squad"—to allow exemptions from the requirements in the ESA. 16 U.S.C. § 1536(e). The Committee consists of seven members including the Secretaries of Agriculture, Army, and Interior, the Administrators of EPA and NOAA, and the Chairman of the Council of Economic Advisors. The seventh member is an individual from the affected state, appointed by the President. Despite the conflicts with the continued existence of a species, the Committee is authorized to allow an action threatening jeopardy to an endangered species to proceed if it finds that there are no reasonable and prudent alternatives and the benefits of the action "clearly outweigh the benefits of each considered alternative course of action [consistent with conserving the species]." 50 C.F.R. § 451.02(5)(ii).

Congress established the Endangered Species Committee—popularly known as the God Squad—to allow exemptions from the requirements in the ESA.

In 1992, the Endangered Species Committee was convened in connection with the controversial northern spotted owl listing. The Director of the Bureau of Land Management (BLM) sought an exemption from the ESA after the Service concluded that planned timber sales on 44 tracts of land in Oregon were likely to jeopardize the continued existence of the northern spotted owl. 56 Fed. Reg. 54562 (October 22, 1991). After public hearing and consideration, the Committee granted an exemption to 13 of the proposed 44 sales, subject to mitigation and enhancement measures to be taken by BLM. 57 Fed. Reg. 23405 (June 3, 1992).

BLM = Bureau of Land Management

In *Portland Audubon Society v. Endangered Species Committee*, the court heard a challenge from environmental groups to the proceedings charging that the White House improperly interfered with the Committee's decision-making process. 984 F. 2d 1534 (9th Cir. 1993). The court held that the deliberations of the Endangered Species Committee are subject to the ban on *ex parte* communications found in section 557(d)(1) of title 5 of the United States Code and that the ban applies to White House communications. *Id.* at 1546. The court remanded the case to the Committee for an evidentiary hearing to determine the nature, content, and extent of any off-the-record communications.

Despite the Endangered Species Committee, and a few instances of special legislation overriding ESA requirements, compliance with the ESA remains a fundamental obligation of federal agencies. It imposes a mandatory duty to consider the effect of their actions on endangered or threatened species and to conserve such species. *See Riverside Irr. Dist. v. Andrews*, 758 F. 2d 508 (10th Cir. 1985) (requiring the Corps to consider the direct and indirect impact on endangered whooping cranes of its actions in approving wetlands fill permits for a dam); *Nat'l Wildlife Fed'n v. NMFS*, 481 F. 3d 1224, 1234 (9th Cir. 2007) (the fact that federal agencies have competing interests as between their statutory mission and the mandates of the ESA does not relieve them from their "affirmative duty to satisfy the ESA's requirements, as a first priority").

Prohibitions Against Takings

Section 9 applies to any person, including natural persons, corporations, and federal, state, and local agencies.

The consultation process in Section 7 of the ESA applies only to actions by federal agencies (including the issuance of permits to private parties). In contrast, Section 9, which concerns prohibited acts, applies to any person, including natural persons, corporations, and federal, state, and local agencies. 16 U.S.C. § 1538(a)(1).

For fish and wildlife species listed as "endangered," Section 9 makes it unlawful to:

- Import any such species into, or export any such species from, the United States
- Take any such species within the United States or the territorial sea of the United States
- Take any such species upon the high seas
- Possess, sell, deliver, carry, transport, or ship, by any means whatsoever, any such species illegally taken
- Deliver, receive, carry, transport, or ship in interstate or foreign commerce, by any means whatsoever and in the course of a commercial activity, any such species
- Sell or offer for sale in interstate or foreign commerce any such species, or
- Violate any regulation pertaining to such species or to any threatened species of fish or wildlife listed pursuant to section 1533 of this title and promulgated by the Secretary

The Section 9 prohibitions applicable to endangered fish and wildlife have been extended to threatened fish and wildlife through regulation.

16 U.S.C. 1538(a)(1). These prohibitions have been extended to threatened fish and wildlife through regulation. 50 C.F.R. § 17.31.

For plant species as "endangered," Section 9 makes it unlawful to:

- Import any such species into, or export any such species from, the United States
- Remove and reduce to possession any such species from areas under federal jurisdiction; maliciously damage or destroy any such species on any such area; or remove, cut, dig up, or damage or destroy any such species on any other area in knowing violation of any law or regulation of any state or in the course of any violation of a state criminal trespass law
- Deliver, receive, carry, transport, or ship in interstate or foreign commerce, by any means whatsoever and in the course of a commercial activity, any such species
- Sell or offer for sale in interstate or foreign commerce any such species, or

- Violate any regulation pertaining to such species or to any threatened species of plants listed pursuant to section 1533 of this title and promulgated by the Secretary pursuant to authority provided by this chapter

16 U.S.C. § 1538(a)(2). The Secretary has adopted regulations extending most of these prohibitions to threatened plants. 50 C.F.R. § 17.71.

The take prohibition applicable to plants is narrower than that applicable to animals, and generally does not prohibit the taking of plants on private lands. In contrast, as discussed below, the California Endangered Species Act prohibits the taking of state-listed plants wherever located. Federally listed plants on private lands also need to be considered in a Section 7 consultation.

The ESA defines the term "take" to mean "harass, harm, pursue, hunt, shoot, wound, kill, trap, capture, or attempt to engage in any such conduct." 16 U.S.C. § 1532(19). The Service further defines "harm" and "harass" by regulation. Land management techniques that result in "harm" to an endangered species constitute a taking within the meaning of the ESA. *See Sierra Club v. Lyng*, 694 F. Supp. 1260, 1272 (E.D. Tex. 1988) (decline in the population of woodpeckers ranging from 22 percent to 76 percent on lands managed by the United States Forest Service in a period of less than 10 years constituted a taking of an endangered species), *aff'd in part and vacated in part, Sierra Club v. Yeutter*, 926 F. 2d 429 (5th Cir. 1991) (upholding takings finding and application of *de novo* review standard).

One key issue that has dominated controversies involving the ESA has been the scope of the takings prohibition in relation to the modification or destruction of species habitat. As noted above, the ESA defines "take" to include "harm," but the ESA does not define what the term "harm" means. The Service created a definition for "harm" in a regulation adopted in 1975. Under that regulation, "harm" is defined to mean "an act which actually kills or injures wildlife." The definition also states that such an act "may include significant habitat modification or degradation where it actually kills or injures wildlife by significantly impairing essential behavioral patterns, including breeding, feeding, or sheltering." As the Service's species protection efforts have become increasingly directed at protecting habitat in recent years, on both public and private property, controversies involving the type and amount of habitat modification that constitutes "take" have increased.

In *Babbitt v. Sweet Home Chapter of Communities for a Great Oregon*, the United States Supreme Court considered a facial challenge to the "harm" regulation. 515 U.S. 687 (1995). Rather than challenge the application of this regulation by the Service in a specific factual situation, the plaintiffs asserted that the regulation itself was inconsistent with the ESA and that the Secretary had exceeded his authority under the ESA in adopting the regulation. The district court rejected these arguments, granting summary judgment for the government. But the appellate court reversed, concluding that the term "harm" in the ESA was limited to a direct application of force against a listed species. Since that ruling conflicted with the Ninth Circuit decision in *Palila v. Hawaii Department of Land and Natural Resources*, 852 F. 2d 1106 (9th Cir. 1988), the Supreme Court granted review to resolve the issue.

By a 6–3 margin, the Court in *Sweet Home* reversed the appellate court, holding that the Secretary's regulatory definition was reasonable. 515 U.S. at

HCP = Habitat conservation plan

693. The Court reasoned that both the ordinary understanding of the word "harm," as well as the broad species protection goals of the ESA, support the Secretary's interpretation. The Court also found support for the regulation in the legislative history of the ESA, and in 1982 amendments to the ESA that allow the Service (under Section 10) to issue permits authorizing the "incidental take" of listed species when a habitat conservation plan (HCP) is first developed that provides the subject species with sufficient protection.

The majority opinion acknowledged the strong concerns of the plaintiffs (and the numerous entities that filed *amicus curiae* briefs) that in any particular case the Service might apply the "harm" regulation in a manner that was inconsistent with the ESA. For example, the opinion states that the plaintiffs had advanced "strong arguments" that activities that cause minimal or unforeseeable harm would not constitute a violation of the ESA, even though the Service might conclude otherwise by deciding that such activities fall within its definition of "harm." However, since the plaintiffs only challenged the validity of the regulation itself and not its specific application, and since, in the words of Justice O'Connor's concurring opinion, the regulation "does not on its terms exceed the agency's mandate, and...the regulation has innumerable valid habitat-related applications," the Court concluded that the Secretary had not exceeded his authority under the ESA and that the regulation is valid. *Id.* at 714.

The Sweet Home *decision did not involve the manner in which the Service applies the harm regulation in its day-to-day mission of implementing the ESA. It is just such day-to-day application, however, that has made this regulation so controversial.*

The *Sweet Home* decision did *not* involve the manner in which the Service applies the "harm" regulation in its day-to-day mission of implementing the ESA. It is just such day-to-day application, however, that has made this regulation so controversial. Indeed, many briefs filed with the Court contained lengthy descriptions of specific instances in which landowners had incurred enormous costs and administrative burdens as a result of the Service's application of the regulation to their property. Many landowners believe that in practice the Service simply ignores that portion of its regulation that states that significant habitat modification or degradation is "harm," and therefore a "take" prohibited by the ESA, only when such habitat modification or degradation "actually kills or injures wildlife." Although the Court could not rule on that concern directly given the limited nature of plaintiffs' claim, it did address the issue. In her concurring opinion, Justice O'Connor discussed at length her understanding that the harm regulation applies only where significant habitat modification proximately (*i.e.*, "foreseeably") causes *actual* ("as opposed to hypothetical or speculative") death or injury to listed species. *Id.* at 708–09. Such concerns leave the door wide open for lawsuits challenging the application of the regulation by the Service in any particular situation.

One such case involved the construction of a high school in Tucson, Arizona, on a site the Service designated as critical habitat for the cactus ferruginous pygmy owl, which at that time was a species listed as endangered by the Service. *See Defenders of Wildlife v. Bernal*, 204 F. 3d 920 (9th Cir. 2000). A biological survey showed that an owl used a section of the site that the school district owned but was not going to develop. No owls, however, used the part of the site that the school district proposed to develop. The Ninth Circuit held that the plaintiff had not met its burden of showing that construction of the school would actually "harm" or "harass" the owl, because no owls actually used the proposed construction site. *Id.* at 924.³ These decisions provide guidance that distinguishes "potential habitat" not actually used by listed wildlife from "actual habitat," which is used by listed wildlife.

Similarly, the Ninth Circuit held that the Service could not impose restrictions on grazing activities that were the subject of a Section 7 consultation, in the absence of evidence that a take was "reasonably certain to occur." *Arizona Cattle Growers Ass'n v. U. S. Fish and Wildlife Serv.*, 273 F. 3d 1229 (9th Cir. 2001). In *Arizona Cattle Growers*, the Service included a conditional incidental take statement in its biological opinion on a grazing program adopted by the Bureau of Land Management. These conditions imposed significant restrictions on the grazing activities, despite the fact that there was no credible evidence that the grazing activities at issue would take a listed species. The court held that the Service exceeded its authority by imposing these conditions without a rational basis for concluding that a take was reasonably certain to occur.

The Ninth Circuit held that the Service could not impose restrictions on grazing activities that were the subject of a Section 7 consultation, in the absence of evidence that a take was reasonably certain to occur.

The listing of threatened and endangered salmon and steelhead habitat in California and the Pacific Northwest may provide the courts with another opportunity to deal with the relationship between destruction of habitat and actual harm to a listed species. In 2000, NOAA listed five evolutionary significant units (ESU) of steelhead and salmon as endangered under the ESA, and another 21 ESUs were listed as threatened. NOAA defines an ESU as a genetically distinct population of fish. The typical ESU includes numerous river basins and covers several counties. For the five endangered ESUs, the Section 9 takings prohibition applied automatically upon listing. For 14 of the threatened ESUs, NOAA issued a rule under Section 4(d) of the ESA that applied the Section 9 no take prohibition to these ESUs effective September 8, 2000.

ESU = Evolutionary Significant Unit
NOAA = National Oceanic and Atmospheric Administration

Following the district court decision in *Alsea Valley Alliance v. Evans*, 161 F. Supp. 2d 1154 (D. Or. 2001), which invalidated NOAA's treatment of hatchery fish, most of these listings were withdrawn and then reissued in slightly modified form in 2005. 70 Fed. Reg. 37160 (June 28, 2005).

NOAA also defined critical habitat within these ESUs. In settlement of a suit brought by the National Association of Home Builders, most of these critical habitat designations were withdrawn in 2002, although designations remained in place for the Sacramento River winter-run Chinook, Central California Coast coho, and Southern Oregon/Northern California Coast coho. *See* 68 Fed. Reg. 55926 (September 29, 2003). NOAA redesignated critical habitat for seven of these ESUs in 2005. 70 Fed. Reg. 52488 (September 2, 2005).

Under the ESA and the new regulations adopted by NOAA, it is illegal to cause harm to listed species of salmon or steelhead within an ESU. According to NOAA, harm is any act that kills or injures a listed species, including modification or degradation of habitat that could significantly impair essential behavioral patterns such as breeding, spawning, rearing, migrating, feeding, or sheltering. 50 C.F.R. § 222.102. Within the ESUs governed by the no take prohibition of Section 9, it is illegal to alter salmon or steelhead habitat in a

Under the ESA and the new regulations adopted by NOAA, it is illegal to cause harm to listed species of salmon or steelhead within an ESU.

---

3. The opinion distinguished the 1995 decision of the Ninth Circuit in *Forest Conservation Council v. Rosboro Lumber Co.*, 50 F. 3d 781, 783 (9th Cir. 1995), which held that a taking could be based on a showing that harm to the species was "reasonably certain." *Cf. Marbled Murrelet v. Babbitt*, 83 F. 3d 1060, 1066 (9th Cir. 1996).

manner that causes harm to the fish. Activities that may cause harm include: "logging, grazing, farming, urban development, road construction in riparian areas and areas subject to mass wasting and surface erosion." 70 Fed. Reg. 37196 (June 28, 2005).

In some cases, the taking of a threatened or endangered species is an historic part of Native American religion and tribal practices. Some wildlife protection acts, such as the Bald Eagle Protection Act, 16 U.S.C. § 668 *et seq.*, provide exceptions for such religious practices, but the ESA contains no exceptions. In *United States v. Billie*, the court found that the prohibitions on taking in the ESA do not constitute a burden on freedom of expression and religious beliefs as applied to the Florida black panther. 667 F. Supp. 1485 (S.D. Fla. 1987). Therefore, the court found that the ESA was not void on its face. *Id.* at 1495. It held that the interest in hunting the panther was not central to the claimed religious belief, and did not outweigh the government's interest in protecting the species. *Id.* at 1497.

> *The courts have decided that the right to protect domestic livestock must give way to the mandates of the ESA.*

The courts also have decided that the right to protect domestic livestock must give way to the mandates of the ESA. In *Christy v. Hodel*, the court upheld a fine of $2,500 against a rancher who shot an endangered grizzly bear that was killing his sheep. 857 F. 2d 1324, 1330 (9th Cir. 1988). Justice White, dissenting from a denial of certiorari, commented that the right to protect one's property was a deeply rooted liberty interest and would have accepted certiorari to consider a possible Fifth Amendment claim. *See Christy v. Lujan*, 490 U.S. 1114, 1116 (1989).

Habitat Conservation Plans

Originally, the ESA provided no opportunity for private persons to obtain advance protection if their activities inadvertently caused a taking. This could occur, for example, if grading or land clearing activities destroyed the habitat of an endangered species. In 1982, Congress amended the ESA to allow the Secretary to issue permits to allow the "incidental" taking of listed, threatened, or endangered species. To qualify, the taking of the species must be "incidental to, and not the purpose of, the carrying out of an otherwise lawful activity." 16 U.S.C. § 1539(a)(1)(B). These incidental taking provisions are of particular interest to the development community. They permit incidental takings pursuant to activities, such as construction of homes, roads, and other facilities.

> *Section 10 of the ESA and the regulations adopted by the Secretary establish a process by which a person may seek a permit to authorize incidental taking of endangered species.*

Section 10 of the ESA (16 U.S.C. § 1539) and the regulations adopted by the Secretary establish a process by which a person may seek a permit to authorize incidental taking of endangered species. To be eligible for a Section 10 permit, the prospective permittee must submit a habitat conservation plan to the Secretary that specifies:

- The impacts that are likely to result from the taking
- The steps the applicant will take to mitigate and minimize the impacts
- The funding that will be available to implement such steps
- What alternative actions to the taking the applicant has considered
- The reason why the alternatives are not being adopted, and
- Such other measures as the Secretary may require

16 U.S.C. § 1539(a)(2)(A)

The Secretary is authorized to issue the incidental takings permit only if the Secretary finds that the applicant, to the maximum extent practicable, minimized and mitigated the impacts of the taking, that adequate funding for the plan will be provided, and that the taking will not appreciably reduce the likelihood of the survival and recovery of the species in the wild. 16 U.S.C. § 1539(a)(2)(B).

The process leading to issuance of a permit for an incidental taking under Section 10 of the ESA can be quite complex. 50 C.F.R. § 17, pts. C, D. The action is treated as a proposed federal action and triggers the requirements of NEPA, including the possible preparation of an EIS. The plans typically take in excess of one year to prepare and require extensive information to be obtained regarding the species and extensive measures to be undertaken to protect the species.

Nevertheless, the Service advocates the use of HCPs as a creative and mutually beneficial way of resolving species concerns while allowing desired development to proceed. For example, in August 1994 the Secretary issued a new policy—commonly referred to as the "No Surprises" policy—which is intended to assure landowners participating in an HCP that no additional land, land use restrictions, or financial compensation will be required from them in connection with their lawful land development activities, so long as the HCP is properly functioning. In settlement of litigation challenging the No Surprises policy on the grounds that it was not subjected to public notice and comment, the Service solicited public comment on the policy in 1997, and promulgated the policy as a rule in 1998. 50 C.F.R. § 17.22(b)(5). In August 2007, the United States District Court in Washington, D.C. upheld the rule. *Spirit of the Sage Council v. Norton*, No. 98–1873 (EGS) (D.D.C. Aug. 30, 2007).

In late 1996, the Service also released a handbook on the Section 10 process, which contains guidance on developing and processing HCPs and Section 10(a) applications for incidental take permits. The handbook is available at **www.fws.gov/Endangered/hcp/hcpbook.htm**. The 1996 handbook was modified by an addendum issued on June 1, 2000, which addresses the issues of biological goals and objectives, adaptive management, monitoring, permit duration, and public participation, in the HCP context. 65 Fed. Reg. 35242 (June 1, 2000).

Despite its complexity, the HCP process is of increasing importance in California, where development often encroaches on territory inhabited by listed species.

Multi-species planning is recognized as an effective way to protect species while minimizing economic disruptions; however, from a practical standpoint, it is difficult to implement. On the state level, to encourage such planning, the California Legislature, at the urging of Governor Wilson, passed the Natural Communities Conservation Planning Act (NCCP Act) (1991 Cal. Stat. ch. 765), which provides for multi-species habitat conservation planning. Fish & Game Code § 2800 *et seq.* The NCCP Act was substantially revised in 2002 to include much greater detail regarding the procedures for the adoption of plans. The goal of the NCCP Act was to enable California to go beyond the single species focus of the ESA and to focus on preservation of entire ecosystems. It includes the use of scientific review panels, and calls for cooperation with the Service and development of interim measures to protect natural communities during the planning process by working closely with affected local communities. In July 1997, the City of San

EIS = Environmental impact statement
NCCP = Natural Communities Conservation Planning

Multi-species planning is recognized as an effective way to protect species while minimizing economic disruptions; however, from a practical standpoint, it is difficult to implement.

Diego completed and obtained approval of one of the largest multi-species plans in the country, covering approximately 90 species over 600,000 acres.

In order to provide take coverage for both state and federally listed species, the major NCCP efforts to date have typically been multi-agency efforts that also include HCPs with incidental take coverage under the federal ESA.

Incidental take authorizations under Section 10 also are available through two other mechanisms. Under the Safe Harbor policy, private landowners may enter into an agreement with the Service whereby if a landowner agrees to manage the land to restore, enhance, or maintain habitats for listed species, the Service will offer incentives in return. Specifically, the Service may authorize certain incidental taking of the covered species, and provide assurances that additional restrictions will not be imposed should the covered species become more numerous as a result of the property owner's voluntary conservation actions. 50 C.F.R. §§ 17.22(c), 17.32(c); 64 Fed. Reg. 32717 (June 17, 1999). The second mechanism is a Candidate Conservation Agreement, through which similar incentives may be offered to a landowner who implements voluntary conservation measures with regard to proposed and candidate species, as well as species likely to become candidate species. 50 C.F.R. §§ 17.22(d), 17.32(d); 64 Fed. Reg. 32726 (June 17, 1999). In 2004, the Service adopted minor revisions to both the Safe Harbor policy and Candidate Conservation Agreement regulations. 69 Fed. Reg. 24084 (May 3, 2004).

In the absence of a Section 10 permit, purely private activity that is near or adjacent to the habitat of a listed species places the developer at risk of civil penalties and injunctive relief. Once it is determined that a threatened or endangered species is in the vicinity of construction activity, there is a risk of "taking" and serious fines. The incidental take permit offers insurance against those penalties.

Judicial Review and Enforcement

The Secretary's decisions under the ESA, including whether to list a threatened or endangered species, the designation of critical habitat, the issuance of a permit, and the results of the Section 7 consultation process are subject to judicial review. The basic standard of judicial review is the arbitrary and capricious test under the Administrative Procedure Act. 5 U.S.C. § 706. Agency actions will be upheld unless they are arbitrary or capricious or otherwise not in accordance with the law. *See Cabinet Mountains Wilderness v. Peterson*, 685 F. 2d 678, 685 (D.C. Cir. 1982); *Oregon Natural Resources Council v. Allen*, 476 F. 3d 1031, 1036 (9th Cir. 2007).

Nonprofit organizations with an interest in threatened or endangered species have standing to challenge decisions under the ESA. *See Palila v. Hawaii Dep't of Land and Natural Resources*, 471 F. Supp. 985, 991 (D. Hawaii 1979), However, like other plaintiffs, they must prove three elements: (1) "injury in fact," (2) a causal connection between the injury and the defendant's conduct, and (3) redressability of the injury by a favorable decision of the court. *See Lujan v. Defenders of Wildlife*, 504 U.S. 555, 560 (1992). Moreover, plaintiffs must allege particular injury to cognizable interests. General grievances, such as a challenge to the Secretary's failure to follow Section 7 procedures, do not confer standing on plaintiffs. *Id.* at 571–79; *see also Morrill v. Lujan*, 802 F. Supp. 424,

432 (S.D. Ala. 1992) (characterizing plaintiff's injury as a generalized grievance for which plaintiff had no standing). Invasion of economic interests protected by contract does not confer standing to challenge restrictions on timber cutting, although a showing of injury to plaintiffs' informational and participational rights is sufficient. *See Region 8 Forest Serv. Timber Purchasers Council v. Alcock*, 736 F. Supp. 267, 271–73 (N.D. Ga. 1990).

In injunctive proceedings, the party seeking a permit from a federal agency is not an indispensable party to a suit seeking an injunction. In *Pacific Legal Foundation v. Andrus*, a legal foundation and some state residents filed suit to require the Service to prepare an EIS on a proposal to list seven species of mussels as endangered species. 657 F. 2d 829 (6th Cir. 1981). The Service defended the injunctive relief sought on the grounds that there was a lack of an indispensable party—the person seeking the permit. The court rejected this argument, stating that complete relief could be granted because the Service was the party who was subject to the action. *Id.* at 833. The court also concluded that no EIS was required because NEPA conflicted with the ESA's mandatory requirements. *Id.* at 836–41.

In injunctive proceedings, the party seeking a permit from a federal agency is not an indispensable party to a suit seeking an injunction.

Violation of the take prohibition of the ESA can result in civil penalties, criminal liability, and/or injunctive relief. Any person who knowingly violates the prohibitions against taking also is subject to a civil penalty of not more than $25,000 for each violation. 16 U.S.C. § 1540(a)(1). Any person who knowingly violates the prohibitions against taking also is subject to a criminal fine of not more than $50,000 or imprisonment for not more than one year in jail or both. With respect to criminal enforcement of the ESA, at least one court has held that the misdemeanor criminal provisions are a general intent crime, and thus it is not necessary that the defendant know of the possession of an endangered species or that such possession was illegal. *See United States v. Nguyen*, 916 F. 2d 1016, 1018–19 (5th Cir. 1990). In *Nguyen*, the defendant, Danh Nguyen, captained a small fishing boat that the Coast Guard boarded for a safety check. During the inspection, the Coast Guard found four flippers from a threatened sea turtle. Mr. Nguyen was charged with a misdemeanor violation of rules on the importation and transportation of this species. The court held specific intent was not required. *Id.* at 1019.

Violation of the take prohibition of the ESA can result in civil penalties, criminal liability, and/or injunctive relief.

Violators of the takings provisions also are subject to injunctive relief. In *United States v. Glenn-Colusa Irrigation District*, the court enjoined the Glenn-Colusa Irrigation District from operating a water pumping facility on the Sacramento River from July 15 through November 15 to protect endangered winter-run Chinook salmon. 788 F. Supp. 1126 (E.D. Cal. 1992). The court rejected arguments that enforcement required compliance with NEPA and that designation of critical habitat and designation of a recovery plan has to precede enforcement. *Id.* at 1135. In *Marbled Murrelet v. Babbitt*, the Ninth Circuit upheld the district court's granting of an injunction that enjoined the defendant from cutting timber in an old-growth forest pursuant to a state-approved timber harvest plan. 83 F. 3d 1060, 1063 (9th Cir. 1996). The district court had found, after an eight-day trial, that the acreage in question was in fact habitat for the marbled murrelet, a threatened seabird, and that the proposed timber harvesting would "harm" and "harass" the bird so as to constitute a prohibited take.

Violators of the takings provisions are subject to injunctive relief.

The ESA specifically authorizes citizens to bring suits for injunctive relief. 16 U.S.C. § 1540(g). The citizen suit provision allows any person to commence a civil suit to enjoin any person, including the United States, who is alleged to be in violation of the ESA or regulations issued under the authority of the ESA. Citizen suits also are allowed to compel the Secretary to carry out the prohibitions against the taking of endangered species and against the Secretary where there is a failure of the Secretary to perform a nondiscretionary act or duty. *See Morrill v. Lujan*, 802 F. Supp. at 432 (plaintiff could not utilize citizen suit provision to force the Secretary to revise a critical habitat designation as that was a matter left to the Secretary's discretion). Suits are to be filed in the district court that has jurisdiction without regard to the amount of the controversy or citizenship of the parties.

No citizen suit may be brought prior to 60 days after written notice of the violation has been given to the Secretary to allege any violation of the Act. The failure to give the required notice requires dismissal of the suit.

No citizen suit may be brought prior to 60 days after written notice of the violation has been given to the Secretary to allege any violation of the Act. 16 U.S.C. §§ 1540(g)(2)(A–C). The failure to give the required notice requires dismissal of the suit. *See Humane Soc'y v. Lujan*, 768 F. Supp. 360, 362 (D.D.C. 1991) (submitting comments to the Service during the notice and comment period of rulemaking does not constitute written pre-suit notice). Initially, the courts differed on the interpretation of the citizen suit provision and whether it is mandatory that the notice be given a full 60 days prior to the filing of suit. *Compare Save the Yaak Com. v. Block*, 840 F. 2d 714, 721 (9th Cir. 1988) (compliance with the 60-day notification provision was jurisdictional, and thus no suit could be brought under the ESA until these requirements were met) *with Sierra Club v. Yeutter*, 926 F. 2d 429, 435 (5th Cir. 1991) (although compliance with the 60-day notification provision is "mandatory," it is not jurisdictional "in the strictest sense of the term," and therefore, may not be raised for the first time on appeal). Another holding on the 60-day notice provision, *Building Industry Association v. Lujan*, 785 F. Supp. 1020 (D.D.C. 1992), strictly construed the provision citing *Hallstrom v. Tillamook County*, 493 U.S. 20 (1989), where the United States Supreme Court upheld a strict construction of a similar section of the Resource Conservation and Recovery Act.

Frequently, litigants do not have the time or anticipate the need to file the 60-day notice before seeking a preliminary injunction. One procedure that has been used is to seek preliminary injunctive relief under NEPA.

Frequently, litigants do not have the time or anticipate the need to file the 60-day notice before seeking a preliminary injunction. One procedure that has been used is to seek preliminary injunctive relief under NEPA.

A six-year statute of limitations generally applies to ESA citizen suits. *See Ctr. for Biological Diversity v. Hamilton*, 453 F. 3d 1331, 1334 (11th Cir. 2006) (dismissing as untimely lawsuit to compel Service to designate critical habitat, since more than six years had passed since the deadline for making the designation).

Parties who are successful in filing suits under the ESA are entitled to attorneys' fees at the court's discretion. 16 U.S.C. § 1540(g)(4). At least in the Ninth Circuit, however, the converse is not true for prevailing defendants; they only can recover fees from the plaintiff if the plaintiff's claims are found to have been frivolous. *See Marbled Murrelet v. Babbitt*, 83 F. 3d 1060, 1094 (9th Cir. 1996).

The California Endangered Species Act

CESA = California Endangered Species Act

The California Endangered Species Act (CESA) (Fish & Game Code §§ 2050–2098) provides the legal authority for the protection of threatened and endangered species by the state. The legislative policy expressed in CESA is "to conserve, protect, restore and enhance" threatened and endangered species and their habitat and to acquire lands for habitat for threatened and endangered species. Fish & Game Code § 2052.

The CESA Listing Process

The California Fish and Game Commission (Commission) is required to establish a list of threatened species and a list of endangered species. The Commission adds or removes species from the lists "upon the receipt of sufficient scientific information...that the action is warranted." Fish & Game Code § 2070. Interested persons may petition the Commission to add or remove a species from the lists. The petitioning process is described in detail in Title 14, California Code of Regulations, section 670.1. Once received by the Commission, a petition is referred to the California Department of Fish and Game (DFG) within 10 days. Fish & Game Code § 2073. The DFG must make a recommendation to the Commission within 90 days that the petition should be accepted and considered or that the petition should be rejected. The DFG's recommendation is based on its determination of the sufficiency of the information in the petition to indicate whether or not the petitioned action may be warranted. Fish & Game Code § 2073.5.

Following DFG's recommendation, the Commission must consider the petition and make a finding based on DFG's recommendation at its next available meeting. If the Commission finds that a petition seeking to add a species to either list is sufficient to indicate that the petitioned action may be warranted, then the Commission publishes a notice to that effect and the species becomes a "candidate" species. Fish & Game Code § 2074.2.

A candidate species is evaluated by the DFG to determine whether listing is warranted, to identify preliminarily habitat that may be essential to the continued existence of the species, and to recommend management activities and other recommendations for recovery of the species. Fish & Game Code § 2074.6. DFG has 12 months from the acceptance of the petition in which to review the status of the species and report to the Commission. Thereafter, the Commission considers DFG's report, and makes a finding to list the species as threatened or endangered or to remove the species from candidacy. Fish & Game Code § 2075. Any finding by the Commission may be reviewed by writ of mandate under section 1094.5 of the California Code of Civil Procedure.

In late 2007, the California Court of Appeal upheld the Commission's decision to list separately two "evolutionary significant units" of the coho salmon. *California Forestry Assn. v. California Fish & Game Commission*, 156 Cal. App. 4th 1535 (2007). The court deferred to the position of the Commission and DFG that the definition of species under the CESA is broad enough to authorize the listing of ESUs. The court also deferred to the agencies' position that the term "range" under the CESA refers to a species' California range *only*, "thereby entitling a species to protection if its threatened with extinction throughout all, or a significant portion, of its California range (as opposed to its worldwide range)." The court therefore rejected the view that the CESA requires the Commission and DFG to consider the coho's *entire* geographic range, including areas outside of the state. Finally, the court determined that the state listings under the CESA were not duplicative, even though the ESUs were already protected under the federal ESA.

The case therefore highlights the fact that the federal and state endangered species lists are distinct, with frequent dual listings under both programs. As a

---

The California Fish and Game Commission is required to establish a list of threatened species and a list of endangered species.

DFG = California Department of Fish and Game

DFG has 12 months from the acceptance of the petition in which to review the status of the species and report to the Commission.

result, the regulatory status of a species needs to be evaluated under both programs in every instance.

"Take" Under CESA

Section 2080 of the California Fish and Game Code prohibits, among other things, the "take" of species listed by the Commission as threatened or endangered. Unlike its federal counterpart, the CESA does not distinguish between plants and wildlife with regard to take prohibitions. Section 86 of the Fish and Game Code defines "take" as meaning to "hunt, pursue, catch, capture, or kill," or to attempt any of these acts. In *Department of Fish and Game v. Anderson-Cottonwood Irrigation District*, a court held that "take" in the context of CESA does not prohibit only hunting or fishing related activities. 8 Cal. App. 4th 1554 (1992). Thus, the court held that section 2080 applied to the incidental killing of winter-run chinook salmon at an irrigation district's pump diversion. *Id.* at 1568. Candidate species also are protected from taking. Fish & Game Code § 2085.

CESA did not expressly provide DFG with the authority to issue permits for the incidental take of CESA species, unlike the federal ESA.

With respect to habitat modification, the California Attorney General concluded in a May 15, 1995 opinion that, in contrast to the federal ESA, CESA does not prohibit indirect harm to CESA-listed species by way of habitat modification. 78 Ops. Cal. Atty. Gen. 137 (1995).

Incidental Take Permits Under CESA

Prior to January 1, 1998, section 2081 provided that the DFG, among other things, may authorize the "take" of threatened or endangered species for "management purposes" through permits or memoranda of understanding. CESA did not expressly provide DFG with the authority to issue permits for the "incidental take" of CESA species, unlike the federal ESA. As a result, DFG historically interpreted the term "management purposes" broadly to include land use or development projects that might impact the habitat, or potentially result in the take, of a threatened or endangered species. It then issued a "Management Authorization" to a project proponent to authorize the anticipated take to occur, and to require mitigation for such take.

DFG's practice was invalidated by a court in 1997. *See Planning and Conservation League v. Dep't of Fish and Game*, 55 Cal. App. 4th 479, 482 (1997). This left DFG without any ability to authorize the take of CESA-listed species in connection with land use or development projects.

Senate Bill 879 expressly authorizes DFG to issue permits allowing the incidental take of CESA species, subject to several conditions.

The Legislature solved this problematic situation by amending CESA in late 1997 to provide DFG with explicit incidental take authority. Senate Bill 879, which took effect on January 1, 1998, expressly authorizes DFG to issue permits allowing the "incidental take" of CESA species, subject to several conditions:

- The impacts of the authorized take must be minimized and fully mitigated
- The mitigation must be "roughly proportional" to the impact
- The applicant must ensure adequate funding to minimize and mitigate impacts, and to monitor the effectiveness of such measures
- Take permits cannot be issued if they would jeopardize the continued existence of the species

For species listed under both the state and federal acts, DFG is authorized to rely on an incidental take statement in a federal permit to confer taking authority for purposes of CESA. Fish & Game Code § 2080.1.

9

Design Review, Historic Preservation, Williamson Act, TDR, Water Supply, Coastal Development, and Other Development Regulations

Introduction

This chapter discusses the following sources of regulation by which local, regional, state, and federal governments protect important resources and interests typically affected by proposed development:

- Design Review and Historic Preservation (aesthetic, cultural, and historic resources)
- Williamson Act Contracts (agricultural lands and the agricultural economy)
- Coastal Development (coastal lands, water and habitat)
- Transfer of Development Rights (preservation of open space, scenic views, agricultural lands, and historical landmarks)
- Water Supply Planning, Storm Water Requirements, and Congestion Management Programs (planning and development of vital infrastructure and utilities)
- Prevailing Wage and Public Bidding Concerns (economic health of the labor force)

Design Review

When a city considers adopting or implementing a design or architectural review process, one of the issues that often arises is the legality of aesthetic control. Aesthetic regulation is permissible if it is reasonably related to the public health, safety, and welfare. Broad latitude is given to cities in exercising this control. *See Metromedia, Inc. v. City of San Diego*, 26 Cal. 3d 848, 863 (1980); *see also Ehrlich v. City of Culver City*, 12 Cal. 4th 854, 881–882 (1996).

Although the design review might limit the use of, diminish the value of, or impose additional costs upon property, it does not impose requirements for either conveyances of land or monetary exactions. As a result, design review is a general regulation of land use that is not subject to the higher scrutiny test employed in *Nollan* and *Dolan*. *See Breneric Assocs. v. City of Del Mar*, 69 Cal. App. 4th 166, 176–77 (1998) (rejecting application of the heightened scrutiny *Nollan-Dolan* standard to design review). For a thorough discussion of *Nollan* and *Dolan*, *see* chapter 12 (Takings) and chapter 13 (Exactions). Therefore, denial of a design review application will be upheld so long as the denial

Aesthetic regulation is permissible if it is reasonably related to the public health, safety, and welfare. Broad latitude is given to cities in exercising this control.

substantially advances a legitimate governmental interest and is supported by substantial evidence.

The leading case in this field is *Novi v. City of Pacifica*, where the court upheld a city's ordinance that precluded "monotonous" developments and uses detrimental to the "general welfare." 169 Cal. App. 3d 678, 682 (1985). Responding to a claim that the ordinance was unconstitutionally vague, the court stated, "[i]n fact, a substantial amount of vagueness is permitted in California zoning ordinances...." *Id.* For a more detailed discussion of the sufficiency of development standards in zoning ordinances, *see* chapter 4 (Zoning).

Similarly, another court, relying on *Novi*, held that a view protection ordinance was not unconstitutionally vague, and that such an ordinance supported denial of a building permit. *See Ross v. City of Rolling Hills Estates*, 192 Cal. App. 3d 370, 376 (1987); *see also Briggs v. City of Rolling Hills Estates*, 40 Cal. App. 4th 637, 643 (1995) (a "neighborhood compatibility" ordinance requiring that designs "respect the existing privacy of surrounding properties" was not void for vagueness); *Echevarrieta v. City of Rancho Palos Verdes*, 86 Cal. App. 4th 472, 484–485 (2001) (an ordinance that prohibited residents from significantly impairing a view by permitting foliage to grow to heights in excess of certain limitations was not unconstitutionally vague).

In Guinnane, the court provided support for a city's concerns regarding neighborhood aesthetics.

In *Guinnane v. City of San Francisco Planning Commission*, the court provided support for a city's concerns regarding neighborhood aesthetics. 209 Cal. App. 3d 732 (1989). Guinnane sought a building permit to construct a four-story, 6,000-square-foot house with five bedrooms, five baths, and parking for two cars. The planning commission rejected Guinnane's application during design review because the proposed building was too massive and thus, "not in character" with the neighborhood. The board of permit appeals also denied the permit.

The court upheld the city's action. It stated that the planning commission and the appeals board had the authority to exercise discretion in deciding whether to issue the permit. *Id.* at 742. The court noted that such a review is not limited to a determination of whether the applicant has complied with zoning ordinances and building codes. The San Francisco Planning Code specifically directed the commission to "protect the character and stability of residential...areas...." Such concern for neighborhood aesthetics has long been justified as a legitimate governmental objective. Sufficient evidence existed to uphold the commission's finding that the proposed house would increase traffic, cause parking problems, and have a negative effect on the neighborhood. *Id.*

Similarly, the court in *Saad v. City of Berkeley* upheld the City of Berkeley's denial of a use permit for a three-story home in a single-family zone because it would impair the view of neighboring property owners, and would have a towering effect. 24 Cal. App. 4th 1206, 1216 (1994). *See also Harris v. City of Costa Mesa*, 25 Cal. App. 4th 963, 973 (1994) (denial of a use permit for second residential unit on one lot based on incompatibility with the neighborhood was proper).

One court clarified that a city can regulate tree growth for aesthetic reasons alone.

Another court clarified that a city can regulate tree growth for aesthetic reasons alone. *See Kucera v. Lizza*, 59 Cal. App. 4th 1141 (1997). In that case, the court upheld the Town of Tiburon's land use ordinance preserving access to views and sunlight by regulating obstructing trees and tree growth as a valid exercise of police power. *Id.* at 1149.

In *Crown Motors v. City of Redding*, the city adopted an urgency ordinance prohibiting electronic reader boards. 232 Cal. App. 3d 173 (1991). The city found the ordinance necessary for the immediate preservation of the public peace, health, and safety under Government Code section 36937(b), which allows cities to designate urgency ordinances that take effect immediately upon final passage. The court held the city council had the right to interpret "public health" to include the quality of life as it is affected by the aesthetics of the city. The court stated that "[m]ental health is certainly included in the public health." *Id.* at 178.

A city council has the right to interpret public health to include the quality of life as it is affected by the aesthetics of the city.

Further supporting cities' power to regulate design of structures is the decision in *Tahoe Regional Planning Agency v. King*, 233 Cal. App. 3d 1365 (1991). There, the court held that *First English Evangelical Lutheran Church v. County of Los Angeles*, 482 U.S. 304 (1987), did not preclude the historic use of legitimate land use regulations for the removal of billboards after a reasonable amortization period. *Id.* at 1397, 1400. For a thorough discussion of the *First English* case, *see* chapter 12 (Takings). The court also held that *Nollan* did not remove aesthetics or scenic zoning as a legitimate focus of such regulations. *Id.* at 1401.

The court in *Friends of Davis v. City of Davis* upheld a city's interpretation of its own design review ordinance. 83 Cal. App. 4th 1004 (2000). In this case, a group of citizens asked the city to use its design review ordinance to prevent a Borders bookstore from locating in the city. The city refused to do so, taking the position that its ordinance did not extend to tenant approval, but was limited to a detailed review of the exterior design and appearance of a proposed project. In upholding the city's interpretation, the court noted that a city is not required to have a design review ordinance, but when it chooses to do so, the scope of such review is determined by the city. *Id.* at 1014.

The court in *Friends of Davis* also clarified some limits with respect to a city's power to regulate aesthetics. A city may not exercise its discretion "carte blanche" to exclude a retailer that some of its citizens do not like. An ordinance proposing to do so "would confer on the City's planning department virtually unrestrained power to decide who may and who may not do business in the City." *Id.*

A city may not exercise its discretion carte blanche *to exclude a retailer that some of its citizens do not like.*

There are other significant limitations on a city's ability to exercise its police power to control aesthetics. For instance, a city cannot unduly infringe on a person's freedom of speech. In fact, the courts scrutinize more closely a city's action in furthering aesthetics when the action could jeopardize a citizen's right to free speech. The United States Supreme Court held invalid a city ordinance enacted to minimize visual clutter caused by signs, which was utilized to prohibit a sign reading "For Peace in the Gulf" on private property. *See City of Ladue v. Gilleo*, 512 U.S. 43, 54–55 (1994). In another case, the court held that an ordinance prohibiting adult cabaret operations near a freeway violated First Amendment free speech rights, because the city did not have a legitimate interest in protecting its "image." *Gammoh v. City of Anaheim*, 73 Cal. App. 4th 186, 191 (1999).

Moreover, a city cannot infringe upon certain registered trademarks. *See Blockbuster Videos, Inc. v. City of Tempe*, 141 F. 3d 1295 (9th Cir. 1998). In *Blockbuster*, the Ninth Circuit held that section 1121(b) of the Lanham Act (15 U.S.C. § 1121 (b)) preempted the City's attempt to require alterations in the depictions of registered trademarks on outdoor signs. *Id.* at 1296. The city required all exterior signs in a shopping center to conform to a shopping center's sign package, which typically

A city cannot infringe upon certain registered trademarks.

specified such things as the color. Individual businesses could apply to the design review board for variances. Blockbuster was denied permission to use the blue awning with yellow letters that is one of its own marks. In ruling partially against the city, the court stated that part of the legislative intent behind the Lanham Act was to protect registered marks from interference by state or local government. *Id.* at 1300. While the city could not require alterations of a registered mark, it retained the power of all municipalities to regulate where and whether signs may be placed and how large they may be.

The court in *Bowman v. City of Berkeley* addressed the relationship between design review and the CEQA process. 122 Cal. App. 4th 572 (2004). The petitioners in *Bowman* challenged a proposed four-story building within a developed area, claiming the city should have prepared an EIR on the aesthetic impacts of the building. The proposed building had undergone the city's thorough design review process. In rejecting the petitioners' CEQA challenge, the court noted that issues relating to the aesthetics of a building "are ordinarily the province of local design review, not CEQA." *Id.* at 593. Indeed, where a project must undergo design review prior to approval, as in *Bowman*, that process itself can be found to mitigate purely aesthetic impacts to a level of insignificance under CEQA. *Id.* at 594.

Historic Preservation
Federal Level

The primary federal statute that addresses historic preservation is the National Historic Preservation Act (NHPA). 16 U.S.C. § 470 *et seq*. The NHPA sets forth a comprehensive program to carry out the national policy of protecting America's historic and cultural resources. It provides the authority for a number of activities that implement the federal historic preservation program, including (1) the National Register of Historic Places (identifying and listing historic and cultural resources), (2) an expanded national register to include sites of state and local significance, (3) the matching grants-in-aid program, encouraging preservation activities at the state and local levels, (4) the Advisory Council on Historic Preservation, providing information on historic properties, and (5) the "section 106" review process.[1] For a thorough discussion of historic preservation at the federal, state, and local levels, *see* Juergensmeyer and Roberts, *Land Use Planning and Control Law*, section 12.6 *et seq*. (1998).

State Level

Public Resources Code section 5020 *et seq*. is California's state historic preservation statute. This statute does not prohibit local control of historic properties. Rather, it assists local entities in encouraging historic preservation. Public

---

[1] Section 106 (16 U.S.C. § 470(f)) provides the basic federal legal protection for historic sites. It requires agencies to identify and assess the effects of federal actions on cultural resources included in or eligible for listing in the National Register of Historic Places. It also requires federal agencies responsible for actions that affect National Register-listed or eligible properties to consult with the State Historic Preservation Office (SHPO), local officials, affected Indian tribes, applicants for federal assistance, and the public. The agency also must allow the Advisory Council to comment on the undertaking. The primary goal of section 106 consultation is to avoid adverse effects on National Register-eligible or listed properties. If avoidance is impossible, consulting parties must attempt to minimize effects, or as a last resort, to mitigate adverse effects.

CEQA = California Environmental Quality Act
EIR = Environmental impact report
NHPA = National Historic Preservation Act

The NHPA sets forth a comprehensive program to carry out the national policy of protecting America's historic and cultural resources.

Resources Code section 5020.1 established the California Register of Historic Resources, which is the authoritative listing and guide to be used by cities to identify existing historic resources deserving of protection. Once an historic site is included in the register, any project that may have an adverse impact on the site is deemed a project for purposes of CEQA. *See* James Longtin, *Longtin's California Land Use*, § 3.11[7] (2003 update). CEQA defines historic resources more broadly than does federal law, and includes both procedural and substantive project review requirements. Agencies must implement feasible mitigation measures or alternatives for projects that would cause significant adverse impacts.

Although California imposes stricter environmental review requirements than required for federal review under NHPA, the state also has created significant financial incentives to help preserve historic resources. The State Historical Building Code (SHBC) is an alternative building code that guides historic building rehabilitations and can offer substantial cost savings over the Uniform Building Code. The SHBC addresses accessibility, seismic, structural, infrastructure, and energy issues. The "triggers" for full upgrading to current standards that exist in other codes are not recognized by the SHBC, which concentrates instead on resolution of safety considerations. Note that the SHBC does not authorize the city to *prevent* changes an historic structure. If the property owner has complied with the Uniform Building Code, the city has no discretion to deny the building permit on historical preservation grounds. *See Prentiss v. City of South Pasadena*, 15 Cal. App. 4th 85 (1993).

SHBC = State Historical Building Code

Local Level

Some of the most important historic preservation work occurs at the local level. Cities have the authority under their general police power to protect property of historical and aesthetic significance. *See* David L. Callies, "Historic Preservation Law in the United States," 32 *Envtl. L. Rep.* 10348 (March 2002).

Cities have the authority under their general police power to protect property of historical and aesthetic significance.

In the leading case of *Penn Central Transportation Company v. City of New York*, the United States Supreme Court affirmed that the broad scope of the general police power provides cities with the authority to regulate property of historical interest. 438 U.S. 104 (1978). In that case, the property owners alleged that New York City's landmark preservation law, which prohibited them from building a 54-story office building on top of Grand Central Station, constituted an unlawful taking. The Court found the local regulation valid, since it provided the owners with a reasonable beneficial use of their property, while fostering an important government interest.

Although the Court never mentioned the police power specifically, it made clear that local regulation of individual landmarks as well as historic districts fall within the scope of permissible government objectives. The Court observed that because it already had recognized "in a number of settings, that States and cities may enact land-use restrictions or controls to enhance the quality of life by preserving the character and desirable aesthetic features of a city," the property owners challenging the law did not even contest the legitimacy of the city's interest in preserving "structures and areas with special historic, architectural, or cultural significance." *Id.* at 129. *See also Bohannon v. City of San Diego*, 30 Cal. App. 3d 416, 423 (1973) (rejecting a takings challenge of a local measure that regulated the use of architectural styles in remodeling and repairs as a means of historic preservation; "[r]egulations and restrictions upon the use of property in an exercise of the police power for an authorized purpose do not constitute the taking of property without compensation or give rise to constitutional cause for complaint").

Local governments have the authority to acquire property for the preservation or development of an historical landmark, as well as the development of recreational purposes and facilities therein.

Under Government Code section 25373 (counties) and Government Code section 37361 (cities), local governments have the authority to acquire property for the preservation or development of an historical landmark, as well as the development of recreational purposes and facilities therein. These provisions also provide broad local authority to impose conditions to protect and enhance "places, building, structures, works of art, and other objects, having a special character or special historical or aesthetic interest or value." This local control "may include appropriate and reasonable control of the use or appearance of neighboring private property within public view, or both." Gov't Code § 31361(b).

Generally, a city will initiate a preservation program through appropriate enabling legislation that establishes a preservation overlay zone, sets forth criteria for inclusion in the district, and creates an administrative body to review proposals. Under this regulatory scheme, property owners of designated historic sites must seek board approval prior to making any changes to the property. Cities also may impose duties on these property owners through local anti-neglect or minimum maintenance ordinances to prevent demolition by neglect.

Careful drafting of local historic preservation ordinances can thwart constitutional challenges.

Careful drafting of local historic preservation ordinances can thwart constitutional challenges. For example, incorporating NHPA review standards, which have received extensive treatment in the case law, can protect an ordinance from a vagueness challenge. Similarly, the insertion of safety valves, which allow for exceptions to the scheme where economic hardship would otherwise result, may address a potential takings challenge. Cities should consider inclusion of three elements when designing and implementing an historic preservation program: (1) a survey to establish the requisite nexus for designation and regulation of historic sites; (2) a way to provide technical and economic assistance to affected property owners; and (3) some means of synchronizing the preservation program with a city's general plan, zoning ordinances, or other regulatory programs.

For a good discussion regarding historic preservation efforts at the local level, *see* Juergensmeyer and Roberts, *Land Use Planning and Control Law*, sections 12.10, 12.11 (1998).

Preservation of Agricultural Lands by Williamson Act Contract

As development expands into areas historically devoted to agricultural uses, it is increasingly important for cities and property owners to be familiar with restrictions on the development of farmland. California's primary farmland preservation law is the California Land Conservation Act of 1965, Government Code § 51200 *et seq.*, commonly known as the Williamson Act. The Williamson Act sets forth a framework based on traditional contract law whereby landowners within locally designated agricultural preserves may voluntarily place restrictions on agricultural lands in exchange for tax reductions and other incentives. *See County of Marin v. Assessment Appeals Board*, 64 Cal. App. 3d 319,

325–326 (1976) (to achieve the objectives of the Act, and give each party the benefit of its bargain, a Williamson Act contract is to be interpreted like any other form of contract).

Roughly 16.3 million of California's 30 million acres of farm and ranch land are restricted by Williamson Act contracts. *See* California Governor's Office of Planning and Research, *California Land Conservation (Williamson) Act*, Technical Advisory Document, Local Government Partnership Rural Policy Task Force, page 7 (2003). The Williamson Act is estimated to save agricultural landowners from 20 to 75 percent in property tax liabilities each year. *See* California Legislative Analyst's Office, Analysis of the 2004–05 Budget Bill (February 2004). For an overview of the Williamson Act and an analysis of its role in shaping national farmland preservation efforts, *see* Joshua Safran, "Contracting for Preservation: An Overview of State Agricultural District Programs," 27 *Zoning and Planning Law Report* 7 (July/August 2004).

Roughly 16.3 million of California's 30 million acres of farm and ranch land are restricted by Williamson Act contracts.

The Williamson Act was adopted by the Legislature to maintain the agricultural economy of the state, to assure sufficient food supplies, to discourage the premature and unnecessary conversion of agricultural lands, to discourage discontiguous urban development patterns, and to preserve the open space and aesthetic values of agricultural lands. Gov't Code § 51220; *See also Kelsey v. Colwell*, 30 Cal. App. 3d 590, 594–595 (1973).

Any city may, by resolution and after a public hearing, establish an agricultural preserve under the Williamson Act. Proposals to establish an agricultural preserve must be submitted to the planning department of the city having jurisdiction over the land. Gov't Code § 51234. Preserves must be established for the purpose of defining the boundaries of those areas within which the city will be willing to enter into Williamson Act contracts. Agricultural preserves generally must consist of no less than 100 acres, but may be smaller if the city finds that smaller preserves are necessary due to the unique characteristics of the agricultural enterprises in the area and are consistent with the city's general plan. Gov't Code § 51230. While agricultural preserves are nominally limited to "agricultural land," the Williamson Act broadly defines this term to include lands within a scenic highway corridor, wildlife habitat areas, saltponds, managed wetland areas, or submerged areas. Similarly, the required dedication of such lands to "agricultural uses" includes recreational and open space uses, and most recently, as of 2005, greenhouses. Gov't Code §§ 51201, 51205. Agricultural preserves generally continue in full effect following annexation, detachment, incorporation, or disincorporation of land within the preserve. Gov't Code § 51235.

Any city may, by resolution and after a public hearing, establish an agricultural preserve under the Williamson Act.

Parcels under Williamson Act contract must be large enough to sustain agricultural uses; parcels are presumed to be large enough if the land is at least 10 acres in size in the case of prime agricultural land or at least 40 acres in size in the case of nonprime agricultural land. Gov't Code § 51222. Every Williamson Act contract must provide for the exclusion of all uses incompatible with agricultural uses. Gov't Code § 51243. While the determination of what uses are "compatible" with agricultural uses is generally left to the discretion of each city, such compatibility determinations must be accompanied by certain findings and conducted in a manner that recognizes that a permanent or temporary population increase often hinders or impairs agricultural operations. Gov't

Parcels under Williamson Act contract must be large enough to sustain agricultural uses.

Code §§ 51220.5, 51238, 51238.1. Williamson Act contracts also must be binding upon and inure to the benefit of all successors in interest of the contracting landowner. Gov't Code § 51243. Where a city filed a protest to a Williamson Act contract with the county board of supervisors prior to the county's execution of the contract, the city may, where certain requirements are met, have the option not to succeed to the county's rights, duties, and powers under the contract upon annexation. Government Code section 51243.5 identifies detailed requirements that must be met for such an option to exist.

Cities are authorized to enter into contracts providing for restrictions, terms, and conditions, including payments and fees, more restrictive than called for in the Williamson Act.

Cities are authorized to enter into contracts providing for restrictions, terms, and conditions, including payments and fees, more restrictive than called for in the Williamson Act. Gov't Code § 51240. While not all contracts affecting land within a preserve need to be identical, discrepancies in terms must relate to differences in location and characteristics of the land, and all contracts must be made pursuant to uniform rules adopted by the city. Gov't Code §§ 51231, 51241.

Williamson Act contracts must provide for an initial term of no less than 10 years and must provide that on the anniversary date of the contract, or such other annual date as specified by the contract, a year will be added automatically to the initial term unless a notice of nonrenewal is given by the landowner or the city. Gov't Code § 51244. Where the initial term of the contract is more than 10 years, the contract may provide that on a specified annual date beginning with the anniversary date on which the contract will have an unexpired term of nine years, a year will be added automatically to the initial term unless a notice of nonrenewal is given. Gov't Code § 51244.5. This requirement means that no matter when the notice of nonrenewal is given, the contract has at least nine additional years to run.

If either the landowner or the city desires not to renew the contract, that party must serve written notice of nonrenewal upon the other before the annual renewal date of the contract. Unless such written notice is served by the landowner at least 90 days before the renewal date or by the city at least 60 days before the renewal date, the contract is considered to be automatically renewed. Gov't Code § 51245. Once the notice of nonrenewal is timely served, the existing contract remains in effect for the balance of the period remaining under the contract. Gov't Code § 51246(a).

Because contract nonrenewals typically take about a decade to become effective, landowners of restricted agricultural lands wishing to develop their lands for nonagricultural uses sooner often seek a contract cancellation.

Because a notice of nonrenewal typically takes about a decade to become effective, landowners of restricted agricultural lands wishing to develop their lands for nonagricultural uses sooner often seek a contract cancellation. Any owner of lands restricted under the Williamson Act may petition the city council for cancellation of any Williamson Act contract as to all or any part of the subject lands. Gov't Code §§ 51281, 51282. The landowner's petition must be accompanied by a proposal for a specified alternative use of the land. Gov't Code § 51282(e). Prior to taking action on the petition for cancellation, the county assessor of the county in which the land is located must determine the current fair market value of the land as though it were free of the contractual restriction. Gov't Code § 51283(a). Because this valuation is the basis for calculating the cancellation fee that will be due if the petition for cancellation is approved, the landowner may contest the assessor's valuation. Gov't Code §§ 51203(b); 51283(a).

Prior to giving tentative approval to the cancellation of the contract, the city must determine and certify to the county auditor the amount of the cancellation fee that the landowner must pay the county treasurer upon cancellation. The fee is calculated as an amount equal to 12½ percent of the current fair market value of the land as though it were free of the contractual restriction. Gov't Code § 51283(b). Under limited circumstances, the city council may waive some or all of the cancellation fee. Gov't Code § 51283(c). Cancellation fees also may be avoided in certain cases if the canceling landowner places an agricultural conservation easement on other land within the county that is of equal size or larger than the land subject to the contract and is equally or more suitable for agricultural use. Gov't Code § 51256(c). Such an "easement exchange" requires approval by the State Department of Conservation. Gov't Code § 51256.1.

The city council may approve cancellation of a Williamson Act contract only if it finds, at a noticed public hearing, that the cancellation is consistent with the purposes of the Williamson Act or is in the public interest. Gov't Code §§ 51282(a); 51284; *Sierra Club v. City of Hayward*, 28 Cal. 3d 840, 852 (1981) (holding that cancellation provisions of Williamson Act were included in the act as a means of dealing with strictly "emergency situations" where the public interest no longer dictates that the contract be continued). Such findings must be supported by substantial evidence. *Friends of East Willits Valley v. County of Mendocino*, 101 Cal. App. 4th 191, 204 (2002).

A determination that cancellation is consistent with the Williamson Act's purposes must be supported by the following findings:

- Cancellation is for land on which a notice of nonrenewal has been served
- Cancellation is not likely to result in the removal of adjacent lands from agricultural use
- Cancellation is for an alternative use that is consistent with the city's general plan
- Cancellation will not result in discontiguous patterns of urban development, and
- There is no proximate noncontracted land which is available and suitable for the use proposed on the contracted land unless the use of such land would provide less contiguous patterns of urban development

Gov't Code § 51282(b)

A determination that cancellation is in the public interest must be supported by findings that other public concerns substantially outweigh the objectives of the Williamson Act, and that there is no proximate noncontracted land that is available and suitable for the use proposed on the contracted land unless the use of such land would provide less contiguous patterns of urban development. Gov't Code § 51282(c).

Upon approval of cancellation, a certificate of tentative cancellation is recorded. Once the landowner has satisfied all conditions and contingencies enumerated in the certificate of tentative cancellation, including payment of the cancellation fee, a certificate of cancellation of contract is recorded. Gov't Code § 51283.4. Judicial review of final city council determinations regarding contract cancellations must be brought within 180 days under Code of Civil Procedure § 1094.5. Gov't Code § 51286.

Landowners may elect to rescind their traditional 10-year Williamson Act contracts by entering into 20-year farmland security zone contracts.

In 1998 the Legislature established a new optional program within the Williamson Act allowing owners of certain important farmlands to create "farmland security zones." Gov't Code §§ 51296, 51296.1, 51296.8. Landowners may elect to rescind their traditional 10-year Williamson Act contracts by entering into 20-year farmland security zone contracts, which afford the benefits of significantly lower property tax bills and exemptions from parcel taxes, annexation, and designation for school use. Gov't Code §§ 51296.1, 51296.2(a); Rev. & Tax. Code § 423.4. For a discussion of recent trends in Williamson Act legislation, *see* R. Clark Morrison and Bradley B. Brownlow, "Keeping Them Down on the Farm—Recent Trends in Williamson Act Legislation," 13 *California Land Use Law & Policy Reporter*, no. 9, page 219 (June 2004).

Coastal Development

The California Coastal Commission was established by voter initiative in 1972 in order to control and regulate the use of land and water in the coastal areas of California. It was later made permanent by the Legislature through the adoption of the California Coastal Act of 1976 (Act). Pub. Res. Code § 30000 *et seq.* Under the Act, the mission of the Coastal Commission is to "protect, conserve, restore and enhance environmental and human-based resources of the California coast and ocean for environmentally sustainable and prudent use by current and future generations." *See* www.coastal.ca.gov. Development activities within the coastal zone generally require a coastal permit issued by or appealable to the Coastal Commission.

The California Coastal Act of 1976

The California Coastal Act created a unique partnership between the state and local governments to manage the conservation and development of coastal resources through a long-term and comprehensive planning program.

The California Coastal Act was enacted by the State Legislature in 1976 to provide long-term protection of California's 1,100 mile coastline. The Act created a unique partnership between the state (acting through the Coastal Commission) and local governments (15 coastal counties and 58 coastal cities) to manage the conservation and development of coastal resources through a long-term and comprehensive planning program.

In addition to creating and authorizing the Coastal Commission, the Act outlines standards for development in the coastal zone. The Act includes specific policies addressing issues such as shoreline public access, recreation, protection of marine and terrestrial habitats, visual resources, landform alteration, agricultural lands, commercial fisheries, industrial uses, water quality, offshore oil and gas development, transportation, development design, power plants, ports and public works. *See generally* Pub. Res. Code § 30200 *et seq.*

The California Coastal Commission

The California Coastal Commission, in partnership with coastal cities and counties, regulates development within the coastal zone. Such development may not commence until a coastal development permit has been issued either by the Coastal Commission or by a local government with a Commission-certified local coastal program. Pub. Res. Code § 30600.

Composition

The Coastal Commission is an independent, quasi-judicial state agency. It consists of 16 members, 12 voting and four non-voting.[2] The 12 voting members are appointed equally (four each) by the Governor, the Senate Rules Committee, and the Speaker of the Assembly. Six out of the 12 voting members are locally elected officials; the other six are appointed from the public at large. Pub. Res. Code § 30301.

The Coastal Commission is an independent, quasi-judicial state agency. It consists of 16 members, 12 voting and four non-voting.

Constitutionality

Until 2003, all Commission members served "at the pleasure of their appointing authority." Pub Res. Code § 30312. In 2002, a lawsuit was filed in which the petitioner claimed that the structure of the Commission unconstitutionally failed to separate the legislative and executive branches of government. *Marine Forests Soc'y v. California Coastal Comm'n*, 36 Cal. 4th 1 (2005). Marine Forests Society argued that because the majority of the Commission's voting members were appointed by and served at the will of the Legislature, the Commission was a legislative body without the authority to grant or deny permits. *Id.* at 13. The appellate court agreed in a published opinion. *Marine Forests Soc'y v. California Coastal Comm'n*, 104 Cal. App. 4th 1232 (2002) (review granted). The Legislature then passed urgency legislation which both lengthened the terms of the Commission members appointed by the Legislature, and provided that they were not removable by their appointing authority. *Id.* at 15. On appeal, the California Supreme Court determined that as revised, the Act was constitutional, concluding that the revised appointment structure and numerous safeguards built into the Act ensured that members would adhere to statutory guidelines and be protected from improper interference by the Legislature. *Id.* at 10.

The Coastal Zone

Excluding the coastal area of the San Francisco Bay (which is under the jurisdiction of the San Francisco Bay Conservation and Development Commission) the coastal zone stretches for the entire 1,100 mile length of the California coastline, from Oregon to the Mexican border. It encompasses approximately 1.5 million acres. The Act defines the coastal zone as the land and water area of the State of California, as specified by the maps identified and set forth in the Section 17 of the chapter enacting the Coastal Act. Pub. Res. Code § 30103(a). In general, the boundaries of the coastal zone extend seaward to the state's outermost line of jurisdiction, including all offshore islands, and inland to the point designated on the maps adopted by the Legislature. Pub. Res. Code § 30103(a). In significant estuary, habitat, and recreational areas, the inland boundary extends to the first major ridgeline paralleling the ocean, or five miles from the mean high tide line of the ocean, whichever is less. In developed urban areas, the boundary generally extends inland less that 1,000 yards. Pub. Res. Code § 30103(a). The Commission may adjust the inland boundary upon the request of a city or county, to avoid the circumstance of the boundary bisecting an individual parcel of property. Pub. Res. Code § 30603.1.

---

2. The non-voting members represent the Resources Agency, the Business, Transportation and Housing Agency, the Trade and Commerce Agency, and the State Lands Commission. Pub. Res. Code § 30301.

Development and Permitting

With certain exceptions, any person intending to undertake development in the coastal zone must obtain a coastal development permit. The Act defines development very broadly:

> "Development" means, on land, in or under water, the placement or erection of any solid material or structure; discharge or disposal or any dredged material or...waste; grading, removing...or extraction of any materials; change in the density or intensity of use of land, including, but not limited to, subdivision... and any other division of land, including lot splits...; change in the intensity of use of water, or of access thereto; construction, reconstruction, demolition, or alteration of the size of any structure, including any facility...[or] utility; and the removal or harvesting of major vegetation....

Pub. Res. Code § 30106

Lot line adjustments also constitute development under the Act. *La Fe, Inc. v. County of Los Angeles*, 73 Cal. App. 4th 231, 240–42 (1999) (coastal development permit required for a lot line adjustment because, like a subdivision or a lot split, it can result in changes in the density or intensity of use).

Despite the Act's broad definition of development, many types of development are statutorily exempt from coastal permitting requirements. Coastal development permits are not required for most repairs and improvements to existing single-family residences. They also are not required for development in areas subject to categorical exclusions, replacement of structures destroyed by disaster, and certain types of temporary development. Pub Res. Code § 30610. Permit requirements also may be waived in cases of emergency. Pub Res. Code § 30611.

The Commission will approve a coastal development permit if it finds that "the proposed development is in conformity with Chapter 3 [the Coastal Resources Planning and Management Policies of the Coastal Act] and that the permitted development will not prejudice the ability of the local government to prepare a local coastal program that is in conformity with Chapter 3." Pub. Res. Code § 30604(a). Responsibility for issuing coastal development permits is shared between the Coastal Commission and local governments. Most coastal development permits are issued by local governments through Commission-approved local coastal programs (discussed below), and subject to appeal to the Commission. Pub. Res. Code § 30603. However, the Commission retains original permit jurisdiction over the immediate shoreline, tidelands, submerged lands, public trust lands, and land within a certain distance of wetlands, estuaries, streams, and coastal bluffs. The Commission also has original permitting authority over developments constituting major public works projects or energy facilities. Pub. Res. Code § 30601.

Local Coastal Programs

LCP = Local coastal program

Local coastal programs (LCPs) contain the ground rules for future development and protection of coastal resources, and are the basic planning tools used by local governments to guide development in the coastal zone, in partnership with the Coastal Commission. LCPs identify the location, type, densities, and intensities of land uses, the applicable resource protection and development policies, and other ground rules for future development in the coastal zone portion of a local government. Each LCP includes a land use plan and its implementing measures (*e.g.*, zoning ordinances and maps). Pub. Res. Code §§ 30108.5, 30108.6. Prepared by local governments, these programs govern decisions that determine the short- and long-term conservation and use of coastal resources. *See generally* www.coastal.ca.gov for a description of LCPs and their function under the Act. The Act requires local governments to submit proposed LCPs to the Coastal Commission for the portion of the coastal zone within their jurisdiction. Pub. Res. Code § 30500. In lieu of preparing an LCP, local governments may request that the Commission prepare one on their behalf.

Local governments may elect to divide their coastal zone jurisdictions into separate geographic segments, and prepare LCPs for each. Pub. Res. Code § 30500. Many of the 74 coastal counties and cities have done this, resulting in 128 certified LCP segments as of June 30, 2005. As of this date, 36 LCPs had been submitted and were awaiting certification. Only 10 segments statewide had failed to file an LCP as of June 30, 2005. *See* California Coastal Commission, Summary of LCP Program Activity (available at www.coastal.ca.gov/lcp/LCP-Summary-2005.pdf).

Local governments may elect to divide their coastal zone jurisdictions into separate geographic segments, and prepare LCPs for each.

The Commission must certify or refuse certification of a proposed LCP within 90 days, based on whether it conforms with the requirements of Chapter 3 of the Act, Pub. Res. Code § 30200 *et seq.* (Coastal Resources Planning and Management Policies). Pub. Res. Code § 30512. In addition to its role in approving LCPs, the Commission must also review and approve any amendments to previously certified LCPs. Pub. Res. Code § 30514.

After final certification of an LCP, with the exception of the limited areas over which the Commission retains jurisdiction, permitting authority under the Coastal Act is delegated to the local government which is implementing the LCP. Pub Res. Code § 30519(a).

Appeals

Any action taken by a local government on a coastal development permit application may be appealed to the Commission. Pub. Res. Code § 30600.5(d). After a local government's LCP is certified, its coastal development permitting decisions may be appealed to the Commission pursuant to Public Resources Code section 30603. The following types of developments approved by local governments are appealable to the Commission:

Any action taken by a local government on a coastal development permit application may be appealed to the Commission.

- Developments between the sea and the first public road paralleling the sea or within 300 feet of the inland extent of any beach or of the mean high tideline of the sea where there is no beach
- Developments located on tidelands, submerged lands, public trust lands, within 100 feet of any wetland, estuary, or stream, or within 300 feet of the top of the seaward face of any coastal bluff
- Developments located in a sensitive coastal resource area
- Any development approved by a coastal county that is not designated as the principal permitted use under the zoning ordinance
- Any development which constitutes a major public works project or a major energy facility

Pub. Res. Code § 30603(a)

The grounds for an appeal of a local government's decision are limited to a claim that the development does not conform to the standards set forth in the certified LCP, or with the access policies set forth in the Act. Pub. Res. Code §§ 30603(b), 30210–30214. Appeals must be filed within 10 days from the date that the Commission receives notice of the local government's decision on a permit. If an appeal is not submitted within this time, the local government's action becomes final. Pub. Res. Code § 30603(c).

Judicial Review of Commission Decisions

Once it issues a decision on a permit, the Coastal Commission may be sued by an aggrieved person under Code of Civil Procedure section 1094.5. Such petition for review must be filed within 60 days of the Commission's decision. Pub. Res. Code § 30801. For a detailed discussion of litigation procedures as they relate to land uses, *see* chapter 21 (Land Use Litigation).

Other Coastal Commission Responsibilities

The Coastal Commission has a variety of additional statutory functions that must be carried out on an ongoing basis:

- **Public Works Plans and University Long-Range Development Plans.** The Commission must review and approve these plans even when an LCP has been certified. Pub. Res. Code §§ 30605–30606
- **LCP, Port Master Plan, University Long-Range Development Plan, and Public Works Plan Amendments.** The Commission must review and approve all amendments to these plans. Pub. Res. Code §§ 30514, 30515, 30716, and 30605
- **Federal Activities.** The Commission must review activities authorized, funded, or carried out by the federal government that affect coastal zone resources for consistency with the federally approved California Coastal Management Program, including the Coastal Act. Pub. Res. Code §§ 30330, 30400
- **Offshore Energy Projects.** The Commission must review all offshore oil and gas exploration, including any development on the federal outer continental shelf and projects in federal waters for consistency with the Coastal Act, and must regulate marine terminals, refineries, oil and gas pipelines, and other energy development in the coastal zone. Pub. Res. Code §§ 30260–30263
- **Oil Spill Program.** The Commission must assist in the implementation of a statewide oil spill prevention and response program for providing the best achievable protection for the state's coastal and marine resources under the California Oil Spill Prevention and Response Act (in coordination with other federal and state agencies)
- **Public Access.** The Commission must implement a public coastal access program for the length of California's coastline, including maintaining and updating an access inventory, keeping records of easements and dedications, and expediting the opening of new accessways for public use. Pub. Res. Code §§ 30530–30534

- **Access Guide.** The Commission has published and must periodically revise the popular Coastal Access Guide. 1979 Cal Stat. ch. 868
- **Energy Projects and Public Works.** The Commission may amend a certified LCP (upon request or on its own motion) to accommodate energy and public works projects if the local government refuses to do so. Pub. Res. Code § 30515
- **LCP Reviews.** The Commission must review each LCP at least every five years to determine whether the program is being effectively implemented in conformity with the Coastal Act. Pub. Res. Code §§ 30519.5
- **Power Plant Siting.** The Commission must update previously adopted maps of areas not suitable for new coastal electric power plants every two years, and must participate in Energy Commission decisions relative to other coastal power plant sites. Pub. Res. Code §§ 30413(c) and (d)
- **Coastal Resources Information Center.** The Commission is required to establish and maintain a centralized information center and clearinghouse of data about coastal resources for public and private use. Pub. Res. Code § 30343
- **Guide to Coastal Resources.** The Commission has published and must periodically revise the Coastal Resource Guide for public use. Pub. Res. Code § 30344
- **Public Participation.** The Commission must make recommendations to state and local agencies to ensure effective public participation in their coastal resources management decisions. Pub. Res. Code § 30339
- **Wastewater Treatment Works.** The Commission must review coastal wastewater treatment works. Pub. Res. Code § 30412(c)
- **Restoration of Wetlands.** The Commission must work on and promote wetland restoration. Pub. Res. Code §§ 30231, 30233, 30411(b), and 30607.1
- **Local Government Costs.** The Commission must review all local government mandated cost claims resulting from Coastal Act duties and must make grants to local governments. Pub. Res. Code §§ 30350–30555 and 30340.5
- **Federal Pass Through Grants.** The Commission is designated, under the federally approved California Coastal Management Program, as the state agency to receive and pass through federal grants to the San Francisco Bay Conservation and Development Commission and State Coastal Conservancy

The San Francisco Bay Conservation and Development Commission

Under the federal Coastal Zone Management Act of 1972, California's federally approved coastal management plan for the state consists of two segments: one for the coastline, administered by the California Coastal Commission, discussed above; and one for the San Francisco Bay, administered by the San Francisco Bay Conservation and Development Commission.

The 27-member San Francisco Bay Conservation and Development Commission (SFBCDC), was created in 1965 by the McAteer-Petris Act, and has land use planning and regulatory authority over both private and public projects in and near the San Francisco Bay and its environs. *See* Gov't Code § 66600 *et seq.*

Composition

SFBCDC is made up of appointees from the following local governments and state and federal agencies: five, including the chairman and vice-chairman,

California's federally approved coastal management plan for the state consists of two segments: one for the coastline and one for the San Francisco Bay.

SFBCDC = San Francisco Bay Conservation and Development Commission appointed by the Governor; one appointed by the Speaker of the State Assembly; one appointed by the State Senate Rules Committee; one appointed by the Director of Finance; one each appointed by the Board of Supervisors of each of the nine Bay Area Counties; one each from a north, east, south, and west bay city appointed by the Association of Bay Area Governments; one from the California Business and Transportation Agency; one from the California Resources Agency; one from the California State Lands Commission; one from the California Regional Water Quality Control Board, San Francisco Bay Region; one from the U. S. Army Corps of Engineers; and one from the U. S. Environmental Protection Agency. Gov't Code § 66620.

Jurisdiction

SFBCDC has jurisdiction over the open water, marshes, and mudflats of the greater San Francisco Bay along with the first 100 feet inland from the shoreline. This jurisdiction includes the bays of Suisun, San Pablo, Honker, Richardson, San Rafael, San Leandro, Grizzly, and the Carquinez Strait. SFBCDC also regulates the Suisun Marsh, portions of most creeks, rivers, sloughs, and other tributaries that flow into San Francisco Bay, as well as salt ponds, duck hunting preserves, game refuges, and other managed wetlands that have been diked off from San Francisco Bay. Gov't Code § 66610.

Permitting Authority

Any person or governmental agency wishing to place fill in, extract materials from, or make any substantial change in the use of any water, land, or structure within the San Francisco Bay must obtain a permit from SFBCDC. Gov't Code § 66604. SFBCDC is charged with the following responsibilities:

- Regulating all filling and dredging in San Francisco Bay (which includes San Pablo and Suisun Bays, sloughs, and certain creeks and tributaries that are part of the bay system, salt ponds and certain other areas that have been diked-off from the bay).
- Protecting the Suisun Marsh, the largest remaining wetland in California, by administering the Suisun Marsh Preservation Act in cooperation with local governments.
- Regulating new development within the first 100 feet inland from the bay to ensure that maximum feasible public access to the bay is provided.
- Minimizing pressures to fill the bay by ensuring that the limited amount of shoreline area suitable for high priority water-oriented uses is reserved for ports, water-related industries, water-oriented recreation, airports, and wildlife areas.
- Pursuing an active planning program to study bay issues so that SFBCDC plans and policies are based upon the best available current information.
- Administering the federal Coastal Zone Management Act within the San Francisco Bay segment of the California coastal zone to ensure that federal activities reflect SFBCDC policies.
- Participating in the region wide state and federal program to prepare a long-term management strategy (LTMS) for dredging and dredge material disposal in San Francisco Bay.

- Participating in California's oil spill prevention and response planning program.

Transfer of Development Rights

In recent years some cities have incorporated the concept of transfer of development rights (TDR) into their general plans, specific plans, and/or zoning ordinances as a means of preserving open space, scenic views, agricultural land, historic landmarks, and ridgelines. However, even though they have been widely discussed, few communities have actually put TDRs to use and very few court cases have discussed their applicability.

TDRs allow a city to assign a development right to a parcel of property that in turn can be transferred to another parcel. Typically, future development potential is transferred from one piece of property (the sending site) to another (the receiving site). The receiving site can be in the immediate vicinity of the sending site or within a specified area citywide, depending on the local regulatory provisions of the city.

Once the transfer has occurred, a legal restriction on the sending site usually prohibits any future use of its transferred development potential. This permits the receiving site to be legally developed with additional floor area, dwelling units, or parking spaces.

Although no California statute or law provides for the use of TDRs, the United States Supreme Court, in the case of *Penn Central Transportation Company v. City of New York* validated the concept. 438 U.S. 104 (1978). In *Penn Central*, the Court upheld the use of TDRs in conjunction with the city's landmarks law to preserve Grand Central Station. Holding that the law did not amount to a "taking," the Court determined that the ability of Penn Central to transfer its development rights to other sites in mid-town Manhattan would sufficiently mitigate any financial burden imposed by the city's Landmarks Preservation Law. *Id.* at 131–32.

In *Suitum v. Tahoe Regional Planning Agency*, the Court held that a land owner, who had been awarded TDRs but denied the right to build on her property, need not attempt to market the TDRs before bringing a takings claim. 520 U.S. 725, 739–40 (1997). In a concurring opinion, Justice Scalia wrote: "TDRs can serve a commendable purpose in mitigating the economic loss suffered by an individual whose property use is restricted, and property value diminished, but not so substantially as to produce a compensable taking." TDRs, the concurrence continued, "may also form a proper part, or indeed the entirety, of the full compensation accorded a landowner when his property is taken." *Id.* at 750 (Scalia, J., concurring).

The adoption of TDR regulations is an exercise of a city's police power that will be upheld if applied in a manner that is not arbitrary, capricious, or unrelated to the public health, safety, and welfare. For a thorough discussion of a city's police power, *see* chapter 1 (Overview).

In striking down a substantive due process challenge to Marin County's TDR regulations for ranching and agricultural areas (which allowed only one residence for every 60 acres of land, but allowed the property owner/developer to acquire other property owners' development rights), the Ninth Circuit held that the regulations were a valid exercise of the police power. The court stated:

TDR = Transfer of development rights

TDRs allow a city to assign a development right to a parcel of property that in turn can be transferred to another parcel. Typically, future development potential is transferred from one piece of property to another.

The adoption of TDR regulations is an exercise of a city's police power that will be upheld if applied in a manner that is not arbitrary, capricious, or unrelated to the public health, safety, and welfare.

The cowboy and the farmer may be friends as the song has it, but not the rancher and the urban commuter, at least not if commuters, with the roads they need and the cars they drive and the tastes they have, begin to predominate in the countryside. Marin's zoning no doubt preserves a bucolic atmosphere for the benefit of a portion of the population at the expense of those who would flow into the county if there was no zoning. The Constitution lets that decision be made by the legislature. The Countywide Plan is a legislative declaration that there will be a corridor in Marin [that is] agricultural in its use. The choice was not irrational, the application to Barancik not arbitrary.

Barancik v. County of Marin, 872 F. 2d 834, 837 (9th Cir. 1988)

In response to plaintiff's claim that the county's TDR provisions violated the nexus-taking law of *Nollan v. California Coastal Commission,* 483 U.S. 825 (1987), the court ruled that such provisions do not constitute a taking since they allow development if one is willing to pay the price. The court stated:

You are being permitted to accumulate development rights in the same area by a price paid to the owner of the rights.

In other words, a finite amount of development is permitted in the area. The County is rightly indifferent as to who does the development. It lets the market decide the price. A purchase of Transfer Development Rights does not increase the total amount of development possible in the rural corridor. The regulation permitting the accumulation of transfer rights is rationally related to the overall purpose of preserving agriculture in the area.

Barancik, 872 F. 2d at 837

A city intending to use TDRs first should consider adopting a program specifying appropriate goals and policies as an integral part of its general plan. This should be then followed by the implementation of a regulatory scheme in the city's zoning ordinance that includes land use designations for sending and receiving sites.

For an excellent discussion of TDRs, *see* R. Pruetz, *Putting Transfer of Development Rights to Work in California* (Solano Press, 1993). The American Planning Association has published a model transfer of development rights ordinance that is available at www.planning.org/smartgrowthcodes/phase1.htm.

Water Supply Planning

Several bills enacted in 2001 address the marriage of land use planning and water supply planning. Key among these were Senate Bill 610, which amended Water Code section 10910 *et seq.*, and Senate Bill 221, which added Government Code section 66473.7. Both bills, which took effect January 1, 2002, require that specific information about water availability be presented and considered by cities in connection with certain large projects. The California Department of Water Resources has released a Guidebook for Implementation of Senate Bill 610 and Senate Bill 221 of 2001.[3]

Both statutes require certain public agencies to contact the water agency proposed to serve a large development project to determine whether water supplies

---

3. The Guidebook (available at www.owue.water.ca.gov/Guidebook.pdf) essentially breaks the requirements for a water supply analysis or verification into several small steps, and walks the reader through compliance with each step.

Table 1. Comparison of SB 610 and SB 221

	SB 610 Assessment	SB 221 Verification
Codified	Water Code (WC) §§ 10631, 10656, 10657, 10910–10912; Pub. Res. Code § 21151.9	Business & Prof. Code § 11010 (report to DRE to include verification); Government Code (GC) §§ 65867.5 (development agreement); 66455.3 (process); 66473.7 (tentative map condition)
Projects Covered	Large projects approved by a city or county—various land uses: • Residential > 500 units • Shopping center or business establishment > 1,000 employees or > 500,000 sf of floor space • Office building > 1,000 employees or > 250,000 sf of floor space • Hotel or motel > 500 rooms • Industrial, manufacturing or processing plant, or industrial park housing > 1,000 persons, > 40 acres or > 650,000 sf of floor space • Mixed-use project that includes one or more of above • Project that would demand water the amount of water required by 500 dwelling units • If public water system has < 5,000 connections, an increase of 10 percent or more, or a project with equivalent water demand WC § 10912	Large subdivisions—residential only: • Residential subdivisions of > 500 units; or if public water system has < 5,000 connections, a residential development that would generate an increase of 10 percent or more in connections. GC § 66473.7(a) • Development agreements that include such a subdivision. GC § 65867.5(c)
Exceptions	None stated	SB 221 does not apply to: • Project proposed for a site within an urbanized area that has previously been developed for urban uses or where the immediate contiguous properties surrounding the site are, or previously have been, developed for urban uses • Housing projects that are exclusively for very low and low-income households GC § 66473.7(i)
Context	*Processing.* An evaluation of a 20-year water supply for the project must be included in an EIR, Negative Declaration, or Mitigated Negative Declaration prepared for the project.	*Map Act.* The tentative map approval must be conditioned on a requirement that water supply be verified before final map approval.
Water Supply Analysis Required	An assessment of water supplies which addresses whether "the total projected water supplies available during normal, single-dry and multiple-dry water years during a 20-year projection will meet the projected water demand associated with the proposed project, in addition to...existing and planned future uses, including agricultural and manufacturing uses." WC § 10910(c).	A verification that a sufficient water supply shall be available, meaning "the total water supplies available during normal, single-dry, and multiple-dry years within a 20-year projection that will meet the projected demand associated with the proposed subdivision, in addition to existing and planned future uses, including, but not limited to, agricultural and industrial uses." GC § 66473.7(a).

Table 1. Comparison of SB 610 and SB 221 *continued*

	SB 610 Assessment	SB 221 Verification
Agency that Analyzes Water Supply and Form of Determination	A public water system, which means a system for the provision of piped water to the public for human consumption that has 3,000 or more service connections. WC § 10912(c). The city or county must identify any public water system that may supply water for the project and request an assessment from each. WC § 10910(b), (c). The governing body of the water supplier must approve the assessment at a regular or special meeting. WC § 10910(g)(1) If there is no public water system, then the city or county prepares the assessment after consulting with any domestic water supplier whose service area includes the project site, LAFCO, and any public water system adjacent to the project site. WC § 10910(b)	A public water system, which means a system for the provision of piped water to the public for human consumption that has 3,000 or more service connections, that may supply water for a subdivision. GC § 66473.7(a)(3); WC § 10912. The public water system must "deliver the written verification" to the local agency. GC § 66473.7(b) If there is no public water system, the local agency approving the map shall make a finding of sufficient water supply based on the same evidence, and identify the mechanism for providing water to the subdivision. GC § 66473.7(e)
Initial Step in Process	The "city or county, at the time that it determines whether an environmental impact report, a negative declaration, or a mitigated negative declaration is required for any project subject to the California Environmental Quality Act..." must identify the water provider. WC § 10910(b); Pub. Res. Code § 21151.9	"Not later than five days after a city or county has determined that a tentative map application for a proposed subdivision...is complete," the city or county must send a copy of the application to the water supplier. GC § 66455.3 For a development agreement, the city or county need only ensure that the agreement requires that the tentative map(s) comply. GC § 65867.5
Timing	The public water system is to provide the assessment not later than 90 days after receiving a request from the city or county. WC § 10910(g)(1). Before that time expires, the public water system may request an extension of up to 30 days from the city or county. WC § 10910(g)(2). If the public water system does not meet these deadlines, the city or county may seek a writ compelling compliance. WC § 10910(g)(3)	Proof of the availability of a sufficient water supply "shall be based on a written verification from the applicable public water system within 90 days of a request." If the water system fails to deliver the verification, the local agency or any interested party may seek a writ compelling compliance. If the water system fails to provide a verification notwithstanding a writ, then the local agency may make a finding—on the record and supported by substantial evidence—that sufficient water supplies are, or will be, available prior to completion of the subdivision. GC § 66473.7(b)
Proof of Supplies	The assessment must identify relevant, existing water supply entitlements, water rights, or water service contracts, and describe the quantities of water received in prior years. The identification shall be demonstrated by providing information related to all of the following: • Written contracts or other proof of entitlement to an identified water supply	In determining a "sufficient water supply," all of the following factors shall be considered: • The availability of water supplies over a historical record of at least 20 years • The applicability of an urban water shortage contingency analysis prepared pursuant to Section 10632 of the Water Code that includes actions to be undertaken by the public water system in response to water supply shortages.

Table 1. Comparison of SB 610 and SB 221 *continued*

	SB 610 Assessment	SB 221 Verification
Proof of Supplies (*continued*)	• Copies of a capital outlay program for financing the delivery of a water supply that has been adopted by the public water system • Federal, state, and local permits for construction of necessary infrastructure associated with delivering the water supply • Any necessary regulatory approvals that are required in order to be able to convey or deliver the water supply If no water has been received in prior years under an existing entitlement, right, or contract, the assessment must identify the other public water systems or water service contractholders that receive a water supply or have existing entitlements, rights, or contracts, to the same source of water. WC § 10910(d)(2), (e)	• The reduction in water supply allocated to a specific water use sector pursuant to a resolution or ordinance adopted, or a contract entered into, by the public water system, as long as that resolution, ordinance, or contract does not conflict with Section 354 of the Water Code. • The amount of water that the water supplier can reasonably rely on receiving from other water supply projects, such as conjunctive use, reclaimed water, water conservation, and water transfer, including programs identified under federal, state, and local water initiatives such as CALFED and Colorado River tentative agreements, to the extent that these water supplies meet the criteria of subdivision (d) [regarding projected supplies] GC § 66473.7(a)(2) In addition, the verification shall be supported by substantial evidence which may include, but is not limited to: • The public water system's most recently adopted urban water management plan • A water supply assessment that was completed pursuant to Part 2.10 (commencing with section 10910) of Division 6 of the Water Code • Other information relating to the sufficiency of the water supply that contains analytical information that is substantially similar to the assessment equired by section 10635 of the Water Code* GC § 66473.7(c)
Other Water Supplies	*Supplies to Remedy Insufficiency.* If the public water system's total projected water supplies available during a 20-year projection are insufficient, then the water agency must identify plans to acquire additional supplies that may include, but are not limited to: • The estimated total costs, and the proposed method of financing the costs, associated with acquiring the additional water supplies • All federal, state, and local permits, approvals, or entitlements that are anticipated to be required in order to acquire and develop the additional water supplies	*Projected Supplies.* For projected supplies not currently available to the public water system, the verification shall be based on all of the following, to the extent each is applicable: • Written contracts or other proof of valid rights to the identified water supply that identify the terms and conditions under which the water will be available to serve the proposed subdivision • Copies of a capital outlay program for financing the delivery of a sufficient water supply that has been adopted by the applicable governing body

* Section 10635 requires that an Urban Water Mangement Plan include "an assessment of the reliability of its water service to its customers during normal, dry, and multiple dry water years. This water supply and demand assessment shall compare the total water supply sources available to the water supplier with the total projected water use over the next 20 years, in five-year increments, for a normal water year, a single dry water year, and multiple dry water years. The water service reliability assessment shall be based upon the information compiled pursuant to Section 10631, including available data from state, regional, or local agency population projections within the service area of the urban water supplier."

Table 1. Comparison of SB 610 and SB 221 *continued*

	SB 610 Assessment	SB 221 Verification
Other Water Supplies *(continued)*	• Based on the considerations set forth in paragraphs (1) and (2), the estimated timeframes within which the public water system, expects to be able to acquire additional water supplies WC § 10910(c)(3), 10911(a)	• Securing of applicable federal, state, and local permits for construction of necessary infrastructure associated with supplying a sufficient water supply • Any necessary regulatory approvals that are required in order to be able to convey or deliver a sufficient water supply to the subdivision GC § 66473.7(d) *Supplies Not Considered by the Water Supplier.* The local agency may make a finding, after consideration of the written verification by the applicable public water system, and based on substantial evidence, that additional supplies not accounted for by the public water system are, or will be, available prior to completion of the subdivision that will satisfy the requirements for a verification of a 20-year water supply. GC § 66473.7(b)(3)
Groundwater	If a water supply for a proposed project includes groundwater, the following additional information shall be included in the water supply assessment: • (f)(1) A review of any information contained in the urban water management plan relevant to the identified water supply for the proposed project • (f)(2) A description of any groundwater basin or basins from which the proposed project will be supplied. For those basins for which a court or the board has adjudicated the rights to pump groundwater, a copy of the order or decree adopted by the court or the board and a description of the amount of groundwater the public water system... has the legal right to pump under the order or decree. For basins that have not been adjudicated, information as to whether the department has identified the basin or basins as overdrafted or has projected that the basin will become overdrafted if present management conditions continue, in the most current bulletin of the department that characterizes the condition of the groundwater basin, and a detailed description by the public water system... of the efforts being undertaken in the basin or basins to eliminate the long-term overdraft condition. • (f)(3) A detailed description and analysis of the amount and location of groundwater pumped by the public water system... for the past five years from any groundwater basin from which the	Where a water supply for a proposed subdivision includes groundwater, the public water system serving the proposed subdivision shall evaluate, based on substantial evidence, the extent to which it or the landowner has the right to extract the additional groundwater needed to supply the proposed subdivision. Nothing in this subdivision is intended to modify state law with regard to groundwater rights. GC § 66473.7(h)

Table 1. Comparison of SB 610 and SB 221 *continued*

	SB 610 Assessment	SB 221 Verification
Groundwater *(continued)*	proposed project will be supplied. The description and analysis shall be based on information that is reasonably available, including, but not limited to, historic use records. • (f)(4) A detailed description and analysis of the amount and location of groundwater that is projected to be pumped by the public water system, . . . from any basin from which the proposed project will be supplied. The description and analysis shall be based on information that is reasonably available, including, but not limited to, historic use records. • (f)(5) An analysis of the sufficiency of the groundwater from the basin or basins from which the proposed project will be supplied to meet the projected water demand associated with the proposed project A water supply assessment shall not be required to include the information required by this paragraph if the public water system determines, as part of the review required by paragraph (1), that the sufficiency of groundwater necessary to meet the initial and projected water demand associated with the project was addressed in the description and analysis required by paragraph (4) of subdivision (b) of Section 10631.** WC § 10910(f)	
Analyses Regarding Issues Other Than Sufficiency	The assessment is to be included in an environmental document, which will address other impacts of the project. WC § 10911(b)	The verification must also include a description, to the extent information is reasonable available based on published records of federal and state agencies, and public records of local agencies, of the impacts of a proposed subdivision on the availability of water resources for agricultural and industrial uses within the public water system's service area that are not receiving water from the public water system, but are taking from the same source. If this issue was evaluated in a prior environmental document, that information may be used. GC § 66473.7(g)
City or County's Ability to Override Public Water Agency's Determination	The city or county may include an evaluation of the assessment in the EIR, Negative Declaration, or Mitigated Negative Declaration. WC § 10911(c).	The local agency may make a finding, after consideration of the written verification by the applicable public water system, and based on substantial

** SB 610 proposed amendments to section 10631(b)(4) to require "A detailed description and analysis of the location, amount, and sufficiency of groundwater that is projected to be pumped by the urban water supplier. The description and analysis shall be based on information that is reasonably available, including, but not limited to, historic use records." Subdivision (b)(4) now provides: "A detailed description and analysis of the amount and location of groundwater that is projected to be pumped by the urban water supplier. The description and analysis shall be based on information that is reasonably available, including, but not limited to, historic use records."

Table 1. Comparison of SB 610 and SB 221 *continued*

	SB 610 Assessment	SB 221 Verification
City or County's Ability to Override Public Water Agency's Determination *(continued)*	The city or county is ultimately responsible for determining whether supplies will be sufficient. WC § 10911(c) (see next cell).	evidence, that additional supplies not accounted for by the public water system are, or will be, available prior to completion of the subdivision that will satisfy the requirements for a verification of a 20-year water supply. GC § 66473.7(b)(3)
City or County Findings	"The city or county shall determine, based on the entire record, whether projected water supplies will be sufficient to satisfy the demands of the project, in addition to existing and planned future uses. If the city or county determines that water supplies will not be sufficient, the city or county shall include that determination in its findings for the project." WC § 10911(c)	The initial requirement is to include as a condition on the tentative map "a requirement that a sufficient water supply shall be available." GC § 66473.7(b)(1) If the water agency reports that supplies are not sufficient, the local agency may find that additional supplies support a verification. This finding "shall be made on the record and supported by substantial evidence." GC § 66473.7(b)(3). If no verification is provided by the water agency despite requests and a court order, the local agency "may make a finding that sufficient water supplies are, or will be, available prior to completion of the subdivision that will satisfy the requirements of this section. This finding shall be made on the record and supported by substantial evidence." GC § 66473.7(b)(4)
Prior and Later Analyses	If the project has been the subject of an assessment that complies with the requirements of SB 610, then no additional water supply assessment shall be required for subsequent projects that were part of a larger project for which water supplies were found sufficient. Exceptions are: • Changes in the project that will substantially increase water demand • Changes in circumstances that substantially affect the ability to provide a sufficient water supply • Significant new information becomes known WC § 10910(h)	A water supply assessment prepared under SB 610 may constitute evidence for the SB 221 verification. GC § 66473.7(c)(2)

are sufficient to serve the project. If the water agency has a current, comprehensive urban water management plan, then obtaining the information may prove to be fairly straightforward. If not, the analysis may be difficult to obtain. For a detailed comparison of SB 610 and SB 221, *see* Table 1.

Senate Bill 610—
Water Supply Assessment
Water Code §§ 10910–10915

Senate Bill 610 (Chapter 643, Statutes of 2001) applies when a city[4] determines that any "project" that meets any of the following criteria is subject to CEQA:

---

4. SB 610 applies only to cities and counties, not to other agencies. SB 221, because it applies only to agencies that have the power to approve tentative subdivision maps, also applies only to cities and counties.

- A proposed residential development of more than 500 dwelling units
- A proposed shopping center or business establishment employing more than 1,000 persons or having more than 500,000 square feet of floor space
- A proposed commercial office building employing more than 1,000 persons or having more than 250,000 square feet of floor space
- A proposed hotel or motel, or both, having more than 500 rooms
- A proposed industrial, manufacturing, or processing plant, or industrial park planned to house more than 1,000 persons, occupying more than 40 acres of land, or having more than 650,000 square feet of floor area
- A mixed-use project that includes one or more of the projects specified in this subdivision
- A project that would demand an amount of water equivalent to or greater than, the amount of water required by a 500-dwelling unit project

Water Code section 10910 *et seq.* were amended to require a city to make inquiries of the proposed water agency for such projects. "At the time that it determines whether an environmental impact report, a negative declaration, or a mitigated negative declaration is required, a city must identify any public water system that may supply water to the project." Those public water systems then assess whether their "total projected water supplies available during normal, single dry, and multiple dry water years during a 20-year projection will meet the projected water demand associated with the proposed project, in addition to the public water system's existing and planned future uses, including agricultural and manufacturing uses." Water Code § 10910(c)(3). If supplies are projected to be inadequate, the water agency "shall provide to the city or county its plans for acquiring additional water supplies, setting forth the measures that are being undertaken to acquire and develop those water supplies." Water Code § 10911(a). If the city cannot identify a public water system, it must provide the water supply assessment itself. Water Code § 10910(b).

The governing body of each identified water supplier must submit the assessment to the city within 90 days from the date on which the request was received. Water Code § 10910(g)(1). The city may grant the water supplier up to a 30-day extension of time to prepare the assessment. Water Code § 10910(g)(2). Should the water supplier fail to submit the assessment, the city may seek a writ of mandate to compel the water supplier to prepare the assessment. Water Code § 10910(g)(3).

SB 610 refers to numerous details the water supply assessment must address, as described in portions of amended Water Code section 10910:

(d) (1) The assessment required by this section shall include an identification of any existing water supply entitlements, water rights, or water service contracts relevant to the identified water supply for the proposed project, and a description of the quantities of water received in prior years by the public water system…, under the existing water supply entitlements, water rights, or water service contracts.

(2) An identification of existing water supply entitlements, water rights, or water service contracts held by the public water system…shall be demonstrated by providing information related to all of the following: (A) Written contracts or other proof of entitlement to an identified water supply.

(B) Copies of a capital outlay program for financing the delivery of a water supply that has been adopted by the public water system. (C) Federal, state, and local permits for construction of necessary infrastructure associated with delivering the water supply. (D) Any necessary regulatory approvals that are required in order to be able to convey or deliver the water supply.

(e) If no water has been received in prior years by the public water system... under the existing water supply entitlements, water rights, or water service contracts, the public water system... shall also include in its water supply assessment... an identification of the other public water systems or water service contract holders that receive a water supply or have existing water supply entitlements, water rights, or water service contracts, to the same source of water....

(f) If a water supply for a proposed project includes groundwater, the following additional information shall be included in the water supply assessment:

(1) A review of any information contained in the urban water management plan relevant to the identified water supply for the proposed project.

(2) A description of any groundwater basin or basins from which the proposed project will be supplied. For those basins for which a court or the board has adjudicated the rights to pump groundwater, a copy of the order or decree adopted by the court or the board and a description of the amount of groundwater the public water system, or the city or county if either is required to comply with this part pursuant to subdivision (b), has the legal right to pump under the order or decree. For basins that have not been adjudicated, information as to whether the department has identified the basin or basins as overdrafted or has projected that the basin will become overdrafted if present management conditions continue, in the most current bulletin of the department that characterizes the condition of the groundwater basin, and a detailed description by the public water system, or the city or county if either is required to comply with this part pursuant to subdivision (b), of the efforts being undertaken in the basin or basins to eliminate the long-term overdraft condition.

(3) A detailed description and analysis of the amount and location of groundwater pumped by the public water system, or the city or county if either is required to comply with this part pursuant to subdivision (b), for the past five years from any groundwater basin from which the proposed project will be supplied. The description and analysis shall be based on information that is reasonably available, including, but not limited to, historic use records.

(4) A detailed description and analysis of the amount and location of groundwater that is projected to be pumped by the public water system, or the city or county if either is required to comply with this part pursuant to subdivision (b), from any basin from which the proposed project will be supplied. The description and analysis shall be based on information that is reasonably available, including, but not limited to, historic use records.

(5) An analysis of the sufficiency of the groundwater from the basin or basins from which the proposed project will be supplied to meet the projected water demand associated with the proposed project. A water supply assessment shall not be required to include the information required by this paragraph if the public water system determines... that the sufficiency of groundwater necessary to meet the initial and projected water demand associated with the project was addressed in [its urban water management plan].

The information required by Water Code section 10910 may come from the public water system's urban water management plan, if the projected water demand associated with the proposed project was accounted for in the most recently adopted plan. Water Code § 10910(c)(2).

The assessment may incorporate less certainty for future supplies. The California Supreme court explained:

> With regard to *existing* supply entitlements and rights, a water supply assessment must include assurances such as written contracts, capital outlay programs and regulatory approvals for facilities construction..., but as to additional *future* supplies needed to serve the project, the assessment need include only the public water system's plans for acquiring the additional supplies, including cost and time estimates and regulatory approvals the system anticipates needing.

Vineyard Area Citizens for Responsible Growth v. City of Rancho Cordova, 40 Cal. 4th 412, 433 (2007)

When the water agency is required to describe its plans for acquiring additional water because it has determined supplies will be insufficient to meet the demands of planned growth and the project, the plans may include, but are not limited to, information concerning the following:

(1) The estimated total costs, and the proposed method of financing the costs, associated with acquiring the additional water supplies.

(2) All federal, state, and local permits, approvals, or entitlements that are anticipated to be required in order to acquire and develop the additional water supplies.

(3) Based on the considerations set forth in paragraphs (1) and (2) the estimated timeframes within which the public water system, or the city or county if either is required to comply with this part pursuant to subdivision (b), expects to be able to acquire additional water supplies.

Water Code § 10911

SB 610 requires a city to include the assessment in "any environmental document prepared for the project pursuant to [CEQA]." Water Code § 10911. The city also may include its own evaluation of the water agency's assessment in that same document. SB 610 then leaves the ultimate determination whether water supplies will be sufficient to the city:

> The city or county shall determine, based on the entire record, whether projected water supplies will be sufficient to satisfy the demands of the project, in addition to existing and planned future uses. If the city or county determines that water supplies will not be sufficient, the city or county shall include that determination in its findings for the project.

Water Code § 10911(c)

Once an SB 610 assessment concluding that supplies will be sufficient has been prepared for a large project, no additional assessment shall be required for subsequent projects that are part of that larger project. Water Code § 10910(h).

Senate Bill 221—Water Supply Verification Gov't Code § 66473.7

Senate Bill 221 (Chapter 642, Statutes of 2001) is more narrow in application than SB 610, but includes similar requirements.

SB 211 requires more certainty in water supplies than does SB 610:

> Taken together, Water Code sections 10910 to 10912 and Government Code section 66473.7 thus demand... that water supplies must be identified with more specificity at each step as land use planning and water supply planning move forward from general phases to more specific phases. The plans and estimates that Water Code section 10910 mandates for future water supplies at the time of *any* approval subject to CEQA must, under Government Code section 66473.7, be replaced by firm assurances at the subdivision map approval stage.

Vineyard Area Citizens, 40 Cal. 4th at 433–434 (quotations omitted)

The substance of SB 221 appears as part of the Subdivision Map Act, at Government Code section 66473.7. SB 221 applies to a "subdivision," which is defined to mean "a proposed residential development of more than 500 dwelling units, except that for a public water system that has fewer than 5,000 service connections, 'subdivision' means any proposed residential development that would account for an increase of 10 percent or more in the number of public water system's existing service connections." Gov't Code § 66473.7(a)(1). Development agreements that include such a subdivision must require that the subdivision map comply with SB 221 requirements. Gov't Code § 65867.5. There are exceptions for certain infill projects in urbanized areas. Gov't Code § 66473.7(i).

SB 221 requires cities to impose a condition on tentative map approval for the "subdivision" requiring written verification from the proposed water agency that sufficient water will be available during normal, single-dry, and multiple-dry years within a 20-year projection to meet the estimated demand associated with the proposed subdivision, in addition to existing and planned future uses, including, but not limited to, agricultural and industrial uses. Gov't Code § 66473.7(b)(1). If this condition is not satisfied, the final map cannot be recorded. Gov't Code § 66473 (local agency shall disapprove a map for failure to meet or perform any of the conditions imposed).

A water supply verification may be requested from the proposed water supplier by the agency or the applicant.

A water supply verification may be requested from the proposed water supplier by the agency or the applicant. Gov't Code § 66473.7(b). The governing body of each applicable water supplier must submit the verification to the city within 90 days from the date on which the request was received. Gov't Code § 66473.7(b)(1). If the supplier fails to submit the verification, the city or any other interested party may seek a writ of mandate. Gov't Code § 66473.7(b)(2). In the event the supplier does not comply with the writ, the city may itself find that sufficient water supplies are, or will be, available prior to completion of the subdivision. Gov't Code § 66473.7(b)(4).

The water supply verification required by SB 221 may be based upon an assessment completed under SB 610.

The water supply verification required by SB 221 may be based upon an assessment completed under SB 610. Gov't Code § 66473.7(c)(2). In determining whether water supply is sufficient, the water agency considers the following factors:

- The availability of water supplies over a historical record of at least 20 years
- The applicability of an urban water shortage contingency analysis... that includes actions to be undertaken by the public water system in response to water supply shortages

- The reduction in water supply allocated to a specific water use sector pursuant to a resolution or ordinance adopted, or a contract entered into, by the public water system
- The amount of water that the water supplier can reasonably rely on receiving from other water supply projects, such as conjunctive use, reclaimed water, water conservation, and water transfer, including programs identified under federal, state, and local water initiatives such as CALFED and Colorado River tentative agreements

Gov't Code § 66473.7(a)(2)(A)–(D)

When the verification rests on supplies not yet available to the water provider, it is to be based on firm indications the water will be available in the future, including written contracts for water rights, approved financing programs for delivery facilities, and the regulatory approvals required to construct infrastructure and deliver the water.

Vineyard Area Citizens, 40 Cal. 4th at 433

The statute provides that if the water agency relies upon projected water supplies not yet available to it, then the written verification shall be based on the following elements, to the extent each is applicable:

- Written contracts or other proof of valid rights to the identified water supply that identify the terms and conditions under which the water will be available to serve the proposed subdivision
- Copies of a capital outlay program for financing the delivery of a sufficient water supply that has been adopted by the applicable governing body
- Securing of applicable federal, state, and local permits for construction of necessary infrastructure associated with supplying a sufficient water supply
- Any necessary regulatory approvals that are required in order to be able to convey or deliver a sufficient water supply to the subdivision

Gov't Code § 66473.7(d)(1)–(4)

If the water supply for the proposed subdivision includes groundwater, the public water system shall also evaluate, based on substantial evidence, the extent to which it or the landowner has the right to extract the additional groundwater needed to supply the proposed subdivision. Gov't Code § 66473.7(h).

The water agency's written verification also must:

[I]nclude a description, to the extent that data is reasonably available based on published records maintained by federal and state agencies, and public records of local agencies, of the reasonably foreseeable impacts of the proposed subdivision on the availability of water resources for agricultural and industrial uses within the public water system's service area that are not currently receiving water from the public water system but are utilizing the same sources of water.

Gov't Code § 66473.7(g)

The water agency may rely upon a prior CEQA document for this analysis. *Id.*

If the water agency determines that water supplies are insufficient, the local agency may override that decision:

The local agency may make a finding [based on substantial evidence], after consideration of the written verification by the applicable public water system,

If the water supply for the proposed subdivision includes groundwater, the public water system shall also evaluate, based on substantial evidence, the extent to which it or the landowner has the right to extract the additional groundwater needed to supply the proposed subdivision.

that additional water supplies not accounted for by the public water system are, or will be, available prior to completion of the subdivision that will satisfy the requirements of this section. The finding shall be made on the record and supported by substantial evidence.

Gov't Code § 66473.7(b)(3)

Storm Water Quality Requirements for California Cities

Water quality issues are becoming increasingly important in the arena of land use.

Water quality issues are becoming increasingly important in the land use arena. Development has permanently altered the hydrological landscape, replacing surfaces made of soil and grasses with impermeable asphalt and concrete. When stormwater drains across these impermeable surfaces, it carries with it a host of pollutants, such as motor oil, heavy metals, and household chemicals that flow into sewers, and sometimes directly into rivers and bays. Because the Clean Water Act (CWA), 33 U.S.C. § 1251 *et seq.*, requires cities to address this problem, land use practitioners should be familiar with the regulatory regime governing storm water runoff. For further discussion of the Clean Water Act, *see* chapter 7 (Federal and State Wetland Regulation).

CWA = Clean Water Act
MS4 = Munipality separate storm sewer system
NOI = Notice of Intent
NPDES = National Pollutant Discharge Elimination System

Section 402(p) of the CWA states that permits for discharges from municipal storm sewers:

[S]hall require controls to reduce the discharge of pollutants to the maximum extent practicable, including management practices, control techniques and system, design and engineering methods, and such other provisions as the Administrator or the State determines appropriate for the control of such pollutants.

33 U.S.C. § 1342(p)(3)(B)(iii)

The California water boards have been national leaders in vigorously implementing the CWA's municipal storm water requirements through the State's Municipal Storm Water Permitting Program.

In California, the National Pollutant Discharge Elimination System (NPDES) is administered by the State Water Resources Control Board and nine regional boards that issue permits and enforce regulations within their respective regions. The California water boards have been national leaders in vigorously implementing the CWA's municipal storm water requirements through the State's Municipal Storm Water Permitting Program (Program).

The Program regulates storm water discharges from municipal separate storm sewer systems (MS4s). MS4 permits have been issued in two phases.

Under Phase I of the Program, which started in 1990, the regional boards adopted NPDES storm water permits for medium and large municipalities.

Under Phase I of the Program, which started in 1990, the regional boards adopted NPDES storm water permits for medium (serving between 100,000 and 250,000 people) and large (serving 250,000 people or more) municipalities. Most of these permits are issued to groups of co-permittees encompassing an entire metropolitan area. For this reason, and for purposes of efficiency, some municipalities with populations of less than 100,000 were permitted under Phase I of the Program, even though they technically fall under Phase II due to their smaller size. In addition to these municipal permits, during Phase I all construction projects over five acres in size were required to obtain coverage under a statewide general permit governing such construction activities, through the filing of a Notice of Intent (NOI) with the appropriate regional board.

Under Phase II of the Program, adopted in 2003, the State Board approved a General Permit for the Discharge of Storm Water from "Small MS4s." Small MS4s include smaller municipalities (populations less than 100,000) located in urbanized areas as defined by the Bureau of the Census, or in areas with high population density (more that 1000 residents per square mile) or high growth potential (more that 25 percent growth between 1990 and 2000). Small MS4s also include governmental facilities such as military bases, public campuses, and prison and hospital complexes. The Phase II regulations also reduced the threshold for the NOI filing requirement to one acre.

Generally, storm water permits issued in Phase I have not required cities to meet a quantified standard for specific pollutants. Rather, the historic focus has been on requiring planning procedures to reduce discharge of pollutants in storm water from areas of new development and significant redevelopment. Recently, however, the State Board increasingly has shown signs of requiring new and redevelopment project sponsors to address numeric design standards for storm water detention and treatment before issuing local land use approvals. In other words, the state is moving towards requiring design standards that would necessitate the capture and treatment of a specific, quantifiable amount of water from each storm event, rather than "best management practices," as a way of meeting the "maximum extent practicable" test of section 402(p). By way of example, the most recent NPDES storm water permit for the Metropolitan Los Angeles[5] and Orange County[6] areas require such design standards. The Contra Costa Clean Water Program's Stormwater C.3. Guidebook[7] also includes a section on numeric criteria for the design of treatment BMPs.

Generally, storm water permits issued in Phase I have not required cities to meet a quantified standard for specific pollutants.

Under the Phase II permit, regulated Small MS4s are required to develop a Storm Water Management Program that describes BMPs, measurable goals, and timetables for implementation in six program areas, including public education and participation, illicit discharge detection and elimination, construction site storm water runoff control, post construction storm water management, and pollution prevention. The permit incorporates specific design standards, which must be incorporated into post-construction programs. The design standards stress low impact design, source controls, and treatment controls, and must be complied with within five years of designation as a Small MS4.[8] It should be noted that while the design standards require the incorporation of BMPs to reduce the pollutant load, they do not impose numeric criteria on cities.

BMP = Best management practice
CMA = Congestion Management Agency
CMP = Congestion Management Plan

Congestion Management and Land Use

Introduction

In June 1990, the voters of California adopted Proposition 111, which triggered the operation of chapter 2.6 (Congestion Management) of Title 7 (Planning and

---

5. The NPDES permit for Los Angeles may be viewed at the State Water Resources Control Board website (www.swrcb.ca.gov/rwqcb4/html/programs/stormwater/la_ms4_final/FinalPermit.pdf). The design standards are on page 36 of the permit.
6. The NPDES permit for the County of Orange, Orange County Flood Control District, and Incorporated Cities of Orange County within the Santa Ana Region may be viewed at the SWRCB website (www.swrcb.ca.gov/rwqcb8/pdf/R8-2002-0010.pdf). The design standards are on page 30 of the permit.
7. The Contra Costa Clean Water Program's Stormwater C.3. Guidebook may be viewed at www.ccleanwater.org/construction/Publications/C3_Guidebook_1st_Draft.pdf. The numeric criteria begin on page 44.
8. A table of submitted SWMPs for Small MS4s is available on the SWRCB website (www.swrcb.ca.gov/stormwtr/sm_municipal_swmp.html). For a list of design standards, *see* Attachment 4 to the Small MS4 General Permit (available at www.swrcb.ca.gov/stormwtr/docs/final_attachment4.pdf).

Land Use) of the Government Code. Gov't Code § 65088 *et seq*. This law created a new regional planning agency for each county called a Congestion Management Agency (CMA). Each agency must prepare an annual Congestion Management Program that requires cities and counties to maintain specified levels of service on identified roadways of regional significance. The statutory scheme includes a powerful enforcement mechanism: If a city fails to comply with the CMP, the state controller is obligated to withhold that city's apportionment of the increased gas tax revenues generated by Proposition 111. Gov't Code § 65089.5.

Adoption of a CMP

Under Government Code section 65089(a), a CMP must be developed, adopted, and biennially updated for every county that includes an "urbanized area," and must include every city in the county. The program must be adopted at a noticed public hearing of the Agency. The program shall be developed either by the county transportation commission, or by another public agency, as designated by resolutions adopted by the county board of supervisors and the city councils of a majority of the cities representing a majority of the population in the incorporated area of the county. In developing the program, the agency is required to consult and cooperate with the transportation planning agency, regional transportation providers, local governments, the Transportation Department, and the air pollution control district or the air quality management district.

"'Urbanized area' has the same meaning as is defined in the 1990 federal census for urbanized areas of more than 50,000 population." Gov't Code § 65088.1(l). Under 1990 census data, the statute will apply in at least 39 counties: Alameda, Butte, Contra Costa, El Dorado, Fresno, Humboldt, Imperial, Kern, Kings, Los Angeles, Madera, Marin, Mendocino, Merced, Monterey, Napa, Nevada, Orange, Placer, Riverside, Sacramento, San Bernardino, San Diego, San Francisco, San Joaquin, San Luis Obispo, San Mateo, Santa Barbara, Santa Clara, Santa Cruz, Shasta, Solano, Sonoma, Stanislaus, Sutter, Tulare, Ventura, Yolo, and Yuba.

The deadline for adopting a CMP is set forth in Government Code section 65082(b), which provides that the CMP "shall be incorporated into the regional transportation improvement program submitted to the commission by December 15 of each odd-numbered year." However, the Agency may gain an additional year if more time is required to prepare an EIR for the CMP. Gov't Code § 65082(c). Many agencies have elected to prepare an EIR, if only to gain an additional year to prepare the CMP. Once adopted, the plan must be updated every two years. Gov't Code § 65089(a).

Recent changes to the CMP law allow cities to create "infill opportunity zones" within one-third of a mile of major public transit routes for new compact residential and mixed use development in population centers over 400,000. These zones are exempt from traffic level of service requirements normally required by a CMP. Instead, the new law requires the CMP to take into account the alternative transit opportunities in the "infill opportunity zones," including pedestrian, bicycle, and public transit, using a "multimodal composite." Gov't Code § 65088.4. The Legislature's intent is to encourage dense infill development near transit where traffic level of service requirements would otherwise preclude higher densities. The idea is that if other forms of transportation are

---

PRACTICE TIP

Attorneys and developers should consult the CMP, especially on large projects, since a city will be referring to it as a tool in reviewing a development project, and it will be a primary source of imposing impact fees.

Recent changes to the CMP law allow cities to create infill opportunity zones within one-third of a mile of major public transit routes for new compact residential and mixed use development in population centers over 400,000.

available and functional, new development should not be restricted by traffic requirements. Attorneys and developers should consult the CMP, especially on large projects, since a city will be referring to it as a tool in reviewing a development project, and it will be a primary source of imposing impact fees.

Failure to Comply with the CMP

If the CMA, after conducting its annual monitoring, determines, following a noticed public hearing, that a city is not conforming with the requirements of the CMP, the CMA must notify the city in writing of the specific areas of nonconformance. Gov't Code § 65089.5(a). If, within 90 days of the receipt of the written notice of nonconformance, the city has not come into conformance with the CMP, the CMA must make a finding of nonconformance and submit the finding to the California Transportation Commission and the California Controller. Upon receiving notice of nonconformance from the CMA, the Controller must withhold apportionments of funds to that nonconforming city until the Controller is notified by the CMA that the city or county is in conformance. *Id.*

Failure to complete or implement a CMP does not give rise to a cause of action against a city for failing to conform with its general plan, unless the city incorporates the CMP into the circulation element of its general plan. Gov't Code § 65089.6.

Prevailing Wage Concerns on Private Development Projects

The California Labor Code generally requires that wage rates on all "public works" projects performed under contract be not less than the general prevailing rate per diem for work of a similar character in the locality in which the public work is performed. Labor Code § 1771. The overall purpose of this prevailing wage law is to protect and benefit employees on public works projects. *Lusardi Construction Co. v. Aubry*, 1 Cal. 4th 976 (1992). More specifically, prevailing wage law is designed to protect such employees from substandard earnings and to protect local craftsmen who were losing work to contractors who recruited labor from distant cheap-labor areas. *O.G. Sansone Co. v. Dept. of Transportation*, 55 Cal. App. 3d 434 (1976) (quoting federal authorities on the purpose of the federal Davis-Bacon Act). Courts will liberally construe prevailing wage statutes. *McIntosh v. Aubry (Pricor)*, 14 Cal. App. 4th 1576 (1993).

"Public works" is defined under the Labor Code to include all "work done under contract and paid for in whole *or in part* out of public funds." Labor Code § 1720(a)(1) (emphasis added). Under this broad language, payment of prevailing wages may be required for all work on an otherwise private development project where only a small, discrete part of the project is paid for out of public funds. Where the publicly funded portion of a project is arguably discrete and separate from the portion of a project funded solely with private funds, questions arise as to whether the project should be characterized: as (1) a single project with privately and publicly funded components, both subject to prevailing wage requirements; or (2) two separate projects, one that is publicly funded and subject to prevailing wage law and a second privately funded project that is not.

DIR = California Department of Industrial Relations

The Labor Code is silent in this regard. Instead, practitioners must look to a series of administrative decisions issued by the California Department of Industrial Relations (DIR) beginning with the DIR's decision in Public Works Case No. 2000-016, *Vineyard Creek Hotel and Conference Center*, Redevelopment Agency, Santa Rosa (October 16, 2000).[9] In *Vineyard Creek*, the DIR established a five-factor test to be applied on a case-by-case basis to determine whether a development undertaking is one project or a set of separate projects. The five factors are:

- **Organization**—the manner in which the construction for the project is organized in view of, for example, bids, contracts, agreements, and workforce
- **Physical Layout**—the physical layout of the project
- **Common Oversight**—the oversight, direction, and supervision of the work
- **Common Financing**—the financing and administration of the construction funds, and
- **General Interrelationship**—the general interrelationship of the various aspects of the construction

Between 2000 and 2004, the DIR generally found that the publicly funded construction undertaking at issue was part of a larger integrated project and that the otherwise privately funded project therefore was entirely subject to prevailing wage requirements. *See, e.g.*, Public Works Case No. 2001-044, *Soledad Canyon Center Shopping Center*, City of Santa Clarita (September 26, 2002) (development of a private shopping center was a public work subject to prevailing wage requirements because the private developer agreed to build a public library within the center and the library and certain off-site improvements were paid for, in part, out of public funds); Public Works Case No. 2001-016, *Development of River Street Historic District*, City of San Jose (May 6, 2002); Public Works Case No. 2001-068, *Field Technician Observation and Testing*, Los Angeles County Sanitation District Sewer Line Project (July 19, 2002); Public Works Case No. 2003-028, *Baldwin Park Marketplace Project*, City of Baldwin Park (October 16, 2003), incorporated by reference into Decision on Administrative Appeal (June 28, 2005).

In more recent decisions, however, the DIR has found that upon application of the five-factor *Vineyard Creek* test, the publicly funded construction undertaking at issue was a separate project and that construction of the privately funded project therefore was *not* subject to payment of prevailing wages. *See* Public Works Case No. 2003-022, *Chapman Heights*, City of Yucaipa (January 30, 2004) (construction of private residential development not subject to prevailing wage requirements because certain related infrastructure work paid for out of public

---

9. The DIR is authorized to make prevailing wage coverage determinations pursuant to Title 8, California Code of Regulations, section 16001(a). These administrative determinations were previously deemed "precedential," meaning that subsequent DIR decisions had to adhere to the standards set in earlier decisions addressing similar issues. In 2007, the DIR advised that its coverage determinations should be considered advice letters directed to specific individuals about whether a specific project is subject to prevailing wage requirements. This change was spurred by the DIR's efforts to comply with Government Schwarzenegger's Executive Order S-2-03, which required that California departments review their regulations to assure that the impact of such regulations on businesses were adequately addressed under this new regulatory scheme. The DIR's coverage determinations remain important guidelines in assessing how the Department will likely view a particular project, but there is less certainty now for the present project proponents with regard to the circumstances under which prevailing wage requirements will be imposed.

funds was a separate project); Decision on Administrative Appeal Re: Public Works Case No. 2003-028, *Baldwin Park Marketplace Project* (June 28, 2005) (construction of a Wal-Mart "super center" found to be a project separate and distinct from a shopping center project in which Wal-Mart was an "anchor tenant" despite the fact that Wal-Mart was required to conform to "unifying design elements" and the site clearance, demolition, and rough grading as well as off-site infrastructure improvements were paid for out of public funds); Public Works Case No. 2003-014, *Phase II Residential Development*, Victoria Gardens, City of Rancho Cucamonga (July 20, 2005) (construction of 500–600 multi-family residential units was considered separate from the remainder of a master planned community and no prevailing wages were required to be paid despite the use of public funds for grading of the site and improvement of border streets).

Because of the broad scope of the "public works" language in the Labor Code and the relative ease with which otherwise privately funded projects can be subjected to prevailing wage requirements, private developers and public agencies alike should carefully consider the risks of using public funds and should design their projects to separate the public and private projects where feasible if they desire to avoid the imposition of such requirements.

Public Bidding Concerns on Private Development Projects

It is common practice for private developers of large parcels of land to construct and dedicate significant public facilities, such as schools, fire stations, and libraries within their developments. Public agencies may require the financing or construction of such facilities before approving the plans for development. *See, e.g.*, 69 Ops. Cal. Atty. Gen. 300, 301 (1986). Of increasing concern to public agencies and private developers alike is the issue of whether such facilities constitute "public works" or "public projects"—for which a public competitive bidding process must be conducted by a public agency—when they are being constructed by a developer on land to be transferred to such agency as a condition of development of a larger project.

Under existing law, there is no express requirement that public bidding be conducted for the construction of public facilities on private lands which will later be transferred to a public entity. However, due to a paucity of reported cases on the subject, private developers should expect that concerns about public bidding will arise and should be prepared to work with public agencies to satisfy such concerns.

The duty to solicit competitive bids for construction of public works is not a rule of general application, rather it is the result of certain specific statutory mandates. "Competitive bidding is necessary only when required by statute." *County of Riverside v. Whitlock*, 22 Cal. App. 3d 863, 878 (1972). There is "no all-pervasive public policy that requires all public entities" to engage in competitive bidding. *San Diego Service Authority v. Superior Court*, 198 Cal. App. 3d 1466, 1469 (1988). Rather, "the Legislature imposes competitive bidding requirements on public entities within its purview when the Legislature determines it is in the public interest to do so." *Id.* "[A]bsent a statutory directive, a public entity is not bound to engage in competitive bidding." *Construction Industry Force Account Council v. Amador Water Agency*, 71 Cal. App. 4th 810, 815 (1999).

The Public Contract Code specifically enumerates the entities that qualify as "public agencies" subject to public bidding requirements, and does not include private entities constructing public facilities as a condition of project approval within the meaning of "public agency." The statute does recognize that certain entities may act as agents of or proxies for "public agencies," but limits the application of the competitive bidding requirements to certain nonprofit transit corporations. Pub. Cont. Code § 22002.

In *San Diego Service Authority*, the court held that absent an express statutory requirement, even a public entity which is an agent of or proxy for another public agency is not bound to engage in competitive bidding. 198 Cal. App. 3d at 1472. In *Service Authority*, San Diego County and a number of area cities established a service authority (which is a public entity) to implement an emergency call box system. Suit was brought against the service authority when it contracted to have the system installed by a party who did not offer the lowest bid. Although the cities and county that established the service authority would have been required to engage in competitive bidding under the Public Contract Code if they had individually let the contract, the court stated that the service authority was a separate legal entity without any express statutory limitations upon its ability to contract. *Id.* The court held that if the Legislature wanted to require competitive bidding in all instances it would have done so specifically. It ruled that a court should not presume the Legislature intended to legislate by implication. *Id.*

In *Service Authority*, the court also concluded that it would be inconsistent with public policy to require the service authority to engage in competitive bidding. *Id.* at 1471. The purpose of competitive bidding is to guard against "favoritism, extravagance, fraud, and corruption; it serves the public by preventing waste and securing the best economic result." *Id.* at 1469. Where public bidding is not cost effective or in the public interest it is unnecessary from a public policy perspective. *Id.* at 1470. Public policy considerations militate against application of public bidding requirements to developer-built facilities because private developers gain nothing by increasing expenditures on their projects. Because construction of public facilities are conditions of project approval and because where some reimbursement is provided by the public agency it is usually capped at certain statutory limits and less than the actual costs incurred, it is in the developer's best interest to diligently complete construction of the facilities as quickly and as cheaply as possible.

Even where projects are subject to the Public Contract Code's public bidding requirements, certain projects may be excused from bidding due to policy considerations. It is "well established that where requests for competitive proposals would be futile, unavailing, or would not produce an advantage, statutes requiring competitive bidding do not apply." *Meakin v. Steveland, Inc.*, 68 Cal. App. 3d 490, 498 (1977) (holding city's disposition of public land was excused from public bidding because the buyers were the only potential purchasers and were willing to pay the full appraised price). This principle has been held applicable by California courts in a variety of situations involving the construction of public improvements and buildings where it has appeared that competitive bidding would be incongruous or would not result in any advantage to the public entity in efforts to contract for the greatest public benefit. *See, e.g., Graydon v. Pasadena Redevelopment Agency*, 104 Cal. App. 3d 631, 636 (1980).

10

Vested Rights—Development Agreements and Vesting Tentative Maps

Vested Rights [1]

On occasion, at planning commission and city council meetings, a property owner will speak in opposition to a proposed general plan and/or zoning change and claim that the city has no right to change the law governing its property because the owner already has completed significant planning, and perhaps some construction work, for development of the project. Unless the property owner previously has obtained statutory vested rights under a development agreement or a vesting tentative map, the property owner will need to establish that sufficient development activities have been undertaken to establish common law vested rights, thereby preventing a change in the law governing the use of the property.

The *Avco* Rule

The common law rule in California is that if a city changes its land use regulations, a property owner cannot claim a vested right to build out a project under existing land use regulations unless the owner has obtained a building permit, performed substantial work, and incurred substantial liabilities in good faith reliance upon the permit. This common law vested rights rule was affirmed in 1976 when the California Supreme Court stated:

> It has long been the rule in this state and in other jurisdictions that if a property owner has performed substantial work and incurred substantial liabilities in good faith reliance upon a permit issued by the government, he acquires a vested right to complete construction in accordance with the terms of the permit. [Citations omitted.] Once a landowner has secured a vested right the government may not, by virtue of a change in the zoning laws, prohibit construction authorized by the permit upon which he relied.

Avco Community Developers, Inc. v. South Coast Reg'l Comm'n, 17 Cal. 3d 785, 791 (1976)

Once a landowner has secured a vested right the government may not, by virtue of a change in the zoning laws, prohibit construction authorized by the permit upon which he relied.

---

1. *See* Daniel J. Curtin, Jr., "Developer Claims of Vested Rights, Current Trends and Practical Strategies," *Land Use Law and Zoning* 31 (Patricia E. Salkin ed., ABA, Sect. of State and Local Gov't Law, 2004); David L. Callies, Daniel J. Curtin, Jr., and Julie A. Tappendorf, *Bargaining for Development: A Handbook on Development Agreements, Annexation Agreements, Land Development Conditions, Vested Rights and the Provision of Public Facilities* (Environmental Law Institute, Wash., D.C. 2003).

The *Avco* court stated further, however, that:

> [N]either the existence of a particular zoning nor work undertaken pursuant to governmental approvals preparatory to construction of buildings can form the basis of a vested right to build a structure which does not comply with the laws applicable at the time the building permit is issued.

Id. at 793

Avco owned approximately 8,000 acres of land in Orange County, a small portion of which was located within the coastal zone. Prior to February 1, 1973, the date on which the coastal development permit requirement became effective under the California Coastal Act (Pub. Res. Code section 30000 *et seq.*), Avco had obtained zoning and tentative and final subdivision map approvals, and had completed or was in the process of constructing storm drains, improvements of utilities, and similar facilities for the subdivision tract. However, no building permits had been issued for vertical unit construction. The company had spent $2,000,000 and incurred additional liabilities of $750,000 for development of the subdivision. Based on this, Avco argued that it should be exempt from the new coastal development permit requirement. Although it had not yet obtained building permits, Avco believed that it had a vested right to proceed with its development because it had obtained all of its discretionary entitlements and had installed extensive utility improvements. The Coastal Commission disagreed, and denied Avco's requests for an exemption from the Coastal Act. The California Supreme Court held that Avco had no vested right to proceed:

> By zoning the property or issuing approvals for work preliminary to construction the government makes no representation to a landowner that he will be exempt from the zoning laws in effect at the subsequent time he applies for a building permit or that he may construct particular structures on the property, and thus the government cannot be estopped to enforce the laws in effect when the permit is issued.

Id. at 793

In summarizing the policy behind the vested right rule, the court stated:

> Our conclusion that Avco has not acquired a vested right under the common law to proceed with its development absent a permit from the commission is not founded upon an obdurate adherence to archaic concepts inappropriate in the context of modern development practices or upon a blind insistence on an instrument entitled "building permit."

> If we were to accept the premise that the construction of subdivision improvements or the zoning of the land for a planned community are sufficient to afford a developer a vested right to construct buildings on the land in accordance with the laws in effect at the time the improvements are made or the zoning enacted, there could be serious impairment of the government's right to control land use policy. In some cases the inevitable consequence would be to freeze the zoning laws applicable to a subdivision or a planned unit development as of the time these events occurred.

> Thus tracts or lots in tracts which had been subdivided decades ago, but upon which no buildings have been constructed could be free of all zoning laws enacted subsequent to the time of the subdivision improvement, unless facts

constituting waiver, abandonment, or opportunity for amortization of the original vested right could be shown. In such situations, the result would be that these lots, as well as others in similar subdivisions created more recently or lots established in future subdivisions, would be impressed with an exemption of indeterminate duration from the requirements of any future zoning laws.

Id. at 797–98

Other cases have applied the same principle. *See Hill v. City of Manhattan Beach*, 6 Cal. 3d 279, 286–87 (1971) (application of a subsequent zoning ordinance to a previously divided parcel that prohibited development or sale of one of the lots was proper); *Oceanic Cal., Inc. v. North Cent. Coastal Reg'l Comm'n*, 63 Cal. App. 3d 57, 70 (1976) (although county repeatedly had approved developer's concept of a planned community development, such general approval was not sufficient basis for a claim of vested rights without securing the necessary coastal permit); *Hermosa Beach Stop Oil Coalition v. City of Hermosa Beach*, 86 Cal. App. 4th 534, 552 (2001) (no right to develop vests until all final discretionary permits have been authorized and significant "hard costs" have been expended in reliance on those permits, *i.e.*, until substantial construction has occurred in reliance on a building permit); *Hafen v. County of Orange*, 128 Cal. App. 4th 133 (2005) (county was authorized to enforce zoning changes that occurred after approval of a tentative parcel map since developer had not obtained a vested right).

Refinements of the *Avco* Rule

Courts subsequently have refined and limited the *Avco* rule. First, the rights that may vest upon reliance on a governmental permit are no greater than those specifically granted by the permit itself. *See Santa Monica Pines, Ltd. v. Rent Control Bd.*, 35 Cal. 3d 858, 866 (1984); *People v. Thomas Shelton Powers*, 2 Cal. App. 4th 330, 337–38 (1992) (holding a city was not estopped from imposing a later-enacted ordinance restricting the resale price of units on a previously approved condominium conversion).

The rights that may vest upon reliance on a governmental permit are no greater than those specifically granted by the permit itself.

Second, an owner of undeveloped land has no vested right in existing zoning, more valuable zoning that may have been anticipated, or zoning for the highest and best use of the property. *See Gilliland v. County of Los Angeles*, 126 Cal. App. 3d 610, 617 (1981).

Third, an invalid permit vests no rights. The California Supreme Court held that a developer cannot claim a vested right in reliance upon a permit he had reason to know might be defective. *See Strong v. County of Santa Cruz*, 15 Cal. 3d 720, 725 (1975). Another court held that a property owner who had constructed improvements in reliance upon an invalid building permit could be required to remove the structure, even though the permit was regular on its face and the property owner acted without actual knowledge of any defect in it. *See Pettitt v. City of Fresno*, 34 Cal. App. 3d 813, 823 (1973). The following year, in *People v. County of Kern*, the court held that a property owner could not obtain vested rights in reliance upon an approval obtained in accordance with the requirements of the county where the rules and practices adopted by the county did not conform strictly to the requirements of state law. 39 Cal. App. 3d 830 (1974).

A property owner also cannot rely on written statements made by a public official unless the official is authorized to make those statements. *See Burchett v.*

City of Newport Beach, 33 Cal. App. 4th 1472 (1995). In *Burchett*, the property owners alleged a breach of a written agreement with the City of Newport Beach, claiming that the city agreed to allow the property owners to improve real property with a two story condominium structure. The allegation was based on a letter from the property owners to the planning department asking for a permit to use an existing, nonconforming driveway, on which an assistant planner had marked a notation that the facts were "correct." *Id.* at 1475.

In denying the petitioner's claim of a contractual right to develop, the court first noted that the city's charter provided that it could not be bound by any contract unless it was in writing, approved by the city council, and signed on behalf of the city by the mayor and the city clerk or by another designated officer. *Id.* at 1479. Second, the assistant planner was neither the person to contact for an "encroachment permit" nor a member of the correct department. The court then cited *Horsemen's Benevolent & Protective Association v. Valley Racing Association* for the proposition that "no government, whether state or local, is bound to any extent by an officer's acts in excess of his authority." 4 Cal. App. 4th 1538, 1564 (1992). Based on this reasoning, the court held that any purported right to develop was invalid. *Burchett*, 33 Cal. App. 4th at 1480. "One who deals with the public officer stands presumptively charged with a full knowledge of that officer's powers, and is bound at his peril to ascertain the extent of his powers to bind the government for which he is an officer, and any act of an officer to be valid must find express authority in the law or be necessarily incidental to a power expressly granted." *Id. See also G.L. Mezzetta, Inc. v. City of American Canyon*, 78 Cal. App. 4th 1087, 1093 (2000) (general law city was not bound by oral contract because it did not comply with Government Code section 40602 and relevant city code provisions).

A vested right may be restricted or revoked if the use would be a menace to the public health and safety or a public nuisance.

Fourth, a vested right may be restricted or revoked if the use would be a menace to the public health and safety or a public nuisance. *See Davidson v. County of San Diego*, 49 Cal. App. 4th 639, 648 (1996) (although a county zoning ordinance conferred a vested right to have a building permit application for a crematorium reviewed and considered in light of the regulations existing on the date of application, the county could require an application for a major use permit for the crematorium because vested rights may be impaired through subsequent police power enactments necessary to protect public health or safety).

Fifth, a city-promulgated administrative regulation relied on by an owner in proceeding with a condominium conversion may be a valid basis for estoppel against the city, even though the city later enacts an ordinance that would have prevented the conversion. *See Hock Inv. Co. v. City and County of San Francisco*, 215 Cal. App. 3d 438, 449 (1989); *see also City of W. Hollywood v. Beverly Towers, Inc.*, 52 Cal. 3d 1184 (1991). In *Beverly Towers*, several apartment building owners had obtained final map approval from Los Angeles County to convert their rental units into condominiums. The owners also had obtained permission to sell individual units as condominiums from the California Department of Real Estate. The owners did not need any further permits to complete the conversion. The California Supreme Court held that a newly incorporated city could not enforce new condominium regulations after final map and Department of Real Estate approval. *Id.* at 1191. The Court further held that it made no difference that the owners had not sold any units. *Id.* at 1190.

While these decisions narrowed the applicability of the *Avco* rule to some degree, California courts continue to rely on *Avco* to define when a property owner has acquired a vested right. For example, subdivision approval for condominium conversions does not give a developer a vested right against later-enacted police power ordinances. *See Santa Monica Pines, Ltd. v. Rent Control Board*, 35 Cal. 3d 858, 866 (1984) (converter had to obtain a permit from the rent control board since reliance upon tentative map approval was inadequate to establish vested rights); *Consaul v. City of San Diego*, 6 Cal. App. 4th 1781, 1794 (1992) (reaffirming *Avco*); *Hafen v. County of Orange*, 128 Cal. App. 4th 133 (2005) (developer required to comply with zoning changes as tentative parcel map did not confer a vested right). In *People v. H & H Properties*, the developer was required to comply with the county's later enacted rent control ordinance even though he already had obtained tentative and final map approval. 154 Cal. App. 3d 894, 900 (1984). "Vested rights is not the question here. H & H is free to proceed. It simply must pay somewhat more than it expected for the privilege of engaging in a condominium conversion in Los Angeles County in the 1980's." *Id.* at 902.

In a California Supreme Court case, developers were ordered to comply with a transit impact development fee even though they had acted on building permits and had begun construction before the fee ordinance went into effect. *See Russ Bldg. Partnership v. City and County of San Francisco*, 44 Cal. 3d 839, 847 (1988). The fee was imposed pursuant to a generally worded condition of approval requiring the developer's participation in some type of transportation funding. The court held that the developers did not have a vested right to develop free of imposition of the transit impact fee under the *Avco* rule because of the "open ended" condition attached to the earlier approval. *Id. See also Blue Jeans Equities W. v. City and County of San Francisco*, 3 Cal. App. 4th 164, 172 (1992).

Development Agreements[2]

A city's general plan, local ordinances, or policies may impose additional exactions or development conditions as a condition to obtaining the benefits of a development agreement. Such local laws should be reviewed carefully before proceeding.

In 1979, in an attempt to soften the impact of the *Avco* decision, the Legislature enacted legislation establishing a property development agreement procedure. Gov't Code § 65864 *et seq.; see also The Legacy Group v. City of Wasco*, 106 Cal. App. 4th 1305 (2003).

The principal provisions of the legislation governing development agreements are as follows:

---

2. *See* David L. Callies, Daniel J. Curtin, Jr., and Julie A. Tappendorf, *Bargaining for Development: A Handbook on Development Agreements, Annexation Agreements, Land Development Conditions, Vested Rights and the Provision of Public Facilities* (Environmental Law Institute, Wash., D.C. 2003); Daniel J. Curtin, Jr., *Exactions, Dedications and Development Agreements Nationwide and in California: When and How Do* Nollan/Dolan *Apply*, ch. 2, 33rd Annual Institute of Planning, Zoning and Eminent Domain (Matthew Bender, 2003); *Development Agreement Manual: Collaboration in Pursuit of Community Interest* (Institute for Local Self Government, 2002). *See also* Brad Schwartz, "Development Agreements: Contracting for Vested Rights," 28 *Boston College Envtl. Affairs L. Rev.*, no. 4, 719 (Summer 2001); David L. Callies and Julie A. Tappendorf, *Annexation Agreements and Development Agreements, Trends in Land Use Law from A to Z*, ch. 14 (Patricia Salkin ed., ABA, Sect. of State and Local Gov't Law, 2001).

- Cities are given express authorization to enter into a development agreement and may adopt procedures to do so by resolution or ordinance. Gov't Code § 65865.
- The development agreement is enforceable by any party to the agreement, notwithstanding a change in any applicable general or specific plan, zoning, subdivision, or building regulation adopted by the city. Gov't Code § 65865.4; *see also Beverly Towers*, 52 Cal. 3d at 1193 n. 6; *Native Sun/Lyon Communities v. City of Escondido*, 15 Cal. App. 4th 892, 910 (1993); *Midway Orchards v. County of Butte*, 220 Cal. App. 3d 769, 773 (1990); 76 Ops. Cal. Atty. Gen. 227 (1994); 77 Ops. Cal. Atty. Gen. 94 (1994).
- Unless otherwise provided by the development agreement, the applicable rules, regulations, and policies are those that are in force at the time of the execution of the agreement. Gov't Code § 65866.
- A city's exercise of its power to enter into a development agreement is a legislative act. *Santa Margarita Area Residents Together ("SMART") v. County of San Luis Obispo*, 84 Cal. App. 4th 221, 227–28 (2000). It must be approved by ordinance, be consistent with the general plan and any specific plan, and is subject to repeal by referendum. Gov't Code § 65867.5.
- There is a 90-day statute of limitations to challenge the adoption or amendment of a development agreement approved on or after January 1, 1996. Gov't Code § 65009(c)(1)(d). An action by either a city or an applicant for breach of a development agreement is subject to the normal breach of contract statute of limitations. *The Legacy Group v. City of Wasco*, 106 Cal. App. 4th 1305, 1312-13 (2003) (holding that the Subdivision Map Act's 90-day statute of limitations to attack or review a "decision" of the city council "concerning a subdivision" does not apply to decisions concerning the adoption or amendment of a development agreement or interpretation of a clause therein).
- A city may terminate or modify a development agreement if it finds, on the basis of substantial evidence, that the applicant or successor in interest thereto has not complied in good faith with its terms or conditions. Gov't Code § 65865.1.
- A city is authorized to enter into a development agreement for property outside the city limits but within its sphere of influence; the development agreement, however, does not become operative until annexation proceedings are completed within the period of time specified by the agreement. Gov't Code § 65865(b).
- A city shall not approve a development agreement that includes a residential subdivision of more than 500 dwelling units, unless the agreement provides that any tentative map prepared for the subdivision will comply with Government Code section 66473.7 relating to the availability of water supply. Gov't Code § 65867.5(c).
- If, prior to incorporation of a new city (or annexation to a city), a county has entered into a development agreement with the developer, that development agreement shall remain valid for the duration of the agreement, or for eight years from the effective date of the incorporation or annexation, whichever is earlier, or for up to 15 years upon agreement between the developer and the city. Gov't Code § 65865.3. This statute applies to incorporations where the development agreement was applied for prior to

circulation of the incorporation petition and entered into between the county and the developer prior to the date of the incorporation election. The statute also allows the newly incorporated or annexed city to modify or suspend the provisions of the development agreement if it finds an adverse impact on public health or safety in the jurisdiction. However, as to annexations, if the proposal for annexation is initiated by a petitioner other than a city, the development agreement is valid unless the city adopts written findings that implementation of the development would create a condition injurious to the public health, safety, or welfare of the city's residents.

- Pursuant to 2007 legislation, a city within the Sacramento-San Joaquin Valley shall make certain general amendments to provide for increased flood protection, and thereafter shall not enter into a development agreement for any property that is located within a flood hazard zone, unless the city makes one of three findings related to the adequacy of the flood protection. Gov't Code §§ 65302.9, 65860.1, 65865.6.

The California Supreme Court described the rights that may be vested pursuant to a development agreement as follows:

> [D]evelopment agreements...between a developer and a local government limit the power of that government to apply newly enacted ordinances to ongoing developments. Unless otherwise provided in the agreement, the rules, regulations, and official policies governing permitted uses, density, design, improvements, and construction are those in effect when the agreement is executed.

City of W. Hollywood v. Beverly Towers, Inc., 52 Cal. 3d at 1193 n. 6

The Court in *Beverly Towers* noted that the purpose of granting vested rights in a development agreement is "to allow a developer who needs additional discretionary approvals to complete a long-term development project as approved, regardless of any intervening changes in local regulations." *Id.* at 1194.

Because a development agreement may offer a property owner or developer substantial assurance that its project can be completed "in accordance with existing policies, rules and regulations, and subject to conditions of approval" (Gov't Code § 65864(b)), it is advisable for the property owner and/or developer to retain a complete set of the local ordinances, policies, and standards in effect when the development agreement becomes effective. Otherwise, should a dispute arise years after the agreement has been executed, it may be difficult to piece together the operative law.

A city's decision to enter into a development agreement is a legislative act, and therefore is subject to repeal by referendum. However, the opportunity for such referendum expires 30 days after the city's adoption of the ordinance approving the agreement; thereafter, the project is immune to subsequent changes in zoning ordinances and land use regulations not consistent with those provided for in the agreement. Elec. Code § 9141. In *Midway Orchards v. County of Butte*, the court set aside the county's adoption of a development agreement because the general plan amendment needed for the agreement to be consistent with the general plan was timely referended. 220 Cal. App. 3d 765 (1990). In setting aside adoption of the agreement, the court stated:

> The development agreement was therefore unlawfully approved and executed. A contract entered into by a local government without legal authority is

PRACTICE TIP

To ensure the validity of a contract entered into with a city, verify that the contract complies with all applicable state and local provisions related to contract formation.

A city's decision to enter into a development agreement is a legislative act, and therefore subject to repeal by referendum.

"wholly void," ultra vires, and unenforceable. [Citation]. Such a "contract" can create no vested rights. Therefore, Midway can claim no right to develop its property based on a development agreement void from the beginning.

Id. at 783. Prior to expiration of the 30 day referendum period, the development agreement is not effective. *See also 216 Sutter Bay Assocs. v. County of Sutter*, 58 Cal. App. 4th 860, 872–74 (1997) (an interim urgency zoning ordinance and a parallel "ordinary" urgency ordinance, adopted by a newly elected board of supervisors within the 30-day "referendum period," successfully stopped a development agreement adopted by the preceding, lame-duck board).

A "fully negotiated" development agreement is a "project" under CEQA (Pub. Res. Code § 21000 *et seq.*), and is subject to environmental review. This is true even when the negotiated development agreement is submitted by the city to the electorate for approval. *See Citizens for Responsible Gov't v. City of Albany*, 56 Cal. App. 4th 1199, 1215 (1997); *see also Friends of Sierra Madre v. City of Sierra Madre*, 25 Cal. 4th 165 (2001) (holding that by voting to place the measure on the ballot, the city council had approved a "project" subject to CEQA, and thus did not fall within CEQA's exemption for proposals submitted to the voters).

CEQA = California Environmental Quality Act

Since entering into a development agreement is a legislative act, a city's decision not to enter into a development agreement need not be supported by findings.

Since entering into a development agreement is a legislative act, a city's decision not to enter into a development agreement need not be supported by findings. Gov't Code § 65867.5; *see also Native Sun/Lyon Communities v. City of Escondido*, 15 Cal. App. 4th 892, 910 (1993).

Not infrequently, those who challenge projects governed by development agreements will argue that the agreements are invalid because the city is "contracting away" its police power. The courts have not been persuaded by this argument.

For example, in *SMART v. County of San Luis Obispo*, an area residents' association contended that because San Luis Obispo County had entered into a development agreement freezing zoning for a five-year period for a project before the project was ready for construction, the county improperly contracted away its zoning authority. 84 Cal. App. 4th 221, 232–33 (2000). In rejecting this contention, the court stated that the development agreement statute should be liberally construed to permit "local government to make commitments to developers at the time the developer makes a substantial investment in the project." *Id.* at 228. The court noted that land use regulation is an established function of local government, providing the authority for a locality to enter into contracts to carry out the function. The county's development agreement required that the project be developed in accordance with the county's general plan, did not permit construction until the county had approved detailed building plans, retained certain of the county's discretionary authority in the future, and allowed a zoning freeze of limited duration only. The court found that the zoning freeze in the county's development agreement was not a surrender of the police power but instead "advance[d] the public interest by preserving future options." *Id.* at 234.

Likewise, settlement agreements between city and developer do not surrender the city's police power. *108 Holdings LTD v. City of Rohnert Park*, 136 Cal. App. 4th 186 (2006). In *108 Holdings*, the court held that the city's execution of a settlement agreement with a preservation committee and subsequent acceptance of the stipulated judgment that bound the city to interpret and apply the general plan in a manner specified by the judgment did not constitute a surrender or bargaining away of the city's police power nor did it constitute an improper general plan amendment. *Id.* at 194. The court noted that the stipulated judgment did not grant any party veto power over future general plan amendments. The court also agreed with the city's argument that the stipulated judgment did no more than set forth the manner in which the city would interpret certain provisions of its general plan, and that the provisions of the stipulated judgment were facially consistent with the general plan. *Id.* at 197. The fact that the city had agreed to include the provisions as an appendix to its general plan did not demonstrate that they were amendments or that they constituted legislation. *Id.* at 202–03.

However, in *Trancas Property Owners Association v. City of Malibu*, the court reached a different result. 138 Cal. App. 4th 172 (2006). After filing a lawsuit challenging the disapproval of its final subdivision maps, Trancas entered into a settlement agreement with the city in which it agreed to dismiss the suit and downsize its development in exchange for the city's approval of the final maps. In addition, the agreement exempted the downsized development from various current and future zoning provisions which would affect the project. The city council entered into the agreement after several closed sessions held under the Brown Act Litigation exemption. *See* Gov't Code § 54956.9.

The court set aside the agreement on two grounds. First, the court recognized that a city may lawfully agree to freeze the zoning governing a project, however numerous procedural and substantive limitations attend the making and performance of such a "development agreement." *Trancas*, 138 Cal. App. 4th at 182. Without following the development agreement statutory process, the court held that the settlement agreement's commitment to refrain from zoning actions was invalid on the basis that it contracted away the city's right to exercise its police power. Second, the court held that the settlement agreement was invalid as a municipal act because it violated the Brown Act. Although the court recognized that the litigation exemption to the Brown Act had previously been construed to permit a local legislative body to approve settlement agreements in closed sessions, the exemption is limited. The court held that the litigation exemption could not be construed to empower a city to enter into a settlement agreement in a closed session that in essence granted a zoning variance—an act that by substantive law requires a public hearing. *Id.* at 186–87. For a further discussion on the Brown Act, *see* chapter 17 (Rights of the Regulated and of the Citizens).

Similarly, in *League of Residential Neighborhood Advocates v. City of Los Angeles*, the court held that a "settlement agreement cannot override state law absent a specified determination that federal law has been or will be violated." 498 F. 3d 1052, 1053 (4th Cir. 2007). In this case, the city had entered into a settlement agreement with Congregation Etz Chaim to resolve the Congregation's lawsuit that denial of a conditional use permit violated the Congregation's federal and state constitutional rights. However, the court determined that the settlement agreement was the functional equivalent of a conditional use permit for which public hearings are required. A city cannot bargain away its police powers by entering a settlement agreement that prevents it from enforcing applicable zoning restrictions. *Id.* at 1057. Thus, the settlement agreement was held invalid and unenforceable.

In *City of Glendale v. Superior Court*, the court held that in entering into a fixed-term lease as a lessor, a city did not contract away its eminent domain

> *In* League of Residential Neighborhood Advocates v. City of Angeles, *the court held that a settlement agreement cannot override state law absent a specified determination that federal law has been or will be violated.*

power to take back the property by condemning the lessee's leasehold interest. 18 Cal. App. 4th 1768, 1780 (1993). In *Glendale*, the issue of possible condemnation was not raised in either the contract or in closing negotiations. Accordingly, the court could not imply a waiver of the eminent domain power.

In *Hermosa Beach Stop Oil Coalition v. City of Hermosa Beach*, the court held that the developer, who had failed to establish entitlement to vested rights to develop an oil business on property leased from the City of Hermosa Beach, could have protected itself from subsequent regulatory changes by insisting that the city enter into a development agreement. 86 Cal. App. 4th 534 (2001). The court noted that it was likely that the city would have demanded additional consideration for either a risk-adjustment provision in the existing lease or a separate development agreement, and that having at least implicitly decided to forego such protection against future regulatory changes, the developer must accept the consequences of this decision. *Id.* at 558.

Development agreements are adopted as a result of negotiations between a city and a developer; and therefore, are not subject to the *Nollan/Dolan* heightened scrutiny standard. *See Leroy Land Dev. Corp. v. Tahoe Reg'l Planning Agency*, 939 F. 2d 696 (9th Cir. 1991); *see also Nollan v. California Coastal Comm'n*, 483 U.S. 825 (1987); *Dolan v. City of Tigard*, 512 U.S. 374 (1994). For further discussion on this issue, *see* David L. Callies and Julie A. Tappendorf, "Unconstitutional Land Development Conditions and the Development Agreement Solution: Bargaining for Public Facilities After Nollan and Dolan," 51 *Case Western Reserve L. Rev.*, no. 4 (Summer 2001), and chapter 13 (Exactions).

In *Leroy*, the developer entered into a settlement agreement, pursuant to which it agreed to certain restrictions on development. *Leroy*, 939 F. 2d at 697–698. After the United States Supreme Court subsequently decided *Nollan*, the developer sought to challenge the restriction as an inverse taking of private property. The Ninth Circuit rejected the challenge, holding that regardless of whether the restriction would have violated the Fifth Amendment Takings Clause if imposed as a condition of development, it could not be found invalid because the developer had voluntarily agreed to its imposition. *Id.* at 697.

The court stated:

> The threshold issue is whether, assuming arguendo that the mitigation provisions would constitute a taking under *Nollan* if imposed unilaterally by [the Tahoe Regional Planning Agency (TRPA)], they can be viewed as a "taking" when consented to as a part of a settlement agreement. We hold that they cannot. The mitigation provisions at issue here were a negotiated condition of Leroy's settlement agreement with TRPA in which benefits and obligations were incurred by both parties. Such a contractual promise which operates to restrict a property owner's use of land cannot result in a "taking" because the promise is entered into voluntarily, in good faith and is supported by consideration. Indeed we have found only one case in which an agreement negotiated before *Nollan* was challenged as a "taking" after *Nollan*, and it reached the same conclusion we reach. *See Xenia Rural Water Ass'n v. Dallas County* [citation omitted]. To allow Leroy to challenge the settlement agreement five years after its execution, based on a subsequent change in the law, would inject needless uncertainty and an utter lack of finality to settlement agreements of this kind. We therefore hold that a takings analysis as articulated in *Nollan* is inapplicable

where, as here, parties choose to terminate or avoid litigation by executing a settlement agreement supported by consideration.

Id. at 698. In *Meredith v. Talbot County*, a Maryland appellate court reached the same conclusion. 560 A. 2d 599, 604–05 (Md. App. 1989). For further discussion, *see* chapter 12 (Takings).

Attempts to challenge a development's fee contained in a development agreement as a taking also is unlikely to be successful. Under a line of cases starting with *Pfeiffer v. City of La Mesa*, acceptance and use of a land use approval waives any right to challenge the condition. 69 Cal. App. 3d 74 (1977). In response, the Legislature enacted the pay-under-protest statute (Gov't Code § 66020), which allows a developer to protest and challenge a fee or condition without waiving the benefit of the permit. However, this provision is part of the Mitigation Fee Act and only applies to development fees as defined in the Act. Because the Act expressly excludes fees imposed under a development agreement, they are not subject to the protections of the Act. *See* Gov't Code §§ 66000 and 66020.

These decisions, coupled with the express exemption in the Mitigation Fee Act for fees imposed under a development agreement (Gov't Code § 66000 *et seq.*), make it difficult to argue that fees or exactions agreed to in a development agreement must meet common law and statutory nexus requirements. Commentators almost uniformly reject the proposition that such fees can later be challenged as excessive, and one of the main attractions of a development agreement for a city is that it can negotiate for mitigation it could not otherwise exact.

Under a line of cases starting with Pfeiffer v. City of La Mesa, *acceptance and use of a land use approval waives any right to challenge the condition.*

Vesting Tentative Maps

In 1984, in another legislative response to the *Avco* decision, the Legislature adopted Chapter 4.5 (Development Rights) of the Subdivision Map Act, which established a new form of tentative map for subdivisions in California—the "Vesting Tentative Map." Gov't Code § 66498.1 *et seq.* The purpose of the vesting tentative map statute is to give a statutory vested right that will be effective earlier in the planning and development process than a common law vested right established pursuant to *Avco*. The vesting tentative map process starts when the subdivider files a tentative or parcel map with the words "Vesting Tentative Map" presented conspicuously on the face of the map. Gov't Code § 66452(c). For a general discussion of the legislative history of the statute and its application, *see Bright Development Company v. City of Tracy*, 20 Cal. App. 4th 783, 788–89 (1993) and *Kaufman & Broad Central Valley, Inc. v. City of Modesto*, 25 Cal. App. 4th 1577, 1587–88 (1994). The rights accruing to a subdivider upon approval of a vesting tentative map are expressly deemed to constitute "vested rights" to proceed with the development in substantial compliance with the local ordinances, policies, and standards in effect at the time the application for approval of the vesting tentative map is found or deemed complete. Gov't Code § 66498.1. The vesting tentative map provisions of the Map Act were designed to "freeze in place" ordinances, policies, and standards in effect at the time the vesting tentative map application is deemed complete. *Bright Development*, 20 Cal. App. 4th at 793. These vested rights extend for a substantial period of time, and therefore add a critical dimension to the approval process connected with such maps. For a detailed discussion of the life of vesting tentative maps, *see* chapter 5 (Subdivisions).

PRACTICE TIP

Obtain copies of local laws in effect when the vesting tentative map application is complete. Otherwise, should a dispute arise years after the vesting tentative map was deemed complete, it may be extremely difficult to determine the operative law.

Vesting Tentative Maps vs. Development Agreements

A vesting tentative map differs in several respects from a development agreement. In particular, a vesting tentative map approval is unilateral, and a development agreement approval is bilateral. This means that cities must process a properly submitted vesting tentative map application and approve or deny it based on statutory criteria, whereas a development agreement is the result of negotiation. A vesting tentative map will vest rights earlier than a development agreement, by vesting rights as of the date the map application is found or deemed complete. In comparison, development agreement rights, which generally vest on the date the agreement is executed, can be significantly later in the process. Finally, as a legislative act, a development agreement is subject to referendum, while approval of a vesting tentative map is not.

A vesting tentative map does not provide a mechanism for controlling a city's future exercise of discretionary approvals. A development agreement may provide negotiable conditions and requirements that will govern and even limit the processing of future discretionary approvals.

A vesting tentative map does not provide a mechanism for controlling a city's future exercise of discretionary approvals. For example, if a subdivider needs a discretionary approval, such as a use permit, after the subdivider's tentative map vests, there is no guarantee of such approval. In approving or denying the use permit, however, a city will be governed by the ordinances, policies, and standards in effect at the time the tentative map application was complete, which may serve to limit a city's exercise of discretion. Gov't Code § 66498.1(b).

A development agreement, by contrast, may provide negotiable conditions and requirements that will govern and even limit the processing of future discretionary approvals. Gov't Code § 65865.2. Thus, its use is likely to provide a broader range of benefits than those obtained solely through the use of a vesting tentative map.

A city's general plan, local ordinances, or policies may impose additional exactions or development conditions (*e.g.*, increased inclusionary affordable housing) as a condition to entering into a development agreement. Local ordinances also may provide additional requirements necessary to obtain approval of a vesting tentative map. As is the case with all land use laws, such local laws should be reviewed carefully before proceeding with either a development agreement or a vesting tentative map.

As with a development agreement, when a vesting tentative map is approved, it is advisable for the subdivider to retain a complete set of the local ordinances, policies, and standards in effect when the vesting tentative map application was deemed complete since the rights vested continue for some time. Otherwise, if a dispute should arise years after the vesting tentative map application was deemed complete, the operative law may be extremely difficult to determine.

Table 2. A Comparison of California's Vested Rights Statutes

Vesting Tentative Map Gov't Code §§ 66498.1–66498.9	Development Agreement Gov't Code §§ 65864–65869
1. Processing mandatory: city cannot refuse application	1. Processing elective: city's discretion whether to enter
2. Exactions subject to statutory and case law restrictions (e.g., "nexus")	2. Ad hoc negotiation—exempt from development project fees requirements (Mitigation Fee Act, Gov't Code §§ 66000–66025); procedures for improvement deposits and accounting of such fees still apply (Gov't Code § 66006); waiver potential
3. Permits are discretionary, subject to vested current law	3. May seek to alter future permit process; have city commit to future issuance of entitlements
4. Locks in rules when application "complete"	4. Locks in rules at execution of agreement unless agreement provides otherwise
5. Subdivision Map Act limits vesting life of tentative and final maps; incorporation exception	5. Longer life for agreement; tentative (or vesting tentative) map and certain permits may be extended for life of agreement
6. Does not limit other agencies (e.g., school districts)	6. Does not limit agencies that are not parties (incorporation/annexation exception)
7. Voters cannot referend (adjudicatory act)	7. Subject to referendum (legislative act)
8. No contrary future rules unless needed to prevent situation "dangerous" to health/safety or changes in state/federal law	8. No contrary rules unless consistent with agreement
9. City must have implementing regulations (if not, Subdivision Map Act governs)	9. Local procedural regulations needed if requested by applicant, otherwise use statute
10. Generally, 90-day statute of limitation after approval to file suit challenging	10. Generally, 90-day statute of limitation to challenge adoption, amendment, or modifications occurring on or after January 1, 1996
11. Incorporating city is subject to county-approved vesting tentative map; annexing city is *not* subject	11. With certain exceptions, both incorporating city and annexing city are subject to county-approved agreement

11

Necessity for Findings

Background

Land use decisions are frequently challenged in court. Accordingly, courts require an adequate "record" upon which to exercise judicial review, especially when the city is acting in an adjudicatory or nonlegislative role. This means that the documentation supporting an adjudicatory approval or denial of a project must include findings that explain how the city processed the evidence presented when reaching its decision. The courts want to see the method by which the city analyzed the facts and applied its policies in reaching a particular conclusion.

The findings requirement applies equally to planning commissions, zoning boards or administrators, design review commissions, and city councils when they act in a nonlegislative, adjudicatory role. Findings also are required for certain legislative acts, as explained below.

Courts require an adequate "record" upon which to exercise judicial review, especially when the city is acting in an adjudicatory or nonlegislative role.

Topanga: The Cornerstone for Adjudicatory Findings Under Code of Civil Procedure Section 1094.5

The California Supreme Court has set forth distinct, definitive principles of law detailing the need for adequate findings when a city approves or disapproves a project while making certain quasi-judicial, administrative decisions. *See Topanga Ass'n for a Scenic Community v. County of Los Angeles*, 11 Cal. 3d 506 (1974). In *Topanga*, the Court interpreted Code of Civil Procedure section 1094.5,[1] which requires that certain adjudicatory decisions be supported by findings, and that the findings be supported by evidence. The Court found that a zoning board did not render findings adequate to support its ultimate ruling in granting a variance. *Id.* at 513. The Court defined findings, explained their purposes, and showed when they are required.

The California Supreme Court has set forth distinct, definitive principles of law detailing the need for adequate findings when a city approves or disapproves a project while making certain quasi-judicial, administrative decisions.

Purpose of Findings

The *Topanga* court outlined the following five purposes for making findings:

---

1. *See* chapter 21 (Land Use Litigation) for a discussion of the types of adjudicatory decisions to which section 1094.5 applies.

- Providing a framework for making principled decisions, thereby enhancing the integrity of the administrative process
- Facilitating orderly analysis and reducing the likelihood the city will leap randomly from evidence to conclusions
- Serving a public relations function by helping to persuade parties that administrative decisionmaking is careful, reasoned, and equitable
- Enabling the parties to determine whether and on what basis they should seek judicial review and remedies
- Apprising the reviewing court of the basis for the city's decisions

11 Cal. 3d at 514

One court emphasized how important it is not only to prepare adequate findings, but to ensure that they are made easily available for a court to review. In *Protect Our Water v. County of Merced*, the court could not determine from the record what the county's findings were and whether they complied with CEQA. "The board of supervisors did appear to adopt [findings], but it is impossible to determine from this record what those findings are." 110 Cal. App. 4th 362, 373 (2003). The consequences were drastic: "Because we cannot discern the required findings under CEQA, we reverse the [county's approval]." *Id. See* chapter 21 (Land Use Litigation) for a discussion of preparation of an adequate record.

Evidence in the Record to Support Findings

There must be evidence in the record to support the findings. Evidence may consist of staff reports, written and oral testimony, the EIR, exhibits, and the like. Findings are proper if they incorporate a staff report. *See McMillan v. American Gen. Fin. Corp.*, 60 Cal. App. 3d 175, 184 (1976). One court held that a summary of factual data, the language of a motion, and the reference in a motion to a staff report can constitute findings. However, the court made clear that the transcript of a council debate was not adequate. *See Pacifica Corp. v. City of Camarillo*, 149 Cal. App. 3d 168, 179 (1983). "The Council debate, although reflective of the views of individual councilmen, is not the equivalent of *Topanga* findings." *Id.*

However, the city's "written findings" are not the sole means by which *Topanga* requirements can be satisfied. *See Harris v. City of Costa Mesa*, 25 Cal. App. 4th 963 (1994). The *Harris* court said that in addition to the findings stated in the city council resolution, it could look to the transcript of the hearing for findings contained in statements made by council members. The court further held that it is proper to look for findings in oral remarks made at a public hearing where both parties were present, which were recorded, and of which a written transcript could be made. *Id.* at 971. The court noted that opinions of neighbors may constitute evidence, and that sufficient evidence can be found in presentations by neighbors seeking to deny a project. *Id.* at 973.

Relevant personal observations also may be evidence. An adjacent property owner may testify to traffic conditions based upon personal knowledge. *See Citizens Ass'n for Sensible Dev. of Bishop Area v. County of Inyo*, 172 Cal. App. 3d 151, 173 (1985). Also, testimony at a public hearing describing various problems posed by the proposed development, including increased flooding and traffic, security problems, and health and safety risks, can support a city's findings in denying a development plan. *See Lindborg/Dahl Investors, Inc. v. City of Garden Grove*, 179 Cal. App. 3d 956, 962–63 (1986); *Placer Ranch Partners v. County of Placer*, 91 Cal. App. 4th 1336, 1342 (2001) (holding that the opinion of area residents was an appropriate factor to consider in making zoning decisions, citing *Stubblefield Construction Co. v. City of San Bernardino*, 32 Cal. App. 4th 687, 711 (1995)). *See also Browning-Ferris Indus. v. City Council*, 181 Cal. App. 3d 852, 865 (1986) (a city may rely upon staff's opinion as substantial evidence in reaching decisions).

Findings must relate to the issue at hand. In striking down findings that were not legally sufficient to justify a variance, the court stated:

> [D]ata focusing on the qualities of the property and Project for which the variance is sought, the desirability of the proposed development, the attractiveness of its design, the benefits to the community, or the economic difficulties of developing the property in conformance with the zoning regulations, lack legal significance and are simply irrelevant to the controlling issue of whether strict application of zoning rules would prevent the would-be developer from utilizing his or her property to the same extent as other property owners in the same zoning district.

Orinda Ass'n v. Board of Supervisors, 182 Cal. App. 3d 1145, 1166 (1986)

Boilerplate or conclusory findings that do not recite the specific facts upon which the findings are based are not legally sufficient. *See Village Laguna, Inc. v. Board of Supervisors*, 134 Cal. App. 3d 1022, 1033–34 (1982). Similarly, a finding that was made "perfunctorily" and "without discussion or deliberation and thus does not show the Board's analytical route from evidence to finding" will be struck down. *Honey Springs Homeowners Ass'n v. Board of Supervisors*, 157 Cal. App. 3d 1122, 1151 (1984).

PRACTICE TIP

Conclusory findings are not acceptable under Code Civ. Proc. § 1094.5. The findings should refer to the specific evidence upon which they are based.

For example, in *City of Poway v. City of San Diego*, the City of Poway alleged that San Diego's findings on a land use project were insufficient under the *Village Laguna* standard. 155 Cal. App. 3d 1037 (1984). The court disagreed and held that San Diego's written findings, as dictated in the record, provided enough comprehensive information and factual discussion of the issues before the city. *Id.* at 1049. This comports with *Craik v. County of Santa Cruz*, in which the court stated that "findings need not be stated with judicial formality. Findings must simply expose the mode of analysis, not expose every minutia." 81 Cal. App. 4th 880, 884 (2000).

Similar findings also were upheld in *Jacobson v. County of Los Angeles*, 69 Cal. App. 3d 374 (1977). In this case, the ordinance pertaining to conditional use permits required the zoning board to reach seven specific subconclusions and described these as the "findings" that must be made. *Id.* at 391 (citing *Topanga*, 11 Cal. 3d 506 (1974)). The court found these specific subconclusions sufficient.

In summary, there is no presumption that a city's rulings rest upon the necessary findings and that such findings are supported by substantial evidence. Rather, cities must expressly state their findings and must set forth the relevant facts supporting them. *See J.L. Thomas, Inc. v. County of Los Angeles*, 232 Cal. App. 3d 916, 926 (1991).

There is no presumption that a city's rulings rest upon the necessary findings and that such findings are supported by substantial evidence.

When Are Findings Required?

Legislative Acts

Findings are not required for legislative acts unless a statute or local ordinance so requires.

Findings are not required for legislative acts unless a statute or local ordinance so requires. *See Mountain Defense League v. Board of Supervisors*, 65 Cal. App. 3d 723, 732, fn.5 (1977). Thus, findings are generally not required for approval of zoning ordinances since they are legislative in nature. *See Ensign Bickford Realty Corp. v. City Council*, 68 Cal. App. 3d 467, 473 (1977) (disapproved on other grounds by *Hernandez v. City of Hanford*, 41 Cal. 4th 279, 297 (2007)); *Towards Responsibility In Planning v. City Council*, 200 Cal. App. 3d 671, 685 (1988) (summary of fiscal finding is not required in a general plan amendment or a rezoning).

Under certain circumstances, however, local ordinances or state law mandate findings for a legislative act. For example, state law requires findings when a general plan limits the number of newly constructed housing units, when a local ordinance has an effect on the housing needs of a region, or when a housing development project that complies with the applicable general plan and zoning is disapproved because it would have an adverse effect on public health or safety. Gov't Code §§ 65302.8, 65863.6, 65589.5(j). *See also Mira Dev. Corp. v. City of San Diego*, 205 Cal. App. 3d 1201, 1222 (1988) (Government Code section 65589.5 does not require findings to support denial of a rezoning application, citing *Arnel Dev. Co. v. City of Costa Mesa*, 28 Cal. 3d 511, 522 (1980)). Findings are not required if the housing limitation is adopted by an initiative. *See Building Indus. Ass'n v. City of Camarillo*, 41 Cal. 3d 810, 823–24 (1986). The Mitigation Fee Act requires that certain determinations be made by the legislative body when it establishes or increases development impact fees. Gov't Code § 66001.

CEQA requires that certain findings be made whenever a project is approved and an EIR has been prepared that identifies significant impacts.

Other statutes require that certain determinations be made regardless of whether the decision at issue is adjudicatory or legislative. For example, CEQA requires that certain findings be made whenever a project is approved and an EIR has been prepared that identifies significant impacts. Pub. Res. Code § 21081. The Water Code requires, for certain large projects, that the city "shall determine, based on the entire record, whether projected water supplies will be sufficient to satisfy the demands of the project, in addition to existing and planned future uses." Water Code § 10911(c).

Nonlegislative Acts

Findings are required whenever a city acts in its nonlegislative (quasi-judicial, adjudicatory or administrative role) as opposed to its legislative capacity. A city usually acts in its legislative capacity when it establishes a basic principle or policy, such as a general plan adoption or amendment, or a rezoning. *See Ensign Bickford*, 68 Cal. App. 3d at 474. The nonlegislative or quasi-judicial capacity usually involves applying a fixed rule, standard, or law to a specific parcel of land. Examples of such nonlegislative actions include granting or denying variances, use permits, subdivision maps, design proposals, and the like. *See* chapter 21 (Land Use Litigation) for further discussion of the difference between adjudicatory and legislative approvals.

The nonlegislative or quasi-judicial capacity usually involves applying a fixed rule, standard, or law to a specific parcel of land.

Dedications or Ad Hoc Impact Fees

In the landmark exaction case *Dolan v. City of Tigard*, the United States Supreme Court for the first time held that a city must prove that development conditions, especially relating to dedications, placed on a discretionary (nonlegislative) permit have a "rough proportionality" to the development's impact. 512 U.S. 374, 391 (1994). If conditions are not roughly proportional, then a "taking" may occur. When imposing conditions to development, the city can meet its burden of proof by making appropriate findings based on the record and by quantifying its findings in support of the particular dedication. The city may not rely on conclusory statements that the dedication "could" offset the burden. This rule also is applicable when a city imposes a fee on an ad hoc basis not based on a generally applicable legislative enactment. *See Ehrlich v. City of Culver City*, 12 Cal. 4th 854 (1996). For a thorough discussion of *Dolan* and claims for an inverse taking, *see* chapter 12 (Takings) and chapter 13 (Exactions).

For excellent discussions on findings, *see* Governor's Office of Planning and Research, *Bridging the Gap: Using Findings in Local Land Use Decisions* (1989) (available at http://ceres.ca.gov/planning/Bridging_Gap/Bridging_Gap.html) and *Special Issues Under Takings Law: Findings, Fees and Dedications*, Institute for Local Self Government (1999).

In Dolan v. City of Tigard, *the U.S. Supreme Court for the first time held that a city must prove that development conditions, especially relating to dedications, placed on a discretionary permit have a rough proportionality to the development's impact.*

12
Takings

Takings[1]
Overview[2]

The ability to regulate land derives from the police power of government to regulate for the public health, safety, and welfare of its citizens. The government's ability to so regulate is, however, limited by the Fifth Amendment to the United States Constitution, which states in part, "nor shall private property be taken for public use, without just compensation." *See also* Cal. Const. art. I, § 19. Thus, if a land use regulation becomes so unduly restrictive that it causes a "taking" of a landowner's property for public use, just compensation must be paid.

A land use regulation or action must not be unduly restrictive such that it causes a "taking" of a landowner's property without just compensation.

The United States Supreme Court has confirmed the import of the "public use provision" by stating "purely private takings could not withstand the scrutiny of the public use requirement." *Hawaii Housing Authority v. Midkiff*, 467 U.S. 229, 245 (1984).[3]

More recently, in the widely discussed United States Supreme Court decision of *Kelo v. City of New London*, the high Court again emphasized the use of a comprehensive land use plan to support the "public purpose" need for the use

---

1. Three theories are used to sue for damages to property interests as a result of a land use regulation: violation of civil rights under 42 United States Code section 1983; denial of due process and equal protection under the Fourteenth Amendment to the United States Constitution; and takings under the Fifth Amendment to the United States Constitution.
2. For a good discussion of key takings decisions, *see Taking Sides on Taking Issues, Public and Private Perspectives* (Thomas E. Roberts, ed., ABA, Sect. of State and Local Gov't Law, 2002) and *Taking Sides on Takings Issues, The Impact of Tahoe-Sierra* (Thomas E. Roberts, ed., ABA, Sect. of State and Local Gov't Law, 2003). See Bill Higgins, *Regulatory Takings and Land Use Regulations: A Primer for Public Agency Staff*, Institute for Local Government (July 2006); Steven J. Eagle, *Regulatory Takings* (2nd ed., Lexis Publishing 2001); Dwight H. Merriam, "Reengineering Regulations to Avoid Takings," 33 *The Urban Lawyer*, no. 1 at 1 (2001); Daniel J. Curtin, Jr., "How the West Was Won: Takings and Exactions California Style," *Trends in Land Use Law from A to Z*, ch. 9 (Patricia E. Salkin, ed., ABA, Sect. of State and Local Gov't Law, 2001); Douglas T. Kendall *et al.*, *Takings Litigation Handbook* (American Legal Publishing Corp. 2000); Robert Meltz *et al.*, *The Takings Issue* (Island Press, 1999). *See also* Bill Higgins and Barbara E. Kautz, *Property Rights and Land Use Regulation: A Primer for Public Agency Staff* (League of California Cities, Institute for Local Government 2005).
3. For an in-depth discussion of the public purpose requirement, *see also* Camarin Madigan, "Taking for Any Purpose?," *Hastings West-Northwest Journal of Environmental Law and Policy*, vol. 9, no. 2 (Spring 2003).

of eminent domain. 545 U.S. 469, 480 (2005). The Court noted that the City of New London had carefully formed an economic development plan that it believed would provide appreciable benefits to the community, including new jobs and increased tax revenue. The Court stated:

> Given the comprehensive character of the plan, the thorough deliberation that preceded its adoption, and the limited scope of our review, it is appropriate for us, as it was in *Berman*, to resolve the challenges of the individual owners, not on a piecemeal basis, but rather in light of the entire plan. Because that plan unquestionably serves a public purpose, the takings challenged here satisfy the public use requirement of the Fifth Amendment.

Id. at 484 [4]

In 1996, the California Supreme Court summarized the takings law as follows:

> Adoption of a zoning ordinance which is not arbitrary and does not unduly restrict the use of private property is a permissible exercise of the police power and does not violate the taking clause of the Fifth Amendment of the United States Constitution and comparable provisions of the California Constitution, even when the law restricts an existing use of the affected property. [Citations omitted.]
>
> A zoning ordinance or land use regulation which operates prospectively, and denies the owner the opportunity to exploit an interest in the property that the owner believed would be available for future development, or diminishes the value of the property, is not invalid and does not bring about a compensable taking unless all beneficial use of the property is denied. [Citations omitted.] However, if the law effects an unreasonable, oppressive, or unwarranted interference with an existing use, or a planned use for which a substantial investment in development costs has been made, the ordinance may be invalid as applied to that property unless compensation is paid. [Citation omitted.]

Hansen Bros. Enters. v. Board of Supervisors, 12 Cal. 4th 533, 551 (1996)

A regulation may effect a taking though it does not involve a physical invasion and leaves the property owner some economically beneficial use of his property.

Although the summary of takings law in *Hansen Brothers* is still generally valid, the California Supreme Court in the 1997 *Kavanau* decision, clarified that "a regulation...may effect a taking though it does not involve a physical invasion *and leaves the property owner some economically beneficial use of his property.*" *Kavanau v. Santa Monica Rent Control Bd.*, 16 Cal. 4th 761, 774 (1997) (emphasis in original). The California Supreme Court further refined the law of takings in *Landgate, Inc. v. California Coastal Commission*, 17 Cal. 4th 1006, 1010 (1998). In that case, the court held that no taking occurred when issuance of a development permit was delayed due in part to a government agency's mistaken assertion of jurisdiction. The court concluded that this was a "normal delay" in the development process and did not amount to a taking.

This book divides the law of takings into two categories: inverse condemnation and exactions. This chapter discusses inverse condemnation, which results when regulations on the use of land amount to a taking, while chapter 13

---

4. For a discussion of the *Kelo* case and the role of the comprehensive plan in establishing public purpose, *see* David L. Callies, "Kelo v. City of New London: Of Planning, Federalism, and a Switch in Time," 28 *U. Haw. L. Rev.* 327 (2005–2006). Dwight H. Merriam and Mary Massaron Ross, *Eminent Domain Use and Abuse: Kelo in Context* (ABA Sect. of State and Local Government Law 2006); Robert H. Freilich, "Kelo Provides Tools to Rebuild, Revitalize Urban America," *San Francisco Daily Journal*, July 26, 2005, page 8; Daniel J. Curtin, Jr., "The Implications of Kelo in Land Use Law," *Santa Clara L.R.* (2006 Symposium).

discusses exactions, and the extent to which conditions on development (*i.e.*, "exactions") may cause a taking.

Federal Constitutional Standard

Determining whether a land use regulation or decision amounts to a taking under the Fifth Amendment to the United States Constitution has been a difficult task for the courts. The United States Supreme Court candidly has admitted that it never has been able to develop a "'set formula' for determining when 'justice and fairness' require that economic injuries caused by public action be compensated by the government, rather than remain disproportionately concentrated on a few persons." *Penn Cent. Transp. Co. v. City of New York*, 438 U.S. 104, 124 (1978). Instead, the Court has observed that "whether a particular restriction will be rendered invalid by the government's failure to pay for any losses proximately caused by it depends largely 'upon the particular circumstances [in that] case.'" *Id*. Thus, the Court in *Penn Central* did not establish a specific, rigid test for determining when a taking has occurred, but rather stated that a takings analysis proceeds on an essentially "ad hoc" basis.

In *Penn Central*, New York City declared Grand Central Terminal historic, thereby barring a proposal that would have constructed a high-rise office building over the station. The landowner claimed that the regulation caused a taking of its property in violation of the Fifth Amendment, but the Supreme Court disagreed. In ruling that the city's regulation did not effect a taking, the Court set forth a three-factor test to be applied in conducting the ad hoc factual inquiries that underlie regulatory takings cases. *Id*. at 124. Under the *Penn Central* test, three factors to be considered are: (1) "the economic impact of the regulation on the claimant," (2) "the extent to which the regulation has interfered with distinct investment-backed expectations," and (3) "the nature of the governmental action." *Id*. Weighing these factors, the Court held that the city's historic preservation ordinance did not effect a taking because it did not have any economic impact upon the station. Nor did the ordinance interfere with the landowner's investment-backed expectations, because there was no physical taking and the railroad could continue to earn a reasonable return under the existing use.

Two years later, in *Agins v. City of Tiburon*, the Supreme Court set forth an additional takings formula, the first prong of which is now, as discussed below, discredited as an independent takings test. 447 U.S. 255 (1980). The dispute involved municipal zoning ordinances that restricted the types of structures the landowners could build on their land. The landowners never sought approval to develop under the changed zoning, instead filing a facial challenge to the ordinances. The Court affirmed a decision of California's highest court that concluded the ordinances did not constitute a taking. The Court held that the application of a general zoning law to a particular property becomes a taking if the ordinance either (1) "does not substantially advance legitimate state interests" or (2) "denies an owner economically viable use of his land." *Id*. at 260. Since the city's ordinances substantially advanced a legitimate governmental goal, that of discouraging premature and unnecessary conversion of open space to urban uses, and was a proper exercise of the city's police power to protect its residents from the effects of urbanization, the Court concluded that no taking had occurred. *Id*. at 261–62.

Determining whether a land use decision amounts to a taking prohibited by the Fifth Amendment to the United States Constitution has been a difficult task for the courts.

Since the Supreme Court's decision in *Agins*, several of its cases have cited the "substantially advances" formula as a test for determining whether a taking has occurred, though none have actually relied upon it to conclude that there has been a taking. *See, e.g., Dolan v. City of Tigard*, 512 U.S. 374, 385–87 (1994); *Lucas v. South Carolina Coastal Council*, 505 U.S. 1033, 1011 (1992); *Nollan v. California Coastal Comm'n*, 483 U.S. 825, 834 (1987); *Keystone Bituminous Coal Ass'n v. DeBenedictis*, 480 U.S. 470, 485 (1987). In citing the "substantially advances" formula, the court treated the "substantially advances" inquiry as a stand-alone test under which a challenged regulation was required to "substantially advance a legitimate state interest." Many legal commentators disagreed with the Court's approach, criticizing the *Agins* test as improperly imposing substantive due process requirements in the context of regulatory takings. *See, e.g., Taking Sides on Takings Issues, the Impact of Tahoe-Sierra*, page 8 (Thomas E. Roberts, ed., ABA, Sect. on State and Local Gov't Law, 2003).

The United States Supreme Court was recently presented with the opportunity to directly address that issue in *Lingle v. Chevron U.S.A. Inc.*, 544 U.S. 528 (2005). In *Lingle*, the Court ruled that the *Agins* inquiry whether a land use regulation "substantially advance[s] a legitimate state interest" is not a valid method for identifying regulatory takings for which the Fifth Amendment requires the payment of just compensation. *Id.* at 539–44. The Court instead reaffirmed its earlier decision that the ad hoc, fact-dependent approach set forth in *Penn Central* is an appropriate method. *Id.* at 538–48.

In *Lingle*, the Supreme Court was asked to reconsider the appropriateness of the "substantially advances" inquiry in a regulatory takings case that did not involve land. The Hawaii Legislature, concerned about the effects of market concentration on the retail price of gasoline, passed Act 257, which limited the rent oil companies could charge lessee-dealers. Under the rent cap of the state statute, oil companies could not charge lessee-dealers more than 15 percent of the dealer's gross profits from gasoline sales plus 15 percent of gross sales of products other than gasoline.

Chevron challenged the rent cap on its face, arguing that it did not substantially advance any legitimate government interest. In defending the statute, Hawaii argued that the rent cap was designed to prevent concentration of the retail gasoline market, as well as the higher gasoline prices that resulted from that concentration, by maintaining the viability of independent lessee-dealers. The federal district court and the Ninth Circuit Court of Appeals sided with Chevron, ruling that the state statute would not substantially advance the stated interest because it would not actually reduce lessee-dealers' costs or retail prices.

The Supreme Court unanimously reversed, writing that the "substantially advances" inquiry is one of due process, that it has no place in takings jurisprudence, and that the language was "regrettably imprecise." *Id.* at 539–42. In other words, the means-ends nature of the inquiry addresses due process considerations, but it has nothing to do with whether private property has been taken under the Constitution. *Id.* at 540–42. The Court reasoned that a valid takings analysis should not demand heightened review of legislative determinations, "a task for which courts are not well suited," but rather should be focused on "help[ing] identify those regulations whose effects are functionally comparable to government appropriation or invasion of private property." *Id.* at

542–44. Consequently, the Court held that the "substantially advances" test is not a valid method of identifying regulatory takings for which the Fifth Amendment requires just compensation. *Id.* at 545.

In noting that its opinion did not affect any of its earlier decisions (since none of the cases citing the "substantially advances" language even actually concluded that there was a compensable taking), the *Lingle* decision clarified the law of regulatory takings. *Id.* at 545-47. In particular, the Court carefully grouped its regulatory takings cases for which just compensation must be paid into four well-defined categories: (1) regulations that cause a physical invasion of land; (2) regulations that deprive a landowner of all economically beneficial use of land; (3) other regulatory takings; and (4) land use exactions.

With respect to physical takings, the Court cited *Loretto v. Teleprompter Manhattan CATV Corporation*, for the proposition that "where government requires an owner to suffer a permanent physical invasion of her property—however minor—it must provide just compensation." 458 U.S. 419 (1982). In *Loretto*, the Court held that a state law that required landlords to permit cable companies to install cable facilities on apartment buildings was a categorical taking. Thus, any government regulation that causes a physical intrusion on private property will be treated as a categorical taking for which just compensation must be paid.

Any government regulation that causes a physical intrusion on private property will be treated as a categorical taking for which just compensation must be paid.

The second type of categorical taking occurs when, as in *Lucas v. South Carolina Coastal Council*, government regulations deprive a landowner of "all economically beneficial use[]" of property. 505 U.S. 1003 (1992). In the event of such a total regulatory taking, government must pay just compensation, except to the extent that "background principles of nuisance and property law" independently restrict the landowner's desired use of the land. *Id.* at 1026–1032. In other words, when an owner of real property is called upon to sacrifice all economically beneficial uses in the name of the common good, *i.e.*, to leave his property economically idle, this may constitute a taking. *Id.* at 1015.

In the *Lucas* decision, the United States Supreme Court considered a landowner's takings challenge to a South Carolina regulation barring development of two beachfront lots in a developed subdivision. The state regulation findings stated that new construction in the coastal zone threatened a valuable public resource. The Court suggested that the property owner was entitled to compensation, and remanded the case back to the state court for a final determination. On remand, the state court held that a taking had occurred, and ordered payment to Lucas.

In practical terms, the *Lucas* decision is a narrow one. The Court limited its holding to situations in which owners are deprived of "all economically beneficial uses" of their property. *Id.* at 1027. The Court itself recognized that such cases are relatively rare. *Id.* at 1018. In dissent, Justice Blackmun stated that the majority opinion "launches a missile to kill a mouse." *Id.* at 1036.

Recent United States Supreme Court takings cases have also emphasized the limited applicability of *Lucas*. See *Tahoe-Sierra Preservation Council, Inc. v. Tahoe Reg'l Planning Agency*, 535 U.S. 302 (2002) (holding that a 32-month moratorium did not permanently deprive the landowners of all economically viable use, and thus was not a categorical taking); *Palazzolo v. Rhode Island*, 533 U.S. 606 (2001) (holding that a regulation permitting a landowner to build a

Recent United States Supreme Court takings cases have also emphasized the limited applicability of Lucas.

substantial residence on an 18-acre parcel did not leave the property "economically idle," and therefore did not result in a per se taking). *See also Blue Jeans Equities W. v. City and County of San Francisco*, 3 Cal. App. 4th 164, 171 (1992) (finding *Lucas'* principles not applicable since all the property was not taken); Anthony Saul Alperin, "Tahoe-Sierra—The Supreme Court Again Rejects Per Se Rules for Regulatory Takings Claims," 34 *Urb. L.*, no. 4, 811 (Fall 2002). At the same time, those cases reaffirmed the ad hoc, case-by-case balancing test of *Penn Central*. *See also San Remo Hotel v. City and County of San Francisco*, 27 Cal. 4th 643, (2002) (citing *Penn Central* factors in upholding a housing replacement provision in a local ordinance); Gregory M. Stein, "Takings in the 21st Century: Reasonable Investment-Backed Expectations After Palazzolo and Tahoe-Sierra," 69 *Tenn. L. Rev.* 891 (Summer 2002) (categorical rule rejected and factors of *Penn Central* must be followed).

General regulatory takings are governed by the three-part test established in Penn Central Transportation Company v. City of New York.

The third category of case, general regulatory takings, is governed by the three-part test established in *Penn Central Transportation Company v. City of New York*, 438 U.S. 104 (1978). If a governmental regulation does not cause a physical invasion or otherwise deprive a landowner of all economically beneficial use, the courts still will engage in an ad hoc, factual inquiry that considers the economic impact of the regulation on the landowner, the extent to which it has interfered with distinct investment-backed expectations, and the nature of the governmental action. *Id.* at 124.

The Court in *Lingle* explained that the *Penn Central* factors serve "as the principal guidelines for resolving regulatory takings claims that do not fall within the physical takings or *Lucas* rules." *Lingle v. Chevron U.S.A. Inc.*, 544 U.S. 528, 539 (citing *Palazzolo v. Rhode Island*, 533 U.S. 606, 617–18 (2001)). *See also Tahoe-Sierra Preservation Council, Inc. v. Tahoe Reg'l Planning Agency*, 535 U.S. 302 (2002) (noting that aside from categorical takings, its regulatory takings cases are characterized by "essentially ad hoc, factual inquiries"). The Court further stated that the inquiries reflected in each of its principal regulatory takings cases (*Loretto*, *Lucas*, and *Penn Central*) "share a common touchstone." 544 U.S. at 539. According to the Court:

> Each aims to identify regulatory actions that are functionally equivalent to the classic taking in which government directly appropriates private property or ousts the owner from his domain. Accordingly, each of these tests focuses directly upon the severity of the burden that government imposes upon private property rights.

Id.

While the determinative factor in a *Lucas* type taking is "the complete elimination of a property's value," the inquiry in a *Penn Central* case depends largely, but not exclusively, on "the magnitude of a regulation's economic impact and the degree to which it interferes with legitimate property interests."[5] *Id.* at 539–40.

---

5. To state a takings claim, a plaintiff must demonstrate the existence of a constitutionally protected "property interest." *See Gammoh v. City of La Habra*, 395 F.3d 1114 (9th Cir. 2005) (landowner challenging city ordinance requiring "adult cabaret dancers" to remain two feet away from patrons during performances failed to show a property interest interfered with by the city's regulation of the dancer's conduct).

The fourth type of regulatory taking claim recognized by the Supreme Court is that of exactions, where the government requires a dedication of property as a condition to issuance of a discretionary permit. These claims are analyzed under the principles set forth in the Court's decisions in *Nollan v. California Coastal Commission*, 483 U.S. 825 (1987), and *Dolan v. City of Tigard*, 512 U.S. 374 (1994). As was well explained in *Lingle*, the issue in both *Nollan* and *Dolan* was whether the government could exact an easement as a condition for granting a development permit that it was entitled to deny, without the payment of compensation to the landowners that would otherwise be required for effecting such a taking.

Exactions claims are analyzed under the principles set forth in the Court's decisions in Nollan v. California Coastal Commission.

In *Nollan*, where a permit to build a larger residence on beachfront property in California was conditioned upon the dedication of an easement to permit the public on a strip of land between the owner's property and the mean high-tide line, the Court ruled that such an exaction is permissible if the exaction would substantially advance *the same* government interest that would furnish a valid ground for denial of the permit. 483 U.S. at 834–37. In *Dolan*, where the government conditioned a permit to expand a store and parking lot on the dedication of a portion of the property for a bicycle and pedestrian path, the Court refined the rule set forth in *Nollan*. The Court held that an adjudicative, or nonlegislative, exaction must also be "roughly proportional" both in nature and extent to the impact of the proposed development. 512 U.S. at 391.

An adjudicative, or nonlegislative, exaction must also be roughly proportional both in nature and extent to the impact of the proposed development.

In *Lingle*, the Court took care to note that while the language it used in *Nollan* and *Dolan* "drew upon the language of Agins...it did not apply the 'substantially advances' test." 544 U.S. at 546. The *Lingle* Court explained the distinction as follows:

> *Nollan* and *Dolan* both involved dedications of property so onerous that, outside the exactions context, they would be deemed *per se* physical takings. In neither case did the Court question whether the exaction would substantially advance *some* legitimate state interest. [Citations omitted]. Rather, the issue was whether the exactions substantially advanced the *same* interests that land-use authorities asserted would allow them to deny the permit altogether.

Id. at 547

In summary, *Lingle* abolished the "substantially advances" inquiry as a valid test for identifying a regulatory takings claim for which just compensation is required.[6] The Court wrote that its takings jurisprudence addresses four types of regulatory takings challenges: (1) permanent physical invasions; (2) denials of all economically beneficial use; (3) partial regulatory takings; and (4) land use exactions. The Court also emphasized that in a partial regulatory taking governed by *Penn Central*, the inquiry focuses largely upon the magnitude of the economic impact of the challenged regulation and the degree to which it interferes with legitimate property interests. *See also Manufactured Home Communities, Inc. v. City of San Jose*, 420 F. 3d 1022 (9th Cir. 2005) (a takings claim based on the "substantially advances" test is foreclosed by *Lingle's* holding that such an inquiry is not a valid takings test); *Los Altos El Granada Investors v. City*

---

6. For a detailed discussion of the takings issue and the "substantially advances" inquiry, *see* Simon Lazar and Dwight H. Merriam, "Ding Dong the Witch Is Dead: O'Connor Drops a House on the Agins Takings Test," 57 *Plan. & Envtl. L.* 3 (2005).

of Capitola, 139 Cal. App. 4th 629, 651 (2006) (error for a court to evaluate whether a rent control ordinance substantially advanced a legitimate government interest since such test is no longer available); *Allegretti & Co. v. County of Imperial*, 138 Cal. App. 4th 1261, 1280 (2006) (whether a county's action substantially advanced a state interest was no longer a valid standard to assess an unconstitutional taking under the Fifth Amendment since *Lingle* decision).

Denial of Economically Viable Use

Government regulations, by their very nature, have an impact on property values. However, mere fluctuations in value are "incidents of ownership," and "cannot be considered a 'taking' in a constitutional sense." *Danforth v. United States*, 308 U.S. 271, 285 (1939). The United States Supreme Court consistently has "recognized, in a wide variety of contexts, that the government may execute laws or programs that adversely affect recognized economic values." *Penn Cent. Transp. Co. v. City of New York*, 438 U.S. at 124; *see also Long Beach Equities, Inc. v. County of Ventura*, 231 Cal. App. 3d 1016, 1030 (1991) (holding that a land use regulation is constitutional on its face if it is substantially related to the public welfare, even where a substantial diminution in value is alleged).

In *Keystone Bituminous Coal Association v. DeBenedictis*, the United States Supreme Court focused on how to evaluate whether the owners had been deprived of "economically viable use." 480 U.S. 470, 495–97 (1987). To determine this issue, the Court looked to the value that was left in the owners' property, rather than the value that was taken. *Id.* The plaintiffs in the case were an association of coal mine owners in Pennsylvania who brought suit alleging that the Pennsylvania Bituminous Mine Subsidence and Land Conservation Act (Subsidence Act) constituted a taking of their property. Although the association alleged that the Subsidence Act required them to forego mining almost 27 million tons of coal in their mines, the Court instead focused on the fact that the total coal in the 13 mines operated by the companies amounted to over 1.46 billion tons. Noting that the Subsidence Act affected less than two percent of the owners' coal, the Court said that the owners "have not shown any deprivation significant enough to satisfy the heavy burden placed upon one alleging a regulatory taking." *Id.* at 493. "[T]here is no showing that petitioners' reasonable 'investment-backed expectations' have been materially affected . . . ." *Id.* at 499.

The Ninth Circuit interpreted Nevada eminent domain law in *Vacation Village, Inc. v. Clark County*, where owners of property near an airport claimed that the county inversely condemned their property by restricting building heights. 497 F. 3d 902, 918 (9th Cir. 2007). The court determined that the ordinances were not a per se taking because the plaintiffs neither suffered permanent damage nor were completely deprived of all economic use.

The California Supreme Court unanimously rejected a takings claim in *Regency Outdoor Advertising, Inc. v. City of Los Angeles*, 39 Cal. 4th 507, 513 (2006), where billboard owners claimed they were entitled to compensation when the city planted trees on city-owned property in the vicinity of their roadside billboards, thereby obstructing the view. The court, after surveying over 100 years of jurisprudence, found the owners' billboards had no "right to be seen" that would justify compensation for the allegedly lessened value of the billboards.

In *Buena Park Motel Association v. City of Buena Park*, a California court of appeal held that a city's restriction on extended stays at motels did not constitute an unlawful taking of private property. 109 Cal. App. 4th 302 (2003). The City of Buena Park adopted ordinances limiting guest stays in motels to 60 days in a 180-day period. A motel association sued the city, alleging the ordinances were an unlawful taking of private property without just compensation. In ruling for the city, the court stated that whether an ordinance constitutes an unlawful taking depends on its economic effects. *Id.* at 309. Although the restrictions on stay length did diminish the motel owners' use of their property, they were not considered unduly restrictive. The court held that while the motel owners undoubtedly would be economically impacted by the enforcement of the ordinances, they would not be deprived of all "economically viable use of their property." *Id.* at 311. The court noted that between 35 and 70 percent of the motel association's business would be unaffected by the ordinances, and that motel owners could modify their properties to meet criteria for allowing extended stays. *Id.*

The courts have repeatedly held that denial of the highest and best use does not constitute a taking of the property. *See Long Beach Equities, Inc. v. County of Ventura*, 231 Cal. App. 3d at 1036; *see also MacLeod v. County of Santa Clara*, 749 F. 2d 541, 548 (9th Cir. 1984).

The courts have repeatedly held that denial of the highest and best use does not constitute a taking of the property.

California courts follow the valuation rule, *i.e.*, the court must examine the use of the property that *remains* to determine whether a landowner has been deprived of economically viable use of his property. For example, in one case, the court held that the owners were not deprived of all use of their property when they could not demolish an existing building and erect a new multistory office structure, because they were not barred from remodeling the existing building. *See Terminals Equip. Co. v. City and County of San Francisco*, 221 Cal. App. 3d 234 (1990). The court stated:

> In every case in which a landowner seeks compensation for burdensome regulation of his or her property, the standard remains whether the regulations in issue have deprived the landowner of all use of the property. "When, as here, the claim is made that the regulation has significantly diminished the property value, the focus of the inquiry is on the uses of the property which remain. (*Penn Cent. Transp. Co. v. New York City*) [citation omitted.] Plaintiff cannot contend he was denied all use of his property. He was neither deprived of his right to exclude others from his land nor denied the right to sell the property." (*Guinnane v. City and County of San Francisco*) [citation omitted.]

Id. at 243 (emphasis in original)

In *Barancik v. County of Marin*, the Ninth Circuit held that a rezoning that permitted only one residence per 60 acres, with a right to buy development rights, was not a violation of substantive due process because it did not deny an owner all beneficial use of his land. 872 F. 2d 834, 837 (9th Cir. 1988). In upholding the ordinance, the court said it was not irrational or arbitrary. The court in *Outdoor Systems Inc. v. City of Mesa* reiterated this position:

> As for the question whether the sign codes deprive an owner of the economically viable use of the land, we recognize at the outset the term "economically viable use" has yet to be defined with such precision. [Citation omitted.] We have

held, however, that "the existence of permissible use [generally] determines whether a development restriction denies a property holder the economically viable use of its property." [Citation omitted]

997 F. 2d 604, 616 (9th Cir. 1993); *see also William C. Haas & Co. v. City & County of San Francisco*, 605 F. 2d 1117, 1119 (9th Cir. 1979) (a zoning ordinance that reduced the value of private property by more than 90 percent, from $2 million to $100,000, was constitutional); *Moore v. City of Costa Mesa*, 886 F. 2d 260, 263 (9th Cir. 1989) (invalid conditional use permit (variance) that caused a landowner a three-year delay in developing his property did not amount to a taking under the Fifth Amendment)

Until the 1997 California Supreme Court decision in Kavanau, *courts had declared that to satisfy the second prong of the* Agins *test, the challenged regulations must deprive the landowner of all, or substantially all, of the use of the land.*

Until the 1997 California Supreme Court decision in *Kavanau*, courts had declared that to satisfy the second prong of the *Agins* test, the challenged regulations must deprive the landowner of *all*, or *substantially all*, of the use of the land. See, e.g., *Moore v. City of Costa Mesa*, 886 F. 2d at 263; *Terminals Equip. Co. v. City and County of San Francisco*, 221 Cal. App. 3d at 243–44; *Long Beach Equities, Inc. v. County of Ventura*, 231 Cal. App. 3d at 1039.

Kavanau v. Santa Monica Rent Control Board involved a property owner's claim that Santa Monica's rent control regulations violated his right to due process and effected a taking. 16 Cal. 4th 761 (1997). The court ultimately ruled that the property owner had no viable inverse condemnation claim because the city's process for adjusting future rents provided an adequate remedy for any compensable due process violation he might have suffered. The decision is significant because the court departed from language previously used by California courts, stating that "a regulation...may effect a taking though it does not involve a physical invasion *and leaves the property owner some economically beneficial use of his property.*" *Id.* at 764. The court observed that the United States Supreme Court in *Lucas* had "expressly rejected the 'assumption that the landowner whose deprivation is one step short of complete is not entitled to compensation.'" *Id.* at 774. Thus, the *Kavanau* court reasoned that such an owner merely loses the benefit of the court's categorical formulation that a taking occurs when a regulation deprives property of all use. The court also concluded that when a regulation does not result in a physical invasion and does not deprive the property owner of all economically beneficial use of the property, a reviewing court must evaluate the regulation in light of the ad-hoc three part test established by the United States Supreme Court in *Penn Central* and discussed in numerous subsequent cases. The court in *Kavanau* also listed ten additional, nonexclusive factors, that might be relevant considerations in determining whether a regulatory taking has occurred. *Id.* at 776.[7]

In *Herzberg v. County of Plumas*, a state appellate court noted that "[e]ven the wisest lawyers would have to acknowledge great uncertainty about the scope of the [the United States Supreme Court's] takings jurisprudence [citation omitted]"

---

7. In *Galland*, the court addressed two questions that had been left unanswered in the *Kavanau* decision. 24 Cal. 4th 1003 (2001). The court first concluded that a *Kavanau* adjustment would preclude damages for violation of the right to due process under 42 U.S.C. section 1983. Next, the court turned from the rent adjustment itself to determine whether unreasonable costs, in the form of administrative and attorneys' fees imposed on landlords seeking rent increases, may themselves be the basis of a section 1983 claim. It concluded that such a claim may lie when one of two conditions is present: (1) the costs imposed are part of a government effort to deliberately flout established law, *e.g.*, obstruct legitimate rent increases; or (2) the landlord suffers confiscation as a result of the imposition of such costs.

but noted that "some general rules have taken shape in recent years and have just been clarified [in *Lingle*] by the United States Supreme Court." 133 Cal. App. 4th 1, 13 (2005). Relying on that clarification, the court in *Herzberg* ruled that a county ordinance which does not cause a physical taking, impose conditions on development, or deprive a landowner of all economically beneficial use of land must be analyzed under the ad hoc balancing test of *Penn Central*. The court also applied and analyzed several of the additional factors described in *Kavanau*.

In *Herzberg*, a group of landowners sued the county alleging that its "fencing out" ordinance, which declared certain areas of land to be devoted primarily to the grazing of livestock, caused a taking of their property under both the state and federal constitutions. The landowners argued that the ordinance, which prohibited landowners from removing grazing animals from the landowners property, unless the animals were found within a fenced area, unconstitutionally shifted the burden of animal grazing from cattle ranchers to private landowners, since the ordinance required landowners to construct fences if they desired to prevent other people's livestock from grazing upon their property.

Under the *Penn Central* ad hoc factual inquiry, the court concluded that the "fencing out" ordinance was not a taking. It did not interfere with the landowners' investment-backed expectations, since the affected land was in a traditional open grazing area and the "occasional use of and damage to property caused by wandering cattle as they move on" could be avoided by fencing. *Id.* at 19. The ordinance also did not, under *Kavanau*, restrict the landowners' use of their property or extinguish any fundamental attribute of ownership. *Id.* at 20. The court noted that the ordinance supported important historic, traditional, and economic uses of rural California property, and held that it "simply does not unconstitutionally 'forc[e] some people alone to bear public burdens which, in all fairness and justice, should be borne by the public as a whole.'" *Id.* [Citations omitted]. As a result, the ordinance did not effect a taking under either the state or federal constitutions.

Similarly, in *Allegretti & Co. v. County of Imperial*, the court rejected a takings claim premised on the imposition of a conditional use permit that limited the total amount of groundwater available for a 2400 acre parcel of land. 138 Cal. App. 4th 1261 (2006). Analyzing the claim under the *Penn Central* ad hoc test, the court found that the regulation was not a physical taking because it did not divert any water or physically invade the property, nor did it deny the landowner of all economic use of the property. In applying the *Penn Central* factors, the court noted that the basis for the factual inquiry is "the owner's entire property holdings at the time of the alleged taking, not just the adversely affected portion." *Id.* at 1277. The court held that the regulation was not a taking because it did not interfere with legitimate property interests to such a degree that would constitute a taking under the third *Penn Central* factor—the only economic impact shown was a diminution in value resulting from the inability to farm the entire 2400 acres, and mere interference with potential expectations of profits gained from farming the entire property was not a compensable interference with a "distinct investment backed expectation." *Id.* at 1278-79.

In *Garneau v. City of Seattle*, the Ninth Circuit reiterated that in noncategorical regulatory taking cases—*i.e.*, cases in which property has not been physically invaded and the property owner has not been deprived of all economically viable use of his land—the two key factors to consider are (1) diminution in

> *In* Allegretti & Co. v. County of Imperial, *the court rejected a takings claim premised on the imposition of a conditional use permit that limited the total amount of groundwater available for a 2400 acre parcel of land.*

value and (2) interference with distinct investment-backed expectations. 147 F. 3d 802, 807–08 (9th Cir. 1998).

In *Santa Monica Beach, Ltd. v. Superior Court*, the California Supreme Court rejected the higher-scrutiny standard for a takings claim based on rent control law, and adopted a "hands off" policy for land use legislation. 19 Cal. 4th 952, 967 (1999). In that case, a landlord sued the city's rent control board for inverse condemnation on the grounds that the goals of the rent control program—providing affordable housing for the poor, elderly, and young families—were not achieved by rent control. The landlord claimed that the city's rent control law had actually reduced, rather than preserved, affordable housing for low-income renters, young families, and the elderly, and thus the law had failed to substantially advance its stated purpose. The court elected not to review the rent control law to determine whether it would achieve the stated goals, holding that the heightened scrutiny under *Nollan* and *Dolan* should not be applied to rent control ordinances. Instead, the court reasoned, such laws should be governed by a standard of review "at least as deferential as for generally applicable zoning laws and other legislative land use controls." *Id.* at 967. While rent control legislation that causes confiscation of private land will be invalidated as an uncompensated taking, the courts will not review such legislation to determine whether it actually achieves desired goals.

The California Supreme Court also rejected the *Nollan/Dolan* test as being applicable to hotel conversion fees adopted by the City and County of San Francisco. *See San Remo Hotel v. City and County of San Francisco*, 27 Cal. 4th 643 (2002), discussed *infra*.

Further, in *Home Builders Association of Northern California v. City of Napa*, the court, in upholding an inclusionary housing zoning ordinance, held that the *Nollan/Dolan* test was not applicable. 90 Cal. App. 4th 188 (2001). The association claimed that the city's ordinance was invalid under *Nollan* and *Dolan* because there was no "essential nexus" or "rough proportionality" between the exaction required by the ordinance and the impacts caused by development of the property.

The court rejected that argument, holding that *Nollan* and *Dolan* were inapplicable under the facts of the case. The court stated that the higher standard of judicial scrutiny formulated by the high court in *Nollan* and *Dolan* was intended to address land use "bargains" between property owners and regulatory bodies—those in which the local government conditions permit approval for a given use on the owner's surrender of benefits which purportedly offset the impact of the proposed development. *Id.* at 196. The court in *Napa* observed that it was not called upon to determine the validity of a particular land use bargain between a governmental agency and an owner who wants to develop his land. Instead, it was confronted with a facial challenge to economic legislation that was generally applicable to *all* development in the city. Therefore, it concluded the heightened standard of review described in *Nollan* and *Dolan* was inapplicable under these facts.[8] For a more detailed treatment of exactions, *see* chapter 13 (Exactions).

---

8. *See* Daniel J. Curtin, Jr. *et al.*, "Inclusionary Housing Ordinance Survives Constitutional Challenge in Post-Nollan-Dolan Era: Home Builders Ass'n of N. Cal. v. City of Napa," *Land Use Law & Zoning Digest* (August 2002, APA); Barbara Kautz, "In Defense of Inclusionary Zoning: Successfully Creating Affordable Housing," 36 *U.S.F. L. Rev.* 971 (2002).

Temporary Takings—Interim Ordinances, Moratoria, and Other Growth Management Measures

When governmental activity deprives an owner of all use of a property, even though the activity is not permanent, a property owner may have a claim for a "temporary taking." Like other actions by local governments, interim ordinances, moratoria, and other growth management measures are lawful exercises of the police power and do not amount to a temporary taking under *First English* so long as they do not "go too far."

An interim ordinance, adopted pursuant to Government Code section 65858, that prohibits approval of new development plans so that a city can re-evaluate its land use policies, is lawful provided the period of delay is reasonable and there are valid governmental reasons justifying its adoption. *See Tahoe-Sierra Preservation Council, Inc. v. Tahoe Reg'l Planning Agency*, 535 U.S. at 353; *First English Evangelical Lutheran Church v. County of Los Angeles*, 482 U.S. 304, 320 (1987).

The United States Supreme Court's decision in *Tahoe-Sierra* reaffirmed the ability of cities to use temporary development moratoria as a planning tool, such as interim ordinances that can be adopted under Government Code section 65858, without necessarily having to compensate property owners for the time period during which development is banned.

In *Tahoe-Sierra*, the Tahoe Regional Planning Agency imposed two moratoria totaling 32 months on development in the Lake Tahoe basin while formulating a comprehensive land use plan for the area. Property owners filed suit, claiming that the moratoria constituted a temporary categorical taking under *Lucas*. In rejecting this argument, the Court stated that because property subject to a temporary moratorium will recover its value when the moratorium is lifted, the moratorium did not permanently deprive the owner of all economically viable use. In effect, a moratorium is not a per se facial taking.

The landowners had also asked the Court to set a bright-line rule that any moratorium of longer than one year was a categorical taking. The Court refused to do so, stating that formulation of a general rule of this kind was more suitable for the state legislatures. The Court noted that many states (including California) have enacted legislation authorizing interim ordinances, including moratoria, with specific time limits. *See, e.g.* Gov't Code § 65858 (authorizing interim ordinances of up to two years).

The Court stated that unlike the "extraordinary circumstances" in which the government deprives a property owner of all economic use, moratoria are used widely among land use planners to preserve the status quo while formulating a more permanent development strategy. Yet even the weak version of the landowners' categorical rule would treat these interim measures as takings regardless of the good faith of the planners, the reasonable expectations of the landowners, or the actual impact of the moratorium on property values. 535 U.S. at 303–304.

The Court stated that the interest in facilitating informed decisionmaking by regulatory agencies counsels against adopting a per se rule that would impose such severe costs on their deliberations. Otherwise, the financial constraints of compensating property owners during a moratorium might force cities to rush through the planning process or to abandon the practice altogether. To the extent that communities are forced to abandon using moratoria, landowners will have incentives to develop their property quickly before a comprehensive plan can be enacted, thereby fostering inefficient and ill-conceived growth.

The Court stated that since a categorical rule tied to the length of deliberations would likely create added pressure on decisionmakers to reach a quick resolution of land use questions, it would only serve to disadvantage those landowners and interest groups who are not as organized or familiar with the planning process. Moreover, with a temporary ban on development there is less risk that individual landowners will be "singled out" to bear a special burden that should be shared by the public as a whole. At least with a moratorium, there is a "reciprocity of advantage," because it protects the interests of all affected landowners against immediate construction that might be inconsistent with the provisions of the plan that is ultimately adopted. "While each of us is burdened somewhat by such restrictions, we, in turn, benefit greatly from the restrictions that are placed on others." *Id.* at 341. In fact, there is reason to believe property values often will continue to increase despite a moratorium.

How much delay is reasonable will vary from case to case, and courts should recognize that limited fiscal resources necessarily would slow the planning process.

How much delay is reasonable will vary from case to case, and courts should recognize the fact that limited fiscal resources necessarily would slow the planning process. Developers may wish (or may be asked) to help fund independent studies that otherwise would have to be delayed for lack of resources. As a preventive measure, a city should consider allowing some use of the property during the interim period. For a thorough discussion of interim ordinances, *see* chapter 4 (Zoning). For further discussion of temporary moratoria, *see* Thomas E. Roberts, "Moratoria as Categorical Regulatory Takings, What First English and Lucas Say and Don't Say," 31 *Envtl. L. Rep.* News & Analysis 110389 (Environmental Law Institute 2001).[9]

Moratoria and other growth management measures that are based on documented health, safety, and general welfare concerns are more likely than other types of measures to withstand constitutional challenges. In cases where the perceived problems of development can be mitigated, those measures that relax restrictions upon attainment of realistic service level goals will be more likely to withstand attack.

Also, properly documented growth management measures generally withstand judicial scrutiny if they allow adequate potential for eventual development or other fruitful use, so that owners are not denied all economically viable use of their property.

In *Landgate, Inc. v. California Coastal Commission*, 17 Cal. 4th 1006 (1998), the California Supreme Court addressed the issue of "temporary takings" as considered in *First English Evangelical Lutheran Church v. County of Los Angeles*, 482 U.S. 304 (1987). In *First English*, the owner operated a campground on which a number of buildings had been destroyed by a flood. An interim Los Angeles County ordinance prohibited construction or reconstruction of any building or structure in an interim flood protection area that included the

---

9. *See also Taking Sides on Takings Issues: The Impact of* Tahoe-Sierra (Thomas E. Roberts, ed., ABA, Sect. of State and Local Gov't Law, 2003); S. Eagle, "Planning Moratoria and Regulatory Takings: The Supreme Court's Fairness Mandate Benefits Landowners," 31 *Florida State L. Rev.* 429 (Spring 2004).

owner's land. The court assumed for purposes of the appeal that the ordinance deprived the owner of all economically beneficial use of its property. It then held that such deprivation constituted a temporary taking of the property for which compensation must be paid. "'[T]emporary' takings which...deny a landowner all use of his property, are not different in kind from permanent takings, for which the Constitution clearly requires compensation." *Id*. at 318. Thus, the court held that "where the government's activities have already worked a taking of all use of property, no subsequent action by the government can relieve it of the duty to provide compensation for the period during which the taking was effective." *Id*. at 321.

In *Landgate*, the plaintiff, Landgate, owned two long, thin parcels of land in the Malibu Hills. In the mid-1980s, the County of Los Angeles planned to provide a road that would run through the two lots. Landgate's predecessor and the county agreed that the county would build the road in exchange for the reconfiguration of the lots into one sloped 2.45-acre lot north of the road, and one flat 1.56-acre lot south of the road. In October 1990, Landgate bought the northern lot and received the county's permission to grade the lot and build a single-family home. However, after an investigation raised objections regarding the grading plan and the height of the proposed home, along with contentions that the lot line adjustment had been illegal, the California Coastal Commission rejected Landgate's application. Landgate sued the Commission seeking damages for a taking, contending it had no jurisdiction over the lot line adjustment. In addition, the trial court granted Landgate's mandamus petition and summary judgment motion on the takings claim, ruling that the Commission had temporarily taken Landgate's property from February 1991 to February 1993. Damages of $155,657 were awarded and the court of appeal affirmed.

In ruling for the Commission, the California Supreme Court reversed and remanded. The majority, in an opinion authored by Justice Mosk, stated that "[v]irtually every court that has examined the issue has concluded...that a regulatory mistake resulting in delay does not, by itself, amount to a taking of property." *Id*. A government agency's error "in the development approval process does not necessarily amount to a taking even if the error in some way diminishes the value of the subject property, any more than the commission of state law error during a criminal trial is an automatic violation of the due process clause." *Id*. at 1016. Although the enforcement of a law or regulation that deprives property of all value is a compensable taking, land use regulations that are part of a reasonable regulatory process designed to advance legitimate government interests are not takings. *Id*. at 1021.

The *Landgate* court also noted that the *First English* Court emphasized the narrowness of its holding. "We...point out that the allegation of the complaint which we treat as true for purposes of our decision was that the ordinance in question denied appellant all use of its property. We limit our holding to the facts presented, and of course do not deal with the quite different questions that would arise in the case of normal delays in obtaining building permits, changes in zoning ordinances, variances, and the like which are not before us." *Landgate*, 17 Cal. 4th at 1017 citing *First English*, 482 U.S. at 321.

The significance of *Landgate* is its holding that an erroneous assertion of jurisdiction by the Coastal Commission, which prevented a landowner's

Although the enforcement of a law or regulation that deprives property of all value is a compensable taking, land use regulations that are part of a reasonable regulatory process designed to advance legitimate government interests are not takings.

development of his property for two years, was merely a "normal delay" in the development process and did not amount to a taking. *See also Buckley v. California Coastal Comm'n*, 68 Cal. App. 4th 178, 183 (1998) (relying on *Landgate*, the court found no taking even though Coastal Commission acted erroneously in assuming jurisdiction over the development).

Landgate was distinguished in *Ali v. City of Los Angeles*, where the court held that a delay in issuing a demolition permit and the eventual denial of the permit was a temporary taking. 77 Cal. App. 4th 246 (1999). The City of Los Angeles took approximately 19 months to issue a demolition permit for the property owner's building (which the city temporarily considered a single-room occupancy hotel), after a fire substantially destroyed the building. In a prior appeal, the court ruled that this delay violated the Ellis Act (Gov't Code § 7060–7060.7), which precludes public agencies from forcing property owners to continue offering accommodations for rent or lease.

On remand, the trial court found a temporary taking. The parties stipulated as to damages, and the judgment awarded Ali $1,199,237 plus interest for inverse condemnation. The appellate court affirmed. In so doing, it looked to the California Supreme Court decision in *Landgate* for guidance. In *Ali*, the court concluded that the city's position, unlike the Coastal Commission's position in *Landgate*, was "so unreasonable from a legal standpoint as to lead to the conclusion that it was taken for no purpose other than to delay the development project before it." 77 Cal. App. 4th at 254–55.

In the earlier, unrelated published decision, the court had held that the Ellis Act preempted local laws, and that property owners were entitled to a demolition permit without having to comply with local conditions. The city's contrary position was arbitrary and unreasonable in light of this precedent. The delay in issuing the permit, therefore, was not a "normal delay" in the development process, and the property owner was entitled to damages for the temporary taking. *Id.* at 255.

> The Landgate *principles were affirmed in* Loewenstein v. City of Lafayette, *where the court held that a two-year delay precipitated by a city's erroneous action was not an unlawful temporary taking.*

The *Landgate* principles were affirmed in *Loewenstein v. City of Lafayette*, where the court held that a two-year delay precipitated by a city's erroneous action was not an unlawful temporary taking. 103 Cal. App. 4th 718, 729 (2002). In *Loewenstein*, property owners applied for a lot line adjustment, which would have allowed the owners to merge a smaller new lot into their existing lot, divide the merged property into two lots, and build an additional home. The landowners sought approval from the City of Lafayette, which refused because it believed that the adjustment would create an extra lot in a restricted subdivision. The city was also concerned that the proposed lot line adjustment would violate municipal ordinances regarding hillside property. Eventually, the property owners obtained a trial court ruling that the city had erred and that they were entitled to compensation. Thereafter, the city rescinded its denial of the request and approved the adjustment, thus rendering the taking temporary.

Upon appeal by the city, the court reversed, holding that *Landgate* precluded a takings finding since the resolution of the threshold issue of the legality of the lot line adjustment was a normal delay in the process of obtaining a permit pertaining to land use. In so doing, it rejected the owners' arguments that the exception noted in *Landgate* and relied upon in *Ali* applied. The delay in this case was not objectively unreasonable; it was not taken solely to delay the proposed project. Rather, the city merely was attempting to carry out reasonable land use policies. Further, the court held that the *Penn Central* factors are negated when *Landgate* applies, since a property owner can have no reasonable expectation that there will be no delays in the processing of his application.

In *Allegretti & Co. v. County of Imperial* (discussed above), the Attorney General, as amicus curiae, argued that Allegretti's claim was not a regulatory taking, but a temporary taking procedurally barred by the *Landgate* decision. Although it was not clear whether Allegretti proceeded on a theory of a permanent or temporary taking, the court nonetheless addressed *Landgate* because Allegretti sought to apply *Agins'* substantially-advances test on the ground that *Landgate* retained its viability. Under this test, Allegretti argued that the county's act of initially imposing the conditional use permit and the subsequent defense against Allegretti's inverse condemnation action were "so unreasonable from a legal standpoint" that they had no legitimate purpose. 138 Cal. App. 4th 1261, 1282 (citing *Landgate* 17 Cal. 4th at 1031). The court concluded that Allegretti's claim could not succeed even under *Landgate's* standards, and assuming the circumstances of this case warrant application of *Landgate* the court's conclusion ends it analysis.

> Once a court determines that a governmental entity engaged in decisionmaking whose purpose is not delay for delay's sake but legitimate oversight, the question of whether a landowner has a reasonable investment-backed expectation that is impacted in a manner requiring compensation is, of necessity, an answered in the negative. A landowner can have no reasonable expectation that there will be no delays or bona fide differences of opinion in the application process for development permits. Sometimes the application process must detour to the court process to resolve genuine disagreement. Because such delay comes within the *Landgate* category of normal delays in the development approval process, there is no taking even if the value of the subject property is diminished in some way.

Id. at 1284–85 (citing *Loewenstein*, 103 Cal. App. 4th at 736–37)

No temporary taking was found where interim delay in acting on a building permit left some beneficial use of the property. *See Guinnane v. City and County of San Francisco*, 197 Cal. App. 3d 862 (1987). In *Guinnane*, the landowner sued for damages, claiming that designation of his land as a possible site for a public park was an unreasonable precondemnation action, and that delays in processing his application for a building permit entitled him to damages for a temporary taking under *First English*.

First, the court rejected the claim that the city's designation of an area including the owner's property as open space, to be studied for possible acquisition as a public park, amounted to unreasonable precondemnation activities. Mere planning activities of the city did not entitle the owner to require the city to condemn the property in question and pay the landowner the market value of the property before the threat of condemnation arose. *Id.* at 86667. The court distinguished the facts in this case from the situation where a city had actually announced or initiated eminent domain proceedings and thus the landowner was entitled to damages for inverse condemnation. *Id.* (citing *Klopping v. City of Whittier*, 8 Cal. 3d 39 (1972)).

The owner in *Guinnane* also relied on *First English* to support a cause of action for damages for a "temporary taking" resulting from delays in the processing of

In Guinnane v. City and County of San Francisco, *no temporary taking was found where interim delay in acting on a building permit left some beneficial use of the property.*

his application for a building permit. The court found that the temporary suspension of land use that occurs during a normal governmental decision-making process, such as environmental review, does not constitute a taking. *Id.* at 866–67. The court rejected the owner's claim that the city's delay in acting on his application was unusual, excessive, and unreasonable. To the contrary, the court found that many of the delays were directly attributable to the owner.

The court also indicated that the landowner had not been deprived of all economically viable use of his land during the period of environmental review, noting that "the focus of the inquiry is on the uses of the property which remain." *Id.* at 868 (citing *Penn Central Transp. Co. v. City of New York*, 438 U.S. 104 (1978)).

> Plaintiff cannot contend he was denied all use of his property. He was neither deprived of his right to exclude others from his land nor denied the right to sell the property.

Id. (emphasis in original)[10]

In *Tensor Group v. City of Glendale*, the court noted, without going into extensive discussion, that because the ordinances in question did not preclude the landowner from "substantially all use of [its] property," no inverse condemnation based upon a regulatory taking occurred. 14 Cal. App. 4th 154, 161 (1993). The court did not consider whether a temporary taking had occurred in light of the myriad of factors referenced in *Penn Central* for determining when a regulation has gone too far.

In 1995, a court held that no taking resulted from a delay caused by the erroneous decision of a regulatory agency. There was no egregious bureaucratic overreaching; the agency's actions "were facially valid and supported by a plausible though erroneous legal argument." *See Littoral Dev. Co. v. San Francisco Bay Conser. & Dev. Comm'n*, 33 Cal. App. 4th 211, 221 (1995).

The California Supreme Court has made clear that "delays" in the development process will not easily be elevated to the level of a taking—permanent or temporary. For instance, in *Landgate*, the court held that a two-year delay in the issuance of building permits, resulting from the Coastal Commission's erroneous assertion of jurisdiction over a lot line adjustment, was a "normal delay" in the development process and did not amount to a taking. 17 Cal. 4th at 1017.

"Partial" Takings; Segmentation— the Relevant Parcel Issue[11]

The determination whether all economically viable use of a given property has been denied will depend on how that "property" is defined. If, for example, a regulation precludes development on 90 percent of a parcel, should the regulation be considered to have deprived the owner of all use of that segment, or should the analysis focus on the uses and value of the parcel viewed as a whole?

---

10. In *Dolan v. City of Tigard*, the United States Supreme Court emphasized the importance of this "right to exclude others" from the land, stating that it is "'one of the most essential sticks in the bundle of rights that are commonly characterized as property.'" 512 U.S. 374, 384 (1994) (quoting *Kaiser Aetna v. United States*, 444 U.S. 164, 176 (1979)).

11. For further discussion of the partial takings/segmentation question, *see* Juergensmeyer and Roberts, *Land Use Planning and Control Law*, section 10.8 (1998).

If a court were to look only at the segment on which all use was prohibited, it would find a categorical taking under *Lucas*, which would shift the burden to the government to justify the regulation. *See Lucas v. South Carolina Coastal Council*, 505 U.S. at 1027. If the parcel is viewed as a whole, however, then the burden remains on the property owner to prove that the city's action unreasonably interferes with the owner's investment-backed expectations under *Penn Central*. Prior to *Lucas*, the United States Supreme Court had not adopted a segmentation approach; instead, it had looked generally to the uses and value remaining in the parcel as a whole. *See, e.g., Penn Cent. Transp. Co. v. City of New York*, 438 U.S. 104; *Keystone Bituminous Coal Ass'n v. DeBenedictis*, 480 U.S. 470. In *Lucas*, however, the Court acknowledged that there was some uncertainty about how it would decide the issue.

> Regrettably, the rhetorical force of our "deprivation of all economically feasible use rule" is greater than its precision, since the rule does not make clear the "property interest" against which the loss of value is to be measured. When, for example, a regulation requires a developer to leave 90% of a rural tract in a natural state, it is unclear whether we would analyze the situation as one in which the owner has been deprived of all economically beneficial use of the burdened portion of the tract, or as one in which the owner has suffered a mere diminution in value of the tract as a whole.

505 U.S. at 1016 n. 7

Likewise, in *Palazzolo v. Rhode Island*, the Court again stated that it had at times expressed discomfort with the idea that parcels must be considered as a whole, but here the high Court refused to allow Mr. Palazzolo to raise this issue for the first time at the certiorari stage. 533 U.S. at 631.

However, the Court directly addressed the segmentation issue in its *Tahoe-Sierra* decision. In the early 1980s, the Tahoe Regional Planning Agency (TRPA) imposed two moratoria totaling 32 months on development in the Lake Tahoe basin while formulating a comprehensive land use plan for the area. Property owners filed suit in federal court claiming that the moratoria constituted a taking of private property without just compensation. Relying on *Lucas*, which declared that a regulation that deprives a landowner of all economically viable use of his or her land constitutes a "categorical" taking, the trial court held that because the moratoria had temporarily prevented any use of the property owners' land, they were automatically entitled to compensation for the loss of the use of their property while the moratoria were in effect. 535 U.S. 302, 316–17.

On appeal, the Ninth Circuit reversed, holding that because the moratoria were only temporary, the landowners had not been permanently deprived of all economically viable use of their land, and therefore no categorical taking had occurred. Instead, the appellate court held that the takings question should be analyzed using the case-by-case balancing test established under *Penn Central*.

The United States Supreme Court upheld the Ninth Circuit's decision. On appeal to the Supreme Court, the landowners argued that property ownership can be divided into discrete temporal segments, and therefore because the moratoria had denied them all use of their land during one such 32-month segment, the moratoria should be declared a categorical taking automatically entitling the landowners to compensation under *Lucas*. The Court rejected this

TRPA = Tahoe Regional Planning Agency

argument, holding that the property interest in question must be evaluated as a whole, and the length of time that a regulation denies an owner the use of its property is only one factor to consider in determining whether or not a taking has occurred. Because property subject to a temporary moratorium will ultimately recover its value when the moratorium is lifted, the moratorium does not permanently deprive the owner of all economically viable use. The Court also noted that an area-wide moratorium often provides a reciprocity of advantage to the affected landowners because they each benefit from protection against hasty construction by their neighbors that may ultimately be inconsistent with the land use plan that is adopted. Based on this reasoning, the Court held that the TRPA temporary moratoria did not constitute a categorical taking, and instead the case-by-case balancing test of *Penn Central* should be applied to the landowners' claims. The trial court had previously determined, however, that the moratoria did not constitute a taking under *Penn Central*, and because the landowners had not appealed that ruling, the judgment against the landowners was upheld.

In arriving at its decision, the high Court stated that the categorical rule applied in *Lucas* requires compensation whenever a regulation deprives an owner of "*all* economically beneficial uses" of his or her land. Under that rule, a statute that "wholly eliminated the value" of Mr. Lucas' fee simple title clearly qualified as a taking. But the Court's holding was limited to "the extraordinary circumstance when *no* productive or economically beneficial use of the land is permitted." *Id.* at 330, citing 505 U.S. at 1012. The emphasis on the word "no" in the text of the *Lucas* opinion was, in effect, reiterated in a footnote explaining that the categorical rule would not apply if the diminution in value were 95 percent instead of 100 percent. Anything less than a "complete elimination of value," or a "total loss," the Court held, would require the kind of analysis applied in *Penn Central*. As a result, the *Lucas* rule is to be narrowly applied in the future.

In summary, the Court in *Tahoe-Sierra* upheld the 32-month moratoria, holding that the analysis prescribed in *Penn Central* applies in the regulatory takings context, and the *Lucas* categorical taking rule should apply only when *no* productive or economically beneficial use of the property remains.[12]

California courts have not squarely decided the segmentation, or relevant parcel, issue. They have stated, however, that the question of whether differently zoned contiguous parcels are considered separately or as a whole depends on the facts, including the potential for development of each of the properties "from the standpoint of both economics and governmental cooperation." *Twain Harte Assocs., Ltd. v. County of Tuolumne*, 217 Cal. App. 3d 71, 87 (1990) (remanding to the trial court the issue of whether an undeveloped 1.7-acre parcel that had

---

12. For an interesting discussion on the *Tahoe-Sierra* case, *see* Dwight H. Merriam, "Tahoe-Sierra: A Takings Time Warp," 25 *Zoning and Planning Law Report* 61 (June 2002) and *Taking Sides on Takings Issues: the Impact of* Tahoe-Sierra (Thomas E. Roberts, ed., ABA, Sect. of State and Local Gov't Law, 2003). For an argument that the "reciprocity of advantage" principle relied on in *Tahoe-Sierra* ought to control takings jurisprudence and should preclude compensation for all but categorical takings that permanently deprive property of all market value or compel physical occupation, *see* Andrew W. Schwartz, "Reciprocity of Advantage: The Antidote to the Antidemocratic Trend in Regulatory Takings," 22 *UCLA J. Envtl. L. & Pol'y* 1 (2003–04).

been downzoned from commercial to open space should be viewed as part of an 8.5 acre parcel on which the owner had built a shopping center). California courts also have identified as an important factor the availability of density transfers or other techniques for shifting burdens and benefits between the parcels. *See Aptos Seascape Corp. v. County of Santa Cruz*, 138 Cal. App. 3d 484, 497 (1982); *see also American Sav. & Loan Ass'n v. County of Marin*, 653 F. 2d 364, 371–72 (9th Cir. 1981).

For a discussion of takings where development is prohibited on a portion of property consisting of wetlands, *see* chapter 7 (Federal and State Wetland Regulation).

Remedies for Excessive Land Use Regulation— Damages

In 1987, the United States Supreme Court held that the just compensation requirement under the Takings Clause of the Fifth Amendment, as applied to the states under the Fourteenth Amendment, mandates that a landowner recover just compensation if the land use restriction constitutes a temporary "taking" of property. *See First English Evangelical Lutheran Church v. County of Los Angeles*, 482 U.S. 304 (1987).

Prior to *First English*, California courts had held that one who claims unreasonable governmental regulation could initially seek only a court order invalidating the regulation, and that compensation was not required until the government decided to continue a regulation in effect after a court had determined it to be excessive. *See First English*, 482 U.S. at 308–09, citing *Agins v. City of Tiburon*, 24 Cal. 3d 266, 275–77 (1979). The court in *Agins*, in explaining its reasoning for holding that mandamus or declaratory relief was more appropriate than a damages award, pointed to the need to preserve flexibility in the land-use planning process and the fiscal impact that requiring compensation would have. The court noted that the utilization of inverse condemnation would have a "chilling effect upon the exercise of police regulatory power at the local level" because the threat of unanticipated financial liability would not only intimidate, but discourage strict or innovative planning. *Agins*, 24 Cal. 3d at 276. The court further noted that requiring compensation for the enactment of a stringent zoning measure would give the voters power to inadvertently spend funds from the public treasury because legislation can be enacted directly by the people through direct initiative and invalidation of a particular land-use control would remedy legislative excess more expediently than forced compensation. *Id.*

In overturning the California rule, the United States Supreme Court held that the United States Constitution requires compensation for any "temporary taking" that may occur while the regulation is in effect prior to a court's takings determination. *First English*, 482 U.S. at 320. In 1957, the First English Evangelical Lutheran Church purchased a 21-acre parcel of land in a canyon along the banks of the Middle Fork of Mill Creek in the Angeles National Forest. The Middle Fork was a natural drainage channel for a watershed area owned by the United States Forest Service. The church operated a campground on the site, known as Lutherglen, as a retreat center and a recreational area for disabled

In overturning the California rule, the United States Supreme Court held that the United States Constitution requires compensation for any "temporary taking" that may occur while the regulation is in effect prior to a court's takings determination.

children. In July 1977, a forest fire destroyed 3,860 acres of mountainous forest upstream from Lutherglen, creating a serious flood hazard. In February 1978, a flash flood killed ten people and destroyed the buildings at Lutherglen.

In response to the flooding of the canyon, the County of Los Angeles adopted an interim ordinance that declared the area a flood zone and prohibited First Lutheran Church from rebuilding. The church sued seeking monetary damages, challenging the county's prohibition as a taking. The California courts dismissed the claim, concluding that invalidation, not money damages, was the only available remedy.

The United States Supreme Court, addressing only the issue of the availability of money damages, reversed the decision of the state courts. The Court held that invalidation of the ordinance, without payment of money damages for the use of the property during the period of time the church was denied all use of its property, would be a constitutionally insufficient remedy. *First English*, 482 U.S. at 320. The Court then remanded the case to the state court on the question of whether such a flood control ordinance actually amounted to a taking.

In *First English*, the Court decided only one issue: whether damages were an available remedy if a temporary taking is found. It did not address the more difficult question of whether Los Angeles County's interim flood control regulation actually constituted a temporary taking.[13] Instead, because of the nature of the appeal, the Court assumed that a taking had occurred and with that assumption, held that the Fifth Amendment required just compensation for all takings, whether temporary or permanent.

While in *First English* the Court held that damages were a proper remedy, it limited its holding to the facts presented where the landowner was denied all use of his property. Further, the Court expressly stated that it was not addressing the "quite different" questions that would arise in the case of normal delays in obtaining building permits, changes in zoning ordinances, and variances. 482 U.S. at 311.

On remand, the California court of appeal held, for two independent reasons, that no taking had occurred:

- The interim ordinance in question substantially advanced the pre-eminent state interest in public safety and did not deny the church all use of its property.
- The interim ordinance only imposed a reasonable moratorium for a reasonable period of time while the county conducted a study and determined what uses, if any, were compatible with public safety.

First English Evangelical Lutheran Church v. County of Los Angeles, 210 Cal. App. 3d 1353 (1989)

In summary, the United States Supreme Court's *First English* decision focused solely on the constitutional remedy required once it has been determined that there has been a taking. If a landowner was deprived of all use of property while the invalid law was in effect, mere withdrawal of the regulation is an insufficient remedy, and compensation for use of the property during the period in which the law was in effect must be paid. 482 U.S. at 321. The Supreme Court in

---

13. Justice Stevens, writing for the dissent, stated that the regulation clearly would not constitute a taking. 482 U.S. at 322.

Tahoe-Sierra Preservation Council Inc. v. Tahoe Regional Planning Agency confirmed that the *First English* decision only addressed the proper remedy for a temporary taking, and expressly disavowed any ruling on the merits of the taking claim. 535 U.S. at 330. If there is no taking, the compensation requirement under *First English* is not an issue. *See Tahoe Reg'l Planning Agency v. King*, 233 Cal. App. 3d 1365, 1393 (1991).

Once a city's obligation to pay just compensation arises, a city might not be able to avoid the obligation by claiming that the spending limits of California Constitution, articles XIII A, XIII B, XIII C, and XVI make the expenditure impossible. *See F&L Farm Co. v. City of Lindsay*, 65 Cal. App. 4th 1345 (1998). In *F&L Farm Company*, the city was compelled to pay a $5 million inverse condemnation judgment when its handling of saline industrial waste caused damage to nearby farmlands. The court concluded that paying an inverse condemnation judgment "does not implement a municipal purpose" within the meaning of article XIIIC, and thus is not covered by the spending limitations. *Id.* at 1355.

Once a city's obligation to pay just compensation arises, a city might not be able to avoid the obligation by claiming that the spending limits of California Constitution, articles XIII A, XIII B, XIII C, and XVI make the expenditure impossible.

However, in *Ventura Group Ventures, Inc. v. Ventura Port District*, the California Supreme Court distinguished its facts from those in *F&L Farm Company*, and found flaws in the reasoning of *F&L Farm Company*. 24 Cal. 4th 1089 (2001). In *Ventura Group*, the plaintiff developer obtained a judgment for damages resulting from the port district's breach of the covenant of good faith and fair dealing in relation to a contract between the developer and the district. The developer asserted that the *F&L Farm Company* decision supported its argument that the district, which was bankrupt, could levy property taxes higher than the one percent ceiling imposed by article XIII of the California Constitution for the purpose of paying judgments against it. The Court found *F&L Farm Company* distinguishable on two grounds and upheld the monetary judgment. First, unlike the inverse condemnation claim in *F&L Farm Company*, the claim at issue in *Ventura Group* was based upon a breach of contract, and thus was not covered by the statutory exemption to article XIII. Second, unlike the city in *F&L Farm Company*, the district was not permitted to avoid satisfaction of the judgment on the grounds that it had no money. To the contrary, as a result of the district's bankruptcy proceeding, the developer already had received payment on nearly one-half of its judgment.

Moreover, *Ventura Group* criticized the reasoning in *F&L Farm Company*:

> The analysis of article XIII A in *F&L Farm Co.* got off on the wrong track because the case focused on whether, rather than how, the City was required to satisfy the judgment. [The court] got the whether right, but the how wrong. That is, article XIII A is most assuredly not a license to "stiff" judgment creditors with impunity.... However, the fact that article XIII A does not absolutely shield a local public entity from a judgment creditor does not mean that a court can compel a county to levy property taxes in excess of article XIII A's one percent limit in order to satisfy the judgment.

The fact that article XIII A does not absolutely shield a local public entity from a judgment creditor does not mean that a court can compel a county to levy property taxes in excess of article XIII A's one percent limit in order to satisfy the judgment.

24 Cal. 4th at 1101

Hensler v. City of Glendale highlights a judicial tendency to invalidate a regulation or give the city the option to rescind the regulation, rather than award monetary damages to be paid by a local government that does not have the resources to pay. 8 Cal. 4th 1 (1994).

In Hensler, *the California Supreme Court ruled that the statute of limitations in an inverse condemnation action alleging a taking of real property by application of a city ordinance was the 90-day limitation period of the Subdivision Map Act.*

In *Hensler*,[14] the California Supreme Court in a unanimous decision ruled that the statute of limitations in an inverse condemnation action alleging a taking of real property by application of a city ordinance was the 90-day limitation period of the Subdivision Map Act (Gov't Code § 66499.37), since the ridgeline regulation under attack was part of the city's subdivision ordinance. 8 Cal. 4th at 22.

In that case, the property owner acknowledged that since development was permitted on part of his property, the city ordinance did not deny him all economically feasible use of the property. Rather, his claim was that a compensable taking of his property occurred when the city's ridgeline ordinance was enacted, because development was limited to less than all of the property. However, the argument that the property owner did not need to pursue administrative and judicial remedies as a prerequisite to a suit in inverse condemnation was rejected by the court. Rather, the court stated that the property owner could not avoid these steps and simply seek to compel the city to purchase the undeveloped portion of the property by seeking only compensation in an inverse condemnation action. *Id.* at 12–13.

When restrictions on use of real property are the basis for a takings claim, the owner must pursue any available administrative permit process before seeking compensation or challenging the statute or regulation.

The Court held that when restrictions on use of real property are the basis for a takings claim, the owner must pursue any available administrative permit process before seeking compensation or challenging the statute or regulation. California's permit process includes both administrative and judicial review. A court can determine whether a taking has occurred only when that review process is completed.

On this remedy issue, the Court noted that,

> The disparity in resources between the federal government and local governmental entities both explains and justifies the state procedure. The likelihood that the impact of a federal regulatory statute may effect a taking of property of such value as to threaten the federal treasury with insolvency is remote. Congress has determined that providing a damage remedy for those cases in which a taking occurs will not cause undue hardship. Few local governments could afford the financial impact of a decision that a widely applicable zoning or regulatory ordinance brought about a taking of all affected property.[15]
>
> The California procedural requirements to which plaintiff objects do no more than ensure to the state its right to a prepayment judicial determination that the ordinance or regulation is excessive and will constitute a taking, thus affording the state the option of abandoning the ordinance, regulation, or challenged action, or exempting parcels from its scope if the regulation on use is excessive. As we noted above, the United States Supreme Court has recognized repeatedly the right of the state to reserve the option of rescinding a statute that imposes excessive regulation, and has reaffirmed the principle that a landowner may not compel the state to initiate an eminent domain action. These requirements extend that principle, to the inverse condemnation context.

Id. at 19

---

14. *See* John A. Ramirez, "The California Supreme Court's Foreclosure of the Compensation Remedy for Takings Claimants: Assuming the Effect of Recent California Supreme Court Opinions," 8 *California Land Use Law & Policy Reporter* 193 (Apr. 1999).

15. The prayer in plaintiff's complaint sought damages of $10 million for the alleged taking of his property alone.

As to the takings claim itself, the court stated that, since the owner acknowledged that development was permitted on part of his property and thus conceded that the Glendale ordinance did not deny him all economically feasible use of the property,

> We...reject both plaintiff's claim that a compensable taking of his property necessarily occurred when the Glendale ridge-line ordinance was enacted because development was limited to less than all of the property and his argument that he need not pursue administrative and judicial remedies as a prerequisite to a suit in inverse condemnation. He may not avoid these steps and compel the defendant to purchase the undeveloped portion of his property by electing to seek only compensation in an inverse condemnation action.

Id. at 13. *See also Carson Harbor Village*, 37 F. 3d 468, 476 (9th Cir. 1994) (mobile home park owner's "as applied" takings claim not ripe, and the owner lacked standing to bring a facial takings claim based on mobile home rent control and conversion ordinances, where the owner did not own the property at the time the ordinances at issue were enacted) (overruled on other grounds by *WMX Tech, Inc. v. Miller*, 104 F. 3d 1133, 1136 (9th Cir. 1997))

In *Border Business Park, Inc. v. City of San Diego*, 142 Cal. App. 4th 1538 (2006), the court of appeal rejected an inverse condemnation takings claim when the landowner failed to produce evidence indicating that the city's action had affected it in any unique manner. In *Border*, the owner purchased land to develop a business park. The city later annexed the area containing the property and announced plans to relocate its international airport there, only to later drop such plans. Border claimed, and trial court agreed, that the city's conduct in announcing its airport proposal was reckless and amounted to inverse condemnation (pursuant to *Klopping v. City of Whittier*, 8 Cal. 3d 39 (1972)) by causing a drop in sales at the business park. The court of appeal disagreed, finding that Border failed to show the city's announcements subjected it to "direct and special injury" or affected it in any unique manner different from other owners in the area. *Border*, 142 Cal. App. 4th at 1548–49. The court also rejected Border's inverse condemnation claim that the city actions limiting truck routes to the property amounted to a compensable interference with the right of access where access, while reduced, still remained. *Id.* at 1557–58.

The court in *Del Oro Hills v. City of Oceanside* held that an invalid regulation is not necessarily an unconstitutional one, and stated that in denying damages, "the only available remedy for Del Oro is invalidation of the ordinance." 31 Cal. App. 4th 1060, 1080 (1995).

Measurement of Damages
Permanent Takings

Historically, diminutions in property value that accrue as the result of governmental regulation have been recognized as legitimate public assessments against private ownership. Only those decreases in value resulting from regulations that are held to be excessively restrictive, and thus invalid, will be compensated as a taking. *See Pennsylvania Coal Co. v. Mahon*, 260 U.S. 393, 419 (1922). The general rule that Justice Holmes first identified in *Pennsylvania Coal*, and that the *First English* majority later cited, sets forth this threshold limitation on the proper

Historically, diminutions in property value that accrue as the result of governmental regulation have been recognized as legitimate public assessments against private ownership.

scope of governmental regulation: "while property may be regulated to a certain extent, if regulation goes too far it will be recognized as a taking." *Id.* at 415.

The diminution-in-value test does not provide much practical guidance. Courts applying this test have found no taking based on disparate valuations.

The diminution-in-value test does not provide much practical guidance. Courts applying this test have found no taking based on disparate valuations. *See, e.g., Keystone Bituminous Coal Ass'n v. DeBenedictis*, 480 U.S. 470, 471 (1987) (state statute requiring plaintiffs to forgo mining 27 million tons of coal was not a taking); *Euclid v. Ambler Realty Co.*, 272 U.S. 365, 384–85 (1926) (75 percent diminution in value was not a taking); *William C. Haas & Co. v. City and County of San Francisco*, 605 F. 2d 1117, 1120 (9th Cir. 1979) (90 percent diminution in value was not a taking); *HFH, Ltd. v. Superior Court*, 15 Cal. 3d 508, 516 (1975) (80 percent diminution in value was not a taking).

The *Lucas* Court failed to provide direction as to how damages for a taking should be determined. Based upon a state court finding that the owner's property was rendered valueless by the state coastal zone regulations, the Court suggested the property owner was entitled to compensation. However, the Court did not decide how the damages should be measured. Rather, it remanded the case to state court for a final decision on this issue. 505 U.S. at 1032.

In a footnote to the *Lucas* opinion, the majority admitted that the rhetorical force of the "deprivation of all economically feasible use" rule is greater than its precision, because it "does not make clear the 'property interest' against which the loss of value is to be measured." 505 U.S. at 1016 n. 7. The Court conceded that it did not know how it would analyze the situation in which a regulation requires a developer to leave 90 percent of a rural tract in its natural state. The Court said it was unclear whether such a situation should be analyzed as one in which the owner has been deprived of all economically beneficial use of the burdened portion of the tract, or alternatively, as one in which the owner has suffered a mere diminution in value of the tract as a whole. *Id.* at 1016. *See Taking Sides on Takings Issues, Public and Private Perspectives* (Thomas E. Roberts, ed., ABA, Sect. of State and Local Gov't Law, 2002) and *Taking Sides on Takings Issues, The Impact of Tahoe-Sierra* (Thomas E. Roberts, ed., ABA, Sect. of State and Local Gov't Law, 2003).

The United States Claims Court addressed this issue when it awarded a developer $933,921 plus interest from the date of the Army Corps of Engineers' denial of a Section 404 permit to place fill in a wetland. *See Formanek v. United States*, 26 Cl. Ct. 332 (1992). The property consisted of 12 acres of upland and 99 acres of wetland. Within the wetland acreage, there were 45 acres of calcareous fen, a rare wetland plant community. The developer wished to construct a multi-lot industrial project for which the Corps directed him to apply for an individual Section 404 permit, which ultimately was denied.

Ruling on the developer's subsequent lawsuit, the court held that the denial of the permit was proper. However, the court noted that "[t]he value before the taking was $933,921; the value after the permit denial was perhaps $112,000. This change clearly exceeds the 'mere diminution-in-value' which our society must tolerate in order for government to effectively operate." *Id.* at 340. After acknowledging that a substantial reduction in value alone will not produce a taking, the court found that the permit denial interfered with the developer's investment-backed expectations and this, in combination with the "dramatic reduction," constituted a taking. *Id.* at 340–41.

The *Formanek* court further held that the government's nuisance exception defense was not persuasive. The proposed development simply did not present the extreme threat to the public health, safety, and welfare that precluded the payment of compensation in *Miller v. Schoene*, 276 U.S. 272 (1928) (destruction of trees to prevent spread of disease), and *Allied-General Nuclear Services v. United States*, 839 F. 2d 1572 (Fed. Cir. 1988) (prohibition of plutonium processing to prevent worldwide nuclear proliferation).

For a thorough discussion of takings where development is prohibited on a portion of property consisting of wetlands, *see* chapter 7 (Federal and State Wetland Regulation).

Temporary Takings

As discussed above, prior to the United States Supreme Court's decision in *First English*, California courts had held that a landowner who had been denied all beneficial use of the property through unreasonable governmental regulation was not entitled to compensation until after an agency had decided to continue in effect a regulation that had been declared excessive by the courts, and could initially seek only a court order invalidating the regulation. *First English*, 482 U.S. at 308–309, citing *Agins v. City of Tiburon*, 24 Cal. 3d 266, 275–77 (1979). In *First English*, the United States Supreme Court reversed the California rule, holding that the just compensation requirement under the Takings Clause of the Fifth Amendment, as applied to the states under the Fourteenth Amendment, mandates that a landowner recover compensation if the land use restriction constitutes a taking of its property. 482 U.S. at 321. In overturning the California rule, the Court held that the Constitution requires compensation "for the period during which the taking was effective." *Id.*

The problem that arises from *First English* is that although the Court decided that damages are an available remedy for a taking, it did not discuss the method of calculation. The *First English* court indicated that there must be "payment of fair value for the use of the property during [the period of the taking]." *Id.* at 322. However, it did not indicate how fair value of the use is to be determined. To date, the number of cases addressing this issue has been scant at best, and the California courts have thus far bypassed the opportunity to clarify this confusing area of law.

The problem that arises from First English *is that although the Court decided that damages are an available remedy for a taking, it did not discuss the method of calculation.*

In *Ali v. City of Los Angeles*, the court affirmed a judgment in favor of the plaintiff landowner and an award for inverse condemnation for $1,199,237, based upon a stipulation as to the amount of damages. 77 Cal. App. 4th at 249. Unfortunately, the court did not discuss the calculation of damages, making the case of little value in clarifying the issue of measurement of damages.

In *Brown v. Legal Foundation of Washington*, the United States Supreme Court held that where a taking occurs, "just compensation" required by the Fifth Amendment is measured by "the property owner's loss rather than the government's gain." 538 U.S. 216, 235–36 (2003). At issue in *Brown* was a rule requiring that all client funds paid to any Washington lawyer or law firm (or non-lawyer who is licensed to act as escrowee in real estate closings), which are insufficient to earn net interest for the client, be pooled into a trust account and the interest paid over to the Legal Foundation of Washington. *Id.* at 224–25. By the terms of the rule itself, the client funds subject to the rule would not

In Brown, *the Court held that where a taking occurs, "just compensation" required by the Fifth Amendment is measured by "the property owner's loss rather than the government's gain."*

have earned interest in any event, thus the requirement that interest be turned over to the Legal Foundation was constitutionally irrelevant. The fact that the plaintiffs suffered no loss meant that just compensation was not owed. *Id.* at 240. For further discussion of *Brown, see* Dwight H. Merriam, "Panning for Gold in the Trickle of Supreme Court Cases This Term: What Can We Learn from the IOLTA and Referendum Cases?," 26 *Zoning and Planning Law Report*, no. 6, 1 (June 2003); *Reading the U.S. Supreme Court's Tea Leaves: What Do Its Decisions This Term on IOLTA and Public Referenda and Initiatives Portend?* (ABA Annual Conference, Real Property and State and Local Gov't Secs., August 9, 2003).

IOLTA = Interest on lawyers' trust account

The Importance of Properly Calculating Damages

Duration of Temporary Taking

The only guidance for computation of takings damages provided by the Court in First English *was that aggrieved property owners must be compensated "for the period during which the taking was effective."*

The only guidance for computation of takings damages provided by the Court in *First English* was that aggrieved property owners must be compensated "for the period during which the taking was effective." 482 U.S. at 321. The emphasis that the Court placed on the duration of temporary takings implies that the calculation of interim damages ultimately must depend on a compensation formula. The variables for such a formula were enunciated in the dissent by Justice Stevens in *First English* as "depth," "width," and "length." *Id.* at 330. Regarding depth, "regulations define the extent to which the owner may not use the property in question. With respect to width, regulations define the amount of property encompassed by the restrictions. Finally, ... regulations set forth the durations of the restrictions." *Id.*

One of the most difficult elements to measure is duration. Specifically, when does the period for which compensation is due begin? The filing of an application for administrative relief has been proposed as the proper event by which to initiate the compensation period. *See* Robert Freilich, "Solving the 'Taking' Equation: Making the Whole Equal the Sum of its Parts," 15 *Urb. Law.* 447, 472–73 (1983). Other possible inaugural "events" include notification that an application for administrative relief has been denied, or a judicial determination that a regulatory taking has occurred. However, each of these takings "events" represents a different value for the duration of the compensation period. In order of their increasing magnitude, the initiating events of a proposed takings period could be listed as follows: the judicial determination that a taking has occurred; the filing by the plaintiff of a complaint; the denial of the plaintiff's application for administrative review; and the date on which the regulation had first been adopted or enforced. *First English*, 482 U.S. at 321.

Some commentators have argued that the *First English* Court intended for compensation to be paid retroactively to the date a regulation was either enacted or first enforced.[16] If this argument accurately reflects the majority view, then there is no incentive for owners to file petitions for review early. There is, however, an incentive for cities to expedite the review of an owner's claim, perhaps at the expense of thoroughness. For example, wealthy developers could wait to file a petition for some time before the expiration of the limitations period, to maximize the duration of the compensation period, thereby increasing the stakes for the city.

---

16. *See, e.g.*, Joseph LaRusso, "Paying for the Change," 17 *Envtl. Aff. L. Rev.* 551 (1990).

Measuring Compensation

One of the frustrating features of the variable classifications set forth by Justice Stevens in his *First English* dissent is that they provide little guidance to assist in the calculation of damages. Instead, the values assigned to these variables are entirely dependent on judicial discretion. Consequently, the values are not merely quantitative because they will depend ultimately on qualitative judgments encompassing a series of policy decisions, which must be incorporated into the valuation of the constituent variables that make up the three-part damage formula. These policy decisions necessarily involve significant considerations: the ease of judicial administration and consistency of result, the need to satisfy community expectations regarding equality of treatment, and the need for the timely resolution of takings claims.

Thus, while the three-part formula is theoretically appealing, its practical application is dubious because it leaves open too many means of calculating damages. For example, an aggrieved owner could be compensated for the market value that its property would have if the property were entirely free of regulation. Alternatively, the owner could be compensated for the value of the property interest improperly infringed, *i.e.*, the difference between the fair market value of the land regulated to the permissible limit less its value subject to the invalid restrictions. Finally, the value of the owner's proposed but restricted use could be factored into the damage formula, and the owner could be compensated for the value of the proposed use less the value that the parcel had before it was downzoned, or the value of the proposed use less the value of the parcel with the invalid restrictions in place.

First English instructs that the measure of damages should be the value of the *use* of the property during the period of the temporary taking. There are many approaches to reaching this determination, including: rental value; reasonable investment-backed expectations; equity interest rate; the probability method; "before-and-after;" and option value. Each of these methods is briefly discussed below. For a more extensive discussion of each approach, *see* Robert Meltz *et al.*, *The Takings Issue*, pages 494–99 (Island Press, 1999).

The rental value approach simply assigns damages at the fair market rental value multiplied by the period of the taking. *See Kimball Laundry Co. v. United States*, 338 U.S. 1, 7 (1949). Though simple, this approach is not readily applicable to property where its *future* use is being restricted, *e.g.*, where development is unreasonably delayed.

The *First English* Court, with reference to the issue of compensation for temporary takings, referred to three World War II cases in which the government had exercised its power of eminent domain for a limited period of time in support of the nation's war effort. 482 U.S. at 318 (citing *Kimball Laundry Co. v. United States*, 338 U.S. 1 (1949); *United States v. Petty Motor Co.*, 327 U.S. 372 (1946); *United States v. General Motors Corp.*, 323 U.S. 373 (1945)). In these cases, compensation was based on the value of a leasehold interest in the property taken.

Even assuming this is the appropriate measure of damages, however, it is not clear how the rental value of the property should be determined. In the regulatory takings context, it would rarely make sense to calculate the rental value on the basis of the use in existence at the time of the taking, because very often no use at all is being made of the property. Should the use for which the rental value is determined be the developer's planned use, or the "highest and best" use, if different? Or, since the developer is not necessarily entitled to use the property according to its desires, should the assumed use for calculation of the rental value be the most profitable use allowed under the most restrictive possible lawful regulation?

Another option is to relate damages to the owner's reasonable "investment-backed expectations."

Given these concerns, rental value may not be the proper measure of damages. Another option is to relate damages to the owner's reasonable "investment-backed expectations." Does this mean that the owner's damages should be based somehow on the owner's investment or on some kind of return on that investment? This would tend toward the unlikely result of favoring those owners who have overpaid (or at least paid top dollar) for their property. This was not likely the Court's intention. Indeed, there is an inherent ambiguity in the reference to interference with "investment-backed expectations." On the one hand, the cases establish that even a substantial diminution in value due to a downzoning is not sufficient, alone, to constitute a taking. *See William C. Haas & Co. v. City and County of San Francisco*, 605 F. 2d 1117, 1120–21 (9th Cir. 1979) (a zoning ordinance that reduced the value of private property by more than 90 percent, from $2 million to approximately $100,000 was valid). On the other hand, such a downzoning will almost surely frustrate the investment-backed expectations of any recent purchaser of the property and likely result in a loss on the investment.

The reasonable, investment-backed expectations argument was discussed in Long Beach Equities, Inc. v. County of Ventura.

The reasonable, investment-backed expectations argument was discussed in *Long Beach Equities, Inc. v. County of Ventura*, 231 Cal. App. 3d 1016 (1991). There, in upholding a local growth control regulation, the court referred to the developer's argument that its reasonable investment-backed expectations to profitably build a residential subdivision had been rendered economically infeasible because of past and future delays caused by the laws and the conduct of the defendants. *Id.* at 1039–40. The court said:

> There is considerable controversy whether the courts should consider a landowner's profit expectations in an inverse condemnation action. [Citation omitted.] Although in some cases it may be a legitimate consideration, here LBE has not stated facts which enable it to proceed on this theory....
>
> Prediction of profitability is essentially a matter of reasoned speculation that courts are not especially competent to perform.... [Citations omitted.] The Fifth Amendment is not a panacea for less-than-perfect investment or business opportunities. [Citation omitted.]

Id. at 1039–40

Other courts also have avoided the reasonable investment-backed expectations approach, instead invoking the equity interest approach. For example, the Eleventh Circuit reaffirmed its mandate expressed in *Wheeler v. City of Pleasant Grove*, 833 F. 2d 267 (11th Cir. 1987) (*Wheeler III*), that an award for a temporary taking be based on the "market rate return computed over the period of the temporary taking on the difference between the property's fair market value without the regulatory restriction and its fair market value with the restriction." *Wheeler v. City of Pleasant Grove*, 896 F. 2d 1347, 1350 (11th Cir. 1990) (*Wheeler IV*). The court in *Wheeler IV* held that it was erroneous for the district court to look to the fair market value of the land on which apartments were to be built. Instead, it should have focused on the "difference in the fair market value of appellants' right to develop their project when they received their building permit, and the fair market value of what remained after the city's actions against appellants." *Id.* at 1351.

Although the equity interest approach is a more accurate statement of the owner's actual losses, this approach has been criticized because it requires the court to assume success on the part of the completed development. It also fails to consider other uses of the land under the restrictive regulations, and ignores other investment opportunities for capital that would have gone into the completed development.

Although the equity interest approach is a more accurate statement of the owner's actual losses, this approach has been criticized because it requires the court to assume success on the part of the completed development.

The probability method to measure compensation is an attempt to strike a balance between avoiding the speculativeness of the above approaches while still protecting a property owner from unreasonable delay in its attempts to develop land. This method assesses the probability that a development permit would have been approved in the absence of the restrictive regulation, taking into consideration the highest and lowest valuations of the property proposed by the parties. The full difference between these values may only be awarded if the landowner can show with 100 percent certainty that its land would have been developed but for the restrictive ordinance. Then, the court determines damages by applying a reasonable rate of return to the difference in the high and low valuations.

The probability method was articulated in *Herrington v. County of Sonoma*, 790 F. Supp. 909, 915–16 (N.D. Cal. 1991). The Herringtons owned a parcel of land in Sonoma County for which they submitted a 32-lot subdivision proposal. After the county determined that their proposal was inconsistent with the county's 1978 general plan, they sued the county for violations of due process and equal protection. Following a jury trial, the Herringtons were awarded $2,500,600 in damages. On appeal, the Ninth Circuit affirmed the finding of liability, but vacated the damages award and remanded for a retrial on this issue. *Herrington v. County of Sonoma*. 834 F. 2d 1488, 1503 (9th Cir. 1987), amended by 857 F. 2d 567 (9th Cir. 1988). The district court then considered the remanded issue of damages and used the probability method to determine that property owners were entitled to a reduced amount of damages for property value that was lost due to the county's rejection of their subdivision proposal. 790 F. Supp. at 915–16.

The district court awarded a much smaller amount of damages to the Herringtons, construing their loss as temporary rather than permanent. Thus, the damages were analogous to those for a temporary taking of property. The lost value of the property, as calculated by the Herringtons, was too high because approval of a 32-lot subdivision by the county was speculative. Furthermore, the Herringtons continued to own the property, which had appreciated substantially. The harm suffered due to the county's conduct was a temporary taking of the ability to use or develop the property. Such harm was valued at $52,123.52 plus interest. The total damages award came to $121,472.06, a far cry from the initial award of $2,500,600. 790 F. Supp. at 924–25. This district court opinion was upheld on appeal. *Herrington v. County of Sonoma*, 12 F. 3d 901, 903 (9th Cir. 1993).

The "before and after" approach is a basic diminution of value approach that works in one of two ways. In the first, the court determines the difference between the value of a piece of property on the date the regulatory taking begins and then again on the date the taking ceases. 790 F. Supp. at 914. In the second, the court finds the difference between the value immediately before the invalid regulation was imposed and the value immediately after its imposition. *See* Robert Meltz *et al.*, *The Takings Issue*, page 495 (Island Press, 1999). However, this approach is rarely used by the courts, likely because it does not address *use value* during the taking, but rather only the value of the *fee interest*.

The option value technique calculates damages based on the value of a fictional option to buy the property in question for the period of the regulatory taking.

The option value technique calculates damages based on the value of a fictional option to buy the property in question for the period of the regulatory taking. Though this may be an accurate way of determining the value of the interest taken, it may not bear any relationship to the property owner's actual losses. *See* Meltz *et al.*, page 496.

Perhaps the lesson to glean from the many approaches used by the courts to determine takings damages is that there is no one formula for measuring a temporary taking. Like the question of liability for a taking, the amount of damages is heavily dependent on the facts of a particular case.

Summary

Wheeler IV held that the accurate measure of damages is based on the difference between the property's fair market value without the regulatory restriction and its fair market value with the restriction.

While courts have worked to clarify the process of calculating damages in takings cases, further guidance is needed. The *Wheeler* cases provide the most significant attempt to define a formula. *Wheeler IV* held that the accurate measure of damages is based on the difference between the property's fair market value without the regulatory restriction and its fair market value with the restriction. *Wheeler IV*, 896 F. 2d at 1350. However, its precedential value is limited. It will not be until the United States Supreme Court addresses damage calculations directly that a formula will be uniformly recognized.

The Ripeness Issue—When Is a "Takings" Claim Ripe for Judicial Determination?

Courts have been strict with property owners in determining when they can bring an action in court. They require a property owner not only receive a final determination from the city, but also seek compensation through the procedures the state has provided before a takings claim is ripe. For a good discussion of these two requirements, *see generally Levald Inc. v. City of Palm Desert*, 998 F. 2d 680 (9th Cir. 1993), and *Suitum v. Tahoe Regional Planning Agency*, 520 U.S. 725 (1997). Note, however, that this ripeness rule generally does not apply when the property owner seeks a declaration that a statute or ordinance controlling development is unconstitutional on its face, rather than "as applied" to a particular parcel of land. *See Rezai v. City of Tustin*, 26 Cal. App. 4th 443, 448 (1994).[17]

The Final Determination of the Agency

As to the first requirement for ripeness, the general rule is that a constitutional challenge to a land use regulation is ripe when the landowner has received the

---

17. The distinction between facial challenges to a regulation and "as applied" challenges is important. A facial challenge presents an issue of law, and case-specific factual inquiry is not required. *See Del Oro Hills v. City of Oceanside*, 31 Cal. App. 4th 1060, 1076 (1995).

agency's "final, definitive position regarding how it will apply the regulations at issue to the particular land in question." *MacDonald, Sommer & Frates v. County of Yolo*, 477 U.S. 340, 351 (1986) (citing *Williamson County Reg'l Planning Comm'n v. Hamilton Bank*, 473 U.S. 172 (1985)). In both *Williamson County* and *MacDonald*, the United States Supreme Court required the submission and resubmission of development plans or the application for variances before the takings claim would be ripe for adjudication, unless such requests would be futile.

In *MacDonald*, the Court held that mere rejection of one development application (in that case, a subdivision map) did not constitute a taking because, with its denial of a single application, the county had not yet reached a final decision as to how land use regulation would be applied to the property in question. 477 U.S. at 342. Therefore, it was too early for the Court to determine whether a taking had occurred. *Id.*

The United States Supreme Court attempted to provide further clarification of the "final decision" aspect of a ripeness inquiry in *Palazzolo v. Rhode Island*, 533 U.S. at 620. Palazzolo owned a waterfront parcel consisting mainly of salt marsh subject to tidal flooding over which the Rhode Island Coastal Resources Management Council had regulatory authority. Starting in 1983, Palazzolo applied to develop the land. Two separate applications for a private beach club were denied by the council. Palazzolo filed an inverse condemnation action claiming the council's action had deprived him of "all economically beneficial use" of his property, thus effecting a taking without just compensation. The Rhode Island State Supreme Court ultimately rejected Palazzolo's takings claim on the grounds that it was not ripe, and that Palazzolo could not recover because he could have had "no reasonable investment-backed expectations that were affected by this regulation" since the regulation predated his ownership of the land. *Id.* at 616.[18]

The United States Supreme Court attempted to provide further clarification of the "final decision" aspect of a ripeness inquiry in Palazzolo v. Rhode Island.

The United States Supreme Court disagreed. The Court stated that the central question in resolving the ripeness issue under *Williamson County* is whether the petitioner obtained a final decision from the public agency, here the council, in determining the permitted use for the land. While a landowner must give a land use authority an opportunity to exercise its discretion, once it becomes clear that the agency lacks the discretion to permit any development, or the permissible uses of the property are known to a reasonable degree of certainty, a takings claim is likely to have ripened. *Palazzolo*, 533 U.S. at 620.

The Court noted, however, that *Palazzolo* is quite unlike those cases where an owner challenged a land use authority's denial of a substantial project, leaving doubt whether a more modest submission or an application for a variance would be accepted. *See MacDonald*, 477 U.S. 340 (1986) (denial of 159-home residential subdivision); *Williamson County*, 473 U.S. at 182 (476-unit subdivision); *cf. Agins v. City of Tiburon*, 447 U.S. 255 (1980) (case not ripe because no plan to develop was submitted). Those cases stand for the important principle

---

18. On the question of whether Palazzolo could assert a takings claim since he did not own the property at the time the regulations went into effect, and therefore acquired the property with knowledge of the regulations (the so-called "notice rule"), the Court held that certain enactments are unreasonable and do not become less so due to the passage of time. *Palazzolo*, 533 U.S. at 627. Therefore, the Court held that the post-regulation acquisition was not fatal either to the claim that Palazzolo had been deprived of all economically viable uses of the property (*Lucas*), or to the claim that Palazzolo had been deprived of his reasonable investment-backed expectations (*Penn Central*).

that a landowner may not establish a taking before a land use authority has the opportunity, using its own reasonable procedures, to decide and explain the reach of a challenged regulation. Under the Court's ripeness rules, a takings claim based on a law or regulation that is alleged to go too far in burdening property depends upon the landowner's first having followed reasonable and necessary steps to allow regulatory agencies to exercise their full discretion in considering development plans for the property, including the opportunity to grant any variances or waivers allowed by law.

Palazzolo took a somewhat innovative position, by placing the burden on the government to indicate possible development options once the landowner has made a reasonable application for development. Nevertheless, this case failed to create predictability as to whether a final decision has been made. The inquiry thus remains an essentially *ad hoc* endeavor, but one that *Palazzolo* indicates may now be resolved in favor of landowners when the record is unclear.

In *Dunn v. County of Santa Barbara*, a court of appeal relied on the analysis in *Palazzolo* to determine that a landowner's regulatory takings claims were ripe for adjudication. 135 Cal. App. 4th 1281 (2006). In *Dunn*, the County of Santa Barbara had denied the landowner's application to subdivide a six-acre parcel into two three acre parcels, each with a residence, concluding that only one residence could be built on the property. The trial court found that the claims were not ripe because the landowner had not sought a final determination from the county regarding the extent of development that would be allowed. The court of appeal reversed, holding that the permissible use of the property was known to a reasonably certain degree because the county had made it clear that its wetland and environmental regulations effectively limited the development to one residence. *Id.* at 1300–01. Dunn's regulatory takings claims and the derivative causes of action therefore were ripe even though he had not yet sought permission to build a single-family residence on his property. *Id.* at 1301.

Other California cases have likewise sought to clarify the final decision rule articulated in *Williamson County* and *MacDonald*. In *Kinzli v. City of Santa Cruz*, the property owner's takings claim was dismissed because there had been no attempt to secure a development permit prior to bringing suit. 818 F. 2d 1449, 1452–53 (9th Cir. 1987). Relying on *Williamson County*, the Ninth Circuit ruled that an inverse condemnation cause of action is not ripe until the landowner has secured a "final decision" on a permit application and a request for a variance. This prerequisite could be waived only upon a showing that such requests would be "futile"—"clear beyond peradventure that excessive delay in such a final determination [would cause] the present destruction of the property's beneficial use." *Id.* at 1454. The *Kinzli* court also suggested another test for futility: "the submission of a plan for development is futile if a sufficient number of prior applications have been rejected by the planning authority." *Id.* Therefore, the *Kinzli* rule holds "that a property owner must make use of the development and variance application procedures even when the statute deprives the property owner of all beneficial uses and the application will therefore be denied....[N]o claim will be heard on the merits until rejection of development and variance applications." *Zilber v. Town of Moraga*, 692 F. Supp. 1195, 1199 (N.D. Cal. 1988); *see also County of Alameda v. Superior Court of Alameda County*, 133 Cal. App. 4th 558 (2005).

A final decision by a city requires at least the following: "(1) a rejected development plan and (2) a denial of a variance or other similar land use relief such as a conditional use permit." *Kinzli*, 818 F. 2d at 1454; *Long Beach Equities, Inc. v. County of Ventura*, 231 Cal. App. 3d at 1016. The courts have stated that the term "variance" is not definitive or talismanic; if other types of permits or actions are available and could provide similar relief, they should be sought.

In *Kawaoka v. City of Arroyo Grande*, the Ninth Circuit held that the property owners' claim was not ripe because they had not filed any development application and, in particular, had not applied for a specific plan. 17 F. 3d 1227, 1231–32 (9th Cir. 1994). With the exception of *Kawaoka*, which involved unusual facts, California courts have not required applications for legislative changes (*e.g.*, rezonings or general plan amendments) in order to ripen a claim.

In Kawaoka v. City of Arroyo Grande, *the Ninth Circuit held that the property owners' claim was not ripe because they had not filed any development application and, in particular, had not applied for a specific plan.*

In *Milagra Ridge Partners Ltd. v. City of Pacifica*, a court further clarified an applicant's obligation to obtain a final determination of its development rights. 62 Cal. App. 4th 108 (1998). In that case, the city denied a developer's original application as being inconsistent with the city's general plan. It later approved a different residential development plan and a corresponding general plan amendment, but the amendment was rejected by the electorate. The developer then sued for inverse condemnation. The court held that the developer's claim was not ripe because the developer had not submitted a development application for the property as it was then zoned. The developer's request for a general plan amendment was not the equivalent of a request for a variance under the regulations then in effect. The court noted that, under the present regulations, a substantially greater portion of the property was zoned commercial, which often carries a higher value than residential use. Thus, it was possible that some combination of commercial and residential use would be approved and would produce an economically viable use of the land. *Id.* at 119. Until a final determination was made under the present regulations, however, the claim was not ripe. *See also Sinclair Oil Corp. v. County of Santa Barbara*, 96 F. 3d 401 (9th Cir. 1996).

In *Toigo v. Town of Ross*, the court rejected a takings claim as not being ripe because, even though a subdivider's plans for five lots had been rejected twice, the owner had not sought approval at a lower density. 70 Cal. App. 4th 309 (1998). The court stated that since Toigo made no attempt to alter its vision of the intensity of the development on its property, no final determination had been made. *Id.* at 326.

Both *Toigo* and *Milagra* were cited in *Calprop Corporation v. City of San Diego*, which confirmed that the futility exception is narrow. 77 Cal. App. 4th at 594 (2000). The *Calprop* court stated that only when a landowner proposes specific development and places a practical matter before a governmental agency defined by that development, may a court then determine whether there has been a taking. *Id.*, *see also County of Alameda v. Superior Court of Alameda County*, 133 Cal. App. 4th 558 (2005) (in order to ripen a takings claim and to rely on the futility exception, a landowner must submit a development proposal that the city has rejected).

The Calprop *court stated that only when a landowner proposes specific development and places a practical matter before a governmental agency defined by that development, may a court then determine whether there has been a taking.*

The Ninth Circuit also addressed the final decision rule in *Hoehne*, holding:

> The [U.S.] Supreme Court has recognized that land use planning is not an all-or-nothing proposition. A government entity is not required to permit a landowner to develop property to the full extent it may desire. Denial of the intensive

development desired by a landowner does not preclude less intensive, but still valuable development. *MacDonald, supra*, 477 U.S. at 353. "The local agencies charged with administering regulations governing property development are singularly flexible institutions; what they take with the one hand they may give back with the other." *Id.* at 350. The property owner has a high burden to prove that the agency reached a final decision before the owner can seek compensatory or injunctive relief in federal court on federal constitutional grounds.

Hoehne v. County of San Benito, 870 F. 2d 529, 532–33 (9th Cir. 1989)

Nevertheless, in *Hoehne*, the court held that the owners were not required to apply for a variance, rezoning, conditional use permit, or other similar variations because, given the facts of the case, the variance procedures were not available and other applications would have been futile:

> [I]n actually rezoning the tract to further restrict development, the supervisors themselves sent a clear, and we believe, final signal announcing their views as to the acceptable use of the property. [I]t would have been futile for the Hoehnes to seek a General Plan amendment in their favor, because the supervisors had amended the General Plan in a manner clearly and unambiguously adverse to the application of the landowners.

Id.

The United States Supreme Court unanimously ruled that a landowner seeking to bring a regulatory takings claim need not attempt to sell her TDRs in order to ripen a takings claim.

The United States Supreme Court unanimously ruled that a landowner seeking to bring a regulatory takings claim need not attempt to sell her transfer of development rights (TDRs) in order to ripen a takings claim. *See Suitum*, 520 U.S. 725, 726 (1997). Many local governments have adopted TDR policies to preclude claims that restrictions on development take the value of property without just compensation. TDRs provide a means by which a property's development rights may be sold or transferred for use on a different property. A landowner who acquires TDRs may be allowed to construct additional floor area, dwelling units, or parking spaces. For a more complete discussion of TDRs, *see* chapter 9 (Design Review and Other Development Regulations).

TDR = Transfer of development right

Bernadine Suitum owned an undeveloped lot in Nevada in a "Stream Environment Zone" designated by the Tahoe Regional Planning Agency. In 1987, the agency adopted a regional plan that barred development of property in Stream Environment Zones but gave owners of such property extra TDRs. The agency later denied Suitum permission to build a house. She sued, alleging an unconstitutional taking of her property. The Ninth Circuit affirmed the trial court's ruling that Suitum's action was not ripe for judicial consideration. The appellate court held that, because Suitum had not attempted to sell her TDRs, it was not possible to know the economic impact of the development denial.

The United States Supreme Court reversed the appellate court's decision and held that Suitum could proceed with her suit. *Suitum v. Tahoe Reg'l Planning Agency*, 520 U.S. at 744. The Court noted that there was a "final decision" in this instance because the agency irrevocably had determined that Suitum could not build on her property. Furthermore, the agency lacked discretion to grant an exception to the development ban. The Court also noted that the trial court could estimate the value of Suitum's TDRs from evidence already presented to it. For these reasons, the Court held there was no need for Suitum to market her TDRs before the trial court could decide her takings claim. *Id.* at 726.

In a concurring opinion, Justice Scalia argued that the availability of TDRs is irrelevant to deciding whether property was "taken," because TDRs can only compensate, after the fact, for a denial of the right to build. *Id.* at 741. (Scalia, J., concurring). He observed that if the availability of TDRs dissuades a court from finding a taking, then it may be that no additional compensation is due, regardless of how little the TDRs are worth. But, if TDRs are viewed as a form of compensation, they must be worth as much as the property that was taken. Allowing TDRs to forestall the ripeness of takings claims means "the government can get away with paying much less." *Id.*

Although it determined that a failure to market TDRs presented no bar to a takings suit, the *Suitum* Court did not resolve an important related issue: Should a court view the availability of TDRs as indicating that a development denial falls short of a taking? Or should a court, after finding that denial of development causes a taking, treat TDRs as compensation? The distinction is significant because if TDRs are viewed as compensation for a taking, they must be worth the full amount that was taken by the development denial.

Ripeness must be distinguished from exhaustion of administrative remedies. The test of ripeness is not one of exhaustion of a particular administrative remedy. Instead, "it is a test of whether a developer has exhausted all administrative appeals regarding a particular application for development. The developer must show that it has submitted the appropriate applications necessary to proceed with the particular project and that it has received a final rejection of those applications." *Long Beach Equities, Inc. v. County of Ventura*, 231 Cal. App. 3d at 1034. For a more thorough discussion of the exhaustion doctrine, *see* chapter 21 (Land Use Litigation).

The test of ripeness is not one of exhaustion of a particular administrative remedy. It is a test of whether a developer has exhausted all administrative appeals regarding a particular application for development.

Seeking Compensation Through State Procedures

The second ripeness requirement is that the owner must seek compensation through the procedures the state has provided. *See Williamson County Regional Planning Commission v. Hamilton Bank*, 473 U.S. 172 (1985); *Schnuck v. City of Santa Monica*, 935 F. 2d 171, 173–74 (9th Cir. 1991) (there is a procedure available to a plaintiff in California for seeking compensation from the state). Unless the attempt would be futile, failure to seek compensation in state court requires dismissal of a federal takings case as unripe.

The second ripeness requirement is that the owner must seek compensation through procedures the state has provided.

The Ninth Circuit applied this rule in *Ventura Mobilehome Communities Owners Association v. City of San Buenaventura*, 371 F. 3d 1046 (9th Cir. 2004). The plaintiffs there challenged as a taking a mobile home rent control ordinance passed by the City claiming that it allowed owners to realize a premium on the sale of their mobile homes amounting to the present value of future rent limitations. While the plaintiffs had engaged in substantial negotiations with the City to make changes to the ordinance and had even mediated their dispute, they had not filed a state court proceeding seeking compensation. *Id.* at 1053. Nor had they applied for relief from the rent restrictions under provisions available in the ordinance itself. *Id.* Plaintiffs' failure to seek such compensation or redress in state court made their claims unripe for review in the Ninth Circuit. *Id.* at 1054.

This second ripeness requirement was highlighted by the United States Supreme Court decision in *City of Monterey v. Dela Monte Dunes*, 526 U.S. 687

(1999). Del Monte Dunes and its predecessor tried to develop a 37.6-acre oceanfront parcel in Monterey. In 1986, after five years, five formal denials, and 19 different site plans, the landowner filed suit in federal district court under section 1983 of title 42 of the United States Code, alleging that the city's denials of its applications constituted an uncompensated regulatory taking. The district court dismissed *Del Monte Dunes*' claims as unripe under *Williamson County* in part because it had not sought just compensation in state court.

The Ninth Circuit reversed, concluding that because the state had not provided a compensatory remedy for temporary regulatory takings when the city issued its final denial in 1986, Del Monte Dunes was not required to pursue relief in state court as a precondition to federal relief. *Del Monte Dunes v. City of Monterey*, 920 F. 2d 1496 (9th Cir. 1990). (At that time, the United States Supreme Court had not yet rendered its decision in *First English Evangelical Lutheran Church v. County of Los Angeles*, 482 U.S. 304 (1987), which reversed the California rule and held that the Fifth Amendment mandates a landowner may recover damages if the land use restriction constituted a taking of property.)

The case proceeded to a federal jury, which awarded Del Monte Dunes $1.45 million on its takings claim. The United States Supreme Court later upheld the jury verdict, holding that it had been proper to submit the claim to a federal jury given that no state remedy had been available at the time. The Court noted, however, that a federal court may not entertain a takings claim under section 1983 unless or until the complaining landowner has been denied an adequate post-deprivation remedy, and that, because such a remedy had since been provided in *First English*, the Court's holding was narrowly limited to its specific facts. *City of Monterey v. Del Monte Dunes*, 526 U.S. at 688–89.

The practical result of the requirement that a property owner first seek just compensation through state procedures is that it will almost always preclude litigation of any taking claim in federal court.

The practical result of the requirement that a property owner first seek just compensation through state procedures is that it will almost always preclude litigation of any taking claim in federal court. The landowner must lose his or her takings challenge in state court in order to ripen a federal constitutional challenge; however, under the Full Faith and Credit Clause of the United States Constitution, the state court judgment usually will be given res judicata effect, precluding litigation of the issue in federal court. *See, e.g., Palomar Mobilehome Park Ass'n v. City of San Marcos*, 989 F. 2d 362 (9th Cir. 1993); Thomas E. Roberts, "Fifth Amendment Taking Claims in Federal Court: The State Compensation Requirement and Principles of Res Judicata," 24 *The Urban Lawyer* 479 (1992) ("The ripeness requirement of Fifth Amendment taking claims, coupled with the law of res judicata, precludes claims seeking compensation from state or local action based on the Fifth Amendment from being pursued in federal court."). *But see Fields v. Sarasota Manatee Airport Auth.*, 953 F. 2d 1299, 1303 (11th Cir. 1992) (describing a procedure for "reserving" federal claims for litigation in federal court); Thomas E. Roberts, "Procedural Implications of Williamson County/First English in Regulating Takings Litigation, Reservations, Removals, Diversity Supplemental Jurisdiction, Rooker-Fildman, and Res Judicata," 31 *Envtl. L. Rep.* News & Analysis, no. 4 at 10353–70 (Environmental Law Institute, April 2001).

The United States Supreme Court illustrated in *San Remo Hotel v. City and County of San Francisco* how "issue preclusion" typically occurs in the context of federal court takings challenges. 545 U.S. 323, 342–47 (2005). At issue in *San Remo* was a hotel conversion ordinance that prevented residential hotel owners from converting their units to tourist use unless they constructed new units, rehabilitated old ones, or paid an in lieu fee. Owners of the San Remo Hotel filed a series of administrative appeals and lawsuits in both state and federal court challenging the validity of the ordinance.

In a proceeding brought by San Remo in Federal District Court, the court held that because San Remo had not sought and been denied just compensation in state court for the alleged taking effected by the ordinance, the claim was unripe under *Williamson County*. San Remo therefore proceeded in state court seeking compensation for the alleged taking and reserved in the state court proceedings its right to later pursue its federal takings claim under the Fifth Amendment in federal court, after the conclusion of the state court proceedings. However, after supposedly "reserving" the claims for a later federal court proceeding, San Remo litigated in the state court proceeding a variety of regulatory takings issues, including whether the ordinance substantially advanced a legitimate state interest.

The San Remo owners then returned to Federal District Court to reassert their reserved claims, having now satisfied the *Williamson County* ripeness requirement that the state have denied just compensation. But the Federal Court found that San Remo had fully litigated all of its claims in state court and was now precluded by the doctrine of issue preclusion from relitigating those claims in state court. This conclusion was in part because the California state courts, in deciding San Remo's state claims for just compensation, had at the same time chosen to address and apply federal takings law standards as well, despite the fact that San Remo had sought to reserve these claims for its later federal court proceedings.

The United States Supreme Court agreed with the Federal District Court, holding that issue preclusion prevented San Remo from relitigating in federal court those claims that had been presented to and decided by a state court of competent jurisdiction. San Remo argued that the doctrine of issue preclusion ought not to apply where a litigant has been forced by *Williamson County* to proceed in state court to ripen a federal claim. The Court rejected this argument, noting that a property owner does not necessarily have a right to try its federal claims in federal court. Rather, the full faith and credit statute requires that federal courts give preclusive effect to issues that were conclusively decided in state courts. *San Remo*, 545 U.S. 343-347; *see also Manufactured Home Communities, Inc. v. City of San Jose*, 420 F. 3d 1022 (9th Cir. 2005) (holding that federal takings claims challenging city's mobile home rent ordinance barred by doctrine of res judicata because those claims "depended on issues identical to those that had previously been resolved in the state-court action") (quoting *San Remo*).

The Court noted, however, that the second ripeness requirement of *Williamson County*—that a property owner first seek compensation in state court—will not always preclude a takings plaintiff from the federal courts. First, to the extent that a property owner asserts a facial takings claim, the relief sought would be "distinct from the provision of 'just compensation'" under the Fifth Amendment and therefore could be raised directly in federal court. Alternatively, the San Remo owners could have refrained from litigating in state court those facial takings challenges that they had indicated they intended to "reserve" for judgment in the federal court. *Id.* at 345.

The second ripeness requirement of Williamson County—*that a property owner first seek compensation in state court—will not always preclude a takings plaintiff from the federal courts.*

A concurring opinion in the *San Remo* case, joined by four justices, questions the appropriateness of continuing to require litigants to seek compensation through state procedures before pursuing takings claims in federal court. While noting that the validity of this requirement was not among the issues before the Court, the concurring opinion reasoned that "it is not obvious that either constitutional or prudential principles require claimants to utilize all state compensation procedures before they can bring a federal takings claim." *Id.* at 349. While this concurring opinion has no binding legal effect, and therefore does nothing to lighten the burden of the second ripeness requirement, it leaves open the possibility that the United States Supreme Court will revisit that requirement sometime in the future.

The Illegal Condition Must First Be Challenged in Court As Invalid Before Damages Are Sought for Inverse Condemnation

A property owner seeking to recover money damages on an inverse condemnation claim against a public entity first must establish the invalidity of the conditions the public entity is seeking to impose through an administrative mandamus proceeding.

A property owner seeking to recover money damages on an inverse condemnation claim against a public entity first must establish the invalidity of the conditions the public entity is seeking to impose through an administrative mandamus proceeding. This rule serves the salutary purpose of promptly alerting the agency that its decision is being questioned and that it may be liable for inverse condemnation damages. See *California Coastal Comm'n v. Superior Court (Ham)*, 210 Cal. App. 3d 1488, 1496 (1989). In *Ham*, the California Coastal Commission approved the demolition and rebuilding of a beachfront house on the condition that the property owner dedicate an easement for public access across a strip of beach in front of his home. The owner did not file a mandamus action, but after some time had passed, sought money damages based on the United States Supreme Court ruling in *Nollan*. The court held that Ham's failure to file a mandamus action precluded him from making a takings claim. See also *Rossco Holdings, Inc. v. State of California*, 212 Cal. App. 3d 642, 657 (1989); *Patrick Media Group Inc. v. California Coastal Comm'n*, 9 Cal. App. 4th 592, 617 (1992); *Serra Canyon Company Ltd. v. California Coastal Commission*, 120 Cal. App. 4th 663 (2004).

In *Rezai v. City of Tustin*, the court held that the property owner must exhaust administrative remedies under Code of Civil Procedure section 1094.5 before suing for damages relating to a conditional use permit. 26 Cal. App. 4th 443, 448 (1994). For a good discussion of the purpose of the rule in *Rezai*, see *Hensler v. City of Glendale*, 8 Cal. 4th 1 (1994), where the court said that since the property owner did not sue within the Subdivision Map Act's 90-day statute of limitations, he was prevented from bringing a takings challenge. *Id.* at 446. (Gov't Code § 66499.37); see also *Ojavan Investors, Inc. v. California Coastal Comm'n*, 26 Cal. App. 4th 516, 524–25 (1994).

In *County of San Luis Obispo v. Superior Court*, the court rejected the owner's inverse condemnation claim, holding that because the owner failed to pursue his claim in ordinary mandamus, he could not then wait until he had lost the property in bankruptcy to initiate his suit. 90 Cal. App. 4th 288, 291 (2001). In that case, the owner sought 577 certificates of compliance with the Subdivision Map Act for an 834-acre parcel for which a subdivision map had been filed a hundred years earlier, prior to the enactment of the Map Act. The planning department took the position that the map did not create a separate parcel under the Map Act, and would allow only 135 lots to be developed. The owner appealed the decision to the Board of Supervisors, which upheld the decision of the planning department following a hearing approximately a year and half after the owner's appeal had been filed.

Following denial of his appeal, the owner filed suit for damages, inverse condemnation declaratory relief, and for a writ of administrative mandate. Around the same time, the owner also filed for bankruptcy. The owner then purchased the right to pursue his action from the bankruptcy trustee. Four days following the filing of the owner's suit, the property was acquired by another party in a foreclosure sale. The new owner filed a complaint in intervention, settled its claim with the county, and dismissed its action. With regard to the owner's remaining action, the trial court ruled that the subdivision map in fact created valid lots, and ordered the county to issue certificates of compliance for all 577 lots. The trial court found that the owner had standing to pursue his suit because, in order for him to obtain damages for inverse condemnation, he must first establish by administrative mandamus that the administrative decision was invalid.

On appeal, the court denied standing, holding that because foreclosure divested the owner of all interest in the property prior to completion of judicial review of the administrative action, it was impossible for the owner to obtain relief. *Id.* at 291–92. The court pointed out that the owner had no more rights than any other stranger to the title, and that it is not within the purview of administrative mandamus to make a hypothetical determination whether the owner would be entitled to the certificates if he were the current owner of the property. Finally, the court noted that had the owner believed that the county was unreasonably delaying the processing of his application, he had a remedy in ordinary mandamus. The owner could not, the court concluded, forego such a remedy and wait until he lost the property to act. *Id.* at 294.

The Direction of the California Courts After the *First English, Nollan, Lucas,* and *Dolan* Decisions

As a result of *First English*, *Nollan*, *Lucas*, and *Dolan*, some observers predicted that various land use regulations adopted or decisions rendered, especially by California cities, would be jeopardized. However, even though the courts in past years reviewed local land use decisions more carefully, under the "substantially advances" inquiry recently abandoned as a relevant regulatory takings inquiry, the great majority of reported cases in California continue to be favorable to cities. For example, the court of appeal recently ruled that a county ordinance that prohibited landowners from seizing grazing livestock unless they are located in a fenced area was not a regulatory taking under either the federal or state constitutions. *Herzberg v. County of Plumas*, 133 Cal. App. 4th 1 (2005). Cities also prevailed in several recent decisions of the United States Supreme Court. *See Kelo v. City of New London*, 545 U.S. 469 (2005); *Lingle v. Chevron U.S.A. Inc.*, 544 U.S. 528 (2005); and *San Remo Hotel v. City and County of San Francisco*, 545 U.S. 323 (2005). Some exceptions to these decisions in favor of the city include the following: *City of Monterey v. Del Monte Dunes*, 526 U.S. 687 (1999) (upholding a jury verdict of $1.45 million against the city);

Herrington v. County of Sonoma, 834 F. 2d 1488 (9th Cir. 1987) (monetary damages for denial of due process were awarded); *Ali v. City of Los Angeles*, 77 Cal. App. 4th 246 (1999) (19-month delay in issuing a demolition permit was a temporary taking); *Surfside Colony, Ltd. v. California Coastal Comm'n*, 226 Cal. App. 3d 1260 (1991) (dedication of easement was held invalid; no legal nexus, because no specific study (discussed further in chapter 13 (Exactions)); *Rohn v. City of Visalia*, 214 Cal. App. 3d 1463 (1989) (street dedication invalid since there was no legal nexus); *Bixel Assocs. v. City of Los Angeles*, 216 Cal. App. 3d 1208 (1989) (fire hydrant fees illegal because there was not a sufficient nexus).

Civil Rights Action [19]

Federal law provides a possible remedy whenever anyone acting under color of state law deprives a person of federal rights, privileges, or immunities.

Federal law provides a possible remedy whenever anyone acting under color of state law deprives a person of federal rights, privileges, or immunities. 42 U.S.C. § 1983. It does not apply to actions taken by federal officers. *See District of Columbia v. Carter*, 409 U.S. 418, 424 (1973). State action of some kind is required; a private person, acting alone, cannot be liable under section 1983. *See Taylor v. Nichols*, 558 F. 2d 561, 564 (10th Cir. 1977). A number of cases have held that damages may be recovered for overregulation of land under section 1983. *See, e.g., San Diego Gas & Elec. Co. v. City of San Diego*, 450 U.S. 621, 654–55 (1981); *Lake Country Estates, Inc. v. Tahoe Reg'l Planning Agency*, 440 U.S. 391, 402–03 (1979). However, a landowner cannot recover under section 1983 when it is shown that that provisions of the substantive statute under which relief is sought provide more limited remedies than those contained in section 1983. *City of Rancho Palos Verdes v. Abrams*, 544 U.S. 113 (2005) (landowner sought injunctive relief and damages under the federal Telecommunications Act of 1986, 47 U.S.C. § 332(c)(7), based on city's denial of permission to construct a radio tower on his property).

A section 1983 claim is not subject to the same ripeness requirements associated with takings claims.

A section 1983 claim is not subject to the same ripeness requirements associated with takings claims. In *Carpinteria Valley Farms, Ltd. v. County of Santa Barbara*, a landowner sought to develop a home and personal polo field in Santa Barbara County. The county imposed numerous conditions on the development, including a requirement that he apply for a conditional use permit for the polo field, even though the county allowed others to build polo fields without such a permit. 334 F. 3d 796, 801(2003), *as modified in* 344 F. 3d 822 (9th Cir. 2003). After a lengthy period of trying to resolve his differences with the county, the landowner sued under section 1983, claiming that the county violated his constitutional rights, primarily because he had been vocal in criticizing a group which supported a county supervisor. The district court characterized these claims to be "as applied" takings challenges. Accordingly, the court applied the *Williamson County* finality rules and held that they were not ripe for review because there had been no final agency decision on the development applications. *Id.* at 798; *see Williamson County Regional Planning Commission v. Hamilton Bank*, 473 U.S. 172 (1985).

On appeal, the Ninth Circuit disagreed with the district court's analysis because the constitutional claims asserted by the landowner pertaining to the development applications were not "as applied" takings claims. Rather, they

---

19. *See* Richard G. Carlisle, *The Section 1983 Land Use Case in Sword and Shield Revisited*, page 416 (Mary Kass ed., 1998).

were separate claims supported by allegations of discrete constitutional violations. *Carpinteria Valley Farms, Ltd. v. County of Santa Barbara*, 334 F. 3d at 801, *as modified in* 344 F. 3d 822 (9th Cir. 2003). The appellate court stated that if the county's requirements were imposed in retaliation for the landowner's exercise of free speech rights to criticize the county, then he had suffered harm and need not wait for further action by the county. The same reasoning applied to the landowner's claims that the county violated his equal protection and due process rights, and the Ninth Circuit found that his claims were ripe for adjudication. 344 F. 3d. at 802.

Although the county had granted eleven development permits, the landowner's challenge was to the procedure he had endured to get those permits. The court held that even if the county relented today and issued all of the permits that had been applied for, the landowner still would have a claim for injury based upon the treatment he allegedly received (*e.g.*, restricting him from playing polo on his property since 1994, forcing him to consider possible county retaliation before he exercised his First Amendment rights, and increasing the time and money necessary to develop his property). *Id.*

The United States Supreme Court has held that local governments are "persons" for purposes of section 1983, and that local governing bodies and local officials can, therefore, be sued directly in their official capacities for monetary, declaratory, and injunctive relief where an allegedly unconstitutional action implements or executes a policy, ordinance, regulation, or decision officially adopted or promulgated by those whose edicts or acts may fairly be said to represent official policy. *See Monell v. Dept. of Social Servs.*, 436 U.S. 658, 688 (1978); *see also Owen v. City of Independence*, 445 U.S. 622, 645–46 (1980) (section 1983 creates a species of tort liability that on its face admits of no immunities; thus, a municipality has no immunity flowing from its constitutional violations and may not assert the good faith of its officers as a defense to such liability).

The United States Supreme Court has held that local governments are "persons" for purposes of section 1983.

In *Lake Country Estates, Inc. v. Tahoe Regional Planning Agency*, the United States Supreme Court entertained an action for inverse condemnation that had been dismissed at the district court level because the planning agency had no power of eminent domain and thus was not properly subject to an action in inverse condemnation. 440 U.S. 391, 401–03 (1979). The Court held that a cause of action could be stated against the agency under section 1983 and opened the doors to litigation of allegations that police power and zoning regulations were excessive. *Id.* at 399–400.

Actions under section 1983 will lie in state courts as well as in federal courts. *See Williams v. Horvath*, 16 Cal. 3d 834, 837 (1976). Therefore, this section authorizes state courts to award monetary damages for improper land use decisions. However, successful use of section 1983 to recover damages, as with claims for damages for inverse condemnation, has not been evident to date, apparently because of the courts' hesitancy to require cities to pay large amounts of compensation to property owners. *See Grupe Dev. Co. v. California Coastal Comm'n*, 166 Cal. App. 3d 148 (1985); *MacLeod v. County of Santa Clara*, 749 F. 2d 541, 544 (9th Cir. 1984).

Actions under section 1983 will lie in state courts as well as in federal courts.

For example, the California Supreme Court, in overturning an $11.5 million jury award, held there was no violation of section 1983 or substantive due process when a city acted in its legislative capacity in adopting new ordinances and regulations that prevented a development project from being approved, where the developer had no vested right to build an apartment complex. *See Stubblefield Constr. Co. v. City of San Bernardino*, 32 Cal. App. 4th 687, 706–07 (1995).

The ripeness doctrine applies equally to a civil rights claim and takings claim. *See Long Beach Equities, Inc. v. County of Ventura*, 231 Cal. App. 3d at 1041. Section 1983 also provides a right to a jury trial for certain takings cases in federal court. *See City of Monterey v. Del Monte Dunes*, 526 U.S. at 707–08. Jury trials in takings cases, however, are extremely rare. Further, since 1992, takings compensation cases have generally been required to be tried in state courts, where jury trials on takings claims usually are not allowed.

Damages Resulting from Constitutional Violations— Due Process and Equal Protection

A claim that a city has damaged property in violation of the owner's rights guaranteed by U.S. constitutional provisions relating to due process and equal protection does not require proof that all use of the property has been denied.

A claim that a city has damaged property in violation of the owner's rights guaranteed by United States constitutional provisions relating to due process and equal protection does not require proof that all use of the property has been denied. *See Herrington v. County of Sonoma*, 834 F. 2d at 1498, *Harris v. County of Riverside*, 904 F. 2d 497, 503–04 (9th Cir. 1990) (a county violated a landowner's due process rights when it deprived him of the commercial zoning on his property without prior notice of its proposed action).

Relying on *Harris*, the court in *Carpinteria Valley Farms* held that a landowner's equal protection and due process claims were not takings claims within the meaning of *Williamson*, but rather independent section 1983 claims which were ripe for review. 334 F. 3d at 798–99, *as modified in* 344 F. 3d 822 (9th Cir. 2003). The fact that the landowner's constitutional claims arose in the context of a county's permitting process did not render those claims "unripe," so long as the landowner otherwise met the ripeness requirements set forth in *Harris*. *Id.* at 802.

A due process claim under the Fourteenth Amendment to the United States Constitution can allege that the contested action was arbitrary and capricious and, thus, not a proper exercise of the police power. *See Lingle v. Chevron U.S.A. Inc.*, 544 U.S. 528, 548 (2005) (Kennedy, J., concurring) (noting that land use regulations that are arbitrary or irrational may violate a landowner's due process rights). However, the California Supreme Court has held that "an ordinance restrictive of property use will be upheld against due process attack, unless its provisions are 'clearly arbitrary and unreasonable, having no substantial relation to the public health, safety, morals or general welfare.'" *Nash v. City of Santa Monica*, 37 Cal. 3d 97, 103 (1984); *see also Kawaoka v. City of Arroyo Grande*, 17 F. 3d 1227, 1234 (9th Cir. 1994).

In *Barancik v. County of Marin*, the Ninth Circuit responded to the owner's argument that the zoning of one residence per 60 acres was a violation of his substantive due process rights by stating:

> The district court found that the County had a reasonable purpose in zoning as it did and applying the zoning as it did to Loma Alta Ranch. We agree. To prove his case Barancik had to show that the County's zoning was arbitrary and irrational. *Usery v. Turner Elkhorn Mining Co.*, 428 U.S. 1, 15 (1976). He attempted to do so by concentrating on the zoning in relation to his own property and arguing that just as many cows would graze there if there were

28 residences as would if there were nine. The argument, of course, is myopic. Zoning is of an area. The planner wants to preserve an area for a given use. Yielding to Barancik's arguments would set a precedent which, followed, would lead to the emulative destruction of agriculture in Nicasio Valley. The cowboy and the farmer may be friends as the song has it, but not the rancher and the urban commuter, at least not if commuters, with the roads they need and the cars they drive and the tastes they have, begin to predominate in the countryside. Marin's zoning no doubt preserves a bucolic atmosphere for the benefit of a portion of the population at the expense of those who would flow into the county if there was no zoning. The Constitution lets that decision be made by the legislature. The Countywide Plan is a legislative declaration that there will be a corridor in Marin agricultural in its use. The choice was not irrational, the application to Barancik is not arbitrary.

872 F. 2d 834, 836 (9th Cir. 1988)

The Ninth Circuit later held that a rent control ordinance restricting rent increases in mobile home parks was not a denial of substantive due process. See *Levald Inc. v. City of Palm Desert*, 998 F. 2d 680 (9th Cir. 1993). In so ruling, the court laid out the rule of judicial deference to the legislative body in such cases:

> In reviewing economic legislation on substantive due process grounds, we give great deference to the judgment of the legislature. "[O]rdinances survive a substantive due process challenge if they were designed to accomplish an objective within the government's police power, and if a rational relationship existed between the provisions and purpose of the ordinances." [T]here is no requirement that the statute actually advance its stated purpose; rather, the inquiry focuses on whether "the governmental body could have had no legitimate reason for its decision." "[T]he law need not be in every respect logically consistent with its aims to be constitutional. It is enough that there is an evil at hand for correction, and that it might be thought that the particular legislative measure was a rational way to correct it." [Citations omitted]

Id. at 690

The Ninth Circuit later held that a rent control ordinance restricting rent increases in mobile home parks was not a denial of substantive due process.

In a very brief opinion, the United States Supreme Court held that the Equal Protection Clause protects not only classes or groups, but also individuals who constitute a "class of one." See *Village of Willowbrook v. Olech*, 528 U.S. 562 (2000). In this case, the owners had asked the Village of Willowbrook to connect their property to the municipal water supply. The village at first conditioned the connection on the owners' granting the village a 33-foot easement. The Olechs objected, claiming that other property owners seeking access to the village's water supply were only required to grant a 15-foot easement. After a three-month delay, the village agreed to connect the owners to the municipal water supply with a 15-foot easement.

The owners sued the village under the Fourteenth Amendment, claiming that the village's demand for a 33-foot easement was "irrational and wholly arbitrary." *Id.* at 1074. In affirming the Seventh Circuit decision, the Supreme Court noted that its prior opinions recognized successful "class of one" equal protection claims where "the plaintiff alleges that she has been intentionally treated differently from others similarly situated and that there is not rational basis for the difference in treatment." *Id.* The Court held that the owners' complaint alleging, among other things, that the village's demand was "irrational and wholly arbitrary," was sufficient to state a claim for relief under traditional equal protection analysis. *Id*. at 1075.

The requirement of securing a "final decision" from the local agency also applies to a substantive or procedural due process claim or denial of equal protection claim. *See Long Beach Equities, Inc. v. County of Ventura*, 231 Cal. App. 3d at 1041–42; *Herrington v. County of Sonoma*, 857 F. 2d 567 (9th Cir. 1988). The second ripeness requirement—seeking state remedies—does not apply, because plaintiffs in such cases are not seeking "just compensation."

There seems to be a distinction in finding a violation of substantive due process when a city acts in its legislative capacity as compared to its nonlegislative, "quasi-adjudicatory" administrative capacity. In *Cohan v. City of Thousand Oaks*, a court held that the cumulative procedural errors committed by the city impaired the adequacy of the appeal hearing on the Cohans' subdivision and that, therefore, their due process rights were violated. 30 Cal. App. 4th 547, 556–57 (1994). Some of the errors involved the council itself appealing the planning commission's decision, failure to inform the Cohans of the grounds for the appeal, and unfairly placing the burden on the Cohans "to convince the Council of the correctness of the Planning Commission's decision." *Id*. at 548. The court held that "this stands due process on its head." *Id*. at 560.

In contrast, another court held there was no denial of civil rights or substantive due process when a city was acting in its legislative capacity and the plaintiff had no vested right to build an apartment complex. *See Stubblefield Constr. Co. v. City of San Bernardino*, 32 Cal. App. 4th 687, 707–08 (1995). In this case, one councilperson used everything in his power to stop the project. While arbitrary zoning actions directed at a specific property may be invalidated (*Arnel Dev. Co. v. City of Costa Mesa*, 126 Cal. App. 3d 330 (1981)), the *Stubblefield* court said the actions it reviewed were general in application. Therefore, the court said that, in its view, there was nothing arbitrary or unreasonable in the zoning actions taken. The city's revised multi-family zoning ordinance applied to all multi-family housing in the city. An urgency ordinance applied to all development applications pending at the time it was adopted, and a moratorium ordinance applied to all foothill property north of a specified line. General plan revisions affected all property in the city, while hillside provisions were based on slope percentages. These, the court said, were all rational classifications. It also noted that it was reluctant to minutely scrutinize the legislative processes of the city in the manner suggested by the Stubblefields. "[T]his is an ordinary dispute between a developer and a municipality and we conclude that the claims asserted simply do not qualify as a deprivation of substantive due process." *Id*. at 712.

The distinction in substantive due process cases between legislative and administrative action disappears, however, in the context of land use referenda. In *City of Cuyahoga Falls v. Buckeye Community Hope Foundation*, the United States Supreme Court held that the subjection of a local land use decision to a city's referendum process did not constitute per se arbitrary government conduct in violation of due process "regardless of whether that ordinance reflected an administrative or legislative decision." 538 U.S. 188 (2003). The City of Cuyahoga Falls, Ohio, passed an ordinance authorizing developers to construct a low-income housing complex. Citizens submitted a referendum petition to the city asking that the ordinance be repealed or submitted to a vote. Pursuant to the city's charter, the referendum petition stayed the project until the voters voted. The city engineer, on advice from the city's law director, denied the developers' request for building permits. The developers sued the city, alleging that submission of the ordinance to voters violated the Equal Protection and Due Process Clauses.

In ruling for the city, the Supreme Court held that the developers failed to present sufficient evidence of an equal protection violation. The Court stated that it is quite clear that the "[p]roof of racially discriminatory intent or purpose is required" to show a violation of the Equal Protection Clause. *Id.* at 1394. The developers, claiming injury from the referendum petitioning process, not the referendum itself, had not presented proof of racially discriminatory intent. Submitting the petition to voters was pursuant to the city's charter, which set out a facially neutral petitioning procedure. Acting on the advice of the city's law director, the engineer performed a nondiscretionary ministerial act consistent with the city charter in refusing to issue permits while the referendum was pending. *Id.*

Nor did subjecting the ordinance to the city's referendum process constitute arbitrary government conduct in violation of substantive due process. First, the city engineer's refusal to issue permits while the petition was pending "in no sense constituted egregious or arbitrary government conduct" denying the developers the benefit of the development ordinance. In light of the charter's provision that no challenged ordinance can go into effect until approved by the voters, the law director's instruction to the engineer represented an "eminently rational directive." *Id.* at 1396.

Secondly, the city's submission of an administrative land use determination to the charter's referendum procedures did not constitute per se arbitrary conduct. The Court noted that the "people retain the power to govern through referendum with respect to any matter, legislative or administrative, within the realm of local affairs." *Id.* Because the developers did not challenge the referendum itself, they derived no benefit from the principle that a referendum's substantive result may be invalid if it is arbitrary or capricious. *Id.* For further discussion of *City of Cuyahoga Falls, see* Dwight H. Merriam, "Panning for Gold in the Trickle of Supreme Court Cases This Term: What Can We Learn from the IOLTA and Referendum Cases?," 26 *Zoning and Planning Law Report*, no. 6, 1 (June 2003); *Reading the U.S. Supreme Court's Tea Leaves: What Do Its Decisions This Term on IOLTA and Public Referenda and Initiatives Portend?* (ABA Annual Conference, Real Property and State and Local Gov't Sects., August 9, 2003).

The Ninth Circuit previously ruled that substantive due process claims could not apply where the government has allegedly effected a taking violative of the Fifth Amendment, since the Takings Clause provided "an explicit source of constitutional protection against the challenged governmental conduct." *Armendariz v. Penman*, 75 F. 3d 1311 (9th Cir. 1996), *see also Squaw Valley Development Co. v. Goldberg*, 375 F. 3d 936, 949 (9th Cir. 2004). Where a regulation has denied economically viable use of property, the claim is one under the Takings Clause and a substantive due process argument based on the same set of facts is preempted by the takings claim.

Recently, however, the Ninth Circuit recognized that the Supreme Court's *Lingle* decision had undermined that rule. *See Crown Point Development, Inc. v.*

Where a regulation has denied economically viable use of property, the claim is one under the Takings Clause and a substantive due process argument based on the same set of facts is preempted by the takings claim.

City of Sun Valley, __ F. 3d __, 2007 WL 31977049 (9th Circ. 2007) (discussing *Lingle*, 544 U.S. at 532). In *Crown Point Development*, a developer alleged that a city's arbitrary and irrational denial of its development applications violated its right to substantive due process. The district court dismissed the claim based on the rule of *Armendariz*, which did not allow substantive due process claims pursuant to the Fourteenth Amendment when the interest at stake was real property.

The Ninth Circuit reversed. It noted that *Armendariz* was based upon a pre-*Lingle* view that a regulation that does not "substantially advance legitimate state interests" is a taking. It further explained:

> However, this understanding of the *Agins'* "substantially advances" language—i.e., that it is a "stand-alone regulatory takings test"—was rejected by the Supreme Court in *Lingle*. 544 U.S. at 540. The Court concluded "that this formula prescribes an inquiry in the nature of due process, not a takings, test, and that it has no proper place in our takings jurisprudence." *Id*. As the Court explained, the "substantially advances" test "does not help to identify those regulations whose effects are functionally comparable to government appropriation or invasion of private property; it is tethered neither to the text of the Takings Clause nor to the basic justification for allowing regulatory actions to be challenged under the Clause." *Id*. at 542.
>
> In this, *Lingle* pulls the rug out from under our rationale for totally precluding substantive due process claims based on arbitrary or unreasonable conduct. As the Court made clear, there is no specific textual source in the Fifth Amendment for protecting a property owner from conduct that furthers no legitimate government purpose.

Id. at *3

Accordingly, the Fifth Amendment would preclude a due process challenge only if the alleged conduct is actually covered by the Takings Clause. *Lingle* indicates that a claim of arbitrary action is not such a challenge. It is therefore no longer possible to read *Armendariz* as imposing a blanket obstacle to all substantive due process challenges to land use regulation.

The Ninth Circuit explicitly held that the Fifth Amendment does not invariably preempt a claim that land use action lacks any substantial relation to the public health, safety, or general welfare. *Id*. at *4.

The California Supreme Court, however, has recognized the viability of a substantive due process claim in the context of rent control ordinances. In *Kavanau v. Santa Monica Rent Control Board*, the Court interpreted and applied substantive due process principles to a local rent control law and held that "a rent control law that merely allows a landlord to recoup the bare cost of a necessary capital improvement runs the risk of being confiscatory and thereby violating the landlord's right to [substantive] due process of law." 16 Cal. 4th at 773. The *Kavanau* court provided a conceptual distinction between takings and substantive due process in the rent control context. "[T]akings protection focuses on the impact of the government's action: whether the government has in effect appropriated private property for its use of the property," whereas "the due process protection focuses on the government's means and purpose: whether the government's method rationally furthers legitimate ends." *Id*. at 770–71.

In a case raising issues of both inverse condemnation and substantive due process in the rent control context, the court in *H.N. & Frances C. Berger Foundation v. City of Escondido*, 127 Cal. App. 4th 1 (2005) (*Berger Foundation*) relied upon the *Galland* and *Kavanau* decisions. In *Berger Foundation*, the owner of a mobile home park challenged a city resolution authorizing a smaller rent increase than the one for which it applied, on the grounds that the authorized rent increase was confiscatory because it would not allow a reasonable return on investment. The court rejected this claim. According to the court, to avoid unconstitutional confiscation, a constitutionally valid rent control ordinance must allow landowners to earn a fair return on their investment. While such a fair rate of return has "a broad zone of reasonableness," it must allow profits to be adjusted for inflation so that the real value of profit does not unconstitutionally diminish over time. *Id.* at 8. However, there is no set formula for determining a reasonable return on investment, and annual rent increases do not have to be indexed so that they are equal to increases in inflation. *Id.* at 14–15. Cities therefore have wide latitude to balance the interests of property investors with those of tenants. Thus, there can be no taking or other civil rights violation if a city allows for future rent adjustments that allow a fair rate of return on investment. *Id.* at 16.

In *Galland v. City of Clovis*, the plaintiff landlord brought a due process claim seeking damages for allegedly confiscatory rent control restrictions, as well as costs in the form of administrative and attorneys' fees, imposed on the landlord in the process of seeking a rent increases. 24 Cal. 4th 1003 (2001). The court held that a future rent adjustment (a "*Kavanau* adjustment") would preclude damages for violation of the right to constitutional due process under 42 U.S.C. section 1983. *Id.* at 1030–31. With regard to the due process claim based on costs incurred by the landlord in seeking rent increases, the court concluded that such a claim may lie when one of two conditions is present: (1) the costs imposed are part of a government effort to deliberately flout established law, *e.g.*, obstruct legitimate rent increases; or (2), the landlord suffers confiscation as a result of the imposition of such costs. *Id.* at 1005.

As the foregoing cases indicate, substantive due process rarely will protect property rights in the land use context. That said, recent California cases seem at least to recognize that substantive due process provides some protections in the rent control arena. Cities employing rent control schemes to regulate rent increases therefore should allow future rent adjustments that give landowners the opportunity to earn a fair rate of return on their investments.

Substantive due process rarely will protect property rights in the land use context. However, recent California cases seem at least to recognize that substantive due process provides some protections in the rent control arena.

13

Exactions: Dedications and Development Fees

Overview[1]

In nearly all aspects of land use approval, significant controversies arise over the amount and type of exactions a city may impose when approving a development, whether they require dedications of property or the imposition of development fees. The concept is simple in theory: The developer, in return for receiving the city's approval to develop the land and realize a profit, agrees to donate to the city an amount of land or money needed to provide certain services and amenities necessitated by the anticipated influx of new residents or employees into the community as a result of such development. *See Associated Home Builders, Inc. v. City of Walnut Creek*, 4 Cal. 3d 633, 644 (1971); *Trent Meredith, Inc. v. City of Oxnard*, 114 Cal. App. 3d 317, 328 (1981).

Cities contend that this arrangement is only fair. Developers create new, sometimes overwhelming burdens on city services; therefore, they should offset the additional responsibilities required of cities through dedication of land or the payment of fees. Developers, on the other hand, argue that these extra expenses drive up the cost of development and result in higher costs for the home buyer or commercial users, thus eliminating affordable housing and/or driving away needed commerce. In an effort to avoid such costs, developers have challenged such fees by claiming that they are special taxes illegally imposed without a vote of the people, or that the dedications are takings of property without just compensation. Through the exercise of its police power, however, a city has

> *In nearly all aspects of land use approval, significant controversies arise over the amount and type of exactions a city may impose when approving a development.*

---

1. For a good overview of exactions, *see* David L. Callies, Daniel J. Curtin, Jr., and Julie A. Tappendorf, *Bargaining for Development: A Handbook on Development Agreements, Annexation Agreements, Land Development Conditions, Vested Rights and the Provision of Public Facilities* (Environmental Law Institute, Wash. D.C. 2003); Daniel J. Curtin, Jr., *Exactions, Dedications and Development Agreements Nationwide and in California: When and How Do Nollan/Dolan Apply*, 33rd Annual Institute of Planning, Zoning and Eminent Domain, ch. 2 (Matthew Bender, 2003); Daniel J. Curtin, Jr., *Dolan and Nollan Takings and Exactions, California Style*, 32nd Annual Institute on Planning, Zoning and Eminent Domain (Matthew Bender, October 2002); William Abbott et al., *Exactions and Impact Fees in California* (Solano Press, 2001); Daniel J. Curtin, Jr., "How the West Was Won: Takings and Exactions—California Style," *Trends in Land Use Law from A to Z*, ch. 9 (ABA 2001). *See also* Ronald H. Rosenberg, "The Changing Culture of American Land Use Regulation: Paying for Growth with Impact Fees," 59 *SMU L. Rev.* 177 (2006).

the authority to impose these exactions, so long as they are reasonable and have the required nexus to the proposed development.

The Proper Exercise of Police Power[2]

A city relies on its authority to exercise its police power to impose conditions on a development project through the dedication of land or the payment of fees. Cal. Const. art. XI, sec. 7; *California Bldg. Indus. Ass'n v. Governing Bd. of the Newhall Sch. Dist.*, 206 Cal. App. 3d 212, 234 (1988). The United States Supreme Court and the California Supreme Court have long held that the regulation of land use does not effect a taking of property if the regulation does not deny the property owner economically viable use of the land. *See Lingle v. Chevron U.S.A. Inc.*, 544 U.S. 528 (2005); *Dolan v. City of Tigard*, 512 U.S. 374, 385 (1994); *Lucas v. South Carolina Coastal Council*, 505 U.S. 1003, 1016 (1992); *Nollan v. California Coastal Comm'n*, 483 U.S. 825, 834 (1987); *Landgate, Inc. v. California Coastal Comm'n*, 17 Cal. 4th 1006 (1998).

Development: A Privilege or a Right?

Over the years, there has been a great deal of controversy over whether development is a privilege or a right. In California, courts repeatedly have held that there is no right to develop and that development is instead a privilege. Examples of such decisions are:

- No right to subdivide. *Associated Home Builders, Inc. v. City of Walnut Creek*, 4 Cal. 3d 633 (1971)
- Development is a privilege. *Trent Meredith, Inc. v. City of Oxnard*, 114 Cal. App. 3d 317 (1981)
- No right to go out of business. *Nash v. City of Santa Monica*, 37 Cal. 3d 97 (1984)
- No right to convert an apartment to a condominium. *Norsco Enters. v. City of Fremont*, 54 Cal. App. 3d 488 (1976); *Griffin Dev. Co. v. City of Oxnard*, 39 Cal. 3d 256 (1985)
- No right to convert residential hotel units to other uses; it is a "privilege." *Terminal Plaza Corp. v. City and County of San Francisco*, 177 Cal. App. 3d 892 (1986)
- Transit fees are "exacted only if the developer voluntarily chooses to create new office space" and are "for the privilege of developing a particular parcel." *Russ Bldg. Partnership v. City and County of San Francisco*, 199 Cal. App. 3d 1496, 1506 (1987)

The United States Supreme Court has sought to clarify this issue: "[T]he right to build on one's own property—even though its exercise can be subjected to legitimate permitting requirements—cannot remotely be described as a 'governmental benefit.'" *Nollan v. California Coastal Comm'n*, 483 U.S. at 833.

---

2. *See Special Issues Under Takings Law: Findings, Fees and Dedications* (Institute for Local Self Government 1999).

While the Court's decision in *Nollan* can be interpreted as stating a right to build *something* on one's own property, it cannot be read as recognizing any right to build a particular project:

> [Plaintiff] relies in particular on footnote 2 of *Nollan*, where the Court, in responding to Justice Brennan's dissent, said that "the right to build on one's own property—even though its exercise can be subject to legitimate permitting requirements—cannot remotely be described as a 'government benefit.'" [Plaintiff] argues that the reference to building on one's property is a "right" and not a "benefit" is somehow inconsistent with the doctrine that a "right" to build a *particular project* vests only after substantial work is performed in reliance on a government permit. (emphasis in original.)
>
> There are two difficulties with this argument. First, the *Nollan* case dealt only with a property owner's right to build a single-family house, traditionally among the most minimally regulated uses [footnote omitted]. Second, and more important, the *Nollan* court's reference to a landowner's abstract "right" to build in no way suggests that a landowner has an unconditional right under the taking or deprivation clauses of the federal Constitution to build any particular project he chooses. The sentence quoted from the *Nollan* footnote is qualified by its reference to "legitimate permitting requirements." The footnote does not imply that a permitting requirement is "illegitimate" simply because it disallows a previously permitted use. It is well established that there is no federal Constitutional right to be free from changes in land use laws.

Lakeview Dev. Corp. v. City of South Lake Tahoe, 915 F. 2d 1290, 1294–95 (9th Cir. 1990)

To date, notwithstanding *Nollan*, California courts have not changed their position that development is merely a privilege. For example, in *Saad v. City of Berkeley*, the court rejected the property owner's "right to build" argument based on footnote 2 of *Nollan* when the city denied a use permit for a home on the grounds that it would impair views and have a towering effect on the neighborhood. 24 Cal. App. 4th 1206, 1212–13 (1994). In another decision also rendered after *Nollan*, the court struck down a school district fee as being an invalid special tax. In so doing, it stated that "[t]ypically, a development fee is an exaction imposed as a precondition for the *privilege* of developing the land." *California Bldg. Indus. Ass'n v. Governing Bd. of the Newhall Sch. Dist.*, 206 Cal. App. 3d 212, 235 (1988) (citing *Candid Enters., Inc. v. Grossmont Union High Sch. Dist.*, 39 Cal. 3d 878 (1985) (emphasis added); *Associated Home Builders, Inc. v. City of Walnut Creek*, 4 Cal. 3d 633 (1971)); *see also Sinclair Paint Co. v. State Bd. of Equalization*, 15 Cal. 4th 866, 874 (1997) (it is a "voluntary decision to develop or to seek other government benefits or privileges"); *Clark v. City of Hermosa Beach*, 48 Cal. App. 4th 1152, 1178–84 (1996) (a denial of a fair hearing on a development application did not violate the owners' procedural or substantive due process rights, since the owners had no protected property right or interest in an application for a specific residence); *California Bldg. Indus. Ass'n v. Governing Bd. of the Newhall Sch. Dist.*, 206 Cal. App. 3d at 236 (the fee is "triggered by the voluntary decision of the developer [to proceed with his development]"); *Russ Bldg. Partnership v. City and County of San Francisco*, 199 Cal. App. 3d at 1505.

Whether development is a privilege or a circumscribed limited right, it is clear from California cases, as well as from *Nollan* and *Dolan* (discussed below)

To date, notwithstanding Nollan, *California courts have not changed their position that development is merely a privilege.*

that a dedication or impact fee condition will be upheld so long as it does not deny an owner economically viable use of the land and the required nexus exists.[3] For a more detailed discussion on the takings issue, *see* chapter 12 (Takings).

Test of Reasonableness/ Nexus Requirement

In General

Given the voluntary or "privileged" nature of development, courts have held that cities may impose conditions on development so long as the conditions are reasonable, and there exists a sufficient nexus between the conditions imposed and the projected burden of the proposed development. *See Nollan v. California Coastal Comm'n*, 483 U.S. at 834–35; *Associated Home Builders, Inc. v. City of Walnut Creek*, 4 Cal. 3d at 644; *Ayres v. City Council*, 34 Cal. 2d 31, 42 (1949).

There is no single, precise rule that is applied by the courts to determine whether a dedication or a fee condition is reasonable and thus valid. Rather, courts use an ad hoc analysis, examining the facts of each case. The determination depends on the size of the development, the demand for services, the burden that will be created by the development, and the development's overall effect on the city and the surrounding community. Courts use a balancing test that examines whether there has been a proper exercise of police power in a reasonable manner such that no taking of property has occurred. As the United States Supreme Court stated in determining what constitutes the required nexus, "no precise mathematical calculation is required, but the city must make some sort of individualized determination that the required dedication is related both in nature and extent to the impact of the proposed development." *Dolan v. City of Tigard*, 512 U.S. at 391.

The major legal issue involving exactions is not whether the dedication or payment of a fee as a condition precedent to development may be required, but to what extent the dedication or fee may be imposed.

As a general rule, California courts have long required a nexus between project conditions and the impacts of development. *See Ayres*, 34 Cal. 2d at 42. In 1971, however, the California Supreme Court moved away from whatever direct nexus requirement previously existed in California. Instead, the Court held that, in the absence of a more restrictive statute, a dedication may be required based on broad public welfare concerns, although some nexus must be present. *See Associated Home Builders*, 4 Cal. 3d at 644. The *Associated Home Builders* test continues to be followed by the California courts. *See Ehrlich v. City of Culver City*, 12 Cal. 4th 854, 865 (1996); *Shapell Indus., Inc. v. Governing Bd.*, 1 Cal. App. 4th 218, 234 (1991); *Balch Enters. v. New Haven Unified Sch. Dist.*, 219 Cal. App. 3d 783, 793 (1990); *Rohn v. City of Visalia*, 214 Cal. App. 3d

---

3. As is further discussed in chapter 12 (Takings), a city's ability to enact land use regulations, to require dedications, and to impose fees under its police power is limited by the Takings Clause of the Fifth Amendment of the United States Constitution, as made applicable to the states by the Fourteenth Amendment. The Takings Clause protects private property rights against governmental action by providing that a city shall not appropriate (take) private property for public use without compensating the owner of the property. Private property need not be physically seized to constitute a taking; regulation of property, such as land use regulation, may constitute a taking if it is determined to be excessive. *See Penn Cent. Transp. Co. v. City of New York*, 438 U.S. 104 (1978).

1463, 1471 (1989). *See also* James Longtin, *Longtin's California Land Use*, sections 8.22[3] (Local Government Publications, 2006 Update).

For example, in one case developers challenged an ordinance adopted by the City of Sacramento that levied fees on nonresidential development to assist in building low-income housing. *Commercial Builders of N. Cal. v. City of Sacramento*, 941 F. 2d 872 (9th Cir. 1991). The court found evidence in the record that the commercial development proposed by the developers indirectly would affect the need for more affordable housing units, and so upheld the ordinance. "A purely financial exaction, then, will not constitute a taking if it is made for the purpose of paying a social cost that is reasonably related to the activity against which the fee is assessed." *Id.* at 876. *See also Garrick Dev. Co. v. Hayward Unified Sch. Dist.*, 3 Cal. App. 4th 320, 337 (1992).

In a line of cases beginning with *Nollan v. California Coastal Commission*, 483 U.S. 825 (1987), and *Dolan v. City of Tigard*, 512 U.S. 374 (1994), the United States Supreme Court also has required an appropriate nexus. The two-prong *Nollan/Dolan* nexus test was interpreted by California's high court in *Ehrlich v. City of Culver City*, 12 Cal. 4th 854, 881 (1996). In 1987, California also passed nexus legislation that codified many of the nexus requirements, particularly those established by *Associated Home Builders, Inc. v. City of Walnut Creek*, 4 Cal. 3d at 640. *See* Gov't Code §§ 66000–66025 (the Mitigation Fee Act).

U.S. Supreme Court Case Law—The *Nollan* and *Dolan* Decisions

Nollan v. California Coastal Commission. In *Nollan*, the Supreme Court considered the constitutionality of a California Coastal Commission development permit condition requiring dedication of a lateral access easement along the owners' private beach. 483 U.S. 825 (1987). The easement purportedly was required to assist the public in viewing the beach and in overcoming a perceived "psychological barrier" to using the beach. The owners challenged the easement, claiming that the condition constituted a taking. The Court agreed and held that since there was no "nexus" between the burdens imposed by the owners' development and the permit condition, the dedication requirement failed to "substantially advance" a "legitimate state interest." *Id.* at 837. The Court reasoned that while protection of the public's ability to see the beach was a legitimate governmental interest, no nexus existed between the identified impact of the project (obstruction of the ocean view) and the easement condition (physical access across the beach). *Id.* at 839.

If there is no such connection, the decision to impose the condition would not be proper and could amount to a taking. *Id.* at 837.

Nollan left unanswered the question of how close the nexus must be for a regulation to "substantially advance" the government's stated interest?[4] However, in the majority opinion authored by Justice Scalia, the Court acknowledged that, while it had not specified the showing necessary to pass the nexus test, a wide variety of land use regulations had met this burden:

In Nollan, *the Supreme Court considered the constitutionality of a California Coastal Commission development permit condition requiring dedication of a lateral access easement along the owners' private beach.*

Nollan *left unanswered a key question: How close must the nexus be for a regulation to substantially advance a legitimate state interest?*

---

4. This issue was addressed seven years later by the United States Supreme Court's decision in *Dolan v. City of Tigard*, 512 U.S. at 386.

Our cases have not elaborated on the standards for determining what constitutes a "legitimate state interest" or what type of connection between the regulation and the state interest satisfies the requirement that the former "substantially advance" the latter. They have made clear, however, that a broad range of governmental purposes and regulations satisfies these requirements." See *Agins v. City of Tiburon*, 447 U.S. 255, 260–62 (1980) (scenic zoning); *Penn Cent. Transp. Co. v. New York City*, supra (landmark preservation); *Euclid v. Ambler Realty Co.*, 272 U.S. 365 (1926) (residential zoning).

Id. at 834–35

Subsequent cases have made clear that so long as there is the required nexus, courts will broadly construe the governmental interests to be advanced. Moreover, several California cases interpreted the *Nollan* nexus requirement—that a regulation "substantially" advance a legitimate governmental interest—narrowly, as applying only where the regulation involves a physical encroachment. See *Saad v. City of Berkeley*, 24 Cal. App. 4th at 1212–13; *City and County of San Francisco v. Golden Gate Heights Invs.*, 14 Cal. App. 4th 1203, 1209 (1993) (and cases cited therein); *Blue Jeans Equities W. v. City and County of San Francisco*, 3 Cal. App. 4th 164, 168–71 (1992). See also *San Remo Hotel v. City and County of San Francisco*, 27 Cal. 4th 663, 664–65 (2002).

In *Long Beach Equities, Inc. v. County of Ventura*, a California appellate court ruled that the *Nollan* test was satisfied because there was a substantial relationship between the regulations and the public welfare. 231 Cal. App. 3d 1016, 1030 (1991). In the case, Long Beach Equities (LBE) purchased 250 acres of land in unincorporated territory adjacent to the city and within an "area of interest" of the city, claiming reliance on promised municipal approval for the building of 1,100 units on the site. After a substantial investment by LBE in public service facilities, the city declared a moratorium on land use permits. The city in 1988 advised LBE that only approximately 325 units had been designated to occupy that property. The county, after amending its general plan to designate LBE's property as OS-160 (one unit per 160 acres), refused to allow LBE to apply to process the project through the county, stating that any such project must occur in the city after annexation. The developer sued both the city and county, arguing among other things, that the governmental changes and delays supported a cause of action for inverse condemnation in that the regulations would so greatly delay development as to render any use of its property economically infeasible.[5]

The court upheld both the county's and city's legislation against LBE's facial attack based on the finding that the required reasonable relationship existed. "Local government legislation is constitutional on its face if it bears 'a substantial relationship to the public welfare...' and inflicts no irreparable injury on the landowner." *Id.* at 1030 (citing *Agins v. City of Tiburon*, 447 U.S. at 261; *Euclid v. Ambler Realty Co.*, 272 U.S. 365, 397 (1926)). The court further held that the city's growth control ordinance was valid because it was designed "'to protect the unique, hill-surrounded environment; enhance the quality of

---

5. The court held that the plaintiff's "as-applied" attack on the ordinances was not ripe because Long Beach Equities had not secured a "final determination" as to uses that would be allowed by the city on its property.

life; promote public health, safety or welfare and the general well-being of the community....' By limiting the rate, distribution, quality, and type of residential development on an annual basis, with periodic reviews of the ongoing situation, City seeks 'to improve local air quality, reduce traffic demands...and ensure that future demands for such essential services as water, sewers and the like are met....'" *Id.*

In *Hotel & Motel Ass'n of Oakland v. City of Oakland*, the federal Ninth Circuit Court of Appeals held that city ordinances enacted to improve conditions in and around hotels were not an unconstitutional taking. 344 F. 3d 959, 967 (9th Cir. 2003). The Oakland City Council enacted two ordinances for the purpose of improving the physical conditions in and around hotels within the city. Studies showed a continued pattern of illegal activity, including prostitution and drug use, associated with poorly maintained hotels. Previous steps such as increased police patrols showed little success, which led Oakland to believe regular maintenance and property management would lead to better outcomes. The hotels that did not abide by the ordinances could face revocation of their approved status. The Hotel & Motel Association of Oakland claimed the ordinances were a taking in violation of the Fifth and Fourteenth Amendments. In ruling for the city, the federal appellate court held that the ordinances advanced a legitimate governmental interest since they were adopted to protect the public from illegal activity and were directed toward protecting the health and welfare of citizens and visitors in Oakland. The court also noted that the ordinances require no substantive change in the Association's use of its property.

In Hotel & Motel Association of Oakland v. City of Oakland, *the federal Ninth Circuit Court of Appeals held that city ordinances enacted to improve conditions in and around hotels were not an unconstitutional taking.*

Other cases have applied *Nollan's* nexus holding with varied results. For example, in one case, a city's requirement for a street widening was struck down since there was no nexus. There was no evidence in the record that the dedication was required to compensate for increased traffic produced by the project. *See Rohn v. City of Visalia*, 214 Cal. App. 3d at 1475. Citing *Associated Home Builders*, the Rohn court held that, although the facilities to be dedicated need not solely benefit the project, they at least must serve it in some capacity. This was not the case in *Rohn*, where no nexus existed between the dedication condition and the alleged traffic burden imposed by the project.

The Rohn *court held that, although the facilities to be dedicated need not solely benefit the project, they at least must serve it in some capacity.*

In another case, the court struck down an easement dedication allegedly required to prevent erosion, because there was no specific report or study to justify the dedication. *See Surfside Colony, Ltd. v. California Coastal Comm'n*, 226 Cal. App. 3d 1260 (1991). The Coastal Commission had relied on general studies of other areas to justify the exaction, but the court found they were inadequate to provide a legal nexus. *Id.* at 1269.

However, in *Commercial Builders of Northern California v. City of Sacramento*, the court upheld a city's ordinance imposing a low-income housing fee on nonresidential development. 941 F. 2d 872 (1991). In so doing, the court applied the "reasonable relationship" test of *Associated Home Builders*, and stated that *Nollan* stands only for the proposition that if there is no nexus, there is a taking. *Id.* at 874. The court rejected the builder's argument that under *Nollan* an ordinance that imposes an exaction can be upheld only if it can be shown that the development in question is directly responsible for the social ill that the exaction is designed to alleviate. Rather, the court held that *Nollan* did not create a stricter standard than prior federal law for judging how close the nexus must be. *Id.* at 874; *see also Tahoe Reg'l Planning Agency v. King*, 233 Cal. App. 3d 1365, 1400 (1991) (*Nollan* does not alter established law that aesthetic values are an appropriate subject of land use regulations; *Nollan* only requires that there be a nexus).

In *Blue Jeans Equities West v. City and County of San Francisco*, the court held that the *Nollan* analysis was not applicable to any exaction that did not involve a physical invasion or "possessory taking." 3 Cal. App. 4th 164, 166 (1992). In this case, the San Francisco Planning Commission approved a building permit for a five-building office, retail, and residential complex in January 1979, in the northeast waterfront section of San Francisco's Levi Plaza. The permit provided that the owner "make a good-faith effort to participate in future funding mechanisms to assure adequate transit service to the area of the city in which the project is located." *Id.* at 171. In May 1981, before issuance of a certificate of completion for the project, the board of supervisors enacted the Transit Impact Development Fee ordinance, which required developers of downtown buildings with new office space to pay a transit impact development fee not to exceed $5 per square foot as a condition to receiving a certificate of completion. The project owner argued that this ordinance could not be lawfully applied to its building project and sued, claiming that the heightened scrutiny test alluded to in *Nollan* should be applied to the ordinance.

In upholding the fee, the court concluded that the nexus required by *Nollan* to determine whether a government condition violated the Takings Clause of the Fifth Amendment did not apply to this ordinance, since *Nollan* was applicable only to possessory takings, not regulatory takings. *Id.* at 172 (citing *Russ Bldg. Partnership v. City and County of San Francisco*, 44 Cal. 3d 839 (1988) "[T]he high court appears to make a distinction between 'regulatory takings', *i.e.*, economic regulation, most forms of zoning, and other restrictions on land use, and 'possessory takings', where the government, or an authorized third person, physically intrudes upon or appropriates the property." *Id.* at 169. Therefore, the court held any heightened scrutiny test in *Nollan* is limited to possessory rather than regulatory takings. *See also Saad v. City of Berkeley*, 24 Cal. App. 4th at 1212; *Golden Gate Heights*, 14 Cal. App. 4th at 1209.

Dolan v. City of Tigard. In 1994, the *Dolan* Court addressed the question left unanswered by *Nollan*, adding the second prong of the Court's nexus test. In *Dolan*, a sharply divided court held that cities must prove that development conditions placed on a discretionary permit have a "rough proportionality" to the development's impact. If not, this action may constitute a taking. 512 U.S. 374, 391 (1994). In this 5–4 decision, the Court held for the first time that in making an adjudicative decision, a city must demonstrate a "required reasonable relationship" between the conditions to be imposed on a development permit and the development's impact. Even though the Court coined a new term ("rough proportionality") for the standard, it was basically the same reasonable relationship test that California and a majority of other states had followed for years.

Florence Dolan owned a plumbing and electrical supply store located in the business district of Tigard, Oregon, along Fanno Creek, which flows through the southwestern corner of the lot and along its western boundary. Dolan applied to the city for a building permit to develop the site. Her proposed plans called for nearly doubling the size of the store and paving a 39-space parking lot.

The planning commission granted Dolan's permit application subject to certain conditions, including the requirement that Dolan dedicate the portion of her property lying within the 100-year flood plain for improvement of a storm drainage system along Fanno Creek. In addition, she was required to dedicate an additional 15-foot strip of land adjacent to the flood plain as a pedestrian/bicycle pathway. In so doing, the city made a series of findings concerning the relationship between the dedicated conditions and the projected impacts on the Dolan property.

The United States Supreme Court granted certiorari "to resolve a question left open" by its decision in *Nollan*—what is the required degree of connection between the exactions imposed by a city and the projected impacts of the proposed development? *Dolan*, 512 U.S. at 377. Significantly, the Court in *Dolan* noted that it was not dealing with a legislative determination regarding land use regulations, but instead with a city having made "an adjudicative decision to condition petitioner's application for a building permit on an individual parcel." *Id*. The Court also observed that "the conditions imposed were not simply a limitation on the use [the] petitioner might make of her own parcel, but a requirement that she deed portions of the property to the city." *Id*.

In evaluating the takings claim, the Court stated that it first must determine whether an "essential nexus" exists between the "legitimate state interest" and the exaction imposed. If a nexus exists, the next step is to determine whether the degree of connection is sufficient. The Court noted that in *Nollan*, there had been no nexus; thus, the Court did not move beyond the first step in the analysis. In *Nollan*, the absence of a nexus between the easement and the ocean view left the California Coastal Commission in the position of simply trying to obtain an easement "through gimmickry," which converted a valid regulation of land use into an "out-and-out plan of extortion." *Id.* at 387. In the *Dolan* situation, however, the Court stated that no such "gimmickry" was evident. Rather, the Court concluded that the required nexus did, in fact, exist. Therefore, it was necessary for the Court to address the question left unanswered in *Nollan*—whether the *degree of exaction* demanded by the city's permit conditions bore the *required relationship* to the projected impact of the development.

Since state courts had a long history of dealing with this question, the Court then reviewed several representative state court decisions. The Court noted that the decisions fell into three categories: first, a generalized nexus requirement, which the Court determined to be too lax; second, an exacting nexus described as the "specific and uniquely attributable test" (the so-called *Pioneer Trust* Rule from Illinois, 22 Ill. 2d 375 (1961)), which the Court rejected; and third, an intermediate position of a "reasonable relationship" nexus (highlighted in *Jordan v. Menomonee Falls*, 28 Wisc. 2d 608, 137 N.W. 2d 442 (1965)).

The *Dolan* Court noted that the intermediate "reasonable relationship test" adopted by the majority of states (including California, *see Associated Home Builders*, 4 Cal. 3d at 640) was closer to the federal constitutional norm than the other two tests. However, it stated, "we do not adopt [the reasonable relationship test] as such, partly because the term 'reasonable relationship' seems confusingly similar to the term 'rational basis' which describes the minimal level of scrutiny

In evaluating the takings claim in Dolan, *the Court stated that it first must determine whether an "essential nexus" exists between the "legitimate state interest" and the exaction imposed.*

under the Equal Protection Clause of the Fourteenth Amendment." 512 U.S. at 391. Instead, the Court coined the term "rough proportionality" to summarize what it holds to be required by the Fifth Amendment.[6] It then attempted to provide some meaning to the phrase. "No precise mathematical calculation is required, but the city must make some sort of individualized determination that the required dedication is related both in nature and extent to the impact of the proposed development." *Id.*

With the rough proportionality requirement in mind, the Court then reviewed the two required dedications and held that the City had not met its burden of demonstrating the required relationship. After analyzing the findings upon which the City relied, the Court stated that the City had not shown the "required reasonable relationship" between the floodplain easement and the petitioner's proposed new building. *Id.* at 395.

Noting that Dolan's proposed development would have increased the amount of impervious surface—which in turn would increase the quantity and rate of storm water flowing from the property, the Court determined that the City could have required that Dolan simply keep the area open. But by requiring complete dedication of the land rather than simply restricting Dolan's ability to build on it, the City limited Dolan's ability to exclude others, which, the Court stated, is "'one of the most essential sticks in the bundle of rights that are commonly characterized as property.'" *Id.* at 393 (quoting *Kaiser Aetna v. United States*, 444 U.S. 164, 176 (1979)).

In addition, regarding the dedication of the pedestrian/bicycle pathway easement, the Court did not accept the City's conclusory statement that the creation of the pathway 'could offset some of the traffic demand...and lessen increase in traffic congestion.'" *Id.* (emphasis added). "No precise mathematical calculation is required," the Court repeated, "but a city must make some effort to quantify its findings in support of the dedication for the pedestrian/bicycle pathway beyond the conclusory statement that it could offset some of the traffic demand generated." *Id.* at 395–96.

The Court concluded by stating:

> Cities have long engaged in the commendable task of land use planning, made necessary by increasing urbanization particularly in metropolitan areas such as Portland. The city's goals of reducing flooding hazards and traffic congestion, and providing for public greenways, are laudable, but there are outer limits to how this may be done. "A strong public desire to improve the public condition [will not] warrant achieving the desire by a shorter cut than the constitutional way of paying for the change."

Id. at 396 (quoting *Pennsylvania Coal Co. v. Mahon*, 260 U.S. 393, 416 (1922))

The dissenting justices stated that the majority had made a serious error by abandoning the traditional presumption of constitutionality, and imposing a novel burden of proof on a city implementing an admittedly valid comprehensive land use plan. "[H]aving thus assigned the burden, the Court concludes that the city loses based on one word ('could' instead of 'would'), and despite

No precise mathematical calculation is required, but the city must make some sort of individualized determination that the required dedication is related both in nature and extent to the impact of the proposed development.

---

6. Interestingly, after coining the term "rough proportionality," the Court, in its majority opinion, never used that term again in applying its analysis to the facts; instead it continued to use the words "required reasonable relationship" or "reasonably related."

the fact that this record shows the connection the court looks for." *Id.* at 413 (Souter, J., dissenting).

Subsequent case law has clarified that the *Dolan* rough proportionality rule applies when a court is determining whether dedications demanded as a condition of development are proportional to the development's anticipated impacts and was not intended to address, and is not applicable to, an analysis of whether or not a complete denial of development is a taking. *See City of Monterey v. Del Monte Dunes at Monterey, Ltd.*, 526 U.S. 687, 703 (1999). In a major victory for cities, the U.S. Supreme Court in *Del Monte Dunes* unanimously held that it had not expanded the rough proportionality test of *Dolan* beyond the "special context of exactions—land use decisions conditioning approval of development on the dedication of property to public use." *Id.* at 702. The rough proportionality test was not designed to address, and is not readily applicable to, the much different questions arising where the landowner's challenge was based on denial of a development permit. California court cases are consistent with the decision in *Del Monte Dunes. See, e.g., Breneric Assocs. v. City of Del Mar*, 69 Cal. App. 4th 166, 175–76 (1998) (rejecting Pacific Legal Foundation's argument in its amicus brief that the *Nollan/Dolan* "test should be applicable to denial of a design review permit").

Subsequent case law has clarified that the Dolan *rule was not intended to address, and is not applicable to, an analysis of whether or not a complete denial of development is a taking.*

In *Lingle v. Chevron U.S.A. Inc.*, the United States Supreme Court reaffirmed the role of *Nollan* and *Dolan* in cases involving challenges to adjudicative land use exactions. 544 U.S. 528 (2005).[7] In so doing, however, the Court clarified the limited holdings of those cases to adjudicative land use exactions only. The issue in both *Nollan* and *Dolan* was whether the government could demand an easement as a condition for granting a development permit. *Id.* at 546–47. The Court in *Nollan* held that the exaction must substantially advance the same government interest that would furnish a valid ground for denial of the permit, while in *Dolan* it held that the required degree of connection must be "roughly proportional" both in nature and extent to the impact of the proposed development. In her unanimous majority opinion, Justice O'Connor emphasized that *Nollan* and *Dolan* do not address whether the challenged exactions "would substantially advance some legitimate state interests..." but rather "whether the exactions substantially advanced the same interests" the government claimed would allow it to deny the permit itself. *Id.* at 547.

In Lingle v. Chevron U.S.A. Inc., *the United States Supreme Court reaffirmed the role of* Nollan *and* Dolan *in cases involving challenges to adjudicative land use exactions.*

What does *Dolan* mean in California? The United States Supreme Court has placed some limitations on a city's exercise of its police power to require dedication of land as a condition for issuing a development permit. *Dolan* requires a city to document the connection between the dedication and the projected impact of the proposed development. Not only must the required nexus exist, but findings must establish the required reasonable relationship between the required dedication and the impact. Thus, a two-part inquiry must be made to determine whether the essential nexus exists between the project and (1) the type of condition and (2) the burden created by of the condition. The "type of impact" nexus

---

7. *See* Daniel J. Curtin, Jr., W. Andrew Gowder, Jr. and Bryan W. Wenter, "Exactions Update: The State of Development Exactions After Lingle v. Chevron U.S.A., Inc.," 38 *Urb. Law.* 641 (Summer 2006).

test requires that the type of condition imposed must address the same type of impact caused by the development (*Nollan*) and the "burden created" nexus test requires an assessment of whether this condition is in reasonable proportion to the burden created by the new development (*Dolan's* rough proportionality). See James Longtin, *Longtin's California Land Use*, sections 8.22[3] (Local Government Publications 2006 Update). In California, the courts always have required a nexus based on a reasonable relationship. *Dolan* reiterates the need for a reasonable relationship, but emphasizes that there must be something more than generalized or conclusory findings to support that connection.

In addition, as a general rule in California, the *Dolan* higher scrutiny standard is not applicable to a general legislative act involving a range of properties, such as a general zoning regulation, rent control law, or other land use law. In *Home Builders Ass'n of Northern California. v. City of Napa*, the plaintiffs claimed that a generally applicable inclusionary housing ordinance, which offered developers a number of alternative modes of compliance and allowed a waiver under certain circumstances, effected a taking under *Nollan* and *Dolan*. 90 Cal. App. 4th 188 (2001). The builder's group contended that the city's ordinance was invalid under *Nollan* and *Dolan* because there was no "essential nexus" or "rough proportionality" between the exaction required by the ordinance and the impacts caused by development of the property.

The court rejected this argument, holding that *Nollan* and *Dolan* were inapplicable under the facts of this case. The court stated that the higher standard of judicial scrutiny formulated by the high Court in *Nollan* and *Dolan* was intended to address land use "bargains" between property owners and regulatory bodies—those in which the local government conditions permit approval for a given use on the owner's surrender of benefits which purportedly offset the impact of the proposed development. It is in this paradigmatic permit context—where the individual property owner-developer seeks to negotiate approval of a planned development—that the combined *Nollan* and *Dolan* test quintessentially applies. But a different standard of scrutiny applies to development fees that are generally applicable through legislative action "because the heightened risk of the 'extortionate' use of the police power to exact unconstitutional conditions is not present." *Id.* at 196–97.

The court in *Napa* observed that it was not called upon to determine the validity of a particular land use bargain between a governmental agency and an owner who wants to develop his land. Instead, the court was confronted with a facial challenge to economic legislation that is generally applicable throughout the city. Therefore, the court concluded the heightened standard of review prescribed in *Nollan* and *Dolan* was inapplicable under these facts.[8]

In other words, a generally applicable ordinance does not warrant the heightened standard of review accorded to the type of individualized land use bargain that creates a heightened risk of extortionate use of the police power to demand unconstitutional exactions. *Id.; see Santa Monica Beach, Ltd. v. Superior*

---

8. For additional discussion of the *Home Builders Ass'n of Northern California v. City of Napa* case, *see* Daniel J. Curtin, Jr., *et al.*, "Inclusionary Housing Ordinance Survives Constitutional Challenge in Post-Nollan-Dolan Era: Home Builders Ass'n of N. Cal. v. City of Napa," *Land Use Law & Zoning Digest* (APA August 2002); Barbara Kautz, "In Defense of Inclusionary Zoning: Successfully Creating Affordable Housing," 36 *U.S.F. L. Rev.* 971 (2002).

Court, 19 Cal. 4th 952, 966 (1999); *San Mateo County Coastal Landowners' Ass'n v. County of San Mateo*, 38 Cal. App. 4th 523, 549 (1995).

As a result of *Dolan*, if a city seeks to require a dedication of land as a condition of approval (*e.g.*, building permits, map approvals) as compared to legislative requirements (*e.g.*, a determination applicable to all large development projects, where no individual bargaining is involved), the following rules should be followed:

- A city has the burden of proving a sufficient nexus exists between the required dedication and the impact of the proposed development.
- No precise mathematical calculation is necessary to show the required reasonable relationship, but a city must make some sort of individualized determination that the required dedication is related, both in nature and extent, to the impact of the proposed development (*i.e.*, it is roughly proportional).
- A city has the burden of proving why a dedication is necessary and why a land use regulation restricting the use of the property cannot suffice.
- A city must tailor the conditions it demands to counter only the types of impacts expected from the development.
- To meet the heightened *Nollan-Dolan* standard, a city should quantify its findings as much as possible, rather than relying on conclusory statements.

For further discussion of the takings issue outside of the context of exactions, *see* chapter 12 (Takings).⁹

Applicability of the *Nollan/Dolan* Test to Impact Fees: *Ehrlich v. Culver City* ¹⁰

In *Dolan*, where the City of Tigard conditioned a development permit on the property owner's dedication of land, the Supreme Court of the United States did not address the question of whether the heightened standard enunciated applies to the situation when a city requires payment of an impact fee rather than a dedication of land. The Court briefly touched on this issue in *Lingle v. Chevron U.S.A. Inc.*, but did not squarely resolve the question of whether the *Nollan* and *Dolan* rules would be applied to development impact fees, especially those that are imposed by generally applicable legislation act such as an ordinance or resolution, as in *San Remo*. 125 S. Ct. 2074 (2005). The Court indicated that *Dolan* addressed only the degree of connection in the context of "adjudicative exactions requiring dedication of private property," specifically citing its decision in *City of Monterey v. Del Monte Dunes at Monterey, Ltd.*, 526 U.S. 687, 702 (1999), "emphasizing that we have not extended this standard 'beyond the special context of [such] exactions.'" Thus, it remains somewhat

In Dolan, *the Supreme Court of the United States did not address the question of whether the heightened standard enunciated applies to the situation when a city requires payment of an impact fee rather than a dedication of land.*

---

9. For a discussion of the applicability of *Nollan/Dolan* heightened scrutiny to development and annexation agreements, as well as to project conditions of approval, *see* Daniel J. Curtin, Jr., W. Andrew Gowder, Jr., and Bryan W. Wenter, "Exactions Update: When Nollan/Dolan Heightened Scrutiny Does Not Apply," 37 *Urb. Law.* 539 (Summer 2005).
10. For further discussion of impact fees and *Ehrlich*, *see* Daniel J. Curtin, Jr. and W. Andrew Gowder, Jr., "Recent Developments in Land Use, Planning and Zoning Law Relating to Exactions," 36 *Urb. Law.* 519 (Summer 2004). *See also* Daniel J. Curtin, Jr., *Update on Exactions: The Legislative Versus Administrative Distinction (Ehrlich v. Culver City and Progeny)*, 34th Annual Institute on Planning, Zoning and Eminent Domain, ch. 8 (LexisNexis 2004).

unclear what standard the United States Supreme Court will employ in examining a challenge to the adjudicative imposition of impact fees.

In contrast, the California Supreme Court affirmatively answered the question of whether higher scrutiny should be used to examine the constitutionality of impacts fees rather than dedications of land in *Ehrlich v. City of Culver City*, 12 Cal. 4th 854 (1996), and then reaffirmed this position in *San Remo Hotel v. City and County of San Francisco*, 27 Cal. 4th 643 (2002). Prior to the decision in *Ehrlich*, courts had concluded that a higher level of scrutiny only applied in cases of possessory takings. *See Blue Jeans Equities W. v. City and County of San Francisco*, 3 Cal. App. 4th 164, 169 (1992). *See also* William Fulton and Paul Shigley, *Guide to California Planning*, ch. 10 (Solano Press, 3rd ed. 2005).

Factual situation. In the early 1970s, Ehrlich acquired a vacant 2.4-acre lot in Culver City. At his request, the city amended its general plan and zoning, and adopted a specific plan to provide for the development of a privately operated tennis club and recreational facility. In 1981, in response to financial losses from operating the facility, Ehrlich applied to the city for a change in land use to construct an office building. The application was abandoned when the planning commission recommended against approval on the grounds that the existing club provided a needed commercial recreational facility within the city. Then, in 1988, Ehrlich closed the facility as a result of continuing financial losses and applied for an amendment to the general plan and the specific plan, as well as a zoning change, to allow construction of a 30-unit condominium complex valued at $10 million. At one point, the city expressed interest in acquiring the property for operation as a city-owned sports facility. However, this idea was later abandoned as unfeasible. At the same time, the city council rejected Ehrlich's application based on concerns about the loss of a needed recreational facility. Ehrlich then tore down the existing improvements and donated the recreational equipment to the city.

After denial of his application, Ehrlich filed suit and then entered into discussions with the city to secure the necessary approvals to restructure the property. After a closed-door meeting, ostensibly to discuss the pending litigation, the city council voted to approve the project conditioned upon the payment of certain monetary exactions, including a $280,000 recreation mitigation fee for the loss of the private tennis facility, payment of $33,200 for art in public places, and a $30,000 in lieu parkland dedication fee. The $280,000 fee was to be used "for partial replacement of the lost recreational facilities" occasioned by the specific plan amendment. The amount of the fee was based upon a city study that showed that the replacement costs for the recreational facilities "lost" as a result of amending the specific plan. After formally filing a protest pursuant to Government Code sections 66020 and 66021, Ehrlich challenged the $280,000 recreation fee and the in lieu art fee, but not the parkland dedication fee.

Government Code sections 66020 and 66021 provide the exclusive method of challenging any fee, dedication, reservation, or other exaction imposed on a housing development. Any challenging party may file a protest by (1) tendering the dedication, fee, or exaction in full and (2) providing the city with written notice that the payment is made under protest. For additional discussion of the procedure for challenging fees and dedications, *see* chapter 21 (Land Use Litigation).

Judicial proceedings. After the trial court struck down the conditions, the appellate court upheld them. *See Ehrlich v. City of Culver City*, 15 Cal. App. 4th 1737 (1993). The United States Supreme Court, after granting a writ, then remanded the matter back to the court of appeal to be re-examined in light of its then recent decision in *Dolan*. Following the remand, the court of appeal, in an unpublished opinion in 1994, again upheld both fees. The California Supreme Court then granted a petition to consider the important and unsettled question concerning the extent to which *Nollan* and *Dolan* applied to development permits that exact a fee as a condition of issuance, as opposed to the possessory dedication of real property.

The decision: new distinction—legislatively formulated vs. ad hoc development fees. Citing *Nollan*, the *Ehrlich* court expressed concern that adjudicative, ad hoc conditions on development presented "an inherent and heightened risk that local government will manipulate the police power to impose conditions unrelated to legitimate land use regulatory ends, thereby avoiding what would otherwise be an obligation to pay just compensation." 12 Cal. 4th at 869. The court emphasized the "extortion[ary]" danger of this "form of regulatory 'leveraging.'" *Id.* at 867. In response to this concern, the court drew a distinction between legislatively formulated development fees imposed on a class of property owners and individually imposed conditions.

> **PRACTICE TIP**
> When a city seeks to require a dedication of land as a condition to development, it has the burden of making affirmative findings to show that the proper nexus exists.

The court held that in the "relatively narrow class of land use cases" that involve individual "land use 'bargains' between property owners and regulatory bodies...where the individual property owner-developer seeks to negotiate approval of a planned development...the combined *Nollan* and *Dolan* test quintessentially applies." *Id.* at 868. The discretionary aspect of conditioning an individual approval heightens the risk that a city may manipulate the police power to impose conditions unrelated to legitimate land use regulatory ends. On this point, the court stated:

> It is the imposition of land-use conditions in individual cases, authorized by a permit scheme which by its nature allows for both the discretionary deployment of the police power and an enhanced potential for its abuse, that constitutes the sine qua non for application of the...standard of scrutiny formulated by the court in *Nollan* and *Dolan*.

Id. at 869

The court next considered whether the *Nollan/Dolan* test applied to general development fees in addition to dedications. In grappling with the decisions of *Blue Jeans Equities West v. City and County of San Francisco*, 3 Cal. App. 4th 164 (1992) (transit fees), and *Commercial Builders of Northern California v. City of Sacramento*, 941 F. 2d 872 (9th Cir. 1991) (affordable housing fees), which had limited the application of the heightened scrutiny standard to possessory takings cases, the *Ehrlich* court reasoned that those cases involved "legislatively formulated development assessments imposed on a broad class of property owners," and therefore did not require heightened scrutiny. 12 Cal. 4th at 876. Based on this reasoning, the court then rejected the city's argument that the *Nollan/Dolan* test only applies to possessory dedications and not to fees. Instead, it found that whether the *Nollan/Dolan* test applied to a fee depends upon whether the fee is an ad hoc or a legislative determination. *Id.* at

906. *See also San Remo Hotel*, 27 Cal. 4th at 669–30 (relying on *Ehrlich*, court held an in lieu fee for conversion of a residential hotel to tourist units was not subject to the *Nollan/Dolan* test); *Loyola Marymount Univ. v. Los Angeles Unified Sch. Dist.*, 45 Cal. App. 4th 1256, 1270–71 (1996) (applying *Ehrlich* to hold that the *Nollan/Dolan* test did not apply to a fee imposed pursuant to the Sterling Act (Educ. Code § 17620; Gov't Code § 65995)).

The $280,000 recreational mitigation fee. In striking down the $280,000 recreational mitigation fee, the court applied the strict scrutiny test of *Nollan/Dolan*, concluding that although there was a nexus, it was not roughly proportional to the impact. *Ehrlich v. Culver City*, 12 Cal. 4th at 864. The court then remanded the matter to the city council to determine an appropriate fee consistent with the court's decision. *Id*. at 885.

With respect to the existence of a nexus, the court stated that "there thus exists a potential basis *in logic* for a connection between a social need generated by plaintiff's condominium project and the $280,000 mitigation fee imposed by the city." *Id*. at 879. The court came to the conclusion that even though the club was a privately operated facility, accessible only to dues-paying members, a zoning change withdrawing the parcel from such a private recreational use still had a public impact. The court then stated that "[t]his principle—that the discontinuation of a private land use may have distinctly *public* consequences—is well accepted in land-use law." *Id*. The court stated:

> [I]t is well accepted in both the case and statutory law that the discontinuance of a private land use can have a significant impact justifying a monetary exaction to alleviate it. We perceive no reason why the same cannot be said of the loss of land devoted to private recreational use through its withdrawal from such a use as a result of being "up zoned" to accommodate incompatible uses.

Id.

Having found a valid governmental interest, the court then concluded that there was an essential nexus between this interest and the imposition of a development fee for park and recreational purposes that substantially advanced that interest. However, despite the existence of an essential nexus, the $280,000 fee was not proper since the record was "devoid of any individualized findings to support the required 'fit' between the monetary exactions and the loss of parcel zoned for commercial recreational use." *Id*. at 883. The court then remanded the matter to the city council to reconsider the amount of the fee in light of the court's decision. In so doing, it observed this type of recreational fee could be proper as long as it was based on (1) the additional administrative expenses incurred in redesignating other property within a city for recreational use or (2) by the monetary incentives needed to induce private recreational development on other land.

Art in public places fee. Another important aspect of the *Ehrlich* decision is the court's holding on the public art fee. The city's ordinance required that new residential projects of more than four units, as well as all commercial, industrial, and public building projects with a building valuation exceeding $500,000, provide "art work" for the project in an amount equal to one percent of the total building valuation, or to pay an equal amount in cash to the city's art fund. In this case, Ehrlich was required to pay $33,200. The court unanimously agreed that such a fee was not a development exaction of the kind subject to the heightened *Nollan/Dolan* standard since it was more akin to traditional land use regulations, such as imposing minimal building setbacks, parking and lighting conditions, landscaping requirements, and other design conditions. The court reasoned that such aesthetic control has long been held to be a valid exercise of a city's traditional police power, and does not amount to a taking merely because it might incidentally restrict a use, diminish the value, or impose a cost in connection with the property. *Id.* at 886.

Mitigation Fee Act. Note one final aspect of the *Ehrlich* decision: the court held that "developers who wish to challenge a development fee on either statutory or constitutional grounds must do so via the statutory framework" of the Mitigation Fee Act (Gov't Code §§ 66000–66025, discussed below), which requires that for a fee to be challenged, it must first have been paid under protest, and then a suit must be brought within 180 days. *Id.* at 867.

Developers who wish to challenge a development fee on either statutory or constitutional grounds must do so via the statutory framework of the Mitigation Fee Act.

Summary of Impacts of *Ehrlich*

- The *Nollan/Dolan* heightened scrutiny test applies only to development fees imposed on an individual, ad hoc basis in a discretionary permit granting process, and not to general legislatively formulated fees.
- *Nollan/Dolan* does not apply to legislative acts applicable to a general class, *e.g.*, transit fees imposed on downtown office developers (*Blue Jeans*), housing fees imposed on nonresidential developers (*Commercial Builders*), art fees (*Ehrlich*), nor or in lieu inclusionary housing fees (*Napa Home Builders Ass'n v. City of Napa*). Applying this standard, it is clear from *Ehrlich* that cities have the authority to impose fees for a wide range of services, including transit fees, housing, and art, and that so long as cities base development conditions on general legislative determinations, the conditions will almost always be within the police power.
- If a developer wants to challenge an individually applied fee either statutorily or constitutionally, it must follow the statutory framework of the Mitigation Fee Act. This means that the challenger must file a written protest, pay the fee under protest, and bring suit within a 180-day time frame.
- A city can legally charge a mitigation fee as a condition of a land use change if the discontinuation of the previous private use has public consequences, as long as the *Nollan/Dolan* test has been met.
- An ordinance enacted for aesthetic purposes alone is well within the scope of a city's police power.

A city can legally charge a mitigation fee as a condition of a land use change if discontinuation of the previous private use has public consequences, as long as the Nollan/Dolan *test has been met.*

San Remo Hotel Reaffirms *Ehrlich*

The California Supreme Court reaffirmed the holding and rationale of *Ehrlich* in *San Remo Hotel v. City and County of San Francisco*, wherein the court said that the in lieu fees required to pay for replacement housing in a hotel conversion from residential to tourist use were not subject to the heightened scrutiny test of *Nollan/Dolan*. 27 Cal. 4th 643 (2002). Here, the San Remo Hotel (Hotel) in San Francisco included both tourist units and residential units for low-income tenants. The Hotel sought to convert the residential rooms to rooms for tourists rather than to longer term residents. The Hotel eventually received approval but in the process was required to (1) comply with zoning laws by obtaining a conditional

HCO = Hotel Unit Conversion and Demolition Ordinance

use permit for use of the property as a tourist hotel, and (2) help replace the residential units the city claimed would be lost by the conversion. Pursuant to the city's Residential Hotel Unit Conversion and Demolition Ordinance (HCO), the Hotel elected to pay an in lieu fee into a governmental fund for the construction of low- and moderate-income housing.

The Hotel challenged the conditional use permit requirement, as well as the housing replacement condition, alleging that these caused a taking of private property without just compensation in violation of article I, section 19 of the California Constitution. In ruling for the city, the California Supreme Court stated that the HCO's purpose was to "benefit the general public by minimizing adverse impact on the housing supply and on displaced low income, elderly, and disabled persons resulting from the loss of residential hotel units through their conversion and demolition." Accompanying the ordinance were findings that the city suffered from a severe shortage of affordable rental housing and that many elderly, disabled, and low-income persons resided in residential hotel units. The HCO made it unlawful to eliminate a residential hotel unit without obtaining a conversion permit or to rent a residential unit for a term shorter than seven days.

An application to convert residential units to tourist use must include, *inter alia*, a statement regarding how one-for-one replacement of the units to be converted will be accomplished. The applicant may satisfy the replacement requirement by constructing or bringing onto the market new residential units comparable to those converted; constructing or rehabilitating certain other types of housing for low-income, disabled, or elderly persons; or paying an in lieu fee equal to the replacement site acquisition costs plus a set portion of the replacement construction costs.

The California Supreme Court stated that because the Hotel allowed both residential and tourist rentals, a conditional use permit was required before it could convert to an exclusively tourist hotel.

The court stated that because the Hotel allowed both residential and tourist rentals, a conditional use permit was required before it could convert to an exclusively tourist hotel. The fact that some of the units were already being used by tourists did not relieve the Hotel from the obligation to obtain a permit to convert the remaining units. Therefore, the city correctly determined that a conditional use permit was required.

Further, the court held that the in lieu fee imposed on the Hotel in the amount of $567,000 did not violate the Takings Clause, and was not subject to the heightened scrutiny test set forth in *Nollan*, *Dolan*, and *Ehrlich*. The court discussed the takings issue under both state and federal law. The Takings Clause of the California Constitution (art. I, § 19) provides: "Private property may be taken or damaged for public use only when just compensation, ascertained by a jury unless waived, has first been paid to, or into court for, the owner." The federal Takings Clause (U.S. Const., amend. V) provides: "nor shall private property be taken for public use, without just compensation."

The court stated that by virtue of including "damage[s]" to property as well as its "tak[ing]," the California clause "protects a somewhat broader range of property values" than does the corresponding federal provision. But aside from that difference, not pertinent here, the court stated that "we appear to have construed the clauses congruently." 27 Cal. 4th at 664.

The court noted that the appellate court held that housing replacement fees assessed under the HCO were subject to *Nollan/Dolan/Ehrlich* heightened scrutiny review because they were exacted discretionarily and applied only to a relatively small number of property owners rather than to "every other property in the City." The Hotel defended this analysis, while the city argued for the more deferential constitutional scrutiny applicable to land use regulations made generally applicable by legislative enactment to a class of property owners.

The court agreed with the city. Contrary to the appellate court's assertion, and unlike *Ehrlich*, the HCO did not provide city staff or administrative bodies with any discretion as to the imposition or size of a housing replacement fee.

The court declined the Hotel's invitation to extend heightened takings scrutiny to all development fees, adhering instead to the distinction it drew in *Ehrlich, supra*, between ad hoc exactions and legislatively mandated, formulaic mitigation fees. The court noted that while legislatively mandated fees do present some danger to improper leveraging, such generally applicable legislation is subject to the ordinary restraints of the democratic political process. A city council that charged extortionate fees for all property development, unjustifiable by mitigation needs, would likely face widespread and well-financed opposition at the next election. Ad hoc individual monetary exactions deserve special judicial scrutiny mainly because, affecting fewer citizens and evading systematic assessment, they are more likely to escape such political controls.

The Ehrlich *Court noted that while legislatively mandated fees do present some danger to improper leveraging, such generally applicable legislation is subject to the ordinary restraints of the democratic political process.*

Nor was the Hotel correct that without *Nollan/Dolan/Ehrlich* scrutiny, legislatively imposed development mitigation fees are subject to no meaningful means-ends review. As a matter of both statutory and constitutional law, such fees must bear a reasonable relationship, in both intended use and amount, to the deleterious public impact of the development. Gov't Code, § 66001; *Ehrlich v. Culver City*, 12 Cal. 4th 854 (1996); *Associated Home Builders, Inc. v. City of Walnut Creek*, 4 Cal. 3d 633, 640 (1971).

In addition, the Hotel attacked the housing replacement provisions of the HCO on their face, asserting that there was no connection between the housing replacement fees assessed and the housing lost by conversion to tourist use. The court rejected this contention, concluding that the housing replacement fees bore a reasonable relationship to loss of housing based on the wording of the ordinance.

The court said that the Hotel failed to demonstrate from the face of the ordinance that fees assessed under the HCO bore no reasonable relationship to housing loss in the generality or great majority of cases, the minimum showing the court has required for a facial challenge to the constitutionality of a statute. Here, the Hotel sought not merely a change in the zoning affecting the site of the Hotel, but permission to change the use of existing residential facilities on the property. A mitigation fee measured by the resulting loss of housing units was thus reasonably related to the impacts of Hotel's proposed change in use.

In a strong dissent, Associate Justice Brown, in espousing the importance of private property ownership, stated "private property, already an endangered species in California, is now entirely extinct in San Francisco. The [city] has implemented a neo-feudal regime where the nominal owner of property must use that property according to the preferences of the majorities that prevail in the political process—or worse, the political powerbrokers who often control the government independently of majoritarian preferences. Thus, 'the lamb [has been] committed to the custody of the wolf.'" 27 Cal. 4th at 692 (Brown,

J., dissenting) (quoting 6 The Works of John Adams, *Discourses on Davila*, page 280 (1851)). Justice Brown continued, stating that "San Francisco has redefined the American dream. Where once government was closely constrained to increase the freedom of individuals, now property ownership is closely constrained to increase the power of government. Where once government was a necessary evil because it protected private property, now private property is a necessary evil because it funds government programs." *Id.* Based on this rationale, Justice Brown said that the HCO was facially unconstitutional under the Takings Clause of the California Constitution.[11]

California's "Nexus Legislation"— The Mitigation Fee Act

In 1987, the Legislature adopted Assembly Bill 1600 (AB 1600), often referred to as the 1987 "nexus legislation." AB 1600 added Government Code sections 66000–66011, which set forth certain requirements that must be followed by a city in establishing or imposing fees. In 1996, the Legislature relabeled AB 1600 and other related sections (Gov't Code §§ 66000–66025) the "Mitigation Fee Act."

In 1996, in an apparent response to the California Supreme Court's decision in *Ehrlich*, the Legislature amended the definition of a "fee" to specifically include both fees established for a broad class of projects by legislation of general applicability and fees imposed on a specific project on an ad hoc basis. Gov't Code § 66000.

In 1996, the Legislature amended the definition of a "fee" to specifically include both fees established for a broad class of projects by legislation of general applicability and fees imposed on a specific project on an ad hoc basis.

Section 66001(a) requires any city that establishes, increases, or imposes a fee as a condition of approval of a development project to do all of the following:

- Identify the purpose of the fee
- Identify how the fee will be used
- Demonstrate that a reasonable relationship exists between the purpose of the fee and the type of development project on which the fee is imposed; and
- Demonstrate that there is a reasonable relationship between the need for the public facility and the type of development project on which the fee is imposed

Next, Government Code section 66001(b) requires that a city show that there is a "reasonable relationship" between the specific amount of the fee

---

11. On April 16, 2003 the United States District Court for the Northern District of California dismissed without leave to amend *San Remo's* federal as-applied taking case. The court essentially held that the California Supreme Court sealed the suit's fate in its decision by deciding a similar dispute. It stated that the California Supreme Court utilized an appropriate level of scrutiny by not applying the *Nollan/Dolan* higher scrutiny list. *San Remo Hotel v. City and County of San Francisco*, No. C-93-1644-DJL, filed April 16, 2003. On April 14, 2004, the Ninth Circuit Court of Appeals affirmed that decision, concluding that adjudication of the facial and as-applied challenges raised by plaintiffs in state court was an "equivalent determination" of the federal takings claim. The federal claims were therefore barred by the doctrine of issue preclusion. *San Remo Hotel L.P. v. City and County of San Francisco*, 364 F. 3d 1088, 1096 (9th Cir. 2004). The United States Supreme Court affirmed that decision, holding that there is no exception to the rules of issue preclusion that would allow a landowner to pursue federal takings claims in federal court where the issues necessary to decide those claims have been fully determined by a state court of competent jurisdiction. *San Remo Hotel L.P. v. City and County of San Francisco*, 545 U.S. 323, 336–38 (2005). For a thorough discussion of the application of ripeness and issue preclusion rules in takings cases, see the discussion in chapter 12 (Takings).

imposed as a condition of approval on a particular development project and the cost of the public facility attributable to that project. Note, however, that impact and development fees imposed pursuant to a development agreement are exempt from the Act. Gov't Code § 60000(b).

The Mitigation Fee Act also contains provisions requiring a city to deposit, invest, account for, and expend such fees (Gov't Code § 66006);[12] to make findings once every fifth year regarding any portion of the fee remaining unexpended or uncommitted (Gov't Code § 66001(d)); to identify, within 180 days of determining that sufficient funds have been collected, an approximate date of commencing construction of improvements, or else to refund unexpended fees (Gov't Code § 66001(e)); and to adopt capital improvement plans (Gov't Code § 66002). Within 180 days of the close of each fiscal year, a city must make available to the public the beginning and ending balance for the fiscal year, the description and amount of fees, interest, and other income, the identification of public improvements on which fees were expended, the amount of expenditure by city, and the amount of refunds made pursuant to section 66001 during the fiscal year. The city council is to review this information at the next regularly scheduled meeting, not less than 15 days after it becomes available. Gov't Code § 66006(b).

Under the Mitigation Fee Act, a developer may challenge the imposition of a fee, dedication, or other exaction if the developer follows a specified procedure that includes protesting the fee in writing, "at the time of approval or conditional approval of the development or within 90 days after the date of the imposition of the... exactions." Gov't Code § 66020(d)(1). A city is required to provide written notice of the 90-day protest period to the developer at the time of project approval or imposition of the fees, though the statute is silent regarding any consequences of a city's failure to provide such notice. *Id*. Any party who files a protest may then file an action attacking the imposition of the fees within 180 days after delivery of the city's notice. Gov't Code § 66020(d)(2).

Under the Mitigation Fee Act, a developer may challenge the imposition of a fee, dedication, or other exaction if the developer follows a specified procedure.

The California Supreme Court distinguished between the Act's remedies pertaining to fees imposed on a development project and fees for building inspections and permits in *Barratt American, Inc. v. City of Rancho Cucamonga*, 37 Cal. 4th 685 (2005). In *Barratt*, a developer challenged a building permit fee and sought relief under Government Code section 66016(a), which provides a prospective fee reduction remedy if building permit fees exceed actual costs and create excess revenues, and sections 66020 and 66021, which authorize a refund of any unlawful part of fees imposed on a development project. The *Barratt* court clarified that building permit fees are not fees imposed on a development project. *Id*. at 696–700.

The California Supreme Court distinguished between the Act's remedies pertaining to fees imposed on a development project and fees for building inspections and permits in Barratt American, Inc. v. City of Rancho Cucamonga.

In 2007, Barratt American challenged yet another fee resolution. *County of Orange v. Barratt American, Inc.*, 150 Cal. App. 4th 420 (2007). The county had resolved to expend its surplus fee revenue by reducing future developer fees and spending a portion of the surplus on related services and expenses. Barratt American argued that instead of spending any of the surplus, the county should further reduce future developer fees. The court held that section 66016(a)

---

12. Government Code section 66006 is applicable to any public improvement fee received pursuant to a development agreement entered into on or after January 1, 2004. *See* Gov't Code § 65865(e).

allowed the county to use any "surplus fee revenue to cover the reasonable and necessary costs of the services rather than merely lowering the fees until the surplus is dissipated." *Id.* at 433. However, the court further held that the county had not shown its spending of $4.5 million of the surplus was reasonable and necessary and, therefore, ordered the county to lower its fees until that amount was dissipated. For a discussion of litigation under the Mitigation Fee Act, *see* chapter 21 (Land Use Litigation).

Documenting the Nexus

In order to meet the constitutional and statutory nexus requirement, a city must have strong factual support.

In order to meet the constitutional and statutory nexus requirement, a city must have strong factual support. A good traffic fee study, for example, will anticipate development that is designated in the city's general plan, and estimate future traffic based upon that level of development. A strong study also will use established trip generation rates, or explain the rationale for deviating from those rates. A typical study then will project needed facilities based upon acceptable traffic levels and public transportation criteria set forth in the general plan, estimate the cost and schedule for building those facilities, then allocate the cost of constructing those facilities to new and existing development on a proportional basis.

Russ Building Partnership v. City and County of San Francisco contains an example of a well-documented fee. 199 Cal. App. 3d 1496, 1496 (1987) (opinion certified for partial publication). In *Russ*, the court upheld a $5-per-square-foot fee imposed on new office development for the San Francisco Municipal Railway System, based on the city's detailed study that documented the need and cost of the facilities. This case was decided before *Nollan* and before the effective date of the Mitigation Fee Act, but follows the principles later enunciated by those authorities.

In contrast, *Bixel Assocs. v. City of Los Angeles* provides an example of a poorly-documented fee. 216 Cal. App. 3d 1208 (1989). The court invalidated the City of Los Angeles' fire hydrant fees because there was no evidence of a proper nexus. The court then cited the proper methodology to analyze such exactions, citing *Russ Bldg. Partnership*, 199 Cal. App. 3d 1496, and *J.W. Jones Cos. v. City of San Diego*, 157 Cal. App. 3d 745 (1984).

Double Taxation

Developers often have argued that the dedication of land or the payment of fees in return for approval of a project is a tax for a public purpose, thereby constituting double taxation. However, the California Supreme Court rejected this argument in *Associated Home Builders, Inc. v. City of Walnut Creek*:

Double taxation occurs when two taxes of the same character are imposed on the same property, for the same purpose, by the same taxing authority within the same jurisdiction during the same taxing period.

> Double taxation occurs only when "two taxes of the same character are imposed on the same property, for the same purpose, by the same taxing authority within the same jurisdiction during the same taxing period." (Rhyne, Municipal Law, p. 673.) Obviously the dedication or fee required of the subdivider and the property taxes paid by the later residents of the subdivision do not meet this definition. If Associated's claim were valid the prior residents of a community could also claim double taxation since their tax dollars were utilized to purchase and maintain public facilities which will be used by the newcomers who did not contribute to their acquisition.

4 Cal. 3d 633, 642 (1971)

Equal Protection

Another course developers have pursued to avoid dedications of land or the payment of fees is to argue that such exactions violate the equal protection provisions of the Fourteenth Amendment to the United States Constitution. However, these arguments generally fail. The Fourteenth Amendment does not require that every law treat every person in exactly the same manner. Reasonable classifications can be established, and it only is necessary that the laws apply equally to persons within such classifications. With respect to economic regulation, the legislative determination of the propriety of the classification controls, so long as it meets the "rational relation" test. Thus, unless the classification is arbitrary or fails to rest upon any substantial distinction or apparent natural reason, such a determination will be upheld. *See Nordlinger v. Hahn*, 505 U.S. 1, 11 (1992) (upholding the acquisition value real property scheme of California's Proposition 13 (1978 ballot measure approving article XIIIA of the California Constitution)); *Old Dearborn Distrib. Co. v. Seagram Distillers Corp.*, 299 U.S. 183, 197 (1936). Strict scrutiny of differential treatment will be applied only where there is a "suspect classification" or where a fundamental right is affected. As the California Supreme Court stated when it upheld a city's comprehensive condominium conversion ordinance:

> The vast majority of cities and counties in California has adopted comprehensive schemes of land use regulation. Except where such regulations have infringed upon fundamental constitutional rights or relied on suspect classifications such as race, they have generally been upheld in the face of due process and equal protection challenges.

Griffin Dev. Co. v. City of Oxnard, 39 Cal. 3d 256, 263 (1985). *See also Candid Enters., Inc. v. Grossmont Union High Sch. Dist.*, 39 Cal. 3d 878, 890 (1985) ("Developers do not constitute a 'suspect class,' and development is not a 'fundamental interest.'").

This equal protection argument was pursued by the developers in *Russ Building Partnership*, but to no avail. In *Russ Building Partnership*, office developers claimed that the $5-per-square-foot municipal railway fee ordinance discriminated against owners of office buildings constructed after 1979, denying them access to government benefits on the same footing as owners of pre-1979 buildings, and that it arbitrarily singled out commercial buildings while giving retail stores in the downtown area a free ride. The court rejected this contention, holding that there was no denial of equal protection:

> Under an equal protection analysis, the transit fee as an economic regulation is presumed to be constitutional.... Likewise, the argument that retail stores, which are also responsible for increased ridership, somehow got a windfall also fails. The Ordinance imposes the fee on the projected ridership directly and reasonably arising from the new office space. The city may rationally conclude that office workers increase the need for transit services during peak hours. The conclusion that it is office space, and not retail stores, that is primarily responsible for the need for improved transit services is properly left to the sound discretion of the local governing body.

199 Cal. App. 3d at 1508

In other cases, developers have claimed equal protection violations based on the contention that a state law or city ordinance that applies only to subdividers and exempts single lot or apartment house developers denies subdividers equal protection. As part of this contention, the subdivider often argues that the occupants of an apartment house can impose as great a burden on the community as occupants of a single-family residential subdivision. However, the California Supreme Court has not been persuaded:

> This point has some arguable merit in the sense that the apartment builder, by increasing the population of an area, may add to the need for public recreational facilities to the same extent as the subdivider. However, the apartment is generally vertical, while the subdivision is horizontal. The Legislature could reasonably have assumed that an apartment house is thus ordinarily constructed upon land considerably smaller in dimension than most subdivisions and the erection of the apartment is, therefore, not decreasing the limited supply of open space to the same extent as the formation of a subdivision. This significant distinction justifies legislatively treating the builder of an apartment house who does not subdivide differently than the creator of a subdivision.

Associated Home Builders, Inc. v. City of Walnut Creek, 4 Cal. 3d at 643

Opportunities for Dedications or Fees [13]

In General

The land use approval process provides many opportunities for a city by using its police power to require dedication of land and payment of fees as conditions of approval of a development project.

The land use approval process provides many opportunities for a city by using its police power to require dedication of land and payment of fees as conditions of approval of a development project. In *Ayres v. City Council*, the California Supreme Court upheld dedication conditions for a subdivision map approval based on the city's general police power, and rejected the subdivider's argument that the city needed an enabling ordinance. 34 Cal. 2d 31 (1949). Such opportunities include, but are not limited to, general and specific plan adoption or amendment, zoning, use permit, variance, subdivision or building permit approval, and approval of property development agreements. Exactions and dedications can be required for a wide range of purposes, such as streets, sewers, drainage, parks, habitat conservation, and off-site improvements, and might include fees for building child day care centers in commercial developments, public art, financing a municipal transit system, or providing library sites, police or fire stations, or affordable housing.

The General Plan

Under the umbrella of its police power, a city can look to its zoning ordinance, subdivision ordinance, and use permit provisions for many of the standard types of dedications.

Under the umbrella of its police power, a city can look to its zoning ordinance, subdivision ordinance, and use permit provisions for many of the standard types of dedications. However, more cities now are relying upon the general plan or applicable specific plan to support dedication or fee requirements. Given that the general plan is considered the constitution for development, it makes sense that dedication requirements can flow from goals and policies contained in such plans. *See J.W. Jones Cos*, 157 Cal. App. 3d at 749. Since all land use approvals must be consistent with the goals, policies, and

---

13. *See* Governor's Office of Planning and Research, *A Planner's Guide to Financing Public Improvements* (June 1997), for an excellent overview of various methods for processing public improvements, including impact fees, Mello-Roos taxes, and school district financing.

objectives of the general plan, conditions can be attached to achieve these goals. For a thorough discussion of general plans and consistency requirements, *see* chapter 2 (General Plan).

For example, in *Soderling v. City of Santa Monica*, the court upheld a city's requirement that smoke detectors be installed in all units in a condominium conversion. In so doing, it reasoned that this requirement flowed from the city's general plan to "promote safe housing for all." 142 Cal. App. 3d 501, 506 (1983). This condition was seen as a valid means to achieve the goals of the city's general plan. Therefore, the power to impose the condition need not be expressed by the specific enactment of an ordinance or promulgation of a regulation, because the Subdivision Map Act requires consistency with the general plan.

Similarly, in *J.W. Jones Cos.*, the court ruled that the City of San Diego properly exercised its police power to impose a facilities benefits assessment (FBA) on developers in order to carry out its general development scheme as "sketched in the general plan" of the City. 157 Cal. App. 3d at 758. An FBA would require the installation of a broad spectrum of public improvements by the developer, such as public libraries and fire stations, which in the past had been financed by general city revenues. The court stated, "[T]he ordinance is the key to implementing San Diego's controlled growth concept as formalized by the general plan and community plan.... The vision of San Diego's future as sketched in the general plan is attainable only through the comprehensive financing scheme contemplated by the FBA." *Id.* at 757–58.[14]

Thus, given the propriety of tying exactions to general plan goals, some cities have amended their general plans to adopt goals and policies relating to the need for child day care centers, public libraries, and fire stations and have, in turn, adopted ordinances requiring developers to pay a fee for those purposes.

Subdivision Process

Dedications and development fees are generated from three basic sources in the subdivision approval process:

- Specific conditions that may be imposed by local ordinance through the specific statutory authorization contained in the Subdivision Map Act (Gov't Code §§ 66410–66499.58) and related statutes
- Environmental mitigation measures that may be imposed through the CEQA process (Pub. Res. Code §§ 21000–21177), and through Government Code section 66474(e), which requires denial of maps likely to cause substantial environmental damage
- Conditions that may be imposed through the definitions of "design" and "improvement" in the Subdivision Map Act and reliance on the general plan. *See* chapter 5 (Subdivisions).

If a dedication or fee requirement is attached to the approval of a map based on the specific statutory authorization of the Subdivision Map Act, then that criterion governs. However, a different rule applies if a dedication or fee is attached to a non-subdivision approval, *e.g.*, a PUD or CUP. In these situations,

The power to impose the condition need not be expressed by the specific enactment of an ordinance or promulgation of a regulation, because the Subdivision Map Act requires consistency with the general plan.

CEQA = California Environmental Quality Act
CUP = Conditional use permit
FBA = Facilities benefits assessment
PUD = Planned-unit development

PRACTICE TIP

If a city plans to attach conditions of dedications to building permit issuance, it should have enabling authority written into the ordinance to ensure that issuance of a building permit is not treated as ministerial.

---

14. For a discussion of infrastructure finance mechanisms and the ability of the general plan to promote fairness and predictability, *see* Edward J. Sullivan and Ian Lester, "The Role of the Comprehensive Plan in Infrastructure Financing," 37 *Urb. Law.* 53 (Winter 2005).

the imposition of the requirement is governed by the city's general police power as interpreted under the nexus rules. For example, if a city wants to impose a condition requiring parkland dedication or payment of fees for park or recreational facilities as part of the subdivision process, a city, by ordinance, may do so. Gov't Code § 66477; *see also Associated Home Builders, Inc. v. City of Walnut Creek*, 4 Cal. 3d 633 (1971). Therefore, if the city attaches this condition to the approval of a map, it must adhere to the limitation of three to five acres per 1,000 residents set forth in the Map Act. But, if a city's general plan calls for six or seven acres per 1,000 residents, then a city may impose this higher standard under its general police power if this condition is attached to a non-subdivision approval, like a PUD or CUP, rather than the map approval, and the city has adopted a regulation to that effect. *See* 73 Ops. Cal. Atty. Gen. 152, 156 (1990).

Building Permits

The dedication of land or the payment of fees can be required as a condition of issuance of building permits. The issuance of building permits once was viewed by developers as a right, so long as the project was in compliance with building codes and zoning regulations. *See Sunset View Cemetery Ass'n v. Kraintz*, 196 Cal. App. 2d 115, 118–19 (1961). However, courts no longer treat the issuance of building permits as ministerial only. Rather, courts consistently uphold local regulations that treat the issuance of building permits as discretionary, which allows cities to impose conditions on their issuance:

> The contention that Avco was entitled to a building permit because the county would have been compelled to issue it upon mere application has no merit. The Orange County Building Code (§ 302(a)) provides that a building permit may not issue unless the plans conform not only to the structural requirements of the Code but to "other pertinent laws and ordinances." This provision codifies the general rule that a builder must comply with the laws which are in effect at the time a building permit is issued, including the laws which were enacted after application for the permit.

Avco Community Developers, Inc. v. South Coast Reg'l Comm'n, 17 Cal. 3d 785, 795 (1976); *see also Friends of Westwood, Inc. v. City of Los Angeles*, 191 Cal. App. 3d 259, 276–77 (1987); *Fontana Unified Sch. Dist. v. City of Rialto*, 173 Cal. App. 3d 725, 732–33 (1985); *Slagle Constr. Co. v. County of Contra Costa*, 67 Cal. App. 3d 559, 563 (1977)

Building fees are also subject to the Mitigation Fee Act. Pursuant to Government Code § 66014, building fees may not exceed the estimated reasonable cost of providing the service for which the fee is charged.

Building fees are also subject to the Mitigation Fee Act. Pursuant to Government Code § 66014, building fees may not exceed the estimated reasonable cost of providing the service for which the fee is charged. In *Barratt*, the California Supreme Court held that because building fees are not development fees, the applicable remedy and limitations period for excessive building fee claims are stated in sections 66016 and 66022. 37 Cal. 4th at 692. Under section 66016, the applicable remedy is a prospective fee reduction and, pursuant to section 66022(a), the applicable limitation period is 120 days from the effective date of the ordinance, resolution, or motion. *Id.* at 694. The court also found that if a city reenacts a building permit fee, even though the fee amount is unchanged, it does constitute a modification or amendment of an existing fee or service charge under section 66022, thus triggering a new limitations period. *Id.* at 703. The court reasoned that the city's reenactment of a permit fee changed the duration of the fee, extending its applicability, and by implication, its validity. Otherwise, without this interpretation, all subsequent reenactments of a fee not initially challenged would be immune from judicial challenges. *Id.*

School District Facilities Fee
Background [15]

In 1985, the California Supreme Court held that a city could impose fees on new construction to mitigate impacts on school districts. *Candid Enterprises, Inc. v. Grossmont Union High Sch. Dist.*, 39 Cal. 3d 878 (1985). In 1986, the Legislature adopted the School Facilities Legislation in an attempt to moderate the effects of the *Candid Enterprises* decision. Former Educ. Code § 17620; Gov't Code § 65995 (Sterling Act). The Sterling Act capped school fees at $1.50 per square foot for residential development and $0.25 per square foot for commercial/ industrial development, subject to biennial adjustments for inflation. *Id.* The California Supreme Court held that Government Code section 65995, relating to school fees, preempted local agencies, including a school district, from imposing other development fees or special taxes on developers. *See Grupe Dev. Co. v. Superior Court*, 4 Cal. 4th 911, 919 (1993).

The Sterling Act declared that the financing of school facilities with development fees is a matter of statewide concern and that the Legislature occupied the subject matter to the exclusion of all local measures. Former Gov't Code § 65995(e). It also prohibited a public agency, acting under CEQA (Pub. Res. Code §§ 21000–21177) or the Subdivision Map Act (Gov't Code §§ 66410–66499.58), from denying approval of a project based on the adequacy of school facilities. Former Gov't Code § 65996; *see also Corona-Norco Unified Sch. Dist. v. City of Corona*, 13 Cal. App. 4th 1577 (1993).

At first it appeared that the Sterling Act strictly limited the power of a city and a school district to deal with impacts of development on schools. However, later judicial decisions interpreted the Act as allowing cities to consider the availability of school facilities when making "legislative" decisions, such as general and specific plan adoptions and amendments and zoning changes. *See William S. Hart Union High Sch. Dist. v. Reg'l Planning Comm'n*, 226 Cal. App. 3d 1612, 1624 (1991); *Murrieta Valley Unified Sch. Dist. v. County of Riverside*, 228 Cal. App. 3d 1212, 1220, 1229, 1234 (1991); *Mira Dev. Corp. v. City of San Diego*, 205 Cal. App. 3d 1201, 1218 (1988). *Mira*, *Hart*, and *Murrieta* limited the Act's application to only "adjudicatory" project approvals (*e.g.*, map approvals, conditional use permits). The courts held that cities therefore could deny or modify legislative approvals (despite the developer's willingness to pay the Act's school fees) based on inadequate school facilities.

Leroy F. Greene School Facilities Act of 1998 (SB 50).[16] In 1998, the Legislature made significant amendments to the statutory scheme for school fees. Most

The Sterling Act declared that the financing of school facilities with development fees is a matter of statewide concern and that the Legislature occupied the subject matter to the exclusion of all local measures.

---

15. For an excellent historical review of the legislative and judicial history of school development fees, *see Grupe Development Co. v. Superior Court*, 4 Cal. 4th 911 (1993). In *Grupe*, the court held that the 1986 legislation preempted the field of school construction financing and declared invalid a special tax ($1,500 per unit) adopted after Proposition 13 and under its provisions by two-thirds vote. *See also* Sandra L. Silberstein, "Financing Schools in the 90's," 2 *CEB Land Use & Env. Forum* 281 (Fall 1993); *Western/Cal. Ltd. v. Dry Creek Joint Elementary Sch. Dist.*, 50 Cal. App. 4th 1461 (1996).
16. For a comprehensive discussion of the Leroy F. Greene School Facilities Act of 1998, *see* Maureen F. Gorsen, *et al.*, *California School Facilities Planning: A Guide to Laws and Procedures for Funding, Siting, Design, and Construction* (Solano Press, 2006), in particular pages 59 *et seq.*

importantly, the legislation sought to override the rule of the *Mira-Hart-Murrieta* trilogy; *i.e.*, that the statutory limitations on school impact fees and mitigation apply only to adjudicative, not legislative, actions.

The express inclusion of "legislative" approvals in the statute evidences a clear legislative intent to overturn the *Mira-Hart-Murrieta* line of cases. The Legislature also included a clear statement of its intent to occupy the field:

> The Legislature finds and declares that the financing of school facilities and the mitigation of the impacts of land use approvals, whether legislative or adjudicative...on the need for school facilities are matters of statewide concern. For this reason, the Legislature hereby occupies the subject matter of requirements related to school facilities levied or imposed in connection with, or made a condition of, any land use approval, whether legislative or adjudicative act...and the mitigation of the impacts of land use approvals, whether legislative or adjudicative...on the need for school facilities, to the exclusion of all other measures, financial or nonfinancial, on the subjects. For purposes of this subdivision, "school facilities" means any school-related consideration relating to a school district's ability to accommodate enrollment.

Gov't Code § 65995(e)

SB 50 included a $9.2 billion state bond measure that was approved by the voters as Proposition 1A in the November 3, 1998 general election. The approval of Proposition 1A, effective November 4, 1998, made operative other provisions of SB 50 that amended the laws governing school impact fees and other mitigation measures. SB 50 amended Government Code section 65995(a) to prohibit state or local agencies from imposing school impact mitigation fees, dedications, or other requirements in excess of those provided in the statute in connection with "any legislative or adjudicative act...by any state or local agency involving...the planning, use, or development of real property...." Consistent with prior statutes, school districts are limited to imposing only the school impact fees authorized by statute. Educ. Code § 17620. *See Warmington Old Town Assos. v. Tustin Unified Sch. Dist.*, 101 Cal. App. 4th 840 (2002) (affirming refund of school fees paid by developer because the fees were in excess of those authorized under Education Code section 17620).

The legislation also amended Government Code section 65996(b) to prohibit local agencies from using the inadequacy of school facilities as a basis for denying or conditioning approvals of any "legislative or adjudicative act...involving...the planning, use, or development of real property...." The former version of this statute extended only to approvals under the Subdivision Map Act or CEQA.

The Government Code sets the base amount of allowable developer fees for residential, commercial, and industrial construction.

The Government Code sets the base amount of allowable developer fees for residential, commercial, and industrial construction. Gov't Code § 65995(b). These base amounts are commonly referred to as Level 1 fees and are subject to adjustment for inflation. Gov't Code § 65995(b)(3). In January 2006, the State Allocation Board authorized its latest adjustment for inflation of Level 1 fees, bringing the base amounts to $2.63 per square foot for residential and $0.42 per square foot for commercial and industrial construction. For updated information regarding statutory developer fees, *see* the State Allocation Board's website (www.opsc.dgs.ca.gov).

In certain circumstances, for residential construction, school districts can impose fees in excess of Level 1 fees. School districts can impose fees equal to 50 percent of land and construction costs (commonly referred to as Level 2 fees) if they prepare and adopt a school facilities needs analysis, and the State Allocation Board determines the district to be eligible to impose Level 2 fees. In addition, the district must meet at least two of the following four conditions to impose Level 2 fees (Gov't Code § 65995.5):

- At least 30 percent of the district's students are on a multitrack year-round schedule.
- The district has placed on the ballot within the previous four years a local school bond that received at least 50 percent of the votes cast.
- The district has passed bonds equal to (1) 15 percent of its bonding capacity prior to November 4, 1998 or (2) 30 percent of its bonding capacity after November 4, 1998.
- At least 20 percent of the district's teaching stations are relocatable classrooms.

Also, if the state's bond funds are exhausted, a school district that is eligible to impose Level 2 fees will be authorized to impose even higher fees, which are commonly referred to as Level 3 fees, equal to 100 percent of land and construction costs of new schools required as a result of new developments.

The 1998 legislation also included various "grandfathering" provisions for projects that were under contract or had obtained certain approvals and building permits before the legislation was passed. The relevant dates and conditions for those "grandfathering" provisions are found in Government Code section 65995(c).

Nonprofit private university is not exempt from school fees. In *Loyola Marymount University v. Los Angeles Unified School District*, the court held that a nonprofit, private university was not entitled to an exemption from school impact fees in connection with construction of its new business school. 45 Cal. App. 4th 1256, 1267–71 (1996).

Loyola Marymount University, a nonprofit Catholic institution, acquired vacant land adjacent to its Los Angeles campus. The university intended to construct a new building to house a postgraduate business school and a new parking structure. Loyola Marymount applied for a building permit, which would not be issued unless it paid the school development fees authorized by the Sterling Act. Loyola Marymount paid $37,483 in school development fees under protest and then petitioned for a writ of mandamus. The trial court ordered the Los Angeles Unified School District to refund the fees with interest.

In ruling for the school district, the appellate court reversed, stating that to offset the burden imposed on school districts by new development, Education Code section 17620 (former Gov't Code § 53080(a)(1)) authorizes school districts to levy a fee to fund the construction of school facilities against all residential, commercial, and industrial development projects that are not subject to exemption. *Id.* at 1261. Loyola Marymount's proposed project qualified as commercial use since the school offered services in exchange for money. Moreover, Loyola Marymount did not qualify for an exemption from school facilities fees for state entities or facilities used exclusively for religious purposes.

Redevelopment construction is not exempt from school fees. In *Warmington Old Town Associates v. Tustin Unified School District*, a case of first impression, the court held that redevelopment construction is not exempt from the imposition of school-impact fees. 101 Cal. App. 4th 840 (2002).

In this case, as part of a redevelopment project, the developer demolished 56 apartment units in the City of Tustin and replaced them with 38 single family homes. The school district then imposed $122,080 in school-impact fees, based on the total square footage of the 38 single family homes, considering them "new residential construction" within the meaning of Education Code section 17620(a)(1)(B). The developer paid the fees under protest, then filed a petition for a writ of mandate, claiming that (1) he was owed a "credit" with respect to the 56 units that were replaced, and (2) the district failed to establish a sufficient nexus between the fee and the purported impact.

With respect to the developer's first contention, the court held that Education Code section 17620 permits school districts to impose school-impact fees to "new residential construction." These fees also apply to the resulting increase in space of "other residential construction." The court acknowledged that including an exemption for redevelopment projects would be consistent with the purpose of the statutory scheme, *i.e.*, to address the impact on the affected school district related to the increase in students generated by the development. However, it rejected this argument because it would render section 17626 (exemption for remodeling projects) superfluous. Therefore, to harmonize the exemptions provided in sections 17620 and 17626, the court concluded that the demolition of apartments and replacement with houses does not fall within the scope of "other residential construction" entitled to a credit. 101 Cal. App. 4th at 850–51.

The court also addressed the question of whether the fee study presented by the district in support of the imposition of school fees established the reasonable relationship required under Government Code section 66001. The fee study evaluated the impact of building new homes, which would generate new students, thereby impacting the district. However, the court held that the fee study was not sufficient to establish the required nexus between the amount of the fee imposed and the burden created. *Id.* at 851. In so holding, the court pointed out the flaws in this study as applied to redevelopment projects:

> [T]he Fee Study gives no thought to the extent of the impact of a tract of homes that are newly constructed in the place of older residential housing previously existing on the same site. It gives no consideration to whether those newly constructed replacement homes in fact generate additional numbers of students over and above those who occupied the previous homes at the site.... It suggests no method for estimating the impact of new construction in the redevelopment context, in which new homes may generate no more students than replaced homes did previously or may even generate fewer students."

Id. at 859

Level of scrutiny for school fees. In its school fee challenge mentioned above, Loyola Marymount also argued that due process requires that fees be imposed only where there is a nexus between the state interest served by the fees and the proposed project. *Loyola Marymount Univ.*, 45 Cal. App. 4th at 1270 (citing *Dolan v. City of Tigard*, 512 U.S. 374 (1994)). Relying on *Ehrlich*, however, the court rejected this

Education Code section 17620 permits school districts to impose school-impact fees to new residential construction. These fees also apply to the resulting increase in space of other residential construction.

argument since the *Nollan/Dolan* test is not applicable to legislatively formulated development fees imposed on a class of property owners, but only to individually applied ad hoc fees. The court then stated:

> Unlike *Ehrlich*, the present case falls within the general category of development fees. In light of *Ehrlich's* discussion, we conclude that the heightened scrutiny standards articulated by the United States Supreme Court in takings clause cases have no application in California cases involving development fees.

Id. at 1271

Loyola Marymount University is consistent with other cases that have held that the action of imposing a school fee was a legislative act reviewable under ordinary mandate (Code Civ. Proc. § 1085), and therefore the fee need only meet the "reasonable relationship" test. *See Western/Cal. Ltd. v. Dry Creek Joint Elementary Sch. Dist.*, 50 Cal. App. 4th 1461, 1492 (1996); *Garrick Dev. Co. v. Hayward Unified Sch. Dist.*, 3 Cal. App. 4th 320, 327–28 (1992).

Habitat Conservation Plans

One area of increasing interest among cities and counties is the use of Habitat Conservation Plans (HCPs) and Natural Communities Conservation Plans (NCCPs) to ensure the protection of certain species and certain types of habitat. Habitat Conservation Plans are the federal mechanism under the Endangered Species Act (ESA) for striking a balance between development and the protection of important habitat. Development and approval of an HCP acceptable to federal agencies would entitle a developer to a permit documenting compliance with the ESA. Natural Communities Conservation Plans are a similar mechanism under state law for complying with the California ESA.[17] Impact fees on development and land exchanges among private, local, state, and even federal entities are among the ways HCPs and NCCPs are proposed to be funded.

ESA = Endangered Species Act
HCP = Habitat Conservation Plan
NCCP = Natural Communities Conservation Plan

Certain local agencies have made moves to combine these federal and state conservation plans with their own local planning mechanisms. For example, Riverside County has coordinated its general plan update, transportation plan, and HCP. Riverside County's Multi-Species Habitat Conservation Plan was adopted by 14 cities and was approved by state and federal regulators in June, 2004.[18] For a thorough discussion of HCPs, *see* chapter 8 (Endangered Species Protections). *See also* Joshua Safran, "Zero Sum Game: The Debate Over Off-Site Agricultural Mitigation Measures," 6 *Vt. J. Envt'l L.* 15 (2004–2005).

Interestingly, as some local governments use their police power and planning authority to help implement the regional conservation goals of HCPs and NCCPs, others are frustrated that these plans circumvent the local planning process. They claim that the plans—with their promise of compliance with the Endangered Species Act—cede too much planning authority to federal and state statutes and authorities. They argue that the result is a patchwork of ineffective conservation that does not reflect local preferences or local circumstances.[19]

As some local governments use their police power and planning authority to help implement the regional conservation goals of HCPs and NCCPs, others are frustrated that these plans circumvent the local planning process.

---

17. For a detailed discussion of Habitat Conservation Plans and Natural Community Conservation Plans, *see* Paul Cylinder, *et al.*, *Understanding the Habitat Conservation Planning Process in California* (Institute for Local Self Government, California League of Cities, 2004).
18. *Id.*, page 4.
19. For a critical view of HCPs and NCCPs, *see* "Drawing New Lines for Conservation," *Contra Costa Times*, April 18, 2004, page A1.

CEQA

Although CEQA does not independently authorize a city to impose dedications or exactions, the statute is intended to be used in conjunction with the police powers or other discretionary powers granted to public agencies by other laws.

Although CEQA does not independently authorize a city to impose dedications or exactions, the statute is intended to be used in conjunction with the police powers or other discretionary powers granted to public agencies by other laws. Cal. Code Regs. tit. 14, § 15040. Therefore, so long as a dedication or exaction is carried out under some other authority, CEQA provides a basis for analyzing and considering the effects of a particular exaction. The CEQA Guidelines provide that "a lead agency for a project has the authority to require feasible changes in any or all activities involved in the project in order to substantially lessen or avoid significant effects on the environment, consistent with applicable constitutional requirements such as the 'nexus' and 'rough proportionality' standards established by case law." Cal. Code Regs. tit. 14, § 15041 (citing *Nollan v. California Coastal Comm'n*, 483 U.S. 825 (1987); *Dolan v. City of Tigard*, 512 U.S. 374 (1994)).

Special Requirements Relating to Imposition of Fees

Waiting Period Before Fees Become Effective; Public Hearing Required

State law requires a 60-day waiting period before new fees or increased fees on development can go into effect. Gov't Code § 66017(a). This waiting period applies not only to processing fees but to development fees, such as circulation and drainage fees. Also, properly noticed public hearing must be conducted pursuant to Government Code section 66016.

In addition, state law imposes a general 10-day newspaper notice and public hearing requirement with respect to the adoption or increase of any fee, if that fee would not otherwise be subject to other statutory notice requirements (*i.e.*, Government Code sections 66017 and 66016). Gov't Code § 66018.

> **PRACTICE TIP**
>
> A developer, before paying a processing fee or a development fee that has been recently increased, should check whether the 60-day waiting period has run.

When Fees Are Required to Be Paid

In general, a city that "imposes fees or charges for the construction of public improvements or facilities on a residential development" cannot require payment of the fee until the date of the final inspection or the date the certificate of occupancy is issued, whichever is first. Gov't Code § 66007.[20] Government Code section 66007 has two purposes: (1) to require cities to defer payment of general development fees so that developers will no longer be required to pay the fees as early in the process; and (2) to encourage cities to specify how money collected from fees will be spent prior to being able to collect such fees.

However, an exception exists. A city may collect fees at an earlier time if the city determines prior to the final inspection or the issuance of a certificate of occupancy that:

- The fees will be collected for public improvements or facilities for which an account has been established and funds appropriated, and the city has adopted a proposed construction schedule or plan for the project, or

---

20. For a detailed discussion of fees in the context of open space programs, *see Funding Open Space Acquisition Programs: A Guide for Local Agencies in California* (Institute for Local Government, League of California Cities, 2005).

- The fees are to reimburse the local agency for expenditures previously made Gov't Code § 66007(b)(1). This exception does not apply, except for developer fees levied for school construction purposes, to units reserved for occupancy by lower income households where: (1) the units are included in a residential development proposed by a nonprofit housing developer; and (2) at least 49 percent of the total units are reserved for occupancy by lower income households at an affordable rent. Gov't Code § 66007(b)(2).

Cities may require applicants for building permits to enter into a contract to pay the required fees. Gov't Code § 66007. The contracts must be recorded, and are enforceable against successors in interest to the applicant. The contracts may require notification to the city when any escrow for sale of a dwelling unit is opened, and may also require the fees to be paid from escrow before any sale proceeds are disbursed to the seller. *Id.*

Another exception involves the collection of utility service fees. Utility service fees may be collected at the time an application for utility service is received. Gov't Code § 66007.

In a 1990 case, a court held that Government Code section 66007 was not applicable to school impact fees. The court stated that the specific provision relating to payment of school development fees (former Gov't Code § 53080) prevailed over the general provisions of Government Code section 66007. Therefore, the fees had to be paid before obtaining a building permit. *See RRLH, Inc. v. Saddleback Valley Unified Sch. Dist.*, 222 Cal. App. 3d 1602, 1611 (1990). The ruling in *RRLH* is probably also applicable to timing of fees specified in the Subdivision Map Act, such as fees for bridges and major thoroughfares. Gov't Code § 66484.

In a 1990 case, a court held that Government Code section 66007 was not applicable to school impact fees.

Reasonableness of Development Fee Amount

As discussed previously regarding the Mitigation Fee Act, when a city imposes any fees or exactions as a condition of approval of a proposed development, those fees or exactions shall not exceed the estimated reasonable cost of providing the service or facility for which the fees or exactions are imposed. Gov't Code § 66005. Furthermore, cities must comply with certain fee-identification and "reasonable relationship" requirements before establishing, increasing, or imposing a fee. Gov't Code § 66001. Cities may not include the cost attributable to existing deficiencies in public facilities, but may include the cost attributable to the increased demand for public facilities reasonably related to the development project. Gov't Code § 66001(g).

Fees Cannot Be Levied for Maintenance and Operation

Fees cannot be levied on development projects for the maintenance or operation of public capital facility improvements. Gov't Code § 65913.8. However, a maintenance and/or operation fee may be required if the improvement is designed and installed to serve only the specific development project on which the fee is imposed, and the improvement serves 19 or fewer lots or units, so long as the city makes a finding based upon substantial evidence, that it is infeasible or impractical to form an assessment district or to annex into one. In addition, this type of fee can be required if the improvement is within a water, sewer maintenance, street

Fees cannot be levied on development projects for the maintenance or operation of public capital facility improvements.

lighting, or drainage district if an assessment district will be created. This section does not affect developer fees for the construction of capital improvements.

Dedication of Land— Reconveyance to Subdivider

Government Code section 66477.5 provides that if a subdivider is required to make a dedication of land in fee (not an easement) for public purposes (other than for open space, schools, or parks), the city to which the land is dedicated must record a certificate with the county recorder identifying the subdivider and the land being dedicated, and stating that the land shall be reconveyed to the subdivider if the same public purpose for which it was dedicated no longer exists, or the land or a portion thereof is not needed for public utilities. The subdivider may request that the city make such a determination and reconvey the land to the subdivider as provided above, but the city may assess a fee for making the determination. The fee may not exceed the cost of making the determination. If land is to be reconveyed, it shall be reconveyed to the subdivider or its successor in interest. The law also provides that the city must give the subdivider whose name appears on the certificate 60 days notice prior to vacating, leasing, selling, or otherwise disposing of the dedicated property, unless the dedicated property will be used for the same public purpose for which it was dedicated.

Development Fee or a Tax?

Historical Background

For many years, in particular before the passage of Proposition 218 in 1996, the courts had upheld a taxing approach by which cities and counties could distribute the burden of supporting community services.

For many years, in particular before the passage of Proposition 218 in 1996, the courts had upheld a taxing approach by which cities and counties could distribute the burden of supporting community services. This approach could, for example, require the payment of a tax computed according to the number of bedrooms in the proposed structure, payable at the time of issuance of the building permit. The monies could then be used for various types of capital facilities. This bedroom tax approach was initially approved by the courts of appeal, which said that a general law city's ordinance imposing such a tax was solely a revenue measure imposing a valid tax, rather than having any regulatory purpose. *See Associated Home Builders, Inc. v. City of Newark*, 18 Cal. App. 3d 107, 111 (1971).

For example, the California Supreme Court upheld a license tax on a company engaged in the business of acquiring, subdividing, improving, selling, and otherwise disposing of real property. *See City of Los Angeles v. Rancho Homes, Inc.*, 40 Cal. 2d 764, 771 (1953). In another case, a court upheld an environmental excise tax ordinance that levied $500 per bedroom with a maximum of $1,000 per dwelling unit. *See Westfield-Palos Verdes Co. v. City of Rancho Palos Verdes*, 73 Cal. App. 3d 486 (1977).

In Centex Real Estate Corporation v. City of Vallejo, *the court held valid a property development excise tax imposed on developers as a condition of the issuance of a building permit.*

In *Centex Real Estate Corp. v. City of Vallejo*, the court held valid a property development excise tax imposed on developers as a condition of the issuance of a building permit. 19 Cal. App. 4th 1358, 1362 (1993). The ordinance provided that the tax of $3,000 per unit of residential development and $0.30 per square foot of nonresidential development was a general tax imposed on the privilege of developing property and benefiting from city services. The revenue derived from the tax went to "the City's general fund to support general community services provided now and in the near future." *Id.* at 1361.

The court held that the tax was not in violation of the Mitigation Fee Act (Gov't Code §§ 66000–66025), which does not prohibit a city from enacting an excise tax. The court stated that an excise tax may properly be imposed on the privilege of developing property, and the tax at issue had all of the characteristics of an excise tax. It was imposed only upon approval and issuance of a building permit, which generally precedes the exercise of the privilege of developing property. Additionally, the purpose of the excise tax was to raise revenue for the city's general fund, and not for the limited purpose of funding public facilities or services related to a new development. In contrast, the court stated that development fees are commonly imposed on developers by local governments in order to lessen the adverse impact of increased population generated by the development. *Id.* at 1358 (citing *California Bldg. Indus. Ass'n v. Governing Bd. of the Newhall Sch. Dist.*, 206 Cal. App. 3d 212, 235 (1988)). For a good discussion of the distinctions between a "tax" and a "regulatory fee," *see Sinclair Paint Co. v. State Board of Equalization*, 15 Cal. 4th 866 (1997).

Effect of Jarvis Initiatives—Proposition 13 (1978), Proposition 62 (1986), and Proposition 218 (1996)

In 1978, the passage of Proposition 13, adding article XIIIA to the California Constitution, dramatically changed local government finance by limiting most property taxes to one percent of the property value. In addition, Proposition 13 made the imposition of new state and local taxes more difficult by requiring (for state taxes) a two-thirds vote of the Legislature, or (for local taxes) a two-thirds vote of the electorate. *See Sinclair Paint Co. v. State Bd. of Equalization*, 15 Cal. 4th at 877–78 (considering whether the "fee" established by the Childhood Lead Poisoning Act, which the Legislature passed by a simple majority vote, was actually a "tax" requiring a two-thirds vote);[21] *see also Howard Jarvis Taxpayers Ass'n v. City of Riverside*, 73 Cal. App. 4th 679 (1999) (overview of Proposition 13). Many cities were hit hard by the resulting loss in revenues and had to cut services sharply. To make up for the losses, cities increasingly turned to benefit assessments, special taxes, development fees, and other new revenue sources.

Proposition 62 (Gov't Code §§ 53720–53730) passed by the voters in November 1986, was designed to fill apparent gaps in Proposition 13. Proposition 62 specifically targeted loopholes through which local governments had continued to levy taxes, *i.e.*, utility user taxes, transient occupancy taxes, and business license taxes simply by a majority vote of the city council or board of supervisors without voter ratification. *See City and County of San Francisco v. Farrell*, 32 Cal. 3d 47, 56–57 (1982); *McBrearty v. Brawley*, 59 Cal. App. 4th 1441, 1448 (1997) (discussing the constitutionality of Proposition 62 and its retroactive application). Proposition 62 classifies all taxes as either "general taxes" or "special taxes." A "general tax" is a tax imposed for general governmental purposes.

In 1978, the passage of Proposition 13, adding article XIIIA to the California Constitution, dramatically changed local government finance by limiting most property taxes to one percent of the property value.

---

21. In *Sinclair*, the California Supreme Court held that a state-imposed charge on paint companies and other businesses that made products using lead was a "fee" and not a "tax" subject to the two-thirds vote requirement of Proposition 13. In November 2000, California voters endorsed the court's opinion by defeating an initiative that would have required a two-thirds Legislative or voter approval for certain regulatory charges like the one in *Sinclair*.

Under Proposition 62, no general tax may be imposed without a two-thirds vote of all members of the legislative body proposing to impose the tax and a majority vote of the local electorate voting on the issue.

All taxes other than general taxes, including taxes for specific purposes, are "special taxes." No special tax may be imposed without a two-thirds vote of the local electorate voting on the question of whether to impose the tax.

All taxes other than general taxes, including taxes for specific purposes, are "special taxes." No special tax may be imposed without a two-thirds vote of the local electorate voting on the question of whether to impose the tax. Gov't Code § 53722; *see also Santa Clara County Local Transp. Auth. v. Guardino*, 11 Cal. 4th 220, 231–32 (1995). The voter-approval requirement of Proposition 62 was upheld by the California Supreme Court, which determined that it did not violate the state constitutional prohibition against subjecting tax statutes to a referendum. *Id.* at 241; Cal. Const. art. II, § 9. Thus, all new "taxes" sought to be imposed by local governments and districts are subject to voter approval.

Proposition 62 did not limit the authority of local governments to impose "special assessments," "fees," or "charges" under their police power in connection with the development of real property.

However, Proposition 62 did not limit the authority of local governments to impose "special assessments," "fees," or "charges" under their police power in connection with the development of real property. This authority already was well established in California. *See, e.g., Russ Bldg. Partnership v. City and County of San Francisco*, 199 Cal. App. 3d 1496, 1503 (1987); *J.W. Jones Cos. v. City of San Diego*, 157 Cal. App. 3d 745, 758 (1984); *Trent Meredith, Inc. v. City of Oxnard*, 114 Cal. App. 3d 317, 325 (1981). Proposition 62 and the cases that followed it also left open the question of whether or not its restrictions and requirements applied to charter cities. *See Guardino*, 11 Cal. 4th at 260.

Proposition 218. California voters approved Proposition 218 in November 1996, adding articles XIIIC and XIIID to the California Constitution.[22] Proposition 218 was drafted by the Howard Jarvis Taxpayers Association, a group comprising many of the same people who championed Propositions 13 and 62. It was intended to close perceived loopholes in those earlier laws by placing in the state constitution the voter-approval requirements of Proposition 62, as well as by requiring voters to approve all locally-imposed special assessments and certain other fees and charges. Significantly, Proposition 218 expressly makes these restrictions and requirements applicable to both general law and charter law cities. *See Burbank-Glendale-Pasadena Airport Auth. v. City of Burbank*, 64 Cal. App. 4th 1217 (1998) (a charter city's enactment of a transient parking tax under Proposition 62 did not require voter approval, but that upon passage of Proposition 218, voter approval was required).

An official report by the Legislative Analyst in 1996 predicted that Proposition 218 would result in short-term local government revenue losses of more than $100 million; the long-term losses would total hundreds of millions of dollars annually. However, it appears that Proposition 218's actual impacts have been varied. Some cities have had significant revenue losses because their electorates have voted against taxes, assessments, fees, and charges needed to provide important municipal services. In other cities, including many in the San Francisco Bay Area, despite causing delays and increased administrative costs,

---

22. For a summary of the historical background that led to the adoption of Proposition 218, *see Howard Jarvis Taxpayers Ass'n v. City of Riverside*, 73 Cal. App. 4th at 681–683. Also, for a good discussion of Proposition 218, *see* Robert E. Merritt and Rajiv Parikh, "The Proposition 218 Odyssey: New Challenges for Real Property Development," 20 *CEB Real Prop. L. Rep.* 70 (May 1997). *See also Proposition 218—Implementation Guide* (League of California Cities 1998-A).

Proposition 218 has had limited impacts on revenue because voters have supported existing and proposed assessments.

Impacts on local general taxes. Proposition 218 answered an important question not addressed in Propositions 13 and 62 by requiring all new or increased local, general taxes, including those in charter cities, to be approved by a majority vote of the local electorate. It also required existing general taxes that were imposed, extended, or increased after January 1, 1995 to be approved by a majority of voters within two years, unless the tax had been approved previously by a majority vote.

Proposition 218 answered an important question not addressed in Propositions 13 and 62 by requiring all new or increased local, general taxes, including those in charter cities, to be approved by a majority vote of the local electorate.

Proposition 218 requires that elections to approve general taxes be held at the same time as the regularly scheduled general election for the members of the local governing body. However, special elections to approve general taxes can be held upon a unanimous vote of the governing body declaring a case of emergency. It also prohibits special purpose districts or agencies, including school districts, from levying general taxes.

Under subsequent legislation clarifying Proposition 218 (Stats. 1997, chap. 38), resolutions presented to voters for taxes may state a range of rates or amounts. In addition, such resolutions may provide for an automatic inflation adjustment pursuant to a clearly identified formula, unless the tax rate itself is determined by a percentage calculation. Gov't Code §§ 53739(a), (b).

Impacts on local special taxes. Proposition 218 reaffirms that special taxes may be imposed, extended, or increased only upon a two-thirds vote of the electorate. As with general taxes, resolutions proposing special taxes may state a range of rates or amounts, and may provide for an automatic inflation adjustment unless the special tax is determined by a percentage calculation.

Impacts on special assessments. Special assessments, also known as benefit assessments, are charges levied on real property to pay for benefits that the property receives from a local improvement. Cities can levy special assessments to finance improvements such as sidewalks, street lighting, parks, open space, and recreational programs.[23] Following passage of Proposition 13, special assessments became popular among local governments because the assessments were exempt from the tax limits of Proposition 13 and usually were not subject to a public vote.

Special assessments, also known as benefit assessments, are charges levied on real property to pay for benefits that the property receives from a local improvement.

Prior to the enactment of Proposition 218, statutory law contained a number of requirements for establishing a valid special assessment. An assessment could not be levied against property that did not benefit from the improvement being financed or against property outside the area receiving the special improvement. Each property within the area subject to the assessment could be assessed only a share of the costs of the improvements that was proportional to the benefits it received from those improvements. Assessment statutes also contained procedural requirements such as notice, hearings, and a right to protest. Proposition 218 supersedes and significantly expands those requirements for existing, new, or increased special assessments.[24]

---

23. For a discussion of open space funding mechanisms, *see Funding Open Space Acquisition Programs: A Guide for Local Agencies in California* (Institute for Local Government, League of California Cities, 2005).
24. For a discussion of what constitutes an "increase," *see* 82 Ops. Cal. Atty. Gen. 35 (1999).

Proposition 218 defines "assessment" as "any levy or charge upon real property by an agency for a special benefit conferred upon the real property."

Proposition 218 defines "assessment" as "any levy or charge upon real property by an agency for a special benefit conferred upon the real property." Cal. Const. art. XIIID, § 2(b). Thus, to constitute an "assessment," the levied amount must be based on property ownership. *See Howard Jarvis Taxpayers Ass'n v. City of San Diego*, 72 Cal. App. 4th at 236–37 (Proposition 218 does not apply to an assessment levied by a Business Improvement District because that assessment was levied on all businesses, not on real property).

The California Supreme Court in *Richmond v. Shasta Community Services District* held that a capacity charge levied on new water connections did not constitute an "assessment" under Proposition 218. 32 Cal. 4th 409, 419–20 (2004). Plaintiffs in *Richmond* were property owners who challenged the local water district's adoption of an ordinance establishing capacity charge for all new water connections. Plaintiffs claimed the capacity charge was an assessment and that its adoption by ordinance had failed to comply with Proposition 218's requirements for such assessments. The court disagreed, noting that the district's capacity charge is not imposed upon particular identifiable parcels. Rather, it is imposed upon a self-selected group of individuals requesting new water service. The charge therefore could not be described as a "charge upon real property" and was not an assessment for purposes of Proposition 218. *Id.* at 419.

Proposition 218 raises to the constitutional level the procedures by which a local government can impose a special assessment.

Importantly, Proposition 218 raises to the constitutional level the procedures by which a local government can impose a special assessment. It also addresses the distinction between general benefits and special benefits by defining a special benefit as a "particular and distinct benefit over and above general benefits conferred on real property located in the district at large," and expressly excludes a "[g]eneral enhancement of property value." Cal. Const. art. XIIID, § 2(i). This provision appears to distinguish the common law definition of special benefit set forth in *Knox v. City of Orland*, in which the court stated that a special benefit is a benefit that "particularly and directly" benefits the assessed property, and is "over and above" any benefit received by the general public. 4 Cal. 4th 132, 143 (1992).

Perhaps most importantly, Proposition 218 requires an assessment ballot proceeding, similar to an election, for every type of assessment previously addressed by existing statutes (*e.g.*, Streets and Highways Code sections 2800–3012 (Majority Protest Act)). *See* Elec. Code § 4000(c)(9) (Proposition 218 Omnibus Implementation Act of 1997). Specifically, Government Code section 53753 sets out notice, protest, and hearing requirements, including procedures in preparation, processing, and counting ballots. In addition, ballots in such proceedings must be weighted based on the proportional financial obligation of each assessed parcel. This is a change from previous law, which required a majority protest of property owners owning more than 50 percent of the area of assessable land in order to block an assessment, but did not require an election or a ballot proceeding. Proposition 218 requires the agency to mail a ballot to each property owner of record. When ballots are counted, a majority of ballots actually received must favor the assessment. Thus, a small group of very interested voters submitting protests can defeat the assessment if the majority of eligible voters favor the assessment, but do not vote. Significantly, in contrast to prior law, the legislative body cannot override a protest. Under Government Code section 53753(c), added in 1997, voters may change or withdraw an assessment ballot at any time prior to the conclusion of the public testimony offered at the required public hearing. *See Not About Water Com. v. Board of Supervisors*, 95 Cal. App. 4th 982, 999–1000 (2002) (use of voting tied proportionally to property ownership in the context of a voting scheme employed by district officials in the formation of a water assessment district does not violate due process).

The notice requirements described above, as clarified by the 1997 legislation, supersede virtually all other existing statutory notice, protest, and hearing requirements. Gov't Code §§ 53753, 53753.5, 53755.

Proposition 218 exempts the following benefit assessments if they existed on or before November 6, 1996:

- Assessments to finance the capital costs or operation and maintenance of sidewalks, streets, sewers, water, flood control, drainage systems, or vector control
- Assessments imposed pursuant to a petition signed by all the owners of the parcels subject to the assessment; and
- Assessments previously approved by a majority vote in an election on the assessment

See Howard Jarvis Taxpayers Ass'n v. City of Riverside, 73 Cal. App. 4th at 683. All other existing assessments that Proposition 218 does not exempt must have been approved by a ballot proceeding held no later than July 1, 1997. *See Consolidated Fire Protection Dist. v. Howard Jarvis Taxpayers Ass'n*, 63 Cal. App. 4th 211, 220 (1998) (district's assessment for fire suppression equipment that was authorized in 1991, but which the district had to levy on an annual basis, required voter approval under Proposition 218).

Impacts on fees and charges. Proposition 218 also creates significant procedural requirements for new and increased fees or charges. "Fee" or "charge" is defined as "any levy other than an ad valorem tax, a special tax, or an assessment, imposed by an agency upon a parcel or upon a person as an *incident of property ownership, including user fee or charge for a property related service*." Cal. Const. art. XIIID, § 2(e) (emphasis added).

While "property related service" is defined as "a public service having a direct relationship to property ownership," the phrase "an incident of property ownership" is not defined. Proposition 218 does clarify that fees for the provision of electrical and gas service are not fees or charges imposed as an incident of property ownership. These ambiguous definitions and the distinctions made among gas, electric, and other basic services (*e.g.*, water and sewer) have been the subject of several California Attorney General Opinions. *See, e.g.*, 82 Ops. Cal. Atty. Gen. 43 (1999) (where a water *usage-based* surcharge is imposed only on property-owners already paying a *property-based* charge for the same service, the usage-based charge is subject to Proposition 218's notice and hearing, but not voter approval, requirements); 81 Ops. Cal. Atty. Gen. 104 (1998) (fees for storm drain maintenance do not fall within Proposition 218's exception to voter approval requirement for sewer or water services because storm drain maintenance is distinct from sewer or water services); 80 Ops. Cal. Atty. Gen. 183 (1997) (certain water charges were not subject to Proposition 218 because they were based on water usage, not imposed as an "incident of property ownership").

> *Fee or charge is defined as any levy other than an ad valorem tax, a special assessment, or an assessment, imposed by an agency on a parcel or a person as an incident of property ownership, including user fees or charges for a property related service.*

The court in *Richmond v. Shasta Community Services District* held that a fire suppression fee imposed on new water connections did not constitute a "fee" subject to Proposition 218. 32 Cal. 4th at 426 (2004). The court reasoned that a water connection charge is not imposed simply by virtue of property ownership, but instead it is imposed as an incident of the voluntary act of the property owner in applying for a water service connection. The fees for connection to the system therefore were not imposed as "an incident of property ownership" and were not subject to Proposition 218. *Id.*

In *Bighorn-Desert View Water Agency v. Verjil*, the California Supreme Court upheld the provisions of a voter-initiative that reduced current water delivery charges, but overturned those provisions that required future voter pre-approval for new increases or charges. 39 Cal. 4th 205 (2006). The Court found that Proposition 218 protects the initiative power in matters reducing any local fee, but that Proposition 218 did not permit an initiative to require further voter approval for future increases in fees or new charges. *Id.* at 218–20. The Court also acknowledged there was a question whether the provision of Proposition 218 at issue applied only to "property-related fees" as do other parts of Proposition 218, but held that it applied to such fees at a minimum, and concluded that ongoing water delivery fees, as opposed to new water connections, are imposed as an incident of property ownership. *Id.* at 216–17.

In 2007, a court of appeal relied upon *Bighorn-Desert* and ruled that a groundwater augmentation charge could not be validly imposed without complying with the provision of Proposition 218 because the fee was imposed "as an incident of property ownership." *Pajaro Valley Water Mgmt. Agency v. Amrhein*, 150 Cal. App. 4th 1364, 1370 (2007).

Like the requirements for assessments, fees and charges on a parcel may "not exceed the proportional cost of the service attributable to the parcel." Cal. Const. art. XIIID, § 1(b)(3). *See* 81 Ops. Cal. Atty. Gen. at 106 (storm drain fees imposed only on property owners connected to a district's sewer system violate Proposition 218; the fees are not proportional to the benefit received by those owners because they are subsidizing other property owners who contribute to storm water flows but who are not charged the fee). However, it is unclear whether the proportionality requirement will prevent cities from subsidizing rates for low-income users with revenues from other ratepayers.

Fees or charges cannot be imposed for general governmental services that are available to the public at large, such as police, fire, and library services. Fees and charges also may be levied only for services that are "actually used or immediately available," therefore, charges based on future use of a service are not permitted.

Proposition 218 further states that fees and charges "shall not exceed the funds required to provide the property related service." Cal. Const. art. XIIID, § 6(b)(1). Although cities may recover all of their costs for particular services through user fees, the limits, under Cal. Const. art. XIIID, § 1(b)(3), on the amount of the fee or charge imposed restrict the manner in which they may do so. As the court explained in *Howard Jarvis Taxpayers Ass'n v. City of Fresno*, a city that seeks "to recover all of its utilities costs from user fees [must] reasonably determine [citation omitted] the unbudgeted costs of utilities enterprises and that those costs be recovered through rates proportional to the cost of providing service to each parcel." 127 Cal. App. 4th 914, 923 (2005).

Proposition 218 imposes procedural requirements for fees and charges that are different from those for assessments in two important ways. First, voters effectively get "two bites at the apple" because they have an opportunity to block the fee or charge first at a public hearing held on the issue, and second at a ballot election held no earlier than 45 days following the hearing. If a majority of the affected property owners files written protests against the proposed fee or charge at the hearing, the agency shall not impose it. If there is not a majority protest against the fee or charge at the hearing, then the agency proceeds to hold a ballot election on the issue (except in the case of fees or charges for sewer, water, and refuse collection services which do not require an election). In conducting the election, a local agency may use procedures similar to those set forth by Proposition 218 for an assessment election. The fee or charge cannot be imposed unless it is approved either by a majority vote of the affected property owners or by a two-thirds vote of the electorate.

The second important way the procedures for fees and charges differ from those for assessments is that the votes on proposed fees and charges are not weighted according to the proportional financial obligation of the affected property as they are for assessments. This means that the majority protest procedure for fees and charges may underrepresent owners of large parcels. For example, it would allow the owners of two parcels that total only five acres and are worth a total of only $500,000 to block a charge supported by the owner of an adjacent 50-acre parcel worth $5,000,000.

Under Proposition 218, votes on proposed fees and charges are not weighted according to the proportional financial obligation of the affected property as they are for assessments.

Possible impacts on new development fees. Proposition 218 states that it shall not be construed to "affect *existing* laws relating to the imposition of fees or charges as a condition of property development." Cal. Const. art. XIIID, § 1(b) (emphasis added). However, it is unclear whether this exemption for development fees will apply to new laws imposing development fees adopted after July 1, 1997. The Attorney General has suggested that school impact fees are not subject to the voter approval requirements of Proposition 218. *See* 81 Ops. Cal. Atty. Gen. 181 (1998). *But see Apartment Ass'n v. City of Los Angeles*, 24 Cal. 4th 830, 844 (2001) (Proposition 218 inapplicable to a housing inspection fee; and stating that the exemption for development fees applies only to fees already in existence).

Impacts on standby charges. Despite its name, a standby charge is an "assessment" for the purposes of Proposition 218. Cal. Const. art. XIIID, § 6(b)(4); *see also Keller v. Chowchilla Water Dist.*, 80 Cal. App. 4th 1006, 1011 (2000). Thus, the procedural rules concerning assessments apply to standby charges. Accordingly, the Attorney General has opined that Proposition 218's exception for increases in fees, charges, or taxes (but not assessments) in accordance with a schedule of adjustments adopted prior to November 6, 1996, does not apply to such increases in standby charges. *See* 82 Ops. Cal. Atty. Gen. 35 (1999). *See also Howard Jarvis Taxpayers Ass'n v. City of Los Angeles*, 85 Cal. App. 4th 79, 83 (2000) (fees for water usage rates are commodity charges rather than fees under Prop. 218, since they were not "levies or assessments" incident to property ownership).

Despite its name, a standby charge is an assessment for the purposes of Proposition 218. Thus, the procedural rules concerning assessments apply to standby charges.

However, as assessments, standby charges are exempt from the procedural rules concerning assessments if they are imposed exclusively to finance certain capital costs or maintenance and operation expenses, *e.g.*, sidewalks and water.

See *Keller v. Chowchilla Water Dist.*, 80 Cal. App. 4th at 1012; Cal. Const. art. XIIID, § 5(a). The court in *Keller* addressed this issue. There, the question was whether a standby charge imposed by the water district for its purchase of water was exempt. The court found that the district's standby charge was an "assessment imposed exclusively to finance the... maintenance and operation expenses for water" and was exempt from Proposition 218's procedures and approval process for assessments. 80 Cal. App. 4th at 1014.

Use of initiatives. Proposition 218 specifically authorizes the use of initiatives to repeal or reduce local taxes, assessments, fees, or charges. Cal. Const. art. XIIIC, § 3. Thus, it appears that virtually all sources of local revenue may be repealed or reduced through the initiative process. As a result, the rating, valuation, and marketing of local agency bonds may be affected significantly if the revenue sources that support these bonds can be repealed or reduced.

It is unclear whether an initiative that affects such a revenue source can withstand a challenge based on an impairment-of-contract theory. The 1997 legislation clarifying Proposition 218 bolsters the impairment-of-contract argument by adding a provision that Proposition 218 "shall not be construed to mean that owners of municipal bonds assume the risk of, or consent to, any action by initiative that constitutes an impairment of contractual rights protected under the Contract Clause of the U.S. Constitution." Gov't Code § 5854. For a discussion of impairment-of-contract doctrine in the context of Proposition 218's balloting requirements as applied to pre-existing assessments, *see Consolidated Fire Protection Dist. v. Howard Jarvis Taxpayers Ass'n*, 63 Cal. App. 4th 211, 219 (1998).

For a more thorough discussion of initiatives, *see* chapter 14 (Initiative and Referendum).

Conditions Attached to Land Use Approvals for Financing and Maintaining Public Facilities

Taxpayers revolted in the late 1970s by passing two constitutional amendments: Proposition 13, which provided property tax relief, and the "Gann limit," which constitutionally restricted state spending. Since then, cities have sought alternative methods for raising funds to finance needed public works projects. This is particularly true when the need is triggered by new development. Since Propositions 13, 62, and 218 limit cities' ability to heavily rely on property taxes, cities have sought to increase impact fees and form districts creating benefit assessments, especially attaching these to development approvals.

In order to relieve themselves of the burden of constructing and particularly of maintaining new infrastructure, cities attempt to establish various funding vehicles through state law to shift the cost to project owners and new inhabitants. For example, a city could form a Mello-Roos district pursuant to the 1982 Mello-Roos Community Facilities Act (Gov't Code § 53311 *et seq.*) and impose special taxes on the developing property to fund the installation of public facilities, including streets, sidewalks, storm drains, fire stations, and other improvements. The city could also form a landscaping and lighting district, or require an annexation into one, pursuant to the Landscaping and Lighting Act of 1972 (Sts. & High. Code § 22500 *et seq.*), or form a geologic hazard abatement district (GHAD) pursuant to

Public Resources Code section 26500 *et seq.*[25] Further, certain cities, such as the City of San Diego, have set up conditions relating to facilities benefits. For a discussion of these and other methods of financing, *see A Planner's Guide to Financing Public Improvements* (Governor's Office of Planning and Research, June 1997).

The assessments levied by these districts must comply with Proposition 218. This is usually easily done, because the developer initially owns all the property in the proposed district, and is therefore the only voter required to cast a ballot in approving the assessments. Today, conditions regarding such financing are just as important as the conditions for exactions relating to fees and dedications.

GHADs in particular.[26] GHADs are local governmental districts formed specifically to address geologic hazards and related concerns. The law authorizing their formation (Pub. Res. Code § 26500 *et seq.*) was enacted in 1979 to address the aftermath of the Portuguese Bend landslides in the Palos Verdes area of Southern California. A GHAD may be formed for the purpose of prevention, mitigation, abatement, or control of a geologic hazard, and also for mitigation or abatement of structural hazards that are partly or wholly caused by geologic hazards. Pub. Res. Code § 26525. A "geologic hazard" is broadly defined as an actual or threatened landslide, land subsidence, soil erosion, earthquake, fault movement, or any other natural or unnatural movement of land or earth. Pub. Res. Code § 26507.

GHADs are local governmental districts formed specifically to address geologic hazards and related concerns.

A GHAD is a political subdivision of the state and is not an agency or instrumentality of a local agency. Pub. Res. Code § 26570. The legislative body of a city or county conducts the formation proceedings. Once the GHAD has been formed, the legislative body must select the district's initial board of directors—either five landowners from the GHAD area, or the legislative body itself. If the legislative body selects five landowners, the initial term shall be four years; thereafter, the landowner board shall be elected from the district. Pub. Res. Code §§ 26567, 26583. Otherwise, the legislative body remains as the board of directors.

A GHAD is empowered to acquire, construct, operate, manage, or maintain improvements on public or private lands. "Improvement" is defined as any activity that is necessary or incidental to the prevention, mitigation, abatement, or control of a geologic hazard, including, but not limited to, the acquisition of property or any interest therein, construction, and maintenance, repair, or operation of any improvement.

A GHAD is empowered to acquire, construct, operate, manage, or maintain improvements on public or private lands.

A GHAD may include property in more than one city or county, and the property may be publicly or privately owned. Pub. Res. Code §§ 26531, 26532. The property comprising the district need not be contiguous so long as all included property is specially benefited by the proposed construction to be undertaken by the GHAD in a plan of control. Pub. Res. Code §§ 26530, 26534. However, no parcel of real property shall be divided by the boundaries of the proposed district. Pub. Res. Code § 26533. Land may be annexed into an existing GHAD following formation; however, the district's board of directors

---

25. GHADs are empowered to finance the prevention, mitigation, abatement, or control of actual or potential geologic hazards by levying and collecting special assessments.
26. *See* Daniel J. Curtin, Jr. and Shawn Zovod, "GHADs: California's Experience with Hazard Mitigation through Special Districts," *Landslide Hazards and Planning*, ch. 4, page 62 (APA, 2005); *see also* S. Jeer, "Weighing the Benefits of GHADs." *Id.*, page 69.

assumes the responsibilities of the legislative body of the city or county. Nonetheless, annexation is subject to the approval of the legislative body that ordered formation of the district. Pub. Res. Code § 26581.

A GHAD is authorized to finance improvements through the Improvement Act of 1911, the Municipal Improvement Act of 1913, and the Improvement Bond Act of 1915. Pub. Res. Code § 26587. It also may accept financial or other assistance from any public or private source (Pub. Res. Code § 26591), and may borrow funds from a local agency, the state, and the federal government. Pub. Res. Code § 26593.

A district may assess landowners for operation and maintenance of improvements acquired or constructed under the GHAD law.

A district may assess landowners for operation and maintenance of improvements acquired or constructed under the GHAD law. Pub. Res. Code § 26650. These assessments, which attach as liens on property, may be collected at the same time and in the same manner as general taxes on real property. Pub. Res. Code § 26654. All assessment proceedings must also comply with the requirements of Proposition 218, adopted by the voters in 1996.

GHADs are public agencies that operate locally for the sole and specific purpose of addressing geologic hazards and related concerns.

GHADs are public agencies that operate locally for the sole and specific purpose of addressing geologic hazards and related concerns. As such, they offer several distinct advantages. Through the development and implementation of a Plan of Control, a GHAD acts to prevent damage resulting from earth movement by identifying and monitoring potential geologic hazards and undertaking improvements as appropriate. When unforeseen hazards arise, GHADs, as existing agencies, are in place with the technical and organizational resources and funding capability necessary to respond quickly and effectively. Since GHADs are authorized to collect assessments along with the general property tax, there is no need for separate collection by a private entity, such as a homeowners' association. Finally, under state law (Gov't Code § 865 *et seq.*), GHADs are given a degree of immunity from liability for actions they undertake. The Legislature intended that these provisions encourage local public entities to take remedial action to abate earth movement. In addition, the Tort Claims Act (Gov't Code § 810 *et seq.*) in general provides immunities to GHADs as it does to other local public agencies.

Proposition 218 shifts the burden to the local government to prove that the fees and assessments are legal.

Burden of proof and interpretation. Courts traditionally have given local governments significant flexibility in determining the amount of fees and assessments. Under previous law, the challenging party in a lawsuit had the burden of proving that the fees were not legal. Proposition 218 shifts the burden to the local government to prove that the fees and assessments are legal. Cal. Const. art. XIIID, § 6(b)(5). *See also Howard Jarvis Taxpayers Ass'n v. City of Fresno*, 127 Cal. App. 4th 914 (2005). It also states that its provisions "shall be liberally construed to effectuate its purposes of limiting local government revenue and enhancing taxpayer consent." Cal. Const. art. XIIID, § 5.

Processing Fees—Land Use and Building Permits

Fees for zoning changes, use permits, building permits, and similar filing and processing fees may not exceed the estimated reasonable cost of providing the service for which they are charged. Gov't Code § 66014. Although Government Code section 66016 provides a prospective fee reduction remedy where fees have exceeded the cost of services, cities are not constitutionally required to conduct annual financial audits of its "proceeds of taxes," including regulatory fees that exceed the costs borne in providing regulatory services. *Barratt American*, 37 Cal. 4th at 702.

Before adopting such fees, a city must make available to the public "data indicating the amount of cost, or estimated cost, required to provide the service for which the fee or service charge is levied...." Gov't Code § 66016(a). Also, a city must hold at least one public meeting at which oral or written presentation can be made. *Id.*

Government Code section 66014 allows cities to include, as part of the fees they may charge, the costs reasonably necessary to prepare and revise the plans and policies they are required to adopt before making any necessary findings and determinations.

Judicial Review

Since the adoption of fees is a legislative act, it is reviewed under the narrow standards of ordinary mandate. Code of Civil Proc. § 1085. The court need only determine whether the action taken was arbitrary, capricious, or entirely lacking in evidentiary support, or whether it failed to conform to procedures required by law. Such a limited review is based on the doctrine of separation of powers, which (1) sanctions the legislative delegation of authority and (2) acknowledges the presumed expertise of the agency. *See Canyon North Co. v. Conejo Valley Unified Sch. Dist.*, 19 Cal. App. 4th 243, 251 (1993) (upholding school fees); *Garrick Dev. Co. v. Hayward Unified Sch. Dist.*, 3 Cal. App. 4th 320, 328 (1992) (upholding school fees); *see also Western/Cal. Ltd. v. Dry Creek Joint Elementary Sch. Dist.*, 50 Cal. App. 4th 1461, 1492 (1996).

Since the adoption of fees is a legislative act, it is reviewed under the narrow standards of ordinary mandate.

A party that wants to challenge the imposition of any fees, dedications, or other exactions must follow the procedures in the Mitigation Fee Act (Gov't Code §§ 66000–66025). Exactions are often challenged under the Mitigation Fee Act, or as aspects of an agency decision challenged in a mandate proceeding. For a detailed discussion of fee challenges, *see* chapter 21 (Land Use Litigation).

Conclusion

In using its authority to impose conditions of dedication or the payment of fees upon a proposed development, a city is relying on one of its most important powers, the police power—that is, the power to adopt ordinances and regulations to protect the public health, safety, and welfare of its residents. *See Berman v. Parker*, 348 U.S. 26, 32 (1954). The police power "extends to objectives in furtherance of the public peace, safety, morals, health, and welfare and 'is not a circumscribed prerogative, but is elastic and, in keeping with the growth of knowledge and the belief in the popular mind of the need for its application, capable of expansion to meet existing conditions of modern life.'" *Birkenfeld v. City of Berkeley*, 17 Cal. 3d 129, 160 (1976).

In exercising its police power, however, a city must comply with both statutory and constitutional requirements. Note that the requirements of the Mitigation Fee Act are applicable to development fees regardless of how they are imposed by the city. Gov't Code § 66000. However, pursuant to *Ehrlich* and *San Remo Hotel*, fees that a city imposes on an individual or ad hoc basis will be subject to a higher level of constitutional scrutiny (under the *Nollan* and *Dolan* tests) than fees imposed pursuant to generally applicable legislation.

In exercising its police power, a city must comply with both statutory and constitutional requirements.

14

Initiative and Referendum

Ballot box planning, the practice of placing land use initiatives before the voters, is common in California. Frequently it is citizens, unhappy with the current state of affairs in their communities, who resort to the ballot box to adopt or repeal general and specific plans or zoning measures. Sometimes a developer will use the ballot box to advance its own proposal. Finally, city councils and boards of supervisors frequently submit land use measures directly to the citizens for their approval or rejection.

The practice of using the ballot box to adopt or repeal normally legislative acts is formally known as the initiative and referendum process, and is reserved in the California Constitution.

Overview [1]

The United States Constitution has no provision for initiative or referendum. Consequently, many states have chosen to adopt one or both of these powers in their state constitutions. California reserved the power of the initiative, referendum, and recall mechanisms in its 1911 Constitution.[2] With respect to local ordinances, local initiatives and referenda are based upon article II, section 11, which provides:

> Initiative and referendum powers may be exercised by the electors of each city or county under procedures that the legislature shall provide. Except as provided in subdivisions (b) and (c), this section does not affect a city having a charter.[3]

Initiative and referendum proceedings provide a way to obtain a direct popular vote on proposed or recently enacted legislation. The California Supreme

California reserved the power of the initiative, referendum, and recall mechanisms in its 1911 Constitution.

---

1. For a good discussion on the use of the initiative process as a means to manage growth, *see* Daniel J. Curtin, Jr. and M. Thomas Jacobson, "Growth Control by the Ballot Box: California's Experience," 24 *Loyola L.A. L. Rev.* 1073 (1991); "Growth Management by the Initiative in California: Legal and Practical Issues," 21 *Urb. Law.* 491 (1989); *California 2025: Taking on the Future* (Ellen Harak and Mark Baldassare eds., Public Policy Institute of California, 2005); *see also* Michael Patrick Durkee *et al.*, *Ballot Box Navigator* (Solano Press, 2003).
2. *See Rossi v. Brown*, 9 Cal. 4th 688 (1995), for an interesting discussion of the historical background of these constitutional provisions.
3. Many charter cities have initiative and referendum procedures similar to those in the general law, but at times the procedures vary from the general law in certain particulars (*e.g.*, number of signatures required, filing deadlines).

Court held that an initiative can be used only to enact a statute—a legislative act—and cannot be used to declare policy or guide lawmakers in future decisions. *See American Fed'n of Labor v. Eu*, 36 Cal. 3d 687, 708 (1984); *see also Marblehead v. City of San Clemente*, 226 Cal. App. 3d 1504, 1509 (1991). In short, the initiative process is used to adopt ordinances or resolutions, and the referendum process is used to reject them.

Since the people reserved to themselves the powers of initiative and referendum through the Constitution, the courts have carefully guarded these rights. For example, when the California Supreme Court upheld Proposition 140 (term limitations on state legislators) in *Legislature v. Eu*, it noted:

> Accordingly, the initiative power must be *liberally construed* to promote the democratic process. (Citation omitted.) Indeed, it is our solemn duty to jealously guard the precious initiative power, and to resolve any reasonable doubts in favor of its exercise. (Citation omitted.) As with statutes adopted by the Legislature, all presumptions favor the validity of initiative measures and mere doubts as to validity are insufficient; such measures must be upheld unless their unconstitutionality clearly, positively, and unmistakably appears.

54 Cal. 3d 492, 501 (1991) (emphasis in original) (citing *Calfarm Ins. Co. v. Deukmejian*, 48 Cal. 3d 805, 814 (1989)); *see also DeVita v. County of Napa*, 9 Cal. 4th 763, 784 (1995) (upholding a county land use element initiative amending the county's general plan); *Rossi v. Brown*, 9 Cal. 4th 688, 702 (1995) (upholding an initiative prospectively repealing a local tax ordinance and barring future adoption of a tax); *Associated Home Builders, Inc. v. City of Livermore*, 18 Cal. 3d 582, 591 (1976) ("If doubts can reasonably be resolved in favor of the use of this reserve power, courts will preserve it.")

In 1978, the California Supreme Court upheld the general validity of Proposition 13 (the Jarvis-Gann Tax Initiative). In so doing, it stated:

> [T]he initiative is in essence a *legislative battering ram* which may be used to tear through the exasperating tangle of the traditional legislative procedure and strike directly toward the desired end. Virtually every type of interest group has on occasion used this instrument. It is deficient as a means of legislation in that it permits very little balancing of interests or compromise, but it was designed primarily for use in situations where the ordinary machinery of legislation had utterly failed in this respect.

Amador Valley Joint Union High Sch. Dist. v. State Bd. of Equalization, 22 Cal. 3d 208, 228 (1978) (emphasis in original)

Wielding this "legislative battering ram," voters in cities across the state have taken matters into their own hands and adopted planning and zoning laws. Most often, they have done so when the city failed to heed their demands for specific legislation.

The Initiative

The California Constitution defines the initiative as "the power of the electors to propose statutes and amendments to the Constitution and to adopt or reject them." Cal. Const. art. II, § 8(a); *see also Marblehead*, 226 Cal. App. 3d at 1509; *American Fed'n of Labor*, 36 Cal. 3d at 708–09. At the local level, this process empowers the voters to enact ordinances through a local election. The local initiative power reserved in a city charter may be even broader than the initiative power reserved in the Constitution. *See Rossi*, 9 Cal. 4th at 696.

The Referendum

The California Constitution defines the referendum as "the power of the electors to approve or reject statutes or parts of statutes...." Cal. Const. art. II, § 9(a). As contrasted with the initiative power, the referendum only applies to newly enacted legislation and is subject to express constitutional limitations, among them the exemption of tax measures from referendum. *See Rossi*, 9 Cal. 4th at 697. For purposes of local government, referendum is the power to reject an ordinance or resolution that a city recently passed to accomplish a legislative act, such as the adoption of a general plan or specific plan.

The California Constitution defines the referendum as the power of the electors to approve or reject statutes or parts of statutes.

Procedural Requirements for Placing an Initiative or Referendum Measure on the Ballot

The California Elections Code sections on measures submitted to the voters in county elections (Elec. Code § 9100 *et seq.*) and municipal elections (Elec. Code § 9200 *et seq.*) set out detailed provisions for the format and circulation of petitions for initiatives and referenda. The Elections Code also contains procedures for qualifying initiative and referendum petitions for the ballot in special districts. Elec. Code § 9300 *et seq.* A ballot measure in a general law city or county is subject to the procedures in the Elections Code. A ballot measure in a charter city whose charter "makes any provision for the direct initiation of ordinances by the voters" is governed by the charter, unless the measure would amend the charter. Elec. Code § 9247. If the charter has no provisions setting forth initiative and referendum procedures, then the Elections Code provisions govern.

> **PRACTICE TIP**
>
> In a charter city, be sure to check whether the charter or the Elections Code governs procedures for placing initiative and referendum measures on the ballot.

The procedures in the Elections Code for submitting an initiative measure are similar for general law cities, charter cities, and counties, although they differ in particular details. In general, the procedural steps to qualify an initiative in either a city or county are:

(1) Submittal of the petition form and initiative measure text to the elections official of the county or city (usually the county or city clerk); request that a ballot title and summary be prepared; and file of notice of intent to circulate the petition. Elec. Code §§ 9103, 9105(a) (counties); 9202, 9203(a) (cities)

(2) Preparation of ballot title and summary by county counsel or city attorney. Elec. Code §§ 9105 (counties); 9203 (cities)

(3) Publication and/or posting of notice of intent to circulate an initiative petition. Elec. Code §§ 9105(b) (counties); 9205 (cities)

(4) Circulation of initiative petitions for signatures. Elec. Code §§ 9108–9110 (counties); 9207–9209 (cities)

(5) Filing of initiative petitions and examination of signatures. Elec. Code §§ 9113–9115 (counties); 9210–9211 (cities)

(6) Optional report on the effect of the initiative measure. Elec. Code §§ 9111 (counties); 9212 (cities)

(7) Adoption of the measure by board of supervisors or city council, or alternatively, placement of the measure on the ballot. Elec. Code §§ 9116, 9117 (counties); 9214, 9215 (cities)

(8) Preparation of impartial analysis and arguments to appear on ballot. Elec. Code §§ 9120, 9160 *et seq.* (counties); 9219, 9220, 9280 *et seq.* (cities)

(9) Election campaign and vote

The steps for qualifying a referendum also are similar in cities and in counties. The steps are:

(1) Circulation of referendum petition (no notice required) and submittal of petition to county or city elections official prior to date when subject legislation would otherwise take effect (usually 30 days after enactment). Elec. Code §§ 9141–9144, 9146 (counties); 9235–9238 (cities)

(2) Examination of petition form and signatures. Elec. Code §§ 9146 (counties); 9239–9240 (cities)

(3) Repeal by board of supervisors or city council of subject legislation, or alternatively, placement of referendum on ballot. Elec. Code §§ 9145 (counties); 9241 (cities)

(4) Preparation of impartial analysis and ballot arguments. Elec. Code §§ 9146 (counties); 9243 (cities)

(5) Election campaign and vote. Elec. Code §§ 9146 (counties); 9243 (cities)

Form of Petition

Initiative petitions in cities and counties must be designed so that each signer may personally affix onto the petition the following:

(a) The signer's signature

(b) The signer's printed name

(c) The signer's residential address, giving street number, or if no street number exists, adequate designation of residence so that the location may be readily ascertained

(d) The name of the incorporated city or unincorporated community in which the signer resides

Elec. Code § 9020

Each "section" of the petition, meaning each separate printed copy of the petition, must include the text of the measure proposed for enactment. Elec. Code §§ 9101 (counties); 9201 (cities). The ballot title and summary must appear across the top of each page of the petition where signatures are to appear. Elec. Code §§ 9105(c) (counties); 9203(b) (cities). Each section of an initiative petition shall also bear a copy of the notice of intention to circulate. Elec. Code §§ 9108 (counties); 9207 (cities).

In a county, the form of a referendum petition is subject to the Elections Code provisions regarding form of initiative petitions.

In a county, the form of a referendum petition is subject to the Elections Code provisions regarding form of initiative petitions. Elec. Code § 9146. Across the top of each page of a county referendum petition there shall be printed the following: "Referendum Against an Ordinance Passed by the Board of Supervisors." Elec. Code § 9147(a). In a city, the form of a referendum petition must be substantially the same as that required for statewide initiative or referendum petitions. Elec. Code § 9238(a). The heading "Referendum Against an Ordinance Passed by the City Council" must appear across the top of each page of a city referendum petition. *Id*. Each section of a referendum petition must contain the ordinance's identifying number or title, and must include the text of the ordinance or the portion of the ordinance that is the subject of the referendum. Elec. Code §§ 9147(b) (counties); 9238(b) (cities). For example, if a resolution adopting a general plan incorporates by reference as an exhibit the text of the general plan, that entire exhibit must be attached to each petition circulated to referend the resolution, even if it consists of several hundred pages and is 2.5 inches thick. *See Nelson v. Carlson*, 17 Cal. App. 4th 732, 738–39 (1993).

The form of a petition need only be in "substantial compliance" with statutory and constitutional requirements. This, however, means "actual compliance" with essential statutory requirements. *See Assembly v. Deukmejian*, 30 Cal. 3d 638, 649–52 (1982). A petition can be deemed in substantial compliance with the Elections Code, despite a technical defect, when the purpose of the technical requirement established by the Elections Code is not frustrated by the defective form of the petition. *See Costa v. Superior Court*, 37 Cal. 4th 986, 1013 (2006) (minor defects that do not affect the integrity of the electoral process do not warrant invalidation of a petition and preclusion of a vote as long as the fundamental purposes underlying applicable statutory and constitutional requirements have been fulfilled).

Courts have reached inconsistent results when evaluating whether a defect is substantial. Nonetheless, courts generally focus on the common sense notion of whether the petition signers were fully informed. For example, in *Hebard v. Bybee*, three words were dropped from the lengthy ordinance title on some, but not all, of the referendum petitions that were circulated for signatures. 65 Cal. App. 4th 1331 (1998). The court concluded that the omission created an ambiguity regarding the effect of the ordinance, and that any voter who did not read the text of the ordinance (which was attached to the petition) was not clearly informed about its full effect. Thus, the court affirmed an order directing the city clerk not to count the signatures on the defective petitions. *Id.* at 1338. *See also Myers v. Patterson*, 196 Cal. App. 3d 130, 136 (1987) (registrar had a duty to reject petitions that did not include the notice of intent to circulate, which was required by statute).

A city elections official's duty to certify petition signatures is limited to the ministerial function of determining whether procedural requirements for submitting an initiative have been met. *Alliance for a Better Downtown Millbrae v. Wade*, 108 Cal. App. 4th 123 (2003). City elections officials are not authorized under state law to consider extrinsic evidence or engage in "discretionary factfinding" to determine whether an initiative petition complies with the Elections Code. *Id.* In *Wade*, the City Clerk of Millbrae found that an initiative petition was circulated in violation of the Elections Code and refused to certify the petition. The clerk's finding was based on a number of factors: the signature page showing greater wear than the full text and notice of intention pages; unidentified persons told her they saw circulation of the petition without the full text and notice of intention; a folder with signature pages by themselves were found; and she believed the circulators had violated the Elections Code in the past. *Id.* at 134. In ruling for the petitioner, the court held that the city clerk impermissibly went beyond the face of the petition, made unauthorized adjudicative decisions based on extrinsic evidence, and violated her ministerial duty to accept the petition. *Id.* at 131–134. If initiative petitions are adequate on their face, the courts, not elections officials, are the proper forum for enforcing the provisions of the Elections Code. *Id.* at 136.

In *Mervyn's v. Reyes*, the court set aside an initiative petition that did not contain the "full text" of the general plan provisions to be enacted by the initiative, as required by Elections Code section 9201, and held that the petition's reference to those sections was not substantial compliance. 69 Cal. App. 4th 93 (1998).[4] Section 9201 requires only the text of the measure proposed to be enacted, not all the information an informed voter would want. *We Care-Santa Paula v. Herrera*, 139 Cal. App. 4th 387, 391 (2006). Section 9201 does not require that a petition include the text of every plan, law, or ordinance the measure might affect. *Id.* at 390.

In contrast, in *Hayward Area Planning Ass'n v. Superior Court*, the court held that the lack of the required title, "Referendum Against an Ordinance Passed by the City Council," did not invalidate the petition because the language of the petition furnished the information that would have been provided by the statutorily required title. 218 Cal. App. 3d 53, 59 (1990).

Notice of Intention to Circulate; Ballot Title and Summary

A notice of intention to circulate an initiative petition must be filed with the clerk prior to circulating copies of the petition for signatures.

A notice of intention to circulate an initiative petition must be filed with the clerk prior to circulating copies of the petition for signatures. Elec. Code §§ 9104 (counties); 9202 (cities). The notice of intention must be accompanied by the written text of the initiative, and may be accompanied by a written statement of up to 500 words giving reasons for the proposed initiative. No notice of intention to circulate is required for referendum petitions.

Sections 9104 and 9202(a) of the Elections Code provide that a notice of intention to circulate shall be in "substantially" the form provided in those sections. The notice of intention in a county must include the names and addresses of at least one, but not more than five proponents. Elec. Code § 9104. In a city, the notice of intention must be signed by at least one, but not more than three, proponents. Elec. Code § 9202(a). A city or county elections official has a ministerial duty to reject an initiative petition that does not include a notice of intention. *See Myers*, 196 Cal. App. 3d at 136.

In counties, when the elections official receives the notice of intention to circulate, the official must immediately transmit a copy of the proposed initiative to the county counsel for preparation of a ballot title and summary.

In counties, when the elections official receives the notice of intention to circulate, the official must immediately transmit a copy of the proposed initiative to the county counsel for preparation of a ballot title and summary. Elec. Code § 9105. In cities, initiative proponents or any other "interested" person shall request preparation of a ballot title and summary upon submission to the city elections official of the notice of intention. The elections official must then immediately transmit the proposed measure to the city attorney. Elec. Code § 9203. The county counsel or city attorney must return the official ballot title and summary within 15 days after the proposed measure is filed. The ballot title and summary must be a "true and impartial" statement of the purpose of the proposed measure, not to exceed 500 words in length. Elec. Code §§ 9105(a) (counties); 9203(a) (cities). The ballot title and summary must appear across the top of each page of the initiative petition where signatures are to appear. Elec. Code §§ 9105(c) (counties); 9203(b) (cities).

An initiative proponent may seek a writ of mandate requiring the ballot title or summary to be amended. A peremptory writ will not issue unless there is clear and convincing evidence that the ballot title or summary is false, misleading, or

---

4. The *Mervyn's* opinion contains a good summary of cases concerning whether an initiative or referendum measure substantially complied with statutory requirements.

otherwise fails to conform to the statutory requirements. Elec. Code §§ 9106 (counties); 9204 (cities).

Publication and Posting

The notice of intention to circulate, ballot title, and summary must be published and posted prior to circulation of an initiative petition for signatures. *See Ibarra v. City of Carson*, 214 Cal. App. 3d 90, 96 (1989). The requirements for publication and posting differ in counties and cities. In counties, the notice of intention, the ballot title, and the summary of the proposed measure must be published in a newspaper of general circulation published in the county. The initiative proponents must file a proof of publication with the county elections official. Elec. Code § 9105(b).

In cities, the notice of intention and the title and summary of the proposed measure must be published or posted or both. The notice, title, and summary must be published at least once in a newspaper that has been adjudicated as being of general circulation in the city in which the petition is to be circulated. If there is no such newspaper in the city, the notice, title, and summary must be published at least once in a newspaper circulated in the city and adjudicated as being of general circulation in the county in which the city is located, and also be posted in three public places within the city that are used for posting ordinances. If there is no adjudicated newspaper of general circulation that is circulated in the city, the notice, title, and summary need not be published, but must be posted in three public places within the city that are used for posting ordinances. Elec. Code § 9205.

These provisions are designed to serve the important purpose of educating the public about the petition campaign before it begins. Therefore, strict compliance with the publication and posting requirements is necessary. *Ibarra*, 214 Cal. App. 3d at 95–96.

> *In cities, the notice of intention and the title and summary of the proposed measure must be published or posted or both.*

> **PRACTICE TIP**
> Publication and/or posting of the notice of intention and the ballot title and summary must occur before any signatures may be collected.

Circulation; Signature

Circulation of an initiative petition may commence after the notice, ballot title, and summary are published and/or posted, as required. Elections Code section 101 requires that petitions for local initiatives contain a notice that the petition may be circulated by either a paid signature gatherer or a volunteer, and that members of the public have the right to ask about the circulator's status. Only a voter who is eligible and registered to vote in the jurisdiction for which an initiative or referendum measure is proposed may sign a petition. Elec. Code § 100. Initiative proponents have 180 days from receipt of a ballot title and summary, or from termination of any action for writ of mandate regarding the title and summary, whichever occurs later, in which to collect sufficient signatures. Elec. Code §§ 9110 (counties); 9208 (cities).

In a county, an initiative petition must be signed by at least 10 percent of the entire vote cast in the county at the last gubernatorial election in order to qualify the initiative for a regular election, and by at least 20 percent of such a vote to qualify for a special election. Elec. Code §§ 9101, 9116, 9117. In a city with more than 1,000 registered voters, initiative petitions must be signed by not less than 10 percent of the city's registered voters to qualify the measure for the regular election, and by not less than 15 percent of registered voters to qualify for a special election. Elec. Code §§ 9201, 9214, 9215. In a city with 1,000 or fewer registered voters, an initiative petition must be signed by 25 percent of the registered voters, or 100 registered voters, whichever is the lesser number. Elec. Code §§ 9214, 9215.

The Elections Code contains a separate article governing city charter amendments. Elec. Code § 9255 *et seq*. For these amendments, 15 percent of the registered voters must sign the initiative petition. In a combined city and county (*i.e.*, San Francisco) only 10 percent of the registered voters' signatures are required. Elec. Code § 9255. If an initiative in a charter city proposes an ordinance, but does not amend the charter, the initiative provisions of the city charter will determine the number of signatures required. If the charter does not contain initiative procedures, then the Elections Code provisions governing general law cities apply. Elec. Code § 9247.

A city or county ordinance may be referended by filing a petition protesting the adoption of the ordinance with the elections official of the local legislative body before the effective date of the ordinance.

A city or county ordinance may be referended by filing a petition protesting the adoption of the ordinance with the elections official of the local legislative body before the effective date of the ordinance (usually within 30 days of adoption of the ordinance). In a county, a referendum petition must be signed by not less than 10 percent of the entire vote cast within the county at the last gubernatorial election. Elec. Code § 9144. In a city with more than 1,000 registered voters, referendum petitions must be signed by not less than 10 percent of the city's registered voters. Elec. Code § 9237. In a city with 1,000 or fewer registered voters, a referendum petition must be signed by 25 percent of the registered voters, or 100 registered voters, whichever is the lesser number. *Id*. When a valid petition is filed, the ordinance does not go into effect, and the legislative body must reconsider the ordinance. Elec. Code §§ 9144 (counties); 9237 (cities).

Filing; Examination of Signatures

The provisions of the Elections Code governing filing and examination of petitions in cities and counties are applicable to petitions for both initiatives and referenda.

The provisions of the Elections Code governing filing and examination of petitions in cities and counties are applicable to petitions for both initiatives and referenda. Elec. Code §§ 9146 (counties); 9239 (cities). After sufficient signatures are collected, a petition may be filed by proponents or any person so authorized in writing by the proponents. All sections of a signed petition must be filed with the elections official of the jurisdiction in which the measure is proposed at one time. Elec. Code §§ 9113 (counties); 9208 (cities). In counties an affidavit, and in cities a declaration, signed by the circulator must be attached to each section. Elec. Code §§ 9109 (counties); 9209 (cities). The forms of the county affidavit and city declaration are provided in the Elections Code. §§ 104 (counties); 9022 (cities).

The local elections official has 30 days, excluding Saturdays, Sundays, and holidays, from the date of filing in which to examine the petition and determine if it contains the required number of signatures. Elec. Code §§ 9114, 9115 (counties); 9211 (cities). Random sampling techniques may be employed to examine petitions bearing more than 500 signatures; however, verification of each signature is required where statistical sampling shows that the number of signatures is between 95 and 100 percent of the number required. Elec. Code §§ 9115 (counties); 9211 (cities). The elections official is to attach a certificate to the petitions showing the results of the examination, and to notify the proponents of the petition as to its sufficiency. *Id*.

If a petition is found to bear an insufficient number of valid signatures, no further action is taken. Elec. Code §§ 9114, 9115 (counties); 9211 (cities). Failure to secure sufficient signatures does not preclude the filing later of an entirely new petition on the same subject at a later date. *Id.* If the number of signatures is sufficient, the elections official certifies the results to the local legislative body at its next regular meeting. *Id.*

The duties of an election official in examining an initiative or referendum petition are ministerial and not judicial. It is not the function of the official to determine whether a proposed measure is within the power of the electorate to adopt or will be valid if enacted. If the petition satisfies formal requirements and contains a sufficient number of valid signatures, the official must certify the petition as sufficient. *See Truman v. Royer*, 189 Cal. App. 2d 240, 243 (1961); *Farley v. Healey*, 67 Cal. 2d 325, 327 (1967).

However, the election official's duties, although ministerial, are not mechanical. The official must exercise some judgment, *e.g.*, when comparing signatures on the petition with those on voter registration affidavits. *See Wheelwright v. County of Marin*, 2 Cal. 3d 448, 455–56 (1970).

For example, in *Truman*, the court recognized that a city clerk may refuse to certify petitions because of noncompliance with election procedures. 189 Cal. App. 2d at 243. Nonetheless, while certain procedural requirements relating to circulators' affidavits and other related items are mandatory, they are only for the convenience of the clerk. Thus, once a clerk has accepted a petition and commenced examination of signatures, "he must certify the petition as sufficient," if the petition contains a sufficient number of valid signatures. *Id.* at 243–44. The court held that the clerk could not refuse to certify the petitions for failure of the circulators to comply with the circulators' affidavit requirement. "The defective affidavits accompanying the referendum petition are not part of the petitions themselves, and failure of such should not invalidate a petition which was in fact signed by the requisite number of qualified voters...." *Id.* at 244.

Truman was distinguished in *Myers v. Patterson*, where the court noted that a failure of a referendum petition to include a notice required by the city charter "directly affected the content of the petition sections circulated to voters... [and] the information was not just for the benefit of the City official." 196 Cal. App. 3d 130, 137 (1987). Accordingly, the *Myers* court held that *Truman* was not applicable since, in contrast to *Truman*, the defect directly affected the content of the petition sections circulated to the voters. *Id.* at 136.

Pre-Election Invalidation of Initiatives and Referenda for Failure to Comply with Procedural Requirements

Pre-election challenges to initiatives and referenda (discussed in further detail later in this chapter) have been upheld because:

- Referendum petition misstated the title of the challenged ordinance. *Hebard v. Bybee*, 65 Cal. App. 4th 1331, 1338 (1998)
- Referendum petition contained only the number and title of the challenged ordinance, rather than its complete text. *Creighton v. Reviczky*, 171 Cal. App.

3d 1225, 1229 (1985); *see also Billig v. Voges,* 223 Cal. App. 3d 962, 968 (1990); Elec. Code § 9238

- Referendum petition failed to include an exhibit setting forth the technical legal description and location of the affected real property. *Chase v. Brooks,* 187 Cal. App. 3d 657, 664 (1986); *see also Nelson v. Carlson,* 17 Cal. App. 4th 732, 739–740 (1993); Elec. Code § 9238
- An initiative petition was signed after notice of intent to circulate the petition was published, but prior to that notice being posted. *Ibarra,* 214 Cal. App. 3d at 95–96; Elec. Code § 9202(a)
- An initiative petition contained indisputably false statements about the reasons for signing the petition. *San Francisco Forty-Niners v. Nishioka (Comstock),* 75 Cal. App. 4th 637, 649–50 (1999); Elec. Code § 18600

Action by Local Legislative Bodies on Initiatives and Referenda

The Elections Code allows the legislative body to refer a proposed initiative measure to staff or any city or county agencies for a report on its fiscal impact, consistency with the general plan, and any other matters.

The Elections Code allows the legislative body to refer a proposed initiative measure to staff or any city or county agencies for a report on its fiscal impact, consistency with the general plan, and any other matters. The report must be completed within 30 days after the initiative petition is certified as having a sufficient number of signatures. Elec. Code §§ 9111 (counties); 9212 (cities). The legislative body may request such a report prior to certification of the petitions, to allow for a longer period for completion of the report.

However, a city council may have the authority to delay the election on an initiative. In *Jeffrey v. Superior Court,* more than 22,000 Huntington Beach residents sought to amend the city charter in 2002 by placing the Fair Apportionment and Individual Representation (FAIR) initiative on the ballot. The initiative proposed to modify the city council's term limits and change the city council from seven members elected at large to five members elected by districts, with changes becoming effective two years in the future, during the November 2004 general municipal election. 102 Cal. App. 4th 1 (2002). Though Huntington Beach had an upcoming general election in 2002, the city council placed the FAIR initiative on the March 2004 ballot instead, for the express purpose of giving the city council more time to defeat the initiative. FAIR supporters petitioned the court to have the initiative placed on the November 2002 ballot. The trial court denied the petition after concluding council members have the authority to delay the initiative. The appellate court affirmed, relying on Elections Code sections 9255(a) and 1415, which detail the minimum time limits but not the maximum time limits in which a proposal must be submitted to voters. The Court noted that nothing in these provisions requires a city council to "order" an election at the next available opportunity. *Id.* at 4.

FAIR = Fair Apportionment and Individual Representation

After receiving a valid petition, the city council must either pass the proposed ordinance without change or submit it, without alteration, to the city electorate.

After receiving a valid petition, the city council must either pass the proposed ordinance without change or submit the ordinance, without alteration, to the city electorate. Elec. Code §§ 9118, 9214, 9215. The city's duty to adopt a qualified voter-sponsored initiative by ordinance or place it on the ballot is ministerial and mandatory. *Native Am. Sacred Site & Envtl. Protection Ass'n v. City of San Juan Capistrano,* 120 Cal. App. 4th 961 (2004). In one case, the court held that the board of supervisors should not usurp a judicial function by refusing to place a duly certified initiative on the ballot; the board had a duty to do so unless it obtained a court order barring the matter from the ballot. *See Save Stanislaus Area Farm Econ. (SAFE) v. Board of Supervisors*, 13 Cal. App. 4th 141, 148 (1993); *but see Worthington v. City Council of the City of Rohnert Park*, 130 Cal. App. 4th 1132 (2005) (court did not address the city's refusal to place a referendum on the ballot based on determination that subject agreement was an administrative act not subject to referendum).

In both cities and counties, the council or board may choose, on its own, to submit proposals to the voters. Elec. Code §§ 9140 (counties); 9222 (cities). The council or board must, however, comply with CEQA before doing so. *See Friends of Sierra Madre v. City of Sierra Madre*, 25 Cal. 4th 165, 194–95 (2001).

If the majority of the voters on a proposed ordinance vote in its favor, the ordinance becomes a valid and binding ordinance. Elec. Code §§ 9122 (counties); 9217 (cities). No ordinance proposed by initiative petition and adopted either by the voters or the city council can be repealed or amended except by a vote of the people, unless the ordinance provides to the contrary. Elec. Code §§ 9125 (counties); 9217 (cities).

Upon submission of a referendum petition, the subject ordinance or resolution must be suspended and the legislative body must reconsider it. Elec. Code §§ 9144, 9237. If the legislative body does not then entirely repeal the ordinance or resolution, it must be submitted to the voters. It shall not become effective unless a majority of the electorate vote in favor of it. Elec. Code §§ 9145, 9241.

Upon submission of a referendum petition, the subject ordinance or resolution must be suspended and the legislative body must reconsider it.

Cities may not avoid this stay provision by reenacting materially identical laws as an interim measure until the referendum election. *Lindelli v. Town of San Anselmo (Marin Sanitary Service)*, 111 Cal. App. 4th 1099 (2003). In *Lindelli*, the Town of San Anselmo maintained a waste management services contract with North Bay Corporation from 1994 to 2002. In August 2002, the town passed a resolution awarding a new franchise grant to a competitor, Marin Sanitary Service (MSS). A referendum petition challenging the award was certified. The town then awarded an interim contract to MSS until the referendum election and set an election for the referendum for November 4, 2003. The terms were identical to the original agreement, except for the duration. Lindelli and North Bay petitioned for writ of mandate, arguing that the interim contract violated the stay provision of Elections Code section 9241.

MSS = Marin Sanitary Service

In ruling against the town, the court held that the function of the stay provision is to enforce the electorate's power to approve or reject legislation provisionally adopted before it takes effect. Granting of a franchise is a legislative act subject to the referendum stay, and the legislative body may not violate the stay by enacting an essentially identical measure on the same subject matter. The interim contract to MSS differed from the original award only in the length of time—one year versus five years. It was the change in provider, not the length of the award, that inspired the referendum advocates. Because the interim contract was essentially the same as the challenged franchise ordinance, the court held that it violated the stay provision. The court further held that the contract did not fall within any exception to the referendum stay, including the urgency exception, because there was no imminent risk that garbage would pile up in the streets without immediate legislative action since alternative waste management providers were available.

The function of the stay provision is to enforce the electorate's power to approve or reject legislation provisionally adopted before it takes effect.

In cities, a municipal ordinance or resolution rejected by referendum cannot again be enacted by the council for a period of one year after the date of its repeal by council or disapproval by the voters. Elec. Code § 9241. However, there is no equivalent statutory or judicial restriction for counties.

Limitations on the Use of Initiative and Referendum

Constitutional Limitations

Single subject rule. The California Constitution places some limitations upon the use of the initiative and referendum. The most significant limitation is that an initiative can embrace only one subject. Cal. Const. art. II, § 8(d). However, the California courts have taken a broad view as to what constitutes a single subject. *See, e.g., Brosnahan v. Brown*, 32 Cal. 3d 236, 248–49 (1982). For instance, in *Raven v. Deukmejian*, the Court held that "an initiative measure does not violate the single subject requirement if, despite its varied collateral effects, all of its parts are 'reasonably germane' to each other and to the general purpose or object of the initiative." 52 Cal. 3d 336, 346 (1990); *but see Senate v. Jones*, 21 Cal. 4th 1142, 1153–54 (1999) (rejecting in a preelection challenge Proposition 24, the "Let the Voters Decide Act of 2000," which would have significantly revised the role of the California Citizens Compensation Commission in setting salaries of legislators and which would also have transferred the power to reapportion congressional, legislative, and Board of Equalization districts from the Legislature to the Supreme Court); *Chemical Specialties Mfg. Ass'n, Inc. v. Deukmejian*, 227 Cal. App. 3d 663, 667–68 (1991) (striking down Proposition 105, the "Public Right to Know Act," enacted by the voters in November 1988, as violating the single subject rule of the California Constitution).

In *Shea Homes L.P. v. County of Alameda*, the court held that an initiative altering a county's solid waste management practices, and designating more land for agriculture and open space and less land for urban growth, did not violate the single subject rule. 110 Cal. App. 4th 1246 (2003). Measure D, a "Citizens for Open Space Initiative Plan to Protect Agriculture and Open Space," was adopted in November 2000 by the electorate of Alameda County, and relocated the urban growth boundary to coincide with existing or proposed city urban growth boundaries, generally redesignating previous urban development use designations with agricultural uses. In addition, Measure D altered the county's solid waste management and planning practice.

Property owners affected by Measure D brought suit and argued that because the initiative constricted the county's urban growth boundary and altered its solid waste policies, it violated the single subject rule of the State Constitution and violated various state housing laws. In ruling for the county, the court held that the purpose of the single subject rule is to avoid voter confusion and subversion of the electorate's will. An initiative that is entitled "Save Agriculture and Open Space Lands" reasonably and naturally encompasses provisions that will (1) limit a use of the land at issue, such as a landfill, that is incompatible with this title, and (2) promote an activity, such as coordination of solid waste recycling and management, that fosters this title by reducing a

---

An initiative measure does not violate the single subject requirement if, despite its varied collateral effects, all of its parts are "reasonably germane" to each other and to the general purpose of the object of the initiative.

cause for encroachment on open space. *Id.* at 1258–59. Consequently, such provisions, even if they may effectively realign agency responsibility for solid waste management, would not mislead a voter as to Measure D's purpose, because, like all the provisions in the measure, they are germane to achieving its clearly stated objective of preserving and enhancing specifically defined open space and agricultural lands within the county. *Id.*

The single subject rule is equally applicable to both state and local measures. *See San Mateo County Coastal Landowners' Ass'n v. County of San Mateo*, 38 Cal. App. 4th 523, 553 (1995).

Other constitutional limitations provide that a referendum may not be used to reject "urgency statutes, statutes calling elections, and statutes providing for tax levies or appropriations for usual current expenses." Cal. Const. art. II, § 9(a); *see also Rossi v. Brown*, 9 Cal. 4th 688, 697–98 (1995) (relating to tax measures).

Cannot conflict with state law. The California Constitution prohibits cities from exercising their police power to enact ordinances that conflict with provisions of general state law. Cal. Const. art. XI, § 7. This limitation applies to measures adopted either by the city council or by the voters directly. *See Legislature v. Deukmejian*, 34 Cal. 3d 658, 675 (1983); *Galvin v. Board of Supervisors of Contra Costa County*, 195 Cal. 686, 692 (1925). This restriction does not apply to charter cities with respect to strictly municipal affairs. *See* Cal. Const. art. XI, § 5(a). With regard to matters of statewide concern, even charter cities are precluded from enacting measures that conflict with state law, whether by council action or initiative. *See Bishop v. City of San Jose*, 1 Cal. 3d 56, 61 (1969).

Thus, for example, a local initiative that granted a franchise for a toll bridge was invalidated because preconditions set by state law, such as obtaining the approval of the state engineer, were not met. *See Galvin*, 195 Cal. at 696–98. In another case, the Court found that Government Code section 66484.3 granted exclusive authority to impose the developer fees at issue to the Orange County Board of Supervisors and to the Orange County city councils, rather than to the voters. The Court held that the voters' imposition of the fees conflicted with state law because of the exclusive delegation by the Legislature to the local legislative body. *See DeVita v. County of Napa*, 9 Cal. 4th 763, 786 (1995).

In *Shea Homes*, as discussed above, the court held that an initiative designating more land for agriculture and open space and less land for urban growth did not violate state housing laws. 110 Cal. App. 4th at 1266. In ruling for the county, the court held that claims alleging that a local ordinance conflicts with a state statutory scheme implicate questions of law, not fact. The first step in the reviewing court's inquiry is to determine whether a genuine conflict exists between the local ordinance and the state law. The court then examined Measure D in relation to the four enumerated Government Code statutes set forth by the property owners to determine if they actually conflicted. Although it concluded that Measure D did reduce the amount of vacant land available for development, the court held that the initiative did not conflict with state law.

The court referred to section 7 of the initiative which stated that none of its provisions would be applied so as to preclude the county's compliance with state law housing obligations. Section 7 also authorized the voters to approve an extension of the East County Area Plan urban growth boundary. The court stated that it could not presume that the county electorate would fail to approve a proper corrective extension if the present boundary proved inadequate to meet mandated housing needs. *Id.* at 1265. Section 7 also authorized the county board of supervisors to approve housing beyond that boundary to meet state housing requirements if certain factors were demonstrated and certain guidelines as to location of that housing were adhered to. In concluding on this point, the court said that clauses such as section 7, together with the rule that initiatives are to be upheld when possible, may defeat a challenged cause of action as a matter of law. *Id.* at 755–56.

Judicial Limitations

As a general rule, the power of the voters to adopt an ordinance by initiative is restricted by the same limitations that restrict the city council's power to do so.

The California courts have fashioned various additional limitations on the voters' initiative and referendum powers. As a general rule, the power of the voters to adopt an ordinance by initiative is restricted by the same limitations that restrict the city council's power to do so. In other words, at least with respect to the substance or content of an ordinance, the voters by initiative have no greater power than does the city council. Accordingly, the courts have held that an initiative ordinance may not (1) invade a duty imposed solely on the city council as an agent of the state (*Simpson v. Hite*, 36 Cal. 2d 125, 133–34 (1950)); (2) violate the California or United States Constitutions (*Howard Jarvis Taxpayers Ass'n v. City of San Diego*, 120 Cal. App. 4th 374, 385 (2004); *Hawn v. County of Ventura*, 73 Cal. App. 3d 1009, 1018 (1977)); (3) be inconsistent with, or make internally inconsistent, the city's general plan (*DeVita v. County of Napa*, 9 Cal. 4th 763, 777–78 (1995); *Lesher Commc'ns, Inc. v. City of Walnut Creek*, 52 Cal. 3d 531, 542–43 (1991)); (4) affect administrative, as opposed to legislative, matters (*McKevitt v. City of Sacramento*, 55 Cal. App. 117, 124 (1921)); or (5) impair an essential governmental function (*Birkenfeld v. City of Berkeley*, 17 Cal. 3d 129, 143 (1976)).

In *Bighorn-Desert View Water Agency v. Verjil*, the California Supreme Court found that, pursuant to section 3 of article XIII C of the California Constitution, an initiative could be used to reduce the rate charged by a public water district for domestic water. 39 Cal. 4th 205 (2006). However, the court found that the State Constitution did not support the premise that the initiative power could be used to grant local voters a right to impose a voter-approval requirement on all future adjustments of, or creation of new, water delivery charges. *Id.* at 218–19.

The initiative process cannot be used to introduce a local measure that would alter a redevelopment plan or interfere with its implementation.

Cannot invade a duty imposed on an "agent of the state." A prime example of "invading a duty imposed on a city as an agent of the state" is that of a city using its redevelopment power. Local redevelopment agencies functioning in a city pursuant to the Community Redevelopment Law (Health & Safety Code § 33000 *et seq.*) are administrative agents of the state. The initiative process cannot be used to introduce a local measure that would alter a redevelopment plan or interfere with its implementation. However, pursuant to legislative amendments adopted in 1977, the deactivation of the redevelopment agency and the adoption or the amendment of a redevelopment plan were made subject to the referendum process. Health & Safety Code §§ 33141, 33365, 33450.

In one case, a citizens' group opposed part of a 1967 redevelopment plan that called for building the West Berkeley Industrial Park. *Redevelopment Agency v. City of Berkeley*, 80 Cal. App. 3d 158 (1978). The group objected to the elimination of numerous old residences in the project area. The initiative would have amended the plan and rezoned a six-square-block area to retain the residences. The court held that the development of the project pursuant to the redevelopment plan was an administrative act carrying out state policy even though adopted by ordinance, and therefore was not subject to amendment by initiative. The court further stated that the 1977 legislative amendments authorizing the use of the referendum on certain redevelopment decisions did not authorize the use of the initiative in the redevelopment field. The court stated that the referendum is a procedure used to invalidate an ordinance adopted by a legislative body, and in this situation, the Berkeley citizens' group was offering its own ordinance through the initiative process. *Id.* at 169.

The same citizens' group had lost an earlier court battle launched to stop the razing of the old residences for development of the West Berkeley Industrial Park. *Kehoe v. City of Berkeley*, 67 Cal. App. 3d 666 (1977). In 1973, the group had secured the adoption of an initiative to restrict the razing of old homes by controlling the issuance of demolition permits. The court held that the provisions of the "Neighborhood Preservation Ordinance" could not be applied to the redevelopment project area because they conflicted with general state law (the Community Redevelopment Law). *Id.* at 674.

Cannot be an improper exercise of the police power. If the content of an initiative ordinance violates the California or United States Constitutions, it is invalid. Constitutional challenges typically involve claims that the initiative, especially a growth management measure, is an improper exercise of the city's police power because it violates the due process or equal protection rights of affected property owners. *See, e.g., Building Indus. Ass'n v. City of Camarillo*, 41 Cal. 3d 810, 824 (1986). For example, in *Hawn v. County of Ventura*, an initiative giving approval power over airport site selection to the voters of a city, but not nearby residents of unincorporated territory, was ruled an unconstitutional denial of equal protection. 73 Cal. App. 3d 1009, 1018 (1977).

If the content of an initiative ordinance violates the California or United States Constitutions, it is invalid.

In adjudicating constitutional challenges, courts hold initiative measures to the same standards as council-enacted measures. In *Arnel Development Co. v. City of Costa Mesa*, which involved a rezoning by initiative, the court held that "[t]he city's authority under the police power is no greater than otherwise it would be simply because the subsequent rezoning was accomplished by initiative." 126 Cal. App. 3d 330, 337 (1981).

In adjudicating constitutional challenges, courts hold initiative measures to the same standards as council-enacted measures.

Developer Arnel had proposed to construct a 50-acre development consisting of 127 single-family residences and 539 apartment units. The city had approved a specific plan for development of the Arnel property, and pursuant to that plan had rezoned the property for planned residential development of both medium and low density. Objecting to the developer's proposal, a neighborhood association circulated an initiative petition to rezone the property as well as two adjoining properties to a lower density single-family residential designation. The initiative passed.

The trial court found that the initiative's purpose was to rezone the property in order to defeat the Arnel project, despite the existence of an acute shortage of moderate-income housing in the city. The court also found that the rezoning designation had been selected without considering the best use of the property or various zoning alternatives.

> *The people may not use an initiative to discriminate against a particular parcel of land, and the courts may properly inquire as to whether the classification scheme had been applied fairly and impartially.*

On appeal, the *Arnel* court found that the measure suffered from two fatal flaws. First, the court noted that the people may not use an initiative to discriminate against a particular parcel of land, and that the courts may properly inquire as to whether the classification scheme had been applied fairly and impartially. *Id.* As the Costa Mesa ordinance clearly would have been held invalid as arbitrary and discriminatory if adopted by the city council, it was also invalid when adopted by initiative.

Second, the initiative failed because it lacked a substantial and reasonable relationship to the public welfare. *Id.* The court first noted the "regional" scope of the inquiry, stating that "municipalities are not isolated islands remote from the needs and problems of the area in which they are located; thus an ordinance, superficially reasonable from the limited viewpoint of the municipality, may be disclosed as unreasonable when viewed from a larger perspective." *Id.* at 338. Accordingly, the relevant question is "whether the ordinance reasonably relates to the welfare of those whom it significantly affects." *Id.* at 339.

Next, applying the three-step analysis from *Associated Home Builders, Inc. v. City of Livermore*, 18 Cal. 3d 582 (1976), the *Arnel* court held that no attempt had been made to accommodate the competing public interests that were present, namely, the acute shortage of moderate-income housing in Costa Mesa versus a desire for lower-density development. The court concluded that "the initiative ordinance, which completely precludes development of multiple family residences in the area, does not effect a reasonable accommodation of the competing interests on a regional basis and is therefore not a valid exercise of the police power." *Id.* For a general discussion of the police power, *see* chapter 1 (Overview).

Two ballot initiatives were held to be invalid in *Howard Jarvis Taxpayers Association v. City of San Diego* because they were inconsistent with the California Constitution and therefore exceeded the city's police power. 120 Cal. App. 4th 374 (2004). The plaintiff taxpayer group in *Howard Jarvis* had placed Proposition E on the ballot, which sought to amend San Diego's charter so as to require a super-majority two-thirds vote in order to approve any new general tax or increase in an existing tax. In response, the city placed onto the same ballot Proposition F, which sought to retroactively require a two-thirds super-majority vote in order to amend the city charter, thus imposing a higher threshold for passage of Proposition E. Both measures received greater than 50 percent affirmative votes. The city declared that voters had approved Proposition F and Proposition E had failed because it had not received an affirmative two-thirds vote.

The appellate court held that both initiatives violated the Constitution and were invalid. Proposition F, by which the city hoped to create a two-thirds super-majority requirement for amendment of its charter, violated article XI, section 3(a) of the California Constitution, which expressly provides that a city may adopt or award its charter by *majority vote* of its electors. The court concluded that this constitutional provision preempted any effort by the city or its voters to establish a different vote requirement for amendment of the city's charter. *Id.* at 385–86.

Proposition E likewise was invalid because its requirement of a two-thirds vote for any new general tax or tax increase conflicted with amendments made to the California Constitution by Proposition 218. Those amendments provide that general taxes may be enacted or increased by a simple majority vote of the electorate. *Id.* at 392–93. For further discussion of Proposition 218, *see* chapter 13 (Exactions).

Cannot Be Inconsistent with the General Plan[5]

Vertical consistency. Under California law, every city must adopt a general plan as the "constitution" for that jurisdiction's physical development. Gov't Code § 65300; *Lesher Communications, Inc. v. City of Walnut Creek*, 52 Cal. 3d 531, 540 (1990). Generally, all other land use regulations, actions, or approvals must be consistent with the applicable general plan. Gov't Code § 65860. Zoning enactments of a charter city (except the City of Los Angeles) do not have to be consistent with the provisions of the city's general plan unless consistency is required by the city's ordinance or charter. Gov't Code § 65803; Gov't Code § 65860(d); *City of Los Angeles v. State of California*, 138 Cal. App. 3d 526, 532 (1982); *see* discussion in chapter 4 (Zoning). Whether a land use initiative is consistent with the applicable general plan is determined by comparing the substance of the initiative with each of the elements of the general plan, including the seven mandatory elements and any optional elements included within the plan, as well as any maps and diagrams within the various elements.

If a subordinate land use regulation, whether enacted by the legislative body or directly by the voters, is inconsistent with the applicable general plan, a legal challenge to the regulation may result in its being found void *ab initio*. For example, a California court held that a proposed referendum, which would have rejected a zoning ordinance adopted by the Norco City Council, was invalid because if passed, the resulting zoning would have been inconsistent with the city's general plan. *deBottari v. City Council*, 171 Cal. App. 3d 1204, 1210–11 (1985); *see also Merritt v. City of Pleasanton*, 89 Cal. App. 4th 1032, 1036–37 (2001); *City of Irvine v. Irvine Citizens Against Overdevelopment*, 25 Cal. App. 4th 868, 873–74 (1994) (local referendum preventing prezoning of unincorporated land in the city's sphere of influence was not inconsistent with the city's general plan).

In 1990, the California Supreme Court affirmed the rule that a zoning ordinance in conflict with a general plan is invalid at the time it is passed. *Lesher*, 52 Cal. 3d at 544. First, the Court found that the city's traffic-based growth management ordinance, which was passed by initiative was, in fact, a zoning ordinance and not a general plan amendment. The Court then held that because the initiative was admittedly inconsistent with the city's general plan, it was void *ab initio*. *Id.* at 545–46.

A court, relying on *Lesher*, held that a numerical residential cap initiative was invalid when passed. *See Building Indus. Ass'n v. City of Oceanside*, 27 Cal. App. 4th 744, 762–63 (1994). Since Proposition A, a zoning ordinance, conflicted with the housing goals of Oceanside's general plan, the initiative measure was void when passed. The opinion in *Oceanside* superseded an earlier decision, *Building Indus. Ass'n v. Superior Court*, 211 Cal. App. 3d 277 (1989) (disapproved in part by *Lesher*), which suggested that inconsistency of an ordinance with a general plan could be remedied with a compliance decree.

Under California law, every city must adopt a general plan as the constitution for that jurisdiction's physical development. Generally, all other land use regulations, actions, or approvals must be consistent with the applicable general plan.

PRACTICE TIP

When drafting a zoning initiative, be sure to consider whether approval could result in vertical inconsistency with the general plan.

---

5. For a detailed discussion of general plans and consistency requirements, *see* chapter 2 (General Plan).

Horizontal or internal consistency. In addition to the requirement that land use regulations be "vertically" consistent with the general plan, "horizontal" or internal consistency within the general plan also is required. Gov't Code § 65300.5. For example, an initiative to amend the general plan to limit growth may be inconsistent with pre-existing general plan provisions relating to affordable housing. Any measure, whether enacted by initiative or the local legislative body, that will result in inconsistency within the general plan is vulnerable to legal challenge. *See DeVita*, 9 Cal. 4th at 796 n.12. For a thorough discussion of general plan internal consistency, *see* chapter 2 (General Plan).

Legal inadequacy of the general plan. A related basis for limiting the voters' ability to enact a growth management or other land use measure is the legal inadequacy of the general plan itself. The consistency requirement is one of consistency with a legally adequate general plan. *See Sierra Club v. Board of Supervisors*, 126 Cal. App. 3d 698, 704 (1981) (cited by *Lesher*, 52 Cal. 3d at 541). Therefore, if the general plan fails to meet all of the statutory requirements, including internal consistency, a measure intended to implement that general plan, whether enacted by the legislative body or the voters, may be found inconsistent. *See Resource Defense Fund v. County of Santa Cruz*, 133 Cal. App. 3d 800, 806 (1982). For example, in *Sierra Club*, the court found the general plan of Kern County to be internally inconsistent, and therefore invalid, and because the zoning ordinance under review could not be consistent with an invalid general plan, the zoning ordinance was also invalid at the time it was passed. 126 Cal. App. 3d at 704.

However, before a court will find that a legally inadequate general plan invalidates an initiative measure, there must be a nexus. A 1991 decision held that the inadequacy of a general plan will invalidate an amendment adopted by initiative only if there is "a nexus between the amendments and the elements or characteristics of the plan claimed to be inadequate." *Garat v. City of Riverside*, 2 Cal. App. 4th 259, 289–90 (1991) (overruled on other grounds in *Morehart v. County of Santa Barbara*, 7 Cal. 4th 725, 743 (1994)); *see also San Mateo County Coastal Landowners' Ass'n v. County of San Mateo*, 38 Cal. App. 4th 523, 535–36 (1995).

Cannot affect non-legislative matters. Judicial restriction precluding direct voter action in administrative matters is based on the fundamental principle that the powers of initiative and referendum extend only to legislative acts. *See Yost v. Thomas*, 36 Cal. 3d 561, 570 (1984); *Arnel Dev. Co. v. City of Costa Mesa*, 28 Cal. 3d at 514–16 (1980). Accordingly, actions that are administrative in nature can be neither enacted nor overturned by initiative or referendum. Additionally, legislative acts of a city for which the legislative power is conferred by statute, such as annexation of territory, are preempted by general law and thus beyond the reach of the local initiative process. *L.I.F.E. Committee v. City of Lodi*, 213 Cal. App. 3d 1139, 1148–49 (1989).

In the land use area, the courts have drawn generic classifications, viewing zoning ordinances as legislative and other decisions, such as variances, use permits, and subdivision map approvals, as nonlegislative or administrative. *See id.* Similarly, the adoption or amendment of general plans, specific plans, or Local Coastal Programs are legislative acts subject to initiative and referendum even though enacted by a resolution rather than by an ordinance. *See Midway Orchards v. County of Butte*, 220 Cal. App. 3d 765, 773–74 (1990); *Yost*, 36 Cal. 3d at 569–70; *DeVita*, 9 Cal. 4th at 775–76; *San Mateo County Coastal Landowners'*, 38 Cal. App. 4th at 534. However, a city's agreement with a Native American tribe to mitigate casino impacts, even though approved by resolution, was held to be an administrative act not subject to referendum. *Worthington v. City Council of the City of Rohnert Park*, 130 Cal. App. 4th 1132, 1143 (2005). The court found that based on the extensive federal regulation of Indian gaming, federal and state governments have sole authority to exercise legislative power in this area, and that the city was acting merely as an administrative agent of the state in its negotiation and approval of the agreement. Further, the court rejected the argument that the city's decision to negotiate with the tribe and then publicly oppose the casino plan was a policy decision subject to referendum, stating that "policy" is a broad term not synonymous with legislation. *Id.* at 1142.

The court in *Pettye v. City and County of San Francisco* held that the enactment of standards for providing general assistance to the indigent was a legislative act that was properly subject to a voter initiative. 118 Cal. App. 4th 233, 244–45 (2004). In November 2003, voters in San Francisco passed the "Care Not Cash" initiative, which called for the city to change the nature of the "general assistance" it is required to provide under state law by replacing most outright cash grants to homeless recipients with in-kind benefits for housing, utilities, and meals. The court noted that by declaring a new goal and public policy with respect to aid and care for the indigent homeless, the San Francisco initiative had a "quintessential legislative character." *Id.* at 244. The court rejected the petitioners' claim that the state general assistance amounted to an exclusive delegation of power to the local legislative body that preempted the involvement of the local electorate. *Id.* at 245–46. Recognizing also that it must "construe constitutional and charter provisions in favor of the people's right to exercise their reserved power of initiative," the court held that the initiative had been a proper exercise of that power. *Id.* at 240.

In a variation on the "legislative acts only" theme, a court struck down an initiative because it directed the city council to adopt legislation, rather than enacting the legislation itself. In *Marblehead v. City of San Clemente*, the court invalidated an initiative that tied future development to the ability to meet specified service levels for traffic and a range of public services. 226 Cal. App. 3d 1504, 1507 (1991). The court held that the initiative, which contemplated amendments to the city's general plan, violated the California Constitution's provisions authorizing initiatives. *Id.* at 1510. The court noted that the measure did not actually enact legislation, which is the constitutional authorization. Rather, the initiative directed the city council to enact legislation, in the form of a general plan amendment, in order to implement the policies in the initiative.

In a variation on the "legislative acts only" theme, a court struck down an initiative because it directed the city council to adopt legislation, rather than enacting the legislation itself.

Cannot impair an essential governmental function. An initiative may not interfere with the efficacy of some essential governmental power, such as a city's power to grant a franchise (*Newsom v. Board of Supervisors*, 205 Cal. 262, 271–72 (1928)) or site a courthouse (*Simpson v. Hite*, 36 Cal. 2d 125, 134 (1950)). For instance, *Citizens for Jobs and the Economy v. County of Orange* involved an initiative measure passed by the voters in Orange County, which placed a number of spending and procedural restrictions upon the Board of Supervisors regarding the planning and implementation process for the conversion of the El Toro

Marine Base to a civilian airport. 94 Cal. App. 4th 1311 (2002). Although "mindful that initiative measures are not to be stricken down lightly," the court found this measure defective. *Id.* at 1324.

The court reasoned:

> Measure F impermissibly intrudes into Board prerogatives, particularly with respect to the functions of the Board in managing its financial affairs and in carrying out the public policy declared by [a prior measure]. The terms of Measure F seek to broadly limit through procedural restrictions the power of future legislative bodies to carry out their duties, as prescribed to them by their own inherent police power. As such, the measure should not be considered to have proper legislative subject matter.

Id. at 1331

This limitation on the impairment of an essential governmental function has been relied upon as the basis for voiding an initiative that would impair a city's fiscal management abilities.

This limitation on the impairment of an essential governmental function has been relied upon as the basis for voiding an initiative that would impair a city's fiscal management abilities. *See, e.g., City of Atascadero v. Daly*, 135 Cal. App. 3d 466, 470 (1982) (initiative is invalid if it will impede city's taxing power). However, in *Rossi v. Brown*, the Court upheld a tax-repeal initiative as not impairing a city's fiscal management, distinguishing the facts from those in *Atascadero*. 9 Cal. 4th 688, 698–99 (1995). The *Rossi* decision stated that it cannot be assumed that every initiative that repeals a tax will impermissibly interfere with a local legislative body's responsibility for fiscal management. It may do so, however, if the repeal initiative eliminates a major revenue source, and no other revenue source is available that may be tapped to offset a resulting budget deficit or to avoid future deficits. *Id.* at 710; *see also Santa Clara County Local Transp. Auth. v. Guardino*, 11 Cal. 4th 220, 235–36 (1995) (the requirement of Proposition 62 for a vote by the people on all general and special taxes did not impair a local government's fiscal powers). The Constitution also limits statewide referenda regarding tax matters. Cal. Const. art. II, § 9(a).

Initiatives and Referenda Are Not Subject to the Same Procedural Requirements as City Council Measures

PRACTICE TIP

Drafters of petition-sponsored initiatives can bypass CEQA.

An exception to the general rule that initiatives must comply with general law is that certain procedural requirements (*i.e.*, notice, hearing, and findings) necessary for adoption of a general plan or amendment, a specific plan adoption or amendment, or a zoning ordinance if proposed by a city council, do not apply if the same measures are enacted by initiative. The California Supreme Court stated: "It is well established in our case law that the existence of procedural requirements for the adoption of local ordinances generally does not imply a restriction of the power of initiative or referendum." *DeVita*, 9 Cal. 4th at 785 (1995). This position is consistent with an earlier case where the Court held that an initiative zoning measure was valid without complying with the general law requirements of public hearings before the planning commission and the city council and notice to affected property owners. *See Associated Home Builders, Inc. v. City of Livermore*, 18 Cal. 3d 582, 596–97 (1976). The same principle applies to general plan and specific plan procedures (*DeVita*, 9 Cal. 4th at 785), or locally enacted plan procedures (*San Mateo County Coastal Landowners'*, 38 Cal. App. 4th at 539).

Another major prerequisite to adoption of most land use ordinances or resolutions is California Environmental Quality Act (CEQA) review. Pub. Res. Code § 21000 *et seq*. Courts have held that this requirement does not apply to voter-sponsored initiatives. *See Stein v. City of Santa Monica*, 110 Cal. App. 3d 458, 460–61 (1980) (initiative ordinance to adopt rent control); *DeVita*, 9 Cal. 4th at 769 (general plan amendment initiative); Cal. Code Regs. tit. 14, § 15378(b)(4).

A court recently held that CEQA compliance was not required where a city adopted a voter-sponsored initiative rather than placing it on the ballot. *Native American Sacred Site & Envtl. Protection Ass'n v. City of San Juan Capistrano*, 120 Cal. App. 4th 961 (2004). The city council of San Juan Capistrano was presented with a petition signed by more than 15 percent of the city's voters supporting an initiative to make certain amendments to the city's general plan and zoning laws. No environmental review under CEQA was conducted on those amendments. The city council ultimately adopted the initiative without putting it on the ballot or conducting such review.

The court rejected the petitioners' arguments that the council's adoption of the ordinance was invalid for lack of CEQA review. The court noted that the duty to either place a voter-sponsored initiative on the ballot or adopt it by ordinance is ministerial and mandatory. Ministerial projects proposed to be carried out or approved by public agencies are exempt from CEQA. The council's adoption of the voter-sponsored initiative therefore did not require compliance with CEQA so long as the material provisions of the Elections Code were followed. *Id*. at 968.

The duty to either place a voter-sponsored initiative on the ballot or adopt it by ordinance is ministerial and mandatory. Ministerial projects proposed to be carried out or approved by public agencies are exempt from CEQA.

In *Citizens for Responsible Government v. City of Albany*, the court held that a city council-sponsored measure to approve and implement a "fully negotiated" development agreement could not be submitted to the electorate without CEQA review. 56 Cal. App. 4th 1199, 1219 (1997). The California Supreme Court affirmed this position in *Friends of Sierra Madre v. City of Sierra Madre*, which held that CEQA compliance was required when a project is proposed and placed on the ballot by a public agency as compared to a voter-sponsored initiative. 25 Cal. 4th 165, 190–91 (2001). In that case, the Sierra Madre City Council, relying on CEQA Guideline 15378(b)(3), which exempts from CEQA "the submittal of proposals to a vote of the people of the state or of a particular community," had placed a land use measure on the ballot without first conducting CEQA review. The Court, noting that the case on which the guideline was based involved a voter-sponsored, rather than a city council-sponsored, initiative, held that by voting to place the measure on the ballot, the city council had approved a "project" subject to CEQA and its action therefore did not fall within the exemption. *Id*. at 192. This holding handicaps a city council in responding to voter-sponsored initiatives with its own initiative, since CEQA review usually cannot be completed before ballot deadlines pass. The Court explained that the Elections Code allows cities to conduct an abbreviated environmental review of voter-sponsored initiatives with its own initiative, and that cities are free to inform the public of any environmental concerns that are revealed during such a study. Any further steps are within the realm of the Legislature, and not the courts, to address. Thus, unless such action is taken by the Legislature, the *Sierra Madre* decision will hinder the ability of cities to present voters with a choice of initiatives.

CEQA compliance is required when a project is proposed and placed on the ballot by a public agency.

could refuse to place a duly qualified initiative on the ballot. *See Save Stanislaus Area Farm Econ. (SAFE) v. Board of Supervisors*, 13 Cal. App. 4th at 148–49 (1993); *but see Worthington v. City Council of the City of Rohnert Park*, 130 Cal. App. 4th 1132 (2005) (court did not address a city's refusal to place referendum on the ballot despite the lack of a court order).

Generally, the courts weigh two competing considerations when deciding whether to undertake pre-election review. On the one hand, courts are concerned with preventing the waste of public funds in pointless elections. *See, e.g., Gayle v. Hamm*, 25 Cal. App. 3d 250, 257 (1972). On the other hand, courts are reluctant to delay exercise of the public's right to vote on a measure while its legality is determined. If a court does find a measure facially invalid, it will order either that the measure be removed from the ballot or that any vote taken be disregarded. Balancing these concerns is relatively straightforward when a measure is invalid on its face. Where the issues are not so apparent, it is difficult to predict when a court will agree to review an initiative or referendum measure prior to an election.

If a court does find a measure facially invalid, it will order either that the measure be removed from the ballot or that any vote taken be disregarded.

Two decisions by the California Supreme Court demonstrate the reluctance of courts to delay exercise of the public's right to vote while the legality of a ballot measure is being determined. *Independent Energy Producers Ass'n v. McPherson*, 116 P. 3d 475 (2005), and *Costa v. Superior Court*, 37 Cal. 4th 986 (2006). In *Independent Energy Producers*, the court vacated a stay issued by the court of appeal restraining Proposition 80 on the November 8, 2005 ballot. The court quoted *Brosnahan v. Eu*, 31 Cal. 3d 1 (1982), which held "[I]t is usually more appropriate to review constitutional and other challenges to ballot propositions or initiative measures after an election rather than to disrupt the electoral process by preventing the exercise of the people's franchise, in the absence of some clear showing of invalidity." 116 P. 3d at 475. Disagreeing with the court of appeal that the initiative, which would have given the Public Utilities Commission additional authority and jurisdiction over the California electricity market, was clearly precluded by the Constitution, the court concluded that its validity should not be determined prior to the election. *Id.* Using similar reasoning, the court issued a stay of a superior court judgment directing the Secretary of State not to place any version of Proposition 77 on the November 8, 2005 ballot. *Costa v. Superior Court*, 37 Cal. 4th 986 (2006). The initiative, which would have amended the State Constitution's redistricting process, was circulated for signatures and received a sufficient number for placement on the ballot. However, the proponents failed to disclose that the measure circulated was a different version than that originally submitted to the California Attorney General as required by law. Despite this discrepancy, the court concluded that it would be inappropriate to deny the electorate the opportunity to vote on Proposition 77, and directed the Secretary of State to place the circulated version on the November ballot. *Id.* at 1004. While Proposition 77 was defeated by the voters, the court issued a full opinion to provide guidance in future cases. The court stated that, even when a pre-election challenge was appropriate—such as a challenge to procedural defects in Proposition 77—considerable caution must be exercised before a court intervenes to remove or withhold a measure with qualified signatures from an imminent election, and should only occur when a court is confident that a pre-election

A legislative body may request a limited "CEQA review" of an initiative measure under the clauses of those sections allowing the legislative bodies to request investigation of "any other matters." Elec. Code §§ 9111(a)(3) (counties); 9212(a)(3) (cities). Although the information gained from that process could presumably assist the voters in passing judgment on the initiative, this review cannot be used to modify the initiative. The board of supervisors or city council is allowed to refer the proposed initiative measure to any county or city agency, respectively, for a report or reports on a number of issues related to the measure. Topics for which reports may be commissioned include the fiscal impact of the measure, its effect on the internal consistency of the county's or city's general and specific plans, including the housing element, consistency between planning and zoning, limitations on city or county actions under various sections of the Government Code, and any other matters the board or council request to be in the report.

Despite a catch-all provision, 2000 legislative amendments further expanded the list of specifically allowable topics to include many quality of life and environmental issues. The expanded list includes the effect of the measure on the use of land, the impact on the availability and location of housing, the ability of the city or county to meet its regional housing needs, the impact of the measure on funding for infrastructure of all types, including whether or not the proposed measure would result in increased infrastructure costs or savings to current residents and businesses, the impact of the measure on the community's ability to attract and retain business and employment, the impact on the uses of vacant parcels of land, and the impacts on agricultural lands, open space, traffic congestion, existing business districts, and developed areas designated for revitalization. Although these sections are useful to governments in ensuring that the public is well-informed as to all the potential impacts of a proposed initiative measure, the measure must be submitted to the voters as drafted by its sponsors, and cannot be modified based on conclusions reached in the course of generating any reports.

The basis for excluding voter-sponsored initiatives from certain procedural requirements applicable to council actions was explained by the California Supreme Court in *Building Industry Association v. City of Camarillo*, 41 Cal. 3d 810 (1986). The voters of the City of Camarillo adopted a restricted growth ordinance limiting the number of dwelling units constructed in the city to 400 per year. The Building Industry Association (BIA) challenged the initiative as failing to meet the requirements of Government Code section 65863.6, which requires a city to balance housing needs against public service needs before passing growth control ordinances, and to list findings in those ordinances as to the public health, safety, and welfare promoted by the ordinance that justify reducing housing opportunities in the region. BIA further argued that the city failed to meet the requirements of Evidence Code section 669.5, which shifts to a city the burden of proving that a growth control ordinance is necessary to promote public health, safety, and welfare. The Court held that Evidence Code section 669.5 applied to initiative measures but that Government Code section 65863.6 did not. It pointed out that the "[p]rocedural requirements which govern *council* action...generally do not apply to initiatives, any more than the provisions of the initiative law govern the enactment of ordinances in council." *Id.* at 823 (citing

Livermore, 18 Cal. 3d at 596). The Court further cautioned that "a statute which made compliance with *procedural* requirements a prerequisite to enactment of local ordinances would be constitutionally suspect if applied to preclude enactment by initiative of an ordinance on a subject on which the city council could legislate." *Id.* at 821. The Court concluded that requiring the electorate to make the findings required by Government Code section 65853.6 would "place an insurmountable obstacle in the path of the initiative process." *Id.* at 824. However, Evidence Code section 669.5 "places no procedural barriers on the ability of the electorate to legislate through the power of initiative." *Id.* at 822. The Court emphasized that limiting the applicability of certain procedural requirements did not affect the general rule that "the people may [not] enact a statute which the Legislature has no power to enact." *Id.* at 821.

The United States Supreme Court gave ballot-box zoning a boost with its decision in *City of Cuyahoga Falls v. Buckeye Community Hope Foundation*, 538 U.S. 188 (2003). The Court held that discriminatory impacts based on race and family status resulting from a facially neutral referendum process are not sufficient to support a violation of the equal protection clause. The Court also held that a referendum may not be challenged as a violation of substantive due process—even where the ordinance at issue reflects an administrative, non-legislative land use decision. *Id.* at 199–200.

Discriminatory impacts based on race and family status resulting from a facially neutral referendum process are not sufficient to support a violation of the equal protection clause.

In *Cuyahoga Falls*, the city passed an ordinance authorizing developers to construct a low-income housing complex. Project opponents submitted a referendum petition to the city asking that the ordinance be repealed or submitted to a vote. Pursuant to the city's charter, the referendum petition stayed the project until the voters voted. The city engineer, on advice from the city's law director, denied the developers' request for building permits. The developers sued the city, alleging that submission of the ordinance to voters violated the Equal Protection and Due Process Clauses.

The developers alleged that by allowing the referendum petition to stay their project, the city gave effect to racial bias reflected in the public's opposition to the project. The Supreme Court held that the developers failed to present sufficient evidence of an equal protection violation, and could not ascribe the motivations of a handful of citizens backing the referendum to the city. The Court stated that it is quite clear that the "[p]roof of racially discriminatory intent or purpose is required" to show a violation of the Equal Protection Clause. *Id.* at 194. The developers, claiming injury from the referendum petitioning process, not the referendum itself, had not presented proof of racially discriminatory intent. Submitting the petition to voters was pursuant to the city's charter, which set out a facially neutral petitioning procedure. Acting on advice of the city's law director, the engineer performed a nondiscretionary ministerial act consistent with the city charter in refusing to issue permits while the referendum was pending. *Id.*

Proof of racially discriminatory intent or purpose is required to show a violation of the Equal Protection Clause.

Nor did subjecting the ordinance to the city's referendum process constitute arbitrary government conduct in violation of substantive due process. The city engineer's refusal to issue permits while the petition was pending "in no sense constituted egregious or arbitrary government conduct" denying the developers the benefit of the development ordinance. In light of the charter's provision that no challenged ordinance can go into effect until approved by the voters, the law director's instruction to the engineer represented an "eminently rational directive." *Id.* at 196.

The Court also held that subjection of the low-income housing development ordinance to the city's referendum process would not constitute per se arbitrary government conduct in violation of due process "regardless of whether that ordinance reflected an administrative or legislative decision." *Id.* The Court noted that the "people retain the power to govern through referendum 'with respect to any matter, legislative or administrative, within the realm of local affairs.'" *Id.* Because the developers did not challenge the referendum itself, they derived no benefit from the principle that a referendum's substantive result may be invalid if it is arbitrary or capricious. *Id.* For further discussion of *City of Cuyahoga Falls*, see Dwight H. Merriam, "Panning for Gold in the Trickle of Supreme Court Cases This Term: What Can We Learn from the IOLTA and Referendum Cases?," 26 *Zoning and Planning Law Report*, no. 6 (June 2003) (predicting that the Court's unanimous decision in *City of Cuyahoga Falls* is likely to encourage more use of referenda and political turmoil); *Reading the U.S. Supreme Court's Tea Leaves: What Do Its Decisions This Term on IOLTA and Public Referenda and Initiatives Portend?* (ABA Annual Conference, Real Property and Local Government Sections, August 9, 2003).

Pre-Election Challenges to Initiatives and Referenda

The California courts have indicated an increased willingness to review an initiative or referendum measure for legal validity *prior* to its submission to the electorate if the measure would conflict with state law or if the drive to qualify the measure is procedurally defective. The effect of a successful pre-election challenge can be substantial. If an initiative is kept off the ballot by a pre-election challenge, and that decision is appealed, the provisions of the ordinance obviously will not become effective unless and until the appeal succeeds and the initiative is subsequently enacted. Compare this to the case of a post-election challenge to a measure that already has been enacted by the voters. The challenged measure remains in effect until the judicial process, including all appeals, has been exhausted. For example, the growth management measure enacted in Walnut Creek in November 1985 and challenged in *Lesher* was found invalid by the trial court in February 1987. 52 Cal. 3d at 535. The measure's limitations remained in effect, however, until the California Supreme Court's decision affirming the trial court in December 1990. Standing to challenge the measure may also be problematic. *See City of Santa Monica v. Stewart*, 126 Cal. App. 4th 43 (2005) (city lacked standing for a post-election challenge to the constitutionality of an initiative amending the city charter as there was no actual or threatened action which would injure the city or violate its rights).

Although courts generally prefer post-election review, at times a court will undertake a case to determine a measure's validity prior to its submission to the electorate. The decision to make such a determination, however, lies wholly within the discretionary power of the court. *See deBottari v. City Council*, 171 Cal. App. 3d at 1209. In one case, the court stated that the opponents of a duly qualified initiative must make a compelling showing that the measure should be removed from the ballot and that only a court, and not a board of supervisors, challenge is meritorious and justifies withholding the measure from the ballot. *Id.* at 1007–08.[6]

Reaching a different result, in *deBottari*, the court of appeal considered the appropriateness of pre-election judicial review in the context of a referendum measure that sought to reject rezoning ordinances enacted by the city council. 171 Cal. App. 3d at 1209–10. After a referendum petition was successfully circulated, the city council refused to either repeal the ordinances or submit the referendum to the voters as required by Elections Code section 9241. The council relied on its determination that rejection of the ordinances would result in zoning inconsistent with the city's general plan. First, the court held that the city council had a mandatory duty under the referendum laws either to repeal the challenged ordinances or to submit them to referendum unless "'directed to do otherwise by a court on a compelling showing that a proper case has been established for interfering with the [referendum] power.'" *Id.* at 1209 (quoting *Farley v. Healey*, 67 Cal. 2d 325, 327 (1967)).

The *deBottari* court assessed whether such a showing had been made by the city council. As an initial matter, the court noted two exceptions to the general rule from *Brosnahan* that "'it is usually more appropriate to review constitutional and other challenges to...initiative measures after an election rather than to disrupt the electoral process by preventing the exercise of the people's franchise.'" *Brosnahan*, 31 Cal. 3d at 4. First, a court may review challenges to initiative measures prior to an election where the electorate "lacks the 'power to adopt the proposal'," as when the initiative proposed would affect an administrative, rather than a legislative, matter. *Id.* Second, a court may review a measure prior to a vote when "the substantive provisions of the proposed measure are legally invalid." *Id.* at 1210.

The court analyzed the referendum at issue in *deBottari* under the second of these exceptions. It held that because rejection of the zoning ordinance would result in the property being zoned in a manner inconsistent with the City's general plan, the "invalidity of the proposed referendum [had] been compellingly demonstrated," and the "referendum, if successful, would enact a clearly invalid zoning ordinance.... Judicial deference to the electoral process does not compel judicial apathy towards patently invalid legislative acts." *Id.* at 1212–13. *See also City of Irvine v. Irvine Citizens Against Overdevelopment*, 25 Cal. App. 4th 868, 875–76 (1994) (permitting a city to bring a pre-election challenge to keep a referendum of a pre-zoning ordinance off the ballot to protect consistency with general plan).

Under the *deBottari* rule, a challenging party might be successful if it could show, for example, that an initiative is inconsistent with a city's general plan or would cause the general plan to become internally inconsistent. *See Lesher*, 52 Cal. 3d at 531, 541; *Concerned Citizens of Calaveras County v. Board of Supervisors*, 166 Cal. App. 3d 90, 95 (1985); *Sierra Club*, 126 Cal. App. 3d at 704. Such

---

6. The court found that the proponents of the initiative had substantially complied with the constitutional and statutory requirements that the version of the initiative submitted to the Attorney General be identical to the version printed on petitions and circulated for signatures. The court found the differences between the two to be relatively minor and did not mislead the public or otherwise defeat purposes of the constitutional and statutory provisions. *Costa v. Superior Court*, 37 Cal. 4th 896, 1022.

inconsistencies could be shown by a report ordered by the city council pursuant to Elections Code sections 9111 or 9212. For example, if the report requested by a city council shows that an initiative would be inconsistent with the city's general plan, the challenger could use that official report as the basis for seeking a court order to keep the initiative off the ballot. *See SAFE v. Board of Supervisors*, 13 Cal. App. 4th 141, 145–46 (1993).

In *Committee of Seven Thousand (COST) v. Superior Court*, the California Supreme Court upheld the pre-election invalidation of a proposed initiative measure, finding that the measure was correctly kept off of the ballot by the trial court because it conflicted with state law. 45 Cal. 3d 491, 495 (1988). A city also may bring a declaratory relief action to keep a referendum of a pre-zoning ordinance off the ballot on the basis that if the referendum passed it would create an inconsistency between the pre-zoning and the general plan. *See City of Irvine v. Irvine Citizens Against Overdevelopment*, 25 Cal. App. 4th at 879.

In addition to substantive flaws in an initiative measure, courts have upheld pre-election challenges based on technical flaws in the initiative petition itself or elsewhere in the initiative procedure. *See Lesher*, 52 Cal. 3d at 542–43. Initiative opponents have frequently looked to procedural deficiencies as a means of accomplishing their ends. *See, e.g., Senate v. Jones*, 21 Cal. 4th 1142, 1153–54 (1999) (California Supreme Court heard pre-election challenge to statewide initiative where challengers demonstrated a "strong likelihood" that the measure violated the single subject rule); *see also Insurance Indus. Initiative Campaign Com. v. Eu*, 203 Cal. App. 3d 961, 964–65 (1988) (plaintiff claimed initiative violated single subject rule). Such procedural flaws will be a basis for invalidation, however, only if the purpose for the technical requirement is frustrated by the flaw. *See Costa*, 37 Cal. 4th at 1012–13; *Assembly v. Deukmejian*, 30 Cal. 3d 638, 652–53 (1982).

In addition to substantive flaws in an initiative measure, courts have upheld pre-election challenges based on technical flaws in the initiative petition itself or elsewhere in the initiative procedure.

Initiatives Limiting Housing: Burden of Proof

As a general rule, zoning and other land use regulations adopted by council-enacted ordinance or initiative are presumed to be valid, and the burden of proving the contrary rests with the person attacking the regulation. Pursuant to Evidence Code section 669.5, however, in any action challenging the validity of an ordinance that limits housing development by number, the burden is on a city to prove that the ordinance is reasonably related to the public health, safety, or welfare. Thus, with respect to measures seeking to limit housing development, the ordinary presumption in favor of the validity of ordinances has been reversed; accordingly, such measures are more susceptible to successful challenge. However, at least one court, in ruling on the validity of a city's housing element, stated that Evidence Code section 669.5 does not come into play unless there is a violation of the "least cost zoning law" contained in Government Code section 65913.1. *Hernandez v. City of Encinitas*, 28 Cal. App. 4th 1048, 1052 (1994).

The California Supreme Court has made clear that Evidence Code section 669.5 applies to ordinances enacted by the initiative process. *Building Indus. Ass'n v. City of Camarillo*, 41 Cal. 3d 810, 817–18 (1986). The Court stated that pursuant to section 669.5, "if the electorate exercises its initiative power, the local government must bear the burden of showing that the ordinance is

As a general rule, zoning and other land use regulations adopted by council-enacted ordinance or initiative are presumed to be valid, and the burden of proving the contrary rests with the person attacking the regulation.

reasonably related to the protection of the public health, safety, or welfare of the affected population." *Id.* at 822.

Conflicting Initiatives on the Same Ballot

A phenomenon that appears to be increasing at the local level, as well as in California's statewide elections, is for competing initiatives to appear on the same ballot. *See, e.g., Taxpayers to Limit Campaign Spending v. Fair Political Practices Comm'n*, 51 Cal. 3d 744 (1990) (considering two measures regulating political campaign contributions and spending). The Elections Code addresses this issue and provides that, if the provisions of two or more ordinances adopted at the same election conflict, the ordinance receiving the highest number of affirmative votes shall control. Elec. Code §§ 9123 (counties); 9221 (cities).

Some initiatives have attempted to ensure applicability of these provisions of state law by including a "killer" clause as part of the initiative. A killer clause will state that the measure's provisions are intended to, and do, conflict with the provisions of a rival initiative. Thus, the initiative receiving the most votes should "kill" the rival initiative, even if both pass. *See Taxpayers*, 51 Cal. 3d at 767.

In Carlsbad, the court ruled that a city can refuse to enforce a citizens' initiative passed by the voters where a city's own ballot measure on the same subject, which was inconsistent with the citizens' initiative, received more affirmative votes.

An example of the efficacy of Elections Code sections 9123 and 9221, and of a killer clause, was provided in *Concerned Citizens v. City of Carlsbad*, 204 Cal. App. 3d 937 (1988). In *Carlsbad*, the court ruled that a city can refuse to enforce a citizens' initiative that had been passed by the voters where a city's own ballot measure on the same subject, which was inconsistent with the citizens' initiative, received more affirmative votes. *Id.* at 941.

Concerned Citizens presented the City of Carlsbad with an initiative (Proposition G) to regulate housing development for a 10-year period. The measure would have created annual limits on new residential construction. In response to Proposition G, the city council placed an alternative measure on the ballot, Proposition E, which tied the rate of development to the development of new public facilities. In its killer clause, Proposition E stated that it was inconsistent with Proposition G. The voters passed both measures, but the council's measure received more votes. Accordingly, the council enacted Proposition E and refused to enact Proposition G.

Concerned Citizens sought to have Proposition G enforced, claiming that it was not inconsistent with Proposition E. The court held that Proposition E was clearly inconsistent with Proposition G, stating that Proposition E expressed "an unambiguous intent to supplant any [annual] numerical limit [on the rate of residential construction.]" *Id.*

The California Constitution states that if provisions of two or more measures approved at the same election conflict, those of the measure receiving the highest affirmative vote shall prevail.

In *Taxpayers to Limit Campaign Spending v. Fair Political Practices Commission*, the California Supreme Court addressed the degree to which the provisions of two measures dealing with political campaign reform should be made operative. 51 Cal. 3d 744 (1990). *Taxpayers* involved rival statewide initiatives passed on the same ballot, but its holding is probably applicable to local initiatives as well. The court relied on the California Constitution, which states that if provisions of two or more measures approved at the same election conflict, those of the measure receiving the highest affirmative vote shall prevail. Cal. Const. art. II, § 10(b). The court noted that both measures established a comprehensive regulatory scheme. *Taxpayers*, 51 Cal. 3d at 768–69.

The Taxpayers group argued that only those provisions from the "losing" measure that conflict with the provisions of the "winning" measure, and those provisions that cannot be severed from the conflicting provisions, need be invalidated. The court rejected that argument, and held that article II, section 10(b) does not permit the court to graft onto one regulatory scheme provisions which are intended to be part of a different one.

> [U]nless a contrary intent is apparent in competing, conflicting initiative measures which address and seek to comprehensively regulate the same subject, only the provisions of the measure receiving the highest affirmative vote become operative upon adoption. If the measures propose alternative regulatory schemes, a fundamental conflict exists. In those circumstances, [the Constitution] does not require or permit either the court or the agency charged with the responsibility of implementing the measure or measures to enforce any of the provisions of the measure which received the lesser affirmative vote.

Id. at 770–71

In a footnote, the court addressed when provisions of a "losing" measure may be given effect:

> Our construction of Section 10(b) [of the Constitution] does not foreclose operation of an initiative measure that receives an affirmative vote simply because one or more minor provisions happen to conflict with those of another initiative principally addressed to other aspects of the same general subject. In the latter circumstance, if the principal purpose of the initiative can be accomplished notwithstanding the excision of the minor, incidental conflicting provisions, the remainder of the initiative can be given effect.

Id. at 771 n.12

In *Yoshisato v. Superior Court*, the California Supreme Court expanded upon its ruling in *Taxpayers*. 2 Cal. 4th 978 (1992). As in *Taxpayers*, the *Yoshisato* court relied on article II, Section 10(b) of the California Constitution to address the problem of two conflicting statewide initiatives. In *Yoshisato*, the question before the court was the degree to which the provisions of two measures that amended portions of the Penal Code should be made operative. The court held that the *Taxpayers* approach to conflicting initiatives should be employed only when the two measures are "competing," as opposed to merely "complementary." *Id.* Under *Yoshisato*, the threshold question is whether the measures are "competing" or whether the measures are "complementary" (*i.e.*, noncompeting). *Id.* at 988. If the measures are "competing," the *Taxpayers* bright-line interpretation of section 10(b) governs and only the provisions of the measure with the highest affirmative vote are operative. *Id.* at 987–88. However, if the measures are "complementary or supplementary," the court held that:

> The measures should be compared "provision by provision," and the provisions of the measure receiving the lower number of affirmative votes are operative so long as they do not conflict with the provisions of the measure receiving the higher number of affirmative votes, and so long as those nonconflicting provisions are severable from any that do conflict.

Id. at 988

In *Yoshisato*, the court considered two factors to determine whether the measures were "competing" or "complementary." It first considered whether

In Yoshisato, *the Court held that the* Taxpayers *approach to conflicting initiatives should be employed only when the two measures are "competing," as opposed to merely "complementary."*

the materials presented to the voters expressly or impliedly indicated if the measures were "competing" or "complementary." *Id.* at 989. The court then considered whether it was the voters' intention when they enacted each measure to create a comprehensive scheme related to the same subject matter. Ultimately, the court found the measures did not seek to create a comprehensive scheme, and the material presented to the voters indicated both measures sought to amend the code in a complementary fashion. *Id.* at 990–91. Based on this assessment, the court employed the more accommodating interpretation of section 10(b), and compared the measures provision by provision to determine which provisions of the measure receiving the lower number of votes were operative. *Id.* at 991.

Restrictions on a City's Role in Campaigns

As a general rule, California law does not allow local governments to campaign either for or against an initiative or referendum.

As a general rule, California law does not allow local governments to campaign either for or against an initiative or referendum. It is a "fundamental precept" of the American democratic electoral process that the government may not "take sides" in election contests or bestow an unfair advantage on one of several competing factions. *Stanson v. Mott*, 17 Cal. 3d 206, 217 (1976) (holding that such partisanship is an "improper distortion" of the democratic process); *League of Women Voters v. Countywide Crim. Justice Coordination Com.*, 203 Cal. App. 3d 529, 546 (1988) (holding that while such partisanship may be allowed in "totalitarian, dictatorial or autocratic governments" it cannot be tolerated in a democracy).

Local governments are authorized to engage in legislative lobbying for or against proposed state, federal, and other legislation.

At the same time, however, local governments are authorized to engage in legislative "lobbying" for or against proposed state, federal, and other legislation. *See, e.g.*, Government Code § 50023 (authorizing city councils to lobby the Legislature, Congress, and state, federal, and local agencies on behalf of or to oppose legislative actions). Rather than attempting to determine whether an activity constitutes impermissible "campaigning" or permissible "lobbying," the courts have adopted an "audience test" whereby it is not the subject of the promotional activities that matters, but the audience to which it is directed. *Miller v. Miller*, 87 Cal. App. 3d 762, 768 (1978). Under the "audience test," local governments may undertake promotional activities directed at other government bodies but not targeting the electorate itself. *Id.*

Although prohibited from targeting the electorate with "promotional" communications, local governments are authorized, and often required, to provide the electorate with educational "informational" materials on pending initiatives and referenda. To determine whether a city's action is proper in this regard depends upon a careful consideration of such factors as the style, tenor, and timing of the communication. *See Stanson v. Mott*, 17 Cal. 3d at 222; *Keller v. State Bar*, 47 Cal. 3d 1152, 1170–71 (1989); 73 Ops. Cal. Atty. Gen. 255 (1990). In general, courts focus on whether the city discussed the concerns of both sides and presented all the facts in a fair manner. *See, e.g., California Common Cause v. Duffy*, 200 Cal. App. 3d 730, 748 (1987) (holding that distribution of postcards to voters was a political and not an informational activity where the postcards presented not merely the facts, both good and bad, regarding the issue, but rather only one side); *Schroeder v. Irvine City Council*, 97 Cal. App. 4th 174, 187 (2002) (holding that a voter registration program was a proper use of public funds where it did not expressly advocate a partisan position and was conducted without regard to political affiliation); *see also Stanson v. Mott*, 17 Cal. 3d at 211.

Citizens alleging misuse of government funds for impermissible promotional activities may bring a taxpayer action against the city or city officials under Code of Civil Procedure section 526a and common law theories. Section 526a is liberally construed to allow "citizens to challenge asserted illegal expenditures of public funds." *See Blair v. Pitchess*, 5 Cal. 3d 258, 268–267 (1971); *California Ass'n for Safety Educ. v. Brown*, 30 Cal. App. 4th 1264, 1281 (1994); *Bledsoe v. Watson*, 30 Cal. App. 3d 105, 108 (1973). Taxpayers may bring an action against a city at common law as well, but only in cases involving fraud, collusion, ultra vires, or failure by the governmental body to perform a duty specifically enjoined. *See Gogerty v. Coachella Valley Junior Coll. Dist.*, 57 Cal. 2d 727, 730 (1962); *Los Altos Property Owners Ass'n v. Hutcheon*, 69 Cal. App. 3d 22, 26 (1977).

Citizens alleging misuse of government funds for impermissible promotional activities may bring a taxpayer action against the city under Code of Civil Procedure section 526a and common law theories.

The general restrictions on promotional or campaign activities directed at the electorate by cities do not prohibit the city council itself or individual members of the city government from taking sides in an initiative or referendum campaign. The city council is entitled to submit ballot arguments for or against a given measure so long as such arguments are included within "informational" materials giving equal voice to the opposite point of view. *See City of Fairfield v. Superior Court*, 14 Cal. 3d 768, 780 (1975) (holding that a councilmember "has not only a right but an obligation to discuss issues of vital concern with his constituents and to state his views on matters of public importance"). For further discussion on this subject, *see California Municipal Law Handbook*, page III-33-39 (League of California Cities, 2004), concerning rules for city participation in ballot measures, lobbying measures, and drafting ballot measures. *See also Ballot Measure Advocacy and the Law: Legal Issues Associated with City Participation in Ballot Measure Campaigns*, League of California Cities (September 2003); Steven Lucas and Betsy Strauss, "Ballot Measure Fund Raising: Some Legal Do's and Don'ts," *Western City*, page 19 (League of California Cities, March 2004).

The general restrictions on promotional or campaign activities directed at the electorate by cities do not prohibit the city council itself or individual members of the city government from taking sides in an initiative or referendum campaign.

Conclusion

A relatively small, but still significant, backlash to the use of initiatives to enact land use measures—particularly those with the far-reaching impacts of growth management measures—recently has begun to surface in California and elsewhere for fear that such measures make good land use planning difficult, if not impossible. The hallmarks of good land use planning are that decisions are well informed, the planning process is flexible and responsive to changing circumstances and values, and decisions reflect a comprehensive planning process and accommodate competing public interests. Arguably, each of these goals is thwarted when land use planning is done via the ballot box.[7]

The hallmarks of good land use planning are that decisions are well informed, the planning process is flexible and responsive to changing circumstances and values, and decisions reflect a comprehensive planning process and accommodate competing public interests.

Critics of land use initiatives claim that voters never have as much information available to them in making land use decisions as compared to the knowledge, information, and resources available to a professional planning staff, planning commission, or city council. More specifically, the fact that initiatives

---

7. *See* Lora A. Lucero, "Ballot Box Zoning," 28 *Zoning and Planning Law Report*, no. 6 (June 2005); Lora A. Lucero, "Ballot Box Zoning: Good Planning or Vigilantism," *Zoning News* (APA, May 2003); S. Meyers and R. Mandleman, "Planning by Plebiscite; The Ballot Box Is the Wrong Forum for California's Growth Wars," 24 *State and Local Law News*, no. 4 (ABA, Summer 2001).

are generally exempt from the requirement of environmental review under CEQA means that decisions with a potentially enormous environmental impact may be made without the extensive review that CEQA requires. *See Stein v. City of Santa Monica*, 110 Cal. App. 3d 458, 461 (1980); *DeVita v. County of Napa*, 9 Cal. 4th 763, 793–94 (1995). Another criticism is that that voters will rely on titles and perhaps summaries of proposed legislation, rather than carefully review the proposed initiative in order to understand and appreciate its impacts. These concerns were highlighted by the California Supreme Court in *Taxpayers*:

> We observed many years ago that even the most conscientious voters may lack the time to study ballot measures with that degree of thoroughness. Noting the tendency of voters to rely on the title to describe the content of an initiative, we agreed implicitly with the Supreme Court of Oregon whose observation we quoted.
>
>> "The majority of qualified electors are so much interested in managing their own affairs that they have no time carefully to consider measures affecting the general public. A great number of voters undoubtedly have a superficial knowledge of proposed laws to be voted upon.... We think the assertion may safely be ventured that it is only the few persons who earnestly favor or zealously oppose the passage of a proposed law initiated by petition who have attentively studied its contents and know how it will probably affect their private interests. The greater number of voters do not possess this information and usually derive their knowledge of the contents of a proposed law from an inspection of the title thereof, which is sometimes secured only from the very meager details afforded by a ballot which is examined in an election booth preparatory to exercising the right of suffrage." [Citation omitted.]
>
> Those observations are no less pertinent today. "Voters have neither the time nor the resources to mount an in depth investigation of a proposed initiative. Often voters rely solely on the title and summary of the proposed initiative and never examine the actual wording of the proposal." [Citation omitted.]

51 Cal. 3d at 770

This issue was addressed to some degree in the 1987 amendments to the Elections Code. *See* Elec. Code §§ 9111, 9212. Under these amendments, which were adopted to establish procedures designed to better equip the local legislative body and the electorate to evaluate initiatives when a petition is circulated (*see DeVita v. County of Napa*, 9 Cal. 4th 763), a city council may request and receive reports from any city agency on such issues as the measure's fiscal impact, its effect on the internal consistency of the city's general and specific plans, the consistency between planning and zoning, environmental impact, and any other matters the council identifies. Elec. Code §§ 9111 (counties); 9212 (cities). The insights that might result from such reports, however, can only influence the council's decision to enact the initiative measure or place it on the ballot, or the voters' decision on whether to enact the measure should it be placed before them. The measure itself may not be changed from its form when circulated for signature. Thus, these council-ordered reports are very different from environmental impact reports prepared under CEQA, which often have the effect of modifying the land use decisions under review.

The charge that land use initiatives frustrate the flexibility and responsiveness to change that are required of good land use planning is supported by the fact that generally, ordinances adopted by local initiative may not be repealed or amended except by a subsequent vote of the electorate. Elec. Code §§ 9125 (counties); 9217 (cities). This statutory provision stands to reason. The purpose for granting the initiative power—empowering an electorate confronted by an unresponsive legislative body—would be vitiated if the legislative body were allowed to "undo" what the people had accomplished through the initiative. The California Supreme Court has emphasized that these sections have their roots in the constitutional right of the electorate to initiative, ensuring that successful initiatives will not be undone by subsequent hostile legislative bodies. See *DeVita*, 9 Cal. 4th at 797.

As a result, however, a land use regulation adopted by initiative may be very difficult to amend. Even though the concerns that prompted the measure's passage may have subsided, generating sufficient voter interest in updating or repealing the measure to conform to changed circumstances may present a real problem. Further, regulations appropriate for a particular period in a city's development may linger well past their usefulness and may, in fact, impede orderly development. On this point, in answering the claim that the rigidity of a general plan initiative amendment frustrates the basic purpose of the planning law, the Court in *DeVita* recognized that some degree of flexibility is desirable in the planning process. *Id.* at 789 (citing Daniel J. Curtin, Jr. and Thomas Jacobson, *Growth Control by the Ballot Box: California's Experience*, 24 Loyola L.A. Law Rev. 1073, 1102 (1991)). However, the *DeVita* court noted, citing Government Code section 65300, that "[o]n the other hand, it is also desirable that plans possess some degree of stability so that they can be 'comprehensive [and] long-term' guides to local development." *Id.*

A land use regulation adopted by initiative may be very difficult to amend.

Another disturbing aspect of land use initiatives is that the balancing of competing public interests may be lost from the land use planning and regulation process. In upholding Proposition 13, California's tax reform initiative enacted in 1978 (Cal. Const. art. XIIIA, § 16), the California Supreme Court characterized the initiative as deficient as a means of lawmaking, in that it permits very little balancing of interests or compromise. *See Amador Valley Joint Union High Sch. Dist. v. State Bd. of Equalization*, 22 Cal. 3d 208, 228–29 (1978) (quoting V. Key and W. Crouch, The Initiative and the Referendum in California, page 485 (1939)). For example, an initiative measure that places numerical restrictions on housing development is exempt from the requirement of findings that address health, safety, and welfare concerns. Likewise, the fact that CEQA's environmental review provisions do not generally apply to initiative measures means that the balancing procedures that are a part of that process are not brought to bear on the formulation of the proposed policies and standards.

Another disturbing aspect of land use initiatives is that the balancing of competing public interests may be lost from the land use planning and regulation process.

Occasionally, a controversial court decision regarding a land use issue will trigger initiatives seeking to reverse the ruling. Such has been the response to the United States Supreme Court's *Kelo v. City of New London*, 545 U.S. 469 (2005) decision, which upheld the use of eminent domain to take property from one private owner in order to further private economic development that the city determined would provide a public benefit. Although *Kelo* did not represent an extension of existing law in terms of takings jurisprudence, it sparked public outcry over the abuse of government power. In response, a statewide initiative, Proposition 90, qualified for the November 2006 ballot in California, but was defeated at the polls. The debate over Proposition 90 went to the heart of concerns over an initiative eliminating local governments' ability to balance competing public interests and respond to changing circumstances and values. Proposition 90 would have prohibited the use of eminent domain to take property and give it to another private party even if such a transfer provided a public benefit, and would have required compensation to owners whose property suffered an economic loss as a result of a city's land use decision.[8]

A blanket statement that initiative measures are completely free of requirements to balance competing interests would, however, be inaccurate. Still, initiative measures often attempt to provide narrow solutions to multifaceted problems.

A blanket statement that initiative measures are completely free of requirements to balance competing interests would, however, be inaccurate. The three-part balancing test set forth in *Livermore* to determine whether the initiative measure bears a reasonable relationship to a legitimate governmental interest, and is thus a valid exercise of the police power, requires post-election inquiry into how competing interests were balanced. *Associated Home Builders, Inc. v. City of Livermore*, 18 Cal. 3d at 601; *see also DeVita*, 9 Cal. 4th at 796 n.12.

Still, initiative measures often attempt to provide narrow solutions to multifaceted problems. To the degree that this is true, they may stand in the way of effective planning, which by nature must be comprehensive and must consider the interrelationship between a host of factors.

---

8. For a further discussion of Proposition 90, *see* Paul Shigley, "Property Rights Measure Reaches Ballot," *California Planning & Development Report* (August 2006); Boalt Hall California Center for Environmental Law & Policy, *Proposition 90: An Analysis* (U.C. Regents, Oct. 2006).

15

What Is Growth Management?

By the year 2020, California's population is expected to increase by more than 15 million people; by 2040, it will have increased by 24 million people. That translates into a new San Francisco every year or another City of Los Angeles every five years.[1] Between 2005 and 2025, California populations are forecasted to increase 45 percent in inland counties and 17 percent in coastal ones. Absolute increases also are predicted to be greater in inland counties (4.8 million) than in coastal ones (4.4 million). The Inland Empire, the San Joaquin Valley, and the Sacramento area in particular, are predicted to experience the state's fastest growth rates, growing by half their current population from 2005 to 2025. The Inland Empire, one of the fastest growing areas in the United States, has a larger population than Cleveland, San Diego, St. Louis, or Denver. In Northern California, as population spills out of the Bay Area, growth rates in the northern San Joaquin Valley are rivaling those of the Inland Empire. Projections show that this region may be the fastest growing in the state between 2005 and 2025.[2] In the Bay Area, the population is expected to grow by two million people, add 750,000 households, and create 1.5 million jobs.[3] In Contra Costa County alone, the 1 million current residents will be joined by an additional 250,000 new residents within 25 years, according to the Association of Bay Area Governments.[4] Because of its generally strong economy, its inviting climate, and its long tradition as a "melting pot," California's population will continue to expand. The question, then, is not *whether* it will grow, but *how* will it grow?

Not surprisingly, many communities in California have been reacting to the effects of growth, which often include traffic congestion, rising cost of housing,

Because of its generally strong economy, its inviting climate, and its long tradition as a "melting pot," California's population will continue to expand.

---

1. See *Contra Costa Times*, May 19, 2002, page A-3. For a full discussion of this growth phenomenon, see Carol Whiteside, "How Should California Grow: Examining Options for Growth in California," *Western City* (July 2007) (published by the League of California Cities). Ms. Whiteside concludes that meeting the needs of an increasing population will be one of the greatest challenges facing California cities in the next few decades.
2. Public Policy Institute of California, *California 2025: Taking on the Future* (Ellen Harak and Mark Baldassare eds., 2005).
3. See *Contra Costa Times*, June 19, 2003, page A-1.
4. *San Francisco Chronicle*, August 8, 2004, page E-1.

environmental degradation, and loss of a sense of place. Many environmental groups have recommended that the State of California take the lead in curbing "urban sprawl."[5]

Regardless of one's opinions on *how* cities should manage the growth California will see in the coming years, one thing is clear: now is the time for cities to think strategically about growth, to find ways to improve growth patterns, and to build vibrant, livable communities.[6] The purpose of this chapter is to provide a brief introduction to the current discussion on growth management in California. First, it provides a brief overview of some of the many techniques communities use to manage growth, with a particular emphasis on the trend toward regulating land use at the ballot box through voter initiatives. Then, it discusses the legality and legal limits of many of these techniques. Finally, the chapter discusses the "Smart Growth" principles espoused by many city and regional planners and land use reform commentators.

Types of Growth Management Measures

Over the past several decades, California cities have enacted a variety of growth management measures, including council-enacted interim ordinances, permanent measures, and voter-initiated measures.

Over the past several decades, California cities have enacted a variety of growth management measures. These measures include council-enacted interim ordinances, permanent measures, and voter-initiated measures. According to a 1989 survey conducted by the League of California Cities in cooperation with the County Supervisors' Association of California, approximately 72 percent of California cities and counties surveyed had enacted at least one growth management measure through the first quarter of 1989.[7]

Cities advance many reasons for adopting growth management measures and growth boundaries. Some are related directly to a lack of adequate infrastructure—limited sewer capacity, water shortages, revenue shortages, school overcrowding, and traffic congestion. Others are adopted to maintain the "quality of life"—the community's unique character, the preservation of open space, lower densities, and preservation of scenic views. A desire to retain agricultural lands has become yet another reason to restrict growth in certain communities. Environmentalists cite growth management as a means of preventing air pollution, reducing fossil fuel dependence, curbing global warming, and stopping the destruction of quickly disappearing habitat for endangered species.

---

5. William Fulton, "Smart Growth Is the Agenda of California National Leaders," *California Planning & Development Report* (Mar. 1999); Paul G. Lewis and Max Neiman, *Cities Under Pressure: Local Growth Controls and Residential Development Policy* (Public Policy Institute of California, www.ppic.org, January 2002). *See also* Ed Bolen et al., "Smart Growth: State by State," *Hastings W.-Nw. J. of Envtl. L. & Pol'y.* (Spring 2002) (identifying range of state smart growth policies, including those calling for promotion of infill development, elimination of subsidies that promote "sprawl," and preservation of farmland and open space); Mark Baldassare, *Statewide Survey: Special Survey on Californians and the Future* (Public Policy Institute of California, www.ppic.org, August 2004) (tracking public opinion and preferences on current conditions and future projections for growth).
6. *See* Assembly Speaker Hertzberg, *The New California Dream: Regional Solutions for 21st Century Challenges* (Speaker's Commission on Regionalism, Final Report, Jan. 13, 2002).
7. *See* Elisa Barbour, *Metropolitan Growth Planning in California—1900–2000* (Public Policy Institute of California 2002) (report tracing the history of regional planning for growth management in California throughout the past century, with a particular focus on transportation, land use, and environmental planning); Gary Binger, *Smart Growth in the San Francisco Bay Area: Effective Local Approaches* (commissioned by the S.F. District Council, Urban Land Institute, June 2003) (http://sfbayarea.uli.org); and *Contra Costa County Smart Growth or Sprawl?* (Greenbelt Alliance, June 2003).

Growth management also touches on other, less noble motivations. Exclusionary zoning occurs where there is a desire to prevent lower-income families from finding affordable housing in the community, stemming from a fear that such households will generate crime and blight, thereby reducing property values. The California courts have expressed their concern over this "drawbridge mentality." As the late California Supreme Court Associate Justice Stanley Mosk stated in his concurring opinion in *Building Industry Ass'n v. City of Camarillo*:

> I must repeat the misgivings I retain about the constitutional validity of no-growth or limited-growth ordinances. An impermissible elitist concept is invoked when a community constructs a legal moat around its perimeter to exclude all or most outsiders. The growing tendency of some communities to arbitrarily restrict housing to present residents appears at odds with Supreme Court pronouncements from *Shelley v. Kraemer* [citation omitted], to the words of Justice Douglas in *Reitman v. Mulkey* [citation omitted]: "housing is clearly marked with the public interest."

41 Cal. 3d 810, 825 (1986) (Mosk, J., concurring). In addition, existing homeowners benefit financially from the increased housing prices that often result when the housing supply is restricted. For a discussion of measures used to combat exclusionary zoning, *see* chapter 20 (Affordable Housing).

Most cities attempt to achieve their growth management goals by using the most basic of land use tools: the general plan, specific plans, and zoning ordinances. Cities commonly have employed traditional "Euclidian" zoning programs that restrict uses, densities, and house sizes in conjunction with the general plan to sketch a "blueprint" for the location and types of development that will occur in a city. For a complete discussion on the many types of land use techniques available, *see* chapter 2 (General Plan) and chapter 4 (Zoning).

Most cities attempt to achieve their growth management goals by using the most basic of land use tools: the general plan, specific plans, and zoning ordinances.

The most drastic of all the growth management techniques is the development moratorium, through which a city completely halts or limits the approval of all development permits. Moratoria are usually used only until the city can adopt a comprehensive development scheme. Cities often use moratoria to prevent a rash of permits from being issued just before new land use regulations take effect.

Although moratoria have been upheld as a valid use of the police power, there is a question as to how long a government may prohibit development before it must compensate landowners for a taking of private property. In *Tahoe-Sierra Preservation Council, Inc. v. Tahoe Regional Planning Agency*, the United States Supreme Court rejected the claim that a combined 32-month moratorium during which all development was prohibited was a per se taking, noting that the question whether the moratorium was invalid as an ad hoc taking had been waived. 535 U.S. 302 (2002) (*see* chapter 12, Takings). Presumably, a moratorium that lasted too long would be an improper use of the police power. But how long is too long? The courts have not yet specifically answered this question. As noted in *Tahoe-Sierra*, however, the California State Legislature has stepped in to impose a two-year time period on interim-moratorium ordinances. Gov't Code § 65858.

Although moratoria have been upheld as a valid use of the police power, there is a question as to how long a government may prohibit development before it must compensate landowners for a taking of private property.

Some cities require that adequate public services and facilities, such as sewer and water systems, police and fire protection, jails, public parks, and

UGB = Urban growth boundary

schools are in place prior to the development of additional residential units. By doing so, cities hope to keep growth from outpacing their ability to provide the traditional services of local government.[8]

One technique that is gaining popularity in California is the urban growth boundary (UGB), by which a city delineates the area beyond which it will not extend municipal services, like sewers and street maintenance. The concept behind establishing a UGB is that the area *within* the UGB will be made available for urban development, while land *outside* the UGB will remain primarily rural for farming, forestry, or low-density residential development. UGBs are meant to provide something to both developers and environmentalists—the developers are given assurance that development will be allowed to occur *somewhere*, while environmentalists are given assurance that there are certain places where development *will not* occur.

Drawing a line on a map, however, is not enough. In order for UGBs to work properly, several supporting factors need to be in place. First, cities should revise their land use laws within the UGB to allow for more dense development. Otherwise the UGB will not provide any mechanism for a city to accommodate new growth. This is the "legal moat" Justice Mosk described in the above quote from the *Camarillo* case.

Second, effective UGBs require some inter-jurisdictional cooperation. In large, highly developed places like the metropolitan areas of California, if a city draws its UGB at the edge of its jurisdiction, what is to stop the county from picking up where the city left off, just on the other side of the line? A truly effective UGB requires regional cooperation on matters such as planning, tax revenue, and transportation.

In addition to limiting residential development, restrictions on commercial and industrial development have become the focus of citizen efforts in cities of all sizes, including Los Angeles and San Francisco.

In addition to limiting residential development, restrictions on commercial and industrial development have become the focus of citizen efforts in cities of all sizes, including Los Angeles and San Francisco. These measures take the form of limits on building height, annual caps on office space development, and moratoria on certain levels of development until specified public service requirements are met or traffic is reduced to identified levels.

California Growth Management Measures—Ballot Box Planning [9]

A large number of growth management measures have been the direct expressions of citizen concern, adopted by popular vote through the initiative process.[10] When polled on who should make important decisions about growth

---

8. See *The Housing Bottom Line: Fiscal Impact of New Home Construction on California Governments*, a report by The Blue Sky Consulting Group, June 2007, studying whether new residential construction can "pay its own way".
9. On the topic of growth management by initiative, *see generally* Daniel J. Curtin, Jr. and M. Thomas Jacobson, "Growth Control by the Ballot Box: California's Experience," 24 *Loy. L.A. L. Rev.* 1073 (1991); Daniel J. Curtin, Jr. and M. Thomas Jacobson, "Growth Management by the Initiative in California: Legal and Practical Issues," 21 *Urb. Law.* 491 (1989); Daniel J. Curtin, Jr. and Ann Danforth, "Looking Beyond the City Limits: Regional Approaches to the Growth Crisis," 22 *Urb. Law.* 701 (1990); William Fulton and Paul Shigley, *Guide to California Planning*, ch. 11 (Solano Press, 3rd ed. 2005); Governor's Office of Planning and Research, *Local and Regional Perspectives on Growth Management* (1992).
10. For a full discussion of land use and initiatives, *see* chapter 14 (Initiative and Referendum).

issues, 73 percent of residents believed that local voters should do so at the ballot box. Among individual groups, there were no significant differences on this question although support for direct democracy did increase slightly with income and education. Public Policy Institute of California, California 2025: Taking on the Future (Ellen Harak and Mark Baldassare eds., 2005), page 240 (in particular, *see* chapter 8). Between 1986 and 2000, a total of 671 growth management measures were placed on local ballots in cities and counties throughout California.[11] Many of these measures require voter approval of a wide variety of land use approvals, including general plan amendments,[12] expenditures for major public works projects,[13] new hotel and motel construction,[14] sewer line extensions, and developments above a certain size. While these provisions do not restrict development *per se*, they have the potential to do so. They are of particular interest because they change the very manner in which land use decisions are made, often removing a city council's ability to plan for the future needs of its citizens.

The use and success of slow-growth initiatives ebbs and flows. In November 1998, for example, Ventura County received national publicity because the ballot drives there represented an unprecedented attempt to use the ballot box to shape a regional land use policy affecting not only the entire county but virtually all its cities. A countywide initiative requiring voter approval for changing the zoning on agricultural and open-space lands passed, and city UGBs were adopted in virtually all of the county's largest cities, including Camarillo, Simi Valley, and Thousand Oaks.

The use and success of slow-growth initiatives ebbs and flows.

In the March 2000 elections, pro-growth advocates won 11 of 15 land use contests in California.[15] Again in November 2002, the pro-growth side won 19 out of 32 local land use ballot measures.[16]

Notable local land use ballot measures in the November 2002 election included a defeated Nevada County property rights initiative that would have required the county to pay compensation to private property owners for regulations that inhibited development. To the relief of many local government officials, the measure failed by only capturing the support of 43 percent of the voters.[17] Two additional initiatives that would have placed a cap on the number of building permits in Galt and Windsor—two rapidly developing communities—were rejected by the voters, signaling a decidedly pro-growth sentiment

---

11. *See* William Fulton, *Trends in Local Land Use and Ballot Measures, 1986–2000* (Solimar Research Group, Inc., October 2, 2000).
12. The California Supreme Court upheld an initiative measure that provided that land use designations could not be changed during a 30-year period except by a majority vote of the electorate. *DeVita v. County of Napa*, 9 Cal. 4th 763 (1995).
13. For example, voters in Valley Center passed an initiative in 1988 (Proposition B) requiring voter approval of expenditures by a water district for major projects. California Ass'n of Realtors, "Summary of Local Land Use Measures," 16 *California Ballot Monitor*, no. 22 (rev. ed. Dec. 1992).
14. Voters in the City of Monterey passed an initiative in 1986 (Measure E) to require voter approval of hotel/motel construction in specified areas. *Id.*, page 9.
15. *See* William Fulton, "Local Slow-Growth Measures Fare Poorly in March Balloting," *California Planning & Development Report* (April 2000).
16. *See* Paul Shigley, "Voters Show Pro-Growth Sentiment," *California Planning & Development Report* (December 2002).
17. *See id.*

in those communities.[18] In Berkeley, voters overwhelmingly rejected a measure that would have limited the permissible height of buildings in commercial districts outside the downtown area. A resounding 80 percent of the voters rejected this proposition, signaling a possible change in opinion in the traditionally slow- or no-growth City of Berkeley.[19]

In the June 2006 election, while fewer slow-growth measures appeared on local ballots, voters showed a slow-growth bent, rejecting a large housing development in the City of Santa Paula and approving a far-reaching growth-control initiative in Yorba Linda. However, voters in the Town of Apple Valley amended a 1999 initiative to no longer require voter approval for zoning changes.[20]

It is difficult to predict whether the pro-growth or the slow-growth sides will be victorious at the ballot box in any given year. What *is* predictable is that Californians will continue to use the initiative process to enact local land use laws at the ballot box.[21]

Problems with Certain Slow-Growth Measures

Local slow-growth measures aimed at specific infrastructure problems, such as traffic or water supply, rarely solve the underlying issue.

Local slow-growth measures aimed at specific infrastructure problems, such as traffic or water supply, rarely solve the underlying issue. Traffic, for instance, is a regional problem. If new office or residential growth is severely restricted in one city, it will simply go elsewhere, often exacerbating traffic problems in the region. Limits on "high rise" buildings force development to spread rather than concentrate densely, so that walking, carpooling, and mass transit—commuting options that might collectively relieve clogged streets—become impractical.

Legality of Growth Management

The Proper Exercise of the City's Police Power

A land use restriction is within the police power if it is reasonably related to the public welfare.

The legal basis for planning and land use regulations, including growth management, is the police power, the power of the city to protect the public health, safety, and welfare of its residents. *See Berman v. Parker*, 348 U.S. 26, 32–33 (1954). A land use restriction is within the police power if it is reasonably related to the public welfare. *See Associated Home Builders, Inc. v. City of Livermore*, 18 Cal. 3d 582, 589 (1976). For a good discussion of the legality of growth management ordinances, especially in California, *see* Robin S. Myran, "Growth Control as a Taking," 25 *The Urban Lawyer* 385 (1993) (analyzing a hypothetical growth management ordinance under the *Lucas*, *Agins*, and *Penn Central* "takings" tests, and concluding that such an ordinance most likely would survive a takings challenge).

---

18. *See id.*
19. *See id.*
20. *See* Paul Shigley, "Voters Reject Road Taxes, Growth," *California Planning & Development Report* (July 2006).
21. For an excellent discussion of recent trends in initiatives dealing with growth management, see Mai T. Nguyen and William Fulton, *Tools and Patterns of Growth Management Ballot Measures in California 1986–2000* (Solimar Research Group, Inc., September 2002).

Planned Growth Ordinances

The rapid expansion of new construction within existing communities is one of the most important issues facing these communities. Problems created by such dynamic growth derive from both the rate and sequence of growth. The rate of growth determines the total demand for new facilities within a city. A rapid growth rate can result in financial pressure on city budgets and capacity pressure on city infrastructure and community facilities, such as parks and open space. The sequence of growth raises slightly different problems. Absent good planning, residential growth typically takes place on a lot-by-lot or subdivision-by-subdivision basis. The sequence of subdivision development may follow no logical pattern, and instead will occur based upon which parcels of available land happen to come on the market at any given time and their relative prices, leading to scattered more or less at random development in open space areas within and adjacent to the urban fringe of cities.

To help address these issues over the past few decades, cities have increasingly adopted various types of "planned growth regulations," often through general or specific plan measures and appropriate implementing ordinances. The seminal case in the United States declaring the validity of a growth management plan, "The Ramapo Plan," is *Golden v. Planning Board of the Town of Ramapo*, 30 N.Y. 2d 359, 369 (1972), where the New York high court upheld the timing of sequential control of residential subdivision activity for periods of up to eighteen years. *See* "The 30th Anniversary of Golden v. Ramapo: A Tribute to Robert H. Freilich," 35 *The Urban Lawyer*, no. 1 (Winter 2003) (this volume contains several excellent articles on planned growth).

The leading California case upholding a planned growth regulation is *Construction Industry Ass'n v. City of Petaluma*, 522 F. 2d 897 (9th Cir. 1975). There, the Ninth Circuit upheld Petaluma's plan, which fixed the housing development growth rate at 500 dwelling units per year for five years and directed that building permits be divided evenly between single-family and multiple-family residential units (*i.e.*, the "housing mix"). *Id.* at 908–09.

The court held that the concept of public welfare contained in the police power was sufficiently broad to encompass Petaluma's desire to preserve its small-town character, its open space, and its low density of population, and to grow at an orderly and deliberate pace. The court also found that the plan was not unconstitutional, since it was rationally related to the environmental welfare of the city and did not discriminate against interstate commerce. *Id.* at 909. *See also Dateline Builders, Inc. v. City of Santa Rosa*, 146 Cal. App. 3d 520, 528 (1983) (upholding the city's refusal to permit a builder to connect its proposed "leap frog" housing development beyond the city's boundaries with the city's existing sewer trunk lines on the basis that the public welfare concept of the police power is sufficiently broad to encompass the city's desire for orderly and compact growth).

The California Supreme Court also has addressed how to evaluate whether a growth management measure, adopted through a voter initiative process as an exercise of the police power, bears a substantial and reasonable relationship to the public welfare. *See Associated Home Builders, Inc. v. City of Livermore*, 18 Cal. 3d 582 (1976). The Court proposed a three-pronged approach using the following questions as guides:

- What is the probable effect and duration of the ordinance?
- What are the competing interests affected by the ordinance (*e.g.*, environmental protection versus the opportunity of people to settle where they choose)?
- Does the ordinance, in light of its probable impact, represent a reasonable accommodation of the competing interests?

Id. at 608–09

In applying this approach, the Court held that the scope of the inquiry must extend to the welfare of those whom the measure would affect significantly, and not just those within the boundaries of the city enacting the measure. For the purpose of decisions affecting housing, as many growth management measures do, this effectively establishes the requirement of a regional analysis.

Utilizing this test, the *Livermore* court upheld the city's growth management ordinance, finding that the challengers of that ordinance had failed to meet their burden of proving that it lacked a reasonable relationship to the regional welfare. *Id. But see Building Indus. Ass'n v. City of Oceanside*, 27 Cal. App. 4th 744, 762 (1994) (an initiative growth control ordinance was inconsistent with the city's general plan housing goals, viewed as distinguishable from the ordinance upheld in *Livermore*).

In a 1991 court decision, growth regulations were upheld against a facial taking claim alleging that the regulations did not promote the public welfare. *See Long Beach Equities, Inc. v. County of Ventura*, 231 Cal. App. 3d 1016 (1991). The court ruled in favor of the county and the city, holding that the growth control legislation satisfied the test of promoting the public welfare without irreparably injuring the landowner. *Id.* at 1030. On this point the court stated:

> Local government legislation is constitutional on its face if it bears "a substantial relationship to the public welfare..." and inflicts no irreparable injury on the landowner. This is true even where a substantial diminution in value of the property is alleged....
>
> City enacted its ordinance: "to protect the unique, hill-surrounded environment; enhance the quality of life; promote public health, safety or welfare and the general well-being of the community...." By limiting the rate, distribution, quality and type of residential development on an annual basis, with periodic reviews of the ongoing situation, City seeks "to improve local air quality, reduce traffic demands... and ensure that future demands for such essential services as water, sewers and the like are met...."
>
> Courts have long recognized the legitimacy of such ordinances because such laws are designed to protect the public weal.

Id. (citations omitted)

The landowner also argued that the legislation was contrary to Government Code provisions that support the development of housing, such as Government Code sections 65580, 65581, and 65583. Although these sections promote the development of residential housing, the court said such development is not encouraged when it fails to conserve needed open space and contributes to urban sprawl. *Id.* Gov't Code § 65560 *et seq.* For further discussion of when a city may be required to compensate a property owner, *see* chapter 12 (Takings), and for a discussion of the tension between providing housing and growth management measures, see chapter 20 (Affordable Housing).

Introduction to "Smart Growth"[22]

In the past several years "urban sprawl" has become not only one of the most hotly debated issues in planning and land use circles, but has gained attention from the population at large. As a reaction to urban sprawl and the ill effects often associated with it—including disinvestment in central cities, environmental degradation, traffic congestion, increasing separation by race and income, conversion of prime agricultural lands, and loss of community character[23]—the Smart Growth movement has exploded onto the scene.

In the past several years "urban sprawl" has become not only one of the most hotly debated issues in planning and land use circles, but has gained attention from the population at large.

What is Smart Growth?[24] Much like its close relative "sustainable development," it turns out that Smart Growth defies simple definition. Because it has become such a fashionable planning concept, the Smart Growth label has been co-opted and manipulated by a wide range of constituents, all of whom have their own interests. Over time, however, a number of principles have emerged that serve as a general guide to Smart Growth decisionmaking.

What is Smart Growth? Much like its close relative "sustainable development," Smart Growth defies simple definition.

The Smart Growth Network provides the following list of ten objectives for the Smart Growth developer or policymaker:

- Create a Range of Housing Opportunities and Choices
- Create Walkable Neighborhoods
- Encourage Community Stakeholder Collaboration
- Foster Distinctive, Attractive Places with a Strong Sense of Place
- Make Development Decisions Predictable, Fair and Cost Effective
- Mix Land Uses
- Preserve Open Space, Farmland, Natural Beauty and Critical Environmental Areas
- Provide a Variety of Transportation Choices
- Strengthen and Direct Development Towards Existing Communities
- Take Advantage of Compact Building Design[25]

These aspirational objectives take many forms. The unique constraints and needs of any particular community demand as much. But the objectives attempt to create continuity and broad guidance to inform decisionmaking. As part of its Smart Growth strategy, the Association of Bay Area Governments (ABAG) states:

ABAG = Association of Bay Area Governments

> The common thread among different views of smart growth is development that revitalizes central cities and older suburbs, supports and enhances public transit, promotes walking and bicycling, and preserves open spaces and agricultural lands. Smart growth is not no growth; rather, it seeks to revitalize the already-built environment and, to the extent necessary, to foster efficient development at the edges of the region, in the process creating more livable communities.[26]

22. *See* Robert H. Freilich, *From Sprawl to Smart Growth* (Sect. of State and Local Gov't Law, ABA 1999).
23. *See* Charter of the New Urbanism (www.cnu.org/charter).
24. *See* Ed Bolen *et al.*, "Smart Growth: A Review of Programs State by State," 8 *Hastings W.-Nw. J. Envtl. L. and Pol'y*, no. 2 (Spring 2002).
25. *See* www.smartgrowth.org/about/default.asp.
26. *See* www.abag.ca.gov/planning/smartgrowth/whatisSG.html (2007).

Barriers to Smart Growth

A move toward the principles of Smart Growth will require reform of the deeply entrenched legal, fiscal, and cultural institutions that support sprawl.

A move toward the principles of Smart Growth will require reform of the deeply entrenched legal, fiscal, and cultural institutions that support sprawl. The Urban Land Institute's California Smart Growth initiative[27] identifies a number of barriers that currently prevent or impede the spread of Smart Growth practices. Among these barriers are:

- **Fiscal zoning.** With the passage of Proposition 13 in 1978, some of California's cities have preferred tax-generating commercial uses over housing. While commercial and retail uses *create* revenue via sales taxes, residential uses *deplete* revenue via government services. The result of this fiscal zoning has contributed to the current housing crisis.

NIMBY = Not in My Back Yard

- **Neighborhood opposition to new development.** NIMBY (Not in My Back Yard) attitudes run rampant throughout communities that fear new development will only exacerbate problems with traffic, loss of open space, or overcrowding. The opportunities to address the symptoms of sprawl through smart design are met with skepticism by surrounding neighbors. Unfortunately, "victories" by neighborhood groups who stop development in existing communities contribute to sprawl and housing shortages.

- **Fragmented decision making.** Piecemeal planning decisions and failure by local officials to develop and adhere to a comprehensive planning framework prohibit the integration of, for instance, a transportation system linked to efficient development. The same problem is repeated on the regional level for lack of coordination between jurisdictions.

- **Insufficient funding for infrastructure.** Infill development requires the updating of sewer, water, street, and public transportation infrastructure. Anticipated infrastructure deficits will hinder efforts to make these necessary improvements.

- **Limited funding for planning.** Funding for Smart Growth planning strategies often falls victim to perennial budget shortfalls in many localities. In addition, there are generally no opportunities for local governments to receive such funding from the state.

- **Brownfield development issues.** The onerous federal, state, and local regulatory regimes governing the development of even slightly contaminated building sites cause uncertainty and delay that discourage developers, lenders, and insurers from investing in them.

- **Construction defect litigation.** The rise in lawsuits brought by homeowners against developers and builders has made the construction of multi-family residential units very expensive and risky. In recent years, construction defect insurance has become prohibitively expensive as a result of litigation, bringing the construction of condominium and townhouse units to a halt.[28]

---

27. *Putting the Pieces Together: State Actions to Encourage Smart Growth Practices in California* (The Urban Land Institute, Washington, D.C. 2002).

28. Notably, the 2002 Legislature enacted a law that seeks to address this problem by setting out clear performance standards for many aspects of construction. In addition, the statute provides pre-litigation dispute resolution procedures to facilitate lower cost solutions to residents' grievances. *See* Civ. Code § 895 *et seq.*

APA's Growing Smart Legislative Guidebook

In addition to the structural reforms described above, proponents of Smart Growth have advocated for legislative reform of state planning and zoning enabling acts in order to address some of the challenges of accommodating continued growth. To this end, in 2006 the American Planning Association (APA) has published drafts of 11 model smart growth ordinances covering topics including mixed-use, zoning, town center, affordable housing density bonus, unified development permit review process, transferable development rights, cluster development, pedestrian overlay district, and several parking ordinances.[29] In 2002, the APA published the two-volume Growing Smart Legislative Guidebook and an accompanying user's manual. The Guidebook is the product of an effort to produce the next generation of model planning and zoning enabling legislation. It contends that reform is needed to address the increasingly intergovernmental nature of planning, society's changing views of land as something other than a commodity that is bought and sold, and a citizenry that is more actively engaged in making land use decisions.

The Guidebook is a thorough survey of the many techniques being employed across the country. It includes topics such as the planning process and implementing plans (at the state, regional, and local levels), infrastructure and capital improvement plans, special and environmental land development regulations and incentives (*e.g.*, historic preservation, transfer of development rights, conservation easements, purchase of development rights), taxation, finance planning, geographic information systems, and public records.

Two sections of the Guidebook that may be of particular interest to legal and planning practitioners of land use are chapters 8 and 10, which discuss local land development regulations, and administrative and judicial review of land use decisions, respectively. Chapter 8 provides model codes for topics including zoning, subdivision, planned unit developments, uniform development standards, development impact fees, vesting, nonconforming uses, and development agreements. Chapter 10 sets out model procedures for making and reviewing land use decisions, including development permits, conditional uses, variances, and mediated agreements.

In addition to the model statutes (and in some cases several alternative model statutes) for each topic, the Guidebook also includes a narrative commentary that explains how the statutes were selected, and what factors the authors considered in arriving at the specific language.

Finally, the User Manual that accompanies the Guidebook provides a "user needs checklist." The checklist is meant to help would-be policymakers identify their goals, then find the corresponding sections in the Guidebook to help accomplish those goals.

Proponents of Smart Growth have advocated for legislative reform of state planning and zoning enabling acts in order to address some of the challenges of accommodating continued growth.

APA = American Planning Association

ABAG's Smart Growth/Regional Livability Footprint Project

The Association of Bay Area Governments is currently engaged in a novel and ambitious effort to address one of the most challenging obstacles to Smart

---

29. The APA model smart growth ordinances are available at www.planning.org/smartgrowthcodes/phase1.htm.

Growth—regional planning and cooperation. In densely populated areas, such as the metropolitan regions of California, individual local governments do not truly operate as independent entities. Rather, the contiguous cities operate as an interdependent socioeconomic unit. Nevertheless, the role of cities in determining land use policy, and the strength of home rule in California have made regional cooperation sometimes difficult.

Smart Growth proponents recognize that the traditional division of land use decisionmaking at the local level is vulnerable to abuse. For instance, regional land use goals are vulnerable to infighting over tax revenues from big retailers. Likewise, local control over affordable housing allocation is inherently ineffective, since it is often strongly opposed by surrounding neighbors, and since it does not generate significant tax revenue for the local government. A "big picture" perspective, *i.e.* a regional perspective, is sometimes needed to overcome local protectionist attitudes.

To foster discussion about regional planning as it relates to the Bay Area's potential Smart Growth objectives, ABAG has undertaken the "Smart Growth/Regional Livability Footprint Project."

In an attempt to foster discussion about regional planning as it relates to the Bay Area's potential Smart Growth objectives, ABAG initiated the "Smart Growth/Regional Livability Footprint Project."[30] The project is a unique effort at public participation in determining regional land use patterns.

ABAG released its Final Report in October 2002, with a vision for future development in the Bay Area. The hope is that this vision will facilitate a regional thought process and inform the next generation of decisionmakers.

The Final Report was based on a series of public workshops in September and October of 2001, in which citizen participants broke into small groups with maps of their county. They were then challenged to create a vision of development that would identify the most appropriate locations for future development in their county, and the most appropriate character of that development, *i.e.*, density and uses. Using a computerized geographic information system (GIS), participants were able to see immediately what impacts their land use decisions would have on housing and jobs, and their proximity to and effects on public transit.

BAAQMD = Bay Area Air Quality Management District
GIS = Geographic information system
MTC = Metropolitan Transportation Commission

Using input from the workshops and a meeting of more than 100 planning directors, ABAG developed three alternatives for future development in the Bay Area. The alternatives sketched out the physical consequences of certain land use decisions relating to density, transportation, agricultural land, and open space preservation.

During a second round of workshops in April and May 2002, participants came together once more to modify their preferred alternative. By the end of the second workshop, each county had created a vision of development that specified the level of housing and job growth, and the density and allocation of that growth within the planning area.

Every two years ABAG makes projections for future population and household change and employment growth throughout the region. These projections are used by the Metropolitan Transportation Commission (MTC) to develop a regional transportation plan, which in turn guides the Bay Area Air Quality Management District (BAAQMD) in developing a regional air quality plan. The related nature of these planning efforts led the Legislature

30. *See* www.abag.ca.gov/planning/smartgrowth.

in 2004 to require creation of a joint policy committee among ABAG, MTC, and BAAQMD to coordinate development and drafting of major planning documents. Gov't Code § 66536.1.

In the past, ABAG's projections were based primarily on growth trends. MTC would then allocate regional transportation funds based on projected demand. In 2003, for the first time, ABAG used the results of the Smart Growth/Livability Project as the starting point for determining its jobs and housing projections. The new projections take into account the policy-based modeling process that grew out of the project. In this way, ABAG's projection and MTC transportation plans can *influence*, rather than merely *react* to, growth patterns. Through the projections, ABAG hopes to take the Smart Growth/Livability Project's vision and turn it into a reality, with real-world effects.[31]

Smart Growth Is Not Going Away

Whether or not one agrees that the objectives espoused by the Smart Growth movement are indeed in California's or the nation's best interests, one cannot deny the impact that the movement is having on the current debate over urban sprawl and land use reform. A series of statutes passed in 2002 and 2004 suggests that the Legislature has endorsed in part some of the principles of Smart Growth. Perhaps most important, symbolically, was the addition of Smart Growth goals to the State Environmental Goals and Policy Report. The new goals include infill development, redevelopment of land already served by infrastructure and transit, efficient development in greenfields, and the preservation of natural resources and agricultural land. Gov't Code § 65041 *et seq.*

Whether or not one agrees that the objectives espoused by the Smart Growth movement are indeed in California's or the nation's best interests, one cannot deny the impact that the movement is having on the current debate over urban sprawl and land use reform.

Apart from the adoption of policy goals, the Legislature also adopted several other statutes to encourage density. In an apparent response to concerns that the construction of second units has not lived up to its promise of increasing housing in the state, the Legislature in 2002 enacted provisions to further encourage the development of second units by making the approval of second units a ministerial act, not subject to discretionary review or a hearing.

Similarly, in 2002, 2004, and 2005, the Legislature amended the state's density bonus law,[32] which requires a city to provide an incentive or concession to developers who agree to construct affordable housing. A city must now grant a density bonus and certain incentives or concessions, unless it makes written findings to show that the development would have an adverse effect on health, safety, or the environment or that the incentive is not required to provide for affordable housing costs. Gov't Code § 65915(d)(1). "In no case may a city... apply any development standard that will have the effect of precluding the construction of a development meeting the criteria of [the density bonus law] at the densities or with the concessions or incentives permitted by this section." Gov't Code § 65915(e). If a city refuses to grant the density bonus and incentive or concession, the developer may initiate judicial proceedings, and may recover reasonable attorneys fees and costs of suit for violation of the statute. Gov't Code §§ 65915(d)(3) and (e).

---

31. *See* www.abag.ca.gov/planning/smartgrowth/projections.html.
32. For an excellent discussion of the density bonus law, *see* Betsy Strauss, *The Density Bonus Law: Changes, Interpretations, and Implementation* (City Attorney Conference of League of California Cities, May 2006) (available at www.cacities.org/attypapers).

There is also increasing pressure on cities to provide their fair share of the region's housing. A city may not reduce the residential density of *any parcel* to a "lower residential density" than was used by the Department of Housing and Community Development for calculating compliance with the housing element law, unless it makes written findings supported by substantial evidence that the reduction in density is consistent with the current general plan, including the housing element, and the city's share of the regional housing need. Gov't Code § 65863(b). Alternatively, the reduction may be approved if a city identifies "sufficient, additional, adequate, and available sites with an equal or greater residential density... so that there is no net loss of residential unit capacity." Gov't Code § 65863(c). If the city has not adopted a housing element for the current planning period, or if the adopted housing element is not in substantial compliance with the housing element law, "lower residential density" means a density below 80 percent of the maximum allowable residential density for that parcel. Gov't Code § 65863(h). Addressing concerns that cities were unfairly requiring project applicants to obtain additional available sites, the Legislature amended the law in 2004 to prohibit cities from holding the applicant responsible for providing such sites, unless the applicant initially requested the reduction in zoning density. Gov't Code § 65863(f). For further discussion of these housing-related provisions, *see* chapter 20 (Affordable Housing).

The law pertaining to Congestion Management Programs (CMPs) also now facilitates dense new development in urban centers, thus further promoting Smart Growth planning principles. Existing law requires counties with an urbanized area to adopt a CMP, including specific traffic level of service standards, consistent with regional transportation plans. The law allows cities to create "infill opportunity zones" within one-third of a mile of major public transit routes for new compact residential and mixed use development in population centers over 400,000. These zones are exempt from traffic level of service requirements normally required by a CMP. Instead, the law requires the CMP to take into account the alternative transit opportunities in the "infill opportunity zones," including pedestrian, bicycle, and public transit, using a "multimodal composite." Gov't Code § 65088.4. For further discussion of CMPs, *see* chapter 9 (Design Review and Other Development Regulations).

Finally, the Subdivision Map Act provides for expanded protection of agricultural and open space land. A city must deny approval of a tentative map if the land proposed for subdivision is subject to a Williamson Act contract, and the resulting parcels would be too small to sustain continued agricultural use or would result in a residential development not incidental to the agricultural use. This provision was amended to apply also to land subject to an open-space easement, agricultural-conservation easement, or conservation easement. Gov't Code § 66474.4.

The Legislature's pattern in expanding these laws in the past few years appears to reflect a concerted effort to apply Smart Growth principles to state law, even if it means taking some discretion out of the hands of cities. The practical effects of Smart Growth may not be detectable for many years. But if the amount of attention it has been receiving by planners and land use practitioners is any indication, it would seem that the pursuit of "Smart Growth" will not soon fade away. For a broad-ranging discussion of growth, development, and infrastructure as well as "Smart Growth" principles, *see California 2025: Taking on the Future* (Ellen Harak and Mark Baldassare eds., Public Policy Institute of California, 2005).

Surviving Growth Management Regulations, Including Initiatives: Tools Developers Can Use

There have been various reactions to the increased use of initiatives in California as a tool to manage growth. For instance, on a practical level, developers have increased their use of development agreements and vesting tentative maps, which are two California statutory mechanisms that allow an early vesting of development rights, thereby providing insulation from subsequently enacted growth management measures. For a detailed discussion of vested rights and development agreements, *see* chapter 10 (Vested Rights) and David L. Callies, Daniel J. Curtin, Jr., and Julie A. Tappendorf, *Bargaining for Development: A Handbook on Development Agreements, Annexation Agreements, Land Development Conditions, Vested Rights and the Provision of Public Facilities* (Environmental Law Institute 2003).

On a policy level, an increasing number of people are questioning the long-term advisability of allowing land use policy to be determined directly by the voters. However, the California Supreme Court, in upholding a local initiative measure to amend a general plan to preserve agricultural land, found no basis for the "contention that this general plan amendment initiative, or amendment initiatives in general, inherently frustrate the fundamental objectives of the planning law." *DeVita v. County of Napa*, 9 Cal. 4th 763, 792 (1995).

An increasing number of people are questioning the advisability of allowing land use policy to be determined directly by the voters.

Once a developer has a vested right to develop, that developer is largely immune from subsequent governmental actions that would preclude that development. *See Avco Community Developers, Inc. v. South Coast Reg'l Comm'n*, 17 Cal. 3d 785, 792 (1976). Consistent with the principle that the voters may not do by initiative what the city council cannot do, an initiative cannot interfere with a vested right to develop. *See Arnel Dev. Co. v. City of Costa Mesa*, 126 Cal. App. 3d 330 (1981). Thus, obtaining an early vested right to develop can be of great importance to protecting a developer from the unforeseen consequences of a voter-enacted "growth control" ordinance.

Initiatives

Although a city is given wide latitude to adopt growth management regulations, a city and its voters should concentrate on solving the problems that generate the need for growth management—whether the issues involve traffic or managed development for the accommodation of increased sewer or water capacities.

The use of voter initiatives to deal with growth issues is not a truly viable solution. While initiatives can serve an important function in allowing the voters to enact legislation when their elected leaders fail to fulfill expectations in the field of growth management, such initiatives often are inadequate, simplistic approaches to complex, multi-faceted problems. Citizens generally lack the ability to perform the in-depth studies that are necessary to resolve the difficult questions and establish the basis for a system that meaningfully addresses the critical issues. These inadequacies are compounded by the fact that most initiatives

The use of voter initiatives to deal with growth issues is not a truly viable solution.

are limited to local growth and are unlikely to positively affect problems that are regional in nature.

At the core of the most valid criticisms of growth management initiatives is the idea that such measures make comprehensive land use planning difficult, if not impossible. The hallmarks of good land use planning are that decisionmakers be well informed, that the planning process be flexible and responsive to changing circumstances and values, and that final decisions reflect a comprehensive planning process that accommodates competing public interests. Arguably, each of these goals is thwarted when land use planning is done through the ballot box.

Critics of land use initiatives claim that the voters will never have as much information available to them in making land use decisions as a professional planning staff, planning commission, or city council. *See Taxpayers to Limit Campaign Spending v. Fair Political Practices Comm'n*, 51 Cal. 3d 744, 770 (1990). More specifically, the fact that initiatives generally are exempt from the requirement of environmental review under CEQA means that decisions with potentially enormous environmental impacts will be made without the extensive review that CEQA requires.

The charge that land use initiatives frustrate the flexibility and responsiveness to change that are required of good land use planning is supported by the fact that, generally, ordinances adopted by local initiative may not be repealed or amended except by a subsequent vote of the electorate. This statutory provision stands to reason; the purpose for granting the initiative power, empowering an electorate confronted by an unresponsive legislative body, would be vitiated by allowing the legislative body to "undo" what the people have accomplished through the initiative. Elec. Code §§ 9125, 9217. As a result, however, a land use regulation adopted by initiative may be very difficult to amend. Even though the concerns that prompted the measure's passage may have subsided, or even if it is shown that the mechanism adopted is not accomplishing its purpose, generating sufficient voter interest in updating or repealing the measure to conform to changed circumstances may present a real problem. Further, regulations appropriate for a particular period in a city's development may linger well past their usefulness and may, in fact, impede orderly development. For a more complete discussion of the initiative process, *see* chapter 14 (Initiative and Referendum).

In summary, a better method to initiate, develop, and implement a growth management system that fairly distributes the burdens and benefits of growth and assures that the least harm is done once the plan is operating, is to build a consensus among all of the different constituents in the community: namely developers, city activists, environmentalists, business, and financial interest groups. This can be achieved through a series of workshops designed to identify and fully address the relevant critical issues. By developing a consensus regarding the important goals and objectives of the plan from the start, a city can devise a plan that continually addresses the relevant issues. Developers and other similar groups must get involved at the city hall level early in the process of any growth management discussion.

16

Local Agency Formation Commissions: Local Agency Boundary Changes

Introduction

Local Agency Formation Commissions (collectively, LAFCOs or Commissions) oversee public agency boundary changes, as well as the establishment, update, and amendment to spheres of influence. Gov't Code §§ 56001, 56375, 56425. In California, each of the 58 counties have LAFCOs, which make determinations regarding the boundary changes of more than 3,500 government agencies comprised of the 58 counties, 477 incorporated cities, and 3,000-plus special districts.[1]

The overarching goal of LAFCOs is to encourage the orderly formation and extension of government agencies.

The primary purposes of LAFCOs are as follows: (1) to facilitate orderly growth and development by determining logical local agency boundaries; (2) to preserve prime agricultural lands by guiding development away from presently undeveloped prime agricultural preserves; and (3) to discourage urban sprawl and encourage the preservation of open space by promoting development of vacant land within cities before annexation of vacant land adjacent to cities. Gov't Code §§ 56001, 56301. *See also Sierra Club v. San Joaquin LAFCO*, 21 Cal. 4th 489, 495 (1999); *Placer County LAFCO v. Nevada County LAFCO*, 135 Cal. App. 4th 793, 798 (2006); *McBail & Co. v. Solano LAFCO*, 62 Cal. App. 4th at 1228; *City of Santa Cruz v. LAFCO*, 76 Cal. App. 3d at 385.

By ensuring that agency boundaries logically relate to one another, inefficiencies in service provision and overlapping in responsibilities are minimized. LAFCOs have been described as watchdogs, guarding "against the wasteful duplication of services that results from indiscriminate formation of new local agencies or haphazard annexation of territory to existing local agencies." *City of Ceres v. City of Modesto*, 274 Cal. App. 2d 545, 553 (1969).

LAFCO = Local Agency Formation Commission

The overarching goal of LAFCOs is to encourage the orderly formation and extension of government agencies.

Legislative Development of LAFCO Law

The Cortese-Knox Local Government Reorganization Act of 1985 consolidated the three major laws previously used by the state's cities and special districts

---

1. For further information on issues relating to LAFCOs, *see* the materials provided by the California Association of Local Agency Formation Commissions (available at www.calafco.org).

to secure boundary changes: (1) the Knox-Nesbit Act of 1963 (former Gov't Code § 54722 *et seq.*); (2) the District Reorganization Act of 1965 (former Gov't Code § 56000 *et seq.*); and (3) the Municipal Reorganization Act of 1977 (former Gov't Code § 35000 *et seq.*).

The next major revision to this body of law began in the late 1990s. In 1997, the Legislature created the Commission on Local Governance for the 21st Century for the purposes of assessing governance issues and making appropriate recommendations regarding LAFCO law. This 15-member commission, which included city, county, special district, and private members, rendered its lengthy report in Spring 2000. Entitled *Growth Within Bounds*,[2] the report recognized that California did not have a plan for growth, and recommended numerous substantive changes to the laws relating to orderly growth and resource protection, LAFCOs' powers, the sphere of influence provisions, and various boundary change procedures. The report listed eight major recommendations:

- The policies and procedures of LAFCOs must be streamlined and clarified
- LAFCOs must be neutral and independent, and provide balanced representation for counties, cities, and special districts
- The powers of LAFCOs must be strengthened to prevent urban sprawl and to ensure the orderly formation and extension of government services
- The LAFCO policies which are designed to protect prime agricultural lands and open space should be strengthened
- The state-local fiscal relationship should be comprehensively revised
- The state should develop incentives to encourage compatibility and coordination of plans and actions of all local agencies within each region, including school districts, as a way to encourage an integrated approach to public service delivery and to improve overall governance
- Enhancements must be made to communication and coordination, and to the procedures of LAFCOs and local governments
- Opportunities for public involvement, active participation, and information regarding government decisionmaking should be increased

In response to the Commission's report, the Legislature again revised the LAFCO laws by enacting the Cortese-Knox-Hertzberg Local Government Reorganization Act of 2000 (Gov't Code §§ 56000–57550) (the "2000 Act"), incorporating many of the Commission's recommendations. Specifically, LAFCO law was amended to include the following significant changes:[3]

- The power of LAFCOs were strengthened to ensure the logical and orderly extension of services and to prevent urban sprawl
- LAFCOs' neutrality, independence, and balance in membership were emphasized

The Commission on Local Governance for the 21st Century report recommended that the powers of LAFCOs must be strengthened to prevent urban sprawl and to ensure the orderly formation and extension of government services.

---

2. A copy of Growth Within Bounds: Report of the Commission on Local Governance for the 21st Century, can be ordered online from the Commission's website (www.opr.ca.gov/publications/PDFs/79515.pdf). *See also* Peter M. Detwiler, "The Challenges of Growth Within Bounds," *Cal. Envtl. Law Rep.* 101 (May 2000).

3. For a more detailed discussion of the changes that resulted from enactment of the Cortese-Knox-Hertzberg Act, *see* the Governor's Office of Planning and Research website (www.opr.ca.gov); California Assembly Committee on Local Government, *Guide to the Cortese-Knox-Hertzberg Local Government Reorganization Act of 2000* (December 2006).

- LAFCOs' policies and procedures were clarified and streamlined
- Additional opportunities for public involvement in LAFCO processes were provided
- Coordination and communication between LAFCOs and local government agencies were enhanced

Government Code section 56001 sets forth the legislative findings and declarations of the 2000 Act, reinforcing policies that encourage orderly growth and development, which are characterized as essential to the social, fiscal, and economic well-being of California. The Legislature recognized that the logical determination of local agency boundaries is an important factor in balancing the state's interest in promoting orderly development with the sometimes competing state interests of discouraging urban sprawl, preserving open space and prime agricultural lands, and efficiently extending government services. The Legislature declared that the policy favoring orderly development should be realized through the logical formation and modification of the boundaries of local agencies. The Legislature also recognized that providing housing for persons and families of all incomes is an important factor in promoting orderly development. A preference is granted to accommodating additional growth within, or through the expansion of, boundaries of the local agencies that can provide necessary governmental services and housing for persons and families of all incomes in the most efficient manner feasible.

Composition and Function of LAFCOs

Each county in the state has a LAFCO. Except as specifically provided by statute with respect to certain counties (Los Angeles, Sacramento, Santa Clara, San Diego, and Kern), each LAFCO is composed of seven members: two members appointed by the county board of supervisors from its own membership; two members selected by the majority vote of cities in the county, each of whom must be a mayor or councilmember; two special district members selected by majority vote of the special districts in the county; and one member of the general public appointed by the other members of the commission. Gov't Code §§ 56325, 56326–56328, 56332.

LAFCOs make determinations regarding boundary changes to local government agencies, including the incorporation and disincorporation of cities, the formation and dissolution of most special districts, and the annexation, consolidation, merger, and reorganization of cities and districts. Gov't Code §§ 56001, 56375. They also establish, update, and amend spheres of influence for cities and districts. Gov't Code §§ 56425, 56428. The nature of LAFCOs' power is generally treated as legislative and political. *Sierra Club v. San Joaquin LAFCO*, 21 Cal. 4th 489, 495 (1999); *City of Santa Cruz v. LAFCO*, 76 Cal. App. 3d 381, 387 (1978). *But see L.I.F.E. Committee v. City of Lodi*, 213 Cal. App. 3d 1139 (1989) (no initiative or referendum power). Accordingly, LAFCOs have broad discretion in making decisions regarding boundary changes and spheres of influence. *Oxnard Harbor Dist. v. LAFCO*, 16 Cal. App. 4th 259, 262 (1993); *City of Agoura Hills v. LAFCO*, 198 Cal. App. 3d 480, 489 (1988). This discretion, however, must be exercised within legislative parameters. LAFCOs are a creation of the Legislature and have only the powers that are expressly granted by

> *LAFCOs make determinations regarding boundary changes to local government agencies, including the incorporation and disincorporation of cities, the formation and dissolution of most special districts, and the annexation, consolidation, merger, and reorganization of cities and districts.*

statute or that are necessarily implied in order to exercise the powers expressly granted. *City of Ceres v. City of Modesto*, 274 Cal. App. 2d 545, 550 (1969); *Tillie Lewis Foods v. City of Pittsburg*, 52 Cal. App. 3d 983, 999 (1975).

Although they operate independently of the state, LAFCOs must act within legislative parameters that encourage planned, orderly, and efficient urban development patterns, the preservation of open space, and the discouragement of urban sprawl.

Pursuant to Government Code section 56325.1, in making determinations, commission members must "exercise their independent judgment on behalf of the interests of residents, property owners, and the public as a whole in furthering the purposes of this division." Members appointed on behalf of local governments "shall represent the interests of the public as a whole and not solely the interests of the appointing authority." *Id.*

Spheres of Influence

Pursuant to Government Code section 56425, LAFCOs must develop and determine a "sphere of influence" for each local government agency within its county.[4] When an agency provides services to more than one county, the LAFCO in the principal county (*i.e.*, the county having most of the assessed value of the district's taxable property) has jurisdiction. *Placer County LAFCO v. Nevada County LAFCO*, 135 Cal. App. 4th 793, 809 (2006).

A sphere of influence is a plan for the probable physical boundaries and service area of a local government agency, as determined by LAFCO. Gov't Code § 56076. Establishment of a sphere of influence is intended to determine which government agencies can provide services in the most efficient way to the people and property in any given area.

Once it has determined and adopted a sphere of influence, the Commission must review and update it as necessary, but not less than once every five years.[5] Gov't Code § 56425(f). The law imposes an initial deadline for LAFCOs to review and update each sphere of influence on or before January 1, 2008, and then every five years thereafter. Gov't Code § 56425(g).

Every boundary change determination made by LAFCOs must be consistent with the sphere of influence established for the local agency affected by such determination. Gov't Code § 56375.5.

Government Code section 56425(a) provides:

In order to carry out its purposes and responsibilities for planning and shaping the logical and orderly development and coordination of local governmental agencies so as to advantageously provide for the present and future needs of the county and its communities, the commission shall develop and determine the sphere of influence of each local governmental agency within the county

---

4. A city and county may agree to recommend to the LAFCO specific changes in the city's sphere of influence boundaries and express their intent to jointly agree to any changes in such boundaries in the future. Gov't Code § 56425. *See also* 84 Ops. Cal. Atty. Gen. 66 (2001).

5. There is some ambiguity in the law about a sphere of influence "amendment," "revision," and "update." These ambiguities have implications for the requirement of LAFCOs to prepare municipal service reviews (as discussed further below). For an interesting discussion on this and related issues, *see* CALAFCO Legislative Comm., MSR/SOI Subcommittee Report (August 2005), available at www.calafco.org/resources.htm.

and enact policies designed to promote the logical and orderly development of areas within the sphere.

Prior to submitting an application to LAFCO to amend or update a sphere of influence, representatives from the city and county must meet to discuss the proposed sphere "to explore methods to reach agreement on the boundaries, development standards, and zoning requirements within the sphere." If an agreement is reached, LAFCO must give great weight to this agreement in making its sphere determination.[6] Gov't Code § 56425(b).

An determining each local agency's sphere of influence, the commission must consider several factors and prepare a written statement of its determinations with respect to the following:

- The present and planned land uses in the area, including agricultural and open space lands
- The present and probable need for public facilities and services in the area
- The present capacity of public facilities and adequacy of public services that the agency provides or is authorized to provide
- The existence of any social or economic communities of interest in the area if the commission determines that they are relevant to the agency

Gov't Code § 56425(e)

LAFCOs may adopt, amend, or revise a sphere of influence after notice and a public hearing called and held for that purpose. Gov't Code § 56427. An amendment may also be requested by any person or local agency, if a proposal for a boundary change is not consistent with the current sphere of influence. Often, this request is made in connection with a specific boundary change request, and the Commission may act on both requests at the same hearing. Gov't Code § 56428.

Municipal Service Review Requirement

When preparing and updating spheres of influence, LAFCOs are required to conduct municipal service reviews. When two counties receive services from a multicounty service district, the LAFCO in the principal county has exclusive jurisdiction over the municipal service review. *Placer County LAFCO*, 135 Cal App. 4th at 808.

These reviews are designed to be a tool for collecting information and evaluating the provision of services from a broader perspective. Pursuant to Government Code section 56430, "the commission shall conduct a service review of the municipal services provided in the county or other appropriate area designated by the commission..., and shall prepare a written statement of its determinations" with respect to each of the following six categories:[7]

(1) Growth and population projections for the affected area
(2) Present and planned capacity of public facilities and adequacy of public services, including infrastructure needs or deficiencies

---

6. Effective January 1, 2008, the 30-day time limit for this consultation is eliminated.
7. The MSR factors to be considered were modified as reflected below pursuant to AB 1744, to become effective on January 1, 2008.

(3) Financial ability of agencies to provide services

(4) Status of and opportunities for shared facilities

(5) Accountability for community service needs including governmental structure and operational efficiencies

(6) Any other matter related to effective or efficient service delivery, as required by commission policy

The Governor's Office of Planning and Research (OPR) has issued municipal service review guidelines that provide direction to LAFCOs in implementing the service review requirements.[8] However, OPR makes clear that these are only advisory "guidelines" not "regulations." The guidelines recommend how LAFCOs should evaluate each of the nine categories for which written determinations must be rendered. They also suggest several methodologies for identifying an appropriate geographic scope for the municipal service review. For example, depending upon local conditions, circumstances, and geography, LAFCOs may choose to use geographic and growth boundaries, geo-political boundaries, existing planning areas, or multi-county study areas when conducting municipal service reviews. The guidelines also discuss environmental justice considerations that may be considered in the LAFCO decision-making process.

The guidelines encourage LAFCOs to collaborate and coordinate with all stakeholders, including other affected and interested LAFCOs and government agencies, as well as members of the public. Several opportunities for public participation during the municipal service review process are identified, including stakeholder meetings, public hearings or workshops to initiate municipal service reviews, a public review period of the draft municipal service review report, and a public hearing to consider that report.

Boundary Changes

LAFCOs regulate local agency boundary changes by making determinations with respect to proposals for such changes brought by individuals or affected public agencies. In general, LAFCOs have the authority to approve or disapprove changes of organization or reorganization. Gov't Code § 56375. Although LAFCOs make determinations regarding boundary changes, they do not have the authority to directly regulate land use density or intensity, property development, or subdivision requirements. Gov't Code § 56375(a)(3).

A "change of organization" is any one of the following boundary changes (Gov't Code § 56021):

- **Annexation**—defined as the annexation, inclusion, attachment, or addition of territory to a city or district. Gov't Code § 56017
- **Detachment**—defined as the detachment, deannexation, exclusion, deletion, or removal from a city or district of any portion of the territory of that city or district. Gov't Code § 56033
- **Incorporation**—defined as the incorporation, formation, creation, and establishment of a city with corporate powers. Gov't Code § 56043

---

8. OPR's municipal service review guidelines are available at www.opr.ca.gov. The guidelines emphasize the importance of LAFCOs retaining flexibility to modify OPR's recommendations to reflect local conditions and circumstances, and the types of services under review.

- **Formation**—defined as the formation, incorporation, organization, or creation of a district. Gov't Code § 56039
- **Disincorporation**—defined as the disincorporation, dissolution, extinguishment, and termination of the existence of a city and the cessation of its corporate powers, except for the purpose of winding up the affairs of the city. Gov't Code § 56034
- **Dissolution**—defined as the dissolution, disincorporation, extinguishment, and termination of the existence of a district and the cessation of all its corporate powers, except as the commission may otherwise provide pursuant to section 56886 or for the purpose of winding up the affairs of the district. Gov't Code § 56035
- **Consolidation**—defined as the uniting or joining of two or more cities located in the same county into a single new successor city or two or more districts into a single new successor district. Gov't Code § 56030
- **Merger**—defined as the extinguishment, termination, and cessation of the existence of a district of limited powers by the merger of that district with a city as a result of proceedings taken pursuant to this division. Gov't Code § 56056

A "change of reorganization" is a proceeding involving two or more changes of organization initiated in a single proposal. Gov't Code § 56073.

A "change of reorganization" is a proceeding involving two or more changes of organization initiated in a single proposal.

LAFCOs do not have the power to initiate boundary changes, except for proposals involving (1) the consolidation of special districts, (2) the dissolution, merger, or establishment of subsidiary districts, or (3) a reorganization that involves any of these changes of organization. Gov't Code § 56375(a).

Agencies that perform governmental or proprietary functions within limited boundaries are, including county service areas, referred to as "districts" or "special districts," and must comply with LAFCO laws when making boundary changes. Certain agencies, however, are expressly excluded from LAFCOs' jurisdiction. Gov't Code § 56036. These include:

- School districts or community college districts
- Special assessment districts
- Improvement districts
- Community facilities districts formed pursuant to the Mello-Roos Community Facilities Act of 1982
- Permanent road divisions formed pursuant to section 1160 of the Streets and Highways Code
- Air pollution control districts or air quality maintenance districts
- Service zones of fire protection districts, mosquito abatement and vector control districts, public cemetery districts,[9] recreation and park districts, and community services districts
- Unified or union high school library districts
- Bridge or highway districts
- Joint highway districts
- Transit or rapid transit districts

---

9. Government Code section 56036 excludes public cemetery districts from LAFCO jurisdiction based on the enactment of the Public Cemetery District Law (Health and Safety Code § 9000 *et seq.*), which specifies the procedures for district formation.

- Metropolitan water districts
- Separation of grade districts

In addition, the enabling statutes for some entities dictate that certain changes of organization are excluded from LAFCO's jurisdiction. *See, e.g.,* Gov't Code § 26550 *et seq.* (formation of geologic hazard abatement districts); *Las Tunas Beach Geologic Hazard Abatement Dist. v. Superior Court,* 38 Cal. App. 4th 1002 (1995) (general provisions of LAFCO law do not apply to the formation of geologic hazard abatement districts, as the law addressing GHADs contains its own more specific formation procedures). The Community Services District law excludes from LAFCO's control the internal zones of community services districts.[10] Gov't Code § 56036.

LAFCO law also encourages the annexation of "islands," since urban service delivery to these islands is very inefficient, if not impossible, and residents generally receive fewer and lower levels of services for which they may pay the same taxes and fees as those in a nearby city. State legislation enacted in 2001 allowed urban islands of less than 75 acres to be annexed without requiring protest proceedings or elections. Gov't Code § 56375.3. The provision has since been expanded to apply to islands of up to 150 acres and has been extended until January 1, 2014.

Procedures for Boundary Changes

LAFCO law sets out detailed procedures for the initiation, processing, and approval or disapproval of boundary change proposals. *See generally* Gov't Code § 56650 *et seq.* In addition to following these procedures, proponents must comply with the local written policies and procedures of the LAFCO reviewing the proposal, as well as the provisions of any relevant enabling statutes. Gov't Code § 56300.

A change of organization or reorganization may be initiated by landowner or registered voter petition (Gov't Code § 56700) or by resolution of application (Gov't Code § 56650) from the legislative body of an affected agency. Gov't Code § 56654. The petitioner or legislative body (as the case may be) must submit an application to the executive officer of the affected LAFCO that contains, at minimum, the following information:

- Petition or resolution of application initiating the proposal
- Description of the proposal
- Map and description of the boundaries of the subject territory
- Names of officers or persons, not to exceed three, to receive copies of the LAFCO report and to be given mailed notice of the hearing
- Any additional data and information pertaining to the proposal required by the executive officer or by any regulation of the commission

  Gov't Code § 56652

In general, proponents should be prepared to take the following steps as part of the application process:

---

10. County Service District law (Gov't Code § 61000 *et seq.*) was recently amended, which has several implications for LAFCO proceedings. *See Community Services District Law Update: CSDs and LAFCO: What's New?* (September 2005), available at www.calafco.org/resources.htm.

(1) Arrange for a presubmittal meeting with the executive officer to discuss the process

(2) Compile information regarding the property site (*e.g.*, map of the affected territory, assessors' parcel numbers, general plan/zoning designations, development plans)

(3) Complete a certified resolution or petition pursuant to Government Code section 56654 or 56700, as applicable

(4) Provide any environmental review documents prepared pursuant to CEQA

(5) Present evidence that a satisfactory property tax exchange agreement is in place[11]

(6) Remit the required processing fees

CEQA = California Environmental Quality Act

If the proposal involves the annexation of territory to a city, there is a prezoning requirement. As a condition of annexation, a city must have prezoned the territory to be annexed or present evidence satisfactory to LAFCO that either the existing development entitlements on the territory to be annexed are vested or that the territory is already at buildout and is consistent with the city's general plan. Gov't Code § 56375(a). Once the territory is annexed, the city may not make any subsequent change to the general plan or the prezoning for the annexed territory for a period of two years after the completion of the annexation, unless it makes a finding at a public hearing that a substantial change has occurred in circumstances that necessitate a departure from the prezoning relied upon in the annexation. Gov't Code § 56375(e).

If the proposal involves the annexation of territory to a city, there is a prezoning requirement.

The executive officer, who is responsible for conducting the day-to-day business of the commission (Gov't Code § 56384), must render a decision on the completeness of the application for a change of organization or reorganization within 30 days of receipt, and must determine the status of CEQA review. Gov't Code § 56658(d).

Immediately after receiving the application to initiate boundary change proceedings (and prior to issuing a certificate of filing), the executive officer must provide mailed notice to each interested and affected agency and all landowners within 300 feet of the subject territory. Gov't Code § 56157, 56658(b). Once the application is deemed complete, the executive officer must immediately issue a certificate of filing to the applicant. Gov't Code § 56658(g). If the application is determined to be incomplete, the executive officer must immediately inform the applicant in writing of the additional information or supplemental documents that are required before the proposal can be heard before the commission. Gov't Code § 56658(h). If the executive officer fails to make a completeness determination within 30 days, and the appropriate fees have been paid, an application is automatically deemed accepted for filing. Gov't Code § 56658(f). Following issuance of the certificate of filing, the executive officer must set the LAFCO hearing within 90 days of the issuance of the certificate of filing, or the date on

Immediately after receiving the application to initiate boundary change proceedings (and prior to issuing a certificate of filing), the executive officer must provide mailed notice to each interested and affected agency.

---

11. *See* Revenue and Taxation Code sections 99 and 99.1 regarding the requirement of a satisfactory property tax exchange. Note that master property tax agreements may be applicable or separate property tax exchange resolutions may be required. The mandatory process for negotiating property tax sharing agreements between a county and city in the event of an annexation of unincorporated land is scheduled to sunset in 2010. *See also* Gov't Code §§ 56810 (determination), 56811 (formation of district), 56812 (incorporation of city), and 56815 (revenue neutrality).

CURTIN'S CALIFORNIA LAND USE AND PLANNING LAW

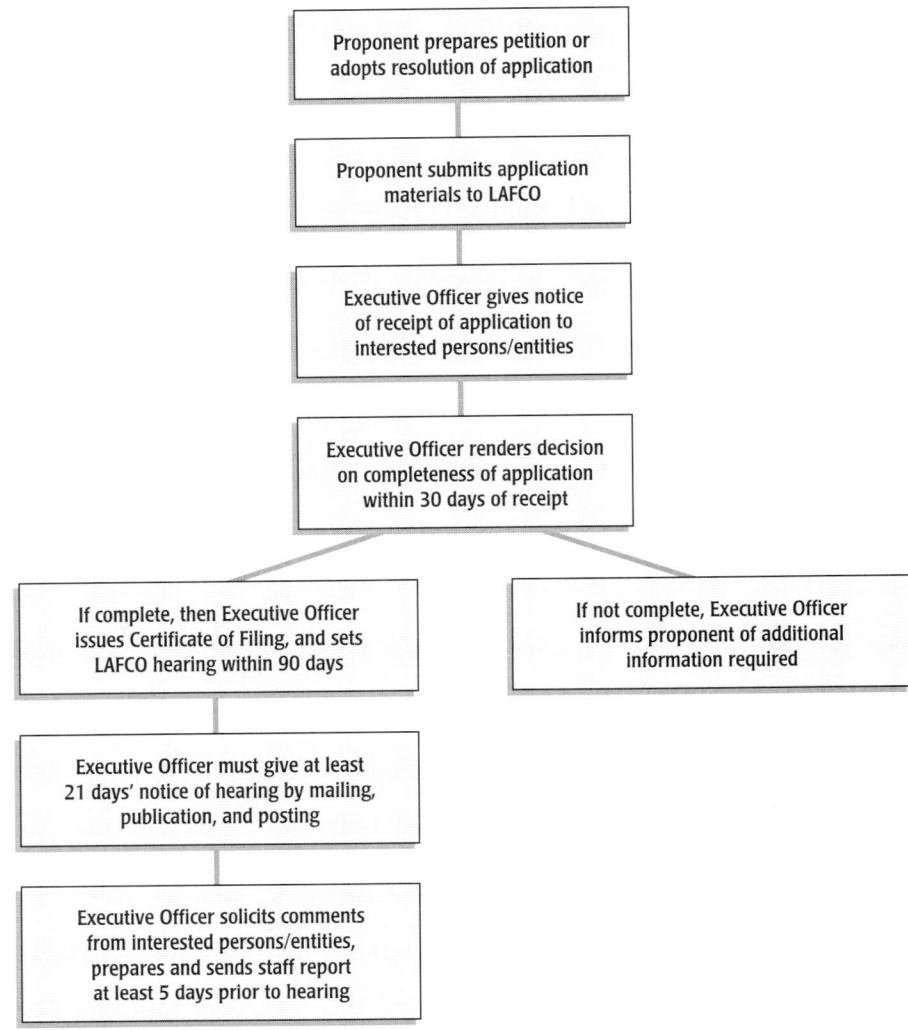

**Figure G
LAFCO Proceedings**

After reviewing the completed application, public or other agency comments, and other relevant information, the executive officer must prepare a staff report, including recommendations, on the application.

which the application was deemed accepted, whichever is earlier. Gov't Code § 56658(i). Except as provided in Government Code section 56662 and 56663, notice of the hearing must be given at least 21 days prior to the hearing by mailing, publication, and posting.[12] LAFCO may continue a hearing up to 70 days from the date on which it is noticed. Gov't Code § 56666(a).

After reviewing the completed application, public or other agency comments, and other relevant information, the executive officer must prepare a staff report, including recommendations, on the application. The staff report must be completed not less than five days before the hearing, and copies must be furnished to each individual designated in the application, each affected local agency[13] requesting a report, each agency whose boundaries or sphere of influence would be changed, the executive officer of another affected county when a district is or will be located in that other county, and each affected city. Gov't Code § 56665.

---

12. In certain limited circumstances, LAFCOs may make determinations without notice and a hearing. Gov't Code §§ 56662, 56663.
13. LAFCO law defines an "affected local agency" as any local agency which contains, or would contain, or whose sphere of influence contains, any territory within any proposal or study to be reviewed by the commission.

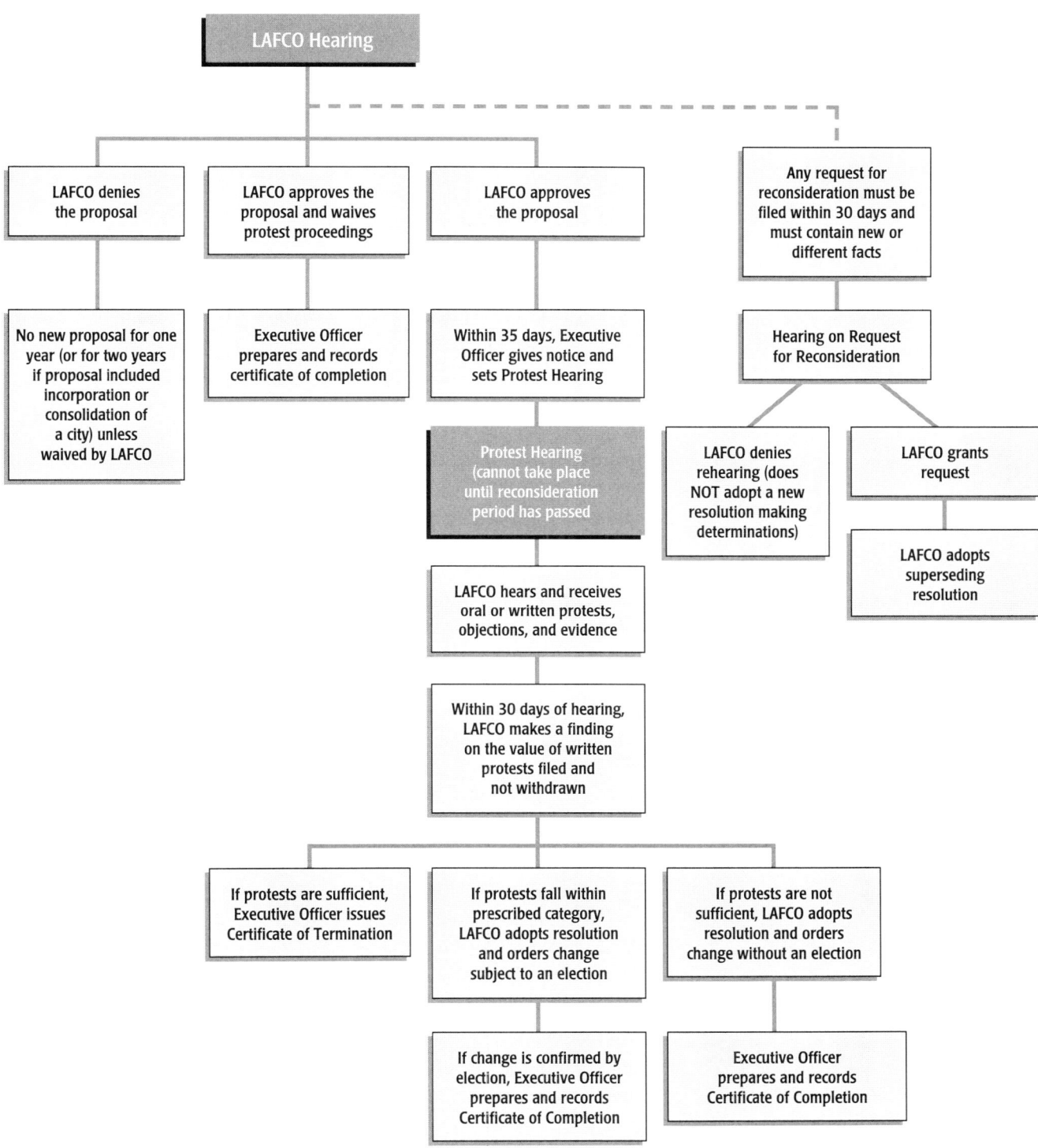

Under certain circumstances, annexation proceedings may be terminated prior to the hearing. Pursuant to Government Code section 56857, any special district to which annexation of territory is proposed may adopt and transmit to the commission a resolution requesting termination of the proceedings. This resolution is subject to judicial review prior to the Commission's termination of proceedings. Gov't Code § 56857(b). If the commission timely receives a resolution requesting termination, but has not received notice that judicial review of the resolution is being sought, the commission must terminate the proceedings no sooner than 30 days from receipt of the resolution. Gov't Code § 56857(c). *See also* Gov't Code § 56751 (a city from which detachment of territory is proposed may adopt and transmit to the commission a resolution requesting termination of the city detachment proceedings).

Factors LAFCOs Must Consider When Reviewing a Boundary Change Proposal

Under Government Code section 56668, LAFCOs must consider the following factors when reviewing a proposal:

- Population and population density; land area and land use; per capita assessed valuation; topography, natural boundaries, and drainage basins; proximity to other populated areas; and the likelihood of significant growth in the area and in adjacent incorporated and unincorporated areas during the next ten years
- The need for organized community services; the present cost and adequacy of governmental services and controls in the area; probable future needs for those services and controls; probable effect of the proposed incorporation, formation, annexation, or exclusion and of alternative courses of action on the cost and adequacy of services and controls in the area and adjacent areas
- The effect of the proposed action and of alternative actions on adjacent areas, on mutual social and economic interests, and on the local government structure of the county
- The conformity of both the proposal and its anticipated effects with both the adopted commission policies on providing planned, orderly, efficient patterns of urban development, and the policies and priorities set forth in Government Code section 56377
- The effect of the proposal on maintaining the physical and economic integrity of agricultural lands, as defined by Government Code section 56016
- The definiteness and certainty of the boundaries of the territory, the nonconformance of proposed boundaries with lines of assessment or ownership, the creation of islands or corridors of unincorporated territory, and other similar matters affecting the proposed boundaries
- Consistency with city or county general and specific plans
- The sphere of influence of any local agency that may be applicable to the proposal being reviewed
- The comments of any affected local agency or other public agency
- The ability of the newly formed or receiving entity to provide the services that are the subject of the application to the area, including the sufficiency of revenues for those services following the proposed boundary change
- Timely availability of water supplies adequate for projected needs as specified in Government Code section 65352.5
- The extent to which the proposal will affect a city or cities and the county in achieving their respective fair shares of the regional housing needs, as

Table 3. LAFCO Protest Proceedings—Effect of Protests

Most changes of organization or reorganization proceed in a three-step fashion: (1) application, (2) LAFCO decision, and (3) protest proceedings. The purpose of protest proceedings (also known as conducting authority proceedings) is to allow landowners or voters to have a say in whether the changes or organization or reorganization will proceed. The conducting authority—LAFCO—holds a hearing to receive protests. The number of protests determine whether LAFCO must terminate proceedings, approve the change, or approve the change subject to an election. This chart details what number of protests trigger which actions.

Registered-Voter Districts[1] or Cities Where the Only Changes of Organization or Reorganization Consist of Annexations, Detachments, or Formation of County Service Areas[2]

	Inhabited	Uninhabited
Who May Protest	Any owner of land within the territory, or any registered voter residing within the territory may protest. Gov't Code § 57026(g)	Any owner of land within the territory may protest. Gov't Code § 57026(h)
Actions That Require Termination of Proceedings	Majority protest by 50% of the voters residing in the territory. Gov't Code §§ 57075(a)(1), 57078(b)	Majority protest by landowners owning 50% of the assessed value of the land within the territory. Gov't Code §§ 57075(b)(1), 57078(a)
Actions That Require Approval of Change Subject to Election	Election of voters residing in the affected territory if written protests from either: 25% but < 50% of registered voters residing within affected territory OR 25% of the number of owners of land who also own at least 25% of the assessed value of land within the affected territory. Gov't Code § 57075(a)(2)	Not provided for
Actions That Require Approval of Change Without Election	Protests from: < 25% of registered voters OR < 25% of the number of owners of land owning AND < 25% of the assessed value of the land within the affected territory. Gov't Code § 57075(a)(3)	Protests from owners of land who own < 50% of the total assessed value of the land within the affected territory. Gov't Code § 57075(b)(2)

Landowner-Voter Districts[3] Where the Only Changes of Organization or Reorganization Consist of Annexations and Detachments

Who May Protest	The provisions of Government Code sections 57026(g) and (h) are written to apply to any protest hearing. These discuss the ability of registered voters and landowners to protest in inhabited territory, and only landowners to protest in uninhabited territory. However, the provisions specifically related to protests in landowner-voter districts, noted below, do not distinguish between inhabited and uninhabited territory, and indicate that only those who hold voting power are entitled to protest.
Actions That Require Termination of Proceedings	Majority protest by 50% of the voters entitled to vote as a result of owning land within the district. (Note that the reference is to the district, not just the affected territory.) Gov't Code §§ 57076(a), 57078(c)
Actions That Require Approval of Change Subject to Election	Election within affected territory if protests from: 25% of the number of owners of land who also own 25% of the assessed value of land within the territory OR 25% of the voting power of landowner voters entitled to vote as a result of owning property within the territory. Gov't Code § 57076(b)
Actions That Require Approval of Change Without Election	Protests from < 25% of the number of owners of land who own < 25% of the assessed value of land within the affected territory. Gov't Code § 57076(c)

1. Registered-voter district means a district whose principal act provides that registered voters residing within the district are entitled to vote for the election of district officers, incurring of bonded indebtedness, or any other district matter. Gov't Code § 56072.
2. Does not include inhabited territory that is proposed to be annexed to a city with more than 100,000 residents and that is located in a county with a population of more than 4 million. Gov't Code § 57075.5.
3. Landowner-voter district means a district whose principal act provides that owners of land within the district are entitled to vote upon the election of district officers, the incurring of bonded indebtedness, or any other district matter. Gov't Code § 56050.

determined by the appropriate council of governments consistent with Housing Element law[13]

- Any information or comments from landowners, voters or residents of the affected territory[14]
- Any information relating to existing land use designations
- The extent to which the proposal will promote environmental justice; as used in this subdivision, "environmental justice" means the fair treatment of people of all races, cultures, and incomes with respect to the location of public facilities and the provision of public services[15]

When considering the above factors, LAFCOs must evaluate proposals with the purposes of the Cortese-Knox-Hertzberg Act in mind. *McBail & Co. v. Solano LAFCO*, 62 Cal. App. 4th at 1227–29; *Simi Valley Recreation and Park Dist. v. LAFCO*, 51 Cal. App. 3d at 668.

Within 35 days of the completion of the hearing, LAFCOs must adopt a resolution making determinations approving or disapproving the proposal. With respect to boundary change decisions, formal written findings of fact are not required. *City of Santa Cruz v. LAFCO*, 76 Cal. App. 3d at 387. To enable a court to scrutinize the substantiality of the evidence supporting the agency's decision, however, the record of the proceedings must adequately reflect the reason for the decision. *McBail & Co. v. Solano LAFCO*, 62 Cal. App. 4th at 1230. LAFCOs have express authority to impose certain conditions specified by statute when approving a change of organization or reorganization. Gov't Code § 56886. *See, e.g.*, AG Opinion, 89 Ops. Cal. Atty. Gen. 173 (2006 (LAFCOs may condition approval of the incorporation of a city upon voters within the proposed city approving a general tax, and may do so by a majority vote). However, these conditions may not directly regulate land use. Gov't Code § 56375(a)(3). If denied, no new proposal can be made for one year unless this restriction is waived by LAFCO. Gov't Code § 56884. If the proposal included incorporation or consolidation of a city, no new proposal can be made for two years unless this restriction is waived by the commission. Gov't Code § 57090.

So long as the commission members exercise their independent judgment on behalf of the public in making determinations on boundary change proposals, the resulting LAFCO action is difficult to challenge.

So long as the commission members exercise their independent judgment on behalf of the public in making determinations on boundary change proposals, the resulting LAFCO action may be difficult to attack.

However, if LAFCOs fail to comply with their statutory mandate, their decisions may be challenged in court. Gov't Code § 56107 (recognizing the judiciary's authority to independently review a LAFCO decision). In any action or proceeding to attack a LAFCO decision, judicial review extends only to whether there was fraud or a prejudicial abuse of discretion. *Id. See also Resource Defense Fund v. LAFCO*, 191 Cal. App. 3d 886, 890 (1987); *City of Santa Cruz v. LAFCO*, 76 Cal. App. 3d at 391. Prejudicial abuse of discretion is established if the court finds that LAFCO's decision was not supported by substantial evidence in light

---

13. This requirement took effect January 1, 2004. Previously, the statute required the commission to consider only the extent to which the proposal would assist the receiving entity in achieving its fair share of the regional housing needs.
14. This factor was modified to include voters and residents of the affected territory by the passage of SB 162, to become effective January 1, 2008.
15. This factor was included by the passage of SB 162, to become effective January 1, 2008.

of the whole record. Gov't Code § 56107. *See also City of Agoura Hills v. LAFCO*, 198 Cal. App. 3d at 489; *Simi Valley Recreation and Park Dist. v. LAFCO*, 51 Cal. App. 3d at 686; *City of Livermore v. LAFCO*, 184 Cal. App. 3d 531, 540 (1986).

The court's role is to ensure that LAFCOs adequately consider all relevant factors and demonstrated a rational connection between these factors, the choice made, and the purposes of the enabling statute. *McBail & Co. v. Solano LAFCO*, 62 Cal. App. 4th at 1228. *See also Ridgecrest Charter School v. Sierra Sands Unified School Dist.*, 130 Cal. App. 4th 986, 1006–07 (2005). The petitioner would have the affirmative burden to establish this is not the case. *CEQUEL III Comm. v. LAFCO*, 149 Cal. App. 4th 310, 329 (2007).

If, at the time the challenge is brought, the reorganization is not "complete," some case law suggests that the LAFCO decision is reviewable by ordinary mandamus.[16] *McBail & Co. v. Solano LAFCO*, 62 Cal. App. 4th at 1227. *See also Bozung v. LAFCO*, 13 Cal. 3d 263, 271 (1975); *Hills for Everyone v. LAFCO*, 105 Cal. App. 3d 461, 466 (1980); *Norlund v. Thorpe*, 34 Cal. App. 3d 672, 676 (1973); *Los Angeles County v. City Council of City of Lawndale*, 202 Cal. App. 2d 20, 26 (1962); *Cothran v. Town Council of Los Gatos*, 209 Cal. App. 2d 647, 650 (1962); *City of Campbell v. Mosk*, 197 Cal. App. 2d 640, 645 (1961); *Hazelton v. City of San Diego*, 183 Cal. App. 2d 131, 135 (1960); *Jefferson Union School Dist. of Santa Clara City v. City Council of City of Sunnyvale*, 129 Cal. App. 2d 264, 267–68 (1954); *American Distilling Co. v. City Council of City of Sausalito*, 34 Cal. 2d 660, 667 (1950). *But see CEQUEL III Communications I, LLC v. Nevada City LAFCO*, 149 Cal. App. 4th at 316 (because LAFCO's approval was not complete until after the certification of completion was issued, a legal challenge filed immediately after the adoption of the resolution and before LAFCO's issuance of a certificate of compliance would have been premature).

If, at the time the challenge is brought, the reorganization is not complete, some case law suggests that the LAFCO decision is reviewable by ordinary mandamus.

LAFCO law requires that any completed boundary change or sphere of influence decision be challenged by a validation action pursuant to Code of Civil Procedure section 860 *et seq.*, which must be brought within 60 days. Gov't Code § 56103. *See also Hills for Everyone v. LAFCO*, 105 Cal. App. 3d 461, 467 (1980); *Environmental Coalition of Orange County, Inc. v. LAFCO of Orange County*, 110 Cal. App. 3d 164, 170 (1980); *City of Campbell v. Mosk*, 197 Cal. App. 2d at 645. *See also Crowl v. Bd. of Trustees of City of Southgate*, 292 P. 985, 215–16 (1930); *Coe v. City of Los Angeles*, 183 P. 822, 480–81 (1919). Some case law indicates this is generally true even if there are allegations that the boundary change is only complete because of a failure to adhere to legal requirements. *Coe v. City of Los Angeles*, 183 P. 822 at 481. *But see City of Anaheim v. City of Fullerton*, 102 Cal. App. 2d 395, 401 (1951) (since the annexation was only "complete" because of "subterfuge and evasion," a validation action was not required based on court's conclusion that the city had neither an actual nor de facto exercise of dominion over the annexed land).

LAFCO law requires that any completed boundary change or sphere of influence decision be challenged by a validation action pursuant to Code of Civil Procedure section 860 et seq., which must be brought within 60 days.

Important policy considerations underlie the validation requirement. A uniform procedure for prompt resolution of the validity of a completed annexation by an *in rem* action is necessary in order to settle any questions respecting the city's jurisdiction over the annexed territory, including any uncertainties

---

16. Pursuant to Government Code section 56102, the reorganization shall be deemed complete and in existence upon execution by the Executive Officer of the certificate of completion.

regarding the applicable land use regulations, or the city's responsibilities to provide police, fire, and other municipal services to the area. The procedure prescribed by the validating statute assures due process notice to all interested persons and settles the validity of the annexation once and for all by a single lawsuit. *Hills For Everyone v. LAFCO*, 105 Cal. App. 3d at 467–68. *See also Katz v. Campbell Union High School Dist.*, 144 Cal. App. 4th 1024, 1028 (2006); *Embarcadero Mun. Improvement Dist. v. City of Santa Barbara*, 88 Cal. App. 4th 781, 789 (2001); *Friedland v. City of Long Beach*, 62 Cal. App. 4th 835, 844 (1998).

Reconsideration Hearing

After LAFCO adopts a resolution approving, modifying, or denying a proposal determining a boundary change, the executive officer is required to send the resolution to the proponents and to each affected agency whose boundaries will be changed by the proposal. Gov't Code § 56882. Any person or affected agency may file a written request with the executive officer requesting amendments to or reconsideration of the resolution. The request must state the specific modification to the resolution being requested, and what new or different facts exist that could not have been presented previously, or what applicable new law is claimed to warrant the requested reconsideration. Gov't Code § 56895(a). The request must be filed within 30 days after adoption of the resolution by the Commission. Gov't Code § 56895(b).

Upon receipt by the executive officer of a timely request for reconsideration, the executive officer shall place the request for reconsideration on the agenda of the Commission's next meeting for which proper notice can be given. The time to file an action, including, without limitation, an action pursuant to CEQA, shall be tolled during the time the Commission takes to act on the reconsideration request. Gov't Code § 56895(d). The executive officer must give notice of the Commission's hearing on the reconsideration request in the same manner as for the original proposal and also may give notice in any other manner that he or she deems necessary or desirable. Gov't Code § 56895(e).

At the reconsideration hearing, the Commission must consider the request and receive any oral or written testimony. The Commission's consideration of the request may be continued from time to time, but such continuances cannot exceed 35 days from the hearing date first specified in the notice. The person or agency that filed the request for reconsideration may withdraw the request at any time prior to the conclusion of the Commissioners' consideration. Gov't Code § 56895(f).

At the conclusion of its consideration, the Commission may approve or disapprove the requested modifications to its resolution, with or without amendment, wholly, partially, or conditionally. If it disapproves the request to modify its resolution, the Commission shall not adopt a new resolution making determinations. If it approves the request, with or without amendment, the Commission shall adopt a new resolution that supersedes the previous resolution. Gov't Code § 56895(g). The determinations of the Commission are final and conclusive, and no person or agency shall make any further request for the same change or a substantially similar change, as determined by the commission. Gov't Code § 56895(h). Since seeking reconsideration is permissive only,

After LAFCO adopts a resolution approving, modifying, or denying a proposal determining a boundary change, the executive officer is required to send the resolution to the proponents and to each affected agency whose boundaries will be changed by the proposal.

pursuing reconsideration of a LAFCO decision is not required for purposes of exhaustion. *Sierra Club v. LAFCO*, 21 Cal. 4th 489 (1999).

Protest Proceedings

After a LAFCO adopts a resolution approving, denying, or modifying a proposed boundary change, it must conduct protest proceedings (except for certain changes of reorganization pursuant to Government Code § 57077), unless the proceedings have been waived pursuant to Government Code sections 56663 and 57002.[17] Gov't Code § 57000. The purpose of the protest hearing is to provide a forum in which registered voters and property owners (if the territory is inhabited[18]) or property owners (if the territory is uninhabited) can formally voice their approval or opposition for the particular change of organization or reorganization. The executive officer must set the proposal for hearing and give proper notice within 35 days of the commission's adoption of its resolution determinations. This hearing shall not be held, however, prior to the expiration of the reconsideration period. Gov't Code § 57002. The date of the protest hearing must be within 60 days, but not less than 21 days, from the date of published notice.[19] Gov't Code § 57002. The hearing may be continued from time to time, not to exceed 60 days from the date specified for the hearing in the notice.

At the protest hearing, the Commission must hear and receive any oral or written protests, objections, or evidence that are presented. Gov't Code §§ 57050, 57051. At any time prior to the conclusion of the protest hearing, any owner of land or any registered voter within the affected territory may file a written protest. Gov't Code § 57051. However, in contrast to the original LAFCO proceedings on the proposal, the commissioners at a protest hearing have no decision-making power. Rather, the action taken at this hearing is based solely on the *number* of written protests received. Written protests may be withdrawn during the protest hearing.

Upon conclusion of the protest hearing, if no written protests have been filed, the Commission must adopt a form of resolution ordering the change of organization or reorganization without an election. However, if written protests have been filed, the commission must, except under certain limited circumstances (see Gov't Code § 57077), make a determination on the value of written protests filed and not withdrawn within 30 days after the conclusion of the hearing.[20] Gov't Code § 57052.

The Commission then must take one of the following actions, depending on the nature of the change of organization or reorganization:

In contrast to the original LAFCO proceedings on the proposal, the commissioners at a protest hearing have no decision-making power.

---

17. These proceedings also are referred to as "conducting authority" proceedings. After approval of a change of organization or reorganization, LAFCOs generally assume the ministerial role of "conducting authority." A conducting authority means the commission of the principal county of the entity proposing a change of organization or reorganization unless another conducting authority is specified by law. Gov't Code § 56029.
18. "Inhabited territory" means territory within which there reside 12 or more registered voters. Gov't Code § 56046.
19. With respect to subsidiary districts, the hearing shall be held not less than 90 days or more than 135 days following notice. Gov't Code § 57002(c).
20. To determine the value of written protests, *see* Gov't Code sections 56707, 56708, and 56710. For an evaluation of the effects of protests, *see* Table 3.

- Issue a Certificate of Termination terminating the LAFCO proceedings[21]
- Adopt a resolution making determinations and ordering the change of organization or reorganization without an election, or
- Adopt a resolution making determinations and ordering the change of organization or reorganization subject to confirmation by the voters

Final Actions, Filings, and Notifications

Immediately after the protest hearing is completed and if the LAFCO proceedings are not terminated, upon satisfaction of any conditions contained in LAFCO's resolution-making determinations that are required to be completed prior to filing a certificate of completion, the executive officer must prepare, execute, and file a certificate of completion. Gov't Code § 57200. The certificate then must be recorded in the county recorder's office within 90 days. Gov't Code § 57203. The change of organization or reorganization is complete on the date the certificate of completion is executed and effective on the dates specified in the resolution. If no effective date is specified in the LAFCO resolution, then the date of recordation of the certificate of completion is the effective date. Gov't Code § 57202. A statement of boundary change or creation will then be issued by the executive officer and filed along with appropriate fees with the State Board of Equalization and the County Assessor. If it is a city change, notice will be provided to the Secretary of State. Gov't Code § 57204. Property tax resolutions, if any, will be forwarded to the County Auditor to enable property tax transfers. The executive officer must provide a notice of completion and effective date to affected agencies and county departments. Gov't Code § 57203. Any other agencies, utilities, and other affected parties also will be notified, as appropriate. Gov't Code § 57204. After receiving notice, affected agencies are required to recognize completion of the jurisdictional changes and implement any amended processes such as the redistribution of property tax.

Processing Multi-County Changes of Organization or Reorganization

More than one LAFCO may be involved in a particular proposal—for example, in the case of a district that is, or as a result of a proposed boundary change would be, located in more than one county. Under these circumstances, exclusive jurisdiction shall be vested in the commission of the principal county. Gov't Code §§ 56123, 56387; *Placer County LAFCO,* 135 Cal. App. 4th at 808. "Principal county" is defined as the county having all or the greater portion of the entire assessed value, as shown on the last equalized assessment roll of the county or counties, of all taxable property within a district or districts for which a change of organization or reorganization is proposed. Gov't Code § 56066.

However, exclusive jurisdiction can be vested in the commission of an affected county other than the commission of the principal county if all of the following occur: (1) the commission of the principal county approves the request

---

21. *But see* Gov't Code § 57077 (law recently revised to eliminate, in certain limited circumstances, the option of issuing a certificate of termination to terminate proceedings for certain changes of organization).

to transfer jurisdiction; (2) the commission of the principal county designates the other affected county to assume jurisdiction; and (3) the commission of the other affected county agrees to assume jurisdiction. Gov't Code §§ 56124, 56388.

Environmental Review

As a public agency, LAFCO must comply with the provisions of the California Environmental Quality Act (Pub. Res. Code § 21000 *et seq.*). As a general proposition, CEQA requires public agencies to assess the potential environmental impacts of their discretionary actions. LAFCO must comply with CEQA when it considers an action that constitutes a "project" as defined by CEQA. As the California Supreme Court noted, "LAFCO must recognize that [LAFCO law] dovetails with CEQA." *Bozung v. Local Agency Formation Comm'n*, 13 Cal. 3d 263, 281–82 (1975). Under *Bozung*, if a LAFCO approval starts in motion a chain of events that ultimately can lead to a development project that will cause environmental impacts, the need for analysis under CEQA is triggered. *Id.* at 278. This is true even though numerous further steps in the approval process will be required prior to any actual development. *Id.* at 282. *See also Pistoresi v. City of Madera*, 138 Cal. App. 3d 284, 287 (1982); *City of Santa Clara v. Local Agency Formation Comm'n*, 139 Cal. App. 3d 923, 930–31 (1983); *People v. Local Agency Formation Comm'n*, 81 Cal. App. 3d 464, 478–79 (1978).

Usually, the city, county, or special district that is involved in the annexation or other boundary change assumes the role of lead agency. This entails the preparation of the required CEQA document, and the certification of any EIR that may be required with respect to the project. For example, prior to annexing territory into a city, that city must prezone the territory (Gov't Code § 56375(a)); this entails the city acting as lead agency for purposes of CEQA.

LAFCO generally will function as a responsible agency, thereby having the opportunity to provide input to the lead agency as to any environmental concerns the commission may have with respect to those project activities that are within LAFCO's area of expertise or which are required to be carried out or approved by LAFCO. CEQA Guidelines § 15096(d).

LAFCOs should be mindful of the potential application of CEQA to changes in LAFCO policies. This is particularly true given the requirement that LAFCOs have policies in place relating to planned urban development patterns and the preservation of open space. Gov't Code § 56300(a). *See also City of Livermore v. Local Agency Formation Comm'n*, 184 Cal. App. 3d 531, 538 (1986) (new guidelines regarding spheres of influence required preparation of an EIR since they would "influence LAFCO decisions about development plans and future growth of cities and service areas").

There are some unsettled questions as to LAFCO's role in the CEQA process. One involves the issue of how amendments or updates to spheres of influence that are not coupled with a change of organization should be treated for purposes of CEQA. *Compare City of Agoura Hills v. LAFCO*, 198 Cal. App. 3d 480, 493 (1988) (such action does not trigger CEQA; "the fact that spheres of influence are recognized as important factors in annexations does not compel the conclusion that they are per se 'projects' subject to [CEQA]") *with* Gov't Code § 56428 (requests for a sphere amendment must be placed on the LAFCO agenda after "compliance" with CEQA).

> *Usually, the city, county, or special district that is involved in the annexation or other boundary change assumes the role of lead agency.*

EIR = Environmental impact report

The question of whether the preparation of a municipal service review triggers CEQA remains unsettled.

The question of whether the preparation of a municipal service review triggers CEQA remains unsettled as well. If a service review is treated as merely "information gathering" or as a "planning and feasibility study," then it is exempt under CEQA. CEQA Guidelines §§ 15262, 15306. However, if it involves something that actually will influence growth patterns or otherwise affect land use in a way that results in environmental impacts, it may trigger application of CEQA. *City of Livermore v. LAFCO*, 184 Cal. App. 3d at 538; and Governor's Office of Planning and Research, Municipal Service Review Guidelines (Aug. 2003).

In the event of a CEQA challenge of a completed boundary change or sphere decision, the validation rule discussed above still applies. For example, in *Hills for Everyone*, the petitioner argued the case should not be dismissed for missing the 60-day statute of limitations period under validation actions because the challenge was grounded in CEQA claims. The court rejected this argument, stating:

> Although grounded on alleged violations of CEQA, petitioner's action is one seeking to invalidate a completed municipal annexation; it is not just an action to review and set aside LAFCO approval of a proposed annexation. Petitioner should have proceeded under the validating statute and its action was subject to dismissal for failure to do so.

Hills for Everyone v. LAFCO, 105 Cal. App. 3d at 468

For a more detailed discussion on the requirements regarding the environmental review process, see chapter 6 (CEQA).

17

Rights of the Regulated and of the Citizens

In General

Property owners are entitled to constitutional due process and equal protection when a city regulates projects through a general plan amendment, specific plan adoption, zoning or subdivision approval, or other similar regulation. Affected citizens also are entitled to have their rights protected. A city must act reasonably in exercising its police power. When acting in its adjudicatory capacity in granting use permits, variances, or subdivisions, a city must ensure that the property owner and affected citizens each receive adequate notice of all hearings, and that the required findings are made regarding the particular decision. For a discussion on damages resulting from a city's violation of an individual's rights to due process and equal protection, *see* chapter 12 (Takings).

Property owners are entitled to constitutional due process and equal protection when a city regulates projects through a general plan amendment, specific plan adoption, zoning or subdivision approval, or other similar regulation.

Citizens also enjoy certain statutory rights relating to the regular business of their local governments. The Ralph M. Brown Act requires that, with certain exceptions, meetings of city bodies be open and public. The Permit Streamlining Act is designed to ensure timely consideration by the city of many types of applications relating to development. These statutes are discussed later in this chapter.

Notice and Hearing[1]

As a general rule, the procedural due process requirements of "notice and opportunity for a hearing" before governmental deprivation of a significant property interest only apply in adjudicatory hearings, and not in the adoption of general legislation. *See Horn v. County of Ventura*, 24 Cal. 3d 605, 612 (1979) (neighbors entitled to due process notice of hearing on subdivision map application); *see also Kennedy v. City of Hayward*, 105 Cal. App. 3d 953, 961–62 (1980). However, the notice-and-opportunity-for-a-hearing requirement extends to certain legislative acts, such as rezonings, because of specific state statutory provisions. Thus, it is imperative that a city notify all city and non-city residents if they fall within the distance requirements of the notice provisions or if,

---

1. *See Public Notice and Land Use Planning: An Overview of the Statutory Requirements for Public Notice, Circulation and Review* (Governor's Office of Planning and Research, 1998). For a good discussion on how public agencies can maximize the effectiveness of public hearings, *see Getting the Most Out of Public Hearings: Ideas to Improve Public Involvement*, Institute for Local Government (2005).

pursuant to *Horn*, the decision will affect their property rights. *See Scott v. City of Indian Wells*, 6 Cal. 3d 541, 549 (1972) (neighbors entitled to due process notice of hearing on conditional use permit application).

The notice given must adequately describe what action is being requested, because the courts view inadequate notice as equivalent to providing no notice at all. *See Drum v. Fresno County Dep't of Pub. Works*, 144 Cal. App. 3d 777, 782 (1983) (notice inadequate because it did not show that a variance request for a garage included a second-story dwelling unit). Notice need not be given by mail unless a statute or ordinance so requires; publication and posting can be constitutionally adequate. *See Hayssen v. Board of Zoning Adjustments*, 171 Cal. App. 3d 400, 405 (1985). If a citizen, developer, or property owner would like to ensure actual notice of a land use matter, he or she should submit a request in writing to the city asking to receive copies of all planning commission and city council notices and agendas. Actual notice of a hearing satisfies due process. *See Benson v. California Coastal Commission*, 139 Cal. App. 4th 348, 354 (2006). In *Benson*, a developer received actual notice of a Coastal Commission appeal hearing regarding his previously approved project, but failed to attend after being told by Commission staff that no substantive action was likely to be taken. In fact, the Commission found that the appeal raised substantive issues. Benson challenged the Commission's finding on the ground that he was denied due process because of inadequate notice. The court held that the written notice given was adequate and Benson could not reasonably rely on staff recommendations and comments. *Id.* at 355. The court noted that predictions and suggestions from staff could be misleading, therefore a party should take such advice with caution.

Failure to receive notice that is properly given may not invalidate an action. *See Newberry Springs Water Ass'n v. County of San Bernardino*, 150 Cal. App. 3d 740, 745–46 (1984). In *Newberry Springs*, the court referred to the uncodified section 4 of Chapter 131 of the 1980 Statutes, which reads in part:

> [T]he Legislature... affirm[s] the general principle that statutory requirements for public notice are fulfilled if the public agency responsible for giving the notice makes a good faith effort to follow the procedures prescribed by law for giving the notice.

Id. at 746

Failure to receive notice can be a factor, however, in a court's decision that a permit application must be reheard because the applicant was denied a fair hearing. *See Clark v. City of Hermosa Beach*, 48 Cal. App. 4th 1152, 1173 (1996). In *Hermosa Beach*, the court found that the applicants had been denied a fair hearing in several respects. First, the city raised issues and concerns for the first time after the public portion of a hearing was closed; the applicants had not received notice of these issues and were not permitted to address them by having the hearing reopened. Second, the city exhibited unfair bias against the project by unsuccessfully attempting to impose a moratorium against construction. Third, a council member with a common law conflict of interest voted on the project. Together, these defects amounted to a denial of a fair hearing. The court's remedy was to have the city council rehear the matter and provide the applicants with a fair hearing. *Id.* at 1169.

In another decision, a court held that the cumulative procedural errors committed by a city and its city council impaired the adequacy of the appeal hearing on the developers' subdivision, thereby violating their due process rights. *See Cohan v. City of Thousand Oaks*, 30 Cal. App. 4th 547, 559–60 (1994). The court in *Cohan* vacated the city council's decision without ordering that further hearings be held. *Id.* at 562. Some of the errors involved the council itself appealing the planning commission's decision without complying with the Brown Act and the local ordinance, failure to inform the developers of the grounds for the appeal, and unfairly placing the burden on the developers "to convince the council of the correctness of the planning commission's decision." The court held that "this stands due process on its head." *Id.* at 560. In ruling for the developer, the court concluded:

> As real estate developers, appellants [developers] took the risk that their proposed project may not be approved or, if approved, may be severely conditioned. They may even incur the risk of a seemingly unfair decision. However, they should not be subjected to the blatant disregard of their due process rights. The Council simply submitted to the roar of the crowd.

Id.

Cohan was distinguished in *BreakZone Billiards v. City of Torrance*, 81 Cal. App. 4th 1205 (2000). The issue in *BreakZone Billiards* was whether a city council member's notice to appeal the approval of a conditional use permit satisfied the city's notice requirements. The court found that, unlike the ordinance in *Cohan*, the applicable ordinance prescribed only that there be a written statement of appeal stating the grounds for the appeal, with which the city council member complied. *Id.* at 1223. Further, the notice of appeal appropriately informed the applicant that it had the burden of establishing to the satisfaction of a majority of the city council that the application should be approved. *Id.* at 1222. Finally, unlike the cumulative effect of procedural errors in *Cohan*, there were no individual procedural errors in *BreakZone Billiards* resulting in a violation of the applicant's procedural and substantive due process rights. *Id.* at 1243. For a discussion of what constitutes a "fair hearing," *see* chapter 21 (Land Use Litigation).

The One Who Decides Must Hear

In a landmark administrative law case, Chief Justice Hughes of the United States Supreme Court made the now oft-quoted statement: "The one who decides must hear." *Morgan v. United States*, 298 U.S. 468, 481 (1936). A frequent problem arises in land use law concerning the legality or propriety of a planning commissioner or a council member voting on a matter that was required to be heard at a prior public hearing at which that member was absent.

California courts have found that a public hearing required to be held by law contemplates a fair hearing at which evidence may be presented. A commentator notes that a proper hearing allows interested parties an opportunity to present evidence. *See* Charles S. Rhyne, *The Law of Local Government Operations*, page 764 (1980). The members of the decision-making body therefore must be present or, if absent, must familiarize themselves with the record before voting. *Id.* at 764–65.

For further discussion on information that local officials may consider in the decision-making process, *see* chapter 4 (Zoning).

Therefore, it is good practice to follow these procedures: If a commissioner or council member is to vote on a matter to be heard at a public hearing, then that individual should not only be present during the public hearing, but should be sure to remain attentive throughout. If an individual is absent and the public hearing has been closed and continued for a decision to another date, or the hearing continued to another date, the absent member should review the tape of the earlier part of the public hearing, read all of the documents involved, examine all aspects of the issue presented, and state on the record that such review and examination was completed. Under these circumstances, the member may vote. *See Old Santa Barbara Pier Co. v. State of California*, 71 Cal. App. 3d 250, 255–56 (1977); Charles S. Rhyne, *The Law of Local Government Operations*, page 765.

Maintaining Separation Between Prosecutorial and Adjudicatory Function

Two decisions reflect a concern among courts that cities establish and maintain adequate separation between prosecutorial and adjudicatory functions in administrative hearings. *See Quintero v. City of Santa Ana*, 114 Cal. App. 4th 810, 816 (2003); *Nightlife Partners, Ltd. v. City of Beverly Hills*, 108 Cal. App. 4th 81, 92 (2002).[2]

In Nightlife Partners, *the plaintiff claimed the city had blurred the lines between prosecutorial and adjudicatory functions and had thereby violated its due process rights.*

In *Nightlife Partners*, the plaintiff claimed the city had blurred the lines between prosecutorial and adjudicatory functions and had thereby violated its due process rights. 108 Cal. App. 4th at 92. Nightlife Partners had submitted an application for renewal of a use permit. On the advice of an assistant city attorney that the application was incomplete, the city refused to renew the permit. At the administrative hearing on the plaintiff's appeal from that decision, the hearing officer announced that the same assistant city attorney would be "advising [him] and assisting [him] as necessary in these proceedings." *Id.* at 85.

In ordering that Nightlife Partners be granted a new hearing, the court held that there had been an "objectionable overlapping of the role of advocate and decision-maker" where the attorney had both advocated the City's position on the denial of the permit and then advised the decisionmaker at the administrative hearing relating to that permit denial. *Id.* at 94.

The court in *Quintero* went a step further than *Nightlife Partners*, holding that due process was violated where a lawyer who had advised the decisionmaker on *other* matters represented the city as an advocate before that decisionmaker. 114 Cal. App. 4th at 817. Quintero, a former detention officer, appealed his termination to the city's personnel board. He claimed that the board's hearing

---

2. For further discussion of the relationship between the roles of advocate and decisionmaker in administrative proceedings, see Michael Jenkins, "How Many Lawyers Does It Take to...? An Analysis of Nightlife and Quintero," *Western City Magazine* (League of California Cities, May 2004) and Manuela Albuquerque, *Procedural Due Process Limitations on the Municipal Lawyer Combining Quasi-Judicial and Prosecutorial or Investigating Functions* (League of California Cities, City Attorney Spring Meeting, May 2004). The City Attorneys Department of the League of California Cities has collected and developed guidelines to assist local officials with issues surrounding separation of prosecutorial and adjudicatory functions. Contact information for the City Attorneys Department is available on the League's website (www.cacities.org; *see also* www.ca-ilg.org).

violated due process because the deputy city attorney who represented the city at the hearing had at times served as a legal advisor to the board on various other matters, including other termination cases as well as the development of new procedural rules for appeals and standards for the adoption of findings. *Id.* at 813.

In granting Quintero's request for a new hearing, the court concluded that, while the deputy city attorney had not acted as both advocate and advisor in Quintero's particular case, the nature and extent of his relationship with the personnel board created the appearance of bias. *Id.* at 814. The court noted that dual representation is not barred so long as there is adequate separation of the two roles and the attorneys performing them. But it held that the totality of the circumstances of the deputy city attorney's relationship with the board created a substantial risk that the board's judgment in Quintero's case was "skewed in favor of the prosecution." *Id.* at 817.

In Quintero, *the court concluded that, while the deputy city attorney had not acted as both advocate and advisor in Quintero's particular case, the nature and extent of his relationship with the personnel board created the appearance of bias.*

Ralph M. Brown Act [3]

The Ralph M. Brown Act (Brown Act) details the various requirements to be followed by local bodies, including city councils and planning commissions, in conducting their meetings.[4] Gov't Code § 54950 *et seq.* The Brown Act states that all meetings of city bodies shall be open and public, and all persons shall be permitted to attend any meeting with certain statutory exceptions, such as meetings for personnel matters and litigation. Gov't Code § 54953. The legislative intent of the Brown Act is contained in Government Code section 54950:

The Ralph M. Brown Act details the various requirements to be followed by local bodies, including city councils and planning commissions, in conducting their meetings.

> In enacting this chapter, the Legislature finds and declares that the public commissions, boards and councils and the other public agencies in this State exist to aid in the conduct of the people's business. It is the intent of the law that their actions be taken openly and that their deliberations be conducted openly.
>
> The people of this State do not yield their sovereignty to the agencies which serve them. The people, in delegating authority, do not give their public servants the right to decide what is good for the people to know and what is not good for them to know. The people insist on remaining informed so that they may retain control over the instruments they have created.

Gov't Code § 54950

The definition of "meeting" includes the following:

- Any congregation of a majority of the members of a legislative body in the same time and place to hear, discuss, or deliberate upon any item that is within the subject matter jurisdiction of the legislative body or the local agency to which it pertains.
- Any use of direct communication, personal intermediaries, or technological devices that is employed by a majority of the members of the legislative

---

3. For further discussion of the Brown Act, *see* League of California Cities, *California Municipal Law Handbook*, pages II-21 to II-50 (2004); Ted Fourkas, *Open and Public III, A User's Guide to the Ralph M. Brown Act* (revised 2003, published by the Open and Public Participants including the League of California Cities); *The Brown Act: Open Meetings for Local Legislative Bodies* (California Attorney General's Office, 2003) (available at http://caag.state.ca.us).

4. A ballot measure approved by voters in November 2004 gives constitutional status to the notion that meetings of public bodies shall be open to public scrutiny. Proposition 59 amended the California Constitution to provide that statutes furthering the people's right of access shall be broadly construed while those limiting the right of access shall be narrowly construed. Cal. Const. art. I, § 3.

body to develop a collective concurrence as to action to be taken on an item by the members of the legislative body.

Gov't Code §§ 54952.2(a), (b)

However, this definition does not impose the requirements of the Brown Act upon any of the following:

- Individual contacts or conversations between a member of a legislative body and any other person.
- The attendance of a majority of the members of a legislative body at a conference or similar gathering open to the public that involves a discussion of issues of general interest to the public or to public agencies of the type represented by the legislative body, provided that a majority of the members do not discuss among themselves, other than as part of the scheduled program, business of a specified nature that is within the subject matter jurisdiction of the local agency. Nothing in this paragraph is intended to allow members of the public free admission to a conference or similar gathering at which the organizers have required other participants or registrants to pay fees or charges as a condition of attendance.
- The attendance of a majority of the members of a legislative body at an open and publicized meeting organized to address a topic of local community concern by a person or organization other than the local agency, provided that a majority of the members do not discuss among themselves, other than as part of the scheduled program, business of a specific nature that is within the subject matter jurisdiction of the legislative body of the local agency.
- The attendance of a majority of the members of a legislative body at an open and noticed meeting of another body of the local agency, or at an open and noticed meeting of a legislative body of another local agency, provided that a majority of the members do not discuss among themselves, other than as part of the scheduled meeting, business of a specific nature that is within the subject matter jurisdiction of the legislative body of the local agency.
- The attendance of a majority of the members at a purely social or ceremonial occasion, provided that a majority of the members do not discuss among themselves business of a specific nature that is within the subject matter jurisdiction of the legislative body of the local agency.
- The attendance of a majority of the members of a legislative body at an open and noticed meeting of a standing committee of that body, provided that the members of the legislative body who are not members of the standing committee attend only as observers.

Gov't Code § 54952.2

As noted above, the Brown Act's definition of "meeting" does not include individual contacts between one member of a legislative body and any other person. However, separate meetings between a member of the public and individual council members do violate the Brown Act if they are used in concert to build consensus between the council members by conveying the opinions of other council members behind closed doors. These meetings, called "seriatim meetings," are identified as a series of closed meetings held between members of a legislative body and members of the public, with the goal of gathering information to be conveyed between respective members of the public body, while ensuring that a quorum of the legislative body is never present at any one meeting. The prohibition is against using intermediaries "to develop a collective concurrence as to action to be taken on an item by the members of the legislative body...." Gov't Code § 54952.2(b). There is no prohibition against individual conversations in which there is no attempt to use such conversations to achieve a collective deliberation between the members.

The Attorney General's office further explained the distinction. It concluded that the Brown Act clearly prohibits seriatim meetings, in which the members of the legislative body are "engaged in '*collective* discussion' and '*collective* acquisition and exchange of facts preliminary to the ultimate decision' albeit they do so in a series of meetings and not in a single meeting." 65 Ops. Cal. Atty. Gen. 63 at 65 (1982), quoting 63 Ops. Cal. Atty. Gen. 820 (1980) (emphasis added). The opinion clarified, however, that there was no intention to preclude individual councilpersons or commissioners from discussing matters of public concern with their constituents, nor to prevent private citizens from approaching and discussing their public business with individual members of the council or commission. Were it otherwise, public agencies effectively would be prohibited from conducting business in an efficient manner; if all communications outside the context of a public meeting were prohibited, then council members would never be permitted even to read correspondence submitted to them on matters of public concern before attending a noticed meeting. *Id. See also Wolfe v. City of Fremont*, 144 Cal. App. 4th 533, 549 (2006) (serial non-public discussions among city council members resulting in collective concurrence on issue prior to public meeting would violate Brown Act).

However, the Brown Act expressly allows a public agency to meet in closed session on a variety of topics, including those concerning personnel. Gov't Code § 54957(b)(1). The purpose of the personnel exception is to allow free and candid discussions of personnel matters by governmental bodies, and to protect employees from public embarrassment. In *Harron v. Bonilla*, a public official admitted that when speaking with a newspaper reporter about the termination of a district employee he revealed matters discussed in closed session. 125 Cal. App. 4th 738 (2005). Ruling that the comments were not protected under the anti-SLAPP statute, which protects speech in connection with an issue of public interest, the court stated that the comments violated the Brown Act. Contrary to the official's assertion that he had a duty to apprise the public of the reason for the termination, he was forbidden under the Brown Act from disclosing such information discussed in closed session. *Id.*

> *The Brown Act expressly allows a public agency to meet in closed session on a variety of topics, including those concerning personnel.*

The Brown Act also allows public agencies to meet in closed session to discuss pending litigation. Gov't Code § 54956.9. This exception from the general open meeting rule is designed to ensure that the local agency's position in the litigation not be prejudiced. However, this exception is not unlimited. The court in *Trancas v. Property Owners Association* invalidated a settlement agreement adopted in a closed meeting held pursuant to the litigation exception, because the agreement, which in essence granted a zoning variance, violated the Brown Act since a zoning variance requires a public hearing. 138 Cal. App. 4th 172, 186 (2006). The court concluded:

> *The Brown Act also allows public agencies to meet in closed session to discuss pending litigation. However, this exception is not unlimited.*

> The statutory exemption of discussions with counsel remains plenary: under section 54956.9, governing bodies may discuss with their counsel, in closed

session, any settlement proposals or terms they deem worthy of consideration. And they generally may agree to such terms and settlements in closed session. What they may not do is decide upon or adopt in closed session a settlement that accomplishes or provides for action for which a public hearing is required by law, without such a hearing.

Id. at 187

The Brown Act's requirements apply to "legislative bodies," which is defined to include the governing body of a local agency as well as decisionmaking or advisory commissions, committees, boards, or other bodies of the agency. Gov't Code §§ 54952(a), (b). It also includes a board, commission, committee, or other multimember body that governs a private corporation, limited liability company, or other entity that either:

- Is created by the elected legislative body to exercise authority delegated by the governing body, or
- "Receives funds from a local agency and the membership of whose governing body includes a member of the legislative body of the local agency appointed to that governing body as a full voting member by the legislative body of the local agency."[5]

Gov't Code § 54952(c)(1)

A member who attends a meeting during which action is taken in violation of the Brown Act, with wrongful intent to deprive the public of information to which it is entitled under the Brown Act, is guilty of a misdemeanor. Gov't Code § 54959. Further, a court can enjoin a city from violating the Brown Act, and can declare null and void an action taken in violation of the Brown Act. Gov't Code §§ 54960, 54960.1.

Ex Parte Contacts

Due process concerns sometimes arise when a developer or a citizen contacts a planning commissioner or councilmember outside of a public hearing or outside the presence of other interested parties concerning projects that may come before the city. Ex parte contacts during the course of a quasi-judicial proceeding may lead to claims of bias on the part of the public official or violation of an interested party's right to know what evidence is used by the council or commission in reaching its decision.[6]

The problem of ex parte contacts in the land use arena has been largely ignored by the Legislature and California courts.[7] The leading California case on

---

5. For example, where a chamber of commerce is funded in part by a city and the mayor is appointed by the city council to sit on the chamber's board of directors, the chamber would be subject to the Brown Act. Ted Fourkas, *Open and Public III, A User's Guide to the Ralph M. Brown Act* (revised 2003).

6. Only those governmental decisions that are adjudicative or "quasi-judicial" in nature are subject to procedural due process principles. Legislative action is not burdened by such requirements. *See Horn v. County of Ventura*, 24 Cal. 3d 605, 612 (1979).

7. Other states such as Oregon and Washington have enacted legislation regulating ex parte contacts with local officials. *See, e.g.*, Oregon's planning procedure guidelines, Or. Rev. Stat. § 227.180, and Washington's "Appearance of Fairness" Statute, Wash. Rev. Code § 42.36.060. The Idaho Supreme Court addressed this issue in *Idaho Historic Preservation Council, Inc. v. City Council*, 134 Idaho 651 (2000). See also Edward J. Sullivan and Carrie Richter, "Out of the Chaos: Towards a National System of Land-Use Procedures," 34 *Urb. Law.* 449 (2002).

this issue is *City of Fairfield v. Superior Court*, 14 Cal. 3d 768 (1975). In *Fairfield*, the California Supreme Court discussed whether three city councilmembers should be disqualified from voting on a land use permit in a quasi-judicial hearing because of previous spoken opposition during an election campaign. The court stated: "that fact would not disqualify them from voting on the application." *Id.* at 779. Because even quasi-judicial decisions may significantly influence the nature and direction of future economic growth, a councilmember "has not only a right but an obligation to discuss issues of vital concern with his constituents and to state his views on matters of public importance." *Id.* at 780. *See also Todd v. City of Visalia*, 254 Cal. App. 2d 679 (1967); League of California Cities, *California Municipal Law Handbook*, page II-63 (2004).

Local officials are not and cannot be held to the same standards that apply to judges.[8] Councilmembers and planning commissioners have a statutory duty to apprise themselves of all of the facts in any given issue. In addition, local officials dealing with land use issues have much more exposure to the public, particularly in smaller cities.

PRACTICE TIP

Although State law provides little guidance concerning ex parte contacts, local ordinances or other policies may regulate such contacts in greater detail. Project applicants and other interested parties should consult local rules before contacting local officials outside of a public hearing.

Permit Streamlining Act

Protecting California's economy, the health of its citizens, and its environment requires a sophisticated system of development project application, review, and permitting. By adopting the Permit Streamlining Act (Gov't Code § 65920 et seq.), the California Legislature declared that the protection of those interests also involves the "statewide need to ensure clear understanding of the specific requirements which must be met in connection with the approval of development projects and to *expedite* decisions on such projects." Gov't Code § 65921 (emphasis added). The Permit Streamlining Act was adopted to relieve permit applicants from protracted and unjustified governmental delays in processing their applications.

Protecting California's economy, the health of its citizens, and its environment requires a sophisticated system of development project application, review, and permitting.

The Permit Streamlining Act applies to certain local land use decisions and requires a city to follow a standardized process with respect to those decisions. It also requires completion of review and decisions on development applications within strict time limits. Gov't Code § 65943. Pursuant to the Act, failure by a city to approve or disapprove a development project within those time limits may result in the project being "deemed" approved, provided that the prescribed public notice requirements have been met. *Id.* Under the Act, a city is required to compile one or more lists specifying in detail the information needed from a project applicant, and to make such lists available to all applicants and also to anyone else who requests them. Gov't Code § 65940; *see also Bickel*, 16 Cal. 4th at 1046. These lists must be revised so that they are current and accurate at all times. Gov't Code § 65942. In general, revisions may be prospective only, and cannot be applied to applications submitted before they are effective. The lists must indicate the criteria that will be applied in determining

PRACTICE TIP

An application may be deemed complete when a city fails to make a determination on its completeness within 30 days of its submission, but only if "the application includes a statement that it is an application for a development permit." Gov't Code § 65943(a). Therefore, those words should be conspicuously placed on the front of any development application.

---

8. For a good overview of the competing approaches to this issue, *see* 32 *Fed. Prac. & Proc. Judicial Review*, section 8260 (2007); Edward H. Ziegle, 2 *Rathkopf's Law of Zoning and Planning*, sections 32:10–11 (4th ed. September 2007); John W. Witt, "The Problem of Ex Parte Contacts," 3 *Land Use & Env. Forum* 24 (CEB Winter 1994); Daniel J. Curtin, Jr., "Ex Parte Contacts: A Less Restrictive View," 3 *CEB Land Use & Env. Forum* 31 (Winter 1994); *see also* William W. Eigner and Robert L. Wernli, Jr., "Lobbying Guidelines and Rules for Ex Parte Contact," 21 *California Real Prop. J.*, no. 2 (Spring 2003).

whether an application is complete, and the time limits for the review and approval of applications. Gov't Code §§ 65941, 65941.5. *See also Beck Dev. Co. v. Southern Pac. Transp. Co.*, 44 Cal. App. 4th 1160, 1198 (1996).

Submittal of a project application is the first step in the streamlined permitting process. Within 30 calendar days of receiving an application, a city must inform the applicant in writing whether the application is complete and accepted for filing. Gov't Code § 65943. If it finds the application incomplete, the city must point out in detail where the application is deficient and specify the additional information needed. Gov't Code § 65943.

Also, before a city accepts an application as complete for any development project, the applicant must consult certain local lists and submit a signed statement indicating whether the project is located on a site that is included on any such lists. Gov't Code § 65962.5. For example, one of those lists, prepared by the California Integrated Waste Management Board, is of all solid waste disposal facilities from which there is a known migration of hazardous waste. Gov't Code §§ 65962.5(d), (f) (Cortese List). The Secretary for Environmental Protection maintains a statewide list and is responsible for distributing this information to any persons upon request. Gov't Code § 65962.5(e). The form of the Hazardous Waste and Substance Statement is contained in Government Code section 65962.5(f).

In addition, a city must include in the information list for development projects, or in the application form for a building permit, specified requirements concerning compliance with statutes regulating hazardous materials and air pollution, the handling of acutely hazardous materials, and the emission of hazardous air emissions. Gov't Code § 65850.2. This section prohibits a city from finding an application complete, or from approving a development project or a building permit for a project that requires only a building permit, if the project meets specified requirements concerning hazardous materials and emissions, unless the owner or authorized agent complies with certain provisions. It also requires the owner or authorized agent to substantially meet the requirements for submitting a risk management and prevention program if the administering agency makes a specified determination. This section does not apply to applications solely for residential construction. Gov't Code § 65850.2(i).

If the city fails to notify an applicant whether the application is complete, the application is deemed "complete and accepted" 30 days after it was received by the city.

If the application is complete, a city proceeds with the evaluation of the development project. As noted, if the city fails to notify the applicant whether it is complete, the application is deemed "complete and accepted" 30 days after it was received by the city. *See Bickel*, 16 Cal. 4th at 1046; *Orsi v. City Council of Salinas*, 219 Cal. App. 3d 1576, 1584 (1990). Once an application is accepted as complete or is deemed complete, the city cannot ask for new information, although it may require the applicant to clarify or supplement the material provided in the accepted application. Gov't Code § 65944; *Bickel*, 16 Cal. 4th at 1046.

All deadlines under the Permit Streamlining Act begin from the day an application is accepted as complete or is deemed complete. The time that an application is complete or deemed complete is important for other reasons as well. For example, at least three specific laws refer to the completion of an application as a triggering device:

- To address the problem of affordable housing, when a proposed housing development project complies with the applicable general plan, zoning, and development policies in effect at the time the application is determined to be complete, a city cannot disapprove it or approve it at a lower density without making written findings stating that certain specific conditions exist. Gov't Code § 65589.5

- With certain exceptions, a city, when approving or disapproving a tentative subdivision map, can apply only those ordinances, policies, and standards that were in effect at the time the application was determined to be complete. Gov't Code § 66474.2
- When a city approves a vesting tentative map, that approval confers a vested right to proceed with development in substantial compliance with the ordinances, policies, and standards that are in effect at the time the application is complete (much like Government Code section 66474.2). Gov't Code § 66498.1(b)

Subject to certain exceptions, under the Permit Streamlining Act, a city acting as the lead agency for a project for which an EIR is prepared shall approve or disapprove the project within 180 days from the date of the EIR's certification. Gov't Code § 65950(a)(1). Certain residential and mixed-use projects providing no less than 49 percent of their units as affordable housing must be approved or disapproved within 90 days of EIR certification. Gov't Code § 65950(a)(2). A city cannot disapprove a project in order to comply with the Act's time limits. Gov't Code § 65952.2. Also, any disapproval must specify reasons for the disapproval other than the failure to act timely in accordance with the time limits of the Act. *Id.* Under CEQA, a city must complete and certify an EIR within one year. Pub. Res. Code § 21151.5. A project applicant may be entitled to a writ of mandate to enforce this time limit. *See Sunset Drive Corp. v. City of Redlands*, 73 Cal. App. 4th 215, 220 (1999). However, failure to adhere to these time limits does not invalidate subsequent agency action. *See Meridian Ocean Sys., Inc. v. State Lands Comm'n*, 222 Cal. App. 3d 153, 168 (1990). For a detailed discussion of CEQA, *see* chapter 6 (CEQA).

A 60-day time limit is provided when a negative declaration is adopted or if the project is exempt from the CEQA. Gov't Code § 65950. The Permit Streamlining Act provides a one-time-only 90-day extension to these deadlines upon consent of the city and the applicant. Gov't Code § 65957. Legislation enacted in 1998 amended Government Code section 65957 so that no other extension, continuance, or waiver of these time limits by either the applicant or the lead agency is permitted. The Legislature included a declaration that it was aware of *Bickel v. City of Piedmont*, which held that an applicant had a common law right to waive the time limits prescribed by the Permit Streamlining Act, and stated its intent to clarify that the Act "does not provide for the application of the common law doctrine of waiver by either the act's purpose or its statutory language." 1998 Cal. Stat. ch. 283, § 5. *See Eller Media Co. v. City of Los Angeles*, 87 Cal. App. 4th 1217, 1220 (2001) (Permit Streamlining Act time limits do not apply when a city fails to timely complete CEQA review).

If approval or disapproval of a project does not occur within certain time limits after the application is determined or deemed complete, the project shall be deemed approved provided that the prescribed public notice requirements have been met. Gov't Code § 65956; *see also Orsi v. City Council of Salinas*, 219 Cal. App. 3d at 1585. However, the deemed approved or automatic approval provisions

Subject to certain exceptions, under the Permit Streamlining Act, a city acting as the lead agency for a project for which an EIR is prepared shall approve or disapprove the project within 180 days from the date of the EIR's certification.

CEQA = California Environmental Quality Act
EIR = Environmental impact report

do not apply to legislative acts, such as rezonings and general plan amendments. *See Landi v. County of Monterey*, 139 Cal. App. 3d 934, 937 (1983). There is a statutory prohibition against a city's requiring extensions or waivers of the time limits for approval or disapproval. Gov't Code § 65940.5. Further, the time period for an appeal is not included within the prescribed time limits. Gov't Code § 65922.

The Act provides two methods for an applicant to ensure that the public notice requirements for a project to be deemed approved are met: (1) the applicant may use the civil mandamus remedy to compel a city to provide the required public notice (Gov't Code § 65956(a)); or (2) the applicant may provide public notice of the project, if the city fails to do so. Gov't Code § 65956(b). Section 65956(b) specifically states that if the applicant provides public notice, the notice must include the fact that failure of the city to act on the application within 60 days will result in the application being deemed approved.

Although not explicitly set out in the statute, a 2006 court of appeal decision held that a local agency's notice must also state that a failure to act will result in the application being deemed approved. *Mahon v. County of San Mateo*, 139 Cal. App. 4th 812 (2006). Mahon applied for design review and building permits for two small projects. The county determined that each project was exempt from CEQA review, starting the 60-day period for the county to approve or disapprove the projects. Neither the mailed nor the posted notices advised that the permits would be deemed approved if the county failed to act within a specified period. The county failed to approve or disapprove the permit applications within this 60-day deadline, and Mahon sued, arguing that the applications had been deemed approved by the Act.

The court held that, although it was undisputed that the county failed to act within the 60-day deadline, the notice given by the county was not the "public notice required by law" necessary for deemed approval under Gov't Code § 65956(b), in that it did not contain language stating that the permits would be deemed approved if the county failed to act within the 60-day period. *Id.* at 822. The court rejected Mahon's argument that this was only applicable to notices that an applicant must give. The court concluded that "we see no reason why 'public notice required by law' would mean one thing if notice is provided by the agency and another if provided by the applicant." *Id.* Since section 65956(b) requires an applicant's notice to include a warning regarding the potential for deemed approval, the court found the requirement must be considered part of "public notice required by law"—a term not otherwise defined in the statute. *Id.* at 821–22.

As to the proper method of noticing under Government Code section 65956(b), the court in *Ciani v. San Diego Trust & Savings Bank* held that an applicant must follow notice distribution requirements under the applicable law that governs the particular permit in question. 233 Cal. App. 3d 1604 (1991). In that case, the court found that a "deemed approved" permit bears all the legal entitlements of a tangible permit issued by the agency, including availability of the statutory appeal provided for agency-issued permits. *Id.* at 1613. In *Ciani*, the 10-day appeal period provided in the statute and regulation for a coastal permit was applicable. Because the applicant failed to provide notice to the Coastal Commission prior to commencement of the 10-day appeal period, its permit was not deemed approved. *Id.* at 1616–1617. For an introduction to some of the issues faced by an applicant when its project is deemed approved, *see* Robert E. Merritt, "The Permit Streamlining Act," 1 *CEB Land Use Forum* 30 (Fall 1991).

Several cases uphold application of the Act's automatic approval provisions to particular projects. In 1986, a court held that the Act was applicable to a development project for a subdivision, conditional use permit, and building permits when a city failed to act within a one-year time limit. In this situation, the general plan and zoning permitted the use. See *Palmer v. City of Ojai*, 178 Cal. App. 3d 280, 293 (1986).

In 1989, a court held that the Act's time limits for acting on a development application were not tolled by a building moratorium. See *Selinger v. City Council*, 216 Cal. App. 3d 259 (1989). The court also rejected the City's argument that the automatic approval provision was not applicable because a tentative map cannot be deemed approved without the city council making the express finding that the map is consistent with the City's general plan as required by the Subdivision Map Act. The court held that the City's duty to make findings cannot be reconciled with the Act's automatic approval provision and that the latter prevailed. Gov't Code §§ 66473.5, 66474.

In 1989, a court held that the Act's time limits for acting on a development application were not tolled by a building moratorium.

In 1990, another court held that there was an automatic approval for a planned unit development when a city failed to notify the developer that the application was incomplete within the first 30 days. See *Orsi v. City Council of Salinas*, 219 Cal. App. 3d at 1586. Also, the court stated that the developer's resubmittal at the request of the City after the time had expired did not change the effect of the automatic approval. In this case, a negative declaration was adopted, notice was given, and hearings were held.

However, the courts also have strictly limited application of the Permit Streamlining Act. One court held that the Act was not meant to impose a rigorous timetable on a city's exercise of its policy-making "legislative" powers, but only on the exercise of its "adjudicatory" powers. See *Landi v. County of Monterey*, 139 Cal. App. 3d 934, 937 (1983). Thus, the Act has been declared not to apply to an application for a legislative approval, such as a general plan amendment or a rezoning. In *Landi*, the court held that because the applicant had requested a rezoning, which is a legislative act, the Act and its time limits for approval did not apply. *Id.*

However, the courts also have strictly limited application of the Permit Streamlining Act.

Further, the Act does not require automatic approval of a nonlegislative or adjudicatory project, *e.g.*, a site plan or map approval permit application, when such permit application would require legislative changes in applicable general plans, zoning ordinances, or other controlling land use regulations. If the nonlegislative or adjudicatory permit is tied to legislative change, then the deemed approved provisions of the Act are not applicable. See *Land Waste Mgmt. v. County of Contra Costa Bd. of Supervisors*, 222 Cal. App. 3d 950, 959 (1990). Significantly, the Act also does not cause an automatic certification of an EIR. *Id*. Nor does the Act appear to provide for automatic approval of a negative declaration or other review required by CEQA.

The Act was found not to apply to a request for a certificate of compliance under the Subdivision Map Act since "development project" as defined in the Permit Streamlining Act does not include ministerial acts. See *Findleton v. Board of Supervisors*, 12 Cal. App. 4th 709, 714 (1993).

The Act also was not applicable to a determination of whether an EIR should be prepared for a permit application involving geophysical research utilizing underwater airguns. *See Meridian Ocean Sys., Inc. v. State Lands Comm'n*, 222 Cal. App. 3d 153, 166 (1990). The court held that this was a policy decision, and thus a quasi-legislative action as defined by *Landi*. Further, the *Meridian* court held that the Act applies only to approval of development projects as defined and not to a permit to operate (Gov't Code § 65428, repealed by 1984 Cal. Stat. ch. 1009, § 16). Thus, the Act was not applicable to an application for a permit to conduct geophysical research.

Other Procedural Matters

A subdivider as well as tenants in condominium conversions are entitled to the city staff's written report at least three days before the hearing on a subdivision. Gov't. Code § 66452.3. Tenants also must be notified by a subdivider when a final map has been approved for a condominium project, community apartment project, or stock cooperative project. Gov't Code § 66459. A planning commission must follow the minimal procedural standards set forth in Government Code section 65804. Also, many cities have enacted local ordinances or resolutions that require that staff reports be made available to the public prior to the hearing.

Developer Misrepresentations

A developer's misrepresentations, unfulfilled promises, and negligent predictions of future actions made to induce political support may be actionable. *See Lacher v. Superior Court*, 230 Cal. App. 3d 1038, 1046–47 (1991). In *Lacher*, the court held that willful and negligent misrepresentations made to a homeowners' association that its members' views would not be affected by the developer's residential beachfront project were actionable since they induced the association to support the proposed development before the local planning commission. *Id.* at 1046.

Significantly, the *Lacher* court also found no merit in the developer's claim that the Planning and Zoning Law and the Subdivision Map Act precluded the homeowners' cause of action for fraud and negligent misrepresentation. The court held that those laws were meant to limit a party's ability to challenge a city's land use decisions, but that the Legislature did not intend to supplant the common law with respect to actions brought against third-party developers. 230 Cal. App. 3d at 1050.

Standing to Sue

Most land use litigation involves a property owner, developer, public interest group, industry association, or some public agency challenging a city's decision or regulation. Those suing must demonstrate that they have standing to sue. In the vast majority of cases, the courts have interpreted standing requirements liberally. For a general discussion of this subject, *see* chapter 21 (Land Use Litigation); James Longtin, Longtin's California Land Use, § 12.20 (2004 update). As a general rule, the challenging party must show that it is adversely affected by the city's decision. *See generally Neighborhood Action Group v. County of Calaveras*, 156 Cal. App. 3d 1176, 1186 (1984) (affected citizens' group had standing to challenge permit issuance on the ground that the permit was issued in violation of the general plan consistency requirement).

18

Legal Liability of Local Agency and Its Personnel

In General

Most land use decisions are challenged in writ of mandate proceedings, in which the challenger asks a court to set aside the decision.[1] Writ proceedings typically raise claims under the land use laws discussed throughout this book: the State Planning and Zoning Law, the California Environmental Quality Act, and the Subdivision Map Act. The takings clauses of the United States and California Constitutions provide another common basis for claims against cities.

However, two other laws are sometimes applied to land use issues—the California Tort Claims Act and the Federal Civil Rights Act. The former limits the liability of government officials and agencies, while the latter renders them liable for violations of federal civil rights. While an in-depth analysis of these laws is beyond the scope of this book, a brief summary is provided below.

Most land use decisions are challenged in writ of mandate proceedings, in which the challenger asks a court to set aside the decision.

California Tort Claims Act

The California Tort Claims Act (Gov't Code §§ 810–996.6) declares that "[e]xcept as otherwise provided by statute, [a] public entity is not liable for an injury, whether such injury arises out of an act or omission of the public entity or a public employee or any other person." Gov't Code § 815; *see also Cochran v. Herzog Engraving Co.*, 155 Cal. App. 3d 405, 409 (1984).

In *Caldwell v. Montoya*, the California Supreme Court described the basic structure of the Act as comprising the following four general rules:

- Public entities are immune from liability except as provided by statute. Gov't Code § 815(a)
- Public employees are liable for their torts except as otherwise provided by statute. Gov't Code § 820(a)
- Public entities are vicariously liable for the torts of their employees. Gov't Code § 815.2(a)

---

1. For an in-depth discussion of all of these topics, including both traditional and administrative mandate proceedings, litigation challenging exactions, fees and dedications, as well as the procedural rules and standards of review that apply to the particular type of land use decision being challenged, *see* chapter 21 (Land Use Litigation).

- Public entities are immune where their employees are immune, except as otherwise provided by statute. Gov't Code § 815.2(b)

10 Cal. 4th 972, 980 (1995)

Liability of Public Employees and Entities

Employees. Government Code section 820 provides that a public employee is liable for any injury caused by his or her act or omission "to the same extent as a private person," except as provided by statute. In general, therefore, employees are liable for their own common law torts just as any other individual would be unless shielded by the immunities, discussed below. *See* Gov't Code §§ 820.2–823.

Entities. The Tort Claims Act provides four principal avenues through which a public entity may be held liable for its actions. These are vicarious liability (Gov't Code § 815.2(a)), liability for independent contractors (Gov't Code § 815.4), liability for breach of a mandatory duty imposed pursuant to enactment (Gov't Code § 815.6), and dangerous condition liability (Gov't Code § 835). Although all four types of liability are equally actionable, breach of mandatory duty is the claim most likely to be asserted in the land use context. The Act describes the mandatory duty theory of liability as follows:

> Where a public entity is under a mandatory duty imposed by an enactment that is designed to protect against the risk of a particular kind of injury, the public entity is liable for an injury of that kind proximately caused by its failure to discharge the duty unless the public entity establishes that it exercised reasonable diligence to discharge the duty.

Gov't Code § 815.6

Whether an enactment is "designed to protect against the risk of a particular kind of injury" is determined under a three-prong test. To impose liability:

- The enactment must impose a mandatory, not discretionary, duty
- The Legislature must have intended that the statute protect against the risk of the kind of injury suffered by the claimant
- The breach of the mandatory duty must be a proximate cause of the injury

State of California v. Superior Court (Perry), 150 Cal. App. 3d 848, 854 (1984)

An "enactment" is defined as "a constitutional provision, statute, charter provision, ordinance or regulation." Gov't Code § 810.6. When alleging a cause of action for breach of a mandatory duty, a claimant must specifically identify the enactment alleged to create the mandatory duty. *Lehto v. City of Oxnard*, 171 Cal. App. 3d 285, 292 (1985).

The enactment must impose a duty that is mandatory, not discretionary. In order to be considered a mandatory duty, the enactment must be obligatory and must require that a particular action be taken. *Haggis v. City of Los Angeles*, 22 Cal. 4th 490, 498 (2000). For cases discussing whether a particular enactment imposes a mandatory duty, *see California Government Tort Liability Practice*, section 9.25 *et seq.* (Cal. Cont. Ed. Bar, 4th ed. 2004).

Immunity of Public Employees and Entities

For purposes of land use practice, the most relevant immunity conferred under the Act is that for discretionary acts and omissions. Under Government Code section 820.2, "[e]xcept as otherwise provided by statute, a public employee is not liable for an injury resulting from his act or omission where the act or omission was the result of the exercise of the discretion vested in him, whether or not such discretion be abused." *See Caldwell v. Montoya*, 10 Cal. 4th 972, 988 (1995) (school board members immune against claims of terminated superintendent as decision to replace school district's highest official was basic governmental policy decision and "quintessential discretionary act of government"). Under Government Code section 815.2(b), public entities have the same immunity for discretionary acts and omissions as public employees.

Whether discretionary immunity applies depends on whether the challenged decision arises in a planning as distinct from an operational context. In *Johnson v. State*, which involved a suit by a foster mother injured by a violent youth placed into her care without a warning, the court recognized a distinction between the planning and operational functions of government. 69 Cal. 2d 782, 793 (1968). The planning function, as described by the court, involves a basic, conscious policy decision, in which an employee can show a deliberate balancing of risks and objectives within the policymaking arena of government. *Id.* at 795. Such decisions are subject to discretionary immunity. In the case at bar, the court determined that the decision to place the youth into parole was a policy decision. However, the decision of whether or not to warn the foster mother of the youth's violent history, was not discretionary, but merely an implementing or "operational" decision, not subject to immunity. *Id.* at 794.

There are a variety of factors to consider when determining whether a public employee or entity has exercised a "discretionary" function which would be eligible for immunity if challenged. The two most important factors are as follows:

- Statutory provisions: When statutory provisions entrust authority and discretion to a branch of government, a court is likely to find that actions taken under those statutes are subject to discretionary immunity. *See Caldwell v. Montoya*, 10 Cal. 4th 972 (1995) (school board decision to fire superintendent immunized due to statute's placement of superintendent's employment within board's authority and discretion); *Leyva v. Nielsen*, 83 Cal. App. 4th 1061 (2000) (parole board decision to deny parole immunized due to statutory powers)

- Distinction between planning and operational functions: Immunity is reserved for occasions when a public employee is making a policy decision, wherein risks and advantages are balanced. *See Johnson v. State*, 69 Cal. 2d 782 (1968); *Barner v. Leeds*, 24 Cal. 4th 676 (2000) (original decision to represent criminal defendant immunized as basic policy decision but services of public defender in actual representation of criminal defendant are operational as merely implementing initial decision to represent, and thus are not immunized)

Attorney's fees may be awarded to the prevailing party in a civil action under the Tort Claims Act. *See* Gov't Code § 800. For an in-depth discussion of public employee and entity liability and immunity under the Tort Claims Act, *see California Government Tort Liability Practice* (Cal. Cont. Ed. Bar, 4th ed. 2004).

Federal Civil Rights Act

The Federal Civil Rights Act of 1871 (42 U.S.C. § 1983) provides another basis on which a city's land use decisions may be challenged. This statute authorizes a court to grant relief when an individual's constitutional or other federally protected rights have been violated by a state or local official or other person acting under color of state law. The basic purpose of section 1983 is to allow redress for injuries inflicted by an official or other person acting on behalf of the government. Two basic questions arise under section 1983: who is a *person* subject to suit, and when does a deprivation of federal rights occur *under color of state law?*

Color of Law

A claim for relief under section 1983 may only be asserted against persons who acted under color of state law.

A claim for relief under section 1983 may only be asserted against persons who acted under color of state law. As a general rule, the official conduct of state and local officials is almost always found to have occurred under color of state law. *See* Schwartz and Kirklin, *supra*, vol. 1A, page 490; *see also United States v. Classic*, 313 U.S. 299, 326 (1941) ("Misuse of power, possessed by virtue of state law and made possible only because the wrongdoer is clothed with the authority of state law, is action taken 'under color of' state law.").

Many state political subdivisions, including cities and counties, are authorized or created by state law and endowed with police powers and/or other authority. *See* Cal. Const. art XI. Thus, anyone acting under local laws enacted pursuant to those grants of authority is acting under color of state law for purposes of section 1983. *See generally Lugar v. Edmondson Oil Co.*, 457 U.S. 922 (1982) (discusses approach to determining whether action is taken under color of state law).

Treatment of Persons and Public Entities Under Section 1983: Municipal Liability and Legislative Immunity

Most relevant in the land use context, local governments, municipal corporations, school boards, special assessment districts, and their agents acting under color of 'state' law (which may encompass implementation or enforcement of a municipal or local law, regulation, policy or custom), are 'persons' subject to liability under section 1983. *Monell v. Dept. of Social Servs.*, 436 U.S. 658 (1978). This liability does not arise under a theory of respondeat superior, but rather "when execution of a government's policy or custom, whether made by its lawmakers or by those whose edicts or acts may fairly be said to represent official policy, inflicts the injury." *Id.* at 694. In *Brandon v. Holt*, the Court held that a suit against a municipal official acting in his official capacity is the same as a suit against the municipal entity. 469 U.S. 464 (1985). A city itself may also be held liable under section 1983 in some instances for failure to comply with land use laws. *See Sunset Drive Corp. v. City of Redlands*, 73 Cal. App. 4th 215, 225 (1999) (developer's allegations that a city had acted arbitrarily in failing to complete and certify an EIR within one year, as required by CEQA, stated valid claim for damages under section 1983).

Liability of individual officials is limited substantially by the doctrine of legislative immunity.

Liability of individual officials is limited substantially, however, by the doctrine of legislative immunity. Of particular relevance to land use decisions is the holding of *Tenney v. Brandhove*, in which the United States Supreme Court held that state legislative officials are absolutely immune from section 1983 liability for official conduct within "the sphere of legitimate legislative activity." 341 U.S. 367, 376 (1951). This absolute legislative immunity applies regardless of the official's motive. *Id.* at 377. *See also Bogan v. Scott-Harris*, 523 U.S. 44, 54 (1998) (city officials were immune from a claim that their legislative act of eliminating a city agency violated the Civil Rights Act, regardless of their subjective motivation); *Chappell v. Robbins*, 73 F. 3d 918, 921 (9th Cir. 1996) (legislator convicted of accepting bribes for sponsoring and voting for legislation was entitled to legislative immunity); *Ogborn v. City of Lancaster*, 101 Cal. App. 4th 448 (2002) (federal qualified immunity applied to bar claims brought under section 1983 against public officials executing a nuisance abatement warrant). Local legislators are also protected by absolute legislative immunity. *See Cinevision Corp. v. City of Burbank*, 745 F. 2d 560, 577 (9th Cir. 1984); *Kuzinich v. Santa Clara*, 689 F. 2d 1345 (9th Cir. 1982).

By contrast, no immunity exists where officials are acting in an administrative rather than a legislative capacity. In *Kaahumanu v. County of Maui*, commercial wedding arrangers filed a section 1983 suit against the Maui County Council for denying a conditional use permit for a commercial wedding business on beach-front residential property. 315 F. 3d 1215 (9th Cir. 2003). The councilmembers argued that they were entitled to absolute legislative immunity under section 1983 because the use permit was formally legislative in character. *Id.* at 1223. In ruling against the county council, the court held that the decision to deny the use permit was administrative and not legislative because it was ad hoc, affected only the plaintiffs, and did not bear all the hallmarks of traditional legislation. *Id.* at 1224. Accordingly, the councilmembers were not entitled to absolute legislative immunity for the use permit denial under section 1983.

Legislative immunity also does not apply to actions merely related to a legislative act. *See San Pedro Hotel Co. v. City of Los Angeles*, 159 F. 3d 470, 478 fn. 11 (9th Cir. 1998) (legislative immunity does not extend to a retaliation claim against a council member under the federal Fair Housing Act, even though the alleged retaliation grew out of a legislative act).

Finally, absolute legislative immunity protects individual legislators and may not be asserted by municipal entities sued under section 1983. *See* Schwartz and Kirklin, *supra* vol. 1B, section 7.2.

Attorneys' fees may sometimes be awarded to a plaintiff under section 1983, and in narrow circumstances, to the defendant. *See* 42 U.S.C. § 1988.

For an in-depth discussion of legislative immunity and municipal liability, along with other relevant provisions of the Federal Civil Rights Act, *see* Schwartz and Kirklin, *supra*; *see also California Government Tort Liability Practice, Federal Civil Rights Act*, ch. 13 (Cal. Cont. Ed. Bar, 4th ed. 2004).

Legislative immunity does not apply where city officials are acting in an administrative rather than a legislative capacity.

19

Enforcement of Land Use Laws

Introduction

This chapter discusses some of the enforcement mechanisms a city may use when confronting violations of its land use regulations or noncompliance with the conditions imposed on a permit approval or development. This chapter also discusses the possible defenses to enforcement actions.

Administrative and Criminal Sanctions

Misdemeanor

The scope of a city's authority to impose administrative or criminal sanctions for violations of ordinances or codes is set by Government Code section 36900, which provides that "[v]iolation of a city ordinance is a misdemeanor unless by ordinance it is made an infraction."

The maximum penalties are set forth in Government Code § 36901, which provides that "a fine shall not exceed one thousand dollars," and "[i]mprisonment shall not exceed six months." However, it allows both penalties to be imposed for the same violation, which is permitted by Penal Code section 19. The violation may be prosecuted by city authorities (or by the district attorney) in the name of the people of the State of California. Gov't Code § 36901.

The right of a municipality to impose multiple penalties for continuous conduct was upheld in *People v. Djekich*, 229 Cal. App. 3d 1213 (1991). There, the conduct at issue involved illegal conversion of a building into a duplex and the disregard of multiple notices of continuing violation. The court then stated that a zoning ordinance may specifically authorize a separate punishment for each violation and define each day's continuance as a distinct offense. Thus, "a penal provision reflecting a clear legislative intent to permit pyramiding of punishment through cumulative convictions by providing for a separate offense for each day a defendant continues his/her criminal conduct is valid...providing the fine imposed is not unconstitutionally excessive or the sentence imposed does not constitute cruel and/or unusual punishment." *Id.* at 1224.

The right of a municipality to impose multiple penalties for continuous conduct was upheld in People v. Djekich.

Infraction

Under Government Code section 36900, a violation of an ordinance or code determined to be an infraction is punishable by (1) a fine not exceeding one hundred dollars for a first violation; (2) a fine not exceeding two hundred dollars for a second violation of the same ordinance within one year; (3) a fine not exceeding five hundred dollars for each additional violation of the same ordinance within one year. As with the misdemeanor violations, these can be cumulated based both on the number of violations and their duration. However, in contrast to misdemeanor prosecutions, infraction proceedings lack procedural protections such as a trial.

The infraction procedure is typically used when dealing with small land use infractions, such as sign violations.

Administrative Penalties

Government Code section 53069.4 permits a city to adopt an ordinance that subjects any person who violates an ordinance to an administrative fine or penalty.

Government Code section 53069.4 permits a city to adopt an ordinance that subjects any person who violates an ordinance to an administrative fine or penalty. Under this law, a city must adopt an ordinance setting forth the administrative procedures that govern the imposition, enforcement, collection, and administrative review of these fines or penalties. Where the violation otherwise would be an infraction, the administrative fine or penalty cannot exceed the maximum fine or penalty for infractions set forth in Government Code sections 25132 and 36900, except in the case of building or safety code violations where the maximum fines are greater. Gov't Code §§ 25132(c), 36900(c). When a code violation pertains to building, plumbing, electrical, or other similar structural or zoning issues that do not create an immediate danger to health or safety, the administrative procedures must give the person responsible for the continuing violation a reasonable amount of time to remedy the violation before imposing fines or penalties.

Warrant

When inspecting private property in the field, enforcement agents step into the domain of law enforcement.

When inspecting private property in the field, enforcement agents step into the domain of law enforcement. Although not police or peace officers, they are public employees seeking to enforce applicable municipal regulations or ordinances. Thus, enforcement agents, like the police, must adhere to legal and constitutional limits of search of private property. *Camara v. Municipal Court*, 87 S. Ct. 1727 (1967).

An administrative inspection warrant must (1) be in writing (Code of Civil Procedure (CCP) § 1822.50); (2) be in the name of the people (CCP § 1822.50); 3) signed by a judge of a court of record (CCP § 1822.50); (4) issued upon "cause" (CCP § 1822.51); and (5) be supported by an affidavit that particularly describes the place, dwelling, structure, etc. to be inspected (CCP § 1822.51). The affidavit must contain either a statement that consent was sought and refused or facts or circumstances reasonably justifying the failure to seek such consent. CCP § 1822.51.

Cause shall be deemed to exist if either reasonable legislative or administrative standards for conducting a routine or area inspection are satisfied with respect to the particular place, dwelling, structure, premises, or vehicle, or there is reason to believe that a condition of nonconformity exists with respect to the particular place, dwelling, structure, premises, or vehicle.

CCP § 1822.52

A warrant will only be valid for a maximum of 14 days. CCP § 1822.55.

Enforcement Under the Revenue and Taxation Code

Where there is a violation of a local code dealing with health, safety, or building conditions associated with rental housing, cities also may use Revenue and Taxation Code sections 17274 and 24436.5 for enforcement. Under these provisions, after following specific procedures set forth in the law, a city may file a written notice of violation with the Franchise Tax Board. If the owner of the rental income property fails to remedy the violation within a certain time period, he or she is then precluded from taking a deduction for interest, taxes, depreciation, or amortization paid or incurred in a taxable year. Rev. and Tax. Code § 24436.5. All state revenue that normally would have accrued to the property owner by way of tax deductions is returned to the city that notified the Franchise Tax Board of the violation. To initiate this procedure, the Franchise Tax Board has adopted a "Notice of Non-Compliance" (SRH 1010 (10-78)) that can be obtained from the Board. *See* Joseph M. Schilling and James B. Hare, *Code Enforcement: A Comprehensive Approach*, pages 104–05 (Solano Press, 1994).

Where there is a violation of a local code dealing with health, safety, or building conditions associated with rental housing, cities also may use Revenue and Taxation Code sections 17274 and 24436.5 for enforcement.

Enforcement Under the Subdivision Map Act

For violation of subdivision regulations, the Subdivision Map Act provides its own detailed enforcement procedures. *See* Gov't Code § 66499.30 *et seq.* In addition to these various remedies for noncompliance, once a city makes a finding that development is contrary to the public health or safety, it must refuse to issue any permit or grant any approval necessary to develop the property that is in violation of the law. Gov't Code § 66499.34.

A city may also encourage compliance with its subdivision regulations through the notice-and-hearing procedure set forth in state law. *See* Gov't Code § 66499.36. Whenever a city has knowledge that property has been illegally subdivided it must inform the property owner of its intention to file a notice of violation. This notice will cloud title to the property, encouraging compliance.

In addition, if fees, costs, and expenses incurred in the enforcement of state or local zoning, building, and housing laws and regulations or in the abatement of a nuisance are not paid within 45 days, a city can impose a lien against the property that is the subject of the enforcement activity. Gov't Code § 54988. However, the power to impose enforcement costs as a penalty in a criminal prosecution of code infractions is not valid under the general law. *See People v. Minor*, 96 Cal. App. 4th 29, 32 (2002).

PRACTICE TIP

Under the Subdivision Map Act, if a city finds that development is contrary to the public health or safety, it must refuse to issue any permit or grant any approval necessary to develop property that is in violation of the law. Gov't Code § 66499.34.

Enforcement Under CEQA

The California Environmental Quality Act (CEQA) also provides cities with a mechanism to remedy a developer's failure to implement mitigation measures required by law. If changes have been incorporated into a development project,

CEQA = California Environmental Quality Act

or conditions have been proposed on the project, to mitigate or avoid significant adverse environmental effects of the project upon the environment (as may be required by an environmental impact report or mitigated negative declaration), an agency must adopt a mitigation monitoring program at the time the project is approved to ensure that the developer complies with the mitigation measures during project implementation. Pub. Res. Code § 21081.6(a); Cal. Code Regs. tit. 14, § 15091(d). As part of the mitigation monitoring program, cities must ensure that mitigation measures are fully enforceable as conditions of development of the project. Pub. Res. Code § 21081.6(b).

The conditions of approval generally are incorporated into the resolution or ordinance approving the project. The conditions must address each of the mitigation measures adopted by the city and must expressly provide that approval of a final map or other approvals is conditioned upon completion of certain mitigation measures. If a developer fails to implement a mitigation measure, the conditions then provide a city with the mechanism for permit revocations, stop work orders, or denial of subsequent approvals that are needed to complete, operate, or occupy the project. For a detailed discussion of CEQA, *see* chapter 6 (CEQA).

Enforcement Under the Business and Professions Code

Another method to enforce land use regulations is found in Business and Professions Code section 17200 (the unfair competition statute). In 1997, a court found that Squaw Valley Ski Resort had engaged in unfair competition by committing unlawful business practices when it violated not only conditions of a conditional use permit, but also the Forest Practices Act (Pub. Res. Code § 4511 *et seq.*) by resorting to self-help and cutting down more than 1,800 trees without a permit. *See Hewlett v. Squaw Valley Ski Corp.*, 54 Cal. App. 4th 499, 520 (1997). The court rejected Squaw Valley's claim that the tree-cutting should not be prosecuted as an unlawful business practice, holding that the intent at the time of cutting, rather than the final use of the timber, controlled. *Id.* at 523–24.

Possible Defenses to a City's Enforcement Action

Denial of Due Process or Equal Protection

At times, a violator will claim as a defense that the relevant laws are not being enforced against similarly situated people. However, the courts generally have rejected this argument. *See City and County of San Francisco v. Burton*, 201 Cal. App. 2d 749, 755 (1962) (unintentional discriminatory enforcement of a zoning ordinance is not a defense to prosecution). In such cases, there is no denial of due process or equal protection. For example, in *City of Banning v. Desert Outdoor Advertising, Inc.*, the court stated that it was not a defense that zoning officials permitted similar violations by others to continue over a number of years. 209 Cal. App. 2d 152, 155–56 (1962); *see also Riggs v. City of Oxnard*, 154 Cal. App. 3d 526, 531 (1984) (zoning enforcement is a discretionary function); *Sutherland v. City of Fort Bragg*, 86 Cal. App. 4th 13, 24 (2000) (a fire chief's duty to enforce fire code was discretionary, and therefore enforcement of the code against one party but not another did not subject him to liability).

Disparate treatment of individual violators of a law or ordinance generally will survive rational basis scrutiny—and therefore not give rise to an equal protection or due process claim—so long as it bears some rational relation to a legitimate state interest. *See Squaw Valley Development Co. v. Goldberg*, 375 F. 3d 936 (9th Cir. 2004) (recognizing that more aggressive enforcement against a violator could be rationally related to a legitimate state interest).

However, to the extent that the "rational basis" used to justify selective enforcement is shown to be merely a pretext for differential treatment, a plaintiff may establish an equal protection violation. *Squaw Valley Development Co.*, 375 F. 3d at 944–45. The plaintiff in *Squaw Valley* claimed an equal protection violation by the executive officer of the regional water quality control board with oversight of the plaintiff's property. Squaw Valley claimed that it was singled out and subjected to stricter enforcement by the board's management because of personal animus on the part of the board's executive officer. *Id.* at 944. The Ninth Circuit held that, while there may have been a rational basis for selective enforcement against Squaw Valley, there also was evidence that could support a conclusion that the purported rational basis was merely a pretext. *Id.* at 948. Most notably, the defendant regulator was unable to recollect a single instance when the plaintiff Squaw Valley had failed to comply with water quality laws so as to arguably justify the stricter enforcement he claimed was necessary. The Ninth Circuit therefore reversed the trial court's grant of summary judgment as to the board's executive officer and allowed Squaw Valley's equal protection claim against him to proceed. *Id.* at 949.

To the extent that the "rational basis" used to justify selective enforcement is shown to be merely a pretext for differential treatment, a plaintiff may establish an equal protection violation.

In *Lim v. City of Long Beach*, owners and operators of adult businesses claimed that the city violated their equal protection rights by forcing existing adult businesses to relocate under a new zoning ordinance, which restricted the locations in which adult businesses could operate, while allowing non-adult businesses to remain in place even when in violation of other city ordinances. In denying the adult business owners' claim, the court stated that the city's actions only needed to be rationally related to a permissible government objective. 217 F. 3d 1050, 1056 (9th Cir. 2000). The court found sufficient the city's proffered reason for enforcing its adult business ordinance as its interest in curbing the secondary effects of adult businesses. The city did not have a similar interest in enforcing its other zoning ordinances. *Id.* at 1057.

However, not all enforcement of planning and zoning provisions is discretionary. In *Terminal Plaza Corporation v. City and County of San Francisco*, Terminal Plaza filed a petition for writ of mandate, contending that the city had refused to enforce a project condition requiring the construction of a mid-block pedestrian way. 186 Cal. App. 3d 814, 831 (1986). The court held that in light of the clear language of the condition, the zoning administrator had a ministerial duty to enforce its requirements. *Id.* The zoning administrator had no discretion to determine whether an express condition had been violated or to interpret it, and did not have the discretionary enforcement authority of a prosecuting attorney. *Id.* at 834.

Not all code enforcement is discretionary.

In *Lockyer v. City and County of San Francisco*, the California Supreme Court held that local officials did not have any judicial or quasi-judicial discretionary authority in their enforcement of the state family law statute that limits the granting of a marriage license to a couple comprised of a man and a woman. 33 Cal. 4th 1055, 1093 (2004). At the Mayor's direction, the San Francisco County Clerk had removed mention of gender from marriage forms created by the State Registrar of Vital Statistics and had begun to solemnize marriages between same-sex couples. The Mayor had directed such action based on his belief that the state law violated the equal protection clause of the California Constitution.

The Lockyer *court held that once a statute is duly enacted, it is presumed constitutional and the scope of a public official's statutorily derived authority to act is defined by the terms of the statute itself.*

The *Lockyer* court held that once a statute is duly enacted, it is presumed constitutional and the scope of a public official's statutorily derived authority to act is defined by the terms of the statute itself. *Id.* at 1086. In this instance, the state law governing the issuance of marriage licenses did not grant city officials discretion in issuing licenses, but rather created a ministerial duty to grant licenses in accordance with the statute. The County Clerk therefore had no authority to disregard the statutory mandate based on her own determination that the statute was unconstitutional. *Id.* at 1092–93.

Estoppel

The estoppel theory is very difficult to use successfully against a city because courts have a strong policy against applying this doctrine where the interests of the public will be adversely affected.

Another defense that may surface in an enforcement action is a claim that the city is estopped from enforcing its own regulations because the city itself has acted contrary to them. The estoppel theory is very difficult to use successfully against a city because courts have a strong policy against applying this doctrine where the interests of the public may be adversely affected.

To establish a claim of estoppel against the government a litigant must prove the same four elements as make up a cause of action for equitable estoppel against a private party as well as a fifth element which applies only to the government. *La Canada Flintridge Development Corporation v. Department of Transportation*, 166 Cal. App. 3d 206, 219 (1985). The first four elements are:

(1) the party to be estopped must be apprised of the facts

(2) it must intend that its conduct shall be acted upon, or must so act that the party asserting the estoppel had a right to believe it was so intended

(3) the other party must be ignorant of the true state of facts, and

(4) the other party must rely upon the conduct to its injury

Driscoll v. City of Los Angeles, 67 Cal. 2d 297, 305 (1967)

The fifth element requires the plaintiff to demonstrate that the injury to its personal interests if the government is not estopped exceeds the injury to the public interest if the government is estopped. Thus an estoppel will not be applied against the government if to do so would effectively nullify "a strong rule of policy, adopted for the benefit of the public...." *La Canada*, 166 Cal. App. 3d at 219, quoting *County of San Diego v. California Water and Telephone Co.*, 30 Cal. 2d 817, 829–30 (1947). As a result of this principle, courts rarely enforce an estoppel defense against local governments, *see County of Sonoma v. Rex*, 231 Cal. App. 3d 1289, 1295 (1991) (county not estopped from enforcing a zoning ordinance against an innkeeper), and *Smith v. County of Santa Barbara*, 7 Cal. App. 4th 770, 775–76 (1992) (county not estopped from revoking erroneously issued land use permit to install microwave dishes).

However, there are several cases where property owners have successfully asserted an estoppel theory. In *Congregation Etz Chaim v. City of Los Angeles*, the Ninth Circuit Court of Appeals estopped the City of Los Angeles from revoking building permits upon which the plaintiff congregation had relied. 371 F. 3d 1122 (9th Cir. 2004). Congregation Etz Chaim and the city had reached a settlement agreement to resolve their disagreement over permit requirements in connection with renovation of the Congregation's facility. The Congregation thereafter submitted renovation plans for the facility. After requiring numerous changes to the plans, the city approved them and issued a building permit. Within a week after the Congregation began work and in response to complaints from neighbors, the city issued a stop-work order and notified the Congregation that it intended to revoke the building permit. The city claimed the permit was issued in violation of other provisions of its code.

The Ninth Circuit held that the city could not revoke the permit, finding that the facts of the case "provide particularly strong support for the Congregation's estoppel argument." *Id.* at 1125. The court found that the city's own grant of the building permit after having reviewed and approved the plans along with the settlement agreement amounted to a representation by the city that the plans complied with the agreement. Moreover, the Congregation had performed substantial work and incurred substantial liabilities in reliance on the permit. *Id.*

In another case, a court held that reliance by a property owner on an administrative regulation of the City and County of San Francisco was a valid basis for an estoppel against the city in enforcing a later-enacted ordinance. *See Hock Inv. Co. v. City and County of San Francisco*, 215 Cal. App. 3d 438, 450–51 (1989). Also, the City of Laguna Beach was estopped from enforcing its second-dwelling unit ordinance because the city did not administer the second-dwelling unit state law correctly in the first place. *See Wilson v. City of Laguna Beach*, 6 Cal. App. 4th 543, 558 (1992).

While cities may be estopped by a property owner's reliance on a permit or administrative regulation, it is important to note that property owners rely on statements made by public officials at their peril. A property owner cannot rely on statements—whether oral or written—made by an official unless the official is authorized to make such statements. In *Burchett v. City of Newport Beach*, the court held: "[N]o government, whether state or local, is bound to any extent by an officer's acts in excess of his [or her] authority." 33 Cal. App. 4th 1472, 1479 (1995).

The *Burchett* court went on to state:

> One who deals with the public officer stands presumptively charged with a full knowledge of that officer's powers, and is bound at his [or her] peril to ascertain the extent of his [or her] powers to bind the government for which he [or she] is an officer, and any act of an officer to be valid must find express authority in the law or be necessarily incidental to a power expressly granted.

Id. (quoting *Horsemen's Benevolent & Protective Ass'n v. Valley Racing Ass'n*, 4 Cal. App. 4th 1538, 1563–64 (1992))

PRACTICE TIP

Enforcement rights cannot be created by public officials acting in excess of their authority. Individuals must make sure that the officials with whom they are dealing have the authority to provide the right they seek.

While cities may be estopped by a property owner's reliance on a permit or administrative regulation, it is important to note that property owners rely on statements made by public officials at their peril.

20

Affordable Housing

Introduction: The Affordable Housing Crisis in California[1]

Communities across California continue to confront the challenges posed by a scarcity of housing, particularly affordable housing. In the last several decades, housing production in the state has lagged behind population and job growth, resulting in a housing deficit.[2] In fact, even with the recent housing slowdown, Census Bureau figures show that housing costs consumed more of the monthly paycheck for millions of Americans in 2006 as compared to 2005.[3]

This lack of adequate supply results in escalating housing prices, making homeownership out of reach for many. California has the highest median home price in the nation, and currently is ranked as the least affordable state in the nation; its homeownership rate is the fourth lowest in the country, with just 58 percent of its residents owning homes.[4] During the second quarter of 2007, nine of the ten least affordable communities in the nation were located in California.[5] According to one recent study, while affordability rose slightly, only 24 percent of households carried the minimum income required to purchase an entry-level home.[6] Since 1980, homeownership rates have increased only among whites in the state (from 60 to 65 percent), while they have declined for blacks (from 40 to 39 percent), and remained stagnant for Latinos (48 percent) and Asian Americans (55 percent).[7] Currently, two million households pay more

Communities across California continue to confront challenges posed by a scarcity of housing, particularly affordable housing.

---

1. For a thorough discussion of local, state, and federal regulatory responses to the issue of affordable housing, see *The Legal Guide to Affordable Housing Development*, T. Iglesias and R.E. Lento, eds. (ABA, State and Local Government Law Section, 2005).
2. See California Budget Project, *Locked Out 2002: California's Affordable Housing Crisis Continues*, pages 8–9, Sacramento (Oct. 2002).
3. See "Housing Costs Consumed More of Paychecks in 2006," *New York Times*, September 12, 2007; U.S. Census Bureau, American Community Survey, 2006.
4. *California Affordable Housing Handbook: Strategies for Building Better Communities*, page 7 (Feb. 2006).
5. NAHB/Wells Fargo Housing Opportunity Index (Aug. 2007).
6. "Home Affordability Rises in State," *San Diego Union-Tribune*, Aug. 30, 2007.
7. *Expanding Opportunity: New Resources to Meet California's Housing Needs*, page 9 (PolicyLink, Winter 2005).

than the recommended 30 percent of their income for housing. In Los Angeles, the fair market rent for a two-bedroom apartment is affordable only to households with earnings equivalent to nearly three full-time minimum wage jobs. In San Francisco, the situation is even more dire, with such housing affordable only to households with earnings equivalent to more than five full-time minimum wage jobs.[8] While all Californians feel the impact of this housing shortage at some level, those with incomes at the lowest end of the economic spectrum, in particular, families with children, and Latino, African American, and immigrant households, bear the brunt of this crisis.

Housing is the linchpin of sustainable development and smart growth, and is inextricably linked to economic and social opportunity.

The impacts are far reaching. The "lack of housing is a critical problem that threatens the economic, environmental, and social quality of life in California." Gov't Code § 65589.5(a)(1). Housing is the linchpin of sustainable development and smart growth, and is inextricably linked to economic and social opportunity.[9] The level of access to quality employment, education, and support systems, as well as the availability of a wide range of services and amenities are, in significant part, determined by where one lives.[10] As the Millennial Housing Commission emphasized:

> Decent, affordable, and accessible housing fosters self-sufficiency, brings stability to families and new vitality to distressed communities, and supports overall economic growth. A lack of affordable housing has significant implications for the environment and growth management policies as well.[11]

Following is a discussion of various aspects of state law that are designed to eliminate unnecessary constraints on residential development and provide housing opportunities to meet the needs of all Californians.

State Housing Element Law

Purpose of the Mandated Housing Element

The Legislature has declared that the availability of housing is a matter of "vital statewide importance," and that "the early attainment of decent housing and a suitable living environment for every Californian, including farmworkers, is a priority of the highest order." Gov't Code § 65580(a).

To facilitate the improvement and development of housing for all economic segments of the community, every city in the state is required to adopt a housing element as part of its general plan.

To facilitate the improvement and development of housing for all economic segments of the community (pursuant to Gov't Code § 65580(d)), every city in the state is required to adopt a housing element as part of its general plan. Gov't Code § 65302(c). This mandate helps to ensure that "counties and cities recognize their responsibilities in contributing to the attainment of the state housing goal" by planning for future housing needs of all income levels.

---

8. *Id.*
9. *See Bay Area Housing Profile: A Report Card on the Supply and Demand Crisis*, page 4 (Bay Area Council, 2003). *See also* Arthur C. Nelson and Susan M. Wachter, "Growth Management and Affordable Housing Policy," 12 *J. Affordable Housing & Cmty. Dev. L.* 173 (2003).
10. *See* Angela Glover Blackwell and Radhika K. Fox, *Regional Equity and Smart Growth: Opportunities for Advancing Social and Economic Justice in America*, the Funders' Network for Smart Growth and Livable Communities, Translation Paper no. 1, ed. 2 (2004). This paper discusses the interplay between regional development patterns and inequality/inequity, and provides a framework for action to advance regional equity.
11. *Meeting Our Nation's Housing Challenge*, page 11 (Millennial Housing Commission, 2002).

Gov't Code § 65581(a). *See Committee for Responsible Planning v. City of Indian Wells*, 209 Cal. App. 3d 1005, 1013 (1989); *Buena Vista Gardens Apartments Ass'n v. City of San Diego*, 175 Cal. App. 3d 289, 295 (1985).

Required Contents of the Housing Element

While cities have considerable flexibility in drafting the other elements of the general plan, the housing element must comply with elaborate statutory provisions. *See* Gov't Code § 65580 *et seq*. In evaluating the adequacy of a housing element, a court will limit its review to determining whether a city has "substantially complied" with the statutory requirements and will not engage in an examination of its merits. *See Hernandez v. City of Encinitas*, 28 Cal. App. 4th 1048, 1067–68 (1994) (a city's housing element withstood attack by low income and homeless petitioners since it substantially complied with statutory requirements). *See also Hoffmaster v. City of San Diego*, 55 Cal. App. 4th 1098, 1111 (1997) (providing guidance regarding what constitutes "substantial compliance").

While cities have considerable flexibility in drafting the other elements of the general plan, the housing element must comply with elaborate statutory provisions.

Government Code section 65583 establishes the required contents of a housing element. Among other things, it must contain an assessment of the jurisdiction's existing and projected housing needs, including special needs of the elderly, the disabled, female-headed households, large families, farmworkers, homeless persons and families, and emergency shelters. The existing and projected needs assessment must include its share of the regional housing need in accordance with Government Code section 65584. Gov't Code § 65583(a). It must also contain a land inventory (Gov't Code § 65583(a)(3)), and must identify adequate sites to provide for the housing needs of households at all income levels. *But see Fonseca v. City of Gilroy*, 148 Cal. App. 4th 1174 (2007) (under the pre-2005 housing law in effect when the City of Gilroy updated its housing element and general plan in 2002, the City was not required to provide a site-specific inventory and analysis). The element also must contain an analysis of governmental and non-governmental constraints, and include a statement of the community's goals, quantified objectives,[12] financial resources, and scheduled programs for the preservation, improvement, and development of housing. *Hoffmaster*, 55 Cal. App. 4th at 1107; *Buena Vista Gardens Apartments Ass'n v. City of San Diego*, 175 Cal. App. 3d at 302.

Government Code section 65583 establishes the required contents of a housing element.

Regional Housing Needs Allocation Process

There has been increasing recognition of the need to evaluate housing and growth issues in a regional context. To that end, state law has established a regional housing needs allocation (RHNA) process, which determines existing and projected housing needs during the planning period for each jurisdiction. Gov't Code § 65584 *et seq*.

RHNA = Regional housing needs allocation

---

12. *See* 88 Ops. Cal. Atty Gen. 84 (2005) (Attorney General opining that a community may, when determining its "quantified objectives," establish its maximum number of housing units by income category that can be constructed, rehabilitated, and conserved over the next planning period below the numbers of units that would meet its regional fair share housing needs if the community demonstrates that its available financial resources are insufficient to meet those needs).

COG = Council of Governments
HCD = Department of Housing and Community Development

The Department of Housing and Community Development (HCD) in consultation with each Council of Government (COG) determines the existing and projected housing needs for each region. Gov't Code § 65584.01. Then, the appropriate COG determines each city's fair share of that regional housing need. COGs are authorized under the law to charge a fee to cities to cover the projected reasonable, actual costs in completing the allocation process. A city also may charge a fee to developers to support the work of the planning agency and to reimburse it for the cost of any fee charged by the COG. Changes in the law limit the fees cities may charge developers to the amount charged to the city by the COG. Gov't Code § 65584.1; Health & Safety Code §§ 17021.6, 18021.7, 50451, 50452, and 50453. Where a COG does not exist, this determination is made by HCD. Gov't Code § 65584(b). Each city's share of the regional housing need is distributed among four income categories to ensure planning for all income levels. These categories are based on the percentage of an area's median income (Gov't Code § 65589.5(h)(4)), as periodically established by HCD pursuant to Health and Safety Code section 50093:

Income level	Percentage of median income
Very low income	0 – 50
Low income	51 – 80
Moderate income	81 – 120
Above moderate income	121+

Gov't Code §§ 65584(a)(1) & (e); Health & Safety Code §§ 50105, 50079.5, 50093

If a city disagrees with the COG's (or HCD's) initial determination, it must follow the procedure contained in Government Code section 65584.05 or 65584.06 to obtain revisions.

If a city disagrees with the COG's (or HCD's) initial determination, it must follow the procedure contained in Government Code section 65584.05 or 65584.06 to obtain revisions.

In 2004, the Legislature significantly revised the allocation process. These modifications included: the establishment of overall policy objectives for the regional allocation; the requirement of COGs to incorporate specific factors into their methodologies; the inclusion of an alternative process to allocate housing needs to subregions; and the provision for a detailed process to determine the allocation, to allow for public participation, and to hear appeals.

The allocation plan must be consistent with the following objectives: (1) increasing the housing supply and the mix of housing types, tenure, and affordability within the region in an equitable manner, which must result in each jurisdiction receiving an allocation for low and very low income units; (2) promoting infill development and socioeconomic equity, the protection of environmental and agricultural resources, and the encouragement of efficient development patterns; (3) promoting an improved intraregional relationship between jobs and housing; and (4) allocating a lower proportion of housing needs to an income category when a jurisdiction already has a disproportionately high share of households in that category. Gov't Code § 65584(d).

To the extent sufficient data is available, the allocation methodology factors must include: existing and projected jobs and housing relationships; opportunities and constraints to development of additional housing in each member jurisdiction; household growth distribution and opportunities to maximize the use of public transportation; market demand for housing; city-county agreements to direct growth toward incorporated areas; loss of existing affordable units; and high housing cost burdens. Further, the law provides that any direct or indirect local growth control ordinances shall not be justification for reducing a community's share of the regional housing need. Gov't Code §§ 65584.01–65584.07.

Government Code section 65584.5 sets forth the rules and procedures for transferring a portion of a city's share of the regional housing need to other jurisdictions. The donor entity may transfer a portion of its regional share under certain specified circumstances, so long as the detailed procedures set forth in that section are followed. Government Code section 65584.07 describes the circumstances under which a county's share of regional housing need may be reduced, where a city within the county has agreed to increase its share in the equivalent amount.

Preparing the Land Inventory and Identifying Adequate Sites

The housing element must demonstrate site development capacity equivalent to, or exceeding, the projected housing need. This requires preparation of a land inventory. Gov't Code § 65583(a)(3). The inventory's purpose is to identify specific sites suitable for residential development in order to compare the city's new construction need with its residential development capacity. If the inventory does not demonstrate adequate site capacity to accommodate the city's regional housing need for all income groups, the element must contain actions designed to address this shortfall. Gov't Code § 65583(c)(1).[13]

The land inventory's purpose is to identify specific sites suitable for residential development in order to compare the city's new construction need with its residential development capacity.

Recent changes in the law more clearly defined what constitutes "land suitable for residential development" for purposes of the land inventory. This includes: (1) vacant sites zoned for residential use; (2) vacant sites zoned for nonresidential use that also allows residential development; (3) underutilized residentially zoned sites that are capable of being developed at a higher density or with greater intensity; and (4) sites zoned for nonresidential use that can be redeveloped for, and as necessary, rezoned for, residential use. Gov't Code § 65583.2(a). The land inventory also must contain information regarding any environmental constraints and the availability of utilities, as well as other detailed site-specific information. Gov't Code § 65583.2(b).

The land inventory also must contain information regarding any environmental constraints and the availability of utilities, as well as other detailed site-specific information.

To substantially comply with the adequate sites requirement under Government Code section 65583(c)(1), a city must identify sufficient sites—with appropriate zoning and development standards to encourage residential development during the planning period—in an amount adequate to meet its regional fair share of housing need. *Hoffmaster v. City of San Diego*, 55 Cal. App. 4th 1098, 1111 (1997). This requires the city to provide specific information to demonstrate that the identified sites will actually be available for development during the planning period, and that these sites will accommodate the amount of development the city has attributed to them. *Id. See also* 70 Ops. Cal. Atty. Gen. 231 (1987). As the *Hoffmaster* court emphasized when it found the City of San Diego's housing element inadequate:

---

13. *See also Housing Element Questions and Answers: A Guide to the Preparation of Housing Elements*, pages 36–57 (Calif. Dep't of Housing and Cmty. Dev., October 2006) (www.hcd.ca.gov).

> Substantial compliance with the legislative mandate requires more than merely designating every unoccupied mote within City's boundaries, each of which is subject to City-imposed developmental and separate restrictions....

Id.

In *Hoffmaster*, the plaintiffs challenged the City of San Diego's housing element on the ground that it failed to identify adequate sites that would be made available as part of a plan designed to facilitate development of homeless emergency shelters and transitional housing. San Diego's housing element merely identified in its land inventory the amount of "available" land zoned at various density levels, and then assumed the maximum possible buildout to support its claim that it could meet its projected housing need. The court acknowledged that as a matter of mathematics, the amount of acreage identified, if truly "available," could satisfy the city's housing need for all income groups. However, the court emphasized that the law requires more. To demonstrate the adequacy of the sites for residential development that it has identified, a site-specific analysis must consider the following:

> An adequate site is one available for immediate development, which is located within reasonable access to public agencies and transportation services; will not require unusually high site development costs; has available public services and facilities; is consistent with the general plan designation and site zoning so as to permit the development of... housing without undue regulatory approval; and is consistent with applicable parking requirements, fire regulations and design standards.

Id.

Adequate sites must be identified to accommodate 100 percent of the need for very low- and low-income households. In instances where the inventory does not identify sites sufficient to meet the city's share of the regional housing need for low and very low income households, sites must be identified in the housing element and rezoned for development within the planning period to make up for the shortfall. Gov't Code §§ 65583(c)(1)(A), 65583.2(h). The rezoning shall allow owner-occupied and rental multi-family residential "use by right." Once a site is rezoned pursuant to the above provisions at sufficient densities to promote affordable housing development, the city shall not require a conditional use permit, planned unit development permit, or other discretionary approval that would constitute a "project" for purposes of CEQA. However, the Subdivision Map Act still applies and cities may require design review subject to certain restrictions. Gov't Code § 65583.2(i).

If a city in a prior planning period failed to identify or make available adequate sites to accommodate its fair share of regional housing needs, then the city shall, in its next housing element, within the first year of the planning period, zone or rezone adequate sites to accommodate the unaccommodated portion of regional housing need allocation from the prior planning period. Gov't Code § 65584.09.

Analysis of Governmental and Non-Governmental Constraints

In preparing a housing element, potential and actual governmental constraints upon the maintenance, improvement, or development of housing for all income levels and for persons with disabilities must be analyzed. Gov't Code § 65583(a)(4). For each policy, requirement, or procedure identified as a governmental constraint, the element must include an appropriate action program to modify or eliminate the constraint or demonstrate how its impacts will be effectively offset. HCD provides a number of strategies that communities may use to reduce or eliminate regulatory barriers, including modifications to land use controls, codes, and enforcement procedures, on and offsite improvement requirements, fees and exactions, and processing and permit procedures.[14]

Housing elements also must identify and mitigate to the extent feasible non-governmental constraints, such as land prices, construction costs, and financing availability. Gov't Code § 65583(a)(5). HCD recognizes that although nongovernmental constraints are primarily market-driven and generally outside direct government control, cities can significantly influence and offset the negative impact of such constraints through responsive programs and policies.[15]

Consistency with General Plan, Preparation of Annual Report, and Notification Requirements

Other housing element requirements that must be satisfied include: (1) maintaining consistency with other elements of the city's general plan (Gov't Code § 65300.5); (2) preparing an annual report to the legislative body, the Office of Planning and Research (OPR), and HCD (Gov't Code § 65400(a)(2)); and (3) notifying retail water and sewer providers upon the completion of an amended or adopted housing element. Gov't Code § 65589.7.

OPR = Office of Planning and Research

With respect to the consistency requirement, Government Code section 65589.5(d) limits a city's discretion to deny certain affordable housing projects unless certain findings are made, such as the project is inconsistent with both the general plan and zoning designations. A city's discretion if further limited by providing that such inconsistency shall not be the basis for denying an affordable housing project if certain requirements are met. "This paragraph cannot be utilized to disapprove or conditionally approve a housing development project if [it] is proposed on a site that is identified as suitable or available for very low, low or moderate income households in the jurisdiction's housing element, and consistent with the density specified in the housing element, even though it is inconsistent with both the jurisdiction's zoning ordinance and general plan land use designation." Gov't Code § 65589.5(d)(5)(A).

Government Code section 65589.5(d) limits a city's discretion to deny certain affordable housing projects unless certain findings are made, such as the project is inconsistent with both the general plan and zoning designations.

With respect to the annual report requirement, each planning agency, after a general plan has been adopted, must provide an annual report, on or before April 1st of each year, to the legislative body, OPR, and HCD on the status of the general plan and its progress in meeting the community's share of regional housing needs and local efforts to remove governmental constraints. The report must include the degree to which the approved general plan complies with OPR's general plan guidelines and the date of the last revision to the general plan. Gov't Code § 65400(b)(3).

---

14. *Id.*, page 37.
15. *Id.*, page 23.

Effective January 1, 2007, a court is required to issue an order or judgment compelling compliance with this reporting requirement within 60 days, if the housing element portion of the report is untimely. Gov't Code § 65400(c).

Special Provisions Regarding Housing Needs Within the Coastal Zone

Special attention is given to housing needs within the state's coastal zone. *See* Gov't Code §§ 65588(d), 65590, and 65590.1. When coastal zone jurisdictions review their housing elements, such reviews must provide the following information:

- The number of new housing units approved for construction within the coastal zone.
- The number of housing units for persons and families of low- and moderate-income required to be provided in new housing developments either within the coastal zone or within three miles of it.
- The number of existing residential units occupied by low- and moderate-income households that have been authorized to be demolished or converted in the coastal zone.
- The number of residential units for low- and moderate-income households that have been required for replacement of those units being demolished or converted in the coastal zone. The location of these replacement units must be designated.

Gov't Code §§ 65588(d)(1–4)

The case of *Coalition of Concerned Communities, Inc. v. City of Los Angeles*, involved a question of the interpretation of a California statute (Gov't Code § 65590(d)) that imposes an inclusionary requirement on new housing developments constructed within the coastal zone. 34 Cal. 4th 733 (2004). Plaintiff citizen groups claimed that this provision applied to a proposed project located partially within the coastal zone, even though no housing units would actually be constructed within that zone.

The court rejected this contention. In so doing, it held that the statute in question is not applicable if the development does not propose to construct any housing or even private amenities within the coastal zone. In the case at hand, the project included only some infrastructure and construction of a public view park within the coastal zone. The court determined that it neither affected existing affordable housing nor had a new housing impact within the zone and therefore the statute did not apply. *Id.* at 739. The court, however, left open the question of whether the inclusionary requirement would apply if the project proposed to build private amenities within the coastal zone, such as a golf course or other sporting facility.

Review and Certification of Housing Elements

The housing element shall be reviewed "as frequently as appropriate" in order to evaluate progress made and any changes in conditions affecting a city's housing needs. It must be revised as necessary, but not less than once every five years. Gov't Code § 65588(a),(b). This revision schedule is unique to the housing element. The remainder of the general plan need be reviewed only periodically and updated only when warranted by changing circumstances. Gov't Code § 65103(a). *See also Citizens of Goleta Valley v. Board of Supervisors*, 52 Cal. 3d 553, 572 (1990); *Garat v. City of Riverside*, 2 Cal. App. 4th 259, 298 (1991). Although the timetable for cities to revise their housing elements is set forth in Government Code sections 65588 and 65588.1, failure to comply does not automatically invalidate a general plan or its housing element. *San Mateo County Coastal Landowners' Ass'n v. County of San Mateo*, 38 Cal. App. 4th 523, 544 (1995) (to invalidate a housing element on the basis that it has not been timely revised, plaintiff must show how the failure to timely revise is connected to a substantive deficiency in the general plan or the housing element).

In preparing the housing element, a city must consider the guidelines adopted by HCD. However, these guidelines are advisory only. Gov't Code § 65585(a). Prior to adopting or amending the housing element, a city must submit a draft of the element to HCD for review. HCD must prepare written findings regarding whether the draft substantially complies with the statutory provisions.[16]

The city must consider HCD's findings before taking action, unless the findings are not available within specified time limits. If HCD finds that the draft does not comply with the law, the city must either change the draft to substantially comply or adopt it without changes. If the city decides not to make changes, then its resolution of adoption must include written findings explaining its conclusions that the draft substantially complies with the law despite HCD's findings to the contrary. Gov't Code § 65585(f).

The city must consider HCD's findings before taking action, unless the findings are not available within specified time limits.

There are several effects of compliance certification. If HCD has found that the element complies with the law, there is a rebuttable presumption of its validity in any court challenge. Gov't Code § 65589.3. Once HCD has certified compliance, the city's ability to deviate from its housing element is limited to a certain extent. Under Government Code section 65863(b), a city, with certain exceptions, is prohibited from reducing, requiring, or permitting the reduction of residential density for *any parcel* to a "lower residential density." Effective January 1, 2007, the definition of "lower residential density" is dependent on whether a city has an adopted housing element for the current planning period that HCD has found to be in substantial compliance with the housing element law. If a city's housing element is in compliance, "lower residential density" means a density below that used in the inventory for sites identified therein, or below that used to determine the housing unit capacity for sites that have been, or will be, rezoned pursuant to the city's housing element program. Gov't Code

---

16. HCD has released a "Housing Element Review Worksheet," which is a checklist that it uses when reviewing housing elements. The worksheet can serve as a helpful guide to cities in ensuring that their housing elements comply with state law. In addition, HCD has published *Housing Element Questions and Answers, A Guide to the Preparation of Housing Elements*, which sets forth clear responses to questions frequently asked by cities in preparing and updating their housing elements. The Association of Bay Area Government's *Blueprint 2001: Housing Element Ideas and Solutions for a Sustainable and Affordable Future* provides further guidance to cities in preparing and updating housing elements. The publication includes a list of ten keys to a successful housing element, as well as practical suggestions for analyzing needs, defining goals, and encouraging participation. It also includes guidelines for an effective monitoring program that, among other things, facilitates the element's compliance with statutory requirements.

§ 65863(h)(1). If the city has not adopted a housing element for the current planning period, or if the adopted housing element does not comply with the housing element law, "lower residential density" means a density below 80 percent of the maximum allowable residential density for the parcel. Gov't Code § 65863(h).

A city may allow for a reduction of residential density if it makes the following findings supported by substantial evidence:

- The reduction is consistent with the adopted general plan, including the housing element.
- The remaining sites identified in the housing element are adequate to accommodate the city's share of regional housing needs.

Alternatively, the reduction may be approved if a city can establish through written findings based on substantial evidence that there are "sufficient, additional, adequate, and available sites with an equal or greater residential density in the jurisdiction so that there is no net loss of residential unit capacity." Gov't Code § 65863(c). An amendment to the "no downzoning" law makes the city solely responsible for compliance, unless the applicant initially requests the reduction in zoning density. Gov't Code § 65863(f). The law also clarifies that development agreements and applications for subdivision maps made prior to January 1, 2003 are not subject to this statute. Gov't Code § 65863. If a plaintiff is successful in challenging a city's action under this statute, the court shall award reasonable attorneys' fees and costs except under limited circumstances. HCD issues a Housing Element Compliance Report, as required by Health and Safety Code section 54059(c).[17]

Anti-Nimby Laws—Restrictions on the Disapproval of Certain Housing Projects

In 1982, in response to the housing crisis, which was viewed as threatening the "economic, environmental and social quality of life in California," the Legislature enacted Government Code section 65589.5. Commonly referred to as the "Anti-Nimby" legislation, but re-named the "Housing Accountability Act" by legislation passed in 2006, this statute restricts a city's ability to disapprove, or require density reductions in, certain types of residential projects.[18]

The basis of this statute is the Legislature's finding that "the excessive cost of the state's housing supply is partially caused by activities and policies of many local governments that limit the approval of housing, increase the cost of land for housing, and require that high fees and exactions be paid by producers of housing." Gov't Code § 65589.5(a)(2). The purpose of the anti-Nimby legislation is to help ensure that a city "not reject or make infeasible housing developments that contribute to meeting the housing need determined pursuant to [Housing Element Law] without a thorough analysis of the economic, social,

---

17. See Dep't of Housing and Cmty. Dev., Div. of Housing Policy Dev., *Housing Element Compliance Report*.
18. See also Gov't Code § 65008 (action by a city is "null and void" if it denies an individual, or a group of individuals, the enjoyment of residence, landownership, tenancy, or any other land use for enumerated reasons including intended occupancy of a residential development by persons of very low, low, moderate, or middle income).

and environmental effects of the action and without complying with subdivision (d)." Gov't Code § 65589.5(b).

Although this statute affords various protections to certain affordable housing projects (Gov't Code § 65589.5(d)) and certain housing projects generally (Gov't Code § 65589.5(j)), it does not relieve a city from complying with provisions of the Congestion Management Program, the California Coastal Act, CEQA, or other state or local requirements. Gov't Code § 65589.5(e). It also does not limit a city's ability to impose fees or exactions otherwise authorized by law that are essential to provide necessary public services and facilities to the project. Gov't Code § 65589.5(f). Further, it does not prohibit a city from enforcing written development standards, conditions, and policies appropriate to, and consistent with, meeting the jurisdiction's share of the regional housing need. However, the standards relied upon must be "objective" and "quantifiable," and must be applied to facilitate and accommodate development at the density permitted on the site and proposed by the project.

The Housing Accountability Act does not limit a city's ability to impose fees or exactions otherwise authorized by law that are essential to provide necessary public services and facilities to the project.

Affordable Housing Projects Under Government Code Section 65589.5(d)

Under Government Code section 65589.5(d), a city may not disapprove a housing development project[19] affordable to very low-, low-, or moderate-income households, supportive housing, transitional housing, or emergency shelters, or condition approval of such a project in a manner that makes the project infeasible, unless it finds, based on substantial evidence, one of the following:

- The city has adopted a housing element that has been revised in accordance with Government Code section 65588, is in substantial compliance with the Housing Element law, and the city has met or exceeded its share of the regional housing need for the income category proposed for the housing development project. If it includes a mix of income categories, and the jurisdiction has not met its fair share housing needs, then this paragraph cannot be used as a basis to deny or condition approval.

- The project as proposed would have a specific adverse impact upon the public health and safety that cannot be satisfactorily mitigated without rendering it unaffordable. Inconsistency with the zoning ordinance or general plan land use designation shall not constitute a specific, adverse impact upon public health and safety.

- The denial of the project or imposition of conditions is required in order to comply with state or federal law (*e.g.*, CEQA), and there is no feasible method to comply without rendering the project unaffordable.

- The project is proposed on land zoned for agriculture or resource preservation that is surrounded on at least two sides by land being used for agriculture

---

19. For purposes of this statute, "housing development project" means a use consisting of either: (1) residential units only, or (2) mixed-use developments consisting of residential and nonresidential uses in which the nonresidential uses are limited to neighborhood commercial uses and to the first floor of buildings that are two or more stories. Gov't Code § 65589.5(h)(2). At least one court has held that a specific plan, rejected by the voters by the referendum process, does not constitute a "housing development project." *Chandis Sec. Co. v. City of Dana Point*, 52 Cal. App. 4th 475, 486–87 (1996).

- or preservation purposes, or the site does not have an adequate water or wastewater facility to serve the project.
- The project is inconsistent with both the city's zoning ordinance and general plan land use designation as specified in the general plan as it existed on the date the application was deemed complete, and the city has adopted a revised housing element in accordance with section 65588 that is in substantial compliance with the Housing Element law.

Section 65589.5(d)(5) of the Government Code cannot be utilized to disapprove a housing development project if it is proposed on a site that is identified as suitable or available for very low, low-, or moderate-income households in the city's housing element and is consistent with the density specified in the city's housing element, even though it is inconsistent with *both* the city's zoning ordinance and general plan land use designation. Moreover, a city cannot disapprove an affordable housing development by declaring it is not needed unless the community has actually met its fair share housing needs. This change is intended to preclude a city from relying on speculative projects not yet approved to justify denial. The 2007 legislative amendments to this section add supportive housing, transitional housing, and emergency shelters to the list of protected housing projects.

To qualify for the protections provided by Government Code section 65589.5(d), the project must propose development of housing for "very low-, low- or moderate-income households," which means that either:

- At least 20 percent of the total units shall be sold or rented to lower income households (as defined in Health and Safety Code section 50079.5); or
- 100 percent of the units shall be sold or rented to moderate income households (as defined in Health and Safety Code section 50093), or to middle income households (as defined in Government Code section 65008).

Gov't Code § 65589.5(h)(3)

Housing units targeted for lower income households must be made available at a monthly housing cost that does not exceed 30 percent of 60 percent of the median income for the area, adjusted for family size. Housing units targeted for moderate-income households shall be made available at a monthly housing cost that does not exceed 30 percent of 100 percent of median income for the area, adjusted for family size. Gov't Code § 65589.5(h)(3). In addition, the developer must provide sufficient legal commitments to ensure continued affordability of low and very low income units for 30 years. Gov't Code § 65589.5(h)(4).

The applicant for the housing development project or any person who would be eligible to apply for residency in the development may bring an action to enforce this law. Gov't Code § 65589.5(k). In any legal action challenging a city's denial or conditional approval of an affordable housing project under Government Code section 65589.5(d), the city shall have the burden of proof to show that its decision is consistent with the requisite findings and supported by substantial evidence. Gov't Code § 65589.5(i). If the city cannot meet this burden, then the court shall issue an order compelling compliance within 60 days, including, without limitation, an order to take action on the proposed project. The court shall retain jurisdiction to ensure its order or judgment is carried out and shall award reasonable attorneys' fees and costs of the suit to the petitioner, except under extraordinary circumstances in which the court finds that awarding fees would not further the purposes of the statute. If the court determines that its order or judgment has not been carried out within 60 days, the court may issue further orders to ensure the purposes and policies of this law are fulfilled, including, but not limited to, vacating the city's decision, deeming the project approved, and imposing fines if the court finds that the city acted in bad faith. Gov't Code § 65589.5(k).

Housing Development Projects Generally Under Government Code Section 65589.5(j)

Under Government Code section 65589.5(j), a city's ability to deny approval or impose conditions on housing development projects that do not contain an affordable housing component is also restricted under certain circumstances. When a proposed housing development project complies with applicable, objective general plan and zoning standards and criteria, the city shall not disapprove the project or condition approval on a density reduction unless it makes written findings based upon substantial evidence that both of the following conditions exist:

- The housing project would have a specific, adverse impact upon the public health and safety unless the project is disapproved or approved only on condition that the project be developed at a lower density. "Specific, adverse impact" is defined as "a significant, quantifiable, direct, and unavoidable impact, based on objective, identified written public health or safety standards, policies, or conditions...." Gov't Code § 65589.5(j)(1).
- There is no feasible way to satisfactorily mitigate or avoid the adverse impact identified, other than the disapproval of the project or the approval conditioned on developing the project at a lower density. Gov't Code § 65589.5(j)(2).

There is no requirement under this subsection (j) that the development project contain any affordable units. *Sequoyah Hills Homeowners Ass'n v. City of Oakland*, 23 Cal. App. 4th 704, 715–16 (1993) (when there are findings that a proposed residential project complies with all general plan and zoning policies, Government Code section 65589.5 prevents a city from requiring a reduction in the density of the project without first establishing that the project poses a "specific adverse impact upon the public health or safety"). *See also North Pacifica, LLC v. City of Pacifica*, 234 F. Supp. 2d 1053, 1057 (N.D. Cal. 2002) (Government Code section 65589.5(j) applies to all "housing development projects" regardless of the income level of the intended occupants).

Under Government Code section 65589.5(j), a city's ability to deny approval or impose conditions on housing development projects that do not contain an affordable housing component is also restricted under certain circumstances.

Prioritization of Services to Certain Affordable Housing Projects

Each public agency or private entity providing water or sewer services must grant a priority for the provision of available and future resources or services to proposed housing developments that help meet a city's affordable housing needs. Effective January 1, 2006, these service providers must adopt a written policy with "specific objective standards" for allocation of water and sewer services to affordable housing developments. In addition, such service providers are prohibited from denying, conditioning approval, or reducing the amount of service for a proposed affordable housing development unless certain findings are made. Gov't Code § 65589.7.

Special Treatment for Affordable Multi-Family Housing Projects

Section 65589.4 applies to a broad range of projects, including all attached housing developments (with the exception of second units and existing structures converted to condominiums) with two or more units.

Pursuant to Government Code section 65589.4, under certain circumstances, attached housing developments shall be a permitted use not subject to a conditional use permit on any parcel zoned for attached housing. This law applies to a broad range of projects, including all attached housing developments (with the exception of second units and existing structures converted to condominiums) with two or more units. This law is applicable to charter cities.

To qualify under this statute, the project must meet one of the following affordability criteria:

- At least 10 percent of the project's units shall be affordable to very low income households, as defined in Health and Safety Code section 50105
- At least 20 percent of the project's units shall be affordable to lower-income households, as defined in Health and Safety Code section 50079.5, or
- At least 50 percent of the project's units shall be affordable to moderate-income households, consistent with Health and Safety Code section 50052.5

Gov't Code § 65589.4(b)

The developer must provide sufficient legal commitments to ensure that the units will remain affordable for a period of at least 30 years.

The developer must provide sufficient legal commitments to ensure that the units will remain affordable for a period of at least 30 years. In addition to satisfying the affordability criteria specified above, the project must either:

- Qualify for one of three CEQA exemptions relating to the development of housing for agricultural employees (Pub. Res. Code § 21159.22), certain small affordable projects (Pub. Res. Code § 21159.23), or certain infill projects (Pub. Res. Code § 21159.24); or
- Meet all of the following criteria:
  - The project is subject to a discretionary decision other than a conditional use permit, and a negative declaration or mitigated negative declaration has been adopted for the project under CEQA.
  - The project is consistent with both the city's zoning ordinance and general plan as it existed on the date the project application was deemed complete, except that a project shall not be deemed to be inconsistent with the general plan only because the project site has not been rezoned to conform with the most recent adopted general plan.
  - The project is located in an area that is covered by one of the following documents that has been adopted by the city within five years of the date the project application was deemed complete: (1) a general plan, (2) a revision or update to the general plan that includes at least the land use and circulation elements; (3) an applicable community plan; or (4) an applicable specific plan.
  - The project consists of not more than 100 residential units with a minimum density of not less than 12 units per acre or a minimum density of not less than eight units per acre if the project consists of four or fewer units.

- The project is located in an urbanized area (as defined in Pub. Res. Code § 21071), or within a census-defined place with a population density of at least 5,000 persons per square mile, or, if the project consists of 50 or fewer units, within an incorporated city with a population density of at least 2,500 persons per square mile and a total population of at least 25,000 persons.
- The project is located on an infill site (as defined in Pub. Res. Code § 21061.0.5).

However, a city is not prohibited from applying design and site review standards in existence on the date the application was determined complete. Gov't Code § 65589.4(c).

Other State Laws Designed to Facilitate Housing Production

In addition to state housing element provisions, the Legislature has provided a number of reforms and incentives to encourage development of affordable housing. Gov't Code § 65582.1 (cataloging such laws).

Least Cost Zoning Law

State laws have been enacted in order to (1) expedite the entitlement process; (2) assure that cities zone sufficient land at densities high enough for affordable housing production; and (3) assure that cities make a diligent effort to significantly reduce development costs and facilitate the development of affordable housing.

Under Government Code section 65913.1, commonly known as the "Least Cost Zoning" law, cities must designate and zone sufficient vacant land with "appropriate standards" for residential use to meet the housing needs of all income levels. Gov't Code § 65913.1. This requirement is in addition to the mandate under Government Code section 65583(c)(1) imposed upon cities to identify adequate sites in their housing elements to meet fair share housing needs.

Under the Least Cost Zoning law, cities must designate and zone sufficient vacant land with appropriate standards for residential use to meet the housing needs of all income levels.

Under Government Code section 65913.1, "appropriate standards" means densities and requirements imposed on residential lots that contribute significantly to the economic feasibility of producing housing at the lowest possible cost including requirements with respect to minimum floor areas, building setbacks, rear and side yards, parking, the percentage of a lot that must be occupied by a structure, and amenities. These standards must take into consideration economic and environmental factors, public health and safety, and the need to facilitate the development of affordable housing.

Density Bonuses

Density bonuses for affordable housing are addressed in Government Code section 65915 *et seq*. This law requires a city to grant a density bonus and a certain number of concessions or incentives to a developer who agrees to construct certain housing developments that provide either affordable or senior housing and meet certain criteria.[20] Gov't Code § 65915(b)(1). A density bonus means a floor area ratio bonus over the otherwise maximum allowable density permitted

---

20. The American Planning Association has published a model affordable housing density bonus ordinance, available on the APA website (www.planning.org).

under the applicable zoning and general plan land use designation. Revisions to the law in 2005 expressed the Legislature's intent that cities "encourage, to the maximum extent practicable, the location of housing developed pursuant to [Density Bonus Law] in urban areas with adequate infrastructure to serve the housing." 2005 Cal. Stat., ch. 496 (S.B. 435), Section 1.[21] Although application of the statute can be complicated, its purpose is fairly simple: When a developer agrees to construct a certain percentage of the units in a housing development for moderate-, low-, or very low-income households, or to construct a senior housing development, the city or county must grant the developer one or more itemized concessions and a "density bonus," which allows the developer to increase the density of the development by a certain percentage above the maximum allowable limit under local zoning and general plan laws. Gov't Code §§ 65915(a), (b); *see also Friends of Lagoon Valley*, 154 Cal. App. 4th 807 (2007). In other words, the Density Bonus Law "reward[s] a developer who agrees to build a certain percentage of low-income housing with the opportunity to build more residences than would otherwise be permitted by the applicable local regulations." *Shea Homes Ltd. Partnership v. County of Alameda*, 110 Cal. App. 4th 1246, 1263 (2003).

Development concessions or incentives under the Density Bonus Law may include, but are not limited to:

- A reduction in site development standards
- A modification of zoning code requirements or architectural design requirements that exceed the minimum building standards
- Approval of mixed-use zoning in conjunction with the housing project if commercial, office, industrial, or other land uses will reduce the cost of the housing development, and if such nonresidential uses are compatible with the project and the existing and planned development in the area
- Other regulatory incentives or concessions proposed by the developer or the city that result in identifiable, financially sufficient, and actual cost reductions

Recent changes in density bonus law provide for greater bonuses for the inclusion of more affordable units.

The Density Bonus Law now provides for greater bonuses for the inclusion of more affordable units. It also reduces the percentage of units required to earn the density bonus, while increasing the level of density bonus and the incentives and concessions that the city must provide. Specifically, the new law lowers the minimum number of affordable housing units required to be provided to qualify for a density bonus as follows:

- From 20 percent to 10 percent of the total units of a housing development for lower-income households
- From 10 percent to five percent of the total units of a housing development for very low-income households
- From 50 percent of the total units for seniors to any senior citizen housing development with at least 35 units as well as including mobile home parks that limit residency based on age; and

---

21. For an excellent discussion of the density bonus law, *see* Betsy Strauss, *The Density Bonus Law: Changes, Interpretations, and Implementation* (City Attorney Conference of the League of California Cities, May 2006) (available at www.cacities.org/attypapers).

- From 20 percent to 10 percent of the units in a common interest development for moderate-income households, provided that all units in the development are offered to the public for purchase

The definition of "housing development" has been expanded as well to include a subdivision or a common interest development, and the density bonus has been lowered from 25 percent to 20 percent for low-income, very low-income, or senior housing. In addition, the number of extra units that may be included for moderate-income over the otherwise maximum allowable residential density under the local zoning ordinance has been lowered to five percent; and the density bonus is required to increase incrementally. Gov't Code § 65915(g)(1) (how to calculate the level of density bonus).

The definition of housing development was expanded as well to include a subdivision or a common interest development.

In terms of calculating the amount of density bonus, a recent case has confirmed that the Density Bonus Law does not impose a cap on the maximum amount a developer may obtain. In *Friends of Lagoon Valley*, petitioners agreed that the city violated state Density Bonus Law when it awarded the developer a 40 percent density bonus. The version of the law in effect at the time of project approval provided for a maximum of 35 percent density bonus that a city could be required to give to a developer. Petitioners in *Friends of Lagoon Valley* argued that this law contained an absolute cap, and therefore the city violated state law when it awarded a developer over 40 percent density bonus. The court, however, rejected this position.

> Because the statute imposes a mandatory duty on local governments, and provides a means for developers to enforce this duty through civil proceedings [Citation omitted], it is clear that 35 percent represents the maximum amount of bonus a city is *required to provide*, not the maximum amount a developer can ever obtain. The entire aim of Section 65915 is to provide incentives to developers to construct housing for seniors and low income families. [Citation omitted.] It would undermine this policy to interpret [this law] as imposing an absolute cap, since such a rule would prevent developers from negotiating to obtain a higher density bonus in exchange for including even more low income or senior housing than is provided for in Section 65915.

Friends of Lagoon Valley, 154 Cal. App. 4th at 825 (emphasis in original)

The provision of direct financial incentives for such housing by the city is not limited or required, and the waiver of fees or dedication requirements may be retained. Gov't Code § 65915(k).

Affordability rates and processing requirements are set forth in Government Code section 65915(c). The requirement that the developer and the city agree to the continued affordability of moderate-income units for 10 years has been removed, although the 30-year affordability requirement for the low- and very low-income units which qualified the applicant for the density bonus has been retained. However, the developer must agree, and the city must ensure, that the initial occupants of moderate-income units meet the moderate-income standard, as statutorily defined. Upon the subsequent sale of such units, the seller is allowed to keep the value of any improvements, the down payment, and an allocated share of appreciation. The city also may recapture an allocated share of appreciation, but must use that share within three years for the promotion of affordable home ownership. Upon the developer's request, the city is prohibited from requiring parking standards greater than one on-site parking space for units with zero to one bedroom, two on-site spaces for two- to three-bedroom units, and 2.5 parking spaces for units with four or more bedrooms. Cities may grant density bonuses greater than what is provided in the statute or lower in cases where the statutory requirements are not met.

The law also provides a 15 percent density bonus for the entire project to the developer of any market rate housing project who donates land to a city that could accommodate housing for very low-income households equal to at least 10 percent of the number of units in the market rate development. To be eligible for this bonus, the applicant must donate and transfer the land no later than the approval of the final subdivision map, parcel map, or development application. The transferred land also must be at least one acre or of sufficient size to accommodate 40 units and be located within, or within one mile of, the proposed development. The land must be subject to deed restrictions ensuring continued affordability and must be donated to the city or to a developer approved by the city. Further, it must have the appropriate general plan and zoning designations, the necessary permits and approvals, and the ability to be served by infrastructure.

In addition, when an applicant proposes to construct a project that conforms to the requirements of the statute and includes a child care facility that will be located on the premises of, as part of, or adjacent to the project, the city shall grant either an additional density bonus equal to or greater than the square footage of the child care facility, or an additional concession or incentive that contributes significantly to the economic feasibility of the construction of the child care facility. Gov't Code § 65915(i)(1). An applicant must meet certain conditions in order to receive the additional child care density bonus, including: (1) continued operation of the facility for a duration of time equal in length to the period of time the affordable units within the project must remain affordable; and (2) a requirement that, of the children who attend the facility, the children of very low-income households, lower income households, and moderate-income households shall constitute a percentage that is equal to or greater than the percentage of affordable units required to qualify for the density bonus. Gov't Code § 65915(i)(2).

To deny a particular density bonus, concession, or incentive requested by the applicant, the city must adopt findings that it is not needed to achieve affordability or would threaten public health and safety or a historic structure.

To deny a particular density bonus, concession, or incentive requested by the applicant, the city must adopt findings that the particular bonus, concession, or incentive is not needed to achieve affordability or would threaten public health and safety or a historic structure. Gov't Code § 65915(d)(1). *See also Building Indus. Ass'n v. City of Oceanside*, 27 Cal. App. 4th 744, 755–66 (1994) (a zoning initiative that imposed a numerical residential growth cap conflicted with Government Code section 65915). If a city is unable to make these findings and still refuses to grant the density bonus or required incentives or concessions, the developer may initiate judicial proceedings. In such a proceeding, a court must award reasonable attorneys' fees and costs of suit if the plaintiff succeeds in showing that a city violated the statute. Gov't Code §§ 65915(d)(1) and (e).

There also are incentives for low income housing development provided for in connection with condominium conversions. Gov't Code § 65915.5.

In *Friends of Lagoon Valley*, the court rejected the petitioners' interpretation of the law, which was based on the detailed legislative history instead of the plain language of the statute. This case is a good indicator of how courts may rule on another significant emerging conflict in the interpretation of the Density Bonus Law. Recently, a few cities have argued that the state law does not apply to affordable units provided to satisfy local inclusionary housing requirements. These cities maintain that inclusionary units do not count for purposes of calculating density bonuses or for the issuance of incentives or concessions. Such cities recognize that state law requires cities and counties to grant density bonuses and incentives or concessions whenever a developer agrees to construct affordable units as a part of a development, and that the bonus is determined based on the percentage of the "total units" in a project that are affordable. Nevertheless, these cities maintain that affordable units provided to satisfy a local ordinance may not be counted as part of the "total units" of a project since the developer has not "agreed" to provide these units; rather, the affordable units are required by local ordinance.

This argument is based on selected legislative history from the State Assembly for SB 435, a Senate bill that recently amended Government Code section 65915. This argument appears to ignore the plain meaning of the word "agreed" since, unless challenged in court, every condition of approval and project component is "agreed" to by a project developer. As with the interpretation proposed by the project opponents in *Friends of Lagoon Valley*, this argument appears to ignore the plain meaning of the statute in favor of excerpts from the legislative history. In addition, the legislative history relied upon by these cities is likely an "isolated" piece of legislative history within the meaning of the *Friends of Lagoon Valley* case because when the identical bill was returned to the State Senate, the Senate Floor analysis stated that "any affordable units in a development count toward meeting density bonus requirements, regardless of whether or not the affordable units are required to be constructed by the local government pursuant to an ordinance."

This case should be read with interest by those applying or seeking affordable housing density bonuses. Under *Friends of Lagoon Valley*, the plain meaning of the words "agreed" and "total units," not the legislative history, should be read to control interpretations of the density bonus law. Excluding inclusionary units when calculating the mandatory density bonus would defeat the aim of the state density bonus law to provide incentives to developers to construct housing for seniors and low-income families.

Second Units

Facilitating the development of second units has been recognized as one way of increasing the supply of affordable housing, and, therefore, laws have been enacted to encourage their development. Gov't Code § 65852.150. For a good discussion of the purposes of the second unit law, *see Wilson v. City of Laguna Beach*, 6 Cal. App. 4th 543, 555–56 (1992); *Sounheim v. City of San Dimas*, 47 Cal. App. 4th 1181, 1191 (1996).

Second unit means an attached or detached residential unit that provides complete independent living facilities for one or more persons. Gov't Code § 65852.2(i)(4). Government Code section 65852.2 sets forth procedures by which second units in single-family and multi-family residential zones may be established. The intent of the Legislature is that any second-unit ordinances

Facilitating the development of second units has been recognized as one way of increasing the supply of affordable housing, and, therefore, laws have been enacted to encourage their development.

adopted by cities have the effect of providing for the creation of second units, and any requirements imposed are not so onerous as to unreasonably restrict the creation of such units. Gov't Code § 65852.150. This section permits a city to establish a procedure by ordinance to allow these types of units. In addition, it requires cities without second unit ordinances to consider these applications ministerially, without discretionary review and a hearing unless they adopt such an ordinance within 120 days after receiving the application. Further, the law requires that the city grant a variance or special use permit for the creation of a second unit if the applicant's proposal meets all of the criteria set forth in Government Code section 65852.2(b)(1). Those criteria also establish the maximum standards that cities are allowed to use in evaluating second unit applications. Gov't Code § 65852.2(b)(3).

Cities are not permitted to restrict the use of second units to specific categories of people.

Cities are not permitted to restrict the use of second units to specific categories of people. *Coalition Advocating Legal Housing Options v. City of Santa Monica*, 88 Cal. App. 4th 451 (2001) (invalidating an ordinance that restricted the creation of second units in single-family residential zones only to those units where either the property owner or the owner's dependent or caregiver would reside). Prior legislation granted a city authority to approve what were commonly referred to as "granny" units. Effective January 1, 2007, that authority has been repealed in favor of the newer law addressing second units. However, such "granny" units constructed or with approved permits issued before this date are legal. Gov't Code § 65852.1(b).

Community Redevelopment Law

Certain provisions under Community Redevelopment Law are designed to facilitate the development of affordable housing.

Certain provisions under Community Redevelopment Law are designed to facilitate the development of affordable housing. Health & Safety Code § 33000 et seq.[22]

Health and Safety Code section 33334.2 requires that, in redevelopment project areas adopted after 1976, not less than 20 percent of the gross tax increment generated from the project area must be used by the redevelopment agency to increase and improve the community's supply of affordable housing. *See also Hogar Dulce Hogar v. Community Dev. Comm'n*, 110 Cal. App. 4th 1288, 1292 (2003). An agency may exempt itself from the set-aside requirement only if it makes written findings annually as to the following:

- No need exists in the community to improve, increase, or preserve the supply of low- and moderate-income housing (including housing for very low income households) in a manner that would benefit the project area and that this finding is consistent with the community's housing element (Health & Safety Code § 33334.2(a)(1)); or
- Some stated percentage less than 20 percent of the tax increment generated by the project area is sufficient to meet the housing needs of the community and that this finding is consistent with the housing element (Health & Safety Code § 33334.2(a)(2)).

There is a 10-year statute of limitations period for actions to compel compliance with a redevelopment agency's set-aside obligation. Such actions

---

22. *See California Affordable Housing Handbook: Strategies for Building Better Communities*, pages 113–138 (Feb. 2006), for a thorough discussion on the legal requirements of affordable housing under Community Redevelopment Law.

accrue on the last day of the fiscal year of the required deposit. Health & Safety Code § 33334.2(j)(1)(A). There is also a 10-year statute of limitations period to bring actions against redevelopment agencies for improper expenditures of set-aside funds, with such actions accruing on the date of the improper expenditure. Health & Safety Code § 33334.2(j)(1)(B). An agency found to have deposited inadequate funds or unlawfully expended funds must repay the funds with interest. Health & Safety Code § 33334.2(j)(1)(C).

In addition to the set-aside requirement, community redevelopment law imposes inclusionary housing requirements. Health and Safety Code section 33413(b)(1) mandates that at least 30 percent of all new and substantially rehabilitated dwelling units developed by a redevelopment agency be affordable. Not less than 50 percent of these affordable units must be available to very low income households. In addition, at least 15 percent of all new and substantially rehabilitated units developed within a redevelopment project area by public or private entities or persons other than the redevelopment agency must be affordable. Not less than 40 percent of these affordable units must be available to very low income households. Health & Safety Code § 33413(b)(2)(A)(i).

At least 30 percent of all new and substantially rehabilitated dwelling units developed by a redevelopment agency must be affordable.

A redevelopment agency may fulfill these inclusionary housing requirements outside of the project area so long as the agency provides for two units for each housing unit that otherwise would have been available inside the redevelopment project area. Health & Safety Code § 33413(b)(2)(A)(ii). Aggregation of new or substantially rehabilitated dwelling units in one or more project areas to meet the inclusionary housing requirements is permitted, so long as the agency finds that such aggregation will not cause or exacerbate racial, ethnic, or economic segregation. Health & Safety Code § 33413(b)(2)(A)(v).

Growth Management and Affordable Housing

Tension Between Environmental Protection and Affordable Housing

Often, as efforts increase to facilitate the production of more housing, antigrowth sentiment may be heightened.[23] Cities, confronted with significant opposition to proposed residential projects because of environmental concerns, are then placed in the untenable position of trying to reconcile these sometimes competing objectives.

Housing advocates point out that when environmental protection laws are used to substantially reduce housing production, a fundamental problem of supply and demand results. Without an adequate supply, unmet demand drives housing costs and rents even higher, thereby further exacerbating the affordable housing crisis.[24] The California courts have expressed their concern over this "drawbridge mentality." As the late California Supreme Court Associate Justice Stanley Mosk stated:

Housing advocates point out that when environmental protection laws are used to substantially reduce housing production, a fundamental problem of supply and demand results.

---

23. See Cecily T. Talbert and Nadia L. Costa, "Inclusionary Housing Programs: Local Governments Respond to California's Housing Crisis," 30 *B.C. Envtl. Aff. L. Rev.*, no. 3, 567 (2003).
24. See *Bay Area Housing Profile: A Report Card on the Supply and Demand Crisis*, page 4 (Bay Area Council, 2003).

> I must repeat the misgivings I retain about the constitutional validity of no-growth or limited-growth ordinances. An impermissible elitist concept is invoked when a community constructs a legal moat around its perimeter to exclude all or most outsiders. The growing tendency of some communities to arbitrarily restrict housing to present residents appears at odds with Supreme Court pronouncements from *Shelley v. Kraemer* [citation omitted], to the words of Justice Douglas in *Reitman v. Mulkey* [citation omitted]: "housing is clearly marked with the public interest."

Building Indus. Ass'n v. City of Camarillo, 41 Cal. 3d 810, 825 (1986) (Mosk, J., concurring)[25]

Enhancing long-term planning and regulatory consistency requirements can serve to appropriately balance the goals of protecting the environment and producing affordable housing.

Rather than environmental protection goals conflicting with affordable housing objections, the latter can be viewed as a key component of protecting the environment and managing growth.[26] Enhancing long-term planning and regulatory consistency requirements can serve to appropriately balance the goals of protecting the environment and producing affordable housing.[27] As a corollary, the elimination of low-density, class-based[28] exclusionary zoning can significantly reduce sprawl and its concomitant harmful effects while increasing affordable housing opportunities. "Smart Growth" is often proffered as the answer to this dilemma. In addition, while not a panacea, "Smart Growth" principles come into play—by promoting more compact development, mixed-use and mixed-income neighborhoods, and creating jobs near housing and transportation, increased housing may be available to meet the demand at affordable costs. *See* Ass'n of Bay Area Gov'ts, *Smart Growth Strategy—Regional Livability Footprint Project Final Report: Shaping the Future of the Nine-County Bay Area* (2002) (available at www.abag.ca.gov/planning/smartgrowth/Final/SmartGrowthRpt_final.pdf) (focusing on three "key goals" of sustainability including a prosperous economy, a quality environment, and social equity, and identifying a housing shortage as a major impediment to economic growth).

Special Legislative and Judicial Requirements for Growth Management Measures

Over the past several decades, cities have enacted a variety of growth management measures, both council and voter-initiated. Although there are often

---

25. *See also Shea Homes L.P. v. County of Alameda*, 110 Cal. App. 4th 1246 (2003) (illustrates tension between environmental concerns and affordable housing concerns); Daniel J. Curtin, Jr., *Cuyahoga County (U.S. Supreme Court) and Shea v. County of Alameda (California) on Referenda, Initiatives, and Affordable Housing—Federal and State Challenges*, Program on Planning, Zoning, and Eminent Domain (San Francisco, 2003).
26. *See* Arthur C. Nelson and Susan M. Wachter, "Growth Management and Affordable Housing Policy, 12 *J. Affordable Housing & Cmty. Dev. L.* 173 (2003).
27. *See, e.g.*, Rusty Russell, "Equity in Eden:Can Environmental Protections and Affordable Housing Comfortably Cohabit in Suburbia?," 30 *B.C. Envtl. Aff. L. Rev.* 437 (2003).
28. Many commentators have emphasized the importance of considering the impact of racial animus on housing patterns and resulting residential segregation. *See, e.g.*, Reginald Leamon Robinson, "The Racial Limits of the Fair Housing Act: The Intersection of Dominant White Images, the Violence of Neighborhood Purity, and the Master Narrative of Black Inferiority," 37 *Wm. & Mary L. Rev.* 69 (1995–96); Jon C. Dubin, "From Junkyards to Gentrification: Explicating a Right to Protective Zoning in Low Income Communities of Color," 77 *Minn. L. Rev.* 739, 773–74 (1993); John Charles Boger, "Toward Ending Residential Segregation: A Fair Share Proposal for the Next Reconstruction," 71 *N.C.L. Rev.* 1573 (1992–93).

legitimate reasons for adopting growth management measures, California law imposes special requirements on such measures to ensure they do not unduly hamper the production of housing.

If a city, including a charter city, adopts or amends a general plan element that operates to limit the number of housing units that may be constructed on an annual basis, such action must be based on findings that justify reducing the housing opportunities of the region. Gov't Code § 65302.8. The findings shall include all of the following:

- A description of the city's appropriate share of the regional need for housing
- A description of the specific housing programs and activities being undertaken by the city to fulfill the requirements of the state housing element law
- A description of how the public health, safety, and welfare would be promoted by such adoption or amendment
- The fiscal and environmental resources available to the city

Any zoning ordinance that, by its terms, limits the number of housing units that may be constructed on an annual basis shall contain findings as to the public health, safety, and welfare of the city to be promoted by the adoption of the ordinance that justify reducing the housing opportunities of the region. Gov't Code § 65863.6. These requirements are not applicable, however, if the numerical restrictions are imposed by initiative. *Building Indus. Ass'n v. City of Camarillo*, 41 Cal. 3d 810, 815 (1986).

When a growth limitation is adopted, the burden of proving that the ordinance or regulation is reasonably related to the protection of public health, safety, and welfare of the affected population is on the city and not the attacking party. Evid. Code § 669.5(b). *See also Building Industry Ass'n v. Superior Court*, 211 Cal. App. 3d 277, 292–93 (1989); *Lee v. City of Monterey Park*, 173 Cal. App. 3d 798, 806–07 (1985). *But see Hernandez v. City of Encinitas*, 28 Cal. App. 4th 1048, 1076 (1994) (Evidence Code § 669.5 does not come into play unless there is a violation of the "least cost zoning law" contained in Government Code § 65913.1). This burden shifting applies even if the restriction is imposed by initiative. *Building Indus. Ass'n v. City of Camarillo*, 41 Cal. 3d at 815 (1986). However, there are certain exceptions. For example, if the initiative exempts affordable housing projects, Evidence Code section 669.5 does not apply.

Any growth management measure also must comply with state law, including substantive requirements for the general plan. HCD has devised a compliance test to determine the validity of a growth management measure under the housing element requirements of state law, taking into consideration the following:

- Is the measure based upon actual and clearly defined environmental or public facility constraints (*e.g.*, limited sewer, water, or school capacity)?
- Does the measure set the city's new construction maximums above its new construction need, including its share of the region's housing needs?
- Does the measure provide adequate incentives to encourage the development of housing affordable to low- and moderate-income households, consistent with the city's share of the region's housing needs for all income levels?
- Is the city taking all reasonable and available steps to relieve the constraints that made the growth limitation necessary?

- Does the measure also equitably limit industrial and commercial development that may increase the need for housing?
- Is the growth limitation measure conditioned to expire upon removal of the justifying constraint?[29]

If a particular measure appears to preclude the locality from meeting its housing element obligations, HCD will report that, in its opinion, the housing element does not comply with state law. Such a finding could serve as evidence in a legal action seeking a judgment that the city's general plan is inadequate. See, e.g., *Buena Vista Gardens Apartments Ass'n v. City of San Diego*, 175 Cal. App. 3d 289, 304 (1985).

Inclusionary Housing
Introduction

In general, inclusionary housing practices either mandate or encourage developers of new residential projects to set aside a certain percentage of a project's residential units for lower and moderate income households.

In general, inclusionary housing practices[30] either mandate or encourage developers of new residential projects to set aside a certain percentage of a project's residential units for lower and moderate income households. These programs are typically effectuated by ordinance, zoning codes, policy statements, or a city's housing element or fair share plan.[31]

Components of inclusionary housing programs may include: the specification that a certain percentage of affordable units must be provided as part of a project; the establishment of affordability criteria for those units based upon a percentage of median income; and the provision for future price or rent restrictions in order to preserve the long-term affordability of such units. In addition, inclusionary housing programs often provide certain incentives and concessions to encourage the provision of affordable units,[32] as well as various alternatives to on-site affordable housing production, such as in-lieu fees, land dedication, and off-site development.[33]

Reliance on the tool of inclusionary housing continues to grow as communities seek ways to increase their affordable housing stock.[34] In the absence of

---

29. Dep't of Housing and Cmty. Dev., Statutory and Constitutional Requirements with Regard to Growth Control Measures (Memorandum) (Nov. 7, 1986).

30. Although the term "inclusionary housing" is sometimes used interchangeably with "inclusionary zoning," not all inclusionary practices are zoning overlays. For a good reference nationwide, *see* "Mandatory Inclusionary Zoning: The Answer to the Affordable Housing Problem," *B.C. Envtl. Aff. L. Rev.*, vol. 33, no. 2 (2006).

31. *See* Cecily T. Talbert and Alison L. Krumbein, "Inclusionary Zoning, How to Strengthen the Defensibility of This Popular Tool to Meet Your Community's Affordable Housing Needs," 46 *The Municipal Lawyer*, page 7 (May/June 2005). *See also* Barbara Ehrlich Kautz, "In Defense of Inclusionary Zoning: Successfully Creating Affordable Housing," 36 *U.S.F. L. Rev.* 973, 983–5 (Summer 2002) for a thorough history of the use of inclusionary housing across the nation.

32. Such benefits to developers may include density bonuses, expedited processing, local tax abatements, waiver of permit fees or land dedication requirements, reduction of required developer-provided amenities, and subsidization or provision of infrastructure by the jurisdiction for the developer's project.

33. *See generally* Dr. Robert W. Burchell and Catherine C. Galley, "Inclusionary Zoning: Pros and Cons," *California Inclusionary Housing Reader* (Institute for Local Self Government, 2003). This publication may be ordered online (www.ilsg.org).

34. *See* Nico Calavita, "Origins and Evolution of Inclusionary Housing in California," in "Inclusionary Housing: The California Experience," *NHC Affordable Housing Policy Rev.*, vol. 3, no. 1 (Feb. 2004). *See also* D. Porter, *Inclusionary Zoning for Affordable Housing*, (Urban Land Institute, 2004), for a considered analysis of these issues as well as case studies of communities that have implemented inclusionary housing programs throughout the nation.

a statewide approach to inclusionary housing, each jurisdiction has the option of whether to implement inclusionary practices and, if so, how to design an inclusionary program to match its local needs and political reality.

Based on currently available information, one-fifth of California localities (107 cities and counties) have adopted some form of inclusionary housing.[35] At least 30 other jurisdictions in the state are considering adopting some kind of inclusionary housing policy. Nearly two-thirds of these programs have been adopted since 1990.[36] Inclusionary practices are also being employed in increasingly diverse kinds of neighborhoods.[37] The growing reliance on inclusionary housing in large cities like San Francisco, San Diego,[38] and Sacramento is of particular note.[39] Other large-city jurisdictions, including Los Angeles and Oakland, are considering the adoption of some form of inclusionary housing.[40]

Determining the actual number of units produced as a result of inclusionary housing is a challenge, due in part to the difficulties faced by implementing jurisdictions in collecting and maintaining the necessary data.[41] However,

> *Based on currently available information, one-fifth of California localities (107 cities and counties) have adopted some form of inclusionary housing.*

---

35. *See* Cal. Coalition for Rural Housing and Non-Profit Housing Ass'n Northern California, *Inclusionary Housing in California* (2003) (available at www.nonprofithousing.org).

36. *Id. See also* the National Housing Conference, "Inclusionary Zoning: the California Experience," *NCH Affordable Housing Policy Review*, vol. 3, no. 1 (Feb. 2004).

37. *See Expanding Housing Opportunity in Washington, D.C.: The Case for Inclusionary Zoning*, page 16 (discussing the potentially positive impact of using inclusionary housing in different kinds of neighborhoods, including those that are gentrifying, new and expanding, expensive, and those that have high concentrations of poverty) (PolicyLink, Winter 2005); Jesse M. Keenan, "Affordable Housing Policy in Miami: Inclusionary Zoning and the Median-Income Demographic," 14 *J. Aff. Housing & Cmty. Dev. Law*, no. 2, page 110 (Winter 2005) (arguing that Miami should institute some form of an inclusionary housing policy).

38. In 2006, a superior court invalidated the City of San Diego's inclusionary housing ordinance, holding that on its face the ordinance did not include a "complete waiver" provision and therefore did not allow the city to avoid the unconstitutional application of the ordinance. San Diego Sup. Ct. Case No. 6JC817064. The city settled the suit by adding a waiver provision to the ordinance and adjusted how in-lieu fees are calculated. Lori Weisberg, "City, Builders Settle Ordinance Fight," *San Diego Union-Trib.*, July 26, 2006.

39. For a historical perspective on development patterns that resulted in metropolitan decentralization, *see* Angela Glover Blackwell and Radhika K. Fox, *Regional Equity and Smart Growth's Opportunity for Advancing Social and Economic Justice in America*, the Funder's Network for Smart Growth and Livable Communities, Translation Paper no. 1, ed. 2 (2004), pages 3–4. *See* Nicholas Brunick, "Inclusionary Housing: Proven Success in Large Cities," *Zoning Practice*, no. 10 (Oct. 2004) (discussing the reasons for the growth of inclusionary housing in large cities, and describing several large-city programs).

40. *See* Bill Higgins, *Inclusionary Zoning and Affordable Housing After Homebuilders Ass'n of Northern California v. City of Napa*, page 3 (Inst. on Planning, Zoning, and Eminent Domain, 2003). *See also* David Paul Rosen and Associates, *Los Angeles Inclusionary Housing Study: Final Report* (2002); *Dellums Housing Task Force Majority Report* (December 2006).

41. Inclusionary housing programs remain controversial, and debate about their level of effectiveness in terms of unit production continues. For differing perspectives regarding the effectiveness of mandatory programs, *see* Nicholas Brunick, Lauren Goldberg, and Susannah Levine, *Voluntary or Mandatory Inclusionary Housing Production, Predictability and Enforcement* (Business and Professional People for the Public Interest, Nov. 2003) (concluding that mandatory programs produce more units for a wider range of income levels); Benjamin Powell and Edward Stringham, *Housing Supply and Affordability: Do Affordable Housing Mandates Work?* (The Reason Public Policy Institute, April 2004) (finding that mandatory programs produce relatively few units at very high costs); Victoria Basolo and Nico Calavita, *Policy Claims with Weak Evidence: A Critique of the Reason Foundation Study on Inclusionary Housing Policy in the San Francisco Bay Area* (refuting claims that inclusionary housing programs are too costly and ineffective). *See also* David Rosen, "Inclusionary Housing and Its Impact on Housing and Land Markets," *NHC Affordable Housing Policy Rev.*, no. 1 (Feb. 2004) (evaluating the effect inclusionary housing policies have on housing production in California cities).

available reports indicate that, in total, inclusionary housing may well have produced as many as 34,000 affordable units in California.[42]

In addition to increasing a community's affordable housing stock, advocates of inclusionary practices point to other related benefits, including: (1) facilitating racial and economic integration;[43] (2) encouraging implementation of smart growth principles; (3) providing housing for a diverse work force, which helps foster a strong economic environment; and (4) protecting against displacement of lower income households when new investment occurs.[44]

Judicial Treatment of Inclusionary Housing

Despite its proliferation, debate regarding the legality and effectiveness of inclusionary housing remains.

Despite its proliferation, debate regarding the legality and effectiveness of inclusionary housing remains.[45] Decisions addressing inclusionary housing challenges have recognized the legitimate governmental interest in promoting affordable housing and in imposing regulations intended to achieve that objective. However, the courts have not yet fully addressed the key question of whether cities can constitutionally burden new development with the obligation to remedy an affordable housing crisis caused in large part by pre-existing market forces that drive up the costs of housing based upon a restricted supply that cannot fulfill demand.

History of Inclusionary Housing— The Pre-*Nollan* and *Dolan* Era

Nationwide, there are relatively few published decisions considering the legality of inclusionary housing. The first court to address this issue was in the Virginia case of *Board of Supervisors v. De Groff Enterprises*, 198 S.E. 2d 600 (Va.

---

42. See California Coalition for Rural Housing and the Non-Profit Housing Ass'n of Northern California, *Inclusionary Housing in California: 30 Years of Innovation*, page 7 (2003).

43. See generally Angela Glover Blackwell, "Urban Equity: Consideration of Race and the Road Towards Equitable Allocation of Municipal Services: It Takes a Region," 31 *Fordham Urb. L. J.* 1303 (2004); Edward G. Goetz, Karen Chapple, and Barbara Lukermann, "The Minnesota Land Use Planning Act and the Promotion of Low- and Moderate-Income Housing in Suburbia," 22 *Law & Ineq. J.* 31 (Winter 2004); Thomas A. Brown, "Democratizing the American Dream: The Role of a Regional Housing Legislature in the Production of Affordable Housing," 31 *U. Mich. J. L. Ref.* 599 (Winter 2004); Christopher Courchesne, "What Regional Agenda?: Reconciling Massachusetts' Affordable Housing Law and Environmental Protection," 28 *Harv. Envtl. L. Rev.* 215 (2004).

44. See Angela Glover Blackwell, "Urban Equity: Consideration of Race and the Road Towards Equitable Allocation of Municipal Services: It Takes a Region," 31 *Fordham Urb. L. J.* 1303 (2004); *Expanding Housing Opportunity in Washington, D.C.: The Case for Inclusionary Zoning*, 9, 16 (PolicyLink, 2003); Nicholas Brunick, *The Impact of Inclusionary Zoning on Development*, pages 2–3 (2003).

45. For a discussion regarding the legal issues, see, e.g., Barbara Ehrlich Kautz, "In Defense of Inclusionary Zoning: Successfully Creating Affordable Housing," 36 *U.S.F. L. Rev.* 973 (Summer 2002); Laura M. Padilla, "Reflections on Inclusionary Housing and a Renewed Look at Its Viability," 23 *Hofstra L. Rev.* 539 (1995). For differing perspectives on the costs and benefits of inclusionary housing, see generally Burchell and Galley, supra note 31; Benjamin Powell and Edward Stringham, *Housing Supply and Affordability: Do Affordable Housing Mandates Work?* (The Reason Public Policy Institute, April 2004) (finding that mandatory programs produce relatively few units at very high costs); Andrew G. Dietderich, "An Egalitarian's Market: The Economics of Inclusionary Zoning Reclaimed," 24 *Fordham Urb. L. J.* 23 (1996); Lawrence Berger, "Inclusionary Zoning Devices as Takings: The Legacy of the Mount Laurel Cases," 70 *Neb. L. Rev.* 186 (1991); Robert C. Ellickson, "The Irony of 'Inclusionary' Zoning," 54 *S. Cal. L. Rev.* 1167 (1981).

1973). In that decision, despite acknowledging the "urgent need for housing units for low and moderate income families," the Virginia Supreme Court invalidated a mandatory inclusionary housing ordinance that required 15 percent of multi-family units in new residential projects be affordable. It did so based on the grounds that the ordinance exceeded the city's police power, as well as constituted a taking under the Virginia State Constitution.

Subsequent cases, however, have not followed suit. New Jersey, where the courts have tended to take on a more legislative role than is typically seen in most states, has been in the forefront. In 1983, in the case of *Southern Burlington County N.A.A.C.P. v. Township of Mt. Laurel* ("*Mt. Laurel I*"), the New Jersey Supreme Court issued the first decision in the country to explicitly recognize the importance of combating exclusionary zoning practices. 336 A.2d 713 (N.J. 1983).[46] In that case, the plaintiffs, representing minority, low-income residents, attacked a local zoning ordinance that had both the intent and effect of excluding low- and moderate-income residents from the city. The ordinance accomplished this goal by: (1) permitting only single-family detached dwelling units in residentially zoned areas; and (2) requiring significant minimum lot sizes and floor areas for new units. The New Jersey Supreme Court found this ordinance to be unconstitutional, violating basic principles of fairness. While the court stopped short of endorsing mandatory price controls on new housing, it ruled that all developing cities have an affirmative obligation, through their local land use regulations, to "make realistically possible" an appropriate variety and choice of housing without excluding low- and moderate-income housing opportunities. *Id.* at 724.

In a subsequent decision that year, *Southern Burlington County N.A.A.C.P. v. Township of Mt. Laurel* ("*Mt. Laurel II*"), the state high court made it clear that it would not back away from its holding in *Mt. Laurel I*. 456 A.2d 390 (N.J. 1983). Rather, it extended the duty to provide an appropriate variety of housing to *all* cities in New Jersey and advocated mandatory set-aside programs as one way for cities to fulfill their *Mt. Laurel* obligations. The court directed cities to accommodate their fair share of housing needs and went so far as to direct certain cities to accommodate certain specific needs.

On the constitutional question regarding the legality of singling out developers of new projects to bear the burden of remedying the affordable housing crisis, the court gave mixed signals. On the one hand, the court recognized the need to "assur[e] developers of an adequate return on their investment." *Id.* at 446. On the other hand, the court held that mandatory set-asides did not suffer from the infirmities identified in an earlier case, which had overturned a rent control ordinance that precluded rent increases for certain tenants. The *Mt. Laurel II* court reconciled these situations by emphasizing that in the case at hand, the inclusionary rental units would not be exempt from rent increases, which would likely track increases in the median incomes of lower income families. Thus, the result could not be considered confiscatory to the developer, since "the

---

46. For recent articles discussing the continuing implications of Mt. Laurel, exclusionary zoning, and potential housing, *see* Adam Gordon, "Making Exclusionary Zoning Remedies Work: How Courts Applying Title VII Standards to Fair Housing Cases Have Misunderstood the Housing Market," 24 *Yale L. & Pol'y Rev.* 437 (2006); Catherine Durkin, "The Exclusionary Effect of "Mansionization": Area Variances Undermine Efforts to Achieve Housing Affordability," 55 *Cal. U. L. Rev.* 439 (Winter 2006).

builder who undertakes a project that includes a mandatory set-aside voluntarily assumes the financial burden, if there is one, of that condition." *Id.* at 446, n.30.

Inclusionary Housing in California in the Post-*Nollan* and *Dolan* Era

> *Heightened scrutiny places the burden of proof on the city to establish an "essential nexus" and a "rough proportionality" between a project's impacts and the particular requirement imposed, a more difficult task.*

Between 1987 and 1994, in the cases of *Nollan v. California Coastal Commission*, 483 U.S. 825 (1987), and *Dolan v. City of Tigard*, 512 U.S. 374 (1994), the United States Supreme Court applied an intermediate level of judicial review referred to as "heightened scrutiny" to examine certain conditions applied to development projects. In contrast to a more deferential standard, heightened scrutiny places the burden of proof on the city to establish an "essential nexus" and a "rough proportionality" between a project's impacts and the particular requirement imposed, a more difficult task. *Nollan*, 483 U.S. at 839–40; *Dolan*, 512 U.S. at 391. A key question then surfaced in the inclusionary housing debate—how does the *Nollan/Dolan* heightened scrutiny standard fit into the legal analysis?

In 1991, a federal appellate court in *Commercial Builders of Northern California v. City of Sacramento*, weighed in on the issue, which involved the connection between commercial development and affordable housing requirements. 941 F. 2d 872 (9th Cir. 1991). In that case, the ordinance at issue conditioned the approval of certain types of non-residential building permits upon the developer's payment of a fee dedicated to an affordable housing trust fund. The plaintiff, citing *Nollan*, argued that the ordinance constituted an impermissible means of advancing the city's legitimate interest in increasing the supply of affordable housing, since it placed a burden of paying for low-income housing on non-residential development without establishing a sufficient nexus between such development and the stated need. However, the court was not persuaded. Refusing to require a direct causal relationship,[47] it held that *Nollan* did not materially change the level of scrutiny in the case at hand. The court then relied on the fact that the ordinance was implemented only after a careful study revealed the amount of low-income housing that would likely become necessary as a direct result of the influx of workers that would be associated with the new non-residential development and held there was a sufficient nexus.

In 2001, in the California appellate case of *Home Builders Association of Northern California v. City of Napa*, the plaintiff challenged the City of Napa's inclusionary housing ordinance, which imposed a mandatory 10 percent affordability requirement on new residential projects. 90 Cal. App. 4th 188 (2001). Plaintiffs contended that the ordinance was facially invalid because it (1) was an impermissible taking under both state and federal law; and (2) violated the federal Due Process Clause. In ruling for the city, the court affirmed the trial court's decision and upheld the ordinance against the facial constitutional attacks.

The plaintiff's principal constitutional claim was that the city's ordinance was invalid under the heightened scrutiny standard required by *Nollan* and *Dolan*. It contended that there was no "essential nexus" or "rough proportionality" between the exaction required by the ordinance and the impacts caused by development of the project.

---

47. This case was decided prior to the *Dolan* decision, which imposes the requirement of "rough proportionality." Therefore, the court did not address the question of "how close a fit" is required between the project and its impacts on the affordable housing supply.

However, the court rejected this argument, holding that the *Nollan/Dolan* heightened scrutiny test was inapplicable to the facts at hand. The court reasoned that this higher level of review was reserved for situations involving land use "bargains" between property owners and regulatory bodies, whereby the city sought to impose *ad hoc* requirements on individual developers in exchange for project approval. The court found that since the ordinance was generally applicable to all development in Napa, and the risk of extortionate behavior on the part of the city was therefore minimized, the more deferential standard of scrutiny applied.

The court reasoned that the Nollan/Dolan *higher level of review was reserved for situations involving land use "bargains" between property owners and regulatory bodies.*

After acknowledging the legitimate governmental interest in encouraging the development of affordable housing, the court rejected the facial challenge to Napa's ordinance. In so doing, it found dispositive the fact that the ordinance contained an administrative relief clause, which allowed for a complete waiver of the inclusionary requirements should the developer establish that they were unconstitutional or unlawful.[48] However, the court did not address the issue of the appropriate standard of review to be applied in the event a developer brought a challenge based on the city's refusal to grant a waiver for lack of nexus or rough proportionality to that developer's specific project.

In 2002, the California Supreme Court, in *San Remo Hotel v. City and County of San Francisco*, addressed a unique situation involving the imposition of affordable housing fees as a condition of approval for a permit to convert a hotel from long-term residential use to tourist use. 27 Cal. 4th 643 (2002). Here, the plaintiff hotel owners were required to pay $567,000 to convert 62 residential hotel rooms to tourist rooms under San Francisco's Hotel Conversion Ordinance. Upon imposition of those requirements, the owners paid the fee under protest and sued the city for inverse condemnation.

The California Supreme Court upheld the fee, declining to extend the heightened scrutiny standard to the San Francisco ordinance. Instead, the court found that challenges to "generally applicable legislation" that imposed fees that were calculated according to a nondiscretionary formula, such as the ordinance at issue, were subject only to a deferential standard of review. The court clarified that "generally applicable legislation" under *Ehrlich v. City of Culver City*, 12 Cal. 4th 854 (1996), need not apply to every property in a city, so long as it applies to "all property in the class logically subject to its strictures." *Id.* at 669. The court then held that because the housing replacement fee bore a reasonable relationship to the loss of housing caused by converting residence hotels to tourist hotels, the fee was valid. In so doing, the decision reaffirmed the ruling in *Ehrlich* which held that the "heightened scrutiny" test for exactions required under the *Nollan* and *Dolan* decisions does not generally apply to fees imposed under an inclusionary housing program enacted by general legislation in California.

Legal Issues to Consider When Adopting and Implementing an Inclusionary Housing Program

Given that several inclusionary housing programs have survived in the face of legal challenge thus far, it is anticipated that inclusionary practices will continue

---

48. *Home Builders* may have paved the way for inclusionary housing programs to be upheld as constitutional. *See* Brian R. Lerman, "Mandatory Inclusionary Zoning—The Answer to the Affordable Housing Problem," 33 *B.C. Envtl. Aff. L. Rev.* 383 (2006).

to proliferate as cities seek to address the lack of affordable housing in their communities. However, as the number of inclusionary programs increases and cities attempt to impose higher affordability requirements on a broader spectrum of developers, it is anticipated that more legal challenges will follow. In addition, the recent trend of cities seeking to prioritize certain groups of individuals, such as firefighters and teachers, for receipt of the benefits of inclusionary housing programs may be subject to challenge.[49] *But see City of Cuyahoga Falls v. Buckeye Community Hope Foundation*, 538 U.S. 188 (2003) (mere discriminatory and detrimental impact of a facially neutral referendum process was not enough for an equal protection claim against a local government; plaintiff must establish discriminatory intent or purpose to show an equal protection violation). Therefore, a number of legal issues should be considered when cities are designing and implementing inclusionary housing programs to reduce the risk of such litigation.

Method of Enactment

Cities enact inclusionary housing programs pursuant to their local police power. *Euclid v. Ambler Realty Co.*, 272 U.S. 365 (1926) (discussing the scope of the local police power). These programs can be implemented in several ways, including through ordinances, zoning codes, general policy statements, a city's housing element, or various permit approval procedures. To date, the majority of jurisdictions in California—approximately 78 percent—have enacted inclusionary housing programs by local ordinances.[50]

Although cities may adopt inclusionary housing in various ways, there are benefits to enacting these programs through a generally applicable ordinance. Adoption of a zoning regulation is a legislative act and is entitled to judicial deference. It is presumed that the enactment of the regulation is justified under the police power and was adopted for the purpose of promoting the public health, safety, and general welfare. Hence, a zoning regulation may be invalidated only if it bears no reasonable relationship to a legitimate public purpose. *Candid Enters., Inc. v. Grossmont Union High School Dist.*, 39 Cal. 3d 878 (1985).

In addition, the adoption of an inclusionary housing program through a generally applicable ordinance reduces its legal vulnerability by helping to avoid the kind of individualized *ad hoc* application that invites takings or other legal challenges. In *Home Builders Association of Northern California v. City of Napa*, the court held that since the ordinance was enacted legislatively, the more deferential standard of scrutiny applied "because the heightened risk of the 'extortionate' use of the police power to exact unconstitutional conditions is not present." 90 Cal. App. 4th at 197. The court emphasized that the heightened scrutiny standard set forth in *Nollan* and *Dolan* is intended to address land use "bargains" between property owners and regulatory bodies where there is a heightened risk of the extortionate use of police power.

---

49. For an interesting discussion about the body of laws that potentially affect a city's authority to impose resident and employee preferences, *see Resident and Employee Preferences in Affordable Housing* (City Attorneys Spring Conference, May 2006).

50. *See* California Coalition for Rural Housing and the Non-Profit Housing Ass'n of Northern California, *Inclusionary Housing in California: 30 Years of Innovation*, page 8 (2003) (available at www.nonprofithousing.org).

It is in this paradigmatic permit context—where the individual property owner-developer seeks to negotiate approval of a planned development—that the combined *Nollan* and *Dolan* test quintessentially applies. *Id.* at 196–97 (quoting *Ehrlich v. City of Culver City*, 12 Cal. 4th 854, 868 (1996)).

Id.

While some flexibility can be retained to allow for discretionary decisions that may be necessary when applying the ordinance to specific projects, it is important to minimize such discretion to the extent possible. The specific requirements—the type and percentage of affordable units to be produced, affordability levels and controls, availability of alternatives to on-site production and developer incentives, and selection of beneficiaries—should be generally applicable and sufficiently detailed rather than individually negotiated.[51] In addition, the ordinance should contain clear definitions and mandates, defining all terms precisely and providing clear statements regarding the applicable standards.

Taking these steps limits the risk of misinterpretation and arbitrary application. Such limits on discretion give the ordinance a better chance of withstanding constitutional challenge. As stated in *San Remo Hotel v. City and County of San Francisco*:

> The "sine qua non" for application of *Nollan/Dolan* scrutiny is...the "discretionary deployment of the police power" in the "imposition of land-use conditions in individual cases." Only individualized development fees warrant a type of review akin to the conditional conveyances at issue in *Nollan* and *Dolan*. [citations omitted.]

27 Cal. 4th 643, 670 (2002)

Factual Record to Support Enactment and Application

Inclusionary housing is less vulnerable to legal attack when it is based on empirical data that justifies the city's policy decisions. In particular, adequate findings supported by substantial evidence should be made to demonstrate a legitimate governmental interest in providing affordable housing in the community and the ways in which inclusionary housing will substantially advance this interest.[52]

Even assuming the general proposition that the creation of affordable housing is a legitimate interest,[53] cities would be well served to show the need for additional affordable housing in their particular communities. There are numerous

---

51. *See* Barbara Ehrlich Kautz, "In Defense of Inclusionary Zoning: Successfully Creating Affordable Housing," 36 *U.S.F. L. Rev.* 973, 1021–22 (Summer 2002).
52. For example, in the *City of Napa* case, the court relied in part on its finding that the inclusionary housing ordinance, which imposed a 10 percent affordability requirement, substantially advanced a legitimate state interest. The court reasoned that both the California Supreme Court and the State Legislature had recognized the creation of affordable housing for low- and moderate-income households as a legitimate state interest. The court then assumed that the city's inclusionary ordinance would necessarily result in the substantial advancement of this important interest by increasing the affordable housing stock in the community. 90 Cal. App. 4th at 195.
53. The assumption that inclusionary housing requirements necessarily leads to the creation of more affordable housing has been questioned. *See* Robert C. Ellickson, "The Irony of 'Inclusionary' Zoning," 54 *S. Cal. L Rev.* 1167 (1981) (concluding that inclusionary housing aggravates housing shortages, which results in less housing "filtering down" to lower-income families and an increase in overall housing prices).

existing sources of data upon which a city can rely. For example, this information can be gathered as the calculation of each community's "fair share" of the regional housing need is made every five years. In addition, cities can rely on public input or may decide to conduct a nexus study to establish such local need.

Developing and collecting evidence demonstrating that imposition of the inclusionary requirements will not deny property owners all economically viable use of their property and will not interfere with their reasonable investment-backed expectations may help further insulate an inclusionary housing program from a takings challenge.

Cities should consider documenting how their inclusionary programs actually increase the affordable housing stock.

Finally, cities should consider documenting how their inclusionary programs actually increase the affordable housing stock. This evidence can be used to counter the argument that inclusionary housing requirements actually diminish the amount of overall residential construction, thereby hampering rather than advancing the interest of providing more affordable housing.[54]

Inclusion of "Safety Valve" Provisions

The inclusion of a provision that would allow a city to waive the inclusionary requirements or permit an alternative means of compliance can reduce the legal vulnerability of an inclusionary housing program. *Home Builders Ass'n of N. Cal. v. City of Napa*, 90 Cal. App. 4th at 199. As discussed above, the potential utility of a waiver provision was emphasized in *City of Napa*. This provision permitted city officials to reduce, modify, or waive the requirements contained in the ordinance if the developer could demonstrate that there was no reasonable relationship or nexus between the impact of the development and the inclusionary requirement. As the court stated, "Since City has the ability to waive the requirements imposed by the ordinance, the ordinance cannot and does not, on its face, result in a taking." *Id.* at 194.

An inclusionary housing program may also contain a provision that permits a developer to comply with the affordable housing requirements without producing units on site. Typical alternatives to on-site production include allowing developers (1) to pay an in-lieu fee that is deposited in an affordable housing trust fund to be used for construction of affordable units; (2) to dedicate land for construction of affordable units; or (3) to build affordable units on another site.

It remains an open question whether an alternative compliance provision is necessary to withstand constitutional scrutiny.

It remains an open question whether an alternative compliance provision is necessary to withstand constitutional scrutiny. In *City of Napa*, the court acknowledged the alternative compliance provision in the ordinance at issue, noting that although the ordinance placed "significant burdens" on developers, it also provided "significant benefits" to developers who complied with its terms. However, it did not rely on this provision to uphold the ordinance. Rather, its key concern was the city's ability to waive the inclusionary requirements if necessary to avoid unconstitutional applications.

From a policy perspective, there is support for the position that permitting such flexibility will result in the construction of more affordable units in the

---

54. *See* Barbara Ehrlich Kautz, "In Defense of Inclusionary Zoning: Successfully Creating Affordable Housing," 36 *U.S.F. L. Rev.* 973 (Summer 2002).

community than on-site production, alone, could attain.[55] Accordingly, numerous jurisdictions include such alternative compliance provisions.

However, providing the option of paying in-lieu fees or dedicating land could increase the likelihood that a court would review the ordinance as an exaction as opposed to a land use regulation and therefore impose a higher level of scrutiny to evaluate the constitutionality of the program. For example, a city could enact an inclusionary ordinance that applies to all residential developments, regardless of size. However, because it would not be feasible to require on-site production where a developer proposes a one-unit project, this ordinance could require that such developer pay an in-lieu fee instead. If the fee is one of general applicability, then the city would need to establish an adequate factual basis to demonstrate a connection between the ordinance's requirements and the impacts of development. *San Remo Hotel v. City and County of San Francisco*, 27 Cal. 4th at 669. However, if the fee is determined on a case-by-case basis, the heightened scrutiny standard may well apply.

In addition, allowing an in-lieu fee option raises two additional issues involving the Mitigation Fee Act and Proposition 218. The Mitigation Fee Act (Gov't Code §§ 66000–66025) provides that a fee or exaction imposed as a mandatory condition for approval of development cannot exceed the estimated reasonable cost of providing the public facility for which the fee is imposed. Gov't Code § 66005. If an in-lieu fee provision in an inclusionary housing program is viewed as a "fee" under the Mitigation Fee Act, then such fee would be subject to said statutory restrictions.[56]

If an in-lieu fee provision in an inclusionary housing program is viewed as a "fee" under the Mitigation Fee Act, then the fee would be subject to said statutory restrictions.

Proposition 218 added Article XIIID to the California Constitution, which prohibits a city from imposing a fee on property owners for services that are available to the public in general. A fee may not be assessed "as an incident of property ownership" except as specified in the article. Therefore, the issue is whether an in-lieu fee option constitutes a "fee" and thus is subject to the constitutional restrictions of Proposition 218.[57] It could be argued that such a fee is subject to Proposition 218, since it imposes a cost on property owners in connection with the development of their property. However, it is important to note that the *City of Napa* court rejected this position. In so doing, it reasoned

---

55. *See, e.g.*, Cal. Affordable Housing Law Project and Western Center on Law and Poverty, *Inclusionary Zoning: Policy Considerations and Best Practices*, pages 15–19 (2002) (discussing potential benefits of providing alternatives to on-site production). This kind of provision may be particularly appropriate in jurisdictions that seek to impose inclusionary requirements on all projects, including those that propose to develop only one unit; otherwise, the inclusionary program could be subject to legal challenge for imposing an entirely economically infeasible requirement. Of course, there also are policy arguments against the broad use of such alternatives. *See, e.g.*, *Expanding Housing Opportunity in Washington, D.C.: The Case for Inclusionary Housing*, pages 33–34 (PolicyLink, Fall 2003).

56. In *City of Napa*, the plaintiff raised this argument, claiming that the ordinance's in-lieu fee provision violated the Mitigation Fee Act. The court did not address the merits of this claim, as it was deemed waived in an unpublished portion of the court's decision. 90 Cal. App. 4th at 198. *See* Cal. Affordable Housing Law Project and Western Center on Law and Poverty, *Inclusionary Zoning: Policy Considerations and Best Practices*, pages 30–31 (2002) for a discussion regarding the applicability of the Mitigation Fee Act to an in-lieu fee option in an inclusionary ordinance.

57. *See* Cal. Affordable Housing Law Project and Western Center on Law and Poverty, *Inclusionary Zoning: Policy Considerations and Best Practices*, page 33 (2002) for a discussion regarding the applicability of Proposition 218 to an in-lieu fee alternative.

that the fees come into play only when an owner acts to develop property and not "solely by virtue of property ownership." 90 Cal. App. 4th at 200. *See also Richmond v. Shasta Cmty. Services Dist.*, 32 Cal. 4th 409, 419–20, 426 (2004) (upholding a water connection fee challenged under Proposition 218, holding that the fee was imposed not on real property as such, but upon individuals who apply for new service connections; it thus is not a fee imposed on incident of property ownership).

Provision of Incentives and Concessions to Developers

Many inclusionary housing programs provide incentives or concessions to developers in order to elicit compliance and further support the position that the program does not constitute an impermissible taking.[58] There are a range of incentives and concessions that jurisdictions can consider, including:

- Waivers of zoning requirements, including density, area, height, open space, use, or other provisions
- Local tax abatements
- Waiver of permit fees or land dedication requirements
- Reduction of required developer-provided amenities
- Fast-track permitting, and
- Subsidization or provision of infrastructure by the jurisdiction for the developer's project

Relationship to the Costa-Hawkins (Anti-Rent Control) Act

Another potential benefit to including incentives or concessions like those listed above is the potential to undermine claims brought under the state rent control statute. *See Town of Telluride v. Lot Thirty-Four Venture, L.L.C.*, 3 P. 3d 30 (Col. 2000) (town's "affordable housing mitigation" ordinance, which required developers to create affordable housing for 40 percent of the employees generated by the new development, as well as setting a base rental rate, constituted "rent control," thereby violating the state's anti-rent control statute). The Costa-Hawkins Rental Housing Act invalidates local rent control ordinances that do not permit owners of residential real property to set initial rents at a certain level or to establish subsequent rents when the unit is later vacated. Cal. Civ. Code §§ 1954.50–1954.535 (2001). Accordingly, inclusionary programs

---

58. The majority of jurisdictions in California provide some kind of developer incentive or concession. About half of the city authorize their councils to grant a density bonus, often on a one-to-one basis (*i.e.*, for each affordable unit provided, the developer is entitled to one additional market rate unit). A number of programs provide a list of possible incentives to be granted only at the city's discretion. Numerous others provide "priority processing" or fast track review, which may have little practical value if every new residential project qualifies. Only one city specifically lists financial assistance as an incentive. About 35 percent of inclusionary programs provide no incentives to a developer providing inclusionary housing. *See* Barbara Ehrlich Kautz, "In Defense of Inclusionary Zoning: Successfully Creating Affordable Housing," 36 *U.S.F. L. Rev.* 973, 981 (Summer 2002).

that impose initial and long-term affordability covenants on rental units[59] may be subject to legal challenge for violating the Act.[60]

It remains an open question whether the Costa-Hawkins Act applies to inclusionary housing programs. To date, this has been presented to at least two courts but neither has reached the merits of the issue.[61] Further, a recent attempt to have the Legislature clarify this issue was not successful.[62]

Until the Legislature or the courts provide clear guidance, the availability of incentives or concessions, especially direct financial assistance, may furnish a basis for avoiding any application of the Costa-Hawkins Act. This is based on an exemption in the Act for rental units that have been built under a contract with a public agency in exchange for a financial contribution or other form of assistance included under California's Density Bonus Law. Gov't Code § 1954.53(a)(2). *See California Inclusionary Housing Reader*, pages 112–117 (Institute for Local Self Government, 2003), for further discussion on this point.

It remains an open question whether the Costa-Hawkins Act applies to inclusionary housing programs.

Policy Issues to Consider When Crafting an Inclusionary Housing Program

Along with legal considerations, there are a number of policy issues that cities must evaluate when designing and implementing inclusionary housing. In so doing, a city can better tailor inclusionary housing[63] to meet specific community needs as well as potentially bolstering the program's legal viability.[64]

Along with legal considerations, there are a number of policy issues that jurisdictions must evaluate when designing and implementing inclusionary housing.

Nature of the Program— Mandatory or Voluntary?

Cities must consider whether the inclusionary housing program they adopt will be mandatory or voluntary.[65] Advocates of a mandatory approach contend that

---

59. The Costa-Hawkins Act only applies to rental units. Accordingly, the Act cannot be applied to inclusionary for-sale units even if such units are subject to lifetime affordability covenants.

60. Several commentators have argued that Costa-Hawkins does not apply to inclusionary ordinances. *See, e.g.,* Nadia I. El Mallakh, "Does the Costa-Hawkins Act Prohibit Local Inclusionary Zoning Programs?," 89 *Cal. L. Rev.* 1849 (2001). *See also* Barbara Ehrlich Kautz, "In Defense of Inclusionary Zoning: Successfully Creating Affordable Housing," 36 *U.S.F. L. Rev.* 973, 1010–11 (Summer 2002).

61. One case was dismissed when the City of Santa Monica amended its ordinance. *See* Nadia L. El Mallakh, "Does the Costa-Hawkins Act Prohibit Local Inclusionary Zoning Programs?," 89 *Cal. L. Rev.* 1849, 1851 (2001). In the other case, a court of appeal decision applied a 90-day statute of limitation to a Costa-Hawkins claim. The California Supreme Court recently reversed that decision in part and remanded to the appellate court, clearing the way for a potential decision on the merits in the future. *Travis v. County of Santa Cruz*, 33 Cal. 4th 757, 766–67 (2004).

62. *See* Senate Bill 178 (stalled in committee as of the end of the 2004 term), which sought to clarify that the Costa-Hawkins Act does not preempt a locality's ability to enact an inclusionary housing ordinance that limits rent or income levels.

63. For a discussion that addresses a variety of practical issues in implementing inclusionary housing programs, see *On Common Ground: Joint Principles on Inclusionary Housing Policies* (July 2005) (collaborative policy brief between the Home Builders Ass'n of N. Cal. and the Non-Profit Housing Ass'n of N. Cal.).

64. For an evaluation of policy considerations, *see Expanding Housing Opportunity in Washington, D.C.: The Case for Inclusionary Housing* (PolicyLink, Fall 2003). *See also* California Affordable Housing Law Project and Western Center on Law and Poverty, *Inclusionary Zoning: Policy Considerations and Best Practices* (2002). *See also California Affordable Housing Handbook: Strategies for Building Better Communities*, pages 87–100 (Feb. 2006) (discussing various policy considerations for inclusionary housing programs).

65. To date, nearly all of the units in California and New Jersey have been produced under mandatory programs. *See* Institute for Local Self Government, "Legal Issues Associated with Inclusionary Housing Ordinances," *California Inclusionary Housing Reader*, page 7 (2003).

voluntary programs lack sufficient incentives over typical market-based conditions to encourage the development of affordable units.[66] They further argue that even if there were enough incentives to offset the costs, other issues may hamper voluntary participation. These can include: (1) a lack of understanding on the part of developers regarding the economics of the inclusionary program; (2) a concern that inclusion of an affordable housing component, particularly when accomplished through higher levels of density than otherwise would be permitted, may heighten public opposition; and (3) issues relating to the administration and enforcement of the inclusionary requirements.[67]

However, there is support for voluntary programs as well. These programs rely solely on incentives to encourage developers to provide the affordable units. To be effective, the incentives must be sufficiently attractive to balance the percentage of units that are affordable and the income ranges they target. Advocates of this approach cite to the fact that voluntary programs are harder to attack legally, and their administration can be more flexible, thereby improving efficiency and effectiveness.[68]

A hybrid voluntary-mandatory inclusionary housing approach has emerged in a number of fast-growing jurisdictions that have adopted growth management ordinances.

A hybrid voluntary-mandatory inclusionary housing approach has emerged in a number of fast-growing cities that have adopted growth management ordinances. In these communities, a growth restriction is imposed by ordinance that limits the number of dwelling units that can be constructed in any given year. To determine which development applications will be approved, the city holds a "beauty contest" whereby project sponsors compete to present the most desirable project. By awarding points for the inclusion of affordable units in the proposed development, the city is able to leverage its growth cap by encouraging developers to "volunteer" to include affordable units so as to enhance their opportunity to be awarded their approvals.[69]

Determining the Classes and Size of Development That Will Be Subject to the Inclusionary Housing Program

The majority of inclusionary programs apply only to new residential developments.

Cities need to consider what classes of development, *i.e.*, residential, mixed-use, commercial, or industrial, will be subject to inclusionary housing. The majority of inclusionary programs apply only to new residential developments. If this approach is taken, a city must then determine whether they apply

---

66. For arguments in support of mandatory inclusionary programs, *see Expanding Housing Opportunity in Washington, D.C.: The Case for Inclusionary Housing*, page 24 (PolicyLink, Fall 2003) (citing a study to demonstrate the superior delivery power of mandatory inclusionary housing); *Inclusionary Zoning: A Primer* (D.C. Office of Planning, 2002) (arguing that the most successful inclusionary housing programs in the country in terms of number of affordable units built are the mandatory programs that also offer incentives to provide some compensation to the requirements); Nicholas J. Brunick, "The Inclusionary Housing Debate: The Effectiveness of Mandatory Programs Over Voluntary Programs," *Zoning Practice*, page 2 (APA, Sept. 2004); "Mandatory Inclusionary Zoning: The Answer to the Affordable Housing Problem," 33 *B.C. Envtl. Aff. L. Rev.*, no. 2 (2006).

67. *See* Barbara Ehrlich Kautz, "In Defense of Inclusionary Zoning: Successfully Creating Affordable Housing," 36 *U.S.F. L. Rev.* 973, 975 (Summer 2002).

68. *See Inclusionary Zoning: Program Design Considerations, An Enterprise Foundation Issue Brief* (available at www.enterprisefoundation.org/model%20documents/e512.htm).

69. *See* Bill Higgins, *Inclusionary Zoning and Affordable Housing After Homebuilders Ass'n of Northern California v. City of Napa*, page 3 (Inst. on Planning, Zoning, and Eminent Domain, 2003).

to single-family or multi-family development, or both, and whether residential components of mixed-use projects will be included.

Some cities also apply inclusionary requirements to commercial or industrial developments. These are often referred to as "linkage programs" because they assume that a link exists between the development of a new commercial or industrial project and an increase in affordable housing needs, presumably from the new workers that the project brings to an area.[70]

In addition to determining the classes of development that will trigger application of inclusionary requirements, cities also must define the size of the project at which those requirements apply. Typically, the threshold ranges from 10 to 50 units, with small projects being exempted. Recently, however, several cities have adopted programs that set a relatively low threshold; still others are applying inclusionary policies to all projects, regardless of size.[71]

The designation of a threshold for triggering application of inclusionary requirements is a policy decision to be based on numerous factors. However, one key consideration must be an understanding of the community development patterns; otherwise, an ineffective inclusionary program may well result. For example, consider a community that has a limited supply of available land, and thus, few development applications for projects over 50 units are submitted. An inclusionary program that applied only to projects with 50 or more units would not result in the production of much affordable housing.[72] Since the success of inclusionary housing depends on the approval and production of market-rate projects, jurisdictions are well advised to assess construction patterns and establish an inclusionary program that captures the majority of that development.

Required Amount and Affordability Levels of Inclusionary Units

There is considerable variation among inclusionary housing programs with respect to the percentage of affordable units required. Affordability levels generally range from 4–30 percent, with most cities imposing requirements from 10–15 percent.[73] Numerous considerations come into play in making this policy determination. Some cities are seeking to require a percentage of affordable units at the higher end of the range, with the goal of further increasing the affordable housing supply.[74] However, there are risks associated with doing so. Among others, this approach will likely heighten the risk of legal challenge and could enhance the plaintiff's chance at success should litigation ensue. Further, it actually may hamper the goals of the inclusionary program by increasing

There is considerable variation among inclusionary housing programs with respect to the percentage of affordable units required.

---

70. *See* "Legal Issues Associated with Inclusionary Housing Ordinances," *California Inclusionary Housing Reader*, page 43 (Institute for Local Self Government, 2003).
71. *See Expanding Housing Opportunity in Washington, D.C.: The Case for Inclusionary Housing*, page 31 (PolicyLink, Fall 2003).
72. Several jurisdictions have recently adjusted the project triggers in their inclusionary ordinances to reflect shifting development patterns. For example, San Francisco recently amended its inclusionary housing program to eliminate the exemption for live-work developments.
73. *See* California Affordable Housing Law Project and Western Center on Law and Poverty, *Inclusionary Zoning: Policy Considerations and Best Practices*, page 5 (2002).
74. *Id.*

the costs of residential construction so much that developers simply cannot afford to build in that community.[75]

In addition to determining the total amount of affordable housing that will be required, cities must also consider whether their inclusionary programs will target certain lower income households. If a program merely sets forth a percentage of affordable units required, but does not specify whether these units will be affordable to very low-, low- or moderate-income households, moderate units are more likely to be produced, given the associated costs of development. Accordingly, many programs designate specific targets for each major income category in order to achieve deeper levels of affordability.[76]

Given the increased costs associated with constructing units affordable to households with low- and very low-incomes, cities may consider decreasing this financial burden by providing income-targeting incentives in their inclusionary programs. For example, the program could provide a credit against part of the moderate income obligation in return for the developers producing a greater number of very low- and low-income units. Thus, if a city requires 20 percent affordability (with a mix of 10 percent moderate-, 5 percent low- and 5 percent very low-income units) and a developer exceeds the 5 percent very low requirement, the 10 percent obligation on the moderate end could be reduced in a commensurate amount.[77]

Timing Issues and Design Standards for Inclusionary Units

Cities may want to consider specifying the timing of when the inclusionary units are planned for completion within the context of the overall development. For a variety of reasons, affordable units may not, in fact, result unless certain timing requirements are imposed. Among others, financing issues can impair a developer's long-term ability to produce such units. In addition, there is a risk of public opposition to the construction of affordable units within the project from new residents, who might not have understood that affordable units were part of the project when they bought their homes. To counter these problems and help ensure that inclusionary units are built, some cities require that the inclusionary units be constructed up front or be phased in a way that is proportional to the rest of the development.

Along with timing issues, cities should consider what design standards will be applied to the affordable units. The inclusionary program should clarify the extent to which these units must be built to the same development standards and design guidelines as the market rate units. Conformity assures that the affordable units will consist of quality construction and will not be stigmatized within the project or the community. However, imposing such requirements can increase the cost of these units tremendously, potentially making their development infeasible.

---

75. See Robert C. Ellickson, "The Irony of 'Inclusionary' Zoning," 54 *S. Cal. L Rev.* 1167, 1215–16 (1981).
76. See Bill Higgins, *Inclusionary Zoning and Affordable Housing After Homebuilders Ass'n of Northern California v. City of Napa*, pages 3, 6 (Inst. on Planning, Zoning, and Eminent Domain, 2003).
77. California Affordable Housing Law Project and Western Center on Law and Poverty, *Inclusionary Zoning: Policy Considerations and Best Practices*, page 6 (2002).

In order to balance these competing concerns, many cities require stricter controls for the exterior of the affordable units, but allow for the use of less expensive (but still quality) materials for interior features and the provision of fewer interior amenities. Another means of addressing this issue is to provide the developer with incentives to construct affordable and market rate units in a uniform manner. For instance, in return for providing affordable homes that mirror the more expensive housing in the project, developers could be permitted to charge an additional amount (perhaps 5 or 10 percent) for the affordable homes.[78]

Preserving Affordability of Inclusionary Units

In order to ensure that inclusionary units remain affordable for a significant period of time, most programs contain some kind of affordability controls. Otherwise, inclusionary units would be "lost" in the system and sold or rented at market rates, thereby creating a windfall to the owner at the expense of lost public and private investment. Avoiding this pitfall may require the establishment of various controls, including: (1) price and rent restrictions; (2) a program for determining eligibility of applicants; (3) the setting of a specific period of time during which the inclusionary units must remain affordable; and (4) enforcement and monitoring mechanisms to ensure these requirements are met.

In order to ensure that inclusionary units remain affordable for a significant period of time, most programs contain some kind of affordability controls.

To effectively implement such affordability controls and related monitoring and enforcement mechanisms, a great deal of staff supervision is required. Accordingly, cities need to consider these administrative issues when crafting their inclusionary programs. Cities take various approaches in this regard based on the amount of supervision required under their specific programs. While some administer inclusionary housing with existing staff, others contract with outside sources such as local housing authorities to administer this staff-intensive activity.[79]

Rent and Price Limitations

Most cities include formulas to calculate the maximum price for housing units, adjusted by bedroom size (which relates to family size) and appropriate income level. Different standards are often used for rental and for-sale housing. In addition, some formulas will include the cost of utilities in the rental price. Ownership units will typically include utilities, homeowners' association dues, taxes, and mortgage insurance.[80]

Most cities include formulas to calculate the maximum price for housing units, adjusted by bedroom size and appropriate income level. Different standards are often used for rental and for-sale housing.

Qualification of Beneficiaries

Criteria need to be established to screen the applicants for the affordable units to ensure their income qualifies them for such units. Inclusionary programs should establish clear guidelines to assist in the administration of the program, reduce confusion, and ensure fairness. Among the issues to consider is how the

---

78. *See* Karen Destorel Brown, *Expanding Affordable Housing Through Inclusionary Zoning: Lessons from the Washington Metropolitan Area*, The Discussion Paper Series, page 26 (The Brookings Institute, Wash., D.C., Oct. 2001).
79. *Id.*
80. *See* Bill Higgins, *Inclusionary Zoning and Affordable Housing After Homebuilders Ass'n of Northern California v. City of Napa*, page 9 (Inst. on Planning, Zoning, and Eminent Domain, 2003).

inclusionary program will define very low-, low-, and moderate-income households. To ensure consistency, most inclusionary ordinances use the definitions provided by the U.S. Department of Housing and Urban Development. Another item to consider is how the income limits will be adjusted for family size and the method by which income limits will be updated.

Length of Time That Inclusionary Units Must Remain Affordable

Typically, units are required to remain affordable for a period of 20 to 30 years, although the length of time can range from five years to perpetuity depending upon the city. Various policy considerations come into play when cities are determining what this time period should be. On the one hand, if affordability is required for only a short period of time, this imposes a significant burden on the community to produce additional affordable units within a relatively short time frame in order to maintain the affordable housing stock. In addition, this approach can increase the legal vulnerability of the inclusionary program by providing support for the argument that it is not, in fact, substantially advancing a legitimate interest since the increase in affordable units is more of an illusion than a reality. On the other hand, perpetuity is a long time and may unreasonably penalize developers and disserve individual owners of inclusionary units by reducing their ability to benefit from the financial opportunities afforded by home ownership or their ability to remodel or refurbish units.[81]

Enforcement and Monitoring Mechanisms

With respect to ownership units, affordability controls generally are implemented, enforced, and monitored through resale restrictions. Such restrictions can include the following: (1) "soft" second mortgages for the difference between the appraised value and the delivered price; (2) terms for repayment of such mortgages upon sale and/or forgiveness over 10 to 20 years; (3) ownership of the underlying land by a land trust; and (4) other related devices such as the city's right of first refusal. Regulatory agreements are another tool that can be utilized to lock in specific commitments of owners, tenants, and inclusionary homeowners over time.

In order to evaluate the effectiveness of their inclusionary programs, some cities have initiated reviews or refinements once they have been in place for a number of years. One way to accomplish this objective is to build in a defined program review milestone to ensure that the inclusionary program is effective and is maximizing inclusionary opportunities.

The recent case of *Dieckmeyer v. Redevelopment Agency*, raises issues of enforcement and monitoring. 127 Cal. App. 4th 248 (2005). In that case, the petitioner purchased a condominium under an affordable housing program (adopted pursuant to redevelopment law), wherein the city helped her finance

---

81. To balance the goals of preserving affordability and promoting wealth-building opportunities of home ownership, many inclusionary programs establish shared appreciation formulas to allow the program and the inclusionary homeowner to share resale profits. *See Expanding Housing Opportunity in Washington, D.C.: The Case for Exclusionary Housing*, page 33 (PolicyLink, Fall 2003).

the purchase of the unit. The parties executed a loan agreement, note, and deed of trust, and certain restrictions were imposed as a condition of purchasing the home through recorded covenants, conditions, and restrictions (CC&Rs). One such condition required the homeowner to pay an "equity share," *i.e.*, a percentage of the profit earned on the sale of the home, under certain circumstances.

The petitioner filed suit when the city sought payment of the equity share at the time petitioner sought to prepay the loan. While the court agreed with the petitioner that the terms of the loan agreement did not require payment of the equity share at the time of prepayment, it refused to eliminate the equity share requirement altogether. Rather, it would remain due upon sale of the unit to a buyer who did not qualify as a low- or moderate-income household, or upon any of the other specific trigger conditions set forth in the agreement.

In so doing, the court rejected the petitioner's argument that imposing the equity share violated a legislative intent to expand housing opportunities for people of all economic levels. It noted that the equity share is designed to recapture some of the profit (which would then be used to support development of additional affordable units) if the unit is sold at a market price during the 30-year affordability period in effect. The court held that the purpose of the programs would be undermined if the equity share could be eliminated by the simple expedient of prepaying the city's small down payment and closing costs loan. Since the petitioner chose to take advantage of the benefits provided by the affordable housing program, the court noted that she could not now complain about terms she accepted.

CC&Rs = Covenants, conditions, and restrictions

21

Land Use Litigation

*by Geoffrey L. Robinson
and Marie A. Cooper*

Introduction

This chapter discusses the procedures most frequently used to challenge local land use decisions in court: traditional mandate and administrative mandate. This chapter also discusses litigation challenging exactions, including dedications and development fees.[1]

Procedural rules and standards of review that apply specifically to the type of land use decision being challenged are discussed in the chapters pertaining to those decisions.

Overview and Terminology

A writ of mandate is the most common method by which courts compel or set aside actions by a local agency.[2] Mandate proceedings—also called "mandamus proceedings" or "writ proceedings"—are commenced with the filing of a petition. A petition functions much like a complaint in an ordinary civil action in that it states the petitioner's claimed bases for relief, and seeks an order directing the respondent agency to implement the remedy sought.

A writ of mandate is the most common method by which courts compel or set aside actions by a local agency.

When land use decisions are challenged, there is often a party with a particular interest that may be affected by the action, who must be named as the real party in interest. For example, a petitioner challenging a city's approval of a development project must name the city as respondent and the developer as real party in interest. Likewise, if a petitioner is challenging a city clerk's decision

---

1. For additional litigation resources, *see California Administrative Mandamus* (Cal. Cont. Ed. Bar, 2006) Smith-Chavez, Stratton, Trembath, and Carrico, 2 *California Civil Practice: Real Property Litigation*, ch. 14 (Thomson-West, 2d ed. 2005); 31 *California Forms of Pleadings and Practice*, ch. 358 (Lexis Publishing, 2006); 5 Manaster and Selmi, *California Environmental Law and Land Use Practice, Administrative Law and Litigation* section 10 (Lexis Publishing, 2006); Eisenberg, Horvitz and Wiener, *California Practice Guide: Civil Appeals and Writs* (The Rutter Group, 2006); Sorgen *et al.*, *California Civil Writ Practice* (Cal. Cont. Ed. Bar, 3rd ed. 2006); Geoffrey L. Robinson, *Handling Administrative Mandamus, Step 28* (Cal. Cont. Ed. Bar, Action Guide, Spring 2000); Kendall, Dowling, Schwartz, *Takings Litigation Handbook* (American Legal Publishing Corp., 2000); Kostka and Zischke, *Practice Under the California Environmental Quality Act*, ch. 23 (Cal. Cont. Ed. Bar 2nd ed. 2008, supplemented annually).
2. In this chapter, the term local agency is used and it includes a city, a county, special district, and other local government agencies. The local agency most often sued in a land use case is a city or county.

A mandate proceeding functions essentially as an appeal to a court of a local agency's decision or failure to act.

to place a citizen-sponsored initiative on the ballot, the petitioner must name the city clerk as respondent and the initiative sponsors as real parties in interest.

A mandate proceeding functions essentially as an appeal to a court of a local agency's decision or failure to act. After the petition is filed, one of the parties (usually the respondent agency) prepares a record consisting of the documents and minutes or transcripts of testimony upon which the local agency based its decision. The parties lodge the record with the court and establish a hearing and briefing schedule. Generally, the petitioner files an opening brief, the respondent and real party in interest file opposition briefs that respond to the petitioner's arguments, and the petitioner files a reply brief.

The court typically does not hold a traditional trial with testimony and exhibits; it instead hears oral argument, reviews the briefs and the record, and issues its decision. Because the trial court is reviewing a local agency's decision in light of the evidence that was presented to the agency, the court's review is similar to an appellate court's review of a traditional trial.

If it finds no merit in the challenge, the court denies the petition and enters judgment in favor of the respondent and real party in interest. If it rules in favor of the petitioner, the court enters a judgment directing that a writ issue. The court clerk then issues a writ of mandate directing the local agency either to vacate its decision or to take some other specified action. The agency then files a return to the writ indicating how it has complied with the writ, or that it has appealed the judgment.

Types of Mandate Proceedings

There are two broad types of mandate proceedings: traditional mandate and administrative mandate.

There are two broad types of mandate proceedings: traditional mandate and administrative mandate. Code of Civil Procedure sections 1084–1097 specify the procedures for both traditional and administrative mandate. Traditional mandate proceedings involve judicial review of legislative and ministerial acts. Administrative mandate proceedings involve judicial review of certain types of quasi-judicial decisions made after a hearing in which the agency received evidence. As explained in more detail below, the two types of mandate proceedings differ primarily in the standard the court employs when reviewing the legality of the agency action.

The type of mandate proceeding to be used to challenge a particular land use decision depends upon whether the agency being challenged was quasi-judicial as distinct from legislative or ministerial.

The type of mandate proceeding to be used to challenge a particular land use decision depends upon whether the agency decision being challenged was quasi-judicial as distinct from legislative or ministerial. Quasi-judicial decisions are reviewable under administrative mandate,[3] whereas legislative or ministerial decisions are reviewable by traditional mandate.

---

3. Administrative mandate is technically a subset of mandate—with specific procedural rules and standards—rather than a separate form of proceeding. As the California Supreme Court observed, "mandamus pursuant to...section 1094.5, commonly denominated 'administrative mandamus' is mandamus still. It is not possessed of 'a separate and distinctive legal personality. It is not a remedy removed from the general law of mandamus or exempted from the latter's established principles, requirements and limitations.' The full panoply of rules applicable to 'ordinary' mandamus applies to 'administrative' mandamus proceedings except where modified by statute." *County of San Diego v. State of California*, 15 Cal. 4th 68, 109 (1997) (even where petitioner pleads the wrong mandate statute—1085 instead of 1094.5—the error does not affect the court's ability to grant mandate relief and a demurrer on this ground should be overruled); *see also Woods v. Superior Court*, 28 Cal. 3d 668, 674 (1981) (ordinary mandate statutes and cases interpreting them govern administrative mandate proceedings unless they conflict with section 1094.5).

The difference between quasi-judicial and legislative decision making is not always easy to discern. The distinction turns on the function being performed by the agency (*see Pitts v. Perluss*, 58 Cal. 2d 824, 834 (1962)), rather than the particular procedure by which the decision was reached. *Wilson v. Hidden Valley Mun. Water Dist.*, 256 Cal. App. 2d 271, 280 (1967); *Pacifica Corp. v. City of Camarillo*, 149 Cal. App. 3d 168, 176 (1983) (classification of a decision as adjudicatory does not depend on the procedural characteristics of the administrative process). In general, legislative decisions involve adoption of local laws, policies, or regulations of general applicability. *See, e.g., Karlson v. City of Camarillo*, 100 Cal. App. 3d 789, 799 (1980) (adoption or amendment of general plan is quasi-legislative). Quasi-judicial decisions, by contrast, involve application of pre-existing laws, policies, or regulations in a specific factual context. *See, e.g., San Diego Bldg. Contractors Ass'n v. City Council*, 13 Cal. 3d 205, 211 (1974).

In practice, however, rather than engaging in a case-by-case determination, courts have tended to classify types of land use decisions as quasi-judicial or legislative according to the subject matter of the decision rather than the procedure employed. *See Arnel Dev. Co. v. City of Costa Mesa*, 28 Cal. 3d 511, 567 (1980) ("[t]he courts have not resolved the legislative or adjudicative character of administrative land use decisions on a case by case basis, but instead have established a generic rule that variances, use permits, subdivision maps, and similar proceedings are necessarily adjudicative").

Traditional Mandate Proceedings Under Section 1085 Challenge
Legislative and Ministerial Acts

Code of Civil Procedure sections 1085–1094 and 1095–1097 create a set of procedures commonly called "traditional" or "ordinary" mandate proceedings. These rules supplement the rules generally applicable to ordinary civil actions. Code Civ. Proc. § 1109 (code provisions pertaining to ordinary civil actions apply to writ proceedings except as otherwise provided in the statutes pertaining to special proceedings such as a writ proceeding). Traditional mandate proceedings are used to review two types of agency decisions: legislative and ministerial actions.

Traditional mandate proceedings are used to review two types of agency decisions: legislative and ministerial actions.

Legislative acts.[4] In general, legislative actions establish rules or standards of general applicability and are political in nature; they involve "the exercise of discretion governed by considerations of public welfare." *Wilson*, 256 Cal. App. 2d at 280. Legislative actions tend to declare a public purpose and make provision for the ways and means of its accomplishment. *See, e.g., Meridian Ocean Sys., Inc. v. State Lands Comm'n*, 222 Cal. App. 3d 153, 167 (1990); *Fishman v. City of Palo Alto*, 86 Cal. App. 3d 506, 509 (1978). Legislative acts involve more than a mere statement of policy, and also carry an implication of an ability to compel compliance. *Worthington v. City Council of the City of Rohnert Park*, 130 Cal. App. 4th 1132 (2005).

In general, legislative actions establish rules or standards of general applicability and are political in nature; they involve the exercise of discretion governed by considerations of public welfare.

The following have been held to be legislative actions:

- The adoption or amendment of a general plan or specific plan. *See, e.g., Yost v. Thomas*, 36 Cal. 3d 561, 570 (1984); *Sierra Club v. Gilroy City Council*, 222 Cal.

---

4. The phrase "legislative acts" as used in this chapter includes quasi-legislative acts.

App. 3d 30 (1990); *O'Loane v. O'Rourke*, 231 Cal. App. 2d 774, 784–85 (1965). See also chapter 2 (General Plan); chapter 3 (Specific Plan).

- Zoning or rezoning. *See Arnel Dev. Co.*, 28 Cal. 3d 511; *San Diego Bldg. Contractors Ass'n*, 13 Cal. 3d at 212–13; *William S. Hart Union High Sch. Dist. v. Reg'l Planning Comm'n*, 226 Cal. App. 3d 1612, 1625 (1991); *but see Southwest Diversified, Inc. v. City of Brisbane*, 229 Cal. App. 3d 1548, 1555–58 (1991) (adjustment of zoning boundaries in accordance with settlement agreement held not to be legislative); *W.W. Dean & Assoc. v. City of South San Francisco*, 190 Cal. App. 3d 1368, 1374–80 (1987) (amendment of development plan not legislative even though adoption of plan was legislative). See also chapter 4 (Zoning).

- Incorporation or annexation decisions. *See Bookout v. Local Agency Formation Comm'n*, 49 Cal. App. 3d 383, 386 (1975); *Richards v. City of Tustin*, 225 Cal. App. 2d 97, 100 (1964) (deannexation). See also chapter 16 (LAFCO).

- Adoption of rules or regulations by a regulatory body. *See Western States Petroleum Ass'n v. Superior Court*, 9 Cal. 4th 559 (1995); *Dunn-Edwards Corp. v. Bay Area Air Quality Management Dist.*, 9 Cal. App. 4th 644, 665 (1992).

Ministerial acts. Ministerial acts involve no judgment by the public official as to the wisdom or manner of carrying out the activity: "The public official merely applies the law to the facts as presented but uses no special discretion or judgment in reaching a decision. A ministerial decision involves only the use of fixed standards or objective measurements, and the public official cannot use personal subjective judgment in deciding whether or how the project should be carried out." *Mountain Lion Found. v. Fish & Game Comm'n*, 16 Cal. 4th 105, 117 (1997).

When a local agency is required by law to make a decision, that duty usually is held to be ministerial, even though the substance of the decision may be wholly within the agency's discretion.

When a local agency is required by law to make a decision, that duty usually is held to be ministerial, even though the substance of the decision may be wholly within the agency's discretion. Thus, a writ of mandate may be used to compel an agency to exercise its discretion, even though the writ may not be used to control the manner in which that discretion is exercised. *See Arnel Dev. Co.*, 28 Cal. 3d 511; *Sunset Drive Corp. v. City of Redlands*, 73 Cal. App. 4th 215 (1999) (writ may issue even if duty is directory, not mandatory); *Mitchell v. County of Orange*, 165 Cal. App. 3d 1185 (1985); *Benny v. City of Alameda*, 105 Cal. App. 3d 1006 (1980); *Ensign Bickford Realty Corp. v. City Council*, 68 Cal. App. 3d 467 (1977).

The following have been held to be ministerial acts:

- Approval of a final subdivision map that substantially conforms to the tentative map. *See Youngblood v. Board of Supervisors*, 22 Cal. 3d 644 (1978)

- Issuance of a building permit for a development that is consistent with the zoning and applicable building codes. *See Prentiss v. City of South Pasadena*, 15 Cal. App. 4th 85 (1993). However, the question of whether issuance is ministerial may depend on the local agency's ordinances or on potential environmental impacts. *See, e.g., Friends of Westwood, Inc. v. City of Los Angeles*, 191 Cal. App. 3d 259 (1987); *Slagle Constr. Co. v. County of Contra Costa*, 67 Cal. App. 3d 559 (1977)

- Issuance of a conditional use permit for second units that meet the requirements of the state's "granny flats" statutes, when the city has not adopted its own ordinance regulating second units. *See Wilson v. City of Laguna Beach*, 6 Cal. App. 4th 543 (1992)

- Adoption of forestry regulations required by statute, even though the contents of the regulations are a matter of agency discretion. *See Redwood Coast Watersheds Alliance v. State Bd. of Forestry & Fire Protection*, 70 Cal. App. 4th 962, 970 (1999)

- Implementation by a local agency or administrator of non-discretionary duties imposed by ordinance or statute. *See, e.g., Terminal Plaza Corp. v. City and County of San Francisco*, 186 Cal. App. 3d 814, 830–32 (1986) (zoning administrator required to enforce permit condition)

Administrative Mandate Proceedings Under Section 1094.5 Challenge Administrative and Quasi-Judicial Decisions

Administrative mandate proceedings, which are governed by Code of Civil Procedure section 1094.5, challenge a third type of agency decision, commonly called "administrative" and sometimes labeled "adjudicatory" or "quasi-judicial."[5]

Administrative decisions are those in which a local agency applies existing policies, laws, or regulations to a given set of facts. *See San Diego Bldg. Contractors Ass'n*, 13 Cal. 3d at 211; *Pacifica Corp.*, 149 Cal. App. 3d at 176.

Administrative decisions are those in which a local agency applies existing law or policy to a given set of facts.

Section 1094.5 applies only when there is a challenge to:

> ... any final administrative order or decision made as the result of a proceeding in which by law a hearing is required to be given, evidence is required to be taken, and discretion in the determination of facts is vested in the inferior tribunal, corporation, board, or officer....

Code Civ. Proc. § 1094.5. Section 1094.5 applies only when all of these specific requirements are met. *See Western States Petroleum Ass'n*, 9 Cal. 4th at 567–68. *See also Topanga Ass'n for a Scenic Cmty. v. County of Los Angeles*, 11 Cal. 3d 506, 514 n. 12 (1974). For section 1094.5 to apply, the hearing must be required by law and the agency must be legally required to take evidence, not merely *permitted* to take evidence. *See Lightweight Processing Co. v. County of Ventura*, 133 Cal. App. 3d 1042, 1049 (1982). *See, e.g., Mahdavi v Fair Employment Practices Comm'n*, 67 Cal. App. 3d 326 (1977). (Applicable law must mandate a hearing; if it gives the agency discretion on whether to hold a hearing, that requirement is not satisfied.)

Many of the decisions that have been categorically held to be subject to administrative mandate review are made after relatively informal proceedings (such as decisions on zoning variances, use permits, and subdivision maps made at city council or planning commission meetings) that have none of the usual indicia of a trial-type proceeding, such as sworn testimony, cross-examination, evidentiary restrictions, or neutral decision makers. *See Topanga Ass'n for a Scenic Cmty.*, 11 Cal. 3d at 518 (land use decisions are often made after procedures that may be characterized as casual).

On the other hand, a proceeding that meets all requirements of section 1094.5 (legally required hearing and taking of evidence and discretion in factual determinations vested in the agency) may nonetheless not be subject to administrative mandate review because it is not defined as "quasi-judicial." *See*,

---

5. These are collectively referred to as "administrative" decisions. Land use decisions, which are typically made by cities, counties, or special districts, seldom involve an adversary proceeding, subject to rules of evidence and decisionmaking by a neutral arbitrator). However, courts commonly refer to them as "quasi-judicial."

e.g., Western States, 9 Cal. 4th at 567 (quasi-legislative actions must be challenged in traditional mandate proceedings even if administrative agency was required by law to conduct hearing and take evidence). The following kinds of land use decisions have been held to be quasi-judicial and hence subject to section 1094.5:

- Variances from zoning ordinances. *See Topanga*, 11 Cal. 3d at 517
- Tentative subdivision maps and parcel maps. *See Horn v. County of Ventura*, 24 Cal. 3d 605, 612 (1979). *See also* chapter 5 (Subdivisions)
- Most types of use permits. *See Horn*, 24 Cal. 3d at 614; *Johnston v. City of Claremont*, 49 Cal. 2d 826, 834 (1958); *Neighborhood Action Group v. County of Calaveras*, 156 Cal. App. 3d 1176, 1186 (1984)
- Many types of planned unit development permits. *See City of Fairfield v. Superior Court*, 14 Cal. 3d 768, 773 (1975)
- Coastal development permits. *See Patterson v. Central Coast Reg'l Comm'n*, 58 Cal. App. 3d 833, 840–41 (1976)
- Cancellations of Williamson Act contracts. *See Sierra Club v. City of Hayward*, 28 Cal. 3d 840, 849 (1981)
- Timber harvesting plans. *See Laupheimer v. State of California*, 200 Cal. App. 3d 440 (1988)

Administrative Mandate Is the Exclusive Procedure for Challenging Administrative Decisions

Administrative mandate generally is held to be the exclusive method for challenging an administrative decision.

Administrative mandate generally is held to be the exclusive method for challenging an administrative decision. *See State of California*, 12 Cal. 3d at 249; *Guilbert v. Regents of Univ. of Cal.*, 93 Cal. App. 3d 233, 244–45 (1979).[6] Failing to bring such a challenge within the applicable statute of limitations renders the agency decision final and immune from attack under the doctrine of administrative res judicata. *See Hensler v. City of Glendale*, 8 Cal. 4th 1 (1994); *State of California v. Superior Court*, 12 Cal. 3d 237 (1974); *Patrick Media Group, Inc. v. California Coastal Comm'n*, 9 Cal. App. 4th 592 (1992); *Rossco Holdings, Inc. v. State of California*, 212 Cal. App. 3d 642 (1989); *California Coastal Comm'n v. Superior Court*, 210 Cal. App. 3d 1488 (1989); *City and County of San Francisco v. Padilla*, 23 Cal. App. 3d 388, 396–397 (1972) (discussing application of doctrine against local agency that made the administrative decision). It also precludes the party involved in the administrative proceeding from relitigating, in any subsequent judicial action, any issue that was raised and expressly or necessarily decided in the administrative proceeding. *See Briggs v. City of Rolling Hills Estates*, 40 Cal. App. 4th 637, 645–46 (1995) (failure to challenge building permit condition by administrative mandate precluded 42 U.S.C. § 1983 federal civil rights action). This principle—known as "administrative collateral estoppel" or "failure to exhaust

---

6. When § 1094.5 was first adopted, its primary purpose was to provide a procedure for prompt judicial review of administrative licensing and discipline of private citizens. *Royal Convalescent Hosp. v State Bd. of Control* 99 Cal. App. 3d 788, 793 (1979); *Brock v. Superior Court*, 109 Cal. App. 2d 594, 599 (1952). Use of administrative mandate has now been expanded beyond these parameters to include the full panoply of land use decisions made by city councils, planning commissions, zoning administrators, and other bodies during relatively informal meetings. *Royal Convalescent Hosp.*, 99 Cal. App. 3d at 794; *see Topanga Ass'n for a Scenic Cmty. v. County of Los Angeles*, 11 Cal. 3d 506, 518 (1974) (commenting on informality of proceedings involving land use decisions).

judicial remedies"—precludes such a party from bringing a subsequent action (whether based on statutory, constitutional, or other grounds) if any issue necessary to the successful prosecution of such action was decided in the administrative proceeding. *See Johnson v. City of Loma Linda*, 24 Cal. 4th 61, 70 (2000) (failure to bring mandate action challenging agency's findings and decision barred later action for violation of Fair Employment and Housing Act); *Knickerbocker v. City of Stockton*, 199 Cal. App. 3d 235, 240–44 (1988) ("Unless the administrative decision is [judicially] challenged, it binds the parties on the issues litigated and if those issues are fatal to a civil suit, the plaintiff cannot state a viable cause of action").

In an appropriate situation, even claims for violations of federal civil rights are subject to this doctrine. *See Mola Dev. Corp. v. City of Seal Beach*, 57 Cal. App. 4th 405, 412 (1997) (rejecting developer's arguments that the administrative collateral estoppel doctrine cannot be applied in federal civil rights actions, and that the doctrine cannot be applied unless the administrative hearing contained procedural safeguards such as the right to cross-examine and subpoena witnesses). Administrative collateral estoppel only applies, however, if the issue sought to be raised in court was one that the administrative agency was qualified to decide. *See State of California*, 12 Cal. 3d at 251 (issue of constitutionality of statute under which agency functioned could be raised for the first time in court action).

One court, however, recognized a limited circumstance in which administrative mandate was not deemed to be the exclusive procedure, and a petitioner was permitted to bring a later claim. In *Uniwill L.P. v. City of Los Angeles*, the court recognized the general rule that conditions of approval must be challenged in a timely mandate proceeding, and that any attempt to bring a later challenge would be barred. 124 Cal. App. 4th 537 (2004). In that case, a developer failed to bring a timely writ action challenging conditions of approval, and later brought suit to overturn a requirement that the city imposed. The court allowed the action to proceed. It explained that the petitioner was not challenging a condition of approval, but instead challenging the city's attempt to impose an easement requirement that had not been included in the conditions of tentative map approval. Accordingly, the failure to timely challenge the conditions of approval did not bar the developer from pursing its claim. *Id.* at 543–544 (also holding that five year statute of limitations applicable to inverse condemnation claims, rather than 90-day statute applicable to map decision, controlled).

If a petitioner brings a timely mandate proceeding together with other claims that are dependent upon the validity or propriety of the agency's decision,[7] the mandate issues must be resolved first. *See Hensler v. City of Glendale*, 8 Cal. 4th 1, 13–15 (1994); *Patrick Media Group, Inc. v. California Coastal Comm'n*, 9 Cal. App. 4th 592, 612 (1992) (challenges to administrative actions allegedly constituting takings must be brought initially by mandate).

If a petitioner brings a timely mandate proceeding together with other claims that are dependent upon the validity or propriety of the agency's decision, the mandate issues must be resolved first.

Standards Courts Apply in Reviewing Land Use Decisions

The standard under which a court reviews a local agency's actions depends upon both the type of agency action involved (legislative or administrative) and

---

7. *See* discussion under heading "Joining Other Causes of Action with a Writ Claim," below.

the rights affected by the agency's decision. Land use decisions ordinarily do not implicate fundamental vested rights, as, for example, those involved in revocation or suspension of a business or professional license (*see Bixby v. Pierno*, 4 Cal. 3d 130, 146 (1971)), or termination of social welfare benefits (*see Harlow v. Carleson*, 16 Cal. 3d 731, 737 (1976)). *See Interstate Brands v. Unemployment Ins. Appeals Bd.*, 26 Cal. 3d 770, 779 n. 5 (1980) (fundamental vested right is one that an individual presently possesses and is so significant that it cannot be extinguished or abridged by any entity lacking judicial power); *see also* chapter 10 (Vested Rights). Rather, they typically involve proceedings relating to issuance of a new permit or entitlement as to which there is no right. *See, e.g., Bank of America v. State Water Resources Control Bd.*, 42 Cal. App. 3d 198, 206 (1974). Accordingly, writ proceedings that challenge land use decisions ordinarily do not employ the independent judgment test, in which a court reweighs evidence and makes its own determination. Code Civ. Proc. § 1094.5(c). Instead, such proceedings are subject to standards of review that grant varying degrees of deference to the agency's decision.[8]

Standard of Judicial Review of Legislative Decisions

Courts cannot interfere with legislative discretion, and may overturn an agency's legislative decision only if that decision is arbitrary, capricious, wholly lacking in evidentiary support, or fails to conform to the procedures required by law.

The "arbitrary-and-capricious" standard of review. When local agencies make legislative decisions, they generally are adopting local laws or policies. The local agency is granted the discretion to make these policy decisions by statute and sometimes by the California Constitution. Courts do not have this discretion. Accordingly, courts cannot interfere with legislative discretion, and may overturn an agency's legislative decision only if that decision is arbitrary, capricious, wholly lacking in evidentiary support, or fails to conform to the procedures required by law. *See, e.g., Fullerton Joint Union High Sch. Dist. v. State Bd. of Educ.*, 32 Cal. 3d 779, 786 (1982) ("In reviewing...legislative decisions, the trial court does not inquire whether, if it had the power to act in the first instance, it would have taken the action taken by the administrative agency. The authority of the court is limited to determining whether the decision of the agency was arbitrary, capricious, entirely lacking in evidentiary support, or unlawfully or procedurally unfair."). This standard often is called the "arbitrary-and-capricious" standard of review.

Courts have consistently refused to substitute judicial judgment for the legislative judgment of the governing body of a local agency. So long as the enactment bears a reasonable relationship to the public welfare, it is upheld.

This limited review is grounded in the doctrine of separation of powers, which sanctions the legislative delegation of authority to the agency and acknowledges the agency's presumed expertise. *See Baldwin v. City of Los Angeles*, 70 Cal. App. 4th 819, 836 (1999). Courts have consistently refused to substitute judicial judgment for the legislative judgment of the governing body of a local agency. So long as the enactment bears a reasonable relationship to the public welfare, it is upheld. *See Associated Home Builders, Inc. v. City of Livermore*, 18 Cal. 3d 582 (1976). *See also California Hotel & Motel Ass'n v. Industrial Welfare Comm'n*, 25 Cal. 3d 200, 212 (1979) (judicial review of legislative administrative decisions limited "out of deference to the separation of powers between the Legislature

---

8. Mandate proceedings involving ministerial acts are an exception to the rule. In most such cases, the court is not reviewing a specific decision by an agency, but is instead determining whether, by law, the agency has a ministerial duty to act. Accordingly, the court does not grant any deference to the agency, but rather simply determines whether the law requires the act to be taken. Stated differently, agencies have no discretion not to follow the law; thus the court accords no deference when the issue is whether the agency has failed to comply with a mandatory legal requirement.

and the judiciary [and] to the legislative delegation of administrative authority to the agency"); *Western/Cal. Ltd. v. Dry Creek Joint Elementary Sch. Dist.*, 50 Cal. App. 4th 1461 (1996); *Canyon North Co. v. Conejo Valley Unified Sch. Dist.*, 19 Cal. App. 4th 243 (1993) (upholding school fees).

A California court explained this general principle by reciting the rules courts must follow when reviewing legislative enactments such as zoning ordinances:

> In considering the scope or nature of appellate review in a case of this type we must keep in mind the fact that the courts are examining the act of a coordinate branch of the government—the legislative—in a field in which it has paramount authority, and not reviewing the decision of a lower tribunal or of a fact finding body.
>
> Courts have nothing to do with the wisdom of laws or regulations, and the legislative power must be upheld unless manifestly abused so as to infringe on constitutional guaranties. The duty to uphold the legislative power is as much the duty of appellate courts as it is of trial courts, and under the doctrine of separation of powers neither the trial nor appellate courts are authorized to "review" legislative determinations.

Carty v. City of Ojai, 77 Cal. App. 3d 329, 333 n. 1 (1978) (citations and quotations omitted)

Individual legislator's motives are irrelevant. The motive of *individual council members* in enacting local land use laws is immaterial absent an unconstitutional motivation, such as racially discriminatory animus, motivation arising from a conflict of interest, or a bias sufficient to deprive an applicant of a fair hearing where one is required. The court explained this principle in *County of Butte v. Bach*:

> The Bachs suggest that, by advancing the interests of the neighbors who opposed commercial use of the corner lots, Supervisor Wheeler, and by attribution the County of Butte, acted improperly. The implication is that Wheeler's affiliation with the cause of those constituents who opposed the commercial use is an illicit motivation for her official acts in the course of the controversy. With few exceptions, *e.g.*, racially discriminatory animus, none of which are made out in this case, the motive of officials enacting a zoning ordinance is immaterial. [Citation omitted.] Absent such an unconstitutional motivation, we discern no legal impropriety in an elected official siding with one faction in what is, so long as the alternative chosen is not unreasonable, ultimately a political contest. [Citation omitted.]

172 Cal. App. 3d 848, 862 n. 1 (1985)

The motive of individual council members in enacting local land use laws is immaterial absent an unconstitutional motivation, such as racially discriminatory animus, a conflict of interest, or a bias sufficient to deprive an applicant of a fair hearing where one is required.

The intent and purpose of the legislative body is relevant. The prohibition against inquiries into the motives and intent of the individual members of the legislative body does not preclude judicial inquiry into the intent, purpose, and effect of local land use laws. Motives and purposes of the legislative body—or even the electorate—are factors to be considered in determining whether a land use law is invalid as discriminatory. *See Arnel Dev. Co. v. City of Costa Mesa*, 126 Cal. App. 3d 330 (1981) (court reviewed ballot arguments in determining that an initiative ordinance discriminated against a particular parcel of land).

In *G & D Holland Construction Company v. City of Marysville*, the court explained that the prohibition against judging the wisdom of legislation does not preclude an inquiry into the discriminatory nature of some local laws:

The prohibition against inquiries into the motives and intent of the individual members of the legislative body does not preclude judicial inquiry into the intent, purpose, and effect of local land use laws.

The principle limiting judicial inquiry into the legislative body's police power objectives does not bar scrutiny of a quite different issue, that of discrimination against a particular parcel of property. "A city cannot unfairly discriminate against a particular parcel of land, and the courts may properly inquire as to whether the scheme of classification has been applied fairly and impartially in each instance." [Citation omitted.]

Every intendment favors the legislative body's action, which will not be overthrown in the absence of physical facts requiring the conclusion that the ordinance is unreasonable and invalid as a matter of law. [Citations omitted.] Nevertheless, where "spot zoning" or other restriction upon a particular property evinces a discriminatory design against the property user, the courts will give weight to evidence disclosing a purpose other than that appearing upon the face of the regulation.

12 Cal. App. 3d 989, 994 (1970)

The legislative body's motive and intent are to be determined from a review of the evidence before the legislative body.

The legislative body's motive and intent are to be determined from a review of the evidence before the legislative body. "Resolution of that question is an objective determination, drawn not from an inquiry into individual motives, but from an analysis of the evidence supporting the government agency's official findings. 'The proper inquiry is not into the subjective motive of the government agency, but whether there is, objectively, sufficient connection between the land use regulation in question and a legitimate governmental purpose....'" *Loewenstein v. City of Lafayette*, 103 Cal. App. 4th 718, 731 (2002) (quoting *Landgate, Inc. v. California Coastal Comm'n*, 17 Cal. 4th 1006, 1022 (1998)). *See also Kissinger v. City of Los Angeles*, 161 Cal. App. 2d 454 (1958) (objective evidence showed that the city's purpose in zoning property was to depress its value so that it might be acquired for airport purposes at a lower cost).

There is no statutory requirement for a fair hearing when a local agency is making a legislative decision. Nonetheless, even legislative actions may be subject to fair hearing or due process requirements under some circumstances.

Due process and fair hearing requirements. There is no statutory requirement for a "fair hearing" when a local agency is making a legislative decision. *Contrast,* Code Civ. Proc. § 1094.5 (fair hearing required for administrative decisions). Courts grant a high degree of deference to the local agency and allow decisionmakers to vote based on predispositions, campaign promises made before the matter has come before the agency, and *ex parte* communications and information.[9] This is because great leeway is required when a council is establishing local policy and addressing political issues. *See* John W. Witt and Daniel J. Curtin, Jr., "The Problem of Ex Parte Contacts," 3 *CEB Land Use & Env. Forum* 24 (Winter 1994). For a discussion of ex parte contacts, *see* chapter 17 (Rights of the Regulated and of the Citizens).

Legislative actions may be subject to fair hearing or due process requirements under some circumstances.

Nonetheless, even legislative actions may be subject to fair hearing or due process requirements under some circumstances. *See Harris v. County of Riverside*, 904 F. 2d 497 (9th Cir. 1990) (procedural due process required when change in land use designation from commercial to residential has particularized effect on

---

9. Decisionmakers who have a conflict of interest (such as ownership of neighboring property) in a matter may be prohibited from involvement in the decision under Government Code section 1090 *et seq.* and the Political Reform Act (Gov't Code § 87100 *et seq.*). *See* California Attorney General's Office, Conflicts of Interest (1998). *See also Providing Conflict of Interest Advice Handbook*, City Attorneys Department, Continuing Legal Education Seminar (League of Calif. Cities, Feb. 2004).

plaintiff); *Scott v. City of Indian Wells*, 6 Cal. 3d 541, 548–49 (1972) (discussing due process notice requirements in the context of a zoning decision); *Clark v. City of Hermosa Beach*, 48 Cal. App. 4th 1152, 1171 (1996) (in holding that the plaintiff had not received a fair hearing under Code of Civil Procedure section 1094.5, court cited with approval a treatise providing that ordinances or bylaws passed by interested legislators are void). Additionally, the public is entitled to certain notices and the right to be heard at most legislative body hearings pursuant to the Ralph M. Brown Act, Gov't Code § 54950 *et seq.*, and, as relevant, specific provisions of the Planning and Zoning Law. *E.g.* Gov't Code §§ 65854, 65856 (notice and hearing requirements for proposed adoption or amendment of zoning ordinance). *See* chapter 17 (Rights of the Regulated and of the Citizens) for a discussion of the Brown Act.

Standard of Judicial Review of Administrative Decisions

Courts grant less deference to administrative decisions than to legislative decisions. Because such a proceeding adjudicates individual rights and interests, findings are required and a reviewing court looks to whether the evidence supports the findings. *Topanga Ass'n for a Scenic Cmty.*, 11 Cal. 3d at 514 (1974); *Shapell Indus., Inc. v. Governing Bd.*, 1 Cal. App. 4th 218, 231 (1991). The standard of review in an administrative mandate proceeding is set forth in Code of Civil Procedure section 1094.5(b), which states that the judicial inquiry extends to:

- Whether the respondent has proceeded without, or in excess of, jurisdiction
- Whether there was a fair hearing
- Whether there was any prejudicial abuse of discretion

It further provides that "abuse of discretion" is established when:

- The respondent has not proceeded in the manner required by law
- The order or decision is not supported by the findings
- The findings are not supported by the evidence

Code Civ. Proc. § 1094.5(b)

The standard of review thus differs according to the specific ground for challenge of the administrative decision, as described more specifically in the following sections.

"Excess of jurisdiction." In determining whether a local agency has proceeded in excess of its jurisdiction, courts generally grant no deference to the agency's determination of whether jurisdiction existed. *See State of California v. Superior Court*, 12 Cal. 3d 237, 248 (1974) (agency decision could not be upheld unless agency had jurisdiction to hear appeal).

In determining whether a local agency has proceeded in excess of its jurisdiction, courts generally grant no deference to the agency's determination of whether jurisdiction existed.

"Fair hearing." Code of Civil Procedure section 1094.5 expressly mandates that there be a "fair trial" when an agency makes an administrative decision. In the land use context, this is generally interpreted to require a fair hearing, since there is no "trial" in the usual sense. In determining whether an agency afforded a "fair hearing" pursuant to section 1094.5, courts generally use due process principles to evaluate the fairness of the agency action. *See Nasha v. City of Los Angeles*, 125 Cal. App. 4th 470, 482 (2004) ("procedural due process principles apply to quasi-judicial decisionmaking"); *Clark v. City of Hermosa Beach*, 48 Cal. App. 4th 1152,

In determining whether an agency afforded a "fair hearing" pursuant to section 1094.5, courts generally use due process principles to evaluate the fairness of the agency action.

1170 ("foundational factual findings must be sustained if supported by substantial evidence; however, the ultimate determination of whether the administrative proceedings were fundamentally fair is a question of law to be decided on appeal"). *See also* Geoffrey L. Robinson, *Handling Administrative Mandamus, Step 15* (Cal. Cont. Ed. Bar, Action Guide, 2000).

Generally speaking, in light of the fundamentally political nature of land use decisions, there is no denial of a fair hearing when council members come to the hearing with pre-determined notions regarding the desirability of the type of project before them. Even when council members have publicly announced their opposition to the very project being considered, there is no denial of a fair hearing, at least when the council hearing does "not turn upon the adjudication of disputed facts or the application of specific standards to the facts found." *City of Fairfield v. Superior Court*, 14 Cal. 3d 768, 780 (1975) (city did not deny developer a fair hearing under section 1094.5 when it denied a PUD permit, even if council members had previously announced their positions on the developer's proposed shopping center, which could significantly influence the nature and direction of future economic growth in the city). *See also Breneric Assocs. v. City of Del Mar*, 69 Cal. App. 4th 166, 184 (1998) (allegations that council members were hostile to the developers seeking design review approval failed to state a claim of arbitrary action because motives for voting on land use issues are irrelevant to assessing validity of the action taken); *Stubblefield Constr. Co. v. City of San Bernardino*, 32 Cal. App. 4th 687 (1995) (no violation of civil rights or substantive due process when city's actions were not arbitrary or irrational, even though one council member sponsored numerous procedural and substantive ordinances designed to stop and delay the project); 78 Ops. Cal. Atty. Gen. 77 (1995) (council member who signs a petition opposing a land use project is not disqualified from participating in the council proceeding regarding that project).

At some point, however, a council member's bias and animus towards a project or a developer may be so extreme as to constitute a denial of a fair hearing. *See Clark*, 48 Cal. App. 4th at 1173 (city denied a fair hearing on application for permits to demolish one duplex and build a bigger one, in part because council member's "personal animosity toward the [applicants] contributed to his conflict of interest; he was not a disinterested, unbiased decisionmaker").

Similarly, a planning commissioner's authorship of a newsletter article characterizing a project site as an "absolutely crucial habitat corridor" while the project was pending before the commission, can result in the denial of a fair hearing, by establishing an unacceptable probability of actual bias. *Nasha*, 125 Cal App. 4th 470. The project at issue was approved by the city planning director and appealed to the planning commission by a group of neighborhood residents. *Id.* at 473–475. Before the planning commission hearing, the residents association, of which one of the planning commissioners was the president, published an unsigned news update on the project, contending that it was a threat to the wildlife corridor. The court overturned the commission's decision, holding that while the standard of impartiality at an administrative hearing is less exacting than that required in judicial proceedings, procedural due process requires that the hearing be conducted before a reasonably impartial uninvolved reviewer. *Id.* at 483. In this case, authorship of the article gave rise to an unacceptable probability of actual bias, and precluded the commissioner from serving as an impartial reviewer. *Id.* at 484.

"Proceeding in the manner required by law." In determining whether a local agency's actions conform to the procedures required by law, the courts simply apply the law at issue to the agency's actions. *See Azusa Land Reclamation Co. v. Main San Gabriel Basin Watermaster*, 52 Cal. App. 4th 1165, 1192 (1997); *Bright Dev. Co. v. City of Tracy*, 20 Cal. App. 4th 783 (1993) (court determined whether agency's denial of a subdivision map conformed to state law requirement that only certain ordinances be applied, without giving deference to agency's decision). The "law" to which the procedure must adhere may be either the applicable statute or ordinance (*e.g.*, *Georgia-Pacific Corp. v. California Coastal Comm'n*, 132 Cal. App. 3d 678, 701 (1982)), or the requirement of due process (*e.g.*, *Negrete v. State Personnel Bd.*, 213 Cal. App. 3d 1160, 1165 (1989)). As discussed more fully below, courts do not grant deference to a city's interpretation of state or constitutional law, but will defer to a city's interpretation of *local* laws and procedures.

In determining whether a local agency's actions conform to the procedures required by law, the courts simply apply the law at issue to the agency's actions.

"Supported by the findings and evidence." In determining whether a local agency's decisions are supported by findings and whether the findings are supported by the evidence, the court accords different degrees of deference to the agency. The court gives substantial deference in determining whether the evidence is *sufficient*:

In determining whether a local agency's decisions are supported by findings and whether the findings are supported by the evidence, the court accords different degrees of deference to the agency.

> In reviewing the evidence... all conflicts must be resolved in favor of the [prevailing party], and all legitimate and reasonable inferences indulged in to uphold the [finding] if possible. It is an elementary, but often overlooked principle of law, that when a [finding] is attacked as being unsupported, the power of the... court begins and ends with a determination as to whether there is any substantial evidence, contradicted or uncontradicted, which will support the [finding]. When two or more inferences can be reasonably deduced from the facts, the reviewing court is without power to substitute its deductions for those of the [agency].

Western States Petroleum Ass'n, 9 Cal. 4th at 571 (quotations and citations omitted)

The court accords less deference in determining whether the decision is supported by proper findings, but still recognizes the expertise of the local agency. In *Topanga Association for a Scenic Community*, the court explained the fundamental rules that apply to judicial review of findings in an administrative mandate proceeding:

> Implicit in [Code Civ. Proc.] section 1094.5 is a requirement that the agency which renders the challenged decision must set forth findings to bridge the analytic gap between the raw evidence and ultimate decision or order.
>
> ... [The agency] must render findings sufficient both to enable the parties to determine whether and on what basis they should seek review and, in the event of review, to apprise a reviewing court of the basis for the board's action.

11 Cal. 3d at 514–15

The substantial evidence test compels courts only to sustain existing findings supported by such evidence, not to hypothesize new findings. As the court explained in *Sierra Club v. City of Hayward*, even the existence of substantial evidence to support a necessary determination will not compel a conclusion that the determination was in fact made. 28 Cal. 3d 840, 859 (1981). Findings do not however, require judicial precision. "[F]indings need not be stated with judicial formality. Findings must simply expose the mode of analysis, not expose every minutia." *Craik v. County of Santa Cruz*, 81 Cal. App. 4th 880, 891 (2000). The court must review the entire record and consider all relevant evidence, including evidence that fairly detracts from the evidence supporting the agency decision. *California Youth Authority v. SP Board*, 104 Cal. App. 4th 575, 585 (2002); *Young v. Gannet*, 97 Cal. App. 4th 209, 225 (1997). For further information regarding the required content of findings, *see* chapter 11 (Necessity for Findings).

Standard of Judicial Review of Agency Decisions with Both Legislative and Administrative Aspects

The case law is unclear as to the applicable standard when agency decisions possess both legislative and administrative aspects.

The case law is unclear as to the applicable standard when agency decisions possess both legislative and administrative aspects. Some courts hold that the nature of the agency's "dominant concern" in making the decision determines the decision's character, which then determines whether review is in traditional or administrative mandate. *See Del Mar Terrace Conservancy, Inc. v. City Council*, 10 Cal. App. 4th 712, 725–28 (1992) (dominant concern of challenged action regarding location of a highway was legislative); *Meridian Ocean Sys., Inc.*, 222 Cal. App. 3d at 167–68 (court looked to an agency's dominant concern in making a decision relating to high energy permits connected with geophysical research and concluded it was legislative); *City of Rancho Palos Verdes v. City Council*, 59 Cal. App. 3d 869, 883–85 (1976) (where city's dominant concern in vacating a public street was the effect on a few individuals, the action was adjudicatory).

Other courts have held that the stricter standard of substantial evidence is controlling where agency decisions involve both judicial and legislative functions.

Other courts have held that the stricter standard of substantial evidence is controlling where agency decisions involve both judicial and legislative functions. *See City of Carmel-By-The-Sea v. Bd. of Supervisors*, 183 Cal. App. 3d 229, 239 (1986) (board action determining a wetlands demarcation line subject to substantial evidence test when action involved a determination of specific rights in regard to a particular factual situation, even though demarcation line was established as part of a zoning decision). *See also Mountain Def. League v. Bd. of Supervisors*, 65 Cal. App. 3d 723, 729 (1977) ("where...an agency in two capacities is simultaneously disposing of two legally required functions with but one decision, review of that determination must be by the more stringent standard").

In general, where an agency's "final act" is legislative, the steps preceding it also are deemed to be legislative. *See Prentis v. Atlantic Coast Line Co.*, 211 U.S. 210, 227 (1908). Holding hearings and taking evidence before reaching a legislative decision do not make the final action administrative. *See Patterson*, 58 Cal. App. 3d at 841; *Wilson*, 256 Cal. App. 2d at 279.

Standard of Judicial Review of an Aspect of an Agency Decision That Interprets or Applies Law

Many local land use decisions involve the interpretation and application of law. The degree of judicial deference afforded these aspects of a local agency's decision depends not so much on whether review is under traditional or administrative mandate as on what law the agency is interpreting. When the issue involves construction of general state law, courts exercise independent judgment without deference to the agency decision. *See County of San Diego*, 15 Cal. 4th at 109; *Baldwin*, 70 Cal. App. 4th at 836. *See also Azusa Land Reclamation Co.*, 52 Cal. App. 4th at 1192 ("The issue is one of law because it turns on the interpretation of the [CEQA] Guidelines. An issue involving a rule of law is one which this court decides de novo.").

CEQA = California Environmental Quality Act

When, however, the contention raises a question of an agency's interpretation and application of its own local laws, courts defer to the agency's interpretation: "[T]here is a strong policy reason for allowing the governmental body which passed legislation to be given a chance to interpret or clarify its intention concerning that legislation." *City of Walnut Creek v. County of Contra Costa*, 101 Cal. App. 3d 1012, 1021 (1980). Courts likewise give deference when an interpretation of state or local law is rendered by an agency that is charged with applying and interpreting the law or regulation at issue. *Id.*; *see also Rizzo v. Board of Trustees*, 27 Cal. App. 4th 853, 861 (1994) (long-standing, consistent construction by the administrative agency is entitled to great weight and should not be disturbed unless it is clearly erroneous).

Courts likewise give deference when an interpretation of state or local law is rendered by an agency that is charged with applying and interpreting the law or regulation at issue.

This distinction is important in land use cases because local agencies frequently interpret and apply their own general plans, zoning ordinances, and other local laws in determining whether to issue a permit or grant a project approval. In these instances, courts will overturn the local agency's interpretation only if "a reasonable person could not have reached the same conclusion." *No Oil, Inc. v. City of Los Angeles*, 196 Cal. App. 3d 223, 243 (1987) (referring to determination that project was consistent with the city's general plan). *See also Sequoyah Hills Homeowners Ass'n v. City of Oakland*, 23 Cal. App. 4th 704, 719–20 (1993) ("once a general plan is in place, it is the province of elected city officials to examine the specifics of a proposed project to determine whether it would be 'in harmony' with the policies stated in the plan. [Citation omitted.] It is emphatically not the role of the courts to micromanage these development decisions.").

Judicial deference does not, however, mean judicial abdication. In *Families Unafraid to Uphold Rural El Dorado County v. County of El Dorado*, the court overturned the county's findings of consistency because the general plan provision at issue was "fundamental, mandatory and unambiguous" in prohibiting the action the County approved. 62 Cal. App. 4th 1332 (1998). Similarly, in *Napa Citizens For Honest Government v. County of Napa Bd. of Supervisors*, the court found a specific plan to be inconsistent with the general plan when the county acknowledged that the specific plan's circulation element did not actually implement the goals and policies identified in the general plan, and recognized that the specific plan required no specific action that would further the general plan's housing goals, policies, or objectives. 91 Cal. App. 4th 342 (2001). *See* chapter 2 (General Plan).

Deadlines for Bringing Actions

Statutes of limitations in the land use area are unusually short, and the statutes sometimes overlap or conflict, or are simply confusing. The purpose of such relatively short limitations periods is to permit and promote sound fiscal planning by state and local governmental entities. *See Hensler v. City of Glendale*, 8 Cal. 4th 1, 27 (1994). Another express legislative purpose is "to provide certainty for property owners and local governments regarding decisions made pursuant to [the Planning and Zoning Law]." Gov't Code § 65009(a)(3). *See Wagner v. City of*

Statutes of limitations in the land use area are unusually short, and the statutes sometimes overlap or conflict, or are simply confusing.

South Pasadena, 78 Cal. App. 4th 943, 948–49 (2000). To achieve these ends, the statutes of limitations applicable to land use decisions—particularly those governing planning and zoning decisions (Gov't Code § 65009), and decisions regarding subdivisions (Gov't Code § 66437)—employ expansive language to describe the scope of decisions covered. *Hensler*, 8 Cal. 4th at 25 (referencing "broad language" in § 66499.37); *Utility Cost Management v. Indian Wells Valley Water Dist.*, 26 Cal. 4th 1185, 1191 (2001) (broad construction required for Gov't Code § 66022, addressing challenges to fees and exactions).

The general rule requiring narrow construction of statutes of limitation does not apply where, as is often the case with land use matters, the governing statute reflects a policy judgment by the legislature in favor of expeditious resolution of disputes.

The general rule requiring narrow construction of statutes of limitation (*see, e.g., Steketee v. Lintz, Williams & Rothberg*, 38 Cal. 3d 46, 56 (1985)) does not apply where, as is often the case with land use matters, the governing statute reflects a policy judgment by the legislature in favor of expeditious resolution of disputes. *Maginn v. City of Glendale*, 72 Cal. App. 4th 1102, 1109 (1999) (rule of narrow construction not appropriate in litigation involving the Subdivision Map Act (Gov't Code §§ 66410–66499.37), which reflects legislative intent that disputes should be resolved as quickly as possible consistent with due process). As a result, not only are the limitations periods in land use cases very short, courts are more likely than in the ordinary civil context to select the *shorter* of two applicable limitations periods if there is any doubt on the subject.

Many land use statutes of limitations require that an action not only be filed but also served within a specific period. When that is the case, the service must be completed—not merely commenced—by the indicated deadline.

Many land use statutes of limitations require that an action not only be filed but also served within a specific period. When that is the case, the service must be *completed*—not merely commenced—by the indicated deadline. See *Royalty Carpet Mills, Inc. v. City of Irvine*, 125 Cal. App. 4th 1110 (2005) (petition dismissed even though it was timely filed, because it was not timely served); *Wagner*, 78 Cal. App. 4th at 948 (because statute applicable to notice and acknowledgment of receipt of the summons provides that service is not complete until the notice is signed, mailing the notice and acknowledgment on the last day to file and serve an action was insufficient); *Gonzalez v. County of Tulare*, 65 Cal. App. 4th 777 (1998) (where Government Code section 65009 required that action be served as well as filed within 120 days (now 90 days), petitioner's mandate proceeding was time-barred where service was not completed within the statutory period). Where, however, the respondent appears in the action before the deadline for serving the action has passed, the respondent likely will be held to have waived any arguments about service. Both *Kriebel v. City Council*, 112 Cal. App. 3d 693 (1980), and *Sprague v. County of San Diego*, 106 Cal. App. 4th 119 (2003), discussed application of the 90-day file and serve statute to claims arising under the Subdivision Map Act and noted that appearance within the 90-day statutory period waived any claims relating to failure to serve the summons.

"To determine the statute of limitations that applies to a cause of action, it is necessary to identify the nature of the cause of action, *i.e.*, the 'gravamen' of the cause of action. [Citations omitted.] [T]he nature of the right sued upon and not the form of action nor the relief demanded determines the applicability of the statute of limitations...." *Hensler*, 8 Cal. 4th at 22–23. In *Hensler*, the plaintiff claimed that the city took his property without just compensation when it applied a ridgeline ordinance to his project. He argued that his lawsuit was timely because the statute of limitations on such "takings" claims is five years. (Code Civ. Proc. §§ 318, 319). However, the court concluded that the plaintiff actually was challenging the adoption and application of a land use ordinance to the proposed project. It held that (1) the plaintiff's as-applied claims were barred by Government Code section 66499.37, which contains a 90-day statute of limitations for proceedings involving the Subdivision Map Act; and (2) the plaintiff's facial challenges to the ordinance were subject to Government Code section 65009, which provided for a 120-day limitation period for actions challenging the facial validity of a land use ordinance. *Id.* at 22.

In *Honig v. San Francisco Planning Department,* the court applied the 90-day statute of limitations governing challenges to zoning actions, to a challenge of a building permit issuance. 127 Cal. App. 4th 520 (2005). It reasoned that the complaint, although nominally seeking rescission of the building permit, was actually challenging the validity of the underlying variance that allowed the issuance of the building permit. The court stated that it "would exalt form over substance to refuse to apply [Section 65009] to a challenge to a different zoning and planning decision where that decision rested entirely on the variance." *Id.* at 528. *See also Gonzales,* 65 Cal. App. 4th 777 (where two statutes of limitation—Gov't Code §§ 65009 and 65860—both governed challenge to zoning enactment for inconsistency with general plan, petitioner was required to comply with service requirements of section 65009, even though section 65860 was the shorter and more specific statute and had no service deadline).

How to Find the Applicable Statute of Limitations

The applicable statute of limitations may be found in the laws that pertain to all decisions made by the agency. For example, Public Resources Code section 30801 directs that actions challenging any decision of the California Coastal Commission be brought within 60 days.

The applicable statute of limitations may be found in the laws that pertain to all decisions made by the agency. Alternatively, the applicable statute may pertain to the type of decision being challenged.

Alternatively, the applicable statute may pertain to the *type* of decision being challenged. For example, Government Code section 65009(c) creates a 90-day statute applicable to many planning and zoning decisions such as amendment of a general plan or zoning ordinance. Similarly, Government Code section 56103 and Code of Civil Procedure section 860 require challenges to annexations, formations, and detachments of property to be brought within 60 days.

A party attempting to determine the applicable deadline should also review Code of Civil Procedure section 1094.6, which applies to decisions to deny or revoke a permit, license or other entitlement, and provides for a 90-day statute of limitations.[10] For section 1094.6 to apply, however, the local agency must provide formal notice to the party that section 1094.6 governs the time within which judicial review of the decision must be sought. Code Civ. Proc. § 1094.6(f). The 90-day limitations period does not begin to run until this notice is given. *Donnellan v. City of Novato,* 86 Cal. App. 4th 1097, 1102 (2001); *El Dorado Palm Springs, Ltd. v. Rent Review Comm'n,* 230 Cal. App. 3d 335, 345 (1991). Code of Civil Procedure section 1094.6(b) requires that a verified or testimonial statement attesting to the date the decision was mailed to the party by first-class mail, postage prepaid, be mailed with the decision. *Donnellan,* 86 Cal. App. 4th at 1102. An after-the-fact declaration stating that the notice was mailed on a particular date does not satisfy the requirements of section 1094.6 because the statute expressly requires that

---

10. The former requirement under Code of Civil Procedure section 1094.6(g) that the local agency formally have adopted an ordinance approving section 1094.6 was deleted by 1993 legislation.

Table 4. Statutes Applicable to Common Land Use Decisions

Time Period	Type of Action Challenged	Authority
30 days of decision to carry out or approve project	Approval of a project pursuant to a specific plan without having previously certified a supplemental EIR for the specific plan	Pub. Res. Code § 65457(b)
30 days after CEQA notice of determination is filed	Adoption of Negative Declaration under CEQA	Pub. Res. Code § 21167(b)
30 days after CEQA notice of determination is filed	Certification of EIR under CEQA	Pub. Res. Code § 21167(c)
30 days after the last date on which reconsideration could have been ordered	Agency proceedings subject to the Administrative Procedure Act	Gov't Code § 11523
30 days after assessment is levied	The validity of an assessment or supplemental assessment against real property for public improvements, the proceedings for which are prescribed by the legislative body of any chartered city	Code Civ. Proc. § 329.5
35 days after CEQA notice of exemption is filed	Determination that project is exempt from CEQA	Pub. Res. Code § 21167(d)
35 days following 30-day period to cure or correct, following demand given within 30 days or 90 days of violation	Open meeting law (Brown Act) violation	Gov't Code § 54960.1
60 days	Completed change of organization or reorganization (LAFCO decisions)	Gov't Code § 56103; Code Civ. Proc. § 860
60 days	Any decision or action of the Coastal Commission	Pub. Res. Code § 30801
90 days to commence action and serve legislative body	Adoption or amendment of general plan*	Gov't Code § 65009(c)
90 days to commence action and serve legislative body	Adoption or amendment of zoning ordinance	Gov't Code § 65009(c) Pub. Res. Code § 21167(d)
90 days to commence action and serve legislative body	Adoption or amendment of any regulation attached to a specific plan	Gov't Code § 65009(c)
90 days to commence action and serve legislative body	Adoption or amendment of a development agreement	Gov't Code § 65009(c)
90 days to commence action and serve legislative body	Decision on conditional use permit, decision of board of zoning adjustment or zoning administrator, authorization for board of zoning adjustment or zoning administrator to decide variances without a public hearing	Gov't Code § 65009(c)
90 days to commence action and serve legislative body zoning administrator	Decision of board of appeals on appeal of decision of board of zoning adjustment or zoning administrator	Gov't Code § 65009(c)
90 days to commence action and serve legislative body	Conditions attached to a variance, conditional use permit, or any similar permit	Gov't Code § 65009(c)
90 days to commence action and serve legislative body	Determination that zoning is consistent with the general plan	Gov't Code § 65860(b)
90 days to commence action and serve summons	Decision concerning a subdivision	Gov't Code § 66499.37
90 days to commence action and serve summons	Written verification of sufficient water supply for certain residential subdivisions	Gov't Code §§ 66473.7(o), 66499.37
90 days from date of decision (or from mailing of decision if a written decision or findings are required)**	Decision revoking or denying an application for a permit, license, or other entitlement	Code Civ. Proc. § 1094.6
120 days	Adoption of ordinance or resolution to establish, increase or modify specified sewer or water fees, capacity charges, or processing fees	Gov't Code § 66022(a)
180 days after imposition; protest must be delivered within 90 days of imposition	Imposition of fees, dedications, or exactions on a development project	Gov't Code §§ 66020(d), 66021
180 days after determination***	CEQA determination made but no notice of determination or notice of exemption filed	Pub. Res. Code § 21167(a); 14 Cal. Code Regs. § 15112(c)(5)

Table 4. Statutes Applicable to Common Land Use Decisions *continued*

Time Period	Type of Action Challenged	Authority
180 days after project approved or agency begins to carry it out	Approval or carrying out of project without CEQA determination	Pub. Res. Code § 21167(a)
180 days after decision on cancellation petition	Cancellation of Williamson Act contract	Gov't Code § 51286
One year to commence action and serve legislative body	Certain challenges to general plan housing element decisions	Gov't Code § 65009(d)
One year	Action alleging violation of federal civil rights under 42 U.S.C. § 1983	*Wilson v. Garcia,* 471 U.S. 261 (1985); *Barancik v. County of Marin,* 872 F. 2d 834 (9th Cir. 1988)
Three years of accrual of action	Challenge to ordinance based on claim it has been preempted by later-enacted statute	*Travis v. County of Santa Cruz,* 33 Cal. 4th 757 (2004)
Three years after assessor establishes cancellation value	State of California's challenge to a cancellation fee made pursuant to a decision to cancel a Williamson Act Contract	*People ex rel. Dept. of Conservation v. Triplett,* 48 Cal. App. 4th 233 (1996)

* Not all general plan provisions are protected by the 90-day statute. Even general plan provisions that were enacted years ago may be challenged in certain instances. A petitioner may claim that a general plan amendment or project approval is invalid because there is no legally adequate general plan to support a determination of general plan consistency. In that instance, the petitioner may challenge the legal adequacy of the portions of the general plan that are relevant to the consistency determination. See *Garat v. City of Riverside,* 2 Cal. App. 4th 259 (1991).

** This period may be extended if the agency has a provision for reconsideration CCP § 1094.6(b) or if petitioner requests the record within ten days of the decision becoming final. CCP § 1094.6(d).

*** *County of Amador v. El Dorado County Water Agency,* 76 Cal. App. 4th 931, 963 (1999) ("If notice of exemption is not filed, or is defective in any material manner, the limitations period is extended to 180 days after the project is approved.") The 180-day period also may apply when an agency determines that no supplemental or subsequent EIR is required, but files no notice of determination. See *Cumming v. City of San Bernardino Redevelopment Agency,* 101 Cal. App. 4th 1229 (Aug. 9, 2002) (petition time-barred because not filed within 180 days after city made finding that no further environmental review was required. See also *Kraus v. Trinity Management Servs., Inc.,* 23 Cal. 4th at 129; *Cortez v. Purolator Air Filtration Products Co.,* 23 Cal. 4th at 168 (2000)).

"the facts of the mailing must be attested to in a written statement *included* with the written decision." *Id.* (emphasis in original).

The party should also determine whether the agency proceedings were subject to the Administrative Procedure Act (APA) (Code Civ. Proc. § 11500 *et seq.*), which applies to most state agencies and any local agency that acts on behalf of a state agency subject to the APA. *See Garner v. City of Riverside*, 170 Cal. App. 3d 510 (1985). If so, the mandate action must be filed within 30 days of the last date on which reconsideration could have been ordered by the agency. Gov't Code § 11523. The statute applies regardless of whether reconsideration actually was sought. *Id.*

APA = Administrative Procedure Act

If no specific limitations period applies to the particular decision or agents, the statute of limitations applicable to the right being asserted will govern. *See* Code Civ. Proc. § 1109; *Peralta Fed. of Teachers v. Peralta Cnty. Coll. Dist.*, 24 Cal. 3d 369, 386 (1979). For example, Code of Civil Procedure section 338(a) creates a three-year statute for "an action upon a liability created by statute...." This three-year limitation runs from accrual of the action, but does not apply "where, in special cases, a different limitation is prescribed by statute." *Travis v. County of Santa Cruz*, 33 Cal. 4th 757, 769 (2004). Accordingly, the three-year statute would apply in the land use context only in the rare instance where land use laws do not prescribe a more specific statute of limitations. *E.g., id.* at 769, (challenge to zoning ordinance, to the extent it was based on preemption by later-enacted state law, held subject to the three-year limit of Code of Civil Procedure section 338 rather than the 90-day limit of Government Code section 65009).

If no specific limitations period applies to the particular decision or agents, the statute of limitations applicable to the right being asserted will govern.

If no other statute of limitations applies, the catch-all statute of Code of Civil Procedure section 343 provides a four-year statute for "an action for relief not hereinbefore provided for."

If no other statute of limitations applies, the catch-all statute of Code of Civil Procedure section 343 provides a four-year statute for "an action for relief not hereinbefore provided for." Code Civ. Proc. § 343. However, administrative mandate is an equitable proceeding in which the defense of laches may be invoked. *Concerned Citizens of Palm Desert, Inc. v. Bd. of Supervisors*, 38 Cal. App. 3d 257, 265 (1974). Laches applies independently of any statute of limitations and may bar an action filed within the appropriate statute. *Holt v. County of Monterey*, 128 Cal. App. 3d 797, 801 (1982) (delay in challenging specific plan, during which developers expended significant sums, warranted dismissal under laches doctrine); *Concerned Citizens*, 38 Cal. App. 3d at 265 (action challenging conditional use permit barred by laches where recipient incurred significant financial liabilities in reliance on permit during period of delay); *People v. Dep't of Hous. & Cmty Dev.*, 45 Cal. App. 3d 185, 195 (1975). Thus, practitioners should be wary of relying on multi-year statutes of limitations if there is any possibility that the local agency will claim prejudice from the delay and assert the defense of laches.

One case suggests that local agencies may establish local statutes of limitations. In *Pan Pacific Properties, Inc. v. County of Santa Cruz*, the court held that a county ordinance that established a 30-day statute of limitations for judicial review of county zoning ordinances was not preempted by state law, since at the time the Planning and Zoning Law contained no statute specifically applicable to such challenges. 81 Cal. App. 3d 244 (1978). However, since *Pan Pacific* was decided, the Legislature has enacted and amended Government Code section 65009 to establish statutes of limitations applicable to most, if not all, planning and zoning decisions. In *Hittle v. Santa Barbara County Employees Retirement Ass'n*, the court overturned a local agency's attempt to establish a shorter period of limitations than allowed under CCP 1094.6 39 Cal. 3d 374, 387 (1985).

Practitioners also should investigate the possibility that a statute has been tolled. *Compare Concerned Citizens of Costa Mesa, Inc. v. 32nd District Agric. Ass'n*, 42 Cal. 3d 929, 937–39 (1986) (CEQA statute tolled when no public notice was given of changes to project) *with Cumming v. City of San Bernardino Redev. Agency*, 101 Cal. App. 4th 1229 (2002) (no tolling of CEQA statute on redevelopment project). Practitioners should ascertain whether a tolling agreement has been entered into. That agreement should be evaluated for compliance with Code of Civil Procedure section 360.5, which refers to a waiver for the commencement of an action being effective for a period not exceeding four years.

Practitioners should investigate whether a seemingly time-barred facial challenge to a legislative enactment may be pursued as a challenge to the application of that legislation to a particular project.

Finally, practitioners should investigate whether a seemingly time-barred facial challenge to a legislative enactment may be pursued as a challenge to the application of that legislation to a particular project. *See, e.g., Travis*, 33 Cal. 4th 757 (court permitted challenge to constitutionality of second unit ordinance because petitioner challenged the application of that ordinance to its project); *Garat v. City of Riverside*, 2 Cal. App. 4th 259 (1991) (court indicated that an otherwise time-barred challenge to the adequacy of certain general plan provisions may be pursued when those general plan provisions have a nexus with a project that was recently approved and timely challenged). Such a challenge may be valid even where the basis for the challenge is some defect in the ordinance as originally enacted, not the validity of the application of the ordinance to the petitioner. *See Travis*, 33 Cal. 4th at 768 ("a challenge to a permit or permit condition, timely under section 65009, subdivision (c)(1)(E), is [not] rendered untimely merely because the theory of challenge is the facial invalidity of the ordinance upon which the permit or condition is based").

Process of a Mandate Proceeding
Prerequisite to Litigation: Exhaustion of Administrative Remedies

The common law exhaustion doctrine. A court has no power to make a land use decision in the first instance; it can act only to review a decision made by a local agency. Accordingly, a court cannot consider a claim unless the petitioner presented that claim to the agency before bringing suit. This requirement is called the exhaustion of administrative remedies doctrine and is a jurisdictional prerequisite to bringing an action that challenges an agency decision. *See Abelleira v. District Court of Appeal*, 17 Cal. 2d 280 (1941). Under this doctrine, where an administrative remedy is provided (*e.g.*, an appeal to the city council), "relief must be sought from the administrative body and this remedy exhausted before the courts will act." *Id.* at 292. The doctrine "is not a matter of judicial discretion...." *Id.* at 292. As one court explained:

> When administrative machinery exists for the resolution of differences, the courts will not act until such administrative procedures are fully utilized and exhausted. To do so would be in excess of their jurisdiction. Because the rule is jurisdictional, the doctrine is not open to judicial discretion. The rule is applicable whether the petitioner is seeking ordinary mandamus or administrative mandamus.

Leff v. City of Monterey Park, 218 Cal. App. 3d 674, 680–81 (1990)

However, courts do not always use the same criteria to prescribe the circumstances under which administrative remedies must be exhausted or precisely what constitutes a "remedy." Some courts use the phrase "exhaustion of administrative remedies" only in its most technical, literal sense. These courts hold that the exhaustion doctrine applies only when there is an administrative process available for the complainant to seek a remedy for a past wrong. *Tahoe Vista Concerned Citizens v. County of Placer* represents this variant of the exhaustion doctrine:

> Ordinarily we use the word remedy as meaning a device to redress a wrong. It is decidedly inappropriate to speak of remedying a wrong that has not occurred and may not occur. Prior to the adoption of a negative declaration under the scheme here in issue there is no wrong to be remediated. Hence, the mere public opportunity to participate in an administrative proceeding prior to the adoption of a negative declaration is not a remedy. The exhaustion of administrative remedies doctrine has never applied where there is no available administrative remedy. [Citations.]

Tahoe Vista, 81 Cal. App. 4th 577, 590 (2000), *quoting California Aviation Council v. County of Amador*, 200 Cal. App. 3d 337, 348 (1988) (conc. opn. of Blease, J.). *See also Lindelli v. Town of San Anselmo*, 111 Cal. App. 4th 1099, 1105–06 (2003) (holding that a public hearing did not constitute a remedy because it was scheduled before any action was taken). By this reasoning, the exhaustion of administrative remedies doctrine has no application to the wide gamut of public hearings preceding approval of development projects because there is no "wrong to be remediated" until the agency has made a decision to which a party objects.

A court has no power to make a land use decision in the first instance; it can act only to review a decision made by a local agency.

A less restrictive approach to the doctrine focuses on the nature of the proceedings, rather than whether there is a wrong to be remedied. Courts adhering to this view hold that the exhaustion requirement may apply even though the agency has not yet committed a wrong, if in fact the agency was required to consider and respond to comments concerning its proposed action. The court in *City of Coachella v. Riverside County Airport Land Use Comm'n*, 210 Cal. App. 3d 1277 (1989), took this approach to the exhaustion doctrine. The opinion dealt with the city's challenge to the County Airport Land Use Commission's adoption of a land use plan. The Commission argued that the challenge was barred because the city had failed to raise its arguments during the public hearings preceding adoption of the plan. The court disagreed, stating:

> The mere fact that the City was entitled to attend the Commission's hearings on the adoption of the TALUP and submit materials relevant to that legislative act does not constitute an administrative remedy. An administrative remedy is provided only in those instances where the administrative body is required to actually accept, evaluate and resolve disputes or complaints. [citation omitted] The public hearings held by the Commission with regard to the adoption of the TALUP did not require that the Commission do anything in response to submissions or testimony received by it incident to those hearings.

City of Coachella, 210 Cal. App. 3d at 1287 (emphasis in original); *accord, Lindelli*, 111 Cal. App. 4th at 1106 (holding that a public hearing did not constitute a remedy because the city council was not "required" to do anything in response to it).

The least restrictive and most widespread approach to the exhaustion doctrine is founded on the twin purposes of avoiding judicial interference into administrative proceedings and promoting judicial economy.

The least restrictive (and most widespread) approach to the exhaustion doctrine is founded on the twin purposes of avoiding judicial interference into administrative proceedings and promoting judicial economy. *See Abelleira*, 17 Cal. 2d at 292 ("[t]o permit the initial consideration of these matters by the courts would not only preclude the efficient operation of the [administrative proceedings], but would overwhelm the courts with cases of a technical, specialized character, and seriously impair their capacity to handle their normal work"). Courts have characterized the doctrine as furthering a variety of practical and policy considerations, including "bolstering administrative autonomy, mitigating damages, giving agencies opportunity to make factual findings, encouraging settlement, filtering out frivolous claims, fostering better prepared litigation, and promoting judicial economy." *Wright v. State*, 122 Cal. App. 4th 659, 666 (2004). The unifying theme of these cases, however, is that a court should not review claims that an agency has not had a full and fair opportunity to resolve. *Coalition for Student Action v. City of Fullerton*, 153 Cal. App. 3d 1194, 1198 (1984) ("the agency should be given an opportunity to meet all the issues and defenses during administrative hearings and offer opposing evidence and argument, so that appropriate rulings and findings may be made.... The essence of the exhaustion doctrine is the public agency's opportunity to receive and respond to articulated factual issues and legal theories before its actions are subjected to judicial review"). Based on those considerations, the exhaustion doctrine has been held to be jurisdictional:

> When the plaintiff is required to seek relief through an administrative remedy first, the administrative claim or "cause of action" is within the special jurisdiction of the administrative agency, and the courts may act only to review the final administrative determination. Allowing a suit prior to such a final determination

would constitute interference with the subject matter jurisdiction of another tribunal. Accordingly, the exhaustion of an administrative remedy is a jurisdictional element in California.

Hayward v. Henderson, 88 Cal. App. 3d 64, 70 (1979). The question, under this application of the exhaustion doctrine, is not whether a remedy existed for a wrong being challenged, but whether the issues were raised in a manner that gave the agency notice of and an opportunity to act on the petitioner's objections. *See, e.g., Corona-Norco Unified School District v. City of Corona*, 17 Cal. App. 4th 985 (1994) (barring petitioner's CEQA claim because he failed to raise the issue in the approval process and in public hearings); *Coalition for Student Action*, 153 Cal. App. 3d 1194 (holding that petitioner's objections during public hearings were too vague to satisfy the exhaustion requirement).

The exhaustion requirement has two components. First, "issue exhaustion" requires that all legal and factual issues be presented to the administrative agency before being asserted in court. Second, "appeal exhaustion" requires that all available administrative appeals be taken before resorting to the court.

Issue exhaustion. Petitioners must submit all factual and legal issues to the administrative agency before seeking judicial review. Generalized concerns or conclusory arguments, unsupported by specific factual or legal arguments against the challenged actions, are not sufficient. *See Corona-Norco Unified Sch. Dist.*, 17 Cal. App. 4th 985; *Coalition for Student Action*, 153 Cal. App. 3d at 1197; *City of Walnut Creek*, 101 Cal. App. 3d at 1020. "Less specificity is required to preserve an issue for appeal in an administrative proceeding than in a judicial proceeding, since citizens are not expected to bring legal expertise to the administrative proceeding." *Citizens Ass'n for Sensible Dev. of Bishop Area v. County of Inyo*, 172 Cal. App. 3d 151, 163 (1985). However, recent cases suggest a stricter trend. *See, e.g., Park Area Neighbors v. Town of Fairfax*, 29 Cal. App. 4th 1442 (1994) (generalized objections to a traffic study are insufficient; specific objections to the methodology employed must be raised administratively); *Resource Defense Fund v. Local Agency Formation Comm'n*, 191 Cal. App. 3d 886 (1987) (the exact issue must have been presented to the agency before it may be raised in court), and *Evans v. City of San Jose*, 128 Cal. App. 4th 1123 (2005) (objections raised regarding the redevelopment plan during the administrative proceedings were too general to alert the agency to the host of alleged technical deficiencies subsequently asserted in court).

Petitioners must submit all factual and legal issues to the administrative agency before seeking judicial review. Generalized concerns or conclusory arguments, unsupported by specific factual or legal arguments against the challenged actions, are not sufficient.

These principles are perhaps best expressed in *Coalition for Student Action*, 153 Cal. App. 3d 1194. There, the Coalition tried to raise in court, for the first time, the issue that CEQA had been violated because a negative declaration was prepared rather than an EIR. The court refused to hear the merits of the case since the Coalition had not raised this issue at the planning commission or city council hearings. The court stated that the doctrine of exhaustion of administrative remedies precludes judicial review of issues, legal and factual, that were not first presented at the administrative agency level. The court then held:

EIR = Environmental impact report

> The essence of the exhaustion doctrine is the public agency's opportunity to receive and respond to articulated factual issues and legal theories before its actions are subjected to judicial review. The doctrine was not satisfied here by a relatively few bland and general references to environmental matters. The

city was entitled to consider any objection to proceeding by negative declaration in the first instance, if there was one. Mere objections to the project, as opposed to the procedure, are not sufficient to alert an agency to an objection based on CEQA. Petitioners, having failed to raise their CEQA claims at the administrative level, cannot air them for the first time in the courts.

Id. at 1198. *See also Corona-Norco Unified Sch. Dist.*, 17 Cal. App. 4th 985 (letters opposed rezoning as inconsistent with the general plan but did not raise any specific CEQA challenges and so did not exhaust CEQA issues).

The petitioner also must obtain a final decision on the merits at the highest available administrative level before seeking judicial review.

Appeal exhaustion. The petitioner also must obtain a final decision on the merits at the highest available administrative level before seeking judicial review. If an appeal can be taken to a higher administrative body—such as from the planning commission to the council—that appeal must be pursued and the issues must be presented to the final decisionmaker before they can be presented in court. For example, in *Tahoe Vista Concerned Citizens*, the petitioner in a CEQA case argued that it had exhausted its administrative remedies by presenting its comments on a negative declaration before the close of the last public hearing, as required by Public Resources Code section 21177, part of CEQA. 81 Cal. App. 4th 577. The court disagreed, noting that while petitioners had presented all their comments to the planning commission, they had appealed only a planning issue, and not the environmental review issues, to the board of supervisors. The court held that compliance with section 21177 did not excuse them from bringing their CEQA concerns to the board of supervisors.[11] *See also Edgren v. Regents of Univ. of Cal.*, 158 Cal. App. 3d 515, 520 (1984).

So long as the issues are presented to the final decision-making body, it does not matter that the petitioner did not appear before or present issues to the lower body.

So long as the issues are presented to the final decision-making body, it does not matter that the petitioner did not appear before or present issues to the lower body. For example, in *Browning-Ferris Industries v. City Council*, the court found it irrelevant that the petitioner did not present comments to the planning commission, when the commission acted only in an advisory role, and comments had been presented to the city council. 181 Cal. App. 3d 852 (1986).

Additionally, the petitioner must comply with all procedural requirements applicable to such an appeal, such as payment of a fee, verification of the application, and provision of proper notice. *See Park Area Neighbors v. Town of Fairfax*, 29 Cal. App. 4th 1442, 1452 (1994). In *Park Area Neighbors*, petitioners challenged the planning commission's approval of a development project. The city's code provided that a planning commission action could be appealed to the town council by verified application. The petitioners did not file such an appeal. Instead, they presented the council with a list of signatures opposing

---

11. The court in *Tahoe Vista* held that the petitioners' presentations of issues to the planning commission conferred standing under section 21177, but held that standing was not sufficient absent appeal of the CEQA issues to the Board of Supervisors. *Tahoe Vista*, 81 Cal. App. 4th at 590–91. In *Waste Mgmt. of Alameda County, Inc. v. County of Alameda*, 79 Cal. App. 4th 1223, 1239 (2000), in contrast, the court ruled that section 21177 addressed only exhaustion, and did not confer standing:

Public Resources Code section 21177 is a statutorily imposed requirement of the exhaustion of administrative remedies before bringing a judicial action. Exhaustion of administrative remedies is an entirely separate issue from the requirement of standing to pursue a judicial action. [Citations omitted.] The exhaustion of administrative remedies does not automatically confer standing to seek judicial review, and nothing in Public Resources Code section 21177 states or implies otherwise.

the project. The court found that the petitioners had not pursued the correct remedy and thus had failed to exhaust administrative remedies. It reached this result despite the petitioners' claims that (1) they were not represented by counsel; and (2) they had relied on erroneous advice by a member of the planning commission that the correct remedy was a petition to the council rather than an appeal. The court stated:

> We conclude that neither lack of legal representation, nor any consequent vulnerability to purported misadvice on matters of administrative procedure, relaxes the requirement that [the petitioners] must have exhausted [their] administrative remedies as a jurisdictional prerequisite to resort to the courts, or excuses [their] failure to do so. The exhaustion doctrine is well rooted in *stare decisis*, and courts should be loathe to carve out exceptions to such established procedural rules absent compelling reasons to do so.

Id. at 1450 (emphasis in original)

Rehearing/Reconsideration. Where a request for reconsideration is mandatory under the applicable statute, such reconsideration must be sought in order to exhaust administrative remedies. There was previously considerable uncertainty as to whether such a reconsideration request was necessary to exhaust when the applicable statute permitted but did not *require* reconsideration. The California Supreme Court resolved this uncertainty in *Sierra Club v. Local Agency Formation Commission*, 21 Cal. 4th 489 (1999). The court, overruling a 50-year-old precedent,[12] held that a reconsideration request was not necessary to exhaust administrative remedies where a reconsideration application was permitted but not required by statute.

The Court cautioned, however, that even where reconsideration is permissive, reconsideration may be necessary to exhaust remedies on issues that have not previously been presented to the local agency:

> We emphasize this conclusion does not mean the failure to request reconsideration or rehearing may never serve as a bar to judicial review. Such a petition remains necessary, for example, to introduce evidence or legal arguments before the administrative body that were not brought to its attention as part of the original decisionmaking process. [Citation omitted.] Our reasoning here is not addressed to new evidence, changed circumstances, fresh legal arguments, filings by newcomers to the proceedings and the like. Likewise, a rehearing petition is necessary to call to the agency's attention errors or omissions of fact or law in the administrative decision itself that were not previously addressed in the briefing, in order to give the agency the opportunity to correct its own mistakes before those errors or omissions are presented to a court. The general exhaustion rule remains valid: Administrative agencies must be given the opportunity to reach a reasoned and final conclusion on each and every issue upon which they have jurisdiction to act before those issues are raised in a judicial forum. Our decision is limited to the narrow situation where one would be required, after a final decision by an agency, to raise for a second time the same evidence and legal arguments one has previously raised solely to exhaust administrative remedies under Alexander.

Id. at 510

---

12. *Alexander v. State Personnel Bd.*, 22 Cal. 2d 198 (1943).

In the case of an administrative decision, if rehearing or reconsideration is not provided for by statute or local ordinance or rule, an agency has no power to rehear or reconsider a final decision. *Heap v. City of Los Angeles*, 6 Cal. 2d 405, 406 (1936) (city civil service commission, having made its final decision on the discharge of a city employee, "had no jurisdiction to retry the question and make a different finding at a later time"); *Olive Proration Program Com. v. Agricultural Prorate Comm'n*, 17 Cal. 2d 204, 209 (1941) (agency could not change its prior final decision without express authorization to do so).

Exceptions to the exhaustion requirement. The courts have developed several exceptions to the exhaustion requirement that may excuse a petitioner from having to present issues to the agency before presenting them to a court.

Exhaustion of administrative remedies is not required where an administrative remedy is not expressly required by statute or rule. *See Endangered Habitats League, Inc. v. State Water Resources Control Bd.*, 63 Cal. App. 4th 227, 238–39 (1997) (State Board provided no opportunity to comment before implementing a plan without a second tier of environmental review); *City of Coachella*, 210 Cal. App. 3d at 1287 (administrative remedy provided only where the agency is required to accept, evaluate, and resolve disputes or complaints); *Environmental Law Fund v. Town of Corte Madera*, 49 Cal. App. 3d 105, 115 (1975) (where petitioners had no statutory right to an administrative appeal of a tentative map approval, no further exhaustion was required).

Exhaustion of administrative remedies is likewise not required when the petitioner challenges the validity of the statute from which the administrative agency derives its authority. *See State of California*, 12 Cal. 3d at 251 ("It would be heroic indeed to compel a party to appear before an administrative body to challenge its very existence and to expect a dispassionate hearing before its preponderantly lay membership on the constitutionality of the statute establishing its status and functions."). However, the exhaustion doctrine applies to the agency's construction and application of its governing statute in the course of exercising its administrative functions.

Exhaustion is not required where the administrative body or official has no power to grant the relief sought. *See Bernstein v. Smutz*, 83 Cal. App. 2d 108, 115 (1947) (zoning administrator lacked power to grant variance).

A petitioner need not exhaust administrative remedies when it would be futile to do so. *See Twain Harte Assocs., Ltd. v. County of Tuolumne*, 217 Cal. App. 3d 71, 91–92 (1990); *see also Furey v. City of Sacramento*, 24 Cal. 3d 862, 871 (1979). However, futility can be shown only if it is certain what the agency's decision in the case would be. *See County of Contra Costa v. State of California*, 177 Cal. App. 3d 62, 77–78 (1986); *Doyle v. City of Chino*, 117 Cal. App. 3d 673, 683 (1981) (the futility exception applies only where a petitioner can positively state that the agency has already declared what its decision will be in a particular case).

A petitioner also is excused from presenting issues to a local agency when the agency did not give proper notice of the action it was considering. In *McQueen v. Board of Directors*, the petitioner was excused from exhausting remedies when the project description the agency gave did not disclose that the property to be acquired contained PCBs. 202 Cal. App. 3d 1136 (1988). However, incomplete notice does not excuse exhaustion unless it is the effective equivalent of *no* notice of the matter at issue. In *Temecula Band of Luiseno Mission Indians v. Rancho California Water District*, the court clarified the rule of *McQueen*, holding that "an incomplete or misleading notice may be treated as equivalent to no notice only to the extent that the notice's deficiencies prevented the petitioner from invoking administrative remedies." 43 Cal. App. 4th 425, 435 (1996). The petitioner still must raise the objections and exhaust the administrative remedies available at the time. In *Temecula*, the court concluded that the petitioner had failed to exhaust its administrative remedies because, although the public notice had failed to state that the project was a modification of the earlier project, the agency had announced this fact at a public hearing attended by petitioner, and petitioner had failed to object that the project description was inaccurate. *Id.*

Finally, petitioners are *not* excused from the exhaustion requirement merely because they comprise a public interest group, provided that they were not actually aware of a duly noticed hearing or administrative process. *Resource Defense Fund v. Local Agency Formation Comm'n*, 191 Cal. App. 3d 886, 895 (1987).

Codification of the exhaustion requirement. The exhaustion of administrative remedies doctrine has been codified in the Planning and Zoning Law and in CEQA. The Planning and Zoning Law provides:

> In an action or proceeding to attack, review, set aside, void, or annul a finding, determination, or decision of a public agency made pursuant to this title[13] at a properly noticed public hearing, the issues raised shall be limited to those raised in the public hearing or in written correspondence delivered to the public agency prior to, or at, the public hearing, except where the court finds either of the following:
>
> (A) The issue could not have been raised at the public hearing by persons exercising reasonable diligence.
>
> (B) The body conducting the public hearing prevented the issue from being raised at the public hearing.

Gov't Code § 65009(b)(1)

In order to rely on this statute, the agency must give notice that the exhaustion doctrine will apply to any subsequent litigation. The notice must be substantially in the following form:

> If you challenge the (nature of the proposed action) in court, you may be limited to raising only those issues you or someone else raised at the public hearing described in this notice, or in written correspondence delivered to the (public entity conducting the hearing) at, or prior to, the public hearing.

Gov't Code § 65009(b)(2)

This statutory codification of the exhaustion of administrative remedies doctrine supersedes the common law doctrine. *See Kings County Farm Bureau v. City of Hanford*, 221 Cal. App. 3d 692, 740 (1990) ("A public agency cannot claim the protection of the exhaustion doctrine despite noncompliance with a statutory mandate to provide notice of the doctrine's application... [t]he provisions

This statutory codification of the exhaustion of administrative remedies doctrine supersedes the common law doctrine.

---

13. The title referenced is Title 7 of the Government Code. Title 7 "may be cited as the Planning and Zoning Law," Gov't Code § 65000, but it includes Division 1, Planning and Zoning; Division 2, the Subdivision Map Act; and Division 3, Official Maps.

of Government Code section 65009 supersede the requirements of the common law doctrine of exhaustion of remedies."). Accordingly, an agency's failure to provide the notice required by Government Code section 65009(b)(2) excuses the petitioner from the exhaustion requirement. *Id.*

Identifying the Proper Parties

Petitioner. Although standing is a general requirement in all cases, it has particular importance in mandate cases. Standing is a jurisdictional issue that may be raised at any time during the proceedings, even on appeal. *See Common Cause v. Board of Supervisors*, 49 Cal. 3d 432, 438 (1989). Thus, it is important for the petitioner to state facts demonstrating standing, either by showing a beneficial interest in the litigation or by establishing some other basis for standing (such as a citizen or taxpayer action), discussed below.

Beneficial interest. Under Code of Civil Procedure section 1086, a writ of mandate may be issued "only upon the verified petition of the party *beneficially interested*." (emphasis added.) The beneficial interest requirement has been construed to require pleading of specific facts showing that the petitioner has a special interest to be served or right to be protected over and above a general interest held in common with the public at large. *See Carsten v. Psychology Examining Com.*, 27 Cal. 3d 793, 796 (1980); *Waste Mgmt. of Alameda County*, 79 Cal. App. 4th 1223; *Braude v. City of Los Angeles*, 226 Cal. App. 3d 83 (1990).

The inquiry involves a two-step analysis:

The first...is whether the plaintiff will obtain some benefit from issuance of the writ or suffer some detriment from its denial. The plaintiff's interest must be direct, and it must be substantial. Also, it generally must be special in the sense that it is over and above the interest held in common by the public at large.

The second prong of the beneficial interest test is whether the interest the plaintiff seeks to advance is within the zone of interests to be protected or regulated by the legal duty asserted.

Waste Mgmt., 79 Cal. App. 4th at 1233–34 (Citations omitted)

These requirements are often met easily in CEQA cases. General allegations that the petitioner is within a class of persons beneficially interested and is a citizen or resident of the affected area normally are sufficient. *See Kane v. Redevelopment Agency*, 179 Cal. App. 3d 899, 904 (1986). While a mere claim of geographic proximity may be insufficient to establish a beneficial interest, *Waste Mgmt.*, 79 Cal. App. 4th at 1236, the courts recognize that "[e]ffects of environmental abuse are not contained by political lines; strict rules of standing that might be appropriate in other contexts have no application where broad and long-term effects are involved." *Bozung v. Local Agency Formation Comm'n*, 13 Cal. 3d 263, 272 (1975). Accordingly, "a property owner, taxpayer, or elector who establishes a geographical nexus with the site of the challenged project has standing." *Citizens Ass'n for Sensible Development of Bishop Area*, 172 Cal. App. 3d at 158.

The petitioner in a CEQA case must, however, assert environmental interests. A petitioner that asserts only commercial interests does not have standing to bring a CEQA claim, because commercial interests are not within the zone of interests CEQA is designed to protect. *See Waste Mgmt.*, 79 Cal. App. 4th 1223 (landfill developer's competitor did not have standing to assert a CEQA claim). As the *Waste Management* court explained, "an interest, including a financial or commercial interest, which is not within the zone of interests to be protected or regulated by the asserted legal duty can only be an indirect interest from the standpoint of the law." *Id.* at 1234. Accordingly, a commercial competitor who does not establish that it is threatened with environmental harm cannot claim the direct interest in CEQA compliance that is required to establish a beneficial interest. *Id. Regency Outdoor Advertising, Inc. v. City of West Hollywood*, 153 Cal. App. 4th 825 (2007) (billboard corporation lacked standing to bring CEQA challenge to zoning amendment regarding outdoor signs, since amendment only affected corporation commercially, and corporation could not rely on "citizen standing" under CEQA).

An unincorporated association may have proper standing to bring a writ of mandate if (1) one or more of its members would have standing individually; (2) the interests at issue are germane to the organization's purpose; and (3) the claim or relief sought does not require individual participation in the suit by the organization's members. *See Brotherhood of Teamsters v. Unemployment Ins. Appeals Bd.*, 190 Cal. App. 3d 1515, 1522 (1987).

Citizen's action. Even if a petitioner does not have a beneficial interest, a court may exercise its discretion to allow the suit to proceed if the public interests are strong enough and the petitioner is acting for the public good:

> The matter of a citizen's action is a long-established exception to the requirement of a personal beneficial interest. The exception applies where the question is one of public right and the object of the action is to enforce a public duty—in which case it is sufficient that the plaintiff be interested as a citizen in having the laws executed and the public duty enforced.... [¶] This exception promotes a policy of guaranteeing citizens an opportunity to ensure that the purpose of legislation establishing a public right is not impaired or defeated by a governmental agency.

Waste Mgmt., 79 Cal. App. 4th at 1236–37. *Accord Laidlaw Environmental Services, Inc. v. County of Kern*, 44 Cal. App. 4th 346, 354 (1996). The propriety of a citizen's suit requires a judicial balancing of interests, and the interest of a citizen may be considered sufficient when the public duty is sharp and the public need is weighty. *Waste Mgmt.*, 79 Cal. App. 4th at 1237.

Citizen's action standing has been denied when the petitioner's action was motivated by factors other than a neutral interest in seeing the laws enforced. *See Carsten*, 27 Cal. 3d at 799 (in denying a member of administrative board standing to pursue a citizen's action, the court noted that "[h]er interest in the subject matter was piqued by service on the board, not by virtue of the neutrality of citizenship"); *Waste Mgmt.*, 79 Cal. App. 4th at 1238 (economic competitor was not pursuing the interest of a neutral citizen).

Even if a petitioner does not have a beneficial interest, a court may exercise its discretion to allow the suit to proceed if the public interests are strong enough and the petitioner is acting for the public good.

Taxpayer suits. Taxpayers have standing under Code of Civil Procedure section 526(a) to challenge any action alleged to involve illegal expenditure or waste of public funds, or injury to funds or property. The purpose of the statute is to permit any individual or corporate taxpayer to challenge wasteful governmental action that might otherwise go unchallenged because of the standing requirement. *See Blair v. Pitchess*, 5 Cal. 3d 258, 267–68 (1971). Although it refers to actions for injunctive relief against cities and counties, the statute has been judicially

Taxpayers have standing under Code of Civil Procedure section 526(a) to challenge any action alleged to involve illegal expenditure or waste of public funds, or injury to funds or property.

extended to all state and local agencies and officials (*Farley v. Cory*, 78 Cal. App. 3d 583, 589 (1978)), and to mandamus actions (*Van Atta v. Scott*, 27 Cal. 3d 424, 449–50 (1980)). The statute has been broadly construed to give taxpayers standing to enjoin enforcement or application of allegedly unlawful or unconstitutional ordinances. *See, e.g., Tobe v. City of Santa Ana*, 9 Cal. 4th 1069 (1995). Standing is permitted under section 526(a) even when the waste is alleged to be simply the time spent by government employees performing illegal acts, and even where the challenged procedures result in a net savings. *See Blair v. Pitchess*, 5 Cal. 3d at 267.

To establish taxpayer standing, a petitioner must cite specific facts and reasons for a belief that some illegal expenditure or injury to public funds is occurring or will occur.

To establish taxpayer standing, a petitioner must cite specific facts and reasons for a belief that some illegal expenditure or injury to public funds is occurring or will occur. General allegations, innuendo, and legal conclusions are not sufficient. *Waste Mgmt.*, 79 Cal. App. 4th at 1240.

Taxpayer organizations also have been held to have standing. *See Common Cause v. Board of Supervisors*, 49 Cal. 3d 432, 439 (1989) (county taxpayer and organizations concerned with voting rights had standing to seek mandate concerning voter outreach program).

Respondent. The correct respondent in a mandate action is:
- If the writ petition seeks review of a decision, the person or entity with final responsibility for making that decision
- If the writ petition seeks to compel a particular act, the person or entity with authority to carry out that act

The identity of the appropriate respondent generally can be derived from the review of the statute or ordinance governing the decision or action in question. In general, the appropriate respondent is:
- The board, council, or commission, not its individual members
- The city council or board of supervisors, not the planning commission (unless there is no provision for appeal to the council)
- The state agency with responsibility for the act, not the state

In an action seeking review of a decision made on behalf of a city, it is common practice to name both the city council and the city itself as respondents in writ petitions.

In an action seeking review of a decision made on behalf of a city, it is common practice to name both the city council (or other city board, department, or agency) and the city itself as respondents in writ petitions. This practice may derive from an early decision, *Dierkes v. City of Los Angeles*, 25 Cal. 2d 938 (1945), in which the court stated that although the City Board of Pensions had exclusive control over the pensions at issue, the writ was appropriately directed at the city as well. Additionally, there may be instances in which the city itself is an indispensable party as, for example, where the petition relies, in part, upon a contractual obligation of the city. *See, e.g., Roccaforte v. City of San Diego*, 89 Cal. App. 3d 877, 888 (1979) (in mandamus action seeking reinstatement of police officer, the "real party in interest was city, which was bound by contractual agreements with officer [and] while city had many departments and sub-departments, it was a single entity in its contractual obligation"). In order to avoid any such issues, the best course is to name the local entity as a respondent in all cases since its inclusion is, at worst, harmless error. *See Shannon v. City of Los Angeles*, 205 Cal. 366, 372 (1928) (in mandamus proceeding challenging petitioner's dismissal by Department of Building and Safety, city was "a proper, though perhaps not a necessary, party" to proceedings).

It is generally not good practice to name *only* the city as respondent. Doing so may create uncertainty regarding appropriate service and enforcement of the writ, responsibility for the return to the writ, and sanctions for noncompliance with the writ. For example, section 1097 of the Code of Civil Procedure, which addresses sanctions for noncompliance with a writ of mandate, specifically refers to disobedience of the writ by "any *member* of [the] tribunal, corporation, or board or such *person* upon whom the writ has been personally served...." (emphasis added). Moreover, it has been held that failure to name the respondent with specific authority to carry out the requested writ may result in dismissal. *See Valley Motor Lines, Inc. v. Riley*, 22 Cal. App. 2d 233, 257 (1937) (failure to name respondent with authority to carry out requested order may lead to dismissal).

When the challenged decision is made by a multi-member board, council or commission, the proper respondent is the board, council, or commission, not its individual members. *See State of California v. Superior Court*, 12 Cal. 3d 237, 255 (1974). However, it also is permissible to name the individual members in their official capacity as respondents. *See, e.g., Moran v. State Bd. of Medical Examiners*, 32 Cal. 2d 301, 314 (1948) (in mandamus action regarding board decision, in the absence of a legislative provision to the contrary, naming of individual members of the board was proper although not necessary); *Harmer v. Superior Court*, 275 Cal. App. 2d 345, 350 (1969) (individual members of commission were proper but not necessary parties to mandamus proceeding; commission itself was the only indispensable party). *See also* 43 Cal. Jur. 3d, *Mandamus and Prohibition*, section 38 (3d ed., 2002).

Real party in interest. Any real party in interest also should be named as a party. *See Inland Counties Reg'l Ctr. v. Office of Admin. Hearings*, 193 Cal. App. 3d 700 (1987); *see also* Code Civ. Proc. § 389(c). The real party in interest usually is the person or entity in whose favor the agency decision operates, or anyone having a direct interest in the result. *See Sonoma County Nuclear Free Zone '86 v. Superior Court*, 189 Cal. App. 3d 167, 173 (1987). Similarly, anyone who received a permit or benefit that would be lost if the petitioner were successful is a real party in interest. A real party in interest has a right to be served with the petition, to file an answer or other pleadings, and to be heard before the trial or appellate court issues a peremptory writ. *Sonoma County Nuclear Free Zone '86 v. Superior Court*, 189 Cal. App. 3d 167 (1987). *See Harris v. Alcoholic Beverage Control Appeals Bd.*, 245 Cal. App. 2d 919, 923 (1966) (real party in interest who did not participate in superior court proceedings had right to appeal trial court's judgment).

The failure to include a real party in interest in the action does not necessarily preclude maintenance of the action, unless that party is "indispensable," in which case the court may refuse to hear the petition unless that party is added before the statute of limitations expires. *See, e.g., Citizens Ass'n for Sensible Dev. of Bishop Area*, 172 Cal. App. 3d 151 (owner of property proposed for shopping center development deemed real party in interest, but not indispensable party); *Sierra Club, Inc. v. California Coastal Comm'n*, 95 Cal. App. 3d 495 (1979). However, the court may limit the relief in order to avoid harm to the real party in interest or restrict the action to avoid potentially inconsistent judgments or collateral attack on the judgment. Therefore, the better practice is to include

Naming only the city as respondent may create uncertainty regarding appropriate service and enforcement of the writ, responsibility for the return to the writ, and sanctions for noncompliance with the writ.

When the challenged decision is made by a multi-member board, council or commission, the proper respondent is the board, council, or commission, not its individual members.

any party whose interests are or may be directly affected by the outcome of the mandate proceeding in the absence of authority indicating that such a party is categorically not an indispensable party.

Failure to name an indispensable real party in interest prior to expiration of the statute of limitations may result in dismissal under the compulsory joinder rules of Code of Civil Procedure section 389(a). *See, e.g., Save Our Bay, Inc. v. San Diego Unified Port Dist.*, 42 Cal. App. 4th 686, 696 (1996); *Beresford Neighborhood Ass'n v. City of San Mateo*, 207 Cal. App. 3d 1180, 1189 (1989). In a broad application of the indispensable party rule, the court in *Save Our Bay* held that an owner whose property would have been acquired for a port marina project was a real party in interest in an action challenging the project. 42 Cal. App. 4th at 695.

The developer of a project whose entitlements are challenged generally is considered an indispensable party to the litigation. However, it is generally not necessary to name the owner of the property a developer has under option as well as the developer. The rationale for this rule is that the developer can and will adequately represent the interests of the property owner in the litigation. *See Citizens Ass'n for Sensible Dev. of Bishop Area*, 172 Cal. App. 3d at 158 (developer could adequately represent interests of property owner); *see also Deltakeeper v. Oakdale Irrig. Dist.*, 94 Cal. App. 4th 1092, 1102 (2001) ("[a] party's ability to protect its interest is not impaired or impeded as a practical matter where a joined party has the same interest in the litigation"). By contrast, courts have held that the city or county issuing the land use approval cannot reasonably be expected to represent the interests of either the landowner or the developer under such circumstances. *See, e.g., Beresford Neighborhood Ass'n*, 207 Cal. App. 3d at 1189; *Buena Vista Gardens Apartments Ass'n v. City of San Diego*, 175 Cal. App. 3d 289 (1985).

In determining whether a party in the land use context is indispensable, courts have drawn a distinction between challenges to quasi-legislative approvals (such as a general plan amendment) and administrative approvals (such as a tentative map approval). In the former case, the owners of the affected property are generally not deemed real parties in interest, and the action may proceed solely against the respondent agency. *See, e.g., Buena Vista Gardens Apartments Ass'n*, 175 Cal. App. 3d 289; *Camp v. Board of Supervisors*, 123 Cal. App. 3d 334 (1981) (sphere of influence plan). The rationale is that unless a challenge is aimed at a specific developer or landowner, the developer or landowner is not exposed to "the prejudice necessary to make it an indispensable party." *Sierra Club, Inc. v. California Coastal Comm'n*, 95 Cal. App. 3d 495. *See, e.g., City of Livermore v. Local Agency Formation Comm'n*, 184 Cal. App. 3d 531, 544 (1986) (in action to prevent a LAFCO from implementing revised sphere-of-influence guidelines, developer who had proposed to build a project outside the city's sphere of influence was not an indispensable party because the developer had the same interest as any other potential developer).

In *Kaczorowski v. Board of Supervisors*, the court held that where an appeal is taken to the Coastal Commission and the Commission conducts a *de novo* proceeding, the Commission is an indispensable party in any subsequent challenge to the administrative decision. 88 Cal. App. 4th 564, 569 (2001). It reasoned that because the Commission is the entity that issues permits or sets conditions, failure to join it in the action would not bind the Commission and would render the decision open to collateral attack.[14]

Joining Other Causes of Action with a Writ Claim

The rules governing joinder of other causes of action with a writ petition can be confusing, as claims for declaratory relief, damages, injunctions, and other remedies sometimes are allowed and sometimes are prohibited in the case law. The key distinction is between non-mandate claims that attempt to seek review of a local agency's decision—which are not allowed—and claims that are based on independent grounds, which are permitted. Thus, for example, a claim for declaratory relief based on the alleged invalidity or impropriety of the agency's action is prohibited, since that is the central issue in the mandate action. By contrast, a request for a declaratory judgment regarding the constitutionality of a statute under which the agency acted may properly be joined with a mandate action. *See State of California*, 12 Cal. 3d at 251 (declaratory relief was the appropriate remedy to challenge constitutionality of Coastal Act but not Commission's application of Act to petitioner).

The key distinction is between non-mandate claims that attempt to seek review of a local agency's decision—which are not allowed—and claims that are based on independent grounds, which are permitted.

When an action that should be brought in mandate is improperly labeled as an action for declaratory relief or injunction, the complaint is subject to demurrer, *State of California*, 12 Cal. 3d at 249, although the court has discretion to treat it as a mandate petition. *See Scott*, 6 Cal. 3d at 546.

A petition for writ of mandate includes an implied claim for injunctive relief. *See Camp*, 123 Cal. App. 3d at 356. Accordingly, the petitioner need not state a separate cause of action for an injunction, nor pray for an injunction as a remedy separate from the writ.

A claim for a writ may be joined with a claim of inverse condemnation. *See Hensler*, 8 Cal. 4th at 13; *Patrick Media Group, Inc.*, 9 Cal. App. 4th at 603. However, when mandate claims questioning the validity or propriety of an agency's administrative decision are joined with an inverse condemnation claim, the mandate issues must be resolved first. *See Hensler*, 8 Cal. 4th at 10; *Patrick Media Group, Inc*, 9 Cal. App. 4th at 606 (challenges to administrative actions constituting takings must be brought initially by mandate). *All* claims must be resolved before any decision on any particular claim may be appealed. *See Morehart v. County of Santa Barbara*, 7 Cal. 4th 725, 743 (1994).

When mandate claims questioning the validity or propriety of an agency's administrative decision are joined with an inverse condemnation claim, the mandate issues must be resolved first.

Preparation of the Record

With rare exceptions, mandate cases are heard and decided on the basis of the record of proceedings before the local agency. In broad terms, the record includes all of the documents presented to or considered by the agency and minutes or transcripts of hearings before the agency. If hearings are held before

With rare exceptions, mandate cases are heard and decided on the basis of the record of proceedings before the local agency.

---

14. Conversely, the Coastal Commission's participation in a writ proceeding may deprive it of authority to hear an appeal of a coastal development permit. In *City of Half Moon Bay v. Superior Court*, the Coastal Commission intervened in a writ proceeding that challenged a city's decision to deny a coastal development permit. 106 Cal. App. 4th 795 (2003). The court issued a writ ordering the City to issue the permit, and the City reluctantly complied. The Coastal Commission then attempted to hear an appeal of the permit and impose additional conditions relating to the issues addressed in the writ proceeding. The court held that the effect of the Commission's action was to overturn a valid court order, which it could not do.

more than one person or body, such as a zoning administrator, planning commission, and city council, the record includes all materials relating to each of the proceedings. For land use decisions, the record normally will include application materials, memos and correspondence to and from staff, notices, agendas, staff reports, minutes, transcripts of proceedings, all documents presented to the decision-making body by staff, applicant, or others, and proposed and final versions of findings, resolutions, and ordinances.

Although the mandate statutes specify the contents of and procedures for the record in actions subject to Code of Civil Procedure section 1094.6, they are silent as to procedures for the record in all other mandate cases.

Although the mandate statutes specify the contents of and procedures for the record in actions subject to Code of Civil Procedure section 1094.6 (applicable to proceedings for revocation or denial of a permit, license, or other entitlement and to employment and retirement benefits), they are silent as to procedures for the record in all other mandate cases. Also, with the exception of CEQA cases, there is no statutory provision for "certification" of the record by the local agency. Thus the timing, scope, and content of the record frequently are matters of negotiation between the parties and motions to the court to limit or augment the record.

The procedures for preparation of the record in a CEQA case are contained in Public Resources Code section 21167.6. These procedures, although not binding in other mandate cases, often serve as a useful reference point for parties and courts dealing with issues regarding the scope and content of the record. *See* Litigation Under CEQA below.

Discovery and Evidence Outside the Record

Whether evidence outside the record may be discovered and admitted depends upon the issue to which the evidence relates.

Evidence outside the record generally is inadmissible and undiscoverable to determine whether a local agency's decision is valid. When the issue in controversy is whether an agency's decision is supported by the evidence or findings, or whether the decision was arbitrary and capricious, the court reviews the agency's decision in light of the matters considered by the agency, as reflected in the record before it. *See Toyota of Visalia, Inc. v. New Motor Vehicle Bd.*, 188 Cal. App. 3d 872, 881 (1987); Standards Courts Apply in Reviewing Land Use Decisions, above. Accordingly, only the evidence in the record is relevant on this issue (Evid. Code § 350), and it is an error for the court to consider any other evidence. *See Gong v. City of Fremont*, 250 Cal. App. 2d 568, 573 (1967). Because discovery directed to evidence outside the record could not possibly lead to the discovery of evidence admissible on this issue (Code Civ. Proc. § 2107), such discovery is not permitted. *State of California*, 12 Cal. 3d 237 (discovery of evidence outside the record not permitted; joinder of claim for declaratory relief did not entitle petitioner to discovery).

The rule limiting evidence to the record before the agency applies in traditional mandate proceedings that challenge legislative decisions.

The rule limiting evidence to the record before the agency applies in traditional mandate proceedings that challenge legislative decisions. *See Western States Petroleum Ass'n*, 9 Cal. 4th 559. It is codified for administrative mandate proceedings that challenge adjudicatory decisions in Code of Civil Procedure section 1094.5(e). *See Cadiz Land Company, Inc. v. Rail Cycle, L.P.*, 83 Cal. App. 4th 74, 120 (2000); *Fort Mojave Indian Tribe v. Department of Health Servs.*, 38 Cal. App. 4th 1574 (1995); *Sacramento Old City Ass'n v. City Council*, 229 Cal. App. 3d 1011, 1039 n.13 (1991).

An exception to this rule exists when there is "relevant evidence which, in the exercise of reasonable diligence, could not have been produced or which was improperly excluded at the hearing." Code Civ. Proc. § 1094.5(e) (administrative mandate); *See also Western States Petroleum Ass'n*, 9 Cal. 4th at 578 (analogizing to section 1094.5(e) in traditional mandate proceeding challenging legislative action). However, in order to conduct discovery aimed at augmenting the administrative record, the moving party must demonstrate to the court:

- What evidence is sought to be discovered for the purpose of augmenting the record
- How that evidence is relevant
- Either that the evidence could not have been produced at the hearing with the exercise of reasonable diligence or that it was improperly excluded

See Pomona Valley Hospital Med. Ctr. v. Superior Court, 55 Cal. App. 4th 93 (1997). If the moving party fails to make this showing, it is an abuse of the court's discretion to allow discovery. *Id.*

This exception does not apply, and evidence is limited to the record, even when the petitioner is claiming that the evidence presented to the decisionmakers was tainted or incomplete. In *Cadiz Land Company, Inc.*, the petitioner propounded discovery intended to solicit information explaining why certain evidence was not presented to the board of supervisors, contending that an individual took actions that tainted the administrative process. 83 Cal. App. 4th 74. The court acknowledged that the individual had received a prison term for conspiring to wiretap, receive, and conceal stolen property, manipulate computer data, misuse trade secrets, and commit fraud in connection with sale of stock, all in matters related to the landfill project before the board. The court nonetheless held the discovery impermissible, because the petitioner could not establish under section 1094.5(e) that the evidence it sought "could not have been produced or... was improperly excluded at the hearing."

The court also upheld a decision not to permit the petitioner to depose the individual. While the petitioner presented evidence that this individual might testify to bribing members of the board of supervisors, there was inadequate evidence that the deposition would lead to evidence of fraud or corruption. *Id.* at 121–23.

Evidence outside the record regarding issues other than the validity of a local agency's decision generally is admissible and discoverable. Evidence outside the record concerning such issues as the court's jurisdiction, or procedural issues or defenses, generally is admissible in mandate cases. *See Running Fence Corp. v. Superior Court*, 51 Cal. App. 3d 400, 424, n. 14 (1975). Unlike the issue of the validity of a local agency's decision, these issues are *not* determined based solely on a review of the record. Evidence outside the record therefore is relevant to the court's decision. Because evidence outside the record often is relevant and admissible on these issues, it also is discoverable.

These issues include such matters as:

- Petitioner's standing (or "beneficial interest")
- Whether petitioner properly exhausted all available administrative remedies, and whether any exception (*e.g.*, futility) applied

Because evidence outside the record often is relevant and admissible on these issues, it also is discoverable.

- Whether the action is barred by laches
- Whether the action is moot (*e.g.*, because of subsequent agency action)
- Whether an injunction or stay is appropriate because of impending irreparable harm
- Issues related to a request for attorneys' fees
- Whether a real party in interest should have been included in the action
- Accuracy and completeness of the record of proceedings
- Any affirmative defense that relies on extra-record evidence

Evidence outside the record in traditional mandate actions challenging ministerial or informal administrative actions is admissible if the facts are in dispute.

Evidence outside the record may be admissible in traditional mandate proceedings that challenge ministerial acts. Evidence outside the record in traditional mandate actions challenging ministerial or informal administrative actions is admissible if the facts are in dispute. *See Western States*, 9 Cal. 4th at 576. As a practical matter, in many such cases, there is no record of proceedings because the agency has not taken any action with regard to the alleged ministerial act at issue.

Evidence regarding the decisionmaker's thought processes is not admissible or discoverable. Evidence regarding the mental processes of individual decisionmakers is not discoverable or admissible. *See City of Fairfield*, 14 Cal. 3d at 772–73; *State of California*, 12 Cal. 3d at 257–58; *County of Los Angeles v. Superior Court*, 13 Cal. 3d 721, 726 (1975). This "deliberative process privilege" means that evidence regarding individual decisionmaker's motives or mental processes cannot be presented to the court, and that discovery regarding these matters is not permitted. *See Bd. of Supervisors v. Superior Court*, 32 Cal. App. 4th 1616, 1623 (1995).

The doctrine prohibits any inquiries "to determine what evidence [the decisionmakers] relied upon, or what reasoning they employed, in voting...." *City of Fairfield*, 14 Cal. 3d at 773. The privilege applies to attempts to determine when a legislator decided to vote a particular way. *Id.* at 774. Discovery seeking to determine what materials were considered and relied upon by a decisionmaker in reaching a decision also is prohibited by the privilege. *See State of California*, 12 Cal. 3d at 257–58 (interrogatories were improper because they sought to determine whether the Commission was aware of certain facts at the time of the hearing).

The privilege also prohibits disclosure of discussions in which local officials participated prior to voting. *See County of Los Angeles*, 13 Cal. 3d at 729. *See also City of Santa Cruz v. Superior Court*, 40 Cal. App. 4th 1146, 1148 (1995) ("discovery into the subjective motives or mental processes of legislators is forbidden, and that this proscription may not be circumvented by deposing others about the factors that may have led to the legislators' votes"). It also prohibits discovery into council members' recollections of a closed session even when there is no other means of ascertaining whether the session was conducted lawfully. *See Kleitman v. Superior Court*, 74 Cal. App. 4th 324 (1999) (court refused to allow the plaintiff to conduct discovery into the council members' recollections, even though there were no other means of proving a violation of the Brown Act).

Discovery regarding whether a council member relied on information acquired outside the hearing room likewise is impermissible. *See Bd. of Supervisors*, 32 Cal. App. 4th 1616 (plaintiff could not conduct discovery concerning whether members of the board of supervisors took a judges' vote into advisement before reaching their decision to consolidate court-related services in the county sheriff instead of in the marshal's office).

The privilege applies to documents as well as testimony. *See Times Mirror Co. v. Superior Court*, 53 Cal. 3d 1325 (1991) (materials reflecting deliberative or decision-making processes are exempt from disclosure under the Public Records Act). Even if the content of a document is purely factual, it still is exempt from public scrutiny if it is "actually related to the process by which policies are formulated or inextricably intertwined with policy-making processes." *Id.* at 1342–43 (the deliberative process privilege protects from disclosure the appointment calendars and schedules of the Governor, and finding that "[d]isclosing the identity of persons with whom the Governor has met and consulted is the functional equivalent of revealing the substance or direction of the Governor's judgment and mental processes").

The privilege applies to both administrative and legislative decisions. *See State of California*, 12 Cal. 3d at 257–58 (applying privilege to decision of state commission to deny land use permit).

Judicial notice of matters outside the record. It is common in land use cases for petitioners or respondents to attempt to supplement the record through a request for judicial notice. However, the doctrine is frequently misused, and care should be taken to ensure that the facts identified are properly subject to judicial notice. Judicial notice is not merely a substitute for introducing or authenticating evidence or a way to eliminate hearsay objections, but instead is a manner of establishing a fact as incontrovertible. "[T]he weight of the authority is that, where notice is mandatory, the effect is substantially that of a *conclusive* presumption; *i.e.*, the fact must be accepted and no evidence can be offered to dispute it." 1 Witkin, *Calif. Evidence, Judicial Notice*, section 3 (4th ed. 2000).

Additionally, judicial notice cannot be used to evade other evidentiary problems. Rather, judicial notice may be taken only of documents, and statements within such documents, that otherwise meet evidentiary requirements. *Mozzetti v. City of Brisbane*, 67 Cal. App. 3d 565, 578 (1977) ("[t]he purpose of judicial notice is to expedite the production and introduction of *otherwise admissible* evidence.") (emphasis added); *Marocco v. Ford Motor Co.*, 7 Cal. App. 3d 84, 89 (1970); *Love v. Wolf*, 226 Cal. App. 2d 378, 403 (1964). Moreover, even if documents are judicially noticeable as official acts of a governmental agency, this merely allows the court to take judicial notice of the fact that an agency generated the document, not of the substance or conclusions of the document. *Beckley v. Reclamation Board of the State*, 205 Cal. App. 2d 734, 741–42 (1962); *see also Mangini v. R. J. Reynolds Tobacco Co.*, 7 Cal. 4th 1057, 1063 (1994) (judicial notice of the authenticity of an official document does not establish the truth of the statements it makes); *People v. Long*, 7 Cal. App. 3d 586, 591 (1970). "The underlying theory of judicial notice is that the matter being judicially noticed is a law or fact that is *not reasonably subject to dispute*." *Lockley v. Law Office of Cantrell, Green, Pekich, Cruz & McCort*, 91 Cal. App. 4th 875, 882 (2001) (emphasis added). "The appropriate setting for resolving facts reasonably subject to dispute is the adversary hearing." *Id.*

Judicial notice of documents is not judicial notice of the truth of statements contained in those documents. "Taking judicial notice of a document is not the

Even if the content of a document is purely factual, it still is exempt from public scrutiny if it is "actually related to the process by which policies are formulated or inextricably intertwined with policy-making processes."

Judicial notice is not merely a substitute for introducing or authenticating evidence or a way to eliminate hearsay objections, but instead is a manner of establishing a fact as incontrovertible.

same thing as accepting the truth of its contents or accepting a particular interpretation of its meaning." *Joslin v. H.A.S. Ins. Brokerage*, 184 Cal. App. 3d 369, 374 (1986); *see also StorMedia Inc. v. Superior Court*, 20 Cal. 4th 449, 456–57 n. 9 (1999) (when judicial notice is taken of a document, the truthfulness and proper interpretation of the document may be subject to dispute); *Mangini*, 7 Cal. 4th at 1063 (truth of government reports not judicially noticeable). At least one court has held that even judicial findings are subject to this rule. *Sosinsky v. Grant*, 6 Cal. App. 4th 1548, 1565 (1992) (disagreeing with Jefferson's California Evidence Benchbook and cases following it, and holding that court cannot take judicial notice of truth of court findings, even though made after a contested adversary hearing).

Finally, care should also be taken when seeking judicial notice of documents alleged to comprise legislative history. The Court of Appeal (Third District) has emphatically renounced the practice of many attorneys of submitting requests contending that "every scrap of paper that is generated in the legislative process constitutes the proper subject of judicial notice." *Kaufman & Broad Communities, Inc. v. Performance Plastering, Inc.*, 133 Cal. App. 4th 26, 29 (2006). The court directed, "This must stop." *Id.* The court produced a list of both documents constituting cognizable legislative history, such as conference committee reports and different versions of the bill, and documents that may not be noticed, such as letters to the Governor urging signing of a bill. *Id.* at 31–39.

Setting a Briefing and Hearing Schedule

There are two procedures for bringing a writ proceeding to hearing: noticed motion made by either party, or application for an alternative writ by the petitioner.

There are two procedures for bringing a writ proceeding to hearing: noticed motion made by either party, or application for an alternative writ by the petitioner. Both procedures allow for short briefing schedules and a prompt hearing date. Both procedures presume that the record will be prepared and presented to the court quickly. In cases challenging a general plan or any element thereof on the grounds that it fails to comply with the Planning Law, the petitioner must request a hearing with 90 days of filing a petition. Gov't Code § 65753.[15]

In practice, many parties stipulate to a hearing and briefing schedule and present the stipulation to the court for approval.

Alternative writ. An alternative writ is an interim order issued by the court, usually at the outset of the case, that commands the respondent to carry out the act requested by the petitioner, or to show cause before the court at a specified date and time why it has not done so. Code Civ. Proc. § 1087. The practical effect of the alternative writ is to establish a hearing and briefing schedule, except in rare instances in which the agency decides, in response to the writ, to carry out the act sought by petitioners.

Additionally, the alternative writ (which must be served in the same manner as a civil summons) constitutes the process whereby the court acquires personal jurisdiction over the respondent and any real party in interest. If no alternative

---

15. This is also true in CEQA cases. Pub. Res. Code § 21167.4(a). *See* Special Procedures for CEQA action below.

writ is obtained, there is no court process to compel the respondent and real party in interest to appear unless a summons is served. Service of the petition itself is not sufficient to bring parties before the court. *See Wagner*, 78 Cal. App. 4th at 947–51. *See also Bd. of Supervisors v. Superior Court*, 23 Cal. App. 4th 830, 840 (1994) (the apparently optional use of summons procedures authorized by Code of Civil Procedure section 1107 for mandate proceedings is actually mandatory).

To obtain an alternative writ, the petitioner submits an application for an alternative writ *ex parte*—*i.e.*, without formal notice. Generally, the petitioner must give at least 24 hours' informal notice to the other parties of the *ex parte* application, to comply with local court rules.

The alternative writ process is detailed, requiring submittal of an application, memorandum, proposed order, and proposed alternative writ, and service upon the respondent agency and real party in interest twice. *See* Geoffrey L. Robinson, *Handling Administrative Mandamus, Step 28* (Cal. Cont. Ed. Bar, Action Guide, Spring 2000). The petitioner must prepare a memorandum of points and authorities to accompany the application, showing the legal basis for the court's issuance of the alternative writ, and specifying the reasons the writ should issue.

The alternative writ process is detailed, requiring submittal of an application, memorandum, proposed order, and proposed alternative writ, and service upon the respondent agency and real party in interest twice.

Alternative writs are a useful vehicle for bringing all parties before the court quickly and establishing a short hearing and briefing schedule. Alternative writs are therefore most commonly issued when time is of the essence.

Noticed motion. A mandate proceeding also may be brought to hearing by a noticed motion "by any party."[16] Code Civ. Proc. § 1094. *See also* Code Civ. Proc. § 1088. A noticed motion in a writ proceeding is governed by the rules applicable to noticed motions generally. Code Civ. Proc. § 1109. These provisions arguably include the 21-day notice provisions of Code of Civil Procedure section 1005, although Code of Civil Procedure section 1088 states only that notice of the application for writ must be given *at least* ten days before the writ issues.

A noticed motion in a writ proceeding is governed by the rules applicable to noticed motions generally.

Because the notice period required for a motion for judgment on the writ is short, and because the noticed motion procedure is not limited to petitioners, it often is used when the respondent or real party in interest wants to bring a case to hearing quickly.

Informal means of obtaining hearing date. Land use practitioners have developed informal means of setting a hearing and briefing schedule. Experienced practitioners generally will enter into a stipulation covering both preparation and lodging of the record and a briefing and hearing schedule, and present it to the court for endorsement. Even when a party brings an *ex parte* application for an alternative writ, the parties often stipulate to a hearing and briefing schedule, which the court then inserts into the alternative writ.

Experienced practitioners generally will enter into a stipulation covering both preparation and lodging of the record and a briefing and hearing schedule, and present it to the court for endorsement.

CERES = California Environmental Resources Evaluation System
OPR = Office of Planning and Research

Some courts assign a specific judge or judges to hear writ proceedings.[17] In that situation, a petitioner often will call the clerks of those departments to

---

16. As noted above, however, a summons should be served with the petition if the matter is to be brought to hearing other than by alternative writ. *See Wagner*, 78 Cal. App. 4th at 947–51.

17. CEQA requires that the superior courts in all counties with a population of more than 200,000 designate one or more judges to develop expertise in CEQA and related land use and environmental laws. Pub. Res. Code § 21167.1(b). A list of CEQA judges can be found at the California Environmental Resources Evaluation System (CERES), a web-based information system developed by the California Resources Agency (http://ceres.ca.gov/ceqa), and in the California Planners' Book of Lists published annually by the Governor's Office of Planning and Research (OPR).

determine the preferred method for setting a hearing date. Other courts hear writ matters on their law and motion calendars, even if the matter proceeds pursuant to an alternative writ. In those courts, the process for obtaining a hearing date in a writ proceeding is the same method specified in the local court rules for other noticed motions.

Summary Judgment

Because a court must review the entire record to determine whether substantial evidence supports the decision, the summary judgment procedure is effectively unavailable.

Although there is no express limitation on the use of summary judgment in mandate proceedings, its applicability is limited by pragmatic considerations. The court's review is limited to the record. Because a court must review the entire record to determine whether substantial evidence supports the decision, the summary judgment procedure (in which review is limited to the evidence tendered in the moving and opposing papers) is effectively unavailable. *Dunn v. County of Santa Barbara*, 135 Cal. App. 4th 1281, 1292 (2006). The court in *Dunn* held that where the requirements for a motion for judgment on the peremptory writ under CCP section 1094 are met (*i.e.*, where the petition presents no triable issue of fact or is based solely on an administrative record), a motion for judgment under Section 1094 "is the proper, and exclusive, procedural means for seeking a streamlined review of an agency's decision." *Id.*

On the other hand, summary judgment may be granted in mandate proceedings where evidence outside of the administrative record disposes of the petition as a matter of law. *See, e.g., Stanton v. Dumke*, 64 Cal. 2d 199 (1966) (summary judgment appropriate in administrative mandate proceeding upon showing that petition was moot); *California Rifle & Pistol Assn. v. City of West Hollywood*, 66 Cal. App. 4th 1302, 1309 (1998) (summary judgment granted in favor of defendant City in mandate proceeding challenging gun control ordinance on grounds of preemption, equal protection, and due process).

Preparing the Briefs

Courts apply myriad rules to briefs in mandate cases. Some consider them subject to the rules normally applicable to law and motion practice. In that case, court permission to file a brief that exceeds the relatively short page limits allowed in law and motion practice usually is required. Other courts consider the briefs to be trial briefs, and impose no page limits. Still others have special rules applicable to mandate cases, "writs and receivers," or CEQA cases. Local rules should be checked. The issue often is addressed in a stipulated order regarding the hearing and briefing schedule. *See* Informal Means of Obtaining a Hearing Date, above.

A petitioner should be especially aware of the burden it faces in preparing a brief, and ensure that all recitations of fact are supported by citations to the record.

A petitioner should be especially aware of the burden it faces in preparing a brief, and ensure that all recitations of fact are supported by citations to the record. In *Jacobson v. County of Los Angeles*, the petitioners brought an administrative mandate proceeding challenging the decision of a zoning board. 69 Cal. App. 3d 374 (1977). The court chastised the petitioners for failing to address the evidence in the record that supported the zoning board's findings. With an analogy to appellate review of trial court proceedings, the court explained how the petitioners failed to establish their case:

> No fair statement of the evidence has been undertaken by petitioners. [¶] Here appellants have made no effort to comply with the rules of court and have failed

to set forth the evidence of the matter under consideration. What is said in *Hickson v. Thielman*, [Citation omitted.], is particularly appropriate: "The first contention of defendants is that the findings are unsupported by the evidence. In this connection, we repeat what every lawyer should know, namely, that when an appellant urges the insufficiency of the evidence to support the findings it is his duty to set forth a fair and adequate statement of the evidence which is claimed to be insufficient. He cannot shift this burden onto respondent, nor is a reviewing court required to undertake an independent examination of the record when appellant has shirked his responsibility in this respect."

Id. at 388. Similarly, in *Stolman v. City of Los Angeles*, the court faulted the City for not providing citations to the record to support its contention, stating that "[i]ts cursory argument on this point, unsupported by citations to the record, is clearly deficient. '[S]tatements of fact contained in the briefs which are not supported by the evidence in the record must be disregarded.'" 114 Cal. App. 4th 916, 926–27 (2003) (quoting *Tisher v. California Horse Racing Bd.* 231 Cal. App. 3d 349, 361 (1991)). *See also Defend the Bay v. City of Irvine*, 119 Cal. App. 4th 1261, 1266 (2004) ("an appellant challenging an EIR for insufficient evidence must lay out the evidence favorable to the other side and show why it is lacking. Failure to do so is fatal. A reviewing court will not independently review the record to make up for appellant's failure to carry his burden."); *Markley v. City Council*, 131 Cal. App. 3d 656, 673 (1982) (quoting *Jacobson*).

A Stay or Preliminary Injunction May Issue Pending a Final Decision on the Writ Petition

A petitioner challenging a development project often will seek to halt construction of the project pending the court's final decision. Two interim orders are available in writ proceedings to maintain the status quo pending a final decision on the merits: a stay and a temporary restraining order followed by an injunction.

Stays. A stay of a local agency's decision is available under Code of Civil Procedure section 1094.5(g). The stay operates to preclude the agency decision from taking effect. A stay may be issued unless the court determines that a stay would be against the public interest. Code Civ. Proc. § 1094.5(g).

A stay operates to preclude the agency decision from taking effect.

The decision whether to issue a stay is discretionary with the trial court. *West Coast Home Improvement Co. v. Contractors' State License Bd.*, 68 Cal. App. 2d 1, 4 (1945).

The court also has discretion to require the petitioner to post a bond when a stay is issued. *See Venice Canals Resident Home Owners Ass'n v. Superior Court*, 72 Cal. App. 3d 675, 679–80 (1977) (bond properly required to protect developer from losses resulting from stay of project issued at request of neighbors). A bond is designed to protect the respondent or real party in interest from the damages that would be caused by the stay if the court later determines the agency action was valid, up to the limit of the bond. *Id.*

The mandate statutes expressly reference a stay only in connection with administrative mandate proceedings. Code Civ. Proc. § 1094.5(g). However, courts often analogize to this provision and grant stays in traditional mandate proceedings, and petitioners in traditional mandate proceedings also can proceed by way of preliminary injunctive relief.[18]

TROs and preliminary injunctions. Temporary restraining orders (TROs) last a few days, and are followed by preliminary injunctions, which generally last until the merits of the writ petition are decided. These orders are permitted in writ proceedings. *See Camp*, 123 Cal. App. 3d at 356; Code Civ. Proc. § 1109. A TRO or injunction typically prohibits the real party in interest—often a developer—from carrying out the activity approved by the local agency. A TRO or injunction requires a showing of a probability of prevailing on the merits and irreparable harm in the absence of an order. *See Cohen v. Board of Supervisors*, 40 Cal. 3d 277 (1985).

A bond is required for an injunction to issue. Code Civ. Proc. §§ 529 (general provisions), 529.1 (bond in action to enjoin a construction project that has received all legally required licenses and permits), 529.2 (bond in action to enjoin low- or moderate-income housing development project). The bond is designed to protect the respondent or real party in interest against damages sustained by reason of the injunction if the court finally decides that the petitioner was not entitled to the injunction. Code Civ. Proc. § 529.

The damages that may be recovered against a bond are those that appear with reasonable certainty to be the necessary and proximate result of the injunction, up to the limit of the bond. 6 Witkin, *Calif. Procedure, Provisional Remedies*, section 413, page 334 (4th ed. 1996). Those damages may include attorneys' fees the respondent or real party in interest incurs in defending the main action, on the theory that defending the main action is necessary to establish that the injunction should not have issued. *Id.*, section 414, page 336. Thus, by seeking an injunction, a petitioner may open itself up to an award of attorneys' fees where none would otherwise be recoverable.

Issuance of the Writ

The writ issued at the end of a case is a peremptory writ of mandate. The writ cannot be granted by default. The case must be heard by the court whether the adverse party appears or not. Code Civ. Proc. § 1088.

If the petition challenges a local agency decision, and the court determines that the petition has merit, it enters a judgment directing issuance of a writ. The clerk of the court then issues the writ. *See* 31 *California Forms of Pleading and Practice*, ch. 358, forms 18 and 20 (Matthew Bender) 2004. The writ typically directs the respondent agency to vacate and set aside the decision, and not to take similar action until there has been compliance with the law. Code Civ. Proc. § 1087. If the petition seeks to compel specific action, the writ directs the respondent agency to take the action. At least one court held that the writ must specify a return date to ensure compliance. It explained:

---

18. In CEQA cases, by statutory mandate, if no stay or injunction is issued, responsible agencies are required to assume that the EIR or negative declaration is adequate, and decide whether to approve the project accordingly. A responsible agency's approval of the project in that circumstance constitutes permission to proceed with the project at the applicant's risk pending final determination of the CEQA action. Pub. Res. Code § 21167.3(b). The same rules implicitly apply in non-CEQA cases by virtue of the presumption of validity that attaches to public agency decisions. Evid. Code § 664 ("it is presumed that official duty has been regularly performed").

A writ of mandate is a piece of paper. If its purpose is to declare the rights of parties, its existence suffices. If its purpose is to compel someone to do something, its existence does not suffice. The proper way to ensure compliance is to require a return on the writ, which commands a party to do something and report to the court that the act has been done. (*See* Cal. Administrative Mandamus (Cont. Ed. Bar 1989) Procedures After Trial, §§ 13.10–13.11, pp. 411–14 [providing form for this purpose].)

Endangered Habitats League, Inc., 63 Cal. App. 4th at 244. Notwithstanding this statement, many peremptory writs do not expressly require a return.

If the court determines that the writ proceeding has no merit, it issues a judgment denying the petition for writ of mandate, and declaring that the petitioner take nothing by its action. A statement of decision ordinarily is not required, since a writ proceeding typically involves only questions of law. *See City of Coachella*, 210 Cal. App. 3d at 1291–92.

> *If the court determines that the writ proceeding has no merit, it issues a judgment denying the petition for writ of mandate, and declaring that the petitioner take nothing by its action.*

Appeal in a Writ of Mandate Case

Appeals of judgments in mandate cases generally are subject to the rules applicable to appeals in civil cases. Code Civ. Proc. § 1109; California Rules of Court, Rules 1–55. However, caution is warranted in applying these general rules to the peculiarities of mandate proceedings.

Time to appeal. In *Laraway v. Pasadena Unified School District*, the court held that the time to appeal was calculated based upon the trial court's ruling on a motion for writ of mandate, rather than the judgment. 98 Cal. App. 4th 579 (2002). The court held that the original order was appealable, since it contemplated no further action and disposed of all issues between all parties. It explained that once a final, appealable order or judgment has been entered, the time to appeal begins to run, and the time cannot be restarted or extended by the filing of a subsequent judgment or appealable order making the same decision. *Id.*

Effect of appeal on judgment. The statutes governing the effect of appeals on judgments in mandate cases also are somewhat confusing, because some provisions address the effect of the appeal on the *trial court's* decision and others deal with the effect on the underlying *agency* action. The guiding principle, however, is simply stated: during appeal from a judgment granting a writ in an administrative mandate case, the agency's decision is automatically stayed. *See Agricultural Labor Relations Bd. v. Tex-Cal Land Mgmt., Inc.*, 43 Cal. 3d 696, 706 n. 9 (1987); Code Civ. Proc. § 1094.5(g). In all other cases (*i.e.*, denial of a writ in an administrative mandate case or denial or grant of a writ in a traditional mandate case), the agency's decision or order remains in effect pending appeal absent a contrary order issued by the trial court or the court of appeal. Code Civ. Proc. §§ 916(a) (general rule is that appeal stays judgment), 917.1–917.9 (exceptions to general rule, which do not include a writ of mandate), 1109 (code provisions pertaining to ordinary civil actions apply to writ proceedings except as otherwise provided in writ statutes), 1110b (court may direct that an appeal of a judgment granting a writ of mandate does not stay the judgment), 1094.5(g) (agency decision not stayed upon appeal of judgment denying administrative writ unless court order otherwise). *See also Union*

> *During appeal from a judgment granting a writ in an administrative mandate case, the agency's decision is automatically stayed.*

Pacific R.R., Co. v. State Bd. of Equalization, 49 Cal. 3d 138, 158 (1989) (traditional writ of mandate automatically stayed pending appeal; writ of prohibition, which maintains status quo, is not automatically stayed pending appeal).

Administrative mandate. Appeal in an administrative mandate case is governed by Code of Civil Procedure section 1094.5(g), under which (1) in an appeal from denial of the writ, the order or decision of the agency is not stayed except upon the order of the appellate court; and (2) an appeal from the granting of the writ automatically stays the order or decision of the agency pending the determination of the appeal unless the appellate court directs otherwise.

Traditional mandate. A petitioner's appeal from the grant or denial of a writ of traditional mandate is governed by general rules on appeals in civil actions. Code Civ. Proc. § 1109 (except as otherwise provided, general rules of civil procedure govern special proceedings). Under Code of Civil Procedure section 916, "an appeal stays proceedings in the trial court upon the judgment or order appealed from...." Thus, if a court either grants or denies a writ of traditional mandate, its order is automatically stayed by appeal. The practical effect in both cases is to leave the agency decision or order in effect pending appeal.

Mandatory injunctions are automatically stayed pending appeal, while prohibitory injunctions are not.

Injunction. The situation is further complicated, however, if the judgment includes a permanent injunction, such as an injunction prohibiting the developer from pursuing its project. Mandatory injunctions are automatically stayed pending appeal, while prohibitory injunctions are not. 1 *Calif. Civil Appellate Practice*, section 6.19 (Cal. Cont. Ed. Bar, 3d ed. 1997); 9 Witkin, *Calif. Procedure*, *Appeal*, section 276 (4th ed. 1997); 6 Witkin, *Calif. Procedure, Provisional Remedies*, section 400 (9th ed. 1997).

Litigation Under CEQA

CEQA actions are brought as mandate actions, but are subject to several unique procedural rules that dictate the pace of the litigation to a significant degree.

Special Procedures for CEQA Actions

The steps in litigation brought under CEQA are as follows:

Steps Required for Litigation Under CEQA

1. **Service of Notice of Proposed Action.** Petitioner must serve the agency with written notice of the proposed action before filing suit. Pub. Res. Code § 21167.5

2. **Petitioner Files Petition and Request re Record.** The petitioner files the petition with proof of service of the notice of the proposed action. Pub. Res. Code § 21167.5. The petitioner must also file notice that the petitioner elects to prepare the record. Pub. Res. Code § 21167.6(a) and (b)(2)

3. **Service of Petition on Attorney General.** The petitioner must serve a copy of the petition on the Attorney General within 10 days of filing. Pub. Res. Code § 21167.7; Code Civ. Proc. § 388

4. **Service of Petition on Agency.** The petitioner must serve the petition on the agency within 10 business days after it is filed. Pub. Res. Code § 21167.6(a)

5. **Serve Request Re Record.** Within 10 business days of filing the petition, the petitioner must also serve on the agency a request that it prepare the record, or the petitioner must notify the agency that it will prepare the record itself. Pub. Res. Code § 21167.6(a) and (b)(2)

Steps Required for Litigation Under CEQA *continued*

6. **Service on Real Parties in Interest.** The petitioner must serve the petition on all Real Parties In Interest within 20 business days following service on the agency. Pub. Res. Code § 21167.6.5(a)

7. **Give Notice of Settlement Meeting.** Within 20 days after the petition is served, the agency must file a notice setting forth the time and place for a settlement meeting. Pub. Res. Code § 21167.8(a)

8. **List of Other Agencies.** Within 10 business days after the petition is served on the agency, the agency must provide the petitioner with a list of responsible and trustee agencies for the project. Pub. Res. Code § 21167.6.5(b)

9. **Service on Responsible Agencies.** The petitioner must provide responsible and trustee agencies with notice of the action within 15 days of receipt of the list of agencies from the agency. Pub. Res. Code § 21167.6.5(c)

10. **Hold Settlement Meeting.** The settlement meeting must be held within 45 days after the petition is served. Pub. Res. Code § 21167.8(a)

11. **Completion of Record.** The record of the administrative proceedings is to be completed within 60 days after service of the request to prepare the record. Pub. Res. Code § 21167.6(b)

12. **Request for Hearing.** Within 90 days of filing the petition, the petitioner must file a request with the court that a date for a hearing on the merits be placed on the court's calendar. Pub. Res. Code § 21167.4(a)

13. **Initial Response to Petition.** The agency and real parties in interest must file their initial response to the petition within 30 days after the record is completed. Code Civ. Proc. § 1089.5

14. **Petitioners' Statement of Issues.** Within 30 days after service and filing of the notice that the record has been completed, the petitioner must file with the court a statement of issues that it intends to pursue in the case. Pub. Res. Code § 21167.8(f)

15. **Agency's and Real Parties in Interest's Statement of Issues.** The agency and the real parties in interest must file a responsive statement of issues 10 days after service of petitioner's statement of issues. Pub. Res. Code § 21167.8(f)

16. **Briefing.** Briefs on the merits should ordinarily be filed in time to allow completion of the briefing within 90 days from the date the hearing request was filed. Pub. Res. Code § 21167.4(c)

17. **Court Hearing on the Merits.** The hearing involves oral arguments by counsel based upon the written record and the briefs submitted to the court. The hearing should ordinarily be held within 30 days after completion of the briefing. Pub. Res. Code § 21167.4(c)

18. **Trial Court Decision.** At the conclusion of the hearing, the court will generally indicate which way it is inclined to rule and will issue a written ruling on the petition within 90 days of the hearing.

The request for hearing is important. The petitioner must request a hearing within 90 days of filing the petition. Pub. Res. Code § 21167.4(a).[19] The hearing need not be held within the 90-day period, but the request for a hearing must be made within that time. *Id.*; *see also Ass'n for Sensible Development at Northstar, Inc. v. County of Placer*, 122 Cal. App. 4th 1289, 1293–1295 (2004) (disagreeing with *McCormick v. Board of Supervisors*, 198 Cal. App. 3d 352 (1988), which held that the mere filing of a request for a hearing was insufficient); *Mitchell v. County of Orange*, 165 Cal. App. 3d 1185 (1985). The hearing

> *The request for hearing is important. The petitioner must request a hearing within 90 days of filing the petition.*

---

19. A similar requirement to request a hearing within 90 days applies to certain challenges to general plans. Gov't Code § 65753.

must be on the merits of the petition itself; setting a hearing on provisional remedies or collateral matters within 90 days of filing the action is insufficient. *See Miller v. City of Hermosa Beach*, 13 Cal. App. 4th 1118, 1135 (1993). The failure to request a hearing can result in dismissal of the case, and relief from that dismissal under Code of Civil Procedure section 473 has been held to be unavailable when the failure to request a hearing was due to an attorneys' inexcusable mistake. *Nacimiento Reg'l Water Mgmt. Advisory Com. v. Monterey County Water Resources Agency*, 122 Cal. App. 4th 961 (2004).

Contents of a CEQA Record

The contents of a record in a CEQA proceeding are specified by statute. Public Resources Code section 21167.6(e) provides that the record must include certain materials. In general terms, it requires the following:

- All project application materials
- All staff reports and related documents prepared by the agency and written testimony or documents submitted by any person relevant to the agency's action on the project, compliance with CEQA, and any related findings adopted by the agency
- Any transcripts or minutes of proceedings at which the decision-making bodies at the agency heard testimony or considered any environmental document on the project, and any transcripts or minutes of proceedings before any advisory body that were presented to the decision-making body prior to taking action on the environmental documents or the project
- Any other written materials relevant to the agency's compliance with CEQA and its final decision on the merits of the project (such as the initial study, copies of studies or other documents relied upon in any environmental document prepared for the project and either made available to the public or included in the agency's files, and all internal agency communications, including staff notes and memoranda related to the project or compliance with CEQA)
- Local court rules sometimes add a myriad of procedural and substantive requirements regarding preparation of a record

CEQA allows a petitioner to prepare the record, presumably to allow the petitioner to keep costs down. Pub. Res. Code § 21167.6(b)(2). The responsibility for an adequate, well-organized, and comprehensive record always remains, however, with the respondent agency, and "the consequences of providing a record to the courts that does not evidence the agency's compliance with CEQA is severe—reversal of project approval." *Protect Our Water v. County of Merced*, 110 Cal. App. 4th 362, 373 (2003).

Protect Our Water presented an extreme example of poor record preparation, with the court assigning blame to the petitioner, the agency, and the project applicant. The petitioner had exercised its election to prepare the record, and had failed to organize or index the documents coherently. The court noted that "it is nearly impossible to locate the pertinent documents... the majority... are neither properly indexed nor coherently organized," and it was not even clear whether the court had complete copies. *Id.* at 372. There was only a master index, which identified only broad categories of documents spanning hundreds of pages. The county, for its part, failed to prepare coherent documents. It failed to properly label documents, and some appeared incomplete. The court could not differentiate between documents and attachments. "We find it inconceivable that, given the scope and magnitude of this project, the documents comprising the administrative record are so defectively drafted. This responsibility fell squarely on the County." *Id.* at 372–373. The project applicant also received court censure on the ground that project applicants often assist in the preparation of the record, as they are the parties with an indisputable interest in upholding an agency action approving a project. *Id.* at 373.

Presenting comments to the local agency. CEQA also contains a statutory requirement that a petitioner present its claims to the agency before raising them in court:

(a) No action or proceeding may be brought pursuant to Section 21167 unless the alleged grounds for noncompliance with this division were presented to the public agency orally or in writing by any person during the public comment period provided by this division or prior to the close of the public hearing on the project before the issuance of the notice of determination.

(b) No person shall maintain an action or proceeding unless that person objected to the approval of the project orally or in writing during the public comment period provided by this division or prior to the close of the public hearing on the project before the issuance of the notice of determination.

Pub. Res. Code § 21177. Note that Public Resources Code section 21177(b) differs from the common law exhaustion requirement in that it requires the person seeking to bring the action to object to the project approval. There is no corresponding common law requirement that an objection be made to the project approval (either by petitioner or any other person).

Public Resources Code section 21177(a) essentially codifies the "issue exhaustion" requirement, discussed above. Although the statute is silent on the "appeal exhaustion" requirement, courts have held that a petitioner also must satisfy the common law exhaustion requirement by appealing to the final decision-making body. *See Tahoe Vista Concerned Citizens*, 81 Cal. App. 4th at 590–91. Section 21177(b) essentially creates an additional "standing" requirement. *Id.* However, compliance with section 21177(b) is not sufficient, by itself, to confer standing. *Waste Mgmt. of Alameda County, Inc.*, 79 Cal. App. 4th at 1239 (compliance with section 21177(b) does not confer standing on a petitioner that has no beneficial interest in CEQA compliance).

CEQA also expressly provides that an organization formed after the approval of a project may sue if a member of that organization exhausted remedies under the statute. Pub. Res. Code § 21177(c). Section 21177 allows for exhaustion through submittal of comments at the last public hearing on a project, even though the comment period provided for by CEQA has passed. *See Galante Vineyards v. Monterey Peninsula Water Mgmt. Dist.*, 60 Cal. App. 4th 1109 (1997).

The CEQA exhaustion requirement does not apply if there was no public hearing or other opportunity for members of the public to raise objections orally or in writing prior to the approval of the project, or if the local agency failed to give the notice required by law. Pub. Res. Code § 21177(e). By its terms, the statute requires exhaustion only "where (1) CEQA provides a public

CEQA also expressly provides that an organization formed after the approval of a project may sue if a member of that organization exhausted remedies under the statute.

comment period, or (2) there is a public hearing before a notice of determination is issued." *Azusa Land Reclamation Co.*, 52 Cal. App. 4th 1165. Accordingly, a petitioner was not required to exhaust administrative remedies before challenging a CEQA exemption for which no comment period had been provided, and where there was no public hearing. *Id.* Note, however, that the common law "appeal exhaustion" requirement applies regardless of whether there is a public comment period or mandatory public hearing. Thus, for example, a petitioner seeking to challenge issuance of a permit by the building department would need to appeal to the city council in order to exhaust administrative remedies if such an appeal were permitted by local code.

Standard of Judicial Review of CEQA Decisions

Judicial review of CEQA decisions made in connection with a legislative decision is governed by Public Resources Code section 21168.5.

Judicial review of CEQA determinations made in connection with a legislative decision is governed by Public Resources Code section 21168.5. That section states that "the inquiry shall extend only to whether there was a prejudicial abuse of discretion. Abuse of discretion is established if the agency has not proceeded in a manner required by law or if the determination or decision is not supported by substantial evidence." Pub. Res. Code § 21168.5.

Judicial review of CEQA decisions made in connection with administrative decisions is governed by Public Resources Code section 21168. That section provides that review "shall be in accordance with the provisions of Section 1094.5 of the Code of Civil Procedure." Pub. Res. Code § 21168.

The courts have explained that while the standards under these two sections appear different, they are essentially the same. *See Laurel Heights Improvement Ass'n v. Regents of Univ. of Cal.*, 47 Cal. 3d 376, 392 n. 5 (1988). Accordingly, review of any CEQA decision will be made under a standard that essentially is the same as the substantial evidence standard of review of an administrative decision under Code of Civil Procedure section 1094.5. The California Supreme Court has described the standard as follows:

> In reviewing agency actions under CEQA, Public Resources Code section 21168.5 provides that a court's inquiry shall extend only to whether there was a prejudicial abuse of discretion. Abuse of discretion is established if the agency has not proceeded in a manner required by law or if the determination or decision is not supported by substantial evidence. Thus, the reviewing court does not pass upon the correctness of the EIR's environmental conclusions, but only upon its sufficiency as an informative document. We may not set aside an agency's approval of an EIR on the ground that an opposite conclusion would have been equally or more reasonable. Our limited function is consistent with the principle that the purpose of CEQA is not to generate paper, but to compel government at all levels to make decisions with environmental consequences in mind. CEQA does not, indeed cannot, guarantee that these decisions will always be those which favor environmental considerations. We may not, in sum, substitute our judgment for that of the people and their local representatives. We can and must, however, scrupulously enforce all legislatively mandated CEQA requirements.

Citizens of Goleta Valley v. Board of Supervisors, 52 Cal. 3d 553, 564 (1990) (citations and quotations omitted)

The high court also has explained that "[i]n applying the substantial evidence standard, 'the reviewing court must resolve reasonable doubts in favor of the administrative finding and decision.'" *Laurel Heights Improvement Ass'n*, 47 Cal. 3d at 393 (citation omitted). *See also National Parks & Conser. Ass'n v. County of Riverside*, 71 Cal. App. 4th 1341 (1999) (limiting inquiry to whether agency had substantial evidence to support decision to approve EIR).

Because this standard of review applies to CEQA issues regardless of whether the CEQA review is challenged in connection with an administrative decision or a legislative decision, an action that challenges a legislative decision on both CEQA and non-CEQA grounds will be reviewed under two different standards of review. For example, a claim that a general plan amendment fails to conform to state law will be reviewed under the arbitrary and capricious standard that generally applies in traditional mandate proceedings. *See, e.g., Karlson v. City of Camarillo*, 100 Cal. App. 3d 789, 803–04 (1980). But a claim that the EIR prepared for the general plan amendment fails to comply with CEQA will be reviewed under the stricter CEQA standard, which requires an evaluation of whether there is substantial evidence to support the agency's certification of the EIR, and whether the agency abused its discretion by failing to proceed in the manner required by law. 2 Stephen L. Kostka and Michael H. Zischke, *Practice Under the California Environmental Quality Act*, sections 12.4, 12.5, 23.33 (Cal. Cont. Ed. Bar, 1993) (Update Oct. 2005).

Remedies in a CEQA Case

Courts are vested with broad discretion to craft an appropriate remedy to ensure compliance with CEQA and simultaneously to ensure that the local agency understands the appropriate corrective action that is necessary to comply with the law. Pub. Res. Code § 21168.9. Public Resources Code section 21168.9 allows the court wide latitude in determining whether to suspend all activity and void a decision or allow part of the project to move forward. This type of specifically tailored remedy was applied in *Laurel Heights Improvement Association*, in which the California Supreme Court allowed the University to continue its existing uses at the project site when the EIR was inadequate only as to future uses. 47 Cal. 3d at 422.

Litigation Under the Mitigation Fee Act

Challenges to fees and exactions are governed by the Mitigation Fee Act, Government Code section 66000 *et seq.*, and are the subject of two potentially applicable limitations periods.

The first, contained in Government Code section 66020, governs "as-applied" challenges to development fees that are imposed as a condition of approval of specific development projects. Under Government Code section 66020, a party wishing to challenge the imposition of development fees on its project must file a written protest "at the time of approval or conditional approval of the development or within 90 days after the date of the imposition of the... exactions." Gov't Code § 66020(d)(1). Fees are deemed imposed "when they are imposed or levied on a specific development." Gov't Code § 66020(h). In addition to serving a written protest setting forth the factual and legal elements of the dispute, the party must either tender any required payment in full or provide satisfactory evidence of arrangements to pay the fee when due. Gov't Code § 66020(a)(1). A party that satisfies these protest requirements may file an action challenging imposition of the fees within 180 days after delivery of a notice from the local agency containing a statement of the amount of the fees and notification that the protest period has begun. Gov't Code § 66020(d)(1). The pay-under-protest procedures and limitations period under Government Code section 66020 apply only to fees imposed on a development project as a condition of approval of development; they do not apply to water and sewer service connection fees and capacity charges or fees and charges for processing of permits, which may only be challenged under Government Code section 66022 (discussed below). *Barratt American Inc. v. City of Rancho Cucamonga*, 37 Cal. 4th 685 (2005).

The pay-under-protest procedures and limitations period under Government Code section 66020 apply only to fees imposed on a development project as a condition of approval of development.

The second statute of limitations, Government Code section 66022, governs challenges to the adoption of an ordinance or resolution levying or increasing specified fees or service charges. Such an action must be filed within 120 days of the effective date of the challenged ordinance or resolution. Gov't Code § 66022(a). The challenge also must be brought as a validation proceeding pursuant to Code of Civil Procedure section 860 *et seq.* Gov't Code § 66022(b). However, Government Code section 66022, by its terms, applies only to (1) sewer and water connection fees and "capacity charges" described in Government Code section 66013, and (2) to fees and service charges for processing of zoning changes, use permits, and other permits described in Government Code section 66014(a). Challenges to these fees and charges may not be brought under the pay-under-protest procedures of Government Code section 66020. A validation action under section 66022 is the exclusive procedure for challenging these fees. *Barratt American Inc.*, 37 Cal. 4th 685 (fees and charges defined in Government Code sections 66014 and 66016 do not qualify as "development project fees" under section 66020). In contrast to section 66020, which provides for a refund of excessive or invalid development fees, there is no right to a refund of fees or charges challenged under section 66022; the sole remedy is the reduction of future fees or charges.

The two statutes of limitation—Government Code section 66020, governing challenges to imposition of development fees, and Government Code section 66022, governing facial challenges to specified water, sewer, capacity, and processing charges—are discussed in further detail below.

Challenge to Imposition of Fees on a Development Project Gov't Code § 66020

A party seeking to challenge the imposition of any fees, dedications, or other exactions on a development project must follow the procedures in Government Code section 66020.

A party seeking to challenge the imposition of any fees, dedications, or other exactions on a development project must follow the procedures in Government Code section 66020. First, the party must protest the fee in writing "at the time of approval or conditional approval of the development or within 90 days after the date of the imposition of the...exactions." Gov't Code § 66020(d)(1). The written protest must be served on the "governing body" of the local agency (such as the city council of a city) and must set forth "the factual elements of the dispute and the legal theory forming the basis for the protest." Gov't Code § 66020(a)(2). Fees are considered to be imposed "when they are imposed or levied on a specific development." Gov't Code § 66020(h).

This is not necessarily the date on which the fees are paid. *See Ponderosa Homes, Inc. v. City of San Ramon*, 23 Cal. App. 4th 1761 (1994) (tentative map condition requiring payment of traffic mitigation fee prior to issuance of building permits constituted "imposition" of such fees for purposes of Government Code section 66020). However, adoption of an ordinance or resolution applying the fee to broad classes of projects does not constitute "imposition" of the fee for purposes of Government Code section 66020. *See N.T. Hill, Inc. v. City of Fresno*, 72 Cal. App. 4th 977, 989–90 (1999) ("section 66020 applies to a developer's challenge to an agency's adjudicative decision to impose upon a particular development project a fee adopted by a generally applicable legislative decision"); *Trend Homes, Inc. v. Central Unified Sch. Dist.*, 220 Cal. App. 3d 102, 111 (1990).

The applicant must follow a specified procedure, including tendering any required payment in full or committing to performance of any necessary conditions. At the time of project approval or imposition of the fees, the local agency is required to provide written notice to the project applicant describing the exactions and notifying the applicant that the 90-day protest period has begun. Gov't Code § 66020(d)(1). The 180-day statute does not begin to run unless the agency provides the required notice. *Branciforte Heights, LLC v. City of Santa Cruz*, 138 Cal. App. 4th 914, 925 (2006).

At the time of project approval or imposition of the fees, the local agency is required to provide written notice to the project applicant describing the exactions and notifying the applicant that the 90-day protest period has begun.

Compliance with the protest procedures allows a party to challenge the exaction within 180 days of delivery of the notice. Gov't Code § 66020(d)(2). By providing for an action that challenges the imposition of a fee or other exaction upon a development project, Government Code section 66020 creates a vehicle for bringing an "as applied" challenge to a fee ordinance.

Other provisions of the Mitigation Fee Act indicate that a facial challenge to an ordinance or resolution establishing a fee may be combined with the as-applied claim. Government Code section 66024 states that a developer upon whom a fee has been imposed may seek to invalidate "any order or resolution providing for the imposition" of such fee if such a fee is an invalid "special tax," *i.e.*, if the fee exceeds the cost of the service or facility for which it is imposed. Government Code section 66021 likewise allows a developer who protests the imposition of a fee also to protest "the *establishment*... of the fee, tax, assessment, dedication, reservation, or other exaction...." (emphasis added). Further, an action filed within the limitations period for challenges to application of a fee to a specific project may include a claim that the ordinance enacting the fee is facially invalid; such a claim need not be brought within 120 days, or other specific period following enactment or amendment of the underlying ordinance. *See Travis v. County of Santa Cruz*, 33 Cal. 4th 757 (2004). By contrast, as discussed below, a facial challenge, brought as a validation proceeding, is the *exclusive* procedure for challenging adoption or amendment of water and sewer connection charges, fees and charges for permits, and other fees and charges described in Government Code sections 66013 and 66014—they cannot be challenged under Government Code section 66020. *Barratt American Inc.*, 37 Cal. 4th 685 (Gov't Code 66020, by its own terms, applies only to "development fees" that mitigate the effects of development on the community and does not include fees for water or sewer connections or specified service charges).

Government Code section 66024 requires that at least 30 days prior to initiating an action asserting that the fee constitutes a special tax the petitioner must have requested that the local agency provide a copy of the documents establishing that the development fee did not exceed the cost of the service for which it was imposed. The purpose of requiring a party to request documents before suing is not to cause the agency to discontinue collecting the disputed fees, but to provide the party with a factual basis for its claim before filing suit. Therefore, a suing party cannot claim it was futile to ask. *See Trend Homes, Inc. v. Central Unified Sch. Dist.*, 220 Cal. App. 3d 102 (1990).

The statutory "pay and protest" procedure was enacted to negate the harsh common law rule under which a developer was forced to choose between accepting a permit in order to pursue development, or giving up the ability to develop under the permit by suing to invalidate unlawful conditions. *See Pfeiffer v. City of La Mesa*, 69 Cal. App. 3d 74 (1977) (acceptance and use of permit waives right to challenge conditions). If a developer follows the statutory protest procedure, a city cannot use the protest as a basis to withhold approval of the project while the protest is pending. Gov't Code § 66020(b). However, a local agency can make certain findings that the construction of public facilities, the need for which is directly attributable to the proposed development, is required for the public health, safety, and welfare, and then suspend the permit or other approval that was granted on condition that the developer construct such facilities, pending withdrawal or resolution of the protest against those conditions. Gov't Code § 66020(c).

The pay-and-protest procedure prescribes the exclusive method for an as-applied challenge to fees and exactions imposed on a development project as a condition of development approval. *See Ehrlich v. City of Culver City*, 12 Cal. 4th 854, 866 (1996) ("The Legislature intended to require all protests to a development fee that challenge the sufficiency of its relationship to the effects attributable to a development project—regardless of the legal underpinnings of the protest—to be channeled through the administrative procedures mandated by the [Mitigation Fee] Act."); *California Ranch Homes Dev. Co. v. San Jacinto Unified Sch. Dist.*, 17 Cal. App. 4th 573 (1993) (Government Code section 66020 describes the exclusive procedure for challenging the imposition of school fees on a project). Accordingly, the statutory protest procedure supplants the common law exhaustion requirement (discussed above), and allows developers to contest imposition of fees within 90 days after project approval without having raised the issue earlier. *See Kings County Farm Bureau v. City of Hanford*, 221 Cal. App. 3d 692, 740 (1990) (statutory codification of exhaustion requirement supersedes common law). It also supplants the more general 90-day limitations period for challenges to "the reasonableness, legality or validity of any condition" attached to a subdivision map. Gov't Code § 66499.37. *See Branciforte Heights, LLC*, 138 Cal. App. 4th at 925 (party challenging fees imposed under Quimby Act may use pay-and-protest provisions of Mitigation Fee Act in lieu of compliance with Map Act procedures and limitations).[20] On

---

20. There is some question about whether *Branciforte* will remain good law since Government Code § 66000 expressly excludes Quimby Act fees and dedication requirements from the scope of the Mitigation Fee Act (an issue apparently not raised by the parties or noted by the court). Nonetheless, the reasoning of the case should apply to other fees imposed specifically under the Map Act or included as conditions of approval to a tentative map.

the other hand, the pay-and-protest procedure is not available to challenge conditions or restrictions that do not involve exactions or dedication requirements. *See Fogarty v. City of Chico*, 148 Cal. App. 4th 537 (2007) (land use restrictions imposed as condition of approval are not "exactions" even if they allegedly render property valueless).

Because lawsuits contesting the imposition of a condition or exaction challenge agency decisions, such actions usually are brought as writ proceedings. *See* discussion above regarding mandate as the exclusive procedure for challenging administrative agency actions.

Challenge to Enactment or Increase of Certain Fees Gov't Code § 66022

Facial challenges to ordinances or resolutions that enact or amend water or sewer fees or capacity charges and processing fees are governed by Government Code section 66022, which established a 120-day limitations period for challenge. No statutes expressly address a facial challenge to fees imposed as a condition of approval of development. Accordingly, facial challenges to enactment or increase of these fees are left to the common law. At least one court has held that under these circumstances, the applicable statute is the four-year "catch-all" limitations period under Code of Civil Procedure section 343. *See Balch Enters. v. New Haven Unified Sch. Dist.*, 219 Cal. App. 3d 783, 787 (1990) (where imposition of school facilities fee on commercial warehouse was not subject either to 180-day as-applied statute or to 120-day statute for challenges to fee ordinances or resolutions, action was governed by four-year catch-all statute of limitations period of Code of Civil Procedure section 343). As discussed above, the California Supreme Court has held that a challenge to the facial validity of an ordinance or resolution enacting or increasing development impact fees (as distinct from water and sewer fees or processing charges) is timely if brought within the limitations period for an as-applied challenge to imposition of the impact fees to a specific project. *Travis v. County of Santa Cruz*, 33 Cal. 4th 757 (2004).

A developer attacking only the facial validity of water, sewer, or processing fees, as required by Section 66022, must bring the action within 120 days of the effective date of the ordinance and cannot wait until the fee is imposed and then rely upon the pay-and-protest procedure described above. *Barratt American Inc.*, 37 Cal. 4th 685 (fees and charges described in Gov't Code §§ 66013 and 66014 are not "fees imposed on a development project" and are not subject to the pay-under-protest procedures and limitations periods of Gov't Code § 66020); *N.T. Hill, Inc.*, 72 Cal. App. 4th 977 (a developer must comply with the procedures of Government Code section 66022, rather than Government Code section 66020, when seeking a court ruling that a legislative decision adopting a capacity charge cannot be enforced due to some substantive illegality in the decision-making process).

The sole remedy upon invalidation of a fee or service charge under section 66022 is a prospective reduction in the amount of the future fee or charge, not a refund. *Barratt American Inc.*, 37 Cal. 4th 685 (remedy upon invalidation of processing fees is *reduction* of such fees based on revenues in excess of actual cost, not a refund of the excess fees); *Capistrano Beach Water*

Facial challenges to ordinances or resolutions that enact or amend water or sewer fees or capacity charges and processing fees are governed by Government Code section 66022, which established a 120-day limitations period for challenge.

District v. Taj Development Corp., 72 Cal. App. 4th 524 (1999) (water and sewer fees and capacity charges not "development impact fees," and no refund remedy is available); *see also* Govt. Code section 66016(a) ("if fees or service charges create revenues in excess of actual cost, those revenues shall be used to reduce the fee or service charge creating the excess").

A facial challenge under Government Code section 66022 must be brought as a validation action pursuant to the procedures described in Code of Civil Procedure section 860 *et seq.* Gov't Code § 66022(b). *Barratt American Inc.*, 37 Cal. 4th 685. The Legislature created the validation procedure to provide finality and protection from attacks for important, usually financial, transactions of public agencies. A validation proceeding is an action *in rem*, in which the court takes jurisdiction over the ordinance or resolution being challenged. Code Civ. Proc. § 860; *See also Bernardi v. City Council*, 54 Cal. App. 4th 426, 439 (1997). The validation statutes provide for publication of the summons in order to serve "all persons interested" in the matter being validated. Code Civ. Proc. § 861.1. The statutes also impose a short, 30-day period within which any party may appeal from the judgment. Code Civ. Proc. § 870(b). Once the appeal period has passed without an appeal being filed, or once an appeal finally is resolved, the judgment is final as against all persons, not merely the parties involved in the action:

> The judgment...shall, notwithstanding any other provision of law,...thereupon become and thereafter be forever binding and conclusive, as to all matters therein adjudicated or which at that time could have been adjudicated, against the agency and against all other persons, and the judgment shall permanently enjoin the institution by any person of any action or proceeding raising any issue as to which the judgment is binding and conclusive.

Code Civ. Proc. § 870(a)

Because a validation proceeding determines the absolute validity or invalidity of the ordinance or resolution at issue, all claims relating to the validity of that ordinance or resolution must be consolidated with the validation proceeding, and a single judgment must be entered in the consolidated action. Code Civ. Proc. § 865; *see also Comm. for Responsible Planning v. City of Indian Wells*, 225 Cal. App. 3d 191, 196 (1990). The resulting judgment then binds all persons not only as to claims that were adjudicated, but as to all claims that "at the time *could have been* adjudicated." Code Civ. Proc. § 870 (emphasis added).

The validation statutes also expressly allow a party who did not appear in the action, in certain circumstances, to appeal the judgment, and they provide that such a party may, on appeal, challenge the trial court's jurisdiction to enter a validation judgment. Code Civ. Proc. § 870(b). However, at least one court has held that parties who do not answer within the time period specified in the published summons have no right to appear in the action later. *See Green v. Cmty. Redev. Agency*, 96 Cal. App. 3d 491, 494 (1979).

Remedy

If a public agency does not calculate its development fee correctly, only the unlawful portion of the fee—*i.e.*, that which exceeds the estimated reasonable cost of providing the service for which the fee is imposed—need be refunded to the developer. *See Shapell Indus., Inc. v. Governing Bd.*, 1 Cal. App. 4th 218, 241 (1991).

The Anti-SLAPP Statute

In 1992, the Legislature enacted Code of Civil Procedure section 425.16, commonly known as the anti-SLAPP statute. "SLAPP" is an acronym for Strategic Lawsuit Against Public Participation, and the statute frequently has been invoked in actions filed by a land developer against those who object publicly to the development project. *See Wilcox v. Superior Court*, 27 Cal. App. 4th 809 (1994). *See generally*, 4 Witkin, *Calif. Procedure, Pleading*, sections 962 *et seq.* (4th ed. 1996). SLAPP suits have been described as:

> ... "civil lawsuits... that are aimed at preventing citizens from exercising their political rights or punishing those who have done so." [Citations omitted.] They are brought, not to vindicate a legal right, but rather to interfere with the defendant's ability to pursue his or her interests. Characteristically, the SLAPP suit lacks merit; it will achieve its objective if it depletes defendant's resources or energy. The aim is not to win the lawsuit but to detract the defendant from his or her objective, which is adverse to the plaintiff.

Church of Scientology v. Wollersheim, 42 Cal. App. 4th 628, 645 (1996). *See also, Wilcox*, 27 Cal. App. 4th at 815–16; *Hull v. Rossi*, 13 Cal. App. 4th 1763, 1769 (1993)

The anti-SLAPP statute is intended to protect those exercising free speech rights. It imposes a procedural burden on plaintiffs who file suits arising from the exercise of a person's right of free speech or right to petition the government. The anti-SLAPP statute allows a defendant who has been unjustly sued to bring a special motion to strike the offending cause of action early in the litigation. The statute also provides for an attorneys' fees award to either the plaintiff or defendant.

Application of the Anti-SLAPP Statute to the Land Use Context

Many SLAPP cases arise in the land use context, or involve issues relevant to land use practice. Cases involving land use initiatives have been the subject of SLAPP decisions. *See Tuchscher Dev. Enter., Inc. v. San Diego Unified Port Dist.*, 106 Cal. App. 4th 1219 (2003) (developer's action against port district for inducing breach of contract, based on alleged interference with agreement between developer and city granting developer exclusive rights to negotiate to develop bayfront property, dismissed as SLAPP suit); *Rosenaur v. Scherer*, 88 Cal. App. 4th 260 (2001) (court granted the SLAPP motion of project opponents sued by a property owner whom they accused of being a thief during a campaign regarding the property owner's pro-development initiative); *City of San Diego v. Dunkl*, 86 Cal. App. 4th 384 (2001) (no SLAPP dismissal of city's lawsuit against initiative proponents regarding the validity of their proposed ballpark redevelopment project initiative).

The statute also has been invoked in a lawsuit between competing developers. In *Ludwig v. Superior Court*, a developer's attacks on a competing mall in nearby Barstow were held subject to the protection of the anti-SLAPP statute. 37 Cal. App. 4th 8 (1995). "The development of the Barstow mall, with potential environmental effects such as increased traffic and impaction on natural drainage, was clearly a matter of public interest." *Id.* at 15.

CEQA issues have also been addressed in SLAPP decisions. The court in *Mission Oaks Ranch, Ltd. v. County of Santa Barbara* applied the SLAPP statute to dismiss a developer's claims against an environmental consultant and a county regarding the county's denial of the developer's project and the accuracy of an EIR's evaluation of the developer's project. 65 Cal. App. 4th 713 (1998), disapproved *on other grounds by Briggs v. Eden Council for Hope & Opportunity*, 19 Cal. 4th 1106, 1193, fn.10 (1999). In *Dixon v. Superior Court*, the firm that had performed the archeological testing of the site sued a university professor who opposed the development through a letter-writing campaign. 30 Cal. App. 4th 733 (1994). The court held that the professor's SLAPP motion should have been granted. It explained that because the professor's comments were made during CEQA's required public comment period, they were made in response to a matter of public concern. It further concluded that because CEQA invites public comment, the statements were entitled to absolute immunity, so the archeological testing firm could not establish a probability of prevailing at trial.

Attorneys' Fees in Land Use Cases

Attorneys' fees may be awarded under the "substantial benefit" doctrine if the lawsuit has conferred a substantial benefit on the public.

Attorneys' fees are often awarded to a winning petitioner in a land use case under one of two legal theories. Fees may be awarded under the "substantial benefit" doctrine if the lawsuit has conferred a substantial benefit on the public. *See Friends of "B" St. v. City of Hayward*, 106 Cal. App. 3d 988 (1980); *Coalition for L.A. County Planning in the Public Interest v. Board of Supervisors*, 76 Cal. App. 3d 241 (1977). The theory "permits the award of fees when the litigant, proceeding in a representative capacity, obtains a decision resulting in the conferral of a substantial benefit of a pecuniary or nonpecuniary nature. In such circumstances the court, in the exercise of its equitable discretion, thereupon may decree that justice dictates that those receiving the benefit of justice should contribute to the costs of its production." *Serrano v. Priest*, 20 Cal. 3d 25 (1977).

Attorneys' fees also may be awarded under Code of Civil Procedure section 1021.5, which allows for award of attorneys' fees in cases resulting in a public benefit under the private attorney general doctrine. *See Margolin v. Regional Planning Comm'n*, 134 Cal. App. 3d 999 (1982). The purpose of the private attorney general doctrine is simple:

> The private attorney general theory recognizes citizens frequently have common interests of significant societal importance, but which do not involve any individual's financial interests to the extent necessary to encourage private litigation to enforce the right. To encourage such suits, attorneys' fees are awarded when a significant public benefit is conferred through litigation pursued by one whose personal stake is insufficient to otherwise encourage the action. Section 1021.5 was not designed as a method for rewarding litigants motivated by their own pecuniary interests who only coincidentally protect the public interest. This last requirement effectuates public policy by focusing "on the financial burdens and incentives involved in bringing the lawsuit."

Beach Colony II Ltd. v. California Coastal Comm'n, 166 Cal. App. 3d 106, 114 (1985) (citations omitted) (fees denied to private developer)

The private attorney general doctrine grants broad discretion to the trial court to award fees, but requires a showing that the litigation:

- Served to vindicate an important public right
- Conferred a significant benefit on the general public or large class of persons
- Imposed a financial burden on the petitioner that was out of proportion to its stake in the matter

Families Unafraid to Uphold Rural El Dorado County v. County Bd. of Supervisors, 79 Cal. App. 4th 505, 511 (2000) *(Families Unafraid II)*

The most controversial factor in this analysis in land use litigation is usually the financial burden criteria. "The issue, in short, is whether the cost of litigation is out of proportion to the litigant's stake in the litigation." *California Licensed Foresters Ass'n v. State Bd. of Forestry*, 30 Cal. App. 4th 562, 574 (1994) (overturning award of fees and holding that the interest of association is to be measured according to the financial interests of the members it was representing).

For purposes of this analysis, the petitioner's stake is not limited to purely financial interests. It is possible for a petitioner to have a noneconomic stake in the litigation that outweighs the public interest and precludes an award of fees. *See Williams v. San Francisco Bd. of Permit Appeals*, 74 Cal. App. 4th 961 (1999) (trial court's discretion to deny fees to a homeowner who had a "large personal stake in the matter in preventing construction of a structure which was incompatible with the Victorian character of his neighborhood" upheld). However, for a noneconomic interest to block an award of fees, the interest must be specific, concrete, and significant, as established by objective evidence. An abstract or subjective interest in aesthetic integrity or environmental preservation will not automatically preclude an award of fees. *See Families Unafraid II*, 79 Cal. App. 4th at 516.

Fees will be limited to those incurred by the petitioner when it obtained its initial victory. Fees incurred in unsuccessful subsequent challenges to an agency's actions regarding the same development project cannot be recovered. *See National Parks & Conser. Ass'n v. County of Riverside*, 81 Cal. App. 4th 234 (2000) (association that recovered fees on successful challenge to EIR held not entitled to recover fees on unsuccessful challenge to the county's return to the writ in the same case). Moreover, the reversal of a judgment pursuant to which a petitioner was awarded fees ensures reversal of the fee award. *See Metropolitan Water Dist. v. Imperial Irr. Dist.*, 80 Cal. App. 4th 1403, 1436 (2000) (citing cases and explaining "[t]he parties have also appealed from the trial court's post-judgment order variously awarding and denying costs and attorney's fees. Our reversal of the judgment in favor of defendants requires we vacate the attorney fee and cost award in their favor.").

The fee award may run against not only the respondent agency, but also a developer that was named a real party in interest. In *San Bernardino Valley Audubon Society, Inc. v. County of San Bernardino*, the court required both the county and developer to pay the attorney's fees incurred by the Audubon Society. 155 Cal. App. 3d 738 (1984). The court reasoned that the developer should share in the blame for the county's failure to follow CEQA requirements since the developer was involved in filing the application and should have been monitoring the process. On the other hand, an *amicus curiae* is not liable for attorneys' fees under CCP section 1021.5 where its role is to advocate a position based on its own views of what is legally correct and beneficial to the public

Fees will be limited to those incurred by the petitioner when it obtained its initial victory. Fees incurred in unsuccessful subsequent challenges to an agency's actions regarding the same development project cannot be recovered.

The fee award also may run against one public agency in favor of another.

rather than out of direct interest in the litigation. *Connerly v. State Personnel Board*, 37 Cal. 4th 1169, 1183 (2006).

The fee award also may run against one public agency in favor of another. In 1993, the Legislature amended Code of Civil Procedures section 1021.5 to provide that "[w]ith respect to actions involving public entities, this section applies to allowances against, but not in favor of, public entities, and no claim shall be required to be filed therefore, unless one or more successful parties and one or more opposing parties are public entities...." *See also City of Hawaiian Gardens v. City of Long Beach*, 61 Cal. App. 4th 1100 (1998) (fees denied to petitioner city because it did not show that its burden of litigation outweighed its interest in the controversy, as case was tried primarily on pre-existing administrative record with brief trial court hearing).

Attorneys' fees are also available to a defendant who prevails in a SLAPP motion, and to a plaintiff who successfully defends against a meritless anti-SLAPP motion. Code Civ. Proc. § 425.16(c).

22
Conclusion

City officials have three roles in land use matters. First, they take on a legislative role, planning for development by adopting the general plan, and perhaps a specific plan or plans, as well as implementing zoning and other ordinances and resolutions. Second, city officials review project proposals in a nonlegislative, quasi-judicial, adjudicatory capacity for consistency with the relevant planning documents and ordinances. Finally, they implement the city's vision of development by ensuring that any project that is approved complies with the applicable laws and conditions imposed. While there is more latitude in the legislative as opposed to nonlegislative role, in each instance specified, proper decision-making processes must be followed to survive judicial challenge.

Court challenges to a city's power to adopt, apply, implement, and enforce land use and planning regulations as violations of the police power are likely to be successful only under very limited circumstances. The United States Supreme Court, federal courts, and California courts generally uphold a city's action so long as it is not arbitrary or capricious, substantially advances a legitimate governmental interest and does not deny an owner economically viable use of its land. In the last 30 years, only a handful of court decisions have struck down a city's land use ordinance or decision because it went beyond the bounds of its police power.

Indeed, in a unanimous decision, the California Supreme Court held that a city's police power is as broad as the police power of the Legislature itself. *See Candid Enters., Inc. v. Grossmont Union High Sch. Dist.*, 39 Cal. 3d 878, 886 (1985). However, if the power is not exercised within constitutional mandates or statutory provisions as set forth by the Legislature, the decision may be overturned. Thus, it is imperative that a city respect constitutional and statutory mandates, such as adopting a valid general plan, conducting the required hearings, making the necessary findings, and following the California Environmental Quality Act. In comparison to the relatively few successful cases brought challenging a city's decision on substantive grounds, many court decisions have invalidated a city's decision on procedural grounds.

One of the most frustrating aspects of land use planning is to see a wise policy decision set aside by the courts because a staff person failed to give

Court challenges to a city's power to adopt, apply, implement, and enforce land use and planning regulations as violations of the police power are likely to be successful only under very limited circumstances.

proper notice, a decision-making body failed to make the necessary findings, or a city failed to have a legally adequate general plan. Not only is it likely that the city or developer will incur additional expenses in the form of substantial attorneys' fees payable to the prevailing party, but the value of the time and money devoted to the project may be lost permanently and unnecessarily.

> *After all, if a policeman must know the constitution, then why not a planner?*
>
> **William J. Brennan, Jr.**
> Former Associate Justice
> United States Supreme Court
> *San Diego Gas & Elec. Co. v.
> City of San Diego*, 450 U.S. 621 (1981)

Glossary*

abandonment

A cessation of the use of the property by the owner with the intention neither of transferring rights to another owner nor resuming use of the property.

abatement

The method of reducing the degree and intensity of a problem or pollution.

abutting

Having property or zone district boundaries in common; *e.g.*, two lots abut if they have property lines in common.

access

A way of approaching or entering a property. In zoning and subdivision regulations, a lot of record usually is required to have direct access to a public street or highway or to a private street meeting public standards. In the context of land use controls, access includes ingress, the right to enter, and egress, the right to leave.

accessory building or use

An activity or structure on a property that is incidental and subordinate to the main use.

adaptive reuse

The development of a new use for an older building. Often used in reference to a proposal to convert buildings of historic significance to a use different from the original intended use.

Administrative Procedures Act (APA)

The procedures for state departments to adopt their administrative regulations. Gov't Code § 11340 *et seq.*

advisory election

Local officials can put nonbinding questions on local ballots. Elec. Code § 9603.

agricultural conservation easement

Landowners and local officials can voluntarily restrict land to an agricultural use. Pub. Res Code § 10260 *et seq. Also see*, "conservation easement" and "open space easement."

air rights

The rights to the space above a property, for development, usually for a dissimilar use.

Alquist-Priolo Earthquake Fault Zoning Act

Local officials must adopt earthquake fault zoning, based on state maps. Pub. Res. Code § 2621 *et seq.*

ALUC (Airport Land Use Commission)

Every county with a public use airport has an ALUC that must adopt binding land use plans. Pub. Util. Code § 21670 *et seq.*

ambient air

The unconfined outside atmosphere.

amendment, zoning (rezoning)

An amendment to or a change in the zoning ordinance.

amortization

The process by which nonconforming uses and structures must be discontinued or made to conform to requirements of the ordinance at the end of a specified period of time.

annexation

The inclusion of a land area into an existing city or special district with a resulting change in the boundaries of that local agency.

anti-NIMBY law

Cities and counties must approve certain housing developments, even if neighbors object. Gov't Code § 65589.5. In 2006, the title of the anti-NIMBY law was changed to the "Housing Accountability Act."

appeal

Request that another, usually higher, authority review or reconsider a decision.

assessed valuation

The value at which property is appraised for tax purposes.

Bagley-Keene Open Meeting Law

The open meeting law for state agencies, similar to the Brown Act. Gov't Code § 11120 *et seq.*

base map

A map having sufficient points of reference, such as state, county or municipal boundary lines, streets, easements, and

---

* Portions of this glossary were derived from "The Quick List," prepared by the staff of the Senate Local Government Committee (www.sen.ca.gov/locgov) and the Planners Pocket Guide published by the League of California Cities.

other selected physical features to allow the plotting of other data.

BCDC (San Francisco Bay Conservation and Development Commission)
The state commission that plans and regulates land use under and around the San Francisco Bay. Gov't Code § 66600 et seq.

benefit assessment (special assessment)
Involuntary charge on property owners to pay for public works that directly benefit property.

biota
All the species of plants and animals occurring within a certain area.

blighted area
In redevelopment law, predominately urbanized area prevalently characterized by the conditions contained in Health and Safety Code section 33031.

Board of Zoning Adjustment
A local body that considers requests for variances, i.e., deviations from normal zoning ordinances.

bond
Most local bonds require voter approval or a property owner's approval; e.g., general obligation bonds for cities, counties, and special districts need two-thirds voter approval. Cal. Const. Art. XVI, § 18(a); general obligation bonds for school districts require 55 percent voter approval. Cal. Const. Art. XVI, § 18(b); revenue bonds require majority-voter approval. Gov't Code § 54300 et seq.; assessment bonds require property owner's approval in a weighted ballot election. Cal. Const. Art. XIII D, § 4 and Gov't Code § 53753.

bond oversight
Local officials must issue annual reports on how they spend bond funds. Gov't Code § 53410 et seq.

Bradley-Burns Uniform Local Sales and Use Tax Law
Counties and cities levy sales taxes for general purposes. Rev. & Tax. Code § 7200 et seq.

Brown Act
Open meeting law for local governments. Gov't Code § 54950 et seq.

buffer zone
A strip of land zoned to protect one type of land use from another with which it is incompatible.

building coverage
The amount of land covered or permitted to be covered by a building, usually measured in terms of percentage of a lot, or floor area ratio.

building envelope
The space remaining on a site for structures after building setbacks, height limits, and bulk requirements are met.

capital improvement program
A governmental budget that schedules the construction of public facilities to fit its fiscal capability into the future. A planning commission reviews the capital improvement program, thereby linking planning to the annual budgeting process.

census tract
A small portion of a populated area in which data is collected for statistical analysis.

Central Business District (CBD)
A major commercial and business area usually located near the center of the community that has historically served as the city's primary commercial district.

CEQA (California Environmental Quality Act)
The statute requiring public agencies to identify and consider the environmental effects of a development project. Pub. Res. Code § 21000 et seq.

CEQA Guidelines
The state regulations that interpret CEQA. 14 Cal. Code Reg. § 15000 et seq.

certificate of compliance
This term has three distinctly different meanings: (1) it is commonly used synonymously with a zoning permit in which an official certifies that the plans for a proposed use conform with the zoning ordinance; (2) certificate issued pursuant to Map Act which states that the division of property is in compliance with the State Subdivision Map Act and local subdivision ordinances; (3) the term may also mean an enforcement device that, in reference to a certain class of structure (usually multiple-family dwellings), incorporates in one document an indication of conformance, or lack thereof, with the several municipal codes—zoning, building, housing, occupancy—that may apply to a specific property.

certificate of occupancy
Official certification that the premises conforms to provisions of the zoning ordinance (and building code) and may be used or occupied. Such a certificate is granted for new construction or for alteration or additions to an existing structure. Unless such a certificate is issued, a structure cannot be occupied.

charter city
A city incorporated under its own charter rather than under the general laws of the state. Charter cities have broader powers than do general law cities in matters of municipal affairs. Cal. Const. Art. XI, § 3 and § 5; Gov't Code § 34400 et seq. and § 34450 et seq.

city council district
Voters can elect city council members "by divisions" or "from divisions." Gov't Code § 34870 et seq.

city council vacancy
A vacancy on a city council is filled by appointment or election. Gov't Code § 1770 and § 36513.

city ordinance
Procedures for adopting city ordinances and penalties for violations. Gov't Code § 36900 et seq.

Clean Air Act
A federal act establishing national air quality standards.

Coastal Act
State law requires special planning and permits for development in the coastal zone. Pub. Res. Code § 30000 et seq.

Coastal Commission
State agency that reviews development plans within the Coastal Zone according to the California Coastal Act of 1976.

common open space
Land within or related to a development, not individually owned or dedicated for public use, that is designed and intended for the common use or enjoyment of the development's residents.

common ownership
Ownership by one or more individuals of two or more contiguous parcels of property in any form of ownership.

Community Facilities District (Mello-Roos)

Local agencies can levy special taxes to pay for public works and some public services. Gov't Code § 53311 *et seq.*

Community Redevelopment Law (redevelopment)

Redevelopment agencies use tax increment revenue and eminent domain in blighted areas. Health & Safety Code § 33000 *et seq.*

comprehensive plan

See general plan.

condemnation

The exercise by a governmental agency of the right of eminent domain to acquire property.

conditional rezoning

The attachment of special conditions to a rezoning that are not spelled out in the text of the zoning ordinance.

conditional use permit (special use permit)

Permit allowing a use under specified conditions which assure that the use will not be detrimental to the public health, safety, and welfare and will not impair the integrity and character of the zoned district.

conditions, covenants, and restrictions (CC&Rs)

The requirements and limitations placed on each lot of a subdivision or condominium project intended to protect the individual property as well as the general public regarding placement, construction, appearance, and maintenance of buildings and common areas.

condominium

A dwelling unit in a residential development (or space in an office or commercial project) that is under a legal arrangement specifying that the unit is individually owned but the common areas are owned, controlled, and maintained through an organization consisting of all the individual owners.

condominium association

The community association that administers and maintains the common property and common elements of a condominium.

conflict of interest

Public officials may not participate in decisions in which they have a financial interest. Gov't Code § 1090 *et seq.* and § 87100 *et seq.*; 2 Cal. Code Reg. § 18700.

conservation easement

Landowners can grant an easement to preserve open space and prohibit future or additional development. Civ. Code § 815 *et seq.*

contract city ("Gonsalves Act")

A city can contract with the county for municipal services. Gov't Code § 51350.

contracts and bidding

State law spells out bidding and contract procedures for cities, counties, and special districts. *See* city (Pub. Cont. Code § 20160 *et seq.*); county (Pub. Cont. Code § 20120 *et seq.* and § 20150 *et seq.*); and district (chart at Pub. Cont. Code § 20100 *et seq.*).

Cortese-Knox-Hertzberg Local Government Reorganization Act (LAFCO)

State law that governs city and special district boundaries; and also creates a LAFCO in every county. Gov't Code § 56000 *et seq.*

Council of Government (COG)

A regional planning agency between counties and cities that prepares regional plans primarily concerned with transportation planning and housing. Gov't Code § 6500 *et seq.*

county charter

A county can adopt and revise its charter giving it limited local autonomy. Cal. Const. Art. XI § 4; Gov't Code § 23700 *et seq.*

county formation

Procedures for forming a new county. Gov't Code § 23300 *et seq.*

county officers, named and classified

State law spells out the names and duties of county officers. Gov't Code § 24000 *et seq.* and § 24300 *et seq.*

county ordinance

Procedures for adopting county ordinances and penalties for violations. Gov't Code § 25120 *et seq.*

culvert

Drain, ditch, or conduit not incorporated in a closed system that carries drainage water under a driveway, roadway, railroad, pedestrian walk, or public way.

cut

A portion of land surface or area from which earth is removed by excavation; also, the depth below the original ground surface.

Davis-Stirling Common Interest Development Act

State law that governs common interest developments (homeowners' associations). Civ. Code § 1350 *et seq.*

decibel (dB)

Unit of sound pressure level that is used to express noise level.

dedication

Action by a property owner that turns over private land for a public use, and its acceptance for such use by the government agency in charge of the public function for which it will be used. Dedications for streets, parks, school sites, or other public uses are often made conditions for approval of a development.

dedication, payment in lieu of

Cash payment required from a property developer as a substitute for a dedication of land.

deed restriction

A private legal restriction on the use of land that is contained in the deed to the property or otherwise formally recorded.

demolition permit

A permit a local authority issues to allow a building or structure to be razed.

density

The average number of families, persons, or housing units per unit of land; usually density is expressed "per acre." Gross density typically includes the area necessary for streets, schools, and parks. Net density does not typically include land for public facilities.

density bonus

Financial incentive to a developer that builds affordable housing. Gov't Code § 65915 *et seq.*

density transfer

Process that permits unused allowable densities in one area to be used in another area. Where density transfer is permitted, the average density over an area would remain constant, but allow for internal variations.

density zoning

Device for averaging residential density over an entire parcel and placing no restrictions on lot size or dwelling type. Under this approach, any type of dwelling is permitted, from a detached house to an apartment anywhere on the site, so long as total density does not exceed the maximum permitted. The only development standards imposed are: distance between buildings, distance between facing windows, amount of parking, and minimum open space. Conventional setback and lot-size requirements are dropped.

detention basin (pond)

An open storage pond for the temporary storage of stormwater runoff.

developer fee or development impact fee

Counties and cities can charge a developer an impact fee to pay for public facilities. Gov't Code § 66000 *et seq.*

development agreement

An agreement adopted by ordinance between a developer and a city or county establishing the conditions under which a particular development may occur. The local government "freezes" the regulations applicable to the site for an agreed-upon period prior to actual development to allow preparation and approval of plans. Gov't Code § 65864 *et seq.*

development rights

Broad range of less-than-fee-simple ownership interests, mainly referring to easements. The property owner would keep title but agree to continue using the land as it had been used in the past, with the right to develop resting with the holder of the development rights. Such rights usually are expressed in terms of the density allowed under existing zoning.

development timing or development phasing

Rate and geographic sequence of the development of a project.

district

Section of a city or county designated in the zoning ordinance text and usually delineated on the zoning map within which certain zoning or development regulations apply.

downzoning

Change in the zoning classification of land to one permitting development that is less intensive or dense, such as from multi- to single-family or from commercial to residential. A change in the opposite direction is called upzoning.

due process

Generally, a requirement that legal proceedings be carried out in accordance with established rules and principles. Procedural due process assures that all parties to a proceeding are treated fairly and equally; citizens have a right to have their views heard; necessary information is available for informed opinions to be developed; conflicts of interest are avoided; and, generally, the appearance, as well as the fact of fairness exists.

easement

The portion of a property for which access or use is allowed by a person or agency other than the owner.

effluent

Discharge of pollutants, with or without treatment, into the environment.

eminent domain

Legal right of public entities to acquire or take private property for public use or public purpose upon paying just compensation and due process to the owner. Cal. Const. Art. I, § 19; Code Civ. Proc. § 1230.010 *et seq.*

emission standard

Maximum amount of a pollutant legally permitted to be discharged from a single source, either mobile or stationary.

encroachment

Any obstruction or protrusion into a right of way or adjacent property, whether on the land or above it.

environmental impact report (EIR)

An EIR is the public document used by government agencies pursuant to CEQA which analyzes the significant environmental effects of a proposed project, compares alternatives and discusses possible methods to reduce or avoid the environmental impacts. When no significant environmental impact will result, a "negative declaration" is issued.

environmental impact statement (EIS)

Environmental impact document prepared in accordance with the National Environmental Policy Act (NEPA).

ethics training

Elected and key appointed officials must take biennial ethics training courses. Gov't Code § 53234 *et seq.*

exclusionary zoning

Zoning regulations that result in the exclusion of low- and moderate-income or minority persons from a community.

Fair Political Practices Commission (FPPC)

The state commission that administers the Political Reform Act. Gov't Code § 81000 *et seq.* and § 83100 *et seq.*

fair share housing plan

Plan designed to promote equitable distribution of low- and moderate-income housing opportunities among all the communities in a region.

final subdivision map

Map of an approved subdivision that is recorded, usually showing surveyed lot lines, street rights-of-way, easements, monuments, and distances, angles, and bearings pertaining to the exact dimensions of all parcels, street lines, etc.

findings

Specific facts and required statements serving as the legal basis for certain actions by the local decision-making body.

fire protection district

Special district that provides fire protection and other emergency services. Health & Safety Code § 13800 *et seq.*

flood plain

The channel and the adjoining area of a natural stream or river that is susceptible to flooding.

floor area, gross

The sum of the gross horizontal areas of all the floors of a building measured from the exterior face of exterior walls, or from the center line of a wall separating two buildings, but not including interior parking spaces, loading space for motor vehicles, or any space where the floor-to-ceiling height is less than six feet.

floor area ratio (FAR)

Gross floor area of all buildings on a lot divided by the lot area.

Glossary

form-based zoning

Zoning regulations emphasizing design and physical form of buildings, streetscapes and public places with less emphasis on allowed uses inside buildings.

general law city

Most cities rely on state laws to spell out their governance structure and duties. Gov't Code § 36501 *et seq.*

general plan

Required legal document adopted by the local legislative body to establish the policies of a city or county regarding its jurisdiction and long-term development in the form of a map and accompanying textual elements. Sometimes called a comprehensive plan or master plan, it is the constitution for development. Gov't Code § 65300 *et seq.*

general plan guidelines

OPR's advisory guidelines on how to prepare a general plan. Gov't Code § 65040.2.

general tax

General tax revenues are used for general purposes and require approval by a majority of the voters. Cal. Const. Art. XIII C, § 2; Gov't Code § 53720 *et seq.*

geologic hazard abatement district (GHAD)

District that finances the prevention, mitigation, abatement, or control of geologic hazards. Pub. Res Code § 26500 *et seq.*

grade

The rate of rise or descent of a sloping surface, usually expressed in degrees or in a percentage calculated by the number of feet of rise or drop per 100-foot horizontal distance.

granny unit

A dwelling unit for the sole occupancy of one or two adults, 62 years or older, comprising less than 30 percent of the existing primary living area or 1,200 square feet. Gov't Code § 65852.1.

gross leasable area (GLA)

Total floor area for which a tenant pays rent that is designed for that tenant's occupancy and exclusive use.

ground coverage

The amount of land covered or permitted to be covered by a building, usually measured in terms of percentage of a lot.

groundwater

Supply of freshwater under the earth's surface in an aquifer or soil that forms the natural reservoir for potable water.

group care facility

Facility or dwelling unit housing persons unrelated by blood or marriage that provides care beyond simply lodging. Such facilities may include halfway houses; recovery homes; and homes for orphans, foster children, the elderly, battered children, and women, etc.

highest and best use

The use of a property that will bring to its owners the greatest profit.

home occupation

Any activity a resident conducts for monetary gain that is an accessory use in the resident's dwelling unit.

homeowner association

Nonprofit organization representing the particular interests of homeowners. Homeowner associations normally operate under recorded legal agreements attached to ownership of land.

housing element

Part of a general plan that spells out housing data, goals, and implementation programs. Gov't Code § 65580 *et seq.*

hydrology

A branch of science that deals with the properties, distribution, and circulation of water and snow.

impervious surface

Any material that prevents absorption of water into previously undeveloped land.

incentive zoning

The granting by local authority of additional development capacity in exchange for the developer's provision of a public benefit or amenity.

inclusionary zoning

A zoning policy and program to require the provision of affordable housing as part of new residential development.

infill development

Development of new housing or other buildings on scattered vacant sites in a built-up area.

infrastructure

Physical facilities and services needed to sustain industry, residential and commercial activities, such as streets, sewers, utilities, etc.

infrastructure finance

State law provides several ways for local governments to pay for public works.

infrastructure financing district (IFD)

District that uses property tax increment revenues to pay for public works in non-blighted areas. Gov't Code § 53395 *et seq.*

initial study

Under CEQA, a preliminary analysis of the potential environmental impacts of a proposed project. Where the lead agency finds that the project may individually or cumulatively have a significant effect on the environment, an EIR must be prepared. The potential environmental impacts identified in the initial study become the focus of the EIR.

initiative

A ballot measure used to enact new legislation. In California, city and county initiative measures may be placed on the ballot by petition of the voters or action of the legislative body.

interim zoning development control

Device to freeze or severely restrict development of an area for a short period, during which a comprehensive plan or new land use regulations are prepared.

inverse condemnation

The effective taking or reduction in value of a property as a result of public action, in contrast to a direct taking through eminent domain.

JPA (joint powers agreement, joint powers agency)

Public agencies can enter into agreements to jointly exercise any common power. Gov't Code § 6500 *et seq.*

just compensation

The appropriate payment made to a private property owner by an agency with power of eminent domain when the private property is taken for public use.

LAFCO (local agency formation commission)

Commission in each county that regulates annexations, detachments, and incorporations. Gov't Code § 56000 *et seq.*

Landscaping and Lighting Act of 1972

Local officials can charge a benefit assessment to pay for public works and public services. Sts. & High. Code § 22500 *et seq.*

lead agency

Public agency with the principal responsibility for carrying out or approving a project. Under CEQA, the lead agency is also responsible for preparing and certifying an adequate EIR.

lot, coverage

Portion of a lot covered by buildings and structures.

lot line, front

The frontage or front of a lot is usually defined as the side nearest the street. The definition used is important because it may affect yard requirements.

lot line, rear

Ordinarily that line of a lot that is opposite and farthest from the front lot line. In triangular or other odd-shaped lots, the planning commission or other public body with jurisdiction may need to define the rear lot line.

lot line, side

Any lot line other than ones for the front or rear of a property.

lot of record

Lot that is part of a subdivision or a parcel of land which has been recorded, usually at a county recorder's office where property tax records are kept.

lot split

See parcel map.

lot, through (or double frontage)

Lot abutting on two parallel or approximately parallel streets.

low-income housing

Housing that is economically feasible for persons whose income level is categorized as low within the standards set by the U.S. Department of Housing and Urban Development or the appropriate state housing agency.

Mello-Roos Community Facilities Act (Mello-Roos Act)

Local agencies can levy special taxes to pay for public works and some public services. *See also* "community facilities district." Gov't Code § 53311 *et seq.*

metes and bounds

System of describing or identifying land using measure (metes) and direction (bounds) from an identifiable point of reference such as a monument or other marker, the corner of intersecting streets, or, in rural areas, a tree or other permanent feature.

Mills Act (historic preservation)

An owner can contract to preserve an historic property and thereby obtain a lower property tax assessment. Gov't Code § 50280 *et seq.*; Rev. & Tax. Code § 439.

minor land division

A division of contiguous property into four or fewer lots.

mitigated negative declaration (MND)

Under CEQA, a negative declaration that includes measures needed to mitigate or avoid a project's significant effects on the environment.

mitigation

Actions, improvements, features, modifications, or requirements intended to eliminate or reduce the significant environmental effects of a project.

mitigation monitoring program

Program adopted as part of a mitigated negative declaration or environmental impact report that establishes a reporting system designed to ensure compliance with the conditions adopted as part of the MND or EIR during project implementation.

mixed use development

Development of a tract of land or building with two or more different uses.

mixed use zoning

Zoning that permits a combination of usually separated uses within a single development. Many planned unit development ordinances permit combinations of various residential densities and commercial uses.

mobile home

A structure transportable in one or more sections that is at least 8 feet in width and 32 feet in length, built on a permanent chassis, and designed for use as a dwelling unit, with or without a permanent foundation, when connected to the required utilities.

moderate-income housing

Housing that is economically feasible for families whose income level is categorized as moderate within the standards set by the U.S. Department of Housing and Urban Development or the appropriate state housing agency.

moratorium

In planning, a temporary freeze or restriction on all new development pending completion and adoption of certain planning or zoning ordinance requirements, *e.g.*, general plan, zoning ordinance amendment, sewer line installations, or growth management programs.

multiple use

Harmonious use of the land for more than one purpose; not necessarily the combination of uses that will yield the highest economic return, *e.g.*, a mix of residential and commercial development in the same area.

National Environmental Policy Act (NEPA)

Enacted in 1969, NEPA contains a declaration of policy expressing a commitment to environmental values and a requirement that federal agencies prepare an environmental impact statement for any project that may adversely affect the environment.

negative declaration

Under CEQA, a statement that describes why a project will not have a significant adverse effect on the environment, and that may propose measures to avoid all possible adverse effects.

net area of lot (net acreage)

The area of the lot excluding those features or areas that the development ordinance excludes from the calculations.

nonconforming lot

Lot that does not meet current zoning requirements.

nonconforming structure or building

Building that does not meet current zoning requirements.

nonconforming use

Land use that does not meet current zoning requirements.

notice of completion (NOC)

A notice issued and properly filed by the lead agency upon completion of a draft EIR. The NOC contains a description of the project and its location, an address where copies of the draft EIR are available, and the period during which comments will be received on the draft EIR.

notice of determination (NOD)

A notice issued and properly filed by an agency upon its approval of a project subject to CEQA regulation indicating whether the project will have a significant effect on the environment and whether an EIR has been prepared. (The NOD is filed with the State Secretary of Resources if the lead agency is a state agency and with the county clerk if the lead agency is a local agency.)

notice of preparation (NOP)

A notice sent by a lead agency announcing its intention to prepare an EIR for a proposed project, inviting responsible and trustee agencies and other interested parties to state their concerns regarding potential impacts. The responses are then used to further define the EIR's scope.

occupancy permit

Permit needed for a new tenant to move into a commercial or industrial building.

Office of Planning and Research (OPR)

Part of the Office of the Governor that works on land use planning and environmental quality. Gov't Code § 65025 *et seq.*

off-site improvement

Improvement or facility that may be required of a project—such as the installation of streets, curbs, gutters, sidewalks, street trees, etc., that are located adjacent to publicly-owned property.

open space easement

A landowner can grant an easement to protect open space and prohibit development. *See also* "conservation easement." Gov't Code § 51070 *et seq.*

ordinance

Law adopted by a city council or board of supervisors. *See* Gov't Code § 36900 *et seq.* (cities); Gov't Code § 25120 *et seq.* (counties).

overlay zone

Set of zoning requirements in addition to those of the underlying district. Developments within an overlay zone must conform to the requirements of both zones or the more restrictive of the two.

parcel

Lot, or contiguous group of lots in single ownership or under single control, and usually considered a unit for purposes of development.

parcel map

A subdivision map that divides a parcel into four or fewer lots.

parcel tax (special tax)

A special tax levied by local governments with two-thirds voter approval. Gov't Code § 50075 *et seq.*

partial taking

The condemnation of part of a property.

payment in lieu

Payment of cash that is authorized in subdivision regulations when requirements for mandatory dedication of land cannot be met because of the site's physical conditions or other reasons.

peak-hour traffic

The largest number of vehicles passing over a designated section of a street during the busiest one-hour period of a 24-hour period.

performance standard

Minimum requirement or maximum allowable limit on the effects or characteristics of a use, usually written in the form of regulatory language. Performance standards in zoning might describe allowable uses with respect to smoke, odor, noise, heat, vibration, glare, traffic generation, visual impact, etc., instead of the more traditional classifications of "light" or "heavy" uses.

Permit Streamlining Act

Public agencies must meet statutory deadlines for decisions on development projects. Gov't Code § 65920 *et seq.*

permitted use

Use specifically authorized in a particular zoning district, in contrast to a conditional use that is authorized only if certain requirements are met and after review and approval by the appropriate public agency.

phased development control (phased control)

Term that refers to programs or techniques to guide the timing and sequence of development. In one form of phased zoning, land designated for residential use but presently undeveloped could receive permission to subdivide only if the developer can show the availability of adequate public services such as sewers, drainage, park sites, and roads.

planned development (P-D)

Self-contained development, often with a mixture of land uses and densities, in which the subdivision and zoning controls are applied to the project as a whole rather than to individual lots. Commercial and even industrial uses are combined with different types of residential uses. A planned development with only residential uses is referred to as a residential planned development (PR-D).

planned unit development (PUD)

Land use zoning that allows for adoption of a set of development standards specific to a particular project. PUD zones usually do not contain the kind of detailed development standards that are established when proposals are being considered and subsequently adopted by ordinance upon project approval.

Planning Commission

The body, appointed by the city council or board of supervisors, charged with developing the general plan, formulating and administering the zoning map and ordinance, and reviewing development applications.

Planning Director

A planning department's chief administrator.

plat

(1) A map representing a tract of land, showing the boundaries and location of individual properties and streets; (2) a map of a subdivision or site plan.

plot

Often an indefinite term usually referring to a piece of usable property; often used synonymously with parcel or site, and mistakenly, to mean plat.

point source

A stationary source of a large individual emission, generally industrial in nature; for example, a waste discharge pipe or a waste dump.

police power

The authority of government to exercise controls to protect the public's health, safety, and general welfare. Cal. Const. Art. XI, § 7.

Political Reform Act of 1974

Prohibits a public official from having an economic conflict of interest. Gov't Code § 81000 et seq.

PPM

Parts per million.

prezoning

The zoning of unincorporated territory by a city before annexation. Gov't Code § 65859.

property tax allocation

Allocation of property tax revenue to local governments and schools. Revenue and Taxation Code § 95 et seq.

Proposition 1A (1998)

Protects local governments' financing from the state government. Cal. Const. Art. XI § 15, Art. XIII § 25.5, and Art. XIII B § 6.

Proposition 13 (1978)

Limits property tax rate to one percent, limits reassessments, requires voter approval for special taxes. Cal. Const. Art. XIII A.

Proposition 62 (1986)

Requires voter approval for local special taxes and most local general taxes. Gov't Code § 53720 et seq.

Proposition 218 (1996)

Requires voter or property owner approval for local taxes, assessments, and fees. Cal. Const. Arts. XIII C and XIII D; Gov't Code § 53750 et seq.

public domain

All land owned by government.

public hearing

A meeting announced and advertised in advance and open to the public, at which the public has an opportunity to talk and participate.

public improvement

Any improvement, facility, or service together with its associated public site or right-of-way intended to provide transportation, drainage, public or private utilities, energy, or similar essential services.

Public Records Act

Requires public access to public records, with limited exceptions. Gov't Code § 6250 et seq.

publication requirements

Laws governing the publication of public notices. Gov't Code § 6000 et seq.

Quimby Act

Cities and counties can require a subdivider to dedicate land for parks. Gov't Code § 66477.

Redevelopment (Community Redevelopment Law)

A redevelopment agency can use tax-increment revenues and eminent domain to revitalize a blighted area. Cal. Const. Art. XVI, § 16; Health & Safety Code § 33000 et seq.

referendum

A citizen challenge to legislative action taken by a city or county. If enough citizen signatures are filed, the city council or board of supervisors must either rescind its decision or call an election on the issue.

responsible agency

Any public agency other than the lead agency with the power of discretionary project approval. A responsible agency sends comments to the lead agency regarding environmental impacts about which they have expertise.

restrictive covenant

A restriction on the use of land usually set forth in the deed.

reuse

A use for an existing building or parcel of land other than the one for which it was originally intended.

right-of-way

Strip of land acquired by reservation, dedication, forced dedication, prescription, or condemnation and that is occupied or intended to be occupied by a road, crosswalk, railroad, electric transmission line, oil or gas pipeline, water line, sanitary storm sewer, and other similar uses.

riparian land

Land traversed or bounded by a natural watercourse or adjoining tidal lands.

riparian rights

Rights of a landowner to the water on or bordering his property, including the right to make use of such waters and to prevent diversion or misuse of upstream water.

"run with the land"

Term for a covenant or restriction—either contained in a deed or imposed by local government through an ordinance—that is binding on the present and all future owners of the property.

scenic easement

Legal device for protecting scenic views and associated aesthetic qualities of a site by restricting change in existing features without government approval.

school developer fees

A school district can levy developer fees to pay for a new school. Education Code § 17620; Gov't Code § 65995.

second unit

Attached or detached residential dwelling providing complete independent living facilities for one or more persons. Gov't Code § 658522.

setback

Minimum distance that zoning requires be maintained between two structures or between a structure and a property line.

site plan

A plan, to scale, showing uses and structures proposed for a parcel of land. The site plan includes lot lines, streets, building sites, public open space, buildings, major landscape features—both natural and man-made—and, depending on requirements, the locations of proposed utility lines.

Soil Erosion and Sediment Control Plan

A plan that indicates necessary land treatment measures, including a schedule for installation, that will effectively minimize soil erosion and sedimentation.

solar access
A property owner's right to have sunlight shine on his land or buildings.

solid waste management
A program providing for the collection, storage, and disposal of solid waste including, where appropriate, recycling and recovery.

special assessment (benefit assessment)
Fee a local authority levies for the financing of a local improvement that is primarily of benefit to the landowners who must pay the assessment.

special district
A local government that provides limited services and facilities to a defined geographic area. Gov't Code § 50077(d); Rev. & Tax. Code § 95(m).

special district's principal acts
State laws that govern each type of special district. For example, Community Services District Law is Government Code section 61000 *et seq.*

special tax
Special tax revenues are restricted to special uses. Special taxes require two-thirds voter approval. Cal. Const. Arts. XIII A, § 4 and XIII C, § 2; Gov't Code § 50075 *et seq.*, § 53722 *et seq.*, and § 53970 *et seq.*

specific plan
Plan adopted by a city or county to implement its general plan for designated areas. A special plan contains the locations and standards for land use densities, streets, and other public facilities in greater detail than the general plan map and text. Gov't Code § 65450 *et seq.*

sphere of influence
The probable ultimate physical boundary and service limits of a local agency as approved by a LAFCO, identifying the area available to a city for future annexation.

spot zoning
Zoning of an isolated parcel in a manner inconsistent or incompatible with surrounding zoning or land uses, particularly if done to favor a particular landowner.

State Clearinghouse
Part of the Governor's Office of Planning and Research that is responsible for distributing environmental documents to state agencies, boards, and departments.

stormwater detention
Any storm drainage technique that retards or detains runoff, such as a detention or retention basin, parking lot storage, rooftop storage, porous pavement, dry wells, or any combination thereof.

street, arterial
A street with access control, channelized intersections, and restricted parking that collects and distributes traffic from one area of a community to another.

street, collector
A street that collects traffic from local streets and connects with arterials.

street, local
A street designed to provide vehicular access to abutting property and discourage through traffic.

strip zone
A zone normally consisting of a ribbon of uses fronting on one or both sides of a major street and extending inward for approximately one-half block. Strip commercial development is the most common form.

Subdivided Lands Act
Land can be divided into five or more parcels for sale, lease, or finance. Bus. & Prof. Code § 11000 *et seq.*

subdivision
Division of any unit or units of land for the purpose of sale, lease, or financing.

Subdivision Map Act
State law regulates the subdivision of land with tentative maps and parcel maps. Gov't Code § 66410 *et seq.*

taking
The appropriation by government of private land for which compensation must be paid.

tentative subdivision map
A map showing the design and improvement of a proposed subdivision of five or more lots that includes existing conditions in and around a subdivision. At this stage a city or county must place on the map all the restrictions deemed necessary. The term "tentative" is misleading, because additional conditions or substantive design changes cannot be required once a tentative subdivision map is approved.

transfer of development rights (TDR)
The separation of development rights from the land where a community wishes to limit development. Because it permits the selling of rights to an area where high-density development is desirable, TDR is promoted as a way to retain farmland, preserve endangered natural environments, protect historic areas, stage development, promote low- and moderate-income housing, and achieve other land use objectives.

transitional area
(1) An area in the process of changing from one use to another or changing from one racial or ethnic occupancy to another; (2) an area that acts as a buffer between two different land uses.

transitional use
Land use with an intermediate intensity between a more and less intensive use.

transportation systems management (TSM)
A program coordinating many forms of transportation (car, bus, carpool, rapid transit, bicycle, etc.) in order to distribute the traffic impacts of new development. Instead of emphasizing road expansion or construction, TSM examines methods of increasing road efficiency.

tribal consultation
Cities and counties must consult with tribes before adopting or amending a general plan. Gov't Code § 65352.3.

trip generation
The total number of one-way vehicle trips produced by a specific land use or activity.

turbidity
A thick, hazy condition of air or water resulting from the presence of suspended particulates or other pollutants.

urban limit line (urban service area)
An area, identified through official public policy, within which urban development will be allowed during a specified time period. Beyond this line—using a

variety of growth management tools such as acreage zoning and limits on capital improvements—development is prohibited or strongly discouraged.

urban service boundary

A defined region, not always coincidental with a municipality's corporate boundary, that defines the geographical limit of government-supplied public facilities and services.

use

Purpose or activity for which a piece of land or its buildings is designed, arranged, or intended, or for which it is occupied or maintained.

validation suit

Lawsuit that asks a court to validate bonds, boundaries, or other decisions. Code Civ. Proc. § 860 *et seq*.

variance

Permission to depart from the literal requirements of a zoning ordinance. For a variance to be granted, the local decision-making body must make findings that a hardship would exist if a variance were not granted and that granting it would not constitute a special privilege.

vested right

A right that has become absolute and fixed and cannot be defeated or denied by subsequent conditions or a change in regulations, unless it is taken and paid for.

water table

The upper surface of groundwater, or that level below which the soil is seasonally saturated with water.

Williamson Act

The California Land Conservation Act of 1965 (Gov't Code § 51200 *et seq*.). The Williamson Act authorizes local governments to designate "agricultural preserves" and allows for taxation of land within those preserves based on agricultural use, rather than the "highest and best use," which might be residential, industrial, or commercial. In return for this preferential tax treatment, the landowner must agree to maintain the land in agricultural uses for a minimum of ten years.

zero lot line

A development approach in which a building is sited on one or more lot lines to allow more flexibility in site design and to increase the amount of usable open space on the lot. Conceivably, three of the four sides of a building could be on the lot lines.

zoning

Ordinances enacted by a city or county that divide a community into districts or zones within which permitted and special uses are established, as well as regulations governing lot size, building bulk, placement, and other development standards. Gov't Code § 65800 *et seq*.

zoning administrator

An appointed official in charge of carrying out public policy regarding zones and empowered to make decisions concerning design permits, administrative use permits, and other permits as stated in the zoning ordinance.

zoning map

The map or maps that are part of the zoning ordinance, delineating the boundaries of zoning districts.

zoning ordinance

A local law that contains detailed standards and procedures to implement the general plan. The ordinance divides the city or county into various zoning districts with different land uses permitted in each.

Suggested Reading

Ballot Box Navigator 2003 edition
A Practical and Tactical Guide to Land Use Initiatives and Referenda in California
Michael P. Durkee et al.

A summary of the constitutionally-established power of initiatives and referenda and their limits at the local government level to effect land use and growth policies in California. Includes practice tips.

Solano Press Books
P.O. Box 773
Point Arena, CA 95468
(800) 931-9373

Bargaining for Development 2003 edition
A Handbook on Development Agreements, Annexation Agreements, Land Development Conditions, Vested Rights, and the Provision of Public Facilities
David L. Callies, Daniel J. Curtin, Jr., and Julie A. Tappendorf

Provides guidance for and explores principles behind development conditions, vested rights, and development/annexation agreements.

Environmental Law Institute
1616 P Street NW, Suite 200
Washington, DC 20036
(202) 939-3800

California Land Use Practice
March 2006

Adam U. Lindgren and Steve T. Mattas, eds.

Provides comprehensive information on the complex world of California land use law, and covers all major topics encountered in land use practice, including general and specific plans, regulatory takings and exactions, constitutional protections, zoning and variances, conditional use permits, environmental review, code enforcement, design review, growth management, land use litigation, vested rights, and development conditions.

Continuing Education of the Bar (California)
300 Frank H. Ogawa Plaza, Suite 410
Oakland, CA 94612
(800) 232-3444
www.ceb.com

California Municipal Law Handbook
w/ annual supplement

An excellent book that provides municipal law practitioners a source of first resort in researching a given area of California municipal law including land use.

League of California Cities
1400 K Street, Suite 400
Sacramento, CA 95814
(916) 658-8200
www.cacities.org

California Permit Handbook
December 2000

Describes all the major local, state, and federal permit requirements. A useful road map to the complex permitting process for development projects.

California Technology, Trade & Commerce Agency, Office of Permit Assistance
1017 J Street
Sacramento, CA 95814
(800) 353-2672
http://commerce.ca.gov/business/
  permits_assist/index.html

California Planners' 2007 Book of Lists

Practical information that is useful to local, regional, and state planners and resource managers.

State of California
Governor's Office of Planning and Research
1400 10th Street, Suite 100
Sacramento, CA 95814
(916) 322-2318
www.opr.ca.gov

California Planning Guide: An Introduction to Planning in California
2005 edition

A lay person's introduction to the world of planning.

State of California
Governor's Office of Planning and Research
1400 10th Street, Suite 100
Sacramento, CA 95814
(916) 322-2318
www.opr.ca.gov

California Subdivision Map Act and the Development Process
2001 (second) edition, supplemented annually
Daniel J. Curtin, Jr. and Robert E. Merritt

A detailed analysis of the Map Act intended for lawyers.

Continuing Education of the Bar (California)
300 Frank H. Ogawa Plaza, Suite 410
Oakland, CA 94612
(800) 232-3444
www.ceb.com

CEQA Deskbook
A Step-by-Step Guide on
How to Comply with the California
Environmental Quality Act
1999–2000 (second) edition
w/ 2001 supplement
*Ronald E. Bass, Albert I. Herson,
and Kenneth M. Bogdan*

Practical user's guide that explains how to proceed from the beginning to the end of the environmental review process. It summarizes the California Environmental Quality Act and the Guidelines, focusing on CEQA's procedural and substantive requirements.

Solano Press Books
P.O. Box 773
Point Arena, CA 95468
(800) 931-9373

Code Enforcement
A Comprehensive Approach
Joseph M. Schilling and James B. Hare

A must for code enforcement officials and local officials responsible for drafting and enforcing code enforcement regulations.

Solano Press Books
P.O. Box 773
Point Arena, CA 95468
(800) 931-9373

Eminent Domain
2002 edition
A Step-by-Step Guide to the
Acquisition of Real Property
Richard G. Rypinski

Practical guide to the eminent domain process, with practice tips, statutes and regulations, checklists, sample letters and forms, a glossary, and an index.

Solano Press Books
P.O. Box 773
Point Arena, CA 95468
(800) 931-9373

Exactions and Impact Fees in California
A Comprehensive Guide to
Policy, Practice, and the Law
2001 edition w/ 2002 Supplement
William W. Abbott et al.

A comprehensive source of information regarding the history, policy, and law of development fees and exactions, including practice tips.

Solano Press Books
P.O. Box 773
Point Arena, CA 95468
(800) 931-9373

General Plan Guidelines October 2003
Complete guide to the planning process and to the preparation of general plans.

State of California
Governor's Office of Planning and Research
State Clearinghouse
P.O. Box 3044
Sacramento, CA 95812
(916) 445-0613

Growing Pains: Airport Expansion and Land Use Compatibility Planning in California
September, 2006
Grant Boyken

The result of Senator Christine Kehoe's request that the California Research Bureau examine opportunities and challenges faced by airport operators throughout the state as they cope with pressures to expand operations to meet future demand, while dealing with local land use impacts including noise, traffic and compatibility issues.

California State Library, California Research Bureau, State Information and Reference Center
P.O. Box 942837
Sacramento, CA 94237
(916) 654-0261
www.library.ca.gov

Guide to California Planning
2005 (third) edition
William Fulton and Paul Shigley

An extensive account of what land use planning is supposed to be and what it is in California, including the processes and laws that must be observed, and how they are used for better or for worse. Written by a well-respected journalist and urban planner, this book is a must for all those students who wish to understand the fundamentals of the practice of land use planning in California.

Solano Press Books
P.O. Box 773
Point Arena, CA 95468
(800) 931-9373

Guide to the California Environmental Quality Act (CEQA)
2006 (eleventh) edition
Michael H. Remy et al.

An overview of existing requirements for adequate environmental review. Included are an examination of the statutes, the implementing guidelines, current case law. Also included: the entire Act, updated through December 1998, and the entire text of the existing CEQA Guidelines, updated through 2006.

Solano Press Books
P.O. Box 773
Point Arena, CA 95468
(800) 931-9373

Longtin's California Land Use
1987 (second) edition,
supplemented annually
James Longtin

This excellent publication should be consulted by those interested in a detailed, strictly legal analysis of California land use law.

Local Government Publications
P.O. Box 10087
Berkeley, CA 94709
(800) 345-0899

The NEPA Book
A Step-by-Step Guide on How to Comply
with the National Environmental Policy Act
2001 (second) edition
*Ronald E. Bass, Albert I. Herson,
and Kenneth M. Bogdan*

Practitioner's handbook on how to comply with the National Environmental Policy Act. Contains environmental update prepared by Jones & Stokes.

Solano Press Books
P.O. Box 773
Point Arena, CA 95468
(800) 931-9373

An Ounce of Prevention: Best Practices for Making Informed Land Use Decisions
Focuses on the underlying procedures common to all land use decisions.

Institute for Local Government
League of California Cities
1400 K Street, Suite 400
Sacramento, CA 95814
(916) 658-8200
www.cacities.org

The Planning Commissioner and the California Dream
Plan It Again, Sam 2004
Marjorie W. Macris, FAICP

Reference and guidelines directed at the practical needs of city and county planning commissioners in California, with practice tips.

Solano Press Books
P.O. Box 773
Point Arena, CA 95468
(800) 931-9373

Planning Commissioner's Handbook 2004 edition
Primary Contributors: Bill Higgins, Anya Lawler, Gary Binger

Identification of the tools available for planning commissioners and others to assist in reaching the community's goal of quality planning.

League of California Cities
1400 K Street, Suite 400
Sacramento, CA 95814
(916) 658-8200
www.cacities.org

Planning, Zoning and Development Laws 2007

An important tool provided by OPR to help land use professionals keep abreast of the ever-changing land use regulatory environment.

State of California
Governor's Office of Planning and Research
1400 10th Street, Suite 100
Sacramento, CA 95814
(916) 322-2318
www.opr.ca.gov

Practice Under the California Environmental Quality Act
1993 edition, supplemented annually
Stephen L. Kostka and Michael H. Zischke

An encyclopedic, step-by-step guide to the California Environmental Quality Act, covering preparation and judicial review of EIRs and other CEQA documents. Features detailed discussion of legal requirements and practical considerations. Indispensable to attorneys and environmental professionals.

Continuing Education of the Bar (California),
300 Frank H. Ogawa Plaza, Suite 410
Oakland, CA 94612
(800) 232-3444

Redevelopment in California 2004 (third) edition
David F. Beatty and Joseph E. Coomes, Jr., et al.

Guide to detailed provisions of the Community Redevelopment Law and the authority given cities and counties to establish and manage redevelopment agencies and to prepare, adopt, implement, and finance redevelopment projects. Includes thorough policy and economic analyses of redevelopment issues. Includes precise practice tips.

Solano Press Books
P.O. Box 773
Point Arena, CA 95468
(800) 931-9373

State and Local Government Land Use Liability
1998, updated annually
Michael A. Zizka, Timothy S. Hollister, Marcella Larsen, Patricia E. Curtin

The goal of this book is to help government attorneys and officials understand, adopt, administer, and enforce land use regulations and ordinances in a way that will minimize their exposure to "liability."

West Group—Liability
Presentation Services

Subdivision Map Act Manual 2003 edition
Daniel J. Curtin, Jr. and Robert E. Merritt, Jr.

A summary of the Subdivision Map Act, including commentary on the latest statutes and case law and including practice tips.

Solano Press Books
P.O. Box 773
Point Arena, CA 95468
(800) 931-9373

Water and Land Use
Planning Wisely for California's Future
2004 edition
Karen E. Johnson and Jeff Loux

First complete guide to address the increasingly important link between land use planning in California and the availability of water.

Solano Press Books
P.O. Box 773
Point Arena, CA 95468
(800) 931-9373

Wetlands, Streams, and Other Waters 2004 edition
Paul D. Cylinder, Kenneth M. Bogdan, April Zohn, Joel Butterworth

Describes how to identify wetlands, how they are regulated, and the federal, state, regional, or local agencies that have jurisdiction.

Solano Press Books
P.O. Box 773
Point Arena, CA 95468
(800) 931-9373

Table of Authorities

CASES

	page(s)
108 Holdings LTD v. City of Rohnert Park, 136 Cal. App. 4th 186 (2006)	276
1119 Delaware v. Continental Land Title Co., 16 Cal. App. 4th 992 (1993)	60
216 Sutter Bay Assocs. v. County of Sutter, 58 Cal. App. 4th 860 (1997)	66, 67, 276
A Local & Reg'l Monitor (ALARM) v. City of Los Angeles, 16 Cal. App. 4th 630 (1993)	36, 47
Abelleira v. District Court of Appeal, 17 Cal. 2d 280 (1941)	545, 546
Agins v. City of Tiburon, 24 Cal. 3d 266 (1979)	309, 315
Agins v. City of Tiburon, 447 U.S. 255 (1980)	291–292, 305, 322, 344, 424
Agricultural Labor Relations Bd. v. Tex-Cal Land Mgmt., Inc., 43 Cal. 3d 696 (1987)	567
Ailanto Props., Inc. v. City of Half Moon Bay, 142 Cal. App. 4th 572 (2006)	96, 98, 127
Alexander v. State Personnel Bd., 22 Cal. 2d 198 (1943)	548
Ali v. City of Los Angeles, 77 Cal. App. 4th 246 (1999)	304, 315, 330
Allegretti & Co. v. County of Imperial, 138 Cal. App. 4th 1261 (2006)	63, 296, 299, 305
Alliance for a Better Downtown Millbrae v. Wade, 108 Cal. App. 4th 123 (2003)	389
Allied-General Nuclear Services v. United States, 839 F. 2d 1572 (Fed. Cir. 1988)	315
Alsea Valley Alliance v. Evans, 161 F. Supp. 2d 1154 (D. Or. 2001)	209, 225
Amador Valley Joint Union High Sch. Dist. v. State Bd. of Equalization, 22 Cal. 3d 208 (1978)	386, 417
American Canyon Community United for Responsible Growth v. City of American Canyon, 145 Cal. App. 4th 1062 (2006)	171
American Distilling Co. v. City Council of City of Sausalito, 34 Cal. 2d 660 (1950)	449
American Fed'n of Labor v. Eu, 36 Cal. 3d 687 (1984)	386

	page(s)
American Sav. & Loan Ass'n v. County of Marin, 653 F. 2d 364 (9th Cir. 1981)	309
Anderson First Coalition v. City of Anderson, 130 Cal. App. 4th 1173 (2005)	25, 162
Anthony v. Snyder, 116 Cal. App. 4th 643 (2004)	125, 125
Anza Parking Corp. v. City of Burlingame, 195 Cal. App. 3d 855 (1987)	59
Apartment Ass'n of Greater Los Angeles v. City of Los Angeles, 90 Cal. App. 4th 1162 (2001)	152
Apartment Ass'n v. City of Los Angeles, 24 Cal. 4th 830 (2001)	379
Aptos Seascape Corp. v. County of Santa Cruz, 138 Cal. App. 3d 484 (1982)	309
Architectural Heritage Ass'n v. County of Monterey, 122 Cal. App. 4th 1095 (2004)	154
Arizona Cattle Growers Ass'n v. U. S. Fish and Wildlife Serv., 273 F. 3d 1229 (9th Cir. 2001)	225
Armendariz v. Penman, 75 F. 3d 1311 (9th Cir. 1996)	335, 336
Arnel Dev. Co. v. City of Costa Mesa, 126 Cal. App. 3d 330 (1981)	45, 46, 52, 334, 399, 400, 433, 533
Arnel Dev. Co. v. City of Costa Mesa, 28 Cal. 3d 511 (1980)	44, 48, 51, 286, 402, 527, 528
Ass'n for a Cleaner Environment v. Yosemite Community College Dist., 116 Cal. App. 4th 629 (2004)	161
Ass'n for Sensible Development at Northstar, Inc. v. County of Placer, 122 Cal. App. 4th 1289 (2004)	569
Ass'n of Irritated Residents v. County of Madera, 107 Cal. App. 4th 1383 (2003)	161
Assembly v. Deukmejian, 30 Cal. 3d 638 (1982)	389, 411
Associated Home Builders, Inc. v. City of Livermore, 18 Cal. 3d 582 (1976)	1, 4, 44, 45, 46, 49, 386, 400, 404, 407, 418, 424, 425, 426, 532

Case	page(s)
Associated Home Builders, Inc. v. City of Newark, 18 Cal. App. 3d 107 (1971)	372
Associated Home Builders, Inc. v. City of Walnut Creek, 4 Cal. 3d 633 (1971)	109, 115, 116, 339, 340, 341, 342, 343, 345, 347, 357, 360, 362, 364
Avco Community Developers, Inc. v. South Coast Reg'l Comm'n, 17 Cal. 3d 785 (1976)	101, 102, 103, 269, 270, 273, 364, 433
Avoyelles Sportsmen's League, Inc. v. Marsh, 715 F. 2d 897 (5th Cir. 1983)	184
Ayres v. City Council of Los Angeles, 34 Cal. 2d 31 (1949)	79, 108, 115, 116, 342, 362
Azusa Land Reclamation Co. v. Main San Gabriel Basin Watermaster, 52 Cal. App. 4th 1165 (1997)	537, 539, 572
B&P Dev. Corp. v. City of Saratoga, 185 Cal. App. 3d 949 (1986)	120, 140
Babbitt v. Sweet Home Chapter of Communities for a Great Oregon, 515 U.S. 687 (1995)	223
Baird v. County of Contra Costa, 32 Cal. App. 4th 1464 (1995)	62
Bakersfield Citizens for Local Control v. City of Bakersfield, 124 Cal. App. 4th 1184 (2004)	162, 163
Balch Enters. v. New Haven Unified Sch. Dist., 219 Cal. App. 3d 783 (1990)	342, 577
Baldwin v. City of Los Angeles, 70 Cal. App. 4th 819 (1999)	532, 539
Ball v. United States, 77 U.S. 557 (1870)	174
Bank of America v. State Water Resources Control Bd., 42 Cal. App. 3d 198 (1974)	532
Bank of the Orient v. Town of Tiburon, 220 Cal. App. 3d 992 (1990)	5, 67
Banker's Hill v. City of San Diego, 139 Cal. App. 4th 249 (2006)	153
Barancik v. County of Marin, 872 F. 2d 834 (9th Cir. 1988)	250, 297, 332–333
Barner v. Leeds, 24 Cal. 4th 676 (2000)	471
Barratt American Inc. v. City of Rancho Cucamonga, 37 Cal. 4th 685 (2005)	359, 364, 383, 574, 575, 577, 578
Bauer v. City of San Diego, 75 Cal. App. 4th 1281 (1999)	62
Bd. of Supervisors v. Superior Court, 23 Cal. App. 4th 830 (1994)	563
Bd. of Supervisors v. Superior Court, 32 Cal. App. 4th 1616 (1995)	560
Beach Colony II Ltd. v. California Coastal Comm'n, 166 Cal. App. 3d 106 (1985)	580
Beck Dev. Co. v. Southern Pac. Transp. Co., 44 Cal. App. 4th 1160 (1996)	43, 66, 93, 120, 464
Beckley v. Reclamation Board of the State, 205 Cal. App. 2d 734 (1962)	561
Benny v. City of Alameda, 105 Cal. App. 3d 1006 (1980)	80, 93, 528
Benson v. California Coastal Commission, 139 Cal. App. 4th 348 (2006)	456

Case	page(s)
Beresford Neighborhood Ass'n v. City of San Mateo, 207 Cal. App. 3d 1180 (1989)	556
Berkeley Keep Jets Over the Bay Committee v. Port of Oakland, 91 Cal. App. 4th 1344 (2001)	161
Berman v. Parker, 348 U.S. 26 (1954)	1, 2, 290, 383, 424
Bernardi v. City Council, 54 Cal. App. 4th 426 (1997)	578
Bernstein v. Smutz, 83 Cal. App. 2d 108 (1947)	550
Bersani v. U.S. Army Corps of Engineers, 850 F. 2d 36 (2d Cir. 1988), cert denied, 489 U.S. 1089 (1989)	197, 198
Bickel v. City of Piedmont, 16 Cal. 4th 1040 (1997)	94, 463, 464, 465
Big Creek Lumber Co. v. City of Santa Cruz, 38 Cal. 4th 1139 (2006)	2
Bighorn-Desert View Water Agency v. Verjil, 39 Cal. 4th 205 (2006)	378, 398
Billig v. Voges, 223 Cal. App. 3d 962 (1990)	394
Birkenfeld v. City of Berkeley, 17 Cal. 3d 129 (1976)	2, 3, 383, 398
Bishop v. City of San Jose, 1 Cal. 3d 56 (1969)	397
Bixby v. Pierno, 4 Cal. 3d 130 (1971)	532
Bixel Assocs. v. City of Los Angeles, 216 Cal. App. 3d 1208 (1989)	330, 360
Black Hills Invs., Inc. v. Albertsons, Inc., 146 Cal. App. 4th 883 (2007)	136
Blackmore v. Powell, 150 Cal. App. 4th 1593 (2007)	83
Blair v. Pitchess, 5 Cal. 3d 258 (1971)	415, 553, 554
Bldg. Indus. Ass'n v. City of Camarillo, 41 Cal. 3d 810 (1986)	44
Bldg. Indus. Ass'n v. City of Oceanside, 27 Cal. App. 4th 744 (1994)	47
Bledsoe v. Watson, 30 Cal. App. 3d 105 (1973)	415
Blockbuster Videos, Inc. v. City of Tempe, 141 F. 3d 1295 (9th Cir. 1998)	235
Blue Jeans Equities West v. City and County of San Francisco, 3 Cal. App. 4th 164 (1992)	273, 294, 344, 346, 352, 353, 355
Blue v. City of Los Angeles, 137 Cal. App. 4th 1131 (2007)	70, 71
Board of Supervisors v. De Groff Enterprises, 198 S.E. 2d 600 (Va. 1973)	508–509
Board of Supervisors v. Superior Court, 32 Cal. App. 4th 1616 (1995)	52
Bodega Bay Concerned Citizens v. County of Sonoma, 125 Cal. App. 4th 1061 (2005)	97, 100
Bogan v. Scott-Harris, 523 U.S. 44 (1998)	473
Bohannon v. City of San Diego, 30 Cal. App. 3d 416 (1973)	237
Bookout v. Local Agency Formation Comm'n, 49 Cal. App. 3d 383 (1975)	528
Borden Ranch Partnership v. U.S. Army Corps of Engineers, 261 F. 3d 810 (9th Cir. 2001)	186, 206
Border Business Park, Inc. v. City of San Diego, 142 Cal. App. 4th 1538 (2006)	313
Bowman v. City of Berkeley, 122 Cal. App. 4th 572 (2004)	153–154, 236

Case	page(s)
Bowman v. City of Petaluma, 185 Cal. App. 3d 1065 (1986)	171
Bozung v. Local Agency Formation Comm'n, 13 Cal. 3d 263 (1975)	151, 449, 453, 552
Branciforte Heights, LLC v. City of Santa Cruz, 138 Cal. App. 4th 914 (2006)	109, 126, 575, 576
Brandon v. Holt, 469 U.S. 464 (1985)	472
Braude v. City of Los Angeles, 226 Cal. App. 3d 83 (1990)	552
Breakzone Billiards v. City of Torrance, 81 Cal. App. 4th 1205 (2000)	95, 124, 457
Breneric Assocs. v. City of Del Mar, 69 Cal. App. 4th 166 (1998)	52, 349, 536
Briggs v. City of Rolling Hills Estates, 40 Cal. App. 4th 637 (1995)	50, 234, 530
Briggs v. Eden Council for Hope & Opportunity, 19 Cal. 4th 1106 (1999)	580
Bright Dev. Co. v. City of Tracy, 20 Cal. App. 4th 783 (1993)	102, 103–104, 105, 279, 537
Bright v. Board of Supervisors, 66 Cal. App. 3d 191 (1977)	85
Brock v. Superior Court, 109 Cal. App. 2d 594 (1952)	530
Brosnahan v. Brown, 32 Cal. 3d 236 (1982)	396
Brosnahan v. Eu, 31 Cal. 3d 1 (1982), 116 P. 3d at 475	409, 410
Brotherhood of Teamsters v. Unemployment Ins. Appeals Bd., 190 Cal. App. 3d 1515 (1987)	553
Brown v. Legal Foundation of Washington, 538 U.S. 216 (2003)	315–316
Browning-Ferris Industries v. City Council, 181 Cal. App. 3d 852 (1986)	161, 285, 548
Buckley v. California Coastal Comm'n, 68 Cal. App. 4th 178, 183 (1998)	304
Buena Park Motel Association v. City of Buena Park, 109 Cal. App. 4th 302 (2003)	297
Buena Vista Gardens Apartments Ass'n v. City of San Diego, 175 Cal. App. 3d 289 (1985)	18, 32, 485, 506, 556
Building Indus. Ass'n v. City of Camarillo, 41 Cal. 3d 810 (1986)	53, 286, 399, 406, 411, 421, 422, 504, 505
Building Indus. Ass'n v. City of Oceanside, 27 Cal. App. 4th 744 (1994)	25, 401, 426, 500
Building Indus. Ass'n v. Lujan, 785 F. Supp. 1020 (D.D.C. 1992)	230
Building Indus. Ass'n v. Superior Court, 211 Cal. App. 3d 277 (1989)	25, 401, 505
Building Indus. Legal Defense Found. v. Superior Court, 72 Cal. App. 4th 1410 (1999)	67
Bullock v. City and County of San Francisco, 221 Cal. App. 3d 1072 (1990)	124
Burbank-Glendale-Pasadena Airport Auth. v. City of Burbank, 64 Cal. App. 4th 1217 (1998)	374
Burchett v. City of Newport Beach, 33 Cal. App. 4th 1472 (1995)	271–272, 481
Cabinet Mountains Wilderness v. Peterson, 685 F. 2d 678 (D.C. Cir. 1982)	228
Cadiz Land Company, Inc. v. Rail Cycle, L.P., 83 Cal. App. 4th 74 (2000)	558, 559
CalBeach Advocates v. City of Solana Beach, 103 Cal. App. 4th 529 (2002)	152
Caldwell v. Montoya, 10 Cal. 4th 972 (1995)	469–470, 471
Calfarm Ins. Co. v. Deukmejian, 48 Cal. 3d 805 (1989)	386
California Ass'n for Safety Educ. v. Brown, 30 Cal. App. 4th 1264 (1994)	415
California Aviation Council v. City of Ceres, 9 Cal. App. 4th 1384 (1992)	28
California Aviation Council v. County of Amador, 200 Cal. App. 3d 337 (1988)	545
California Bldg. Indus. Ass'n v. Governing Bd. of the Newhall Sch. Dist., 206 Cal. App. 3d 212 (1988)	340, 341, 373
California Coastal Comm'n v. Granite Rock Co., 480 U.S. 572 (1987)	72
California Coastal Comm'n v. Quanta Inv. Corp., 113 Cal. App. 3d 579 (1980)	80
California Coastal Comm'n v. Superior Court (Ham), 210 Cal. App. 3d 1488 (1989)	328, 530
California Common Cause v. Duffy, 200 Cal. App. 3d 730 (1987)	414
California Country Club Homes Ass'n, Inc. v. City of Los Angeles, 18 Cal. App. 4th 1425 (1993)	100
California Forestry Assn. v. California Fish & Game Commission, 156 Cal. App. 4th 1535 (2007)	231
California Hotel & Motel Ass'n v. Industrial Welfare Comm'n, 25 Cal. 3d 200 (1979)	532
California Licensed Foresters Ass'n v. State Bd. of Forestry, 30 Cal. App. 4th 562 (1994)	581
California Oak Foundation v. City of Santa Clarita, 133 Cal. App. 4th 1219 (2005)	162–163
California Ranch Homes Dev. Co. v. San Jacinto Unified Sch. Dist., 17 Cal. App. 4th 573 (1993)	576
California Rifle & Pistol Assn. v. City of West Hollywood, 66 Cal. App. 4th 1302 (1998)	564
California Sportfishing Protection Alliance v. Federal Energy Regulatory Commission, 472 F. 3d 593 (9th Cir. 2006)	215
California v. Cabazon Band of Mission Indians, 480 U.S. 202 (1987)	75
California Youth Authority v. SP Board, 104 Cal. App. 4th 575 (2002)	538
Californians for Alternatives to Toxics v. Dept. of Food and Agriculture, 136 Cal. App. 4th 1 (2006)	161
Call v. Feber, 93 Cal. App. 3d 434 (1979)	101
Calprop Corporation v. City of San Diego, 77 Cal. App. 4th 594 (2000)	323
Camara v. Municipal Court, 87 S. Ct. 1727 (1967)	476
Camp v. Board of Supervisors, 123 Cal. App. 3d 334 (1981)	12, 13, 17, 18, 20, 22, 30, 32, 36, 121, 556, 557, 566

Case	page(s)
Candid Enterprises, Inc. v. Grossmont Union High Sch. Dist., 39 Cal. 3d 878 (1985)	2, 341, 361, 365, 512
Canyon North Co. v. Conejo Valley Unified Sch. Dist., 19 Cal. App. 4th 243 (1993)	383, 533
Capistrano Beach Water District v. Taj Development Corp., 72 Cal. App. 4th 524 (1999)	577–578
Carabell v. U.S. Army Corps of Engineers, 391 F. 3d 704 (6th Cir. 2004)	178
Cardin v. De La Cruz, 671 F. 2d 363 (9th Cir. 1982)	75
Carmel Valley View, Ltd. v. Board of Supervisors, 58 Cal. App. 3d 817 (1976)	122
Carpinteria Valley Farms, Ltd. v. County of Santa Barbara, 334 F. 3d 796 (2003)	330, 331, 332
Carson Harbor Village v. City of Carson, 37 F. 3d 468 (9th Cir. 1994)	313
Carsten v. Psychology Examining Com., 27 Cal. 3d 793 (1980)	552, 553
Carty v. City of Ojai, 77 Cal. App. 3d 329 (1978)	45, 533
Catron County v. U.S. Fish and Wildlife Serv., 75 F. 3d 1429 (10th Cir. 1996)	212
Center for Biological Diversity v. Bureau of Land Management, 422 F. Supp. 2d 1115 (N.D. Cal. 2006)	217
Center for Biological Diversity v. Norton, 240 F. Supp. 2d 1090 (D. Ariz. 2003)	213
Center for Biological Diversity v. Norton, 254 F. 3d 833 (9th Cir. 2001)	211
Center for Biological Diversity v. U.S. Fish and Wildlife Service, 450 F.3d 930 (9th Cir. 2006)	213
Centex Real Estate Corp. v. City of Vallejo, 19 Cal. App. 4th 1358 (1993)	372
CEQUEL III Communications I, LLC v. Nevada City LAFCO, 149 Cal. App. 4th at 316	449
Cf. Marbled Murrelet v. Babbitt, 83 F. 3d 1060 (9th Cir. 1996)	225
Chandis Sec. Co. v. City of Dana Point, 52 Cal. App. 4th 475 (1996)	493
Chappell v. Robbins, 73 F. 3d 918 (9th Cir. 1996)	473
Chase v. Brooks, 187 Cal. App. 3d 657 (1986)	394
Chemical Specialties Mfg. Ass'n, Inc. v. Deukmejian, 227 Cal. App. 3d 663 (1991)	396
Christward Ministry v. County of San Diego, 13 Cal. App. 4th 31 (1993)	170
Christward Ministry v. Superior Court, 184 Cal. App. 3d 180 (1986)	150
Christy v. Hodel, 857 F. 2d 1324 (9th Cir. 1988)	226
Christy v. Lujan, 490 U.S. 1114 (1989)	226
Church of Scientology v. Wollersheim, 42 Cal. App. 4th 628 (1996)	579
Ciani v. San Diego Trust & Savings Bank, 233 Cal. App. 3d 1604 (1991)	466
Cinevision Corp. v. City of Burbank, 745 F. 2d 560 (9th Cir. 1984)	473
Citizen Action to Serve All Students v. Thornley, 222 Cal. App. 3d 748 (1990)	154
Citizens Ass'n for Sensible Dev. of Bishop Area v. County of Inyo, 172 Cal. App. 3d 151 (1985)	23, 153, 284, 547, 552, 555, 556
Citizens for a Megaplex-Free Alameda v. City of Alameda, 149 Cal. App. 4th 91 (2007)	172
Citizens for Jobs and the Economy v. County of Orange, 94 Cal. App. 4th 1311 (2002)	403–404
Citizens for Responsible Equitable Environmental Development v. City of San Diego Redevelopment Agency, 134 Cal. App. 4th 598 (2005)	158
Citizens for Responsible Government v. City of Albany, 56 Cal. App. 4th 1199 (1997)	276, 405
Citizens of Goleta Valley v. Board of Supervisors, 52 Cal. 3d 553 (1990)	10, 11, 15, 24, 31–32, 161, 166–167, 491, 572
Citizens of Lake Murray Area Ass'n v. City Council, 129 Cal. App. 3d 436 (1982)	172
Citizens to Enforce CEQA v. City of Rohnert Park, 131 Cal. App. 4th 1594 (2005)	77
City and County of San Francisco v. Burton, 201 Cal. App. 2d 749 (1962)	478
City and County of San Francisco v. Farrell, 32 Cal. 3d 47 (1982)	373
City and County of San Francisco v. Golden Gate Heights Invs., 14 Cal. App. 4th 1203 (1993)	344, 346
City and County of San Francisco v. Padilla, 23 Cal. App. 3d 388 (1972)	530
City Council v. Taxpayers for Vincent, 466 U.S. 789 (1984)	3
City of Agoura Hills v. LAFCO, 198 Cal. App. 3d 480 (1988)	437, 449, 453
City of Anaheim v. City of Fullerton, 102 Cal. App. 2d 395 (1951)	449
City of Arcadia v. State Water Resources Control Bd., 135 Cal. App. 4th 1392 (2006)	154
City of Atascadero v. Daly, 135 Cal. App. 3d 466 (1982)	404
City of Bakersfield v. Miller, 64 Cal. 2d 93 (1966)	63
City of Banning v. Desert Outdoor Advertising, Inc., 209 Cal. App. 2d 152 (1962)	478
City of Boerne v. Flores, 521 U.S. 507 (1997)	57
City of Buena Park v. Boyar, 186 Cal. App. 2d 61 (1960)	116, 117
City of Campbell v. Mosk, 197 Cal. App. 2d 640 (1961)	449
City of Carmel-by-the-Sea v. Board of Supervisors, 137 Cal. App. 3d 964 (1982)	22, 59, 538
City of Ceres v. City of Modesto, 274 Cal. App. 2d 545 (1969)	435, 438
City of Coachella v. Riverside County Airport Land Use Comm'n, 210 Cal. App. 3d 1277 (1989)	546, 550, 567
City of Cuyahoga Falls v. Buckeye Community Hope Foundation, 538 U.S. 188 (2003)	334, 407, 408, 512

Case	page(s)
City of Del Mar v. City of San Diego, 133 Cal. App. 3d 401 (1982)	45, 46
City of Fairfield v. Superior Court, 14 Cal. 3d 768 (1975)	51, 52, 415, 463, 530, 536, 560
City of Glendale v. Superior Court, 18 Cal. App. 4th 1768 (1993)	278
City of Goleta v. Superior Court, 40 Cal. 4th 270 (2006)	107, 128
City of Half Moon Bay v. Superior Court, 106 Cal. App. 4th 795 (2003)	557
City of Hawaiian Gardens v. City of Long Beach, 61 Cal. App. 4th 1100 (1998)	582
City of Irvine v. Irvine Citizens Against Overdevelopment, 25 Cal. App. 4th 868 (1994)	23, 24, 46, 47, 53, 66, 401, 410, 411
City of Ladue v. Gilleo, 512 U.S. 43 (1994)	235
City of Lafayette v. East Bay Mun. Util. Dist., 16 Cal. App. 4th 1005 (1993)	73
City of Las Vegas v. Lujan, 891 F. 2d 927 (D.C. Cir. 1989)	210
City of Littleton, Colo. v. Z.J. Gifts D-4, LLC, 541 U.S. 774 (2004)	56
City of Livermore v. LAFCO, 184 Cal. App. 3d 531 (1986)	449, 453, 454, 556
City of Los Altos v. Barnes, 3 Cal. App. 4th 1193 (1992)	50
City of Los Angeles v. Alameda Books, Inc., 535 U.S. 425 (2002)	54
City of Los Angeles v. Amwest Surety Ins. Co., 63 Cal. App. 4th 378 (1998)	132
City of Los Angeles v. Gage, 127 Cal. App. 2d 442 (1954)	64
City of Los Angeles v. Rancho Homes, Inc., 40 Cal. 2d 764 (1953)	372
City of Los Angeles v. State of California, 138 Cal. App. 3d 526 (1982)	401
City of Los Angeles v. Wolfe, 6 Cal. 3d 326 (1971)	63
City of Marina v. Bd. of Trustees of the Cal. St. Univ., 39 Cal. 4th 341 (2006)	164
City of Merced v. American Motorists Ins. Co., 126 Cal. App. 4th 1316 (2005)	132
City of Monterey v. Del Monte Dunes at Monterey, Ltd., 526 U.S. 687 (1999)	326, 330, 332, 349, 351
City of National City v. Wiener, 3 Cal. 4th 832 (1992)	54
City of Pasadena v. State of California, 14 Cal. App. 4th 810 (1993)	152
City of Poway v. City of San Diego, 155 Cal. App. 3d 1037 (1984)	285
City of Poway v. City of San Diego, 229 Cal. App. 3d 847 (1991)	30, 31
City of Rancho Palos Verdes v. Abrams, 544 U.S. 113 (2005)	330
City of Rancho Palos Verdes v. City Council, 59 Cal. App. 3d 869 (1976)	538
City of Renton v. Playtime Theatres, Inc., 475 U.S. 41 (1986)	53
City of Sacramento v. Trans Pac. Indus., Inc., 98 Cal. App. 3d 389 (1979)	132
City of Salinas v. Ryan Outdoor Adver., Inc., 189 Cal. App. 3d 416 (1987)	64

Case	page(s)
City of San Diego v. Dunkl, 86 Cal. App. 4th 384 (2001)	579
City of Santa Ana v. City of Garden Grove, 100 Cal. App. 3d 521 (1979)	10
City of Santa Clara v. Local Agency Formation Comm'n, 139 Cal. App. 3d 923 (1983)	453
City of Santa Cruz v. LAFCO, 76 Cal. App. 3d 381 (1978)	437, 448
City of Santa Cruz v. Santa Cruz Bd. of Educ., 210 Cal. App. 3d 1 (1989)	74
City of Santa Cruz v. Superior Court, 40 Cal. App. 4th 1146 (1995)	51, 560
City of Santa Monica v. Stewart, 126 Cal. App. 4th 43 (2005)	408
City of Santee v. County of San Diego, 214 Cal. App. 3d 1438 (1989)	161
City of Sausalito v. County of Marin, 12 Cal. App. 3d 550 (1970)	53
City of Tiburon v. Northwestern Pac. R.R. Co., 4 Cal. App. 3d 160 (1970)	80, 138
City of Vernon v. Board of Harbor Comm'rs, 63 Cal. App. 4th 677 (1998)	149
City of W. Hollywood v. Beverly Towers, Inc., 52 Cal. 3d 1184 (1991)	60, 101, 272, 274, 275
City of Walnut Creek v. County of Contra Costa, 101 Cal. App. 3d 1012 (1980)	25, 539, 547
Clark v. City of Hermosa Beach, 48 Cal. App. 4th 1152 (1996)	341, 456, 535–536
Cmty. Dev. Comm'n v. City of Fort Bragg, 204 Cal. App. 3d 1124 (1988)	61
Coalition Advocating Legal Housing Options v. City of Santa Monica, 88 Cal. App. 4th 451 (2001)	502
Coalition for L.A. County Planning in the Public Interest v. Board of Supervisors, 76 Cal. App. 3d 241 (1977)	580
Coalition for Student Action v. City of Fullerton, 153 Cal. App. 3d 1194 (1984)	124, 546, 547
Coalition of Concerned Communities, Inc. v. City of Los Angeles, 34 Cal. 4th 733 (2004)	490
Cochran v. Herzog Engraving Co., 155 Cal. App. 3d 405 (1984)	469
Coe v. City of Los Angeles, 183 P. 822 (1919)	449
Cohan v. City of Thousand Oaks, 30 Cal. App. 4th 547 (1994)	95, 124, 334, 457
Cohen v. Board of Supervisors, 40 Cal. 3d 277 (1985)	566
Comm. for Responsible Planning v. City of Indian Wells, 225 Cal. App. 3d 191 (1990)	578
Commercial Builders of Northern California v. City of Sacramento, 941 F. 2d 872 (1991)	343, 345, 353, 355, 510
Committee for Responsible Planning v. City of Indian Wells, 209 Cal. App. 3d 1005 (1989)	15, 36, 37, 485
Committee of Seven Thousand (COST) v. Superior Court, 45 Cal. 3d 491 (1988)	411
Common Cause v. Board of Supervisors, 49 Cal. 3d 432, 438 (1989)	552, 554
Communities for a Better Environment v. California Resources Agency, 103 Cal. App. 4th 98 (2002)	147, 164

Case	page(s)
Concerned Citizens of Calaveras County v. Board of Supervisors, 166 Cal. App. 3d 90 (1985)	14, 18, 23, 31, 32, 410
Concerned Citizens of Costa Mesa, Inc. v. 32nd District Agricultural Association, 42 Cal. 3d 929 (1986)	172, 544
Concerned Citizens of Palm Desert, Inc. v. Board of Supervisors, 38 Cal. App. 3d 257 (1974)	62, 544
Concerned Citizens v. City of Carlsbad, 204 Cal. App. 3d 937 (1988)	412
Concerned Citizens v. McCloud Community Services Dist., 147 Cal. App. 4th 181 (2007)	149
Congregation Etz Chaim v. City of Los Angeles, 371 F. 3d 1122 (9th Cir. 2004)	480–481
Connerly v. State Personnel Board, 37 Cal. 4th 1169 (2006)	582
Consaul v. City of San Diego, 6 Cal. App. 4th 1781 (1992)	101, 273
Conservation Council v. Babbitt, 2 F. Supp. 2d 1280 (D. Hawaii 1998)	211
Conservation Law Found. v. Watt, 560 F. Supp. 561 (D. Mass. 1983)	216
Consolidated Fire Protection Dist. v. Howard Jarvis Taxpayers Ass'n, 63 Cal. App. 4th 211 (1998)	377, 380
Consolidated Rock Prods. Co. v. City of Los Angeles, 57 Cal. 2d 515 (1962)	4
Construction Indus. Ass'n v. City of Petaluma, 522 F. 2d 897 (9th Cir. 1975)	425
Construction Indus. Force Account Council v. Amador Water Agency, 71 Cal. App. 4th 810 (1999)	267
Cormier v. County of San Luis Obispo, 161 Cal. App. 3d 850 (1984)	51
Corona-Norco Unified Sch. Dist. v. City of Corona, 13 Cal. App. 4th 1577 (1993)	27, 121, 365
Corona-Norco Unified Sch. Dist. v. City of Corona, 17 Cal. App. 4th 985 (1993)	24, 121, 547, 548
Cortez v. Purolator Air Filtration Products Co., 23 Cal. 4th at 168 (2000))	543
Costa v. Superior Court, 37 Cal. 4th 986 (2006)	389, 409, 410, 411
Cothran v. Town Council of Los Gatos, 209 Cal. App. 2d 647 (1962)	449
County of Alameda v. Superior Court of Alameda County, 133 Cal. App. 4th 558 (2005)	323
County of Amador v. City of Plymouth, 149 Cal. App. 4th 1089 (2007)	149
County of Amador v. El Dorado County Water Agency, 76 Cal. App. 4th 931 (1999)	149, 543
County of Butte v. Bach, 172 Cal. App. 3d 848 (1985)	51, 533
County of Contra Costa v. State of California, 177 Cal. App. 3d 62 (1986)	550
County of Imperial v. McDougal, 19 Cal. 3d 505 (1977)	59, 100
County of Kern v. Edgemont Dev. Corp., 222 Cal. App. 2d 874 (1963)	132
County of Los Angeles v. Superior Court, 13 Cal. 3d 721 (1975)	560
County of Marin v. Assessment Appeals Board, 64 Cal. App. 3d 319 (1976)	238-239
County of Orange v. Barratt American, Inc., 150 Cal. App. 4th 420 (2007)	359
County of Riverside v. Whitlock, 22 Cal. App. 3d 863 (1972)	267
County of San Diego v. California Water and Telephone Co., 30 Cal. 2d 817 (1947)	480
County of San Diego v. Grossmont-Cuyamaca Community College District, 141 Cal. App. 4th 86 (2006)	164
County of San Diego v. McClurken, 37 Cal. 2d 683 (1951)	64
County of San Diego v. State of California, 15 Cal. 4th 68 (1997)	526, 539
County of San Luis Obispo v. Superior Court, 90 Cal. App. 4th 288 (2001)	138, 328
County of Sonoma v. Rex, 231 Cal. App. 3d 1289 (1991)	480
County of Yuba v. Central Valley Nat'l Bank, Inc., 20 Cal. App. 3d 109 (1971)	132–133
County Sanitation Dist. No. 2 v. County of Kern, 127 Cal. App. 4th 1544 (2005)	154
Craik v. County of Santa Cruz, 81 Cal. App. 4th 880 (2000)	60, 285, 538
Creighton v. Reviczky, 171 Cal. App. 3d 1225 (1985)	393–394
Crowl v. Bd. of Trustees of City of Southgate, 292 P. 985 (1930)	449
Crown Motors v. City of Redding, 232 Cal. App. 3d 173 (1991)	235
Crown Point Development, Inc. v. City of Sun Valley, __ F. 3d __, 2007 WL 31977049 (9th Circ. 2007)	336
Ctr. for Biological Diversity v. Hamilton, 453 F. 3d 1331 (11th Cir. 2006)	230
Cucamongans United for Reasonable Expansion v. City of Rancho Cucamonga, 82 Cal. App. 4th 473 (2000)	170
Cumming v. City of San Bernardino Redevelopment Agency, 101 Cal. App. 4th 1229 (Aug. 9, 2002)	543, 544
Danforth v. United States, 308 U.S. 271 (1939)	296
Daro v. Superior Court, 151 Cal. App. 4th 1079 (2007)	80
Dateline Builders, Inc. v. City of Santa Rosa, 146 Cal. App. 3d 520 (1983)	425
Davidon Homes v. City of Pleasant Hill, No. 297988 (Superior Court, Contra Costa County, April 3, 1987)	105
Davidon Homes v. City of San Jose, 34 Cal. App. 4th 106 (1997)	151
Davidson v. County of San Diego, 49 Cal. App. 4th 639 (1996)	272
deBottari v. City Council, 171 Cal. App. 3d 1204 (1985)	47, 53, 401, 410
Defend the Bay v. City of Irvine, 119 Cal. App. 4th 1261 (2004)	167, 565
Defenders of Wildlife v. Bernal, 204 F. 3d 920 (9th Cir. 2000)	224
Defenders of Wildlife v. Flowers, 414 F. 3d 1066 (9th Cir. 2005)	219

Case	page(s)
Defenders of Wildlife v. Lujan, 792 F. Supp. 834 (D.D.C. 1992)	211
Del Mar Terrace Conservancy, Inc. v. City Council, 10 Cal. App. 4th 712 (1992)	538
Del Monte Dunes v. City of Monterey, 920 F. 2d 1496 (9th Cir. 1990)	326, 349
Del Oro Hills v. City of Oceanside, 31 Cal. App. 4th 1060 (1995)	313, 320
Delta Wetlands Properties v. County of San Joaquin, 121 Cal. App. 4th 128 (2004)	73
Deltakeeper v. Oakdale Irrig. Dist., 94 Cal. App. 4th 1092 (2001)	556
Deltona Corp. v. Alexander, 504 F. Supp. 1280 (M.D. Fla. 1981)	195
Deltona Corp. v. United States, 657 F. 2d 1184 (Ct. Cl. 1981)	195
Denny's Inc. v. City of Agoura Hills, 56 Cal. App. 4th 1312 (1997)	64
Department of Fish and Game v. Anderson-Cottonwood Irrigation District, 8 Cal. App. 4th 1554 (1992)	232
DeVita v. County of Napa, 9 Cal. 4th 763 (1995)	2, 9, 10, 12, 30, 32, 116, 386, 397, 398, 402, 403, 404, 405, 416, 417, 418, 423, 433
Dieckmeyer v. Redevelopment Agency, 127 Cal. App. 4th 248 (2005)	522
Dierkes v. City of Los Angeles, 25 Cal. 2d 938 (1945)	554
District of Columbia v. Carter, 409 U.S. 418 (1973)	330
Dixon v. Superior Court, 30 Cal. App. 4th 733 (1994)	580
Dolan v. City of Tigard, 512 U.S. 374 (1994)	35, 108, 233, 278, 287, 292, 295, 300, 306, 329, 340, 341, 342, 343, 346, 347, 349, 350, 351, 353–354, 355, 368, 370, 510, 511, 512, 513
Donnellan v. City of Novato, 86 Cal. App. 4th 1097 (2001)	541
Douglas County v. Babbitt, 48 F. 3d 1495 (9th Cir. 1995)	212
Doyle v. City of Chino, 117 Cal. App. 3d 673 (1981)	550
Driscoll v. City of Los Angeles, 67 Cal. 2d 297 (1967)	480
Drum v. Fresno County Dep't of Pub. Works, 144 Cal. App. 3d 777 (1983)	456
Dunn v. County of Santa Barbara, 135 Cal. App. 4th 1281 (2006)	322, 564
Dunn-Edwards Corp. v. Bay Area Air Quality Management Dist., 9 Cal. App. 4th 644 (1992)	528
East Bay Asian Local Dev. Corp. v. State of California, 24 Cal. 4th 693 (2000)	58, 59
East Bay Mun. Utility Dist. v. Department of Forestry & Fire Protection, 43 Cal. App. 4th 1113 (1996)	163
Echevarrieta v. City of Rancho Palos Verdes, 86 Cal. App. 4th 472 (2001)	234
Economy Light & Power Co. v. United States, 256 U.S. 113 (1921)	174

Case	page(s)
Edgren v. Regents of Univ. of Cal., 158 Cal. App. 3d 515 (1984)	548
Ehrlich v. City of Culver City, 12 Cal. 4th 854 (1996)	3, 233, 287, 342, 343, 351, 352, 353, 354, 355, 357, 368–369, 511, 513, 576
El Dorado Palm Springs, Ltd. v. Rent Review Comm'n, 230 Cal. App. 3d 335 (1991)	541
El Patio v. Permanent Rent Control Bd., 110 Cal. App. 3d 915 (1980)	100
Eller Media Co. v. City of Los Angeles, 87 Cal. App. 4th 1217 (2001)	465
Embarcadero Mun. Improvement Dist. v. City of Santa Barbara, 88 Cal. App. 4th 781 (2001)	450
Employment Div. v. Smith, 494 U.S. 872 (1990)	57
Endangered Habitats League, Inc. v. County of Orange, 131 Cal. App. 4th 777 (2005)	26, 164
Endangered Habitats League, Inc. v. State Water Resources Control Bd., 63 Cal. App. 4th 227 (1997)	550, 567
Enos v. Marsh, 769 F. 2d 1363 (9th Cir. 1985)	212
Ensign Bickford Realty Corp. v. City Council, 68 Cal. App. 3d 467 (1977)	286, 528
Environmental Coalition of Orange County, Inc. v. LAFCO of Orange County, 110 Cal. App. 3d 164 (1980)	449
Environmental Council v. Board of Supervisors, 135 Cal. App. 3d 428 (1982)	23, 35
Environmental Law Fund v. Town of Corte Madera, 49 Cal. App. 3d 105 (1975)	550
Envtl. Prot. Info. Ctr. v. Simpson Timber Co., 255 F. 3d 1073 (9th Cir. 2001)	220
Essick v. City of Los Angeles, 34 Cal. 2d 614 (1950)	62
Euclid v. Ambler Realty Co., 272 U.S. 365 (1926)	314, 344, 512
Eureka Citizens for Responsible Gov't v. City of Eureka, 147 Cal. App. 4th 357 (2007)	150
Evans v. City of San Jose, 128 Cal. App. 4th 1123 (2005)	547
Ewing v. City of Carmel-by-the-Sea, 234 Cal. App. 3d 1579 (1991)	3, 45, 50
F&L Farm Co. v. City of Lindsay, 65 Cal. App. 4th 1345 (1998)	311
Fairbank v. City of Mill Valley, 75 Cal App. 4th 1243 (1999)	152
Fall River Wild Trout Found. v. County of Shasta, 70 Cal. App. 4th 482 (1999)	155
Families Unafraid to Uphold Rural El Dorado County v. County Bd. of Supervisors, 79 Cal. App. 4th 505 (2000)	581
Families Unafraid to Uphold Rural El Dorado County v. County of El Dorado, 62 Cal. App. 4th 1332 (1998)	25, 27, 34, 539
Farley v. Cory, 78 Cal. App. 3d 583 (1978)	554
Farley v. Healey, 67 Cal. 2d 325 (1967)	393, 410

Case	page(s)
Federation of Hillside & Canyon Ass'ns v. City of Los Angeles, 126 Cal. App. 4th 1180 (2004)	23, 166
Federation of Hillside & Canyon Ass'ns v. City of Los Angeles, 83 Cal. App. 4th 1252 (2000)	169
Federation of Hillside and Canyon Assns. v. City of Corona, 126 Cal. App. 4th 1180 (2004)	11
Felice v. City of Inglewood, 84 Cal. App. 2d 263 (1948)	62
Fields v. Sarasota Manatee Airport Auth., 953 F. 2d 1299 (11th Cir. 1992)	326
Findleton v. Board of Supervisors, 12 Cal. App. 4th 709 (1993)	467
First English Evangelical Lutheran Church v. County of Los Angeles, 210 Cal. App. 3d 1353 (1989)	310
First English Evangelical Lutheran Church v. County of Los Angeles, 482 U.S. 304 (1987)	64, 67, 235, 301, 302, 303, 305, 306, 309, 310, 313–314, 315, 316, 317, 326, 329
Fishback v. County of Ventura, 133 Cal. App. 4th 896 (2005)	138, 139
Fishman v. City of Palo Alto, 86 Cal. App. 3d 506 (1978)	527
Flavell v. City of Albany, 19 Cal. App. 4th 1846 (1993)	21, 22
Fogarty v. City of Chico, 148 Cal. App. 4th 537 (2007)	577
Fonseca v. City of Gilroy, 148 Cal. App. 4th 1174 (2007)	485
Fontana Unified Sch. Dist. v. City of Rialto, 173 Cal. App. 3d 725 (1985)	364
Forest Conservation Council v. Rosboro Lumber Co., 50 F. 3d 781 (9th Cir. 1995)	225
Formanek v. United States, 26 Cl. Ct. 332 (1992)	314
Fort Mojave Indian Tribe v. Department of Health Servs., 38 Cal. App. 4th 1574 (1995)	558
Friedland v. City of Long Beach, 62 Cal. App. 4th 835 (1998)	450
Friends of "B" St. v. City of Hayward, 106 Cal. App. 3d 988 (1980)	22, 23, 580
Friends of Davis v. City of Davis, 83 Cal. App. 4th 1004 (2000)	235
Friends of East Willits Valley v. County of Mendocino, 101 Cal. App. 4th 191 (2002)	241
Friends of H Street v. City of Sacramento, 20 Cal. App. 4th 152 (1993)	27
Friends of La Vina v. County of Los Angeles, 232 Cal. App. 3d 1446 (1991)	159
Friends of Lagoon Valley v. City of Vacaville, 154 Cal. App. 4th 807 (2007)	11, 24, 25, 498, 499, 501
Friends of Sierra Madre v. City of Sierra Madre, 25 Cal. 4th 165 (2001)	148, 276, 405, 395
Friends of Sierra Railroad v. Tuolumne Park & Recreation Dist., 147 Cal. App. 4th 643 (2007)	150
Friends of the Eel River v. Sonoma County Water Agency, 108 Cal. App. 4th 859 (2003)	73, 163
Friends of Westhaven and Trinidad v. County of Humboldt, 107 Cal. App. 4th 878 (2003)	98
Friends of Westwood, Inc. v. City of Los Angeles, 191 Cal. App. 3d 259 (1987)	364, 528
Fullerton Joint Union High Sch. Dist. v. State Bd. of Educ., 32 Cal. 3d 779 (1982)	150, 532
Fund for Envtl. Defense v. County of Orange, 204 Cal. App. 3d 1538 (1988)	171
Furey v. City of Sacramento, 24 Cal. 3d 862 (1979)	550
G & D Holland Construction Company v. City of Marysville, 12 Cal. App. 3d 989 (1970)	4, 52, 533–534
G.L. Mezzetta, Inc. v. City of American Canyon, 78 Cal. App. 4th 1087 (2000)	272
Galante Vineyards v. Monterey Peninsula Water Mgmt. Dist., 60 Cal. App. 4th 1109 (1997)	571
Galland v. City of Clovis, 24 Cal. 4th 1003 (2001)	298, 337
Galvin v. Board of Supervisors of Contra Costa County, 195 Cal. 686 (1925)	397
Gammoh v. City of Anaheim, 73 Cal. App. 4th 186 (1999)	54, 235
Gammoh v. City of La Habra, 395 F. 3d 1114 (9th Cir. 2005)	294
Garat v. City of Riverside, 2 Cal. App. 4th 259 (1991)	12, 15, 21, 22, 23, 24, 31–32, 36, 46, 402, 491, 543, 544
Gardner v. County of Sonoma, 29 Cal. 4th 990 (2003)	139, 140, 141
Garneau v. City of Seattle, 147 F. 3d 802 (9th Cir. 1998)	299–300
Garner v. City of Riverside, 170 Cal. App. 3d 510 (1985)	543
Garrick Dev. Co. v. Hayward Unified Sch. Dist., 3 Cal. App. 4th 320 (1992)	343, 369, 383
Gayle v. Hamm, 25 Cal. App. 3d 250 (1972)	409
Gentry v. City of Murrieta, 36 Cal. App. 4th 1359 (1995)	151, 154
Georgia-Pacific Corp. v. California Coastal Comm'n, 132 Cal. App. 3d 678 (1982)	537
Gifford Pinchot Task Force v. U.S. Fish and Wildlife Serv., 378 F. 3d 1059 (9th Cir. 2004)	217
Gilliland v. County of Los Angeles, 126 Cal. App. 3d 610 (1981)	271
Gilroy Citizens for Responsible Planning v. City of Gilroy, 140 Cal. App. 4th 911 (2006)	158, 159, 162
Gobin v. Snohomish County, 304 F. 3d 909 (9th Cir. 2002)	75
Gogerty v. Coachella Valley Junior Coll. Dist., 57 Cal. 2d 727 (1962)	415
Golden State Homebuilding Ass'n v. City of Modesto, 26 Cal. App. 4th 601 (1994)	101, 120
Golden v. Planning Board of the Town of Ramapo, 30 N.Y. 2d 359 (1972)	425

Case	page(s)
Gomes v. County of Mendocino, 37 Cal. App. 4th 977 (1995)	139, 143
Gong v. City of Fremont, 250 Cal. App. 2d 568 (1967)	558
Gonzalez v. County of Tulare, 65 Cal. App. 4th 777 (1998)	47, 540, 541
Graydon v. Pasadena Redevelopment Agency, 104 Cal. App. 3d 631 (1980)	268
Green v. Cmty. Redev. Agency, 96 Cal. App. 3d 491 (1979)	578
Greenbaum v. City of Los Angeles, 153 Cal. App. 3d 391 (1984)	26, 161
Greenpeace Action v. Franklin, 982 F. 2d 1342 (9th Cir. 1992)	216
Griffin Dev. Co. v. City of Oxnard, 39 Cal. 3d 256 (1985)	3, 80, 340, 361
Griffis v. County of Mono, 163 Cal. App. 3d 414 (1985)	80, 97
Groch v. City of Berkeley, 118 Cal. App. 3d 518 (1981)	61
Grupe Dev. Co. v. California Coastal Comm'n, 166 Cal. App. 3d 148 (1985)	331
Grupe Dev. Co. v. Superior Court, 4 Cal. 4th 911 (1993)	365
Guardians of Turlock's Integrity v. City Council, 149 Cal. App. 3d 584 (1983)	22
Guardians v. Johanns, 450 F. 3d 455 (9th Cir. 2006)	220
Guilbert v. Regents of Univ. of Cal., 93 Cal. App. 3d 233 (1979)	530
Guinnane v. City and County of San Francisco, 197 Cal. App. 3d 862 (1987)	297, 305, 306
Guinnane v. City of San Francisco Planning Commission, 209 Cal. App. 3d 732 (1989)	234
Guru Nanak Sikh Society of Yuba City v. County of Sutter, 456 F. 3d 978 (9th Cir. 2006)	58
H.N. & Frances C. Berger Foundation v. City of Escondido, 127 Cal. App. 4th 1 (2005)	337
Hafen v. County of Orange, 128 Cal. App. 4th 133 (2005)	101, 120, 271, 273
Haggis v. City of Los Angeles, 22 Cal. 4th 490 (2000)	470
Hall v. City of Taft, 47 Cal. 2d 177 (1956)	73
Hallstrom v. Tillamook County, 493 U.S. 20 (1989)	230
Hansen Bros. Enters. v. Board of Supervisors, 12 Cal. 4th 533 (1996)	64, 290
Harlow v. Carleson, 16 Cal. 3d 731 (1976)	532
Harmer v. Superior Court, 275 Cal. App. 2d 345 (1969)	555
Harris v. Alcoholic Beverage Control Appeals Bd., 245 Cal. App. 2d 919 (1966)	555
Harris v. City of Costa Mesa, 25 Cal. App. 4th 963 (1994)	234, 284
Harris v. County of Riverside, 904 F. 2d 497 (9th Cir. 1990)	332, 534
Harroman Co. v. Town of Tiburon, 235 Cal. App. 3d 388 (1991)	34, 122
Harron v. Bonilla, 125 Cal. App. 4th 738 (2005)	461
Hawai'i Housing Authority v. Midkiff, 467 U.S. 229 (1984)	289
Hawn v. County of Ventura, 73 Cal. App. 3d 1009 (1977)	398, 399
Hayssen v. Board of Zoning Adjustments, 171 Cal. App. 3d 400 (1985)	456
Hayward Area Planning Ass'n v. Superior Court, 218 Cal. App. 3d 53 (1990)	390
Hayward v. Henderson, 88 Cal. App. 3d 64 (1979)	547
Hazelton v. City of San Diego, 183 Cal. App. 2d 131 (1960)	449
Headwaters, Inc. v. Talent Irr. Dist., 243 F. 3d 526 (9th Cir. 2001)	178
Heap v. City of Los Angeles, 6 Cal. 2d 405 (1936)	550
Hebard v. Bybee, 65 Cal. App. 4th 1331 (1998)	389, 393
Hellweg v. Cassidy, 61 Cal. App. 4th 806 (1998)	88
Hensler v. City of Glendale, 8 Cal. 4th 1 (1994)	125, 311–312, 328, 530, 531, 539, 540, 557
Hermosa Beach Stop Oil Coalition v. City of Hermosa Beach, 86 Cal. App. 4th 534 (2001)	271, 278
Hernandez v. City of Encinitas, 28 Cal. App. 4th 1048 (1994)	13, 15, 18, 32, 36, 44, 411, 485, 505
Hernandez v. City of Hanford, 41 Cal. 4th 279 (2007)	46, 286
Herrington v. County of Sonoma, 12 F. 3d 901 (9th Cir. 1993)	319
Herrington v. County of Sonoma, 790 F. Supp. 909 (N.D. Cal. 1991)	319
Herrington v. County of Sonoma, 834 F. 2d 1488 (9th Cir. 1987)	319, 330, 332, 334
Herzberg v. County of Plumas, 133 Cal. App. 4th 1 (2005)	298–299, 329
Hewlett v. Squaw Valley Ski Corp., 54 Cal. App. 4th 499 (1997)	478
HFH, Ltd. v. Superior Court, 15 Cal. 3d 508 (1975)	314
Hickson v. Thielman, 147 Cal. App. 2d 11 (1956)	565
Hill v. City of Clovis, 80 Cal. App. 4th 438 (2000)	114
Hill v. City of Manhattan Beach, 6 Cal. 3d 279 (1971)	271
Hills for Everyone v. LAFCO, 105 Cal. App. 3d 461 (1980)	449, 450, 454
Hittle v. Santa Barbara County Employees Retirement Ass'n, 39 Cal. 3d 374 (1985)	544
Hock Inv. Co. v. City and County of San Francisco, 215 Cal. App. 3d 438 (1989)	101, 272, 481
Hoehne v. County of San Benito, 870 F. 2d 529 (9th Cir. 1989)	323–324
Hoffman Group, Inc. v. U.S. EPA, 902 F. 2d 567 (7th Cir. 1990)	205
Hoffman Homes, Inc. v. U.S. EPA, 999 F. 2d 256 (7th Cir. 1993)	176
Hoffmaster v. City of San Diego, 55 Cal. App. 4th 1098 (1997)	15, 33, 485, 487, 488
Hogar Dulce Hogar v. Community Dev. Comm'n, 110 Cal. App. 4th 1288 (2003)	502

Case	page(s)
Holt v. County of Monterey, 128 Cal. App. 3d 797 (1982)	544
Home Builders Ass'n of N. Calif. v. City of Napa, 90 Cal. App. 4th 188 (2001)	300, 350, 510, 512, 513, 514, 515
Home Builders Ass'n of N. Calif. v. Norton, 293 F. Supp. 2d 1 (D.D.C. 2002)	213
Home Builders Ass'n of N. Calif. v. U.S. Fish and Wildlife Serv., 268 F. Supp. 2d 1197 (E.D. Cal. 2003)	213
Homebuilders Assn. of N. Calif. v. U.S. Fish and Wildlife Serv., 2006 U.S. Dist. LEXIS 80255 (E.D. Cal. Nov. 2, 2006), *on reconsideration*, 2007 U.S. Dist. LEXIS 5208 (E.D. Cal. Jan. 24, 2007)	212
Honey Springs Homeowners Ass'n v. Board of Supervisors, 157 Cal. App. 3d 1122 (1984)	285
Honig v. San Francisco Planning Department, 127 Cal. App. 4th 520 (2005)	541
Horn v. County of Ventura, 24 Cal. 3d 605 (1979)	48, 93, 95, 128, 134, 455, 462, 530
Horsemen's Benevolent & Protective Association v. Valley Racing Association, 4 Cal. App. 4th 1538 (1992)	272, 481
Hotel & Motel Ass'n of Oakland v. City of Oakland, 344 F. 3d 959 (9th Cir. 2003)	50, 345
Hough v. Marsh, 557 F. Supp. 74 (D. Mass. 1982)	197
Howard Jarvis Taxpayers Ass'n v. City of Fresno, 127 Cal. App. 4th 914 (2005)	378, 382
Howard Jarvis Taxpayers Ass'n v. City of Los Angeles, 85 Cal. App. 4th 79 (2000)	379
Howard Jarvis Taxpayers Ass'n v. City of Riverside, 73 Cal. App. 4th 679 (1999)	373, 374, 377
Howard Jarvis Taxpayers Ass'n v. City of San Diego, 120 Cal. App. 4th 374 (2004)	376, 398, 400
Howell v. U.S. Army Corps of Eng'rs, 794 F. Supp. 1072 (D. N.M. 1992)	205
Hull v. Rossi, 13 Cal. App. 4th 1763 (1993)	579
Humane Soc'y v. Lujan, 768 F. Supp. 360 (D.D.C. 1991)	230
Hunt v. County of Shasta, 225 Cal. App. 3d 432 (1990)	125, 138
Ibarra v. City of Carson, 214 Cal. App. 3d 90 (1989)	391, 394
Idaho Farm Bureau Fed'n v. Babbitt, 58 F.3d 1392 (9th Cir. 1995)	210
Idaho Historic Preservation Council, Inc. v. City Council, 134 Idaho 651 (2000)	462
Independent Energy Producers Ass'n v. McPherson, 116 P. 3d 475 (2005)	409
Inland Counties Reg'l Ctr. v. Office of Admin. Hearings, 193 Cal. App. 3d 700 (1987)	555
Insurance Indus. Initiative Campaign Com. v. Eu, 203 Cal. App. 3d 961 (1988)	411
Interstate Brands v. Unemployment Ins. Appeals Bd., 26 Cal. 3d 770 (1980)	532
Isbell v. City of San Diego, 258 F. 3d 1108 (9th Cir. 2001)	55
J.L. Thomas, Inc. v. County of Los Angeles, 232 Cal. App. 3d 916 (1991)	285
J.W. Jones Cos. v. City of San Diego, 157 Cal. App. 3d 745 (1984)	34, 35, 360, 362, 363, 374
Jacobson v. County of Los Angeles, 69 Cal. App. 3d 374 (1977)	285, 564
James City County v. U.S. EPA, 12 F. 3d 1331 (4th Cir. 1993), *cert. denied*, 513 U.S. 823 (1994)	200
James City County v. U.S. EPA, 955 F. 2d 254 (4th Cir. 1992)	200
Jefferson Union School Dist. of Santa Clara City v. City Council of City of Sunnyvale, 129 Cal. App. 2d 264 (1954)	449
Jeffrey v. Superior Court, 102 Cal. App. 4th 1 (2002)	394
John Taft Corp. v. Advisory Agency, 161 Cal. App. 3d 749 (1984)	142
Johnson v. City of Loma Linda, 24 Cal. 4th 61 (2000)	531
Johnson v. State, 69 Cal. 2d 782 (1968)	471
Johnston v. City of Claremont, 49 Cal. 2d 826 (1958)	530
Jones v. City Council, 17 Cal. App. 3d 724 (1971)	62
Jordan v. Menomonee Falls, 28 Wisc. 2d 608, 137 N.W. 2d 442 (1965)	347
Joslin v. H.A.S. Ins. Brokerage, 184 Cal. App. 3d 369 (1986)	562
Kaahumanu v. County of Maui, 315 F. 3d 1215 (9th Cir. 2003)	473
Kaczorowski v. Board of Supervisors, 88 Cal. App. 4th 564 (2001)	556
Kaiser Aetna v. United States, 444 U.S. 164 (1979)	306, 348
Kalway v. City of Berkeley, 151 Cal. App. 4th 827 (2007)	142
Kane v. Redevelopment Agency, 179 Cal. App. 3d 899 (1986)	552
Karlson v. City of Camarillo, 100 Cal. App. 3d 789 (1980)	23, 527, 573
Katz v. Campbell Union High School Dist., 144 Cal. App. 4th 1024 (2006)	450
Kaufman & Broad Central Valley, Inc. v. City of Modesto, 25 Cal. App. 4th 1577 (1994)	104, 105, 279
Kaufman & Broad Communities, Inc. v. Performance Plastering, Inc., 133 Cal. App. 4th 26 (2006)	562
Kaufman & Broad-South Bay, Inc. v. Morgan Hill Unified Sch. Dist., 9 Cal. App. 4th 464 (1992)	149
Kavanau v. Santa Monica Rent Control Board, 16 Cal. 4th at 773	290, 299, 298, 336, 337
Kawaoka v. City of Arroyo Grande, 17 F. 3d 1227 (9th Cir. 1994)	41, 323, 332
Kehoe v. City of Berkeley, 67 Cal. App. 3d 666 (1977)	71, 399
Keller v. Chowchilla Water Dist., 80 Cal. App. 4th 1006 (2000)	379, 380
Keller v. State Bar, 47 Cal. 3d 1152 (1989)	414

Case	page(s)
Kelo v. City of New London, 545 U.S. 469 (2005)	3, 289–290, 329, 417
Kelsey v. Colwell, 30 Cal. App. 3d 590 (1973)	239
Kennedy v. City of Hayward, 105 Cal. App. 3d 953 (1980)	95, 455
Kern County Farm Bureau v. Allen, 450 F.3d 1072 (9th Cir. 2006)	210
Kern River Pub. Access Com. v. City of Bakersfield, 170 Cal. App. 3d 1205 (1985)	113
Keystone Bituminous Coal Association v. DeBenedictis, 480 U.S. 470 (1987)	292, 296, 307, 314
Kieffer v. Spencer, 153 Cal. App. 3d 954 (1984)	67
Kimball Laundry Co. v. United States, 338 U.S. 1 (1949)	317
Kings County Farm Bureau v. City of Hanford, 221 Cal. App. 3d 692 (1990)	21–22, 31, 124, 163, 164, 551, 576
Kinzli v. City of Santa Cruz, 818 F. 2d 1449 (9th Cir. 1987)	322, 323
Kissinger v. City of Los Angeles, 161 Cal. App. 2d 454 (1958)	52, 534
Kleitman v. Superior Court, 74 Cal. App. 4th 324 (1999)	51, 560
Klopping v. City of Whittier, 8 Cal. 3d 39 (1972)	305, 313
Knickerbocker v. City of Stockton, 199 Cal. App. 3d 235 (1988)	531
Knox v. City of Orland, 4 Cal. 4th 132 (1992)	376
Kraus v. Trinity Management Servs., Inc., 23 Cal. 4th 116 (2000)	543
Kriebel v. City Council, 112 Cal. App. 3d 693 (1980)	127, 540
Kucera v. Lizza, 59 Cal. App. 4th 1141 (1997)	234
Kuzinich v. Santa Clara, 689 F. 2d 1345 (9th Cir. 1982)	473
L&M Professional Consultants, Inc. v. Ferreira, 146 Cal. App. 3d 1038 (1983)	114
L.I.F.E. Committee v. City of Lodi, 213 Cal. App. 3d 1139 (1989)	402, 437
La Canada Flintridge Development Corporation v. Department of Transportation, 166 Cal. App. 3d 206 (1985)	480
La Fe, Inc. v. County of Los Angeles, 73 Cal. App. 4th 231 (1999)	87, 244
Lacher v. Superior Court, 230 Cal. App. 3d 1038 (1991)	468
Laguna Village, Inc. v. County of Orange, 166 Cal. App. 3d 125 (1985)	120
Laidlaw Environmental Services, Inc. v. County of Kern, 44 Cal. App. 4th 346 (1996)	553
Lake Country Estates, Inc. v. Tahoe Reg'l Planning Agency, 440 U.S. 391 (1979)	330, 331
Lakeview Dev. Corp. v. City of South Lake Tahoe, 915 F. 2d 1290 (9th Cir. 1990)	341
Lakeview Meadows Ranch v. County of Santa Clara, 27 Cal. App. 4th 593 (1994)	138, 142
Land Waste Mgmt. v. County of Contra Costa Bd. of Supervisors, 222 Cal. App. 3d 950 (1990)	95, 467
Landgate, Inc. v. California Coastal Commission, 17 Cal. 4th 1006 (1998)	290, 302, 303, 304, 305, 306, 340, 534
Landi v. County of Monterey, 139 Cal. App. 3d 934 (1983)	95, 466, 467, 468
Langrutta v. City Council, 9 Cal. App. 3d 890 (1970)	124
Laraway v. Pasadena Unified School District, 98 Cal. App. 4th 579 (2002)	567
Las Tunas Beach Geologic Hazard Abatement Dist. v. Superior Court, 38 Cal. App. 4th 1002 (1995)	442
Las Virgenes Homeowners Federation, Inc. v. County of Los Angeles, 177 Cal. App. 3d 300 (1986)	164
Laupheimer v. State of California, 200 Cal. App. 3d 440 (1988)	530
Laurel Heights Improvement Ass'n v. Regents of the Univ. of Cal., 47 Cal. 3d 376 (1988)	147, 151, 161, 166, 572, 573
Laurel Heights Improvement Ass'n v. Regents of Univ. of Cal., 6 Cal. 4th 1112 (1993)	167
Lawler v. City of Redding, 7 Cal. App. 4th 778 (1992)	75
League of Residential Neighborhood Advocates v. City of Los Angeles, 498 F.3d 1052 (4th Cir. 2007)	61, 277
League of Women Voters v. Countywide Crim. Justice Coordination Com., 203 Cal. App. 3d 529 (1988)	414
Lee v. City of Monterey Park, 173 Cal. App. 3d 798 (1985)	44, 505
Leff v. City of Monterey Park, 218 Cal. App. 3d 674 (1990)	545
Legacy Group v. City of Wasco, 106 Cal. App. 4th 1305 (2003)	125
LeGault v. Erickson, 70 Cal. App. 4th 369 (1999)	137
Legislature v. Deukmejian, 34 Cal. 3d 658 (1983)	397
Legislature v. Eu, 54 Cal. 3d 492 (1991)	386
Lehto v. City of Oxnard, 171 Cal. App. 3d 285 (1985)	470
Leroy Land Dev. Corp. v. Tahoe Reg'l Planning Agency, 939 F. 2d 696 (9th Cir. 1991)	278
Lesher Communications, Inc. v. City of Walnut Creek, 52 Cal. 3d 531 (1990)	10, 11, 21, 47, 53, 398, 401, 402, 408, 410, 411
Leslie Salt Co. v. United States, 896 F. 2d 354 (9th Cir. 1990)	176
Levald Inc. v. City of Palm Desert, 998 F. 2d 680 (9th Cir. 1993)	320, 333
Leyva v. Nielsen, 83 Cal. App. 4th 1061 (2000)	471
Lighthouse Field Beach Rescue v. City of Santa Cruz, 131 Cal. App. 4th 1170 (2005)	154
Lightweight Processing Co. v. County of Ventura, 133 Cal. App. 3d 1042 (1982)	529

Case	page(s)
Lim v. City of Long Beach, 217 F. 3d 1050 (9th Cir. 2000)	479
Lincoln Property Co. No. 41 v. Law, Inc. 45 Cal. App. 3d 230 (1975)	69
Lindelli v. Town of San Anselmo (Marin Sanitary Service), 111 Cal. App. 4th 1099 (2003)	395, 545, 546
Lingle v. Chevron U.S.A. Inc., 544 U.S. 528 (2005)	292, 293, 294, 295, 329, 332, 336, 340, 349, 351
Littoral Dev. Co. v. San Francisco Bay Conser. & Dev. Comm'n, 33 Cal. App. 4th 211 (1995)	306
Livingston Rock & Gravel Co. v. County of Los Angeles, 43 Cal. 2d 121 (1954)	63, 64
Lockard v. City of Los Angeles, 33 Cal. 2d 453 (1949)	44
Lockley v. Law Office of Cantrell, Green, Pekich, Cruz & McCort, 91 Cal. App. 4th 875 (2001)	561
Lockyer v. City and County of San Francisco, 33 Cal. 4th 1055 (2004)	479–480
Loewenstein v. City of Lafayette, 103 Cal. App. 4th 718 (2002)	304, 305, 534
Long Beach Equities, Inc. v. County of Ventura, 231 Cal. App. 3d 1016 (1991)	296, 297, 298, 323, 325, 332, 334, 344, 318, 426
Loretto v. Teleprompter Manhattan CATV Corporation, 458 U.S. 419 (1982)	293, 294
Los Altos El Granada Investors v. City of Capitola, 139 Cal. App. 4th 629 (2006)	295–296
Los Altos Property Owners Ass'n v. Hutcheon, 69 Cal. App. 3d 22 (1977)	415
Los Angeles County v. City Council of City of Lawndale, 202 Cal. App. 2d 20 (1962)	449
Los Angeles Unified School Dist. v. City of Los Angeles, 58 Cal. App. 4th 1019 (1997)	164
Love v. Wolf, 226 Cal. App. 2d 378 (1964)	561
Loyola Marymount University v. Los Angeles Unified School District, 45 Cal. App. 4th 1256 (1996)	354, 367, 368, 369
Lucas v. South Carolina Coastal Council, 505 U.S. 1003 (1992)	292, 293, 294, 298, 301, 307, 308, 314, 321, 329, 340, 424
Ludwig v. Superior Court, 37 Cal. App. 4th 8 (1995)	579
Lugar v. Edmondson Oil Co., 457 U.S. 922 (1982)	472
Lujan v. Defenders of Wildlife, 504 U.S. 555 (1992)	228
Lusardi Construction Co. v. Aubry, 1 Cal. 4th 976 (1992)	265
MacDonald, Sommer & Frates v. County of Yolo, 477 U.S. 340 (1986)	321, 324
Mack v. Ironside, 35 Cal. App. 3d 127 (1973)	53
MacLeod v. County of Santa Clara, 749 F. 2d 541 (9th Cir. 1984)	297, 331
Madrigal v. City of Huntington Beach, 147 Cal. App. 4th 1375 (2007)	153
Magan v. County of Kings, 105 Cal. App. 4th 468 (2002)	152
Maginn v. City of Glendale, 72 Cal. App. 4th 1102 (1999)	124, 540
Mahdavi v Fair Employment Practices Comm'n, 67 Cal. App. 3d 326 (1977)	529
Mahon v. County of San Mateo, 139 Cal. App. 4th 812 (2006)	466
Malibu Mountains Recreation, Inc. v. County of Los Angeles, 67 Cal. App. 4th 359 (1998)	62
Mangini v. R. J. Reynolds Tobacco Co., 7 Cal. 4th 1057 (1994)	561, 562
Mani Brothers Real Estate Group v. City of Los Angeles, 153 Cal. App. 4th 1385 (2007)	171
Manufactured Home Communities, Inc. v. City of San Jose, 420 F. 3d 1022 (9th Cir. 2005)	295, 327
Marbled Murrelet v. Babbitt, 83 F. 3d 1060 (9th Cir. 1996)	229, 230
Marblehead v. City of San Clemente, 226 Cal. App. 3d 1504 (1991)	386, 403
Margolin v. Regional Planning Comm'n, 134 Cal. App. 3d 999 (1982)	580
Marine Forests Soc'y v. California Coastal Comm'n, 104 Cal. App. 4th 1232 (2002)	243
Marine Forests Soc'y v. California Coastal Comm'n, 36 Cal. 4th 1 (2005)	243
Markley v. City Council, 131 Cal. App. 3d 656 (1982)	565
Marocco v. Ford Motor Co., 7 Cal. App. 3d 84 (1970)	561
Martin v. City and County of San Francisco, 135 Cal. App. 4th 392 (2006)	150
Maryland-Nat'l Capital Park Planning Comm'n v. U.S. Postal Serv., 487 F. 2d 1029 (D.C. Cir. 1973)	72
Massachusetts v. Watt, 716 F. 2d 946 (1st Cir. 1983)	216
Mayo v. United States, 319 U.S. 441 (1943)	72
McBail & Co. v. Solano LAFCO, 62 Cal. App. 4th 1223 (1998)	435, 448, 449
McBrearty v. Brawley, 59 Cal. App. 4th 1441 (1997)	373
McCormick v. Board of Supervisors, 198 Cal. App. 3d 352 (1988)	569
McIntosh v. Aubry (Pricor), 14 Cal. App. 4th 1576 (1993)	265
McKevitt v. City of Sacramento, 55 Cal. App. 117 (1921)	398
McManus v. KPAL Broad. Corp., 182 Cal. App. 2d 558 (1960)	62
McMillan v. American Gen. Fin. Corp., 60 Cal. App. 3d 175 (1976)	284
McMullan v. Santa Monica Rent Control Bd., 168 Cal. App. 3d 960 (1985)	80, 100, 101
McPherson v. City of Manhattan Beach, 78 Cal. App. 4th 1252 (2000)	106, 127
McQueen v. Board of Directors, 202 Cal. App. 3d 1136 (1988)	550
Meakin v. Steveland, Inc., 68 Cal. App. 3d 490 (1977)	268

Table of Authorities

Case	page(s)
Melton v. City of San Pablo, 252 Cal. App. 2d 794 (1967)	62
Meredith v. Talbot County, 560 A. 2d 599 (Md. App. 1989)	279
Meridian Ocean Sys., Inc. v. State Lands Comm'n, 222 Cal. App. 3d 153 (1990)	465, 468, 527, 538
Merritt v. City of Pleasanton, 89 Cal. App. 4th 1032 (2001)	401
Mervyn's v. Reyes, 69 Cal. App. 4th 93 (1998)	389–390
Metromedia, Inc. v. City of San Diego, 26 Cal. 3d 848 (1980)	1, 3, 64, 233
Metropolitan Water Dist. v. Imperial Irr. Dist., 80 Cal. App. 4th 1403 (2000)	581
Midrash Sephardi, Inc. v. Town of Surfside, 366 F. 3d 1214 (11th Cir. 2004)	58
Midway Orchards v. County of Butte, 220 Cal. App. 3d 765 (1990)	29, 274, 275, 402
Mikels v. Rager, 232 Cal. App. 3d 334 (1991)	130
Milagra Ridge Partners Ltd. v. City of Pacifica, 62 Cal. App. 4th 108 (1998)	323
Miller v. City of Hermosa Beach, 13 Cal. App. 4th 1118 (1993)	570
Miller v. Miller, 87 Cal. App. 3d 762 (1978)	414
Miller v. Schoene, 276 U.S. 272 (1928)	315
Mira Dev. Corp. v. City of San Diego, 205 Cal. App. 3d 1201 (1988)	117, 118, 286, 365, 366
Mira Mar Mobile Community v. City of Oceanside, 119 Cal. App. 4th 477 (2004)	11, 167
Mission Oaks Ranch, Ltd. v. County of Santa Barbara, 65 Cal. App. 4th 713 (1998)	159, 580
Mitchell v. County of Orange, 165 Cal. App. 3d 1185 (1985)	25, 41, 528, 569
Mitcheltree v. City of Los Angeles, 17 Cal. App. 3d 791 (1971)	62
Mola Dev. Corp. v. City of Seal Beach, 57 Cal. App. 4th 405 (1997)	531
Monell v. Dept. of Social Servs., 436 U.S. 658 (1978)	331, 472
Moore v. City of Costa Mesa, 886 F. 2d 260 (9th Cir. 1989)	298
Moores v. Mendocino County, 122 Cal. App. 4th 883 (2004)	142
Moran v. State Bd. of Medical Examiners, 32 Cal. 2d 301 (1948)	555
Morehart v. County of Santa Barbara, 7 Cal. 4th 725 (1994)	4, 5, 13, 81, 144, 402, 557
Morgan v. United States, 298 U.S. 468 (1936)	457
Morrill v. Lujan, 802 F. Supp. 424 (S.D. Ala. 1992)	228–229, 230
Mountain Defense League v. Board of Supervisors, 65 Cal. App. 3d 723 (1977)	286, 538
Mountain Lion Found. v. Fish & Game Comm'n, 16 Cal. 4th 105 (1997)	148, 528
Mozzetti v. City of Brisbane, 67 Cal. App. 3d 565 (1977)	561
Mt. Graham Red Squirrel v. Madigan, 954 F. 2d 1441 (9th Cir. 1992)	219
Murrieta Valley Unified Sch. Dist. v. County of Riverside, 228 Cal. App. 3d 1212 (1991)	117, 118, 365, 366
Muzzy Ranch v. Solano County Airport Land Use Comm'n, 41 Cal. 4th 372 (2007)	27, 150, 151
Myers v. Patterson, 196 Cal. App. 3d 130 (1987)	389, 390, 393
N.L. Neilson and Assoc. For Legal Desert Development, et al. v. City of California City, 145 Cal. App. 4th 633 (2007)	70–71
N.T. Hill, Inc. v. City of Fresno, 72 Cal. App. 4th 977 (1999)	103, 757, 577
Nacimiento Reg'l Water Mgmt. Advisory Com. v. Monterey County Water Resources Agency, 122 Cal. App. 4th 961 (2004)	570
Napa Citizens for Honest Gov't v. Napa County Bd. of Supervisors, 91 Cal. App. 4th 342 (2001)	26, 39, 163, 167, 170, 539
Napa Home Builders Ass'n v. City of Napa, 90 Cal. App. 4th 188 (2001)	355
Nash v. City of Santa Monica, 37 Cal. 3d 97 (1984)	46, 332, 340
Nasha v. City of Los Angeles, 125 Cal. App. 4th 470 (2004)	52, 535, 536
Nat'l Adver. Co. v. County of Monterey, 1 Cal. 3d 875 (1970)	63
Nat'l Ass'n of Home Builders v. Defenders of Wildlife, 127 S. Ct. 2518 (2007)	214
Nat'l Ass'n of Home Builders v. Norton, 340 F. 3d 835 (9th Cir. 2003)	209
Nat'l Assn of Home Builders v. U.S. Army Corps of Eng'rs, 453 F. Supp. 2d 116 (D.D.C. 2006)	191
Nat'l Ass'n of Home Builders v. U.S. Army Corps of Eng'rs. Not Reported in F. Supp. 2d, 64 ERC 2050, 2007 U.S. Dist. LEXIS 6366 (D.D.C. Jan. 30, 2007)	185
Nat'l Mining Ass'n v. U.S. Army Corps of Eng'rs, 145 F. 3d 1399 (D.C. Cir. 1998)	184
Nat'l Parks & Conser. Ass'n v. County of Riverside, 71 Cal. App. 4th 1341 (1999)	573
Nat'l Parks & Conser. Ass'n v. County of Riverside, 81 Cal. App. 4th 234 (2000)	581
Nat'l Wildlife Fed'n v. Coleman, 529 F. 2d 359 (5th Cir.), cert. denied, 429 U.S. 979 (1976)	214, 215
Nat'l Wildlife Fed'n v. NMFS, 481 F. 3d 1224 (9th Cir. 2007)	215, 217, 218, 222
Native American Sacred Site & Envtl. Protection Ass'n v. City of San Juan Capistrano, 120 Cal. App. 4th 961 (2004)	148, 394, 405
Native Sun/Lyon Communities v. City of Escondido, 15 Cal. App. 4th 892 (1993)	98, 274, 276
Natural Resources Defense Council v. Kempthorne, 506 F. Supp. 2d 322 (E.D. Cal. 2007)	217
Natural Resources Defense Council v. Rogers, 381 F. Supp. 2d 1212 (E.D. Cal. 2005)	217

Case	page(s)
Negrete v. State Personnel Bd., 213 Cal. App. 3d 1160 (1989)	537
Negron v. Dundee, 221 Cal. App. 3d 1502 (1990)	139
Neighborhood Action Group v. County of Calaveras, 156 Cal. App. 3d 1176 (1984)	21, 22, 34, 59, 468, 530
Nelson v. Carlson, 17 Cal. App. 4th 732 (1993)	389, 394
New Mexico Cattle Growers Ass'n v. U.S. Fish and Wildlife Serv., 248 F. 3d 1277 (10th Cir. 2001)	213
Newberry Springs Water Ass'n v. County of San Bernardino, 150 Cal. App. 3d 740 (1984)	456
Newsom v. Board of Supervisors, 205 Cal. 262 (1928)	403
Nightlife Partners, Ltd. v. City of Beverly Hills, 108 Cal. App. 4th 81 (2002)	458
No Oil, Inc. v. City of Los Angeles, 13 Cal. 3d 68 (1974)	154
No Oil, Inc. v. City of Los Angeles, 196 Cal. App. 3d 223 (1987)	25, 151, 539
Nollan v. California Coastal Commission, 483 U.S. 825 (1987)	64, 108, 233, 235, 250, 278–279, 292, 295, 300, 329, 340, 341, 342, 343, 345, 347, 350, 353, 355, 370, 510–512
Nordlinger v. Hahn, 505 U.S. 1 (1992)	361
Norlund v. Thorpe, 34 Cal. App. 3d 672 (1973)	449
Norsco Enters. v. City of Fremont, 54 Cal. App. 3d 488 (1976)	118–119, 340
North Pacifica, LLC v. City of Pacifica, 234 F. Supp. 2d 1053 (N.D. Cal. 2002)	495
Northern California River Watch v. City of Healdsburg, 496 F. 3d 993 (9th Cir. 2007)	179
Northern Spotted Owl v. Hodel, 716 F. Supp. 479 (W.D. Wash. 1988)	209
Northern Spotted Owl v. Lujan, 758 F. Supp. 621 (W.D. Wash. 1991)	212
Northwest Ecosystem Alliance v. U.S. Fish & Wildlife Service, 475 F.3d 1136 (9th Cir. 2007)	209
Not About Water Com. v. Board of Supervisors, 95 Cal. App. 4th 982 (2002)	377
Novi v. City of Pacifica, 169 Cal. App. 3d 678 (1985)	49–50, 234
NRDC v. Callaway, 392 F. Supp. 685, 686 (D.D.C. 1975)	176
NRDC v. Kempthorne, 506 F. Supp. 2d 322 (E.D. Cal. 2007)	218, 219, 220
O'Loane v. O'Rourke, 231 Cal. App. 2d 774 (1965)	43, 528
O.G. Sansone Co. v. Dept. of Transportation, 55 Cal. App. 3d 434 (1976)	265
Oceanic California, Inc. v. North Cent. Coast Reg'l Comm'n, 63 Cal. App. 3d 57 (1976)	101, 271
Ogborn v. City of Lancaster, 101 Cal. App. 4th 448 (2002)	473
Ojavan Investors, Inc. v. California Coastal Comm'n, 26 Cal. App. 4th 516 (1994)	328

Case	page(s)
Old Dearborn Distrib. Co. v. Seagram Distillers Corp., 299 U.S. 183 (1936)	361
Old Santa Barbara Pier Co. v. State of California, 71 Cal. App. 3d 250 (1977)	458
Olive Proration Program Com. v. Agricultural Prorate Comm'n, 17 Cal. 2d 204 (1941)	550
Oregon Natural Resources Council v. Allen, 476 F. 3d 1031 (9th Cir. 2007)	217, 218, 228
Orinda Ass'n v. Board of Supervisors, 182 Cal. App. 3d 1145 (1986)	61, 150, 285
Orinda Homeowners Comm. v. Board of Supervisors, 11 Cal. App. 3d 768 (1970)	69
Orleans Audubon Soc'y v. Lee, 742 F. 2d 901 (5th Cir. 1984)	186
Orsi v. City Council of Salinas, 219 Cal. App. 3d 1576 (1990)	94, 464, 465, 467
Outdoor Systems Inc. v. City of Mesa, 997 F. 2d 604 (9th Cir. 1993)	297-298
Owen v. City of Independence, 445 U.S. 622 (1980)	331
Oxnard Harbor Dist. v. LAFCO, 16 Cal. App. 4th 259 (1993)	437
Pacific Coast Fed'n of Fishermen's Ass'ns v. Bureau of Reclamation, 426 F. 3d 1082 (9th Cir. 2005)	220
Pacific Legal Foundation v. Andrus, 657 F. 2d 829 (6th Cir. 1981)	210, 229
Pacific Rivers Council v. Thomas, 30 F. 3d 1050 (9th Cir. 1994)	214
Pacifica Corp. v. City of Camarillo, 149 Cal. App. 3d 168 (1983)	284, 527, 529
Pajaro Valley Water Mgmt. Agency v. Amrhein, 150 Cal. App. 4th 1364 (2007)	378
Pala Band of Mission Indians v. County of San Diego, 68 Cal. App. 4th 556 (1998)	149
Palazzolo v. Rhode Island, 533 U.S. 606 (2001)	293, 294, 307, 321
Palila v. Hawaii Dep't of Land and Natural Resources, 471 F. Supp. 985 (D. Hawaii 1979)	228
Palila v. Hawaii Dep't of Land and Natural Resources, 852 F. 2d 1106 (9th Cir. 1988)	223
Palmer v. Board of Supervisors, 145 Cal. App. 3d 779 (1983)	101
Palmer v. City of Ojai, 178 Cal. App. 3d 280 (1986)	467
Palomar Mobilehome Park Ass'n v. City of San Marcos, 989 F. 2d 362 (9th Cir. 1993)	326
Pan Pacific Properties, Inc. v. County of Santa Cruz, 81 Cal. App. 3d 244 (1978)	544
Park Area Neighbors v. Town of Fairfax, 29 Cal. App. 4th 1442 (1994)	547, 548
Patrick Media Group Inc. v. California Coastal Comm'n, 9 Cal. App. 4th 592 (1992)	328, 530, 531, 557
Patterson v. Central Coast Reg'l Comm'n, 58 Cal. App. 3d 833 (1976)	530, 538

Case	page(s)
Penn Central Transportation Company v. City of New York, 438 U.S. 104 (1978)	3, 67, 237, 249, 291–292, 294–295, 296, 297–299, 305, 306, 307, 308, 321, 344, 424
Penn-Co v. Board of Supervisors, 158 Cal. App. 3d 1072 (1984)	61
Pennsylvania Coal Co. v. Mahon, 260 U.S. 393 (1922)	313, 348
People ex rel. Deukmejian v. County of Mendocino, 36 Cal. 3d 476 (1984)	4
People v. County of Kern, 39 Cal. App. 3d 830 (1974)	271
People v. Dep't of Hous. & Cmty Dev., 45 Cal. App. 3d 185 (1975)	544
People v. Djekich, 229 Cal. App. 3d 1213 (1991)	475
People v. Gates, 41 Cal. App. 3d 590 (1974)	49
People v. H & H Properties, 154 Cal. App. 3d 894 (1984)	101, 273
People v. Local Agency Formation Comm'n, 81 Cal. App. 3d 464 (1978)	453
People v. Long, 7 Cal. App. 3d 586 (1970)	561
People v. Minor, 96 Cal. App. 4th 29 (2002)	477
People v. Thomas Shelton Powers, 2 Cal. App. 4th 330 (1992)	271
Peralta Fed. of Teachers v. Peralta Cmty. Coll. Dist., 24 Cal. 3d 369 (1979)	543
Personal Watercraft Coalition v. Marin County Board of Supervisors, 100 Cal. App. 4th 129 (2002)	50
Pescosolido v. Smith, 142 Cal. App. 3d 964 (1983)	83, 87
Pettitt v. City of Fresno, 34 Cal. App. 3d 813 (1973)	271
Pettye v. City and County of San Francisco, 118 Cal. App. 4th 233 (2004)	403
Pfeiffer v. City of La Mesa, 69 Cal. App. 3d 74 (1977)	100, 279, 576
Pistoresi v. City of Madera, 138 Cal. App. 3d 284 (1982)	453
Pitts v. Perluss, 58 Cal. 2d 824 (1962)	527
Placer County LAFCO v. Nevada County LAFCO, 135 Cal. App. 4th 793 (2006)	435, 438, 439, 452
Placer Ranch Partners v. County of Placer, 91 Cal. App. 4th 1336 (2001)	285
Planning & Conserv. League v. Dep't of Fish and Game, 55 Cal. App. 4th 479 (1997)	232
Planning & Conserv. League v. Dep't of Water Resources, 83 Cal. App. 4th 892 (2000)	148, 162, 166
Platte River Whooping Crane v. F.E.R.C., 876 F. 2d 109 (D.C. Cir. 1989)	219
Pomona Valley Hospital Med. Ctr. v. Superior Court, 55 Cal. App. 4th 93 (1997)	559
Ponderosa Homes, Inc. v. City of San Ramon, 23 Cal. App. 4th 1761 (1994)	575
Pongputmong v. City of Santa Monica, 15 Cal. App. 4th 99 (1993)	94
Portland Audubon Society v. Endangered Species Committee, 984 F. 2d 1534 (9th Cir. 1993)	221
Pratt v. Adams, 229 Cal. App. 2d 602 (1964)	83, 86
Prentis v. Atlantic Coast Line Co., 211 U.S. 210, 227 (1908)	538
Prentiss v. City of South Pasadena, 15 Cal. App. 4th 85 (1993)	237, 528
Presenting Jamul v. Board of Supervisors, 231 Cal. App. 3d 665, 670 (1991)	125
Preservation Action Council v. City of San Jose, 141 Cal. App. 4th 1336 (2006)	168
Protect Our Water v. County of Merced, 110 Cal. App. 4th 362 (2003)	284, 570
Protect the Historic Amador Waterways v. Amador Water Agency, 116 Cal. App. 4th 1099 (2004)	161
Quintero v. City of Santa Ana, 114 Cal. App. 4th 810 (2003)	458
Qwest Communications, Inc. v. City of Berkeley, 433 F. 3d 1253 (9th Cir. 2006)	5
Rancho La Costa v. County of San Diego, 111 Cal. App. 3d 54 (1980)	2
Rapanos v. United States, 126 S. Ct. 2208 (2006)	178, 179, 180, 181, 202
Rapp v. County of Napa Planning Comm'n, 204 Cal. App. 2d 695 (1962)	62
Rasmussen v. City Council, 140 Cal. App. 3d 842 (1983)	119
Raven v. Deukmejian, 52 Cal. 3d 336 (1990)	396
Redevelopment Agency v. City of Berkeley, 80 Cal. App. 3d 158 (1978)	398
Redwood Coast Watersheds Alliance v. State Bd. of Forestry & Fire Protection, 70 Cal. App. 4th 962 (1999)	529
Regency Outdoor Advertising, Inc. v. City of Los Angeles, 39 Cal. 4th 507 (2006)	296
Regency Outdoor Advertising, Inc. v. City of West Hollywood, 153 Cal. App. 4th 825 (2007)	553
Regents of Univ. of Cal. v. City of Santa Monica, 77 Cal. App. 3d 130 (1978)	73
Region 8 Forest Serv. Timber Purchasers Council v. Alcock, 736 F. Supp. 267 (N.D. Ga. 1990)	229
Reitman v. Mulkey, 41 Cal. 3d 810 (1986)	421, 504
Remmenga v. California Coastal Comm'n, 163 Cal. App. 3d 623 (1985)	4
Renton v. Playtime Theatres, Inc., 475 U.S. 41 (1986)	55
Residents Ad Hoc Stadium Com. v. Board of Trustees, 89 Cal. App. 3d 274 (1979)	149, 166
Resource Defense Fund v. County of Santa Cruz, 133 Cal. App. 3d 800 (1982)	21, 34, 47–48, 402
Resource Defense Fund v. Local Agency Formation Comm'n, 191 Cal. App. 3d 886 (1987)	448, 547, 551
Resources Ltd. v. Robertson, 35 F. 3d 1300 (9th Cir. 1993)	216

Case	page(s)
Rezai v. City of Tustin, 26 Cal. App. 4th 443 (1994)	320, 328
Rice v. Harken Exploration Co., 250 F. 3d 264 (5th Cir. 2001)	178
Richards v. City of Tustin, 225 Cal. App. 2d 97 (1964)	528
Richmond v. Shasta Community Services District, 32 Cal. 4th 409 (2004)	376, 378, 516
Ridgecrest Charter School v. Sierra Sands Unified School Dist., 130 Cal. App. 4th 986 (2005)	449
Riggs v. City of Oxnard, 154 Cal. App. 3d 526 (1984)	478
Rio Vista Farm Bureau Center v. County of Solano, 5 Cal. App. 4th 351 (1992)	170
Riverside Irrigation District v. Andrews, 758 F. 2d 508 (10th Cir. 1985)	214, 215, 222
Rizzo v. Board of Trustees, 27 Cal. App. 4th 853 (1994)	539
Robertson v. Seattle Audubon Soc'y, 503 U.S. 429 (1992)	219
Robinson v. City of Alameda, 194 Cal. App. 3d 1286 (1987)	81, 83
Roccaforte v. City of San Diego, 89 Cal. App. 3d 877 (1979)	554
Rohn v. City of Visalia, 214 Cal. App. 3d 1463 (1989)	330, 342–343, 345
Roosevelt Campobello Int'l Park Comm'n v. U.S. EPA, 684 F. 2d 1041 (1st Cir. 1982)	214, 216, 219
Rosenaur v. Scherer, 88 Cal. App. 4th 260 (2001)	579
Ross v. City of Rolling Hills Estates, 192 Cal. App. 3d 370 (1987)	50, 234
Rossco Holdings, Inc. v. State of California, 212 Cal. App. 3d 642 (1989)	100, 328, 530
Rossi v. Brown, 9 Cal. 4th 688 (1995)	385, 386, 387, 397, 404
Royal Convalescent Hosp. v. State Bd. of Control, 99 Cal. App. 3d 788 (1979)	530
Royalty Carpet Mills, Inc. v. City of Irvine, 125 Cal. App. 4th 1110 (2005)	540
RRLH, Inc. v. Saddleback Valley Unified Sch. Dist., 222 Cal. App. 3d 1602 (1990)	371
Running Fence Corp. v. Superior Court, 51 Cal. App. 3d 400 (1975)	559
Russ Bldg. Partnership v. City and County of San Francisco, 44 Cal. 3d 839 (1988)	273, 346
Russ Bldg. Partnership v. City and County of San Francisco, 199 Cal. App. 3d 1496 (1987)	340, 341, 360, 361, 374
Saad v. City of Berkeley, 24 Cal. App. 4th 1206 (1994)	62, 234, 341, 344, 346
Sabek, Inc. v. County of Sonoma, 190 Cal. App. 3d 163 (1987)	64
Sacramento Old City Association v. City Council, 229 Cal. App. 3d 1011 (1991)	164, 558
SAFE v. Board of Supervisors, 13 Cal. App. 4th 141 (1993)	411
Salmon Protection and Watershed Network v. County of Marin, 125 Cal. App. 4th 1098 (2004)	152
San Bernardino Assoc. Governments v. Superior Ct., 135 Cal. App. 4th 1106 (2006)	148
San Bernardino Valley Audubon Society, Inc. v. County of San Bernardino, 155 Cal. App. 3d 738 (1984)	166, 581
San Diego Bldg. Contractors Ass'n v. City Council, 13 Cal. 3d 205 (1974)	527, 528, 529
San Diego Gas & Elec. Co. v. City of San Diego, 450 U.S. 621 (1981)	330
San Diego Service Authority v. Superior Court, 198 Cal. App. 3d 1466 (1988)	267, 268
San Dieguito Partnership, L.P. v. City of San Diego, 7 Cal. App. 4th 748 (1992)	88
San Franciscans Upholding the Downtown Plan v. City and County of San Francisco, 102 Cal. App. 4th 656 (2002)	25, 168
San Francisco Baykeeper v. Cargill Salt Division, 481 F. 3d 700 (9th Cir. 2007)	179
San Francisco Forty-Niners v. Nishioka (Comstock), 75 Cal. App. 4th 637 (1999)	394
San Joaquin Raptor Rescue Center v. County of Merced, 149 Cal. App. 4th 645 (2007)	164
San Joaquin Raptor/Wildlife Rescue Ctr. v. County of Stanislaus, 27 Cal. App. 4th 740 (1994)	163
San Jose Christian College v. City of Morgan Hill, 360 F. 3d 1024 (9th Cir. 2004)	57–58
San Lorenzo Valley Community Advocates for Responsible Education v. San Lorenzo Valley Unified School Dist., 139 Cal. App. 4th 1356 (2006)	152
San Mateo County Coastal Landowners' Ass'n v. County of San Mateo, 38 Cal. App. 4th 523 (1995)	15, 351, 397, 402, 404, 491
San Pedro Hotel Co. v. City of Los Angeles, 159 F. 3d 470 (9th Cir. 1998)	473
San Remo Hotel L.P. v. City and County of San Francisco, 545 U.S. 323 (2005)	358
San Remo Hotel v. City and County of San Francisco, 27 Cal. 4th 643 (2002)	294, 300, 344, 351, 352, 354, 355, 511, 513, 515
San Remo Hotel v. City and County of San Francisco, 545 U.S. 323 (2005)	326–327, 328, 329, 358
Santa Clara County Contractors and Homebuilders Ass'n v. City of Santa Clara, 232 Cal. App. 2d 564 (1965)	80
Santa Clara County Local Transp. Auth. v. Guardino, 11 Cal. 4th 220 (1995)	374, 404
Santa Clarita Organization for Planning the Environment v. County of Los Angeles (SCOPE 1), 106 Cal. App. 4th 715 (2003)	162

Case	page(s)
Santa Clarita Organization for Planning the Environment v. County of Los Angeles (SCOPE 2), 2007 WL 2773399 at *10	163
Santa Margarita Area Residents Together (SMART) v. County of San Luis Obispo, 84 Cal. App. 4th 221 (2000)	274
Santa Monica Beach Ltd. v. Superior Court, 19 Cal. 4th 952 (1999)	4, 300, 350–351
Santa Monica Pines, Ltd. v. Rent Control Board, 35 Cal. 3d 858, 866 (1984)	80, 91, 101, 127, 271, 273
Santa Rosa Band of Indians v. Kings County, 532 F. 2d 655 (9th Cir. 1975)	75
Santiago County Water Dist. v. County of Orange, 118 Cal. App. 3d 818 (1981)	151, 161, 162
Save El Toro Ass'n v. Days, 74 Cal. App. 3d 64 (1977)	17, 22
Save Our Bay, Inc. v. San Diego Unified Port Dist., 42 Cal. App. 4th 686 (1996)	556
Save Our Carmel River v. Monterey Peninsula Water Mgmt. Dist., 141 Cal. App. 4th 677 (2006)	152, 153
Save Our Neighborhood v. Lishman, 140 Cal. App. 4th 1288 (2006)	171
Save Our Peninsula Comm. v. County of Monterey, 87 Cal. App. 4th 99 (2001)	25, 160, 164
Save Our Residential Env't v. City of W. Hollywood, 9 Cal. App. 4th 1745 (1992)	166
Save San Francisco Bay Ass'n v. San Francisco Bay Conserv. and Dev. Comm'n, 10 Cal. App. 4th 908 (1992)	166
Save Stanislaus Area Farm Econ. (SAFE) v. Board of Supervisors, 13 Cal. App. 4th 141 (1993)	395, 409
Save the Yaak Com. v. Block, 840 F. 2d 714 (9th Cir. 1988)	230
Schaeffer Land Trust v. San Jose City Council, 215 Cal. App. 3d 612 (1989)	163-164
Schnuck v. City of Santa Monica, 935 F. 2d 171 (9th Cir. 1991)	325
Schroeder v. Irvine City Council, 97 Cal. App. 4th 174 (2002)	414
Scott v. City of Indian Wells, 6 Cal. 3d 541 (1972)	456, 535, 557
Scrutton v. County of Sacramento, 275 Cal. App. 2d 412 (1969)	2, 68
Sea & Sage Audubon Soc'y, Inc. v. Planning Comm'n, 34 Cal. 3d 412 (1983)	124
Segundo v. City of Rancho Mirage, 813 F. 2d 1387 (9th Cir. 1987)	75
Selinger v. City Council, 216 Cal. App. 3d 259 (1989)	94, 467
Senate v. Jones, 21 Cal. 4th 1142 (1999)	396, 411
Sequoyah Hills Homeowners Ass'n v. City of Oakland, 23 Cal. App. 4th 704, 707 (1993)	26, 27, 121, 495, 539
Serra Canyon Company Ltd. v. California Coastal Commission, 120 Cal. App. 4th 663 (2004)	328
Serrano v. Priest, 20 Cal. 3d 25 (1977)	580
Shannon v. City of Los Angeles, 205 Cal. 366 (1928)	554
Shapell Indus., Inc. v. Governing Bd., 1 Cal. App. 4th 218 (1991)	342, 535, 578–579
Shea Homes Ltd. Partnership v. County of Alameda, 110 Cal. App. 4th 1246 (2003)	396, 397, 498, 504
Shelley v. Kraemer, 344 U.S. 1(1948)	504
Shelter Creek Dev. Corp. v. City of Oxnard, 34 Cal. 3d 733 (1983)	79–80
Sierra Club v. Board of Supervisors, 126 Cal. App. 3d 698 (1981)	13, 20, 21, 24, 31, 402, 410
Sierra Club v. California Coastal Comm'n, 35 Cal. 4th 839 (2005)	168
Sierra Club v. California Coastal Comm'n, 95 Cal. App. 3d 495 (1979)	555, 556
Sierra Club v. California Dept. of Forestry, 150 Cal. App. 4th 370 (2007)	154
Sierra Club v. City of Hayward, 28 Cal. 3d 840 (1981)	241, 530, 537
Sierra Club v. County of Contra Costa, 10 Cal. App. 4th 1212 (1992)	169
Sierra Club v. County of Napa, 121 Cal. App. 4th 1490 (2004)	41, 168
Sierra Club v. Gilroy City Council, 222 Cal. App. 3d 30 (1990)	527–528
Sierra Club v. Local Agency Formation Commission, 21 Cal. 4th 489 (1999)	451, 548
Sierra Club v. Lyng, 694 F. Supp. 1260 (E.D. Tex. 1988)	223
Sierra Club v. Marsh, 816 F. 2d 1376 (9th Cir. 1987)	215, 219
Sierra Club v. San Joaquin LAFCO, 21 Cal. 4th 489 (1999)	435, 437
Sierra Club v. Westside Irrigation Dist., 128 Cal. App. 4th 690 (2005)	161
Sierra Club v. Yeutter, 926 F. 2d 429 (5th Cir. 1991)	218, 219, 223, 230
Silvera v. City of S. Lake Tahoe, 3 Cal. App. 3d 554 (1970)	67
Simi Valley Recreation and Park Dist. v. LAFCO, 51 Cal. App. 3d 648 (1975)	448, 449
Simpson v. Hite, 36 Cal. 2d 125 (1950)	398, 403
Sinclair Oil Corp. v. County of Santa Barbara, 96 F. 3d 401 (9th Cir. 1996)	323
Sinclair Paint Co. v. State Board of Equalization, 15 Cal. 4th 866 (1997)	341, 373
Sladovich v. County of Fresno, 158 Cal. App. 2d 230 (1958)	52
Slagle Constr. Co. v. County of Contra Costa, 67 Cal. App. 3d 559 (1977)	364, 528
SMART v. County of San Luis Obispo, 84 Cal. App. 4th 221 (2000)	276
Smith v. County of Santa Barbara, 203 Cal. App. 3d 1415 (1988)	72
Smith v. County of Santa Barbara, 7 Cal. App. 4th 770 (1992)	480
Snow v. City of Garden Grove, 188 Cal. App. 2d 496 (1961)	62
Socialist Party v. Uhl, 155 Cal. 776 (1909)	6

Case	page(s)
Soderling v. City of Santa Monica, 142 Cal. App. 3d 501 (1983)	35, 79, 115, 116, 119, 124–125, 127, 363
Solid Waste Agency of Northern Cook County (SWANCC) v. U.S. Army Corps of Eng'rs, 531 U.S. 159 (2001)	176, 177, 178, 180–181, 202
Sonoma County Nuclear Free Zone '86 v. Superior Court, 189 Cal. App. 3d 167 (1987)	555
Sosinsky v. Grant, 6 Cal. App. 4th 1548 (1992)	562
Sounheim v. City of San Dimas, 47 Cal. App. 4th 1181 (1996)	501
Sounhein v. City of San Dimas, 11 Cal. App. 4th 1255 (1992)	49
South Cent. Coast Reg'l Comm'n v. Charles A. Pratt Constr. Co., 128 Cal. App. 3d 830 (1982)	131
Southern Burlington County N.A.A.C.P. v. Township of Mt. Laurel (Mt. Laurel I), 336 A.2d 713 (N.J. 1983)	509
Southern Burlington County N.A.A.C.P. v. Township of Mt. Laurel (Mt. Laurel II), 456 A.2d 390 (N.J. 1983)	509
Southern Pines Ass'n v. United States, 912 F. 2d 713 (4th Cir. 1990)	205
Southwest Diversified, Inc. v. City of Brisbane, 229 Cal. App. 3d 1548 (1991)	528
Spirit of the Sage Council v. Norton, No. 98–1873 (EGS) (D.D.C. Aug. 30, 2007)	227
Sprague v. County of San Diego, 106 Cal. App. 4th 119 (2003)	124, 540
Squaw Valley Development Co. v. Goldberg, 375 F. 3d 936 (9th Cir. 2004)	335, 479
Stanislaus Natural Heritage Project v. County of Stanislaus, 48 Cal. App. 4th 182 (1996)	158, 162
Stanson v. Mott, 17 Cal. 3d 206 (1976)	414, 415
Stanton v. Dumke, 64 Cal. 2d 199 (1966)	564
State of California v. Superior Court (Perry), 150 Cal. App. 3d 848 (1984)	470
State of California v. Superior Court, 12 Cal. 3d 237 (1974)	530, 531, 535, 555, 557, 558, 560, 561
Stein v. City of Santa Monica, 110 Cal. App. 3d 458 (1980)	405, 416
Steketee v. Lintz, Williams & Rothberg, 38 Cal. 3d 46 (1985)	540
Stell v. Jay Hales Dev. Co., 11 Cal. App. 4th 1214 (1992)	125, 138, 143
Stevens v. City of Glendale, 125 Cal. App. 3d 986 (1981)	164
Stoddard v. Edelman, 4 Cal. App. 3d 544 (1970)	62
Stoeco Dev. Ltd. v. U.S. Army Corps of Eng'rs, 792 F. Supp. 339 (D. N.J. 1992)	204
Stolman v. City of Los Angeles, 114 Cal. App. 4th 916 (2003)	565
Stop H-3 Ass'n v. Dole, 740 F. 2d 1442 (9th Cir. 1984)	216
StorMedia Inc. v. Superior Court, 20 Cal. 4th 449 (1999)	562
Strong v. County of Santa Cruz, 15 Cal. 3d 720 (1975)	271
Stubblefield Construction Co. v. City of San Bernardino, 32 Cal. App. 4th 687 (1995)	52, 285, 332, 334, 536
Suitum v. Tahoe Regional Planning Agency, 520 U.S. 725 (1997)	249, 320, 324
Sukut-Coulson, Inc. v. Allied Canon Co., 85 Cal. App. 3d 648 (1978)	134
Sundstrom v. County of Mendocino, 202 Cal. App. 3d 296 (1988)	153
Sunny Slope Water Co. v. City of Pasadena, 1 Cal. 2d 87 (1934)	74
Sunset Drive Corp. v. City of Redlands, 73 Cal. App. 4th 215 (1999)	94, 160, 465, 472, 528
Sunset View Cemetery Ass'n v. Kraintz, 196 Cal. App. 2d 115 (1961)	364
Surfside Colony, Ltd. v. California Coastal Comm'n, 226 Cal. App. 3d 1260 (1991)	330, 345
Sutherland v. City of Fort Bragg, 86 Cal. App. 4th 13 (2000)	478
Sylvester v. U.S. Army Corps of Engineers, 882 F. 2d 407 (9th Cir. 1989)	196
Tahoe Regional Planning Agency v. King, 233 Cal. App. 3d 1365 (1991)	64, 235, 311, 346
Tahoe Vista Concerned Citizens v. County of Placer, 81 Cal. App. 4th 577 (2000)	124, 545, 548, 571
Tahoe-Sierra Preservation Council, Inc. v. Tahoe Regional Planning Agency, 535 U.S. 302 (2002)	67, 293, 301, 307, 308, 311, 421
Taschner v. City Council, 31 Cal. App. 3d 48 (1973)	43
Taxpayers to Limit Campaign Spending v. Fair Political Practices Comm'n, 51 Cal. 3d 744 (1990)	412, 413, 416, 434
Taylor v. Nichols, 558 F. 2d 561 (10th Cir. 1977)	330
Temecula Band of Luiseno Mission Indians v. Rancho California Water District, 43 Cal. App. 4th 425 (1996)	551
Tennessee Valley Authority v. Hill, 437 U.S. 153 (1978)	220
Tenney v. Brandhove, 341 U.S. 367 (1951)	472
Tensor Group v. City of Glendale, 14 Cal. App. 4th 1541 (1993)	306
Terminal Plaza Corp. v. City and County of San Francisco, 177 Cal. App. 3d 892 (1986)	340
Terminal Plaza Corp. v. City and County of San Francisco, 186 Cal. App. 3d 814 (1986)	479, 529
Terminals Equip. Co. v. City and County of San Francisco, 221 Cal. App. 3d 234 (1990)	297, 298
The Legacy Group v. City of Wasco, 106 Cal. App. 4th 1305 (2003)	273, 274
The Pines v. City of Santa Monica, 29 Cal. 3d 656 (1981)	80, 91
Tillie Lewis Foods v. City of Pittsburg, 52 Cal. App. 3d 983 (1975)	438

Case	page(s)
Times Mirror Co. v. Superior Court, 53 Cal. 3d 1325 (1991)	561
Tisher v. California Horse Racing Bd. 231 Cal. App. 3d 349 (1991)	565
Tobe v. City of Santa Ana, 9 Cal. 4th 1069 (1995)	554
Todd v. City of Visalia, 254 Cal. App. 2d 679 (1967)	463
Toigo v. Town of Ross, 70 Cal. App. 4th 309 (1998)	323
Topanga Ass'n for a Scenic Cmty. v. County of Los Angeles, 11 C3d 506 (1974)	60–61, 123, 283–285, 529, 530, 535, 537
Topanga Ass'n for a Scenic Cmty. v. County of Los Angeles, 214 Cal. App. 3d 1348 (1989)	113–114, 118
Towards Responsibility in Planning v. City Council, 200 Cal. App. 3d 671 (1988)	51, 286
Town of Groton v. Laird, 353 F. Supp. 344 (D. Conn. 1972)	72
Town of Norfolk v. U.S. Army Corps of Eng'rs, 968 F. 2d 1438 (1st Cir. 1992).	194, 197
Town of Telluride v. Lot Thirty-Four Venture, L.L.C., 3 P. 3d 30 (Col. 2000)	516
Toyota of Visalia, Inc. v. New Motor Vehicle Bd., 188 Cal. App. 3d 872 (1987)	558
Trancas Property Owners Association v. City of Malibu, 138 Cal. App. 4th 172 (2006)	277, 461
Travis v. County of Santa Cruz, 33 Cal. 4th 757 (2004)	517, 543, 544, 575, 577
Trend Homes, Inc. v. Central Unified Sch. Dist., 220 Cal. App. 3d 102 (1990)	575–576
Trent Meredith, Inc. v. City of Oxnard, 114 Cal. App. 3d 317 (1981)	108, 340, 339, 374
Tribal Village of Akutan v. Hodel, 869 F. 2d 1185 (9th Cir. 1988)	219
Truman v. Royer, 189 Cal. App. 2d 240 (1961)	393
Tuchscher Dev. Enter., Inc. v. San Diego Unified Port Dist., 106 Cal. App. 4th 1219 (2003)	579
Tuolumne County Citizens for Responsible Growth, Inc. v. City of Sonora, 2007 WL 2834230 (2007)	161
Turlock Irrigation Dist. v. Zanker, 140 Cal. App. 4th 1047 (2006)	152
Twain Harte Assocs., Ltd. v. County of Tuolumne, 217 Cal. App. 3d 71 (1990)	309, 550
Twain Harte Homeowners Ass'n v. County of Tuolumne, 138 Cal. App. 3d 664 (1982)	12, 13, 18, 32
Union Pacific R.R., Co. v. State Bd. of Equalization, 49 Cal. 3d 138 (1989)	567–568
United Outdoor Adver. Co. v. Business, Transp. and Hous. Agency, 44 Cal. 3d 242 (1988)	21
United States v. Hanousek, 176 F. 3d 1116 (9th Cir. 1999), cert. denied, 528 U.S. 1102 (2000)	204
United States v. Appalachian Elec. Power Co., 311 U.S. 377 (1940)	175
United States v. Billie, 667 F. Supp. 1485 (S.D. Fla. 1987)	226
United States v. Chevron Pipe Line Co., 473 F. Supp. 2d 605 (D. Tex. 2006)	179
United States v. Ciampitti, 669 F. Supp. 684 (D. N.J. 1987)	204
United States v. City of Fort Pierre, 747 F. 2d 464 (8th Cir. 1984)	176
United States v. Cooper, 482 F.3d 658 (4th Cir. 2007)	204
United States v. Cumberland Farms, 826 F. 2d 1151 (1st Cir. 1987)	204
United States v. Deaton, 209 F. 3d 331 (4th Cir. 2000)	206
United States v. Ellen, 961 F. 2d 462 (4th Cir. 1992)	183
United States v. General Motors Corp., 323 U.S. 373 (1945)	317
United States v. Gerke Excavating, 464 F.3d 723 (7th Cir. 2006)	179
United States v. Glenn-Colusa Irrigation District, 788 F. Supp. 1126 (E.D. Cal. 1992)	229
United States v. Johnson, 467 F. 3d 56 (1st Cir. 2006)	179
United States v. Larkins, 852 F. 2d 189 (6th Cir. 1988)	186
United States v. Moretti, 478 F. 2d 418 (5th Cir. 1973)	175
United States v. Nguyen, 916 F. 2d 1016 (5th Cir. 1990)	229
United States v. Petty Motor Co., 327 U.S. 372 (1946)	317
United States v. Rapanos, 339 F. 3d 447 (6th Cir. 2003), cert. denied, 541 U.S. 972 (2004)	178
United States v. Rapanos, 376 F. 3d 629 (6th Cir. 2004)	178
United States v. Riverside Bayview Homes, Inc., 474 U.S. 121 (1985)	176, 177, 182
United States v. Classic, 313 U.S. 299, 326 (1941)	472
Uniwill L.P. v. City of Los Angeles, 124 Cal. App. 4th 537 (2004)	125, 531
Uphold Our Heritage v. Town of Woodside, 147 Cal. App. 4th 587 (2007)	168
Upton v. Gray, 269 Cal. App. 2d 352 (1969)	61, 62
Usery v. Turner Elkhorn Mining Co., 428 U.S. 1 (1976)	332
Utility Cost Management v. Indian Wells Valley Water Dist., 26 Cal. 4th 1185 (2001)	540
Vacation Village, Inc. v. Clark County, 497 F. 3d 902 (9th Cir. 2007)	296
Valley Motor Lines, Inc. v. Riley, 22 Cal. App. 2d 233 (1937)	555
Van Atta v. Scott, 27 Cal. 3d 424 (1980)	554
Van Sicklen v. Browne, 15 Cal. App. 3d 122 (1971)	62
Van't Rood v. County of Santa Clara, 113 Cal. App. 4th 549 (2003)	139
Venice Canals Resident Home Owners Ass'n v. Superior Court, 72 Cal. App. 3d 675 (1977)	565
Ventura County v. Gulf Oil Corp., 601 F. 2d 1080 (9th Cir. 1979)	72
Ventura Group Ventures, Inc. v. Ventura Port District, 24 Cal. 4th 1089 (2001)	311
Ventura Mobilehome Communities Owners Association v. City of San Buenaventura, 371 F. 3d 1046 (9th Cir. 2004)	325

Case	page(s)
Verdugo Woodlands Homeowners Ass'n v. City of Glendale, 179 Cal. App. 3d 696 (1986)	46
Viacom Outdoor, Inc. v. City of Arcata, 140 Cal. App. 4th 230 (2006)	5
Village Laguna, Inc. v. Board of Supervisors, 134 Cal. App. 3d 1022 (1982)	166, 285
Village of Belle Terre v. Boraas, 416 U.S. 1 (1974)	2
Village of Euclid v. Ambler Realty Co., 272 U.S. 365 (1926)	2
Village of False Pass v. Clark, 733 F. 2d 605 (9th Cir. 1984)	219
Village of Willowbrook v. Olech, 528 U.S. 562 (2000)	333
Vineyard Area Citizens for Responsible Growth v. City of Rancho Cordova, 40 Cal. 4th 412 (2007)	162, 163, 259, 260, 261
Vo v. City of Garden Grove, 115 Cal. App. 4th 425 (2004)	63
W.W. Dean & Assoc. v. City of South San Francisco, 190 Cal. App. 3d 1368 (1987)	69, 528
Wagner v. City of South Pasadena, 78 Cal. App. 4th 943 (2000)	539–540, 563
Wal-Mart Stores, Inc. v. City of Turlock, 138 Cal. App. 4th 273 (2006)	3, 158
Walt Rankin & Assocs., Inc. v. City of Murrieta, 84 Cal. App. 4th 605 (2000)	131
Warmington Old Town Associates v. Tustin Unified School District, 101 Cal. App. 4th 840 (2002)	366, 368
Waste Mgmt. of Alameda County, Inc. v. County of Alameda, 79 Cal. App. 4th 1223 (2000)	548, 552–554, 571
We Care-Santa Paula v. Herrera, 139 Cal. App. 4th 387 (2006)	390
Wells Fargo Bank v. Town of Woodside, 33 Cal. 3d 379 (1983)	84
West Coast Home Improvement Co. v. Contractors' State License Bd., 68 Cal. App. 2d 1 (1945)	565
Western Placer Citizens for An Agricultural and Rural Environment, 144 Cal. App. 4th 890 (2006)	168
Western States Petroleum Ass'n v. Superior Court, 9 Cal. 4th 559 (1995)	528–530, 537, 558–560
Western Watershed Project v. Matejko, 468 F. 3d 1099 (9th Cir. 2006)	215
Western/Cal. Ltd. v. Dry Creek Joint Elementary Sch. Dist., 50 Cal. App. 4th 1461 (1996)	365, 369, 383, 533
Westfield-Palos Verdes Co. v. City of Rancho Palos Verdes, 73 Cal. App. 3d 486 (1977)	372
Wetlands Action Network v. U.S. Army Corps of Engineers, 222 F. 3d 1105 (9th Cir. 2000)	192–193
Wheeler v. City of Pleasant Grove, 833 F. 2d 267 (11th Cir. 1987)	318
Wheeler v. City of Pleasant Grove, 896 F. 2d 1347, 1350 (11th Cir. 1990)	318–319, 320
Wheelwright v. County of Marin, 2 Cal. 3d 448 (1970)	393
Whitman v. Board of Supervisors, 88 Cal. App. 3d 397 (1979)	161
Wilcox v. Superior Court, 27 Cal. App. 4th 809 (1994)	579
William C. Haas & Co. v. City & County of San Francisco, 605 F. 2d 1117 (9th Cir. 1979)	298, 314, 318
William S. Hart Union High Sch. Dist. v. Reg'l Planning Comm'n, 226 Cal. App. 3d 1612 (1991)	117, 118, 365, 366, 528
Williams v. Horvath, 16 Cal. 3d 834 (1976)	331
Williams v. San Francisco Bd. of Permit Appeals, 74 Cal. App. 4th 961 (1999)	581
Williamson County Regional Planning Commission v. Hamilton Bank, 473 U.S. 172 (1985)	321, 325–327, 330, 332
Wilson v. Block, 708 F. 2d 735 (D.C. Cir. 1983)	214
Wilson v. City of Laguna Beach, 6 Cal. App. 4th 543 (1992)	481, 501, 528
Wilson v. Hidden Valley Mun. Water Dist., 256 Cal. App. 2d 271 (1967)	527, 538
Withrow v. Larkin, 421 U.S. 35 (1975)	124
WMX Tech, Inc. v. Miller, 104 F. 3d 1133 (9th Cir. 1997)	313
Wolfe v. City of Fremont, 144 Cal. App. 4th 533 (2006)	461
Woodland Hills Residents Ass'n, Inc. v. City Council, 44 Cal. App. 3d 825 (1975)	94, 121–122
Woodland Hills Residents Ass'n, Inc. v. City Council, 23 Cal. 3d 917 (1979)	121
Woods v. Superior Court, 28 Cal. 3d 668 (1981)	526
Woodward Park Homeowners Ass'n v. City of Fresno, 150 Cal. App. 4th 683 (2007)	162
Worthington v. City Council of the City of Rohnert Park, 130 Cal. App. 4th 1132 (2005)	77, 395, 403, 409, 527
Wright Dev. Co. v. City of Mountain View, 53 Cal. App. 3d 274 (1975)	120
Wright v. State, 122 Cal. App. 4th 659 (2004)	546
Xenia Rural Water Ass'n v. Dallas County, 445 N.W. 2d. 785 (1989)	278
Yamasaki v. Stop H-3 Ass'n, 471 U.S. 1108 (1985)	216
Yoshisato v. Superior Court, 2 Cal. 4th 978 (1992)	413
Yost v. Thomas, 36 Cal. 3d 561 (1984)	30, 40, 402–403, 527
Young v. American Mini Theatres, Inc., 427 U.S. 50 (1976)	44, 53, 55
Young v. Gannet, 97 Cal. App. 4th 209 (1997)	538
Youngblood v. Board of Supervisors, 22 Cal. 3d 644 (1978)	27, 127, 528
Zabel v. Tabb, 430 F. 2d 199 (5th Cir. 1970), cert. denied, 401 U.S. 910 (1971)	174
Zack v. Marin Emergency Radio Auth., 118 Cal. App. 4th 617 (2004)	74
Zilber v. Town of Moraga, 692 F. Supp. 1195 (N.D. Cal. 1988)	322–323

Table of Authorities

UNITED STATES CONSTITUTION

	page(s)
Article IV, Sec. 2	72
Article IV, Sec. 3	72
Fifth Amendment	278, 289, 290, 291, 293, 296, 298, 309, 310, 318, 326, 327, 335, 336, 345, 346, 348, 356
First Amendment	50, 53, 55, 56, 331
Fourteenth Amendment	289, 333, 336, 345, 348, 361
Commerce Clause	175, 176, 177
Contract Clause	380
Equal Protection Clause	55, 333, 335, 348, 407
Establishment Clause	59
Free Exercise Clause	59
Freedom of Speech Clause	53
Full Faith and Credit Clause	326
Property Clause	72
Supremacy Clause	5, 72
Takings Clause	278, 309, 335, 336, 346, 356, 358

FEDERAL STATUTES

	page(s)
5 U.S.C. Sec. 557(d)(1)	221
5 U.S.C. Sec. 706	228
15 U.S.C. Sec. 1121 (b)	235
15 U.S.C. Sec. 1701 *et seq.*	201
16 U.S.C. Sec. 470	201
16 U.S.C. Sec. 470 *et seq.*	236
16 U.S.C. Sec. 470(f)	236
16 U.S.C. Secs. 661–666(c)	200
16 U.S.C. Sec. 668 *et seq.*	226
16 U.S.C. Sec. 1456(c)	201
16 U.S.C. Sec. 1531 *et seq.*	200
16 U.S.C. Sec. 1532(5)	214
16 U.S.C. Sec. 1532(6)	208
16 U.S.C. Sec. 1532(16)	208
16 U.S.C. Sec. 1532(19)	223
16 U.S.C. Sec. 1532(20)	208
16 U.S.C. Sec. 1533	207, 222
16 U.S.C. Sec. 1533(a)(1)	208
16 U.S.C. Sec. 1533(a)(3)	211
16 U.S.C. Sec. 1533(b)(1)(A)	208
16 U.S.C. Sec. 1533(b)(3)	211
16 U.S.C. Sec. 1533(b)(6)(C)	212
16 U.S.C. Sec. 1533(f)	211
16 U.S.C. Sec. 1536	207, 208, 214
16 U.S.C. Sec. 1536(a)(2)	214
16 U.S.C. Sec. 1536(a)(4)	216
16 U.S.C. Sec. 1536(b)(3)	216
16 U.S.C. Sec. 1536(c)(1)	216
16 U.S.C. Sec. 1536(e)	221
16 U.S.C. Sec. 1536(h)	216
16 U.S.C. Sec. 1538	207
16 U.S.C. Sec. 1538(a)(1)	222
16 U.S.C. Sec. 1538(a)(2)	223
16 U.S.C. Sec. 1539	208, 226
16 U.S.C. Sec. 1539(a)(1)(B)	226
16 U.S.C. Sec. 1539(a)(2)(A)	226
16 U.S.C. Sec. 1539(a)(2)(B)	227
16 U.S.C. Sec. 1540(a)(1)	229
16 U.S.C. Sec. 1540(g)	229
16 U.S.C. Sec. 1540(g)(1)(A)	218
16 U.S.C. Sec. 1540(g)(2)(A–C)	230
16 U.S.C. Sec. 1540(g)(4)	230
16 U.S.C. Secs. 3821–22	201
25 U.S.C. Sec. 2701 *et seq.*	76
25 U.S.C. Sec. 2703(6)	76
25 U.S.C. Sec. 2703(7)	76
25 U.S.C. Sec. 2710	76
25 U.S.C. Sec. 2710(d)(1)(B)	76
25 U.S.C. Sec. 2710(d)(3)	76
25 U.S.C. Sec. 2710(d)(7)	76
25 U.S.C. Sec. 2710(d)(7)(B)(iii)	76
31 U.S.C. Sec. 6506	72
33 U.S.C. Sec. 1251 *et seq.*	262
33 U.S.C. Sec. 1251(a)	175
33 U.S.C. Sec. 1311	175
33 U.S.C. Sec. 1319	204
33 U.S.C. Sec. 1319(b)	204
33 U.S.C. Sec. 1319(c)	204
33 U.S.C. Sec. 1319(c)(1)	204
33 U.S.C. Sec. 1319(c)(2)	204
33 U.S.C. Sec. 1319(c)(3)	204
33 U.S.C. Sec. 1319(d)	205
33 U.S.C. Sec. 1319(g)(3)	205
33 U.S.C. Sec. 1341	200
33 U.S.C. Sec. 1342	175
33 U.S.C. Sec. 1342(p)(3)(B)(iii)	262
33 U.S.C. Sec. 1344	175
33 U.S.C. Sec. 1344(c)	186, 197
33 U.S.C. Sec. 1344(f)	185
33 U.S.C. Sec. 1344(f)(2)	186
33 U.S.C. Sec. 1362(7)	175
33 U.S.C. Secs. 402–403	174
33 U.S.C. Sec. 404(c)	199
42 U.S.C. Sec. 1983	289, 298, 330, 337, 471, 530
42 U.S.C. Sec. 1988	473
42 U.S.C. Sec. 2000cc *et seq.*	57
42 U.S.C. Secs. 2000cc–5(7)(B)	58
42 U.S.C. Sec. 4321 *et seq.*	72
42 U.S.C. Secs. 4321–4347	200
47 U.S.C. Sec. 253	5
47 U.S.C. Sec. 332(c)(7)	330

FEDERAL REGULATIONS

	page(s)
7 C.F.R. Sec. 400.47(c)	201
33 C.F.R. Parts 320–331	198
33 C.F.R. Part 325, Appen. B	200
33 C.F.R. Part 325, Appendix B, Paragraph 7(b)(1)	200
33 C.F.R. Part 325, Appen. C	189, 201
33 C.F.R. Part 328	176
33 C.F.R. Part 329	175
33 C.F.R. Part 330	186, 200
33 C.F.R. Part 331	183
33 C.F.R. Sec. 209.120	174
33 C.F.R. Sec. 320.1(c)	186
33 C.F.R. Sec. 320.4(a)(1)	193
33 C.F.R. Sec. 320.4(a)(2)	193
33 C.F.R. Sec. 321	184
33 C.F.R. Sec. 322	184
33 C.F.R. Sec. 323	184
33 C.F.R. Sec. 323.2(f)	184
33 C.F.R. Sec. 323.3(c)	184
33 C.F.R. Sec. 323.4	185
33 C.F.R. Sec. 324	184
33 C.F.R. Sec. 325.1(b)	192
33 C.F.R. Sec. 325.1(c)	192
33 C.F.R. Sec. 325.1(d)(1)	192
33 C.F.R. Sec. 325.1(d)(2)	192
33 C.F.R. Sec. 325.1(d)(3)	193
33 C.F.R. Sec. 325.2	192
33 C.F.R. Sec. 325.9	206
33 C.F.R. Sec. 326.3(b)	205
33 C.F.R. Sec. 326.3(c)	205
33 C.F.R. Sec. 326.3(d)	205
33 C.F.R. Sec. 326.3(e)	205
33 C.F.R. Sec. 326.3(g)	205
33 C.F.R. Sec. 326.5(a)	205
33 C.F.R. Sec. 328.3(a)	176
33 C.F.R. Sec. 328.3(a)(3)	178
33 C.F.R. Sec. 328.3(b)	182
33 C.F.R. Sec. 329.4	175
33 C.F.R. Sec. 330	184
33 C.F.R. Sec. 330.1	186
33 C.F.R. Sec. 320.1(b)	184
40 C.F.R. Part 230	186, 192
40 C.F.R. Part 231	199
40 C.F.R. Sec. 230.10	194
40 C.F.R. Sec. 230.10(a)	193, 194
40 C.F.R. Sec. 230.10(a)(2)	194, 197
40 C.F.R. Sec. 230.10(a)(3)	194
40 C.F.R. Sec. 230.10(b)	193
40 C.F.R. Sec. 230.10(c)	193
40 C.F.R. Sec. 230.10(d)	193
40 C.F.R. Sec. 230.3(q)	194, 196
40 C.F.R. Secs. 230.41–230.45	194
50 C.F.R. Sec 17.32(c)	228
50 C.F.R. Sec. 17, Part C	227
50 C.F.R. Sec. 17, Part D	227
50 C.F.R. Sec. 17.11	210
50 C.F.R. Sec. 17.22(b)(5)	227
50 C.F.R. Sec. 17.22(c)	228
50 C.F.R. Sec. 17.22(d)	228
50 C.F.R. Sec. 17.31	222
50 C.F.R. Sec. 17.32(d)	228
50 C.F.R. Sec. 17.71	223
50 C.F.R. Sec. 222.102	225
50 C.F.R. Sec. 402.01	214
50 C.F.R. Sec. 402.02	214, 215, 216, 217
50 C.F.R. Sec. 402.11	219
50 C.F.R. Sec. 402.11(e)	219
50 C.F.R. Sec. 402.11(f)	220
50 C.F.R. Sec. 402.14(a)	215, 220
50 C.F.R. Sec. 402.14(c)	216
50 C.F.R. Sec. 402.14(d)	216
50 C.F.R. Sec. 402.14(g)	216
50 C.F.R. Sec. 402.14(i)(1)	218
50 C.F.R. Sec. 402.14(i)(2)	218
50 C.F.R. Sec. 402.14(i)(3)	218
50 C.F.R. Sec. 402.14(i)(5)	218
50 C.F.R. Sec. 402.16	220
50 C.F.R. Sec. 424.02(d)	212
50 C.F.R. Sec. 424.12(a)	212
50 C.F.R. Sec. 424.16	209
50 C.F.R. Sec. 424.16(b)	209
50 C.F.R. Sec. 424.16(b)(3)	209
50 C.F.R. Sec. 424.16(c)(2)	209
50 C.F.R. Sec. 424.17(a)	210
50 C.F.R. Sec. 424.17(b)	212
50 C.F.R. Sec. 424.19	212
50 C.F.R. Sec. 424.20	210
50 C.F.R. Sec. 451.02(5)(ii)	221
42 Fed. Reg. 31722 (June 22, 1977)	176
45 Fed. Reg. 85338–85339 (December 24, 1980)	195
45 Fed. Reg. 85339 (December 3, 1980)	194

	page(s)
46 Fed. Reg. 7644 (January 23, 1981)	201
51 Fed. Reg. 19926 (June 3, 1986)	214
51 Fed. Reg. 19932 (June 3, 1986)	215
51 Fed. Reg. 41216 (Nov. 13, 1986)	176
55 Fed. Reg. 9210 (March 12, 1990)	195
56 Fed. Reg. 2408 (January 22, 1991)	183
56 Fed. Reg. 2411 (January 26, 1991)	206
56 Fed. Reg. 54562 (October 22, 1991)	221
57 Fed. Reg. 23405 (June 3, 1992)	221
58 Fed. Reg. 45008 (Aug. 25, 1993)	184
58 Fed. Reg. 45035 (Aug. 25, 1993)	184
59 Fed. Reg. 15520 (Mar. 28, 2006)	198
63 Fed. Reg. 3835 (January 27, 1998)	210
63 Fed. Reg. 54938 (October 13, 1998)	212
64 Fed. Reg. 32717 (June 17, 1999)	228
64 Fed. Reg. 32726 (June 17, 1999)	228
65 Fed. Reg. 3096 (January 19, 2000)	210
65 Fed. Reg. 16486 (March 28, 2000)	183
65 Fed. Reg. 35242 (June 1, 2000)	227
66 Fed. Reg. 4550 (Jan. 17, 2001)	185
67 Fed. Reg. 47726 (July 22, 2002)	210
68 Fed. Reg. 1995 (Jan. 15, 2003)	177
68 Fed. Reg. 55926 (September 29, 2003)	225
69 Fed. Reg. 24084 (May 3, 2004)	228
70 Fed. Reg. 37160 (June 28, 2005)	225
70 Fed. Reg. 37196 (June 28, 2005)	226
70 Fed. Reg. 49739 (Aug. 23, 2005)	213
70 Fed. Reg. 52488 (Sept. 8, 2005)	213, 225
71 Fed. Reg. 19244 (Apr. 13, 2006)	213
71 Fed. Reg. 53756 (Sept. 12, 2006)	211
71 Fed. Reg. 58176 (Oct. 2, 2006)	213
72 Fed. Reg. 11092 (March 12, 2007)	186
72 Fed. Reg. 11195 (March 12, 2007)	191
72 Fed. Reg. 30279 (May 31, 2007)	212, 213
72 Fed. Reg. 40956 (July 25, 2007)	213
72 Fed. Reg. 48178 (Aug. 22, 2007)	213

OTHER FEDERAL SOURCES

Regulatory Guidance Letters

	page(s)
02-2 (December 24, 2002)	195
07-01 (June 5, 2007)	183
07-02 (July 4, 2007)	185
90-5 (July 18, 1990)	184
90-6 (Aug. 14, 1990)	183, 206

Executive Order

Exec. Order No. 12,372	72

Federal Statutes by Common Title

	page(s)
Bald Eagle Protection Act	226
Clean Water Act	
Sec. 301	175
Sec. 309	204
Sec. 401	200, 202
Sec. 402	175, 214
Sec. 402(p)	262
Sec. 404	175, 176, 184, 185, 197, 202, 206, 214, 215
Sec. 404(B)(1) Guidelines	174, 192, 193, 194, 196, 198, 199
Sec. 404(c)	196–197
Endangered Species Act	
Sec. 4(d)	218, 225
Sec. 7	214, 217, 220, 222
Sec. 7(a)(2)	216
Sec. 9	218, 222, 225
Sec. 10	227
Energy and Water Development Appropriations Act of 1992	182
Federal Civil Rights Act of 1871	471
Federal Telecommunications Act	5
Forest Practices Act	478
Intergovernmental Coordination Act of 1968	72
Lanham Act , Sec. 1121(b)	235
Marine Protection, Research and Sanctuaries Act of 1972	
Sec. 302	201
National Environmental Protection Act	72
National Historic Preservation Act, Sec. 106	230
Natural Communities Conservation Planning Act	227
Religious Freedom and Restoration Act of 1993	57
Religious Land Use and Institutionalized Persons Act	57
Rivers and Harbors Act of 1899	
Sec. 9	174
Sec. 10	174
Telecommunications Act of 1986	330

Reports/Memoranda

Report on Application for Department of Army Permit, Marco Island (April 15, 1976)	195
Memorandum from SWRCB Chief Counsel Craig Wilson, Effect of SWANCC v. United States on the 401 Certification Program, January 25, 2001	181

CALIFORNIA CONSTITUTION

	page(s)
Article I, Sec. 3	459
Article I, Sec. 19	289, 356
Article II, Sec. 8(a)	386
Article II, Sec. 8(d)	396
Article II, Sec. 9	374
Article II, Sec. 9(a)	387, 397, 404
Article II, Sec. 10(b)	412, 413
Article II, Sec. 11	385
Article IV, Sec. 19(f)	76
Article XI	472
Article XI, Sec. 1(b)	6
Article XI, Sec. 3(a)	400
Article XI, Sec. 5(a)	6, 397
Article XI, Sec. 7	1, 79, 340, 397
Article XIII	311
Article XIIIA	311, 361, 373
Article XIIIA, Sec. 16	417
Article XIIIB	311
Article XIIIC	311, 374
Article XIIIC, Sec. 3	380, 398
Article XIIID	374, 515
Article XIIID, Sec. 1(b)	379
Article XIIID, Sec. 1(b)(3)	378
Article XIIID, Sec. 2(b)	376
Article XIIID, Sec. 2(e)	377
Article XIIID, Sec. 2(i)	376
Article XIIID, Sec. 5	382
Article XIIID, Sec. 5(a)	380
Article XIIID, Sec. 6(b)(1)	378
Article XIIID, Sec. 6(b)(4)	379
Article XIIID, Sec. 6(b)(5)	382
Article XVI	311
1911 Constitution	385
Equal Protection Clause	480
Takings Clause	356, 358

CALIFORNIA STATUTES

Business and Professions Code

Sec. 5490 et seq.	64
Sec. 5499	65
Sec. 8762	88
Sec. 11000 et seq.	80, 86
Sec. 11003	109
Sec. 11010	251
Sec. 17200	478

Civil Code

Sec. 659	82
Sec. 815 et seq.	84
Sec. 895 et seq.	428
Sec. 1351(e)	90
Secs. 1954.50–1954.535	516
Sec. 3109 et seq.	134
Sec. 3114 et seq.	133
Sec. 3179 et seq.	134

Code of Civil Procedure

Sec. 318	540
Sec. 319	540
Sec. 338	543
Sec. 338(a)	543
Sec. 343	544, 577
Sec. 360.5	544
Sec. 388	568

	page(s)
Sec. 389(a)	556
Sec. 389(c)	555
Sec. 425.16	579
Sec. 425.16(c)	582
Sec. 473	570
Sec. 526(a)	415, 553, 554
Sec. 529	566
Sec. 771.010	130
Sec. 771.020	130
Sec. 860	541, 578
Sec. 860 *et seq.*	449, 574, 578
Sec. 861.1	578
Sec. 865	578
Sec. 870	578
Sec. 870(a)	578
Sec. 870(b)	578
Sec. 872.040	83
Sec. 916	568
Sec. 916(a)	567
Secs. 917.1–917.9	567
Sec. 1005	563
Sec. 1021.5	580, 582
Sec. 1084 *et seq.*	47
Secs. 1084–1097	526
Sec. 1085	36, 41, 369, 383
Secs. 1085–1094	527
Sec. 1086	552
Sec. 1087	562, 566
Sec. 1088	563, 566
Sec. 1089.5	569
Sec. 1094	563, 564
Sec. 1094.5	231, 241, 246, 283, 328, 526, 529, 530, 534, 535, 572
Sec. 1094.5(b)	535
Sec. 1094.5(c)	27, 532
Sec. 1094.5(e)	558, 559
Sec. 1094.5(g)	565, 567, 568
Sec. 1094.6	541, 558
Sec. 1094.6(b)	541, 543
Sec. 1094.6(d)	543
Sec. 1094.6(f)	541
Sec. 1094.6(g)	541
Secs. 1095–1097	527
Sec. 1097	555
Sec. 1107	563
Sec. 1109	527, 543, 563, 566, 567, 568
Sec. 1110b	567
Sec. 1822.50	476
Sec. 1822.51	476
Sec. 1822.52	477
Sec. 1822.55	477
Sec. 2107	558
Sec. 11500 *et seq.*	543

Education Code

Sec. 17620	354, 365, 366, 367, 368
Sec. 17620(a)(1)(B)	368
Sec. 17626	368

Elections Code

Sec. 100	391
Sec. 104	392
Sec. 1415	394
Sec. 4000(c)(9)	376
Sec. 9020	388
Sec. 9022	392
Sec. 9100 *et seq.*	387
Sec. 9101	388, 391

	page(s)
Sec. 9103	387
Sec. 9104	390
Sec. 9105	387, 390
Sec. 9105(a)	387, 390
Sec. 9105(b)	387, 391
Sec. 9105(c)	388, 390
Sec. 9106	391
Sec. 9108	388
Secs. 9108–9110	387
Sec. 9109	392
Sec. 9110	391
Sec. 9111	387, 394, 411, 416
Sec. 9111(a)(3)	406
Sec. 9113	392
Secs. 9113–9115	387
Sec. 9114	392, 393
Sec. 9115	392, 393
Sec. 9116	387, 391
Sec. 9117	387, 391
Sec. 9118	394
Sec. 9120	387
Sec. 9122	395
Sec. 9123	412
Sec. 9125	395, 417, 434
Sec. 9140	395
Sec. 9141	275
Secs. 9141–9144	388
Sec. 9144	392
Sec. 9145	388, 395
Sec. 9146	388, 392
Sec. 9147(a)	388
Sec. 9147(b)	388
Sec. 9160 *et seq.*	387
Sec. 9200 *et seq.*	387
Sec. 9201	388, 389, 390, 392
Sec. 9202	387, 390
Sec. 9202(a)	394
Sec. 9203	387, 390
Sec. 9203(a)	387, 390
Sec. 9203(b)	388, 390
Sec. 9204	391
Sec. 9205	387, 391
Sec. 9207	388
Secs. 9207–9209	387
Sec. 9208	391, 392
Sec. 9209	392
Secs. 9210–9211	387
Sec. 9211	392, 393
Sec. 9212	387, 394, 411, 416
Sec. 9212(a)(3)	406
Sec. 9214	387, 392, 394
Sec. 9215	387, 392, 394
Sec. 9217	395, 417, 434
Sec. 9219	387
Sec. 9220	387
Sec. 9221	412
Sec. 9222	395
Secs. 9235–9238	388
Sec. 9237	392
Sec. 9238	394
Sec. 9238(a)	388
Sec. 9238(b)	388
Sec. 9239	392
Secs. 9239–9240	388
Sec. 9241	388, 395, 396, 410
Sec. 9243	388
Sec. 9247	387, 392
Sec. 9255 *et seq.*	392
Sec. 9255(a)	394
Sec. 9280 *et seq.*	387
Sec. 9300 *et seq.*	387
Sec. 18600	394

	page(s)
Evidence Code	
Sec. 350	558
Sec. 664	566
Sec. 669.5	44, 406, 407, 411, 505
Sec. 669.5(b)	505
Fish and Game Code	
Sec. 1602	203
Secs. 2050–2098	230
Sec. 2052	230
Sec. 2070	231
Sec. 2073	231
Sec. 2073.5	231
Sec. 2074.2	231
Sec. 2074.6	231
Sec. 2075	231
Sec. 2080	232
Sec. 2080.1	232
Sec. 2085	232
Sec. 2800 *et seq.*	227
Sec. 5653	203
Government Code	
Art. 10.6	14
Sec. 800	471
Sec. 810 *et seq.*	382
Secs. 810–996.6	469
Sec. 810.6	470
Sec. 815	469
Sec. 815(a)	469
Sec. 815.2(a)	469, 470
Sec. 815.2(b)	470, 471
Sec. 815.4	470
Sec. 815.6	470
Sec. 820	470
Secs. 820.2–823	470
Sec. 820(a)	469
Sec. 820.2	470-471
Sec. 835	470
Sec. 865 *et seq.*	382
Sec. 6509	74
Sec. 1090 *et seq.*	534
Secs. 7060–7060.7	304
Secs. 8875–8876	18
Sec. 8875.2	18
Sec. 8875.3	18
Sec. 11523	543
Sec. 12012.40	77
Sec. 12012.45	77
Sec. 1954.53(a)(2)	517
Sec. 23005	6
Sec. 25131	50
Sec. 25132	476
Sec. 25132(c)	476
Sec. 25373	58, 238
Sec. 26550 *et seq.*	442
Sec. 27281.5	60
Sec. 31361(b)	238
Sec. 34900	6
Sec. 35000 *et seq.*	436
Sec. 36501	6
Sec. 36801	6
Sec. 36802	6
Sec. 36900	475, 476
Sec. 36900(c)	476
Sec. 36901	475
Sec. 36934	50
Sec. 36937(b)	235
Sec. 37361	58, 238

CURTIN'S CALIFORNIA LAND USE AND PLANNING LAW

	page(s)		page(s)		page(s)
Sec. 40602	272	Sec. 54960	462	Sec. 56751	446
Sec. 40605	6	Sec. 54960.1	462	Sec. 56800	107
Sec. 50023	414	Sec. 54988	477	Sec. 56810	443
Sec. 51200 et seq.	238	Sec. 54999.1(d)	73	Sec. 56811	443
Sec. 51201	239	Sec. 56000 et seq.	436	Sec. 56812	443
Sec. 51203(b)	240	Secs. 56000–57550	436	Sec. 56815	443
Sec. 51205	239	Sec. 56001	435, 437	Sec. 56857	445
Sec. 51220	239	Sec. 56016	446	Sec. 56857(b)	445
Sec. 51220.5	239–240	Sec. 56017	440	Sec. 56857(c)	446
Sec. 51222	239	Sec. 56021	440	Sec. 56882	450
Sec. 51230	239	Sec. 56029	451	Sec. 56884	448
Sec. 51231	240	Sec. 56030	441	Sec. 56886	448
Sec. 51234	239	Sec. 56033	440	Sec. 56895(a)	450
Sec. 51235	239	Sec. 56034	441	Sec. 56895(b)	450
Sec. 51238	239–240	Sec. 56035	441	Sec. 56895(d)	450
Sec. 51238.1	239–240	Sec. 56036	441, 442	Sec. 56895(e)	450
Sec. 51240	240	Sec. 56039	441	Sec. 56895(f)	450
Sec. 51241	240	Sec. 56043	440	Sec. 56895(g)	450
Sec. 51243	239, 240	Sec. 56046	451	Sec. 56895(h)	450
Sec. 51243.5	240	Sec. 56050	447	Sec. 57000	451
Sec. 51244	240	Sec. 56056	441	Sec. 57002	451
Sec. 51244.5	240	Sec. 56066	452	Sec. 57026(g)	447
Sec. 51245	240	Sec. 56072	447	Sec. 57026(h)	447
Sec. 51246(a)	240	Sec. 56073	441	Sec. 57050	451
Sec. 51256(c)	241	Sec. 56076	438	Sec. 57051	451
Sec. 51256.1	241	Sec. 56102	449	Sec. 57075(a)(1)	447
Sec. 51281	240	Sec. 56103	449, 541	Sec. 57075(a)(2)	447
Sec. 51282	240	Sec. 56107	448, 449	Sec. 57075(a)(3)	447
Sec. 51282(a)	241	Sec. 56123	452	Sec. 57075(b)(1)	447
Sec. 51282(b)	241	Sec. 56124	453	Sec. 57075(b)(2)	447
Sec. 51282(c)	241	Sec. 56157	443	Sec. 57075.5	447
Sec. 51282(e)	240	Sec. 56300	442	Sec. 57076(a)	447
Sec. 51283(a)	240	Sec. 56300(a)	453	Sec. 57076(b)	447
Sec. 51283(b)	241	Sec. 56301	435	Sec. 57076(c)	447
Sec. 51283(c)	241	Sec. 56325	437	Sec. 57077	451, 452
Sec. 51283.4	241	Sec. 56325.1	438	Sec. 57078(a)	447
Sec. 51284	241	Secs. 56326–56328	437	Sec. 57078(b)	447
Sec. 51286	241	Sec. 56332	437	Sec. 57078(c)	447
Sec. 51296	242	Sec. 56375	66, 440, 435, 437	Sec. 57090	448
Sec. 51296.1	242	Sec. 56375(a)	65, 441, 443, 453	Sec. 57200	452
Sec. 51296.2(a)	242	Sec. 56375(a)(3)	440, 448	Sec. 57202	452
Sec. 51296.8	242	Sec. 56375(e)	443	Sec. 57203	452
Sec. 53069.4	476	Sec. 56375.3	442	Sec. 57204	452
Sec. 53080	371	Sec. 56375.5	438	Sec. 5854	380
Sec. 53080(a)(1)	367	Sec. 56377	446	Sec. 60000(b)	359
Sec. 53090	74, 75	Sec. 56384	443	Sec. 61000 et seq.	442
Sec. 53090 et seq.	73	Sec. 56387	452	Sec. 65000	551
Sec. 53091	73, 75	Sec. 56388	453	Sec. 65000 et seq.	53
Sec. 53094	74	Sec. 56425	435, 437, 438	Sec. 65008	492, 494
Sec. 53096	73	Sec. 56425(a)	438	Sec. 65009	36, 41, 124, 540, 541, 543, 544, 552
Sec. 53096(a)	73	Sec. 56425(b)	439		
Sec. 53311 et seq.	380	Sec. 56425(e)	439	Sec. 65009(a)(3)	539
Secs. 53720–53730	373	Sec. 56425(f)	438	Sec. 65009(b)(1)	551
Sec. 53722	374	Sec. 56425(g)	438	Sec. 65009(b)(2)	124, 551, 552
Sec. 53739(a)	375	Sec. 56427	439	Sec. 65009(c)	36
Sec. 53739(b)	375	Sec. 56428	437, 439, 453	Sec. 65009(c)(1)(d)	274
Sec. 53753	376, 377	Sec. 56650	442	Sec. 65009(c)(1)(E)	544
Sec. 53753(c)	376	Sec. 56650 et seq.	442	Sec. 65009(d)	47
Sec. 53753.5	377	Sec. 56652	442	Sec. 65010	53
Sec. 53755	377	Sec. 56654	442, 443	Sec. 65010(a)	53
Sec. 54722 et seq.	436	Sec. 56658(b)	443	Sec. 65010(b)	53
Sec. 54950 et seq.	6, 8, 459, 535	Sec. 56658(d)	443	Sec. 65030.2	51
Sec. 54952(a)	462	Sec. 56658(f)	443	Sec. 65040.2	7, 11, 30
Sec. 54952(b)	462	Sec. 56658(g)	443	Sec. 65040.2(g)	12
Sec. 54952(c)(1)	462	Sec. 56658(i)	444	Sec. 65040.5	32
Sec. 54952.2	460	Sec. 56662	444	Sec. 65041 et seq.	431
Sec. 54952.2(a)	460	Sec. 56663	444, 451	Sec. 65082(c)	264
Sec. 54952.2(b)	460, 461	Sec. 56665	444	Sec. 65088 et seq.	264
Sec. 54953	459	Sec. 56666(a)	444	Sec. 65088.1(l)	264
Sec. 54956.9	277, 461	Sec. 56668	446	Sec. 65088.4	264, 432
Sec. 54957(b)(1)	461	Sec. 56700	442, 443	Sec. 65089(a)	264
Sec. 54959	462	Sec. 56704	107	Sec. 65089.5	264

Table of Authorities

	page(s)		page(s)		page(s)
Sec. 65089.5(a)	265	Sec. 65403	7		465, 492
Sec. 65089.6	265	Sec. 65428	468	Sec. 65589.5(a)(1)	484
Sec. 65090	95, 134	Sec. 65450	39	Sec. 65589.5(a)(2)	492
Sec. 65091	95, 134	Sec. 65451(a)	39	Sec. 65589.5(b)	493
Sec. 65100	6	Sec. 65451(b)	39	Sec. 65589.5(d)	15, 27, 489,
Sec. 65100 et seq.	5	Sec. 65452	40		493, 494
Sec. 65101	6, 7	Sec. 65455	39	Sec. 65589.5(d)(5)	20, 24, 494
Sec. 65103	7	Sec. 65456(a)	40	Sec. 65589.5(d)(5)(A)	489
Sec. 65103(a)	15, 31, 491	Sec. 65457	40	Sec. 65589.5(e)	493
Sec. 65300	11, 12, 23, 31,	Sec. 65457(a)	151	Sec. 65589.5(f)	493
	401, 417	Sec. 65560	17	Sec. 65589.5(h)(2)	493
Sec. 65300 et seq.	5, 10, 80	Sec. 65560 et seq.	426	Sec. 65589.5(h)(3)	494
Sec. 65300.5	12, 23, 31, 33,	Sec. 65560(b)	16	Sec. 65589.5(h)(4)	486, 494
	402, 489	Sec. 65560(b)(5)	16	Sec. 65589.5(i)	494
Sec. 65300.7	20	Sec. 65561	31	Sec. 65589.5(j)	286, 493, 495
Sec. 65300.9	20	Secs. 65561(a)–(b)	17	Sec. 65589.5(j)(1)	495
Sec. 65301	13	Sec. 65562.5	16, 33	Sec. 65589.5(j)(2)	495
Sec. 65301(a)	20	Sec. 65563	16, 17, 22	Sec. 65589.5(k)	494, 495
Sec. 65301(c)	31	Sec. 65564	16, 17, 33	Sec. 65589.7	489, 496
Sec. 65302	11, 13, 21, 33, 70	Sec. 65567	17	Sec. 65590	16, 490
Sec. 65302(a)	13, 14, 18, 32	Sec. 65580	31, 426	Sec. 65590(d)	490
Sec. 65302(a)(2)	14	Sec. 65580 et seq.	14, 485	Sec. 65590.1	16, 490
Sec. 65302(b)	13, 14, 18, 32	Sec. 65580(a)	15, 484	Sec. 65700	23
Sec. 65302(c)	484	Secs. 65580(b)–(d)	15	Sec. 65750 et seq.	32
Sec. 65302(d)	16	Sec. 65580(d)	484	Secs. 65750–65763	36
Sec. 65302(f)	17	Sec. 65580(e)	14	Sec. 65753	36, 562, 569
Sec. 65302(g)	17, 18, 33	Sec. 65581	426	Sec. 65754	36
Sec. 65302(g)(2)	17	Sec. 65581(a)	485	Sec. 65755	36
Sec. 65302.3	31	Sec. 65582.1	497	Sec. 65800 et seq.	5, 43, 80
Sec. 65302.3(a)	27	Sec. 65583	14, 426, 485	Sec. 65803	23, 24, 43, 46, 401
Sec. 65302.3(b)	28	Sec. 65583(a)	14, 485	Sec. 65804	43, 49, 468
Sec. 65302.4	14	Sec. 65583(a)(3)	14, 485, 487	Sec. 65850	48, 50
Sec. 65302.5	18	Sec. 65583(a)(4)	489	Sec. 65850.2	93, 464
Secs. 65302.5(a)(1)–(a)(2)	18	Sec. 65583(a)(5)	489	Sec. 65850.2(i)	93, 464
Sec. 65302.5(a)(3)	18	Sec. 65583(a)(8)	32	Sec. 65850.4	56
Sec. 65302.5(b)	18	Sec. 65583(c)(1)	32–33, 487, 497	Sec. 65852.1	88
Sec. 65302.5(c)	18	Sec. 65583(c)(1)(A)	488	Sec. 65852.1(b)	502
Sec. 65302.8	51, 286, 505	Sec. 65583(c)(3)	7, 30	Sec. 65852.150	501, 502
Sec. 65302.9	275	Sec. 65583(c)(4)	18	Sec. 65852.2	501
Sec. 65302.9(a)	13, 47	Sec. 65583.2(a)	487	Sec. 65852.2(b)(1)	502
Sec. 65303	20	Sec. 65583.2(b)	487	Sec. 65852.2(b)(3)	502
Sec. 65350	33	Sec. 65583.2(h)	488	Sec. 65852.2(i)(4)	88, 501
Sec. 65350 et seq.	28	Sec. 65583.2(i)	488	Sec. 65853	48
Sec. 65351	7	Sec. 65584	7, 14, 485	Sec. 65854	7, 49, 535
Sec. 65352	7, 29	Sec. 65584 et seq.	485	Sec. 65854 et seq.	48
Sec. 65352.2	74	Sec. 65584(a)(1)	486	Sec. 65855	49
Sec. 65352.3	33	Sec. 65584(b)	486	Sec. 65856	49, 535
Sec. 65352.5	446	Sec. 65584(d)	486	Sec. 65857	49
Sec. 65353	7	Sec. 65584(e)	486	Sec. 65858	5, 48, 66,
Sec. 65353(a)	28	Sec. 65584.01	30, 486		67, 301, 421
Sec. 65354	28	Secs. 65584.01–65584.07	487	Sec. 65858(g)	67
Sec. 65354.5	28	Sec. 65584.05	486	Sec. 65858(h)	67
Sec. 65356	29	Sec. 65584.06	486	Sec. 65858(b)	66
Sec. 65357	31	Sec. 65584.09	488	Sec. 65858(d)	66
Sec. 65357(b)	30	Sec. 65584.1	486	Sec. 65858(e)	67
Sec. 65358(b)	29	Sec. 65585(b)	30, 33	Sec. 65858(f)	67
Sec. 65358(c)	29	Sec. 65585(f)	491	Sec. 65859	65
Sec. 65360	33	Sec. 65587(a)	33-34	Sec. 65860	9, 401, 541
Sec. 65361	121	Sec. 65587(b)	36	Sec. 65860(a)	46, 47
Sec. 65361 (c)	33	Sec. 65587(c)	36	Sec. 65860(b)	47
Sec. 65361(a)	33	Sec. 65588	15, 493	Sec. 65860(c)	47
Sec. 65361(b)	33	Secs. 65588	491	Sec. 65860(d)	23, 46, 401
Sec. 65361(d)	34	Sec. 65588(a)	15, 491	Sec. 65860.1	23, 47, 275
Sec. 65361(e)	34, 122	Sec. 65588(b)	15, 491	Sec. 65863	492
Sec. 65361(f)	33	Sec. 65588(d)	16, 490	Sec. 65863(b)	432, 491
Sec. 65400	7, 30	Secs. 65588(d)(1–4)	490	Sec. 65863(c)	432, 492
Sec. 65400(a)(2)	489	Sec. 65588.1	15, 491	Sec. 65863(f)	432, 492
Sec. 65400(b)(3)	489	Sec. 65589.3	491	Sec. 65863(h)	432, 492
Sec. 65400(c)	490	Sec. 65589.4	496	Sec. 65863(h)(1)	491–492
Sec. 65401	7	Sec. 65589.4(b)	496	Sec. 65863.6	51, 286,
Sec. 65402	7	Sec. 65589.4(c)	497		406, 407, 505
Sec. 65402(b)	75	Sec. 65589.5	5, 43, 286,	Sec. 65863.9	101

	page(s)		page(s)		page(s)
Sec. 65864	96	Sec. 65996	27, 365	Sec. 66413(b)	107
Sec. 65864 et seq.	5, 273, 102, 103	Sec. 65996(a)	121	Sec. 66413.5	128
Sec. 65864(b)	275	Sec. 65996(b)	117, 118, 366	Sec. 66413.5(a)	107
Sec. 65865	274	Sec. 66000	279, 383, 576	Sec. 66413.5(c)	107
Sec. 65865(b)	274	Sec. 66000 et seq.	6, 573	Sec. 66413.5(e)	107
Sec. 65865(e)	359	Secs. 66000–66011	358	Sec. 66413.5(f)	107
Sec. 65865.1	274	Secs. 66000–66025	343, 355, 358, 373, 383, 515	Secs. 66418–19	114
Sec. 65865.2	280			Sec. 66418.2	85
Sec. 65865.3	274	Sec. 66001	286, 357, 359, 368, 371	Sec. 66423	81
Sec. 65865.4	274			Sec. 66424	81, 82, 83, 84, 87, 136
Sec. 65865.6	275	Sec. 66001(a)	358		
Sec. 65866	274	Sec. 66001(b)	358	Sec. 66424.1	82
Sec. 65867.5	39, 251, 252, 260, 274, 276	Sec. 66001(d)	359	Sec. 66424.2	89
		Sec. 66001(e)	359	Sec. 66424.6	136
Sec. 65867.5(c)	251, 274	Sec. 66002	359	Sec. 66424.6(a)	86, 87
Sec. 65869.5	96	Sec. 66005	371	Sec. 66424.6(d)	87
Sec. 65901	61	Sec. 66006	359	Sec. 66426	85, 91, 92
Sec. 65906	60, 61	Sec. 66006(b)	359	Sec. 66426.5	87, 89
Sec. 65910	16	Sec. 66007	370, 371	Sec. 66427	91
Sec. 65912	16	Sec. 66007(b)(1)	371	Sec. 66427.1	122, 130
Sec. 65913.1	411, 497, 505	Sec. 66007(b)(2)	371	Sec. 66428	73, 75, 103
Sec. 65913.2	114	Sec. 66013	574, 575, 577	Sec. 66428(a)(2)	89
Sec. 65913.8	371	Sec. 66014	364, 382, 383, 574, 575, 577	Sec. 66428(b)	92
Sec. 65915	500, 501			Sec. 66428(c)	92
Sec. 65915 et seq.	497	Sec. 66014(a)	574	Sec. 66428.1	92
Sec. 65915(a)	498	Sec. 66016	364, 370, 382, 574	Sec. 66429	126
Sec. 65915(b)	498	Sec. 66016(a)	359, 383, 578	Sec. 66430	126
Sec. 65915(b)(1)	497	Sec. 66017	370	Sec. 66433 et seq.	126
Sec. 65915(c)	499	Sec. 66017(a)	370	Sec. 66434	126
Sec. 65915(d)(1)	431, 500	Sec. 66018	370	Sec. 66434(e)	86
Sec. 65915(d)(3)	431	Sec. 66020	125, 126, 279, 352, 359, 573, 574, 575, 576, 577	Secs. 66435–66443	126
Sec. 65915(e)	431, 500			Sec. 66436	126
Sec. 65915(g)(1)	499			Sec. 66437	540
Sec. 65915(i)(1)	500			Sec. 66439	126, 130
Sec. 65915(i)(2)	500	Sec. 66020(a)(1)	574	Sec. 66440	126
Sec. 65915(k)	499	Sec. 66020(a)(2)	574	Sec. 66442(a)	126
Sec. 65915.5	500	Sec. 66020(b)	576	Sec. 66442(b)	126
Sec. 65919 et seq.	29-30	Sec. 66020(c)	576	Sec. 66445(d)	86
Sec. 65919.3	30	Sec. 66020(d)(1)	359, 573, 574, 575	Sec. 66445(d)(3)	86
Sec. 65920 et seq.	6, 80, 93, 94, 463	Sec. 66020(d)(2)	359, 575	Sec. 66445(e)	135
		Sec. 66020(h)	573, 574	Sec. 66447	134
Sec. 65921	463	Sec. 66021	352, 359, 575	Sec. 66451 et seq.	94, 122
Sec. 65922	466	Sec. 66022	364, 540, 574, 577, 578	Sec. 66451.3	135
Sec. 65922(b)	94			Sec. 66451.3(a)	95, 134
Sec. 65940	463	Sec. 66022(a)	364, 574	Sec. 66451.4	122
Sec. 65940.5	466	Sec. 66022(b)	574, 578	Sec. 66451.7	92
Sec. 65941	464	Sec. 66024	575	Sec. 66451.10	141, 143
Sec. 65941.5	464	Sec. 66410 et seq.	5, 26	Sec. 66451.10 et seq.	89, 144
Sec. 65942	463	Secs. 66410–66499.37	540	Sec. 66451.11	143, 144
Sec. 65943	119, 463, 464	Secs. 66410–66499.58	363, 365	Sec. 66451.13	143
Sec. 65943(a)	93	Sec. 66411	79, 80, 112, 114	Sec. 66451.14	143
Sec. 65944	464	Sec. 66411.1	134	Sec. 66451.30 et seq.	145
Sec. 65950	94, 465	Sec. 66411.1(a)	134	Sec. 66451.301	143
Sec. 65950(a)(1)	465	Sec. 66412(a)	82, 89	Sec. 66451.302	143
Sec. 65950(a)(2)	465	Sec. 66412(b)	91	Sec. 66452	106
Sec. 65952.2	465	Sec. 66412(c)	91	Sec. 66452(b)(1)	98
Sec. 65956	465	Sec. 66412(d)	136, 142	Sec. 66452(c)	106, 279
Sec. 65956(a)	466	Sec. 66412(f)	87, 88	Sec. 66452.1	7, 93
Sec. 65956(b)	466	Sec. 66412(g)	90	Sec. 66452.1(b)	94
Sec. 65957	465	Sec. 66412(h)	90	Sec. 66452.1(c)	94
Sec. 65961	120	Sec. 66412(i)	91	Sec. 66452.2	93
Sec. 65962.5	464	Sec. 66412(j)	91	Sec. 66452.2(c)	94
Sec. 65962.5(d)	93, 464	Sec. 66412(k)	91	Sec. 66452.3	96, 468
Sec. 65962.5(e)	93, 464	Sec. 66412.1	89, 90	Sec. 66452.4	94
Sec. 65962.5(f)	93, 464	Sec. 66412.2	88	Sec. 66452.5(a)	123
Sec. 65995	354, 365	Sec. 66412.3	121	Sec. 66452.5(d)	123, 124
Sec. 65995(a)	118, 366	Sec. 66412.5	91	Sec. 66452.6	96, 97
Sec. 65995(b)	366	Sec. 66412.6	81, 145	Sec. 66452.6(a)	96
Sec. 65995(b)(3)	366	Sec. 66412.6(a)	144	Sec. 66452.6(a)(1)	96, 127
Sec. 65995(c)	367	Sec. 66412.6(b)	144	Sec. 66452.6(a)(2)	96
Sec. 65995(e)	365, 366	Sec. 66412.7	141	Sec. 66452.6(b)	98, 100
Sec. 65995.5	367	Sec. 66413(a)	107	Sec. 66452.6(b)(1)	98

Table of Authorities

	page(s)		page(s)		page(s)
Sec. 66452.6(c)	98, 100	Sec. 66474(e)	108, 117, 118, 122, 363	Sec. 66499	131
Sec. 66452.6(d)	97, 127			Sec. 66499.3	131
Sec. 66452.6(e)	96, 100	Sec. 66474.01	122	Sec. 66499.3(c)	131
Sec. 66452.6(f)	98	Sec. 66474.1	107, 123, 127	Sec. 66499.4	131
Sec. 66452.11	97	Sec. 66474.2	107, 119, 122, 465	Sec. 66499.7	133
Sec. 66452.11(c)	97			Sec. 66499.7(a)	133
Sec. 66452.12(a)	101	Sec. 66474.2 (c)	102	Sec. 66499.7(b)	133
Sec. 66452.13(c)	97	Sec. 66474.2(a)	119	Sec. 66499.7(c)	133
Sec. 66453	95, 96	Sec. 66474.2(b)	102	Sec. 66499.7(d)	133
Sec. 66454	107	Sec. 66474.4	432	Sec. 66499.7(h)	133
Sec. 66455	95	Sec. 66474.4(a)	123	Sec. 66499.7(i)	133
Sec. 66455.1	95, 96	Sec. 66474.4(b)	123	Sec. 66499.8	133
Sec. 66455.3	95, 252	Sec. 66474.5	123	Sec. 66499.9	133
Sec. 66455.7	95, 96	Sec. 66474.6	123	Sec. 66499.10	133
Sec. 66456.1	96, 126, 127	Sec. 66474.7	123	Sec. 66499.11 et seq.	132, 139
Sec. 66458	127	Sec. 66474.9	113	Secs. 66499.11–66499.20G	140
Sec. 66458(b)	128	Sec. 66474.9(a)	113	Sec. 66499.16	139
Sec. 66458(d)	128	Sec. 66474.9(b)(1)	113	Sec. 66499.17	120
Sec. 66459	468	Sec. 66474.9(b)(2)	113	Sec. 66499.19	120
Sec. 66462(a)	131	Sec. 66474.10	114	Sec. 66499.20½	139, 136, 140, 142
Sec. 66462.5	114	Sec. 66474.60(c)	121		
Sec. 66462.5(b)	114	Sec. 66475.1	111	Sec. 66499.21 et seq.	139
Sec. 66463	134	Sec. 66475.2	111	Sec. 66499.30	136, 141
Sec. 66463(a)	134	Sec. 66475.3	113	Sec. 66499.30 et seq.	477
Sec. 66463.1	134	Sec. 66477	109, 110, 116, 119, 364	Sec. 66499.30(e)	136
Sec. 66463.5	97			Sec. 66499.31	86, 133
Sec. 66463.5(e)	98	Sec. 66477(a)	120	Sec. 66499.32(a)	137
Sec. 66463.5(g)	103	Sec. 66477(a)–(e)	120	Sec. 66499.32(b)	137
Sec. 66464(a)	128, 129	Sec. 66477(a)(6)	120	Sec. 66499.33	137, 138
Sec. 66464(b)	129	Sec. 66477(a)(9)	110	Sec. 66499.34	138, 477
Sec. 66464(c)	129	Sec. 66477(b)	120, 140	Sec. 66499.35	138
Sec. 66465	129	Sec. 66477(d)	120	Sec. 66499.35(a)	138
Sec. 66466	129	Sec. 66477(e)	109, 110	Sec. 66499.35(b)	138, 139
Sec. 66466(f)	129	Sec. 66477.1	130	Sec. 66499.35(f)(1)(e)	139
Sec. 66468	128	Sec. 66477.5	372	Sec. 66499.36	138, 477
Sec. 66469	135, 136	Sec. 66478	110	Sec. 66499.37	113, 124, 125, 144, 312, 328, 541, 576
Secs. 66469(a)–(c)	135	Sec. 66478.1 et seq.	112		
Sec. 66469(d)	135	Secs. 66478.1–66478.14	108, 113		
Sec. 66469(e)	135	Sec. 66478.2	113	Sec. 66499.50 et seq.	140
Sec. 66469(f)	136	Sec. 66479 et seq.	110, 111	Sec. 66536.1	431
Sec. 66469(g)	135	Sec. 66483	111	Sec. 66600 et seq.	247
Sec. 66470	135, 136	Sec. 66483.1	111	Sec. 66604	248
Sec. 66471	136	Sec. 66483.2	111, 120, 140	Sec. 66610	248
Sec. 66472	136	Sec. 66484	111, 371	Sec. 66620	248
Sec. 66472.1	135, 136	Sec. 66484.3	397	Sec. 87100 et seq.	534
Sec. 66473	122, 127, 128	Sec. 66484.5	111	Title 7	263-264, 551
Sec. 66473.1	108, 113, 121, 122	Sec. 66485 et seq.	111		
		Sec. 66487	112	**Harbors and Navigation Code**	
Sec. 66473.5	22, 26, 115, 116, 121, 467	Sec. 66490	112		
		Sec. 66491	112	Secs. 100–107	113
Sec. 66473.7	108, 110, 250, 259, 260, 274	Sec. 66492	129	**Health and Safety Code**	
		Sec. 66493	128, 129		
Sec. 66473.7(a)	251	Sec. 66493(a)(1)	128		
Sec. 66473.7(a)(1)	260	Sec. 66493(a)(2)	129	Sec. 1566.3	5
Sec. 66473.7(a)(2)	253	Sec. 66493(d)	129	Sec. 1597.40(a)	5
Sec. 66473.7(a)(2)(A)–(D)	261	Sec. 66494.1	129	Sec. 9000 et seq.	441
Sec. 66473.7(a)(3)	252	Sec. 66495 et seq.	112	Sec. 17021.6	486
Sec. 66473.7(b)	252	Sec. 66498.1	103, 105, 279	Sec. 17958.1	88
Sec. 66473.7(b)(1)	256, 260	Sec. 66498.1 et seq.	102, 279	Sec. 18007	88
Sec. 66473.7(b)(2)	260	Secs. 66498.1–66498.9	102	Sec. 18021.7	486
Sec. 66473.7(b)(3)	254, 256, 262	Sec. 66498.1(b)	102, 106, 280, 465	Sec. 33000 et seq.	70, 398, 502
Sec. 66473.7(b)(4)	256, 260	Sec. 66498.1(c)	103	Sec. 33030	70
Sec. 66473.7(c)	253	Sec. 66498.2	106	Sec. 33031	70
Sec. 66473.7(c)(2)	256, 260	Sec. 66498.3(a)	106	Sec. 33031(a)(1)	71
Sec. 66473.7(d)	254	Sec. 66498.5(b)	106	Sec. 33031(a)(4)	71
Sec. 66473.7(d)(1)–(4)	261	Sec. 66498.5(c)	106	Sec. 33141	398
Sec. 66473.7(e)	252	Sec. 66498.5(d)	106	Sec. 33300	70
Sec. 66473.7(g)	255, 261	Sec. 66498.7	103	Sec. 33320.1	70
Sec. 66473.7(h)	254, 261	Sec. 66498.8	103	Sec. 33324(d)	71
Sec. 66473.7(i)	251, 260	Sec. 66498.8(d)	106	Sec. 33331	70, 71
Sec. 66474	116, 122, 123, 135, 467	Sec. 66498.9	103	Sec. 33333(b)	71
		Sec. 66498.9(b)	104, 105		

CURTIN'S CALIFORNIA LAND USE AND PLANNING LAW

	page(s)		page(s)		page(s)
Sec. 33333.2	70	Secs. 21080.01–21080.03	151	Sec. 21167.7	568
Sec. 33333.4	70	Secs. 21080.05–21080.08	151	Sec. 21167.8(a)	569
Sec. 33334.2	502	Sec. 21080.1	106, 153	Sec. 21167.8(f)	569
Sec. 33334.2(a)(1)	502	Sec. 21080.1 *et seq.*	155	Sec. 21168.5	572
Sec. 33334.2(a)(2)	502	Sec. 21080.3	153	Sec. 21168.9	573
Sec. 33334.2(j)(1)(A)	503	Sec. 21080.4	159, 172	Sec. 21177	548, 571
Sec. 33334.2(j)(1)(B)	503	Secs. 21080.7–21080.33	151	Sec. 21177(a)	571
Sec. 33334.2(j)(1)(C)	503	Sec. 21080.14	152	Sec. 21177(b)	571
Sec. 33346	71	Sec. 21081	168, 169, 286	Sec. 21177(c)	571
Sec. 33365	398	Sec. 21081.6	169, 170	Sec. 21177(e)	571
Sec. 33367(d)(4)	71	Sec. 21081.6(a)	478	Sec. 22002	268
Sec. 33413(b)(1)	503	Sec. 21081.6(b)	478	Sec. 25540.5	20
Sec. 33413(b)(2)(A)(i)	503	Sec. 21082.1	159	Sec. 26500 *et seq.*	381
Sec. 33413(b)(2)(A)(ii)	503	Sec. 21082.1(c)(1)	169	Sec. 26507	381
Sec. 33413(b)(2)(A)(v)	503	Sec. 21082.1(c)(3)	169	Sec. 26525	381
Sec. 33450	398	Sec. 21082.2(b)	154	Sec. 26530	381
Sec. 33500	70	Sec. 21082.2(c)	154	Sec. 26531	381
Sec. 33501	70	Sec. 21083(b)	160	Sec. 26532	381
Sec. 33501.1	70	Sec. 21083.3	151, 158	Sec. 26533	381
Sec. 50052.5	496	Sec. 21083.9(a)	159	Sec. 26534	381
Sec. 50079.5	486, 494, 496	Sec. 21084(a)	152	Sec. 26567	381
Sec. 50093	486, 494	Sec. 21091	159	Sec. 26570	381
Sec. 50105	486, 496	Sec. 21092	159	Sec. 26581	382
Sec. 50451	486	Sec. 21092(b)	154	Sec. 26583	381
Sec. 50452	486	Sec. 21092(b)(3)	159	Sec. 26587	382
Sec. 50453	486	Sec. 21092.1	167	Sec. 26591	382
Sec. 54059(c)	492	Sec. 21092.2	154	Sec. 26593	382
		Sec. 21092.4	159	Sec. 26650	382
Labor Code		Sec. 21092.5	160	Sec. 26654	382
Sec. 1720(a)(1)	265	Sec. 21093	158	Sec. 30000 *et seq.*	31, 87, 242, 270
Sec. 1771	265	Sec. 21100	160	Sec. 30103(a)	243
		Sec. 21100(b)(3)	164	Sec. 30106	244
Penal Code		Sec. 21100(b)(5)	160	Sec. 30108.5	245
Sec. 19	475	Sec. 21100(c)	160	Sec. 30108.6	245
		Sec. 21104	160	Sec. 30200 *et seq.*	242, 245
Public Resources Code		Sec. 21104.2	159	Secs. 30210–30214	246
		Sec. 21151.5	94, 465	Sec. 30231	247
Sec. 2621 *et seq.*	112	Sec. 21151.5(a)	160	Sec. 30233	203, 247
Sec. 2622	112	Sec. 21151.9	251, 252, 160	Sec. 30233(a)	203
Sec. 2623	112	Sec. 21152	172	Secs. 30260–30263	246
Sec. 2712	31	Sec. 21152(a)	172	Sec. 30301	243
Sec. 2761 *et seq.*	16	Sec. 21152(c)	172	Sec. 30312	243
Sec. 3715.5	20	Sec. 21153	160	Sec. 30330	246
Sec. 4511 *et seq.*	478	Sec. 21156	155	Sec. 30339	247
Sec. 5020 *et seq.*	236	Secs. 21156–21159.9	40	Sec. 30340.5	247
Sec. 5020.1	236–237	Sec. 21157.1	155	Sec. 30343	247
Sec. 21000	147	Sec. 21157.6	157	Sec. 30344	247
Sec. 21000 *et seq.*	5, 80, 117, 276, 405	Sec. 21158.5(a)	152	Secs. 30350–30555	247
		Secs. 21159.21–21159.24	151	Sec. 30400	246
Secs. 21000–21177	363, 365	Sec. 21159.22	496	Sec. 30411(b)	247
Secs. 21000–21178.1	122	Sec. 21159.23	496	Sec. 30412(c)	247
Sec. 21001	147	Sec. 21159.24	496	Sec. 30413(d)	247
Sec. 21002	168, 169	Sec. 21161	172	Sec. 30413(c)	247
Sec. 21002.1	148, 155, 169	Sec. 21166	170	Sec. 30500	245
Sec. 21002.1(a)	164	Sec. 21166(c)	171	Sec. 30512	245
Sec. 21002.1(b)	168	Sec. 21167	571	Sec. 30514	245, 246
Sec. 21004	117, 168	Sec. 21167(a)	172	Sec. 30515	246, 247
Sec. 21060.5	150	Sec. 21167(b)	172	Sec. 30519(a)	245
Sec. 21061	155	Sec. 21167(d)	153	Sec. 30519.5	247
Sec. 21061.0.5	497	Sec. 21167.1(b)	563	Secs. 30530–30534	246
Sec. 21064	154	Sec. 21167.3(b)	566	Sec. 30600	203, 242
Sec. 21064.5	154, 155	Sec. 21167.4(a)	562, 569	Sec. 30600.5(d)	245
Sec. 21065	149, 150	Sec. 21167.4(c)	569	Sec. 30601	244
Sec. 21068	37, 118	Sec. 21167.5	568	Sec. 30603	244, 245
Sec. 21068.5	158	Sec. 21167.6	558	Sec. 30603(a)	245
Sec. 21071	497	Sec. 21167.6(a)	568	Sec. 30603(b)	246
Sec. 21080	148, 155	Sec. 21167.6(b)	569	Sec. 30603(c)	246
Sec. 21080(a)	148	Sec. 21167.6(b)(2)	568, 570	Sec. 30603.1	243
Sec. 21080(b)	151	Sec. 21167.6(e)	570	Sec. 30604(a)	244
Sec. 21080(c)	153, 154	Sec. 21167.6.5(a)	569	Sec. 30605	246
Sec. 21080(e)	154	Sec. 21167.6.5(b)	569	Secs. 30605–30606	246
		Sec. 21167.6.5(c)	569		

Table of Authorities

	page(s)		page(s)		page(s)
Sec. 30607.1	247	1984 Cal. Stat., ch. 1009, Sec. 16	468	Secs. 15091–15093	169
Sec. 30610	244	1991 Cal. Stat., ch. 765	227	Secs. 15091–15094	168
Sec. 30611	244	1998 Cal. Stat., ch. 283, Sec. 5	465	Sec. 15091(d)	478
Sec. 30716	246	1998 Cal. Stat., ch. 407	117	Sec. 15092	168
Sec. 30801	246, 541	2005 Cal. Stat., ch. 496, Sec. 1	498	Sec. 15094	172
Public Utilities Code				Sec. 15094(a)	169
Sec. 21670	27			Sec. 15094(f)	169
Sec. 21675	27, 31, 40	**CALIFORNIA REGULATIONS** (including CEQA Guidelines)		Sec. 15096(d)	453
Sec. 21676	27			Sec. 15097(c)	170
Sec. 21676(b)	28, 48	8 Cal. Code Regs., Sec. 16001(a)	266	Sec. 15105	159
Revenue and Taxation Code		14 Cal. Code Regs., Sec. 670.1	231	Sec. 15112(c)(5)	172
Sec. 99	443	14 Cal. Code Regs., Sec. 720	203	Sec. 15122	160
Sec. 99.1	443	23 Cal Code Regs., Sec. 3859	189	Sec. 15123	160
Sec. 327.5	82			Sec. 15124	160
Sec. 423.4	242	**CEQA Guidelines**		Sec. 15125	160
Sec. 2050	82	App. G	153	Sec. 15125(a)	162
Sec. 2052	82	Art. 18	151	Sec. 15125(d)	160
Sec. 17274	477	Art. 19	152	Sec. 15126	160
Sec. 24436.5	477	Sec. 15000 et seq.	147	Sec. 15126(d)(1)	166
Streets and Highways Code		Secs. 15000–15387	5	Sec. 15126.2	160
Sec. 1160	441	Sec. 15040	370	Sec. 15126.2(d)	160, 167
Secs. 2800–3012	376	Sec. 15041	370	Sec. 15126.4	160
Sec. 22500 et seq.	380	Sec. 15051	148	Sec. 15126.4(a)	164
Water Code		Sec. 15051(b)	148	Sec. 15126.4(a)(1)(B)	164
Sec. 354	253	Secs. 15060–15061	148	Sec. 15126.4(a)(1)(D)	164
Sec. 3400 et seq.	112	Sec. 15061	148	Sec. 15126.6	160
Sec. 10631	251	Sec. 15061(b)(3)	151	Sec. 15126.6(a)	166
Sec. 10631(b)(4)	255	Sec. 15062	148, 151	Sec. 15126.6(c)	166
Sec. 10632	252	Sec. 15062(a)	153	Sec. 15126.6(d)	167
Sec. 10635	253	Sec. 15062(d)	153	Sec. 15126.6(e)	166
Sec. 10656	251	Sec. 15063	153	Sec. 15126.6(f)	166
Sec. 10657	251	Secs. 15063–15065	153	Sec. 15128	160
Sec. 10910	253, 257, 259	Sec. 15064(f)(1)	154	Sec. 15129	160
Sec. 10910 et seq.	160, 250, 257	Sec. 15064(f)(4)	154	Sec. 15130	160
Secs. 10910–10912	251, 260	Sec. 15070 et seq.	154	Sec. 15130(b)(1)(A)	163
Secs. 10910–10915	256	Sec. 15070(b)	154, 155	Sec. 15130(b)(1)(B)	163
Sec. 10910(b)	252, 257	Sec. 15070(b)(2)	154	Sec. 15132	159
Sec. 10910(c)	251, 252	Sec. 15071	154	Sec. 15152	158
Sec. 10910(c)(2)	259	Sec. 15072(a)	154	Sec. 15162	158
Sec. 10910(c)(3)	254, 257	Sec. 15073.5	155	Sec. 15162(a)	170
Sec. 10910(d)(2)	253	Sec. 15075(a)	154	Sec. 15162(a)(3)	171
Sec. 10910(e)	253	Secs. 15080–15081.5	155	Sec. 15162(d)	171
Sec. 10910(f)	255	Sec. 15082	159, 172	Sec. 15164(a)	171
Sec. 10910(g)(1)	252, 257	Sec. 15082(a)	159	Sec. 15164(b)	171
Sec. 10910(g)(2)	252, 257	Sec. 15082(b)	159	Sec. 15164(c)	171
Sec. 10910(g)(3)	252, 257	Sec. 15082(c)	159	Sec. 15164(d)	171
Sec. 10910(h)	256, 259	Sec. 15083	159	Sec. 15164(e)	171
Sec. 10911	259	Sec. 15084	159	Sec. 15168	157, 158
Sec. 10911(a)	254, 257	Sec. 15085	159, 172	Sec. 15168(c)	157
Sec. 10911(b)	160, 255	Sec. 15086	159	Sec. 15168(c)(1)	158
Sec. 10911(c)	255, 256, 259, 286	Sec. 15087	159	Sec. 15168(c)(2)	158
Sec. 10912	252	Sec. 15088	159	Sec. 15168(c)(3)	158
Sec. 10912(c)	252	Sec. 15088(b)	160	Sec. 15183	158
Sec. 13000 et seq.	181, 202	Sec. 15088.5(a)	167	Sec. 15183(a)	158
Sec. 13050(d)	202	Sec. 15088.5(b)	167	Secs. 15260–15285	151
Sec. 13050(e)	202	Sec. 15088.5(e)	167	Sec. 15262	454
Sec. 13260(1)	202	Sec. 15089	159	Sec. 15300	152
Session Laws		Sec. 15089(b)	167	Secs. 15300–15332	151
1971 Cal. Stat., ch. 1446	9	Sec. 15090(a)(1)	169	Sec. 15300.2	152
1977 Cal. Stat., ch. 234, Sec. 19	89	Sec. 15090(a)(2)	169	Sec. 15306	454
1979 Cal. Stat., ch. 868	247	Sec. 15090(a)(3)	169	Sec. 15352(a)	149
		Sec. 15091	169	Sec. 15352(b)	149
				Sec. 15355	163
				Sec. 15357	148
				Sec. 15360	150
				Sec. 15365	153
				Sec. 15378	150
				Sec. 15378(a)	149, 150
				Sec. 15378(b)(3)	405
				Sec. 15378(b)(4)	405
				Sec. 15384(a)	154
				Sec. 15385	158

CALIFORNIA RULES OF COURT

	page(s)
Rules 1–55	567

CALIFORNIA ATTORNEY GENERAL OPINIONS

	page(s)
17 Ops. Cal. Atty. Gen. 79 (1951)	81
39 Ops. Cal. Atty. Gen. 82 (1962)	81
40 Ops. Cal. Atty. Gen. 243 (1962)	74
55 Ops. Cal. Atty. Gen. 414 (1972)	82, 86
56 Ops. Cal. Atty. Gen. 274 (1973)	122
57 Ops. Cal. Atty. Gen. 556 (1974)	84
58 Ops. Cal. Atty. Gen. 21 (1975)	9, 20
58 Ops. Cal. Atty. Gen. 408 (1975)	84
58 Ops. Cal. Atty. Gen. 41 (1975)	115, 119
59 Ops. Cal. Atty. Gen. 129 (1976)	26, 115, 122
59 Ops. Cal. Atty. Gen. 581 (1976)	82
61 Ops. Cal. Atty. Gen. 299 (1978)	79, 82
62 Ops. Cal. Atty. Gen. 136 (1979)	81, 89
62 Ops. Cal. Atty. Gen. 140 (1979)	81, 89
62 Ops. Cal. Atty. Gen. 147 (1979)	82
62 Ops. Cal. Atty. Gen. 175 (1979)	134
62 Ops. Cal. Atty. Gen. 410 (1979)	73, 119
63 Ops. Cal. Atty. Gen. 820 (1980)	461
64 Ops. Cal. Atty. Gen. 328 (1981)	113, 122
64 Ops. Cal. Atty. Gen. 762 (1981)	83
64 Ops. Cal. Atty. Gen. 814 (1981)	81
65 Ops. Cal. Atty. Gen. 63 (1982)	461
66 Ops. Cal. Atty. Gen. 120 (1983)	111
66 Ops. Cal. Atty. Gen. 258 (1983)	29
67 Ops. Cal. Atty. Gen. 75 (1984)	21
68 Ops. Cal. Atty. Gen. 108 (1985)	118
68 Ops. Cal. Atty. Gen. 310 (1985)	72
69 Ops. Cal. Atty. Gen. 300 (1986)	267
70 Ops. Cal. Atty. Gen. 231 (1987)	487
71 Ops. Cal. Atty. Gen. 163 (1988)	112
71 Ops. Cal. Atty. Gen. 326 (1988)	124
73 Ops. Cal. Atty. Gen. 152 (1990)	110, 117, 364
73 Ops. Cal. Atty. Gen. 255 (1990)	414
73 Ops. Cal. Atty. Gen. 338 (1990)	123
73 Ops. Cal. Atty. Gen. 78 (1990)	21
74 Ops. Cal. Atty. Gen. 149 (1991)	138, 141
74 Ops. Cal. Atty. Gen. 89 (1991)	131
75 Ops. Cal. Atty. Gen. 98 (1992)	73, 89
76 Ops. Cal. Atty. Gen. 227 (1994)	274
77 Ops. Cal. Atty. Gen. 185 (1994)	79, 87
77 Ops. Cal. Atty. Gen. 231 (1994)	88
77 Ops. Cal. Atty. Gen. 94 (1994)	274
78 Ops. Cal. Atty. Gen. 137 (1995)	232
78 Ops. Cal. Atty. Gen. 158 (1995)	134
78 Ops. Cal. Atty. Gen. 31 (1995)	74
78 Ops. Cal. Atty. Gen. 77 (1995)	52, 536
80 Ops. Cal. Atty. Gen. 183 (1997)	377
81 Ops. Cal. Atty. Gen. 104 (1998)	377
81 Ops. Cal. Atty. Gen. 144 (1998)	139, 142
81 Ops. Cal. Atty. Gen. 166 (1998)	94
81 Ops. Cal. Atty. Gen. 181 (1998)	379
81 Ops. Cal. Atty. Gen. 293 (1998)	110
81 Ops. Cal. Atty. Gen. 57 (1998)	48
81 Ops. Cal. Atty. Gen. 106 (1998)	378
82 Ops. Cal. Atty. Gen. 35 (1999)	375, 379
82 Ops. Cal. Atty. Gen. 43 (1999)	377
83 Ops. Cal. Atty. Gen. 190 (2000)	75
84 Ops. Cal. Atty. Gen. 66 (2001)	438
85 Ops. Cal. Atty. Gen. 21 (2002)	114
86 Ops. Cal. Atty. Gen. 70 (2003)	81, 145
87 Ops. Cal. Atty. Gen. 102 (2004)	28
87 Ops. Cal. Atty. Gen. 96 (2004)	40
88 Ops. Cal. Atty Gen. 84 (2005)	485
89 Ops. Cal. Atty. Gen. 173 (2006)	448
89 Ops. Cal. Atty. Gen. 178 (2006)	6
90 Ops. Cal. Atty. Gen. 69 (2007)	85
307 Ops. Cal. Atty. Gen. 172 (2005)	112

CALIFORNIA PUBLIC WORKS CASES

	page(s)
No. 2000-016, *Vineyard Creek Hotel & Conf. Ctr., Redev. Agency,* Santa Rosa (Oct. 16, 2000)	266
No. 2001-016, *Devel. of River St. Hist. Dist.*, City of San Jose (May 6, 2002)	266
No. 2001-044, *Soledad Canyon Ctr. Shopping Center*, City of Santa Clarita (Sept. 26, 2002)	266
No. 2001-068, *Field Technician Observ. & Testing*, Los Angeles County Sanitation District Sewer Line Project (July 19, 2002)	266
No. 2003-014, *Phase II Res. Devel., Victoria Gardens*, City of Rancho Cucamonga (July 20, 2005)	267
No. 2003-022, *Chapman Heights*, City of Yucaipa (Jan. 30, 2004)	266
No. 2003-028, *Baldwin Park Marketplace Project* (June 28, 2005)	267
No. 2003-028, *Baldwin Park Marketplace Project*, City of Baldwin Park (Oct. 16, 2003), incor. by reference into Dec. on Admin. Appeal (June 28, 2005)	266

COMPACTS

	page(s)
Tribal-State Gaming Compact Between the Coyote Valley Band of Pomo Indians and the State of California Secs. 11.1, 11.2	77

EXECUTIVE ORDERS

	page(s)
Exec. Order S-2-03	266

OTHER STATUTES

Illinois Statutes

	page(s)
Pioneer Trust Rule, 22 Ill. 2d 375 (1961)	347

Oregon Statutes

	page(s)
Or. Rev. Stat., Sec. 227.180	462

Washington Statutes

	page(s)
Wash. Rev. Code, Sec. 42.36.060	462

Supreme Court of Ireland Decisions

	page(s)
In the Matter of Art. 26 of the Const. and In the Matter of Part V of the Plan. & Devel. Bill 1999, Supreme Court of Ireland, Aug. 28, 2000	69

SECONDARY SOURCES

	page(s)
Calif. Adminis. Mandamus, Procedures After Trial, Sec. 13.10–13.11	525n1, 567
1 *Calif. Civil Appellate Prac.*, Sec. 6.19 (CEB, 3d ed. 1997)	568
31 *Calif. Forms of Pleading & Prac.*, ch. 358, forms 18 & 20 (Matthew Bender) 2004	525n1, 566
Calif. Gov't Tort Liability Prac. (CEB, 2004), Sec. 9.25 *et seq.*	470–471, 473
43 Cal. Jur. 3d, Mandamus and Prohibition, Sec. 38	555
Calif. Mun. Law Handbook	415
pp. II-20–II-50	459
p. II-63	463
Calif. SMA Practice (CEB, 1987)	140
Sec. 6.28	104-105
Sec. 6.31	102, 104-105
32 *Fed. Prac. & Proc. Jud. Rvw.*, Sec. 8260 (2007)	32, 463n8
2 Kostka & Zischke, *Practice Under CEQA*	41, 147n1, 525n1
Sec. 5.5	151
Secs. 12.4, 12.5, 23	573
5 Manaster and Selmi, *Calif. Envt'l Law & Land Use Practice, Admin. Law and Litigation*, Sec. 10 (Lexis, 2006)	525
1 Witkin, *Calif. Evid., Judicial Notice*, Sec. 3 (4th ed. 2002)	561
4 Witkin, *Calif. Proc., Pleading*, Sec. 962 *et seq.* (4th ed., 1996)	579
6 Witkin, *Calif. Proc., Provis. Remedies*, Sec. 400 (9th ed. 1997)	568
6 Witkin, *Calif. Proc., Provis. Remedies*, Sec. 413 (4th ed. 1996)	566
9 Witkin, *Calif. Proc., Appeal*, Sec. 276 (4th ed. 1997)	568

OTHER SOURCES

"Affordable Housing Policy in Miami," Keenan (*J. Aff. Hsg. & Cmty. Dev. Law*, Winter 2005), 507n37

Airport Land Use Comms., Detwiler (*CEB L. U. & Env. Forum*, Winter 1994), 28

American Indian Law Deskbook (Western Attys. Gen., 2nd ed., l998), 75

"Amortization in the 22nd Century," Campbell (*Zon. & Plan. Law Rpt.*, Feb. 2004), 63n7

"Annexation Agreements & Dev. Agreements," Callies/Tappendorf, *Trends in Land Use Law from A to Z* (ABA, 2001), 273n2

"Antiquated Subdivisions," Merritt et al., *L. U. & Envtl. Forum* (CEB, Winter 1996), 145

"Ballot Box Zoning," Lucero, *Zoning News* (APA, May 2003), 415n7

"Ballot Box Zoning," Lucero (*Zon. & Plan. Law Rpt.*, June 2005), 415n7

Ballot Measure Advocacy and the Law (League of Calif. Cities, Sept. 2003), 415

Bridging the Gap (OPR, 2nd ed. 1989), 123

Calif. Aff. Housing Handbook (Feb. 2006), 483n4, 502n22, 517n64

Calif. Airport Land Use Planning Handbook (Caltrans, Jan. 2002), 48

Calif. Civil Prac.: Real Property (Thomson-West, 2nd ed. 2005), 525n1

Calif. Civil Writ Prac., Sorgen et al. (CEB, 3rd ed. 2006), 525n1

"Calif. Enacts Form-Based Zoning Legis.," Retzlaff, *Zon. Prac.* (APA, Jan. 2005), 14n6, 65n10

Calif. Evidence Benchbook, Jefferson, 562

Calif. Inclusionary Housing Reader (Inst. for Local Self Gov't, Winter 2003), 69n12, 517n65, 519n70

"Calif. Supreme Court's Foreclosure of the Compensation Remedy for Takings Claimants," Ramirez (*Calif. Land Use Law & Pol. Rptr.*, Apr. 1999), 312n14

Calif. 2025, Harak/Baldassare, eds. (Pub. Pol. Inst. of Calif., 2005), 385n1, 419n2, 423, 433

"Challenges of Growth Within Bounds," Detwiler (*Calif. Envtl. Law Rpt.* 101, May 2000), 436n2

"Changing Culture," Rosenberg (*SMU L. Rvw.*, 2006), 339n1

"Churches Use New Federal Statute to Win Zoning Cases," Dam, *Lawyers Weekly*, Aug. 20, 2001, 59n5

Cities Under Pressure, Lewis/Neiman (Pub. Pol. Inst. of Calif., Jan. 2002), 420n5

"City, Builders Settle Ordinance Fight," Weisberg, *San Diego Union-Trib.*, July 26, 2006, 507n38

Table of Authorities

Calif. Prac. Guide, Eisenberg et al. (Rutter Group, 2006), 525n1
"Compensating for Wetland Losses under the Clean Water Act" (Nat'l Acad. of Science), 198
"Comprehensive Plan as Constitution," Curtin, *Zon. & Plan. Law Handbook* (Clark, Boardman & Callaghan, 1992), 10n3
"Condominium Conversions," *Advising Calif. Common Inter. Dev.* (CEB, 2006), 90n7
Contra Costa County Smart Growth or Sprawl? (Greenbelt Alliance, June 2003), 420n7
"Contracting for Preservation," Safran (*Zon. & Plan. L. Rpt.*, July/Aug. 2004), 239
"Current Issues in Inclus. Zoning," Talbert/Costa (*Urb. L.*, Summer 2005), 69n12
Cuyahoga County, Curtin (Program on Plan., Zon. & Emin. Domain, 2003), 504n25

"Democratizing the Amer. Dream," Brown (*U. Mich. J. L. Ref.*, Winter 2004), 508n43
"Denial of Religious College's Rezoning Bid Was Not Illegal," Curtin/Safran, *S. F. Daily J.*, May 12, 2004, 58n4
"Developer Claims to Vested Rights," Curtin, *Land Use Law and Zoning* (Salkin ed., ABA, 2004), 269n1
"Developers to the Rescue," Dallarda/Cold (*Calif. L. U. Law & Pol. Rptr.*, 2001), 114
Development Agreement Manual (Inst. for Local Self Gov't, 2002), 273n2
"Development Agreements," Schwartz (*Bos. C. Envtl. Aff. L. Rvw.*, Sum. 2001), 273n2
"Ding Dong the Witch Is Dead," Lazar/Merriam (*Plan. & Envtl. L.*, 2005), 295n6
"Does the Costa-Hawkins Act Prohibit Local Inclus. Zon. Programs," El Mallakh (*Cal. L. Rev.*, 2001), 517n60, 517n61
Dolan and Nollan Takings and Exactions, Calif. Style, Curtin (Matthew Bender, Oct. 2002), 339n1
"Drawing New Lines for Conservation," *C.C. Times*, Apr. 18, 2004, 369n19
"An Egalitarian's Market," Dietderich (*Fordham Urb. L. J.*, 1996), 508n45
Eminent Domain Use and Abuse, Merriam/Ross (ABA, 2006), 290n4
"Equity in Eden," Russell (*B.C. Envtl. Aff. L. Rvw.*, 2003), 504n27
"Ex Parte Contacts," Curtin (*CEB Land Use & Env. Forum*, Winter 1994), 463n8
Exactions, Dedications and Development Agreements, Curtin (Matthew Bender, 2003), 273n2, 339n1
"Exactions Update," Curtin et al. (*Urb. L.*, Summer 2006), 349n7, 351n7
"Exclusionary Effect," Durkin (*Cal. U. L. Rvw.*, Winter 2006), 509n46
Expanding Aff. Housing Through Inclus. Zon., Brown (Brookings, Oct. 2001), 521n78
Expanding Housing Opportunity in Washington, D.C. (PolicyLink, Winter 2005), 507n37, 508n44, 515n55, 517n64, 518n66, 519n71, 522n81
Expanding Opportunity (PolicyLink, Winter 2005), 69n12, 483n7
"Fifth Amendment Taking Claims in Federal Court," Roberts (*Urb. L.*, 1992), 326
"Financing Schools," Silberstein (*CEB L.U. & Env. Forum*, Fall 1993), 365n15
Form-Based Land Development Regulations, Sitkowski/Ohm (*Urb. L.*, Winter 2006), 14n6, 65n8
"Form-Based Zoning Is Not the (Whole) Answer," Moore (*APA Northern News*, May/June 2006), 14n6, 65n10

Forming Calif. Common Interest Development (CEB, 2006), 80n2
"From Junkyards to Gentrification," Dubin (*Minn. L. Rvw.*, 1993), 504n28
From Sprawl to Smart Growth, Freilich (ABA, 1999), 427n22
Funding Open Space Acquisition Programs (Inst. for Local Gov't, 2005), 370n20, 375n23

Getting the Most Out of Public Hearings (Inst. for Local Gov't, 2005), 455n1
"GHADs," Curtin/Zovod, *Landslide Hazards and Planning* (APA, 2005), 381n26
Governor's Strategy Growth Rpt. (OPR, 1993), 28
"Growth Control as a Taking" (*Urb. L.*, 1993), 424
"Growth Control by the Ballot Box," Curtin/Jacobson (*Loyola L.A. L. Rvw.*, 1991), 385n1, 417, 422n9
"Growth Management and Aff. Housing Policy," Nelson/Wachter (*J. Aff. Hsg. & Cmty. Dev. L.*, 2003), 484n9, 504n26
"Growth Management by the Initiative," Curtin/Jacobson (*Loyola L.A. L. Rvw.*, 1991), 385n1, 422n9
"Growth Management by the Initiative in California," Curtin/Jacobson (*Urb. Law.*, 1989), 385n1, 422n9
Guidance on Compens. Mitigation Projects for Aquatic Res. Impacts (RGL 02-2) (USACE, Dec. 24, 2002), 195

Handling Administrative Mandamus, Robinson (CEB, Spring 2000), 525n1, 536, 563
"Historic Preservation Law in the U.S.," Callies (*Envtl. L. Rep.*, Mar. 2002), 237
"Home Affordability Rises in State," *San Diego Union-Trib.*, Aug. 30, 2007, 483n6
Housing Bottom Line (Blue Sky Consulting Group, June 2007), 422n8
"Housing Costs Consumed More of Paychecks in 2006," *NYT* (Sept. 12, 2007), 483n3
Housing Element Questions & Answers (HCD, Oct. 2006), 487n13, 489n14, 491n16
Housing Supply and Affordability, Powell/Stringham (Reason Pub. Pol. Inst., Apr. 2004), 507n41, 508n45
"How Many Lawyers Does It Take to…?" Jenkins (*Western City*, May 2004), 458n2
"How Should California Grow," Whiteside (*Western City*, July 2007), 419n1
"How the West Was Won," Curtin, *Trends in Land Use Law from A to Z* (Salkin, ed., ABA, 2001), 289n2, 339n1

Impact of Incl. Zoning, Brunick (2003), 508n44
"Implementing Form-Based Zoning in Your Municipality," Moynihan (*Mun. L.*, July/Aug. 2006), 14n6, 65n10
"Implications of Kelo in Land Use Law," Curtin (*S. C. L. R.*, 2006), 290n4
"In Defense of Inclusionary Zoning," Kautz (*U.S.F. L. Rvw.*, 2002), 300n8, 350n8, 506n31, 508n45, 513n51, 514n54, 516n58, 517n60, 518n67
Inclusionary Housing in California (Calif. Coalition for Rural Hsg., 2003), 69n12, 507n35, 508n42, 512n50
"Inclusionary Housing Debate," Brunick, *Zon. Prac.* (APA, Sept. 2004), 518n66
"Inclusionary Housing and Its Impact," Rosen (*NHC Aff. Hsg. Pol. Rvw.*, Feb. 2004), 507n41
"Inclusionary Housing Ordinance Survives Constitutional Challenge…," Curtin et al., *L.U. Law & Zon. Digest* (APA, Aug. 2002), 300n8, 350n8
"Inclusionary Housing Programs," Talbert/Costa (*B.C. Envtl. Aff. L. Rvw.*, 2003), 503n23

"Inclusionary Housing: Proven Success," Brunick, *Zon. Prac.* (Oct. 2004), 507n39
Inclusionary Zoning (APA, Mar. 2003), 69n12
"Inclusionary Zoning" Burchell/Galley, *Calif. Inclus. Hsg. Reader* (Inst. for Local Self Gov't, 2003), 506n33, 508n45, 506n33
Inclusionary Zoning (Calif. Aff. Hsg. Law Project, 2002), 515n55, 515n56, 515n57, 517n64, 519n73, 520n7
Inclusionary Zoning (Enterpr. Found.), 518n68
"Inclusionary Zoning" (*NCH Aff. Hsg. Pol. Rvw.*, Feb. 2004), 507n36
"Inclusionary Zoning," Talbert/Krumbein (*Mun. L.*, May/June 2005), 506n31
Inclusionary Zoning and Aff. Housing, Higgins (Inst. on Plan., Zon. & Emin. Domain, 2003), 507n40, 518n69, 520n76, 521n80
Inclusionary Zoning for Aff. Housing, Porter (ULI, 2004), 506n34
"Inclusionary Zoning Devices as Takings," Berger (*Neb. L. Rvw.*, 1991), 508n45
Inclusionary Zoning: A Primer (D.C. Office of Plan., 2002), 518n66
Initiative and the Referendum in California, Key/Crouch (1939), 417
"Irony of 'Inclusionary Zoning,'" Ellickson (*S. Cal. L. Rvw.*, 1981), 508n45, 513n53, 520n75

"Keeping Them Down on the Farm," Morrison/Brownlow (*Calif. L. U. Law & Pol. Rptr.*, June 2004), 242
"Kelo Provides Tools to Rebuild, Revitalize Urban America," Freilich, *San Francisco Daily J.*, July 26, 2005, 290n4
"Kelo v. City of New London," Callies (*U. Haw. L. Rvw.*, 2005–06), 290n4

Land Use Planning and Control Law, Juergensmeyer/Roberts (1998), 236, 238, 306n12
Law of Local Gov't Oper., Rhyne (1980), 457–58
Legal Guide to Aff. Housing Development, Iglesias/Lento, eds. (ABA, 2005), 483n1
"Legal Issues Associated with Inclusionary Housing Ordinances," *Calif. Inclusionary Housing Reader* (Inst. for Local Self Gov't, 2003), 517n65, 519n70
"Lobbying Guidelines & Rules," Eigner/Wernli (*Calif. Real Prop. J.*, Spring 2003), 463n8
Local Regulation of Adult Business, Gerard (West, 2005), 56
Local and Regional Perspectives on Growth Management (OPR, 1992), 422n9
"Local Slow-Growth Measures," Fulton (*CPDR*, Apr. 2000), 423n15
Locked Out 2002 (Calif. Budget Project, Sacramento, Oct. 2002), 483n2
"Looking Beyond the City Limits," Curtin/Danforth (*Urb. Law.*, 1990), 422n9
Los Angeles Inclusionary Housing Study, Rosen et al. (2002), 507n40

"Making Excl. Zon. Remedies Work," Gordon (*Yale L. & Pol. Rvw.*, 2006), 509n46
"Mandatory Inclusionary Zoning," Lerman (*B.C. Envtl. Aff. L. Rvw.*, 2006), 506n30, 511n48, 518n66
Meeting Our Nation's Housing Challenge (Millennial Hsg. Comm., 2002), 484n11
Merger and Local Governments (OPR, 1986), 143n13, 145
Metropolitan Growth Planning in California—1900–2000, Barbour (Pub. Pol. Inst. of Calif., 2002), 420n7
"Minnesota Land Use Planning Act & the Promotion of Low- and Moderate-Income Hsg. in Suburbia," Goetz et al. (*Law & Ineq. J.*, Winter 2004), 508n43

Mitigation and Monitoring Proposal Guidelines (Corps, Dec. 2004), 198

Municipal Law, Rhyne, 360

Municipal Service Review Guidelines (OPR, Aug. 2003), 454, 440n8

On Common Ground (Home Builders Ass'n of N. Cal., July 2005), 517n63

Open and Public III, Fourkas (Open & Pub. Participants, rev. 2003), 459n3

"Origins and Evolution of Inclusionary Housing in California," Calavita, *Inclusionary Hsg.* (Feb. 2004), 506n34

"Out of the Chaos," Sullivan/Richter (*Urb. Law.*, 2002), 462n7

"Panning for Gold in the Trickle of Supreme Court Cases This Term," Merriam (*Zon. & Plan. Law Rpt.*, June 2003), 316, 335, 408

"Paying for the Change," LaRusso (*Envtl. Aff. L. Rvw.*, 1990), 316n16

"Permit Streamlining Act," Merritt (*CEB L. U. Forum*, Fall 1991), 467

"Planning by Plebiscite," Meyers/Mandleman (ABA, Summer 2001), 415n7

Planner's Guide to Financing Public Improvements (OPR, June 1997)

Planner's Guide to Spec. Plans (OPR, Jan. 2001), 41

Planning Commissioner's Book (OPR, 1998), 6n4

"Planning Moratoria and Regulatory Takings," Eagle (*Flor. St. L. Rvw.*, Spring 2004), 302n9

Policy Claims, Basolo/Calavita, 507n41

Preemption of Local Land Use Authority in California (OPR, 1989), 4n1

"Problem of Ex Parte Contacts," Witt (*Land Use & Env. Forum*, CEB, Winter 1994), 463n8, 534

Procedural Due Process Limitations, Albuquerque (League of Calif. Cities, May 2004), 458n2

"Procedural Implications of Williamson County/First English," Roberts (*Envtl. L. Rep. News & Analysis*, Apr. 2001), 326

Property Rights & Land Use Regulation, Higgins/Kautz (Inst. for Local Gov't, July 2006), 289n2

"Property Rights Measure Reaches Ballot," Shigley (*CPDR*, Aug. 2006), 418n8

Proposition 218—Implementation Guide (League of Calif. Cities), 374n22

"Proposition 218 Odyssey," Merritt/Parikh (*CEB Real Prop. L. Rep.*, May 1997), 374n22

Protecting Free Speech and Expression, Mandelker/Rubin (ABA, 2001), 53n3

Providing Conflict of Interest Advice Handbook (League of Calif. Cities, Feb. 2004), 534n9

Public Notice and Land Use Planning (OPR, 1998), 455n1

Putting the Pieces Together (ULI, Wash., D.C., 2002), 428n27

"Racial Limits of the Fair Housing Act," Robinson (*Wm. & Mary L. Rev.*, 1995–96), 504n28

"Ramapo's Impact on the Comprehensive Plan," Curtin (*Urb. L.*, Winter 2003), 10n3

Rathkopf's Law of Zoning and Planning, Ziegler (Sept. 2007), 463n8

Reading the U.S. Supreme Court's Tea Leaves (ABA, Aug. 9, 2003), 316, 335, 408

"Recent Developments Concerning RLUIPA," Weinstein, *Current Trends & Practical Strategies in Land Use Law & Zoning* (Salkin ed., 2004), 59n5, 269n1

"Recent Developments in Inclusionary Zoning," Talbert et al. (*Urb. Law.*, Summer 2006), 69n12

"Recent Developments in Land Use, Planning and Zoning Law Relating to Exactions," Curtin/Gowder (*Urb. Law.*, Summer 2004), 351n10

"Reciprocity of Advantage," Schwartz (*UCLA J. Envtl. L. & Pol'y*, 2003–04), 308n12

"Reconciling Liability Standards After Iverson and Bestfoods," Reed (*Ecol. L.Q.*, 2000), 204

"Reengineering Regulations to Avoid Takings," Merriam (*Urb. L.*, 2001), 289n2

"Reflections on Inclusionary Housing and Renewed Look at Its Viability," Padilla (*Hofstra L. Rvw.*, 1995), 69n11, 508n45

Regional Equity and Smart Growth, Blackwell/Fox (Transl. Paper no. 1, ed. 2, 2004), 484n10, 507n39

"Regulating Big Box Stores," Curtin (*Vt. J. Envtl. L.*, 2005), 35

Regulatory Takings, Eagle (Lexis Publ., 2nd ed. 2001), 289n2

Regulatory Takings and Land Use Regulations, Higgins (Inst. for Local Gov't, July 2006), 289n2

Report on Second Units (HCD, Dec. 1990), 88n6

"RLUIPA," Weinstein (*Plan. & Envtl. Law*, Apr. 2004), 59n5

"RLUIPA Is Constitutional," Picarello (*Plan. & Envtl. Law*, Apr. 2004), 59n5

"RLUIPA Is Unfair, Unwise, and Unconstitutional," Hamilton (*Plan. & Envtl. Law*, Apr. 2004), 59n5

"RLUIPA," Weinstein (*Plan. & Envtl. Law*, Apr. 2004), 59n5

"Role of the Comprehensive Plan in Infrastructure Financing," Sullivan/Lester (*Urb. L.*, 2005), 34, 363n14

Sect. 1983 Land Use Case, Carlisle (Kass ed., 1998), 330n19

Smart Growth in the San Francisco Bay Area, Binger (ULI, June 2003), 420n7

"Smart Growth Is the Agenda," Fulton (*CPDR*, Mar. 1999), 420n5

"Smart Growth: State by State," Bolen et al., *Hastings W-Nw. J. of Envtl. L. & Pol'y* (Spring 2002), 420n5, 427n24

"Solving the 'Taking' Equation," Freilich (*Urb. Law.*, 1983), 316

Special Issues Under Takings Law (Inst. for Local Self Gov't, 1999), 287, 340n2

"Summary of Local Land Use Measures" (*Calif. Ballot Monitor*, rev. ed. Dec. 1992), 423n13

"Tahoe-Sierra" (*Urb. L.*, Fall 2002), 294

"Tahoe-Sierra," Merriam (*Zon. & Plan. Law Rpt.*, June 2002), 308n12

"Taking for Any Purpose?," Madigan (*Hastings W-Nw J. Envtl. Law & Policy*, Spring 2003), 289n3

Taking Sides on Takings Issues, the Impact of Tahoe-Sierra (Roberts, ed., ABA, 2003), 289n2, 292, 302n10, 308n13, 314

Taking Sides on Takings Issues, Public and Private Perspectives (Roberts, ed., ABA, 2002), 289n2, 314

Takings in the 21st Century, Stein (*Tenn. L. Rev.*, Summer 2002), 294

Takings Issue, Meltz et al. (Island Press, 1999), 289n2, 317, 320

Takings Litigation Handbook, Kendall et al. (American Legal Publishing Corporation, 2000), 289n2, 525n1

"The 30th Anniversary of Golden v. Ramapo," (*Urb. L.*, Winter 2003), 425

Tools and Patterns of Growth Management Ballot Measures in California 1986–2000, Nguyen/Fulton (Solimar Res. Group, Inc., Sept. 2002), 424n21

"Toward Ending Residential Segregation," Boger (*N.C. L. Rev.*, 1992–93), 504n28

"Transition Away from Suburbia Bolsters Form-Based Zoning Movement," Fulton (*CPDR*, Apr. 2006), 14n6, 65n9

Trends in Local Land Use and Ballot Measures, 1986–2000, Fulton (Solimar Res. Group, Inc., Oct. 2, 2000), 423n11

"Unconstitutional Land Development Conditions and the Development Agreement Solution," Callies/Tappendorf (*Case W. Res. L. Rvw.*, Summer 2001), 278

Understanding the Habitat Conservation Planning Process, Cylinder (Inst. for Local Self Gov't, 2004), 369n17

Update on Exactions, Curtin (LexisNexis 2004), 351n10

"Urban Equity," Blackwell (*Fordham Urb. L. J.*, 2004), 508n43, 508n44

"Using Certificates of Compliance to Help Clients Under the Subdivision Map Act," Merritt/Fox, *Real Prop. Law Rptr.* (CEB, July 2003), 87n4, 138n10

"Utility and Efficacy of the RLUIPA," Smolik (*Boston Col. Envtl. Aff. L. Rvw.*, 2004), 59n5

Variance, The (OPR, July 1997), 60n6

Voluntary or Mandatory Inclus. Hsg. Production, Brunick et al. (Bus. & Prof. People for Public Interest, Nov. 2003), 507n41

"Voters Reject Road Taxes, Growth," Shigley (*CPDR*, July 2006), 424n20

"Voters Show Pro-Growth Sentiment," Shigley (*CPDR*, Dec. 2002), 423n16

"Weighing the Benefits," Jeer, *Landslide Hazards and Planning* (APA, 2005), 381n26

"What Regional Agenda?," Courchesne (*Harv. Envtl. L. Rvw.*, 2004), 508n43

"Where Does APA Stand on RLUIPA?," Lucero (*Plan. & Envtl. Law*, APA, Apr. 2004), 59n5

"Windfalls, Wipeouts, Givings, and Takings in Dramatic Redevelopment Projects," Curtin/Witten (*B.C. Envtl. Aff. L. Rvw.* 325, 2005), 34

"Zen and the Art of Zoning," Hall (*Calif. L. U. Law & Policy Rptr.*, Mar. 2004), 59n5

"Zero Sum Game," Safran (*Vt. J. Envtl. L.*, 2004–05), 369

"Zoning Churches," *Western City* (July 2004), 59n5

Zoning of Religious Land Use and Institutionalized Persons Act of 2000, Hills (ABA, 2001), 59n5

Index

A

AB 1600, 358
AB 1744, 439n7
ABAG. *See* Association of Bay Area Governments
abuse of discretion, 448–449, 535, 572–573
  See also judicial review
addiction treatment facility, CUP allowed for, 62
"adjudicatory" act, 118, 286, 346, 455, 467, 529–530
  See also administrative act
administrative act
  See also legislative act
administrative mandate proceedings, 328–329, 530–531, 544, 558, 564–565
  section 1094.5 challenges, 529–530
  findings requirements, 286, 535
  initiative/referendum may not affect, 402
  judicial review
    administrative/ legislative act, 538
    "excess of jurisdiction," 535
    "fair hearing," 535–537
    "findings and evidence," 537–538
    in general, 535
    "proceeding in manner required by law," 537
  "quasi-adjudicatory" capacity, 334
Administrative Procedure Act, 205, 228, 543
  statute of limitations, 542
administrative record, 199
  See also evidence; findings requirements; judicial review
  preparation, 557–558
adult business regulation, 53–56, 479
  See also zoning ordinance
  not upheld, 235
  as takings claim, not upheld, 294n6
Advisory Council on Historic Preservation, 201, 236

aesthetics
  See also art; design; urban form and design
  does not trigger EIR, 155
  historic preservation and, regulations promoting, 345
  allowed under police power, 3
  freedom of speech, 235
  permissible if related to health, welfare, and public safety, 233
affordable housing
  See housing; inclusionary zoning
"agent of the state," 398–399
Agins test, takings, 291–292
agricultural association, Map Act application to, 81
agricultural conservation easement, 123, 241
agricultural easement, 123
  See also easement
agricultural employee
  housing for, 485, 496
  identification of, in housing element, 15
agricultural land, 91, 123, 238–242, 420, 446, 493–494
  See also agriculture; Williamson Act contract
  conservation element addresses, 16
  initiative, 433
  land clearing activities, 184–185
  prime agricultural land, preservation of by LAFCO, 435, 437
  Williamson Act definition, 239
agricultural lease. *See also* lease
  Map Act application to, 91
agricultural preserve, 238–239
"agricultural purposes," defined, 91
agricultural uses, under Williamson Act, 239
agricultural zone, 493
agriculture
  See also agricultural land
  CWA exemption for, 185
  irrigation, 178, 185
  Subdivision Map Act protection of, 432
airguns. *See* underwater airguns

air pollution, 420
  conservation element addresses, 16
  hazardous waste emissions, 93, 464
  requirements under PSA, 464
air pollution control district, LAFCO jurisdiction, 441
air quality management district, LAFCO oversight of, 441
airplane hangar, CUP allowed for, 62
airport, military activity, 14
airport land use commission, 27–28, 40, 48
Airport Land Use Plan (ALUP)
  adoption as CEQA project, 150
  consistency with general plan, 27–28, 31
  consistency with specific plan, 40, 48
  consistency with zoning ordinance, 48
  overruled by city, 27–28
airspace. *See also* condominium conversion
  division of and Map Act, 82, 109, 111
Alameda County
  Measure D, 396–398
  UGB, 396
  "urbanized area," 264
Alameda whipsnake, 213
Alquist-Priolo Special Studies Zones Act, 112
alternatives. *See also* environmental impact report; mitigation
  project alternatives, 147, 154, 160, 166, 168–169, 216, 219, 237
  density, 166
  infeasibility, 168
  "no project" alternative, 166
  "range of reasonable alternatives," 166–167
  "rule of reason," 166
  wetlands
    availability, 197–198
    "market entry approach," 198
    EPA's 404(b)(1) Guidelines, 193–194
    practicability, 193–195, 196–197, 199–200
    sequencing, 194–196

ALUP. *See* Airport Land Use Plan
American dream, 358
American Planning Association (APA)
  density bonus ordinance,
    website, 497n20
  Growing Smart Guidebook, 429
  smart growth ordinances,
    website, 429n29
  TDR ordinance, web address, 250
amortization, discussed, 63–65
Angeles National Forest, 309
annexation, 239, 402
  See also boundary changes; local
    agency formation commission
  challenged as inverse
    condemnation, 313
  deannexation,
    as legislative act, 528
  development agreements
    and, 274–275, 281
  effect on vesting tentative
    map, 107, 281
  is legislative act, 281, 528
  LAFCO review, 437, 440, 443, 445
    prezoning requirement, 65, 443
  statute of limitations, 541
anti-demolition ordinance, 46
APA. *See* American
  Planning Association
apartment
  See also apartment building;
    apartment conversion;
    community apartment project
  Map Act does not apply
    to leasing of, 82n3, 89–90
apartment building/complex,
  no vested right to build, 334
  occupancy restriction, 60
apartment conversion. *See also*
  condominium conversion
  new regulations may
    not prevent, 272
  no right to convert, 340
  no vested right, 273
Apple Valley, 424
"aquatic resources of national
    importance" (ARNI), 199
  See also wetlands
"arbitrary and capricious" test,
  26, 35, 41, 197, 209,
  218–219, 228, 332, 573
  See also judicial review;
    reasonableness
  EPA veto overturned under, 200
  land use regulation, 4, 35, 41
    discussed, 26, 532–533
architectural review board, 6n3
  See also design review board
ARNI. *See* "aquatic resources
  of national importance"
art. *See also* aesthetics
  dedications allowed for, 116, 362
  public art fee ordinance,
    3, 352, 354–355
assessment
  See also assessment ballot
    proceeding; assessment district;
    assessment roll; taxes
  challenges to, statute
    of limitations, 542
  definition, 376
  facilities benefit assessment,
    363, 380–381

assessment *continued*
  special assessment, 88, 128, 374
    Jarvis propositions
      impacts, 375–377
    Subdivision Map Act and, 82–83, 88
    standby charge as, 379–380
assessment ballot proceeding, 376–77
  See also Proposition 218
assessment district
  fire suppression assessment, 377
  formation, 380
  GHAD, 380–382
  LAFCO jurisdiction, 441
  landscaping and lighting district, 380
  Mello-Roos district, 380
  water assessment district, 377
assessment roll, 82
  See also Subdivision Map Act
Associated Home Builders test, 342, 345
Association of Bay Area
  Governments (ABAG), 419, 427
  Blueprint 2001, 491n16
  population projections,
    website, 431n31
  Regional Livability
    Footprint, 429–431
  website, 504
athletic stadium, EIR for, 149
attorney. *See also* attorneys'
  fees; judicial review
  city attorney, 458–459
attorneys' fees
  See also judicial review
  discussed, 580–582
  ESA suits, 230
  in general, 131, 431,
    471, 495, 500, 566
  private attorney general
    theory, 580–581
  SLAPP suits, 582
  "substantial benefit" theory, 580
"audience test," 414
auto service station, CUP
  not allowed for, 62
auto test track facility,
  land for not blighted, 70–71
Avco rule, 102
  See also vested rights
  in general, 269–271
  refinements, 271–273
Azusa, form-based zoning, 65

B

BAAQMD. *See* Bay Area Air Quality
  Management District
"balancing." *See* general plan
Bald Eagle Protection Act,
  section 668 *et seq.*, 226
ballot box planning
  See also ballot box zoning;
    growth management
  discussed, 385, 415–418, 422–424
ballot box zoning, 407–408
  See also initiative
Barstow, 579
BART. *See* San Francisco Bay Area
  Rapid Transit District
Bay Area Air Quality Management
  District (BAAQMD),
  29, 430–431
Bay Area Council, 484n9, 503n24
bay checkerspot butterfly, 213

Berkeley, 234
  building height measure, 424
  telecommunications
    ordinance, pre-emption of, 5
  West Berkeley
    Industrial Park, 398–399
BIA. *See* Building Industry Association
bias. *See also* judicial review;
    motives; public official
  by public agency, 456
  by public official, 51, 462, 536–537
  "excess of jurisdiction," 535
bicycle facility
  See also bicycle path; transit facility
  circulation element may address, 14
bicycle path,
  dedications allowed for, 111, 295
  dedications not allowed for, 347–348
big box retail stores, zoning
  ordinance concerning, 3, 158
Big Sur, 72
billboard. *See* sign
birds, 176–178, 220, 229
  See also endangered species
Blackmun, Harry, 293
blight, 70–71, 421
  determination upheld, 71
  determination not upheld, 70–71
  findings by
    redevelopment agency, 70
BLM. *See* Bureau of Land Management
Blockbuster Video, 236
board of supervisors, 6n2
  rezoning procedure, 50
board of zoning adjustment, 60
  See also zoning law
  challenges to, 542
bog, 182
  See also wetlands
Borders, 235
boundary changes
  See also annexation; local
    agency formation commission
  change of organization,
    types of, 440–441
  factors LAFCO must
    consider, 446–450
  in general, 440–442
  procedures, 442–446
  protest hearing, 451–452
  reconsideration hearing, 450–451
Brennan, William J., Jr., 584
bribery, 473
bridge district
  See also bridges
    and thoroughfares
  LAFCO jurisdiction, 441
bridges and thoroughfares
  See also roads; streets
  dedications allowed for, 111
Brown, Janice Rogers, 357–358
Brown Act. *See* Ralph M. Brown Act
brownfields, 428
Buena Park, 297
building code
  applicability to
    federal government, 72
  State Historical Building
    Code, 237
  Uniform Building Code, 237
building height ordinance,
  not a taking, 296
Building Industry Association
  (BIA), 406

building intensity, land use
     element must address, 13, 32
building permit, 93, 464, 481
     challenges to, 541
     dedications/conditions
          allowed for, 347, 362, 364–365
     fee, challenges to, 359, 364–365
     fee contracts, 371
     issuance conditions, 363
     issuance is discretionary, 364
     issuance is ministerial, 89, 528
     must be consistent
          with open space plan, 17
     subject to Mitigation Fee Act, 364
Bureau of the Census, 263, 483
Bureau of Land Management
     (BLM), 215, 221
     grazing policy, 214
bus used as restaurant, CUP
     not allowed for, 62
business, no right to go
     out of business, 340
Business Improvement District, 376
Butte County, 213
     "urbanized area," 264

C

cactus ferruginous pygmy owl. *See* owl
calcareous fen, 314
CALFED, 253
     See also water supply
California
     electricity market, 409
     ESA listed species, 207
     home rule, 430
     housing crisis, 483–484, 492
     population growth, 419–420
California Attorney General,
     28, 32, 40, 48n2, 73, 75, 81–83,
     86–87, 89, 111, 115–116, 119,
     139, 142, 232, 305, 379, 409, 461
California Budget Project, 483n2
California Citizens Compensation
     Commission, 396
California Coalition for Rural Housing,
     69n12, 507n35, 508n42, 512n50
California Coastal Act,
     31, 242–247, 270, 493, 557
     development,
          defined, 244
     lot line adjustment as, 87n4, 244
     web address, 242
California Coastal Commission,
     72, 97, 168, 173, 201, 203–204,
     242–244, 270, 303, 306, 328,
     343, 345, 347, 456, 556–557
     Coastal Access Guide, 247
     Coastal Resource Guide, 247
     Coastal Resources Information
          Center, 247
     composition, 243
     constitutionality, 243
     grant administration, 247
     and NWPs, 189
     other responsibilities, 246–247
     publications web address, 204
     statute of limitations, 542
     website, 242
California Coastal Management
     Program, 246–247
California Community Redevelopment
     Law, 70–71, 398–399
     See also redevelopment law
     discussed, 502–503

California Constitution,
     1–2, 4, 95, 356
     Takings Clause, 356, 358
California desert tortoise, 210
     See also endangered species
California Endangered
     Species Act (CESA)
     See also Endangered Species
          Act; Habitat Conservation Plan
     in general, 230, 368
     listing process, 231–232
     "take," 223, 232
     incidental take permits, 232
California Environmental
     Quality Act (CEQA),
     284, 365, 469, 488, 493, 548, 551
     See also environmental impact
          report; National Environmental
          Policy Act; design review
     agricultural employee housing,
          exempt from CEQA, 496
     CEQA Flow Chart for
          Local Agencies, 156
     CERES. *See* California
          Environmental Resources
          Evaluation System
     code enforcement, 477–478
     determining if activity
          is exempt, 148, 151–153, 156
          categorical exemption, 152–153
          challenges to exemption, 153
          finding of no significant
               effect, 151, 155, 160
          notice of exemption,
               148, 156–157
          statute of limitations, 542
          statutory exemption, 151–152
     environmental change, 150–151
     environmental impact report
          (EIR), 94, 148, 151, 154–168
     exactions opportunities,
          108, 117–118, 363, 370
     findings requirements, 155, 168–169
     historic resource definition, 237
     Indian gaming,
          not subject to CEQA, 77
     initial study, 151, 153–157, 165
     interplay with general plan, 22, 33
     interplay with initiative
          process, 394, 405–406
     interplay with LAFCOs, 443
          discussed, 453–454
     interplay with Map Act, 80, 94, 122
          development conditions,
               108, 117–118
     interplay with PSA, 465–466
     interplay with specific plan, 40–41
     judicial review,
          552–553, 563n17, 566n18
          contents of record, 570–572
          exhaustion requirement, 571–572
          in general, 568
          presenting comments, 571–572
          remedies, 573
          SLAPP suits, 580
          special procedures, 568–570
          standard of review, 572–573
     lead agency, 148n3, 156, 158–160,
          167–169, 171, 453, 465
     ministerial acts/projects,
          exempt from CEQA, 148, 156
     mitigation, 117, 147, 152,
          154–155, 157, 160, 168–169
          discussed, 164, 166

California Environmental
     Quality Act (CEQA) *continued*
     negative declaration,
          151, 153–158, 165, 170, 496
          discussed, 154–155
          mitigated negative declaration,
               151, 154, 157, 169–171, 496
     overview, 147–148
     process, 151
     project approval, 149
     project definition, 148–149, 276
          whole of the action, 150–151
     public comments, 159
     residential development projects,
          exempt from CEQA, 40
     school site requirements, 74
     "significant effect" definition, 36–37
     Statement of Overriding
          Considerations, 169
     statute of limitations, 542
     statutory authority for, 5
     tiering, 158
     Time Periods for Review of
          Environmental Documents, 165
     water supply assessment,
          160, 256–257, 259
California Environmental
     Resources Evaluation System
     (CERES), website, 563n17
California Fish and Game
     Commission, 231–232
California Integrated Waste
     Management Board, 93, 494
California Land Conservation
     Act of 1965, 238
     See also Williamson Act
California Oil Spill Prevention
     and Response Act, 246
California Outdoor Advertising Act, 5
California Planners'
     Book of
     Lists (OPR), 20, 43, 563n17
California red-legged frog. *See* frog
California Register of
     Historic Resources, 237
California Resources Agency, 563n17
California Secretary of State, 409
California State Legislature, 4
California tiger salamander, 210, 213
     See also endangered species
California Tort Claims Act
     of 1963, 469–471
California Water District Law, 112
Caltrans. *See* Department
     of Transportation
Camarillo, 406
     UGB, 423
canal, 82
capacity charge
     See also Proposition 218; water
     challenges to, 376
Carlsbad,
     Prop. E and Prop. G, 412
cellular facility, Map Act
     exemption for, 91
cemetery. *See also* cemetery district
     CUP allowed for, 62
     Map Act exemption for, 91
cemetery district, LAFCO
     jurisdiction, 441
Central Valley Flood Protection
     Board, 13
Central Valley Project
     biological opinion for water
          pumping invalid, 218

CEQA. *See* California
Environmental Quality Act
CEQA Guidelines,
5, 147, 151–153, 197, 370
Appendix G, 153
CERES. *See* California Environmental
Resources Evaluation System
certificates of compliance,
87, 137–139, 144
conditional, 87, 95, 137–139, 144
Flow Chart, 137
Map Act enforcement, 138–139
do not grant right
to develop, 138–139
charge. *See also* assessment; fee
capacity charge, 376
commodity charge, 379
defined, 377
standby charge, 379–380
charter city, 70, 73, 374–375
See also city
city council of, 6
consistency requirements, 22–24
public works projects, 23
subdivision map approvals, 23
flood protection
requirements, Sacramento-
San Joaquin Valley, 23
housing limits, findings
requirement, 505
initiative/referendum
process, 385n3, 387
Map Act application to, 80
multi-family housing,
specific treatment, 496
variances, state law
does not apply, 60
zoning law application
to, 23, 43, 46, 401
child day care center
allowed as development
condition, 35
dedications allowed
for, 116, 362–363
Childhood Lead
Poisoning Act, 373
circulation element,
11, 23, 26, 111
See also general plan
CMP, 265
discussed, 14
fiscal responsibility, 32
must be correlated with
land use element, 13–14
city. *See also* charter city; flood
protection; new city
adoption of ordinance
is ministerial, 148
authority to
regulate land use, 1–4
"character," "stability," and
"soul" of, protection
under police power, 3–4
growth limitation,
burden of proof on city, 406
need not create a
planning commission, 6
not bound by own
zoning ordinance, 74
refer "proposed action" by, 29
as respondent, 554–555
city attorney, 7
city clerk,
43, 128–129, 389

city council, 30, 128, 283, 459
See also city council measure;
"legislative body:" public
entity; public official;
Ralph M. Brown Act
appeals under the
Map Act, 123–124
appointment/interaction with
planning commission, 6–7, 28
composition of, 6
duties and responsibilities, 6–7
not an interested person, 124
interim ordinance, adoption of, 66
city council measure
See also administrative act;
legislative act; ministerial act
compared to initiative, 404–408
city council member
See public official
city engineer,
114, 127–128, 335, 407
city planner, 7
civil engineer, 112, 126, 135
Civil Rights Act
See also civil rights action
discussed, 471–473
civil rights action, 531
See also due process; takings
ripeness, 332
statute of limitations, 543
takings, 289n1, 330–332
Clean Water Act (CWA), 173, 185
See also water supply
section 301, 175
section 309, 204
section 401, 190, 200
section 402, 175, 214
section 402(p), 262–263
"maximum extent
practicable" test, 263
section 404, 175–176, 184
permit, 191, 197,
206, 214–215, 314
section 404(b)(1)
Guidelines, 192, 198
section 404(c), 197, 199
storm water and, 262
wetlands regulation,
175–181, 190
cluster development, 69
See also planned-unit
development
CMA. *See* Congestion
Management Agency
CMP. *See* congestion
management program
coastal development permit,
101, 189, 203, 244, 270
appeals, 245–246
challenges to, 114, 343
exemptions, 244
granting of is
quasi-judicial, 527, 530
coastal zone, 168, 242–245, 270
defined, 243
housing element
provisions, 16, 490
public access
easement, 112–113
wetlands, 203
Coastal Zone Management Act,
201, 203, 247–248
consistency certification
and NWPs, 189–190

code enforcement
administrative and criminal sanctions
infraction, 476
misdemeanor, 475
penalties, 476
warrant, 476
Business and Professions Code, 478
CEQA procedures, 477–478
"citation hearing,"
discussed, 475–471
is discretionary, 478–479
is not discretionary, 479–480
Map Act procedures, 477
"Notice of Non-Compliance," 477
possible defenses
denial of due process, 478–480
estoppel, 480–481
Revenue and Taxation Code, 477
COG. *See* Council of Governments
Cold, K., 114
commercial building
See also commercial development
Map Act exemption for, 91
commercial development,
See also development;
planned-unit development
Map Act application
to, 85, 89, 91, 103
PUD procedure, 68
Commission on Local Governance
for the 21st Century, 436
commodity charge, 379
See also charge; fee
common law, 1, 103, 269, 551
See also exhaustion of
administrative remedies; waiver
communication,
"promotional," compared
to "informational," 414–415
community apartment project
See also apartment;
condominium conversion
conditions allowed for, 118–119
Map Act application to,
85, 90–91, 109, 111, 118–119
tenant notification
requirements, 129–130, 468
community college district,
LAFCO jurisdiction, 441
community development
department, 39
community facilities district
formation not a project, 149
LAFCO jurisdiction, 441
community goals, housing element must
address, community plan, 151
See also specific plan
EIR prepared for, 158
planning commission relation to, 7
Community Redevelopment Law
See California Community
Redevelopment Law
community services district,
LAFCO oversight of, 441–442
Community Services District law, 442
Update, web address, 442n10
"compelling government interest," 59
See also "substantial
government interest"
condemnation
See also takings
dedications and, 114
upheld as exercise
of police power, 3

Index

conditional use permit (CUP), 22, 59–63, 95, 117, 298, 323–324, 328, 363–364
    See also use permit; variance
    delay challenged as taking, denial of as substantial burden under RLUIPA, 58
    discussed, 59–60, 61–63
        expiration, 61
        violations, 62
    issuance is ministerial, 59, 528
    must be consistent with general plan, 59
    recordation requirement, 60
    statute of limitations, 542
conditions
    See dedications; exactions
condominium conversion, 500
    See also apartment conversion; housing; stock cooperative conversion
    affordability requirements, 496
    conditions allowed for, 118–119
    Map Act application to, 80, 85, 90–91, 101, 109, 111, 118–119
        right to appeal, 123
    no right to convert apartment, 340
    regulations for upheld, 119
    under police power, 3, 91
    tenant notice requirements, 96, 122, 129–130, 468
Congestion Management Agency (CMA), 264
congestion management program (CMP), 264, 432, 493
    adoption, 264–265
    "infill opportunity zones," 264, 432
    "urbanized area," 264, 432
    failure to comply, 264–265
    in general, 263–264
Congregation Etz Chaim, 277
conservation easement, 84–85, 123, 198
    See also conservation element
conservation element, 11
    See also general plan
    discussed, 16
    mineral resource management policies, 16
consolidation, LAFCO review of, 437, 441
construction, interim ordinance may not authorize, 67
Contra Costa County, 419
    form-based zoning, 65
    "urbanized area," 264
contract, impairment-of-contract doctrine, 380
coral reef, as special aquatic site, 194
Cortese-Knox-Hertzberg Local Government Reorganization Act of 2000, 65, 436–437, 448
Cortese-Knox Local Government Reorganization Act of 1985, 435
"Cortese List," 93, 106, 464
Costa-Hawkins Act, 516–517
    See also rent control law
Costa Mesa, 400
Council of Economic Advisors, Chairman, 221
Council of Governments (COG) determination of housing needs, 486

county airport land use commission, 27–28
county assessor, 240, 452
county auditor, 442
county clerk, 129
county engineer, 128, 136
county recorder, 452
    Map Act duties, 126, 128–129, 136, 143
County Service District law, 442n10
County Supervisors' Association of California, 420
county surveyor, 126–129, 136
courthouse site, 403
crematorium, use permit and setback requirements, 272
critical habitat. *See* habitat
cultural resource, 236
    approval, 201
    survey, 201
Culver City, 352
CUP. *See* conditional use permit
cyber-cafe, CUP requirement not upheld for, 62–63

D

dam, 222
    collapse inundation areas, mapping of under safety element, 18
    CWA exemption for, 185
    CWA permit required for, 214
    EPA veto of overturned, 200
    ESA review, 214–215, 222
    flood control dam, 214
Davis-Bacon Act, 265
day care center, allowed as development condition, 35
deBottari rule, 410
dedications. *See also* exactions; fee
    affordable housing, 69n11, 362, 514
    challenges to, 343, 352, 359, 383
    findings requirements, 287, 349, 351
    general plan provisions for, 34–35, 116–117, 362–363
    Map Act provisions for, 89, 100–101, 107–118, 130, 134
    indemnification, 113–114
    off-site improvements, 114
    residential subdivisions, 114
    no nexus for, 330, 343–345
    offer of dedication, 130
    reservations, 110–111
    rezoning and, 68, 101
deed. *See also* deed of trust
    subdivision created by, 81
deed of trust, 88
    subdivision created by, 81 84
deep ripping, no CWA exemption for, 186, 206
Delta smelt, 217–219
demolition permit
    delay in issuance is taking, 304, 330
    preemption, 71
Density Bonus Law, 517
    See also housing
    APA model ordinance, web address, 497n20
    discussed, 431, 497–501
    "housing development," 498

Denver, CO, water supply, 196
Department of Conservation, 241
Department of Fish and Game (DFG), 97, 231
    must be notified of negative declaration, 155
    Streambed Alteration Agreement, 203
Department of Housing and Community Development (HCD), 489
    determination of housing needs, 486
    growth control compliance test, 505–506
    housing element review, 30, 33, 432, 490–491
Department of Industrial Relations (DIR), 266
    Vineyard Creek test, 266
Department of Real Estate, 80, 86, 130, 272
    report allows condominium conversion, 101
Department of Transportation (Caltrans), 48
    city must refer maps to, 95
    local code application to, 73
    Map Act application to, 81, 89
Department of Water Resources, 250, 250n3
    city must refer maps to, 94
    flood plain maps, 14
desert tortoise
    See California desert tortoise
design. *See also* aesthetics; "design" and "improvement:" design review; urban form and design
    "monotonous" design, 234
"design" and "improvement," 114–116
    See also design review; improvements
    Map Act definitions, 115
    Map Act regulation, conditions imposed under, 114–116, 119
design review, 488
    CEQA relation to, 236
    discussed, 233–236
    ordinance, 235
    permit, denial of, 52, 349
design review board, 6n3, 283
detachment, 239, 446
    LAFCO review of, 440
    statute of limitations, 541
developer, 39, 104, 265, 267, 468
    See also subdivider
    negligence and fraud, 468
    not a "suspect class," 361
    as representative of owner in litigation, 556
development
    See also commercial development; development agreement; development fee
    coastal zone, 242
    definitions, 87n5
    general plan and, 9, 36
    lot line adjustment as, under Coastal Act, 244
    not a "fundamental interest," 361
    police power for control or organization of, 3
    as privilege or right, 340–342

development agreement,
102, 251–252, 260,
359, 405, 433, 492
See also vested rights
compared to vesting
tentative map, 280
dedications/conditions
allowed for, 273, 280, 362
discussed, 273–279
entering into, is legislative
act, 274–275, 280
flood protection
adequacy, Sacramento-
San Joaquin Valley, 275
interim ordinance
may cancel, 66–67
interplay with Map Act, 96, 99
is a CEQA project, 276
is a contract, 275
must be consistent
with general plan, 10, 25, 274
must be consistent
with specific plan, 39, 274
not subject to *Nollan/Dolan*
heightened scrutiny
standard, 278
statute of limitations, challenges
of breaches, 125, 274, 542
statutory authority for, 5
subject to referendum,
275–276, 281
Development Agreement Act, 102–103
development application,
336, 341, 463, 467, 492
See also Permit Streamlining Act
submittal/completion, 464
interim ordinance and, 67
development fee,
69n11, 120, 272, 278, 286,
359, 370, 372–380, 573
See also exactions; fee
capital facilities, 371–372
general plan provisions for, 34–35
no nexus, 279
refund, 120
development moratorium,
98–100, 421
See also moratorium ordinance
development plan
adoption, is legislative act, 528
amendment, is not
legislative act, 528
development project,
6, 24, 27, 93, 97, 167
See also project
approval of, challenged, 548–549
CMP, 265
fees, challenges to, 125, 574–577
statute of limitations, 542, 574–575
"housing development
project," 286, 493n19
interim ordinance to disallow, 67
Map Act application to, 93
PSA
approval process, 463–464
definition, 467
DFA. *See* Department of
Food and Agriculture
DFG. *See* Department
of Fish and Game
diagram. *See also* map
in general plan,
11, 13–14, 21, 23, 33
in specific plan, 39

DIR. *See* Department
of Industrial Relations
disabled persons
residential facilities, preemption
of local zoning, 5
discount superstores
See big-box retail stores
discovery, not allowed, 558
discretionary actions
CEQA application to, 148
discretionary project,
CEQA application to, 157
disincorporation, 239
See also incorporation
LAFCO review of, 437, 441
dissolution, LAFCO review of, 441
district agricultural association,
subject of Map Act, 89
District Reorganization
Act of 1965, 436
ditches
CWA exemption for, 185
draining to "navigable waters,"
as subject of controversy, 178
upland ditch, NWP 46 and, 191
Division of Aeronautics, 28
Division of Mines
and Geology, 17–18, 33
Dolan decision
exactions, 287, 295, 346–351
in general, 306n11
Douglas, William O., 1–2
drainage
See also drainage facility
Map Act consideration of, 111
drainage facility
circulation element
may address, 14
dedications allowed for, 111
drainage fee ordinance, 111
dredged/fill materials, state program
CWA exemption for, 185
dredging. *See also* wetlands
Corps regulation of,
184–185, 193, 203
SWRCB regulation of, 181
discharge of dredged
materials, 184, 205–206
"dredged material," 184
"incidental fallback," 184–185
revised definition
held invalid, 185
navigation dredging permit, 203
pilings as, "sidecasting," 206
due process, 53, 93, 292,
336, 341, 399, 478–480
See also civil rights
action; judicial review
damages from violations,
319, 330–337
"class of one," 333–334
equal protection,
319, 333–334,
361–362, 399, 455
land use regulation must
meet principles of, 4, 455
requirements, 95
discussed, 534–535
notice/hearing,
95, 455–457, 535–537
rezoning/zoning
amendment, 48–49
violation of,
46, 124, 458–459

E

earthquake fault zone mapping, 112
See also seismic hazard
easement, 134, 333
agricultural easement, 123
agricultural conservation
easement, 123, 432
conservation easement,
84–85, 123, 198, 432
as conveyance, 87–88
dedication required for,
held invalid, 330, 348
easement exchange, 241
erosion easement, no nexus, 345
not subject to Map Act, 83–84
open space easement, 123, 432
public access easement,
112–113, 122, 295, 328, 343
solar access easement, 113
subdivision not created by, 83–84
wind power easement, 91
economic development,
condemnation upheld for, 3
economic factors,
critical habitat designation
must consider, 212
housing element must address, 14
economic impact not within
purview of CEQA, 162
economic interest, regulations
affecting are appropriate
exercise of police power, 3
"economic segments of the
community," housing
element must address, 15
efficiency unit
See "second" unit
Ehrlich decision,
exactions, 351–355
EIR. *See* environmental
impact report
EIS. *See* environmental
impact statement
El Dorado County,
"urbanized area," 264
El Toro Marine Base, 403–404
Elections Code,
387–389, 392,
394, 405, 412, 416
electric transmission line, circulation
element may address, 14
electrical generation facility,
zoning law does not apply to, 73
electricity market, in California, 409
electronic reader boards, 235
Ellis Act, 304
emergency evacuation routes
safety element must address, 17
emergency shelters, restrictions
of disapproval, 493–494
eminent domain, 417–418
See also condemnation; takings
"public purpose" need, 289–290
redevelopment and, 70
subdivision created by, 81, 145
takings considerations, 296, 317
endangered species,
200, 207–208, 219,
221–222, 231–232, 420
See also Endangered Species Act
conservation element addresses, 16
definition, 208
NWPs and, 188

Endangered Species
    Act (ESA), 188–189
    See also California
        Endangered Species Act;
        Habitat Conservation Plan
  consultation process
    "action agency,"
        215–216, 218
    "action area," 215
    agency action, 214
    biological
        opinion, 216–220
    "but for" test, 215
    critical habitat designation,
        211–214, 220
    "destruction of
        critical habitat,"
        214, 216–217
    duty to reinitiate
        consultation, 216, 220
    "effects of the action," 215
    Endangered Species Committee
        (God Squad), 216, 221
    in general, 214
    "jeopardize the
        continued existence,"
        214, 216–218, 220–221
    "may affect" trigger, 215
    "no effect," 219
    "non federal" actions, 214
    "scope of the action," 215
    "survival and recovery"
        standard, 217
  exemptions, 220–222
  Habitat Conservation Plans
    (HCP), 224, 226–228, 369
    Candidate Conservation
        Agreement, 228
    Natural Communities
        Conservation
        Planning Act, 227
    Safe Harbor policy, 228
  introduction, 207–208
  judicial review/
    enforcement,
    209, 228–230
    citizen suits, 229–230
    penalties, 229
  listing process, 207–220
    "any subspecies of fish
        or wildlife or plants," 208
    "candidate" species, 211, 228
    "critical habitat"
        designation, 211–214
        legal challenges to, 213
    "emergency listing," 210
    "No Surprises" policy, 227
    notice, 209
    petition process, 209–211
    public comments, 209–210
    public hearing, 209
    "recovery plan," 211
    website, 214
  section 4(d), 218, 225
  section 7,
    190, 214–215, 217–220,
    222, 225, 228
    applies only to discretionary
        actions, 214–215
    handbook web address, 214
  section 9, 218, 222, 225
  section 10, 224
    permit, 226–228
  section 10(a), 227

Endangered Species
    Act (ESA) *continued*
  takings prohibitions,
    207–208, 228
    discussed, 222–226
    evolutionary significant
        units (ESUs), 225, 231
    "harass," defined, 223
    "harm," discussed, 223–225
        NOAA interpretation, 225
    "incidental take
        statement," 218, 220
    incidental take permit,
        224, 226–227
  threatened species definition, 208
  transfer of water pollution
    control, no ESA review, 214
  wetlands regulation, 173, 190, 200
Energy and Water Development
    Appropriations Act of 1992, 182
Energy Commission, 247
energy conservation
    dedications allowed for, 113
    Map Act provisions for, 113
environment
    CEQA definition, 150
    Map Act consideration of, 80, 85,
        92, 94, 108, 117–118, 122–123
environmental excise tax, 372
    See also taxes
environmental factors
    See also environmental impact
    housing element must address, 14
environmental impact
    See also environmental
        impact report
    cumulative impacts,
        152, 155, 160, 163–164
    evaluation, 160
environmental impact report (EIR),
    94, 117, 122, 154, 165, 284,
    286, 416, 453, 467, 478, 573
    See also California Environmental
        Quality Act; environmental
        impact statement
    addendum, 171
    in CEQA process, 148
    "significant effect
        on the environment,"
        118, 147, 152–155,
        160, 162, 164, 168
    "substantial environmental
        damage," 118, 147
    certification, 167
    failure to complete and certify, 94
    statute of limitations, 172, 542
    CMP, 264
    comments, response
        to comments, 160
    contents
        cumulative impacts,
            160, 163–164
        environmental impact
            evaluation, 160–162
        extent of discussion, 167
        in general, 160
        growth inducement,
            155, 160, 167
        mitigation, 164, 166
        project alternatives, 160, 166
        project description, 160–161
        range of alternatives, 166–167
    deadlines/required notices, 172
    total time, 156

environmental impact
    report (EIR) *continued*
    discussed, 22, 40–41, 94, 117
    draft EIR, 156, 159–160, 167
    expert testimony, 154
        disagreement among experts, 161
    failure to complete
        and certify, 94, 160
    final EIR, 156, 159–160, 169
    findings, 156, 168–169
    interplay with PSA, 465
    lead agency decision
        to prepare an EIR, 157
    master EIR, 40, 155, 157
    matrix, 167
    mitigation monitoring
        and reporting, 155, 169–170
    notice of completion, 172
    notice of determination,
        155–156, 165, 169, 172
    notice of preparation,
        156, 159–160, 162, 165, 172
    preparation, 155–158
    procedure
        certification, 160
        draft EIR, 159
        final EIR, 159–160
        scoping, 159
    program EIR, 157–158
    project approval, 168–169
    public review, 159–160, 165
    recirculation, 167–168
    supplemental/subsequent
        EIR (SEIR), 157, 170–171
    tiered EIR, 157–158
    total time, 156, 465
        extensions, 156
    tribal EIR (TEIR), 76
    water supply consideration,
        162–163, 251, 255, 257
environmental impact statement
    (EIS), 190, 200, 227
    See also environmental
        impact report; National
        Environmental Policy Act
environmental justice
    addressed by general plan, 11
    addressed by LAFCO, 448
Environmental Protection Agency
    (EPA). *See also* wetlands
    Clean Water Act
        enforcement, 204–206
    pesticide registration, 214
    role in wetland regulation,
        173, 191–192, 199–200
        Corps/EPA MOA, 195, 199
        404(b)(1) Guidelines, 192–199
        wetlands website, 174
environmental setting in EIR, 160
environmental subdivision
    Map Act application to, 85
EPA. *See* Environmental
    Protection Agency
equal protection, 455, 478–480
    See also civil rights; due process
    discussed, 333–334, 361–362
    "suspect class," 361
    "suspect classification," 361
erosion, 183
    See also erosion control;
        seismic hazard; soils
    conservation element addresses, 16
    easement dedication struck down, 345
    land clearing activities, 188

erosion control, Map Act
    provisions for, 112
error
    effect of procedural
        error, 53, 95, 334, 457
    not a taking, 304
ESA. *See* Endangered Species Act
essential government function
    See also "legitimate
        state interest"
    initiative may not
        impair, 403–404
estoppel theory
    See also judicial review
    "administrative collateral
        estoppel," 530–531
    discussed, 480–481
evidence, 152
    See also findings requirements
    ESA listing, 210
    judicial notice, 561–562
    judicial review
        admissible and
            discoverable, 559–560
        "deliberative process
            privilege," 560
        in general, 537–538
        generally inadmissible
            and undiscoverable, 558–559
        thought processes, 51, 560–561
    no formal rules of evidence, 53
    substantial evidence
        argument and controversy
            not substantial evidence, 154
        for CEQA action,
            151, 153–155, 158,
            162, 169–170, 572–573
        CUP, 62
        definition, 154
        to document nexus, 360
        LAFCO decision, 448
        to support findings,
            123, 284–285, 493–494, 537
        to support zoning ordinance, 55
        to support action, 234
evolutionary significant
    unit (ESU), 225, 231
ex parte contacts, 462–463, 534
    See also Ralph M. Brown Act
    ban, 221
exactions. *See also* dedications; fee;
    school district facilities fee
    challenges to, 339, 352,
        355, 359, 383, 573–578
    as double taxation, 360
    equal protection, 361–362
    statute of limitations, 542
    conditions imposed on
        Map Act extensions, 100
    development as privilege
        or right, 340–342
    as fee or tax
        background, 372–373
        Jarvis initiatives, 373–380
    judicial review, 383
    nexus requirement
        Dolan decision, 346–351
        Ehrlich decision, 351–355
        in general, 339
        legislatively formulated vs.
            ad hoc fees, 353–354
        Mitigation Fee Act, 279
        Nollan decision, 344–346
        San Remo Hotel, 355–358

exactions *continued*
    opportunities for
        building permit, 364–365
        CEQA, 370
        in general, 362
        general plan,
            34–35, 273, 362–363
        HCPs, 369
        school district facilities
            fees, 365–369
        subdivision process,
            100, 107–108
    overview, 339–340
    proper exercise of police
        power, 108, 340
    as regulatory takings, 295–296
"excess of jurisdiction"
    See also bias; motives; public official
    discussed, 535
exclusionary zoning, 421, 504, 509
    See also housing;
        zoning ordinance
exhaustion of administrative remedies
    See also judicial review
    codification, 551–552
    common law exhaustion
        doctrine, 545–547
    components
        "appeal exhaustion,"
            548–549, 571–572
        "issue exhaustion,"
            547–548, 571–572
    distinguished from ripeness, 325
    exceptions, 550–551
    Map Act challenges, 124
    rehearing/reconsideration, 549–550

F

facilities benefit assessment (FBA), 363
    See also assessment
fair argument standard, 153, 155, 162
Fair Employment and Housing
    Act, 531
"fair hearing." *See also* due
    process; public hearing
    requirements for, 457, 534–537
Fair Housing Act, 473
family day care home
    preemption of zoning for, 5
family law, 489
farm. *See* agricultural land; agriculture
farm equipment repair shop
    CUP allowed for, 62
farm worker
    housing for, 485, 496
        identification of,
            in housing element, 15
FBA. *See* facilities benefit assessment
federal activities, Coastal
    Commission review of, 246
federal agency, 29, 72
    ESA interplay with, 214
Federal Bureau of Reclamation, 82
    ESA review of water
        contract invalid, 217
Federal Emergency Management
    Agency (FEMA),
        flood plain maps, 14
Federal Energy Regulatory Commission
    (FERC), relicensing, 219
federal government, zoning
    law application to, 72
federal lands, states may impose
    environmental controls on, 72

federal lessee
    must comply with
        local ordinance, 72
    not required to comply
        with local ordinance, 72
federal patent, parcel created by, 142
Federal Register, 199, 201, 209–212
Federal Water Pollution
    Control Act of 1972, 175
    See also Clean Water Act
fee, 107–108, 111, 116–117, 351, 493
    See also dedications; development
        fee; exactions; school district
        facilities fee; school impact fee
    building permit fee, 359, 382–383
    challenges to, 104, 352, 355,
        359–360, 383, 573–578
        burden of proof on
            local governments, 382
        "catch-all" limitation, 577
        facial challenges, 575, 578
        "pay under protest" procedure,
            279, 352, 355, 367–368, 574–577
        statute of limitations,
            125, 355, 574–575
    city assessment on state, 73
    COG, 486
    definition, 358, 377
    developer fee, 359–360, 486
    development fee,
        34–35, 69n11, 120, 272,
        278, 286, 359, 574–577
        challenged as "tax," 372–380
        Prop. 218 impacts, 379
    findings requirements, 108, 286, 287
        "nexus," 108, 117
        "rough proportionality,"
            108, 117, 287
    housing inspection fee, 379
    impact fee and CMP, 265
    imposition, 574–577
    legislatively formulated vs. ad
        hoc fees, 3, 353–354, 357
    in lieu fee, 110–111, 352,
        354–358, 506, 514–515
    low-income housing,
        343, 345–346, 352
    as mitigation, 164
    park, 109
    refund, 120
    processing fee, 382–383, 577–578
    public art fee, 3, 352, 354–355
    refunds, 120, 140, 366, 578
    regional traffic fees, 164
    "regulatory fee," compared to tax, 372
    requirements
        not allowed for general
            governmental services, 378
    requirements
        not allowed for maintenance
            and operation, 371–372
        public notice/publication, 370
        reasonableness, 371
        reconveyance of land, 372
        waiting period/public hearing, 370
        when fees are to
            be paid, 370–371
    specific plan fee, 34
    storm drain fee, 111, 140, 377–378
        refund, 120
    transit, relation to office
        space, 340, 346, 353
    utility service fee, 371
    Williamson Act cancellation, 240–241

fee interest, as conveyance, 87–88
FEMA. *See* Federal Emergency Management Agency
"fencing out" ordinance, not a taking, 299, 329
FERC. *See* Federal Energy Regulatory Commission
final map
    See also Subdivision Map Act
    accept/reject map for filing, time frame, 129
    approval is ministerial, 127–128, 528
    approval procedures, 127–128
    certificates/security, 128–129
    condos, stock cooperatives, community apartments, 85, 90–91, 129–130
    consent of record title holders, 126, 129
    dedications, 108–111, 130
    form and filing, 126–127
    improvement agreements, 130–132
    local ordinances requirements, 80
    Map Act requirements, 79, 81, 85, 89–92, 107, 126–134, 142–143
    multiple final maps, 96, 126–127
    phased, 96, 99, 127
    valid when recorded, 128–131
    vs. parcel map, 84
financing plan
    in general plan, 14
    Map Act application to, 84
findings requirements, 404, 535
    See also evidence
    adequacy of flood protection, 123
    for ALUP, 27, 40
    background, 283
    for blight, 70–71
    for CEQA action, 118, 155, 168, 286
    conclusory findings not legally sufficient, 285, 287, 547
    for condominium conversion, tenant notice, 122
    density bonus denial, 500
    for "design" and "improvement," 115
    for ESA listing, 211
    evidence in record to support, 123, 284–285
    in general
        for dedications/fees, 287, 349, 371
        for legislative acts, 51, 268
        for nonlegislative acts, 283, 286
    for general plan extension, 33
    for housing element, 15, 51, 286, 431–432, 465, 489, 492–494, 505
    for inclusionary housing, 513–514
    for interim ordinance, 66
    judicial review, 537–538
    Map Act
        amendment of recorded map, 135
        approval, 121, 123, 127–130
        "housing balance finding," 121
        violation, 138
    for map waiver, 92
    for OPR extension, 33
    purpose of findings, 283–284
    for redevelopment, 71
    tentative map, 94
    Topanga, 118, 123, 283–285

findings requirements *continued*
    for Williamson Act, 239 cancellation, 241
    water supply assessment/ verification, 255–256, 286
    for zoning ordinance, 47, 286
fire code enforcement, 478–479
fire hydrant fee, 330, 360
    See also dedications
fire protection district LAFCO jurisdiction, 441
fire severity zone, 18
fire station, 380
    allowed as development condition, 35, 110, 362
    dedication allowed for, 116, 267, 362–363
fire suppression
    assessment for, 377
    fee for, 378
firefighters, 512
First English decision, 302–303, 309–311, 315–317
fiscal factors, housing element must address, 14
fiscal zoning, 428
fish. *See also* endangered species
    protections for, 222
    salmon/steelhead protections, 207, 225–226
Fish and Wildlife Coordination Act, 200–201
flood control dam, 214
    See also dam; flooding
flood protection
    Sacramento-San Joaquin Valley cities findings requirement, 123
    must address in general plans, 13, 23
    must address in zoning ordinances, 47
flood zone, 123
flooding
    conservation element addresses, 16
    groundwater recharge/ storm water management, 16
    land use element must address, 13–14, 32
    Map Act consideration of, 92, 99
    safety element addresses, 17
floodplain, 188
Florida black panther, 226
Food Security Act of 1985, 201
forest, conservation element addresses, 16
    See also logging
Forest Practices Act, 478
forestry regulation, adoption is ministerial, 529
formation
    LAFCO review of, 441
    statute of limitations, 541
franchise granting
    initiative may not interfere with, 403
    is legislative act, 395
    state preemption, 397
Franchise Tax Board, "Notice of Non-Compliance," 477
fraud
    developer fraud, 468
    LAFCO determination, 448
Fresno County, "urbanized area," 264

frog. *See also* endangered species
    California red-legged frog, 213
furniture, ordinance prohibiting sale of upheld, 46

G

Galt, initiative capping permits, 423
"GANN limit," 380
gas lease, Map Act exemption for, 91
gas transmission line, circulation element may address, 14
general law
    "no conflict with general laws," 4
general law city, 6, 272, 374
    See also city
general plan, 115, 151, 163, 421, 562
    See also general plan amendment; specific plan
    adequacy, remedies relating to, 36
    adequacy requirements, CEQA, 22
    challenges to, 13, 51
    charter cities, 22–23
    in general, 12–13
    initiative, 402
    judicial review, 13, 35–37
    "territory," 31
    adequacy requirements
        checklist, 30–33
        action plan/implementation plan, 33
        address all issues, 13, 31
        adoption, 33
        allowable uses for land use districts specified, 32
        completeness, 30
        consistent with state policy, 31
        cover all territory, 31
        currency, 31–32
        density ranges specified, 32
        diagrams and maps, 33
        flood protection, 13, 32
        internal (horizontal) consistency, 12, 23–24, 31
        long-term perspective, 12, 31
        readability and availability, 30–31
        statutory criteria, 12–13, 32
        yardstick, 33
    adoption, 28–30, 121–122
        agency comment period, 29–30
        is legislative act, 29, 35, 402, 527
        procedures, 28–30
        statute of limitations to challenge, 29, 542–543
        subject to initiative and referendum, 29, 402
        timeframe for newly incorporated cities for, 33–34
    advisory status, 9
    availability to public, 30–31
    big box development, regulation of, 3, 35
    charter city, zoning does not have to be consistent with general plan, 22–24
    circulation element, 11, 32, 111
        discussed, 11
        must be correlated with land use element, 13–14
    CMP, 265
    compliance with Government Code, annual report, 7
    conservation element, 11, 16
    consistency doctrine, 9–10

general plan *continued*
  consistency requirements
    with ALUP, 27–28
    for approvals of future
      development only, 27
    deference to city
      findings (vertical
      consistency), 24–27, 401
    "balancing," 26
    internal (horizontal) consistency,
      12, 23–24, 31, 33, 402
  as constitution for
    development, 9–11, 362, 401
  contents, 11–12
    diagrams, 11, 21, 23
    specificity/level of detail, 21
    "statement of development
      policies," 11
  dedications and development
    fees, opportunities for,
      34–35, 273, 362–363
  development approvals,
    12, 25, 34, 280
  dwelling unit limits,
    findings required for, 44
  economic development, support
    of by general plan, 20
  EIR prepared for, 158
  energy element, 11
  environmental justice and, 11
  extensions, OPR extensions,
    33–34, 121–122
    conditions attached to, 34
    not retroactive, 34
    reasons for granting, 33
  as growth control tool, 35
  housing element,
    11, 31, 33, 36, 484–492
    adoption, 14, 30
    challenges to, 15, 36
    closer judicial review of, 36
    discussed, 14–16
    growth management and, 432
    homeless shelters
      and housing, 32
    within coastal zone, 16, 490
  housing limits, findings
    requirement, 286, 505
  inadequacy, 21–23, 36, 402
    actions that may
      be suspended, 36
    development may or may
      not proceed despite, 36–37
  implementation, 30
    annual report on, 30
  initiative must be
    consistent with, 401–402
  judicial review, 35–37
  land use element, 11, 32
    circulation element must
      be correlated with, 13–14
    discussed, 13–14
    low-income housing
      development and, 24, 27
  mandatory elements, 11, 13, 30
    all elements have
      equal legal status, 13, 20
    amendment limit
      per calendar year, 29
    combined element, 20
    organization, 20
    requirements, 19, 21
    statutory criteria, 19–20
    update requirements, 31

general plan *continued*
  Map Act
    actions must be consistent
      with general plan, 9, 22–23, 121
    interplay with
      general plan, 80, 92, 108
  maps, 33
  new cities and, 33–34
  noise element, 11, 17, 32
  open space element, 11, 16–17
  optional elements, 11, 20
  permissive elements
    See optional elements
  planning commission relation to, 6–7
  presumption of validity, 13, 23
  progress report, 12
  public review process, 28–29
  purposes, 11–12
  redevelopment
    law and, 70–71
    plan and, 25, 71
  review, 11, 15, 31–32
  revision, 11, 15, 31–32
    as legislative act, 6
  safety element, 11, 17–19
  specific plan must be
    consistent with, 39–40
  as statement of a city's interest, 34
  statutory authority for, 5
  "substantial compliance," 35–36, 485
  TDRs and, 249–250
  update requirements, 31
  water element, 11
  zoning and, 46–48, 48n2
general plan amendment,
  7, 35, 121–122, 286,
  323, 352, 423, 466
  affordable housing projects and, 29
  availability to public, 29–31
  EIR required for, 150
  following ALUP amendment, 28
  initiative/referendum
    allowed for, 29–30, 402
  judicial review, 35–37
  is legislative act, 29, 402, 527
  procedures, 28–30
  review period, 29–30
  statute of limitations, 29, 542
  subject to CEQA, 150
General Plan Guidelines (2003)
  (OPR), 11–12, 13n5,
  20n9, 28n10, 31, 37, 47
  advisory, not mandatory, 12
geologic hazard
  See also geological hazard
    assessment district; seismic hazard
  definition, 381
  safety element must address, 17
geological hazard assessment district
  (GHAD). *See also* assessment
    district; seismic hazard
  discussed, 381–382
  formation, 381
  LAFCO law does not apply, 442
geophysical research, 538
  permit for, PSA does
    not apply, 467–468
GHAD. *See* geological hazard
  assessment district
gift, subdivision created by, 83
Gilroy, 485
Glenn-Colusa
  Irrigation District, 229
global warming, 420

golf course
  construction of, as
    part of project purpose, 196
Governor's Office of Planning and
  Research (OPR), 30, 159, 489
  general plan
    extensions, 33–34, 121–122
    revisions, 32
  General Plan Guidelines
    (2003), 11–12, 13n5,
    20n9, 28n10, 31, 37
    advisory, not mandatory, 12
    consistency test, 12, 47
  LAFCO "guidelines," 440
  website, 436n3
grading
  Map Act provisions
    for, 101, 112, 115
  separation of grade district, 442
granny unit
  See also housing; "second" unit
  discussed, 88, 501, 528
gray wolf recovery plan, 211
  See also endangered species
grazing limits, 219, 225
grazing policy, 214
grizzly bear, 226
groundwater, 254–255, 261
  See also groundwater
    recharge; water supply
  augmentation charge not valid, 378
  CUP limiting use of,
    not a taking, 63, 299
groundwater recharge
  See also water supply
  conservation element
    must address, 16
  dedications allowed for, 111
growth inducement
  See also growth management
  EIR discussion of, 155, 160, 167
growth management. *See also*
  growth management ordinance
  affordable housing and, 503–506
  "drawbridge
    mentality," 421, 503
    special requirements, 504–506
  conclusion, 433–434
  in general, 419–420
  general plan role in, 35, 421
  "Growth Within Bounds," 436
  legality
    "drawbridge mentality," 421
    housing requirements, 431–432
    planned growth
      ordinance, 425–427
    proper exercise of
      police power, 424
  measures, types of, 420–422
    HCD compliance
      test, 505–506
    NIMBY attitude, 428, 492–493
    planned growth
      ordinance, 425–427
    Ramapo Plan, 425
    slow-growth measures,
      problems with, 424
    Smart Growth, 504
      barriers to, 428
      discussed, 427
      is not going away, 431–433
    tools developers can use, 433
  urban growth boundary, 422
  urban sprawl, 420, 427, 504

growth management initiative, 425–426, 433–435
    See also growth management ordinance; initiative
    ballot box planning, 385, 415–418, 422–424
    problems with, 399
    struck down, 10, 401
    types of, 420–422
    upheld, 49, 406–407
growth management ordinance, 10, 406–407
    burden of proof, 49
    on cities, 13
    upheld as valid, 344–345, 426
gun control ordinance, 564

H

habitat, 207, 369, 420
    See also Endangered Species Act; Habitat Conservation Plan
    critical habitat, 189, 200, 225
        definition, 211–212
        designation, 211–214, 220
        and NEPA compliance, 212
    destruction or modification of, 216–217
    economic factors, consideration of, 212–213
    environmental protections for, 117, 122, 188–191, 200
    mitigation, 220
    NWPs and, 188
    "potential" vs. "actual," 225
Habitat Conservation Plan (HCP), 224
    See also Endangered Species Act
    Candidate Conservation Agreement, 228
    discussed, 226–228
        exactions allowed for, 362, 369
    multi-species planning, 227
    Natural Communities Conservation Plan, 227–228, 369
    Natural Communities Conservation Planning Act, 227
    Safe Harbor policy, 228
Hanford
    ordinance prohibiting sale of furniture upheld, 45
Hawaii, 207
Hawaii Legislature, Act 257, 292
hazard areas
    See also seismic hazard
    open space element overlay requirements, 16
hazardous waste
    See also waste
    air pollution as, 93, 464
    identification of migration of, 93, 464
    requirements under PSA, 464
    risk management and prevention program (RMPP), 93, 464
hazardous waste management plan
    mitigation and monitoring program upheld for, 170
Hazardous Waste and Substance Statement, 93, 464
HCD. See Department of Housing and Community Development
HCP. See Habitat Conservation Plan
hearing. See public hearing
height variance, held invalid, 61

Hercules, form-based zoning, 65
Hermosa Beach, 278
Herzberg decision, 298–299
high school library districts, LAFCO jurisdiction, 441
highway district
    joint highway district, LAFCO jurisdiction, 441
    LAFCO jurisdiction, 441
highway project, federally-financed, ESA review of, 214
historic landmark
    See also historic preservation
    Landmark Preservation Law New York City, 3, 237, 249, 291
    religious freedom and, 57
historic preservation
    See also historical resource
    certification, 190
    federal level, 236
    local level, 237–238
    state level, 236–237
historic property, NWP and, 189
historical resource
    CEQA definition, 237
    National Historic Preservation Act, 236–237
    National Register of Historic Places, 236
    State Historical Building Code, 237
Holmes, Oliver Wendell, 313
Home Builders Association of Northern California, 212
homeless persons, 485
homeless shelters, 32
    See also housing; housing element
hotel, 345
    initiative allowed for, 423
    residential hotel, no right to convert, 340
Hotel and Motel Association of Oakland, 345
hotel conversion fees, 300, 352, 355–358, 511
housing, 31
    See also condominium conversion; redevelopment law; rent control law
    affordable housing, 20, 24, 27, 29, 36, 464–465, 493–495
        challenges to, 36, 47
        conserving and improving, 19
        crisis in, 483–484, 503
        dedications allowed for, 69n11, 362, 54
        density bonus, 69n11, 429, 431, 497–501, 506n32, 516n58
        environmental protection and, 503
        general plan adequacy and, 32
        growth management and, 503–506
        special requirements, 504–506
    Housing Accountability Act and, 5, 492–493
    housing element purpose, 484–485
    requirements for, 15, 485
    incentives for, 497–501
    inclusionary
        dwelling units, 116
        zoning, 69–70, 512

housing
    affordable housing continued
        low-income housing ordinance, 343, 345–346
        repeal by referendum, 334–335, 407–408
        prioritization of services, 495–496
        projects under section 65589.5(d), 24, 27, 493–495
        SB 221 and, 251
        trust fund, 510, 514
    "Anti-NIMBY" legislation, 492–497
    assisted housing
        analysis of restrictions on, 32
        preserving, 32
    burden of proof on housing limits, 51, 411–412
    CEQA review, 152
    density bonus law, 431, 497–501
    EIR discussion of, 167
    emergency shelters, restrictions of disapproval, 493–494
    enforcement/monitoring, 522–523
    exclusionary zoning, 421
    findings requirements, 51, 286
    for-sale on-campus housing, 73, 89
    granny unit, 88, 502, 528
    "housing balance finding," 121
    inclusionary housing, 116, 501, 503
        affordability duration, 522
        affordability preservation, 521
        amount and affordability, 519–520
        "beauty contest," 518
        beneficiary qualification, 521–522
        Costa-Hawkins Act, 516–517
        determining development size, 518–519
        discussed, 69–70
        enactment, 512–513
        enforcement/monitoring, 522–523
        factual record, 513–514
        incentives, 516
        introduction, 506–508
        judicial treatment, 508
        legal issues, 511–512
        "linkage program," 519
        mandatory/voluntary program, 517–518
        ordinance, 510, 512
        post-Nollan/Dolan, 510–511
        pre-Nollan/Dolan, 508–510
        rent/price control, 521
        "safety valve" provisions, 514–516
        timing/design, 520–521
    limits on dwelling units, 44
    matter of "vital statewide importance," 15, 484
    multi-family, special treatment, 66–67, 496–497
    regional housing needs, 432, 446, 514
        annual report, 7, 30, 489
        COG determination, 486
        findings requirement, 489, 505
        housing element, 14, 32, 485, 493
        land inventory, 485, 487–488
        "land suitable for development," 487–488
        regional housing need allocation (RHNA), 485–487
        transfer of share, 487
    residential land inventory, 14

housing *continued*
    restrictions on disapproval of housing projects, 20, 27, 492–497
        affordable housing projects under section 65589.5(d), 489, 493–495
        in general, 492–493
        least cost zoning law, 411, 497
        "second" unit, 501–502
        "senior citizen" housing development, 498
        specific plans and, 40
        state housing goals, 15
        supportive housing, restrictions of disapproval, 493–494
        transitional housing, restrictions of disapproval, 493–494
Housing Accountability Act, 5, 492–493
housing code enforcement
    program exempt from CEQA, 152
housing element, 5, 11, 14–16, 33, 36
    See also general plan
    adoption, 30
    affordable housing and, 15, 20, 484, 506
    annual report, 30, 489
    assisted housing, preservation of, 32
    certification
        discussed, 490–492
        "substantial compliance," 15, 485, 487, 493
    challenges to, 15, 36
    constraints, 488–489
    contents and purposes, 14, 484–485
    city must confer with HCD, 30, 33, 486
    discussed, 14, 485
    needs assessment, 14, 485
    emergency shelters, development of, 32
    general plan, consistency with, 24, 489
    growth management and, 432
    homeless shelters and housing, 32
    Housing Accountability Act and, 5
    land inventory, 485, 487–488
    judicial review, 36
    responsibility to contribute to state housing goals, 15, 32, 484
    review, discussed, 15, 490–492
    revision, 15
    update requirements, 15, 31–32
    within coastal zone, 16, 490
housing inspection fee, 379
    See also fee
Howard Jarvis Taxpayers Association, 374
H.R. 2427, 182
Hughes, Charles Evans, 457
Humboldt County "urbanized area," 264
Huntington Beach, FAIR initiative, 394
hydroelectric project, no ESA review, 215
hydrology. *See also* wetlands
    wetlands, 182–183

I

Idaho Supreme Court, ex parte contacts consideration, 462n7
IGRA. *See* Indian Gaming and Regulatory Act
immunity. *See also* judicial review; liability
    legislative immunity, 472–473
    qualified immunity, 473

impact fee. *See* exactions; fee; school impact fee
Imperial County, "urbanized area," 264
Improvement Act of 1911, 382
improvement agreements
    See also "design" and "improvement;" improvements
    Map Act procedures, 130–132
Improvement Bond Act of 1915, 382
improvement district
    LAFCO jurisdiction, 441
improvement security
    See also dedications; Subdivision Map Act
    faithful performance/performance bond, 131–133
    how much is required?, 131
    releasing security, 133
    remedies, 133–134
    rights and requirements, 131–133
    types of security, 131
improvements, 89, 130, 134
    See also "design" and "improvement"
    definition, for GHAD, 381
    public improvements, 99n1, 133
        fee, 359n12, 370
        off-site improvements, 506
            dedications/conditions allowed for, 114, 362
            standards and criteria, 114
    supplemental improvements/reimbursement agreement, 111–112
    tentative map life and, 96, 99
inclusionary housing zoning ordinance, *Nollan/Dolan* test does not apply, 299, 350
inclusionary zoning. *See* zoning
incorporation, 128, 239, 281, 448
    See also local agency formation commission; new city
    development agreements and, 274–275
    effect on new city, 107
    is legislative act, 528
    LAFCO review of, 437, 440
Indian Gaming and Regulatory Act (IGRA), 76
Indian Gaming in California, 76
industrial development
    See also development
    Map Act application to, 85, 89, 103, 109
    PUD procedure, 68
"infill opportunity zones," 432
    discussed, 264
    "multimodal composite," 264, 432
infill projects, exempt from SB 221 requirements, 260
initial study, 151, 155–157, 165, 433
    See also California Environmental Quality Act
    discussed, 153–154
initiative, 286, 505
    See also referendum
    allowed for general plan amendment, 30
    CEQA and, 405–406
        petition-sponsored initiative, 405
    city has duty to place on ballot, 148, 394, 405
    city's role in campaign, restrictions, 414–415
    conclusion, 415–418

initiative *continued*
    conflicting initiatives on same ballot, 412–414
    definition, 386
    in general, 385–386
    housing initiative, burden of proof, 44, 411–412
    limitations
        cannot affect non-legislative matters, 402–403
        cannot affect vested rights, 105, 433
        cannot be improper exercise of police power, 399–401
        cannot be inconsistent with general plan, 401–402
        cannot conflict with state law, 397–398
        cannot impair essential government function, 403–404
        cannot invade duty of "agent of the state," 398–399
        judicial, in general, 398
        single-subject rule, 396–397
    must be consistent with general plan, 401–402
    not subject to same requirements as city council measures, 404–408
    placing on ballot
        action by local legislative bodies, 394–396
        ballot title and summary, 390–391
        circulation; signature, 391–392
        filing; examination of signatures, 392–393
        form of petition, 388–390
        is a ministerial duty, 394, 405
        notice of intent to circulate, 390–391
        procedural requirements, 387–388
        publication and posting, 391
        "substantial compliance," 389
    pre-election challenges, 47, 408–411
    pre-election invalidation, 394–395
    in general, 393
    Prop. 218 and, 378, 380
    rezoning ordinance held invalid, 46, 52, 105–106
    for zoning ordinance, 52–53
injunction. *See also* interim ordinance
    in mandate proceedings, 568
    preliminary injunction, 565
    temporary restraining order, 565
Inland Empire, 419
insects, ESA protection for, 207
Intergovernmental Coordination Act of 1968, 72
Intergovernmental Coordination Executive Order, 72
interim ordinance, 66–67, 301–302
    See also injunction; "moratorium" ordinance
    challenged as taking, 302–303, 309–310
    discussed, 66–67
    maximum duration, 5, 66–67, 421
    may not authorize construction, 67
    notice and hearing, 48
    not required for first adoption of interim ordinance, 66
    state preemption of, 5, 67
    report, 66
    urgency measure, 48, 235, 276, 334
    to stop development project, 66

interstate commerce. *See also* wetlands
  Corps protection of waterways, 174
inverse condemnation, 125, 304–305,
  311–313, 330, 337, 557
  See also takings
  illegal condition must first be
    challenged in court, 328–329
irrigation
  See also agriculture; water
  CWA exemption for, 185
irrigation canal, 178
Irvine, zoning consistency rule, 23, 46
issue preclusion, 327
  See also judicial review

J

Jarvis-Gann Tax Initiative
  See Proposition 13
joint powers agency (JPA), local
  code application to, 74
JPA. *See* joint powers agency
judicial decision, "quasi-judicial" decision,
  6, 283, 462n5, 527, 529–530
judicial review
  See also immunity; land use
    litigation; nexus requirements;
    rights of the regulated; "rough
    proportionality" test;
    statute of limitations
  administrative act
    "abuse of discretion," 535
    "excess of jurisdiction," 535
    "fair hearing," 535–537
    "findings and evidence," 537–538
    in general, 535
    "proceeding in manner
      required by law," 537
  administrative/legislative act, 538
  administrative record, 557–558
  CEQA, 552, 566n18, 568–573
  coastal development permit, 246
  conditional use permit, 62
  court standards
    "arbitrary and capricious"
      test, 532–533
    for decision that interprets
      or applies law, 538–539
    decisions with legislative/
      administrative aspects, 538
    due process/fair hearing
      requirements, 534–535
    heightened scrutiny,
      57, 233, 278, 300, 346, 351n9,
      353, 355–356, 359, 510–512, 515
    higher scrutiny,
      233, 300, 350, 352
    intent and purpose of
      legislative body, 533–534
    "*Livermore*" test,
      45–46, 400, 418, 425–426
    rational basis test, 46, 347
    religious exercise and, 57–59
    strict scrutiny, 57, 354, 361
    "substantial compliance," 485
    defined, 36
    motives, 533
  deadlines for bringing
    actions, 539–541
  deference to city findings, 24–27,
    41, 333, 512, 532–535, 537–539
  Endangered Species Act, 209, 228–230
    citizen suits, 229–230
  estoppel theory, 480–481

judicial review *continued*
  evidence, 558–562
  evidence outside record
    generally inadmissible
      and undiscoverable, 558–560
    judicial notice, 561–562
  exactions, 383
  exhaustion of administrative remedies
    "appeal exhaustion,"
      548–549, 571–572
    codification, 551–552
    common law exhaustion
      doctrine, 545–547
    components, 547
    distinguished from ripeness, 325
    exceptions, 550–551
    "issue exhaustion,"
      547–548, 571–572
    Map Act challenges, 124
    rehearing/reconsideration, 549–550
  facial challenge, compared to
    "as applied" challenge, 320n18
  findings, 537–538
  general plan, adequacy
    requirements, 35–37
  housing element, 36
  identifying proper parties
    beneficial interest, 552–553
    citizen's action, 553
    petitioner, 552
    real party in interest,
      525–526, 555–557
    respondent, 554–555
    taxpayer suits, 553–554
  initiative/referendum
    process, 408–411
  mandate proceedings
    "administrative collateral
      estoppel," 530–531
    administrative mandate,
      328–329, 535–538, 544, 566
    alternative writ, 562–563
    appeal of writ, 567–568
      effect on judgment, 567–568
      time to, 567
    brief preparation, 564–565
    CEQA actions, 568–573
    evidence, 557–562
    in general, 526–527
    hearing date, 563–564
    injunction, 568
    issuance of writ, 566–567
    joining other causes
      with writ claim, 557
    noticed motion, 563
    stays, 565–566
    summary judgment, 563
    traditional mandate, 35, 41, 44,
      125–126, 369, 383, 558, 565
    TRO/preliminary
      injunction, 566
    writ of mandate,
      36, 94, 231, 260, 367, 390,
      465, 469, 525–526, 528, 557
  Map Act, 124–126
    exhaustion of
      administrative remedies, 124
    statute of limitations, 124–126
  Mitigation Fee Act, 573–578
  of police power, 4
  specific plan, 41
  standing to sue, 468, 552–557
  Willamson Act cancellation, 241
  wetlands regulation, 199

judicial review *continued*
  zoning ordinance, 47, 51, 53
    any resident or property
      owner may bring suit, 47
    limited role of court review, 44–45
    presumption of validity, 43–44

K

Kavanau decision, discussed, 298, 336
Kennedy, Anthony, 178–179, 332
Kern County, 437
  general plan, 402
  "urbanized area," 264
Kings County, "urbanized area," 264
Klamath River, 220
Knox-Nesbit Act of 1963, 436

L

Labor Code, 265–267
Lafayette, 304
LAFCO. *See* local agency
  formation commission
Laguna Beach, second-dwelling
  unit ordinance, 481
Lake Tahoe, 301, 307
lakes, public access easement, 112–113
land installment contract
  subdivision created by, 84
land partition. *See* Subdivision
  Map Act (Map Act)
  Map Act application to, 83
Land Sales Full Disclosure Act, 201
land surveyor, 126, 135
land use element, 11, 23
  See also general plan;
    land use regulation
  circulation element must
    be correlated with, 13–14
  discussed, 13–14
  flooding, land use element
    must address, 13–14, 32
  initiative, 30, 386
  text and diagrams and
    urban form and design, 14
land use litigation
  See also judicial review
  court standards, 531–539
  introduction, 525
  overview/terminology, 525–526
  standing to sue, 468, 548n11, 552
land use regulation
  must be consistent
    with general plan, 24, 362
  nexus for, 342–343
  police power as basis for,
    1–4, 44, 79, 289, 424
  relationship to regional welfare, 45
  statutory framework for, 5–6
  vagueness and uncertainty, 49–50
landfill, 150, 552
  See also waste
landmark preservation law
  See also historic landmark
  New York City, 3, 237, 249, 291
  religious organization exemption, 58
Landscaping and Lighting
  Act of 1972, 380
landscaping and lighting district, 380
  See also assessment district
landslide. *See also* seismic hazard
  Portuguese Bend landslides, 381
Lanham Act, 235–236
large-lot zone, 16

Las Vegas, Nevada, 210
LCP. *See* Local Coastal Program
lead agency, 148n3, 156, 158–160, 167–169, 171, 453, 465
  See also California Environmental Quality Act
Lead Agency Decision to Prepare an EIR, 157
League of California Cities, 420
lease
  agricultural lease, Map Act application to, 82–85
  Map Act exemption for, 89–90
  subdivision created by, 81
leasehold interest, as conveyance, 87–88
least cost zoning law, 411, 497, 505
  See also housing; zoning law
  discussed, 497
  "appropriate standards," 497
legislative act
  See also administrative act
  compared to ministerial/quasi-judicial act, 6, 527
  defined, 6
  discussed, 527
  due process violations, 334
  exercise of police power is, 4
  findings requirements, 286
  initiative/referendum application to, 402
  judicial review, administrative/legislative act, 35
  Mira-Hart-Murrieta cases, 118, 365–366
  Nollan/Dolan does not apply, 355
  notice and hearing requirements, 455
  quasi-legislative act, 527,
  rules/regulations by regulatory body as, 528
  school facilities, 365
  traditional mandate proceedings, 35, 41, 44, 369, 383, 527–528, 558, 565
"legislative body"
  See also city council; public agency
  Brown Act meeting requirements, 462
  motives, 51–52, 533–534, 536
"legitimate state interest,"
  See also essential government function; nexus requirements
  discussed, 34, 291–292, 327, 336, 343–344, 347, 400, 478, 513n52
Leroy F. Greene School Facilities Act of 1998 (SB 50), 117–118
  discussed, 365–367
liability, of local agency
  California Tort Claims Act of 1963, 469–471
  Federal Civil Rights Act, 471–473
    color of law, 472
    section 1983 persons, 331
    treatment of public entities, 472–473
  immunity of public employees and entities, 470–471
    discretionary immunity, 471
  in general, 469
  public employees, 470
  public entities, 470
    breach of mandatory duty, 470
    enactment, definition of, 470

library. *See also* library district
  allowed as development condition, 35, 110, 362
  dedication allowed for, 116, 267, 362–363
  license, as conveyance, 87–88
    See also license tax; permit
license tax, 372
lien, 88
  Map Act enforcement, use of, 128–129, 477
litigation stay, 98–100
  See also tentative map
Little Tennessee river, 221
Littleton, CO, adult business licensing requirement, 56
"*Livermore*" test, 45–46, 400, 418, 425–426
  See also judicial review
live/work space, 519n72
lobbying, 414
local agency. *See also* public agency
  "affected local agency," LAFCO definition, 444n13
  zoning ordinances and, 73
  recommendations concerning subdivisions, 95
local agency formation commission (LAFCO), 29, 252, 556
  See also annexation; incorporation
  boundary changes
    factors LAFCO must consider, 446–450
    in general, 440–442
    "islands," 442
    Landowner-Voter Districts, 447
    procedures, 442–446
    protest
      hearing, 445, 447
      proceedings, 447, 451–452
    reconsideration hearing, 450–451
    Registered-Voter district, 447
  challenges to decisions of, 448
  composition and function
    in general, 437–438
    powers, 437–438
local agency formation commission
  conditions of annexation, 65
  environmental review, 453–454
    LAFCO as responsible agency, 453
    municipal service review, 454
  final actions, filings, notifications, 452
  introduction, 435
  LAFCO Proceedings, 444–445
  LAFCO Protest Proceedings- Effect of Protests, 447
  legislative development, 435–437
  multi-county change of organization/ reorganization, 452–453
  "principal county," 438, 452
  municipal service review requirement, 439–440
  spheres of influence, 438–439
  statute of limitation, 449, 542
local coastal program (LCP), 11, 101, 242, 244–246
  adoption, subject to initiative and referendum, 402
  Coastal Commission amendment of, 247
    review of, 245
  web address, 245

logging. *See also* forest
  conservation element addresses, 16
  effect on wetlands, 186
  Northwest Timber Compromise, 219
  timber harvest plan, 217, 229, 530
Long Beach, 344
Los Angeles, 54, 422, 481, 507
  See also charter city; Los Angeles County
  City Board of Pensions, 554
  demolition permit, 304, 330
  Department of Building and Safety, 554
  fire hydrant fee, 330, 360
  housing cost, 484
  NPDES permit, 263
    web address, 263n5
  zoning law application to, 23, 46, 401
Los Angeles County, 272, 437
  interim flood control ordinance, 302–303, 310
  "urbanized area," 264
Los Angeles Unified School District, 367
Los Padres National Forest, 72
lot
  antiquated lot, merger provisions, 5
  large-lot zone, 16
  lot line adjustment, 136, 142–143, 304
    discussed, 87–88
    not exempt from California Coastal Act, 87n4, 244
    not a taking, 303–304
Lower Lagoon Valley Policy Plan Implementation Project, 24
Loyola Marymount University, 367–368
Lucas decision, 293

M

Madera County, "urbanized area," 264
Majority Protest Act, 376
Malibu, 303
mandamus. *See* mandate proceedings
mandate proceedings. *See also* judicial review; land use litigation
  administrative mandate, 328–329, 535–538, 544
    "administrative collateral estoppel," 530–531
    discussed, 529–531
  alternative writ, 562–563
  appeal of writ, 567–568
  brief preparation, 564–565
  CEQA actions, 568–573
  evidence, 558–562
  in general, 526–527
  hearing date, 563–564
  injunction, 568
  issuance of writ, 566–567
  noticed motion, 563
  summary judgment, 564
  stays, 565–566
  traditional mandamus, 36
  traditional mandate, 125–126
    in general, 527
    legislative acts, 35, 41, 44, 369, 383, 527–528, 558
    ministerial acts, 528–529, 532n8, 560
  TRO/preliminary injunction, 566
  writ of mandate, 36, 94, 231, 260, 367, 390, 465, 469, 479, 525–526, 528, 557

manufactured home, 88
　See also mobile home
map. *See also* diagram;
　　Subdivision Map Act
　compared to diagram, 21
　in general plan, 13–14, 18
　seismic hazard, 17
　zoning map, 7, 45
Map Act. *See* Subdivision Map Act
marbled murrelet, 229
　See also endangered species
Marco Island, FL, 195
Marin County
　Countywide Plan, 250
　Marin Emergency Radio
　　Authority (MERA), 74
　personal watercraft prohibition, 50
　TDR regulations upheld, 249–250
　"urbanized area," 264
Marine Forests Society, 243
Marine Protection, Research
　and Sanctuaries Act
　Section 302, 201
"marine sanctuary," 201
marriage license, 480
marsh, 182
　See also wetlands
master-planned community, 69
　See also planned-unit
　　development
Maui County Council, 473
mayor,
　appointment of planning
　　commissioners, 6
　city council and, 6
McAteer-Petris Act, 247
McCarthy legislation, 115–116
meeting. *See also* Ralph M. Brown Act
　planning commission, 7
Mello-Roos Community
　Facilities Act, 380, 441
memorandum of
　understanding (MOU)
　between cities and tribes, 77
Mendocino County, 143
　general plan challenge, 19
　"urbanized area," 264
MERA. *See Marin County*
Merced County,
　"urbanized area," 264
merger, 5, 142–144
　See also Subdivision Map Act
　automatic merger upheld, 142–143
　LAFCO review of, 437, 441
　ordinance struck down, 144
Metropolitan Transportation
　Commission (MTC), 430–431
Mexican spotted owl. *See* owl
microwave dish, 480
"migratory bird rule," 176–177
　See also wetlands
military
　activity, land use element
　　must address, 11, 14
　installations, open space
　　element addresses, 16
Millbrae, City Clerk, 389
Millennial Housing
　Commission, 484
mineral
　lease, Map Act exemption for, 91
　resource management policies, 16
minerals. *See also* mining
　conservation element addresses, 16

mining
　conservation element address, 16
　CUP allowed for, 62
　EIR requirements, 161
　permit required for, 72
　surface mining, 31
ministerial act, 6, 127, 479
　See also legislative act
　compared to legislative/
　　quasi-judicial act, 6
　discussed, 528
　traditional mandate
　　proceedings, 528–529 532n8
ministerial project
　not subject to CEQA,
　　148, 156–157, 405
Mira-Hart-Murrieta cases, 118, 365
　See also school district
　　facilities fee; school impact fee
mitigation, 85, 237, 279, 352–354
　See also alternatives; Mitigation
　　Fee Act; mitigation monitoring
　　and reporting; wetlands
　casino impacts, 403
　challenged as taking, 278
　housing element
　　requirements, 489
　under CEQA, 117, 147, 152, 154–155,
　　157, 160, 164, 166, 168–169, 478
　school impact fees not
　　allowed as mitigation, 117
　under ESA, 219–220
　wetlands, 189, 191–192,
　　198–199, 203–204
Mitigation Fee Act, 6, 281, 286,
　　358–360, 364, 372, 515, 515n56
　challenges to fees
　　under, 279, 355, 383
　exactions, 343
　judicial review
　　development project fees, 574–577
　　enactment of fee,
　　　364–365, 577–578
　　in general, 573–574
　　remedy, 577–578
　statutory authority for, 6
mitigation monitoring
　and reporting, 155
　See also environmental
　　impact report
　discussed, 169–170, 478
　"performance standards," 164
mobile home park, 325, 327, 337
　See also rent control law
　conversion, 92
　CUP allowed for, 62
Monterey, 326
　Measure E, 423n14
Monterey County,
　"urbanized area," 264
monuments, Map Act
　provisions for, 112
MOU. See memorandum
　of understanding
"moratorium" ordinance
　See also development
　　moratorium; interim ordinance
　challenged as taking, 301–302, 344
　discussed, 67, 334
　effect on tentative map, 34, 98
　limit, 301
　not a taking, 293, 301–302, 307–308
　OPR extensions and, 34
　state preemption of, 5

mortgage, 88
　subdivision created by, 84
Mosk, Stanley, 303, 421, 503
mosquito abatement district
　LAFCO jurisdiction, 441
motel
　initiative allowed for, 423
　limit on guest stays not a taking, 297
motives. *See also* bias; public official
　of public officials, 51–52, 533, 536, 560
MTC. *See* Metropolitan
　Transportation Commission
mudflat, 182
　See also wetlands
　as special aquatic site, 194
mudslides
　mapping of as part of
　　safety element, 17
Municipal Improvement
　Act of 1913, 382
Municipal Reorganization
　Act of 1977, 436
municipal service review, 439–440, 454
Municipal Storm Water Permitting
　Program, MS4s, 262
　notice of intent, 262–263
mussels, 229
　See also endangered species

N

Napa,
　City, inclusionary housing
　　ordinance, 510–511, 513n52
　County,
　　specific plan, 26
　　"urbanized area," 264
National Academy of Science, 198
National Association of
　Home Builders, 191, 225
National City
　ordinance regulating
　　adult businesses upheld, 54
National Environmental
　Policy Act (NEPA)
　See also California
　　Environmental Quality Act
　interplay with ESA,
　　210, 212, 227, 230
　interplay with local regulation, 72
　wetlands regulation,
　　190, 192, 199–200
　alternatives analysis, 197
　environmental assessment, 200
National Forest Land and Resource
　Management Plan, 214
National Historic Preservation Act
　(NHPA), 189–190, 201, 236–238
　Section 106, 236
National Housing Conference, 507n36
National List of Plant Species
　That Occur in Wetlands, 183
　See also wetlands
National Marine Fisheries
　Service (NMFS), ESA
　administration, 207, 209
National Oceanic and Atmospheric
　Administration (NOAA),
　207, 221, 225
National Pollutant Discharge
　Elimination System (NPDES), 175
　See also wetlands
　discussed, 262–263
National Register of Historic
　Places, 189, 201, 236

National Research Council (NRC), 198
National Wild and Scenic River System, 188
Native American church, 57
    See also Native Americans
Native American sites, open space element addresses, 16
Native Americans. See also CEQA
    consultation with required, 12, 16, 29, 33, 236n1
    gaming, 76–77
        impact mitigation agreement as "administrative act," 402
        restricted in densely populated areas, 77
    fishing and hunting rights, NWPs and, 188
    religious exercise, interplay with ESA, 226
    water quality certification, 189
    zoning law application to, 57, 75–77
Natural Communities Conservation Plan, 228
Natural Communities Conservation Planning Act (NCCP), 227–228, 369
    See also Habitat Conservation Plan
natural resource element, 23
natural resources
    conservation element addresses, 16
    open space element addresses, 16
Natural Resources Conservation Service (NRCS), 183
Natural Resources Defense Council (NRDC)
    wetlands issues, 176
navigable waters
    See also non-navigable waters; wetlands
    "continuous surface connection" test, 178–180
    CWA definition, discussed, 175–181
    Corps/EPA joint guidance, 179–180
        traditional navigable waters, 179–180
    history of federal regulation, 174–175
    Rivers and Harbors Act definition, 174–175
    "significant nexus test," 177–180
    as "waters of the United States," 175
navigation dredging permit, 203
    See also dredging
NCCP. See Natural Communities Conservation Planning Act
negative declaration, 94, 148, 153–158, 165, 170–171, 465, 467, 547
    See also California Environmental Quality Act
    adoption, 94, 155
        public notice, 155–156
    challenges to, 542
    mitigated negative declaration, 154, 157, 169–171, 478
        addendum to cannot be relied on, 171
        water supply consideration, 251, 255, 257
    public review, 155–156
    recirculation, 155
    statute of limitations, 542
    total time, 156
        extensions, 156
    water supply consideration, 251, 255, 257

"neighborhood compatibility" ordinance upheld, 50, 234
NEPA. See National Environmental Policy Act
Nevada County
    property rights initiative, 423
    "urbanized area," 264
new city, 128, 272, 274
    See also city; incorporation
    general plan
        extensions, 33–34
        timeframe for adoption of, 33
    incorporation effect on, 107
New Jersey
    inclusionary zoning, 509
    Supreme Court, 509
New London, Conn., 289–290
New York, N.Y.
    Landmark Preservation Law, 3, 237, 249, 291
newly incorporated city. See new city
Newport Beach, 272
"nexus legislation." See Mitigation Fee Act; nexus requirements
nexus requirements
    See also judicial review
    for challenges, generally, 250
    exactions
        Dolan decision, 346–351
        Ehrlich decision, 351–355
        in general, 351
        Nollan decision, 343–346
        Pioneer Trust rule, 347
        San Remo Hotel, 355–358
        "specific and uniquely attributable test," 347
    for general plan challenges, 13, 21
    initiative invalidation, 402
    Map Act conditions, 108, 364
    takings, 117, 279, 330, 342–343, 510
        "legitimate state interest," 344, 479
NHPA. See National Historic Preservation Act
NIMBY attitude, 428
    "Anti-Nimby" legislation, 492–497
NMFS. See National Marine Fisheries Service
NOAA. See National Oceanic and Atmospheric Administration
noise element, 11, 17
    See also general plan
    noise contours, 32
Nollan/Dolan decision
    higher scrutiny test, 233, 278, 299–300, 351–355, 510, 512
    exactions, 295, 343–358
non-discharge site, 199
nondiscrimination requirement
    See also due process; judicial review
    for land use regulation, 4
non-navigable waters, 177
    non-navigable tributaries, Corps/EPA joint guidance 180
    non-navigable water bodies, Corps/EPA joint guidance 180
nonprofit organization
    nonprofit university not exempt from fees, 367
    security determination, 131
    standing to sue, 228
Norco, 401
northern spotted owl. See owl

Northwest Timber Compromise, 219
notice. See public notice
notice of completion, 172
notice of conveyance, 88
notice of determination, 155–156, 165, 169, 172
    See also environmental impact report
notice of exemption, 148, 153, 156–157
    See also California Environmental Quality Act
notice of preparation, 156, 159–160, 162, 165, 172
    See also environmental impact report
NPDES. See National Pollution Discharge Elimination System
NRC. See National Research Council
NRCS. See Natural Resources Conservation Service
NRDC. See Natural Resources Defense Council
nuisance
    nuisance abatement, 477
    public nuisance, 63, 272

O

Oakland, 507
    hotel ordinances upheld, 345
Oceanside
    Proposition A, 401
O'Connor, Sandra Day, 224, 349
office, Map Act does not apply to leasing of, 82n3, 89–90
office building, 72, 194, 257
    See also commercial development
office space
    development limits, 422
    transit fees as exactions, 346, 353
Office of Emergency Services, 17
Office of Noise Control, 17
offshore energy programs, Coastal Commission review of, 246
oil drilling zone, 25
oil exploration, 72
oil facility, EIR requirements, 161
oil lease, Map Act exemption for, 92
oil refinery, ESA review of, 214
oil spill program
    Coastal Commission review of, 242
    SFBCDC participation, 249
Open Meeting Act
    See Ralph M. Brown Act
open space, 16, 39, 120, 432
    See also open space element; parkland dedication
    credit, 109–110
    general plan and, 31
    initiative, 423
    preservation of by LAFCO, 435, 437–438
    property, inventory of, 17
    ridgeline ordinance, 125, 312, 540
    special assessment for, 375
open space easement, 123
open space element, 11, 16–17, 23
    See also general plan
    defined, 16
    "shall contain an action program," 16
optional element. See general plan

Orange County, 270
  Board of Supervisors, 397
  El Toro Marine Base conversion
    initiative, 403–404
  NPDES permit, 214, 263
    web address, 263n6
  "urbanized area," 264
Oregon
  ESA listed species, 212, 221, 225
  ex parte legislation, 462n7
owl. *See also* endangered species
  Arizona pygmy owl, 209
  cactus ferruginous
    pygmy owl, 224–225
  Mexican spotted owl, 213
  northern spotted owl,
    209, 213, 220–221

P

Pacific Legal Foundation, 349
Pacifica, anti-monotony ordinance,
  49–50, 234
parcel. *See also* parcel map
  assessment and
    Subdivision Map Act, 82
  contiguous parcel, 82
  counting, 85–87
    remainder parcels, 86–87
    successive subdivisions, 85–86
  divided parcel, 81
  legal parcel, 136, 140–142
    presumption of
      legal parcel, 144–145
    merger/unmerger, 142–145
  reconveyance, 84
  relevant parcel,
    TDR, 249
  Williamson Act, 239
parcel map, 75, 142–143
  See also Subdivision Map Act
  four or fewer parcels, 81, 134–135
  local ordinance requirements, 80, 134
  Map Act requirements,
    79, 90–92, 103, 126, 128, 134–135
  multiple parcel maps, 134
  must be consistent
    with general plan, 121
  parcel map requirements, 134
  quasi-judicial, 527, 530
  special case, 134–135
  vs. final map, 84
  waiver requirement, 92
parcel numbers, 82
park, 120
  dedications/conditions
    allowed for, 110, 362, 364
  special assessment for, 375
parking
  circulation element may address, 14
  mitigation addressed by EIR, 164
  transient parking tax, 374
parkland dedication
  See also dedications; open space
  in lieu fees, 110, 352
  Map Act provisions for,
    109–110, 140, 364
partisanship, 414
passive or natural heating or cooling,
  Map Act provisions for, 121–122
PCBs. *See* polychlorinated biphenyls
PD. *See* planned-unit development
Pennsylvania Bituminous Mine
  Subsidence and Land
  Conservation Act, 296

performance guarantee, 133
permit, 81, 203, 290, 343, 349, 351, 421
  See also building permit
  automatic approval, 465, 467
  invalid permit vests no rights, 271
  issuance of is ministerial act, 6, 528
  Map Act application to,
    84, 101, 111, 120, 137
  PUD, 69, 100–101
  statute of limitations, 542
Permit Streamlining Act (PSA), 455
  deadlines, 94–95, 464
  discussed, 463–468
  does not apply to legislative acts, 467
  interplay with Map Act,
    80, 94–101, 119
  "deemed" approval and
    completion, 93–94, 463–466
  notice and hearing, 463
  statutory authority for, 6
"person," definition, 472
personal watercraft prohibition, 50
pesticide registration,
  ESA applies to, 214
Petaluma
  form-based zoning, 65
  growth measure, 425
peyote, Native American
  religious use of, 57
Pioneer Trust rule, 347
  See also nexus requirements
Placer County, "urbanized area," 264
planned development, 69
  See also planned
    residential development;
    planned-unit development
planned growth ordinance
  See also growth management
  discussed, 425–427
"planned local drainage
  facilities fund," 111
"planned local sanitary
  sewer fund," 111
planned residential development.
  See also development;
    planned-unit development
  conditions on permit for, 19
  CUP allowed for, 62
planned-unit development
  (PUD/PD), 363–364, 467
  See also commercial
    development; development
  discussed, 68–69
  permit for, 100–101
  granting of is
    quasi-judicial, 527, 530
planning, ballot box
  planning, 385
planning agency, 29–30, 264
  See also planning commission
  statutory authority for, 5
Planning and Zoning Law,
  23, 469, 535, 544, 551, 562
planning commission,
  28, 48, 93, 95, 123–124, 283
  See also planning commissioner
  city need not create, 6
  duties and responsibilities, 6–7
  annual report, 7
  in general, 6–7
  number of members needed for
    approval of general plan, 28
  public hearings, 7
  redevelopment plans and, 71

planning commission *continued*
  staff, 7
  report, 49
  statutory authority for, 5
planning commissioner, 458
  See also planning
    director; public official
  appointment, 6
  suggested reading material for, 6n4
planning department, 7, 39
  statutory authority for, 5
planning director
  See also planning commissioner
  can be an "interested
    person adversely affected," 124
plants. *See also* soils
  facultative plants, 183
  facultative upland plants, 183
  facultative wetland plants, 183
  habitat mitigation, 220
  hydrophytic vegetation, 183
  National List of Plant Species
    That Occur in Wetlands, 183
  obligate wetland plants, 183
  protections for, 222–223
  wetlands plants, 183
  wetland vegetation, defined, 183
Plumas County
  "fencing out" ordinance
    not a taking, 299, 329
police power
  aesthetic concerns and, 3, 355
  as basis for dedications and
    development fees, 34, 68, 108,
      117, 340, 342, 362–363, 374
    limitations, 108, 349–351
  as basis for economic
    development regulation, 3
  as basis for land use regulation,
    1–4, 44, 79–80, 100, 289, 424
  as basis for protection of
    property of historical and
    aesthetic significance, 237
  city cannot contract away, 277
  for inclusionary housing
    programs, 69, 512
  is elastic power, 2
  improper exercise of,
    limits on, 4–6
  proper exercise of, 291, 332, 340
    growth management, 424
police station,
  allowed as development
    condition, 35, 362
  dedication allowed for, 116, 362
policies, in general plan, 11
Political Reform Act, 534n9
polo field, 330
polychlorinated biphenyls (PCBs), 550
population density, land use
  element must address, 13, 32
population growth, 419–420
  See also growth management
Porter-Cologne Water Quality
  Control Act, 181
  See also wetlands
  discussed, 202–203
port master plans, Coastal
  Commission review of, 246
Portuguese Bend landslides, 381
Poway, 285
power plant siting, Coastal
  Commission review of, 247
precedence clause, 20, 24

■ 647

preemption, 71, 235, 304, 365, 543
  effect on local ordinance, 4–5, 67
  federal, 72
  of local ordinance by
    Map Act, 80–81, 144
  of subdivision ordinance
    by Probate Law, 84
prevailing wage
  in general, 265–267
  public bidding concerns on
    private projects, 267–268
prezoning. *See also* zoning ordinance
  for annexation, 443
  discussed, 65–66
  must be consistent with
    general plan, 53, 66, 401
privacy protection, 50
private property, 357–358
  See also public property
private sector, role in housing, 15
Probate Law, 84
project. *See also* California
    Environmental Quality Act;
    public works project
  approval
    during OPR extension, 34
    under PSA, 463–466
  CEQA definition, 148–149
    development agreement
      is a "project," 276
    whole of an action, 150
  definition, for water
    assessment, 257
  development project,
    6, 24, 27, 93, 97, 125, 167, 565
  statewide, regional,
    areawide significance, 159
  wetlands, water-dependent/
    non-water-dependent
    project, 194–195
property rights. *See also* takings
  Map Act considerations of, 136
property rights initiative, 418
property taxes. *See* taxes
property tax exchange agreement, 443
Proposition 1A, 76, 118, 366
Proposition 13, 361, 365n15
  in general, 373–374, 380, 386, 417, 428
Proposition 24, 396
Proposition 59, 459n4
Proposition 62, 373–374
  in general, 375, 380, 404
Proposition 77, 409
Proposition 80, 409
Proposition 90, 418
Proposition 105, 396
Proposition 111, 263–264
Proposition 140, 386
Proposition 218, 372, 382
  assessment ballot
    proceeding, 376–377, 379
  "assessment" definition, 376
  fee increases, 378
  in general, 374, 380, 515, 515n57
  impacts on fees and
    charges, 377–379
  impacts on local general taxes, 375
  impacts on local special taxes, 375
  impacts on new fees, 379
  impacts on special
    assessments, 375–377, 381
  impacts on standby
    charges, 379–380
  initiatives, 378, 380, 399

Proposition 218 Omnibus Implementation
    Act of 1997, 376
PSA. *See* Permit Streamlining Act
public, general plan availability to, 30–31
public access, to coast, 112–113
  Coastal Commission review of, 246
public access easement, 328
  See also easement; takings
  Map Act provisions for, 112–113
public agency, 148, 268, 365
  See also lead agency; local agency
  "advisory agency," definition, 93
  land conveyance to, 87, 89
  as "legislative body," 462
  Subdivision Map Act
    application to, 81, 87, 89
Public Cemetery District Law, 441n9
public comment
  CEQA, 159
  ESA listing, 209–210
  wetlands permit process, 190, 192
Public Contract Code, 268
public entity
  See also city council; liability
  land conveyance to, 87
public health, 5, 233, 235, 272,
    286, 411, 497, 505, 576
  open space element addresses, 16
  Map Act consideration of,
    120, 122, 134, 137–138
  police power as basis for
    protection of, 1, 289, 424
  "specific, adverse impact," 66, 493, 495
public hearing, 51, 284, 404, 462–463
  See also "fair hearing"
  for CEQA matters, 569–570
  CMA, 264–265
  due process requirements,
    48–49, 455, 535
  for ESA listing, 209
  exhaustion, doctrine of, 124
  for fee, 370
  for general plan adoption, 28
  LAFCO, 439, 443–445, 451
  interim ordinance, 66
  for land use matters, 7
  Map Act requirements,
    93, 95–96, 139, 143
  planning commission and, 7
  sphere of influence, 439
  wetlands permit process, 190
  Williamson Act cancellation, 241
  zoning ordinance/amendment/
    rezoning, 43, 48–49, 535
public meeting
  See meeting; public hearing
public notice, 404, 550–551
  CEQA requirements, 155–156, 159
  due process requirements,
    48–49, 455, 535
  ESA requirements, 209, 230
  exhaustion, doctrine of, 124, 551–552
  for fees, 370
  interim ordinance, 66
  LAFCO, 439, 444, 451
  for land use matters, 7
  Map Act requirements,
    93, 95–96, 134, 139, 143, 372
  newspaper publication, 159, 370
  under PSA, 463, 466
  requirements, 25
  sphere of influence, 439
  wetlands permit process, 192
  Williamson Act cancellation, 241

public notice *continued*
  for zoning ordinance/amendment/
    rezoning, 48–49, 535
public nuisance, 63, 272
  See also nuisance
public official. *See also* mayor;
    planning commissioner
  bias, 51, 456
  "cannot use personal
    subjective judgment," 528
  ex parte communications, 462–463
  federal officer,
  may not rely on statements
    of, 271–272, 456, 481
  motives, 51–52, 533, 536
  thought processes, 51
  judicial review, 560–561
public opinion,
  consideration of, 284
public property, ordinance
  prohibits sign posting on, 3
"public purpose" need
  See eminent domain
Public Records Act, 561
public safety, 5, 233, 272,
    286, 411, 497, 505, 576
  Map Act consideration of, 120,
    122, 134, 137–138
  police power as basis for
    protection of, 1, 289, 424
  "specific, adverse
    impact," 66, 493, 495
public transit. *See also* transit facility
  circulation element
    may address, 14
Public Utilities Commission, 409
public utility, Map Act application
  to, 87, 89, 120, 130
public welfare, 233, 342, 411,
    425–426, 505, 576
  land use ordinance must
    be related to, 45–46, 532
  police power as basis for
    protection of, 1, 289, 424
"public works," definition, 265
  See also public works project
public works department, 7
public works plans, Coastal
    Commission review of, 246
public works project, 149
  See also project
  charter cities, 23–24
  compared to "public project," 267
  expenditures, addressed
    by initiatives, 423
  funding, 380
  must be consistent with
    general plan, 7, 22–23
    future, not existing, 27
  specific plan, 39
  prevailing wage concerns, 265
PUD. *See* planned-unit
  development
pygmy owl. *See* owl

Q

quality of life, 235, 420
quarry. *See also* mining
  CUP allowed for, 62
quartering (4x4), 85–86
quasi-judicial proceeding, 286, 462
  due process, 48
Quimby Act, 109, 125, 576

R

radio tower, 330
    CUP allowed for, 62
Ralph M. Brown Act (Brown Act),
    95, 455, 457, 535, 560
    discussed, 7, 459–462
    litigation exemption, 277
    "meeting"
        definition, 459–460
        "seriatim meeting," 460–461
    public meeting requirements, 462
    statute of limitations, 542
    statutory authority for, 6
ranching. *See also* agriculture
    CWA exemption for, 185
raven, 210
real estate development, 109
    See also development
reasonableness requirement, 342–343,
    See also arbitrary and capricious
        test; judicial review; "rule of reason"
    Associated Home Builders test, 342, 345
    for land use regulation,
        2, 4, 45, 54, 108–109
    exactions, 371
    "rational relation" test, 361, 479
    "reasonable relationship" test,
        344–347, 349–350, 357–359,
        368, 418, 512, 532
recession, 97
reconveyance, 84, 120, 372
    release agreements, 84
record. *See* administrative record
recreation. *See also* parkland
        dedication; recreational facility
    dedication for, 109
    challenged, 352
    open space element addresses, 16
    recreational mitigation
        fee, 16, 352, 354
    special assessment for, 375
recreation and park district
    LAFCO jurisdiction, 441
recreational area, EPA
    consideration of, 186
recreational facility, allowed as
    development condition, 110, 364
red-cockaded woodpecker
    See woodpecker
redevelopment law. *See also* housing;
    redevelopment plan
    blight, 70
    California Community
        Redevelopment Law, 502–503
    inclusionary housing
        requirement, 503
    set-aside requirement, 502
    relation to general plan/zoning
        law, 70–71
    "blighted area," 70
redevelopment plan
    adoption, status of zoning, 71
    initiative may not address, 398
    must be consistent
        with general plan, 71
    not exempt from school
        district facilities fee, 368
referendum, 275, 374, 395–396
    See also initiative
    compared to city
        council measures, 404–408
    definition, 387
    due process, 334–335, 407–408

referendum *continued*
    in general, 385–386
    for general plan, 29–30
    limitations, 396–404
    procedural requirements, 387–388, 392
    "Referendum Against
        an Ordinance Passed
        by the City Council,' 388, 390
    pre-election challenge, 47, 408–411
    redevelopment plans and, 398
    "referendum period," 275
    time period for passage, 29
    for zoning ordinance, 52–53
Regents of the University of California,
    exempt from local codes, 72–73
Regional Water Quality Control Boards,
    97, 123, 173, 200, 202–203, 262
    North Coast region,
        website, 181
    "Report of Waste Discharge," 202
    San Francisco region website, 181
    "Water Discharge
        Requirements" permit, 202
Regulatory Guidance Letter (RGL)
    See also wetlands
    discussed, 183–185, 195, 201–202
    web address, 202
release agreement, 84
religion, protection of
    religious exercise, 57–59
    defined under RLUIPA, 58
    "substantial burden," discussed, 57–59
Religious Freedom and Restoration
    Act of 1993 (RFRA), 57
Religious Land Use and
    Institutionalized Persons
    Act (RLUIPA), 57–59
    Nondiscrimination provision, 58
    "religious exercise," defined, 58
"removal permit," 80
rent control initiative. *See also* rent
        control law; rental property
    requirements, 405
    upheld without express
        statutory authority, 2
rent control law. *See also* housing
    affordable housing, 509
    condominium conversion, 3, 91
    Costa-Hawkins Act, 516–517
    in general, 273, 296, 325. 333
        due process claim, 298, 336
    "*Kavanau* adjustment," 298n8, 337
    mobile home park,
        313, 325, 327, 333, 337
    police power and, 3
    not subject to *Nollan/Dolan* heightened
        scrutiny standard, 300, 350
reorganization, LAFCO
    oversight of, 437
replacement project, CEQA
    exemption for, 152
report. *See* staff report
reservations, 352
    See also dedications
    discussed, 110–111
reservoir, 81, 145
    EPA veto of overturned, 200
    public access easement, 112–113
residential character of neighborhood
    See also housing
    "neighborhood compatibility"
        ordinance, 50
    ordinance protecting upheld, 3–4, 45
    residential zoning, 344

residential facility,
    preemption of zoning for, 5
residential hotel,
    no right to convert, 340
residential property, transient commercial
    use of prohibited, 3–4, 50
residential zoning, 344
resolution, adoption/
    amendment of general plan,
        time period to take effect, 29
resort, EIR rejected for, 158
Resource Conservation
    and Recovery Act, 230
responsible agencies, 159, 566n18
"responsible corporate
    officer" doctrine, 204
retail center
    tiering allowed for, 158
reversion to acreage, 120, 132, 143
    See also Subdivision Map Act
    discussed, 139–140
Reynolds, Malvina, 50
rezoning, 6–7, 45, 57–58, 68, 101, 117,
    286, 323–324, 410, 466, 488, 548
    See also initiative; zoning ordinance
    initiative struck down,
        46, 52, 105–106, 399–400
    is legislative act, 48, 528
    notice and hearing
        requirements, 48–49, 455
    ordinance not a taking, 296–297
RFRA. *See* Religious Freedom
    and Restoration Act
RGL. *See* Regulatory Guidance Letter
Rhode Island Coastal Resources
    Management Council, 321
ridgeline ordinance
    See also open space
    challenged as taking, 125, 312, 540
rights of the regulated. *See also* judicial
        review; Ralph M. Brown Act
    developer misrepresentations, 468
    ex parte contacts, 462–463
    in general, 455
    notice and hearing, 455–457
    the one who decides
        must hear, 457–458
    other procedural matters, 468
    Permit Streamlining Act, 463–468
    prosecutorial/adjudicatory
        separation, 458–459
    standing to sue, 468
risk management and prevention
    program (RMPP), 93
river. *See also* dredging;
        water; waterway
    public access provisions, 112–113
    "study river," 188
    wild and scenic river, 188
    withdrawals from,
        cumulative impacts analysis
        held inadequate, 163
Rivers and Harbors Act of 1899, 174
Riverside, charter did not
    require consistency, 46
Riverside County
    HCP, 369
    "urbanized area," 264
Riverside County Airport Land
    Use Commission, 546
RLUIPA. *See* Religious Land Use and
    Institutionalized Persons Act
RMPP. *See* risk management
    and prevention program

roads
    allowed as development condition, 111
    farm/forest roads, CWA exemption for, 185
    Map Act consideration of, 92
    permanent road divisions, LAFCO oversight of, 441
Roberts, John, 178
"rough proportionality" test, 117, 510
    See also judicial review
    exactions, 287, 295, 346, 348–351
    Map Act conditions, 108
    takings, 295
"rule of reason." *See also* reasonableness requirement
    CEQA determination, 166–167
Russian River, 179

S

Sacramento, 419, 507
    commercial development, 343
    fees for low-income housing upheld, 343, 345–346, 352
Sacramento County, 437
    "urbanized area," 264
Sacramento River, 229
    See also salmon
Sacramento-San Joaquin Valley, flood protection, general plans of cities
    must address, 13, 23
    zoning must address, 47
safety element, 11, 17–19
    See also general plan
    review by Division of Mines and Geology, 17–18, 33
    review by State Office of Forestry and Fire Protection, 18, 33
    "state responsibility area," 18
saline waste, 311
salmon. *See also* endangered species; fish
    chinook, Sacramento River winter-run, 225, 229, 232
    coho, 209, 231
    Central California Coast, 225
    Southern Oregon/Northern California Coast, 225
    critical habitat designation, 213, 225
    protections for, 207, 220, 225–226
    hatchery-raised, 209, 225
San Anselmo, 395
San Antonio, TX
    preservation ordinance upheld, 57
San Bernardino County,
    "urbanized area," 264
San Bernardino kangaroo rat, 210
    See also endangered species
San Bernardino Valley Audubon Society, 581
San Diego, 285
    facilities benefit assessment, 363, 381
    housing element, 487–488
    inclusionary housing element, 507n38
    NCCP, 227–228
    ordinance banning offsite advertising billboards, 3
    prevailing wage, 267–268
    Prop. E/Prop. F, 400
    water assessment,
San Diego County, 268, 437
    "urbanized area," 264
San Diego North City, West Housing Development Plan, 46

San Francisco, 422, 507
    "Care Not Cash" initiative upheld, 403
    City and County, 58, 481
    cost of housing, 484
    County Clerk, 480
    growth control measures, 422
    hotel conversion ordinance, 300, 326–327, 355–358, 511
    housing costs, 484
    inclusionary housing program, 519n72
    marriage license, 480
    Municipal Railway fees, 360–361
    private property, 357–358
    transit fee ordinance, 346, 353
San Francisco Bay, 243, 247–248
San Francisco Bay Area Rapid Transit District (BART), 73
San Francisco Bay Conservation and Development Commission, 173, 243, 247–249
    composition, 247–248
    jurisdiction, 248
    and NWPs, 189
    permitting authority, 248–249
San Francisco County
    "urbanized area," 264
San Francisco Municipal Railway System, 360
San Francisco Planning Code, 234
San Francisco Planning Commission, 234, 346
San Joaquin County,
    "urbanized area," 264
San Joaquin Valley, 419
San Juan Capistrano, 404
San Luis Obispo County, 276
    "urbanized area," 264
San Marcos, 150
San Mateo County
    "urbanized area," 264
San Remo Hotel decision, 326–328, 355–358, 511
sanitary facilities, Map Act consideration of, 92, 111, 115
Santa Barbara County, 322
    California tiger salamander, 210
    due process claim, 330–331
    "urbanized area," 264
Santa Clara County, 437
    "urbanized area," 264
Santa Cruz County,
    "urbanized area," 264
Santa Monica
    amendment to city charter by initiative, 408
    anti-demolition ordinance, 46
    rent control ordinance, 91, 298, 300, 517n61
Santa Paula
    measure opposing large development, 424
SB 50. *See* Leroy F. Greene School Facilities Act of 1998
SB 162, 448n14, 448n15
SB 178, 517n62
SB 221
    compared to SB 610, 251–256
    discussed, 250, 259–262
SB 435, 498, 501

SB 610, 260
    See also water supply adequacy
    compared to SB 221, 251–256
    discussed, 250, 256–259
SB 879, 232
SB 2166, 116
Scalia, Antonin, 178–179, 249, 325, 343
scenic zoning, 344
school district, 375
    See also school district facilities fee; school site
    city must refer maps to, 95
    LAFCO jurisdiction, 441
    reimbursement for benefit to, 112
    zoning applicability to, 73–74
school district facilities fee. *See also* exactions; school impact fee
    background, 365
    Leroy F. Greene School Facilities Act, 365–367
    Level 1 fees, 366–367
    Level 2 fees, 367
    Level 3 fees, 367
    level of scrutiny, 368–369
    Mira-Hart-Murrieta cases, 365–366
    nonprofit university not exempt from fees, 367
    redevelopment construction not exempt from fees, 368
school facilities, 121
    . *See also* school site
    adequacy considerations, 27, 365–366
    athletic field exempt from zoning ordinance, 74
    dedications for, 267
School Facilities Legislation, 121, 365
school impact fee, 120, 365, 367–368, 371, 379, 576
    See also fee; school district facilities fee
    imposition without statutory authorization, 2
    Mira-Hart-Murrieta trilogy, 118, 366
    special rules, 117–118
    voter approval requirements, 379
school site, dedication allowed for, 110
scope. *See also* scoping
    "scope of the action," 215
scoping, for EIR preparation, 159
sea turtle, 229
    See also endangered species
"second" unit. *See also* granny unit; housing
    discussed, 88, 501–502
    ordinances, 481, 502, 528
secondary effect
    adult businesses and, 54–56, 479
Secretary of Agriculture, 221
Secretary of the Army, 221
Secretary for Environmental Protection, 93, 494
Secretary of Commerce, 201
Secretary of the Interior, 201, 207–208, 210–211, 221, 223–224, 226–227–228, 230
Secretary of Resources, 147, 152
sedimentation, prevention, 112
    See also sedimentation basin
sedimentation basin, CWA exemption for, 185

seismic hazard
　　See also earthquake; geological
　　　　hazard; geological hazard
　　　　assessment district
　　safety element must address, 17
"senior citizen" housing
　　development, 498
　　See also housing
separation of grade district
　　LAFCO jurisdiction, 442
Service. See U.S. Fish
　　and Wildlife Service
settlement agreement,
　　278, 481, 528
　　does not surrender
　　　　police power, 276–277
　　held invalid, 277, 461
sewage
　　See also sewage facility;
　　　　sewer line; waste
　　circulation element may address, 14
sewage facility. See also sewer line;
　　waste discharge
　　dedications allowed for, 111, 362
　　housing element notification, 489
sewer charge. See also charge
　　challenges to, 575, 577–578
　　statute of limitations, 574
sewer drainage easement, 114
sewer line
　　fees, 140
　　initiative for, 423
Shasta County, "urbanized area," 264
SHBC. See State Historical
　　Building Code
shellfish
　　CWA consideration of, 186, 188
　　EPA consideration of, 186
shooting range, EIR requirements, 161
shopping mall, EPA veto of Corps
　　permit for, 197
shorelines, public access
　　easement, 112–113
SHPO. See State Historic
　　Preservation Office
sidewalk, special assessment
　　for, 375, 380
Sierra Madre, land use measure
　　subject to CEQA, 405–406
Sierra Nevada bighorn sheep, 213
sign, 236, 553. See also San Diego
　　ban of advertising signs
　　　　upheld under police power, 3
　　billboards
　　　　obstruction of view
　　　　　　not a taking, 296
　　　　permit for rebuilding
　　　　　　not preempted, 5
　　electronic reader boards, 235
　　First Amendment and, 235
　　"on-premises sign," 64–65
　　ordinance prohibiting sign
　　　　posting on public
　　　　　　property upheld, 3
　　ordinance requiring
　　　　removal of upheld, 64, 235
"significant new information," 167, 171
silviculture. See also forest; logging
　　CWA exemption for, 185
Simi Valley, UGB, 423
site requirements, 122
　　See also Subdivision Map Act
ski resort, 478
　　ESA review, 214

SLAPP suit
　　anti-SLAPP statute attorneys'
　　　　fees, 580–582
　　CEQA issues, 580
　　defendant's burden, 579–580
　　in general, 461, 579
　　land use context
　　　　application, 579–580
　　persons protected by, 579
SMARA. See Surface Mining
　　and Reclamation Act
Smart Growth, 504
　　See also growth management
　　barriers to, 428
　　California Smart
　　　　Growth initiative, 428
　　discussed, 427
　　is not going away, 431–433
smoke detectors, allowed
　　as development condition,
　　　　34–35, 79, 115, 363
snail darter, 221
soils. See also erosion; plants;
　　　　soils investigation
　　aerobic soil, 183
　　conservation element addresses, 16
　　hydric soils, 182–183
　　land clearing activities, 134–185
　　wetlands soils, 182–183
soils investigation, Map Act
　　provisions for, 112
Solano County, "urbanized area," 264
solar access, dedications
　　allowed for, 113
Sonoma County, 141, 319
　　Board of Supervisors, 97
　　California tiger salamander, 210
　　"urbanized area," 264
Souter, David, 349
special assessment district
　　LAFCO oversight of, 441
special district
　　LAFCO oversight of, 437, 441
"specific and uniquely
　　attributable test," 347
　　See also nexus requirements
specific plan, 352
　　See also community
　　　　plan; general plan
　　adoption, 40
　　　　is legislative act,
　　　　　　40–41, 402, 527
　　　　subject to initiative
　　　　　　and referendum, 402
　　CEQA actions must be
　　　　consistent with, 40, 151
　　challenges to, 41
　　contents, 39–40
　　　　statement of relationship
　　　　　　between specific plan
　　　　　　and general plan, 39
　　　　text and diagrams, 39
　　dedications and
　　　　development fees, 34, 362
　　deference to city findings, 41
　　fee allowed for, 40
　　as growth management tool, 421
　　interplay with
　　　　CEQA, 40–41, 151
　　judicial review, 41
　　Map Act
　　　　actions must be consistent
　　　　　　with specific plan, 39, 123
　　　　interplay with specific plan, 80, 92

specific plan continued
　　must be consistent
　　　　with ALUP, 28, 40
　　must be consistent with
　　　　general plan, 26
　　overview, 39
　　planning commission
　　　　relation to, 6–7
　　statute of limitations, 41, 542
　　statutory authority for, 5
　　TDRs and, 249
　　as zoning, 68
specific plan amendment, 7, 40–41, 352
　　is legislative act, 40, 527
sphere of influence, 556
　　See also local agency
　　　　formation commission
　　discussed, 438–439
staff report
　　availability, 96, 468
　　due process requirements, 49
　　as evidence supporting
　　　　findings, 123, 284
standards for operation
　　in general plan, 14
standby charge. See also charge
　　Proposition 218 effects, 379–380
Stanislaus County, 199
　　"urbanized area," 264
State Allocation Board, 96n8, 366–367
　　website, 366
State Board of Equalization, 396, 442
State Board of Forestry and
　　Fire Protection, 18, 33
State Clearinghouse, 155, 165
State Coastal Conservancy, 247
State Controller, 264–265
State Environmental Goals
　　and Policy Report, 431
state geologist, 16
　　fault zones report, 112
state government
　　Indian tribal-state compacts, 76
　　preemption, 4–5
　　zoning law application to, 72–73
　　fees, 73
State Historic Preservation
　　Office (SHPO), 236n1
State Historical Building
　　Code (SHBC), 237
State Mining and
　　Geology Board, 112
State Registrar of Vital Statistics, 480
"state responsibility area," 18
State Water Project
　　biological opinion for
　　　　water pumping invalid, 218
State Water Resources Control
　　Board (SWRCB), 180–181, 262
　　"Effect of SWANCC v. United
　　　　States," web address, 181n2
　　role in wetlands regulation,
　　　　173, 180–181, 202–203
　　storm water management program
　　　　table, website, 263n7
　　design standards,
　　　　website, 263n7
　　waste discharge permit, 181, 202
　　web address, 181
　　water quality certification
　　　　and NWPs, 189
　　"wetland and riparian area
　　　　protection policy," 181
　　website, 181n3

State Water Resources
  Development System, 95
statement of intent,
  not project approval, 149
Statement of Overriding
  Considerations, 169
  See also California
    Environmental Quality Act
"Statewide Survey" (Baldassare), 420n5
statute of limitations
  See also judicial review
  administrative decision
    challenges, 530
  Administrative Procedure
    Act challenge, 542
  applicable statute of
    limitations, 541–545
  assessment challenges, 542
  CEQA challenges,
    153, 542, 562n15
  to certify EIR, 169, 172
  civil rights action, 543
  Coastal Commission
    decision/action, 542
  coastal development
    permit challenges, 246
  CUP challenges, 542
  development agreement
    challenges, 274–275, 281, 542
  EIR certification
    challenges, 169, 172, 542
  ESA, 230
  fee challenges,
    355, 359, 542, 573–574
  general plan challenges, 29, 542, 562
  housing element
    challenges, 36, 543
  interim ordinance, 66
  LAFCO decision
    challenges, 449, 542
  Map Act challenges,
    124–126, 137, 312, 542
  negative declaration
    challenges, 542
  permit, license, or entitlement, 542
  redevelopment agency,
    set-aside compliance, 502–503
  specific plan challenges, 41, 542
  subdividers notice of
    reconveyance, 120, 372
  takings, 540
  vesting tentative map, 281
  Williamson Act cancellation, 241, 543
  zoning ordinance/zoning
    amendment ordinance,
    challenges, 47, 542
stay. See also judicial review
  discussed, 98, 565–566
steelhead. See also Endangered
    Species Act; fish
  protections for, 207
Sterling Act, 354, 365, 367
  See also school district facilities
    fee; school impact fee
Stevens, John Paul, 310n14, 316–317
stock cooperative conversion
  See also condominium
    conversion; housing
  conditions allowed for, 118–119
  Map Act application
    to, 79, 85, 90–91,
    109, 111, 118–119
  tenant notification, 129–130, 468
stock pond, CWA exemption for, 185

storage yard, CUP
  not allowed for, 62
store, Map Act does not apply
  to leasing of, 82n3, 89–90
storm drain fee,
  111, 140, 377–378, 380
storm drainage easement, 114
storm water, 262–263, 348
  See also waste water
  management of, conservation
    element must address, 16
Storm Water Management Plan, 263
stream. See also river; water;
    "waters of the United States"
  not a "navigable water," 178
  public access
    provisions, 112–113
  as special aquatic site, 194
  streambed alteration permit, 203
street, 380
  dedications allowed
    for, 111, 130, 362
  nexus requirement, 330
street improvements
  See also improvements
  allowed as development
    condition, 79
street lighting, special
  assessment for, 375
street widening, nexus
  requirements, 345
Subcommittee on Premature
  Subdivisions, 121
Subdivided Lands Act, 86
  See also Subdivision Map Act
  distinguished from
    Subdivision Map Act, 80
subdivider. See also developer;
    Subdivision Map Act
  Map Act definition, 81
  reconveyance of
    land to, 120, 372
subdivision. See also subdivision
    approval; Subdivision Map
    Act; subdivision process
  antiquated subdivision, 140–142
  Corps permit for, 201
  definition, water
    supply assessment, 260
  development as privilege, 340–342
    no right to subdivide, 340
  environmental subdivision, 85
  Map Act definition, 81–85
    five or more parcels, 81
    four or fewer parcels, 81
  no right to subdivide, 340
  planning commission
    relation to, 6–7
  process, discussed, 362–364
  regulation by city, 80
  successive, 85–86
subdivision approval, 95
  city's authority for, 80
  must be consistent with
    general plan, 9, 22–23, 121
  must be consistent with
    open space plan, 17
  must be consistent
    with specific plan, 39
  opportunities for
    exactions, 34, 79, 362–364
  statute of limitations, 542
  water supply consideration,
    251–252, 259–262

Subdivision Map Act (Map Act),
  281, 365, 371, 469, 488, 540
  See also tentative map
  agricultural land, protection of, 432
  antiquated subdivision
    federal patent, 142
    legal parcels?, 140–141
    post-1893 map, 141
    pre-1929 map, 141
    presumption of
      legal parcel, 144–145
    U.S. Survey Map, 142
  appeals, 123–124
  charter city, application to, 80
  code enforcement, 477
  consistency requirement,
    exceptions to, 27
  determining type required, 85–87
    exceptions allowing
      parcel map, 85
    counting parcels, 85–87
    conveyance to
      public entities, 87
    "quartering," 85–86
    remainder parcels, 86–87
    successive subdivisions, 85–86
  distinguished from
    Subdivided Lands Act, 80
  enforcement
    certificates of compliance, 138–139
    prohibition, 136
    remedies of city, 138
    remedies of private persons, 137
  exclusions/reversions, 139–140
    reversion to acreage, 120, 132, 143
  final map
    accept/reject map for
      filing, time frame, 129
    approval
      is ministerial act, 127–128, 528
      notice and hearing
        requirements, 129–130
      procedures, 127–128
    certificates/security, 128–129
    condos, stock cooperatives,
      community apartments,
      85, 90–91, 129–130
    consent of record title
      holders, 126, 129
    dedications, 108–111, 130
    form and filing, 126–127
    in general, 79, 81, 85, 89, 92,
      107, 126–134, 142–143
    local ordinances requirements, 80
    improvement agreements, 130–132
    multiple final maps, 96, 126–127
    phased, 96, 99, 127
    valid when recorded, 128–131
    vs. parcel map, 84
  goals, 79
  in general, 79–80
  "arm's length" agency
    relationship, 86
  improvement agreements, 130–132
  improvement security
    how much is required?, 131
    releasing security, 133
    remedies, 133–134
    rights and requirements, 131–133
    types of security, 131
  judicial review, 124–126
    exhaustion of administrative
      remedies, 124
    statute of limitations, 124–126

Subdivision Map Act
(Map Act) *continued*
map
effect of annexation
to city upon maps, 107
effect of incorporation
into new city, 128
hearings, 93, 95–96
must be consistent
with general plan, 122, 363
must be consistent
with specific plan, 123
"official map," 140
map amendment, 135
map approval
automatic approval,
93–94, 128, 465–467
charter cities not exempt from
consistency requirements, 24
conditions, challenges to, 531
conditions, in general, 107–108
conditions and general plan
standards, 108–109, 116–117
conditions imposed for
condominium/stock
cooperative conversion, 118–119
conditions imposed through
CEQA, 108, 117–118, 363
conditions imposed through
Map Act and local
ordinance, 108–114, 363
conditions imposed through
subdivision process, 108, 116
conditions imposed
through "design" and
"improvement," 114–116, 363
conditions, reconveyance
of land, 84
conditions, refunds, 120, 140
conditions, timing, 119–120
final map, 127
findings, 121–123, 127–128
grounds for approval, 121–122
grounds for denial,
119, 122–123, 365
"housing balance finding," 121
indemnification, 113–114
no automatic approval, 94, 466
parcel map, 134
specific conditions
allowed, 108–114
time periods, 93–94
"timely filing," 127
vested rights, 101–102
map correction
changed circumstances, 135
changes affecting property
rights, 136
errors and omissions, 135
map amendment, 135–136
"certificate of
correction," 135–136
map exemption
agricultural lease, 91
condominium conversion, 90–91
conveyances to/from
public entities, 87, 89
financing/leasing of units, 89–90
in general, 87
"granny" unit, 88
lot line adjustment, 87–88
other exemptions, 87, 91
"second" units, 88
three-dimensional division, 91

Subdivision Map Act
(Map Act) *continued*
map extension, 80, 96–97
discretionary extension, 96–97, 99
statutory extension, 97
map waiver
condominium project, 92
mobile home park conversion, 92
other parcel map waivers, 92
merger
in general, 5, 81, 89, 136
merging parcels under
one owner, 142–144
presumption of legal
parcels, 144–145
unmerger, 145
parcel
legal parcel,
136, 140–142, 144–145
merger/unmerger, 142–145
parcel map, 75, 79, 90–92,
126, 128, 142–143
four or fewer parcels, 81, 134–135
local ordinance
requirements, 90, 134
multiple parcel maps, 134
parcel map requirements, 134
quasi-judicial, 527, 530
special case, 134–135
vs. final map, 84
waiver, 92
performance security,
partial release of, 133
preemption, 80–81, 84
process, 92–94
PSA time limits
in general, 94–95
notice and hearing, 95–96
refund after recordation, 140
statute of limitations, 124–126
statutory authority for, 5
subdivisions covered by
assessment roll, 82
contiguous units, 82
division of land, 81
for sale, lease, financing, 82–85
improved or
unimproved land, 82
subdivider, 81
subdivision definition, 81–85
SB 221, 260
tentative map, 92–94, 107, 127
approval, 93–94, 432
no automatic approval, 94
notice and hearing
requirements, 94–96
challenges to, 121
consistency with general
plan, 10, 26, 94, 121
environmental review, 117
filing requirements, 93
general requirements, 79–81, 85
local ordinances, 80, 92–93
necessity for, 92
"one bite at the apple"
rule, 119–120
no protection from subsequent
conditions, 119–120
OPR extension, 34, 125
other regulations, 93
quasi-judicial, 527, 530
time periods, 93–94
under PSA, 93, 96
vesting tentative map, 102–107

Subdivision Map Act
(Map Act) *continued*
tentative map life
calculating life of
tentative map, 99
conditions imposed
on extensions, 100
development agreements, 96
discretionary extension,
96–97, 99
expiration of permits
issued with, 100–101
initial life, 96
litigation stay, 98–100
maximum life, 98–99
moratoria, 98–100
multiple final maps,
96, 126–127
OPR extension, 125
statutory extension, 97
summary, 98–101
tolling period, 99
tolling provision, 100
water supply assessment, 252
water supply verification, 252
subdivision powers
See also police power
of city in relation to the state, 73
parcel map requirement, 75
subordination clause, 24
subsidiary districts
LAFCO oversight of, 441
"substantial compliance," 36, 389
housing element, 15, 485, 487
"substantial government
interest," 53–54, 57
Suisun Marsh Preservation Act, 248
Surface Mining and Reclamation
Act (SMARA), 31
Surfside, 58
Sutter County, "urbanized area," 264
swamp, 182
See also wetlands
SWANCC decision, 176–178
Sweedens Swamp, 197
SWRCB. *See* State Water
Resources Control Board
synagogue
CUP allowed for, 62
CUP not allowed for, 61

T

Tahoe Regional Planning
Agency, 301–302, 307–308
"stream environment zone," 324
take
CESA prohibitions, 223, 232
ESA prohibitions, 207–208, 228
discussed, 222–226
incidental take, 208, 226
"incidental take
statement," 218, 220
"take," defined, 223
permit, 220, 224, 226–227
NWP and, 189
takings, 67, 223, 342n3, 421
See also condemnation;
property rights
aesthetic regulation
is not a taking, 355
Agins two-part test, 291–292
"as applied" taking,
313, 320, 330, 344n5, 575
categorical taking, 293–294

takings *continued*
  CESA prohibitions, 223, 232
  incidental take
    permits, 220, 232
  civil rights action,
    289n1, 330–332
  claim
    "property interest," 294n6
  conditional use permit
    not a taking, 63, 298–299
  damages
    "before and after"
      approach, 319–320
    calculation, 315
    from due process
      violation, 319, 330–337
    duration of taking, 316
    equity interest
      approach, 318–319
    in general, 309–313
    measurement, 313–316
    measuring
      compensation, 317–320
    option value technique, 320
    probability method, 319
    reasonable investment-
      backed expectations, 318
    rental value approach, 317–318
    seeking compensation through
      state procedures, 325–328
    theories, 289n1
  delay challenged as, 290, 304, 306
  exactions challenged as, 287
  federal constitutional
    standard, 291–296
  First English, *Nollan*, *Lucas*,
    Dolan decisions, 329–330
  Herzberg decision, 298–299
  landmark law is not a taking,
    237, 249
  Lingle decision, 292–293, 295
  nexus requirements, 344
    "legitimate state
      interest," 344, 479
    "rough proportionality,"
      346, 348–349
  overview, 289–291
    ad hoc approach,
      291–292, 294, 342
    "reciprocity of advantage"
      principle, 308n13
  owner may not be denied economic
    use of land, 293–294, 296–300
  owner may not be denied
    investment-backed
    expectations, 294, 299–300, 318
  partial taking/segmentation, 306–309
  permanent takings, 313–315
  permit denial was not a taking, 195
  possessory taking, 346, 352–353
  regulatory taking, 295–296, 298, 346
    denial of Corps permit, 314
    investment-backed expectations,
      291, 294, 299–300
  ridgeline ordinance challenged
    as, 125, 312, 540–541
  ripeness
    distinguished from exhaustion
      of administrative remedies, 325
    final agency determination,
      293, 320–325, 344n5
    in general, 320
    illegal condition must first
      be challenged in court, 328–329

takings *continued*
  TDR
    as taking, 324–325
    not a taking, 250
  temporary taking, 309, 317, 319
    discussed, 301–306, 315–316
    moratorium challenged as,
      301–302, 307–308, 421
  "total taking," 293
tax collector, not a subdivider, 81
tax lien, security, 128–129
taxes. *See also* assessment
  ad valorem tax, 377
  city taxes, 91
  compared to "regulatory fee," 372
  development excise tax, 372–373
  double taxation challenge, 360
  environmental excise tax, 372
  fiscal zoning, 428
  "general taxes," 373–374
    Prop. 218 impacts, 375
  license tax, 372
  local revenue taxes, Map Act
    does not preempt, 80
  property taxes, 380, 382
  "special taxes," 374, 377
    Prop. 218 impacts, 375
  tax repeal, initiative
    allowed for, 404
  tax-repeal initiative, 404
  transient parking tax, 374
  Williamson Act contract, 239
taxpayer suits, 553–554
  See also judicial review
TDR. *See* transfer of development right
teachers, 512
TEIR. *See* Tribal Environmental
    Impact Report
Telecommunications Act of 1986, 5, 330
telecommunications ordinance
  pre-emption of, 5
temporary restraining order (TRO), 566
  See also injunction; judicial review
Tennessee Valley Authority, 220
tentative map, 79–81, 92–94, 127, 432
  See also Subdivision Map Act;
    vesting tentative map
  consistency with general
    plan, 10, 94, 121
    agreement or harmony, 26, 121
  filing
    during OPR extension, 34
    requirements, 85, 93
  life
    calculating life of
      tentative map, 99
    conditions imposed on
      extensions, 100
    development agreements, 96
    discretionary extensions, 96–97
    expiration of permits
      issued with, 100–101
    initial life, 96
    litigation stay, 98–100
    maximum life, 98–99
    moratoria, 98–100
    multiple final maps, 96, 126–127
    OPR extension, 34, 122
    statutory extensions, 97
    summary, 98–101
    tolling period, 99
    tolling provision, 100
  local ordinances, 80, 92–93
  Map Act requirements, 79–81, 85

tentative map *continued*
  necessity for, 92
  no protection from subsequent
    conditions, 119–120
  notice and hearing/processing, 95–96
  OPR extension, 34, 122
  other regulations, 93
  quasi-judicial, 530
  time periods, 93–94
    under PSA, 93–101
  water supply verification, 251, 260
term limits, 386
text amendment, 45
  See also zoning ordinance
theater, in lieu fees used for, 110
Thousand Oaks
  UGB, 423
threatened species,
  200, 207–208, 219, 231–232
  definition, 208
  NWPs and, 188
three-story home,
  CUP not allowed for, 62
Tiburon, 74
  land use ordinance upheld, 234
Tigard, OR, 346, 351
timber. *See also* forest;
    logging; timberland
  clearing, no CWA
    exemption for, 186
  harvest plan
    challenges to, 217, 229
    quasi-judicial, 530
timberland
  See also timberland production
  conservation element addresses, 16
timberland production,
  land use element must address, 13
  zone, 145
"time, place, and manner"
  regulation, 53–54
toll bridge, 397
Topanga test, 118, 123
  See also findings
Tort Claims Act, 382
  discussed, 469–470
trademark, on signs, 235–236
traffic impact
  mitigation of addressed by EIR, 164
  fee, 164, 575
traffic study, 547
  See also circulation element
transfer of development
    right (TDR), 429
  adoption is exercise
    of police power, 249
  discussed, 249–250
  provisions not a taking, 250
  as taking, 324–325
transient parking tax, 374
  See also taxes
transit district, LAFCO
  jurisdiction, 441
transit facility
  See also bicycle facility; public
    transit; transit impact fee
  dedications allowed for, 362
transit impact fee. *See also*
    dedications; exactions; fee
  relation to office space
    construction, 340, 346
  requirements for upheld, 273
transit system
  dedications allowed for, 362

tree growth, regulation of, 234
Tribal Environmental Impact
    Report (TEIR), 76
Tribal-State Gaming Compact Between
    the Coyote Valley Band of
    Pomo Indians and the State
    of California, website, 77
TRO. *See* temporary restraining order
truck route, circulation
    element may address, 14
trustee agencies, 159
Tucson, AZ, 224
Tulare County, "urbanized area," 264
Tustin, 368
Two Forks Dam, 196
2000 Act. *See* Cortese-Knox-
    Hertzberg Local Government
    Reorganization Act of 2000

U

UGB. *See* urban growth boundary
underwater airguns, 467–468
university long-range
    development plans, Coastal
    Commission review of, 246
University of California,
    exempt from Map Act, 89
unsubdivided property
    sale contract must be conditioned
        on map recordation, 136
upland ditch. *See* ditch
urban form and design
    See also aesthetics; design
    land use element
        consideration of, 14
urban growth boundary (UGB)
    See also growth management
    discussed, 422
Urban Land Institute
    California Smart
        Growth initiative, 428
urban sprawl, 420, 427
    countering, 435, 437–438, 504
urban water management plan, 259
urgency measure, 48, 66, 235, 276, 334
    See also interim ordinance
    referendum may not reject, 397
U.S. Army Corps of
    Engineers (Corps), 314
    See also wetlands
    District Engineer, 188, 190–191
    Division Engineer, 189
    jurisdiction, 206
        includes dredge spoil
            disposal site, 193
    1993, Memorandum,
        web address, 197
    review of determinations
        and permit denials, 183
    Sacramento District, "Mitigation
        and Monitoring Proposal
        Guidelines," 198
    San Francisco District, 183
        "Mitigation and Monitoring
            Proposal Guidelines," 198
    Scope of Regulatory
        Jurisdiction, 177
    wetlands definition, 182
    wetlands regulatory activities, 184–193
        administrative review process, 183
        Corps/EPA MOA, 195, 199
        wetlands delineation
            process, 182–183
U.S. Coast Guard, 229

U.S. Constitution, 95
    Commerce Clause, 175–177
    Due Process Clause, 335
    Establishment Clause, 59
    Fifth Amendment,
        291–293, 296, 326–327, 336, 348
    First Amendment,
        53–59, 63, 235, 331
    Fourteenth Amendment,
        289n1, 309, 315, 332, 342, 361
    Freedom of Speech Clause, 53
    Free Exercise Clause, 59
    Equal Protection Clause, 333, 335
    Full Faith and Credit Clause, 326
    Property Clause, 72
    Supremacy Clause, 5, 72
    Takings Clause, 34, 289,
        309, 315, 335, 342n3
U.S. Department of Agriculture
    (USDA), 207
    "Swampbuster Provisions"
        of Food Security Act, 201
U.S. Department of Defense, 207
U.S. Department of Housing
    and Urban Development, 522
U.S. Department of the Interior, 207
U.S. Department of Justice, 205
U.S. Fish and Wildlife Service,
    191–192, 200–201, 205,
    207–220, 223–224, 227–228
    grazing regulations invalid, 225
    Section 10 handbook,
        web address, 227
U.S. Forest Service, 213–214, 219, 309
    National Forest Land and Resource
        Management Plan, 214
U.S. Postal Service, 72
U.S. Survey Map, does not
    "create" parcels, 142
use permit, 21, 59–63, 234, 286, 341
    See also conditional use permit
    challenges to, 574
    fee for, 34, 362, 382–383
    granting/denial of is quasi-
        judicial administrative
        59, 402, 473, 527, 530
    must be consistent
        with general plan, 59
    planning commission
        relation to, 6–7
    runs with the land, 59
used car business, CUP
    not allowed for, 62
utilities
    dedications allowed for, 130
    Map Act application to, 87, 89

V

vagueness, allowed in land use
    measure, 49–50, 234
Valley Center
    Proposition B, 423n13
variance, 7, 59–61, 285–286, 323–324
    See also conditional use permit
    challenges to, 542
    charter cities and, 60
    dedications/conditions
        allowed for, 362
    defined, 60
    delay challenged as taking, 298
    discussed, 60–61
    in general, 59–60
    granting of is quasi-judicial/
        administrative, 59, 402, 527, 530

variance *continued*
    must be consistent
        with general plan, 59, 61
    runs with the land, 59
    standards, 60–61
    statute of limitations, 542
vector control district
    LAFCO jurisdiction, 441
vegetated shallows, as
    special aquatic site, 194
Ventura County, 213
    growth initiatives, 423
    "urbanized area," 264
vernal pool species, 212–213
    See also endangered species
vested rights, 279, 433
    See also development agreement;
        vesting tentative map
    Avco rule, 102
    in general, 269–271
    refinements, 271–273
    Comparison of California's
        Vested Rights Statutes, 281
    conditional use permit, 62
    development agreements, 275
    in general, 101–102, 269
    Map Act provisions, 101–102
vesting tentative map,
    96n8, 97–98, 100, 279, 433
    See also tentative
        map; vested rights
    background, 102–106
    compared to development
        agreement, 280
    effect of annexation, 107
    effect of newly
        incorporated city, 107
    procedures, 106
Vesting Tentative Map
    statute, 102–103
view protection ordinance, 234
Virginia Supreme Court, 509
voter registration program, 414

W

waiver, common law
    doctrine of waiver, 94
WalMart, 3, 162, 267
Walnut Creek, growth management
    measure (Measure H), 10, 408
Washington
    ex parte legislation, 462n7
    IOLTA program, 315–316
Washington, D.C., 177
waste. *See also* hazardous waste; sewage
    Porter-Cologne definition, 202
waste discharge. *See also* sewage
    Map Act consideration of, 123
    NPDES permit, 214
    SWRCB permit, 181, 202
    saline waste, 311
waste management plan, 149
waste water
    See also NPDES; sewage
    storm water quality
        requirements, 262–263
    MS4s, 262
    small MS4s, 262–263
        design standards,
            web address, 263n8
wastewater treatment
    facilities, Coastal
        Commission review of, 247

water. *See also* "aquatic resources
of national importance";
groundwater; navigable
waters; waste water
 aquatic resources, 193
 conservation element addresses, 16
 "critical resource waters,"
  defined, 189
  NWPs and, 191
 irrigation, 178
water agency, 256–257, 259–260
water assessment district, 377
 See also assessment district
water charge. *See also* charge
 capacity charge,
  challenges to,
   376, 575, 577–578
  statute of limitations, 574, 577
 commodity charge, 379–380
 rate changes and
  initiatives, 376, 398
 water connection fee,
  377, 516, 574–575
  challenges to, 577–578
Water Code, 286
water connection,
 capacity charge, 376
water contract, 217
water district, 112, 152
 See also water
  supply; water system
 housing element notification, 489
 LAFCO jurisdiction, 442
 zoning ordinance application to, 73
water pollution, 214
 See also Clean Water Act;
  water quality certification
 conservation element
  addresses, 16
water pumping operations, biological
 opinion not valid, 217–218
water quality certification, 189
 See also water supply
water right transfers, as
 separate projects, 161
water supply. *See also* water
 supply adequacy
 CALFED, 253, 261
 Colorado River
  agreements, 253, 261
 CWA protections for, 188
 fire fighting, safety element
  must address, 17
 groundwater recharge, 111
 municipal water supplies, EPA
  consideration of, 186
 planning, 250–262
 program, 149
 "project" definition,
  under SB 610, 257
water supply adequacy
 CEQA consideration
  of, 162–163, 257
 challenges to, statute
  of limitations, 542
 in general, 250, 256
 Map Act consideration of, 92, 143
  discussed, 110
 SB 221, 250–256, 259–262
 SB 610, 250–259
water supply
 assessment, 160, 250–259
water supply verification, 251–256
 statute of limitations, 542

water system
 public water system, 29
  city must refer maps to, 95
  definition under
   SB 610/SB 221, 252
 urban water management plan, 259
 zoning law does not apply to, 73
waterfowl, 173
 See also birds; endangered species
 "migratory bird rule," 176–177
"waters of the state"
 See also "waters
  of the United States"
 definition, 202
"waters of the United States"
 See also wetlands
 defined, 176
 discussed, 175
 "isolated waters," 176–177
 "phone home" rule, 177
 navigable waters, 174–175
 prohibition of discharge of fill into, 193
waterway. *See also* river
 circulation element may address, 14
 conservation element addresses, 16
 public access provisions, 112–113
welfare, 3–4, 34–35, 49, 63
 See also public welfare
Western Attorneys General, 75
western gray squirrel, denial of
 listing petition upheld, 209
wetlands, 314
 Corps permitting
  process, 186–194, 200
  activity-specific permit, 191
  application time schedule, 190
  "aquatic resources of
   national importance," 199
  Corps, 1993, Memorandum,
   web address, 197
  EPA/Corps MOA, 195, 199
  EPA role, 173, 192, 195, 199–200
  EPA's 404(b)(1)
   Guidelines, 192–197, 199
  in general, 186
  "general" permit, 184, 186
  "individual" permit, 186, 200, 206
   application, required
    information, 192
   environmental assessment
    under NEPA, 200
   flow chart, 190
   process, 191–193
   time periods, 192
  "market entry approach," 198
  mitigation, 189, 198–199, 203–204
  nationwide permits (NWPs),
   184, 186–193, 200, 206
   comments, 191
   NWP 26, 191
   NWP 39, 191
   NWP 41, 191
   NWP 42, 191
   NWP 43, 191
   NWP 44, 191
   NWP 46, 191
  permit denial is not a taking, 195
  pre-construction notification
   (PCN), 189, 191–192
  public comment period, 190
  "public interest
   review standard," 174, 193
  water-dependent/non-water-
   dependent project, 194–195

wetlands *continued*
 Corps regulatory activities
  "discharge of fill material,"
   175, 184, 193
  "dredged material," 184
  "fill," 184
  in general, 174–175
  "incidental fallback," 184–185
   revised definition
    held invalid, 185
  land-clearing activities, 184
  statutory exemptions, 185–186
 definition
  Corps definition, 182
  Corps/EPA joint
   guidance, 179–180
   website, 179n1
  CWA definition, 175
  hydrology, 182–183
  legal definition, 175–181
  1987 Manual, 182–183, 203
   Regional Supplements,
    website, 182
  1989 Manual, 182
  1991 Manual, 182
  "phone home" rule, 177
  Rapanos decision, 178–179
  scientific/technical
   definition, 181–183
  soils, 182–183
 enforcement
  after-the-fact permits, 205–206
  federal penalties
   administrative
    penalties, 204–205
   burden of proof on
    government, 204
 EPA vetoes of Corps
  decisions, 186, 197, 199
 EPA's 404(b)(1) Guidelines
  alternatives analysis, 193–194
  availability, 197–198
  Corps regulation, 193
  in general, 192
  "Least Environmentally
   Damaging Practicable
   Alternative," (LEDPA), 196
  practicability,
   193–195, 196–197, 199–200
  project purpose and
   wetlands avoidance
   (sequencing), 194–196
 federal statutes
  Clean Water Act, 173, 175
   section 401, 200
    certification, 190, 200
  Coastal Zone Management
   Act, 189–190, 201, 203–204
  Endangered Species Act,
   173, 190, 200
  Fish and Wildlife
   Coordination Act, 200–201
  Food Security Act, 201
  Land Sales Full
   Disclosure Act, 201
  Marine Protection, Research
   and Sanctuaries Act,
   Section 302, 201
  National Historic Preservation
   Act, 189–190, 201
  NEPA, 190, 192, 199–200
 history of federal program, 174–175
 inadvertently created wetlands, 176
 introduction, 173–174

wetlands *continued*
  National List of Plant Species
    That Occur in Wetlands, 183
  National Pollutant Discharge
    Elimination System, 175
  practical considerations, 206
  Regulatory Guidance
    Letters, 183, 201–202
  restoration, Coastal Commission
    promotion of, 247
  seasonal wetlands/creek
    not ARNIs, website, 199
  as special aquatic site, 194
  state authority
    Coastal Zone Management
      Act, 189, 203–204
    in general, 202
    Navigation Dredging
      Permit, 203
    Porter-Cologne Water
      Quality Control
      Act, 181, 202–203
    Regional Water Quality Control
      Boards, 181, 200, 202–203
    Streambed Alteration
      Agreement, 203
    SWRCB, 180–181,
      189, 202–203
whales, 219
Wheeler decision, 318–320
White, Byron, 226
White House, 221
whooping crane, 222
  See also endangered species
  critical habitat, 215
wildfire, safety element
  must address, 17
wildlife
  conservation element addresses, 16
  EPA consideration of, 207–208, 210
  habitat mitigation, 220
  protections for, 222–224
Williamson Act contract, 91, 123, 432
  See also agricultural land
  discussed, 238–242
    contract cancellation, 240–241
      is quasi-judicial, 530
    "farmland security zone," 242
    statute of limitations, 241, 543
Willowbrook, 333
Wilson, Pete, 227
wind-powered electrical generation,
  Map Act exemption for, 91
Windsor, initiative capping
  permits, 423
winery, use permit upheld for, 41
woodpecker. *See also*
  endangered species
  decline of as taking, 223
  red-cockaded woodpecker, 219
writ of mandate,
  36, 94, 231, 260, 367, 390, 465,
  469, 525–526, 528, 557, 562–568
  See also judicial review;
  mandate proceedings

Y

Yellowstone Park, gray wolf
  recovery plan, 211
Yolo County, "urbanized area," 264
Yorba Linda, growth-
  control initiative, 424
Yuba County, "urbanized area," 264

Z

"zero trash" water
  run off standard, 154
  See also storm
  water; waste water
zoning
  ballot box zoning, 407–408
  board of zoning adjustment, 60
  challenges to, 542
  challenges to zoning decisions,
    statute of limitations, 47, 542
  defined, 43
  "Euclidian" zoning, 421
  planning commission
    relation to, 6–7
zoning administrator,
  6n3, 283, 479,
  529, 542, 550
zoning law
  applicability
    charter city,
      23, 43, 46, 401
    federal/state
      government, 72–73
    Indian lands, 57, 75–77
    joint powers agencies, 73–74
      school districts, 73–74
      other districts, 73–75
    joint powers authority, 74
  conditional zoning, 68
  "contract zoning," 68
  due process, 48–49, 53
  enforcement, 522–523
  fiscal zoning, 428
  form-based, discussed, 65
  inclusionary zoning, 512
    affordability
      duration, 522
    affordability
      preservation, 521
    amount and
      affordability, 519–520
    beneficiary
      qualification, 521–522
    Costa-Hawkins Act, 516–517
    determining development
      size, 518–519
    discussed, 2, 69–70, 506n30
    enactment, 512–513
    factual record, 513–514
    incentives, 516
    judicial treatment, 508
    legal issues, 511–512
    mandatory/voluntary
      program, 517–518
    post-*Nollan/Dolan*, 510–511
    pre-*Nollan/Dolan*, 508–510
    rent/price control, 521
    "safety valve"
      provisions, 514–516
  interim ordinance, 5, 66–67
  interplay with
    Map Act, 80
  "least cost zoning law," 411, 505
    appropriate
      standards, 497
    discussed, 497
  prezoning, 53, 65–66
  redevelopment law and, 70–71
  rules of evidence/
    procedural errors, 53, 95
  variances, 60–61
zoning map, 7, 45

zoning ordinance, 2–4, 151, 286
  See also conditional
  use permit; variance
  adoption procedure, 50–51
  adult business
    regulation, 53–56, 479
  amendment
    is a legislative act, 48, 51, 59
    public notice and
      hearing required, 48–49, 535
    rezoning, 45
    "text amendment," 45, 48
  big box retail stores and, 3
  classes of, 43
  CUPs and, 61–62
  dedications and
    development fees, 34–35
  defined, 43
  downzoning/density reduction,
    432, 465, 490, 492–493
  "lower residential
    density," 490–491
  dwelling units, limits on,
    findings required for, 44
  EIR prepared for, 158
  enactment
    challenges to, 47
    due process requirements, 48–49
    in general, 45
    is legislative act, 6, 43, 402, 528
    must be consistent
      with ALUP, 48
    must be consistent with
      general plan, 9–10, 46–48
    inconsistency as
      result of amendment
      to general plan, 47
    must be consistent with
      specific plan, 39, 46–48
    must be reasonably related
      to public welfare, 45–46
    necessity of valid
      general plan for, 47
    statute of limitations, 47
  exclusionary zoning, 421
  as growth management tool, 421
  housing limits, findings
    requirement, 505
  by initiative or referendum, 52–53
  judicial review, 47, 51
    burden of proof not
      generally on cities, 44
    limited role of court
      review, 43–44
    presumption of validity, 43
    statute of limitations, 47, 542
  as minimum standards
    of practice, 2
  motives, 51–52, 533
  multi-family, 334
  must be consistent
    with open space plan, 17
  nonconforming use, 63–65
  not a taking, 291
  protection of religious
    exercise, 57–59
  redevelopment plan affecting, 71
  specific plan as, 68
  statutory authority for, 5
  TDRs and, 249–250
  vagueness and
    uncertainty, 49–50
zoning regulation
  See zoning ordinance

Other Guides and References

PLANNING . LAND USE . URBAN AFFAIRS . ENVIRONMENTAL ANALYSIS . REAL ESTATE DEVELOPMENT

Arthur L. Littleworth and Eric L. Garner
2007 (second) edition

California Water II
This all-new second edition covers key developments in water law: the implementation of the historic Bay-Delta Accord, the crisis in the Delta, settlement of critical issues on the Colorado River, global warming, and the emergence of new water supplies such as water transfers, conservation, recycling, and the conjunctive use of groundwater.

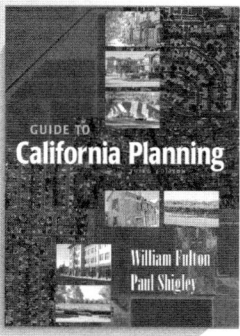

William Fulton and Paul Shigley
2005 (third) edition

Guide to California Planning
Describes how planning really works in California, how cities, counties, developers, and citizen groups all interact with each other to shape California communities and the California landscape, for better and for worse. Recipient of the California Chapter APA Award for Planning Education.

Marjorie W. Macris, FAICP • 2004

The Planning Commissioner and the California Dream
An easily readable reference and set of guidelines directed to the on-the-job needs of California's city and county planning commissioners. With interviews, case studies, tips on how to do the job well, photos, illustrations, and a glossary of common terms.

Ballot Box Navigator
The authoritative resource on securing a ballot title, qualifying an initiative or referendum for the ballot, and submitting a measure for an election. With short articles, practice tips, drawings, an index, glossary, and a table of authorities.
Michael Patrick Durkee et al. • 2003

California School Facilities Planning
A single-source reference that offers a thorough discussion of laws and regulations that govern planning, funding, siting, design, and construction of educational facilities. The book will guide the reader through every stage of the planning process—from initial conception through construction.
Maureen F. Gorsen et al. • 2005

California Public Contract Law
Easy-to-use, concise reference on laws governing the public contracting processes used by federal, state, regional, and local agencies. Suggests model provisions and provides extensive references for relevant statutes and regulations. Includes a list of useful legal research sites on the Internet and a summary of frequently used provisions of the Public Utilities Code.
Jeremy G. March • 2007

CEQA Deskbook
The practitioner's definitive guide to CEQA, explaining in clear language how to traverse the environmental review process, from beginning to end. Contains the full text of the Statutes and Guidelines. Recognized by the California Association of Environmental Professionals with an Award of Excellence. Cited as an Authoritative Source by the California Courts.
Bass, Herson, and Bogdan • 1999–2000 w/ 2001 Supplement

CALL TOLL-FREE
(800) 931-9373 OR FAX (707) 884-4109

Solano Press Books
www.solano.com . spbooks@solano.com . facsimile 707 884-4109

Eminent Domain

Explains the processes California public agencies must follow to acquire private property for public purposes through eminent domain. Includes case law, legal references, tips, a table of authorities, sample letters and forms, a glossary, and an index.
Richard G. Rypinski • 2002 (second) edition

Guide to the California Environmental Quality Act

The professionals' guide to the California Environmental Quality Act presents an understandable, in-depth description of CEQA's requirements for adequate review and careful preparation of environmental impact reports and other environmental review documents. Includes extensive analyses of statutes, provisions of the CEQA Guidelines, and voluminous case law.
Remy, Thomas, Moose, and Manley • 2006 (eleventh) edition

Guide to the California Forest Practice Act

A comprehensive treatise on state and federal legislation that regulates timber harvesting on private lands in California. Includes short articles, charts, graphs, appendices, a table of authorities, and an index to help understand complex regulatory processes and how they interrelate.
Sharon E. Duggan and Tara Mueller • 2005

The NEPA Book

Practitioner's handbook that takes you through the critical steps, basic requirements, and most important decision points of the National Environmental Policy Act. With short articles, practice tips, tables, illustrations, charts, and sources of additional information.
Ronald E. Bass et al. • 2001 (second) edition

CALL TOLL-FREE
(800) 931-9373 OR FAX (707) 884-4109

Planning for Child Care in California

Presents basic child care information and guidelines for municipal, county, and school district planners, and for child care professionals and their advocates. Includes numerous examples of real child care projects, designs, and partnerships, along with sources of funding and other implementation strategies.
Kristen M. Anderson • 2006

Redevelopment in California

Definitive guide to both the law and practice of redevelopment in California cities and counties, together with codes, case law, and commentary. Contains short articles, notes, photographs, charts, graphs, and illustrative time schedules.
David F. Beatty et al. • 2004 (third) edition

Subdivision Map Act Manual

A comprehensive reference containing information needed to understand Subdivision Map Act legal provisions, recent court-made law, and the review and approval processes. With the full text of the Map Act, practice tips, a table of authorities, and an index.
Daniel J. Curtin, Jr. and Robert E. Merritt • 2003 edition

Telecommunications

Detailed summary and analysis of federal and state laws governing the location and regulation of physical facilities including cable, telephone, and wireless systems (cellular, paging, and Internet), satellite dishes, and antennas. With practice tips, photos, a glossary, table of authorities, and an index.
Paul Valle-Riestra • 2002

Water and Land Use

First complete guide to address the link between land use planning in California and the availability of water. Summarizes key statutes, policies and requirements, and current practices. With illustrations and photos, tables, flow charts, case studies, sample documents, practice tips, a glossary, references, and an index.
Karen E. Johnson and Jeff Loux • 2004

Wetlands, Streams, and Other Waters

A practical guide to federal and state wetland identification, regulation, and permitting processes. Provides detailed information, commentary, and practice tips for those who work with federal and state laws and are engaged in wetland conservation planning.
Paul D. Cylinder et al. • 2004 edition

Solano Press Books

www.solano.com • spbooks@solano.com • facsimile 707 884-4109

Solano Press Books

Current Titles

Guide to California Planning
by William Fulton and Paul Shigley

Since first published in 1991, *Guide to California Planning* has served as the authoritative textbook on city and county planning practice. It is used as a textbook in virtually every college- and graduate-level planning program in California.

In this revised, expanded third edition, the authors lay out planning laws and processes in detail, describing how planning really works—how cities and counties and developers and citizen groups all interact on a daily basis to shape California communities and the California landscape, for better and for worse. Easy to read and understand, *Guide to California Planning* is far more than a textbook. It's also an ideal tool for members of allied professions in the planning and development fields as well as citizen activists.

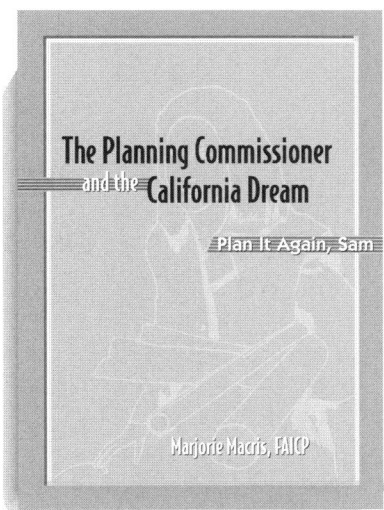

The Planning Commissioner and the California Dream: Plan It Again, Sam
by Marjorie W. Macris, FAICP

Tackling a serious subject with whimsy and humor, as well as seriousness of purpose, *The Planning Commissioner and the California Dream* offers specific guidelines on how to function as an effective planning commissioner in the face of complex issues, special interests, committed advocates, and intricate planning and environmental laws.

Describing the roles and responsibilities of commissioners, and how to make sure things go smoothly, the book includes interviews with a variety of commissioners, a glossary of common terms, and tips on how to do the job well. Peppered with amusing references to selected motion pictures that convey the significance of California and its unique environment.

Solano Press Books

www.solano.com

spbooks@solano.com

Redevelopment in California

by David F. Beatty, Michael L. F. Buck, Joseph E. Coomes, Jr., T. Brent Hawkins, Edward J. Quinn, Jr., Gerald J. Ramiza, Iris P. Yang, Seth Merewitz, and Ethan Walsh with Calvin E. Hollis and Kathleen H. Head of Keyser Marston Associates

The definitive guide to both the law and practice, this third edition of *Redevelopment in California* is a comprehensive, clearly written reference and practitioner's handbook for policymakers, officials, developers, investors, attorneys, citizens, and students.

The book contains the full text of the law, with legislation adopted through January 1, 2004, including SB 1045, SB 114, SB 966, SB 109, and AB 1731, as well as discussion of recent cases. In addition, the book covers such topics as toxics and military base reuse, plan adoptions, tax-increment financing, affordable housing, and plan implementation. The 2007 Supplement, also available, reflects a number of recent significant changes to the law.

California Public Contract Law: Basic Principles and Special Requirements

by Jeremy G. March

California Public Contract Law is an easy-to-use, concise reference on the laws governing the public contracting processes used by federal, state, regional, and local agencies in California. The book reviews key requirements, suggests model provisions, and provides extensive references for relevant statutes and regulations. An important resource for agency administrators, contractors, and bidders involved in public contracting law in California.

Includes a list of useful legal research sites on the Internet, a summary of frequently used provisions of the Public Utilities Code and the Public Contract Code, as well as a table of authorities, a list of acronyms, and an index.

California Water II

by Arthur L. Littleworth and Eric L. Garner

This all-new second edition of *California Water* is the first book since Wells Hutchins' 1956 "bible," *California Law of Water Rights,* to serve as a comprehensive guide to historical, legal, and policy issues that affect the use of water in California.

The book is a major resource for local officials—in water districts, cities, and counties—as well as for lawyers, judges, engineers, planners, community leaders, environmentalists, developers, and farmers. *California Water II* addresses the question, "Do we have enough water?" and covers key developments in water law: the implementation of the historic Bay-Delta Accord, the crisis in the Delta, settlement of critical issues on the Colorado River, global warming, and the emergence of new water supplies such as water transfers, conservation, recycling, and the conjunctive use of groundwater.

Water and Land Use: Planning Wisely for California's Future

by Karen E. Johnson and Jeff Loux

Water and Land Use is the first complete guide to address the increasingly important link between land use planning in California and the availability of water. Summarizes key statutes, governmental policies and requirements, and current practices. Presents methods for evaluating water demand, supply, reliability, and quality, and for meeting legislative requirements for linking water supplies and land use decisions.

A valuable, useful "how to" handbook for environmental and land use planners, engineers, water resource planners, government officials, and attorneys. With illustrations and photos, tables, flow charts, case studies, sample documents, practice tips, a glossary, references, and an index.

PLANNING

LAND USE

URBAN AFFAIRS

ENVIRONMENTAL ANALYSIS

REAL ESTATE DEVELOPMENT

CALL TOLL-FREE
(800) 931-9373
OR FAX (707) 884-4109

Solano Press Books

www.solano.com

spbooks@solano.com

Guide to CEQA

by Michael H. Remy, Tina A. Thomas, James G. Moose, and Whitman F. Manley

The non-legal and legal professionals' guide to the California Environmental Quality Act, this book includes extensive analyses of the statutes, CEQA Guidelines provisions, and voluminous case law. Presents an understandable, in-depth description of CEQA's requirements for adequate review and careful preparation of EIRs and other environmental documents.

Of particular significance is the authors' interpretation of the Court of Appeal decision entitled *Communities for a Better Environment v. California Resources Agency*. Attention is given to day-to-day CEQA practice, such as regulatory standards and significant thresholds, as well as the requirement that water supply issues be addressed in EIRs. Cited as an Authoritative Source by the California Courts.

Wetlands, Streams, and Other Waters: Regulation, Conservation, and Mitigation Planning

by Paul D. Cylinder, Kenneth M. Bogdan, April I. Zohn, and Joel B. Butterworth

Wetlands, Streams, and Other Waters explains the complex laws and regulations that govern our nation's waters. Written in clear, understandable language, the book guides the reader through the intricacy of federal and state permitting requirements, discussing conservation plans and suggesting strategies to plan and protect resources.

The authors exhaustively dissect Section 404 of the Clean Water Act and Section 10 of the Rivers and Harbors Act, also introducing other related federal laws and comprehensively summarizing regulations in all 50 states. *Wetlands* is an invaluable resource for permit applicants, public agencies, environmental organizations, and attorneys confronting these issues.

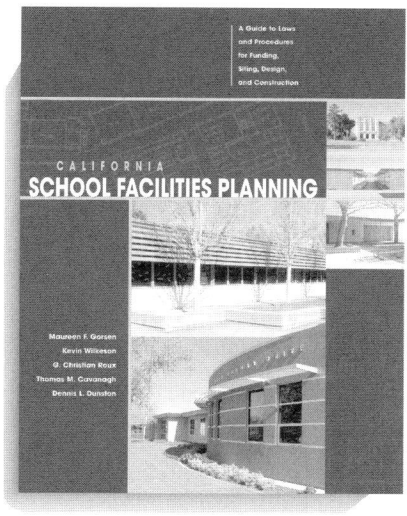

California School Facilities Planning

by Maureen F. Gorsen, Kevin Wilkeson, G. Christian Roux, Thomas M. Cavanagh, and Dennis L. Dunston

School Facilities Planning is a single-source reference that offers a thorough discussion of laws and regulations that govern the planning, funding, siting, design, and construction of educational facilities.

The book will guide the reader chronologically through every stage of the planning process—from initial conception through construction. Topics include the history of school facilities nationwide; funding sources and financing methods; planning and design, both for individual schools and district-wide; and school siting issues, including acquisition of property and compliance with land use and environmental laws. Includes sidebars, tables, figures, photographs, a table of authorities, a glossary, and an index.

Planning for Child Care in California

by Kristen M. Anderson

Presents basic information and guidelines for municipal, county, and school district planners, and for child care professionals and their advocates. It features strategies for ensuring that child care needs are met locally, with resource material that explains how it is regulated in its various forms through the General Plan and zoning.

Planning for Child Care in California discusses guidelines for incorporating child care goals into the public planning process, with specific attention to the location, planning, and design of housing, centers of employment, and transit-based facilities. Numerous examples of real child care projects, designs, and partnerships are presented, along with sources of funding and other implementation strategies. Includes tables, figures, photographs, a glossary, and an index.

PLANNING

LAND USE

URBAN AFFAIRS

ENVIRONMENTAL ANALYSIS

REAL ESTATE DEVELOPMENT

CALL TOLL-FREE
(800) 931-9373
OR FAX (707) 884-4109

Order Form

ORDERED BY / SHIP TO _____ **TELEPHONE** (___) _____
FIRM / AGENCY _____
STREET OR PO BOX _____
CITY _____ **STATE** _____ **ZIP** _____
YOUR UPS DELIVERY ADDRESS (IF DIFFERENT FROM ABOVE) _____
CREDIT CARD: ☐ VISA ☐ MC ☐ AMEX **EMAIL ADDRESS** (OPTIONAL) _____
CARD NUMBER _____ **EXP. DATE** _____ **V CODE** (REQ'D)* _____
NAME ON CARD (IF DIFFERENT) _____ **SIGNATURE** _____
STREET _____ **CITY** _____ **STATE** _____ **ZIP** _____

QTY	CODE	TITLE	UNIT COST	TOTAL
____	BB	Ballot Box Navigator 2003	$50.00	$_____
____	CC	Planning for Child Care in California 2006	$50.00	$_____
____	CL	Contract Law 2007	$65.00	$_____
____	C26	Guide to CEQA 2006 (11th) edition	$85.00	$_____
____	DR	Understanding Development Regulations 1994	$26.00	$_____
____	ED2	Eminent Domain 2002 (2nd) edition	$50.00	$_____
____	FP	The Forest Practice Act in California 2005	$79.00	$_____
____	G25	Guide to California Planning 2005 (3rd) edition	$30.00	$_____
____	L	Curtin's California Land Use and Planning Law (revised and republished annually in March)	$70.00	$_____
____	N20	The NEPA Book 2001	$65.00	$_____
____	PC	The Planning Commissioner and the California Dream 2004	$50.00	$_____
____	Q21	CEQA Deskbook 1999–2000 (2nd) edition w/ 2001 Supplement	$60.00	$_____
____	R21	Redevelopment in California 2004 (3rd) edition	$60.00	$_____
____	RS21	2007 Supplement to Redevelopment in California	$20.00	$_____
____	S22	Subdivision Map Act Manual 2003 edition	$45.00	$_____
____	SF	California School Facilities Planning 2006	$65.00	$_____
____	TE	Telecommunications 2002	$50.00	$_____
____	TL	California Transportation Law 2000	$50.00	$_____
____	TR	Putting TDRs to Work in California 1993	$25.00	$_____
____	WA2	California Water II 2007	$75.00	$_____
____	WE2	Wetlands, Streams, and Other Waters 2004	$50.00	$_____
____	WL	Water and Land Use 2004	$50.00	$_____
			SUBTOTAL	$_____

Sales tax. Add California sales tax of 7.25% (California only). $_____
Domestic shipping. To continental United States, add $8 per book (but not more than $24 for any one order). To Hawaii and Alaska, please inquire. $_____
Supplement shipping. Add $4 per copy; max. $8; no add'l charge when shipped with at least one book. $_____
Foreign shipping. Please inquire. $_____

* **V code required.** On Visa and MasterCard, the V code is on the back (last three digits of card number on signature line); on American Express, above right of the credit card number.

ALL SALES ARE FINAL. NO RETURNS FOR CREDIT. **GRAND TOTAL** $_____

TELEPHONE ORDERS: (800) 931-9373
or **FAX THIS FORM TO:** (707) 884-4109
ORDER BY EMAIL, USING A CREDIT CARD:
spbooks@solano.com

If paying by regular mail, send this form and a check payable to:
SOLANO PRESS BOOKS, PO Box 773, Point Arena, CA 95468

Solano Press Books